ADVANCED CUSTOM ROD BUILDING

Dale P. Clemens

Winchester Press
An Imprint of NEW CENTURY PUBLISHERS, INC.

Printing code
    19
Library of Congress Catalog Card Number: 82-62340

ISBN 0-8329-2587-X
Printed in the United States

Dedication

To my wife, Donna—who originally said there would be no ''son of fishing rod,'' but who subsequently encouraged, helped, and did everything in her power to provide me with the necessary time.

Acknowledgments

Very few books are written by one person alone and this one is certainly no exception. I am deeply indebted to those RodCrafter Associates who unselfishly shared their ideas and methods so that others might learn. Rather than list their names here, I felt it would be more meaningful to mention each of them in the text along with the particular technique discussed. Beyond those individuals cited by name, I want to thank all RodCrafter Associates who shared their thoughts in our journal and participated in our seminars. Their efforts have done much to advance the craft of custom rod building, and will continue to do so in the future.

Much help of all kinds was provided by my very close friend and manager of my rod-building supply business, John Sawyer. Most of the drawings were done by the gifted pen of Charles M. Armontrout, who operates his own custom rod shop in Covington, Virginia. Other drawings were made by one of our crew at Custom Tackle, Drew Strawbridge. Still other drawings and photos were the work of RodCrafter Associates themselves. A great deal of photographic and darkroom assistance was rendered by Ron Dunn.

There is a very special person without whose assistance I could never complete half the projects I tackle, my secretary, Karen George. She caught the spark of enthusiasm for the book and gave most generously of her personal time in typing and retyping the manuscript from my nearly illegible handwriting.

Special thanks to Gary Loomis, chief rod designer of Lamiglas, Inc., for assistance in the technical area and to Jon Sivertsen, Dick Posey, and the entire Lamiglas staff for allowing me free rein to photograph the steps in manufacturing a rod blank.

Contents

Introduction

More than any other piece of fishing tackle, the rod is constantly in hand. It is, in fact, the extension of the angler's hand and the primary instrument through which he transmits his fishing skill. With it he casts to the precise spot chosen, manipulates the lure to entice his quarry, retrieves through the selected water, and finally plays and fights his fish. It is irrefutable logic that the better the rod is matched to the angler, the water, and the specific fishing at hand, the greater will be the expression of the angler's skill, the more he will enjoy his fishing, and the greater will be his chances of success.

Away from the water, fishing rods are frequently a great point of discussion among anglers. Brought out for examination, admiration, and criticism, they are the subjects for debate and the reminders of fishing exploits past and anticipated. In short, rods are accorded the attention and respect they deserve. The reader of this book does not need to have explained that the well-designed and well-made custom rod is always superior to a factory-made rod. The enjoyment of fishing—which, when all is said and done, is really more important than the actual catching of fish—is enhanced tremendously for the angler using a custom rod.

This all became apparent to me years ago when I built my first rod. I didn't invent that experience—many before me had discovered the same thing. And certainly many more have discovered it since, for today increasing numbers of people are discovering the joys and rewards of this fascinating craft. There is much evidence to suggest that custom rod building is presently the fastest-growing segment of the entire tackle industry. To me this is exhilarating, and I only hope that more of the millions of fishermen will try building their own.

For some years before I wrote *Fiberglass Rod Making*, I found myself increasingly on a course of trying to convince fishermen that they could build a better rod than they could buy. The initial suggestion that I write a book for the beginner took me by surprise, but in all honesty I must admit that once started it was a labor of love. Here was an opportunity to encourage many more people to build their own rods. As I took the plunge with the book, I went all the way and expanded my rod-building-supply business to a national mail-order venture.

The response went far beyond what I could have hoped for. Within three years the book was in its fifth printing and scheduled for a softcover edition. My mail-order business grew to become one of the largest. What was perhaps most exciting was the incredible number of letters I received from rod builders both new and experienced. It soon became apparent that (1) I could not personally handle the volume of correspondence, nor was I necessarily qualified to do so, and (2) there was an obvious need for a forum where ideas, methods, and techniques could be exchanged on the subject. Thus was RodCrafters born—an international organization for custom rod builders, both hobbyists and professionals. It has grown by leaps and bounds. Its purpose is "to encourage and improve the development of rod making as a craft through the exchange of ideas and techniques." The key to the whole concept is sharing.

This unselfish and exciting give-and-take occurs in the bimonthly *RodCrafters Journal*. Since the first issue in January 1975, I have had the pleasure of publishing the *Journal* and the rewards of learning from the many outstanding articles. All of the material is submitted by our Associates (that's what we chose to call ourselves), and my staff and I merely edit and rewrite as necessary. The *Journal* is printed on heavy book paper for retention as a permanent reference library. Each year we have held a national seminar with custom builders from all across the country attending. Our future plans include regional seminars so that more of our Associates can participate.

Many of the ideas presented in this book were first shared in the *RodCrafters Journal*. In each case I have tried to credit the individual Associate. None of us is naive enough to think that he necessarily invented the technique or was the first rod builder ever to use it. However, the willingness to share publicly certainly deserves recognition, for from it we all learn and advance the development of our craft.

Personally, I believe that anyone who enjoys building custom rods and who wants to learn more about the subject should become associated with RodCrafters. Through this forum he can probably learn more about some aspects than he could in a lifetime of experimenting on his own. Then too, as our numbers grow, so will the exchange of meaningful and helpful ideas. If you would like more information write:

Dale P. Clemens
RodCrafters, Suite 500
14 Chippewa Drive
Allentown, PA 18104

As the title states, this book is on "advanced" rod making. Advanced, however, only in the sense that it attempts to take over where *Fiberglass Rod Making* left off. In no way is it meant to be construed as the final word on the subject. No one will ever write such a book. Even as this is written, our RodCrafter files are full of new ideas awaiting editing and publishing in future issues of the *Journal*. New techniques, materials, and ideas are constantly being developed. It has been my observation that few people are as creative and innovative as are custom rod builders. They will continue to evolve new methods and place increasing demands upon manufacturers for ever better quality components.

Manufacturers are keenly interested in the tremendous growth occuring in custom rod making. In it they see an entirely new market developing. I know this from personal experience, since I have been fortunate enough to serve as consultant to a number of them. Some are beginning to recognize that the custom builder wants the highest-quality components and that he will not necessarily accept some of the compromises that are inevitable on factory rods. To certain companies this poses a dilemma, since their production is geared of necessity to the economies of large scale. They cannot afford to make two different sets of components—one for their production rods and one for the custom builder. Companies that have always concentrated on quality are in a better position to respond. The small, highly specialized manufacturer is in some cases better able to turn his attention to the custom market. We and other large dealers have seen this to be true, as we have had special parts made exclusively for us. If our craft continues to grow, as I have every reason to expect it will, then we will have available increasing numbers of higher-quality components and materials.

So, on every horizon the future of custom building looks brighter than ever. It is my hope, then, that in this book you will find ideas that will enable you to build even better rods and more fully enjoy the many rewards.

—Dale P. Clemens
September 1977

ADVANCED CUSTOM ROD BUILDING

ONE

The Blank

Any discussion of custom rod building has to start with the blank and its proper selection for the rod to be built. Today we are blessed, although at times confused, with a huge assortment of all kinds of blanks from an increasing number of manufacturers. With the tremendous upsurge in custom rod making, the market for blanks has become so large that sizable sums can be spent in advertising and sales promotion. This is a definite advantage in keeping the crafter of rods informed, but a basic knowledge of the construction of the blank is helpful and in some cases necessary for proper selection.

FIBERGLASS

Primarily because of the cost factor, more rods are built of fiberglass than graphite. So, let's first explore the construction of hollow fiberglass blanks. There are two primary methods in use: the conventional process and the Howald process.

Conventional process

By far the largest number of blanks are made by what is commonly referred to as the conventional process. While there are variations among manufacturers, the system employed consists of the same essential steps. To start with, special chrome-treated, resin-impregnated fiberglass cloth is used. On quality blanks, the weave of this special cloth is made so that there are more fibers running in one direction than the other. This allows most of the fibers to be aligned along the axis of the blank, with just enough cross fibers circling the blank to provide the required hoop strength. Basically, there are two fabrics used, light and heavy. The light fabric used has about 75% to 80% of the fibers placed longitudinally and weighs 5.42 ounces per square yard. The heavier cloth has about 85% to 90% of the fibers in one direction and weighs 8.65 ounces per square yard.

Various thermosetting resins are used to impregnate the glass cloth and to bind the fibers together. One of the earliest was a nylon-plasticized phenolic resin. It does an excellent job, but is more difficult for the manufacturer to handle and has a shorter shelf life after impregnation, but before curing, than the newer resin systems. Also, it has the disadvantage of darkening in color with age. It should be explained here that the term "shelf life" refers to the storage of pre-impregnated fiberglass cloth by the manufacturer before the blanks are made. The large blank companies order their cloth pre-impregnated from the makers of glass. They specify the weave desired, the resin to be used, and the amount of resin in the mixture. Purchases are made in large quantities and then stored for use in production over a period of time. The length of time that the resin-impregnated cloth can be stored, or its shelf life, is thus important to the manufacturer.

Epoxy resins were developed with slightly longer shelf life and more ease in handling. Certain attributes of epoxy allow a lower amount of resin in the finished blank if handled under very carefully controlled manufacturing processes. While generally too costly for fiberglass, these extra controls are compatible with the graphite process. Epoxy resin is therefore used more with graphite than with fiberglass.

The predominate resin system used in today's glass rods is polyester. Its development allowed higher-density laminations containing less total resin. It also has the longest shelf life after impregnation and is the easiest with which to work —both important considerations to the manufacturer and to the final cost of the rod blank.

In the conventional process of making hollow fiberglass blanks, a pattern is cut from the impregnated cloth. Heat is used to tack one side of the pattern

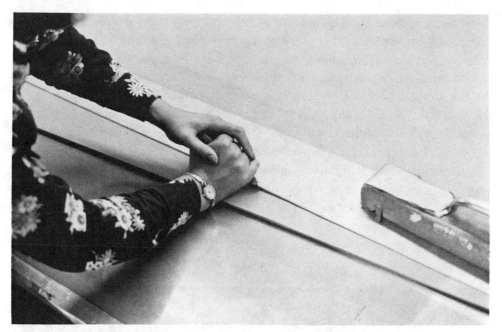

Pattern is cut from fiberglass cloth.

to a tapered steel mandrel, and it is rolled under pressure around the mandrel. In order to create a high-density lamination, it is important that the wrapping pressure be high and uniform all along the length of the mandrel. There are different techniques for performing this operation, and some of them are very much trade secrets. Precision equipment is required and usually consists of heated platens

Pattern is tacked to mandrel before wrapping.

that can be adjusted for the contours of different blanks. As the cloth is wrapped around the mandrel, the high pressure forces air out, resulting in a porosity-free blank of high density and thin walls. In fiberglass, this type of blank is preferable to one of thicker-walled construction for its greater strength and responsiveness. As one would expect, it will be more expensive than the less-desirable and easier-to-make thick-walled blank. It should be noted that the amount of fiberglass contained in a thin- and thick-walled blank is often the same. The thin wall blank has been ''squeezed'' for a higher density and greater strength.

After the cloth is tightly wrapped around the mandrel, the outside of the mold for the blank must be added. This consists of spirally wrapped cellophane tape of ½ to 1 inch in width. The term ''cellophane'' is generally used, although some companies use different polyester or FEP fluoroplastic films. As when wrapping the cloth, high uniform pressure is the objective for top quality, and precision equipment is required for the best results.

Fiberglass cloth and mandrel are wrapped with cellophane.

This cellophane film applies pressure to the laminate not only when it is wrapped, but during the curing process. This happens when the blank is baked and the cellophane shrinks. At that point the resin temporarily liquefies, and the tape provides a smooth suface inside of which the resin is free to flow for even distribution.

Wrapped mandrels are placed in huge oven for curing.

The blanks are hung vertically in an oven for 30 to 60 minutes at a temperature of 300° to 350°F. The variables depend upon the resin system used and are precisely controlled. The resin first turns into a low-viscosity liquid, at which time it is free-flowing. It next becomes a gelatin, and then finally hardens to the desired degree for a full cure.

After the blank has cured, the mandrel, which is longer than the blank and has a notch in its base, is removed from the tapered blank by a rap from a power ram. It is cleaned for reuse and carefully handled to preserve its true shape. The cellophane film must now be removed from the outside of the blank. Various techniques can be used. One of the most common is a short "soak" followed by running the blank against a revolving large-diameter soft-wire-mesh brush. Other methods include high-pressure steam, splitting or stripping the film, or a tumbling process.

7

Holed plate retains blank while notched bottom of mandrel fits in hydraulic ram for removal of mandrel.

Mandrels are meticulously cleaned for reuse.

Wire mesh wheels strip cellophane from cured blank.

With the cellophane removed, the blank contains the slight indentations or spiral marks left by the film. These ridges of extra resin can be removed by carefully controlled sanding to produce a smooth, finished appearance. Precision equipment that automatically adjusts the speed of the sander to the changing diameter of the blank is required, and its operator must be highly skilled.

Since there have been advertising claims for the added strength of unsanded blanks, this aspect of construction warrants further explanation. If two identical blanks had the cellophane removed and one was sanded and the other unsanded, we would find these differences. The unsanded blank would be about 5% heavier, but would also be up to 20% stronger. The reason for this is that no matter how fine the sanding equipment and how talented the operator, some of the exterior glass fibers will be removed or fractured. If we simply left it at that, it would be true that the unsanded blank is indeed stronger.

Rod designers are well aware of this fact and can plan on offsetting the loss from sanding by calculating the additional amount of glass to be added to the original pattern. When this is done by a top-quality manufacturer, any difference in strength or weight becomes rather insignificant. Sanding can also be a form of quality control by revealing any "blisters" or bubbles in the wall resulting from incomplete lamination. It must be remembered, too, that in many types of rods pure strength is not the most important criterion for judging the performance of the blank.

Other factors being equal, the unsanded blank is less expensive to make simply because an entire step utilizing costly equipment can be eliminated. By many, it is also judged less pleasing in appearance. Perhaps the best approach is to make unsanded blanks for those fishing situations where strength is most important and slight weight increase insignificant. These would include bass rods for plastic worm fishing over structure, saltwater rods, and IGFA trolling rods.

Color is given a blank by one of two methods. In those of the highest quality, the pigment is added to the resin. The color is constant throughout the blank; any imperfections occurring during the manufacturing process are easily seen, and the blank is rejected. On less expensive blanks, the color consists of a layer or two of paint squeeged on the surface. Imperfections and blemishes are easily hid, permitting fewer blanks to be classed as rejects. In use, rods made from such blanks are more apt to show signs of wear from scratches, abrasion and nicks.

In recent years translucent blanks have enjoyed increasing popularity among some companies and fishermen. Fiberglass and cured resin are naturally translucent if no color is added. To make a blank of this type, a clear rather than opaque color pigment is added. Because of the chemical properties of these clear pigments, or dyes, and their reaction with the resins, some colors seem to be slightly stronger than others, and they are preferred by the manufacturers. However, the translucent blank has no decided advantages or disadvantages over other quality blanks to which an opaque pigment has been used. It is a matter of cosmetics and personal choice.

Within the industry the approach used to design a given fiberglass blank has often been referred to as the "cut and hack" method. Such a term seems unduly harsh and implies a crude approach to design, which it really is not. A better description would be "trial and error based on experience."

Once the action and performance characteristics of the desired blank are defined, the designer selects a mandrel. He knows that the amount of fiberglass at any point will determine the action and power of the blank. He then proceeds to cut what he feels will be the correct pattern from impregnated cloth, and the blank is made. A rod is built on the blank and testing begins. Careful notes are made of performance. If the blank is too stiff in total or in certain sections, a new pattern is tried with less material. The new blank is then tested. If the desired action is obtained but the blank is too weak, work starts over again with a new mandrel. In the process it may be necessary to have an entirely new mandrel made rather than use one of the company's existing stock mandrels. Obviously, the experience of the designer plays a great part in projecting results and eliminates what could otherwise be hundreds of steps in repeated trial and error. The designer occupies a position of importance to the manufacturer, and each develops certain approaches and individual philosophies to the design of a given company's blanks. This is why even though a manufacturer may produce a great number of different blanks for many different fishing situations, their action and tapers will frequently be similar or of the same general class.

Howald process

The Howald process is an older, patented machine process utilizing separate resins and fiberglass yarn. The yarn is saturated with resin and first spirally wound around the removable mandrel. This forms the core of the blank and provides the necessary hoop strength. Over this core is automatically placed yarn, also saturated with resin, but aligned with the axis of the blank. This is followed

Howald process of blank construction.

by a spiral wrap of cellophane tape to seal the outside and hold the fibers in place while the blank is cured. The cellophane is, of course, subsequently removed. As I understand it, small-diameter hollow tip sections are incompatible with this process, and they are made of solid fiberglass.

Blanks made by this process have excellent durability and adequate performance for most fishing situations. Definitely lighter than solid fiberglass, they are nevertheless a bit heavier than hollow glass blanks made under the conventional method. Economies of production are possible, since it is a machine process and separate yarn and resin are used rather than the more expensive resin-impregnated fiberglass cloth.

GRAPHITE

In 1974, Fenwick introduced the first rods made of an entirely new material, graphite. Within a relatively short time other companies were producing rods of this space-age material. Not since the introduction of fiberglass, over twenty-five years before, was the attention of fishermen focused so sharply on rods and rod building. So acute was the awareness and interest of the fishing market, that new companies were formed to jump on the graphite bandwagon.

While a graphite rod will not cure all angling ills, a good one does possess some remarkable attributes that produce increased performance and make it the best fishing instrument yet devised. Chief among them is sensitivity, or the ability to transmit feel. Because graphite is a stiffer material than fiberglass, it transmits even the faintest of messages along the blank from the tip to the angler's hand. When casting, he can feel precisely the tug of the line or lure, and more accurate timing is possible. The angler also receives a broader spectrum of vibrations from the line as he fishes the rod, and can better feel and differentiate the bottom and the lightest of "pick-ups" by the fish. When hooked, the increased sensitivity of the rod accentuates every movement of the fish. Not only is pleasure enhanced, but the fisherman is better prepared to counter every challenge of his quarry.

Graphite is also more responsive than either fiberglass or cane. It stores and releases energy more decisively. Combined with the increased sensitivity, it enables a higher degree of control in casting. Better accuracy is more easily obtainable. The fly fisherman will find it easier to cast tight loops, and the spin and plug caster will be able to cast with less loft. This responsiveness and sensitivity will also enable the angler to set the hook quicker, resulting in fewer missed strikes.

At the completion of a cast, graphite dampens better than any other rod-building material. This means the top stops vibrating quickly, eliminating distance-robbing waves in the line.

On a weight basis, graphite is four times stronger than steel and two and a half times stronger than fiberglass. To the designer, this means that less material is needed than in a fiberglass rod of the same strength, and smaller diameters are possible. To the fisherman, smaller diameters mean less air resistance as the rod is moved through the casting arc. With air resistance reduced, more of the force applied by the casting hand is converted into usable energy. The tip speed is increased for greater distance, or less effort is required to cast the same distance.

Comparing bare blanks of graphite and fiberglass, there is a weight savings of 25% to 33%. The finished rod must contain reel seat, handle assembly, guides, and wrapping finish. All contribute weight. Add next the weight of the reel and line, and it can be seen that the weight savings in finished *short* rods is rather insignificant. The longer the rod, the greater the effect of the reduced weight of graphite. It is most noticeable and most applicable in surf rods and the longer fly rods.

As a blank is made longer, a disproportionate amount of weight is added. To keep power equal in the longer rod, the increments of weight added seem way out of proportion to the added length. The tip must remain the same on the two rods, long or short, to handle the same fly line or lure weight. Since the total lever is longer, the added butt must support its own weight. This means the butt must be of a larger diameter and a continuation of the taper of the shorter rod. This is the problem with fiberglass and especially with bamboo. If a lighter-weight material, such as graphite, is used, possessing the same strength, great weight saving can be achieved. Also, on the longer rod, the smaller diameter of graphite encounters considerably less air resistance than would a long rod of equal length in fiberglass. This is why the weight savings of graphite becomes important on long rods.

Quality graphite blanks also soften less from material fatigue. In a test of 30,000 mechanical flexes designed to simulate casting, fiberglass softened 8%, bamboo 6%, and graphite less than 1%. A well-made graphite rod can therefore be expected to retain its original action, strength, and feel longer than a rod made of other materials.

The danger in viewing the attributes of graphite is that one assumes all graphite blanks or rods are alike. Nothing could be further from the truth. It has been estimated that a graphite blank is about fifty times more difficult to make than a fiberglass blank. Entirely new technology is required. The total performance of any graphite rod depends upon (1) a design that fully utilizes all the advantages of graphite, combined with (2) the production technology that can accurately produce that design.

Both of these subjects can be quite technical and complex. The problem of comparison is further complicated, from the rodcrafter's view, by the fact that both the design and technology of the companies producing graphite blanks are well-guarded trade secrets.

I have been fortunate in this regard in that I serve as a consultant to a number of rod companies, and have been privy to much confidential information. Naturally, I cannot violate that confidence, but we can discuss here many of the problems associated with graphite construction and the conceptual solutions. Additionally, I can call upon personal experience derived from my rod-building-supply business, where we have tested and purposely broken a great many graphite blanks made by most all manufacturers.

Graphite fiber is made by starting with a synthetic polyacrylonitrile fiber. This is heated first to 200° to 300°C. for stabilization and oxidation, then to 1200° to 1500°C., where carbonization occurs. A series of heating stages follows during which decreasing amounts of oxygen are present. At 2000° to 3000°C. in the complete absence of oxygen, graphitization takes place, forming clusters of crystals. These are then oriented by stretching to make the graphite fiber.

This fiber is extremely fine, as small as .0003 inch. At this writing the fiber cannot be woven into a cloth as is fiberglass. Instead, it is produced in continuous lengths of unidirectional fibers. For blank construction, the fibers are impregnated with inert epoxy resin, which holds them in place, and temporarily backed with paper for ease in handling. A 100-foot-by-12-inch roll of this "tape," as it is called, will have each fiber running the entire 100-foot length.

To make a blank, the desired pattern is cut from the tape. The paper backing is removed, and the fiber is wrapped around the mandrel. In order to derive all of the performance characteristics from graphite in a rod, the fibers must all be aligned with the axis of the blank. Herein lies one of the greatest problems in making graphite blanks. Let's examine some of the aspects of this problem.

The mandrel for a graphite blank is much thinner than one for fiberglass—at some points only ten times the diameter of a human hair! Since the fibers must run absolutely parallel with the mandrel, wrapping under the required great pressure pushes the thin mandrel into the graphite. When this happens, wall thickness does not remain constant, and weak spots are formed in the blank. It might help to visualize a sheet of plastic drinking straws held together only by a tacky substance. Now, try to wrap layers of this around a thin dowel. You will find it impossible to keep the straws from piling up along one side.

In an attempt to solve this problem, the pattern can be cut from the graphite tape so that the fibers are not aligned with the axis of the blank. Since the fibers and the mandrel are not parallel, the mandrel will not be pushed into the graphite and will remain centered. However, if this off-axis alignment is used—and some companies do use it—the exceptional performance attributes of graphite in a fishing rod are reduced.

Off-axis alignment has other disadvantages. Graphite fibers are extremely stiff and resist bending. If the fibers are not parallel with the mandrel, they must of necessity be bent and wrapped around the mandrel. At the very small tip diameters the fibers are bent severely and may tend to separate from the resin, or delaminate in later fishing use. To try to compensate for this, some companies add fiberglass to the tip section, or even make the tip entirely of fiberglass. When this is done, we really no longer have a graphite rod. The prime attribute of graphite—sensitivity—is lost. So, too, is the ideal dampening property of graphite.

So wrapping graphite fibers off-axis in order to keep the mandrel centered and the wall thickness constant results in a rod with reduced performance characteristics and a rod that may not hold up very well in hard use.

The solution to keeping the mandrel centered is to create a barrier between it and the parallel graphite fibers while they are being wrapped around the mandrel. If there was a layer of light fiber running at right angles to the graphite, it would be impossible for the mandrel to be pushed into the graphite. This has been the approach taken by the best manufacturers.

A fairly open weave of very light fiberglass, generally referred to as scrim, is placed on the side of the graphite tape that will be next to the mandrel. This fiberglass scrim should not be confused with regular rod-building fiberglass, which has a diameter of .005 to .009 inch and weighs from 5.5 to 9 ounces per square yard. Scrim has a fiber diameter of from .001 to .002 inch and weighs from .58 ounce to 1.43 ounces per square yard. The companies with the best production technology can use the lightest of the fiberglass scrim. They also can use graphite tape that is thicker—i.e., has more fibers.

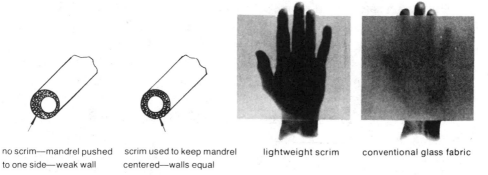

no scrim—mandrel pushed to one side—weak wall   scrim used to keep mandrel centered—walls equal   lightweight scrim   conventional glass fabric

The inclusion of the above small amount of light fiberglass scrim is solely for production purposes to maintain constant wall thickness. It has no effect on rod performance. There is a popular misconception that scrim is added to soften the action of graphite blanks. While the first graphite rods did tend to be too stiff, the stiffness was a result of the tapers used, and has been corrected by taper design—not by additional fiberglass scrim. In fact, the first rods made by Fenwick contained more fiberglass than do their later, more highly refined models.

Graphite-fiberglass blends

There have been attempts by some companies that lacked the production technology to properly handle graphite to blend regular rod-building fiberglass cloth in about equal proportions with graphite tape. The results have been unsatisfactory because of the great difference in the modulus of elasticity (stiffness) of the two materials. Graphite is four times as stiff as fiberglass. It therefore takes four times as much pressure to make a graphite blank attain a certain bend than it would to make a fiberglass blank attain exactly the same bend. Graphite can handle just as great a stress as fiberglass, but the bend or arc will be less. Viewing it another way, graphite loads sooner.

If the two materials are combined in a blank, the graphite fibers are loaded when the fiberglass is only 25% loaded. This means the fiberglass is not yet really performing any significant work. Since these blanks are made for marketing reasons with the same small diameters as graphite blanks, there simply is not enough graphite present to do the job. By the time the blank is flexed far enough to load the fiberglass significantly, the graphite can be considerably overloaded and fail.

"100% graphite"

Some companies advertise that their rods and blanks are made of 100% graphite. This can be misleading and bears closer examination. What they are saying is that graphite is the only fiber used. The term "100% graphite" does not tell us how much resin is in the blank. Nor does it tell us how much total graphite fiber the blank contains. To make a complete comparison we would need to know the "volume fraction" of graphite. This fraction consists of the volume of the graphite fibers contained in the blank, divided by the total volume of the blank. It indicates the percent of the total blank that is made up of graphite fibers. If we multiply this percentage by the total volume, we find how much actual graphite is in the blank.

Perhaps we can simplify this by a rough analogy. Suppose we had a box in which there were 100 balls, 50 of which were black (graphite) and 50 of which were white (resin). Let this box represent the "100% graphite" blank. In another box we also had 100 balls, but 60 were black (graphite), 35 were white (resin), and 5 were red (scrim). While the first box could claim to be 100% graphite, since that is the only fiber used, it clearly has less graphite than the second box, which also contains scrim for production purposes. The blank represented by the first box may have some or all of the fibers off-axis to maintain constant wall diameter. If so, we know the associated problems. Or, if the fibers are aligned with the axis of the blank, the wall diameter may vary, making for erratic action and a weaker blank. So, the statement that a blank is 100% graphite is no indication whatsoever that it is a better blank.

High modulus and low modulus

Another area that can be confusing is the use of the terms "high-modulus" and "low-modulus" graphite. Modulus is merely the technical term for the stiffness of a material, or its resistance to deflection. The higher the modulus the more it resists bending. As mentioned earlier, the graphite used in rod construction has a modulus about four times higher than fiberglass, and about three times higher than bamboo. When compared to these materials, it definitely is "high-modulus."

There is another graphite fiber made with an even higher modulus—about 1.4 times higher. However, it has only about half the flexural break strength and is totally unsuited for fishing rods. If these two fibers are compared, it could be said that the second one is "high-modulus" and the first—the one used for fishing rods—is "low-modulus." The comparison, although great for advertising purposes, is totally invalid because no one builds rods of the higher-modulus graphite fiber. As we have seen, there are many factors that can vary in the construction of a graphite blank with differing results, but the basic graphite fiber used is the same on all rods. In my opinion, any claim that a certain rod is better because it is made of "low-modulus" graphite is misleading.

Ferrules for graphite blanks

There are a great many different ferruling systems employed in the manufacture of graphite blanks. There is only one that is unique enough as of this writing to be patented. The Lamiglas all-graphite integral ferrule is presently patent pending and should be discussed here. The blank is made on two mandrels, one for each rod section. When the butt section is formed, additional graphite fibers are wrapped around the last few inches of the upper end. After curing, this section is precision-bored to make the female ferrule. The male ferrule is similarly constructed on the bottom few inches of the tip section, except that the cross fibers are present internally as thicker walls. The male ferrule is formed by precision grinding on centerless grinding equipment for a perfect fit into the female ferrule. The result is a bare graphite-to-graphite connection with no glue lines or different material to interrupt the flow of maximum sensitivity from tip to butt. Additionally, the design allows for further seating of the ferrule from wear. There is always more than a ⅛ inch gap for this purpose. If a rod were assembled and disassembled three times a week, it would take over 100 years to move the ferrule seating slightly less than ⅛ inch.

Ideally, ferrules should flex the same as the rest of the rod or a dead spot is created in the action. Lamiglas all-graphite ferrules, as well as their graphite rods, have been designed on a large-scale computer program. Incidentally, this is the first such application of computer technology to the design of fishing rods. The computer program designed these unique ferrules on a continuous bending theory compatible with the design characteristics of the rest of the rod in order to totally preserve rod action.

"S" GLASS

Seeing the inroads that graphite was making into the fiberglass market, the. fiberglass manufacturers conducted extensive research in an attempt to improve their products. The result was the development of a special fiberglass designated "S" glass. Fenwick was the first rod company to use this new product in a line of production rods and blanks. For their initial marketing they chose to use the material only on their casting rods and blanks, and selected the trademark name of Fenglass for their line.

The new "S" glass has a higher modulus than regular fiberglass and is lighter. It therefore is more sensitive than regular fiberglass. While it is an improvement over regular fiberglass, it should not be confused with graphite; there is not the dramatic difference that there is between graphite and fiberglass.

"S" glass can be produced in the same type of woven fabric as regular fiberglass. Therefore, essentially the same manufacturing processes for making blanks can be used as are employed for fiberglass—a decided advantage to a blank maker. Fenwick had an exclusive for the 1977 tackle year. After that time "S" glass will be available to any blank manufacturer. It is expected that Fenwick and other companies will continue research and production of this exciting new material.

BLANK ACTION

Before getting into a discussion of the different tapers and their effects on action, we should first review the basic definitions of action. This way we will be sure we are referring to the same terms. Extra-fast action means that just the top 25% of the blank bends in casting the weight for which it is designed. Fast action means the top 33% bends, moderate action means the top 50% bends, and slow action means a progressive curve along the entire blank and all the way

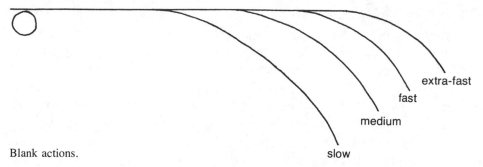

Blank actions.

down into the top of the grips. Over the years there have been many other terms used to define action, particularly on fly rods. Many, as we will see, were combinations of compound tapers—some successful and some not. For our purposes in evaluating today's blanks, the definitions given above are best used.

As noted earlier, the amount of material composing the wall of the blank at any given point determines its stiffness at that point, and therefore the overall action. This is achieved by cutting the cloth or tape into patterns of different shapes. A straight taper has an even progression of additional fiber added to the walls of the blank from tip to butt. As the illustration of the pattern shows, the angled side of the pattern is straight. In its purest form, a straight-tapered blank

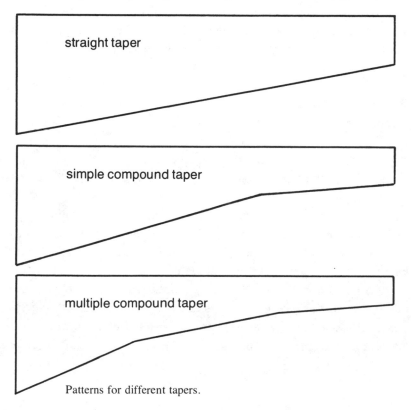

Patterns for different tapers.

will have a slow to medium action with flexing occurring progressively over all or almost all of its length.

A compound taper is one in which there is at least one change in the angle along the side opposite the straight side of the pattern. The taper changes along the length of the blank. If a fast-action blank were being made, the pattern would have comparatively less material in the top third. At that point the pattern would widen rapidly to provide more stiffness over the remaining length of the blank.

There can be many variations and/or combinations of different individual tapers in a compound-tapered blank. For example, the tip could be light and fast, then the midsection and the upper part of the butt section could have an even progression of additional fiber, and finally the butt itself could be made quite stiff by the rapid addition of material.

A number of different techniques can be used to identify the action of a bare blank and judge its applicability for the rod to be built. With all of them, experience is required. Top-quality manufacturers provide not only the statistical measurements of butt, mid, and tip, but also terms regarding the action of each blank. Mail-order companies specializing in rod-building supplies will often add further descriptive information. My experience has been that this information is an excellent basis on which to make a selection. Keep in mind that both the manufacturer's and the dealer's reputations are at stake. The last thing either wants is to mislead you. Your repeat business is dependent upon their ability and willingness to be of assistance. This is particularly true of the dealer specializing in rod-building components.

In examining the statistics and information provided in a catalog, you can tell quite a bit about the blank. The description of action from extra-fast to slow will generally be indicative of the type of taper. Faster actions are made with compound tapers and slower actions with straight tapers. Assuming the blanks are made from the same material, such as high-density fiberglass, you can compare two different blanks of the same length designed to handle the same lure weights.

For example, if you found two 6½-foot spinning blanks, both designated for lure ranges of ⅛–⅜ ounce, you would check the statistics. The first has a butt diameter of .635 inch, a mid diameter of $^{20}/_{64}$ inch, and a size 5½ tip. The second blank has a .555-inch-diameter butt, the same mid diameter of $^{20}/_{64}$ inch, and takes a size 6 tip. Since the first has a comparatively larger butt diameter and a smaller tip diameter, you would expect its action to be faster than the second. You would also reason that the first has to be of a compound-taper design with changes occurring somewhere both in the butt section and in the tip section. This would be borne out by the company's listing for the action—the first is rated extra-fast and the second moderate to slow.

Judging blank action

Once you have the blank in hand you can judge its action by the following process. Hold the blank parallel to the floor, with the butt firmly against your stomach. Start a side-to-side motion with minumum strength and pressure. Then progressively increase the pressure until the maximum flex is attained. By observing the curvature of the blank during this process you will get a fairly accurate

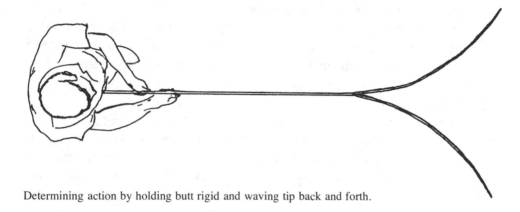

Determining action by holding butt rigid and waving tip back and forth.

picture of the action as we have previously classified it. You will also see how the blank reacts under increasing loads (see drawing).

Some experienced rod builders with an "educated hand" can get an indication of the action by holding the blank by the butt and pointing it up at about a 45° angle. They then press the tip against the ceiling and increase pressure with the hand to put a bend in the blank. The need for an "educated hand" comes into the picture to determine how much pressure to apply to simulate a blank fully loaded with the weight for which it was designed.

A smiliar method used far less today than it once was is the static deflection test. Here a large wall area is employed with two pegs or similar braces that hold the butt on a flat horizontal plane. A fairly heavy weight is then suspended from the tip—this weight is considerably heavier than the weight to be cast by the rod. The arc described by the blank from the weight is supposedly indicative of the action of the rod.

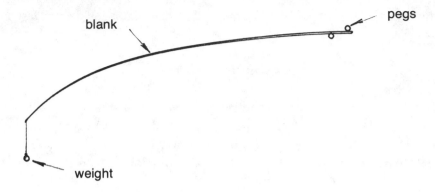

Static deflection test.

Both of these last two static methods are helpful to only certain rod builders. The amount of hand pressure in the first and the amount of weight suspended in the second obviously have to vary with light and heavy rods, and all the subtle gradations in between. It should be kept in mind that both are *static* tests in which the rod is not flexing. Such methods of evaluation will not necessarily indicate how the blank will perform when it is actually used in casting.

The casting property of a rod is really a matter of *dynamics* rather than static mechanics. When a rod is moving, as in casting, it becomes subject to the effects of acceleration, momentum, impact, and even rotation. It could then be described as a beam with cantilevers, or supports, at both ends. The first support is the hand holding the butt. The second is the nodal point near the tip. The nodal point can be easily seen if the rod is set in fairly rapid motion by a loose side-to-side wig-

grip   nodal point

Dynamic properties of blank.

gling of the hand. It is the point where the force applied to the rod is translated into tip motion.

Since dynamics are key, the initially described test of moving the blank from side to side will tell you more about the *action* than will the static methods. The best policy is to use all the tests you feel necessary to help evaluate the many properties of the blank such as strength, stiffness, weight, etc.

Another technique to help evaluate a blank and classify its taper is to locate the "drops." As we have seen, on compound-tapered blanks there will be one or more points where the wall thickness changes rather rapidly because of a change in the angled side of the pattern. By running your fingers along the blank these rapid changes, or "drops," can often be felt. It helps to place a thin piece of cloth (preferably slippery synthetic) over the blank and between thumb and forefinger. This reduces friction from bare fingertips yet will permit the sensitive feel necessary. In and of itself, this test will certainly not tell you how the blank will cast. It will aid in directing your attention to appropriate sections when you perform a dynamic flex test. It can be quite helpful in evaluating whether or not to trim a blank, which will be discussed later.

Choosing a blank taper

Having defined tapers of blanks, we need to understand what generally can be expected in performance from each type, since each has its advantages. Compound tapers are used on extra-fast and fast-action blanks. They will handle a slightly wider range of lure weights than will slower, straight tapers. If too fine a tip is used, there will be a tendency for the tip to vibrate at the end of the cast. Tip vibration causes waves in the line and added friction of the line against the guides. Casting distance will be reduced as a result. As the load, or weight cast, is increased beyond the range for which the blank was designed, the lighter tip breaks up the progressive, uniform bend. Unable to handle the excess weight, the tip "collapses" and becomes useless and a disadvantage in casting. Another aspect of compound tapers is that it is more difficult to predict the results of trimming a blank.

Straight tapers, or tapers very similar, are used on slow- or moderate-action blanks. They form the basis for the progressive class of actions. They are slightly more restrictive in the range of lure weights they will cast. Tip vibration is rarely a problem. While they will reach the upper limit of their ideal lure weight range sooner, the tip will not "collapse," and a lobbing, more slowly timed cast can then be used with fair success. If you are contemplating trimming the blank, the results are easier to predict than with compound tapers.

In the final analysis a blank should be selected for maximum performance with the lure or line weight normally to be cast and at the distance normally cast. It should not be chosen, for example, for maximum casting distance—unless that is the primary function of the rod to be built. Selection should be based on how efficient the rod will be for the work that is to be done by it in the hands of the person who will fish it.

When evaluating blanks from which to build a given rod, knowledgeable builders do not confine themselves to just one classification of blanks. For example, many exceptionally fine ultralight and light spinning rods are built on blanks designated as fly-rod blanks by the manufacturer. In order to get some idea of the general lure weight range of a fly blank used to build a spinning rod, you can refer to the table below. This is simply the conversion derived from the mid-point in the range of acceptable weights for fly lines as designated by the American Fishing Tackle Manufacturers Association (AFTMA). The weights for fly lines are given in grains, which have been converted into ounces at the rate of 437½ grains = 1 ounce.

Fly Line No.	Grains	Ounces
1	60	9/64
2	80	3/16
3	100	7/32
4	120	9/32
5	140	21/64
6	160	3/8
7	185	27/64
8	210	31/64
9	240	35/64
10	280	41/64
11	330	3/4
12	380	7/8

In using the table, treat it as a rough guide only, since manufacturers may adjust their lure- or line-weight rating for a particular action. The tapers used for fly blanks are more often in the general classification of straight tapers and are more likely to have moderate to slow actions. This is what makes certain rod builders prefer them, especially if they cannot locate this type of action in blanks designated for spinning.

In *Fiberblass Rod Making* I made a plea for more moderate, progressive-action blanks. A tremendous number of custom rod builders wrote me that they shared my preference and requested a source. Quite a few mentioned that until they could locate blanks of this type, they were using fly blanks where possible. Finally, this led to our development of the Custom Builder series of blanks in both spinning and fly categories. It was not long before they were among our biggest-selling line of blanks all across the country. Perhaps we will see other manufacturers producing more blanks along the same design lines.

It is, of course, also possible to build fly rods from blanks designated for spinning. In the lighter spinning blanks the action usually tends to be too fast for a fly rod. However, if you encounter a customer who has a strong preference for a stiff, fast-action fly rod, you might consider starting with a spinning blank.

Usually the finished fly rod will be for heavier, saltwater use with fly-line weights of 9 and up. Those blanks that work best for the average caster are of moderate to slow action. Tournament casters, on the other hand, may prefer the faster-action stiffer rod. They have the necessary skill to handle the more critical timing and bring out the full power in the blank. Distance is, of course, their game, not fishing pleasure, and their requirements are therefore different.

Variations from blank to blank

Most custom builders know that no two blanks of the same model will flex or perform exactly the same. The differences will range from very slight to occasionally sizable. This is, of course, why it is necessary for the custom rod crafter to evaluate *each blank* as he builds the rod, making various adjustments to ensure that he ends up with exactly the performance desired. I have received quite a few inquiries about why these variations exist among even the highest-quality blanks. It is often helpful for the custom craftsman who sells his rods to be able to explain something about these differences so that the customer better understands why a custom rod is superior.

First off, the mandrels are longer than the patterns which are wrapped around them. Some patterns for the same blank will be wrapped a bit higher on the mandrel, and others a bit lower. Also, blanks are made slightly longer on each end than the length of the finished size. This makes it easier to handle them through the various steps and controls quality. The ends are then nicely cut to produce the given size. However, the final trimming will not always be in exactly the same place on each blank. For example, one 7-foot blank could be cut with more of the finer tip section while another 7-foot blank of the same model might have been cut with more of the stiffer butt section.

Despite the most modern sophisticated equipment and best-trained operators, there will be slight variations in exactly how tightly the pattern was wrapped around the mandrel. The pressure might not be precisely the same all along the blank, or at all times while this wrapping is performed. Similarly, the pressure can vary slightly as the cellophane is wound in place.

When the blank is sanded, the possibility for yet another small deviation comes into play. The objective is to remove just the excess resin that molded itself to the shape of the cellophane wrap. But as we have seen, a small number of the fibers are also sanded and, in the process, fractured. This can occur the least bit more on one side of the blank than the other, or more at one end than at the other.

On factory-ferruled blanks—or those installed by the custom builder—there are bound to be small differences from one blank to another. If a sleeve-type ferrule is used it consists of a piece of molded material similar to the blank. The molded sleeves themselves can vary a tiny bit, and the section of the blank over which they are fitted can similarly vary. As a result, the sleeve on one blank will fit farther over the male end on one blank than another. This can often be seen on light-colored blanks if the joined rod sections are held against a strong light such as a 100-watt bulb. On internal ferrules there can be similar variables, even among those which are individually precision-ground and hand-fitted.

Keep in mind that all of the deviations discussed are quite small. When accumulated together in the finished blank, it depends upon how many tend to cancel each other and how many amplify each other. Viewed in this perspective, it is easy to see why it is rare indeed for two blanks to be exactly the same.

ALIGNING THE BLANK

Before proceeding further with our exploration of the blank, and with ways to adjust and modify its action, we should first discuss what every custom rod maker does first with a blank: align it. Just about every blank has a ''high side''— a stiffer side. Of the 360 degrees around the circumference of the blank, there is one point running along the axis that is more powerful than any other point on the rod. This is generally referred to as the ''spline,'' or by some as the ''spine,'' of the blank. It can, in some cases, be slight and barely detectable. In others it is quite pronounced. It can be caused by any combination of the production deviations just discussed. Those factors contributing most are (1) the fact that there has to be a point where the pattern overlaps when wrapped on the mandrel, and (2) the subsequent sanding of the blank.

Since the spline is more powerful it must be placed in a position on the finished rod so that it is directly in the plane which the rod moves through in a casting stroke. For example, if a blank is held parallel to the ground with the spline exactly on top, and then the rod is flexed up and down at a 90° angle to the ground, the action of the blank will follow the exact 90° angle. If the blank is held so that the spline is slightly off to one side or the other, and again flexed the same way, the blank's arc will *not* be exactly 90°. Visualize this perpendicular motion to the ground as being the plane through which the angler moves the rod when casting. You can see that if the spline is off to one side, the rod will cast slightly off-center. In some cases there will also be a tendency for the rod to twist as it moves through the casting plane.

If we repeat the above exercise, but this time hold the blank so the spline is exactly on the bottom, we will find that the action of the blank will again describe an exact 90°. Thus, there are really *two positions,* exactly opposite each other, in which the spline can be placed relative to the casting plane, and the rod will still cast accurately. In both cases, the spline is aligned exactly with the plane the rod moves through when a cast is made.

This makes it necessary to align the blank so that when the guides and handle are mounted, the fisherman will automatically move the rod through a casting plane that will be in line with the spline. This is the principle involved in splining a rod, or aligning it. We will return to it later. First, let's examine ways to locate the spline.

Keep in mind that because of production variables, in some cases the spline will be quite pronounced, and therefore will have a greater effect on casting accuracy. This will be most noticeable in lighter rods and in longer rods. In other cases the spline will be less pronounced, and harder to locate. It also follows that in those cases it will have less effect on casting. So, if after checking a blank you cannot locate the spline, don't worry about it. You have an "accidentally perfect" blank.

Locating the spline

The method I find the best to locate the spline is to hold the blank so the butt rests on a smooth surface and the blank is inclined at about a 45° angle. Support the blank toward the tip with the open palm of the left hand. Place the right hand, palm down, on the blank at a point about halfway between your left hand and the butt. Press down with the right hand in order to flex the rod slightly, and feel some resistance against your right hand. Now, roll the blank with your right

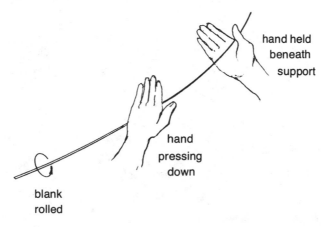

Locating spline.

hand. As you do, you will find a point where the rod seems to jump or produce increased resistance against your right hand. That point is the spline. A variation of this method is to use a stool or countertop of a convenient height to support the tip section of the blank. The butt is placed on a smooth floor so that the blank is at about 45°. The blank is then rolled with the right hand as above (see drawing).

The blank should be marked with a line along the spline. On light-colored blanks a grease pencil or dark-colored crayon can be used. On dark blanks, use a yellow or white crayon. I have a habit of checking for the spline three times to make sure I am as accurate as possible. If you want a mark that will not be inadvertently rubbed off, use a very narrow ($^1/_{16}$-inch or less) strip of masking tape over the crayon mark.

It should be mentioned that when using the above method, the butt end should be cleanly cut at a right angle. Most blanks are. Some, however, have not been trimmed at the factory, and it is expected that the custom builder will do so. Make the cut with a fine-tooth saw, then square the cut with a coarse, flat bastard file.

Another method of locating the spline is to hold the rod by the very tip in the right hand. The left hand is held at a right angle to the floor with fingers straight and joined. (The position of the hand is similar to that in a karate chop made down toward the floor.) The blank is rested on the straight edge along the top of the index finger. The point along the blank where the left-hand support is placed is dependent upon the length and weight of the blank. It will be anywhere from 4 to 18 inches from the tip—close enough to put a good bend in the blank, but not so close as to risk breaking or straining the blank from the weight put on the fragile tip. Now, with the blank supported but flexed, twist the tip in your right hand so that it rolls along the top of the left hand. The butt of the rod

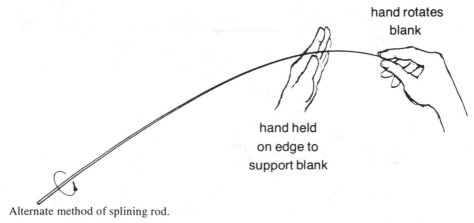

hand rotates
blank

hand held
on edge to
support blank

Alternate method of splining rod.

will move lower toward the floor at the weakest point of the blank. It will be highest from the floor at the strongest point—the spline (see drawing).

A setup for a static deflection test, as described previously, can also be used to locate the spline. The blank is supported parallel to the floor against a large wall. It can be held in place at the butt by two pegs a few inches apart. The one toward the tip is beneath the blank, and the one toward the butt is on top of the blank. A tip-top will have to be temporarily mounted with ferrule cement so that a heavy enough weight can be suspended from the tip to put a good substantial bend in the blank. Hang the weight on a loop of string so it can rotate against the tip-top tube. Again, the rod is slowly rotated to determine the strongest side of the blank. As in the previous method, the end (this time the tip) will be lowest at the weakest point, and highest at the strongest point—the spline.

Some rod builders have made test stands that hold the blank vertically. A pressure-sensitive device is placed against the tip and the blank is rotated slowly in place as it rests in the butt support. For practical reasons this arrangement is most applicable to shorter blanks such as those for casting and spinning rods. When the greatest amount of pressure is recorded, that is the spline. I have never used one of these test stands, but I have always suspected that there is the chance that the pressure registered could just as likely come from any curvature in the blank as from the resistance of the spline. I feel this is particularly true of those setups where the pressure-sensing plate is placed lightly against the blank when it is straight and not flexed. Blank curvature frequently follows the spline—but not always. I therefore prefer the other methods, particularly the one described first.

Positioning guides and reel seat

Having located and marked the spline, we need to discuss the alignment of the blank. This is the proper position of the guides, and fixed reel seat if one is to be used, relative to the spline. Remember the principle is to have the spline be in line with the movement of the rod as it passes through the casting plane.

On fly and spinning rods, the angler holds the rod with the guides on the underside of the blank. When he casts, the guides are in line with the casting plane. Therefore, the guides can be mounted either directly on the spline or on the exact opposite side, 180° around the blank. As we determined earlier, both of these points are in line with the casting plane. Since most rods have some natural curvature, and are not perfectly straight, we determine whether to use the spline or the point exactly opposite it by checking the curvature. Sight along the rod while rotating it to see in which direction it curves. Select the spline or the point opposite it (180° around the blank) *closest* to the convex (outside) of the curve for fly and spinning rods. Placing the guides on the convex side helps to straighten the blank. Notice we said to select either of the two points *closest* to the convex side of the curve. If one of those happens to fall in line with the curve, well and good. If not, pick the *closest*. Obviously, if the blank curves off to the side precisely midway between the spline or the point opposite it, it does not matter which we select. You will, however, rarely find this to be the case.

On casting rods, alignment depends upon how the person that fishes the rod holds it when he casts. Supposedly, the proper way to hold a casting rod is not with the reel and guides directly on top. Instead, they face to the side—90° to the left for a right-handed caster. In that situation the guides are *not* in line with the casting plane. They are at right angles to it, 90° to the left. If we want the spline and the point opposite it to be in line with the casting plane, we need to mount the guides 90° to the spline. This is exactly halfway between the spline and the point opposite it on the blank. Or, to put it another way, the spline should face the water.

Despite what is supposed to be the ''proper'' way to hold a casting rod when casting, many fishermen hold the rod so that the reel *is* on top. If the person for whom the rod is being built casts in this manner, then the guides will be in line with the casting plane. In that case the blank should be aligned, and the guides placed on the side closest to the *concave* side. The angler's casting style must be determined before the rod is built. This is just another example of why a custom rod is superior to a factory rod.

Trolling rods are not used for casting, hence alignment relative to the casting plane is of no concern. The preferred method is to mount the guides directly on the spline. The guides sit on top of the rod, and this places the strongest part of the rod, the spline, on top. The extra strength and resistance of the blank in this position helps fight the pull of the trolled lure, as well as the fish. If curvature follows the spline, the tip will be pointing up, toward the angler.

MODIFYING THE BLANK

Despite the large variety of blanks available, it will not always be possible to locate exactly the perfect one to fit either the fishing situation or the desires of the angler. However, the knowledgeable custom rod builder is able to modify or alter an available blank. This skill is certainly at the very heart of custom rod work.

One method of changing the performance characteristics of a blank is by trimming it from the butt, the tip, or both ends. In fact, this technique is often used by blank and rod manufacturers. To make two different rods, they may actually trim one blank, or accomplish the same thing by merely shortening the same pattern used on the same mandrel.

Let's first examine what happens when the rod builder removes some of the tip of a blank. Regardless of the amount removed, the blank will always become stiffer. The effect is that the blank will no longer cast as light a lure weight or line as it did originally. Depending upon the strength of the butt section, it may also handle a heavier lure weight. However, if the butt section is not strong enough the maximum weight will remain the same, but the minimum will increase. For example, a blank that originally handled ½ to 1 ounce may, after trimming the tip, handle ¾ ounce to 1¼ ounces. However, if the butt is not strong enough, removal of the same length from the tip may result in a blank that will cast ¾ to only 1 ounce.

The amount or length removed from the tip obviously determines the degree of the effect. On a straight taper, the stiffening is fairly proportional. The removal of each inch from the tip will make the blank that much more stiff in an even geometric progression. On the other hand, trimming a compound taper may produce rather sudden and dramatic changes. Regardless of the taper it is best to remove only small increments at a time, and to test the blank by casting with guides temporarily attached. Careful notes will enable you to know in the future just what the effects will be on the action of that particular blank. They will also be an aid if you ever decide to trim similar blanks.

The rather sudden changes in action occurring when trimming compound tapers result from the rapid changes in wall thickness over a short area. In an extra-fast-action blank we have, in effect, a stiff blank except for the very tip, which has thinner walls and is comparatively limber. If half of the limber section is removed, it could be comparable to cutting off a much longer length from a straight taper. If the amount trimmed comprises *all* of the limber section, we are left with an entirely different blank—one which is stiff over its entire length. Its use as a casting instrument will change tremendously.

When you are contemplating cutting back the tip of a compound-tapered blank, it is best to locate the "drop" as previously mentioned. If you cannot be certain from feeling along the blank, use a calipers or micrometer and measure at 1-inch intervals. Record each measurement so you can determine at just what point the taper of the tip changes. While exact measurements would only be needed of the tip section itself, it is a good practice to feel the entire blank for the location of other "drops." When you have an understanding of the entire taper you will be better able to predict the results of any trimming.

Thanks to the excellence of today's factory-installed ferrules, most custom rod builders now work with these two-piece blanks. They are a tremendous improvement over the ferrules available only a few years ago. Additionally, the designers of quality blanks take into account the small resistance of the finest ferrules and, by small adjustments in taper, attain a blank which is remarkably similar to the feel of a comparable one-piece rod. When you are trimming a factory-ferruled blank you must remember that there is a certain amount of resistance to bending at the ferrule, and that this can be used creatively by the custom builder. When only the tip is cut back, the location of the ferrule is moved toward the tip. The stiffening of the rod is thus the combined total of that from removal of tip material, plus advancing the ferrule resistance closer to the tip. When only the butt is trimmed, the opposite is true. The position of the ferrule is moved closer to the hand and there results a proportionately longer, more limber tip section.

Let's turn our attention now to the other effects of trimming the butt. The first thing to keep in mind is that no matter how much of the butt is cut off, it will not lower the ideal lure-weight range. Varying amounts of stiffness will be removed from the butt of the rod, but the range of lure weights or fly-line weights is a function of the tip section—so they will remain essentially unchanged.

The removal of butt material will slow the action of the rod if no trimming is done to the tip. Simple arithmetic illustrates this. If we start with an extra-fast 8-foot fly-rod blank, the top 25%, or top 2 feet, does most of the bending. Cut 1 foot from the butt and the bending occurs over the same 2 feet of the tip section. However, the 2 feet is now 29% of the resultant 7-foot rod. This is an action midway between extra-fast (25%) and fast (33%).

The example is for illustrative purposes only. To work out exactly the blank would have to be one-piece and with a straight taper its entire length. If it were factory-ferruled, the final action would be somewhat slower, since the resistance of the ferrule was lowered along the blank. If it were a compound taper, the action might be slowed more *or* less depending upon the pattern used to make the blank.

Again we encounter the predictability of trimming a blank, this time from the butt. The same general guidelines can be applied, but to the effect on *action,* not lure-weight range. On a straight taper the effect on action will be fairly proportional to the amount of material removed. On a compound taper it will depend upon where the "drops" are located. For example, a blank built with a reinforced lower butt section will change considerably when the butt is trimmed. As in cutting back the tip, if too much is removed for the design of the blank, its casting characteristics cannot only be altered drastically, but it can be rendered useless as a casting instrument. The rule in trimming, then, is to first evaluate the blank carefully, think through the probable results, and remove material in small increments, checking performance along the way.

Keep in mind that we are examining techniques to alter a blank when there is not a ''stock'' blank available to meet our specific needs. We are not advocating trimming all blanks, or even suggesting that many of the blanks with which we work need to be trimmed. It is comparable to surgery in the practice of medicine and, in similar fashion, is used only when other techniques will not effect a cure.

Some of the more common uses for cutting back certain blanks include the following situations. Surf-fishing conditions vary greatly along our coasts, sometimes within rather short distances. In some areas tidal flow and currents are moderate and less sinker weight is needed to hold bottom. In other areas, quite heavy sinkers must be used. Similarly, the weight of the bait required can vary greatly. Or, one fisherman prefers a stiffer rod to deliver and work his artificials in the surf compared to another angler fishing the same area. When a stiffer rod, or one to handle heavier weights, is required, it is common for the custom maker of surf rods to cut back the tip of fairly straight-tapered blanks. Lamiglas surf blanks have long been very popular on the Northeast Coast. The bulk of Lamiglas sales to this part of the country is made up primarily of only three of the many Lamiglas models. Each is essentially a straight-taper design, and all are 11½ feet in length. However, the different rods built from these few blanks is amazing. Lengths range from 9 feet to 11½ feet, and most, but not all, of the trimming is done from the tip.

There is a school of freshwater anglers who use a technique of relatively high-speed trolling for locating the fish. Once fish are located, they switch to casting with spinning or plug-casting rods. Trolling at high speed requires a stiff rod, preferably fairly short. Some of the best tools for this purpose are made by cutting back the tip of compound-tapered casting blanks designed for heavy lure weights. Other rod builders start with IGFA trolling blanks and trim the butts.

Some muskie fishermen, as well as certain saltwater anglers, cast large whole baits. The stiff rod needed for this kind of casting is frequently built by cutting back the tip of a blank with a strong butt section. The popularity of revolving-spool casting tackle has spread from freshwater bassing to saltwater in many areas. Longer rods are preferred than those used in fresh water, and they are crafted by trimming the butts of saltwater blanks.

Custom builders of fly rods sometimes select a factory-ferruled blank of moderate to fast action in a length longer than the rod to be built. They then remove the desired length from the butt. The finished rod is of slightly slower action and has a different feel in hand because of the comparatively longer tip section. Incidentally, this technique of building rods with tip sections longer than the butt sections has been in use for many years. Over sixty years ago split-cane casting rods were customarily made with the tip half again as long as the butt, and three-piece fly rods had a butt shorter than the mid or tip sections.

In recent years factory rods have almost all been center-ferruled. One of the main reasons has been concern over breakage of a longer tip section in transit and storage, not while fishing. If you or your customer share this concern, but prefer a rod with a longer tip, you can solve the problem by building a traveling extension for the butt. This can be of any material, such as wood dowel, or a piece from an old rod or blank. Size the diameter at one end so it fits the ferrule on the butt section, and make it long enough so when combined with the butt section it is equal in length to the tip section. When the rod is taken apart after fishing, the butt section and extension are placed together in one pocket of the rod bag. The tip section, in the other rod bag pocket, is then protected over its entire length.

Modifying effects of guides

There are a number of techniques for modifying the action that involve the guides. Since they are all interrelated, we will first list the factors, then discuss the general effects upon action of each, and finally examine how they can be used in various combinations to achieve a desired result. They are:
1. The weight of the guides and tip-top
2. The resistance to bending the guide imparts to the blank
3. The length of the guide feet
4. The length of the wraps holding the guides

It is important to first note that the lighter the blank being used, the more pronounced will be the effect of each of the above. If an ultralight rod is being built, each of these variables can materially alter the action. On the other hand, a saltwater blank for heavy lure weights will be considerably less affected by each variable.

The weight of the guides and tip-top. The basic effect here is that the heavier the guides and tip-top, the more the action of the blank will be slowed. If you find the action of a certain blank too fast, use heavier guides and tip-top to slow it down. Depending upon the length of the rod, you might even consider adding one or two more guides than usual in order to add more weight. If doing so, add them at the tip end of the rod where they will have the most effect. In unusual situations a rod builder could even use an oversize or heavier tip-top to slow the action.

On the other side of the guide-weight coin, the lighter the guides and tip-top, the more rapid will be the rate of recoil of the blank. So, to keep the action of a blank as fast as possible, use the lightest guides, and especially the lightest tip-top, available. To further reduce weight, use as few guides as you can to adequately distribute the stress along the blank. Also, use a thin coating of a wrapping finish that is light in weight, since a thick, heavy finish adds a surprising amount of weight to a light rod.

The remaining three of the above four factors deal primarily with adding *stiffness* to the blank. As we all know, the guides are placed progressively closer together toward the tip of the rod to distribute stress properly over the increasingly lighter and more limber tip. Thus, most of the guides will be on the top one-third of the blank—and that is the section that does most of the bending in casting. The effect of the following three factors will, then, be primarily on the tip section.

The resistance to bending the guide imparts to the blank. Later, in the chapter on guides, we will classify guides by their weight and also by the degree of resistance they impart to the free flexing of the rod. Here, we want to explore the general effect. For example, a single foot guide offers the least resistance to the bending or flexing of the blank. The finished rod will flex most like the bare blank. By contrast, a guide of high resistance, such as a rigid type of two-footed guide, will add stiffness to the tip section of the blank. Try to keep the weight factor out of your mind as you visualize this effect. You must compare guides of equal weight. As stiffness is added to the blank, particularly at the tip, the rod will assume a different configuration, or shape, in casting the same weight.

The length of the guide feet. Guides are wrapped tightly in place and the feet are held securely against the blank. In effect, each guide is like a splint at that point of the rod. The longer the feet of the particular guide used, the greater the length of the blank that is restricted from freely bending. If we want to reduce the stiffening effect we would use guides with the shortest possible feet, or grind the feet shorter. On the other hand, if we wanted to add stiffness to the blank, we would choose guides with longer feet.

The length of the wraps holding the guides. When a hollow blank flexes it does not stay perfectly round. There is tension across the top of the bent section and compression on the bottom. The blank assumes a slightly oval configuration when it is fully loaded. If a thread wrap is made along a section of the blank, then covered with wrapping finish, it has practically the same effect as adding to the wall thickness of the blank. As we have seen earlier, the thickness of the wall at any given point determines its stiffness at that point, and therefore the overall action. The thread wrap, by adding considerable hoop strength to the blank, helps keep it from becoming oval—thus stiffening it. The longer the wrap beyond the end of the guide feet, the more stiffness will be added. The shorter the wrap, the less stiff and more free-flexing will be the rod.

Using guides to stiffen action

Since the last three factors just listed affect the stiffening of the blank, primarily the tip section, let's examine just how they can be used to modify the action. We would add *maximum stiffness* if we used (1) the lightest possible guides, (2) guides of the most rigid two-foot construction, (3) guides with the longest available guide feet, and (4) considerably longer guide wraps than needed just to hold the guides in place. This is a more or less theoretical situation, since it would be difficult to locate a type of guide that would both be as light as possible, yet be constructed of rigid two-foot construction and have extra long feet. About the lightest two-footed guide with any degree of rigidity in its construction is the Fuji Model BSHG. Both Foulproof and snake guides (applicable only for fly rods) are lighter, but lack rigidity. The length of the feet on Fuji BSHG guides is also not longer than normal. The point is that we will rarely be able to combine all four factors for their maximum effect. Nevertheless, we could stiffen a light rod considerably—if that was our objective—by applying the principle of each to the extent possible. For example, on a light spinning rod we would use the Fuji BSHG guides and make the wraps just as long as possible without destroying the appearance of the finished rod.

While we are exploring the methods of making a rod more stiff, let's examine an actual creative example. I know of a custom rod builder who builds unique fly rods on compound-tapered fast-action blanks. He likes all aspects of the blanks except the tip-oriented action. So what he does is take a blank designed for a certain weight fly line and add more than the usual number of light-weight snake guides with the longest feet he can find. The extra guides are added on the tip section. The length of his wraps, instead of being proportionate to the size of each guide, *increases* toward the tip. The guides near the tip have the longest wraps, while those at the butt end have the shortest wraps. What he has done is to restructure the action of the fast-tip blank. No longer is the action confined primarily to the tip. His objective is to spread out and shift the flexing lower on the rod, and to have the last 1 or 2 feet next to the tip-top remain comparatively stiff. To achieve this action it is generally necessary to use a fly line one size heavier on his rods. He plans for this by simply starting with a blank designated for one size lighter line than is to be cast with the finished rod. If he is building a rod for a 6-weight line, he uses a blank designated for a 5-weight line. He, and his customers, maintain that there is considerably less tip vibration at the end of the cast, and that line shoots more easily. He compares the stiffer tip section to a rifle barrel through which the line is shot with greater accuracy and distance. Probably not all fly fishermen would agree, but for those whose styles of casting it fits, the action is a great improvement over available factory rods.

It might be helpful here to examine the development of this same builder's rods when one of the factors we have been discussing is changed. For quite a time after the Fuji single-foot fly guide first came on the market, he had no interest in it because it did not offer the resistance he desired on his rods. As the advantages of this guide were discovered by custom builders and fishermen, he turned his attention to it, attempting to see if somehow it could be worked into his technique. Since his rods never had a traditional appearance, he was not limited in his approach. As of this writing, he has found that on light blanks for lightweight lines, he can utilize the single-foot guide if he makes his wraps the same length as he did with snake guides, but as one long single wrap instead of two individual wraps. He therefore wraps these guides up over the guide foot and, rather than end the wrap at the guide ring, continues wrapping over the blank alone for an equal distance. He only has one guide foot instead of two for resistance on the blank, but this has largely been offset by (1) the length of the single, solid wrap, (2) the fact that snake guides were certainly not the most rigid guides in the first place, and (3) the better shooting qualities of the O-shape of the Fuji guide and its lower coefficient of friction versus the U-shape of the snake guide. This craftsman understands the factors that affect rod action and uses them creatively.

Let's take another case of stiffening the tip section, but one where it is desired to move more of the bending even lower on the blank, to the middle of the butt section. This type of action is desired by a certain few anglers on spinning and fly rods. For this purpose it would be best to select a blank of fairly straight taper with a tip size of medium to slightly larger diameter. Stiffness could again be given the tip by using available combinations of long wraps and fairly rigid guides. However, here we want to add slightly more weight to the tip section to slow its rate of recoil and force the bending lower on the blank. Thus, for the blank selected, we would use a bit more guide weight on the tip section. When casting the finished rod we will find that to a certain degree we are casting the weight of the tip section itself. This often enables this combination to handle lure or fly-line weights a fraction lower than that for which the blank is designated, and can be useful for that purpose alone.

A word of caution about developing this type of action in a rod. If you carry it too far by adding too much weight on the tip section while proportionately stiffening it, a "hinge" type of action will result. This occurs when practically all of the bending is forced into a small area along the lower part of the blank. This point on the blank acts much like the hinge on a door. Needless to say, it then becomes a poor casting instrument. Too much stress is also being confined to a small area of the blank, and that section will "soften" or grow weaker with use.

As of this writing, we are considering having made for us a special series of fly blanks to effect this particular action. In essence we are testing what could be called a "reverse taper" blank. The external diameter of the blank will retain a normal (or near-normal) taper. But the wall thickness will increase rather than decrease from a point low on the blank toward the tip. This will be accomplished by the shape of the pattern and the design of the mandrel. There will be more weight at the tip of the rod than usual, producing a feel in hand comparable to many bamboo rods. Flex will be greater lower on the blank (without a "hinge" effect) and in casting. The angler will, to a certain degree, be casting the weight of the tip. If all works out as hoped for, the blanks will cast a wider range of fly-line weights, particularly at the lower end of the scale. Our tests and experiments are not yet complete.

Using guides to soften action

We have been discussing the application of our four factors relating to guides for the purpose of stiffening the blank. Let's now look on the other side of the ledger and see how they might be applied to make a blank more flexible. If we found the blank with which we were working to be stiffer than desired, we could make it flex more and slow the action by (1) using heavy guides and tip-top, (2) selecting guides that offered the least resistance to bending, (3) grinding the guide as short as practical, and (4) using short wraps. Here again we are faced with a situation where we are dealing with the theoretical maximum effect, since most heavy guides are quite rigid in construction while the guides that offer the least resistance to bending are also light.

We would have to evaluate the blank and make a compromise on the weight and rigidity factors, then use each of the other factors to maximum advantage. On a very light blank we might gain sufficient weight with the SP series of Foulproof guides, their heaviest series for this purpose. The feet could be ground just a bit shorter and the guide wraps kept short. We definitely would use a heavier tip-top than the Foulproof model. If we preferred aluminum-oxide ceramic guides, the Fuji Model NHG (or BNHG) might be enough weight, or we could go to the heavier American-made wire-frame ceramics. These are certainly not the only possibilities for guides, just illustrations. The objective would be to add as much weight as needed for the blank, and the desired slower action, without using a very restrictive guide.

In order to keep the foregoing discussion in proper perspective, remember these are techniques for using guides to *modify* or change the action of a given blank. This is a change away from the normal action that was built into the blank by the manufacturer. I do not mean to imply that such modification or change is necessary or even desirable. The best solution to building a rod with a certain action is to build it on a blank which already possesses that action. Guides can then be selected and wrapped on a more normal basis to complement the blank.

If a custom rod builder understands the principles involved in using guides and length of wraps, he can tune the action of a blank to his desires, or those of his customer. Initially it will require some experimenting. The effect of guide weight alone can be roughly determined by taping the guides and tip-top to the blank. This is best done after the handle is completed, since the feel of the smaller-diameter bare blank in the hand can be deceiving. For a more precise evaluation, the guides would have to be wrapped on and left unfinished for the testing. To develop skill in predicting results beforehand, it is suggested that you first think the problem through and make a note of your estimate of the effect. Then, after running your test, record the results. If you were off your mark, again estimate the corrective steps, run your tests, and record them. These notes will be of great help in the future and you will master the process much more quickly.

COUNTERBALANCING

Counterbalancing is not a technique for actually modifying the action of a blank, but it will change the feel of the rod in the caster's hand. Counterbalancing is the addition of weight at the extreme butt end of the rod in order to shift rearward the point where the rod could be balanced on a fulcrum. Most spinning and fly rods, other than the shorter ultralights, will feel slightly tip-heavy in the hand even with the reel mounted. Many anglers maintain that just a bit of tip weight is a desirable help in casting, since it adds an element of feel and promotes better timing. On some rods, however, the tip weight is too heavy and will tire the top of the caster's wrist in a long period of fishing. It is not the total weight of rod and reel that tires a fisherman—rather it is the imbalance of too heavy a tip that exerts a pull on the forward cast and especially during the retrieve. This type of rod should be counterbalanced.

Many fishermen have a preference for a certain balance in a rod. A person casts best and enjoys his fishing most when a rod possesses the perfect balance *for him*. Except by pure chance, he will not find this balance in a factory rod. The custom rod maker can build any balance into a rod to exactly fit the desires of the person who will fish it. This is just another one of the many examples of why a custom-built rod is superior.

We should note here that on fly rods, while an angler may definitely have a preference for where the balance point is located, this is generally interpreted by him to be the balance when he is simply holding the rod with reel mounted. In actual fishing, the balance point shifts. This is due to, and dependent upon, the amount of fly line that is out beyond the tip-top of the rod. Fly line has weight. After all, that is what is being cast. When a long length of weight-forward line is past the guides, that weight has been *subtracted* from the reel weight and *added* to the tip weight.

My own experience has been that on fly rods, where the reel is located below or behind the hand on the grip, balance does appear to affect the apparent action of the rod. A rod that is heavy in the butt, and this includes the weight of the reel used, will have a slightly slower action because of the pendulum effect of the weight behind the hand. A rod with the balance point farther up on the rod will appear to liven up the rod's response.

Small pieces of any heavy material can be glued inside the very butt of the blank. For years many of us used bits of lead, slugs from shooting ranges, etc. Then RodCrafter Dave Hartranft introduced us to the perfect material, Shape-A-Wate. This is a moldable putty consisting of 90% lead. It is made for adding small amounts of weight to lures and flies, and is, incidentally, ideal for this purpose.

To counterbalance a rod, fit, but do not glue, the butt cap, butt plate, or closed-end fly-reel seat to the handle assembly until after all other work on the rod, including the finishing of the wraps, has been completed. Mount the reel to be used. Pinch off what you estimate to be the correct amount of Shape-A-Wate and lay it along the top of the butt end. Now, check the balance. If the tip feels too light, remove some of the Shape-A-Wate. If the tip is still too heavy, add another piece. Don't worry about accumulating small pieces of the lead putty. It never gets hard and can be rejoined just like modeling clay. When you have the right amount of weight, roll it into a tube or ball slightly larger than the inside diameter of the blank butt. Place some epoxy glue well up inside the blank, push in the Shape-A-Wate, and glue on the butt cap. Set the rod vertically overnight. The epoxy will run down the inside of the blank, forming a seal to hold the putty in place permanently.

MOUNTING BUTT FERRULES

Ask a bass fisherman what he'd most likely want improved on his favorite rod and he'll probably answer, "The butt ferrule." In the vast majority of cases, when a casting rod breaks it does so at this stress point. The assembly of most factory-made rods does not permit the time necessary to add additional strength

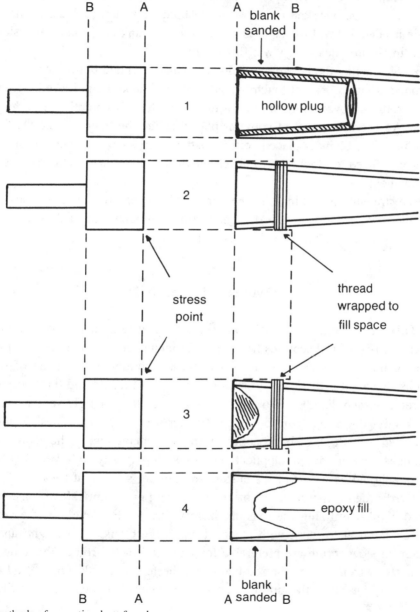

Four methods of mounting butt ferrules.

at this critical point. The custom rod builder can improve on the mounting of butt ferrules in a number of ways. RodCrafter Ken Lane summarized the various methods used by custom men. In reviewing these, it will help to view the accompanying drawing.

1. Seat #1 requires sanding off the bottom of the blank to level the taper. This slightly weakened wall section is then reinforced with a hollow or solid wood plug extending beyond the lip of the ferrule.

2. This is perhaps the most popular technique. A narrow band of thread of the size needed to level the taper is wound on the blank at a point just inside the ferrule lip. It provides a tight yet flexible fit.

3. This is like the above but includes a small rounded button plug of wood. The rounded plug does not touch the sides of the blank. Its purpose is to ensure that the round-to-oval configuration of the blank doesn't come loose at the butt.

4. An excess amount of epoxy is placed inside the blank before the ferrule is mounted. The blank is placed vertical as the epoxy curves. Note that the blank has been sanded at the butt to level the taper, and that the epoxy acts as reinforcement.

The strength needed in all of these installations requires a quality epoxy glue —not the five-minute variety. After the ferrule is mounted on each method, tape the blank vertically along a wall or corner.

COMPACT PACK ROD

There are a number of pack-rod blanks already ferruled. However, most all of these consist of rod sections from 18 to 22 inches in length. These are fine for attaching outside a pack, but many backpackers prefer a rod made of shorter sections. RodCrafter F. Yates Borden designed a 6-foot fly rod that meets these requirements and handles a 6 or 7 weight line. It is a lightweight rod with surprisingly good action considering the five ferrules needed. It is designed for the small fish which the backpacker normally encounters. The construction techniques have numerous applications in developing any lightweight sectional rod, and should be a part of the custom rod builder's "bag of tricks."

Dr. Borden constructed his original rod from two identical two-piece 6-foot fly rod blanks, utilizing the existing factory ferrule. However, it is easier and more economical to work with identical one-piece blanks. A straight taper and medium to slow action are preferable for a multi-ferruled rod of this type.

Select which will be the rod blank and the ferrule blank. On the rod blank, mark the spline from the tip at 6 inches, 18 inches, 30 inches, 42 inches, 54

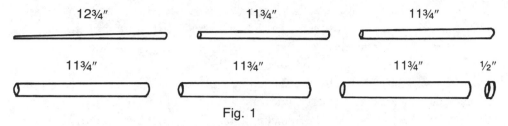

Fig. 1

Rod blank cut into sections. Lengths are shown, plus ½″ waste.

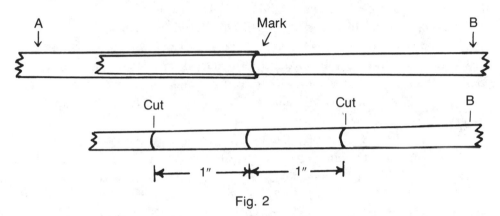

Fig. 2

Making ferrule: Insert female blank (B) into rod blank (A) for snug fit. Mark where ferrule blank emerges. Measure 1″ on each side of mark and cut.

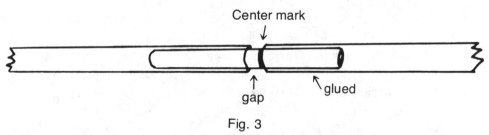

Fig. 3

Ferrule construction. Ferrule is glued into lower section of rod blank. Gap of $^{1}/_{16}″$ to $^{1}/_{8}″$ is made by filing bottom of tip section of rod blank.

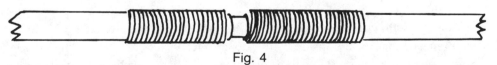

Fig. 4

Ferrule wrapped with size "A" thread for reinforcement.

inches, and 66 inches. Use masking tape and make a permanent mark on the tape. This must be done at this time since the spline cannot be determined once the sections are cut. The marks must withstand handling until the guides are positioned near the end of the construction.

Still working with the blank selected for the rod, cut it into sections. In order to have each finished section the same length, including ferrule, proceed from the tip and cut the first section 12¾ inches long. Each of the succeeding sections should be 11¾ inches long. You will end up with a "waste piece" ½ inch long at the butt end of the blank (See Fig. 1). Sand the carefully cut surfaces square and smooth. This must be done before gluing the ferrules in place.

Turn now to the other blank from which the ferrules will be constructed. Five internal, or inside-fitting ferrules must be made. They will each consist of a section of the hollow fiberglass blank. For a normal, heavier rod these would be considered rather fragile ferrules. However, for the ultra light pack rod designed for small fish they will prove equal to the task. Additionally they will help preserve the action.

Each ferrule will be approximately 2 inches in length; 1 inch will be glued inside the blank and the other inch will project from the rod section forming the internal ferrule. Starting with the tip section of the rod blank, insert the tip section of the ferrule blank. Insert until the fit is quite snug. Mark the point on the ferrule blank where it emerges from inside the rod blank (See Fig. 2).

Remove the ferrule blank from inside the rod blank. Measure 1 inch in each direction from the previously made mark, and cut the ferrule blank at these second marks for a 2 inch ferrule. Using sandpaper, gently round just the very edge of each end of the resulting ferrule. This internal ferrule will have a mark in the center which will be of importance in the subsequent gluing. Proceed down the rod blank in exactly the same manner in order to form the other four ferrules. On the last ferrule you might want to make it a bit longer—say 4 inches—for added reinforcement. In that case, two inches would then be glued into the butt section.

One half of each ferrule will be glued into the lower section of the rod blank. A plug will project out the end which will provide a detachable joint inside the tip-most section of the finished rod. To glue each ferrule in place, *lightly* sand the finish on the half *below* the previously made center mark. This will provide a stronger glue bond. *Do not sand the upper half of the ferrule* since that will destroy the fit.

Smear a light coat of epoxy on the lower half of the ferrule. Also coat a bit more than one inch of the inside of the upper end of the rod section. Insert the ferrule from the *opposite* end (the larger end) of the rod section. Using an old piece of blank, wood dowel, or steel rod, push the ferrule up inside the rod section until it emerges from the upper end. Rotate the ferrule to spread the glue and carefully align your center mark on the ferrule at the point where it just emerges from inside the blank (See Fig. 3). Dampen a rag with epoxy thinner and carefully remove all glue from the projecting plug portion of the ferrule.

After the epoxy has cured, check each ferrule for a good snug fit. You may find that some joints are too loose. To tighten a joint, file a bit off the female (tip) section of the rod blank. A small gap ($^{1}/_{16}$ to $^{1}/_{8}$ inch) should exist between rod sections to allow for future wear. Apply a wrap over both tip and butt sections of each ferrule joint for reinforcement. If you want the tip section of the rod exactly the same length as the others, cut off about ¼ inch before mounting the tip-top. Proceed with building the rod as you would with any blank.

CUTTING BLANKS

There are various rod-building processes that require cutting or trimming blanks. Obviously, we want a clean, straight cut with no splinters. Let's examine some of the methods that can be used. A fine-tooth saw such as an X-Acto miter saw works quite well. There is even a small matching miter box available. Of course, you can make your own from wood or a length of aluminum I-beam. A hack saw can also be used, particularly on heavier blanks. It is recommended that you first wrap the blank with a piece of masking tape to prevent splintering. Some people find it easiest to make the cut through one wall, then rotate the blank as they progressively cut through the wall around the blank. On lighter blanks, or small diameters, a jeweler's saw or fine-tooth coping saw can be used in the same manner.

Another technique is to use a pipe cutter of the type used to cut copper pipe and tubing. It clamps around the blank and a round cutting wheel is fed into the blank as the tool is rotated. Do not feed the cutting wheel too rapidly or internal splintering will occur. The pipe cutter will work well except where there is a sharp taper in a blank.

Regardless of the cutting tool used, the cut should be squared with a file. Use a flat bastard file. You will find that coarse works better than fine. Depending on the purpose for the cut, it is also a good idea to lightly round the edge with sandpaper.

TWO

Glues and Gluing

The single most important ingredient of a well-made custom rod is not any of the components, but the manner in which it is assembled. While this is not a book on fishing, allow me to illustrate with a personal story.

Some years ago I built a two-handed spinning rod, the design of which particularly pleased me. Each of the cork grips was inlaid with a ½-inch walnut trim ring faced with a pair of ⅛-inch white plastic rings. The brown-and-white theme was repeated in the wraps on the gold blank. A few years ago, just before a fishing trip, I decided to replace the guides with aluminum-oxide ceramics. Since I always liked the handle assembly, and it seemed sound, I outdid myself on the new wraps, especially the decorative butt wrap.

The trip was to the Caribbean coast of the Yucatán Peninsula in Mexico. While there, we discovered the sailfishing was hitting its seasonal peak in the channel between the island of Cozumel and the mainland.

We decided to give it a try, and it was understood that I would try casting to my share of any fish we teased within range. I was excited about the prospects and hoped to give my refurbished spinning rod a workout.

As we were told, the fish were there, and finally after a number of unsuccessful attempts, I did get a hookup. The battle started with those breathtaking leaps and tailwalks for which sails are noted. The carefully set drag on my reel was working smoothly, and I was in my glory. What could be better—a beautiful fish and a beautiful custom rod of my own craftsmanship. While the finish was still some time away, I could already visualize a color photo of the fish and me with my rod.

A few minutes later my ego received a jolt. The cork foregrip so lovingly glued in place had come loose, and now rotated on the blank. It just couldn't happen, but it had. I slid my right hand onto the blank just above the foregrip. Not nearly as good a handhold, small and slippery, but it would have to do.

The jumps were now less frequent, and the fish and I were settling into a give-and-take battle. He'd run while I stood at the stern with the rod in a full brace. Then I would slowly pump him toward me and gain back the line a few feet at a time. Without a usable foregrip it was a bit uncomfortable, but I was still in command, albeit with bruised pride.

I shouldn't have worried about the foregrip, because that was nothing compared to what happened next. The glue joint between the cork reel-seat bushings and the blank gave way. Now I was in definite trouble. My spinning reel was a moderate-sized saltwater model with a long handle. Every time I tried to turn the handle against the pressure of the fish, the whole reel seat rotated. On the down stroke of the handle the reel would swing to the right of the rod. On the up stroke the reel would ride up on the left side of the rod. It was almost impossible to gain line.

Now, I'm a stubborn cuss, and I wasn't about to give up, especially since the problem was of my own doing. If I had been using the charter boat's equipment it would have been easy to become quite indignant, throw in the towel, and blame the captain for faulty equipment. But *I made the rod*—the one everyone had admired when we came on board. Then I had bragged a little about the advantages of a quality custom rod. To put it mildly, my ego was smashed. If I was to have any left I would have to land the fish.

Both arms ached, and my hands were cramped to the point where I believed they would never open again. I tried wedging the long rear grip between my legs in an attempt to bring my hands closer to my body and try to offset the rotating reel seat. Fortunately, the fish never sounded, and in a much longer time than it should have taken, I finally—and luckily—landed the fish. I felt none of the glory I had envisioned earlier, just embarrassment.

For the rest of the day I was noticeably quiet while I resolved to learn a lot more about gluing components together. For the next three days my aching hands, arms, and pride served to intensify that resolve. The only good thing was that it had happened to me instead of to one of my customers.

Later when I carefully cut off the cork, I found I had used a glue which dried by evaporation, rather than catalytic action. I also found the surface of the blank had been left smooth rather than roughened for a good glue bond. It was impossible to tell, but I also may not have done a good job of fitting the cork to the blank. All of these are really inexcusable in a custom rod. They are also the most important aspects of gluing. So, with my experience in mind, let's examine carefully the all-important techniques of creating a strong, permanent glue joint.

There are many glues available, and various ones can be used in different rod-building processes. Regardless of the type, it must be waterproof, very strong, and somewhat resilient (not brittle). In all but two applications I believe it should also be permanent. These two exceptions are metal rod ferrules for joining rod sections (not butt ferrules), and non-roller tip-tops.

NONPERMANENT BONDS

Rod ferrules may wear in time and have to be replaced. Therefore a thermoplastic glue such as ferrule cement is generally used. It is not the strongest type, but when the metal ferrules are heated the glue will melt and the parts can be disassembled. If the parts become loose in use, repair is simple. The application of heat alone will often redistribute the cement, forming a good bond again. If that does not work, heat and disassemble. Scrape away the old glue and melt the end of a stick of cement and quickly smear it on the blank. Heat the ferrule section and the glue on the blank, and quickly assemble while hot. Once again heat the ferrule after it is on the blank to distribute the cement evenly inside the joint. If you carry a stick of ferrule cement in your tackle box or vest, these repairs are easily made in the field.

For years ferrule cement was also used on tip-tops, since in time they grooved and had to be replaced. Today, with aluminum-oxide ceramics, grooving is practically nonexistent. Replacement is largely limited to damaged tip-tops. The ceramic rings are mounted inside a plastic shock-absorbing ring. Too much heat applied to the tip-top tube will be conducted to the plastic ring, causing it to melt. The ring becomes loose and either then or later pops out. If ferrule cement is preferred, care must be taken to use only minimal heat. To keep the ring assembly cool, it helps to hold it in a wet cloth.

Personally, I prefer five-minute epoxy glue. This is a fairly brittle adhesive, not nearly as strong as regular curing epoxy. However, it is stronger for tip-top installation than ferrule cement. If you use it sparingly, you will later be able to break the bond with heat. For that purpose I use an electric soldering gun. At that time, you are removing a damaged tip and it doesn't matter if the plastic shock ring melts.

To mount a tip-top with five-minute epoxy, use only a few drops. Immediately after joining, lay the blank on a flat surface with your alignment mark facing up. Place a piece of masking tape over the blank to keep it from rolling and carefully align the top-top. Five minutes later you can proceed with placing the guides in position.

As mentioned, I believe all other assemblies should be permanent. Not everyone will agree with me. RodCrafter Bob Dupont is one who feels saltwater reel seats should be removable. He finds that these are not always given the proper care and can become frozen from saltwater corrosion. Since we just discussed one application of thermoplastic cement, let's see Bob's ingenious technique.

He first builds up the blank in the usual manner to fit the reel seat. Using a propane torch, he melts the end of a large stick of ferrule cement and smears it generously all over the reel-seat bushings. Holding the chrome/brass reel seat with tongs, he heats the seat thoroughly and completely in the flame of the propane torch. A quick pass of the flame over the cement previously applied to the bushings, and he slides the seat into position. A squirt bottle of water, or a faucet, is used to cool the seat. If the seat does ever become corroded and has to be replaced, heat from a torch will melt the glue.

PERMANENT BONDS

My own experience convinces me that just about every other glued assembly on a rod, except the two previously mentioned, should be permanent, including reel seats. The strongest glue for a permanent bond in these situations is epoxy. Again, let me point out that I am not speaking of the quick-setting epoxies—rather, those that take about two hours to set up and overnight to cure. Actually, a full cure will take thirty-six to forty-eight hours, but 90% of the strength is achieved overnight.

One of the important advantages of epoxy is that it cures by catalytic or chemical action between the two parts that are mixed, rather than by evaporation of solvents. In a tight-fitting joint, such as a reel seat or grip, air does not easily penetrate to the glue and evaporation is slowed considerably, sometimes taking many days. Also, evaporative-type adhesives will frequently "skin over," i.e., first the outside dries, but the inside takes much longer to dry. During that time the parts may be moved slightly, resulting in a much weaker joint. This is one of the reasons evaporative glues require clamping. One of the problems is knowing how long the pieces being joined should remain clamped together, since the accessibility of air, temperature, and humidity all affect drying time. In rod building it is often impossible to effectively clamp components together and apply any pressure. Some examples would be joining a reel seat to cork arbors, cork grips to the blank, and a gimbal to a butt.

Many evaporative-type cements tend to crystallize over a period of time. When they do, they will no longer accept stress and the joint will fail. This is particularly true if the film of glue between the two rod components is not kept to the required minimum. Evaporation also causes the volume of the glue to shrink. Parenthetically, this is one of the reasons that clamping is recommended by the manufacturers of these glues. Clamping the parts together squeezes out excess glue and keeps the film of glue as small as possible. As noted, this is often impossible to do in rod building. Epoxy does not shrink when it solidifies, and it does not require clamping pressure. It is only necessary that the parts not be moved while the glue goes through its initial curing stage.

Epoxy glues are not all the same. In fact, there are a great many different formulations. The best for rod work are those that do not become brittle and retain a slight elasticity. Also preferred are those that are clear, since any glue line on the surface of the rod is then practically invisible.

While epoxy is my preference, some other glues can be used for certain applications. Liquid Rod Cement marketed by Gudebrod Brothers Silk Company is frequently employed in joining cork rings to each other. I have found this to be satisfactory if the rings are being joined for the purpose of making a preformed grip. The directions provided should be carefully followed, and the cement should be given plenty of time to dry.

Cork rings can also be joined together with contact cement. A cement with a thin consistency is preferable or the glue line between rings will be evident. When using contact cement it is not necessary to clamp the rings together under pressure. It is important to allow adequate time for the coated surfaces to dry *before* the rings are joined. Since they must be aligned perfectly when they are brought into contact with each other, it is best to slip them over a dowel or metal rod one at a time. To assure complete contact, press each in place as firmly as possible. A helpful tool is a board with a hole just larger than the largest O.D. of the blank. When the cork cylinder is completed, remove the dowel, stand the cork cylinder vertically on the workbench, and place a flat board over the top. Give the board a few sharp raps with a hammer. The grip can be shaped at once on a rod lathe, then taper-reamed to fit the blank. Mount with epoxy.

Epoxy does not bond well with rubber and certain plastics. Keep in mind that many components such as butt caps, Cust-O-Hosels, etc. may appear to be rubber, but are actually man-made synthetics generally of butrate or polyolefin. If the surfaces of these materials are properly roughened, epoxy will bond them. For real rubber, use one of the various adhesives designed for rubber and follow directions. If, by testing a small area, you find that a certain plastic will not bond well with epoxy, use one of the special plastic cements. The situations where these special adhesives are required will be relatively few.

The most important factor in obtaining a good bond with epoxy is proper preparation of the surfaces to be joined. Always roughen both surfaces to provide a "tooth" or "toehold" for the glue. If you could view a cross section of a glued joint under great magnification, you would see that the glue fills every tiny scratch and pore in each surface. This has the effect of increasing the actual glued surface for a much stronger bond. Also, each tiny scratch filled with epoxy serves as a lock to prevent the parts from moving in any direction.

Let me inject here a word about fitting the parts to be joined. For glues other than epoxy, it is frequently recommended that a very tight fit be obtained, such as by forcing a taper-reamed grip into place on the blank. This is *not* the case when using epoxy. If the fit is too tight, much of the epoxy will be forced out of the joint. It is better to make an easy fit—one in which the grip, in the above example, could be just slid into place. The same would be true of a reel seat being fitted to slide over cork arbors. The joint should not be so loose that there is any side play, just an easy fit requiring no forcing or pressure.

As a rule of thumb, the smoother the initial surface, the more it must be roughened. In rod building we work with many smooth, highly polished surfaces. A blank is a prime example. When mounting anything on a blank, mark off the area of the blank to be covered. Use a finely pointed metal scriber, or needle, to scribe lines around the blank. Next, use coarse sandpaper to scratch that section of the blank. Cut through the factory-applied finish to just the surface of the fiberglass or graphite. Move the sandpaper both along the axis of the blank and at right angles to the axis. Also make some passes at a 45° angle in each direction. Wipe the roughened area clean using a rag dampened with acetone or alcohol.

The inside surfaces of reel seats are also extremely smooth and must be scratched and roughened. I use taper reamers made for cork work. These are sections of a blank to which coarse grit has been previously epoxied. A dowel or metal rod wrapped with very coarse sandpaper or emery cloth can also be used.

In fact, any tool with a sharp cutting surface that can be inserted into a reel seat will do the job. Move the tool in and out along the axis, as well as around the circumference. Make scratches at as many different angles as possible all over the inside surface of the reel seat. Again, use a solvent-dampened rag for cleaning.

The inside surfaces of gimbals and butt ferrules can be similarly roughened. Use a piece of very coarse sandpaper over your index finger to scratch the insides of all butt caps, especially those made of resilient material. A taper reamer or thin rasp works well on the inside of hosels. Remember also to roughen the end surface which will be glued to the grip.

Trim rings and reel-seat inserts of wood, both regular or impregnated, need to be scored on the inside. In addition to roughening the inside, I frequently use a small three-cornered file to make about six or eight grooves the length of the

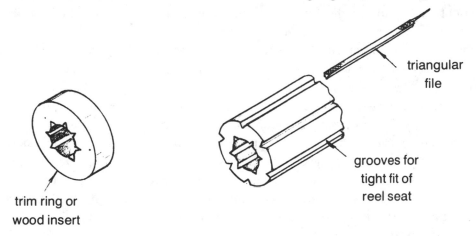

triangular file

grooves for tight fit of reel seat

trim ring or wood insert

Preparing wood parts for gluing.

hole. When filled with epoxy, these really serve to lock the part in place. On trim rings, each side face should be scratched thoroughly with very coarse sandpaper. Make the scored lines at least at right angles to each other, but be careful not to allow any deep scratches to extend to the outside edge where they will show on the finished rod. Exactly the same treatment is given plastic trim rings.

Natural cork is porous and needs less scratching. Reel-seat arbors of composition cork and grips of burnt cork (also a compressed material) are smoother and definitely should be roughened. Regardless of the type of cork, I roughen both the inside hole and the outside surface of reel-seat arbors. I also use the small three-cornered file to make grooves on the inside the same as described for wood inserts and rings. The same file can be used to make a series of short grooves at various angles on the outside of cork arbors.

Arbors made of bands of masking tape on the blank, over which a freshwater reel seat is mounted, should also have their surface improved for a good glue bond. Since they consist of thin layers of paper, general overall roughening with coarse sandpaper does not work very well. I have found that carefully made short grooves cut at random angles with the edge of a small three-cornered file work well. Epoxy should cover the sides of these arbors, as well as the surface, for increased strength.

Any smooth material used to shim a blank to fit a reel seat should be roughened. For example, if you have built up the blank with string or thread wrapped on a film of wet epoxy, then covered the outside with epoxy and allowed the glue to cure, it must be roughened before gluing the seat in place. The smooth surface and fiberglass shims must be treated the same as a blank.

Epoxy glue should be mixed of equal portions of both resin and hardener. Do not attempt to mix them in a container of any type, or on a sheet of plastic. The best mixing surface is a piece of paper laid on a hard, flat surface. It can subsequently be discarded. An excellent mixing tool is a flat popsicle stick.

Squeeze out equal amounts of the two parts from the tubes. The hardener will usually be thicker than the resin, so care is needed to get an equal volume of each. It's best to squeeze a line of the hardener onto the paper first, since it will not spread out as rapidly as the thinner resin. Then when the resin is placed on the paper it is easier to judge an equal volume. Mix the two parts with a linear or straight motion of the stick. Scrape from the outside of the mass toward the center, and progress all the way around. Then use a circular mixing motion. Alternate between the two mixing strokes until mixing is complete. This will usually require a minimum of two minutes. The flat stick used for mixing also makes a good applicator.

Once the surfaces to be glued have been properly roughened and the glue completely mixed, it can be applied. Where possible, such as on butt caps, butt ferrules, gimbals, etc., spread a film of epoxy on *both* surfaces to be joined. The object is to completely fill all the small scratches with glue. On components that must be slid over the blanks, it is generally not practical to first coat the inside with epoxy. No matter how careful you are, you will smear some epoxy onto the surface of the blank before you get the component into the position where it will be glued. If you do not mind cleaning the blank immediately afterward with a rag moistened with epoxy thinner, you can coat the inside of the hole with epoxy. A less messy approach is to place a fairly thick coating of glue on the fixed surface. This will be the blank itself when mounting a grip, or the arbors in the case of a reel seat. Slide the uncoated component over the blank. As it starts to come in contact with the epoxy-coated surface, push it slowly in place with a constant rotating motion. This will spread the glue into all the scratches and pores on the inside of the component being mounted.

You will notice a bulge of excess glue being pushed ahead of the component. If it builds to a size where it may drip or come back over the component being mounted, stop and use a narrow flat stick to remove the excess epoxy. Wood coffee stirrers or Popsicle sticks are good for this purpose. Just before the component reaches its final position, stop and remove the excess glue in the same way. Doing so will eliminate a large amount of glue from being squeezed out as the component is finally seated. Then only a small bead of glue will exist at the glue line. This is easily removed with a rag, preferably an old towel with texture, or a pipe cleaner.

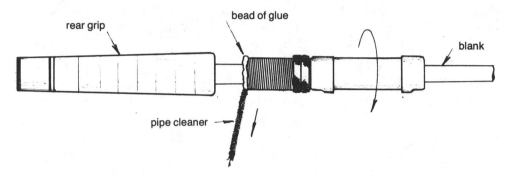

Removing bead of glue with pipe cleaner.

To remove the bead of epoxy without smearing it over adjacent surfaces, place the rag or pipe cleaner underneath the rod to serve as a pickup. Draw the pickup toward you as you rotate the rod down against the pickup. If the speed of the two movements is coordinated, the glue bead will be transferred in a line to the rag or pipe cleaner. Any small amount of glue remaining can be wiped clean with a rag moistened with epoxy thinner.

As noted previously, an epoxied joint need not be clamped. However, it is important that the parts not be moved while the initial cure takes place. Carefully set the rod aside where it will not be accidentally bumped. The glue will flow from gravity inside the joint at first, so give some thought to the position of the rod while the glue sets up. For example, a rod on which you have just glued a butt ferrule, butt cap, or gimbal should be placed vertically. This can often be best done in a corner of the shop. A few strips of masking tape will hold it to the walls.

Heat can be used to accelerate the cure of epoxy. A good source is a heat lamp or a large photo bulb in a reflector. Do not place either source too close to the rod assembly. A temperature of about 150°F. works well with most epoxies. I frequently use a No. 2 photo bulb in a 10-inch polished reflector and place it no closer than 2 feet away. About every five minutes I rotate the rod so that the opposite side is facing the heat. Initially, heat will thin the epoxy a bit, causing it to flow more easily. For this reason it is good practice to check the exterior of the joint frequently at first to see if any additional glue has flowed to the outside. If it has, use the technqiue explained earlier to remove the bead of glue. Heat is not needed during the entire curing process. Remove the heat source when the glue has set up and become firm.

There are some special epoxy adhesives applicable to certain rod-making procedures. The main one is a nonflowing paste type. Various brands are available; I am most familiar with a formulation sold under the name of PC-7. Since they do not flow, they can be used to fill a larger than normal space between surfaces to be joined. This might be encountered in mounting a reel seat that almost fits the blank, but not quite. The space is too small to really build up the blank, but regular epoxy may flow out of the joint. A similar situation may be found when mounting the butt ferrule on a saltwater trolling or boat rod.

Prepare the surfaces the same as for regular epoxy. Be sure to mix the two parts completely. Since each part is a heavy paste, mixing is more difficult. Instead of a piece of paper, mix the parts on a smooth surface such as a board, tile, or piece of glass. The mixture is quite sticky and adheres to all surfaces. It therefore must be pushed into the joint with a flat tool or stick. Make repeated applications until the joint is completely packed with the mixture. PC-7 can be easily cleaned from surfaces with a rag moistened with alcohol. In fact, if it ever becomes necessary to smooth or level an exposed area of the adhesive, it is easily done with a tool or finger dipped in alcohol.

It should be mentioned that all epoxy glues can be quite irritating to the skin. If, after any application, there is any glue on your hands, immediately clean them with a rag dampened with epoxy thinner, or in the case of PC-7, alcohol. Follow this with a complete washing with soap and water. I make a habit of washing my hands twice using Lava soap.

THREE

Reel Seats

There are reel seats made especially for inexpensive rods where every penny of cost is shaved to the minimum. Better rods use better-made reel seats, and recently we have seen the introduction of the highest-quality reel seats designed almost solely for the custom rod builder. The usual objective in making a custom rod is to produce the finest rod possible. When we consider that the biggest investment is in time, skill, and labor, it only makes sense to use the very best components available. Reel seats, as is true of other components, vary greatly in quality, and the rod builder must be able to judge which to use. It is foolish economy to use any but the highest-quality seats, since replacement of one that becomes defective is a major, time-consuming repair.

ALUMINUM REEL SEATS

More rods are built using aluminum reel seats, so let's examine these first for the factors that determine quality. Aluminum itself is rather difficult to machine and to stamp. It is therefore made in a wide variety of alloys for ease of processing. Each of these alloys is designated by a code number. For example, 6061-T832, one of the finest possible alloys for aluminum seats, could be broken down as follows. The first four digits represent the aluminum content in the alloy, in a series from 1000 to 7000. An alloy with a higher aluminum content will have to be machined at slower speeds, but will be more corrosion-resistant, accept a better polish, have higher tensile strength, and take anodizing better. The first digit following the letter represents the hardness on a temper scale of 0 to 8 (for aluminum). The last two digits denote the method used to temper the alloy.

A rod builder doesn't have to be a metallurgist, but he should understand that there is a difference in aluminum alloys used for reel seats. A less expensive alloy that can be machined faster (lower production cost) might be used for a less expensive seat. However, we get what we pay for, and the cheaper seat is simply not as good as one made from a better alloy. Similarly, softer, lower-aluminum-content alloys must be used for stampings and rolled threads.

One easily discernible difference between reel seats is the wall thickness. Some seats have walls so thin that there is barely any metal at the bottom of the threads. Over a period of time with repeated locking and unlocking of the nuts, such seats can actually wear through. Wall thickness is particularly important on the hoods. Thin walls are apt to split if the hood is screwed onto the reel foot too tightly, or if they are forced over larger-than-normal reel feet.

The threads on aluminum seats can be formed by rolling or by machining. Large-volume manufacturers are more apt to use high-speed automated equipment to roll the threads. Economies of scale help keep the cost to the rod builder lower on these seats. A good example of a medium-priced seat made in this manner is the Varmac aluminum line. As a rule, rolled threads will hold up well in normal usage, but not as well as machined threads. Rolled threads are usually found on thin-walled seats, while machined threads can only be made on thicker walls. If, as occasionally happens, a nut is jammed, the damage stands a good chance of being greater on rolled threads than it would be on machined threads. Different types of threads are also used from fine to coarse. Threads too fine will tend to bind if dirt or grit gets on them. If too coarse, however, the nuts will be too loose.

There are two hoods on a reel seat, one fixed and one sliding. The fixed aluminum hood is always stamped. However, the quality of the stamping and the wall thickness can vary. A quality seat will have a fairly thick-walled stamped hood, large enough to accommodate any reel to be used with that size seat. The edge and body of the hood will be nicely finished with no stress marks or ''orange peel'' (indicating that the die was used longer than it should have been). The sliding hood can be either stamped or machined. If stamped, the same criteria apply as to the fixed hood. Machined hoods are more expensive to make, but will have thicker walls and greater strength. If placed in stress situations, the machined hood is far less likely to deform or split.

If you examine a variety of different seats you will find that there is a difference in the way in which the fixed hood is attached. The cheapest and poorest-quality seats have the thin wall of the hood merely rolled over the end of the barrel. If you place your finger inside you can feel the sharp, rolled-over edge. The better-quality seats have the hood tightly pressure-fitted onto the barrel. Viewed from the end you will see both the wall of the barrel and the wall of the hood.

Milled-slot fly-reel seat. The slot helps hold the reel securely and reduces side pressure on the hoods.

On fly-reel seats the best-quality models have a milled slot the entire length. This slot is more expensive to produce, since it involves an additional cutting operation after the barrel has been threaded. It also requires thicker walls to start with. The slot does the best job of holding the reel foot in place and reduces the side pressure on the hoods.

While technically not reel seats, sliding reel bands are used on some ultra-light fly and spinning rods to hold the reel onto the grip. The most distinguishing feature of top-quality models is that the inside is not only smooth, but has a slight taper on the leading edge. Again, this is a case where cost is increased because of the extra machining operation. However, this design will fit better over the reel foot without causing the other end of the band to be levered into the cork, forming dents. The best-quality fly models are made of nickel silver. They also have a narrow band of raised, fine knurling to facilitate tightening them onto the reel feet. On spinning bands the hand encircles both grip and the reel feet, and raised knurling would be uncomfortable. Also, the angler can detect if the bands work loose. The fly reel is mounted behind the hand grip in a position where it acts like a pendulum. It can more easily work loose without being noticed.

Spinning-reel bands are made in straight-taper design and in swaged models. The latter have a bulge in one side to accommodate the reel feet. Provided that both types are of a smooth, chafe-proof design on the inside, selection is best made on the basis of the size of the reel feet on the reel to be used. I have found that on average and small reel feet the straight taper holds well and longest as the cork becomes depressed from use. If the reel feet are quite thick, then it seems best to use the swaged models.

The final aspect of aluminum seats is the quality of the finish. It should be pointed out that only the finest aluminum alloys can be given a high polish that will hold up in use instead of being anodized. This finish is highly prized by many rod builders. These seats will not corrode in fresh water, but will in salt water. They can be used in salt water, but must be rinsed clean with fresh water immediately after use. Anodizing places a protective coating on any aluminum-alloy reel seat that keeps it from corroding. It also has the advantage of adding color of just about any hue.

CHROMED BRASS REEL SEATS

Reel seats normally used on saltwater rods and some heavy-duty freshwater rods are made of noncorrosive brass, then chrome-plated. As with aluminum seats, there are design features that distinguish the better ones, as well as variations in overall quality.

Many saltwater and trolling rods disassemble at the reel seat. Two kinds of ferrules are used for this purpose: a simple friction type and a screw-locking type. On the friction type, the male ferrule is a smooth cylinder that slips tightly into the open end of the reel seat. The better ones have close tolerances so that there is no wobble or rotation when joined. Friction ferrules should really be used only on comparatively light-duty rods. For the strongest, most secure connection, the locking type are decidedly superior.

On the locking type, the end of the reel-seat barrel projects beyond the fixed hood and is threaded. The male ferrule which fits over the butt of the blank has a threaded and knurled collet nut on the rod end. When the male ferrule in inserted into the reel seat, the collet nut engages the threads on the body of the reel seat and is tightened to lock the ferrule in place. To automatically align the blank with the reel seat, there is a V-notch in the bottom of the male ferrule. This slips over a pin across the inside diameter of the reel seat. When the locking nut is tightened the V-notch is seated securely over the pin. This makes it impossible for the blank to turn or rotate inside the reel seat.

An excellent example of a high-quality seat of this type is the Varmac Lock-top. On it the pin inside the reel seat is entirely internal, and there is no evidence of it on the smooth outside of the reel-seat barrel. On less expensive seats, the pin is inserted via a hole drilled through each of the two barrel walls. Even though the ends of the pin are smoothed and plated, there is a groove in which salt deposits and dirt can accumulate.

Another design feature that appears on only the top-quality saltwater seats is a keyed rear hood. In this arrangement there are two lock nuts behind the sliding hood. One is attached to the hood and runs in a track cut in the threads. In this manner the rear hood always remains in line with the front, fixed hood for ease in mounting the reel. Since the rear hood is attached to one of the nuts, it is also easier to move back when the reel is removed from the rod. An entirely free sliding hood will frequently jam over the reel foot after being pushed tightly in place with the locking nuts.

While most reel-seat manufacturers will supply seats with either one or two locking nuts, saltwater rods should always be built with seats employing two nuts. The first one tightens the hood over the reel foot. The second locks the first in place for maximum security.

The strain given saltwater rods is considerably greater than that given freshwater rods. Therefore, the wall thickness and shape of the reel-seat hoods are of particular importance. For lighter rods stamped hoods are satisfactory provided the walls of the hood are thick enough, and the hood is large enough to fit over the reel foot of any reel that might be used with the rod. Avoid chrome/brass reel seats with thin-walled hoods.

For big-game offshore trolling rods the best seats are made with heavy machined hoods. The massive strength of these hoods will hold up under any fishing pressure. Some other component making up the chain from angler to fish will break before the machined hood. Also, the machined hood does a better job of eliminating any side-to-side wobble of the reel.

Top-quality brass/chrome seats will have a round thread design rather than the common V-shaped threads. This construction increases wall strength of the threads and helps prevent binding or freezing up from dirt in the grooves.

It is worth repeating that the custom rod builder should always consider using the very best-quality reel seats obtainable. A poor-quality seat will only cheapen and detract from the rod.

MOUNTING REEL SEATS

The inside diameter of a reel seat is generally quite a bit larger than the outside diameter of the blank over which it must be mounted. Also, the blank is tapered and the seat is not. Various materials can be used to fill this space while keeping the blank centered.

Reel-seat arbors or bushings are cork cylinders usually 1⅛ inches long made for this purpose. They are available in various outside and inside diameters to fit different-size reel seats and blanks. The most common technique is to select an outside diameter that will fit the reel seat, taper-ream the inside, and glue the bushing in place on the blank. If the outside diameter is a bit too large to fit the seat it can be reduced before gluing to the blank. Select a dowel or metal rod on which the arbor can be forced so that it will not rotate. If necessary, the O.D. of the dowel can be built up with masking tape or string. With the arbors in place, chuck the dowel or rod into a lathe or electric drill and sand them down to the proper diameter.

Another approach is to taper-ream and glue them to the blank first, Then, if a rod lathe is available, the outside diameter can be reduced by sanding to fit the reel seat. The outside can also be hand-sanded to reduce the diameter. Care must be taken to remove the same amount of cork all around the arbor, or the seat will not be centered on the blank.

Rod builders who build many rods may find it advantageous to fit and glue cork arbors inside a number of reel seats beforehand. Then when a customer selects a certain seat, all that needs to be done is to taper-ream the cork inside the seat to fit the blank. This saves time by eliminating the wait while the glue dries during one additional step.

The best bond of cork to reel seat will occur if both surfaces are rough and space is provided for a film of glue. For this reason many custom rod builders file a few small grooves in the surface of the cork. For additional strength, the arbors should be mounted with a space between each. When the glue is applied, a generous amount is placed in the spaces between the arbors. Instead of cork reel-seat arbors, regular cork rings can be substituted with any of the above methods.

Not quite as strong as cork, but totally suited to most light freshwater rods, is the technique of building up bands of masking tape. This is one of the faster ways to fill the space between the reel seat and the blank. Many rod companies use special glued paper in much the same way. The tape should be wound as tightly as possible for strong, firm support. A rod lathe that is geared low enough for adequate power and has a variable-speed foot control can be used to speed the job even more. When wrapping the tape, leave space between each band. When epoxy is applied to the surface, also spread some along the side of each tape arbor and in the spaces between to act as a reinforcing brace.

Another material that is fast to work with and which provides good support is cork tape. This is available in 1-inch-width of various lengths. It has an adhesive back which eliminates the need for glue when mounting it on the blank. Bands or arbors 1 inch wide are built up in the same manner as with masking tape. Since it is considerably thicker than masking tape, it builds to the desired diameter more quickly. If the completed cork arbor is slightly oversize, it can be reduced with a rasp worked in the same direction the cork was wound. From that point it is treated the same as bands of masking tape.

If the space between reel seat and blank is not very large, a piece of sheet cork or gasket material can be utilized. I first saw RodCrafter Joy Dunlap of A&J Custom Rods in Destin, Florida, use this technique. From a sheet of cork he cut a piece just a bit shorter than the length of the reel seat. He then wrapped it around the appropriate point on the blank and trimmed it so the ends would just meet. A small gap is permissible. Rubber contact cement was then spread on the blank and on the piece of sheet cork. This was allowed to dry for the required time (about fifteen or twenty minutes) while Joy attended to other matters. Being careful to align the cork sheet first, since it cannot be moved once the surfaces are in contact, he wrapped it around the blank. The bond was permanent immediately, and he chucked the blank into his rod lathe and sanded the cork to fit the inside of the reel seat. Using a rasp, he made some random strokes at intervals around the cork. These grooves were to provide a better bonding surface. A film of epoxy was spread over the cork and the reel seat was slipped in place.

Another material employed in similar situations where the space to be filled is not very great is fiberglass. I learned of this method from the late RodCrafter Clyde Pollard. Clyde used boat-building fiberglass cloth and resin, readily available in kit form at most boat dealers. By wrapping the dry cloth around the blank, the required width and length of the "pattern" is determined. The resin is mixed and applied, following the directions in the kit, and the blank is built up. After the resin has cured, the fiberglass can be sanded to reduce the diameter if necessary. Either a coarse file or coarse sandpaper is used both for rapid removal of material and to provide a good bonding surface for the epoxy glue. Clyde built a lot of saltwater rods, and this is one of the strongest methods of mounting the reel seat.

On heavy rods where the space to be filled is greater, pieces of PVC pipe can be used. The pipe is made in several diameters and each has a number of different wall thicknesses. A good assortment can be obtained by a few visits to a plumber's scrap pile. If there is much taper in the blank where the seat will be mounted, the loose end of the pipe can be filled with a paste type of nonflowing epoxy, such as PC-7. After the PVC is glued to the blank, the outside diameter can be turned down to fit the reel seat.

One of the oldest methods to fill a small space and level the taper of the blank is with string and heavy thread. This is quickly done on a rod lathe, but can be done almost as rapidly by hand. First place a good film of epoxy on the blank. Then make a wrap of the desired length over it. To level the smaller end of the blank another layer of the same size string may be required, or smaller-diameter string or heavy thread may be used. Before applying the second layer to the one end, spread another layer of epoxy. When the wrap is complete, use a flat stick or narrow spatula to work a layer of epoxy into the string, then spread a coat on top. At this point if there is a good fit to the reel seat it can be slipped in place. If the wrap is too thick, allow the epoxy to cure. Then use a rasp, file, or coarse sandpaper to reduce the diameter. This step can be performed in a rod lathe or by hand. Spread a coat of epoxy and mount the reel seat.

SPECIFIC INSTALLATIONS

All-cork reel seats

Let's now direct our attention to the installation of some specific types of reel seats. The lightest is the all-cork seat with sliding bands used on fly rods. This is flared on the bottom end to keep the reel bands from sliding off. The other end butts against the grip. As is true with all cork work, the cork seat can be fabricated separately by the rod builder, then taper-reamed and glued to the blank. Or it can be built up of cork rings glued directly to the blank, then shaped in a rod lathe or by hand. In either case, complete the work on the seat before going on to the cork hand grip so the reel bands can be slid in place.

The outside diameter of the straight cork cylinder is determined by the inside diameter of the reel bands. They can therefore be used as templates. For the bands to slide up over the reel feet, the cork will have to be cut flat on one side. This flat surface also seats the reel and prevents it from turning on the cork. Use a coarse flat file and clamp the cork so that it cannot rotate. Make sure this flat side is aligned with the blank and the future position of the guides. The flat will extend all the way to the end of the cork seat that fits against the grip. On the butt end it will feather into the enlarged flare. Create the flat in small increments and check the depth by attempting to mount the reel. You have cut deep enough when the reel bands can just be forced up over the edge of the reel feet. Finish sanding with fine-grit paper, rounding the edges of the flat just slightly.

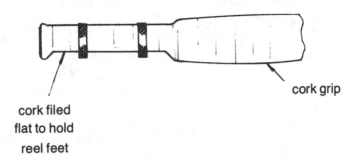

cork grip

cork filed
flat to hold
reel feet

All-cork fly-reel seat with sliding reel bands must be filed flat on one side to hold reel.

There are a number of ways the butt end of an all-cork seat can be finished. A plug of cork can be cut to size to fit into the open end. After it is glued in place, it can be sanded flush with the end of the cork seat. This is light, simple, and neat. The only drawback is that the cork can be damaged and crumbled when the rod is rested vertically on the butt. Better protection and a more finished appearance results with a butt plate. The easiest type to use is of one-piece aluminum, machined so that a plug projects. This plug is mounted inside the butt of the blank. Either use a nonflowing epoxy such as PC-7 to fill out the space around the plug, or build up the O.D. of the plug with masking tape. Instead of a metal butt plate, a flat round piece of rubber (such as a holeless washer) can be glued over a cork plug previously sanded flush. Use rubber cement, since epoxy does not bond well to rubber. The bond with any type of cement is the biggest problem here. Too often the rubber comes loose in use.

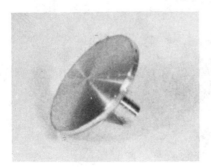

Machined aluminum butt plate is ideal for finishing end of all-cork fly-reel seat.

65

The same techniques apply to finishing the butt end of an all-cork spinning-reel seat with sliding bands. A nice touch in delivering a rod with sliding rings is to wrap thin bands of masking tape at the ends of the straight cork cylinder. The sliding metal rings can then be pushed over the tape and remain stationary instead of clanking about loosely.

A cork fly-rod seat can be built with a fixed hood cap and only one sliding reel band. The technique is much the same except the butt end of the cork is not flared. It is sanded to the correct outside diameter so that the fixed hood cap can be slipped on and glued. Depending on the size of the single sliding reel band you may or may not have to file a flat side in the cork. Some rod builders glue a flat rubber washer on the back of the fixed hood cap. However, as mentioned earlier, it is difficult to get a good bond with rubber.

Classic wood fly-reel seat

A variation of this type of seat was found on many of the old classic split-cane fly rods. Instead of the seat being made of cork, it was of hardwood such as walnut. A fixed hood cap was mounted on the end and there was a single reel band of nickel silver. While the reel is not held as securely on this classic seat as it is on a threaded seat, it will retain light reels, is very attractive, and evokes feelings of nostalgia among many fly fishermen.

To make this seat, turn down a cylinder of hardwood small enough so that the fixed hood cap will just fit over the end. A flat can be cut on one side with a saw, then finished with sandpaper. As with the all-cork seat, make the flat only deep enough so the sliding reel band will fit tightly over the reel foot. Depending upon the diameter of the hole through the center of the wood cylinder relative to the outside diameter of the blank, you may have to build up the blank. This is most easily done with string and epoxy as explained earlier. After gluing all parts in place on the blank, use your favorite protective finish.

Classic wood fly-reel seat with milled slot instead of simple flat side.

Cork-and-wood fly-reel seat

As noted, the hardwood "classic" seat will not hold reels as securely as an all-cork seat, since it lacks the resilience of cork for better gripping. A famous RodCrafter, Don Phillips of Granby, Connecticut, makes a seat that combines the beauty of wood and the gripping resilience of cork. Don was the inventor of the boron rod, and later the boron/graphite hybrid fly rod. Since his blanks are of solid construction, they have very small diameters, usually $3/16$ to $\frac{1}{4}$ inch at the butt. He created his seat of a sliding fly-reel band and a pocket butt cap to keep the size proportionate to his unique rods. The creative addition of wood stems from the fact that he is "partial to the aesthetics of wood grain."

Don builds his seat and hand grip together in one unit on a mandrel. He uses nineteen cork rings with a thin hardwood spacer added between the seventh and eighth corks. After the glue has dried on his cork cylinder, he uses a hacksaw to carefully cut away about the top one-third of the cork on one end. This longitudinal cut is made up to the hardwood spacer. The mandrel is left in the cylinder

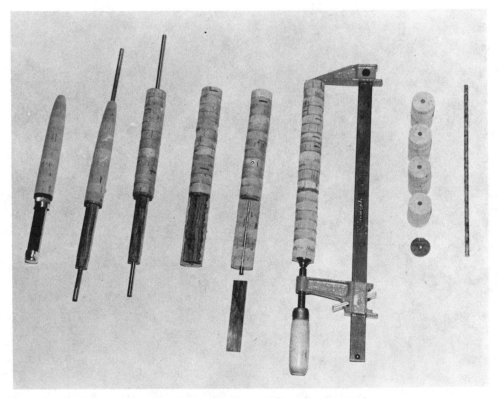

Steps Don Phillips uses in making his cork-and-wood fly-rod seat and grip.

67

during the cutting operation to provide a straightedge against which to guide the hacksaw blade during the longitudinal cut. This is similar to making a deep flat in the cork, but because of the amount of material being removed, it is cut away instead of filed.

Still with the mandrel in place, a hardwood block is glued onto the area where the cork segment was removed. The size of this hardwood block matches the size of the cork cylinder. After the glue has cured, Don removes the mandrel and replaces it with a longer turning mandrel. This is mounted in a modified Unimat lathe for turning the cork-and-wood composite.

When properly finished, the end result is a reel seat that has a good firm base for the reel feet, attractive wood-grain segments, and a resilient cork shank that aids in anchoring the sliding reel band. Don points out that his approach is designed for small-diameter blanks, such as his own boron/graphite blanks and regular graphite blanks. Large-diameter fiberglass blanks might require some intricate cutting and notching of the cork and wood to accommodate relatively small-diameter reel bands.

Turning the cork-and-hardwood seat section.

Reverse-locking fly-reel seat

In recent years there has been a great deal of interest in reverse-mounted, or up-locking, fly-reel seats. Instead of the fixed hood being located at the butt end, it is on the front end of the seat. The fixed hood can be against the cork grip, or it can be recessed inside the end of the grip. Whether you are using an all-metal seat or a skeleton seat with an insert of cork or wood, you will need a model on which the fixed hood is not made as a one-piece end cap. The preferred seats for this kind of installation have a removable metal end cap which can be placed inside the threaded end of the barrel. The metal cap is best, since it affords maximum protection to the butt of the seat—especially if it is of the type that is mounted on a short plug. Seats with a flat rubber button can be used by switching the rubber button to the threaded end. However, the button is rather thin and will neither hold up as well as metal nor protect the seat as well. If the fixed hood is to be mounted against the end of the cork grip, installation is the same as for a conventionally mounted fly-reel seat.

A more unusual effect is created if the fixed hood is recessed under the grip. For it to fit under the cork, the outside of the grip will have to be shaped so that

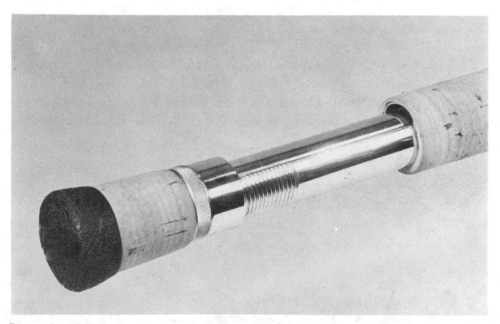

Recessed, up-locking fly-reel seat with short extension butt.

it is rather large at the butt end. The length of the fixed hood will dictate whether one or two cork rings will be required to cover it.

Fit the cork ring, or rings, to the fixed hood before the seat is mounted on the blank. Use a small round file to enlarge the center hole in the cork so that it can just be forced over the round end of the fixed hood. Next, enlarge the hole on one side to barely fit over the pocket portion of the fixed hood. Work slowly, checking your progress frequently. The finished hole in the cork should be slightly on the small side so that the cork must be forced over the hood for a tight fit. When the reel seat is mounted on the blank, glue the cork ring, or rings, over

The hole in the cork ring was shaped with a Dremel tool to fit over the fixed hood. It will be glued in place for a recessed, up-locking fly-reel seat.

the fixed hood. When you are ready to build the rest of the grip from cork rings, simply glue the first ring to the one in place over the fixed hood.

Fly-rod extension butts

On fly rods designed to be used in the pursuit of heavier fish, it is best to plan a short extension below the reel seat. One of the problems encountered in

Parts for wood seat and matching fixed fly-rod extension butt.

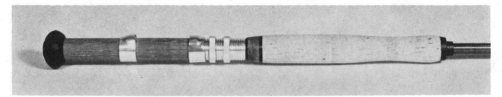

Inlaid-wood fly-reel seat with matching wood extension butt.

taking large fish on a fly is that the reel seat is at the very bottom of the rod. Unless the rod has a short extension, it is difficult and uncomfortable to brace the rod against your body and turn the reel at the same time. The extension can be a permanent one built right on the blank, or it can be detachable.

For a permanent, mounted extension you will need either a slipover-type small spinning seat, or a fly seat with removable end cap or button. Mount it on the blank ahead of the few cork rings needed to form the extension. A regular butt cap of your choice is glued over the bottom of the extension.

A detachable butt is preferred by many fly fishermen. It can be carried in the pocket or vest and inserted after the fish is hooked. The removable butt extension can be made entirely by the rod builder, or he can use one of the prefabricated units now on the market.

To make your own detachable fighting butt you need a small slipover reel seat, or a fly seat with a removable end cap or button. The seat is mounted in the normal manner flush with the end of the blank butt, and the end cap is left off. An alternative is to allow the seat to extend just far enough beyond the blank to permit insertion of the end cap or button when the fighting butt is not going to be called for.

The shaft on which the extension is built can be a length of hollow glass blank, solid fiberglass, or a hardwood dowel. The end of this shaft will be inserted a few inches inside the butt of the rod blank. If hollow fiberglass, the tapers will therefore have to match. Solid glass or hardwood can be shaped to fit the inside taper of the rod blank.

It is suggested you work with a length of shaft material a few inches longer than your planned needs. Then when the proper fit inside the blank's butt is completed, draw a circle around the shaft at the point where it is flush with the end of the reel seat. Using this reference mark, then cut the other end to the length desired for your extension butt. This section of the shaft is then covered with cork or resilient grip material and shaped, and the chosen butt cap is mounted. If you use a skeleton seat with a wood insert, consider also covering the shaft of the extension butt with the same wood. It makes a strikingly handsome combination.

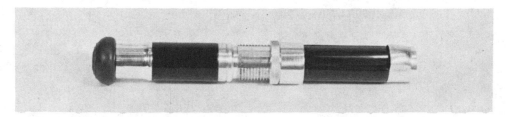

Skeleton seat and detachable extension butt, both fitted with hardwood.

The prefabricated detachable butts generally consist of an aluminum piston with O-rings that fits inside the reel seat. There is also a solid shaft between the piston and the butt cap. Avoid units with a small butt cap, since it is uncomfortable when fighting a fish. The shaft can be covered with any desired material, the same as described above. Since the piston fits inside the reel seat, adequate space must be provided to accommodate it when the reel seat is mounted on the blank. In other words, the reel seat must extend beyond the end of the blank.

To measure for this space, or extension, insert the butt into the reel seat before the seat is mounted. Slide the combination seat and butt over the butt of the blank as far as it will go. Use a scriber to make a small light scratch on the blank at the forward end of the seat. Remove the seat and measure ¼ to ½ inch *toward the butt* from the scratch just made. At this point scribe a circle around the blank. When gluing the seat on the blank, have the forward end of the seat line up with this scribed circle.

Blank Position for Fighting Butt

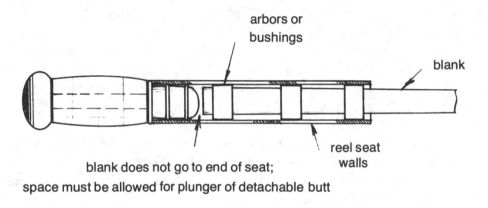

arbors or
bushings

blank

reel seat
walls

blank does not go to end of seat;
space must be allowed for plunger of detachable butt

With piston-type detachable butt, adequate space beyond end of blank must be allowed for insertion of piston.

When mounting the seat you also want to be sure that no excess glue accumulates in the space just provided. This is inside the end of the seat projecting past the blank, and into which the butt's piston slides. Mount the reel-seat arbors and allow to dry. Spread glue on the surface of the *arbors only* and slide the seat in position from the butt end. Rotate the seat as you slowly slide it in place up to the scribed circle on the blank and stop. Do not allow the seat to move past the circle. Use a pipe cleaner to remove excess glue from inside the projecting portion of the seat. Carefully set it aside in a horizontal position so that it will not move while the glue cures.

With some detachable extension butts, a pneumatic effect results which can make it difficult to insert the butt into the seat rapidly. This occurs more frequently on an extension butt made with a tight-fitting piston and rubber O-rings, and a blank whose upper end is sealed. What happens is that there is no way for the air trapped inside the hollow blank to escape when the piston is inserted into the seat. The trapped air compresses, then exerts a pushing force against the piston, which tends to push the fighting butt back out of the seat. Since many anglers carry the butt in their pocket and insert it only after a fish is on, this pneumatic effect can create problems when the fisherman is his busiest, or with a really large fish, when all hell is breaking loose!

To eliminate this problem you only have to create an outlet, or escape route, for the air. The seal in the top of the butt section of the blank can be removed, or opened by a small hole in some cases. Some rod builders prefer to drill the smallest hole possible in the barrel of the reel seat. This hole should not go through the blank, but be located just beyond the end of the butt—in the space where the piston is inserted.

Featherweight makes a completely assembled detachable fighting butt that comes with a double-locking ¾-inch-I.D. reel seat. The extension is 4 inches long and covered with cork. The end is fitted with one of their kraton butt caps. The other end is a piston with an O-ring that fits inside the barrel of the reel seat.

Skeleton seats—wood inserts

In *Fiberglass Rod Making* it was explained how the custom rod builder could cut out the unthreaded barrel portion of an aluminum reel seat and replace it with an insert (or spacer) of attractive hardwood or cork. The idea became so popular that we had such skeleton seats made for us. Now there are a number of companies making these seats, giving us all an even larger choice.

Walnut is the most popular hardwood for reel-seat inserts, but many other beautiful woods can be used. A simple cylinder of the desired length and outside diameter can be made and assembled in sequence on the rod. The wall thickness of the wood must be enough so there is no danger of the wood splitting in the future. You can buy a ready-made wood insert from a reputable rod-building-supply house and thus be assured of adequate wall thickness. If you make your own, bore the hole just large enough to fit the blank.

When making your own wood insert, start by boring the desired size hole. Saw off the square edges for a rough octagonal shape. Slip the wood over a length of threaded rod with a small washer and two nuts at each end. This can then be chucked in a lathe or drill for the final shaping. Turn the wood insert to a diameter just a hair smaller than the O.D. of the skeleton seat. This difference allows for the thickness of the wood finish, which should be applied before the insert is mounted.

One of the best finishes I have found is called Birchwood Casey's Tru-Oil, a gunstock finish available from some rod-building-supply dealers and most good gun shops. Simply follow the directions on the container, with one exception. If you have chosen a dense, oily wood such as rosewood, first apply a thinned sealer coat of clear white shellac. The first coat of Tru-Oil is supposed to dry in a few hours, but depending upon the type of wood it may require twenty-four to forty-eight hours—but the results are well worth the wait.

Another approach to making a wood insert is to make it long enough to fit under the two sections of the skeleton reel seat. In this case, the portions that will be placed under the seat must be turned down so that the seat will fit. This has the advantage of automatically centering the seat components and eliminating bushings or arbors. However, it reduces the wall thickness of the wood beneath the seat. It therefore should only be used when the blank diameter is small enough to allow adequately thick wood walls.

There are a number of ''wood reel seats'' on the market. These are pre-assembled combinations of skeleton seats and wood as described above. A *small* amount of filing (it's hard work) can be done to enlarge the hole to fit the blank. However, on most the wall thickness of the wood under the metal portions of the seat is minimal. If you remove much wood you run the risk of future splitting. My advice is not to risk it. This does not mean you cannot use a wood reel seat on which the hole size (inside diameter) is too small for the butt of the chosen blank. Instead, it means you need *a method other than mounting the seat over the blank*.

The technique is to fit and glue a dowel *inside* the butt of the blank, allowing a long enough extension on which to mount the reel seat. Before starting an installation of this type you must determine whether or not you want to add the length of the reel seat to the total length of the completed rod. In many cases it is desirable to do so. In others, it is preferred to keep the length of the finished rod the same size as the original blank length.

Let's suppose you have a 9-foot blank and a reel seat that is 5 inches long. If you fit a dowel into the existing blank you would end up with a rod 9 feet, 5 inches long. To make a finished rod 9 feet long you would need to trim 5 inches from the butt of the blank before proceeding to fit the dowel. To do this, measure the length of the seat and carefully measure that length from the butt end of the blank. Mark the blank and cut it with a fine-tooth saw. Square the end of the cut with a coarse flat file.

The dowel can be of hardwood, such as common birch dowels, or it can be of solid fiberglass. Measure the length of the reel seat and add 4 to 6 inches for the portion that will fit inside the butt of the blank. Cut the dowel to the combined length.

First turn down the diameter of the end of the dowel which will fit inside the reel seat. This should be a constant diameter and fit the full length of the seat. Next, taper the end of the dowel which will fit inside the blank and round that end slightly. Check the fit of the parts to make sure the end of the reel seat will be flush with the end of the blank. Mark the dowel at that point with a pencil line.

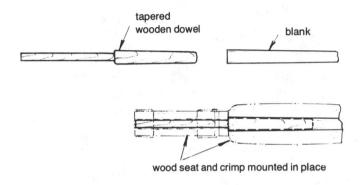

Fitting a wood fly-reel seat whose inside diameter is smaller than the butt diameter of the blank. Dowel is first fitted to seat on one end, then tapered to fit inside of blank on opposite end. Parts are all epoxied together.

Roughen the shaped dowel for a better bond. Place a generous amount of epoxy on the inside of the blank with a pipe cleaner. Spread a layer of epoxy on the section of dowel that goes into the blank. Insert the dowel into the blank with a twisting motion up to the previously made pencil line.

After the epoxy has cured, roughen the inside of the reel seat and the dowel over which it fits. Coat both with epoxy and mount the seat.

As long as care is taken to obtain a good fit, and slow-setting epoxy glue is used, this technique will result in a rod as strong as any. There should be no concern that the reel seat and butt section of the rod is weaker than on a conventional installation. The grip, glued as it is directly over the dowel projecting from the reel seat, acts as reinforcement and provides great hoop strength at that portion of the blank. I have taken 100-pound-plus tarpon on a rod made in this manner and never experienced even the least hint of weakness or failure.

Skeleton fly-reel seats, whether made by the rod builder or purchased, can be mounted over the blank in conventional style or in reverse (up-locking) fashion. Obviously, for a reverse installation the cap on the end of the fixed hood must be removable. To mount a skeleton fly seat in an up-locking manner, proceed as explained for regular one-piece fly-reel seats.

Skeleton seats—cork inserts

If cork is used to form the center barrel in a skeleton seat, either of two methods of assembly can be followed. In the first, each component of the seat is fitted and mounted separately on the blank. An arbor sized for the fixed hood is first glued to the butt and the hood section glued over it. Then, the center cork section is constructed as a preformed piece, taper-reamed, and glued to the blank, or cork rings are glued directly to the blank and then turned down on a rod lathe to fit the sections of the seat (cover the fixed hood with masking tape to prevent scratching it during this operation). Finally, arbors for the threaded portion of the barrel are glued to the blank and the threaded section glued over them.

The other method is to construct the cork skeleton seat as a unit. The total desired length of the finished seat is first established. A cylinder of glued cork rings of this length is slipped on a dowel, metal rod, or some other mandrel, and chucked into a lathe or electric drill. The total length of the cylinder is then

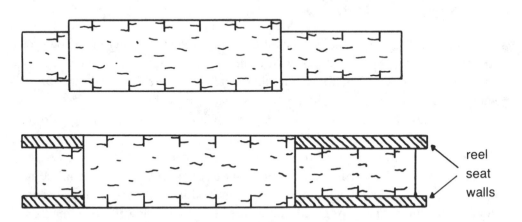

Skeleton seat with cork insert can be made by first shaping cork cylinder, over which sections of seat are glued.

sanded to achieve the finished diameter of the center portion of the seat. A careful measurement is made of the length of the fixed hood. A length to match is then turned down on one end of the cork cylinder. The depth of this cut is just enough to allow the fixed hood to be slipped in place on the cork cylinder. Work slowly and check your progress frequently. Next, the length of the threaded section of the seat is measured, and the same steps as for the fixed hood are repeated on the other end of the cork cylinder. The two sections of the skeleton seat are glued in position on the cork. When dry, the cork is taper-reamed to fit the blank and the entire unit is glued in place on the blank. For the rod builder making many rods, this method is faster, since a number of complete reel seat units are made at one time. Later, as needed, each can be taper-reamed to fit the particular blank. Some rod builders also feel that aligning all of the reel-seat components is easier using this technique.

Wood-button fly-reel seat

A very handsome wood fly-reel seat with a distinctive appearance can be made by the use of a matching wood button. For this you again need a skeleton seat on which the end cap is removable, since it will be replaced by the button. Rod builders who saw these finished seats on rods created enough of a demand for the shaped button that we had them made for us to include in our catalog.

However, anyone with access to a lathe can easily make one. Only a short length of solid wood, of the same type as the insert on the seat, is needed. The diameter of the largest part of the button is made exactly the same size as the wood insert in the seat. The length is generally about ½ to ¾ inch. A short plug is turned on one end of the button to fit inside the fixed hood. The outside diameter of the plug is determined by the inside diameter of the fixed hood. The length of the plug should be such that it will fit about one-third of the way into the end of the hood.

Cut a narrow groove around the plug to make a better glue joint inside the

Wood button to replace end cap on fly-reel seat.

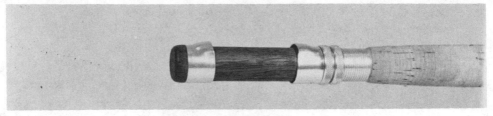

Skeleton seat with wood insert and matching wood button.

hood. Use epoxy to glue the plug into the hood. When completed, the finished reel seat has the appearance of one solid piece of hardwood from the button to the insert. The fixed hood looks as if it has been inlaid into this solid piece of wood.

If you do not have a lathe, you can make a wood button on an electric drill. Start with a piece of wood a few inches longer than the desired finished length. Saw or plane the oversized square piece of wood into an octagonal shape by removing the corners. Locate the center *on the end that will be the plug* and insert a long wood screw partway into the wood. Cut off the screw head with a hacksaw. This provides a shaft which can be chucked into the drill. Make a tool rest of a block of scrap wood so that its height is in line with the center of the wood. Use woodworking lathe tools, or just common wood chisels, to turn the button to shape. When completed, cut off the balance of the wood screw flush with the end of the plug portion of the button.

Inlaid wood reel seat

An eye-catching variation of this, or any wood reel seat, is one in which plastic trim rings have been inlaid. The appearance is definitely custom, and if the inlay matches the wrap design a beautifully integrated rod is the result. I have used this approach on one of my own personal fly rods. It is built on a brown blank with a brown skeleton seat containing a walnut insert and walnut button. The brown guide wraps are each "triple-tipped" with narrow bands of white, black, and white. These match the same sequence of white, black, and white plastic trim rings in the center of the walnut reel-seat insert.

The construction of this seat is exactly the same as that of any skeleton seat with a wood insert. The only difference is that the wood insert is cut exactly in half for insertion of the plastic trim rings. Use a hole saw to cut the plastic rings from ⅛-inch-thick sheets of Plexiglas as described in *Fiberglass Rod Making*. Enlarge the center holes and glue the three rings together. Slip them on a mandrel or threaded rod and turn them to the exact outside diameter of the wood insert. Just include the trim ring in the sequence when mounting on the blank.

It should be mentioned here that all the techniques previously discussed for skeleton reel seats are just as applicable to spinning as to fly rods. The obvious exception is the use of a wood button on the end. The only difference between a spinning-reel and a fly-reel seat is that the spinning model is larger and has both ends open for slipover installation.

Skeleton casting seats

Skeleton seats can also be employed on rods built for conventional, revolving-spool reels. An excellent example is the very functional model created by Gary Loomis, rod designer for Lamiglas. I first saw it on one of Gary's personal graphite steelhead rods. Since these rods are frequently fished in cold weather, the design was developed to place the caster's hand in touch with the maximum of cork and the minimum of cold metal. The fixed hood is completely covered with cork and is "buried" in the top part of the butt grip. The only exposed metal is the short threaded barrel containing the sliding hood and locking nuts. This is forward of the reel and therefore less likely to be held in the fisherman's hand. The cork spacer is unusual in that it is contoured to form the curved portion of the top end of the butt grip, with the rounded taper ending at the base of the threaded barrel. It is flattened on one side, flush with the "buried" fixed hood, to accommodate the feet of the reel.

To construct this assembly you can either work with preformed grips or cork rings. A skeleton fly-reel seat is the size seat to use. Let's first examine the use

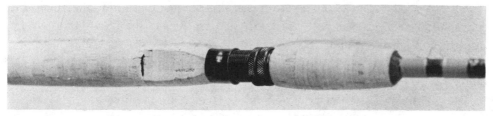

Skeleton casting-reel seat with fixed hood completely recessed beneath cork.

of preformed grip segments. The butt grip is cut square at the top end and is first taper-reamed to fit the blank. Then the hole at the upper end is enlarged so that the fixed hood will just fit inside it. Power tools work best to make this blind hole, but care must be exercised, since cork is removed so rapidly. A small round abrasive cylinder or piston can be chucked into a stationary drill and the grip fed into it. Or a flexible power shaft or Dremel tool can be used.

The preformed cork spacer is made next. The outside diameter at one end should be the same size as the top of the butt grip. It is then tapered and curved slightly to an outside diameter just slightly larger than the threaded reel-seat barrel. Include a tang, or reel-seat arbor, on each end that will just fit inside each of the reel-seat parts—the fixed hood on the bottom end and the threaded barrel on the top end. Fit another separate arbor for the balance of the space beneath the threaded barrel. Next, taper-ream this cork spacer and the separate reel-seat arbor to fit the blank. Carefully clamp the contoured cork spacer in a vise and file one side flat down to the diameter of the tang on each end. Check the fit of all parts assembled without glue on the blank. When satisfied with the fit, epoxy them in place, taking care to align the flat side of the spacer with the pocket in the fixed hood. After the glue dries, sand the cork to blend the surfaces of the butt grip and the spacer.

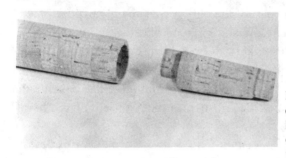

Preformed cork grips shaped for skeleton casting-reel seat. Fixed hood fits inside large hole in upper end of butt grip. Tang on shaped spacer fits inside fixed hood with flat side aligned.

The assembly can also be built of cork rings glued directly to the blank. Fit and glue the rings for the butt grip up to the point where the fixed hood will be located. Next, make a small round cork arbor to fit inside the fixed hood. It must be round so that there is space for the reel foot to slip inside the expanded pocket on the hood. Glue it onto the fixed hood, making sure no glue is on the cork surface under the pocket. When the glue dries, taper-ream the hole to fit the blank. The next step is to shape the hole of a cork ring to fit over the fixed hood. This is done with a round file. Depending upon the length of the fixed hood, you may have to use two cork rings. If so, cut the second one so it is just long enough to cover the hood. Glue the shaped cork over the hood, and glue the hood with previously installed and fitted arbor to the blank.

Work on the cork spacer comes next. Taper-ream a single cork ring to fit the blank, but do not glue it in place. Instead, file one side of the ring flat. Remove a small amount of material at a time and keep checking the depth of your flat until it is level with the cork inside the fixed hood pocket. When it is just flush, glue the ring to the blank and to the adjacent cork surface of the end of the butt grip. This single cork ring will serve as your template for filing the flat on the other rings that make up the spacer. Taper-ream the desired number of rings and glue them to the blank.

To mount the threaded barrel of the seat, fit and glue the necessary arbors to the blank. Then glue the threaded barrel over the arbors. Now go back and file the remaining cork rings of the spacer flat on one side, using the previously flattened single cork ring as a guide. The depth of the flat side should be flush with the first ring and with the surface of the threaded barrel.

Taper-ream the desired number of cork rings to make the foregrip and glue them to the blank. When the glue dries you can shape the butt and foregrip either by hand or in a rod lathe. With some creative imagination different variations of this type of reel seat can easily be developed. Just follow the basic techniques for working with preformed segments or individual cork rings.

Custom "grooved" seats

The hoods on any dark-colored anodized-aluminum reel seat can be given a custom touch by removing the anodizing in a narrow band around the base of each hood. These small stripes of bright metal add desirable accents and highlights. I have found them particularly attractive on black reel seats now so much

Custom "grooved" seat with decorative rings made by removing anodizing.

in vogue with graphite rods. They are also very handsome on all brown seats used with brown blanks. But let your own tastes and preferences dictate their use. After all, that's what custom rod building is all about.

To scrape away the anodizing in a narrow stripe around the base of the hood, you will need to mount the hood so that it can be turned in a lathe. First remove the nuts and sliding hood from the seat so you can work on the attached fixed hood. On a steel rod longer than the seat, build up a series of masking-tape arbors. The object is to make the outside diameter of the arbors just large enough so that the seat can be forced over them. Use a twisting motion in the same direction of rotation as the masking tape is wrapped. It may take some experimenting to get the proper size of the arbors. I find it helps to wind on slightly more tape than needed, then cut it off a bit at a time until a tight fit is obtained.

Chuck the projecting end of the steel rod into the lathe, or lacking one, into an electric drill. The leading edge of your cutting tool should be no wider than $1/16$ inch. A smaller size is preferred. This can be a miniature wood-turning chisel, or you can grind a tool from any piece of steel. You will be scraping the anodizing from the surface and cutting as shallowly as possible into the soft aluminum. Hence, a particularly hard cutting edge is not necessary. If you grind your own tool, first grind to the desired width, then square off the leading edge. Finally, round the edges just slightly.

Adjust your tool rest so that it is as close as practical to the seat. You will have to allow for the projection of the pocket into which the reel foot slips. Use a slow speed of rotation and with your cutting tool braced on the tool rest, feed it carefully into the hood. The cut forming the stripe is made at the base of the hood just below the end of the projecting pocket. Cut only deep enough to expose the bare aluminum.

If the center of rotation is at the exact center of the seat, and there is no wobble, you will get a clean cut of even depth and width all the way around the hood. If not, resist the temptation to feed your cutting tool further into the material to cut the "low side." By doing so you may cut too deeply into the "high side" of the hood. Instead, hold the cutting tool firmly in your right hand and use your left hand to rotate the chuck. In this way you can carefully scrape away the anodizing on the "low side."

After the fixed hood on the seat body is finished, proceed to the sliding hood. You can probably use one of the masking-tape arbors you made for the seat body. Since the sliding hood has a larger inside diameter, wind more tape on the arbor to increase its size for a tight press fit. When placing the sliding hood on the arbor, make sure it is straight. Proceed in exactly the same manner as you did for the fixed hood.

Shortening reel seats

Reel-seat manufacturers quite naturally make their seats long enough to mount a reel with the longest conceivable feet. In some cases, this results in a seat which is longer than practically required. As a custom rod builder you can reduce the length of an aluminum seat to proportions you feel are appropriate. To shorten a seat, use a fine-tooth saw, or hacksaw, to carefully cut off the desired amount from the threaded end of the barrel. A miter box will help keep the cut at a 90° angle to the axis of the seat. Use a flat file to square and smooth the end. Any metal burrs projecting inside the seat can be removed with a round file, or emery cloth held over the index finger. Care must be exercised to avoid scraping any anodizing from the outside of the seat.

The bare metal end resulting from the cut will be seated against the grip, and will not show on the finished rod. Nevertheless, some rod builders prefer to cover the thin cut edge with paint. A close color match is usually obtainable from the wide assortment of model paints found in a hobby store. To make sure the solvents in the glue will not smear the paint, it is a good idea to cover the painted edge with a coat of clear shellac. This same technique can be used when cutting out the center, unthreaded barrel portion of an all-metal seat to make your own skeleton seat.

On spinning seats the question frequently arises whether the seat should be mounted with fixed hood toward the butt or toward the tip. There really is no correct answer. It depends upon the preference of the angler, and is just another way in which the custom rod can be tailored to the person who will fish it.

No reel seat

No discussion of reel seats would be complete without considering the fact that some custom rods are made without any seat. Instead the reel is taped or clamped directly onto the cork handle. The handle can be built of cork rings or of cork tape.

The reasons for building a rod without a seat are varied, with tradition in a given area often contributing greatly. New England surf rods are an example. Many fishermen there find that a reel seat is biting cold to the hand when wading deep in a cold surf. They have also found that unless a seat is washed in fresh water after fishing and the threads are occasionally given a light coat of oil, the seat can become jammed from saltwater corrosion. It is then a major repair job to replace the seat. In other parts of the country, some anglers feel that a freshwater spinning rod is lighter without a reel seat. They prefer a straight cork grip long enough to allow the fisherman to mount the reel at whatever point balances best for him. It should also be mentioned that a few rod builders do not know how to properly glue a reel seat to the blank and, having had some seats come loose, omit the seat as a method of avoiding the problem. The chapter on gluing in this book should enable them to return to using reel seats if they want to.

If no reel seat is provided, the reel can be mounted in a number of ways. Perhaps the most common for spinning rods is to use plastic tape wrapped in a figure-eight around the reel feet and the grip. For conventional reels, the reel can be held either with clamps that come with the reel, or with a small pair of stainless hose clamps. With clamps, the grip beneath the reel must be thick enough to provide a cushion. Too much pressure when tightening the clamps can damage the blank.

A more recent method of mounting reels on seatless rods was pointed out by RodCrafter Paul Winston. Inexpensive nylon straps available at electrical-supply houses are used. These are $3/16$-inch wide and come in 5-inch and 7-inch lengths. Electricians use them for tying groups of wires together. They are most ingenious, with ridges all across the face of one side (the outside when installed). At one end of the strap there is a tiny ratchetlike mechanism inside a small, square head. This engages the ridges and locks the strap tight.

To mount a reel, a strap is wrapped around each reel foot and the grip, and pulled up tight with a pair of pliers. The excess is cut off, leaving a small tab to grab hold of if it becomes necessary to tighten again. The straps are amazingly strong, and care must be exercised when pulling them tight or they will bury themselves in a cork handle. On spinning rods they should be placed so that the small head does not end up beneath the angler's palm.

They are small and light; a supply is easily carried in a tackle box or pocket. To remove, cut them off with a diagonal wirecutter or knife. It is thus possible to reposition a reel in a minute or two.

FOUR

Grips and Handles

MATERIALS FOR GRIPS AND HANDLES

Cork, the most commonly used material for grips and handles, is light in weight, firm yet slightly compressible, and easily worked and shaped. It is provided to the tackle industry in the form of rings ½ inch wide and of various diameters, with the most common size being 1⅛ inches. There are two kinds of cork rings: specie, which is cut so that the pits run parallel to the axis of the hole in the center, and mustard, which is cut so that the pits run at 90° to the axis. By far the better and stronger for grips is the specie cork. You can spot it on a grip by the frequent light wavy lines around the exterior. These are from the annular growth rings.

A number of factors determine the quality of cork rings, and it takes a well-trained eye and knowledge of cork to determine exact classification. The grades are designated by letters of the alphabet from A (the best) to E (the worst used for tackle). The primary factors of quality for the custom rod builder are density, freedom from pits, and absence of dark particles of the exterior bark.

Grade AA cork ring and regular extra-select specie cork ring.

The quality of available cork has deteriorated in recent years, and the price has risen substantially. What today is called extra-select specie cork would merely have been termed specie cork ten or fifteen years ago. Obviously, the designations for the grades have also changed. The present A grade would have been a C grade in years past. When making a grip from cork rings, the rod builder must today select and position each ring carefully. The larger-diameter portions of the grip can be made from rings of which most of the pits are near the center hole and the rim is relatively clear. Similarly, the smaller-diameter grip sections should be made of rings as free as possible of pits toward the center of the ring. On these the pits and blemishes near the outer edge of the ring will be sanded away.

Preformed grips. Most rod companies and many custom rod builders use grips that have been assembled and shaped by the cork companies abroad. These grips have the pits and holes filled with a paste made of cork dust and an adhesive, prior to the finish sanding of the grip. They are also graded by alphabetical designation reflecting both the grade of cork rings used and the quality of workmanship. Most are grades B, C, and D. When using preformed grips only light finish sanding and slight exterior fitting can be done. If more material is removed, you will expose the subsurface, unfilled pits. This will destroy the appearance of the grip or necessitate hand-filling of the new holes.

Compressed cork. This is a very poor substitute for cork grip on fishing rods. Found on only the cheapest of factory rods, it is made of small bits of waste cork that have been ground up, combined with an adhesive, and compressed in a mold. Even if finely sanded, the particles are still quite visible. It does not wear as well, does not feel as good in the hand, and is slightly heavier.

What is commonly referred to as burnt cork by rod builders has not been burned at all. It is made of special particles of dark cork that are compressed into rings under tremendous pressure. No adhesive is added. The great pressures utilize the natural resins in the cork as a bonding agent. The rings are pressed (or glued) into cork cylinders. When sanded, a beautifully even, grain-free finish results.

Cork tape. This is also a form of compressed cork. It is made of ground-up particles of both cork and rubber (or synthetic plastics). An adhesive is added and the composition is pressed into flat sheets. It resembles some common gasket materials. For the tackle industry it is provided in 100-foot rolls, 1 inch wide, with an adhesive backing so that it can be spirally wrapped around the blank.

Man-made resilient materials

Initially, the development of these materials was prompted by a need for something that would wear better than cork on heavier saltwater rods. Weight was not a primary consideration, and the early grips were considerably heavier than cork. The better ones had a good nonslip surface even when wet, and were impervious to gasoline and most common solvents. They could take far more abuse than cork, and retained their original appearance much longer. While there were various formulations, one of the best to emerge was Hypalon, fairly heavy but very rugged. This is a registered trade name of a product developed by DuPont consisting of rubber and synthetic plastics. All of these materials are extruded as long cylinders which are then cut to the desired length and ground to shape.

As the quality of cork declined while the price increased, more and more interest has been given the development of lighter-weight resilient grip materials. Opinions differ as to how resilient the ideal material should be. Some want it as firm as cork, while others want the material to be softer and more cushionlike. In recent years a number of new materials have been introduced. Some proved unsatisfactory after prolonged exposure to weather, particularly the ultraviolet rays of the sun. On these, the surface forms a crust which lacks resiliency and then develops cracks. It should be noted that a custom rod builder can often rejuvenate these grips by sanding them with the rod in a power-driven lathe. However, this is only a temporary measure which will have to be repeated again in time, and it reduces the diameter.

Other new materials are excellent, weighing about the same as cork. They will not dent, nor will pieces break away at the ends or from sharply contoured points as happens with cork. The surface does not become slippery when wet, even with fish slime. Texture and color are consistent throughout. Usually dark in color, they do not show the dirt as does cork. Nor are there any filled pits to erode as with cork.

At the time of this writing, some characteristics of the new materials can be identified to help the custom builder in his selection. Lightweight Hypalon is lighter than regular Hypalon, but is one of the heaviest of the new materials. It is best used on saltwater rods or heavy freshwater rods, and will give very dependable service. Foamlite was quite soft initially, but has changed a number of times. Currently it is of about medium firmness. One of the problems for the rod builder is that this particular manufacturer changes material frequently and the custom builder cannot be sure exactly what he will get. Cellite is a very firm material which, as I understand it, was developed for the handles of ski poles. It is a bit harder to install and does not stretch as much or as easily as some of the other materials. Some rod builders believe it is too firm and lacks the luxurious feel possible with lightweight resilient grips, but this is a matter of personal preference. At the present time it is the only material offered in a two-tone, swirled pattern. Customgrip was designed exclusively for fishing-rod grips. It is of closed-cell construction and will not absorb water. While all the materials under discussion can be shaped by grinding in one fashion or another, Customgrip is by far the easiest to work with. In fact, it is the only grip material available to the custom builder in unshaped lengths, as well as shaped grips. Of medium firmness, it stretches quite well and is adaptable to a wide range of blank diameters.

These new lightweight resilient grips do an exceptional job of filling the need for a cork substitute. They can be used on practically all kinds of rods with the possible exception of fly rods. Here, there is a school of anglers which feels that some of the subtle finger pressures applied to the grip when casting are absorbed by the material and not conducted to the blank. Another consideration is tradition. There are those fishermen who think a fishing rod should have grips made of cork simply because they have always been made of cork. Another future consideration will be cost. The materials are made from petrochemicals and the increasing price of oil will undoubtedly be reflected in the cost.

Wood

Hardwoods, particularly straight-grained hickory, have long been used for the butts on trolling rods and boat rods. Some of the older surf rods frequently had butts of wood, and many older boat rods were made with hardwood foregrips. Wood butts will undoubtedly be with us for a long time. However, on more expensive IGFA trolling rods wood is being replaced with stronger aluminum. As a foregrip on boat rods, wood weathers badly in the salt and sun, and tends to be slippery when wet. Many other materials are more suitable. On freshwater custom rods a few talented builders are using exotic hardwoods. They are occasionally seen in shaped and checkered fashion as the grip on casting rod handles, and in round smooth style on spinning rods.

Miscellaneous materials

Cloth foregrips are rarely seen today. Construction basically consisted of layers of felt glued one on top of the other. It is a very old method, and such grips did not wear very well.

Flocked grips are very modern. They are frequently referred to as Felt Flocked Foregrips. They should not be confused with the previously mentioned old-style felt cloth grips. First a cork grip of the desired size is shaped. It is then coated with epoxy and tiny, short synthetic fibers are imbedded in the glue by an electrostatic process. After the epoxy cures, the fibers are so firmly anchored that they cannot be removed even by rubbing with a wire brush. The fibers stand out from the grip like a brush with extremely short bristles. This provides an excellent nonslip gripping surface for big-game trolling rods. The appearance is quite plush, denoting the high price of these grips. Installation is the same as for cork grips.

There are less common materials used by skilled rod builders to make excellent and unusual grips. For the most part these are used on saltwater rods, and are either wrapped directly onto the blank or over a shaped cork form. They are held in place by one or more layers of epoxy. Nylon or plastic cord of various diameters is used, as well as long strips of vinyl and synthetic leather.

INSTALLING CORK GRIPS

Cork rings can each be individually reamed to fit their respective position, and glued directly to the blank and to each other. After the glue dries, the cork cylinder is shaped into the desired grip.

Fitting each cork is most often done with a round file. The hole must not only be enlarged, but kept centered. The sides of the hole should theoretically conform to the taper of the blank. Since a cork ring is only ½ inch long, the taper over that short a length will be rather insignificant. It is therefore suggested that you file the sides of the hole so they are parallel to the outside surface of the ring. Attempting to match a taper generally results in too large a hole at one end, and a poor glue joint.

To keep the hole centered it is easiest for most people to make a reference mark on the cork, rest it on the workbench, and file horizontally. The reference mark is for turning the cork one-eighth of a rotation at a time. The same number of file strokes is made in each of the eight positions. The hole will then be enlarged evenly, and the fit should be checked on the blank. This technique is explained in detail in *Fiberglass Rod Making*.

Pattern makers have long done much of their intricate filing by moving the file vertically. Some rod builders have found the same system works well for enlarging the hole in cork rings. They work over a wastebasket to catch the cork crumbs and hold the ring low. In this way they can look down on the cork and visually keep the hole centered as they move the file up and down and move it progressively around the hole.

Still other rod builders fit individual cork rings with a power reamer. This can consist of any one of a number of kinds of tapered reamers chucked into a drill or lathe. Generally, quite a bit of experience is required to know how far along the tapered reamer to move the cork ring so that it fits properly in its place on the blank. The cork ring must also be held absolutely parallel with the axis of the reamer or the hole will be at an angle.

Regardless of the technique used to fit the rings, it is important that they be reassembled in the same sequence when actually glued. The most foolproof method is to number the corks with a felt-tipped pen. Do this while they are still in place on the blank, just after the last one has been fitted.

As noted in the chapter on gluing, the blank should be roughened where the grip will be glued. If you spread glue on the entire area of the blank to be covered by the grip, each cork ring slipped over the blank will scrape more of the glue away. There will not be enough glue remaining when the last corks are slipped in place. To eliminate this possibility, spread glue on the blank for only a couple of corks at a time. No glue should be placed on the end faces of the first and last cork rings. On all others, spread an even coat of glue on both faces, making sure you have worked glue into any pits. If epoxy is used, clamping is really not necessary, but the assembly should be pushed together to seat all the rings and left undisturbed while the glue cures. If the rings do not all join evenly, clamping under mild pressure will hold them together. Evaporative cements should be clamped tightly, but will take longer to dry completely. Clamping techniques will be found later in this chapter and in the chapter on tools.

It should be mentioned here that if your handle design includes any inlays of trim rings of hardwood, plastic, or impregnated walnut, as well as hosels, these pieces should first be shaped to the finished size. They are then roughened on each face and the inside of the hole. When the individual cork rings are glued to the blank, these inlaid pieces are also glued to the blank and to the adjacent cork rings in their respective positions on the grip. When the cork cylinder is shaped to form the grip, the cork is blended into the edges of the previously sized inlays. Burnt-cork trim rings can be glued along with regular cork and all sanded at the same time.

Narrow trim rings of about ⅛ inch do not need to have the blank built up to fit a larger hole size. Wider inlays, such as ½ inch, with a hole size greater than the blank are best anchored by building up the blank beneath them. This can be done with epoxy and thread (or light string), or the space can be filled with a nonflowing epoxy such as PC-7. If the latter is used, it is a good idea to file a number of narrow notches or grooves along the inside of the hole with a small three-cornered file. When the epoxy cures these act like key slots to firmly anchor the trim ring.

Shaping cork grips

Cork can easily be shaped by hand. It is just slower than power shaping and requires more care to keep the finished grip centered around the blank. First reduce the rough cylinder of cork rings to an even diameter slightly larger than the widest portion of the grip. If much cork is to be removed, a coarse file or rasp can be used. Cork crumbles and gouges easily, so do not use much pressure and stop considerably short of the finished diameter. If you want to play it safe, use very coarse sandpaper (50 or 60 grit) backed by a small block.

A technique which may help keep the blank centered is to first slightly flatten four sides equally. Next slightly flatten the four corners equally. You now have a rough octagonal shape. It is an easy step to round the eight corners into a cylinder. To reduce the diameter at any point further, such as on the end of a tapered grip, make a reference mark on the cork and make the same number of filing strokes for each one-eighth rotation.

When you have created the desired shape, but oversize, switch to finer-grit sandpaper (100 or 150 grit) and develop the final contours. The last bit of cork is removed with medium-fine sandpaper (200 or 250 grit). When you are satisfied with the shape and diameter, finish with extra-fine paper (300 to 400 grit).

There are some custom shapes that can only be made by hand shaping. One that is eye-catching, as well as surprisingly functional, is a tapered square spinning handle assembly. The first of these grips that I saw was developed by Rod-Crafter Jimmie D. York. As is often the case in custom rod work, Jimmie came up with the first model as an experiment on one of his own rods. A customer saw it and insisted on purchasing the rod. He was so pleased with it, he ordered another with the same handle design. Word got around, and soon Jimmie was building many rods utilizing this style.

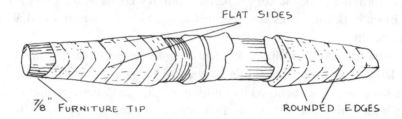

FLAT SIDES

⅞" FURNITURE TIP   ROUNDED EDGES

Tapered square cork spinning handle.

To make the handle, first glue the desired number of rings to the blank along with the reel seat. File or coarse-sand the cork cylinder of each grip into a square shape. Next, taper the square over the length of each grip. Make the square configuration less severe and more round at the extreme butt end where the butt cap will be placed. A soft, pliable type of butt cap works best, since it will mold itself to the slightly squared-off shape. Jimmie uses ⅞-inch soft plastic furniture leg tips. The diameter of the butt cap will, of course, be determined by the amount of taper you use on the grip.

After the rough tapered square shape is made, switch to medium-grit paper backed by a small block, and smooth the four flat sides. Using the same sandpaper without the block, gently round the four edges. The degree to which they are rounded is a matter of personal preference. Finish sanding with progressively finer paper.

Another grip that can only be done by hand shaping is a "hammer handle" fly-rod grip. This is an extremely functional shape. One of the problems in fly casting is to keep the rod in proper alignment throughout the cast. This grip is a great aid in this regard. It is equally adaptable to a hand position where the thumb is placed on top of the grip, or one where the thumb is along the side. The shape of handles on hammers was designed long ago to permit a good strong grasp and control accuracy. These are the requirements of a fly-rod grip, and the shape is a natural. It probably has not been used more since it does not lend itself to mass-production techniques. It is also a departure from tradition, and fly fishermen are frequently the most tradition-bound members of the angling fraternity. The longer the rod and the heavier the fly line to be cast, the more applicable is the design. It has been my experience that the majority of fly fishermen prefer the grip after they have had an opportunity to fish with a rod so equipped.

To determine the shape of the grip you only need a quality hammer as a model. Inspecting and measuring it will tell you far more than I can describe here.

The techniques previously described are used after gluing the cork rings directly on the blank. Naturally, you can adjust the size to fit the hand of the person who will fish the rod.

Fly-rod grips that have depressions for the caster's thumb and/or contours to fit other fingers must also have the final shaping done by hand. The overall configuration of the grip is done by whatever technique you normally use, be it hand shaping or power turning, but with the cork glued directly to the blank. In this type of grip the diameter is critical and should be made so that it is most comfortable for the person who will fish the rod. It really is necessary for that person to be present when the final diameter and the contours are made.

Have the angler hold the rod in his normal casting position. With a soft lead

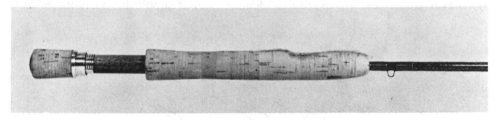

Fly-rod grip with depression for caster's thumb.

pencil, trace the outline of his thumb or fingers. Use a large round file held at an angle across the grip to make the depression. Remove only a small amount of cork at a time and constantly check the fit with the fisherman. As you near the desired depth of the contour, switch to a piece of medium sandpaper wrapped around a length of wood dowel. When the final shape is achieved, finish with a piece of fine sandpaper.

A few hints may be of help. If there is to be more than one depression or contour, work on both of them at the same time as you constantly check the fit against the caster's hand. He will be better able to feel the shape of the grip develop, and you will be less likely to remove too much cork. In general, it is better to make the contours too shallow than too deep. After the angler fishes with the rod for a while, the contours can always be made deeper. Always use a round file or dowel wrapped with sandpaper for the shaping. A few years ago one of the leading magazines carried an article on making this type of grip, and they suggested making the shape with a penknife. It is quite easy to cut too far into the cork, and also much more difficult to control the shape of the depression with a knife. Slicing cork can frequently cause it to crumble, so use a filing technique.

Grips on which the cork rings have been glued directly to the blank can also be shaped by power turning. This really is the best method for obtaining a perfectly round grip with the blank in the exact center. Various types of rod lathes can be used; you will find descriptions in the chapter on tools. Before you start turning a handle assembly, place a layer or two of masking tape on the ends of the reel seat to protect it from scratches. Power shaping will produce cork dust, which will float through the air and ultimately settle on everything in the shop. This can be eliminated by using a vacuum cleaner while shaping. Some sort of temporary or permanent support will be needed to hold the hose and a wide nozzle just below the revolving grip. A homemade support and clamp can be built from scrap wood, or the hose can be held over any convenient object with long strips of masking tape. The hose should come from behind the lathe, and it is helpful to rig an extension cord with an on-off switch to the lathe operator's position. Whenever cork is being sanded the vacuum cleaner should be operating.

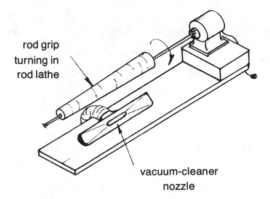

rod grip
turning in
rod lathe

vacuum-cleaner
nozzle

Vacuum-cleaner nozzle picks up cork dust from shaping grips.

If a file or rasp is used for rough shaping, extreme care must be used, especially if the lathe revolves at high speed. Chunks of cork can inadvertently be gouged from the grip, ruining it. Cork is removed quickly on a lathe, and 50-60 grit sandpaper is quite coarse enough for rough shaping. As a rule of thumb, the higher the speed at which the cork is revolved, the finer the grit which should be used. Some rod builders work freehand with strips of this paper. Others feel they have more control when the paper is glued on long, flat strips of wood and used much like a file.

When using sandpaper boards, files, mild rasps, or any similar tool, it is best not to hold the tool horizontally on top of the revolving grip. More control will be obtained by resting the end of the tool on the bench or lathe bed behind the grip. Place it far enough behind so that when the portion that will do the cutting is lowered onto the grip, the tool will be at an angle rather than vertical. Making shallow cuts, the tool can be slid along the bench and the grip in this position, and a straight cylinder of constant diameter can easily be made. Use the tool in the same fashion for precisely controlled tapers, as well as cutting recesses for butt caps, etc. Ends of grips are best rounded with finer grit, 100 to 150. While shaping, use a pair of calipers frequently to check the diameter.

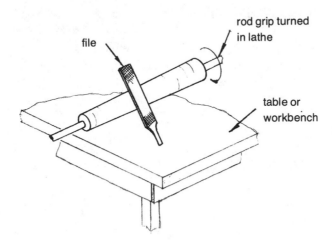

Rest end of file, or similar shaping tool, on bench for best control during rough shaping.

Curves and contours are often made by working freehand with various-width strips of sandpaper. Another technique that affords more precise control and predictable results is to make a number of curved shaping tools. These are quite easy to make by shaping a piece of wood to the desired curvature, coating it with epoxy, and embedding cutting grit. Lengths of stock wood molding can be used, or a piece of soft wood can be shaped by hand. If such tools are made long, like a file, they can be used by supporting them in exactly the same manner as just described.

Cutting grit is available in various sizes from some rod-building-supply houses. A small quantity goes a long way. You might also purchase it locally by looking under abrasives in the Yellow Pages. Use a quality, slow-curing epoxy and spread a fairly thick coat. Lay a piece of household wax paper on your workbench. Sprinkle the grit liberally over the epoxy-coated form. When the tool is fully covered with grit, roll it under light pressure in the accumulated grit on the wax paper, and set it aside until the epoxy cures. Pour the grit remaining on the wax paper back into the container for future use.

This technique has almost limitless uses for making your own abrasive tools. Flat files of all sizes are quickly made. Curved boards of various widths and degrees of curvature can be prepared to develop any shape in a grip. Small custom sanding wheels or cylinders of different sizes are easily made to chuck into a drill or Dremel tool. One of the advantages of these tools is that if they ever become dull, they can be recharged with another coat of epoxy and cutting grit.

If many grips of the same shape are to be made, a form that will make the entire grip in one cutting operation can be developed. One way of doing this is to cut the end of a flat board, ¼ to ½ inch thick, to the desired contour and coat the shaped end with cutting grit. Build a small table rest for your shaping board at a height that will feed the shaper into the center of the revolving grip. This

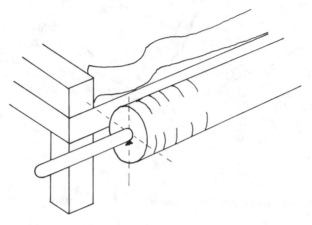

Height of table is made so that center of cutting board is aligned with center of mandrel holding cork.

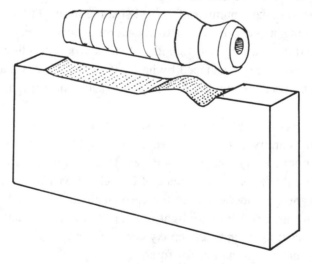

Edge of cutting board is cut to desired contours and coated with coarse, abrasive grit.

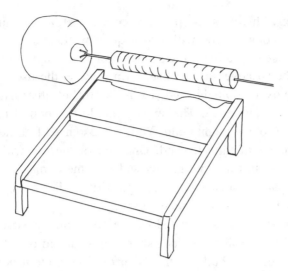

Side rails on table keep cutting board aligned as it is fed into revolving cork.

table should be longer than the grip and have alignment strips or channels on the top into which the cutting board can be slipped. The small table is clamped to the workbench in front of the lathe, making sure it is parallel to the axis of the grip. The cutting tool is slowly fed into the revolving cork until the rough shape is complete. Finish sanding is then done with strips of fine sandpaper.

If you do not have a rod lathe, you can still shape your grips by power turning. In this case, instead of gluing the cork rings to the blank, you make your own preformed grips. When completed, these are taper-reamed to fit the blank. Turning is accomplished by any available power head, such as an electric hand drill. This can be held in a special stand (Sears Roebuck has an excellent one), or you can make your own. Another possibility is to hold the drill in a vise.

Quite a few different methods can be used to hold the cork rings while the glue cures and for turning. A simple method described in *Fiberglass Rod Making* is to make a wrap of string on a length of straight dowel. The diameter should be such that a tight fit exists and each cork ring (with glue on the two faces, but not in the hole) has to be twisted in place. When the grip is finished, the end of the string is picked out with a needle and unraveled from beneath the grip. Hardwood dowels are not always as straight as desired, and metal rods will revolve more true. Instead of a wrap of string, a layer of masking tape can be wrapped on the metal rod for a tight fit of the cork rings. Do not make the fit so tight that the finished grip cannot be removed. The object is to just keep the glued cork cylinder from revolving on the metal rod while it is being sanded. If you are working with cork stick (preglued cork rings), a few thin layers of masking tape spaced along the rod will hold it quite well.

A method used by quite a few RodCrafter Associates and explained in the *Journal* by Robert Ludke and Michael Grimshaw is the use of threaded rod as an arbor. The most commonly used size is ⅜-16, but other handy sizes to have are ¼-20, ⁵/₁₆-18, and ½-13. The lengths should be about 4 to 6 inches longer than the longest grip you might build. You will also need four nuts and two washers to fit each piece of threaded rod. One end of the rod will be chucked into an electric drill, so in time the threads will become damaged. Either mark that end with some paint so that you always place it in the chuck, or have one end of each rod turned by a local machine shop.

The length of rod to be covered by the cork rings is first determined, and a layer of masking tape about ⅛ inch shorter is wrapped over that section of the threaded rod. If need be, build up this layer of tape to the inside diameter of the cork rings you are using. Rub the tape with a piece of paraffin to form a moderate coat of wax. This prevents the glue from attaching the cork to the arbor.

A washer is placed at one end of the tape, followed by two nuts. From the opposite end of the rod, slide on a cork ring, seating it against the washer. Apply glue to the face opposite the washer. Each succeeding cork ring has a film of glue spread on both faces and is slid in place against the preceding cork. On the last cork, no glue is placed on the outer face; otherwise it would become glued to the washer which is placed against it. After the washer is slipped over the rod, the two nuts are added. These nuts are tightened as required for the type of glue being used. It is a good idea to wipe off any glue squeezed out to make it easier to turn the grip later.

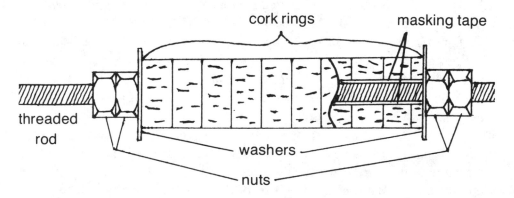

Threaded rod is used to hold cork cylinder for shaping.

After the glue has cured, one end of the threaded rod is chucked into a drill or other power head. If tight clamping pressure was not used while the glue dried, the nuts can be tightened more before turning. While not absolutely necessary, it is recommended that some sort of support be used for the other end of the rod. This could be a simple V-shaped block of wood of the correct height. The techniques for shaping the preformed grip are exactly the same as those discussed above for shaping a grip directly on the blank rotated in a rod lathe. When the grip is completed, it is removed from the arbor and taper-reamed to fit the blank.

A word about the washers and finishing the ends of the grips. Some rod builders prefer to use washers at least as large as the cork rings in order to provide equal pressure and to prevent the washer from digging into the face of the cork rings on each end. If you use this approach, you cannot shape the end of each grip flush against the washer. One technique is to add one or two extra cork rings when placing them on the rod. These are to be waste cork and will subsequently be removed. The grip is shaped, including the ends, which will be located ¼ to ½ inch from each washer. The final step in making the grip is to hold a sharp knife against the revolving cork at each end and cut through to the arbor.

The other approach is to use washers that are smaller in diameter than the finished size of the end of the grip. The end of the grip can then be shaped free of any interference from the washers. After the shaped grip is removed from the threaded rod, the end of the foregrip can be lightly hand-dressed with sandpaper if needed. Similarly, the end of the butt grip that has been recessed for the butt cap can be hand-dressed and any flashing trimmed away.

This same style assembly on a threaded rod is an excellent method to use

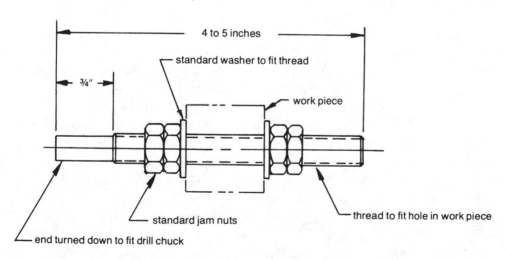

Threaded rod, washers, and lock nuts hold wood and plastic parts for shaping.

to turn and shape hardwood and plastic trim rings and hosels. A shorter length of rod can be used and no end support is required. If you are combining hardwood and plastic, the setup can be used for clamping the pieces until the glue cures.

When turning these parts you will need washers smaller in diameter than the finished diameter of the piece being shaped. You will also need a tool rest. One can be made by clamping a block of scrap lumber to the workbench in front of the mounted pieces. Its height should be to the center line of the grip. If you have wood-turning chisels, fine. If not, use a regular wood chisel and shape with a light scraping action. The drill should be positioned so that the work revolves from over the top and down against the cutting edge of the chisel. The tool rest thus holds the chisel steady for precise control. Do not try to remove too much material at one time. After the desired shape or size is achieved, smooth with fine sandpaper or emery cloth.

Plastic parts can be buffed using a polishing compound or toothpaste. Hardwood parts should have the finish applied and dried before being glued along with the cork rings forming the grip. In this manner you can sand the surrounding cork rings to the exact same diameter. If you apply the finish after the grip is completed, there is danger of staining the cork with the finish. Also, the finish adds slightly to the diameter of the wood and, if it is applied beforehand, the cork can be sanded perfectly flush.

Taper-reaming the grip

There is one method of making preformed grips, used by RodCrafter George L. Dietz, that eliminates the need for taper-reaming after the grip is made and assures a very good fit of the grip to the blank. First, each cork ring is individually filed or reamed for a perfect fit on the blank. When all of the corks are on the blank, but not glued, a felt-tip pen is used to number them. An arbor of threaded rod is used as was previously described. However, the cork rings have already been fitted to the blank, and the hole in each one is slightly larger than the cork preceding it as viewed from tip to the butt. In order to keep the rings centered on the arbor, the threaded rod is wrapped with masking tape to build a tapered form that duplicates the blank. From that point, you proceed exactly the same as for making any preformed grip as discussed earlier, being sure to glue the corks in place on the arbor in the proper sequence. When the grip is shaped and finished, it is removed from the arbor and, since it already fits the taper of the blank, is glued in place on the blank.

All other methods of making preformed grips will have a hole of constant diameter, which will have to be taper-reamed to fit the taper of the blank. The most common method of doing this is with a round tapered file. If you do not attach a handle to the file it can be held by either end. This makes it easier to use either end of the file and work from either end of the grip—a definite aid in removing any high spots that develop inside the grip.

This method is described in detail in *Fiberglass Rod Making*. Briefly, it consists of placing a reference mark on each end of the grip and laying the grip on a flat work surface. The file is inserted at an angle approximating that of the blank's taper. The reference marks are used to make the same number of file strokes for each one-eighth rotation of the grip. In this manner the hole is kept centered inside the grip while it is enlarged. As mentioned earlier in this chapter, some builders prefer filing vertically. As cork is removed from inside the hole, the grip is repeatedly slipped over the blank to check progress and to make sure that not too much cork is being removed from one end. This is easily detected by a wobble in one end of the grip. If this occurs, remove more material from inside the other end, until the grip again matches the taper. Small amounts of cork should be removed, and frequent checks made, until the grip slides into its final position. A light scratch is then made around the blank at the upper end of the grip, and the grip is removed. The blank is roughened and coated with glue, and the grip is slipped into position with a twisting motion to spread the glue evenly.

Final fitting of preformed cork grips can sometimes be a problem. If the grip is too long to conveniently file, it can be cut or broken into two pieces and the hole in each filed to fit the blank. The two sections are rejoined when they are glued to the blank. If the grip is cut in two, use a fine-tooth saw and place a mark across the cut. This mark is later used to perfectly align each section when it is glued. Advocates of the technique of breaking the cork into two pieces point out that the irregularly shaped ends of the break will automatically provide perfect alignment at the gluing stage. The only danger in breaking a long grip is that some small pieces of cork may crumble and be broken loose completely.

Another problem that can occur in fitting a preformed grip when the hole has been enlarged and tapered with a file is that of one or more high spots inside the grip. These can often be removed or leveled by using a dowel wrapped with sandpaper. Another technique has been developed by RodCrafter Walter H. Wesner. He suggests using Scotch double-stick tape No. 400, and applying it to the blank *above the location* where the grip is to finally be glued. The tape is then covered with an open spiral strip of sandpaper. The combined thickness of the tape and the sandpaper determines how far above the gluing location the tape is placed. The idea is to have the outside diameter of the tape and sandpaper on the blank be the same as the outside diameter of the blank at the point where the grip is to be glued.

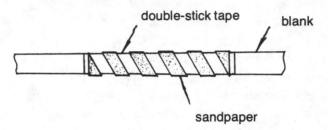

Sandpaper wrapped over double-stick tape can be used to remove high spots when fitting preformed grip.

The previously filed grip is then slipped over the blank and slowly worked over the taped sandpaper. It is rotated in the same direction as the spiral. In the process any high spots will be removed along with the last bit of cork. As the grip is worked off the lower end of the sandpaper, it should form a perfect fit on the blank at the point where it will be glued. The sandpaper and tape are peeled off the blank and the normal gluing process is followed.

Sometimes aggressive use of a file on a preformed grip enlarges the very ends of the hole a bit too much. The grip as a whole may fit well, but the undisguised presence of an unsightly gap at the top end of the grip ruins everything. A number of techniques can be used. A winding check that fits the blank snugly at that point will hide the slightly larger hole. Some rod builders will first fill the hole with a mixture of cork dust and Cork Filler Adhesive or other glue before installing the winding check.

RodCrafter Dan Abramson feels the best way to correct this problem, if it occurs, is to cut off the end of the grip squarely and add a single cork ring. This individual ring can be carefully filed for a perfect, snug fit on the blank. The grip and the fitted ring are glued simultaneously to the blank and to each other. After the glue has hardened the cork ring is filed and sanded to blend into the shape of the original grip. By using the preformed grip as a template of sorts, near-perfect roundness should be achieved without hazard. Dan also uses this technique to modify the appearance of a "store-bought grip" and give it a dimension of originality. These grips are already squared off at the end, although depending upon the shape desired, a bit may have to be removed.

If it is found that too much material was removed from inside a preformed cork grip at one end, it need not be discarded. To eliminate the wobble at that end and attain a proper fit, the blank can be built up slightly with masking tape or thread and epoxy. Glue is applied over this shim and the remainder of the blank where the grip is to be glued.

The rod builder who frequently works with preformed grips, either those that he buys or those that he makes himself, will find it worthwhile to make a set of taper reamers. They can be for hand or power use. Obviously, they can also be used to taper-ream cork reel-seat bushings. If you have previously glued the bushings inside the reel seats, you can quickly taper-ream and glue an entire handle assembly.

The easiest method to make tapered reamers is with abrasive cutting grit of Size 24 to 46, and quality epoxy glue. The grit is epoxied to a tapered mandrel over an area slightly longer than the longest grip to be reamed. Any sturdy material can be used for the tapered mandrel; the most common is a length of rod blank. My own reamers are made from sections of blanks, and when a customer saw them he purchased an 11½-foot medium-action surf blank with a fairly level taper—and proceeded to cut it into lengths right in our shop! Other materials that can be used for the mandrel include solid fiberglass blanks, solid aluminum rod, and hardwood dowels. The solid fiberglass can have the taper changed by sanding while it is revolved under power. Both aluminum rod and hardwood can be turned to the desired taper on a wood lathe. A more expensive but exceptionally durable mandrel can be made from steel rod machined by a local machine shop to the required taper. Whatever the mandrel, it must be remembered that the addition of the glue and grit will increase the outside diameter uniformly over the length of the reamer. The increase must be allowed for when selecting the tapered mandrel.

After the piece of blank or other mandrel has been selected, make a widely spaced spiral of masking tape over the area to be covered with cutting grit. Allow an uncoated length for a handhold, or shorter space to fit in a chuck. The tape should be ¼ to ½ inch wide. If you plan to use the reamer in a power head, such as a lathe or drill, make certain you spiral the tape in the same direction that your motor rotates. Next, coat this section of the reamer with epoxy glue. The glue should not be so thin in consistency that it is runny, and the coating should be moderately thick.

Spread a sheet of kitchen wax paper on a flat work surface. Hold the reamer a few inches above the wax paper and liberally sprinkle the grit onto the glue-covered mandrel, rotating it for complete coverage. When the reamer is entirely covered with grit, roll it in the accumulated grit on the wax paper. This will imbed the abrasive in the epoxy. Set the reamer aside, preferably by clamping the uncoated end in a vise. Wait until the epoxy has just started to set up. This usually requires about a half-hour to an hour. Then, starting at one end, carefully peel off the spiral of tape. The resultant open space provides a channel to carry away the cork dust much like the spiral grooves in a drill bit. Return the reamer to the vise until the glue has hardened completely.

Taper reamers of cutting grit epoxied to pieces of blanks.

As mentioned initially, it is best to have a set of these reamers of various diameters. You can then start with a size which will just fit into the hole of the grip and progressively move up to larger sizes as required. For power reaming, some rod builders prefer to mount a metal butt ferrule on the end of the reamer if a piece of rod blank was used. This eliminates the hazard of crushing if the chuck is tightened too much.

Reamers work best in a power head if revolved at medium to high speed. The grip must be held firmly in the hand, directly in line with the reamer. Accuracy here is important if the hole is to be straight and centered in the grip. The grip is slid onto the revolving reamer until it begins to bite into the cork. After a small amount of cork has been removed, the grip is backed off a bit to allow the cork dust to fall out and the reamer to cool. This is important, since reaming cork generates tremendous heat, which can break down the epoxy bond. If this heat is not controlled it can also cause a piece of rod blank to disintegrate. So work slowly, removing only a small amount of cork at a time and progressing from small-diameter reamers to larger-diameter reamers.

Tapered reamers will not in every case exactly match the taper of some blanks. There are those very occasional blanks that have a sharp "drop" in the taper where the grip is to be placed. Fortunately, there are relatively few of these. If you encounter this situation you can often easily adjust the hole in the grip with a bit of judicious hand filing, or build up the blank at one end with masking tape or thread and epoxy.

Filling the cork

All cork, no matter how good the quality, contains some small pits that will appear as the grip is shaped. On poor-grade cork some large, obvious pits may exist. These should be filled both for appearance's sake and to prevent future crumbling of the cork at the edge of the hole. Some rod builders make a practice of filling practically all pits in the surface of a grip. The best filler is a combination of cork dust obtained from *sanding* cork and Cork Filler Adhesive. Duco cement can be used as a substitute, but is more difficult to work with.

The pits should be filled *before* the final sanding with medium and fine sandpaper. Use a common dust brush to completely remove the cork dust that has settled in the pits. Unless this is done, the adhesive will not have a firm surface on which to bond and the filling will later come out of the pits. Two methods can be used. In the first, a few drops of adhesive are applied to the inside of the hole with a dubbing needle or similar tool. Then, more than enough cork dust to fill the hole is poured on top of the glue and pushed into the hole with the finger. Use a generous amount of cork dust and none of the adhesive will stick to your finger. When all the pits have been filled, lightly brush away the excess cork dust. On particularly deep holes, a second application may be needed to fill it flush with the surrounding surface.

The second method is to mix small quantities of cork dust and Cork Filler Adhesive together to form a paste or slurry. This is then pushed into the pits with a small flat stick. If there are many pits to be filled, make only enough of the mixture to fill a few at a time. After the glue has dried, proceed with the last bit of sanding with medium-grit sandpaper to remove any excess glue on the grip and to smooth the surface. Finish with fine sandpaper.

Cork tape

The most common use of cork tape is on saltwater rods for surf and boat use. The tape is ideally suited to the larger-diameter blanks used for these rods. In some parts of the country cork-tape grips are also used for freshwater spinning rods. However, the smaller the diameter of the blank the less applicable is the tape. When bent around too small a radius it tends to split or crack, and the adhesive backing is less likely to hold it on the blank.

The typical handle assembly consists of a long grip with no reel seat. The reel is either clamped or taped in place where desired on the grip. Proponents of cork tape point out that the grip is rapidly made, light in weight, and has increased sensitivity since it feels as if you were holding the blank itself.

Cork tape can also be used on rods containing reel seats. Here it is normally used to cover a long butt section for two-handed casting. Regular cork or resilient grip material is used in short sections below and above the reel seat.

The tape is usually available in 25- to 100-foot rolls. To estimate the amount needed you can assume 3½ to 4 feet of tape for each foot of blank to be covered. Naturally, this varies somewhat with the diameter of the blank.

RodCrafter David Rader frequently makes saltwater rods for use in southern California waters and has written of his cork-tape technique in the *RodCrafters Journal*. From the other end of the country, Bob Dupont builds similar rods for the New England area, and has demonstrated his methods at a National RodCrafters Seminar. Both suggest that the end of the tape be cut at approximately a 45° angle depending upon the diameter of the blank on which you are working, and application started at the butt end of the blank. Peel the paper backing from only a short length of the total piece of tape.

The cut end is aligned with the bottom end of the blank, and the taper is wound in spirals at a 45° angle to the axis of the blank. It helps to use heavy-duty rod rollers or similar supports to hold the blank while wrapping the tape. It is important that each spiral of the tape butt tightly against the previous one. There should be no gap between each width of tape. Continue peeling away the backing in short lengths. Use the thumb and fingers to apply pressure over the entire surface as you wind. This brings the adhesive in firm contact with the blank, eliminating the chance of it later becoming loose or of water seeping between the blank and the tape. The technique is not difficult to master, but it is advisable to first practice on scrap pieces of blank until you get the hang of it.

After you have made the initial few spirals on the butt end, it is a good idea to wrap a band of electrician's tape around the butt to prevent it from coming

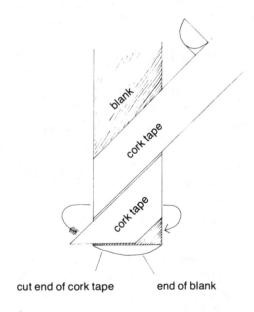

cut end of cork tape   end of blank

Cork tape is spiraled on blank.

loose while you are working. Later, the installation of the butt cap with epoxy glue will permanently bind the end of the tape.

When you reach the point where your grip will end, again cut the tape at an angle so that it goes completely around the blank forming a squared-off end. This end should be pressed firmly in place and temporarily held with a band of electrician's tape.

Dave favors only one layer of cork tape, while Bob builds many rods with a double layer. He feels the second layer gives a fuller appearance to the grip, offers more protection to the blank, and provides a better cushion if the reel is clamped in place. To apply a second layer on top of the first, remove the electrician's tape from the butt end and repeat the entire procedure. When applying the second layer, particularly firm finger pressure is required all along the surface for a good adhesive bond.

As noted, the butt end is finished with a butt cap. Depending upon the diameter, it may be necessary to build up the grip a bit at that point to fit the butt cap. This can be done with a piece of cork tape, or with epoxy and string. The other end of the grip can be finished as desired. Some rod builders use a Turk's-head knot of nylon cord for a decorative effect. This can be finished the same as the guide wraps. Another method is to taper the end, particularly if two layers of cork tape are used, and cover it with a thread wrap which continues a

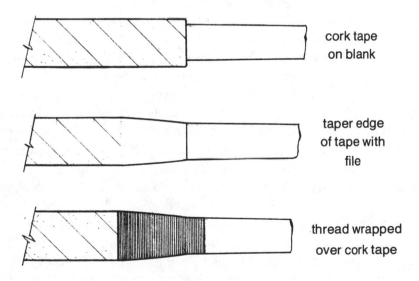

cork tape
on blank

taper edge
of tape with
file

thread wrapped
over cork tape

Cork tape trimmed with thread.

short distance up the blank. A coarse abrasive tool such as a file or sandpaper backed with a block can be used to taper the end of the cork. If you experience difficulty in winding wrapping thread over the tapered end, first give it a few coats of your wrapping finish. After the finish dries it will provide a surface more similar to the blank and on which the thread will better slide into place.

INSTALLING RESILIENT GRIPS

There are a variety of preformed resilient grips available today. Depending upon their chemical composition some are easier to install than others. Generally, those that more readily stretch or expand will be found the easiest to mount. Custom rod builders are a most ingenious and creative group, and there have been a great many techniques developed for mounting resilient grips. So that you might develop your own method to fit your particular needs, we will discuss the most popular of these techniques. For all methods the hole in the grip should be slightly smaller than the smallest diameter of the blank to be covered.

Rod companies use compressed air for rapid installation, as do many custom builders. If you have an air compressor or bottled air in your shop, this is an ideal method. Even if your shop is not so equipped, do not rule it out. You can use the air hose at your local gas station or perhaps can get the use of compressed air at a local garage or industrial shop.

A ¼-inch airgun with a $1/16$-inch or $1/32$-inch nozzle is ideal. Use ¼-inch rubber air hose and about 125 pounds line pressure. Place the grip on the blank and slide it down to the point where it is snug without forcing it. One hand will operate the air nozzle. The free hand can be used to hold the blank *above* the grip, or used to *very lightly* hold the grip and guide it on the cushion of air.

Put the nozzle of the airgun against the junction of the blank and the grip. The nozzle should be placed at approximately a 45° angle to the blank. Do not attempt to place the end of the nozzle into the end of the grip. Instead, keep it just against the grip and blow air down between the blank and the grip. This will slightly expand the grip and it can be floated down the blank on a cushion of air. The grip can be guided down the blank by the air pressure from the nozzle alone, or the free hand can be used to *gently* guide it along the blank *without squeezing the grip*. In either case, once the grip is moving try to keep it moving. The procedure may seem awkward at first, but with a bit of practice can be easily mastered.

Some rod makers use this technique with no adhesive, relying on the basic elasticity of the material to keep the grip snugly in position on the blank. Unless there is a very tight fit, I believe it is better to use epoxy. This will help slide

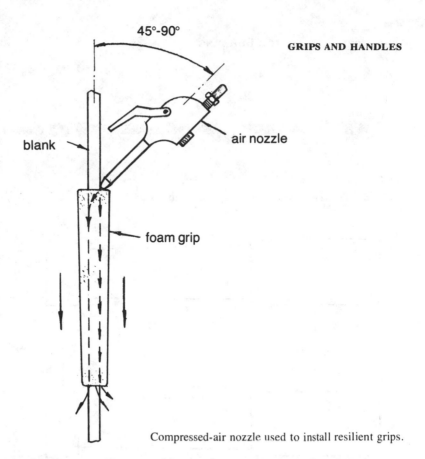

45°-90°

blank

air nozzle

foam grip

Compressed-air nozzle used to install resilient grips.

the grip along the blank, as well as provide a more permanent and secure assembly. Solvent-evaporative glues will also act as a lubricant, but are not especially recommended, since in this particular application they will take quite long to dry. Epoxy can be applied to just the top half of the mounting area. The wiping action of the grip will spread the glue into the lower half of the area and will reduce or eliminate the glue cleanup.

When using compressed air or any method of mounting resilient grips, it is necessary to have some way of stopping the grip at the desired position on the blank. This is necessary because the grip is slid in one continuous motion along the blank. In many cases the grip will naturally come to rest at the end of the rod (against the workbench) or against the reel seat. In some situations, such as when mouting a short grip below the reel seat on a surf rod, you will need to devise a "stop." This is done by winding a number of layers of removable tape on the blank immediately below the point where the bottom of the grip is to be placed.

Obviously there are a great many custom builders who do not have access to compressed air and who mount a large number of resilient grips. One technique is to spread a thin coat of glue on the blank from the point where the grip fits

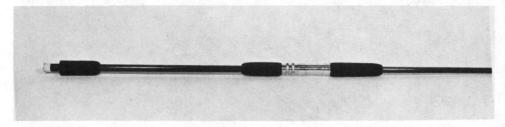

Split-grip surf handle design. Butt cap not yet in place.

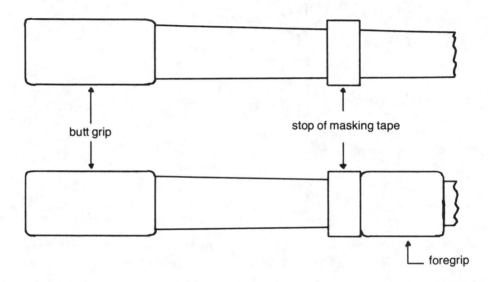

Stop of masking tape used to mount resilient grip on split-grip design surf-rod handle. After grip is in position, masking tape is removed.

snugly all the way to the place where it is to be mounted. Stand the blank, butt down, on the workbench or the floor. Put the grip over the top of the blank and grasp the grip at the very top ½ inch or so with both hands. Push the grip down into position with a strong, fairly rapid motion. Once the grip starts to move, *do not stop*, or you probably will not be able to move the grip again. By holding just the very top end of the grip shut and forcing the grip downward, you create your own small cushion of air, causing the grip to expand slightly. If you pause and allow the cushion to be lost, it is almost impossible to recreate it by hand.

After the grip is in its final position, clean the blank above it with a rag moistened with thinner. If epoxy was the adhesive, use epoxy thinner. To protect the finish on some blanks it is a good idea to follow this by wiping the blank with an acetone-moistened rag. Also carefully clean your hands and wash them imme-

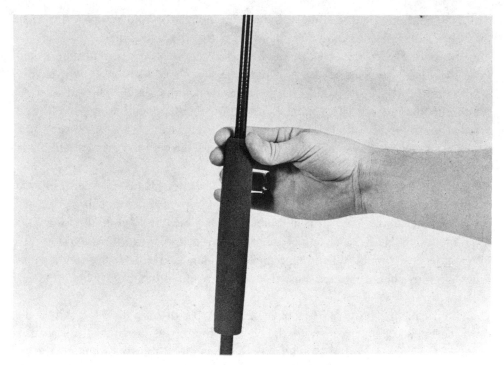

When sliding grip along the blank, hold only by the very top.

diately with soap and water. Then go back and check the length of the grip just installed. It may have been compressed and now be shorter than it was originally. If so, grasp the grip firmly in both hands and pull your hands apart with a slight twisting motion. This will elongate the grip and return it to its original length.

There are certain limitations to all hand-mounting techniques. The smaller the hole in the grip compared to the diameter of the blank, the more difficult it becomes to mount it. The longer the grip, the more difficult. And the less resilient the material, the more difficult. It is therefore best to use a hole size only slightly smaller than the smallest diameter of the blank over which it is to be installed. With some materials, such as Customgrip, the hole size can be enlarged using a homemade coarse-grit (25 to 50) reamer or very coarse sandpaper wrapped around a dowel. Most of the present grip materials can be made a bit more resilient and pliable by placing them in boiling water for fifteen to twenty minutes just before mounting.

Hand mounting requires the use of a lubricant to aid in sliding the grip along the blank. As noted, glue meets this need and also serves to anchor the grip. Another method of lubricating the grip and the blank is with lacquer thinner or a mild ketone solution. Hold a finger over one end of the grip to seal off the hole.

From the other end pour in some of the lacquer thinner or mild ketone. Now block this end of the hole with another finger to confine the liquid inside the grip. Tip the grip back and forth, end to end, for a few minutes to distribute the liquid. Pour the liquid from inside the grip onto the blank. You probably will have to pour more liquid on the blank. The grip is then immediately slipped over the blank and the previously explained procedure for hand mounting is followed. Here again the object is to keep the grip moving. However, if it stops it can sometimes be started again by injecting lacquer thinner through the grip (to the blank) with a hypodermic syringe.

RodCrafter Associate Joy Dunlap of A & J Custom Rods in Destin, Florida, builds a great many saltwater rods with resilient grips. He favors using grips with a hole size relatively small for the blank, and has developed a method for quick hand mounting. He has a strong board, about ¾ inch thick, in which various-size holes have been bored. When he prepares to mount a grip he selects the smallest hole size in the board that will just fit over the blank at the top of where the grip will finally rest.

Lubrication is provided by squeezing a couple of long beads of white glue onto the blank. The grip is then slipped over the top of the blank, followed by the board using the previously selected hole. The board thus rests against the end of the top of the grip. With the blank braced on the workbench or the floor, and both hands on the board, he makes one long powerful push to slide the grip in

Left: Blank is lubricated with white glue, grip is in place, and push board ready.
Above: Joy Dunlap uses push board to mount resilient grip.

place. Since the white glue is water-soluble while wet, cleanup is simply a matter of washing the blank and grip in running water. He then pulls and twists the grip to return it to its original length.

For really large-diameter blanks and grips with small holes, his system is even more ingenious. There is a security gate of iron bars on the shop's back door that is brought into play. In this case the blank is also lubricated with white glue and the proper hole in the board slipped over the blank on top of the grip. The blank is held *horizontally* and the top placed between the bars of the gate. The board is longer than the space between the iron bars. This allows the blank to be pushed through, between the bars, but the board and the grip are held stationary. Another strong board, but one without any holes, is held across the butt end of the blank and braced against Joy's chest. In this position Joy can lean against the board with a great deal of his body weight and push the blank through the bars in the gate. With a long blank he digs in his feet and walks the butt up to the grip. In the process the grip is slid along the blank to its final resting place. Lacking a security gate, you can use this technique with a strong wrought-iron fence or railing, or any similar narrow space that can be straddled by a board with a hole in it.

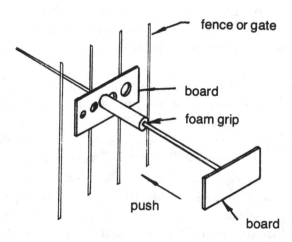

Mounting resilient grips. Push board with hole straddles fence and blank with grip is slipped through push board. A flat board is held against butt and weight of body is used to push butt into grip.

Custom-shaping resilient grips

In quite a few cases the preformed shape of the resilient grip is fine and, once it is installed, the job is finished. On the other hand, there are many situations where the appearance of the rod is enhanced by custom-shaping the grip. All resilient materials are tough and none are shaped as easily as cork. Some, such as Customgrip, are formulated to be shaped, and most can be shaped to at least a certain extent.

Shaping can be done before the grip is installed on the blank, or afterward on a rod lathe. As a general rule, if the hole in the grip is rather small compared to the diameter of the blank, and if reshaping will reduce the wall thickness by much, it is best to shape the grip before mounting. This will allow the grip to expand more easily during installation. A good example is unshaped Customgrip which is provided as a constant-diameter, thick-walled cylinder, just as it comes from the extruder. If a very tight fit exists on the particular blank, it is best to first shape the grip. Mounting will be easier since there is less total material to be stretched over the blank.

To preshape a grip of straight extruded material, force it on a short section of scrap blank, a metal rod, or strong dowel. Chuck this into a power head and preferably support the other end. If you are using a wood or metal lathe, a small blind hole in the center of one end of a metal rod can be mated to the tail stock (preferably ball-bearing) for perfect alignment and support. If you have a rod lathe, an adjustable-height ball-bearing rod lathe support is ideal (see the chapter on tools).

Shaping is best done at high speed. Use very coarse-grit (40-60) sandpaper or homemade epoxy/grit abrasive tools. On some particularly tough materials, I have even used a coarse curved-tooth flat file. If you are working with unshaped Customgrip, you will encounter more initial resistance until you break through the smooth outside "skin" formed during the extrusion process. Once past that you will find it comparatively easy to shape. The same techniques for bracing sanding tools discussed above under shaping cork should be applied. You will just need higher speed, coarser grit, and more pressure. Finish sanding can be done with strips of coarse sandpaper. Some materials will respond to the use of medium-fine paper.

For fast removal of very tough material, RodCrafter Mac Kelley uses a combination of two power tools. The grip is rotated on a rod lathe or similar device. A separate electric hand drill is fitted with a hard-rubber sanding disk faced with very coarse sandpaper. Both the lathe and the hand drill are run at high speed

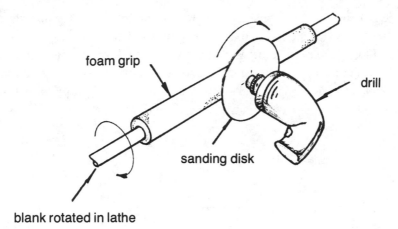

foam grip

drill

sanding disk

blank rotated in lathe

Shape very tough resilient grip with coarse sanding disk in electric drill with grip revolving in lathe.

as the edge of the sanding disk is moved across the rotating grip. If a reversible electric drill is used, the direction of rotation can be selected that is opposite to the rotation of the lathe. This technique is excellent for rough shaping. Keep the sanding disk moving across the surface of the grip for even removal of material. With practice, a fair degree of control can be developed. Intricate contours can be made, as well as recesses cut for butt caps. Final finish shaping is done with strips of very coarse sandpaper.

Some decorative custom work can be performed on resilient grips. One method I use frequently is to make small V-grooves in the surface. These grooves form circles all the way around the grip, providing an interesting contrast to the otherwise smooth material. They look best when done in groups of three closely spaced rings. On a long butt grip I may place a group near the butt cap and another near the reel seat. The foregrip, being shorter, would have only one group in the center.

Resilient grip with V-grooves.

I use a set of dividers whose pointed metal tips are set for the desired spacing between the grooves. The rod is mounted in my rod lathe and I use a tool support made of a block of scrap wood. As the rod is revolved, the points of the dividers are carefully fed into the grip just deep enough to scribe two circles on the grip. The dividers are then repositioned so that one point rides in a previously scribed circle while the outboard point scribes the third circle.

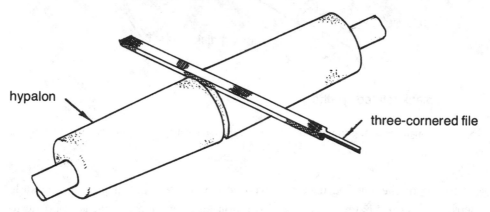

hypalon

three-cornered file

Cutting V-groove in resilient grip.

Now that the position of the grooves is marked, I use a small three-cornered triangular file. One end is supported on the tool rest and the other on a scribed circle to enlarge the circle into a shallow groove. Next, I bend and hold a piece of coarse sandpaper over one of the corners on the file and lay it in the groove. This cuts more rapidly. When the desired depth is reached I tilt the sandpaper-covered file to each side to round off the top edges of the V-groove. The process is repeated on each of the remaining two circles to form matching grooves. The finished cuts are not very deep—just enough to be easily visible. Incidentally, this would be an ideal place to use a homemade epoxy/grit tool. It would be made just like the three-cornered file, but would cut faster.

Another custom touch can be given resilient grips by including narrow inlays of grip material of another color. These trim-ring inlays can also be made of sheets of rubber or similar composition materials. If grip material is used, the trim rings can be cut by slipping the grip on a piece of scrap blank or rod and rotating it under power. Use an X-Acto knife or other sharp knife to make a square cut, 90° to the grip's axis. Use a tool rest of some sort and carefully feed the blade straight into the grip until it cuts all the way through. A second cut is made according to the width of the trim ring inlay desired. I personally find very thin rings most appealing.

Determine where the inlay will be placed in the grip and make a square cut in the grip by the same cutting method just described. The grip is then assembled on the blank in sections with epoxy glue on the face of each section and trim ring. When the glue has cured, shape the grip to smoothly blend in the diameter of the trim ring.

Sheets of rubber or a similar composition can also provide contrasting narrow trim rings. They are most easily cut out by using a piece of pipe or metal tubing of the needed diameter. One end can be sharpened with a file or grinder. The sheet of rubber is laid over a flat metal surface, and the sharpened pipe is placed on top. A few sharp raps with a hammer will stamp out the thin trim ring.

Adjusting resiliency

One other technique of working with resilient grips certainly should be mentioned. This finds application with the softer, more cushiony grip materials. When these grips are forced over larger-diameter blanks the material becomes compressed, and they have a slightly firmer feel. Usually this is desirable, especially on foregrips, since the larger rods are used to fight bigger fish. However, some people also like the firmer feel on lighter, smaller-diameter blanks. Rod-Crafter Don Skodny is one of these. He likes the construction advantages of Customgrip, but wanted a harder feel. He solved the problem by reaming the hole in the grip larger so it would fit over a $^{15}/_{16}$-inch cork reel-seat bushing. The area of the rod to be covered by the grip was first fitted with lengths of $^{15}/_{16}$-inch cork reel arbors, end to end, and epoxied to the blank. The surface of the cork was then coated with epoxy and the grips slipped in place. After the glue cured he customized the shape. The result was a nonslip grip with a firmer feel, exactly what he had been searching for.

WOOD FOREGRIPS

Saltwater rods with foregrips made of wood are preferred by fewer fishermen each year. Since their use has declined, they are more difficult to locate, but some dealers still have a supply. If you cannot find any, they are not too difficult to make on a wood lathe. Use the finest straight-grained, air-dried hickory or ash obtainable. Start with a turning square of the desired length and locate the centers on each end. Saw or plane off the corners to make a rough octagonal shape. Bore a hole of the desired diameter the length of the piece of stock. Drilling the hole first assures that the grip will be round and centered on the rod.

Place a length of threaded rod, with a diameter that will just fit, through the hole. Place a small washer and two lock nuts on each end to tightly hold the octagonal block of wood. Chuck this in a lathe, support the other end, and proceed to shape the grip with woodworking-lathe cutting tools. Use a slow speed and a ½-inch gouge until the stock has been completely rounded. You can then increase the rotation speed and develop the preferred shape, using various lathe cutting tools. Usually the grip has some narrow decorative grooves cut into the surface. A parting tool works well for forming these grooves. Smooth by sanding at very high speed with fine sandpaper.

Brush away the sanding dust, then wipe clean with a tack rag so that all dust is removed. Apply a number of coats of a tough, durable finish such as clear epoxy or marine polyurethane varnish, lightly sanding between coats.

Whether you have made or purchased your wood foregrip, it will have a level hole of constant diameter through the center. It is too difficult to attempt to taper this hole to fit the taper of the blank. A much easier approach is to level the taper of the blank with epoxy and string.

CORD AND OTHER MATERIALS

Interesting foregrips can be made of nylon cord wound on the blank. Many fishermen feel the rough texture of the cord makes an excellent gripping surface on large offshore trolling rods. RodCrafter Scooter Barefield has had excellent results using braided nylon trotline of about ⅛-inch diameter. His method of installation requires the help of an assistant.

First coat the desired section of the blank with a thick coat of slow-curing epoxy glue. The starting end of the cord is unbraided, or frayed, to reduce the bulk where it is wrapped over. The wrap is started the same as for a conventional guide wrap. The assistant turns the rod while you guide the cord onto the blank under moderate tension. Make sure the cord lays flat and untwisted. To end the wrap insert a tie-off loop of the same cord, and pull the short cut end under the wrap. As an extra bit of security to hold the end of the wrap securely, Scooter puts a coat of fast-curing epoxy over about ½ inch of the end.

Scooter points out that any length grip is possible, and that if the cord ever wears out it is easy to replace. The latter is important, since the guides will not have to be replaced as would be the case with conventional foregrips.

An interesting variation of this technique that results in a larger-diameter foregrip preferred by some anglers is to build it on top of a preformed cork grip.

While the entire cork surface could be covered from end to end, the easier method is to leave the ends of the cork exposed. First build a cork foregrip of the desired dimensions. Then evenly sand down all but about ½ to ¾ inch of each end of the cork. The depth of this recess should be just slightly less than the diameter of the cord to be used. After the cork form is mounted on the rod, use Scooter's technique to wind the cord the length of the recess.

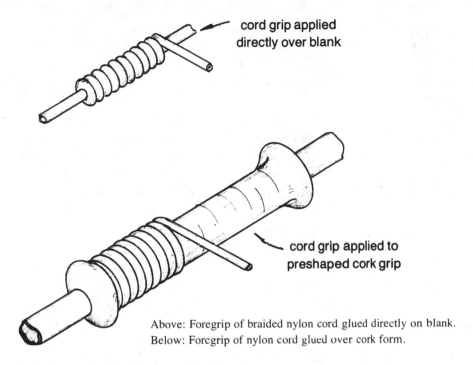

cord grip applied
directly over blank

cord grip applied to
preshaped cork grip

Above: Foregrip of braided nylon cord glued directly on blank.
Below: Foregrip of nylon cord glued over cork form.

When viewed under a microscope, nylon is actually very porous. It thus accepts common dye (such as Rit) quite readily, with the results being colorfast. This provides the rod builder with another variable with which to achieve a color-coordinated, custom appearance. Dyes can even be mixed for special colors. Select a color to complement the guide wraps or another component on the rod. For example, you can match dyed nylon shock rings on some ceramic guides, as well as dyeable winding checks and dyeable plastic trim rings. Dye and completely dry the cord first, then proceed with making the wrap. If desired, the exposed ends of the cork can be painted a matching or contrasting color after filling the pits. The painted cork is protected with a few coats of epoxy wrapping finish. To ensure that the wrapping finish will not lift the paint, place a coat of clear white shellac over the dried paint. After it dries, apply the epoxy.

This same technique of wrapping cord on a prepared cork form can also be used with other materials. Flat nylon braid is available in solid colors, as well as two-tones. Leather can be cut in long narrow strips, or narrow rawhide strips used. Various imitation leathers such as naugahyde and other plastics will make attractive, serviceable foregrips. Keep your eyes peeled for other materials that can give your rods that unique, custom appearance. A lot of custom rod building consists of creative trial-and-error experiments. After all, that is really one of the things that makes rod crafting so exciting.

We have found that cord grips are also used by some custom builders for the butt grip on surf rods and two-handed pier and jetty rods. Still other builders use the technique for fashioning both fore and butt grips on freshwater spinning rods.

Another more intricate and very decorative method of working with nylon cord was developed by RodCrafter Norma B. Stirrup. A few years ago her son attended Farragut Academy Summer Naval Camp and was introduced to the nautical knot work used by sailors on the old sailing ships. They used rope work and knots to dress up and identify their belongings. Her son became very adept at the craft, and as Norma watched him decorate lamps and landing nets, the idea of using it on custom rods emerged.

Her first applications of the technique were on the long butt grips of surf rods. Here it provides a secure grip during the cast and protects the blank against nicks and gouges. The latter is of special consideration when fishing from rocky shorelines such as found in New England where the rod often gets tucked into crevices between casts. The cord she uses is nylon, which is available in many different sizes. Cord diameter is not critical as long as it is not too fine. It should be chosen for compatibility with rod type and size, as well as the effect desired.

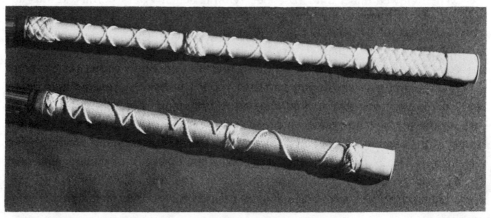

Cord-wrapped rear grips. Note Turk's-head knots.

Norma's nautical-style wrap is put on over the bare blank after the reel seat is installed. Since the wrap is one continuous length, it is worked directly from the spool of cord. The base is a series of simple half hitches worked from the bottom edge of the seat down toward the butt end of the blank. Nylon stretches, so care should be exercised to avoid pulling the wrap too tightly. Use only enough tension to achieve a firm wrap.

A pattern ridge is formed by the crossover of the half hitch. It is controlled by the placement and direction in which the hitch is made. It can be a continuous spiral when the half hitch is formed in the same way each time, or it can form a zigzag pattern by reversing the direction in which the half hitch is looped over the end of the blank after a number of hitches have been made in one. The zigzag can be the same size each time or varied to achieve a widening effect as the butt end is approached. The zigzag can also be placed so the ridges form a thumb/finger grip at the butt.

For still more variation, a crossover pattern can be achieved by starting at the center of a very long cord (or use two cords), and alternating half hitches on each one. By doing this, two opposite spirals meet to form an X on opposite sides of the rod with diagonals on the sides of the rod. This is similar in appearance to the familiar diamond pattern. When using two cords on crossover, the long ends extend in opposite directions—the right-hand cord extends to the right when forming a half hitch, and the left-hand cord extends to the left at the completion of each half hitch.

Another design of the crossover could be a double zigzag by reversing the direction of the half hitches at the point where the ridges meet, or just before or just after. It can be seen that creative design comes into play. And play it is, for this rope work is fun.

Continue along the blank with whatever pattern you have selected until the end of the butt is reached. Trim the ends longer than needed, and tape them temporarily in place. Sear the nylon ends near flame to prevent unraveling of the cord.

Turk's-heads

To cover the start and finish of the nautical wrap, call upon the sailors and use their Turk's-head knot, which was used for just this purpose. The same size cord can be used, or a heavier one selected for emphasis. A short, simple Turk's-head will do the job, but longer, more elaborate ones will be more decorative and, in many cases, provide better balance in the overall design of the rod. A long rear Turk's-head adjacent to the butt cap makes a good rear hand grip. These

121

knots have many other rod-building applications and the technique is worth learning. This knot work can be somewhat complicated, and there is not room to explain it here. The best reference book with detailed instructions and photographs is *Art of Knotting & Splicing* by Cyrus Laurence Day, available from the U.S. Naval Institute, Annapolis, Maryland.

A   B

Pattern for forming Turk's-head knot.

The Turk's-heads are initially formed on a section of dowel or broomstick with a larger diameter than the already wrapped blank. They are constructed loosely, slid into place, and then snugged up tight. Here again you are dealing with a single length of cord. A few trials will enable you to determine the length of cord needed. Naturally, it varies with the diameter of the cord and the blank. As a rough guide, you can wrap the cord loosely around the blank the number of times it will circle the blank in the finished knot and allow for a bit more length. Such estimating comes with experience, since the cord circles the blank more times than it appears to at first.

A simple Turk's-head can be formed by following the drawing. Lay the cord flat as in Diagram A. Keep the loops open and the crosses orderly. Take the long end and follow the thin line in Diagram B—over, under, over, under, over, under, and over. A large-diameter empty plastic pill container makes a good form on which to work. Leave the lid in place and use it for a handle. After laying out the basic knot, insert the pill container into the center. Follow the first "lead" around again in the under, over pattern, laying the cord alongside the first round as indicated by the dotted line in the drawing. To complete the simple Turk's-head, follow the lead around a third time. If a longer knot is desired, you just continue the procedure.

Snugging up is done by gradually taking up the slack from the beginning point of the knot. Work round and round, pulling on the cord until the Turk's-head is snug and even. Like any knot work, it is easier to learn by using a large-diameter cord when practicing.

When the knot is in place on the rod, the ends of the cord are tucked under the Turk's-head after first being trimmed and seared. At the butt end, the cord ends can be tucked into the open end of the blank and held there by the butt cap and the epoxy glue used to mount it. Make sure you allow adequate space for the butt cap when positioning the Turk's-head.

To finish and protect the cord, Norma applies many generous coats of thin color preserver. Her experience has been that the necessary thick buildup of rod varnish and most epoxy wrapping finishes will give the white nylon an amber cast. While this might blend well with the color scheme on a gold blank, she generally prefers the nylon to remain white. To build up more protection after the generous application of color preserver, multiple coats of a heavier clear lacquer can be applied.

I have attempted to present here merely the essence of the fascinating nautical style of custom cord work developed by Mrs. Stirrup. For the creative craftsman it presents many opportunities for further experimentation and self-expression in building custom rods. The possibilities for variations appear practically endless.

For example, as mentioned earlier about nylon cord, it can easily be dyed any color. For Turk's-heads you might want to consider a heavier flat braided nylon sold under the name Dimensional Macrame Cord, available in various colors from American Handicrafts. You can find an assortment of different cords and applicable instructional material at local handcraft shops that carry materials for macrame work. Gudebrod's Butt Wind is a flat nylon braid that can also be used. The only caution when making Turk's-heads of any flat braid is to keep it flat and untwisted while making the knot.

The use of these knots is not limited to surf rods. They can be used to cap a cord foregrip on a trolling rod or add a custom touch ahead of any foregrip on a freshwater rod. Considering all aspects, it is a fascinating technique for developing truly custom rods.

FIVE

Handle Assemblies

The design and construction of the handle assembly on a rod is an area ideally suited to creative craftsmanship. There are really few if any rules, as long as the handle functionally fulfills the needs of the angler. It can be, and generally is, a focal point of the custom rod.

To put this chapter into perspective, it should be mentioned that the basic assembly steps in building all types of rod handles are covered in *Fiberglass Rod Making*. That book also covers various designs and construction techniques for making and using skeleton reel seats, as well as trim rings of wood, plastic, and burnt cork inlaid into handles. Some additional techniques on the subject are also covered in this book in the chapters on reel seats and grips.

The principal classic shapes of fly-rod grips were depicted in *Fiberglass Rod Making,* along with some methods and ideas for custom-designed fly-rod handles utilizing inlays of various materials. In the chapter on reel seats in this book will be found additional designs for fly rods, including extension butts, both fixed and detachable.

This chapter, then, is devoted to more advanced methods of making custom handles, many of which are applicable to specific rods, but can be adapted on an individual basis by the creative rod designer. There are also presented additional basics, as well as advanced information on various saltwater handle assemblies not covered in *Fiberglass Rod Making*. I repeat that none of the material discussed in this chapter, or in this book, is in any way meant to be the last word on the subject. Far from it! Custom rod building by its very nature will continue to evolve, and custom rod builders will continue to create new ideas and methods. I hope some of the material presented here will help spark and accelerate that creativity and hasten future development.

The advent of graphite rods has presented us with much smaller-diameter butt sections of blanks on which to build our handle assemblies. On the lighter rods we are frequently working with diameters in the neighborhood of ¼ inch. This is, indeed, a small bonding surface for a grip or handle assembly when we consider the twisting and other dynamic forces applied thereto. It is not too uncommon to have the grip or handle on these rods work loose after many hours of casting. What is needed to remedy this problem is a larger surface area to which we can glue cork grips.

A technique that works quite well and that has been mentioned previously for other purposes is to build up the diameter of the blank. The method employed must itself form a strong glue bond with the blank. The best way I have found of doing this is to apply a tight wrap of fine string imbedded in epoxy. If desired, the process can be used to level the small amount of taper on the butt of the blank. Doing so eliminates the need to taper-ream the cork rings or preformed grip, affording the opportunity for a better fit of the cork. Although this technique has been mentioned before, I feel it warrants repeating here.

First roughen the surface of the blank to be covered. Apply a fairly thick coat of regular, slow-curing epoxy glue spread over the entire area just roughened. Make a regular wrap of light string, pulling under the end with the usual tie-off loop. Using a flat stick, work another layer of epoxy glue into the wrap, thoroughly saturating it for a strong, permanent bond. The smaller end of the blank can be wrapped immediately on top with thread of a diameter to level the taper, if that is your objective. It too is covered with a layer of epoxy. At this point, if the hole in the grip or rings fits the new blank diameter, they can be glued in place. If the resulting diameter is a bit too large, allow the epoxy to cure.

After hardening, the epoxy and string/thread matrix can be reduced slightly in diameter by sanding in a rod lathe. Using calipers, it is easy to develop a constant diameter over the entire built-up area. If the preformed grip or rings still need to have the hole enlarged, it can be done without taper by using a length of constant-diameter threaded rod in the same manner as you would use a tapered round file. Another tool for the purpose is a chain-saw file. This has a constant diameter, and is not tapered as are other round files.

At the upper end of the foregrip the built-up blank will show next to the cork. This can be completely hidden by a winding check that tightly fits the blank at that point. If your design calls for tapering the front of the foregrip without using a winding check, a different approach is called for. Plan the built-up area of the blank to be ½ inch short of the length of the grip. That is the length of a single cork ring. Carefully fit that one cork ring to the diameter of the blank, then epoxy it to the blank and the adjacent cork. The top ½ inch of the grip is rarely subject to any hand pressure, so there is no danger of it twisting loose from the smaller blank diameter.

This method of building up the butt end of a very small-diameter graphite blank has another use as well. In some quality graphite blanks the female ferrule is located at the top end of the butt section of the blank. On the larger models of these blanks there is no problem, since the diameter of the female ferrule is smaller than the diameter of the butt section, where the handle will be located. However, on the shorter ultralight models, the ferrule diameter may be larger. This presents a problem if the grip is to be slipped down over the top of the blank in the traditional manner. With the blank built up to a bigger, constant diameter the assembly of the handle is simplified.

COMBINATION FLY/SPINNING-ROD HANDLES

In recent years there has been a tremendous increase in the number of people involved in hiking and backpacking. Existing sporting-goods stores have added whole new departments, and new stores devoted exclusively to this interest have opened. A great many of the devotees are fishermen who want combination fly/ spinning backpacking rods. Blank manufacturers have responded with multisectional blanks designed for this purpose. It should be mentioned that the market is not limited to backpackers. Often a fisherman wants a combination rod that breaks into small enough sections so that it can be kept in the car on a more or less permanent basis. Then if during his travels he encounters some fishable water, he is always equipped. It falls to the custom rod builder, however, to design handles ideally suited to each specific rod and the needs of the particular fisherman.

One of the simplest designs is a long straight cork handle, flared slightly at the ends and equipped with sliding spinning-reel bands. Generally this is about

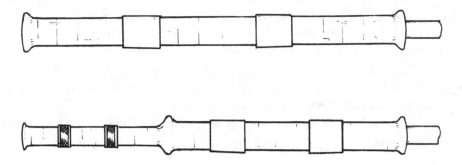

Above: Straight cork combination fly/spinning handle.
Below: Reduced diameter for fly reel.

12 inches long. When a spinning reel is used it is mounted near the middle, or at the point of preferred balance, in the conventional manner. When the angler switches to fly fishing, the fly reel is mounted as far to the rear of the handle as possible. The remaining cork in front of the reel then serves as the fly-rod grip. This is a functional design in most cases, provided the thickness of the reel feet of the fly and spinning reels is the same. One problem frequently experienced is that the fly reel, with shorter feet, tends to twist or move around the handle. The larger diameter of the cork required for the spinning bands is not ideally proportioned for a good fit of the fly reel. Additionally, many custom rod builders would share the sentiment of John Sawyer, my manager, who comments that "it is—well—boring."

In an effort to provide a more secure and proportionately designed mounting for the fly reel, the butt end of the handle can be changed. The diameter of approximately the rear 4 inches is reduced to the size normally used for an all-cork fly-reel seat. One side of the cork is filed flat to provide a seat for the fly reel, and sliding fly-reel bands are installed. The balance of the cork handle is of the necessary diameter for spinning-reel bands.

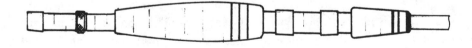

Fixed hood and single-reel band for fly reel.

A variation of this design is to use a fixed fly-reel seat hood (or pocket) on the extreme butt, and one sliding fly-reel band. Both of these arrangements are an improvement, since the fly reel has its own secure seat. Fishing with one of these handles will reveal a distracting and disturbing aspect, more irritating to some than to others. The sliding bands of the "seat" not in use will click together —constantly. A small piece of wood or plastic can be fashioned with a taper on each end. This simulates the reel feet, and the bands of the "seat" not in use are slid over this piece. As long as this piece is not lost or misplaced, the annoying clicking noise is eliminated.

For slightly heavier rods where a more secure mounting for the reels is desired, or in an attempt to eliminate the clicking together of sliding bands, fixed reel seats can be used. Skeleton seats with the metal center barrel removed are often used. They can be made from all-metal seats or purchased. You will need a fly-reel seat and a spinning-reel seat. To keep the assembly light in weight, the centers of each seat can be made of cork. Some rod builders feel the weight savings of skeleton seats are negligible and use all-metal seats for this assembly.

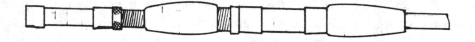

Fly and spinning skeleton seats with cork inserts.

Any of the combination seats described can be built from cork rings directly on the blank, or the individual sections can be preformed separately. These are then taper-reamed and glued on the blank. Remember that when sliding reel bands are used, the cork section over which they slide must be made in two sections to permit the bands to be fitted and slid on to the cork.

RodCrafter Norma Stirrup came up with another solution to the problems of a handle assembly for the combination fly/spinning rod. Basically, she built a conventional fly-rod handle of cork grip and fly-reel seat. Then a detachable rear or butt grip of the type usually found on spinning rods was designed so that it would slide inside the open-ended fly-reel seat. The construction techniques were similar to those used in making a detachable fighting butt for a fly rod. In this case, the detachable section was in reality the butt grip of a spinning handle.

She started with a fly-rod blank slightly longer than desired and cut a short piece off the butt. A suitable piece of scrap blank that would fit inside the taper of the butt of the rod was selected. If a piece of hollow fiberglass is not available

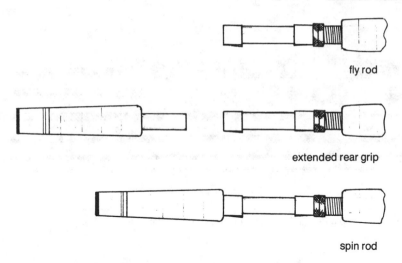

fly rod

extended rear grip

spin rod

Detachable rear grip converts fly handle to spinning handle.

to fit, a length of solid fiberglass can be used, and one end tapered. She now had a piece of fiberglass with a male ''spigot'' or plug ferrule on one end. On the lower end of this piece was built a rear spinning-rod grip. When the rod is used in the fly-rod mode, the rear grip section is carried in the pocket or the pack. When the fisherman switches to a spinning reel, he merely plugs in the rear half of the spinning grip for a comfortable, normal handle.

When making this handle it is important to select a reel seat with hoods large enough to hold both the spinning-reel feet and the fly-reel feet. Assuming that an ultralight spinning reel will be used, this should not present a problem with one of the larger-diameter fly-reel seats. However, check both reels before starting.

Many rod builders feel that no matter how well designed, a combination handle is still a compromise. They argue that balance is never as good, nor the grips as comfortable, as on a handle built for a single purpose. In order to meet their needs we had the manufacturer of our 7½-foot pack rod blanks build *two butt sections* for what we called Dual Versatility. This is a five-section blank with hollow fiberglass internal ferrules. The walls of the ferrules are thicker than the walls of the blank, so they can be individually precision-ground. We were therefore able to have two butt sections made for each blank, with the male ferrules on each one precision-ground to fit the existing female section. The custom rod builder can then build a fly-rod handle on one section and a spinning-rod handle on the other. To switch from fly to spinning, the angler simply unplugs the one butt section and substitutes the other. The idea has been well received, and the custom builder is able to offer his customer a ''one-of-a-kind'' rod.

Pack rod with two separate handle assemblies built on special blank.

SPINNING HANDLES

When spinning was first introduced in this country from Europe, all the rods had handles of straight cork grips equipped with sliding bands or rings to hold the reel. Perhaps the greatest advantage of this handle was that it enabled the fisherman to mount the reel at any point along the handle. He could thus achieve a balance that was most comfortable to him. He could also move the reel to the front of the grip when casting heavier lures, and toward the butt of the handle when working with the lightest lures. Both adjustments helped in casting control. If he switched to a spool of heavier or lighter line he could also move the reel to the best position to eliminate or minimize line slap. The handle design really gave the knowledgeable angler an element of control over his equipment to make it perform to best advantage in different fishing situations.

On the negative side, the sliding bands often tended to loosen while fishing. This was due to a lack of friction between the reel foot and the cork, and between the sliding bands and the cork. A contributing factor to the problem was that after long usage, the cork often became compressed, and the sliding bands therefore worked loose more easily. As a result, American rod manufacturers switched to fixed reel seats on many spinning rods.

RodCrafter Harry Crusenberry of Saltville, Virginia, recognized and preferred the advantages of the straight handle and sliding reel bands. Of necessity, he developed a handle design that, in his words, "holds the reel like a leech." In the process he not only eliminated the problem of the spinning rings working loose, but he was able to add custom color-coordinated trim to his rods.

His approach was to include soft rubber washers between the cork rings on that portion of the handle where the reel might sit. The friction between the rubber and the reel foot does away with all movement. Both the reel feet and the sliding bands stay in place. Over long use the cork does not become compressed, since the washers, although flush with the surface of the cork, are stronger and act as supports to the reel feet.

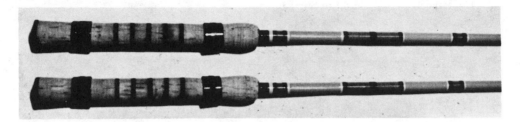

Rubber-inlaid spinning handles to grip reel feet.

The color of the washers can be selected to complement the wrappings or other components. There is a surprisingly large variety available in hardware stores and plumbing-supply houses. Thin "close coupled washers" are very flexible and can be stretched to fit many sizes of rod blanks. They are made in red, black, and white. Many other types of washers in assorted thicknesses will also be found.

It is also an easy matter to make your own washers from sheets of rubber or soft composition plastic. Knife-building-supply houses sell sheets of a composition material that shapes and finishes quite well and is frequently available in a variety of colors. To cut a washer from a sheet of material, make a hole punch from a piece of 1-inch steel conduit or similar tubing as explained earlier. The center hole of the desired size can be made the same way or rough-cut with a sharp blade. Using this technique, thin washers of one color can be cut to bracket thicker washers of another color.

If an attempt is made to sand the cork and rubber at the same time, the results will be unsatisfactory and the experience frustrating. The washers are much tougher and must be ground to shape. The system that Harry uses is to glue the handle together in two sections, as is typical to enable the sliding bands to be fitted. When each section is glued, the selected washers are glued to the adjacent cork rings where desired and to the blank. First glue the butt half to the blank. Plan a design that places a washer at the end of the butt half of the grip where it will be located in the center of the finished handle. Allow the glue to cure completely.

To grind each rubber washer separately to approximately the finished outside diameter, use the edge of a disk sander chucked into an electric drill. One approach is to mount the drill in a vise or drill stand. The rod is then held loosely in your hands and allowed to rotate slowly as the edge of the sanding disk grinds away the rubber. The rod handle is held at an angle to the disk so that only the edge of the sandpaper just touches the rubber.

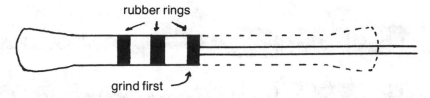

Building washer-inlaid handle.

Another approach is to mount the rod in a rod lathe and hold the electric drill in your hands. As the rod revolves, just the edge of the spinning sanding disk is brought in contact with the rubber washer.

Regardless of which of the two approaches is taken, start with the rubber washer at the center end of the butt half of the handle. Concentrate on reducing the diameter of the washer to the point where one of the sliding reel bands will just fit tightly over it. Then, roughly sand down the cork between that and the next washer. Since the cork will be removed more easily, you may want to use strips of sandpaper for the cork sections, leaving them a bit oversize. Again, grind that washer to the same diameter. A pair of calipers can be used to assure the same diameter, or one of the sliding bands can be used as a template.

Proceed until all the washers are ground to size and the handle is roughly shaped. Slip on both of the sliding reel bands, making sure that each faces properly toward the center. The other half of the handle is now glued to the blank and to the first half. The process is repeated on the second half of the handle after the glue is completely dry.

The rough-shaped handle is then mounted in a rod lathe for final turning and finishing. Since the rubber washers are at approximately the final diameter, the cork and rubber can be sanded together. Use a high speed on the lathe to make the job easier. For the final, velvet finish use fine-grit white cabinetmaker's sandpaper. Do not be concerned if the color of the washers appears to be staining the cork. When finished, the handle is easily cleaned with soap and water.

Although the job of grinding the rubber without inadvertently cutting too deeply into the adjacent cork is a bit ticklish, it can be mastered with care and practice. An alternate method is to tightly mount all of the rubber washers (before gluing to the cork handle) on a length of threaded rod, and grind them to the precise diameter together. Large metal washers will be needed at each end along with a "waste washer" at each end. Because of the metal washers it will not be possible to grind these end washers exactly. Therefore, they are discarded. The problem with this method is that the washers located at the larger-diameter end of the blank will expand outwardly more than those at the smaller-diameter end of the blank. To eliminate this you must first level the taper of the blank where the portion of the handle containing the washers will be located. This can be done with string or thread and epoxy as described previously. The diameter of the built-up section of the blank must exactly match the diameter of the threaded rod. If not, the washers will expand differently on either the built-up blank or the threaded rod. Once ground to the proper diameter to fit the sliding reel bands, the washers can then be glued to the blank along with the cork rings. All that remains is to sand down the cork so that it is flush with the presized rubber washers.

The design does work extremely well and "holds the reel like a leech." Beautifully color-coordinated handles, either bright or subtle, can give the rod a distinctive custom appearance.

Fixed spinning-reel seats

Let's turn our attention now to a unique handle design using a fixed reel seat. On light freshwater spinning rods the grips are most commonly made of cork or resilient materials. One RodCrafter not tradition-bound is Michael Grimshaw of Fort Wayne, Indiana. He developed a short hollow-wood handle assembly of custom beauty. He chose rosewood for the butt and foregrips, but any interesting hardwood could be used.

The handle built to Mike's dimensions is surprisingly light and was first employed by him on a Fenwick HMG graphite blank, Model GSP541. Weight was kept to a minimum by the short length of the grips, the hollow construction, and a small reel seat. The sizes of all the parts are comparable to those used in ultralight rods.

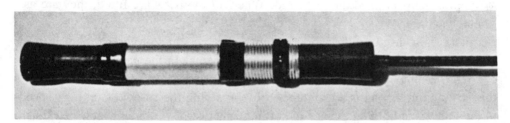

Grimshaw's finished handle.

In the accompanying diagram it is clear that no cork arbors or reel-seat bushings are used. Instead, the reel seat is supported on each end by a ½-inch-long tang, or turned-down recess, in each wood grip. Nor is there a butt cap or winding check. The simple beauty of the wood stands by itself, accented only by the reel seat.

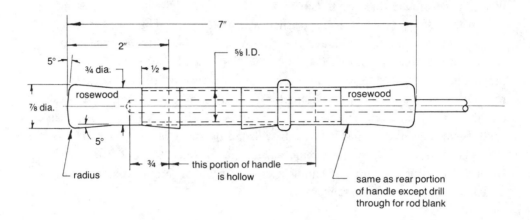

Wood ultralight handle.

The wood grips are each turned on a lathe from blocks 1 × 1 × 2 inches. They are identical in shape except that the foregrip is bored all the way through for the blank. The rear grip has a blind hole only ¾ inch long into which the butt of the blank is epoxied. The end of each grip is flared to a diameter of ⅞ inch. The diameter of the balance of the grip matches the barrel of the reel seat.

When the grips are turned on the lathe, the shape and outside diameters are first developed. Calipers are used to match the outside diameter of the grip to the outside diameter of the reel-seat barrel. Smoothing is done with progressively finer sandpaper, ending with 400 grit. Next, the ½-inch-long recess on the end of the grip is turned. The reel seat must just slip over this tang for support and to keep all parts aligned and centered. When all the parts are fitted, they are assembled with epoxy glue.

The finish used on the wood is a matter of personal preference, but it must be an exterior type that will withstand the elements. In the case of rosewood, it can just be burnished, if desired. This is possible because of the natural oils in this wood. Burnishing is accomplished by revolving the rosewood at high speed in the lathe, and holding a piece of soft pine against it. A smooth, polished finish will result.

CUSTOM HANDLE TRIM

Cork handle assemblies are frequently given a custom appearance reflecting the tastes of the builder or customer by inlaying with trim rings of wood, impregnated walnut, plastic, or burnt cork. Hosels and butt caps can be fabricated from combinations of the same materials. The basic techniques for making and using these accent pieces are covered in detail in *Fiberglass Rod Making*. New methods and techniques are constantly being developed for adding custom trim to handles. These are the subject of this section.

Burnt-cork trim on handle.

Walnut trim ring (½ inch) is bracketed by black plastic trim rings (⅛ inch) glued in place.

Hosel is shaped on lathe.

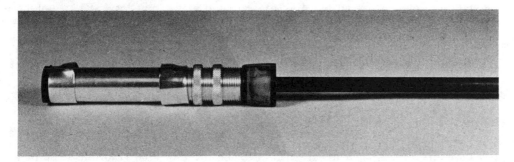

Glued in place on blank and ready for cork rings forming grip.

135

Dyeing trim components

Everyone's taste is different when it comes to handle trim. However, one of the important aspects is color coordination, and developing a color scheme that can be carried throughout the rod. Colored plastic trim rings can be used to pick up the color of the guide wraps. Unfortunately, not all reds, or blues, or any specific color are exactly the same. For example, the red plastic may be different enough from the red wrapping thread to actually clash and detract from the rod. Then again the match may be close enough to attain exactly the desired result. In an attempt to provide a definite color match, dyeable trim components were developed by us and others.

At the present time there are three rod components that can all be dyed to match. By mixing different-color dyes and giving careful attention to time in the dye bath, all can be made to match one another, as well as another component or the wrapping thread used. The dyeable components currently available are plastic trim rings, slightly expandable winding checks (called Dye-Checks), and the shock rings of certain aluminum-oxide ceramic guides. All of these are color-fast when dyed in common household dyes such as Rit.

Dyeing is a fast, economical technique that is easily mastered. There are certain variables that will increase or decrease the intensity or depth of color. Intensity of color will be increased by: (1) the strength of the dye solution, and (2) the amount of time the parts are immersed in the dye bath. Therefore, for optimum control it is best not to make the dye solution too strong, and to keep the parts in the dye bath for relatively short periods of time. If a darker, more intense color is desired, the parts may again be placed in the dye bath. This can be repeated a number of times until the exact color is achieved.

If you are using powdered dye such as Rit, mix the powder with at least two cups of water in a pan and bring to a simmer while stirring periodically. Incidentally, liquid dyes are about twice as concentrated as the powders. Darker colors will develop color intensity most rapidly, so more water can be used with them than with lighter colors. The pan needs to be small enough so that the depth of the dye mixture will completely cover any component placed therein.

Place the pieces to be dyed into the mixture for about three to six minutes. Keep the temperature at a simmer, but do not allow it to come to a full boil. Periodically stir the dye and the parts. Remove the components and rinse in cool flowing water under a faucet. When all trace of color disappears in the rinse water, dry the parts with a paper towel. Inspect to see if the desired color has been obtained. If it is still too light, again place them in the dye mixture and repeat the process. If you keep a simple record of the strength of the dye mixture and the immersion times, you will quickly learn to estimate just what combination is needed for any desired color.

There are some points to keep in mind when working with dye. Since it is simmered, a certain amount of water is disappearing from the solution in the form of steam. The longer the mixture is simmered, the stronger it becomes. If your working time turns out to be very long, it is best to keep an eye on the level in the pan. If it goes down by very much, add water to return it to the original level and the original strength. By the same token, if you initially mixed the dye with too much water and find it difficult to get the color intensity you desire, allow some of the water to escape by simmering for a while. This will concentrate the strength of the dye.

Dye is just what it says it is, and care must be taken to keep clothing and other porous materials in the area from becoming stained. Wear a shop apron or old clothes and keep valuable objects away from the dyeing materials. Metal such as stainless spoons, pans, and guide frames will not absorb the dye and can be rinsed clean.

Dyeable plastic trim rings should be turned to the desired outside diameter and shaped before they are dyed. Also finish them with fine sandpaper before immersing in the dye bath. If they are left in the dye long enough, the color will penetrate throughout. However, to balance with immersion times and intensity of the Dye-Checks and shock rings, they will be in the bath only long enough for the dye to penetrate the outer surface. Thus, if they are shaped and finished beforehand, no problems will be encountered.

Initially it was mentioned that dyeing parts was inexpensive. Even with inflation, I doubt very much that a pack of dye will sell for $1 by the time you read this. An added advantage is that the dye can be saved in an airtight jar and used repeatedly. It is a good idea to label the color and the amount of water used in the mixture for future reference.

Colored-thread trim

The use of dye is only one way to achieve color coordination. A simple method of adding a touch of exactly the same color as the wrapping thread to the handle is to make a trim band of thread on the cork. Since this wrap plus the thickness of the finish on top of it must be flush with the surface of the surrounding cork, a recess must first be made in the cork. Cut the recess while the rod is revolved in a rod lathe, or while the preformed grip is revolved in an electric drill. While very narrow strips of sandpaper can be used, this is another ideal place for a homemade abrasive tool of cutting grit imbedded in epoxy. With it, straight square-cut edges are much more easily made. A flat stick can be shaped to the exact width desired, then coated with epoxy and grit. It is then braced on a tool rest and held against the cork to cut the recess to the desired depth. This cut should be deep enough to allow for a coating of wrapping finish, the thread, color preserver, and finally the wrapping finish.

The reason a coat of wrapping finish (or a few coats of color preserver) is applied to the bare cork is to provide a hard, smooth base on which the thread will "slide" as it does on the blank. Otherwise, it may be difficult to eliminate slight gaps between the individual threads. If the recess is very narrow (for a narrow trim band), lay the tie-off loop in position before the wrap is started, and wind thread over it for the entire width of the wrap.

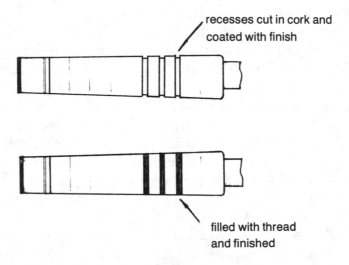

recesses cut in cork and coated with finish

filled with thread and finished

Making thread trim bands.

Thread trim rings.

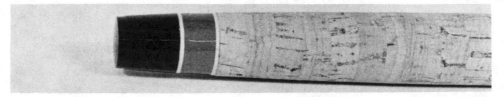

Trim band of thread next to butt cap.

138

A number of coats of wrapping finish will be applied to the thread both for protection and to bring the finished trim band up level with the adjacent cork surface. Care should be exercised here to keep the finish off the cork. In some cases, only the edge of the brush will be used to apply the finish. If, when completed, you find some of the finish did get on the cork, use the fine-grit side of an emery board or a bit of fine sandpaper to carefully remove it without scratching the finished thread.

The thread hosel. Essentially the same technique is used to wrap thread from the blank, up over the end of a tapered foregrip. This is what I refer to as a "thread hosel." Here the foregrip is shaped in a taper that blends in with the diameter of the blank. Then a recess is cut over the desired length of the leading edge of the cork. The length of the recess is the length that will be covered by the thread. It is important that the front cork ring of the foregrip be tightly fitted and glued to the blank beforehand. Even so, when feathering the edge of the cork into the blank, a few bits of cork may crumble away. If so, don't be too concerned; just continue to blend the cork edge as best you can.

The spots where any cork crumbled away can be filled with wrapping finish when it is applied to form a base on the bare cork. If sizable pieces of cork broke away, or if there is a noticeable ridge of cork rather than a smooth taper to the blank, it is best to fill the space with a nonflowing epoxy such as PC-7. The advantage of PC-7 is that while it is sticky when applied, a tool or finger dipped in alcohol can be used to smooth the surface and blend the taper. When it dries, coat it and the bare cork with wrapping finish to form the hard base.

Start your wrap at the desired point on the blank and wind the thread up over the tapered cork. This will prove to be much easier than winding from the cork down onto the blank. Continue wrapping up to the square-shouldered edge of

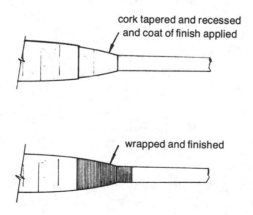

Steps in Making "Thread Hosel".

the recess where the wrap is terminated as close to the edge as possible. Use a thread-burnishing tool or your fingernail to spread the thread evenly, with no gaps, up to the shoulder in the cork. Finish as described for making a trim-ring wrap of thread.

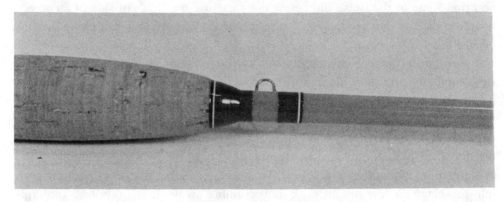

"Thread hosel" made by wrapping over tapered cork.

Painting winding checks

A frequently frustrating point of color coordination is found in the use of the common aluminum winding check. Most dealers stock these only in anodized gold or silver. In many instances, those colors fit in quite well. In other cases they stand out like a sore thumb. Rod companies that might order 50,000 winding checks at a time can have them anodized any color. Your dealer faces a different problem and simply cannot afford to stock the quantities required for a large selection of colors. This was one of the reasons that led us to develop the previously mentioned Dye-Checks. However, you may have a supply of the aluminum checks on hand, or not find the size you need in available Dye-Checks.

If you follow the right procedure, an aluminum check can be painted any color to blend with reel seat, butt cap, or thread wraps. The secret to a chip-free, scratch-free colored finish is to use an overcoat of clear epoxy wrapping finish. You will undoubtedly have some kind of threadwork on the blank next to the winding check. So, when you build up a number of coats of epoxy finish over both, you end up with a smooth, glasslike sheath that adds greatly to the finished appearance.

A huge variety of different colors is readily available in model paints. They are put up in small bottles, and any hobby store will have a large selection. Both glossy and flat finishes are made. Either will work fine, but the "flats," as they are called, have more pigment and will provide better coverage. No need to be concerned with the dull finish, since your epoxy will impart a high gloss. These paints can be mixed to get a specific color, and cleanup is easy with paint thinner. Stir them well before using and keep the bottles tightly capped for long shelf life.

The first step is to fit the winding check to the blank. I customarily use checks that are a bit too small, then enlarge them so they fit tightly around the blank. To enlarge a check, use an X-Acto blade or a Rod Builder's Knife, and carefully carve thin peelings of aluminum from around the inside hole. If the blade is held at the proper angle, the hole in the check will be enlarged with a cut that tapers outward on the underside. This assures that the cut edge will not show on the finished rod. This is mentioned in case you are enlarging a gold-anodized check which is not going to be painted.

With the winding check fitted, wipe it clean with a cloth dipped in thinner, and place it on some kind of support for painting. Since you want to paint the outer surface including both outer and inner edges, this support could be fashioned from a pipe cleaner or be the top of an old medicine dropper. Apply the paint with a small brush, making sure that the edges are covered and that the original color does not show through. As the paint dries, inspect the check and touch up any spots not completely covered. The paint appears to dry rapidly, but it is best to allow a few hours.

The solvents in most epoxy finishes will cause the paint to lift. For this reason, a coat of thinned white shellac is applied over the dry paint. When dry, the shellac will act as a barrier between the paint and the epoxy. After one coat of epoxy has cured, you can mount the winding check. When you later apply the epoxy finish to the adjacent thread, just continue right up over the check. The high luster of your blank, wraps, and colored winding check will all blend together in a unified, professional finish.

Transparent-plastic trim

Another approach to using color creatively in the handle trim is the use of "see-through" plastic trim. Usually the plastic trim rings you make or purchase are of the opaque type. However, Plexiglas is also made in transparent colors. This material presents many opportunities for different effects. I first saw it used by RodCrafter John Sawyer when he was operating his own custom rod-making business and before he became manager of my rod-building-supply business.

Variations in the effects possible with transparent colored Plexiglas depend upon (1) how deep or pale the color built in by the manufacturer is, (2) how rough or how highly polished the edge of the inside hole in the ring is, (3) how bright and what color the material placed beneath the ring is, and (4) how dark or how light the material adjacent to the ring is. The term "ring" is used here to mean a round piece normally cut with a hole saw from ⅛-inch-thick sheet of plastic. Rings can be cut from both thicker and thinner sheets, and a number of rings can be glued together for a thicker piece from which a hosel or butt cap is turned.

By manipulation of the above four factors, the plastic can be made to appear quite transparent or just to have depth of color. Similarly, the color of the material can be changed slightly by the adjacent color and the color beneath it. The effects are many and, for the adventuresome, it is worth experimenting with. Use it alone or combine it with regular opaque Plexiglas or wood.

Making handle components by casting

Many custom rod builders are content to use the stock parts found in rod-building-supply catalogs. Some make their own trim pieces by turning rings of Plexiglas or wood. And a few fabricate their own parts by casting them. The first craftsman with whom I communicated who used this technique was the late Rod-Crafter Clyde E. Pollard. He had built fishing rods for more years than most of us can remember, and finally arrived at the point where he wanted custom-made parts such as winding checks, butt caps, hosels, and trim rings. He naturally had his own ideas about the design of these parts and, after considerable experimentation, developed a method of casting them from polyester resin.

The first step in making a casting is to fabricate a suitable pattern from which a mold can be made. Any easily worked material such as hardwoods or soft metals can be used. Perhaps a material whose characteristics are more familiar to the rod builder—cork—will be easier for some to work with. Satisfactory patterns can be made of cork if you use a select quality, fill all the pits, and seal the surface with two or more coats of casting resin. If you can work comfortably with one of the other materials, less finishing of the pattern is required.

If, for example, you are making a pattern for a winding check, you would proceed as follows. Start with a piece larger than needed and drill a hole slightly smaller than the outside diameter of the blank where the check will later be fitted. Place the piece on a suitable mandrel and turn to the shape desired. Pay particular attention to obtaining a smooth finish. Remove from the mandrel and ream the inside hole to the exact final size. Carefully smooth the hole.

The next step is to make a mold. An ideal material is the liquid plastic for making soft plastic lures, such as worms. Select the smallest possible container, with adequate depth, in which to make the mold. Plastic lure boxes, hook boxes, etc. work very well. Heat the liquid plastic as per the instructions and pour a thin layer in the bottom of the container. Set aside to cool. Once the plastic has set up, place the pattern you have made in the center of the container. Heat more plastic and fill the container around the pattern to a level above the pattern. After cooling, remove the pattern from inside the two-piece mold. It will be easier to manipulate if you remove the entire mold from the container. Be particularly careful not to damage the soft plastic core that forms the hole in the winding check. You now have a mold in which you can cast many duplicates of your original pattern.

Estimate the amount of resin needed and add the coloring pigment. Lay two or three individual strands of fiberglass in the mold cavity, wrapping them around the core. These act as reinforcing material and strengthen the casting. Add the catalyst to the resin and immediately fill the cavity of the mold. The setup time is very short once the catalyst has been added. As a rule of thumb, one drop of catalyst is used with a teaspoonful of resin. The higher the temperature the quicker will be the setup, and the less catalyst will be required.

Cast winding check removed from mold.

How well you have made your pattern will determine how much final finishing, if any, has to be done to the cured casting. If you find some finishing is needed, slip the casting on an arbor and turn it in a lathe. Generally, only fine sanding is required. If the bottom or flat side is uneven, a few strokes on a sanding block should even it off for a snug fit on the rod. After installation a coat of clear resin will restore the color and provide a high gloss.

Clear polyester casting resin and catalyst are available in most hobby stores. They also carry the various-colored pigments. Clear parts with no pigment can be made and a small item imbedded in the casting. One of the photographs shows a butt cap containing a hook and two salmon eggs made in this manner. Another RodCrafter, Gerry Lipka, makes clear plastic butt plates for fly-reel seats that contain an actual fly.

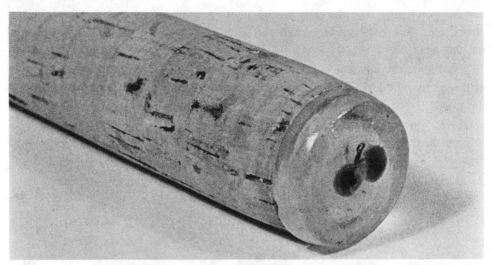

Clear, cast butt cap containing salmon eggs and hook.

Cast butt cap on wood plug for mounting.

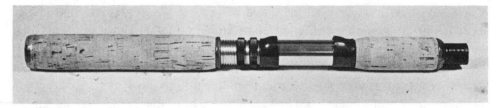

Handle with cast butt cap, cast rings on each end of reel seat, and cast winding check.

Casting unique components is thus still another way for the custom rod builder to add personal expression to his rods. As is true of many rod-building ideas, it is not for everyone. It will find its greatest application with the craftsman who builds many rods and does not want to fabricate the same part from scratch each time. With a mold of his own design, he can quickly and easily duplicate the component as needed. Color can be varied on each casting to coordinate with the colors of any rod, yet the part used is uniquely his.

Cust-O-Checks and Cust-O-Hosels

Focusing our attention on the front end of the foregrip, there are some dandy little components that offer the custom rod builder a host of options for unique design. The parts I am referring to are sold under the names Cust-O-Checks and Cust-O-Hosels. These are made of rubberlike material, enabling them to stretch considerably. In fact, only two sizes of the checks are needed to fit all blank diameters from $^{26}/_{64}$ to $^{46}/_{64}$ inch. In the hosels, four sizes cover the range from $^{20}/_{64}$ to $^{46}/_{64}$ inch. The checks are ¼ inch long (or thick) and of a doubling-ring design with a groove in the center. The hosels are ½ inch long and have a slight straight taper. Both are available in either black or brown.

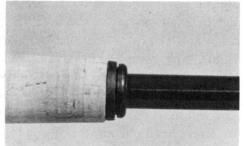

Resilient Cust-O-Checks and Cust-O-Hosels.   Cust-O-Check on foregrip.

Naturally, these components can be used just as they are for a handsome finish to a handle. Since they fit snugly around the blank they do an excellent job of hiding reaming errors in the cork, and the resilient material provides good protection. After being glued in place, the cork can be sanded to blend the grip taper. However, it is their almost limitless versatility that makes them so valuable.

Starting with the Cust-O-Checks, the simple addition of wrapping thread in the groove will serve as an accent in the handle to pick up the color of the wraps. If you prefer a shorter (thinner) check, slip one over a dowel and chuck it into a drill. A sharp knife or X-Acto blade will easily slice it into two checks. The rear piece will have a slightly larger diameter . . . and now you can do two rods.

Another way to use these checks is with an aluminum butt cap (such as the A303) mounted on the front of the foregrip as a hosel. These caps are anodized different colors and yield a professional touch when used in pairs. One serves as a butt cap and the other as a matching hosel. To make a hosel, simply remove the solid rubber cap from the end and replace it with a check with the desired hole size. Turn down the cork or Customgrip foregrip so the "hosel" fits flush with the grip. Save the end cap you removed from the butt cap. It can be trimmed and glued to another rod as a butt plate.

Aluminum butt cap (rubber end cap removed) and Cust-O-Check.

Butt cap and Cust-O-Check used as hosel on foregrip.

The Cust-O-Hosels are just as versatile, perhaps more so. They too can be slipped on a dowel and cut to any desired length. The smallest-size hosel fits tightly inside the largest-size hosel. By combining two in this manner you have a larger-O.D. hosel for a small-diameter blank. The O.D. of the resultant hosel is now large enough to blend the taper of the grip into the taper of the hosel.

A stepped-down design can be achieved by allowing the smaller hosel (used on the inside) to protrude slightly. Then, instead of a flat front edge on the hosel, you will have a small step on the face. If you want a more pronounced step, cut the larger hosel (the one that fits on top) shorter. By adjusting the length of both hosels, some very interesting and unusual effects can be produced.

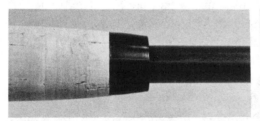 

Large Cust-O-Hosel with cork foregrip blended to fit.

Large Cust-O-Hosel cut short and fitted over small Cust-O-Hosel.

Using just one hosel, you can cut it to any desired length to fit the proportions of the rod being made. Whenever you cut a hosel, save the piece you cut off. Even a thin slice from a hosel can be used very effectively on some rods. I suppose at that point the "hosel" becomes a "check"! Anyway, who cares what we call it as long as it enables us to build attractive, unique custom rods.

 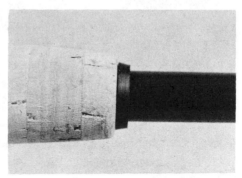

Small Cust-O-Hosel cut short.   Thin slice of Cust-O-Hosel.

Inlaid wood from pool cues

In the constant search for interesting materials to use in handle trim, Rod-Crafter Paul R. Winston discovered a source of quality, inlaid wood. The source? Broken pool cues! They are usually made of well-seasoned maple and walnut, often with elaborate inlaying, or splicing, where the two different woods are joined together. Since they are round and tapered, they are easy for the rod builder to work with. Many times the taper will be in proportion to the handle being built. In other cases, they can easily be turned and sanded to the desired diameter.

First cut the piece to the desired length and as accurately as possible bore a hole through the exact center. The piece is then slipped on a length of threaded rod and locked in place with a washer and two nuts on each end. The rod is chucked into a lathe or electric drill and the piece trued around the center hole by turning. If the piece is to be used as a reel-seat insert (or spacer) with a skeleton reel seat, the outside taper is leveled to the required diameter. If it is to be used in the handle itself, the taper is adjusted as needed. The accompanying sketch shows a trolling-rod handle built on a "blank through design" complete with gimbal that Paul made from a piece of broken pool cue. It was augmented by some trim rings of walnut and burnt cork.

For a source of these handy bits of fancy wood, check local pool halls. Usually a friendly request to the owner to save any broken cues will be rewarded;

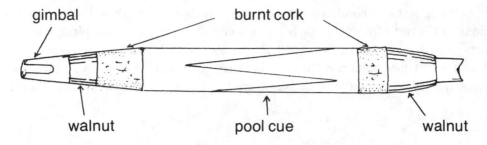

gimbal   burnt cork

walnut   pool cue   walnut

Pool cue used in "blank through" trolling handle.

since they are normally just thrown away. Home pool tables have become quite popular, so it might also pay to check with your pool-playing friends. Whatever your source, I think you will find that a broken pool cue can be an asset in fashioning a custom rod.

Miscellaneous handle-trim techniques

As noted earlier, making your own skeleton seats as explained in *Fiberglass Rod Making* is no longer the only way of obtaining these desirable components. However, RodCrafter Fred C. Rote has found that making your own provides a bonus in the form of the straight piece of unthreaded barrel that is removed from an anodized-aluminum reel seat. He uses this piece to fashion a matching butt hosel.

After cutting out the center of the seat, file the ends to make them square and smooth. Set this piece aside temporarily. Refer to the accompanying diagram for the steps in making the matching butt hosel.

The first step is to cut a recess in the end of the butt grip (A). The diameter of the recess (B) should be sized so that the piece cut from the reel seat (C) will just fit over it. Make the length of the recessed section (B) ¼ inch *shorter* than the section cut from the seat (C). Check the parts for the proper fit, and epoxy the piece from the seat (C) over the recess (B) on the butt grip. Allow the epoxy to cure.

Matching butt cap made from removed section of reel seat.

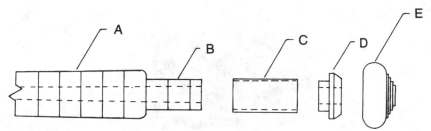

Custom butt cap using section removed from reel seat.

Take a single cork ring (½ inch long), slip it on a mandrel or arbor, and sand down one half of it so that it will just fit the inside diameter of the section removed from the reel seat (C). Shape the other end of the cork ring to a slight chamfer and of a diameter over which you can just fit a Model RB-1 rubber butt cap (E). The shape of the cork ring should be as shown in the diagram as Part D. The Model RB-1 butt cap is the type used on the end of boat-rod handles.

With the remaining parts fitted, all that has to be done is to glue the shaped cork ring (D) into the reel-seat section (C) and to the end of the recessed cork butt grip (B). Then, epoxy the rubber butt cap (E) over the top of the protruding end of the shaped cork ring (D). The large butt cap is quite functional; it makes a nice "belly bumper" and also protects the end of the handle from chipping. Incidentally, this idea is not limited to spinning rods, but can also be adapted to a fly rod on which a fixed fighting butt is being built.

Some other comments regarding butt caps are in order here. Sometimes a molded rubber or rubberlike butt cap will have small bits of material on the open end. This is known as flashing and is left from the molding process. The best way that I have found to trim this away without marring the cap is to place the cap, open end down, on a flat work surface. Do this in such a way that the thin flashing will be spread outward. Use an X-Acto knife or a Rod Builder's Knife to trim away the flashing by making the cut straight down, parallel and as close to the side of the cap as possible without cutting into the side of the cap itself.

Anodized-aluminum butt caps can also have narrow custom grooves of bare aluminum cut in them. This procedure was explained in the chapter on reel seats. Using the same methods, the shallow, decorative grooves can be made to match the reel seat. It is easiest to perform if the butt cap has already been glued onto the butt grip, since it is then centered and will revolve fairly true. To mount in a rod lathe, remove the rubber button from the end of these caps. This will provide access to the blank just inside. Use a "Crusenberry mandrel" (described in the chapter on tools) inserted into the end of the blank to securely hold the rod in the lathe chuck. If the same butt cap was used on the end of the foregrip as

Trim rings made by removing anodizing.

a matching hosel, the narrow, shallow grooves can be similarly cut in it. Such treatment of reel seat, butt cap, and matching hosel (if used) can do a great deal for carrying the trim theme throughout the entire handle assembly. An integrated design always enhances the appearance of a quality custom rod.

CASTING-ROD HANDLES

There is a tremendous amount of custom design work performed in the crafting of spinning-rod and fly-rod handles, and in saltwater rods of all kinds. It has always mystified me that, by comparison, there is relatively little creative effort put forth in building custom casting-rod handles. This seems to be borne out by the fact that when I speak before groups which fish principally with this type of rod, I am more often than not introduced as a "rod wrapper" who has written a book on "rod wrapping" and who will address the group on "how to wrap rods." The implication is clear: On a casting rod you simply select a handle of your choice and wrap on the guides. Relatively few rod builders I have encountered make custom casting-rod handles, and many fishermen have never even seen one.

I have asked myself such questions as "Do builders of casting rods consider the existing handles so perfect in all respects that they feel they cannot be improved upon?" Or "Do many rod builders lack information on how a casting handle is constructed, so they are reluctant to attempt customizing?" Or "Do they feel rebuilding a casting-rod handle is not worth the effort?" I certainly don't have the answers to these questions.

On the other hand, I have been approached by a respectable number of fishermen to build them a longer casting-rod handle, to design a handle for them that better color-coordinates with a custom rod, to make them a handle (usually longer) with a large "belly bumper" butt cap for comfort in fishing crankbaits, and to repair stock handles from which the last inch or two has broken off.

In some geographical areas and in certain economic markets the added price for a custom handle is obviously a deterrent. However, in many areas where the bass boat is king, the high investment in these rigs speaks loudly in support of the fact that the ardent fisherman can afford and is willing to pay substantial sums for his fishing equipment. So another question has popped into my mind: "Why hasn't the bass fisherman, who has paid a lot of money for his boat and all the other fishing tackle he owns, been desirous of owning a unique bevy of rods that match his boat, in color and style, the same as many of his saltwater brethren?" I have met a few that have, but by and large it seems the overwhelming majority have never even entertained the idea until some rod builder suggested it.

By contrast, the casting-rod fisherman is one of the most demanding when it comes to intricate threadwork on the custom rods he builds or buys. This is true for guide wraps, as well as the more obvious elaborate butt wraps. But when it comes to the handle, he seems more than willing to accept a stock handle for an otherwise beautiful and unique rod.

Let's examine how a handle is made. The basic factory construction of a casting-rod handle is a reel-seat frame made of metal or plastic, below which there is a solid or hollow rod. This rod or tube varies from 4 to 6 inches long, with most being 4½ or 5 inches. The hand grip is built or molded around this straight rod. At the opposite end of the reel-seat frame, the fore end, there is usually a collet of some sort that clamps on the butt ferrule. On some handles, there is a female receptacle for a friction fit with a smooth butt ferrule. The handle on many factory-made spin-casting rods differs only in that there is no ferrule connection at the fore end of the reel-seat frame. Instead, the handle is permanently attached to the butt of the blank, and a rod ferrule is installed about midway along the rod.

As is true of many rod components, quality can vary widely. As a general rule, the better models are made of stronger materials and engineered for longer, trouble-free service. Two different rod companies might build quite different-looking handles on the same reel-seat frame purchased from the same supplier. A rod company might change the style and finish of its handles from one tackle year to another, but build the handles on the same frame. My point here is that what lies beneath the skin of most casting-rod handles is quite similar, and the custom rod builder has essentially the same options as a rod company when it comes to designing and building the finished handle.

Creating a custom handle is really no more difficult for a casting rod than it is for any other type rod. Many of the same ideas of various trim design and materials apply, as does the fitting of the handle shape, diameter, and length to the hand of the angler. A superior fishing instrument can result, and the owner can have the pride of possessing something truly unique—something custom in all respects.

Since handles are often made by rod companies on the same frame, a common problem frequently exists. The length of the solid or hollow rod around which the grip is built does not run the entire length of the grip. As RodCrafter Ken Lane has pointed out, this is why a sharp blow to the butt of the handle often results in easy and sudden breakage. Some rod manufacturers have attempted a quick and cheap solution by sticking on a short piece of aluminum tubing to fill the gap. Since the tubing often barely fits over the end of the frame rod, a sharp blow frequently knocks it off too.

This is pointed out since the custom builder is in a position to build a much stronger handle. After stripping away the existing grip material, determine the length of the finished custom grip to be installed. Extend the frame rod to the full length of the planned grip. This can be done by epoxying a piece of aluminum tubing of the proper length over the entire rod. If the frame rod is made of hollow tubing, then use a solid rod epoxied to the inside.

factory handle with center shaft too short

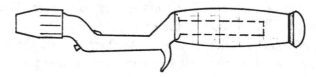

stripped handle with aluminum tubing to extend shank

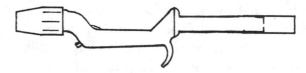

grip installed over extended shank

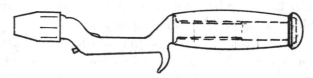

Rod grip lengthened for stronger and/or longer grip.

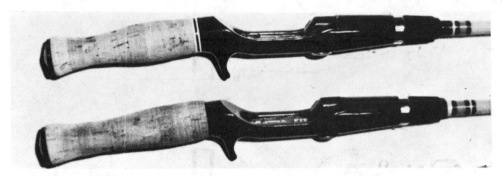

Custom-shaped cork grip on Fuji frame.

It was mentioned earlier that the diameter, length, and shape of the custom grip can be made to fit the hand of the angler and his particular fishing style. If your design calls for a round grip primarily of cork or resilient grip material, then it can be constructed by any of the previously discussed methods of making a preformed grip. Turn and shape the grip to slightly larger than the planned diameter. Slip it on the frame rod and have the angler try it on for size. Remove it from the handle and, working in small increments, reduce the diameter to the size that fits his hand and feels most comfortable to him. At the same time, slight variations in the diameter along the grip can be fit. With the proper size determined, inlays of various trim materials can be made. These will generally be placed where the grip joins the reel-seat frame and at the butt end. The desired butt cap has probably been previously selected and the butt end shaped to blend into the cap. Don't overlook the use of a metal butt plate instead of a butt cap. On it can be engraved the angler's initials. The grip assembly is epoxied in position on the frame rod in the same way any grip is mounted on a rod blank.

Round grips are certainly not the only possibilities. A lighter-than-normal ''pistol'' or similarly shaped grip can be hand-shaped from cork. Fairly large-diameter cork rings will probably be used to glue up a cylinder of cork directly on the frame rod. Working with a file, mild rasp, or coarse sandpaper backed with wood (or a homemade cutting-grit-and-epoxy tool), the basic contours are developed. The angler grasps the grip and soft lead pencil is used to trace the contours of the recesses for his fingers. A round file is then used to slowly work down the recesses at the same time, periodically checking the fit in the fisherman's hand. When the perfect shape for him is achieved, finish with fine sandpaper. It might help here to refer to the procedure explained earlier for shaping fly-rod grips to fit the hand.

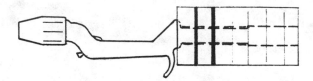

large cork rings glued on shank

cork pistol grip shaped by hand

Lightweight cork pistol grip.

If trim is desired in this type of shaped handle, burnt-cork rings of various thicknesses can be combined for some very handsome and interesting effects. Use the burnt-cork rings sparingly and, for the most part, keep them thin (narrow). When the final, contoured shape is made, the burnt cork may sometimes appear not just as round rings, but as slightly contoured dark lines throughout portions of the grip. Don't overlook the reverse of this process. You can make a grip of all burnt cork. The color blends particularly well with the color schemes used on some rods. It can also be inlaid with thin (narrow) rings of regular cork. Burnt cork when finished has a good-looking smooth appearance, free from pits. It also shows the dirt and soil far less than regular cork.

Some other ideas that have been used successfully would include replacing the white plastic trim rings in the Fuji handles with rings of aluminum or another color plastic. Beautiful handles can be made on Fuji frames by stripping the molded plastic and replacing it with resilient grips or cork. The entire reel-seat frame of any casting handle can be painted to color-coordinate with the rod. First sand the existing frame to provide a tooth for the paint and wipe it clean with a rag moistened with a mild solvent. Use a high-quality, two-part epoxy paint. Just before applying, wipe the surface lightly with a tack rag or finishing cloth to remove any dust, and work in a dust-free atmosphere. For additional protection and depth of gloss, a coat or two of clear epoxy, such as Crystal Coat, can also be applied.

The custom rod builder particularly skilled in working with wood, and perhaps with some experience in making gunstocks, can also fashion a grip from hardwood. Regardless of the shape, the hole for the frame rod should be bored first. If the grip is to be round, it is then turned to shape. If it is to be of the "pistol grip" type, the wood is cut roughly to shape with a saw. A Dremel tool or similar small powered cutting tool is the fastest way to further refine the necessary contours. However, hand carving works just as well. Checkering (as on gun stocks) is a possibility if you have the skill.

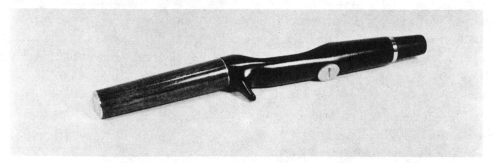

Hardwood grip, aluminum trim ring, and butt plate built on Fuji frame.

Another material from which grips can be made is that used for knife handles, as recommended earlier in this chapter for making decorative washers. Various formulations of synthetic materials have been developed, and some have excellent properties for rod-handle grips. The hobby of building custom knives has grown tremendously in recent years, and there are mail-order houses, such as Indian Ridge Traders, that specialize in this field. The composition material is generally available in different colors and shapes easily. Most of it comes in sheet form.

If building a round grip, large disks similar to washers can be cut from the sheets and cemented together. The resulting cylinder is then turned to shape. Use coarse sandpaper or the edge of a sanding disk chucked into another drill. Strips cut from the sheets can also be cemented together to form a turning square with the plies (or layers) running the length of the grip. The hole for the frame rod is bored and the grip turned on an arbor as above. By alternating different thicknesses of different colors, then shaping the grip so that the outside diameter varies, some beautiful swirled patterns are possible.

Thus far we have discussed just the grip portion of the handle along with painting the frame. Some casting-rod handles are made with the fore end of a hollow metal tube covered with cork or resilient grip material. Such construction lends itself to stripping off the existing covering from the tube and building a new foregrip. It can be built with trim of cork, burnt cork, resilient material such as Customgrip, plastic, wood, etc. to match the hand grip. A tapered "hosel" of such materials is particularly handsome.

Some casting handles, such as the Fuji, use a special fiberplastic adaptor (butt ferrule). These too present opportunities for custom design. The outside shape of the Fuji butt ferrule (or one of the American imitations) can be modified somewhat without affecting strength. I am referring here to the portion of the ferrule which is adjacent to the fore end of the handle when assembled. It is decorative, not functional. Since 2 inches of the blank is epoxied into the ferrule below this point, there is enough strength present for modification. The ferrule can be chucked into a lathe and turned to a different configuration. You can even make a straight taper to the blank and wrap thread from the blank up over the ferrule. If you have a metal lathe or have a friend who owns one, it is also possible to make aluminum ferrules that will fit a Fuji handle. The fore-end portion of the ferrule can then be made to any shape desired.

Fuji adapter (butt ferrule) turned to new, smooth shape.

So, if you build casting or spin-casting rods, don't overloook the many possibilities for custom handles. By doing so, you will be lifted out of the "rod wrapper" category and you will build better fishing instruments, tailored to the needs and desires of the angler—be that you or a customer.

SURF-ROD HANDLES

The term "surf rod" is quite general and broad. There are differences in the rods used from the beach along all our coasts. Further, some "surf rods" are specifically for use from jetties or piers. The lure-weight range of "surf rods" can be anywhere from ½ ounce up to as much as 16 ounces, and the length of the rods run from about 7½ feet to as long as 14 feet. Since we are concerned in this discussion with handle assemblies, a better definition might be "two-handed saltwater rods for either spinning or conventional reels."

Since we are talking about rods on which both hands are used when casting, one of the most important aspects of design is the distance from the butt end to the reel seat. This translates into the distance between the fisherman's hands as he holds the rod during the cast. A fair amount has been written on this subject over the years, and much more has been passed by word of mouth among fishermen, and even from one generation to another. Prescriptions of specific lengths in inches, as well as all sorts of formulas, abound.

While some of these specifications may have made sense when applied to a specific rod and a specific fisherman, there are simply too many factors to be considered to accept fixed standards when building a custom two-handed rod. Those who say that a rod handle must be a prescribed number of inches long or that the reel seat must be a certain number of inches from the butt end are saying in essence that we all should wear the same size shirt.

A custom rod of the type under discussion should always be superior to a factory-made rod simply because the distance between the butt and the reel seat can be tailored to fit the fisherman. Just a partial list of the factors that will determine that distance include: the height of the angler, the length of his arms, the size of his hands, his strength, his style of casting, and, of course, the length and weight of the rod. This is the reason a custom rod builder is not ready to begin designing a two-handed rod until the person who will fish the rod is present.

As RodCrafter Clifford G. Webb explains it, "The custom builder needs to determine, among other things, the proper position of the reel seat and the length of the butt grip *for this particular customer*. On a rod of a given length and weight, two different fishermen may have vastly different preferences. One might like a wide spread between butt and reel seat, while another prefers to cast with his hands placed much closer together."

The best method I have found to determine this spacing is to first have the customer hold the bare blank (with tip-top attached) as if he were casting the rod. If it is a two-piece blank the sections are joined. I make a grease-pencil mark on the blank where his reel-seat hand feels most comfortable. This serves as a starting point for the next step. The customer's own reel is attached to a specially prepared test reel seat. This seat has a layer of plastic foam glued to the inside. This permits sliding it over various blanks and taping it and the reel to the blank. In lieu of this test seat, the reel can be taped directly to the blank.

I first tape the seat centered over the previously made grease-pencil mark and have the customer go through some casting motions. The seat is then retaped in both directions along the blank, and the "false casting" again performed. This is repeated until he finds the point which feels most comfortable to him. The distance is carefully measured and recorded.

If the customer does not feel certain about the best point, you can go further.

Or, you may feel better if you conduct further tests. To do so, tape the guides to the blank in rough, approximate positions. Run line from the reel through the guides, attach the proper weight, and have the customer do some trial casting. It is important that you emphasize to him that he should concentrate on what distance from butt to reel feels best—not on his casting or the performance of the unfinished rod.

Cliff Webb has developed this test procedure to an even finer degree. He has an adjustable (telescoping) fiberglass handle complete with reel seat, split grip, and even interchangeable butt grips and caps. He attaches a finished rod tip to his adjustable handle and has the fisherman experiment with the feel of the handle in different lengths. By this method the customer determines the most comfortable spacing for him and his casting style.

The next decision regarding the handle assembly is the reel seat. In the vast majority of cases a brass/chrome seat is used. However, there are some few situations where an anodized-aluminum model is desired for a light rod. Whichever type is decided upon, the proper diameter must be selected. This will depend upon the diameter of the blank, the reel to be used, and the "feel" the fisherman prefers. His reel is attached to a number of applicable-sized reel seats and he determines which feels best to him. At the same time I explain the differences of weight, strength, and convenience of a heavier seat where the sliding hood moves in a keyed slot versus a lightweight seat. On Varmac seats this would be the difference between the NF series and the LW series.

The custom rod builder and his customer also have a choice of the material used for the grips, their diameter, and their length, as well as the handle design. The various materials have already been discussed elsewhere. However, it should be noted here that resilient materials such as Customgrip and Lightweight Hypalon are the best-wearing for this type of rod. A surf rod is sometimes carried in a vertical pipe holder on the front of a beach buggy, and the grips will be subject to chafing. Or, in some parts of the country, the fisherman will be operating from rock jetties and the rod will be wedged among the rocks between casts. This is pretty brutal treatment for any grip material, and if the rod will be used under such conditions, a tough grip material will be required. The angler who uses only a sand spike or a leather rod holder worn around his waist can get by with cork, if that is his choice.

The rear grip can be one long piece from butt cap to reel seat. Or, a combination of butt cap and grip length sufficient to accommodate the fisherman's hand may be used on the butt. No grip is used between it and a point just below the reel seat, where a short length is attached to the blank. This is known as a split rear grip and is preferred by many anglers. Whichever style is chosen, the diameter of the grip and butt cap at the bottom of the rod should be sized to provide a comfortable feel to the fisherman. Some sample grips of various diameters are a definite help here. Thought should also be given to the selection of the proper butt cap. On a good-sized surf rod it must be tough and functional rather than just decorative. Polyolefin rubber is an excellent material. The walls should be thick and preferably molded with a knurled inside for solid gluing. I have found the best to be 2 inches long with smooth contours, such as Models BC-02 and BC-06.

Depending upon the fish being sought, the dimensions of the foregrip can be quite important. If the angler's fishing requires the use of the foregrip in fighting a fish, it must be long enough (8 to 12 inches) and of the proper diameter to be functional. If, on a lighter rod, the foregrip will rarely be brought into play, then the decisions can be based largely on appearance. The material used will normally be the same as for the rear grip.

Admittedly, this process of fitting the handle assembly of a two-handed rod to the angler is a bit more time-consuming, but it pays handsome dividends in the form of satisfied customers and superior fishing instruments. In my opinion, the nearest to correct theory on how to design a surf-rod handle is that theory which provides the fisherman a finished product with which he is happy and comfortable—or with which he can most efficiently cast a baited hook or an artificial lure to the fish he is seeking.

Any of the previously discussed trim materials and construction methods can be used to add a custom flair to a surf rod. When selecting trim material, give some thought, again, to how the rod will be used. If it will be hand-held or supported in a leather rod support, trim can be placed anywhere on the grips.

If the rod will frequently be placed in a sand spike, you have some options. If hard trim rings such as plastic, impregnated walnut, or wood are used, they can purposely be placed at that point on the grip which will be in contact with the top edge of the spike. This will protect the cork from becoming dented and, in time, possibly chipped. However, the customer should realize that with long use, the surface of the trim ring will become chafed. This may be preferable to damaged cork, especially since trim rings can be refinished. On the other hand the customer may not want marred trim rings at some future time. In that case he has to make a decision between cork and the tougher resilient grips. The same options apply to a rod that will be carried in a pipe holder on a beach buggy.

On a rod subject to rough handle wear, trim rings can be placed right next to, and on either side of, the reel seat. Another possibility for trim that will not easily become damaged is the use of a shaped hosel on the top end of the foregrip. On handle assemblies where resilient grips are used and hard, rugged use is expected, consider sanding some well-placed shallow circular grooves around the grips. This technique is discussed in the chapter on grips.

Handles on surf rods can, of course, also be made of cork tape as explained in the chapter on grips. Here, less time is required in fitting the handle to the fisherman, since the reel is taped or clamped wherever desired. This type of handle was a longtime favorite with New England surf casters. In recent years, increasing numbers of quality custom rod builders in that part of the country have been switching to conventional handles built around a reel seat. With them, the resilient grips have gained in popularity, especially the lighter-weight materials such as Customgrip and lightweight Hypalon.

On occasion the rod builder is faced with the problem of making a specific blank into a longer rod. This arises when all the characteristics of a certain blank are exactly what is required, except that it is too short—and a comparable blank is not available in a longer model. This rare situation is always frustrating, but can be dealt with by building an extension on the butt end of the blank. The long, two-handed handle is assembled over this extension.

One way to build an extension is to use a piece from another blank that can be fitted and epoxied inside the butt. The tapers will have to match over the length to be glued. This length, or the amount of the extension blank that fits inside the primary blank, should be at least 4 inches. If a piece of hollow blank is not available that will fit, a section of a solid fiberglass blank can be used. While it is a bit heavier, it has the advantage of shapeability. The end that will fit inside the butt of the primary blank can be shaped into a matching taper. This is best done by *scraping* with a sharp knife blade held at 90° to the axis. Care must be taken to keep the shaped section round, and material must be removed slowly. The technique for fitting the taper is exactly the same as that described in *Fiberglass Rod Making* for making a solid-glass plug ferrule. When fitted, the extension is epoxied into the butt.

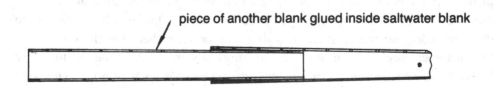

piece of another blank glued inside saltwater blank

Rod length extended by inserting length of matching taper blank into butt.

With either of these methods of building an extension a "step" or sudden change in the outside diameter will arise at the point where the two pieces join. Depending upon what part of the handle is built over this point, it may present no problem. If it does, this step can be eliminated by wrapping a length of the smaller diameter (the extension) with epoxy and string as described at the beginning of this chapter. A smooth taper is thus built up with which it is easier to work.

Another technique for building an extension is to use a length of thick-walled aluminum tubing. The inside diameter of the tubing should fit tightly over the butt of the blank. Again, at least 4 inches of overlap is required. In order to level the taper of the blank over which the tubing will be glued, string or thread and epoxy can be used. The outside diameter of the butt can similarly be built up to fit the inside diameter of the aluminum tubing if necessary.

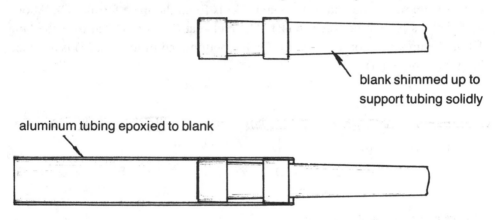

blank shimmed up to
support tubing solidly

aluminum tubing epoxied to blank

Aluminum tubing used to extend blank length.

Depending upon the length desired for the extension and the length of the handle assembly, a detachable extension can be built from a section of another blank. Ideally, the length of the handle should be the same as the extension. In this case, the outside diameter of the upper end of the extension should be just about the same as the outside diameter of the butt. Metal ferrules can then be installed on each, and the entire handle becomes removable. Since there may be some slight difference in the diameters of the two pieces, it may be necessary to shim, or build up, the smaller diameter to fit the ferrule. You can again fall back on a wrap of epoxy and thread to do this. Another possibility is a detachable handle assembly similar to a trolling-rod or boat-rod handle. Here, you would use a friction ferrule and matching reel-seat combination, or a locking-type stamped hood seat.

OFFSHORE TROLLING-ROD AND BOAT-ROD HANDLE
ASSEMBLIES

It has been my experience that many custom rod makers are hesitant to attempt construction of big-game trolling rods for themselves or for customers. Judging from the number of inquiries I receive on this subject, it would seem that there has not been enough how-to information available. Unfortunately, *Fiberglass Rod Making* provided only the barest of essentials. In this book we will therefore be discussing the construction of these important rods in greater detail. Let's start here with the handle assembly.

To see how the various components go together to make up the handle, refer to the diagram. On the butt of the blank (A) is fitted the male ferrule (C). Above the ferrule is placed the foregrip (B). The reel seat (D) is mounted over the tang (E) on the upper end of the butt (F). On the bottom end of the butt (F) is attached the gimbal nock (G).

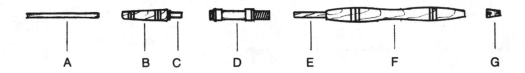

Offshore-trolling-rod handle assembly.

Offshore-trolling-rod handles must be the strongest of all rod-handle assemblies. Usually the rods are trolled from a rod holder. The impact of the strike must be absorbed by the handle, levered against the immobile holder. The handle, as well as the entire rod, is also subjected to tremendous strain in a prolonged fight with a heavy fish during which the extreme butt end is immobilized by the gimbal nock fitted into the fighting chair. Because of the punishment dealt them, specially designed, strong components are used. With a possible trophy fish at stake in the rod's future, it is well to heed the old adage that a chain is only as strong as its weakest link. Use only the best for *all* of the required handle components.

The reel seats used are of the locking type on which a collet nut on the top of the ferrule screws onto the top of the reel seat. For a complete discussion of these seats, refer to the chapter on reel seats. They are available with extra-strong stamped hoods or massive, heavy machined hoods. The choice is somewhat a matter of personal preference dictated by the size reel to be used, the fish caught, and the extra weight added by a heavier seat. Either type will be found on many classes of rods. Generally, however, IGFA rods of under-30-pound class are built with a stamped hood seat and those of over-30-pound class with a machined hood seat. You will find that on 30-pound-class rods the two types of seats are divided about equally.

The ferrule has a V-notch at the bottom which fits over a pin inside the body of the reel seat. This means that when the blank is mounted in the seat it cannot be twisted. When assembling these components the fixed hood on the reel seat must be perfectly aligned with the guides. Since the slotted ferrule is glued to the blank, it must be positioned to ensure this alignment.

The gimbal nock has two deep slots in the bottom. These are at 90° to each other, forming a cross. When the angler is fighting a fish, a slot in the gimbal nock fits over a pin in the gimbal ring of the fighting chair. In some cases, the angler fights the fish from a standing position and wears a harness or belt containing a gimbal ring. In either case, it is imperative that the gimbal nock be mounted on the butt so that when it fits over the pin, the entire rod is aligned properly with the reel exactly on top of the rod.

Alignment of components

It can be seen, then, that alignment of the various components forming the entire rod, including the parts of the handle assembly, is critical. Because of its importance, let's review exactly what parts have to be aligned. First, the guides and tip-top should be placed on the "high side" or spline of the blank. This will ensure that the stiffest, strongest side of the blank will be in direct opposition to the trolled bait and a fish being fought. Since the V-notch in the ferrule determines the position of the guides relative to the fixed hood of the reel seat, the ferrule and the reel seat must be aligned. The heaviest-class rods may be built with a curved butt. This style butt will have to be aligned with the fixed hood of the reel seat so that the curve is centered away from the angler, and the reel sits directly on top. Curved and straight aluminum or steel butts have the gimbal nock mounted as an integral part so that no alignment of the gimbal nock is required. When the gimbal nock is separate, one of the crossed slots in the gimbal nock's base must be aligned with the fixed hood on the reel seat.

Any sequence of assembling the components that provides this alignment throughout the rod is fine. From my own years of trial and error I have evolved a sequence which seems to be the easiest for me to work with. In talking with other custom rod builders I found that many of them have developed the same assembly sequence from their own experiments. This will be the procedure that I will discuss for assembling the offshore trolling rod. We'll go into it in detail, but first let's list the basic steps. (1) Spline the blank. (2) Fit but do not mount the ferrule to the blank. (3) Install the foregrip. (4) Mount the tip-top and wrap the guides. (5) Attach the gimbal nock to the butt. (6) Glue the reel seat to the butt. (7) Align and epoxy the ferrule.

Splining the blank has been covered in the chapter on the blank, so let's see what is involved in fitting the ferrule. It is obvious that since the ferrule fits over the blank, the outside diameter of the blank cannot be larger than the inside diameter of the ferrule. To reduce the wall thickness of the blank would weaken it at precisely the point where it must be the strongest. This is the reason that when selecting a reel seat you refer to the *inside diameter of the ferrule*. You then choose a seat on which the inside diameter of the ferrule is larger than the outside diameter of the butt of the blank. There is no problem if the ferrule is larger than the blank, since the butt can be built up to the required diameter with a bushing.

Many blank manufacturers recognize this problem of fitting the ferrule to the trolling blank and provide the blank with a fiberglass bushing. On some blanks, such as Fenwick, the fiberglass bushing is an integral part of the blank, molded onto the butt when the blank is made. Fenwick has chosen to make the diameter of the bushing correspond with the generally appropriate sizes of the ferrules on Varmac Locktop reel seats. At the time of this writing, the molded bushing on Fenwick blanks is a bit larger in diameter than specified and a bit longer in length. This is to allow you to make a good fit.

First check to see if the ferrule will fit over the bushing. Since it probably will not, reduce the diameter of the bushing with a coarse file. If done in a rod lathe, the reduction will be consistent around the blank, and the ferrule will be centered on the blank. If you file down the bushing by hand, make a reference mark on the end and use the same number of file strokes for each one-eighth rotation of the blank. This will remove material evenly so the ferrule will be centered. In either case, do not file off too much material from the bushing at one time, and keep checking the fit. When the ferrule will slide easily in place, stop filing.

With the bushing now reduced to the proper diameter, you turn your attention to the length. The ferrule should fit all the way up on the bushing so that when the foregrip is installed, the bottom edge of the foregrip is tight against the top edge of the ferrule. You will probably find, however, when the ferrule is slid to this position, the bushing is too long—it projects below the V-notch in the bottom of the ferrule. This would not allow the internal pin in the reel seat to engage the V-notch, or allow the collet nut on the ferrule to be screwed down on the top of the reel seat. This is easily remedied by cutting off the excess length from the butt of the blank. Hold the ferrule alongside the bushing and make a mark on the bushing *at the top of the V-notch*. Remove the ferrule and measure ¼ inch up the ferrule from your mark. Scribe a circle around the blank (bushing) at this point. Cut off the excess blank at the scribed circle, using a fine-tooth saw or hack saw. The ferrule will now properly fit both top and bottom of the bushing.

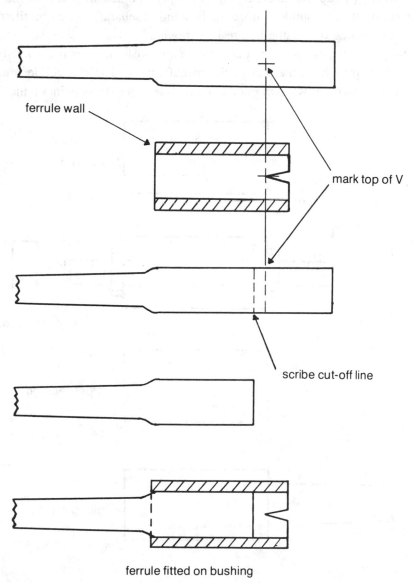

ferrule wall

mark top of V

scribe cut-off line

ferrule fitted on bushing

Fitting a molded bushing on a trolling blank to accept the ferrule.

Lamiglas blanks are provided with a choice of two bushings. One is sized to fit Varmac seats and the other is sized to fit Lakeland seats (also sold by some dealers under other names). In fact, some of the Lamiglas blanks can even be provided with two different-sized bushings for Lakeland seats. This highly desirable versatility for the custom rod builder is achieved by the more expensive process of molding the fiberglass bushings separately and grinding the butt of the blank level. The appropriate bushing is simply epoxied in place on the butt of the blank by the rod builder. Since the bushing is separate, it can be fitted to the ferrule by turning on a lathe before it is mounted.

Some trolling blanks do not come with any bushing. This is obviously a less expensive approach on the part of the manufacturer. The rod builder must then make and fit his own. Keep in mind that this is a major stress point on the finished

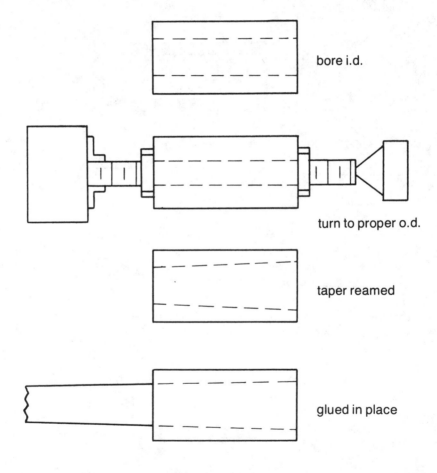

bore i.d.

turn to proper o.d.

taper reamed

glued in place

Making a hardwood bushing for the ferrule on a trolling rod.

rod, and the bushing must be strong and rigid enough to hold up under the pressure. The strongest homemade bushings are either of hardwood or fiberglass. The next strongest are tough fiber composition bushings. Also acceptable is a bushing, really a filler, of nonflowing epoxy such as PC-7. This provides adequate strength, but is difficult to apply and position so that the ferrule remains absolutely centered on the blank while the epoxy cures.

When making your own bushings, keep in mind that the inside diameter will have to be tapered slightly to conform to the taper of the blank. The outside diameter will be constant to fit inside the ferrule. To make a hardwood bushing, first cut the wood to the required length. Then drill a hole just slightly smaller than the size of the *smallest* diameter of the taper. Next, clamp on a mandrel of threaded rod and turn the outside to the required diameter to fit inside the ferrule. Use a very coarse round file or rasp to taper-ream the inside hole to fit the taper of the blank. When a satisfactory fit is obtained, glue the wood bushing onto the butt of the blank. At this point do not glue on the ferrule.

In building a fiberglass bushing you will need some fiberglass cloth and matching resin and catalyst. These are readily available at boat dealers and some automotive stores as body-patching kits. First determine the correct length of blank to be covered to fit your ferrule. Scribe a circle around the top end of the blank, marking the point to which the fiberglass bushing will extend. Follow the directions for saturating the cloth with resin and catalyst, and wrap it tightly around the blank. Build it to a diameter slightly larger than needed to fit the ferrule. Make sure you have built up sufficient material at the upper end of the blank where the diameter is smallest because of the taper. Tape can be wound over the impregnated fiberglass cloth to hold it tight while the resin cures. After the resin has completely cured, file down your fiberglass bushing to a constant diameter that will fit inside the ferrule. The technique to use is the same as described for that used on Fenwick and other blanks which contain an integral molded-fiberglass bushing.

One of the problems with tough fiber composition bushings is that you can only rarely find one with the needed inside and outside diameters to fit the blank and the ferrule. When obtainable, the procedure for fitting them is the same as for a hardwood bushing. Glue the fit bushing to the blank, but do not glue the ferrule in place at this time.

You have now fitted the ferrule to whatever type of bushing is used on the butt of the blank. Remember, the ferrule *should not be glued* in place at this time. The next step is to mount the foregrip. Follow the normal procedure for mounting the particular type of grip being used. The bottom of the foregrip should fit tightly against the top of the bushing now installed on the butt of the blank.

The roller top is mounted with epoxy glue for the needed strength, and aligned with the high side of the blank. Occasionally the tip of the blank will be too large for the tube of the tip-top. You undoubtedly ordered a size tip-top to correspond with the blank manufacturer's specifications—and it is very frustrating to find the tip larger (thicker in diameter) than it was supposed to be. Many times the roller-top tube can be made to fit by sanding off just the finish on the blank. Since the walls are generally quite thick on a trolling blank, strength will not be affected if you sand off just the very smallest amount of fiberglass. However, you must be careful here. Sanding away much fiberglass will weaken the tip. Rather than risk that, exchange the roller top for the next largest size. Doing so will delay assembly of the rod, but it is the best course to follow.

Incidentally, this is a good example of where a quality dealer in rod-building supplies is so important to you. On your order to him you can request that he select the proper size roller top to *actually* fit the blank, regardless of the manufacturer's specifications. Since the price of roller tops increases with size, plan on having to use the next size larger and include that price with your order. Ask your dealer for a refund if the smaller size (the one specified by the manufacturer) does fit. It obviously takes the dealer more time to check this fit for you and select the proper size roller top. However, this is what "service" is all about, and may be the reason the service-conscious dealer has to charge a bit more. In the final analysis you benefited, since you didn't have the expense and annoyance of sending the wrong size top back to him. Nor did you have to delay assembly of the rod. There are many similar problems encountered in building any rod, and in the long run it will pay you to buy from a dealer knowledgeable in custom rod building who places high value on service. I realize I have digressed from the assembly of a trolling rod, but I feel the point warrants it.

You may have to use a roller top that is larger than the tip of the blank, and one on which the fit is rather loose. A wrap of thread imbedded in epoxy will build up the tip for a good, strong fit. After the top is mounted, proceed to position and wrap the roller guides on the blank. Spacing and wrapping are covered in the chapters on guides and wraps. While the coats of color preserver and/or wrapping finish are drying, you can return to working on the handle assembly.

Unless you are working with a factory-assembled handle, you will have to mount the reel seat on one end of the butt and the gimbal nock on the other. I prefer to mount the gimbal nock first, since I find it makes the alignment process easier. If you are using an aluminum or steel butt, this step is omitted, since the gimbal nock is already installed. The gimbal nock supports the rod in the gimbal ring and is subject to a great deal of twisting force. If it comes loose during a fight with a fish, the angler is at a definite disadvantage, and the fish may be lost. For this reason I believe the gimbal nock should always be fastened to a wood butt with a screw through a hole in the side of the gimbal nock, as well as epoxy. Even if the glue bond breaks, the screw will hold the gimbal nock in the proper position, preventing the rod from twisting. Top-quality gimbal nocks are made with the hole drilled in the side before they are heavily chrome-plated, and the proper-size plated screw is provided. Some people refer to these as two-piece gimbal nocks. They are decidedly superior to those without a hole that are only glued to the butt.

Slip the gimbal nock over the recess on the bottom of the wood butt. Check the fit. If too tight, sand the recess where needed. With the gimbal nock in position, mark the spot for the screw with an awl or pencil. Remove the gimbal nock and drill a small pilot hole in the wood for the screw. This hole should be smaller than the screw and a bit shorter. Roughen the inside of the gimbal nock, as noted earlier in the chapter on gluing. Also roughen the recess on the butt over which the gimbal nock fits. Apply a film of epoxy to both the inside and bottom of the gimbal nock and to the recess on the butt. Slide the gimbal nock into position with a twisting motion, then wipe off any excess glue squeezed out. Immediately mount the screw in the pilot hole and tighten. Now, more carefully, wipe off all excess glue squeezed out of the joint.

The next step is to mount the reel seat on the butt. You will recall that the reel seat must be aligned properly with the gimbal nock on the opposite end of the butt. A trick that I find helpful is to tape a good-sized nail or a length of rod in one of the notches in the bottom of the gimbal nock. This serves as a sight, much like that on a rifle, to aid in perfect alignment with the fixed hood of the reel seat.

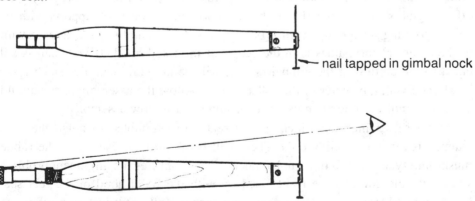

nail tapped in gimbal nock

sighting along nail to align stationary hood on reel seat

Use a nail or piece of rod as a sight to align gimbal nock with fixed hood of reel seat.

169

First slip the seat over the tang on the upper end of the butt to check the fit. Make any necessary adjustments. The tang should have some small grooves around it for a good glue bond. If there are none, now is the time to make them. While you are at it, roughen the surface of the tang. Measure the approximate length of the tang, and roughen the inside of the reel seat for that length. Apply a film of epoxy glue to the entire surface of the tang, making sure the small grooves are filled. Place a film of epoxy on the inside of the reel seat to the length previously roughened (the length of the tang). Slide the tang into the reel seat with a twisting motion to spread the glue, and wipe off any excess glue.

Now, place the butt horizontally in a vise padded with cloth. The vise need only be tightened enough to hold the butt horizontally. Use the nail or rod taped in the gimbal nock as a sight to align the gimbal nock with the hood on the seat. To do this, position the butt so that the nail "sight" is straight up. Without changing the position of the butt, rotate the reel seat on the tang until the hood is centered on the nail. You can view this best if you put your head at the reel-seat end and sight along the assembly as you would along a rifle barrel. When it is perfectly aligned, do not touch the assembly again until the epoxy has cured.

The last step in the assembly sequence is to mount the ferrule on the blank. This was left until the end so that the roller guides could be most easily lined up with the fixed hood on the reel seat. The bushing over which the ferrule is glued was previously fitted. All that remains is to roughen the inside of the ferrule, coat it and the bushing with epoxy, and slide the ferrule in place. Don't slide the ferrule quite all the way up the bushing. Stop about ½ inch short, and wipe off any large bead of glue that has formed on the edge of the ferrule. Then, continue sliding the ferrule until it is tight against the bottom of the foregrip. Wipe off any glue squeezed out. Place the rod horizontally on two supports with the guides pointing straight up. Sight from the handle end and twist the assembly until the center of the guides is in the center of the fixed hood. If your nail is still taped to the bottom of the gimbal nock it will be an additional aid, since it can be aligned with the center of the roller guides. Allow the assembly to remain undisturbed until the epoxy cures. Your trolling rod is now assembled.

Boat rods which have locking reel seats are assembled in much the same manner as offshore trolling rods. There will be a butt cap, usually of the rubber mushroom type, instead of a gimbal nock. This simplifies the alignment problem, since only the guides have to be lined up with the fixed hood of the reel seat. It is suggested that the same assembly sequence be followed; just omit references to the gimbal nock. The rubber mushroom cap can be glued onto the end of the butt at any time.

Lighter boat rods are sometimes made with a friction ferrule and matching reel seat. The ferrule simply slips into the upper end of the reel seat. There is no V-notch in the bottom of the ferrule, no alignment pin inside the reel seat, and no locking collet nut on the ferrule. Alignment of the guides with the fixed hood of the reel seat is done "by eye" each time the rod\is assembled by the fisherman. There are therefore no alignment steps in the assembly of the handle section of the rod. Do fit the ferrule to the blank first, and glue it in place. Then mount the foregrip. From that point you can work on either the guides or the handle assembly.

An entirely different method of construction is sometimes used on offshore trolling rods and on boat rods. Instead of a short blank and a reel seat with a ferrule, permitting the rod to be disassembled at the handle, a longer blank and a slipover reel seat are used. This is known as "straight-through" construction. Basically, it is quite similar to the construction of a spinning rod. Like the spinning rod, assembly starts at the butt and progresses forward as components are fitted and glued into position.

If a wood butt and gimbal nock are used on this type of rod, the butt must be hollow. That is, it must have a hole bored through the center axis. This permits the wood butt to be slipped over the blank. It is difficult to taper-ream a long hardwood butt to fit the taper of the blank. It is much easier to select a hollow butt with a center bore large enough to fit over the largest outside diameter of the blank. Then, level the taper of the blank with string and/or thread imbedded in epoxy. After the wood butt is glued in place on the blank, the gimbal nock is mounted.

Next the slipover reel seat is mounted over the required reel-seat bushings of cork. Instead of cork, the blank beneath the reel seat can be built up with fiberglass cloth and resin as described earlier. When the reel seat is epoxied in place the fixed hood must be aligned with the gimbal nock. Use the previously described technique of taping a nail or metal rod to one of the notches in the bottom of the gimbal nock. Sight along the rod and twist the reel seat until the nail is centered on the fixed hood. After the epoxy cures under the reel seat, the foregrip is mounted.

There is a special blank made for "straight-through" handle construction where the builder does not want to install any kind of butt. It is called a Bottle Blank and made by Shakespeare. The name is derived from its wider, bottlelike tapered shape below the point where the reel seat is mounted. The butt of the rod is thus large-diameter fiberglass. No butt work is needed on this blank except for installation of a butt cap or gimbal nock. The slipover reel seat is mounted immediately above where the butt shape swells. Construction thereafter follows the same sequence as for any rod of "straight-through" design.

Some boat rods and a very few offshore trolling rods are of "straight-through" construction with the butt covered with Hypalon or other resilient grip material. A regular blank, longer than a conventional trolling blank, is used. First the resilient butt grip is installed, and a butt cap is mounted on the end. Then, in the usual manner, a slipover chrome-plated-brass reel seat is mounted, followed by a foregrip of the same resilient material as used on the butt.

Butt materials

Having discussed the construction methods of trolling and boat rods, it may be helpful to review the different materials used for the butts, since this is not mentioned elsewhere in this book. For years, one material predominated—wood. Air-dried, straight-grained hickory was the first choice, and ash the second. In recent years butts have been made of aluminum and hollow stainless steel.

Let's examine wood first. The finest-quality hickory butts are available preformed and prefinished from Varmac and other manufacturers. A variety of shapes and sizes are made for both offshore trolling rods and boat rods. The more venturesome rod builder who has access to a lathe can make his own. In so doing he can make a custom shape and/or vary the pattern of trim grooves usually cut in the surface.

These trim grooves can be left plain, or they can be accented by burning them with an electric wood-burning pencil or a soldering gun equipped with a fine-pointed tip, or by painting them with model paint. After the paint dries, seal it with a coat of clear white shellac. This will prevent the finish applied to the butt from lifting the paint.

The entire wood butt can be painted to match other components used in the rod. RodCrafter W. T. Head does this and then places narrow thread wraps in the grooves. He first paints the butt with two coats of Weber Lacquer Finish of the desired color. To make the wrap of NCP thread in each groove, he starts the thread on top of his tie-off loop. He finishes the butt with five coats of tough marine varnish. At least the recommended drying time is allowed between coats. He suggests that when using this technique, the grooves be checked beforehand to make sure they are deep enough so that the wrap does not come all the way to the surrounding surface of the butt. If you are making the butt yourself, you can cut the grooves sufficiently deep. If you are using a store-bought butt, the grooves can be carefully deepened if necessary with a hack saw or coping saw, then shaped a bit with a triangular file.

Another technique for painting a wood butt is to accent the grain of the wood with a contrasting color. Dark colors such as black, dark blue, and dark brown look good as the base color with the grain highlighted with white. Before applying the base color, carefully brush any sanding dust out of the open grain with a dust brush. Make sure the base paint is dry before applying the accent color to the grain. You should also test the two paints on a piece of scrap wood to be certain the accent color will not lift the base color. To apply the accent color, brush on a coat, then wipe it off with a rag, allowing paint to remain in the grain.

The rod builder experienced in woodworking may also want to make laminated wood butts with the top layer of a beautiful hardwood. Start with a turning square of air-dried, straight-grained hickory or ash. It should be large enough in width so that after turning it will compose the only wood forming the tang that fits inside the reel seat. The piece of hickory should be square, with the sides planed perfectly flat. Onto the four sides are glued four pieces of the selected hardwood. Their surfaces must also be planed perfectly flat for a good glue bond. The thickness of the hardwood will depend upon the effect desired, as well as the planned maximum diameter of the finished butt. After the glue dries, the resulting turning square is shaped in a lathe. If the butt is tapered toward the gimbal end, the lighter-colored hickory or ash will come to the surface for a handsome inlaid effect.

Many rod builders delight in working with wood, and many custom ideas can be incorporated in making a butt. For strength, the center should always be of hickory or ash. Wood also requires the very toughest of finishes to hold up under the sun and salt air. Consider the new two-part clear epoxy finishes, as well as the modern marine varnishes. Use four to six coats. Allow each to dry thoroughly and lightly sand each coat with extra-fine sandpaper.

One of the problems associated with wood butts is that even the best will break at unpredictable pressures. This is due to variations in the grain patterns, contours, and other factors. From extensive tests on a specially designed testing machine, it has been found that most wood butts made for 80-pound-class rods break at about 550 pounds of stress. However, as noted, this is not entirely predictable and some snap at considerably less pressure, some withstand more. This was one of the reasons anodized-aluminum butts were originally introduced.

The first aluminum butts were solid and tended to be too heavy. To reduce weight, a straight hole was bored through the center axis, producing hollow aluminum butts. While lighter, boring caused a loss of strength, since the more vulnerable smaller-diameter portions also had the thinnest walls. To provide high strength with light weight, AFTCO developed a unique "swaging" process. Premium 6061-T6 aluminum tubing is pressed under great pressure into the shape of the butt. This puts extra thickness into the walls of the butt where the outside diameter is smallest. Where the diameter is larger (and naturally stronger), the walls are thinner. The butt is thus uniformly strong from end to end, yet has no unnecessary, nonfunctional weight. Proof of their strength is obtained on a testing machine where the 80-pound-class butt shows no sign of failure at 1,200 pounds of stress.

The gimbal nocks in the AFTCO aluminum butts are precision-machined and fitted to the butt with epoxy. Additional strength is provided by making the final ¼ inch a tight press-fit. There is the possibility of electrolysis when an aluminum butt is mounted inside a chrome/brass reel seat. To eliminate this, AFTCO and other high-quality aluminum butts have a sturdy PVC "insulator" epoxied over the tang. Small grooves are formed into the exterior surface of the PVC for a strong glue bond when the reel seat is attached.

At the time of this writing a new hollow butt of stainless steel has been on the market only a short time. It is marketed by Fenwick, which also uses it on its own line of finished trolling rods. While no stress figures are available, it seems highly likely that it is the strongest butt of all. Like the aluminum butts, it is available in straight models for all classes, and in curved models for the heaviest classes. A company such as Fenwick has undoubtedly done extensive testing of this design. However, especially in light of its quite high price, it needs the test of time with marine anglers and rod builders.

In addition to the earlier-mentioned problem of the unpredictable strength of wood, the cost for quality hickory has been skyrocketing. These two factors have resulted in some extensive research by Varmac. Their objective is to design butts for both offshore trolling rods and boat rods that will be consistently stronger, attractive, yet not as expensive as anodized-aluminum butts. At the time this is written, they are about to introduce a line of Hypalon-covered aluminum butts. I have not yet seen any of the prototypes, but it is my understanding that heavy-walled aluminum tubing will be used for the core. The shape of a butt will be determined by the tough, resilient Hypalon.

SIX

Guides

PREPARATION OF GUIDE FEET

All guide feet should be checked before wrapping. Most will benefit from some dressing. Any rough spots on the underside of the guide feet may, in time, damage and weaken the blank, and finally result in a mysterious break. Consider for a moment the rather obvious fact that the blank bends on each and every cast. It also changes configuration slightly from round to oval, then back to round, each time it is flexed. The metal feet of the guide do not bend exactly the same as the rod. Therefore, there is a very tiny amount of movement between the guide and the blank. If the bottoms of the guide feet are not silky-smooth, abrasion will take place. A rough spot of metal will, from thousands and thousands of casts, dig into the fiberglass. This movement between the two parts is also the reason guides should not be wrapped under heavy thread tension. Tension up near the breaking point of the thread will cause the guide to dig itself into the blank and, in time, cause the wall to collapse.

If you doubt that this movement between the two parts exists, or is significant, the following examination may convert you. Take a medium-light rod that has seen good service for a year or two. To make it easier to find what we're looking for, select one that has guides of average stiffness and preferably received a rather thick coat of finish over the wraps. Now examine the finish at the point just next to and beyond the edge of the guide feet. The chances are excellent that you will find small cracks and checks in the finish. They occur at that particular point, since that is where the end of the guide foot is moving the greatest distance on each cast. It is alternately being levered up and down, back and forth—and the finish is constantly being put under stress, causing it to crack and check as it breaks down.

The top of the guide feet, especially where the ends have been ground, must also be as smooth as glass. The thread binding the feet to the blank is in direct contact with the metal. A rough spot or a sharp edge will, in time, cut the thread. For a handsome wrap, the top, leading edge of the guide foot should form a taper, and is therefore often filed or ground by the rod builder. Unless it is polished smooth afterward, you will eventually encounter trouble. If the taper is ground to a razor edge, as we are encouraged to do by some, it will cut the thread and cut into the finish from the tiny, but constant, movement.

These are the reasons why all guide feet should be checked, and must be dressed to a silky smoothness. Let me trace the steps that I take in the preparation of guides.

The first thing I check for is to make sure the guide feet are both flat and in line. When they are, they will distribute the stress equally along the blank, look much better on the rod, and be much easier to wrap in position. Set the guide on a smooth, hard, flat surface so that you can view it from the side. Both feet should sit flat along the surface. If they point upward at the tip, the guide will be difficult to wrap. After one foot is wrapped flat on the blank it will spring the other foot in the air off of the blank. (This is the reason many rod builders

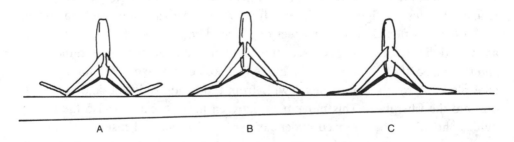

A   B   C

Prepare guide feet by bending so they sit flat on blank.

have to tape both guide feet.) If the ends of the guide feet touch the surface, but the portions nearest to the guide ring are not touching the surface, the ends will have a tendency to dig into the blank. It is an easy job to bend the guide feet if needed so that they sit flat.

I then sit the guide on a flat file and make about three or four back-and-forth movements. This automatically removes any tiny rough spots that might exist on the bottoms of the guide feet. Depending upon the thickness of the guide feet and the taper on the ends, I decide whether to grind or file the leading edge of each foot. In most cases I do. The one exception I have always found is with Aetna Foulproof Guides. They have a perfectly shaped taper.

The best advice on grinding or filing the feet is not to overdo it! We just want a nice taper over which the thread can easily climb as it is wrapped on the guide. It can be made with a small fine-toothed triangular file. A grinder is faster, but requires a bit more control. Avoid high-speed bench grinders with large, fast-cutting wheels. They can remove metal much too quickly and burn the metal, and it can be very difficult to manipulate a small guide on them. Instead, try a small cutting wheel that can be chucked into an electric drill held in a stand. Another good tool is a converted knife sharpener of the type used on electric can openers. Remove the housing for easy access, and the small fan blade to protect your fingers. When grinding the end of the guide feet, first file a flat taper. Then rotate the guide from side to side while holding it against the cutting wheel at a slight angle. This will round, or crown, the top of the tapered foot. Remember, don't grind to a razor edge.

With the increasing use of graphite blanks of very small diameters, I also check the width of the guide feet. I sit the guide on the blank in the general vicinity of where it will be positioned. If the feet of the guide are too wide for the blank, I grind a little off each side. I then round off the top of the foot so there are no sharp, flat edges along the side, and the configuration looks good on the finished rod.

The guide feet have now been tapered and shaped if required. The next step is to smooth all surfaces—top, bottom, and sides of the feet—with fine emery cloth. I follow by polishing all feet surfaces with crocus cloth, especially the tapered edges. Some rod builders use a hone for this final polishing operation. The last step is to wipe the guides clean with a tack rag to remove any residue from the cutting or polishing.

As I write these steps, they seem a lot more lengthy than they really are. It actually takes very little time for what is a truly important operation. After you have done a few sets of guides and have all materials handy, you breeze through in a matter of minutes.

Preparing one-footed guides

The above procedure is for any type of two-footed guides. The Fuji single-footed guides require a slightly different approach. If you have worked with these guides and ground or filed the leading edge both to taper them and to moderate the small cross grooves, you probably encountered a problem. No matter how much you taper the top of the guide foot, it still sits a slight distance off the blank. This becomes noticeable when wrapping with Size A thread, since there is a definite step from the blank to the guide foot. This is caused by the design on the *underside* of the foot. It has a wafflelike surface. The guide therefore sits on the high spots, or bumps. In order to get the leading edge of the guide to sit flush with the blank, I have found it necessary to grind or file the underside of the foot. So as not to reduce the thickness of the guide foot to the point where it loses strength, I grind the underside on a long, flat taper over its entire length. By smoothing away the waffling on the tip end, only a bit in the middle, and not at all near the guide ring, the guide can be made to sit on a slight angle on the blank. The leading edge is now flush with the blank, but the entire foot is in flat contact with the blank.

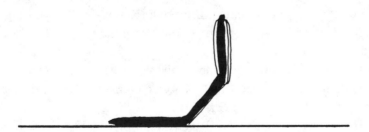

Single-foot guide sits on wafflelike bottom, raising tip of foot.

Single-foot guide with bottom filed on taper sits with tip flush against blank.

178

Many models of Fuji guides, as well as some other brands, now have a black finish. When grinding or smoothing the surface, this black finish is removed in some spots. If you use color preserver or NCP thread there will be no problem. However, if you plan to use regular thread (not NCP) *without color preserver,* the thread becomes translucent. This results in the bright metal spots showing through the wraps. To correct this, cover the bright spots with black model paint. When the paint is dry, seal it with a coat of clear white shellac so the paint will not be lifted by the wrapping finish. If you happen to have black latex paint, you can skip the shellac.

GUIDE SPACING

The selection of the proper guides, their number, and especially their placement are the key elements in producing a superior custom rod. Mass-production techniques simply do not allow time to determine the proper guide spacing for each individual blank to be used with a specific reel and a certain line and lure weight. Instead, guide spacing is plotted for an *average* blank with an *average* reel and an *average* line and lure weight. Every rod of that model is then wrapped with the guides spaced accordingly. By contrast, the custom rod builder can take the time to fit the guides and spacing to the variations of the *specific* blank to be used with a *specific* reel and *specific* line and lure weight. Then, and only then, will the rod cast the maximum distance with maximum accuracy, have stress distributed properly, and keep line wear to a minimum. This is in addition to functionally fitting the rod to the angler and modifying the action to best fit his style of casting.

The important element we are concerned with in this section is the proper number of guides and their correct spacing. I receive more inquiries and questions on this subject than on any other aspect of rod building. The staff of my rod-building-supply business have the same experience and spend many hours each day on the telephone and writing letters in an attempt to answer these questions. From this I can only conclude that there is a real thirst for knowledge in this area.

Many of the people requesting information on guide spacing expect a simple table that will show where each guide is placed on a certain model blank. Or, they would like an ironclad formula that will always indicate exactly where guides should be placed on any blank. Without realizing it, they want a factory approach to guide spacing. In so doing they are surrendering one of the most important controls the custom builder has for making a better rod.

Perhaps I am partly to blame for this, since I did list some tables in *Fiberglass Rod Making* as starting points for the beginning rod builder. I tried to emphasize that they were only "suggested locations" and stated that "it is best if you treat these and all such charts as only starting points, since no two rods bend exactly alike." Since that book was for people new to the art of custom rod building, I tried to simplify things—perhaps too much so. In any event, here we are concerned with advanced techniques and therefore need to fully understand the factors and principles that determine proper spacing. Once these concepts are understood, we can space guides for maximum performance on any rod.

Let's start with the number of guides to be used on a rod. Before I throw any numbers around, let me emphasize that the precise number of guides will not be determined by the knowledgeable rod builder until he is making the tests to determine proper spacing. In other words, it is rarely possible to know beforehand exactly how many guides will be required. All anyone can know at the start is the probable range of numbers of guides. The numbers given below, then, indicate that range and are offered only as a point from which to start.

Conceptually, it must be remembered that the number of guides used is always a compromise. Within practical limits, the more guides we use the better we can distribute stress along the rod blank. On the other side of the coin, the fewer guides we use, to a practical limit, the less friction is present and the greater the distance we can cast and the less wear there is on the line. And there are other limiting factors. The more guides, the more weight is added to the rod. The action can be slowed too much, or even ruined entirely. If there are too few guides, the line will slap against the blank, creating friction. This reduces casting distance and line control and increases line wear.

With the above cautions firmly established in your mind, the *probable ranges* for the number of guides can be considered. *Fly rods* using snake guides generally require slightly more than one guide per foot of rod length. For fly rods of from 6 feet to 9 feet in length, this will translate to about seven to eleven guides. Fly rods using Fuji single-foot or Foulproof guides generally require one guide per foot of rod length. *Ultralight spinning rods* most often have four to five guides. *Standard spinning rods* up to 7 or even 7½ feet usually require five to six guides. *Surf spinning rods,* those rods over 7½ feet, can vary considerably with a range of six to ten guides. About the same range exists for *conventional surf rods. Regular casting rods* for typical bass work usually are mounted with five to six guides. *Longer casting rods* for heavier freshwater and light saltwater use will need one or two more guides, depending upon rod length. *Trolling rods* of most kinds will use four to six guides, with *offshore trolling rods* employing five to six guides. Again, let me repeat, these numbers are only "for starters."

To determine the proper spacing of the guides you will need to make both static tests and casting tests. The static tests will help you first determine a tentative position for the critical placement of the butt guide, as well as place the remaining guides for proper stress distribution. The casting tests allow you to fine-tune the placement for maximum distance. With the exception of fly rods, you should make your tests using the same reel that will be fished on the rod. The reel should be equipped with the weight or pound-test line that will usually be employed with the rod. For the casting tests the proper range of lure weights, for which the rod is designed, is used.

While conducting the tests it will be necessary to move the guides, particularly the butt guide. The guides can be held in position with strips of masking tape. Cellophane tape is not as good, since it can leave a sticky residue on the blank and the guide feet which will later interfere with wrapping and finishing. Masking tape works well, but it does require removal and reapplication each time a guide is to be moved. Taping and untaping the guide feet many times, as is often necessary, can become a nuisance. RodCrafter Jim Cunningham introduced me to a better way that you might want to try.

Jim uses $^3/_{16}$-inch-O.D. latex surgical tubing. He cuts this into lengths of ¼ to ½ inch to form small, wide rubber bands. The pieces of tubing are moistened and slipped over the tip of the blank. From there they are slid or rolled down the blank to the starting position for the butt guide. While the I.D. of the tubing is only ⅛ inch, it has great elasticity. The procedure is continued until there are two bands for each intended guide in the approximate starting positions. It is a simple matter to place a guide where desired and slip a latex band over each foot. Moving the guide from spot to spot now becomes easy. Just roll the tubing in the desired direction, one roll at a time, slide the guide in that direction, and roll the remaining band onto the guide foot. During test casting the guides are held firmly in place. On extremely small-diameter tip sections the band can be doubled over itself to provide sufficient tension on the guide feet. When perfect spacing is achieved, you have the option of leaving the latex holding the guide. Then when wrapping, push the band toward the guide ring, start the wrap up over the foot, and snip the latex with a small pair of pointed scissors.

Now, let's discuss the techniques of working out the actual guide spacing. We will consider each type of rod separately and place a good deal of emphasis on locating the proper position for the butt guide. Before starting, locate the high side of the rod and determine on which side of the blank the guides will be located as explained in the chapter on the blank. Mount the tip-top.

Spinning rods

As we all know, the spool of a spinning reel is stationary, and the line unfurls from it as it is pulled through the guides. This is why we need a large and/or high frame guide as the butt guide, and progressively smaller and lower frame guides toward the tip. The unfurling line must be conducted through a funnel-shaped path on its way to the tip-top. This has given rise to the "cone-of-flight theory" of guide placement advocated by some sources. This is an excellent concept with which to visualize the general path the line travels. However, if it is adhered to too strictly in the placement of guides, improper positioning and too large a size guides will result. Let me illustrate.

Cone of flight theory for spinning rods.

Advocates suggest that the butt guide be secured to the blank one-third of the distance from the reel lip to the tip-top. The line is then strung from the lower lip of the reel through the butt guide and to the outside of the tip-top ring with all the remaining guides hung on the line. Most rod builders who have tried this find the weight of the guides pull against the line, preventing it from forming the desired straight line. If you are going to attempt to follow this approach, at least first attach all the guides temporarily to the blank and *then* run the line from the spool lip to the tip-top. The guides will then not dangle loosely in a mass on the line, distorting it.

The cone-of-flight theory then suggests that each guide be positioned along the rod so that the line just misses touching the inside of the guide ring that is farthest from the blank. It is suggested that the butt guide be the first to be slid along the blank to this desired position. If the butt guide must be moved more than 6 inches from its starting point toward the tip, or if it must be moved onto the tip section of a two-piece rod, then the butt guide is too small and we must use a larger size.

If you try this on most of the common rod-and-reel combinations, you will find an exceptionally large butt guide and adjacent guides are needed—so large, in fact, that their weight is too much for the blank and slows the action greatly, or destroys the action. If you try to solve the problem by using a reel that sits close to the blank (thereby bringing the angle of the "cone of flight" closer to the blank) you introduce another problem—line slap. The spool of a spinning reel must be held far enough from the rod to keep the line from slapping against the rod as it unfurls.

To be fair to the advocates of this system, they do point out that as an ideal method it is not attainable every time. They also state that compromise must be exercised for many reasons. Certainly I have no right to criticize further, for they are attempting the simplification of a complex problem, the same as I tried to do in *Fiberglass Rod Making*. As stated initially, it is an excellent concept with which to visualize the general path the line travels. Let's see if we cannot expand on it to help our understanding of proper spacing.

First of all, the line does not follow the exact straight line from outer edge of reel lip to tip-top. It unfurls, or billows out, in wider loops than the diameter of the spool. It must in order to leave the spool. Otherwise it would generate a great deal of resistance and friction as it crossed the lip of the spool. Also, the diameter of the unfurling line increases slightly as it moves away from the reel. The butt guide must, of necessity, choke the unfurling line somewhat and start the process of reducing the diameter. Each successive guide continues the process so that the line is traveling in a straight path when it goes through the tip-top.

The initial choking of the unfurling line by the butt guide must be done with as little friction as practical. This is why it is fairly large in diameter, and why both the material and the design of the guide ring are important. The height of the guide ring, or the distance it stands off from the blank, is at least as important as its diameter—perhaps more so. If the ring sits too close to the blank it pulls the coils of line in toward the blank and increases the chance that the coils will slap against the blank between the reel and the guide. In extreme cases a low-sitting butt guide can also set up friction on the lip of the spool farthest from the blank. This is especially true as the level of the line on the spool is reduced as a cast is made. The most desirable butt guide, then, is one that has a high frame.

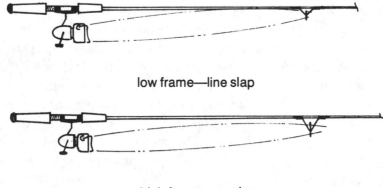

low frame—line slap

high frame—no slap

Height of butt guide is important. Top: Guide sits too low, causing line to slap against blank. Bottom: High guide eliminates line slap.

There are more variables that enter the picture here, some of which we should be aware of. The smaller is the diameter of the reel spool, the smaller are the coils of unfurling line. The greater the "stand-off" or the distance of the spool from the rod, the less the chance that the coils will slap against the blank, assuming the height of the butt guide is appropriate. Lighter pound-test line and softer (limper) line unfurls in smaller-diameter coils and is more easily choked with less friction by the butt guide. Heavier test and stiffer line forms larger coils and creates more friction at the butt guide.

It is no wonder, then, that proper spacing of the butt guide can be determined only by test casting. There are simply too many variables to provide for in a simple formula. This is also why the spacing must be done with the reel and line which will be used on the rod. However, before test casting, we have to put the guides *someplace* on the blank. These are what I keep referring to as "starting points"—tentative, educated guesses from which we will reposition the guides as necessary by further tests.

Starting points for the butt guide on spinning rods can be in the vicinity of one-third of the distance from the reel spool to the tip-top. In terms of inches from the center of the reel seat, you might try: 18 to 25 inches for short ultralights, 22 to 30 inches for medium spinning, and 28 to 36 inches for surf spinning. The distance of the first guide below the tip-top should not be more than 5½ inches. The guides in between can simply be placed by eye with the distance increased progressively toward the butt. Or you can use a mathematical calculation for an even progression. Examples of some formulas are given later. However, most rod builders who use both casting and static tests do not find it necessary.

With the guides at their starting points, the line strung through the guides, and the proper lure weight attached, start casting on flat, clear land. The first thing to check for is line slap against the blank between the reel and the butt guide. This can often be heard, or if the light is right so that it reflects off the line, it can be seen. Two probable places where the line might slap are about two-thirds of the distance between the reel and the butt guide, or right in front of the foot of the butt guide. Some rod builders place a length of cellophane tape on the blank at these two spots as an aid. If the line is slapping against the blank, it will leave marks on the tape. If you detect line slap, move the butt guide a short distance and repeat your casting. Try moving the butt guide in both directions from the starting point. Obviously, if the butt guide gets moved very far from its starting point, you must adjust the other guides accordingly.

Occasionally while testing, especially with longer rods and heavier line, you might hear a pinging sound coming from the reel spool. If so, it means that the butt guide is too close to the reel. The line is being choked too much and too soon, and the line is setting up friction as it is pulled over the lip of the spool. Move the butt guide farther from the reel and repeat your tests.

If, during your testing, you find that you cannot eliminate either line slap or pinging without moving the butt guide onto the tip section of the rod, you probably need a larger-diameter and/or higher frame guide. The same would be true if you cannot attain the casting distance normally expected from that specific rod. If you change to a larger butt guide, also adjust the sizes of the other guides, especially those closest to the butt guide.

Test casting and repositioning of the butt guide, and sometimes the other guides, continues until you find the point where maximum distance is achieved. It helps if your casting field has some reference points to help ascertain relative distance. A lined football field is ideal, but rocks, sticks, shrubs, etc. will work just about as well. After a little experience with this test-casting technique, you will be surprised at how quickly you will determine the correct distance for the butt guide.

Leave the guides in exactly the final position from test casting for the next step, the static test for proper stress distribution. The reel remains mounted and a few feet of line should extend beyond the tip. Either have someone hold the rod for you, or mount it at about a 45° angle with the guides on *top* of the blank (upside down from normal). Turn the reel so that the line pickup roller is away from the blank, and lock the reel with the anti-reverse lever.

Pull down on the line so that the rod is placed in a moderate bend. For a light rod, this would be about the maximum flex reached in a powerful cast. With heavier or stiffer rods, the rod should be flexed a bit more. Now check along the line to see if there are any flat spots. These are points at which the line is touching the rod. The line should run from guide to guide without touching the blank. If you find a flat spot, then the guides are too far apart and you will have to move one of the guides closer. Always move the guide nearest the butt end (but not the butt guide itself) toward the tip. When you shorten the distance from one guide to another in order to eliminate a flat spot, you are also lengthening the distance between the guide you moved and yet another guide—possibly creating another flat spot. For this reason it is best to work from the tip of the rod back toward the butt. You can see how handy Jim Cunningham's latex bands are when you move a number of guides.

Flat spot

Guides too far apart   Guides moved closer

To determine stress distribution, position rod with guides up in a workable arc.

When making this final adjustment in guide spacing *do not move the butt guide*. Also, you will probably find that you could move the first guide below the tip-top farther away from the tip-top than 5½ inches and still not have the line touch the blank. Don't do it! You need that support on the fragile tip section. It can be as close as 4 inches, but not farther away than 5½ inches. The only exception would be on quite heavy, stiff blanks with a large-diameter tip.

If, when conducting this test, you find that you cannot eliminate all the flat spots with the rod bent as suggested, you need to add another guide. Or, you may be able to eliminate the flat spots, but only with a wildly exaggerated pattern of spacing that obviously looks wrong to you. Here again, you should add another guide. Add the smallest-size guide possible at the tip end, and once more work back toward the butt in establishing the new spacing. Sometimes the addition of a guide makes it necessary to change the sizes on a few other guides. Try to confine such changes to the small guides.

Fly rods

There is no "cone of flight" of unfurling line on a fly rod. In fact, the line does not even come from the reel, but comes instead from the left hand (for a right-handed caster). At least it is initially fed from the left hand. It ultimately may be shot from loose line on the water, the boat deck, or stripping basket. It therefore must pass through the stripping (butt) guide at an angle. The farther away from the reel the stripping guide is placed, the less the angle at which the line passes through the guide, and the less is the friction. However, there are definite limits to how far up the rod the stripping guide can be placed. If it is too far, the line will slap against the blank, greatly reducing the casting distance. Again, a compromise is necessary. We want to keep friction on the stripping guide at a minimum (for distance and line wear), but we don't want to run the chance of the line slapping the blank on a powerful cast. A good starting point for locating the stripping guide is 28 to 35 inches from the base of the reel seat. This distance will vary with the length of the rod, with the shorter measurements applicable to shorter rods. It may also vary somewhat with the preference of the angler and his particular casting style. A fly fisherman who shoots line usually prefers the stripping guide a bit higher on the blank.

The first guide should be about 4 to 5 inches below the tip-top. The balance of the guides should be spaced proportionate to the taper for even stress distribution. On blanks that have basically a straight taper, this means the spacing can usually be of evenly increasing increments. Thus a mathematical formula for progressive guide spacing works out quite well. On the other hand, if the blank is

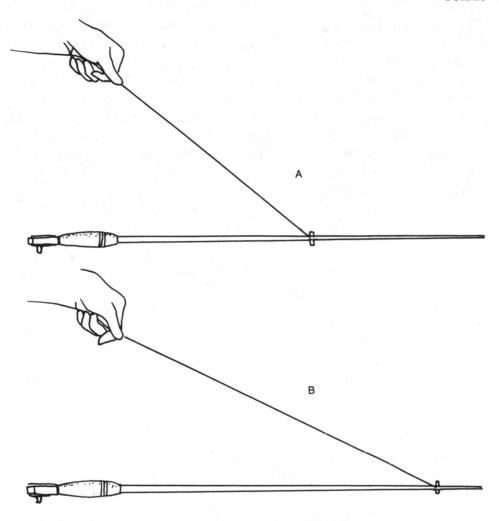

A: Stripping guide on fly rod placed too close to grip, resulting in sharp angle, excess friction, and unnecessary line wear. B: Stripping guide moved farther from grip reduces angle and accompanying problems.

a compound taper with an action that is mostly tip-oriented, then the guides should be spaced closer together near the tip. This type of rod will generally cast better if it has an additional guide over the norm, and if that guide is spaced among the first few below the tip-top.

After attaching the guides, do some test casting to check the position of the stripping guide. If the rod does not seem to cast as well as you think it should, try adding a guide near the tip section. Also, if you detect line slap or excessive line friction against the blank, it may help to add an additional guide.

While the rod is strung with line, run a simple stress-distribution test. This does not have to be as elaborate as for spinning rods. The technique of checking for flat spots will not work here, since the guides sit too close to the blank. Instead, support the rod up at about a 45° angle with the guides below the rod in their normal position. Lock the line to the reel with a rubber band, or have someone hold it while they hold the rod. Pull down on the line projecting beyond the tip and place the rod in a bend comparable to that produced in fighting a fish for which the rod is intended. Check to see that the line follows the pattern of the bend in the rod. There should be no excessive line angle. Where the rod bends the most, the line should be supported with the most guides. Move any guides necessary to achieve an even distribution of stress. In the final analysis, this should be used to determine the spacing between each guide.

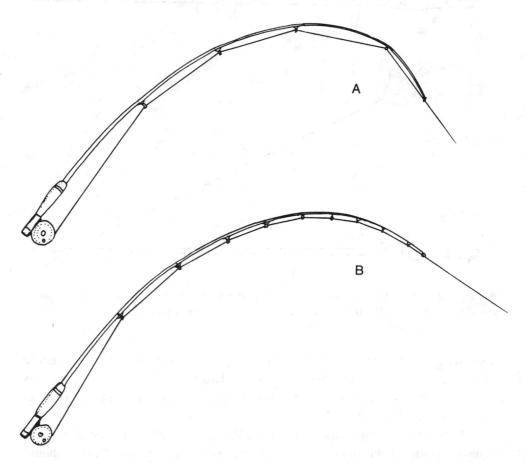

Fly-rod stress-distribution test. A: Too few guides and excess stress on rod blank. B: Proper number and spacing of guides distributes stress properly.

Casting and trolling rods

Some rod builders believe that placement of the butt guide on casting and trolling rods is not a particular problem, since the line comes from a single point source directly through the center of the butt guide. If we stop and look at a reel we find the line comes off of it in a side-to-side motion over the width of the spool. (The only reel that does release line from a single point is a closed-face spin-cast reel.) Since the line from a casting reel is unwinding from side to side, it intersects the butt guide at various angles. The wider the reel spool the greater the maximum angle, and the more friction against the sides of the butt-guide ring. Friction, of course, is what we have to minimize for maximum casting distance and minimum line wear. While the wider reel spool frequently has greater line capacity (often more than needed), it automatically creates more friction at the butt guide. Incidentally, this is one of the reasons why the Lew's Speed Spool reel with its narrow-spool design casts so well.

Proper placement of the butt guide is critical for the custom rod builder. If the guide is placed too close to the reel the angle of the line at the guide is great, and too much friction is generated. On the other hand, the angle of the line to the butt guide is reduced the farther away from the reel that the guide is placed. If this was the only problem we had to contend with, we could solve the problem by mounting the butt guide at a great distance from the reel. However, if we place the butt guide too far away, the line will slap against the blank. Also, when the rod is bent sharply from a heavy fish, the line will be pulled down across the blank, the foregrip, and possibly the hand. So, once again, it is necessary to compromise. The object is to position the guide as far from the reel as possible *without* having the line slap the blank or be pulled across it when the rod is sharply bent.

All of the above assumes that we use a certain-size butt guide. We can do much to help solve the problem by using a larger butt guide. The bigger diameter of the guide ring chokes the line less in its side-to-side travel. Or, to put it another way, it reduces the angle from the side of the reel spool to the side of the guide ring. This helps reduce friction on the cast. Another aspect of guide design can by employed in the solution to our problem. If we use a high frame guide which holds the ring higher off the blank, it helps prevent the line from touching the blank when the rod is bent sharply. The higher frame also helps eliminate line slap against the blank. This means a high frame guide can be placed farther from the reel, which, you will remember, reduces friction on the line. There is no doubt that a larger-size butt guide on a higher frame will increase casting distance, reduce line wear, and even provide more comfort and ease in fighting a large fish.

At this point you might ask why factory rods are not so equipped. Keep a number of points in mind. Tradition is hard to break, and factory rods must be

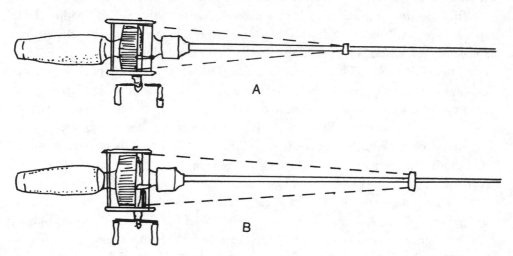

Size and placement of butt guide on casting rod are critical. A: Too small a guide placed too close results in sharp angle from sides of spool and excess friction. B: Larger guide farther from reel reduces friction.

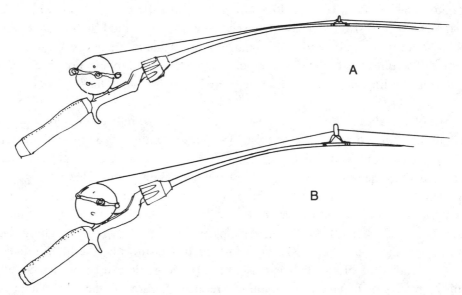

Advantage of higher and larger butt guide on casting rod. A: Too low and too small a guide allows line to rub against blank. B: Higher, larger guide holds line away from blank.

190

made to look sleek for sales purposes. The average fisherman is not knowledgeable enough about this problem, and he'll be more likely to pick the sleek-looking rod from the dealer's rack. The sales departments of rod companies realize this. Also, from a financial standpoint, the larger guide costs a bit more. When you are marketing many thousands of rods on a relatively small margin of profit, every factor of cost must be considered.

To determine guide spacing we need to attach the guides, mount the reel to be used with the rod, and run line through the guides. As always, we need to have some starting points at which to place the guides. For the butt guide try 16 to 24 inches from the reel on casting rods, and 20 to 28 inches on longer trolling or boat rods. The balance of the guides can be placed by eye, or by using a formula for an evenly increasing spacing progression. Use a high-frame butt guide about one size larger than normal. The wider the reel spool, the larger should be the butt guide. Fasten the end of the line to a fixed object on the floor.

Revolve the reel while keeping light tension on the line and observe the angle of the line as it intersects the butt guide. If, as the line travels back and forth, it seems to be choked quite a bit by the butt guide, move the guide farther up the rod. Now put your thumb on the reel to lock the line and lift the rod. Put a bend into the rod comparable to fighting the largest fish that will probably be encountered with that particular rod. With the rod so bent, check to see if the line touches the blank or the foregrip. If it does, you will have to move the guide closer to the reel and try again. If the line does not touch, try moving the guide a bit farther away from the reel and repeat the test. You want to place the guide as far from the reel as practical without having it touch the blank or the foregrip when the rod is bent sharply.

When you conduct this test, the previously discussed advantages of a larger-diameter butt guide that sits higher off the blank will become obvious. You may want to switch to such a guide to achieve the desired results. Keep in mind that there are practical limits to the size of the butt guide because of increased weight. Too heavy a butt guide can damage or destroy the casting action of the rod. On comparatively light boat and trolling rods that will be used in the pursuit of large saltwater game fish, you will find that a Fuji Model CHG or BCHG high-frame folding guide may be an ideal solution. This type of rod will be severely bent under a large fish. The high-frame guide will keep the line from rubbing across the foregrip, introducing friction that could cause the light line to break. It will also protect the angler from a severe line burn on the hand grasping the foregrip.

When you have the correct position for the butt guide determined on the casting rod, make some test casts. You want to look for any possible line slap which would indicate you moved the butt guide too far from the reel. Chances are good that you will not find any. If you do, move the butt guide closer a bit at a time until the slap is eliminated.

All that remains is to perform a static test for even stress distribution. This is exactly the same as that described for spinning rods. The object is to remove any flat spots without changing the position of the butt guide. In the process you will find out if it is necessary to add an additional guide, and also determine your final guide spacing.

Roller guides. Offshore trolling rods are designed and built to do battle with fast, powerful fish utilizing a given class of pound-test line. The all-important factor is *line wear*, and that is the reason roller guides are used. The placement of the butt guide is again critical, but this time entirely for the purpose of keeping line wear to the minimum. If the butt guide is placed too close to the reel, the line traveling from side to side of the spool will rub against the edge of the guide housing. This obviously defeats the whole purpose of the roller guides and a line can be quickly worn and broken.

Therefore, the same two factors apply in placing the butt roller guide as apply with a casting rod or light trolling rod: The guide must be far enough away from the reel to eliminate any danger of the line touching the housing, but close enough (and high enough) to prevent the line from touching the foregrip or blank when the rod is bent to its maximum.

To determine proper placement, tape the guides in estimated positions and, using the reel that will be used with the rod, run the proper test line through the guides. As in the test for casting rods, revolve the spool with the line under tension so that line comes off both sides of the spool. Move the butt guide as close as possible to the reel to the point where there is no danger that the line could come in contact with the guide housing. Allow a bit of a safety margin here. Test to see if the guide is high enough by bending the rod to the maximum with the end of the line anchored.

To place the remaining guides, keep the line anchored to the floor and the rod bent to maximum. Do not move the butt guide. Adjust the guides so that the line does not touch the blank at any point. If this cannot be achieved, you need to add an additional guide near the tip. It should be of the smallest size, and the spacing of all guides except the butt guide should be adjusted.

FORMULAS FOR APPROXIMATE SPACING

As explained in the previous section on guide spacing for each type of rod, it is helpful to many rod builders to have a spacing formula to use for *starting points*. This is for the initial placement of guides *before* the applicable casting and stress-distribution tests are performed. It cannot be emphasized too strongly that the tests don't determine the final placement of guides. In some cases where a level-taper blank is used, the formulas will be quite close. In others, considerable adjustments will be required as a result of the tests. Some rod builders place the guides at the starting points solely by eye and by experience. If you keep a record of the *final placement* of guides on each rod you build, you will accumulate a data bank that will aid you in determining starting points for similar rods.

The small, compact calculator is becoming more available in households across the country. For those who prefer using a formula, it can be computed very quickly once you are familiar with the formula. Two formulas are listed below. Both require knowing the number of guides to be used. The first also requires a starting point for the butt guide only. The second requires starting points for both the butt guide and the first guide below the tip-top.

This first formula is the work of RodCrafter Victor M. Cutter of Greensboro, North Carolina. He first places the butt guide at the previously determined starting point. Then he measures the distance from the butt guide to the tip-top, and plugs that measurement into his formula. The example given is for a 7-foot spinning rod using a total of six guides with the butt guide spaced 32 inches from the butt of the rod.

$$
\begin{array}{ll}
X & \text{1st guide} \\
X+1 & \text{2nd guide} \\
X+2 & \text{3rd guide} \\
X+3 & \text{4th guide} \\
X+4 & \text{5th guide} \\
\underline{X+5} & \text{6th guide} \\
6X+15 = 52 & \text{(distance from tip to butt guide)}
\end{array}
$$

$$
\begin{array}{ll}
6X & = 37 \\
X & = 6^1/_6
\end{array}
$$

To determine the *increasing space between* each guide, return to the formula. You now know that $X = 6^1/_6$ inches. Thus, the distance from the tip to the first guide is X, or $6^1/_6$ inches. The distance between the first and second guide is X plus 1, or $6^1/_6$ plus $1 = 7^1/_6$ inches. The space between the second and third guide will be X plus 2, or $6^1/_6$ plus $2 = 8^1/_6$ inches. Continuing with the formula, you will find successive spacings to be: $9^1/_6$, $10^1/_6$, and $11^1/_6$ inches. We can chart the results on the following page.

Guide	Formula	Space between guides (inches)	Space from tip (inches)
1	X	$6^1/_6$	$6^1/_6$
2	X + 1	$7^1/_6$	$13^2/_6$
3	X + 2	$8^1/_6$	$21^3/_6$
4	X + 3	$9^1/_6$	$30^4/_6$
5	X + 4	$10^1/_6$	$40^5/_6$
6	X + 5	$11^1/_6$	52

The second formula was worked out by RodCrafter Jeffrey D. Baehre of Depew, New York. As noted above, the formula is predicated on knowing the starting points for the distance from the tip of both the first guide and the butt guide. The example is based on a 7-foot spinning rod using six guides, and the starting point for the first guide is 4 inches from the tip, while the starting point for the butt guide is 32 inches from the butt. Subtracting the 32 inches from the 84-inch (7-foot) length of the rod, we find the butt guide is 52 inches from the tip.

We now can assign these values to letters, which we will use in our formula:

B = 52 (distance from tip to *butt* guide)
N = 6 (*number* of guides to be used on the rod)
T = 4 (distance from *tip* to first guide)

The formula which will be used to determine the *distance* (let's call that d) from which we will construct our geometric progression is:

$$B = NT + \frac{N(N-1)d}{2}$$

For those of you who have been away from algebra for some time, that simply means: B equals N times T plus the product of N times N−1 times d, all divided by 2.

Assigning the numerical values listed above (which we previously set) for the letters in the formula, it now looks like this:

$$B = NT + \frac{N(N-1)d}{2}$$
$$52 = 6 \times 4 + \frac{6(6-1)d}{2}$$
$$52 = 24 + \frac{6 \times 5 \times d}{2}$$
$$52 = 24 + \frac{30d}{2}$$

$$52 - 24 = \frac{30d}{2}$$

$$28 = 15d$$

$$\frac{28}{15} = d$$

$$1.866 = d$$

Since d comes out to be an odd number and difficult to work with, we can change it slightly, since our initial values used are not absolutes. We found d equal to 1.866 and 1⅞ is 1.875. That's close enough, so we "round off" 1.866 to 1.875.

We now set up our basic formula to determine the distance or spacing from the tip to each respective guide. The letter S is used to represent the *spacing*, and the formula becomes:

$$S = NT + \frac{N(N-1)d}{2}$$

In applying the formula each of the letters have the following values:

N = the number of each respective guide. Thus, for the first guide, N = 1, for the second guide, N = 2, for the third guide, N = 3, etc.

T = 4 (number of inches to first guide, as above)

d = 1.875 (rounded from 1.866, as above)

The computation for the spacing of each guide looks like this:

$$\text{1st guide: } S = 1(4) + \frac{1(1-1)(1⅞)}{2}$$

$$S = 4''$$

$$\text{2nd guide: } S = 2(4) + \frac{2(2-1)(1⅞)}{2}$$

$$S = 9⅞''$$

$$\text{3rd guide: } S = 3(4) + \frac{3(3-1)(1⅞)}{2}$$

$$S = 17⅝''$$

$$\text{4th guide: } S = 4(4) + \frac{4(4-1)(1⅞)}{2}$$

$$S = 27¼''$$

$$\text{5th guide: } S = 5(4) + \frac{5(5-1)(1⅞)}{2}$$

$$S = 38¾''$$

$$\text{6th guide: } S = 6(4) + \frac{6(6-1)(1\frac{7}{8})}{2}$$

$$S = 52\frac{1}{8}''$$

TYPES OF GUIDES

Having discussed proper spacing and placement of guides, let's turn our attention now to the guides themselves. There are a number of principal manufacturers, and each produces quite a variety of different types of guides. There have been claims and counterclaims of why each is better than the others, but few specifics about the guides themselves and how they relate to performance on a given type of rod. We have already discussed some of the factors that affect performance when we covered guide spacing. Other performance factors were explored in connection with modifying the action of a blank in the chapter on the blank. Our job now is to examine the specifications so we can select the right guides for any rod we might build.

Today, aluminum-oxide ceramic guides have become by far the most popular for high-quality rods. Only a few years ago controversy raged hot and heavy over the advantages and disadvantages. With the introduction of American-made ceramics, the fires died in many quarters, but not all. There are still beds of smoldering embers on this issue. It must be remembered that to a great extent custom rod builders must construct their rods from the same components available to, and primarily made for, the rod companies. It may therefore help to understand what has taken place in the general marketplace for guides.

Let's go back in time to agate as a material for guides. This semiprecious kind of chalcedony is extremely hard, can be polished to a smooth surface, and will not be grooved by fishing line. As such, it seemed to be ideal for guide rings and was encased in metal frames. It was excellent in all respects except one: It was too brittle and fragile. If the guide received a good rap, the agate ring fractured and became useless. Guide makers turned to metal and finally rings of stainless steel.

Tungsten carbide was the next material tried. It greatly resisted grooving by monofilament lines. However, its very name, *tung sten* meaning "heavy stone," is a clue to its biggest drawback. The heavy weight slowed the action of the blank. This prohibited its use on ultralight rods. Over a period of time the compressed tungsten-carbide surface also tended to erode, causing it to become microscopically rough and abrasive to lines. The composition ring had to be soldered to the metal frame, and in time the joint often became brittle and broke, especially when the rod was used in saltwater.

Very hard, so-called industrial, chrome plating was found to resist grooving almost as well as tungsten carbide. Guide rings so made had the decided advantage of being much lighter in weight. The radius of the ring itself (when viewed as a cross-sectional cut of the ring) could be made smaller than for tungsten-carbide rings. This presented less surface to the line, thereby reducing line friction as it passed through the guides. Industrial chrome plating was more expensive and not necessarily recognized by rod buyers. This led some companies to use less expensive and less hard types of plating, which naturally did not wear as well.

The most recent step in the evolution of guides was the application of a ceramic material of aluminum oxide. The material itself was developed for missile nose cones and does an excellent job of dissipating heat, the major cause of line wear from friction. Additionally, it is extremely hard and cannot be grooved by monofilament line. It can be diamond-polished to an incredibly slick surface, and is quite light in weight. As is true of agate, it tends to be fragile. This problem was solved by encasing the ring in an outer plastic shock-absorbing ring.

Guides of aluminum-oxide ceramic were first introduced by the Japanese firm, Fuji, and imported by Lew Childre & Sons, Inc. Initially used on bass casting rods, their use soon spread like wildfire. Their appearance was distinctive and easily recognized, and quality-conscious fishermen wanted rods equipped with the new guides. Rod manufacturers were soon climbing over each other to get them. At this point, American guide makers were caught flatfooted. Many wrongly assumed the new guides were a fad and would soon fade from the scene. Instead of developing guides of the new material, they contented themselves with pointing out the faults, real and imagined, of the Fuji guides. These were the fires of controversy I spoke of earlier.

A number of things happened that brought the American guide makers into the aluminum-oxide arena. First, the Fuji guides were not a fad. Fishermen that used them loved them. Second, for whatever reason, the rod companies frequently received late delivery on the guides, causing very expensive production delays, production changes, and broken promises to jobbers and dealers. Anger and hostility developed among quite a few rod companies against the Fuji guides and their importer. They wanted an aluminum-oxide guide on which delivery would be certain. In other words, we had a classic case where demand exceeded supply. As any beginning student of economics knows, this brings forth competition. So the earlier hesitant American guide makers now quickly tooled up for ceramic guides.

The Fuji guide frames were made by a premium-quality stamping process. They were lighter in weight than wire-frame guides, yet possessed more than adequate strength. Historically, stamped-frame guides made in America were of inferior quality, cheaply made for cheap rods. Thus, to American guide makers the bad connotations of "stamped frame" meant something inferior. They already had the technology and tooling for making wire frames, so their new aluminum-oxide guides were made with heavier wire frames silver-soldered or welded together.

In making the new ceramic guides, the American manufacturers also fell back upon their old designs and, in most cases, to the exact same frames for which they had existing tooling. Thus, shape and especially the height of the guide ring from the blank were comparable to their former models. Please understand that some of these statements have to be only speculation on my part. Whether the new ceramics were made lower because of existing tooling or to keep down the weight of a wire-frame guide doesn't really matter. What is important is that we recognize that, for the most part, American ceramics are heavier and, in the larger sizes, sit lower. The rod manufacturers, the primary market, needed ceramics on which delivery could be assured—so they gladly bought the American models. At the present moment, the American guide makers have more business than they can handle, so they do not have the time or the need for further research or expensive retooling.

The tests explained for spacing guides point out the obvious advantages for higher-frame butt guides on spinning, casting, trolling, and boat rods. I do not mean to imply that every rod you or I might build will always need the highest-frame guide made in that size. There are other factors already discussed that affect the selection of guides for a specific rod. However, as a generalization where other factors are equal, it is safe to say that the higher frame is going to be the better choice.

Many custom surf-rod builders have come to the conclusion that the height of the guide ring above the blank is really more important than the inside diameter. Using Fuji high-frame folding guides and spending extra time to fine-tune the placement, they can achieve as much casting distance as with the traditional very large-diameter wire guides. This is an extreme example, but it makes the point. The high-frame, smaller-diameter guide is not original with Fuji. Some years ago before ceramics were available, Heddon did extensive tests with high-mounted smaller rings and found no significant difference in casting distance. They tried marketing rods so equipped, but fishermen could not be convinced to try them, since they looked too unconventional. Mildrum at one time also made some tests along similar lines. According to Ted Bensen, owner, they worked fine in experiments conducted by himself and his son. But again they were unable to gain the confidence of the fishing public because the anglers *expected* a spinning rod to have a large-diameter butt guide. These two experiences may be why American guide makers chose to fall back on lower-frame butt guides.

As we have discussed, the weight of the guides should be appropriate for the blank on which the rod is being built. Heavier or lighter guides can be used creatively to attain certain preferences in action. Or if needed, weight or lightness can be used along with other techniques to modify a blank's action when that action is not otherwise obtainable. It is fairly safe to generalize, however, that as we work with today's lighter, more moderate-action fiberglass and graphite blanks, the lighter-weight guides are preferable.

Earlier I mentioned some of the arguments and controversy surrounding aluminum-oxide ceramic guides. To be complete in our evaluation of guides and to enable you to investigate on your own, the primary arguments should be briefly presented.

Some people maintain that while the ceramic guide will not be grooved by monofilament line, it does cause more line wear. From actual fishing use I cannot prove either side of the argument. I do know that millions of ceramic guides have been in use for some years. Certainly if line was wearing noticeably faster, it seems to me fishermen would be objecting. Even if we assume ceramics do wear lines a bit more—and the difference would have to be very slight—I personally do not see a problem. Fishermen need to change their monofilament line periodically in any event because of wear on the terminal end, twisting of the line from use, and exposure to sunlight. It would seem to me that since line has to be changed at some point anyway, it is much cheaper to change line than to replace grooved guides. This is especially true on custom-made rods.

The only tests to my knowledge of the effect of guides on line wear were conducted by AFTCO, makers of excellent-quality roller guides. As Bill Shedd, president of AFTCO, has said, "Line wear is really our business." He is referring to the use of roller guides vs. any other guides for offshore trolling rods, and he couldn't be more on target for this specialized type of fishing. Their tests are made on a machine which moves line back and forth over two actual offshore rods equipped with different guides. A heavy weight is suspended from the end of each line, placing the heavy rod in a moderate bend. As anyone would expect, the roller guides are the undisputed leader because a rolling surface is much better than any stationary surface. Their tests also show that the ceramics wear line faster than industrial chrome-plated wire in *this kind of simulated offshore situation*. I, however, am not convinced that their tests actually simulate the same fishing conditions existing in typical spinning and casting situations. It seems to me that if they did, we would have heard many loud objections from millions of fishermen by now.

Another argument against ceramic guides is that the cross-sectional radius of a ceramic ring is larger than the radius on a light-wire guide ring. The ceramic ring is made by fusing together two halves. The inner surface of the ring is then diamond-polished. This leaves a larger radius, or a larger area that will contact the line as it passes through the guide rings. I have no sophisticated measuring equipment to check this out. Although the inner ceramic ring is thicker, I do know it is not ground or polished flat. You can check that as easily as I did. Place a thin metal straightedge through the guide ring and hold it up to a light. It can be seen that the ring surface is curved and the straightedge touches the ceramic at only one tiny point—the same as the line would do.

If, as the argument goes, the radius of the ceramic ring is larger, then more friction will be developed. Friction slows down the line and reduces distance. Without elaborate equipment I cannot measure the difference in the size of the actual contact—that tiny point where the line touches. However, it seems to me and to hundreds of other fishermen I've talked to that casting distance is certainly not reduced with ceramic guides. If anything, it seems just the opposite is true. Perhaps the slick, diamond-polished ceramic material is more friction-free.

Still another criticism against ceramic guides is that since the rings are press-fit they will pop out easily. My experience from my rod-building-supply business is that the inner ceramic rings on quality guides pop out no more frequently than do defectively soldered wire rings. One manufacturer long noted for concern for quality, Mildrum, has designed a ceramic guide (Linesavers) so built that it is impossible for the shock ring or the ceramic ring to pop out. This is achieved by a unique design of interlocking shaped rings. Even the outer metal ring is a band of metal that is cupped around the shock ring.

So much for the arguments. It is obvious I am prejudiced, and I acknowledge that I could be wrong. I do not believe that aluminum-oxide guides are always better than the various wire guides, but I cannot find fault with them that would prove they are not at least as good as wire guides.

Before presenting the comparative statistics of various guides, I would like to discuss the application of different guides to certain types of rods. Starting with fly rods, we find fly fishermen in many respects the most tradition-bound of all anglers. Perhaps this is due to their love of the classics and the rich lore and history of fly fishing. The traditional fly guide has been the very light snake guide, a simple piece of wire shaped to form a U relative to the blank. Since the guides hang beneath the rod, the guides tend to hold the comparatively large-diameter fly line close to the blank. Actually, this causes undue friction of the large line against the blank. It reduces shooting distance and increases line wear.

Quite a few custom rod builders found that very light wire Foulproof guides enabled them to shoot line easier and farther. The O-shape of the guide and the fact that it held the fly line away from the blank were the obvious explanations. Still, many of their customers refused to try Foulproof guides because "they didn't look right." A couple of years ago the rod designer for one of the most respected rod companies confided to me that his company believed the Foulproof guides performed better on its fly rods, but could not risk trying to market a line of rods that were so "unconventional."

When Fuji introduced their single-footed ceramic fly guides, the public was more willing to defy tradition because of all the good things they had heard about aluminum oxide. Fuji fared better, and we have had some customers remove their old snake guides from expensive split-cane rods and replace them with the new Fuji fly guides. There is still a large group of fly-fishing traditionalists who insist on snake guides. However, when you analyze it, the Fuji single-footed fly guide has much to recommend it. Like the Foulproof, the perfect-circle ring holds the line away from the blank. It has the added advantage of not being as fragile as the thin-diameter-wire Foulproof and is just about as light in weight. Its biggest advantage is that it has but a single foot. This permits maximum free flexing of the blank and eliminates the extra weight of wrapping finish from the absent second foot. This weight saving can be significant, since on a typical rod using two-footed guides, the finish will weigh up to 115 grains for a heavy finish (Envirotex) and 31 grains for a light finish (Crystal Coat).

On light trolling rods and boat rods we already mentioned the possible advantage of using a Model CHG or BCHG Fuji high-frame folding guide. However, the regular heavy-duty boat-rod guides, Model DHG by Fuji, leave a bit to be desired. They sit too low on the blank. This makes it far too easy for the line to rub against the blank when the rod is bent fighting a fish. They are also quite heavy. This weight is not a great problem on a heavy, stiff rod, but can be excessive on a light rod. When Perfection brought out its heavy-duty boat guide it was lighter but, for my money, it still sits too low. The strong new Fuji Model NHG or BNHG may be a better choice on lighter rods. Another possibility is the Varmac Model AGB ceramic braced guide. These can be combined with the high-frame folding butt guide in chrome finish.

For rods using wire line, especially braided wire line, ceramic guides are not recommended. The best guide by far for this type of fishing is the roller guide with special case-hardened roller. RodCrafter Joy Dunlap showed me an unusual set of locally made roller guides used by commercial fishermen with braided wire guides. The rollers are made of nylon and the guide is rather primitive in appearance. The notch in the roller is a sharper V-shape than usual. The reason they work so well is that the uneven surface of the braided wire line actually grabs hold of the nylon roller as it passes over it. This causes the roller to turn and eliminates both roller and guide wear.

As an aid in helping you evaluate different guides for different purposes, I have prepared tables showing a number of important specifications on each. The figures used in the tables were not provided by the manufacturers. Instead I personally weighed and measured each guide myself. The guides were selected at random, so they may vary from the norms. The weight shown is in grains and was obtained by using an Ohaus Triple Beam Loading Scale, Model 314. The other measurements are in millimeters. I was careful to be as accurate as possible, but when making over 400 separate measurements there are bound to be some errors, for which I accept full responsibility.

The only measurement that may need further clarification is the length of the guide feet. This is the length from the leading edge of one guide foot to the leading edge of the other guide foot and includes the space beneath the guide ring. On all guides except Foulproof, this space is quite similar and in proportion to the guide. The measurement itself is given as one indication of the resistance to flexing the guide feet impart to the blank. As noted earlier, the guide feet can be ground shorter if desired. On Foulproof guides the space between guide feet is longer. For example, on the SP-7/8 the total length is 80mm, but each guide foot is only 20mm long. On their MSP-5/8 the total length is 58mm while each foot measures only 14mm. In addition, the Foulproof guide is designed of one continuous piece of monel wire with the guide ring resembling a coil. This permits the guide to flex more freely than other types of guides, reducing the resistance imparted to the blank.

The tables, as I have explained, cannot be considered absolute, ironclad facts. Instead, they are meant to be used as relative figures for the basis of comparison. When used in this manner they can serve you well. I have also excerpted from the tables and listed comparisons of the height of spinning-rod butt guides and weight comparisons of typical spinning-rod guide sets and fly-rod guide sets. The analytical rod builder will realize that the distribution of weight in a given guide set can be an important factor. When comparing two guide sets of approximately the same weight, the one with a greater percentage of the weight at the butt end will have less effect upon rod action than will the one with a comparatively high percentage of weight at the tip end.

Finally, to complete the picture on guides, let me add some personal comments and observations about some of the specific guides. These comments could not be included in the tables, and it is hoped they will add useful data for the selection of guides by the custom rod builder.

Fuji BSPHG. Originally called BMKHG, these lightweight single-footed ceramic guides have the frames made of tempered spring steel. They therefore will absorb bumps and knocks without deforming or breaking. The height of the guide ring can be increased, which is especially helpful on the larger sizes. This is done by careful bending to increase the angle of the two side supports where they join together to form the foot. The angle at which the guide ring sits can then be similarly adjusted by bending. The butt guide can also be reversed from its normal position so that the foot faces toward the tip. The unfurling spinning line can then not slap against the guide frame, since it encounters only the guide ring. This flexibility makes them exceptional choices for ultralight spinning rods. They can also be used on the light tip section of any rod (particularly graphite) in combination with BNHG or BSHG guides on the butt end. On fly rods they are rapidly taking over as one of the obvious signs of a custom-made rod. I use BSHG guides for stripping guides on fly rods. Depending upon the length of the rod I will use from one to three BSHG models in sizes from 8 to 12.

Fuji BSHG. Do not make the mistaken assumption that these are merely black versions of the originally introduced SHG model. The metal braces forming the guide frame have been reduced in thickness to shave weight. I have noted that these thinner frames will dent or bend from a sharp rap or pressure, particularly on the larger guides. When they do, they cannot be straightened, and either look bad or must be replaced. Where lightness is a factor, the BSPHG is far superior and preferred in my opinion.

Fuji NHG and BNHG. Thicker metal is used throughout the frame than on the old SHG, but there is less total bracing. The weight remains about the same as on the SHG, but the strength is achieved from curvature of the braces. This well-engineered design makes use of the strength of the arch. The single foot coming directly down from the metal guide ring is also arched for added strength and presents the opportunity to further eliminate line slap against the guide frame. To accomplish this, mount the guide with the short, center-derived foot facing toward the butt. This presents the minimum of frame to the unfurling line coming from the reel. A very strong guide for its weight, Fuji needs to make Size 30 in this model. A Size 40 would be helpful in some saltwater rods and be better than the BSHG-40 for this purpose.

Fuji MHT and BMHT tip-tops. These are extremely lightweight ceramic tip-tops—only half the weight of the PHT and BPHT and lighter than any other aluminum-oxide tip-tops. While designed for fly rods, they can be used quite advantageously on any rod where a light tip is indicated. They work exceptionally well on ultralight spinning rods (and graphite) equipped with BSPHG guides. Varmac is coming out with a comparable unbraced ceramic guide.

Fuji BCHG. The folding aspect of these extra-high-frame guides protects them from damage when the rod is in transport or storage (when most guide damage occurs). Their extra weight is normally not a problem, since they are used at the butt end of the rod. However, they are too heavy for use on very light rods. If the rod builder is willing to spend the time fine-tuning the placement, they can be used to advantage on surf rods. Here, the butt guide will be farther than normal from the reel. In fact, on a two-piece 11-foot surf blank, the butt guide will often be all the way to the ferrule. Fuji would do well to also add larger ring sizes to the model. When used on surf rods, use BCHG-25, 20, and 16. Then use a BNHG-16 followed by a BNHG-12 and as many 10s (and possibly 8s) as needed.

Fuji guides in general. There is a serious problem on delivery of all Fuji guides. From sad experience I know that even the biggest dealers often have to wait eight to twelve months for delivery of a particular size or sizes. This is very bad business for the dealer, since he listed the guides in good faith in his catalog. When he cannot deliver he loses the good will and future business of his customers. Additionally, he has the expense of carrying the other sizes in his inventory—but he cannot sell them because of the missing size. Despite excellent quality and an outstanding choice of models, Fuji will lose business, and rod builders will lose access to great guides, as dealers are forced to recommend other guides on which they know they can count for delivery. You will recall that this is what happened with many rod manufacturers. My immediate advice is to not be too harsh in your judgment of your dealer. Remember, he's human too, so list an alternate choice when ordering.

Varmac Ceramics AG and AGB. Varmac and Perfection originally imported the same aluminum-oxide guide rings from Japan that Fuji uses. Both companies are now using American-made rings. The Varmac AG guides are the lightest American-made ceramics, and the butt guides also sit quite a bit higher than the Perfection guides. The extra-strong, braced Model AGB weighs only slightly more than Perfection's unbraced guide. This weight can be reduced in a total set, and especially where it is critical at the tip end, by using regular AG models on the tip.

Perfection Ceramics ACS. These are strong guides with hydraulically coined feet and welded joints. Their biggest disadvantage is the low height of the guide ring and their heavier weight. They are also sold under the names Duro-Slick and Perfect-O.

Mildrum Linesavers Ceramics. A most innovative design makes it impossible for either the ceramic ring or the shock ring to come loose from the outer metal band. The ceramic material used has a slightly higher content of aluminum oxide (I understand it is in the vicinity of 97% vs. 92%). The manufacturer also claims the combination of higher aluminum-oxide content and finer polishing produces the smoothest, slickest ring surface. Height of the butt guide is quite good, as is the I.D. of the ring. The feet are longer than on other guides; if they are used without grinding them shorter, they will restrict the blank from flexing freely. The only disadvantage is weight; they are the heaviest of the ceramic guides. Otherwise, they are exceptionally well engineered and well made.

Foulproof. These are the lightest of all guides and are available in a very large variety of sizes and wire diameters. Foulproof guides flex more with the blank than any other comparable two-footed guide. Until recently there were problems with the plating being too soft, resulting in easily grooved guides. A new plating is now being used, but it will require the test of time. The ends of the feet are the best shaped of any guide and rarely need any dressing. The design permits reversing the butt guide so that the long brace is toward the tip. This helps eliminate line slap against the frame by presenting the shorter brace toward the unfurling line. The biggest disadvantage is the low height of the guide ring. It is the lowest height of all guides tested.

WEIGHT COMPARISON
SPINNING-ROD SETS

Sets generally applicable for 6½–7-fot rods. Five guides: 25, 20, 16, 12, and 8 or closest to those sizes made. Listed from lightest to heaviest.

Name	Material	Weight (grains)
Foulproof GT-11	monel wire	120.0
Varmac SG	stainless steel	130.3
Fuji BSPHG	aluminum oxide	159.3
Varmac SGB	stainless steel	147.3
Perfection WCSL	stainless steel	172.9
Fuji BSHG	aluminum oxide	222.6
Varmac AG	aluminum oxide	245.0
Fuji BNHG	aluminum oxide	245.6
Perfection ACS	aluminum oxide	270.9
Varmac AGB	aluminum oxide	270.0
Mildrum MAC	aluminum oxide	322.9

WEIGHT COMPARISON
TIP-TOPS

Where applicable, tip-tops used were Size 6. Smaller sizes would be proportionately lighter.

Name	Material	Weight (grains)
Fuji MHT & BMHT	aluminum oxide	7.0
Perfection Fly PCF	stainless steel	8.0
Foulproof CTT	monel wire	9.2
Fuji PHT & BPHT	aluminum oxide	13.9
Mildrum MAT	aluminum oxide	18.9
Perfection ACS	aluminum oxide	21.4
Varmac AT	aluminum oxide	21.5
Mildrum MATS	aluminum oxide	22.1

HEIGHT COMPARISON
SPINNING-ROD BUTT GUIDES

Sizes are all 25 or as close thereto as possible. Height is to bottom of inside of guide ring. Listed from highest to lowest.

Name	Designated size	Height (mm)
Fuji BSPHG	25	19.0
Fuji BSHG	25	17.5
Fuji BNHG & NHG	25	17.5
Mildrum Linesavers	24	17.3
Varmac AG & AGB	25	16.0
Perfection ACS	25	12.3
Varmac SG & SGB (wire)	24	10.0
Perfection WCSL (wire)	24	9.5
Foulproof (wire)	7/8	9.0

WEIGHT COMPARISON
FLY-ROD GUIDE SETS

Sets consist of applicable number of guides for 8-foot fly rod. Stripping guides (butt) vary as noted. Listed from lightest to heaviest.

Name	Stripper	Weight—guides only (grains)	Tip weight (grains) & model	Total weight (grains)
Fuji BSPHG	BSPHG	42.5	7 (MHT)	49.5
Foulproof	Foulproof	40.5	9 (LTT)	49.5
Snake	light wire	46.7	8 (Pear)	54.8
Fuji BSPHG	two BSHG	52.9	7 (MHT)	59.9
Snake	Carboloy	81.9	8 (Pear)	89.9

FUJI NHG & BNHG

Size	Weight (grains)	I.D. (mm)	Height (mm)	Feet (mm)
25	110.7	16.8	17.5	53
20	58.3	12.1	14.5	42
16	39.6	9.4	11.0	36
12	24.8	7.5	8.5	29
10	18.2	6.7	7.3	28
8	12.1	5.1	7.0	23
Tip (PHT & BPHT)	13.9			
Tip (MHT & BMHT)	7.0			

FUJI BSHG

Size	Weight (grains)	I.D. (mm)	Height (mm)	Feet (mm)
40	248.8	27.0	25.0	94
30	143.7	21.4	20.5	75
25	101.6	16.8	17.5	61
20	59.0	12.1	14.5	54
16	37.2	9.4	11.0	46
12	21.1	7.5	8.3	39
10	15.7	6.7	7.3	34
8	9.6	5.1	6.0	29
Tip (PHT & BPHT)	13.9			
Tip (MHT & BMHT)	7.0			

FUJI BSPHG

Size	Weight (grains)	I.D. (mm)	Height (mm)*	Feet (mm)
30	96.6	21.4	20.5	23
25	72.5	16.8	19.0	23
20	42.9	12.1	15.0	21
16	23.1	9.4	11.0	17
12	14.4	7.5	8.5	15
10	8.9	6.7	8.0	14
8	6.0	5.1	5.0	11
7	4.5	4.4	4.0	10
6	3.1	3.7	3.5	9
Tip (PHT & BPHT)				
Tip (MHT & BMHT)				

*Height is as received. Can be bent higher.

FUJI FOLDING-FRAME CHG & BCHG

Size	Weight (grains)	I.D. (mm)	Height (mm)	Feet (mm)
25	204.8	16.8	38	54
20	167.7	12.1	30	53
16	84.0	9.4	21.5	45

VARMAC ALUMAC AG

Size	Weight (grains)	I.D. (mm)	Height (mm)	Feet (mm)
30	126.8	21.5	16.7	61
25	96.6	15.0	16.0	51
20	68.2	11.0	13.0	47
16	41.6	9.0	9.5	40
12	26.6	6.3	8.0	35
10	20.8	5.2	7.0	32
8	12.0	4.2	6.0	25
Tip (AT)	21.5			

VARMAC ALUMAC BRACED AGB

Size	Weight (grains)	I.D. (mm)	Height (mm)	Feet (mm)
30	134.9	21.5	16.7	61
25	103.3	15.0	16.5	50
20	75.8	11.0	13.0	47
16	46.3	9.0	10.5	39
12	29.5	6.3	8.0	34
10	23.7	5.2	7.7	33
8	14.3	4.2	7.0	29
Tip (AT)	21.5			

PERFECTION ACS

Size	Weight (grains)	I.D. (mm)	Height (mm)	Feet (mm)
30	130.8	21.5	14.0	65
25	103.5	15.0	12.3	56
20	68.0	11.4	11.7	53
16	48.4	9.0	9.5	48
12	34.3	6.3	9	43
10	25.8	5.2	8	38
8	16.3	4.2	6	32
Tip (ACRS)	21.4			

MILDRUM LINESAVERS MAC

Size	Weight (grains)	I.D. (mm)	Height (mm)	Feet (mm)
24	165.5	19.5	17.3	86
17	72.3	11.3	12.5	73
12	39.3	7.5	9.0	54
10	28.1	6.3	8.3	43
8	18.1	4.5	6.5	37
Tip (MATS)	22.1			
Tip (MAT)	18.9			

VARMAC WIRE SG

Size	Weight (grains)	I.D. (mm)	Height (mm)	Feet (mm)
28	53.6	22.7	10.7	50
24	45.4	19.0	10.0	47
20	33.6	15.6	8.2	44
17	27.6	13.5	8.2	40
13	17.9	10.0	6.7	35
11	15.0	8.0	6.0	32
9	9.1	7.2	5.3	26
7	6.8	4.9	3.2	22

VARMAC BRACED WIRE SGB

Size	Weight (grains)	I.D. (mm)	Height (mm)	Feet (mm)
28	58.6	22.7	10.7	50
24	51.2	19.0	10.0	47
20	38.5	15.6	8.3	44
17	29.1	13.5	8.2	40
13	19.5	10.0	6.7	35
11	17.4	8.0	6.0	32
9	11.1	7.2	5.3	26
7	10.9	4.9	3.2	22

PERFECTION WIRE WCSL

Size	Weight (grains)	I.D. (mm)	Height (mm)	Feet (mm)
24	57.9	20.1	9.5	56
20	47.7	17.3	9.5	53
16	35.0	12.6	8	48
14	26.1	10.6	7.5	43
12	22.8	8.9	6.9	38
10	13.3	7.1	5.3	32
8	9.4	5.8	5.3	28

FOULPROOF

Size	Weight (grains)*	I.D. (mm)	Height (mm)	Feet (mm)†
SP-1 1/8	95.2	28.6	9.5	95
SP-7/8	58.6	22.2	9.0	80
SP-3/4	55.8	19.0	9.0	73
SP-5/8	30.6	15.9	6.7	69
SP-1/2	23.9	12.7	5.0	54
FM-3/8	12.8	9.5	4.7	49
FM-5/16	10.8	7.9	4.3	48
FM-1/4	10.0	6.4	4.0	45
FC-3/16	4.9	4.8	3.0	38
FC-5/32	4.6	4.0	1.7	38

*Also made in additional series of smaller-diameter wire.
†Feet are widely spaced and guide flexes, hence distance is not good measure of restrictiveness.

FOULPROOF WRAP-ON TIP-TOPS

Size	Weight (grains)	I.D. (mm)
LST-5/16	19.4	8.0
CTT-7/32	9.2	5.5
LTT-3/16	8.8.	4.8
MLTT-3/16	5.2	4.8

SEVEN

Wraps and Wrapping Techniques

Wrapping techniques and wrap designs are of great interest to the majority of custom rod builders. While there are those who prefer to keep wraps quite simple and subdued, intricate designs and patterns are a creative means of expression to a great many of us. I have noticed that the first thing examined when someone is handed a custom rod is invariably the wraps. This is not only true with bright or fancy wraps, but with those which are quite plain as well. Possibly this is the one area of craftsmanship which the nonbuilder feels he is qualified to evaluate. It is also interesting to note that the wraps are one of the first specific areas of workmanship that the custom rod builder either points out to the novice or expects him to examine. Whatever the reasons, it certainly seems important that we, as custom builders, develop a firm mastery of wrapping techniques.

It should be pointed out that this chapter is written under the assumption that the reader already knows the very basic steps involved in making wraps. I do not mean we will not be touching on some very fundamental techniques, for to improve in any skill it is often necessary to return periodically to the basics. How-

211

ever, for the reader who has not already wrapped some rods, I would strongly suggest he read *Fiberglass Rod Making*, where step-by-step, detailed instructions are given. Basically, I have tried here to pick up where I left off in the first book, and to cover areas either not covered there or not covered in depth. The fundamentals which we will explore are those on which I have received numerous questions.

PREPARATION AND MATERIALS

Removing the factory logo from the blank. On some occasions we find ourselves working with a blank on which the company's logo has been placed beneath the final finish, and we would prefer to remove it. Normal solvents such as alcohol, acetone, and lacquer thinner will have no effect. In fact, if we use a solvent strong enough to remove the factory-applied finish we run a real risk of having that solvent also attack the resin bonding the fibers together. In some situations the logo presents no problem because the design and layout permits placing a decorative butt wrap over it. If this is not the case, then the best method I have found is to carefully scrape away the factory finish. Use a fairly sharp, thin blade such as a single-edge razor blade, a Rod Builder's Knife, or an X-Acto knife. Hold the blade at right angles to the axis of the blank. This is important to prevent slicing or digging into the blank. Work with single strokes long enough to cover the area of finish to be removed. Scrape only deep enough to remove the finish and the imprinted logo, making certain you are not scraping the fibers of the blank. You can smooth the scrape marks and feather the ends with very fine sandpaper or fine steel wool. Wipe with a cloth moistened in a mild solvent and, when dry, lightly wipe with a tack rag. The first coat of your wrapping finish can be extended from the butt wrap to cover the scraped area, and it will be restored to like-new condition. A thin finish such as Crystal Coat works best here, since the end can be brushed out and feathered into the unscraped factory finish.

Installing tip-tops. The old standby for installing tip-tops was a daub of thermoplastic ferrule cement. Then came the advent of ceramic tops and their plastic shock-absorbing ring. The heat needed to melt the ferrule cement and then to heat the top (to achieve a good internal flow of the cement) often melted or weakened the shock ring. Some rod builders hold the ring of the top in a wet cloth to keep it cool while heating the tube. I have settled on five-minute epoxy as the best method.

Use only a very small amount of this glue. After slipping the tip-top over the blank's tip, immediately wipe off any excess. Lay the blank on a flat surface with your mark indicating the side on which the guides will be placed facing straight up. A couple of pieces of masking tape will hold the blank in that position. Rotate the tip-top until it is exactly in line with your mark. Within a few more minutes the glue will set and you can untape the blank and proceed. If the tip-top ever becomes damaged and must be replaced, heat from a soldering gun applied to the tube will break the bond. Of course, at that time it doesn't matter if the shock ring on the damaged top melts. The one exception to this method is when mounting roller tops. Then the bond should be as strong as possible and permanent, so use regular long-setting epoxy. The roller frame will never need to be removed, since replacement roller parts are available.

Taping on guides. Robert "Mac" McCowan, a fine rod builder and a good friend of mine, once sent me a humorous poem stating that the single most important component in building rods was masking tape. For many of us, he wasn't too far wrong, since there are so very many applications. One of its primary uses is in taping guides in place while being wrapped, and in temporarily holding threads while making intricate wraps. Very narrow tape can be used to mark the spline on a rod, and some builders prefer a band of narrow tape on each guide foot. Tape in various widths, especially the narrow sizes, can be purchased at auto paint supply dealers.

It you do any amount of wrapping you will find a heavy tape dispenser invaluable. These are readily available in office-supply stores, and I know many rod builders who use two—one for narrow and one for regular. Think of how many times you pick up a roll of tape and either cut or tear off a piece. With a tape

Heavy tape dispenser holds wide and narrow masking tape.

213

dispenser handy all you need to do is reach up with one hand, pull off the desired length, and pull it across the cutting edge on the front. The weight of these units keeps them from tipping over or moving beneath your hand. Let me make another suggestion on a time-saving tool. Instead of small scissors, use a pair of snips of the type with no finger holes and an internal spring that pushes them back open. They come with replaceable blades and are an excellent investment. Check your rod-building-supply dealer.

Thread

Size. In my travels I am surprised at how many rod builders use thread of a heavier size than needed. Naturally, heavier thread is a mite easier to wrap, but it does not give nearly the beauty and visual appeal of finer thread. Some people erroneously assume that heavier thread is needed for added strength. Size A thread is amazingly strong and should be used on freshwater rods of all kinds. If you are using anything heavier, try A on your next rod and see how much better it looks. There will be less bulk around the guides and the individual threads will be almost invisible after finishing. Your intricate butt wraps will also be less bulky and look better. Size D is plenty strong enough for all kinds of saltwater rods, even offshore trolling rods. By comparison, E or EE looks like rope on the finished product.

NCP thread and regular thread. NCP, of course, stands for "No Color Preserver," meaning that the thread so designated will retain its color when any kind of finish is applied directly. A better explanation is that NCP thread has been treated so that it is opaque. You cannot see through it, nor will light pass through it. Most important, the color underneath NCP thread will not show through or "bleed." Light-colored NCP thread on a dark blank will retain its original light color. This is not true for regular thread. If the finish is applied directly to it, without color preserver, it becomes translucent and the color underneath shows through. Light-colored regular thread on a dark blank will lose just about all color and go "muddy" if no color preserver is used. Darker colors of regular thread without color preserver will become a bit darker, but the guide feet will be visible through the wrap. As we will see later when discussing some intricate patterns, these characteristics of both regular and NCP thread can be used quite creatively. However, for now, let's see if we can't more fully understand the differences between these two types of thread.

When using a dark blank or a dark underwrap, light-colored regular thread must have color preserver. However, even with the required number of coats, the light color loses some of its snap. White doesn't look pure white. Instead, it takes on a slight grayish cast. Nor will the color be even. It will look different just along the sides of the guide feet. This dull, mottled effect is what is referred to as blushing. The easiest way to correct it is to use NCP thread for white and all light colors, such as yellow and light blue. Not only will it eliminate the problem associated with dark blanks or dark underwraps, but it will look much better on gold and other light-colored blanks.

You might be thinking that if this is the case, why not use NCP thread in all colors and be done with it? The reason is that in the medium and darker colors NCP looks flat. It lacks the sparkle and snap of regular thread. You can easily see this difference when comparing samples of both finished threads in the sunlight. So a good rule to follow for wraps, as well as trim bands, is to use NCP for light colors and regular thread for medium and dark colors. You'll be surprised at how much better your wraps will look.

Since we have brought up the subject of NCP thread, you should be aware that it should never be stored in sunlight or fluorescent light. The chemicals used to make this thread opaque will cause it to lose strength and deteriorate from prolonged exposure to either of these light sources. In extreme cases the exposed thread will pull apart in your hands. Once NCP thread has been finished, this problem no longer exists.

Storage and handling. All thread should be stored where it will be dust-free. Minute particles of dust adhere to thread, making it next to impossible to get a smooth, glasslike finish. Another suggestion when working with thread is to always wash your hands in soap and water beforehand. If your wrapping session is a long one, stop and again wash your hands in the middle of your work. Perspiration contains body oils. These are absorbed by the thread, but do not make their appearance known until the finish is applied. Then the thread mysteriously becomes mottled.

BASIC WRAPPING TECHNIQUES

Guide alignment. Thread tension should be moderate. After wrapping a guide, you should be able to adjust its position slightly. A by-product of proper tension is that it eliminates the need for a lot of time spent beforehand in getting the guides all perfectly aligned. Instead, try only a rough, estimated alignment initially. Then, after the first guide foot below the tip-top is wrapped, move the guide to either side as needed. After the second foot is wrapped, again make any needed adjustments. Continue in this manner until all guides are wrapped. Just before applying the color preserver, make a final, accurate check.

Instead of the traditional method of sighting along the blank and looking through the guides, I have changed to sighting from the back side of the blank. It is faster and much more accurate. Hold the blank out at arm's length with the guides on the far side and the blank tilted up, nearly vertical. Twist the blank slightly in your hand until the tip of the blank exactly bisects the ring on the tip-top. Without moving the blank, glance at the first guide below the tip-top. The blank should once again be in the exact center of the guide ring. If not, move it as required. Just continue down the blank from guide to guide in the same fashion. When you have f ished, each guide will be perfectly aligned with the tip-top.

Aligning guides by viewing from back.

Wrap length. One sign of good craftsmanship is that the length of each guide wrap is directly proportionate to the size of the guide. (This is, of course, for the normal rod where wraps are not being adjusted to modify the action.) As the sizes of the guides diminish, so do the lengths of the guide feet. We can maintain proper proportion, then, if we make the length of the wrap in front of each guide foot the same on all guides. The total length of the wraps will automatically be shorter on the smaller guides.

To determine this constant length in front of each guide foot, select a guide near the middle of the rod. Make a test wrap to decide on a length that looks appropriate. Take a piece of white card stock or fairly stiff paper and hold it along the blank next to the wrapped guide. On the card place a small pencil mark at the beginning of the wrap, and another at the beginning of the guide foot. This is the distance in front of each guide foot that you want to start each wrap. To use your simple measuring card, hold it next to the blank so one pencil mark is at the leading edge of a guide foot. Use a scriber to make a small scratch in the surface finish of the blank opposite the second pencil mark. Now, all you need to do is start your wrap on the scratch and continue wrapping up over the guide foot. Make sure you end the wrap at the same point on each guide.

This technique is applicable if you are already in the habit of measuring a given distance in front of each guide foot with a ruler. Simply measure the distance once, on the white card, and you will find you can work much faster than measuring each wrap individually. A white card can also be used to keep open

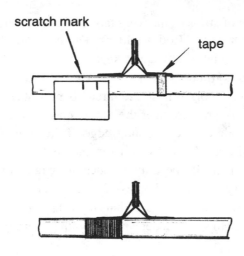

scratch mark

tape

Keeping wraps equal.

spiral wraps exactly the same. Measure the distance between each spiraled thread and mark it on the card. The card is then used to scratch the blank where each spiral of thread is to be placed. As you get more proficient at open spirals, you can make them freehand, then use the card to check their spacing. A fine-pointed "thread tool" or needle can be used to push any spiraled threads into perfect spacing.

Concealing and trimming thread ends. When a wrap is made it is started by wrapping the thread over itself for a number of turns. Then the loose end is trimmed off. Similarly, when a wrap is ended, the thread is pulled under the previous winds. This automatically produces two small humps in the wrap, one at the beginning and one at the end. In order to minimize their obviousness on the finished rod, always plan on hiding them. By that I mean locate the start and the tie-off loop opposite the side of the rod normally seen by the person fishing it. On fly rods and spinning rods this is on the same side as the guides. On casting rods and trolling rods it is on the side opposite the guides.

If you are not careful, a small nub of thread will protrude where the thread has been trimmed after being pulled under by the tie-off loop. This will usually not be noticeable until the finish is applied. Then it stands up like a stiff flag, destroying the beauty of the wrap. A couple of techniques can be used to eliminate these ends from poking through. First, trim the thread as close as possible with a decisive cut of a *sharp* blade made parallel with the wrap. Single-edge razor blades are not as sharp as double-edge blades. However, the edge dulls faster on a double-edge blade. You can cut a double-edge blade in half lengthwise with a pair

217

of scissors. A couple of strips of masking tape folded over the cut edge will make it easy to handle. Or use a Rod Builder's Knife or an X-Acto knife with a relatively new blade which is still quite sharp.

After the thread is trimmed as close as possible, use your thumbnail (or the angled edge of a thread tool) to push the thread beneath the wrap in the direction of the windings. Apply pressure near the thread end, where it was just trimmed, and at about a 45° angle toward the outer edge of the wrap. The idea is to move the hidden, wrapped-over thread away from the spot where it was trimmed. In doing so it will automatically be drawn under the wrap. Some rod builders use an alcohol lamp with a clean, carbonless flame to very quickly singe the wrap. This eliminates any fine strand of fuzz that might have extended from the thread when it was trimmed. However, a decisive cut with a sharp blade should not leave any such fuzz.

Another technique is used by RodCrafter Jim Conaty. He uses a tie-off loop of fine monofilament about 2 inches long and knotted at the end. Several knots jammed against each other provide a bit of a handle to assist when pulling the loop under. Instead of inserting his tie-off loop at the usual 6 to 8 turns before the end, Jim inserts his much earlier in the wrap, and continues wrapping over it. When the end of the wrap is reached, the winding thread is cut as usual and the end inserted into the tie-off loop. He then *slowly* withdraws the loop until it is just barely drawing the end under the wrap. At this point the thread is taut and will not loosen when the tie-off loop is temporarily released. The end of the thread is cut as closely as possible to the loop, and the loop withdrawn. The cut end of the thread will drop out of the loop underneath the wrap instead of coming all the way out with the loop. No trimming is necessary since the end is buried beneath the wrap.

A   tie off loop of fine monofilament

Eliminating nubs. A: Tie-off loop of fine monofilament. B: Loop inserted early in wrap. C: Thread drawn taut and cut short. D: Loop withdrawn and end buried.

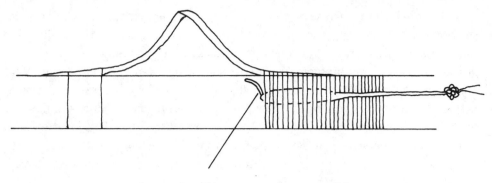

B insert tie-off loop as early as possible

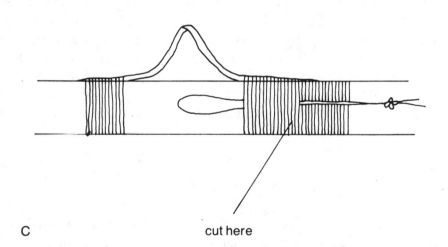

C cut here

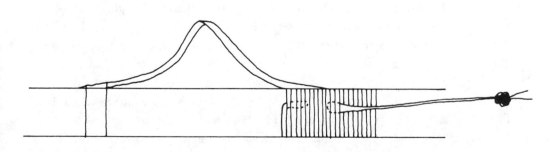

D end of thread is lost under the wrap leaving no end to trim

Avoiding gaps. One very obvious sign of the neophyte rod builder is the small gaps and spaces between individual threads in a wrap. If the thread is wound on evenly there will be very few of these, but even the most experienced professional has some present. The way to eliminate them is to burnish the wrap after it is complete. With underwraps this should be done before the overwrap is started. I formerly used my thumbnail for this until I was introduced to the slick little thread tool—and burnisher—by RodCrafter George Fish. This handy, dandy little gadget is described in the chapter on tools. Here, we'll just discuss using it as a burnisher. Actually, any small-diameter, rounded, highly polished piece of metal will work as a burnisher. Russ Jacobs uses a large darning needle, Richard Jankauskas the finger loops on a pair of surgical scissors, and Joy Dunlap an anodized-aluminum knitting needle. I am sure there are many more objects similarly used.

To burnish a wrap, rub the tool back and forth along the wrap while slowly rotating the supported blank. You must be careful at the ends of the wrap or you will open new gaps between the threads. If you are right-handed, use your left thumbnail placed against the left end of the wrap as a stop. A small-diameter tool will enable you to stroke all the way to the left end until the burnisher automatically stops against your thumbnail. On the end of the wrap to your right, stroke the tool from right to left with light pressure over the end and continuing into the center of the wrap.

UNDERWRAPS

The technique of underwrapping guides probably originated with heavier saltwater rods. The idea is to provide a cushion beneath the feet of the guide to protect the blank. Since larger guides with longer feet are used on these rods, the amount of movement between the inflexible guide and the flexing blank is increased. The underwrap therefore provides a buffer against abrasion in this situation. Because of the design of the feet, the weight of the guides, and the stress present, roller-guide manufacturers recommend that this particular type of guide always be underwrapped.

Over the years, underwrapping spread to other rods, including those for freshwater use. My guess is that at least a couple of things contributed to this. First, the same principle of protecting the blank with a cushion seemed to make good sense. Second, the appearance of an underwrapped guide was attractive to many rod builders and fishermen. Three complementary colors could be brought into use for an appealing design. There was the basic color of the blank, the color of the underwrap which appeared in the interior space beneath the guide ring and at the ends of the wrap, and finally the color of the guide wrap itself. We have all seen very handsome examples of this. Some rod builders have become so convinced of the merits of underwrapping that they regard any rod except the lightest of spinning rods and fly rods as inferior if they are not made with underwraps. Inevitably, there developed two school of thought on the subject and many heated debates have ensued.

Now, don't get me wrong. I am not against underwraps. I personally believe custom rod building is a creative means of expression, and each rod builder should therefore do his own thing. Nor do I think I am expert enough to take up the cause for either side in defense of that position. I do believe that before a person makes a decision on which course to follow he should at least hear the other side of the argument.

Underwraps do add stiffness to the blank. A great deal of pressure is exerted from a wrap of even Size A thread, adding hoop strength to the blank at that point. This principle of restrictiveness to flexing was discussed in connection with modifying the action in the chapter on the blank. When we add two layers of thread it is more restrictive than one layer. It is like adding wall thickness to the blank. Usually the top layer (the guide wrap) is of a size larger thread than the underwrap. Larger thread requires a heavier finish, so we compound the stiffening factor. If our objective is to stiffen the rod, underwrapping will help. But if we want to retain the original action, it would be better not to underwrap.

The cushioning and protective aspects of an underwrap are not needed on most rods if the guide feet are properly prepared by a technique similar to the one explained in the chapter on guides. Underwraps add bulk to the appearance of guide wraps. This is less noticeable on large-diameter saltwater rods, but fairly apparent on most freshwater rods. The smaller the diameter of the blank, the more noticeable is the increased bulk. Underwrapped guides on light graphite blanks begin to look out of proportion to many people.

Those are the main arguments advanced or defended by each side of the question.

False underwraps. If you like the appearance of an underwrapped guide but do not want the bulk or the stiffening effect on a light rod, let me suggest what I call "false underwraps." This is a wrap that has only one layer of thread throughout, but visually is the same as an underwrapped guide.

Let's assume you want to imitate the effect of a silver underwrap with dark-blue guide wraps. You need a band of silver between the guide feet. This must be wrapped on the blank before the guide is wrapped on. Hold the guide in the exact position where it will later be wrapped. With a scriber, carefully place a scratch at each point where the guide wraps will end nearest the guide ring. Remove the guide and make your silver wrap between these two scratches—begin and end the wrap exactly on each mark.

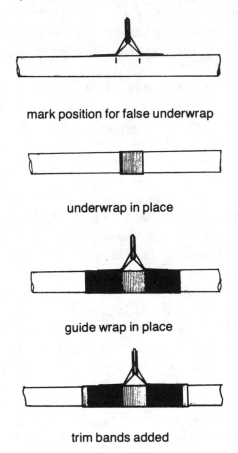

mark position for false underwrap

underwrap in place

guide wrap in place

trim bands added

Making false underwraps.

Next, carefully center the guide over the band of silver thread, and tape one foot to the blank. Make a dark-blue wrap over the untaped foot. Remove the tape and make a matching dark-blue wrap over the remaining guide foot. All that remains to be done is to place a trim band of silver on each end of the wrap.

The underwraps

When making true underwraps, you have to be very careful to maintain proper proportions for each different-size guide. The guide wrap should start at exactly the same distance from the leading edge of every guide foot. The width of the trim band on each end of the wrap (the extended underwrap) should be exactly the same on all wraps. When we consider that (1) the underwrap must be made first, (2) it must be precisely centered on the spot where the guide ring is to be placed, and (3) it must be exactly the right length for that size guide, it's easy to see why many underwrapped rods lack the precision expected of custom work.

Below is a procedure which will ensure perfect results. Let me suggest you use the metric system, since it is so much easier to work with. Small rulers marked in millimeters are readily available. You will need a sheet of paper on which you can list vertically each of the guides by size, and space for five more vertical columns. You also should have the blank marked with a scratch at the point where each guide ring is to be placed.

1. Measure the span of each guide from the end of one foot to the end of the other. Write this figure next to the guide size in Column 1.

2. Determine the length of the guide wrap you want to have in front of each guide foot. Since there are two guide feet, multiply this number by 2 and write it in Column 2 after each size guide.

3. Determine the length of the trim band (extended underwrap) you want on each end of the wraps. Again, since there are two ends to a wrap, multiply by 2 and list in Column 3 after each size guide.

4. To determine the total length of the entire underwrap, add the figures in Columns 1, 2, and 3 and write the result in Column 4. This figure will naturally be different for each size guide.

5. To find the center of the underwrap, or rather the length on each side of the center, divide the figure in Column 4 (total length of underwrap) by 2. Write it in Column 5.

6. Now go to the blank and locate the scratch for the guide ring position of the first guide. Opposite that guide size in Column 5 of the table is the length on either side of the center scratch. Measure that length and make a scratch on each side. This is the length and position of your underwrap for that size guide.

7. Start your underwrap (Size A) precisely on one scratch mark and wrap, over the center scratch, to the other scratch mark. End the wrap exactly on the scratch.

8. If you are going to include a "guide-ring trim band" in the center of the underwrap (directly below where the guide ring will be located), make it now. Measure to the center of the underwrap and place a pencil dot on the thread. Center your narrow guide-ring trim band over the dot. Next position the guide over the trim band and tape one foot. Measure the distance from the end of each guide

foot to the end of the underwrap to make sure the guide is exactly centered. (If no guide-ring trim band is used, center the guide by measuring the space at each end and tape one foot of the guide. Check again to make sure the guide is in the exact center of the underwrap.)

9. On a piece of card stock, measure and mark the length of the trim band (exposed underwrap) that is to be on the end of each wrap. This is one-half of the figure in Column 3. Hold this card next to the blank and the taped guide. Align one mark with the edge of the underwrap, and start your guide wrap (Size D) at the other mark. *This card and this measurement will be used for all guides,* since the length of the trim band is to be the same on each wrap.

UNDERWRAP TABLE*

Size	1 Guide foot length	2 Undergrip length	3 Trim Band length	4 Total	5 Length each side of center
NHG-8	24	10	4	38	19
NHG-10	28	10	4	42	21
NHG-12	29	10	4	43	21.5
NHG-16	36	10	4	50	25
NHG-20	42	10	4	56	28
NHG-25	53	10	4	67	33.5

*All measurements in millimeters.

Always save the table you constructed for future reference. The next time you use that model guide and those sizes, just refer to the table. It is then a snap to mark the ends of the underwraps. Such tables can be prepared ahead of time for the guides you use most frequently. While the procedure will seem a bit cumbersome the first time, you will quickly get the hang of it and be able to work quickly. After you have a few tables prepared as well, you'll breeze through the job. Most important, your guide wraps and underwraps will all be perfectly proportioned and sized to fit the guides. Your work will look like—and be—the work of a master craftsman.

It should be mentioned here that some rod makers find a self-centering ruler of help when locating the midpoint of an underwrap. These are generally short rulers with zero in the middle and the figures running in each direction out from zero. If you decide to try one, make sure it is marked in millimeters rather than inches. They are available at all graphic-arts-supply stores.

Power underwrapping. If you build many rods with underwraps you may want to consider making them with a powered rod-wrapping lathe. On short underwraps on smaller-diameter blanks, the time saving is not very great unless you do enough of it to become quite proficient. On longer underwraps used on larger-diameter saltwater rods you can save time and eliminate boredom! In the chapter on tools you will find ideas for a powered rod-wrapping lathe. Here, we want to concern ourselves primarily with technique.

There are probably almost as many different techniques for power wrapping as there are rod builders who use it. All that we can do here is hit some of the highlights that may help you in developing your own comfortable style. The wrap is started the same as any wrap, by winding the thread over itself. If your wrapping lathe lacks gearing resistance and permits you to rotate the blank by hand, just use the same method you always have. If the blank can only be rotated by the variable-speed foot control, you will have to develop a new way of starting the wrap. Some rod builders attach the end of the thread to the blank temporarily with a piece of masking tape. Others make a wide, loose spiral in the opposite direction of the wrap, then double back over this spiral for a few turns until the thread is anchored.

You must have the underwrap start precisely on your scratch mark. Watch out for the tendency of the thread to "walk" up the blank away from your scratch. Judicious use of your thumbnails will move the first few winds back to the scratch. There is also the possibility that the thread will bunch up the least bit as it is first wound over the loose end. If allowed to remain a slight bump will be present in the wrap. To eliminate this possibility, after about the first five winds, pull on the loose end of the wrapped-over thread while holding the wrap. Then cut it close to the windings.

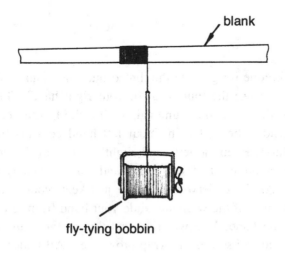

Power underwraps.

The thread can be fed to the rotating blank under tension by many methods. Those who use 50-yard spools of thread find a fly tyer's bobbin works nicely. Some just hold a 1-ounce spool loosely in their cupped hand so that it can rotate by bouncing around inside the hand. Tension will automatically be controlled as needed by your hand. Still other rod builders use their regular thread tension device placed behind the blank. They pull the thread out in a long loop to the front of the lathe where it passes through the thumb and index finger so that it can be guided on to the blank. Another method is to make a thread holder big enough for the size spools you use, and slide it along the workbench in front of the lathe.

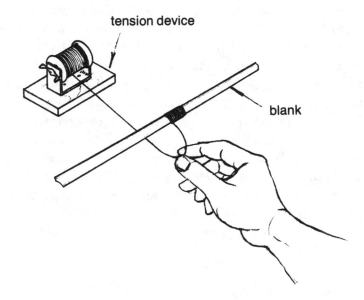

tension device

blank

Power underwraps.

One good technique for guiding the thread onto the blank so that it does not climb over itself is to use the thumbnail of your right hand. This assumes you wrap from left to right. Place the thumbnail against the leading edge of the wrap just where the thread is being fed in. Your left hand controls the angle of the thread and the tension. Keep the left hand slightly ahead of the developing wrap so the angle is never quite 90°. Your right hand can be loosely cupped around the rotating blank. As the underwrap is made just keep your thumbnail pressed against the leading edge of the wrap and slide your hand from left to right in time with the speed of the lathe. You will find that this method automatically packs the thread tightly against itself as the wrap progresses. All underwraps should be burnished.

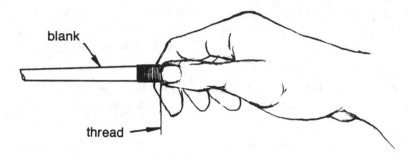

blank

thread

Using the thumbnail to guide thread into place.

If you really do a lot of rod work and you find you have a knack for power underwraps, you may want to give power guide wrapping a try. Rod companies tell me it takes at least two weeks to train a worker in this function—and that is a concentrated forty-hour week with lots of instruction. So, if you can't get the hang of it, don't be discouraged. Most of us just don't have the time to devote to both learning it and maintaining proficiency. I watch those wrappers with fascination as they make it look so easy, but I gave up trying a long time ago.

WRAPPING FERRULES

Any internal ferrule of the plug or spigot type should be wrapped for additional hoop strength. On thin-walled, high-density blanks such as our Custom Builder series and the Lamiglas fiberglass blanks, it is an absolute necessity. The primary section to be wrapped is the female ferrule, but wrap both for added insurance and appearance. The length of the wrap should be slightly greater than the length of the plug that fits inside the blank. Normally, on a precision-ground, factory-installed ferrule one layer of Size A thread is sufficient. Actually this will add tremendous hoop strength, especially after the thread is finished. When wrapping the female ferrule do not apply great tension on the thread. If you do, you run the risk of reducing the diameter of the blank, and the male plug may not fit into it properly. This is merely further evidence of the pressure that can be exerted by a wrap of Size A thread.

This type of ferrule is made so that when the rod sections are joined there should be a gap. This is there by design, and its purpose is to allow for wear. Do not try to sand the male plug to reduce the size of the gap. You will only ruin the precision grinding that formed a perfect taper-to-taper fit. If the gap seems excessive to you, make a very short wrap of thread on the male plug itself.

This little wrap should be placed right against the blank into which the plug is glued. It should not be long enough to eliminate the gap entirely. In time the surface will wear and the gap will be reduced. When the female end gets close to your tiny trim band on the male ferrule, that small wrap should be removed. In anticipation of this, give this little band of thread only one coat of thinned-down finish. It can then be nicked with a razor blade and easily unwound.

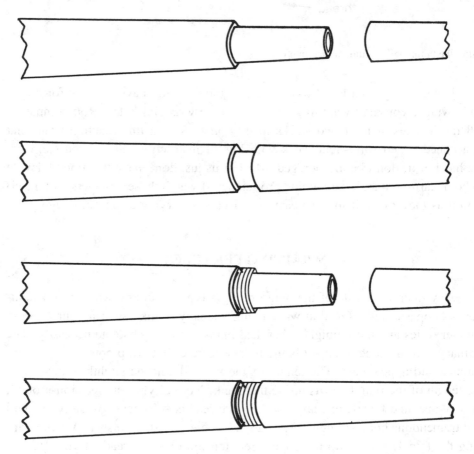

Wrapping large gap on internal ferrule. Male and female sections of blank would also be wrapped for needed reinforcement.

If the original gap between the sections, when joined, is quite small you know that the future wear will close the gap entirely, resulting in a loose fit. Again, you can anticipate this when you wrap the female ferrule. In this situation do not make the wrap extend all the way to the very edge of the female ferrule. Instead, terminate it about ⅛ to ¼ inch short of the end. When the gap has closed completely from wear you can then file off a bit of the end of the blank at the female ferrule without damaging your wrap. Removing a bit of the blank by filing will then allow the plug to penetrate farther into the blank for a strong joint.

Sleeve ferrules made by fitting a section of fiberglass or graphite partway over the end of one section of the blank do not need wrapping for reinforcement. This is the type of ferrule used on Fenwick Gold blanks and on Fenwick graphite blanks. Since the end of the sleeve glued to the blank has been ground at a taper to feather the profile into the blank, the appearance can be improved quite a bit by wrapping at least the feathering taper. You can, of course, wrap the entire ferrule if you prefer. Sometimes you will find that the feathering is not complete and a small step exists between the end of the ground sleeve and the blank. This can be eliminated by careful sanding of the end of the sleeve. Place a single band of thin masking tape or cellophane tape on the blank next to the sleeve. This will prevent inadvertent sanding of the blank itself, which might weaken it. A rod lathe makes quick work of this, but it can also be done by hand. An emery board or similar abrasive-covered flat stick will help. Final finish sanding can be done with fine sandpaper.

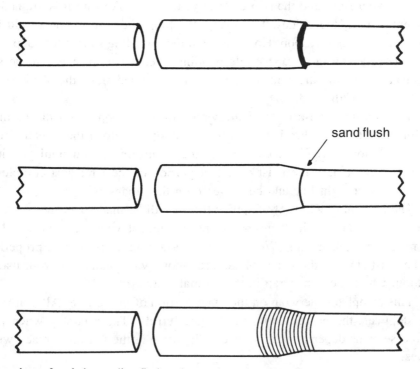

sand flush

Finishing sleeve ferrule by sanding flush and wrapping.

Thread index

When wrapping ferrules you may want to consider incorporating a bit of thread detail to serve as reference marks in aligning the rod sections when they are joined. Such detail is both functional and ornamental. RodCrafter Tom Logan adds a short length of twisted thread on both the male and female ferrule wraps. Here is the procedure he uses.

Cut a 12-inch length of the same size thread in a contrasting color to that being used for your wraps. In all probablility this will be the same color used for trim bands at the ends of the guide wraps. For the moment, set this thread aside where it will be handy.

Beginning with the reinforcing wrap on the male ferrule (butt section), start the wrap about 1¼ inches to the left of where the male ferrule emerges from inside the blank. We will be winding from left to right. As normal, make six winds over the thread itself and cut off the short end. Now make six more winds of threads.

At this point, pick up your previously cut 12-inch length of thread and fold it in half, making a 6-inch loop. Lay the loop against the wrap so that the loop is toward your right and the two ends to your left. Make sure it is aligned with, and centered on, the guides. Wind over the loop end just as you would if you were inserting a tie-off loop. However, continue winding so that the loop is completely covered by the wrap. While winding over the loop, check to be sure it remains aligned with the guides. The wrap is continued along the blank to within about ¼ inch of the end.

Take the two loose ends of the wrapped-under loop. With the thumb and forefinger of the right hand, held about the midpoint along the threads, roll the two strands together. Continue twisting them into one strand until you have a fairly tight twist. Lay the twist over that portion of the wrap just completed. It must lie in a straight line and be centered on the guides.

The remaining winds of wrapping thread will be made over the twist. Make three winds to anchor it, then check final alignment with the guides and make any necessary adjustments. When you are certain that it is aligned properly, cut off the twist close to the wrap. Make three more winds and insert your usual tie-off loop. Complete your wrap in the normal fashion.

This completes the wrap on the male portion of the ferrule. All that remains is to duplicate the procedure on the female ferrule. The accuracy when joining the rod sections depends upon your care in aligning the twisted threads with the guides.

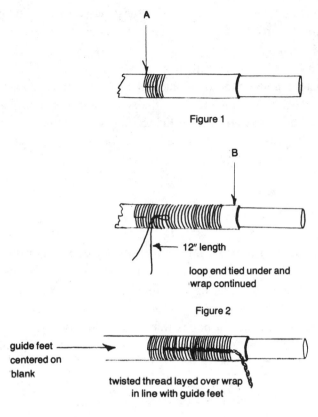

Figure 1

B

12″ length

loop end tied under and
wrap continued

Figure 2

guide feet
centered on
blank

twisted thread layed over wrap
in line with guide feet

Figure 3

this portion of twist is visible

wrapped over twist

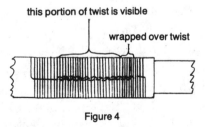

Figure 4

Ferrule thread index. 1: Basic wrap started. 2: Insert 12″ loop and wind over. 3: Thread twisted and aligned with guide feet, then end wrapped over. 4: Ends of twisted thread cut and wrap completed.

A word about finishing the wraps. Since the twist lies on top of the wrap, it is a bit more fragile. To protect it from abrasion it is best to give the ferrule wraps one or two additional coats of finish.

Instead of using a twisted loop of thread with which to make the alignment mark, you can use just a single strand of thread for less bulk. This style is used by RodCrafter Eugene Miller. The procedure is the same, but it is suggested that you make the length of the thread overlay a bit shorter, since it is more fragile in longer lengths.

GUIDE WRAPS

Much of the elaborate and intricate threadwork that is done on custom rods is placed on the butt wrap. There are, however, many opportunities for this decorative craftsmanship on the wraps securing the guides. Quite a few of these were explained and pictured in *Fiberglass Rod Making*. In this section I would like to expand a bit on these techniques in hopes that it will both add to your ideas and encourage you to experiment further on your own. Threadwork is fun, and all of us keep learning from our experiments.

Very narrow trim bands

Very narrow trim bands of a contrasting color look especially handsome on each end of a guide wrap. Their extremely small size adds just a subtle dash of color, and speaks highly of the rod maker's skill with thread. Their proportions are ideally suited to fly rods, light spinning rods, and all small-diameter blanks, but they can be used effectively on all size rods. There are a number of ways of making them, but I will detail the one I use.

Start by increasing thread tension slightly. Since the wrap is quite narrow, all turns of thread must be placed over the tie-off loop. We'll assume you are wrapping from left to right. Hold the tie-off loop in place on top of the blank with your left thumb and forefinger. Use your right hand to bring a generous length of thread from your tension device over the top of both the tie-off loop and the blank. Temporarily hold it in place by slipping it under the thumb of your left hand. Reach over the top of the blank with your right hand and pick up the loose end of the wrapping thread. Bring it up over the blank and lay it beside the previous wind. Keep tension on the end of this thread with your right hand.

Rotate the blank a quarter-turn. Use your left thumb to push the wrapping thread coming from the tension device over the top of the wind just made. While doing this you were keeping tension on the end of the wrapping thread with your right hand. Now, place your left thumb across the wrap made to this point in order to hold it tight. Once again reach over the top of the blank with your right hand and pick up the loose end of the wrapping thread. As before, bring it up over the blank and lay it beside the previous winds. Keep tension on the wrap by pulling with your right hand.

Repeat the rotation of the blank by a quarter-turn, and again use your left thumb to push the thread coming from the tension device over the wind just made. At this point the wrapping thread is secured to the blank and wrapped over the tie-off loop. Make one complete rotation of the blank so the thread crosses over the loose end a third time.

While keeping tension on the thread coming from the spool, use a *very sharp* razor blade or X-Acto knife to cut the loose end flush with the wrap. The trick here is to hold the blade at 90° against the blank and against the previously made winds. Use a rocking motion of the blade to sever the thread with a clean cut. There should be no end of the thread sticking out from beneath the wrap. You can then rotate the blank the remaining half-turn to the tie-off loop, and complete the wrap in the usual fashion. If, back at the point where you severed the thread with the blade, there was a tiny bit of thread sticking out from beneath the wrap, make one and a half turns instead of just one-half turn. This extra wind of thread should cover the bit of thread projecting from the end of the wrap.

When completing the wrap by pulling the tie-off loop through with your left hand, grasp the narrow trim band on each side with the thumb and index finger of the right hand. This keeps the pulled-under end of the thread in position and prevents the band of thread from coming loose. Before cutting the pulled-under thread, press your right thumbnail against the right edge of the trim band and rotate the blank a couple of times. This will compress the threads and make the trim band even more narrow. Again, hold the trim band tightly with your right thumb and index finger and pull any slack out of the loose thread. Then cut it close to the wrap as usual. You can firm up the wrap by again running your thumbnail around the edge. On very small-diameter tip sections, such as graphite, you might want to immediately ''glue'' the fragile band together with a coat of color preserver.

Instead of just a single narrow trim band on each end of a guide wrap, they can be used in twos and threes for really fine detailing. Bands in a sequence of white, black, and white look good with most any color guide wrap. Narrow trim bands also can be isolated and not touching any other wrap. These isolated bands can be a short distance from the ends of guide wraps, in front of butt wraps, or as decoration between the foregrip and first guide. The last is a fine way of putting detail on a conservatively wrapped fly rod.

The easiest way of making an isolated narrow band is to first place a strip of masking tape around the blank. The trim band is wound against the edge of the tape just as if the tape were a guide wrap. This provides support while making the fragile wrap and gives you something to press against as you compress the winds with your fingernail. Put a coat of color preserver on the band before removing the tape.

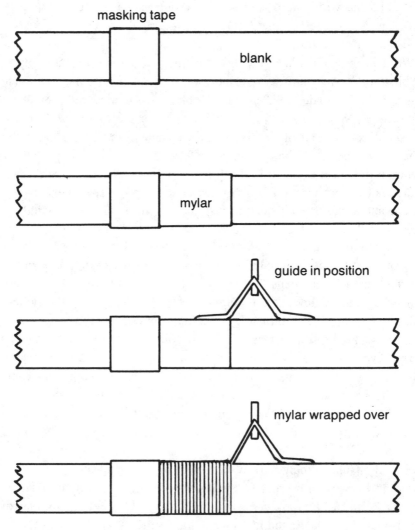

Use of masking tape as brace for aligning edge of mylar and thread.

Mylar or paint under solid wraps

Bright metallic mylar tape is frequently seen beneath open spiral wraps. Not too many people realize it can also be used beneath solid wraps for interesting color variations. To get a bleed-through of the mylar, no color preserver is used and the medium or dark thread becomes translucent. When used on guide wraps the guide feet should be chrome rather than black. Carefully lay out the area to be covered by the wrap and mark it on the blank with a dubbing needle. Cut the mylar to fit the space and glue it around the blank. Position the guide precisely over the two mylar bands and tape one foot. Place a piece of masking tape around the blank just next to the leading edge of the mylar. The tape will act as a brace against which the wrap will be started. This helps keep the leading edge of the thread exactly on top of the leading edge of the mylar. When you end the wrap, make certain it is flush with that edge of the mylar.

Instead of using masking tape to align the leading edge of both mylar and thread, you can make the mylar just a tiny bit longer in front of the guide foot. Start your wrap of regular thread on top of the mylar, but in from the leading edge by the width of one or two winds of thread. After the guide wrap is complete, make a trim band on the end *of NCP thread* in any color desired. The NCP is opaque, and the mylar will not bleed through.

In similar fashion, special rod-wrapping underpaint, or latex paint, can be used beneath wraps. The underpaint is available in white, gold, aluminum, and copper and will not be lifted by any wrapping finishes. When laying out the areas to be painted, mask off the ends with strips of masking tape. When the paint is brushed on, the edges will then be straight. The paint dries within fifteen to thirty minutes and you can then follow the procedures outlined for mylar. You can even carefully paint the portion of the guide feet that will be covered by the wrap for true color fidelity.

For even more varied results, make a solid wrap over mylar or underpaint with fine monofilament instead of thread. Monofilament in small diameters is quite tough and fray-resistant. It is available in clear and various tints. Since it is translucent, the finished color will be a combination of the tint in the mono and the color placed beneath it. Mylar will result in bright wraps, especially if the monofilament is clear, or nearly so. Underpaint with mono will produce more subdued colors. Monofilament can also be wrapped directly over the blank. In this case the color of the blank bleeds through. For example, slightly blue-tinted mono over a gold blank produces a light-green, semitransparent wrap. Use trim bands of NCP thread on the ends of monofilament wraps.

Amazing wraps

If you are bored with conventional wraps and want to make something that will never be duplicated in a factory rod, let me suggest you experiment with a technique I called "amazing wraps" in a *RodCrafter Journal* article. The idea originally came from RodCrafter Louis Hersh, and quite a few rod builders have added it to their bag of tricks. The technique is quite simple in concept, but extremely broad in the variety of results to be obtained. All that is required to give it a try are some felt-tipped marking pens of permanent ink and an assortment of 50-yard spools of thread.

In a way, you could say that you will be making your own custom "space dyed" thread. Simply make lines or bands of ink across the face of a spool of thread. The width of the bands can be varied, as well as their placement and number around the spool of thread. When the thread is wrapped on the blank it will produce different patterns. A third variable is the diameter of the blank. This is very much of a free-form art as you initially experiment. However, if you keep records of the three variables—(1) the width of the ink lines, (2) the space between lines on the spool of thread, and (3) the diameter of the blank—you will soon be able to control and duplicate your results.

There are some generalities that I'll try and pass along. The ink dries almost instantly, so there is little danger of smudging things. Narrow bands of ink pro-

Use of felt-tipped pen to draw lines on thread.

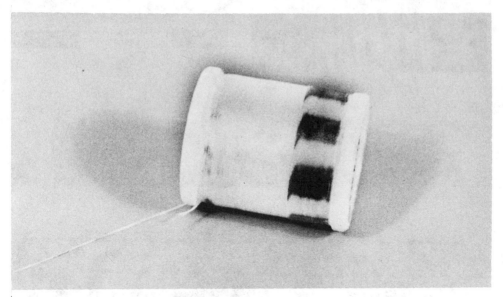

Ink penetrates only one layer of thread.

duce narrow lines in the wrap. Broad ink bands produce correspondingly wider lines in the wrap. When the width of the ink bands is held constant they produce comparatively wider bands when wrapped on a small-diameter blank, and narrower bands when wrapped on a large-diameter blank. Usually, the pattern produced in the finished wrap spirals around the blank to various degrees.

The fact that a blank tapers and has various diameters along its length causes a banded spool of thread to produce different patterns at the butt and the tip. These changes are progressive and subtle as you move along the rod, and sometimes produce an interesting and desirable effect. If you find the changes objectionable and want to keep the pattern the same as you move from butt to tip, it is relatively easy to adjust your markings on the thread. Just strip off the previously inked thread from the spool and make new bands slightly smaller and slightly closer together.

In addition to varying the number of ink markings on the spool and their width, you can vary their placement around the spool. An interesting effect results from alternating wide ink bands with narrow ink lines. The wrap, as you would expect, will have broad bands with narrow lines between. You can make your own custom ''tweed,'' ''jasper,'' or two-tone color combinations by placing many narrow ink lines close together on the spool.

Now that I have broached the subject of color, we have opened the door for still more expressions of your creativity. Felt-tipped pens, both narrow and broad,

Samples of "amazing wrap" effects.

are available in a huge assortment of permanent ink colors. Combine this with all the thread colors at our disposal, and you begin to get an idea of the possibilities. You can do a great job just using black ink on any color thread. Any dark ink looks good on white thread. Start mixing various inks with different-colored thread and you will be amazed at the rainbow of hues afforded.

Finishing the wraps usually requires no different treatment if you used permanent ink. To make certain, test your color preserver and finish on one of your experimental wraps. If you find the color does run or smear, get an aerosol can of spray lacquer that puts out a fine mist. Since it may be handy, you can try women's hair spray of the "hold" variety. The idea is to *lightly* dust the wrap with a fine mist of spray. Just make a few quick passes, trying not to get the surface wet. A very light coat like that dries in a few minutes and you can repeat.

238

After a few coats of the spray lacquer let it fully dry overnight, then apply your favorite finish in the usual manner.

Inlaid single wind

A definite aid to communication is established if we can label new things, or give them names. In that spirit, let's call the next wrap we will discuss an inlaid single wind. This is a wrap where one single strand of contrasting-colored thread appears in the midst of a solid wrap of another color. It is a wrap on which I have received many compliments and one which is quite versatile. I usually make three such inlaid single winds, spaced five turns apart, in a guide wrap or a simple hookkeeper wrap. It is equally at home on a brightly decorated rod, or as a distinctive touch on a conservative fly rod.

The basic technique is to wrap over the end of a single thread so that it is anchored. Then, make a single wind around the blank with the thread. The other end is then wrapped over until it is held in place, trimmed off, and the basic wrap continued. To make three such inlays grouped together, one length of thread is used and it is merely wrapped over between winds two and three.

To start, cut about a 10-12-inch piece of the desired color thread. It should

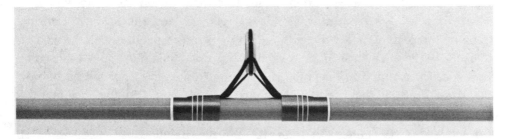

Inlaid single wind: Single thread spaced five winds apart.

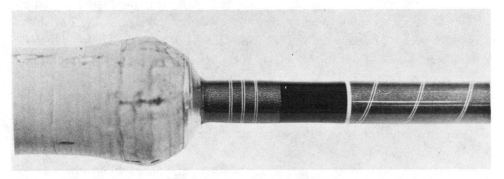

Inlaid single wind: Three threads treated as one, spaced five winds apart on hookkeeper wrap.

be Size A, the same as the basic wrap into which it will be inlaid. Plan where you want the three winds to be located on the wrap. Make your basic wrap from left to right up to a point about five turns before where the first wind will be located. Rotate the blank on your rod rollers until the back side of the rod is facing up. This is the side *opposite* the side usually seen by the angler as he fishes with the rod. For example, on a fly rod or spinning rod it would be the side of the blank on which the guides are located, since they are on the underside of the rod.

Now take your thread to be inlaid and lay it on top of the blank and along the axis of the blank. Place it so the end is just about up against the basic wrap. Use a small piece of masking tape placed about ⅛ inch from the end of the thread to temporarily hold it in position. Continue making your basic wrap, using a bit more tension than usual, so that it is wound right over the top of the end of the thread for five turns. Remove the masking tape. Keep tension on the wrapping thread coming from the spool, but push the wrapping thread a bit to the right. This provides space for you to inlay the single wind.

Hold the inlaid thread to the left of the main wrapping thread. With your right thumb and forefinger, hold both the inlaid thread and the wrapping thread together under tension as you rotate the blank one single turn. When the inlaid thread has come around the blank to the exact point from where it emerged, hold only the inlaid thread in your right hand. Keep tension on the basic wrapping thread from the spool, but turn the inlaid thread 90° and slip it underneath the wrapping thread. The inlaid thread should now be again parallel with the axis of the blank. Wrap three turns of the basic thread over the inlaid thread. At this point place your left thumb over the point where the inlaid thread completed its journey around the blank and met itself. With your right hand, gently pull the inlaid thread at a slight angle toward you. The object of this is that after two more winds over it, it will be directly in line with the point where the first inlay started. Make those two more winds.

Now repeat exactly the procedure you used for making the first inlaid single wind to make the second. When it has encircled the blank precisely one time, repeat the process of wrapping over it for five turns of the basic wrapping thread. At this point you can repeat the inlaid single wind process for the third wind. When it is completed, pull the inlaid thread under the wrapping thread and wrap over the end for about five turns. Trim the end of the inlaid thread close to the basic wrap and wind over it as you proceed with the wrap.

An area to check carefully as you make the wrap is that the inlaid thread should make precisely only one turn. It must come all the way up to the point where it started, but it must not go past it. Another potential problem area is keeping the points where each inlaid thread starts and stops exactly in line with each other along the axis of the blank. With a little practice you will find the wrap easy to make, and a very rewarding technique to use.

Banded spiral underwrap

An entirely different type of wrap that is eye-catching and distinctive on rods that are underwrapped is the banded spiral underwrap. Again, it is a wrap that demonstrates a high level of craftsmanship and attention to detail on the part of the rod builder. Fundamentally it consists of making a solid underwrap beneath each of the guide feet, but wrapping narrow banded spirals in the open area between the guide feet (under the guide ring). As such it employs both the color of the underwrap thread and that of the blank itself.

To make the wrap follow the procedure outlined earlier for determining the exact length of the underwrap. Using that procedure, you will have three scratches on the blank. One will be in the center and one will be at each end, indicating the start and finish of the underwrap. Before starting the underwrap, hold the guide in position on the blank so that the guide ring is directly over the center scratch. Note where each guide wrap will end at the frame supports for

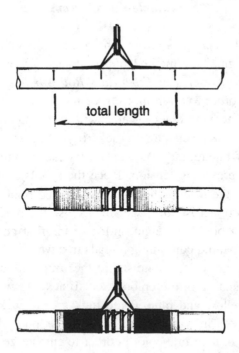

Banded spiral underwrap.

241

the guide ring. Make an accurate scratch on the blank beneath each of these points.

Start your underwrap in the usual manner at the first scratch and make a solid wrap up to the second scratch—the point where the guide wrap will end. Select the side of the blank on which you want the spiraled thread to show as it connects the bands. Now change your underwrap from solid to open, narrow-banded spirals. To do this, spiral the wrapping thread over the desired space, then make three winds tight together. At the conclusion of the third wind, again spiral the thread over the same amount of space and make three more tightly packed winds. Repeat this process of making narrow-banded spirals across the scratch marking the center of the wrap and up to the next scratch. This indicates the point where the other guide wrap will end. Here, return to making a continuous solid wrap all the way to the last scratch marking the spot where the underwrap ends. Check to make sure all the threads spiraling from band to band are in a line and identical. Adjust any as needed with the point of a thread tool or needle. With the underwrap completed, place the guide carefully in position and tape one foot. Make the guide overwrap in the normal manner.

Multiple-thread wraps

Multiple-thread techniques present the rod maker with a host of opportunities for unique design. This method of simultaneously wrapping two or three threads was explained briefly in *Fiberglass Rod Making,* but can be explored more fully here. In order to wrap up to three threads at the same time you need a thread holder and tension device which will accommodate that number. You will find ideas on this in the chapter on tools. If your present setup will not handle this many spools of thread and you want to try the technique, fall back on the "book method" of providing tension. Place the spools in teacups to keep them from rolling and set the teacups behind a good-sized book. Open the book, lay the thread all the way across the page, then close the book. If more tension is needed place another book or weight on top of the first book.

The basic idea behind combining threads in a wrap is to create an interesting visual effect. When viewed from a distance the wrap will appear to be of a color derived from the blending of the colors used. Black and white would look gray, for example, and yellow and blue would look green. Different shades of color than are normally seen in wrapping thread are thus possible. When using three threads, two can be of the same color in order to emphasize that color in the final shade. For example, two blue and one yellow would produce a blue-green shade.

It is just like mixing paint. A white or black thread can be used for the third thread to lighten or darken the final color.

A different effect results when the multiple-thread wrap is viewed at close range. The wrap takes on an almost iridescent quality from the tiny lines of individual thread. From quite close up the intricate nature of the work is apparent and immediately distinguishes it as being custom. Many rod builders who use this technique prefer Size D thread, since the separation of the colors is a bit more pronounced. Combinations of Size A thread will blend the colors more when viewed from moderate distances. A lot depends on the individual colors selected, but I have found that Size A often works well with three colors. Then, two of the three can be the same color, or black or white can be employed as the third thread. This aids in separating the colors, if that is desired. Some experimental test wraps will help you achieve the effect you want. Vary not only the colors of the threads used, but their sequence as well. Trim bands at the end of a wrap most often look best if made of one of the colors used in the mixture. They are quite easily made as part of the wrap. Start the wrap a bit farther from the leading edge of the guide foot. First wrap just the single colored thread you want for the trim band. After the desired number of turns, add the second thread by looping it singly over the blank for one turn, then winding both threads over the loose end. From there, just continue wrapping both threads together.

This process of adding a second thread (or two threads at once) is the key to mastering the multiple-thread technique. It may therefore be helpful to describe in detail the step-by-step process I use. Let's assume we are wrapping from left to right and the colors are black and white. We'll further assume the trim band is to be black. Start the black thread by wrapping it over itself and wind on five turns. Do not trim off the loose end of wrapped-over thread.

Holding the rod on your rollers with your left hand, rotate it so that the loose end is directly on top. Take the white thread in your right hand, place it over the top of the rod and alongside of the last black thread. Bring the white thread down over the front of the rod. Just move your left thumb over and clamp the white thread to the front of the rod, allowing the end to hang loosely. With your right hand, reach over the top of the rod and pick up the end of the white thread. Bring it up around the back, across the top, then down in front. Keep tension on the white thread with your right hand. (At this point the white thread has completely encircled the rod.)

You can now release the clamping pressure of your left thumb, since your right hand is pulling the white thread tight. Shift your left index finger to the right, and use it to push both black and white threads together over the top of the previous turn of white thread. This starts to lock the white thread in place. To keep the threads from slipping, place your left thumb over the threads where they crossed the white thread. Use your right hand to rotate the rod one-half turn—all the while keeping your left thumb in place holding the threads. After one-half turn, press your right thumb on top of the threads on top of the rod to hold them. Use your left hand to rotate the rod another one-half turn until the black and white threads together cross the loose end of the white thread for the second time. This locks the white thread in place. You can trim the ends of both black and white threads and continue wrapping with both threads together.

I said this process of adding a different-colored thread to a wrap in progress is the key to the multiple-thread technique. Let's examine just a few of the things that can be done with it. We can make a guide wrap that will change shade, or depth of color, over its length. This is a style sometimes used by RodCrafter Vaughn Corbridge. Let's suppose we want a wrap that will start as light blue and get darker in three stages as it progresses toward the guide ring. The first one-third of the wrap would be made of light-blue thread. Then a dark-blue thread would be added and the two threads wrapped together for the middle third of the wrap. A black thread would be added last and all three threads wrapped simultaneously to the end. There they would be inserted in a single tie-off loop and pulled under.

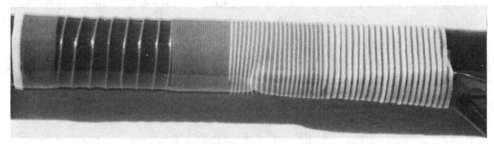

Multiple thread wrap. Single dark color for open spiral and first section of wrap; medium color added for middle; white added for last section.

The above wrap was described in thirds for an even progression of color. It could just as easily have been made in different proportions for a more rapid change of color at one end or the other. The colors used can each be quite different for dramatic, bold changes in shades. An example would be white, red, and black. Or, the colors can be quite similar for subtle, more subdued shifts in color. An example of this approach would be beige, brown, and dark brown.

So far we have only talked about adding colors as the wrap is made. Colors can also be dropped out of the pattern. This would enable you to make a wrap in reverse of the earlier example. It would then progress from dark blue, to medium blue, to light blue, as it moved toward the guide ring. We would start all three threads together—black, dark blue, light blue—in that sequence from left to right. First the black would be dropped, then the dark blue, and the wrap would be finished in light blue only.

To drop a thread, plan the arrangement of threads coming from the spools so that the thread to be dropped will be on your left. Let's suppose we are wrapping black and white together and we want to drop the black. Use your left thumb to clamp the threads in place against the rod. With your right hand reach up and cut the black thread about four inches above the rod, and pull the end to the right and under the white thread. Rotate the blank so the white thread lies over the top of the loose black end. A couple of more turns will lock it securely, and you can trim the end.

Being able to add or drop threads at any point increases the variations possible. We could make a wrap that starts light, gets darker in stages, then in reverse order gets lighter and returns to the original color. Naturally we are not limited to combinations of thread color that simply appear to get lighter or darker. We can also change the basic color itself. For example, from yellow to green (yellow and blue) to blue-green (yellow, blue, and blue) to green (yellow and blue) to yellow.

One or two narrow bands of color can be inserted in a wrap by the same technique. Make the wrap almost entirely of one base color. At the point you want the narrow band, add the second color. Drop it after the desired width of the band is made, and continue with the wrap in the base color. I think by this time you can see that there are an almost infinite number of variations of colors and patterns possible by using the multiple-thread technique.

The only other specific suggestions I can make which may be of help are as follows. When wrapping two or three threads at one time it helps to rotate the rod with your left hand. Place your right thumb and index finger about 2 inches above the rod and grasp the threads coming from the spools. This enables you to keep the threads in the proper sequence, adjust the tension, and lay the threads tightly against the previous winds. It also will help you to keep one of the threads from slipping between previously wound threads. When ending the wrap use a length of strong thread (or mono) as a single tie-off loop. Cut the threads and insert them in the loop. Before pulling the tie-off loop under, make sure the threads are still in the same sequence. After the tie-off loop has been pulled out, pull each thread tight, and trim it individually. Next, check the edge of the wrap where the threads were pulled under. It probably will be indented from the pressure of pulling the threads tight before trimming. Use a thread tool, burnisher, or your fingernail to carefully push the edge of the wrap out so that it is straight. In the process you will probably pull the trimmed ends under, eliminating any nubs in the finished wrap.

WRAPPING SINGLE-FOOTED GUIDES

Because of their many advantages the Fuji BSPHG single-footed guides (formerly designated BMKHG) are being used increasingly on fly rods, all but the heavy spinning rods, and on the tip end of fine-diameter casting rods, especially graphite rods. Various techniques of wrapping these guides are evolving and we will benefit from discussing some of them. Basic preparation of the guide feet has already been discussed under the section on preparation in the chapter on guides. I also carefully bend the guide ring up at a 90° angle. Instead of filing the underside of the foot flat and on an angle toward the leading edge (to keep the tip of the foot from sitting up on the wafflelike underside), RodCrafter Thomas D. Campbell files the bottom of the foot concave. He uses round, Swiss-pattern (needle) files on the smaller guides and a modified chain-saw file for the larger sizes.

Tom has also found that an excellent way to hold these guides on the blank for wrapping is to use short (⅛-inch) pieces of the smallest-diameter surgical tubing. These are placed on the blank beforehand by first slipping them over a pencil point. The point is slipped into the tip of the blank and the surge-tube bands are rolled off onto the blank. They are then positioned according to the guide spacing and slipped over the guide foot as far as they will go while still holding the leading edge of the foot tight against the blank. If, on the small-diameter tip section of a graphite rod, the surge bands are too large, a round toothpick is slipped between the tubing and the blank on the side of the blank opposite the guide. Strong thread is used to tie around the surge band, and as the thread is drawn tight and knotted, the toothpick is withdrawn. Tom then wraps the guides in the usual manner until enough thread is over the leading portion of the foot to hold it firmly. The surge band is then cut off and the wrap is completed over the rest of the foot.

Some people have advocated attaching the guide feet to the blank with instant contact cement, or Super Glue. Personally, I do not recommend this, since it is almost impossible to get the guides perfectly aligned in this manner. To do so would take much too much time. If they are wrapped under the proper tension, final adjustments can be made by moving the guides slightly as discussed earlier. Super Glue is permanent and a mistake once made cannot be corrected.

I started wrapping these guides when they first became available. At that time the shape of the guide was slightly different. I found that, for me at least, I got the best results from taping the guide foot with a piece of masking tape a bit longer than the guide foot, but placing it so that it covered only about two-thirds to three-quarters of the length of the foot from the leading edge to the guide ring. I then wrapped the guides starting at the guide ring and winding toward the end of the foot. As I progressed I peeled back the tape in stages. Today, the shape of the foot is improved, but I still use this method. You may want to give it a try.

A single or double trim band is easily placed on the end of the guide foot in the usual manner. Matching trim bands can also be placed at the guide-ring end. The only catch is that they must be put on the blank before the guide is wrapped in place. This requires a little planning.

First mark the position of the guide ring with a faint scratch from a scriber on the surface finish of the blank. From this mark *toward the tip*, measure the distance that will be occupied by your trim wrap or wraps. Make another faint scratch. Next to this second scratch wrap a small piece of masking tape all the way around the blank. It can be two layers thick if you prefer. This will be the temporary "wall" or "stop" against which you will start your trim wrap.

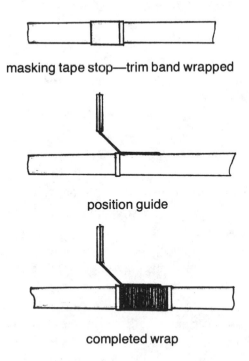

masking tape stop—trim band wrapped

position guide

completed wrap

Trim bands on both ends of single foot guide.

Place the blank (without the guide) with the tape to your left. Hold your tie-off loop in place (with the open ends to your left), and start your trim wrap directly over the loop, and against the tape. After three or four turns, when the wrapping thread is secure, cut off the excess end of the thread as close as possible. Complete the trim band with the desired number of turns and insert the end as usual into the tie-off loop. If a second trim band is planned, just duplicate the procedure to the right of, and against, the first trim band. If you feel these bands of thread are fragile—as they may well be at the tip end of the blank—set them with a single coat of color preserver, temporarily leaving the tape in position for protection.

To position the guide for wrapping, slide it along the blank until it is against the trim band. The guide ring will actually slide up over the trim band. This is necessary because of the design of the angled support from the flat foot to the guide ring. The end of the wrap closest to the guide ring must be against the trim band, with no space between. If a space does result, you know you did not move the guide ring far enough up over the trim band.

Some rod builders are wrapping the foot and then continuing the wrap for an equal distance on the tip side of the guide ring. This is fine if your objective is to modify the blank action by adding stiffness to the blank. Since this is not usually the case, it is better to wrap only the foot. In this way you are using the guide for the purpose for which it was intended and for which it is so outstanding—maximum unrestricted flexing of the blank. If the newness of the appearance concerns you, try adding a trim band at both ends of the wrap as outlined above. It will help provide visual balance.

WRAPPING ROLLER GUIDES

Offshore trolling rods are built on strong, thick-walled blanks for fighting powerful fish. Roller guides are a necessity on these rods, and the comparatively heavy guide feet must be attached securely. This is one situation where an under-wrap is required. It provides a nonslip base on which the guide feet rest and helps resist any twisting force that may push the guides out of alignment.

There was a time when extra-heavy thread was thought to be necessary. Sizes E, EE, and FF were used. This may have arisen in part from the use of silk thread, which was weaker and would rot in time if not adequately protected. Today's strong, rotproof nylon thread in Size D is more than adequate for the job, especially when combined with our modern wrapping finishes. The improved appearance of the wraps made with Size D thread is quite obvious and much more desirable. In those situations where the insurance of additional binding strength is desired by either the rod builder or the customer, the guide wrap is made of two layers. This is stronger and far better-looking than a wrap of EE or FF.

The size of the thread used for the underwrap is not important as far as the strength of the wrap is concerned. Its function as a cushion to protect the blank is minimal. One look at the heavy wall thickness of these blanks will prove this. As noted earlier, its job is to provide a textured gripping surface for the underside of the guide feet. Size A thread meets these requirements and makes a better surface on which to wrap a Size D guide wrap. It also looks better than heavier thread on the exposed portions of the underwrap.

To make the underwraps follow the same technique described earlier in this chapter for layout. There is one difference in the usual wrapping pattern on an offshore trolling rod. The underwrap for the decorative butt wrap often extends all the way to the butt guide, where it also serves as the underwrap for that guide wrap. With long underwraps on a rather large-diameter blank, hand work gets rather tedious and boring. For this reason, rod builders who make more than the occasional rod of this type use power wrapping equipment for the underwraps.

Wrapping technique with roller guides is essentially the same as used on other guides. The exception already noted is double-wrapping the guide feet (two layers) in some situations. A practiced and accomplished rod maker will often make these two layers from one continuous length of thread. He starts the wrap from in front of the guide feet and wraps up over the foot to the end nearest the roller. Instead of ending the wrap there, he then reverses his wrapping direction and wraps the second layer directly over the first. Each turn of thread must lie precisely on top of the turn of thread beneath it. Wrapping the same-size thread over itself is more difficult than wrapping over a smaller-size thread. It is much easier to have small gaps occur.

If you experience difficulty with this, let me suggest you tie off the first guide wrap at the end. Then give the wrap a number of coats of color preserver to fill in the valleys between individual threads. In this situation you can apply the color preserver at comparatively short intervals, since it will not receive any wrapping finish. With the valleys filled, it will be much easier to wrap the same-size thread on top.

As a general rule, trolling rods tend to be brighter and more decorated than other rods. The larger diameter of the blank and the larger roller-guide frames lend themselves to more intricate wraps. The underwrap automatically introduces a different color than the blank, and one around which the color scheme can be designed. For example, most guide wraps have at least one trim band of color beneath the center of the guide and over the underwrap. Often there are three bands of color, the two on the ends being different from the one in the middle. Naturally, such trim bands must be made before the guide is wrapped in place. If three bands of color are used, they can each be wrapped individually, or one longer band can be made with a narrow band overwrapped in the center. The rod builder who enjoys threadwork and color design will find offshore trolling rods a joy to wrap.

DECORATIVE BUTT WRAPS

It seems safe to say that the majority of custom rod builders enjoy making intricate decorative butt wraps. Some work with a number of bright, bold colors and patterns, while their more conservative brethren prefer fewer, muted colors and more delicate versions of essentially the same patterns. However, it has been my experience from holding seminars and speaking to groups all across the country that some of the greatest interest lies in threadwork—particularly at the butt end of the rod.

Butt wraps can become incredibly complex, both to make and to explain to another rod builder. Once a person understands the basic principles and techniques, he can develop and evolve his own unique wraps. I therefore feel that the most helpful and instructive approach we can take here is to first confine our discussion to the concepts and fundamentals common to making intricate wraps. We can then cover some specific wraps as examples of technique and to spark your own creativity.

CROSS WRAPS

It will help if we define a few terms. Diamond, chevron, and many other wraps, whether single or double, all have one thing in common: They are built around a series of crosses formed by thread spiraled up and down the blank. Many of the techniques used are the same. Therefore, let's give this family of wraps a name and call them "cross wraps."

Single cross wraps have crosses on only two sides of the rod, top and bottom (as viewed by the angler when fishing the rod). These could also be called the 0° axis and the 180° axis. Double cross wraps have crosses on four sides of the rod—the top, right side, bottom, and left side. We could also refer to these positions as the 0°, 90°, 180°, and 270° axes. Cross wraps can be made on more sides, or axes, but since the same principles apply to them that apply to double cross wraps, we'll use only those two terms.

Single cross wraps: 0° and 180°. Double cross wraps: 0°, 90°, 180°, and 270°.

Cross wraps can be made by spiraling a length of thread up the blank, then turning the same thread around and spiraling it back down. The threads forming the wrap are bound down with a base wrap only at the bottom. Cross wraps can also be made so that there are two base wraps binding down the threads, one at the top of the wrap and one at the bottom. Single cross wraps can be made in either style, but for practical purposes double cross wraps should only be made with two base wraps, one at each end.

When making any of the styles in the family of cross wraps you can elect to place them over an underwrap or directly on the blank. The underwrap is generally suggested for the beginner, since the friction between it and the wrap being applied helps hold the threads in position as they are wrapped. As the wrap gets more complex this same friction can work against the rod builder, since it is more difficult to slide threads to make slight adjustments. While the underwrap adds a contrasting color it also adds more bulk to the wrap. You will have to weigh these pros and cons against the effects desired when you plan the wrap.

Another thing you will have to decide on when you plan and lay out the wrap is the space between crosses. As a rule, if you want the threads to cross at a 90° angle (which would produce a square diamond, for example), use a measurement of about 3.5 times the blank's diameter for *single* wraps. This means that if the average diameter over the length of the single wrap was ½ inch, then the distance between crosses sould be 1¾ inches (½×3.5). On a *double* wrap use about 1.75 times the blank's diameter. For the same ½-inch-diameter blank you would place the crosses ⅞ inch apart (½×1.75).

If you use a longer measurement on a diamond wrap, the diamonds can be made to elongate *along the axis* of the blank. If you use a shorter measurement, the diamonds will elongate *across the axis*. This is a valuable control you have in making the shape of the diamonds just the way you want them to be.

Another option you have when planning a cross wrap is where on the pattern to locate the inner edge of the base wrap binding down the threads. The usual

251

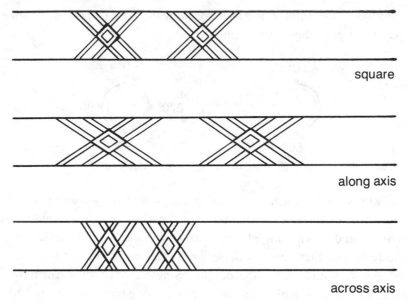

square

along axis

across axis

Spacing between crosses determines shape.

position is to start the base wrap right across the center of one of the crosses. While this is neat and symmetrical in appearance, it does place the base wrap over the thickest, bulkiest part of the pattern—making the base wrap itself bulkier. For this reason some craftsmen prefer to locate the base wrap between two crosses. Once again, you must make this decision before planning your layout.

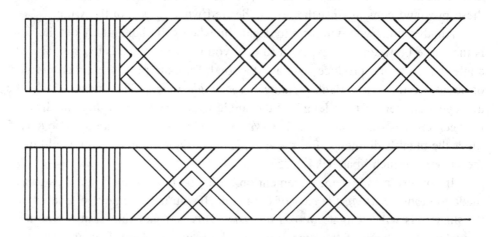

Above: Base wrap across center of crosses.
Below: Base wrap between center of crosses.

Layout for cross wraps

The quality and visual appeal of any cross wrap is based on a number of criteria. The first is how straight along the axis of the blank the crosses lie. They obviously should not angle off to either side. The second criterion is how accurate the space between each cross is. It should be exactly the same throughout. The third area of evaluation is how accurately around the blank the lines of crosses are placed. On a single wrap they should be precisely on top and bottom, or 0° and 180°. On double wraps each line of crosses sould be one-quarter of the circumference, or 0°, 90°, 180°, and 270°. If any of these criteria are not met, the wrap looks out of balance, the shape of some of the patterns will be different, and workmanship is judged to be sloppy. If time is spent beforehand in careful layout, making the wrap itself will be simplified and the results will be outstanding.

The layout, then, is just as important as the actual threadwork. There are undoubtedly a number of good methods to use to plan and lay out a cross wrap. Let me share with you the system that for me, at least, has produced the best results. The first thing to determine is the length along the blank that the wrap will occupy. If a hookkeeper is going to be included, the uppermost wrap holding the foot of the hookeeper will also serve as the base wrap at the bottom end of the cross wrap. This must be planned for in the layout. To simplify things I usually wrap the foot of the hookkeeper closest to the grip before doing the layout of the cross wrap. I then measure the length of the base wrap/hookkeeper wrap and scribe a circle around the blank. This marks exactly where the leading edge of the base wrap will be located.

You can then proceed with determining the length of the cross wrap itself. To do this first calculate the distance between centers of your crosses. If you want

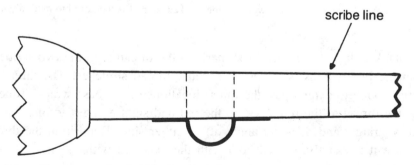

Locating edge of base wrap when hookkeeper is used.

the wrap to be about 5 inches long and the distance between crosses worked out to be 1 inch, you can plan on 5 inches exactly for the wrap. If the measurement between crosses did not divide evenly into the 5 inches, adjust the *length of the wrap* for an even number of crosses. When you have the length of the wrap, measure that distance along the blank from your previously scribed circle, and scribe another circle. You now have marks showing exactly where the wrap will be placed—a definite aid in the following layout steps.

We next need a method of marking the exact distance between centers of the crosses, and they must be on a straight line along the axis of the blank. The easiest, most accurate way to do this is with a length of thread temporarily taped on the blank, and on which the position of each cross is marked. A thread is better than trying to scribe a line along the blank, since minor adjustments can be made with the thread until it lies exactly straight on the axis. I use Size A white NCP thread and mark the location of the crosses with a pencil (ink bleeds along the thread and is less accurate).

First take a piece of paper, draw a line on it, and measure and mark the space between crosses. Lay the paper on your workbench. Cut a piece of thread longer than the wrap, and tape each end so the thread lies along the line on your paper. With a pencil carefully mark the thread at each point where a cross will be located. Untape the thread from the workbench and lay it along the top (0° axis)

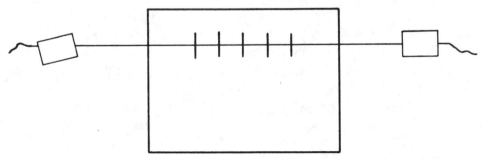

Alignment thread taped across paper with spacing marked. Pencil is then used to mark alignment thread.

of the blank. Align the first and last mark on the thread with the two scribed circles on the blank. This is important because thread stretches. The thread must be long enough to extend past the future locations of the base wraps. Tape each end of the thread to the rod. Pick up the rod and sight along it to make sure the thread is straight and does not angle off to either side. Reposition the thread to make sure it is exactly aligned both with the axis and with the scribed circles. See the top view of the blank on the layout diagram.

top view of blank

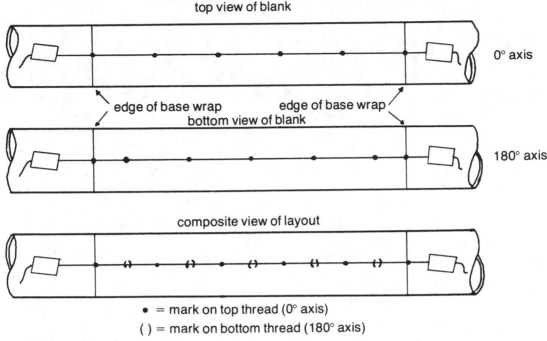

0° axis

edge of base wrap   edge of base wrap
bottom view of blank

180° axis

composite view of layout

• = mark on top thread (0° axis)
( ) = mark on bottom thread (180° axis)

Single cross-wrap layout of marked alignment threads. Note that points marking crosses on bottom view (180° axis) are halfway between those on top view (0° axis). Composite view shows position of both threads.

If you are making a *single* cross wrap, the crosses on the bottom (180° axis) of the rod will be located exactly halfway between each of the crosses on the top (0° axis). You must allow for this when you mark the second thread. The distance from each scribed circle to the nearest cross will be one-half the distance between crosses. For example, if your crosses are 1 inch apart, the measurement from the scribed circle to the first cross will be ½ inch. So, this time when you lay out the location of the crosses on your paper, first measure ½ inch and make a mark. Then make marks at 1-inch intervals until you get to the last cross mark. Follow this with another ½-inch measurement. Untape the thread and line it up along the bottom of the rod exactly as you did with the thread on top. See the bottom view of the blank on the layout diagram, and also the composite view showing both top and bottom alignment threads.

To make sure the two threads are precisely 180° apart, line up one of them with the guides. Then hold the rod vertically in front of you at arm's length so that each thread is along the *side* of the blank. Rotate the rod 180° so that you can view it from either side. In both positions the threads should be exactly on the edge. If not, reposition the thread not lined up with the guide.

If you have trouble placing the alignment threads exactly opposite each other on the top (0° axis) and bottom (180° axis), here is a clever method used by Rod-Crafter Thomas D. Campbell. Cut a narrow strip of paper so that it is *exactly* long enough for the ends to just touch when it is wrapped around the blank. You will do best to cut the strip a bit longer, then snip it shorter bit by bit until the ends meet precisely. Now, carefully fold the paper in half. The crease will be exactly 180° when the paper strip is again wrapped around the blank with the two ends meeting at the top. You can align the first thread with the guides, then use the paper to locate the second thread and mark the blank. For a double wrap you will need to locate the 90°, 180°, and 270° axes. Just fold the paper strip twice.

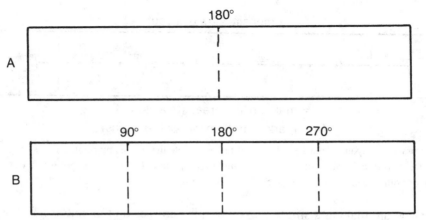

Strip of paper cut to exact circumference of blank. A: Folded in half for single cross wrap. B: Folded in quarters for double cross wrap.

You are now ready to spiral the first thread up and down the blank by simply following the marks on the alignment threads. See diagram showing the composite view of threads wrapped. Your wrapping thread should cross each alignment thread precisely on the marks. When the wrapping thread is in position, just snip each alignment thread at the end. Grasp one end with tweezers and carefully pull it out from beneath the wrapping thread at a shallow angle, so as not to disturb the crosses. If you want, you can fasten each cross in position with a small drop of color preserver.

The above procedure is for a *single* cross wrap. Let's see where it would differ if you were laying out a *double* wrap. First of all you will need four threads instead of two, and they will be placed on each side in addition to top and bottom. This would be on the 0°, 90°, 180°, and 270° axes. On a double wrap the crosses on top and bottom are directly opposite each other. It is the crosses on each side

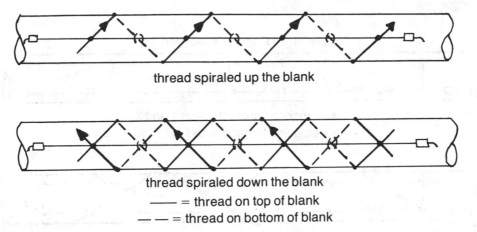

thread spiraled up the blank

thread spiraled down the blank

——— = thread on top of blank

— — = thread on bottom of blank

Composite view of single wrap. Top: First wrapping thread spiraled up blank. Bottom: Wrapping thread spiraled back down blank.

that are halfway between the crosses on top and bottom. This means that when marking the threads, you can do two at a time. The top and bottom ones will both be marked at even intervals—the 1-inch example used above. After they are taped in place on the rod, you can mark the two side threads (90° and 270° axes) at the same time. Since these must have the crosses halfway between the crosses on top and bottom, you will measure half the normal distance at the beginning and end of each thread. This will be ½ inch in the example above—the same as we did there (single wrap) for the bottom thread. They are then taped in place on the rod.

To get an idea of just what this looks like, let's again use a composite-view diagram. However, in order to see all four alignment threads, the diagram is made as if the blank had been rotated 45°. What had been the top alignment thread (0° axis) on our earlier diagram is now labeled #1. In the same fashion, our previous bottom thread (180° axis) is now labeled #3.

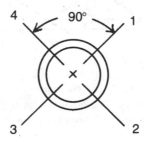

Double cross wrap, composite view. Blank rotated 45° in order to show all four alignment threads.

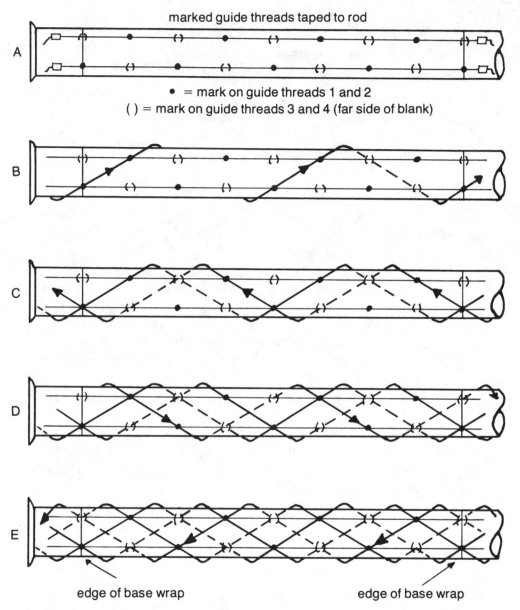

marked guide threads taped to rod

• = mark on guide threads 1 and 2
( ) = mark on guide threads 3 and 4 (far side of blank)

edge of base wrap   edge of base wrap

Double cross wrap composite view. A: All four alignment threads taped in place. B: First wrapping thread spiraled up blank. C: Second thread spiraled down blank. D: Third thread spiraled up blank. E: Last thread spiraled down blank.

The first drawing shows all four marked threads taped in their proper position on the rod. The second drawing is of the first wrapping thread after it has been spiraled up the blank. The third drawing shows the second wrapping thread spiraled down the blank. The fourth drawing shows the addition of the third wrapping thread spiraled up the blank, and the fifth is of the fourth wrapping thread spiraled down the blank. At this point the four alignment threads are snipped at each end and removed the same as we did for the single wrap. We now have an accurate layout for making a *double* cross wrap.

Techniques for cross wraps

With the layout completed we can turn our attention to some of the other common techniques and options for making cross wraps. Most rod builders learn these wraps by taping each course of thread in position with pieces of masking tape. A faster method is to use a fairly wide piece of double-stick tape (coated both sides) or carpet tape. It is first necessary to wrap the blank, hosel, or cork grip beneath with a layer of regular masking tape. This makes removal of the double-stick tape easier without damaging the rod. As each course of thread is wrapped, the ends are just pressed tightly in place on the double-stick tape with your thumbnail. The loose ends are then cut nearly flush with the edge of the tape. This keeps them from falling back on the tape and forming a tangle of imbedded thread. If for any reason, such as crowding or handling, the threads are not sticking properly to the tape, apply another layer over the top. Do the same if stopping for a prolonged period in the middle of the wrap. When the wrap is completed, cover the thread and double-stick tape with a layer of regular masking tape. This is just good insurance to prevent a thread or two from coming loose during the subsequent handling.

To remove the layers of double-stick tape after the wrap is bound down by the base wraps, use a pair of thin pointed scissors or snips. Slide the open point between the bottom layer of masking tape and the first layer of double-stick tape. Make small, snipping cuts across the tape. You will probably find that the cut proceeds in a small spiral rather than straight across. After the cut you can peel off the entire layer of tape. This is much easier than trying to peel off individual layers of uncut double-stick tape.

When first learning cross wraps, most rod builders use Size D thread because it seems somewhat easier to work with. After a bit of experience they will do well to switch to Size A. The smaller size will produce less distracting bulk and permit more intricate, finer-detailed patterns. It can be spiraled on the blank one thread at a time, or in bands up to four threads wide, just as easily as Size D.

If you frequently wind bands of up to four threads wide, and experience problems with it twisting as it is laid in position, here are some helpful hints. Always cut the threads longer than needed. Place the ends firmly on the double-stick tape two at a time and spread them fanlike on your workbench surface. Grasp them close to the tape where they are in proper position, and slide your thumb and forefinger up the threads a good distance from the blank. They should feed into your hands without tangles. Keep your hand at this distance as you wrap the band of threads, and move it to the right so that the thread is fed to the blank at the same angle as the spiral. Pressure of your thumbnail against your index finger should eliminate any tangles. However, even if a twist does slip through, the distance of your hand from the blank should enable the thread to lie in a flat, untwisted band.

A trick used by RodCrafter Harold L. Titus is to use a fine-tooth comb to separate the threads. He holds the comb in his right hand, teeth up, and runs the threads through the individual teeth. He places his thumb against the threads at the base of the comb. A jig designed by RodCrafter Don Dewey is also listed in the chapter on tools.

The base wrap which binds down the threads is common to all cross wraps. It should be smooth, tapered, and not bulky-looking. Use Size A thread with greater than normal wrapping tension. After about one-quarter to one-third of the length is covered, stop wrapping, but keep tension on the wrapping thread. Use fine-pointed scissors to first cut the threads just in front of the double-stick tape. Use the pointed end of a thread tool to comb the threads of the pattern straight. Again use the scissors to cut the thread, but this time close to the edge of the base wrap. Cut them on about a 45° angle. Take a razor blade or an X-Acto knife and trim the threads at an angle while fraying their ends. This will create fuzz, which can be removed with a piece of masking tape pressed over and then removed. Continue winding the base wrap over the angled and frayed ends of the threads and complete it with a tie-off loop. When burnishing the base wrap to close any gaps, always burnish *away* from the center of the cross wraps.

In just about every case you can improve the appearance of a completed cross wrap before the color preserver and wrapping finish is applied. A pair of thread tools, or one tool and a dubbing needle, can be used to push loosely packed threads into position. For example, on a diamond wrap push on opposing points of a diamond. Do this on both sides of an individual diamond to pack the threads together and to define the shape properly. If you cannot get the outer threads to stay in place, try pushing or burnishing threads from the diamond's interior toward the outside. This technique often works on larger diamonds. If neither of the above approaches works and the outside thread will not lie against the pattern, use the following. Put a drop or two of color preserver on the threads. Use a tool in each hand to push the thread in place along two points. Now blow on the thread to dry the color preserver more rapidly, all the while holding the thread in place.It only takes a minute or two until the preserver acts like glue.

A different technique and sequence for completing a cross wrap is used by RodCrafter Ken Wiebe. At the point where the wrap is ready to be bound down with the base wraps, Ken first gets all the threads in place as just described. Then, while the threads are still held in place by the tape, he gives the wrap three coats of color preserver. When dry, the wrap is glued in place. He then uses a sharp blade to cut the threads at an angle, forming a neat, smooth taper. Lastly, the base wrap is wound in position over the tapered ends.

SOME SPECIFIC WRAPS

Some specific wraps and the techniques used in making them are presented to add to your knowledge of patterns, as well as to provide ideas from which you can create your own new wraps. The patterns progress from the more simple to the more complex. Also, a technique explained in one wrap is frequently used in a succeeding wrap. As mentioned at the beginning of this chapter, it is assumed that the reader is already familiar with how to make a basic diamond wrap and chevron wrap. If not, he should refer to *Fiberglass Rod Making*, where detailed directions are given.

Mylar-accented diamonds

This is a wrap that requires no special threadwork beyond that employed in making a regular diamond wrap, yet it is quite striking in appearance. The center of each diamond is a tiny metallic highlight made of mylar. Mylar is a space-age foil, quite thin and pliable, yet tough and tarnish-proof. It is readily available from most fly-tying-supply houses, as well as art and graphic-arts stores. It comes in silver, gold, and many metallic colors. Silver is a good choice if you are using chrome-plated guides. Gold ties in well with the many anodized-aluminum gold reel seats.

Usually only a tiny diamond in the center of each regular diamond is desired. The mylar will stand out best if it is surrounded by darker-color threads. Therefore, you will want to plan your pattern so that the center colors are light (these are the ones covered by the mylar) and the next band is dark in order to border the mylar. For example, I recently wrapped a pattern in Size A thread on a gold blank that started with one center white NCP thread, bordered on each side by two metallic-gold threads. At this point the wrap was stopped and the mylar applied over the five threads forming the tiny diamond.

To apply the mylar, first cut it into a strip about three times as wide as the width of the threads to be covered. In our above example this was five threads. Give the back of the mylar strip a thin coat of Duco cement or a similar adhesive. Immediately cut the strip into squares. Place a square, adhesive side down, over each of the tiny diamonds thus far formed in the wrap. Press the mylar in place so the adhesive holds it there. You do not need a firm glue joint, just enough to temporarily hold the mylar in place while you wrap over the edges. The thread will hold it securely once the balance of the wrap is made. Incidentally, you can sometimes find mylar with an adhesive already on one side, which simplifies the job.

With the mylar squares in place on each diamond, proceed with making the wrap. In our example I next used a band of four dark-brown threads on each side and over the top of the mylar edges. As this band was applied it bound down the mylar. To give you an idea of what the rest of the wrap looked like, I then applied bands on each side consisting of the following: two brown, two metallic gold, one white NCP, two metallic gold, two brown, and two dark brown.

When you tighten up the wrap with a thread tool or your fingernails, first push the outside threads of each diamond toward the center, as usual. Then, to accurately shape and define the mylar centers, use a thread tool to push the inner dark threads around the mylar toward the *outside*. Apply a few coats of color preserver at the prescribed time intervals and finish wrapping finish.

Transparent mylar diamonds

This is the same kind of wrap just described, except that the creative technique of omitting color preserver is used. With no color preserver, the wrapping finish turns the medium-colored and dark-colored threads transparent. A square of mylar is placed over the first four or five threads. This mylar square should be almost as big as the diamond will be when it is finished. Any light-colored threads used in the wrap (white, yellow, goldenrod, light blue, etc.) must be NCP, or they will lose their color and become muddy. The medium and dark colors are all regular thread.

An example may help. The first course of Size A thread consisted of one white NCP bordered on each side by four white NCP. Over these white "crosses" were placed silver mylar squares. The wrap then proceeded with bands of each side of : four brown, two orange, one white NCP, two orange, and finally four brown. No color preserver was used and Crystal Coat two-part epoxy finish was applied directly to the wrap. You must use a thin finish about the consistency of varnish. A thick epoxy or polymer finish will not penetrate rapidly enough to displace the air trapped among the threads. The air will escape while the thicker finish is curing, and tiny bubbles will be trapped within it.

The finished diamonds have a unique three-dimensional effect. There is, of course, a tiny highlight of mylar in the center. The balance of the threads wrapped over the mylar square are all transparent except for the thin square of one white NCP Size A thread. This appears to float on top. The mylar square beneath the threads reflects light and increases the transparency effect.

A variation of this transparent wrap could be made without the tiny mylar diamonds showing in the center. In this case the mylar would be used only to reflect light through the diamonds, heightening their transparency. To do this you would have to glue the mylar squares on the blank (in exactly the proper positions) before any threads were wrapped. This can be done by carefully sliding the squares underneath the single thread forming the initial cross pattern.

Diamonds with trim threads

This style of diamond wrap is quite easy to make. In its simplest form it starts with an already completed diamond wrap. Additional threads are added a short space away from the outside edge of the diamond pattern. They are always parallel with the basic diamond wrap as they spiral up and down the blank. The number of these threads and how close or wide they are spaced, both to the diamond and to each other, is up to the person making the wrap and the effect he wants to achieve.

One version might consist of just a narrow band of two or three threads a very short space away from the outer edge of the diamond. This acts like an accent border surrounding, but not touching, the diamonds. Just one such band might be used, or two bands with a space between them might look better to the creator.

A different approach would be to place a band of threads exactly halfway between the existing diamonds. To do this, start a thread so that it crosses the base-wrap mark at a point exactly in line (on the same axis) as the centers of the existing diamonds. It should spiral up and down the blank at the same angle as the threads forming the diamonds. This will keep it centered in the open space. The crosses formed by this thread will be on the same line (axis) as the existing diamonds, and precisely midway between them. This can be simply a narrow band of thread, or it presents the option of using the first thread spiraled up and back as the center for a second, small diamond pattern.

Let's consider the first alternative, simply a narrow band of thread. Rod-Crafter Al Clark of A&J Custom Rods makes a very handsome wrap using this technique. Since he builds a great many custom saltwater rods, his wrap is often on blanks with a moderate to large butt diameter. Yet, his variation retains a delicate and intriacte appearance. He starts by making small diamonds, usually on a multiple pattern, such as double diamonds. He then places one single two-tone thread (''jasper'' or ''tweed,'' as it is sometimes called) between each of the diamonds. The tiny, repetitive color changes along the single thread make it almost look like fine wire. Combined with the many small diamonds it makes a most unusual wrap.

Small diamonds with single two-tone thread wound between diamonds.

Staying with the single, narrow band of thread between the diamonds, another effect is possible. In addition to that band, we could wrap another narrow band of thread (perhaps two threads wide) *over the top* of the previously made diamonds. This band would cross in exactly the center of each diamond. When the finished wrap was examined we would have a plaidlike pattern. Perhaps you are beginning to see the whole family of wraps that can be built around the basic diamond format.

Alternating diamonds

When we first discussed the technique of adding a thread midway between the existing diamonds, we said it presented the option of using that thread as the center for a second, small diamond pattern. Let's explore this further. To make a small, second set of diamonds, lay a thread or a band of threads to the right of this first thread, then an exact duplicate to the left—the same as for building any diamond wrap. A pattern can thus be developed of tiny diamonds alternated between the regular larger diamonds. The bands of thread forming the small diamonds will cross *over* the midpoint of the bands forming the larger diamonds. If it is preferred to have them underneath, then the small diamond pattern must be wrapped on the blank first. You would provide for this in your original layout.

Let's expand this idea even further. We could make the second set of diamonds identical to the first set, in both size and color pattern. However, if we used normal spacing between diamond centers to produce square diamonds, the wrap would get rather crowded and a lot of the effect would be lost. It would be better to increase the space between diamond centers when we laid out the first diamond wrap. This space could be as much as twice the normal measurement. The shape of the diamonds will naturally elongate along the axis of the blank, but this will add to the overall effect. Assuming this was a single diamond to start with (rather than a double diamond, which would probably get too crowded-looking), we would end up with a pattern of diamonds on the top and bottom (0° and 180° axes) and crossover bands of thread on each side (90° and 270° axes).

Solid line of diamonds

This particular pattern is made using exactly the same techniques as just described above for alternating diamonds. The difference is that the space between diamond centers on the layout is kept small enough so that the alternating diamonds will touch against each other, and the entire blank will be covered with thread. In this case, since the distance between diamond centers is smaller than normal, the diamonds will elongate across the axis of the blank.

Again, proper layout is the key. The trick is to determine beforehand the measurement across the diamonds in the first diamond wrap that will be made. We are referring here to the length of each diamond from one outside point to the other outside point, as measured along the axis of the blank. This does not have to be exact, since the sizes of the two sets of diamonds do not have to be exactly the same. In fact, the pattern looks more interesting if one set of diamonds is just slightly larger than the other. I have no formula for determining this. You can probably estimate closely enough by measuring some other diamond wrap previously made on which diamonds are approximately the same size and shape. If the diamonds on the other rod are closer to square, reduce the measurement proportionately for the elongation (and compression) of the new diamonds across the axis. Another approach is to make a single, sample diamond on a piece of card stock covered with double-stick tape. This technique for planning is explained further along in this chapter.

Once you have your estimated measurement, use it for marking the centers on your layout threads. Then proceed to make the first diamond wrap. When it is completed, carefully measure the space between the outside points between two diamonds. You want to place the initial thread on which your second diamond wrap will be built precisely in the center of the space between the first two diamonds. This is critical. You can use a long ruler which can be kept in perfect alignment along the axis of the centers of the first set of diamonds. Locate the exact center between each diamond and mark it precisely on the blank.

The second diamond wrap is made by first spiraling a thread up and down the blank so that it crosses exactly on the marks just made. Now proceed to build the second set of diamonds around that thread. As the width of the diamond expands you will reach a point where the diamonds touch. Unless you are extremely fortunate, there will still be gaps at many points where at least one more thread can be fitted into the pattern to completely cover the blank. Now comes some careful manipulation of the threads—the second trick involved in this wrap.

While good strong fingernails can be used, I strongly recommend the pointed end of a thread tool. Using it, you can force some threads farther apart so as to make way for the last thread or two needed to cover the blank. In some spots you may have to burnish, or push, threades from the *inside* of adjacent diamonds to fill a gap. Between opening or creating space in some spots of the wrap (for the last thread), and closing the gaps in other spots, you will get the wrap to fit together. A final burnishing of the entire wrap will close any small gaps, and your masterpiece is completed. It will be an impressive-looking wrap, sure to draw compliments and closer examination.

Lattice diamonds

We just discussed the technique of spacing the patterns and the threads so close together that the entire blank section was covered with thread. Not a bit of the blank showed through. Now, let's examine just the opposite technique—purposely allowing a lot of open space within the diamond pattern itself. The effect reminds me of old-fashioned garden trellises made of latticework, hence the name. It might look like lace to someone else. In any event, it is a light, airy pattern, both delicate and intricate-looking.

The basic idea is to form the regular diamond pattern, but not to lay each thread or band of threads against the previous thread. Instead, varying amounts of space are left between threads, or narrow bands of threads. Each must be exactly parallel to the previous thread and remain at the same distance as it is spiraled up and down the blank.

Variety is the key in designing and making these wraps. The center can be solid, forming a tiny diamond, or it can be completely open with the diamond being formed outside the center. The color of the blank can be allowed to show in the open spaces, or the blank can be first underwrapped. The large open pattern can be formed entirely of bands of thread in twos or threes, or these bands can be alternated and interspersed with single threads. A little experimenting will reveal some very interesting patterns quite applicable to certain rods.

Split-center diamonds

So far all our discussions of diamond wraps have been of conventional-shaped diamonds. Regardless of the manner in which it has been utilized, the pattern itself has been the same. The center has been of one color, formed in the shape of a diamond. Around it are concentric diamonds formed of alternating or different colors. It is possible to make the center of the diamond of two colors, splitting the pattern in half. The split can be either along the axis, or across the axis.

I first saw this pattern in wraps done by RodCrafters Al Clark and Joy Dunlap. To anyone used to seeing conventional diamond patterns, it is immediately intriguing. Joy and Al's offshore trolling rods are built for affluent customers all over the world. These anglers have seen a lot of diamond wraps, and the split center captures their attention and increases their pride of ownership.

The technique of making a split center is all in the sequence in which the threads are added. A base wrap is required at both ends, and in order to get an

Split-center diamonds—along axis.

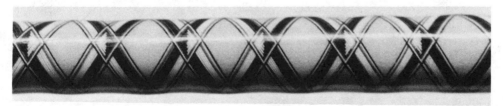

Split-center diamonds—across axis.

even effect, one thread at a time is wrapped rather than bands of thread. The best way to explain this is by way of examples.

Let's suppose we wanted to make a split center of black and white, and we wanted the split to be *across the axis* of the rod. First spiral your initial cross threads of either white or black. This is your center thread, as in any diamond pattern. We will first add a thread to the right spiraling up the blank, then a thread to the right spiraling down the blank. Next, we will shift to the left side of the center thread and spiral a thread up the blank, then spiral a thread to the left back down the blank. The color sequence would be as follows:

SPLIT ACROSS THE AXIS

Side	Direction	Color
right	up	black
right	down	black
left	up	white
left	down	white

This would be repeated as many times as necessary to build the center of the diamond to the size desired. Obviously, the split will not show up very well unless the center is reasonably large. Next, in order to define the outside of the diamond pattern, another color is added as a border and wrapped in the conventional manner. If it is red, then red threads (or bands of threads) are wrapped to the right *up and down* to the left. This could be followed by another border, possibly white or black, the same as making any diamond. In other words, once the size split center is made, the technique for the balance of the wrap is the same as any diamond.

If we wanted to make a split center of black and white, but wanted the split to run *along the axis* of the rod, the following sequence would be used:

SPLIT ALONG THE AXIS

Side	Direction	Color
right	up	black
right	down	white
left	up	white
left	down	white

Double diamonds

The real trick to perfect-looking double diamonds is in the layout. We have already covered this and diagrammed what the layout of the four marked alignment threads would look like. Also using a diagram, we traced the path of each of the four center wrapping threads. From here, it is simply a matter of wrapping the threads around the four center threads *in the proper sequence*. The sequence is emphasized because that is what makes exactly the same diamond pattern at each point where the initial wrapping threads cross.

Perhaps it might help to view the technique as making two separate diamond wraps, but constructing each stage simultaneously. To keep track of this process when making a double wrap, select one of the four threads forming the crosses and label it #1. Do this by placing a small square of masking tape on which you have penned "#1" on the outside of your piece of double-stick tape. A duplicate piece of tape labeled the same way is also placed on the other end of the wrap. Then make a #2 label and place it opposite the next thread forming the crosses. This too is labeled at both ends of the wrap. Now consider the #1 thread as your first diamond wrap, and the #2 thread as your second diamond wrap.

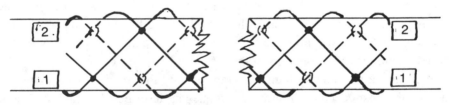

Double-cross wrap, labeling each set of crosses with masking tape to keep track of sequence.

Select the color and width of the first band of thread that will be placed around the center thread to form your diamond pattern. Let's suppose it is four threads wide and gold. Start your wrap with the #1 wrap. Spiral a band of gold to the *right of the #1 thread*, up the blank and back down. Now move over to your #2 wrap and spiral a band of gold to the *right of the #2 thread*, up the blank and back down. Go back to your #1 wrap and spiral a band of gold to the *left of the #1 thread* up and down the blank. Once again return to your #2 wrap and spiral a gold band to the *left of your #2 center thread* up and down the blank.

Get the idea? First to the right of #1, then to the right of #2. Next to the left of #1, then to the left of #2. This is the important sequence mentioned earlier. With it you are making two diamond wraps simultaneously. Always use this sequence and the individual diamonds of your double diamond wrap will be identical.

To simplify things we have said to spiral a band of thread up the blank and then back down. You will be using a base wrap at each end to bind down the wrapping threads, and will start the band by laying it across the double-stick tape at the bottom of the wrap. When you get to the double-stick tape at the opposite end of the wrap you will lay the threads over it. At that point you can trim the thread ends forming the band and start another band of threads to go back down the blank. Just be sure you place it to the right side of the #1 center thread. On some patterns, such as split diamonds, this method is necessary.

Another approach is to use a band of thread long enough to be spiraled up and down the blank. In this case when you reach the upper piece of double-stick tape, lay the band across it to anchor the band of thread. Then take a turn around the blank just past the double-stick tape, reverse direction and spiral the band back down the blank to the right of the #1 center thread. This method is fine for regular diamond patterns.

Labeling the center threads at each end of the wrap is important. It will allow you to always bring your band of thread back down the blank by bordering the proper thread. As you do, always place the band on the *same side* of the center thread as you did when you spiraled the thread up the blank. If you went to the right when going up, you must go to the right when coming back. If you went to the left going up, you must go to the left when coming back.

To complete the double diamond wrap just add the required bands or single threads of the desired color. Follow the sequence described for each additional color. When you have added all the colors and bands desired, place a piece of masking tape over the thread-covered pieces of double-stick tape. This will lock them securely in place. The pattern will extend past the scribed circle marking the inner edge (toward the center) of each base wrap. All that remains is to bind down the pattern at each end with a base wrap.

Double chevrons

The layout and general method of forming a double chevron pattern is essentially the same. The sequence of going first from the #1 thread (or #1 wrap) to the #2 thread (or #2 wrap) is the same. The difference is that you do not make a chevron wrap by bordering a center thread with bands to the right and then to the left. Instead, each succeeding band of thread is always placed *to the right* of the preceding thread or bands of thread.

Thus, when making a double chevron wrap the overall sequence would be as follows. The first band would be spiraled up and back *to the right* of the #1 thread. Then you would move to the #2 thread and spiral a band up and back *to the right*. At this point you would change color and spiral a band *to the right* of the #1 wrap. The same color just used would then be spiraled *to the right* of the #2 wrap.

Colors and width of bands would be changed as needed to develop your pattern. Each succeeding band would always be placed to the right of the preceding band until the pattern is complete. By using this sequence each individual chevron would be identical. The wrap would be bound down with a base wrap at each end, the same as for a double diamond pattern.

A very interesting "full" wrap can be made of a double chevron by spacing the patterns close together. You provide for this when you mark your alignment threads. Use a measurement of no more than one-half of that required for a 90°, or square, crossing of threads. Depending on how wide a band of wrapping thread you use, and the space between patterns, you can make a wrap that allows only a small amount of the blank (or underwrap) to show through. The appearance is one of a relatively tight and full weave.

On chevron wraps in general I see quite a few that are made with bands of exactly the same width. While this undoubtedly has its place, I think you will find more interesting designs can be made by varying the width of the colored bands. For example, here is a pattern I made recently of Size A thread on a gold blank: two brown, two dark brown, one white, two dark brown, four metallic gold, one dark brown, four metallic gold, two dark brown, one white, two dark brown, two brown. Another effective use of color on chevron wraps is to separate different bands of medium and dark colors with a single white thread. Or, if the wrap is mostly of lighter threads, to use black or a very dark color as a single thread divider. This brings out the arrowpoint shape of the chevrons.

When making a double chevron you will be using base wraps at each end, and pieces of double-stick tape to hold the threads. Instead of running each of the two chevron wraps in the same direction from the butt end, consider running one from the tip end. The resulting design will have points facing each direction. Use the same sequence of alternating from the #1 wrap to the #2 wrap. The only difference is that the #2 wrap starts at the tip end and spirals down toward the butt, then up toward the tip end.

Multiple chevrons to produce "diamonds"

Our discussion of layout and wrapping sequence have been for the double cross wraps. As we have seen these are built on four axes around the blank: 0°, 90°, 180°, and 270°. To put it another way, we have made a pattern for each one-quarter of the blank's circumference. Naturally, a rod builder is not limited to just a single cross wrap (two axes) or a double cross wrap (four axes). If the diameter of the blank is large enough and/or the size of individual patterns is small enough, you can make a wrap built on any even number of axes. As long as you lay out the alignment threads properly and follow the sequence of moving from the first wrap (#1) to the second wrap (#2) to the third wrap (#3), etc., you will experience no difficulties.

A favorite wrap of mine consists of a pattern of chevrons on eight axes, or eight times around the circumference. I find the wrap generally fools people into thinking it is some kind of a diamond wrap. This results because I place a light underwrap on the blank first, then make the chevrons of medium and dark colors. The small spaces between the chevrons are diamond-shaped. They stand out because of the light-colored underwrap. It is a comparatively simple wrap to make, yet it looks quite complex.

Multiple chevrons to produce "diamonds."

Multiple chevrons are easier to make in one regard than multiple diamonds. If you were to make a wrap of eight diamonds around the blank you would really be making four diamond wraps. As we have seen, you would have to follow the sequence described and make all four simultaneously. However, because of the nature of the chevron pattern itself, you can first lay out the wrap for a double chevron (four axes). After completion of the first double chevron wrap you can add another double chevron wrap consisting of four more axes. This second pattern is shifted 45° around the blank. If the thread pattern is identical to that used on the first double chevron, they both will blend together perfectly.

To make this wrap, first determine the total length, including base wraps, and make a light-colored underwrap of that length. Following the procedure explained earlier, measure and mark four alignment threads and tape them in place along the four axes of the blank. After four threads are spiraled to form the crosses, snip the alignment threads and carefully remove them. Build a double chevron wrap by adding bands of thread alternately to the right of the first (#1) and second (#2) wraps. Record the number of threads of each color in each band.

To add the second double chevron you probably will not need new alignment threads, since you can align it around the wrap just completed. However, if in doubt, make four new alignment threads and tape them to the blank so they divide the wrap already on the rod. After the first four wrapping threads are spiraled to form crosses, the alignment threads are removed. If you do not use alignment threads you can shift the pattern 45° by sighting on the existing wrap. Now, refer to your notes. Wrap the exact same bands as to number of threads and color as you used on the first wrap. Remember to shift back and forth between your new #1 and new #2 wraps, but always wrap to the right.

When the entire wrap is finished, bind down each end with a base wrap. Use a pair of thread tools or your fingernails to push the threads together. You want to make sure that the light-colored diamond spaces from the underwrap are all the same size and shape.

Diamonds surrounding diamonds

This is a wrap I have used mostly on medium- to large-diameter saltwater blanks, but the technique is applicable to most rods except those of very small diameter. As is true of so many wraps, there are quite a few variations possible. If you understand one specific version you will know the fundamentals and can then make your own designs.

Visually the wrap consists of four small diamonds surrounding, but separate from, another identical diamond. This main pattern is alternated with small diamonds. From a construction standpoint it consists first of a double diamond wrap of small diamonds on four axes. Over top of this, on just two axes, is built the pattern of the four surrounding diamonds.

To make the wrap, first make the double diamond pattern, using small individual diamonds. Keep notes on the numbers of threads, their color, and their sequence so you can duplicate the pattern exactly in the balance of the wrap.

The border diamonds surrounding every other diamond in the initial wrap are formed by first spiraling a thread on each side of *one* of your original two diamond wraps. These threads must be the same color as the center thread used in your original pattern. Since they will be the center threads for your border diamonds, they must be placed far enough from the edges of the initial wrap to allow a space between the border diamonds and the center diamond *after* the border diamonds are completed. This means you must allow for the width of the border diamonds as they are wrapped on each side of the center thread. When wrapping these center threads, take care to keep this distance from the edge constant.

As we did when we wrapped the double diamond, it will help to label the center thread on one side #1 and the center thread on the other side #2. Refer to the notes you made on your initial pattern, and repeat the steps exactly. First wrap to the right of your #1 center thread, then to the right of your #2 center thread. Next, wrap to the left of #1, then to the left of #2. The sequence is the same as the one you used in making the initial double diamond.

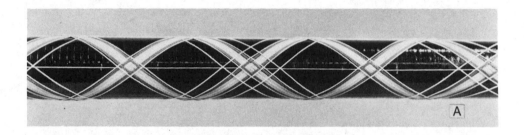

Diamonds surrounding diamonds. A: Small double diamonds completed. Alignment thread and two center threads in place. B: Alignment thread removed and center bands of surrounding diamonds made. C: Completed wrap.

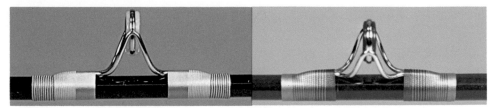

Multithread wrap of dark blue, light blue, and gun-metal silver.

Multithread wrap of green to dark blue, with guide shock ring dyed blue.

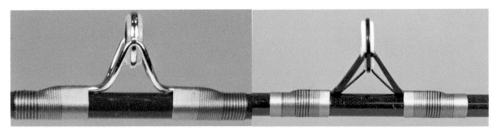

Multithread wrap of dark brown, brown, and beige.

Multithread wrap of green, dark green, and black.

Single inlaid red thread spaced five threads apart. Artificial underwrap done in banded spiral fashion with matching red trim and dyed guide shock ring.

Banded spiral underwrap.

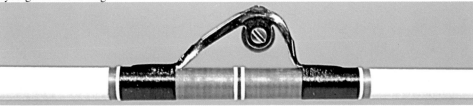

Gold metal underwrap with triple guide trim ring of white and red. White trim at end of black guide wraps.

Triple trim bands of black, red, and white on each end of gun-metal silver single foot wrap.

Transparent mylar diamonds done with no color preserver.

Single diamond wrap with small diamonds between.

Line of diamonds of solid thread wrap done in black, gold metal, and red.

Typical double diamond wrap.

Typical double chevron of green, dark blue, and black with single white threads separating colors.

Double chevron done with very short spacing between centers. Gold metal, dark brown, and orange on gold blank.

Chevrons done on eight axes to produce white diamonds from underwrap.

Double chevron on short spacing with single cross thread over centers of goldenrod diamonds showing through from underwrap.

Diamonds surrounding diamonds on single pattern. The small center diamonds are done on a double pattern.

Single pattern of four diamonds.

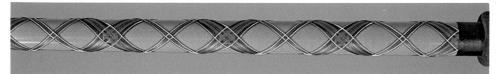

Split diamonds surrounding tiny center diamonds with no space between each. Small diamonds alternating in space between.

Snakeskin pattern.

Tartan wrap.

Tartan wrap.

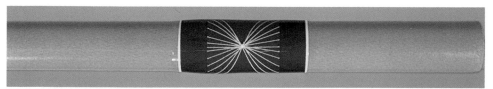

Radial pattern.

Tartan wrap.

Handle assembly of Customgrip with Vee grooves, walnut trim rings, and reel seat and butt cap with Vee grooves cut through anodizing.

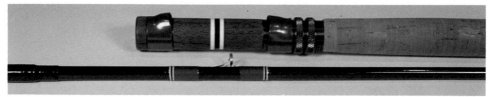

Walnut fly seat and matching walnut button. Center of seat inlaid with white and black plastic trim rings. Trim at end of guide wraps repeats theme of white, black, white.

Handle assembly with walnut insert in skeleton spin seat and matching walnut hosels. Cork has burnt-cork trim rings.

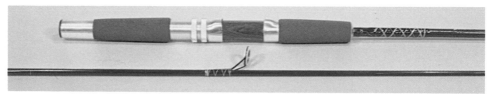

Handle assembly of polished skeleton spin seat (anodizing removed) and polished butt cap. Walnut insert and Customgrips.

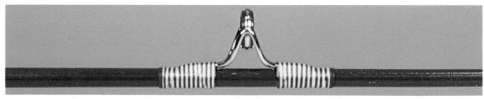

''Amazing'' wrap of red and black Flair pen markings on goldenrod thread. Guide shock ring dyed red.

One of the variations possible is to eliminate the space between the border diamonds and the center diamonds. This can be done by carefully measuring the width of the band of thread forming the original diamonds. Place your center threads for the border diamonds one-half this width from the edge. The last thread on the outside edge of the border diamonds should then fit against the edge of the center diamonds. You will probably have to push some threads to one side, at spots, to make it fit. It will also be necessary to push the entire finished wrap together tightly with a pair of thread tools or your thumbnails.

Other variations would be to make the sizes of the individual center diamonds different from those of the border diamonds. They could be larger or smaller. Another possibility is to make the color pattern of the center diamonds different from the center diamonds. You can use the same colors, but change the pattern. Once again, if you understand the basic technique you can easily design your own unique wraps.

Combining techniques. Split diamonds surround a small center diamond but no space is provided between diamonds.

Straight cross (reverse diamond)

Regular diamonds are made by adding threads alternately to each side of a center thread. Or, to put it another way, we work from the inside (center) to the outside. If you are not already familiar with it, I would like to introduce you to a different technique that is fundamental to another series of wraps. It is working from the outside to the inside. That's why some people call it a "reverse diamond"—it is built in reverse order.

The simplest form is a straight cross surrounded by concentric crosses. Since you work from the outside toward the center, you will have to first spiral a pair of *parallel* threads up and back down the blank. These threads will become the outside edges of the pattern.

To lay out this pattern use two alignment threads as you would for any single cross wrap. After you measure your spaces for centers on a sheet of paper, also measure a fixed distance on each side. The pair of marks surrounding each center will be the ones marked on your alignment threads. They represent the outside edges—or the width—of your pattern. Therefore, they should be adjusted to the size of the blank and the width of the wrap you want to make.

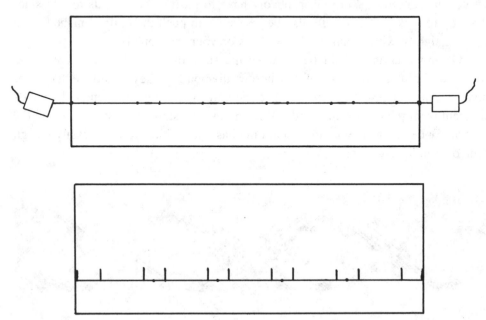

Marking alignment threads for straight cross. Top: Paper with centers and space on each side for initial parallel wrapping threads. Bottom: Thread taped across paper and outside marks made on thread.

With the alignment threads taped on top (0° axis) and bottom (180° axis), spiral a thread of the desired color up the blank and back down. The thread should cross the second mark in each pair. Take another thread of the same color and this time cross the first mark in each pair. Snip the alignment threads and carefully withdraw them.

The wrap will be built by laying threads toward the inside of each of these threads. As in making a regular diamond wrap, a standard sequence is important. The first band of thread should border the upper thread (the one toward the tip of the rod), both going up the blank and coming back down. The second band, the same color and width as the first, should border the lower thread. Keep repeating this sequence, changing colors and widths of the band to form your pattern.

The wrap sequence shown in the photos was done by RodCrafter Sandy

Stein. The pattern he used *on each side,* from the outside in, was: one yellow, four dark blue, two light blue, and three dark blue. At this point there was space for four more threads to fill the center. He used a band of two yellow threads spiraled up, then down the blank.

The addition of the final band of threads to fill the center can be a bit tricky. Before wrapping it, check the pattern to make sure there is enough space in the

Straight cross (reverse diamond) wrapping sequence.

277

center at all points. If not, open the center by pushing the threads outward with a thread tool or your thumbnails. When the center is open, wrap the final band of thread in place. It may be necessary to open the center more as you squeeze in the last threads. Now go over the wrap and push all the threads toward the center from each side. This will pack them tightly and eliminate any gaps.

The final photo shows an easy variation to dress up the wrap. It consists of some open diamonds placed over the top of the straight cross. Bands of dark blue and yellow were used.

Four diamonds

Now that you have the hang of working from the outside to the inside, let's move on to a bit more complex wrap. On this, four small diamonds, all touching together, are formed from one band of thread. At least that is the visual effect. From a construction standpoint, you build two diamond patterns side by side in the conventional manner (from the center of each, outward). However, they have been carefully spaced apart so that they come together in the center forming a straight cross as in the previous wrap.

Since each of the two diamond patterns is made in the conventional manner, you will need two center threads. They must be parallel, and the space between them should be the marks used on your layout alignment threads. The wider the space, the larger will be the overall pattern. To determine this space you can measure the width of an existing normal diamond wrap, or you can make a test pattern on a card faced with double-stick tape as explained later in this chapter. From making my share of various wraps, I have found that nine Size A threads are 2mm wide. Perhaps this will be of help.

Lay out the pattern on the rod in the same manner as for the straight cross. After spiraling your two center threads up and down the blank, you will have an initial guide pattern similar to the one used for the straight cross. The difference will be that the two parallel threads will be a bit closer together. These, however, are center threads, so proceed to build a conventional diamond around each. As always, sequence is important. Add a band of threads to the right of the #1 center thread, then to the right of the #2 center thread. Repeat the process first to the left of the #1 thread, then to the left of the #2 thread.

Continue building the wrap until you get to the point where there is only a narrow space between the two patterns. As in the straight cross, open the center to accept the final band of thread both up the blank *and* back down. Work this band of thread into the wrap, then push all the threads together from the outside. This defines the shape and eliminates any gaps.

An observation may help in making both of these last two wraps. Work as carefully as you can, but do not be overly concerned about having the exact amount of space in the center to accommodate the last band of thread. It is better if the space is slightly larger than needed, since the final step of pushing the threads together toward the center will tighten everything and allow you to accurately form the outer shape.

Snakeskin (nine diamonds)

Sometimes I wonder if I'm the only rod builder who has a habit of giving his wraps pet names. The first time I made this pattern it was of brown, gray, and black, and to me it looked like snakeskin. So, that's what I labeled my notes, and that's what it has been to me ever since.

The appearance is of rather large diamonds, the centers of which contain nine tiny diamonds. Basically, it is made in a double-cross-wrap style of three conventionally built diamonds. The three lie side by side so that as they are built out from the center, they meet forming one solid pattern. Borders are then added around this solid center to make large diamonds.

In our exploration of some specific wraps we have been more or less progressing from the simple to the complex. Let's pause a minute and see what combination of techniques is employed in making this wrap.

1. It is a double cross wrap with diamonds on four sides (0°, 90°, 180°, and 270° axes). We therefore will be making two wraps simultaneously.

2. There are three center threads to each individual pattern, and diamonds are built conventionally (from the center out) around each center thread.

3. Careful spacing between the three parallel center threads is necessary so the pattern fits together.

4. Since the three parallel diamond patterns meet, there are two center spaces into which final bands of thread must be fitted. (There was only one such center space in the previous four diamonds pattern.)

To make the wrap, mark your four alignment threads with three sets of marks at each center space. Since this is a double wrap, remember the top (0° axis) and bottom (180° axis) threads will be the same. The two side threads (90° and 270° axes) will have the marks shifted one-half the distance between centers. Following the marks, spiral three sets of threads up and back for the one wrap, and three sets up and back for the other wrap. Remove the alignment threads and label one set #1 and the other #2—the same as you would for any double pattern.

Starting with the middle center thread on the #1 wrap, place a band of thread on each side. Move over the #2 wrap and repeat the process. The first photo in the sequence shows the wrap at this stage.

Add bands of thread on each side of the uppermost center thread on the #1 wrap. Shift over to the #2 wrap and do the same. Now add bands on each side of the center thread nearest the butt on the #1 wrap, and repeat on the #2 wrap. This is the stage pictured in the second photo.

A darker color (I used red) is chosen to complete and define the tiny diamonds. The number of threads used will be determined by the space remaining that must be filled. Before wrapping make sure the center spaces are opened sufficiently throughout the wrap. Add the dark bands to the center spaces *and* to the outside. This forms the nine tiny diamonds. Push all threads tightly together. The result is shown in the third photo.

From this point on you treat the wrap the same as any double diamond. Add a border of light-color thread by alternating first to the right of the #1 wrap, then to the right of the #2 wrap, followed by the left of the #1 wrap and the left of

Snakeskin (nine diamonds) wrapping sequence.

the #2 wrap. Following this sequence add individual threads, or bands of thread, until the diamonds are of the size desired. The fourth photo shows all but the last border in place.

This wrap generally looks best if the size of the diamonds is rather large. On the example pictured I added a final band of four black threads. Since the blank was also black, this tied the pattern together nicely. The final result is seen in the last photo.

Tartans

We mentioned earlier that we can get a more or less plaid effect by adding bands of thread to the open spaces between individual diamonds, and even by adding some directly on top and through the center of individual diamonds. This effect can be quite interesting and beautiful.

Actual plaid fabric, on the other hand, is made by weaving different-color threads at right angles. This weaving produces a pattern that is dark (where dark threads cross with dark threads), light (where light threads cross with light threads), and a color halfway between (where dark threads cross with light threads). You can see this by examining a piece of plaid cloth. The mixture of light and dark colors, or "bleeding" of the two colors, is the problem in making plaid or tartan butt wraps.

Tartan, incidentally, refers to the specific plaids woven originally by the Scottish Highlanders, where each clan had its own pattern. Personally, I have always been attracted to these tartans with their rich heritage. They are true classics and will always endure. Some of the patterns are frequently used in more expensive clothing, and the connotations seemed ideal to me for custom rod work.

My own experience has been that the best way to wrap a facsimile of a tartan or any plaid is to have an example in front of you. I use articles of clothing, but you can also get books and charts in full color. By studying the tartan, you can determine the proportions of the various parts of the design, as well as the colors used.

To reproduce the bleeding effect of a mixture of light and dark threads, we need to fall back on a technique of threadwork discussed earlier. When we talked about making transparent mylar diamonds, we found that if no color preserver is used on regular thread it becomes transparent. We also found that NCP thread with no color preserver remained opaque. In making a tartan we will make creative use of these characteristics. No color preserver will be applied to the wrap, just the wrapping finish.

A tartan wrap is made in two layers. The first is entirely of regular thread, and this is where the bleeding of colors takes place. The second layer, wrapped on top, consists only of a few trim threads. If medium or dark colors are used as trim threads they can be regular thread. However, any light-color trim threads must be NCP to remain opaque.

To obtain the necessary bleed of colors in the first layer, *regular white* (not NCP) is wrapped over darker colors. When the wrapping finish is applied, the white becomes transparent enough to lighten the darker colors underneath. You're probably saying, "That's fine for the bleedthrough of darker colors, but how do you keep the regular white thread white when there is nothing but the blank beneath it?" The answer—paint the blank underneath the wrap white. Then, the transparent white regular thread will allow the white paint to show through. You must use white wrapping underpaint, or a white latex or acrylic paint. Otherwise, the solvents in the wrapping finsih will lift the paint and ruin the wrap.

The first step, then, is to determine the length of the tartan wrap alone (without the binding base wraps). Measure this on the rod, in the proper location, and scribe two circles. Paint a full coat of white underpaint between the circles. It dries and can be wrapped over in fifteen minutes to a half hour. Measure and make note of the distance from the end of the foregrip to the nearest edge of paint, and also the length of the painted area. You will need these measurements later.

The wrap is built around a double diamond wrap, so place your alignment threads accordingly and spiral the desired center colored threads up and down the blank. After removing the alignment threads, start building your wrap in the normal sequence for a double diamond. The first photo shows the painted section of the blank with the initial bands of thread attached over double stick tape.

As you build your diamond pattern, concentrate on reproducing only the main background of the tartan—the portion where the bleedthrough of colors occurs. Do not be concerned with the fine trim lines, since they will be added afterward on top of the first layer.

When you examine a tartan closely you will frequently find that the colors woven at right angles are not always the same in each direction. This was true in the tartan reproduced in the wrap photographed. The medium-color bands were green, but the darker lines in one direction were black while those at right angles were blue. Unfortunately, a black-and-white photograph reproduces blue and green as just about the same shade of gray. All the threads forming the dark bands were black when spiraled up the blank, but the same bands were blue when spiraled down the blank.

Build your diamonds to resemble the dark portion of the tartan as closely as possible. Study not only the pattern, but the relative proportions of the overall dark area to the light area. When the dark area is complete, stop and push all the threads tightly together. This is the stage of the wrap shown in the second photo.

From here on you use *regular* white thread and keep adding bands around the outside of the diamond pattern. The third photo shows the initial white bands in place. White thread is added until all space between the diamonds is completely covered. You will reach a point where only a narrow space exists between

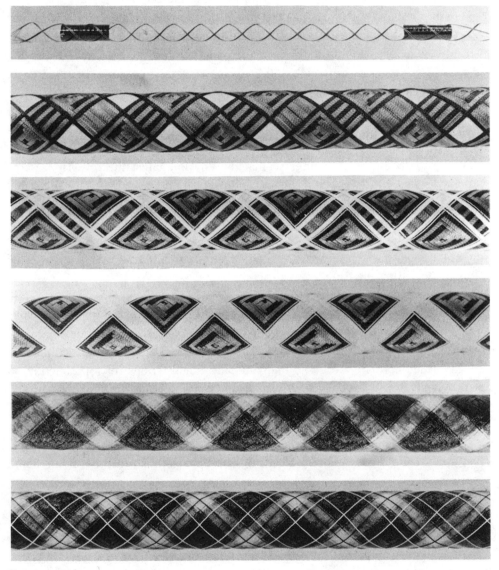

Tartan wrapping sequence.

patterns. Quite probably the space will not be exactly the same throughout the wrap. You will have to open this space by pushing against the threads as explained in previous wraps. The size of the remaining space determines how many white threads are needed to fill it. Don't be concerned if the space along one spiral needs more threads than another. Use whatever number of threads are needed and push and shove until all is covered with white thread. In particularly tight spots, push the point of a thread tool directly ahead of the last white thread to open a space for it. The fourth photo shows all of the white threads in place.

You are now ready to apply the wrapping finish to create the desired bleed of colors. Please note this *must* be a thin-consistency finish such as Crystal Coat two-part epoxy. You need complete penetration of all the Size A threads, and the finish must be thin enough to displace air trapped among the wrappings. Heavier epoxy and polymer finishes will not do the job.

Since you have compeltely covered the blank with thread, you will no longer be able to see where your white underpaint is located. Refer back to your previously made notes to find the distance from the end of the foregrip to the edge of the white paint. Hold a ruler so that the end is against the foregrip. At the proper distance for the edge of the underpaint, brush a coat of your finish around the blank by rotating the rod with the ruler held in front. Follow the same procedure for measuring the opposite end of the underpaint. Cover the entire wrap between these two points with a coat of your finish. As it is applied you will see the color bleed through the white thread. Your wrap will now look similar to the fifth photo. Allow the finish to cure completely.

The next step is to add the trim lines. These are wrapped over the existing pattern. Mostly they will be single Size A threads. Only on large-diameter blanks will some of them consist of a very narrow band of thread. Medium and dark colors can be regular thread, but light colors must be NCP. It should be pointed out here that there are too many lines in some acutal tartans for reproduction on a rod. If all of them were added, the wrap would contain too much detail and the overall pattern would become lost in a maze of thread. Select only the significant ones to create the desired effect.

The completed wrap is shown in the sixth photo. Use no color preserver. Just apply the required number of coats of wrapping finish to provide a smooth coating.

Cross-wrap summation

We have discussed the method for laying out any type of cross wrap and explored some specific wraps. The wraps used were selected to provide us with examples of different techniques. By now it would be obvious that the number of variations possible is limited only by a rod builder's imagination. Each of the techniques can be combined in different ways to design a multitude of wraps. I hope I have opened the door a bit farther to the creative design of your own cross wraps.

I think it is safe to say that most of us do not simply want to be imitators. So much of the fun of threadwork is found in creating. The really outstanding wraps are not necessarily the most complicated. Instead, they are outstanding because a perfect sense of proportion in the design is combined with a tasteful, pleasing use of color.

Radials

Here is a wrap that is made by an entirely different technique. It can be used as a single small decorative wrap, or it can be used in pairs, separated on the butt section. You may well find other uses, variations, and combinations. It's appearance is simply of threads radiating from a midpoint.

When making the wrap it is first necessary to make a Size A underwrap of the desired length for the background. Leave space on either side for each of the base wraps which will bind down the radiating threads. Then place a band of double-stick tape over a layer of regular masking tape. This is pictured in the first photo.

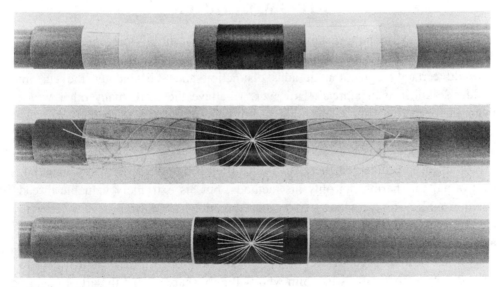

Radial wrapping sequence.

The thread used to form the radials can be either Size A or D. The choice depends somewhat on the diameter of the blank. While the larger-size thread stands out a bit more, it also requires more finish to protect it—especially over the hump that forms in the center. Make the first radial by laying a thread straight along the axis of the blank. The thread should be long enough to reach past the band of-double-stick tape on each end. After pressing one end of the thread firmly into the double-stick tape, stretch the thread just slightly so it is taut when the other end is pressed onto the other band of tape. Lay another thread next to it at a slight angle, crossing the first thread in the center of the pattern. Move to the other side of the first thread and repeat with a thread angled in the other direction. The radials are thus laid in place, alternately, on each side of the first thread. The last few threads will spiral from around the back of the blank, over the center, and again around the back of the blank. The wrap, ready for the base wraps, is shown in the second photo.

Make the base wraps from the center outward. Start them right against the outside edge of the underwrap so that no space or gap shows. When the base wrap is about one-third completed, cut the radial threads and fray their ends to flatten them. Complete the base wraps by wrapping over the ends. Peel away the tape and add a narrow trim band of the same color as the radial threads. The completed wrap is seen in the third photo. You will have to apply more coats of wrapping finish than usual to provide a smooth, protecitve coating.

WRITING WITH THREAD

Have you ever noticed how some people look with awe at a name written in thread on a rod? To a certain group this is the epitome of thread craftsmanship. I would certainly agree that it adds distinction and substantiates the custom builder's skill in using thread. However, I believe there are many other wraps that call for more artistic talent in the use of pattern, proportion, and color. Nevertheless, writing a name in thread is a technique that all rod makers should be able to call upon. It is a unique custom touch.

I am deeply indebted, here, to RodCrafter Bill A. Heckman of Anaheim, Calfiornia, for sharing not only his methods, but his extremely valuable thread position table. This provides step-by-step directions for forming every letter in the alphabet, as well as numbers. It represents a great amount of work on his part, and will save the rod builder countless hours of trial and error. There are those who would jealously guard such a laboriously developed tool. It is a tribute to Bill and other RodCrafters like him who willingly share so that the art of custom rod building may be furthered and enjoyed by all of us.

"Alphabetizing with thread," as Bill calls it, is not particularly difficult. What it does require is great attention to detail, and a measure of patience until one becomes familiar with the process. The basis of the technique is composing block letters generally with a 7:6 ratio. This forms most letters seven threads high and from two to seven threads wide. Using Size D thread you will get about twelve letters to the inch, depending, of course, upon the make-up of the characters. With seven Size D threads the letters will be about ⅛ inch high. A space of three winds of thread between letters works well, as does a space of six winds between words.

The technique is really one of weaving. A band, seven threads wide, is laid along the axis of the blank. These individual threads are woven in and out among the normal wrapping thread. Wrapping progresses from left to right. The weaving threads (which form the letters) are woven over and under the wrapping thread each time one wind of the wrapping thread is made. When a weaving thread is placed on top of the wrapping thread it is visible and forms part of a letter. When a weaving thread is placed under the wrapping thread (by winding over it), it cannot be seen. The block letters are thus formed of individual weaving threads passing over the top of the regular winding thread. In some cases the weaving thread will be on top for only the width of one wind of the wrapping thread. In other cases it will be on top of a number of winds of the wrapping thread.

A simple example will illustrate this process. Let's suppose we wanted to make the numeral 1. This consists of a straight line the height of all seven weaving threads, and it is only one wind of the wrapping thread wide. With the seven weaving threads firmly anchored by previously wrapping over them (and therefore not visible), we would bring all seven threads to the left. This allows us to make one wind of the wrapping thread around the blank. The band of seven weaving threads is now placed over the top of the wind just made by moving them to the right. They are now on top of the wrapping thread and visible. To make the weaving threads "disappear" we again wrap over them with the wrapping thread. This is shown in the accompanying drawing.

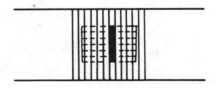

Numeral 1 is one wind of wrapping thread wide. Dotted lines show wrapped-over band of seven weaving threads.

From this example we can conclude that when we move a weaving thread *to the left* it will be on top of the wrapping thread. It will remain on top, and visible, for as many winds of the wrapping thread as we leave it on the left. Conversely, when we move a weaving thread *to the right* it will be under the wrapping thread. It will remain underneath, and invisible, for us as many winds of the wrapping thread as we leave it on the right. So remember:

Left—on top—visible

Right—underneath—hidden

These are the principles. Now, let's fill in the necessary details of this fascinating technique. Since you will need to have both hands free, your rod-wrapping supports will have to be set up to hold the rod stationary with the wrapping thread

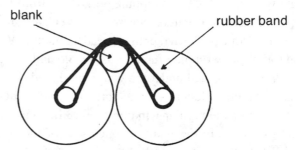

blank   rubber band

To hold blank stationary, a rubber band can be stretched over blank and attached to each roller axle support.

Third roller, under tension from elastic, holds rod stationary for weaving.

under tension. If you use one of the many forms of rod roller wrapping jigs, you can easily modify it for this one kind of threadwork. A rubber band can be placed over the axle supports of the rollers, on your left side, and stretched over the top of the rod (see drawing). When you want to rotate the blank, pull up on the rubber band with your left hand and rotate the blank with your right. Another possibility is to place a third roller with a center groove in the rim on top of the blank, and attach it to the other rollers with elastic. This is the arrangement Bill Heckman uses and is shown in the photo of his rig.

Start the basic wrap into which your letters will be woven. Stop about ten turns short of where you want the first letter to start. At this point you will wrap over the ends of the seven weaving threads.

The easiest way to prepare the weaving threads is to first wrap a single thread of the desired color seven times around a 4- or 5-inch piece of cardboard. Wrap them tightly against each other so they form a neat band. On *each side of the card* place a piece of masking tape across the threads, about ¼ inch from the edge. Now cut the seven threads in a straight line along the edge (see drawing).

cut threads here

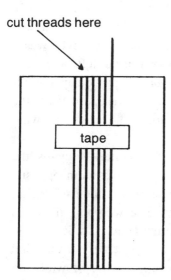

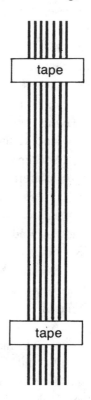

Above: Band of weaving threads prepared by making seven wraps around a card. Pieces of masking tape placed across threads near one end and on each side of card. Cut band of thread at end.
Right: Band of weaving thread after cutting from card.

Presto, you now have a band of seven individual threads held together at each end with a piece of masking tape. Carefully peel the tape from the card without disturbing the position of the threads.

To tape the band of weaving threads on the blank, hold it along the axis of the blank to the right of your previously started basic wrap. Place it so the ends of the threads are almost against the edge of your basic wrap, and tape that end to the blank. Keeping the threads striaght, lay the band to the right and tape the other end to the blank. Now, continue your basic wrap (with a little extra thread tension) by wrapping over the ends of the band of weaving threads. When you reach the tape, peel it away carefully so you do not pull any of the threads out from under the wrap just made. Continue the wrap until you reach the point where you want the first letter to start.

For convenience and reference we will number the seven weaving threads from #1 at the top to #7 at the bottom. Bill has worked out the weaving pattern on his thread position table. Let's examine this blueprint for writing in thread. Across the top you will find columns headed by the number 1 through 8. These rperesent the individual winds of the regular wrapping thread that are used in making the width of each letter. Along the side are listed each letter in the alphabet, as well as numerals. Each box shows the position of each of the seven weaving threads. "L" means those numbered threads are taped ot the left, and "R" means those numbered threads are taped to the right—for that particular individual wind of wrapping thread. The designation "do" (ditto) means to leave the weaving threads in the same position as the previous block, and make one wind of wrapping thread.

Earlier we explained how the numeral 1 is woven. Let's check it against the table. Referring to the table we see that the block in the first column opposite the numeral 1 indicates "1-7L." This means that threads #1 through #7 (or all of the threads) are moved to the left, then the first wind of wrapping thread is made around the blank. The second column, opposite numeral 1, indicates "1-7R." This instructs us to move threads #1 through #7 to the right (over the wind of wrapping thread just made), and to make another single wind of wrapping thread around the blank. The remaining columns are blank indicating that the numeral is now complete.

As you follow the instructions in the table, always use this sequence:

1 First move the designated threads to the left or right.

2. Make one wind of the regular wrapping thread around the blank.

3. At the completion of a letter make three winds of wrapping thread around the blank (and over all seven weaving threads).

4. At the completion of a word make six winds of wrapping thread.

	1	2	3	4	5	6	7	8
A	1-7L	14L 235 67R	do	do	do	1-7L	1-7R	
B	1-7L	147L 235 6R	do	do	do	234 56L 17R	1-7R	
C	1-7L	17L 234 56R	do	do	do	do	1-7R	
D	1-7L	17L 234 56R	do	do	do	2345 6L 17R	1-7R	
E	1-7L	147L 235 6R	do	do	do	do	1-7R	
F	1-7L	14L 235 67R	do	do	do	do	1-7R	
G	1-7L	17L 234 56R	do	157L 234 6R	do	156 7L 234R	1-7R	
H	1-7L	4L 1235 67R	do	do	do	1-7L	1-7R	
I	145 67L 23R	1-7R						
J	156 7L 234R	157L 234 6R	17L 234 56R	1-7L	1L 234 567R	do	1-7R	
K	1-7L	4L 1235 67R	do	35L 124 67R	26L 1345 7R	17L 234 56R	1-7R	
L	1-7L	7L 1234 56R	do	do	do	do	1-7R	
M	1-7L	12L 345 67R	3L 1245 67R	45L 123 67R	3L 1245 67R	12L 345 67R	1-7L	1-7R
N	1-7L	12L 345 67R	3L 1245 67R	4L 123 567R	5L 1234 67R	67L 1234 5R	1-7L	1-7R
O	234 56L 17R	17L 234 56R	do	do	do	234 56L 17R	1-7R	
P	1-7L	14L 235 67R	do	do	do	123 4L 567R	1-7R	
Q	234 56L 17R	17L 234 56R	do	157L 234 6R	167L 234 5R	234 567L 1R	7L 1234 56R	1-7R
R	1-7L	14L 235 67R	do	145L 236 7R	146L 235 7R	123 47L 56R	1-7R	

	1	2	3	4	5	6	7	8
S	123 47L 56R	147L 235 6R	do	do	do	145 67L 23R	1-7R	
T	1L 234 567R	do	do	1-7L	1L 234 567R	do	do	1-7R
U	123 456L 7R	7L 123 456R	do	do	do	123 456L 7R	1-7R	
V	12L 345 67R	34L 125 67R	56L 1234 7R	7L 1234 56R	56L 123 47R	34L 125 67R	12L 345 67R	1-7R
W	1-7L	67L 123 45R	5L 123 467R	34L 125 67R	5L 123 467R	67L 123 45R	1-7L	1-7R
X	17L 234 56R	26L 134 57R	35L 124 67R	4L 1235 67R	35L 124 67R	26L 134 57R	17L 234 56R	1-7R
Y	1L 2345 67R	2L 1345 67R	3L 1245 67R	456 7L 123R	3L 1245 67R	2L 1345 67R	1L 2345 67R	1-7R
Z	17L 234 56R	167L 234 5R	157L 234 6R	147L 235 6R	137L 245 6R	127L 345 6R	17L 234 56R	1-7R
1	1-7L	1-7R						
2	145 67L 23R	147L 235 6R	do	do	do	123 47L 56R	1-7R	
3	147L 235 6R	do	135 7L 246R	do	126 7L 345R	do	1-7R	
4	123 4L 567R	4L 1235 67R	do	1-7L	4L 1235 67R	do	1-7R	
5	7L 234 56R	do	123 47L 56R	147L 235 6R	do	145 67L 23R	1-7R	
6	1-7L	47L 123 56R	do	do	do	456 7L 123R	1-7R	
7	1L 2345 67R	do	do	do	do	1-7L	1-7R	
8	1-7L	147L 235 6R	do	do	do	1-7L	1-7R	
9	123 4L 567R	14L 235 67R	do	do	do	1-7L	1-7R	
0	234 56L 17R	17L 234 56R	do	do	do	234 56L 17R	1-7R	

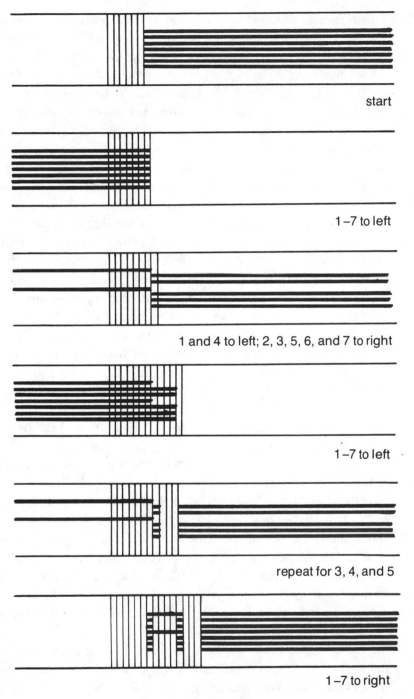

start

1–7 to left

1 and 4 to left; 2, 3, 5, 6, and 7 to right

1–7 to left

repeat for 3, 4, and 5

1–7 to right

Weaving the letter A by following steps in the thread position table. Winding thread is shown outlined in white; weaving threads in black. First drawing shows band of weaving threads with one end wrapped over and ready to start.

Let's take another example to make sure we understand the table and the process. At the start of any letter all seven weaving threads will have been wrapped over and will be taped to the right. To make the letter A, untape threads #1 through #7 and bend them to the left as indicated in Column 1. Straighten them out along the blank and tape them at their ends. Make one wind of wrapping thread. Next, as instructed in Column 2, leave threads #1 and #4 taped to the blank on the left. The remaining threads, #2, 3, 5, 6, and 7, are moved over to the right, straightened, and taped to the blank. Make one wind of wrapping thread. Column 3 indicates "do," so we leave the threads in the same position and make one wind of wrapping thread. The same instructions are given in Columns 4 and 5, so we would make one wind of wrapping thread for *each* of those columns. Column 6 tells us to move all seven weaving threads to the left. Make one wind of wrapping thread. Finally, Column 7 indicates that all seven threads go to the right. Since this is the end of a letter we would make three winds of wrapping thread (over the top of the seven weaving threads). We would then be ready to start the next letter. This sequence is shown in the drawings.

Got it? Good. Let me see if I can add a few helpful hints. At the beginning of the wrap when making the first part of the first letter, do not pull too hard on the weaving threads or you may pull them out from beneath their binding wrap. After you have the first letter almost formed (depending upon its width) you can gently pull any slack out of the winding threads composing the letter. The longer the wrap becomes, the more the weaving threads are bound and locked into position. You can then safely apply enough tension to pull the thread tight before taping them to the blank.

As each wind of wrapping thread is made, use your thumbnail to push the winds together and avoid small gaps. To count down the seven weaving threads to locate a certain one, the pointed end of a thread tool is very helpful. It can also be used to help loosen that thread from the band.

Alignment along the axis of the blank is critical to keeping all the letters in a straight line and of the same height. Check this alignment after each wind, and especially at the completion of each letter. Corrections can usually be made by moving threads #1 and #7. If some of the threads went out of alignment before you noticed it, you can sometimes go back and move them with a thread tool or your thumbnail.

As you move threads back and forth from side to side, try to keep them in position and not twisted. At some points you will invariably find that twists have crept in. In that case, use your thumbnail held against the band of threads and slide it *away from* the wrap. This will push any twists out toward the tape, and you can safely make your wind of wrapping thread across a flat band of thread.

Since you will be constantly taping and retaping threads, have a number of cut pieces of masking tape at hand. I keep a couple on each end of the blank just beyond where the threads will be taped—and a couple of spares on the front edge of the worktable. At the end of the name, wrap over the weaving threads for the same length as was wound over to start the wrap. Cut the weaving threads close to the wrap, and continue wrapping over them. Extend the wrap so that it is of equal length on each side of the name, and tie off in the normal manner.

I have tried to give rather detailed instructions so that you can more easily grasp the technique. After a little experience you will find that the process goes fairly rapidly, and that you can even eliminate some of the tapings.

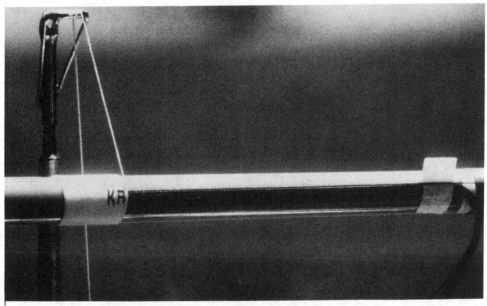

First two letters completed on name being woven on Bill's rig.

Completed name woven in thread.

295

Further weaving

This technique of weaving is not limited to making letters with thread. The rod builder who understands the process and who is venturesome and creative will see some of the other possibilities. Just as the basic diamond wrap was an open door to all varieties of cross wraps, so can weaving lead you to devise all kinds of designs in thread. Sunbursts, crosses, stars—you name the design—they can all be produced by this technique. Use a grid of crossed lines on a paper, and work out the design. Then write yourself a table of instructions, or steps, the same as Bill did in the construction of his table.

CREATING AND PLANNING WRAPS

There have been many times when I wondered what a certain pattern would look like, but I did not want to make an entire wrap to find out. On other occasions I had an idea for a different technique, but needed to experiment with the sequence of threads. Then, of course, there are the times when I needed to see how specific color combinations looked. Fianlly, in desperation, I hit upon a method which allowed me to run all of these tests and experiments comparatively quickly. It may be of help to you also.

Take a piece of card stock such as lightweight poster board. I find a size of roughly 8 × 8 inches about right. Cover about two-thirds of the center portion with adjacent strips of double-stick tape or carpet tape. On this you can place threads in any combination and sequence to form an individual cross wrap pattern. Use lengths of thread longer than needed to span the tape. Press one end of the thread in place, pull any slack out of the thread, and press it in place. A thread tool will allow you to even shift the position of a thread slightly. It can also be used to push the length of the thread into the tape. If your idea needs to be adjusted, just grasp one end of a thread and peel it off.

If you are working out a specific technique or experimenting on a new wrap, keep notes of the construction steps. When an idea works out, plan on saving the card and wrap for future reference. In order to keep the card you will have to trim the ends of the threads and cover the exposed portions of sticky tape with pieces of regular masking tape. Place a border of masking tape around the edges to bind down the ends of the thread. You can transfer your notes to the back of the card so you can repeat the pattern at any time in the future.

Planning patterns on double-stick tape
(four diamonds).

Experimental chevron pattern on double-stick tape.

COLOR COORDINATION

It has surprised me how often I have been asked about color combinations. Color is a very personal thing, and everyone has his own natural preferences. For that reason I always require a customer to select the colors used for all the components, and especially the wraps. Some people like bright colors, and lots of them, while others prefer only a few muted colors throughout.

Sometimes we have a tendency to place people in categories and assume we know what they like. I have been wrong enough times to now resist that temptation. For example, I erroneously assumed that an Orvis dealer for whom I built a graphite rod would want it to be quite plain with a minimum of threadwork. I therefore confined my discussion accordingly. He subsequently saw another customer's fly rod on which I had wrapped an intricate double diamond of conservative (in my opinion) colors. In short order I was confronted by him asking why I had not offered him the same thing. I replaced the butt wrap, and he liked it so much that he had me add similar threadwork to some of his Orvis rods. He now offers my custom wraps as an extra-cost option on the Orivis rods he sells. Granted, he does not have a great many takers, but there have been enough to convince me not to place people in categories.

Because of the very personal nature of color, I do not know just how much help I can provide the reader. Let me try, however, at least to suggest some guidelines. Just remember they are only one man's opinions! My first suggestion is to try for a unified color theme throughout the rod. This will, of necessity, start with the color of the blank. From there you make a decision to go with either the warm or cool family of colors.

Warm colors are often referred to as earth colors. They consist of browns, yellows, and reds. Naturally, there are many shades and mixtures of these colors. Cool colors are blues, greens, and silver. Warm and cool colors can be mixed, but one family should definitely predominate with the other used only as small accents. Black and white are neutral colors and can be used at will with either of the other two color families. They therefore are excellent choices when it is felt desirable to add another color as trim.

The two main areas of color besides that of the blank are the reel seat and the wraps. They should all be selected to complement each other and carry your color theme. Usually the rod will look best if all are from the same family of colors. Brown blanks, for example, look best in a color scheme of warm colors. A brown reel seat on a brown blank allows any combination of warm-colored wraps. If a gold reel seat is used, gold will look good as either the main wrap or as trim bands. A polished silver seat can, of course, also be used on a brown blank. It will, however, look best if the silver is repeated in the small trim bands. Here silver or white will serve as complementary accents.

Black blanks often look best with predominantly cool colors. Silver or black seats are better on these blanks than warm anodized colors. A black blank with silver or black seats can serve as the background for any color combination, but most people will find cool-color wraps more to their liking. White blanks are completely neutral and an excellent base for brightly decorated rods. This is one of the reasons they are preferred for off-shore trolling rods. If brightness is not your objective on a white blank, pick a main color from either the warm or cool family and use only small accents of one other color from the same family. Gold blanks are fairly neutral and can handle warm or cool colors. If cool colors are used, then a black reel seat blends nicely. I have found, however, that most people prefer a gold blank with warm-color wraps and a gold or brown reel seat.

Cork grips are neutral in color. Black resilient grips seem to look better with cool colors. They also provide a good background on a black or white blank for bright wraps. Very dark brown resilient grips work well with either warm or cool colors, but have an edge in the warm department.

Small trim pieces should either be used as accents to repeat part of the total color scheme, or be neutral. These would inlcude winding checks, butt caps, handle trim rings, and the whole new family of dyeable parts: guide shock rings, Dye-Checks, and dyeable plastic trim rings.

Rod builders often have trouble deciding on the colors to be used in decorative butt wraps. They naturally look best when the color of the guide wraps is the main color used. For the second color the trim-wrap color is a natural. If a small amount of a third color is needed, black or white will not upset the theme of the rod. Any other third color will have to be chosen carefully and used in the smallest possible quantity.

A good color scheme for some decorative butt wraps is one that contains the same color as that of the blank or the underwrap. Some very appealing and integrated wraps can be made using this principle. Personally, I have found that large expanses of white thread in either the butt wrap or the guide wraps stand out too much and detract from most rods.

Well, there are my thoughts—for what they are worth. As I said initially, they represent only one man's opinions, and color is a highly personal thing. Custom rod work is a creative endeavor, so that in the final analysis you should do your own thing.

EIGHT

Wrapping Finishes and Finishing Techniques

INSCRIPTIONS

After the wraps are completed the appropriate inscription should be placed on the rod. This is done before the wrapping finish is applied, since it will also be used to protect the inscription. A custom rod deserves the signature of the builder. It helps to set it apart as something special, and indicates pride of craftsmanship. If the rod is made for a customer or as a gift, that person's name should occupy the most prominent position.

The method I use is to place the customer's name along the axis of the rod which will be on top (0° axis) when it is fished. His name is made slightly larger than the other writing. On one side of the rod (270° axis) I write "Custom built for" in smaller script. On the other side of the rod (90° axis) appears "by Dale P. Clemens," also in the smaller script. Sometimes on the bottom of the rod (180° axis) I will place the fly-line weight, lure-weight range, or date. This, too, is done in smaller script. The entire inscription is placed next to the forward edge of the butt wrap. The exact wording is worked out with the customer beforehand.

There are a great many different methods that can be used for placing whatever inscription is desired on the rod. To cover all of them would simply require too much space, here. The *RodCrafters Journal* has had many articles and tips, shared by Associates, on unique techniques. Undoubtedly, future issues will present many more such methods. Here we will confine our discussion to the highlights of some of the more common ways of inscribing a rod.

One of the easiest and, in my opinion, one of the most effective is to write directly on the blank. In order to provide a tooth for the ink, first dull the finish with fine steel wool. Use a tack rag to remove all traces of the steel wool. Follow by degreasing the blank with an acetone-moistened rag. Black india ink looks good on any light-colored blank. Drawing pens with interchangeable tips are inexpensive and work very well. Get a variety of tips for different line widths. A draftsman's reservoir-type pen, such as a Rapidograph by Koh-i-noor, is also great for black, but does not work well with light, opaque inks.

Dark-colored blanks require white or light-colored ink. Unfortunately, india ink and other drawing inks in these colors are semitransparent and do not yield acceptable results. You need a fluid that is completely opaque. Latex or acrylic paint can sometimes be thinned with water. If the proportions are correct, it will flow from the pen point and not be transparent. The best "ink" I have found for dark-colored blanks is Opaque White and Opaque Gold. They come in a small plastic bottle with a brush in the cap for easy application to a drawing-pen point. They are water-soluble for easy clean-up.

Some combinations of pen point and ink will start to flow easier than others. If you experience difficulty, try holding the point at different angles to start the flow. If the ink starts to dry on the point (and it does so fairly quickly), wipe the point with a water-moistened rag and apply fresh ink. If all else fails, switch to a different point. Once the ink flows, keep the pen moving.

Try to keep your writing in a line along the axis of the rod. Don't let it curve off to one side. I lay the rod flat on the workbench and pick up a highlight from the overhead light. Another method is to scribe a line along the axis with a ruler and dubbing needle. Still another approach is to place a piece of masking tape along the axis, but *below* the intended writing. This can serve as a reference line. If you make a mistake you can generally wipe it off with a damp rag, if you do it soon enough. If the ink has already dried, use steel wool and start over.

Despite many attempts, some people find it difficult to write on a curved surface. If you are one of these, use Scotch Magic Tape, as does RodCrafter John J. Racketa. Place a strip on a flat, smooth surface such as a piece of glass. Leave a tab overhanging the edge as a handle for peeling it off. Write on the tape with pen and ink, then transfer the tape to the rod. Smooth it carefully so no air bubbles exist, then apply wrapping finish over it.

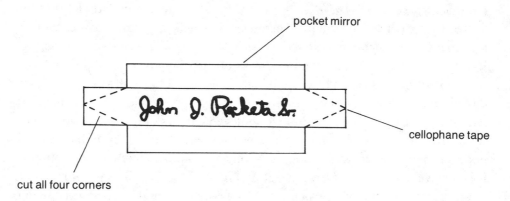

Signature written on Scotch Magic Tape ready to be applied to rod.

Some rod builders prefer printed letters to handwriting. These can be placed on a rod by using one of the many kinds of press type available from graphic-arts dealers. The sheet containing the letter is placed over the rod and burnished to transfer it. If you have trouble working with the large sheets, cut out the individual letter and place it on the underside of a piece of Scotch Tape. Put the tape in position on the rod and burnish the tape and the paper. When the letters are transferred to the rod, peel the tape away.

Custom-printed small strips of paper or mylar can also be used. These are glued to the rod with epoxy and any bubbles carefully smoothed away. They, as well as any form of inscription, can be wrapped over with Size 00 or A regular white thread. No color preserver is used on the thread so that the thin wrapping finish used makes it transparent. On light-colored blanks the thread will be clear. On darker blanks it will have a slight gray color.

FINISHES

With the recent boom in custom rod building, there has been an increase in the various materials used as a wrapping finish. The naturally creative and innovative person involved in rod making has experimented with new coatings, always searching for the perfect one. And well he should, because this is how improvements are made. Too often, however, *initial appearance* is the only criterion applied in determining if a particular material will make a good finish. This can sometimes lead to later problems when it is found that the finish changes with time and exposure. It then can prove to be worse than some of the finishes for which it was substituted.

A topnotch wrapping finish must look good, but let's see what else it must be. First off, it needs to be flexible. As we noted earlier, the blank bends more than the guide feet, so a certain amount of elasticity is required of the finish. If the finish is too rigid it will act to restrict the blank from bending. If too brittle, it will crack or crumble.

A quality finish must have good adhesion properties. If it does not it will separate from the thread and/or blank, and in time will peel. The finish also needs to be abrasion-resistant both, for its continued good appearance and for protection of the wraps.

A good finish should be light in weight. It also should be capable of being spread thinly on a wrap so that it does not add unnecessary weight because of uncontrollable volume. Two finishes might weigh the same, but if one can be applied only in a thick coating it will add extra weight. This can be a problem on the tip section where there are more guides and the blank is more flexible. A heavy finish, or one heavily applied, can slow the action of the rod.

Since some people may doubt this, I weighed two different finishes. Each was applied to identical rectangular sheets of foil whose surface area approximated that of the wrappings on a 7-foot spinning rod. The light finish (Crystal Coat) weighed 31.8 grains, and the heavy finish (Envirotex) weighed 115.5 grains. The test may not have been exact enough for some purposes, but the ratio of 3.6 to 1 is significant. No matter how you look at it, the heavier finish is about 3½ times as heavy. The lighter the rod, the more significant is the effect of the added weight.

While on this subject of weight and the degree of control the rod builder has over the thickness of the coating, let's examine some other aspects of thick versus thin finishes. Some rod makers apply any finish so that it forms a thick blob over all the wraps. If they are using a light, thin finish, they simply apply more coats. These are the same people who complain that their finish forms cracks and checks around the guide feet, particularly on the more flexible tip section. There is a simple rule at work here. The thicker the finish, the more easily it cracks and checks. The wraps at the tip section should be given only enough finish to level the thread and provide a smooth, protective surface—no more. A finish whose thickness can be controlled as it is applied is thus much preferred.

Thick finishes, or multiple coats of finish, should be saved for the decorative butt wraps. Here the added weight is closer to the fulcrum of the rod and has less effect. Also, this portion of the blank flexes much less, and there are no guide feet to cause checking and cracking.

Heavy finishes are almost always comparatively thick in consistency. This makes it more difficult to accurately measure the two parts, a necessity for the proper characteristics of the cured finish. Since they are not thin enough to quickly displace air trapped in the wrappings, thick finishes require more coats of color preserver. Any time saved in applying the finish itself is offset by the time required for extra coats of color preserver. If not enough color preserver is used, the trapped air escapes slowly and appears as bubbles in the finish. Thin-consistency finishes, on the other hand, can be applied directly to thread which has had no color preserver.

Basic types of finishes

Varnish. This old standby has some improved, modern versions. It has good flexibility, but only moderate abrasion resistance and adhesion. Its consistency is thin to start with, but it can be thinned more with neutral spirits. The best way to use it is really by thinning it, and in some cases heating it slightly. Multiple coats in this state (ten to fifteen if you are willing to spend the time) will produce a beautiful glasslike finish. Its biggest drawback is that it has an amber cast initially, and yellows with age. If applied over dark, warm colors this will not be nearly as noticeable.

Epoxy. So many formulations of epoxy finish have come on the market that it is difficult to lump them together. True two-part epoxies have the strongest adhesion of any finish. Their resistance to abrasion is also very high. The good formulas are flexible and elastic. However, some are not. A rough indication is often the cure time, with the fast-curing types tending to be more brittle. Both thin and thick types are available. Those that are thin flow easily and require no rod rotation while curing.

True epoxy finishes with all their advantages share one common drawback: When used over color preserver they take on a slight amber cast. If the amount of white or silver thread is kept to small trim areas, this is not objectionable. However, the amber will become apparent if large areas of white, and to a slightly lesser degree silver, are used on the rod.

Polymers. There are many kinds of clear polymer coatings which are also two-part mixtures. Most were never intended for use on fishing rods, yet some rod builders use them. In trying to describe their common properties, I will consider those in frequent use regardless of their purpose. Their biggest attraction is that they are clear and do not amber when applied over color preserver. Over a period of time when exposed to the sun, some will amber. Another advantage, at least viewed that way by some rod builders, is that they are thick and generally require only one coat. They are among the heaviest finishes in weight alone, and usually cannot be thinned easily.

They have good flexibility, but rate relatively low in adhesion and abrasion resistance. The exceptions would be those formulated solely for fishing rods. Those that are not made for rod work also tend to not weather well.

Miscellaneous. There are basically two other families of finishes with which I have some familiarity. Clear acrylic is excellent in just about all respects except it is a single liquid and, once exposed to the air, starts to cure. Even when placed in small bottles with the best of air-seal caps, the problem occurs as soon as the bottle is opened a few times. This just about eliminates it as a marketable wrapping finish. Clear polyester casting resin is very tough and durable. It has good abrasion resistance and fairly good adhesion. Its big drawback is that it is relatively inflexible and heavy, and therefore suited only to heavy, stiff rods.

Testing finishes

You will, no doubt, at one time or another want to compare finishes or test new ones. This is the best way to learn firsthand about some of the important properties of a wrapping finish. It is certainly better than accepting the manufacturer's claims, or the opinions of others such as myself.

Start with flat pieces of aluminum foil, about 20 square inches (10 × 2 or 3 × 7 inches). Give each piece of foil two coats of the finish with the recommended time between coats. Allow the finish at least a few days to a week to cure thoroughly. For a weight comparison use a good reloading scale, or get help from your friendly pharmacist. Abrasion resistance is fairly difficult to test at home, or even compare. You can try rubbing one spot on each finish for a certain number of minutes with a mildly abrasive rubber eraser. Then compare to see if there is any apparent difference.

To test flexibility and adhesion, first pull the strips repeatedly at a 90° angle over the square edge of a table. A good finish should be able to stand up to a great many such flexes. Next, crumple the piece of foil into a tight ball, then open it flat on a table. Check for cracks and separation. Here again, a quality finish should show no deterioration after many such crushings.

Next take scrap pieces of medium- to large-diameter blanks. Wrap bands of different-colored thread, about ¼ to ½ inch wide, against each other. Use a variety of colors and make sure NCP white is one of them. Apply three coats of color preserver in the usual manner to just *one side* of each blank (along the axis). Wait twenty-four hours after the last coat, then give the entire blank a couple of coats of the wrapping finishes being tested. After they have cured, examine the colors. See if the side with the color preserver retained the original color. Compare the color-preserver side to the other side to determine how much color shift occurred. To see if there is a color cast to the finish, or if one occurs as a result of reacting with the color preserver, check the white band on both sides of the blank. Finally, place the pieces of blanks outside in the sun and weather for a few weeks to see what changes or reactions occur, if any.

Mixing and storing finishes

Epoxy and polymer finishes must be measured precisely in the proportions given in the instructions. If not, the finish may not cure properly and remain tacky, or the properties of the finish will change. Any number of methods of measuring the parts can be used. Just keep in mind that the smaller the quantity that is measured, the more difficult it becomes to be accurate. This is one of the advantages of a finish that can be stored in the freezer after it is mixed. You can measure larger quantities more accurately, yet not waste the finish.

Inexpensive metal kitchen measuring sets are available. They usually come in sizes from 1 tablespoon to ¼ teaspoon. Use two sets—one for the resin and the other for the catalyst. When pouring the liquids into the measurers, make sure both are flush with the surface. On thicker liquids you will have to wait a minute or two for the fluid to flatten in the measurer. Use a flat stick to scrape each spoon completely clean and into the mixing container. Mix the parts thoroughly, scraping the edges and bottom of the mixing container.

Another method of measuring is to use small clear plastic medical measuring cups. These have various calibrations accurately marked along the sides, and generally have a capacity of 2 tablespoons. You can carefully pour each part directly into the cup, using the appropriate calibration marks, then mix it right there. Just discard them after use. The only possible problem with these is that the plastic may react with some finishes, affecting the cure. Run a test first.

Laboratory-supply houses have small glass containers with flat bottoms and straight sides. You can carefully measure the quantity wanted and scribe a mark on the side. Then measure one-half this height on the side of the container, and scribe another mark. Fill the container to the first mark with one part, then add the other part until it reaches the top mark. These must be carefully cleaned afterward. Use solvent and do so before the finish starts to cure.

While I do not personally recommend as a wrapping finish the polymer formula sold under the name of Envirotex (nor does the manufacturer), I do know that a number of rod builders use it. Despite my prejudice, I can possibly help. To thin the mixture slightly, cut down on the number of bubbles, and extend the pot life, you may want to try the following. After measuring the resin, add about one-eighth to one-quarter the same quantity of acetone. Stir completely. Next measure and add the catalyst and immediately stir for about two minutes. Pour the mixture into a shallow container so that it spreads out and exposes more surface. Blow on the surface for about two minutes. The carbon dioxide will help break up the many bubbles.

Some thin epoxies such as Crystal Coat can be stored in the freezer after they are mixed. They must be placed in tightly capped, airtight bottles. Rod-Crafter Albert Jones uses the canisters in which 35mm film is packed. When a container is removed from the freezer, do not remover the cap until the mixture has returned to room temperature. If you do, condensation will form inside the container and the moisture will retard the cure. I hold the capped bottle under running hot water while rotating it on its side. In a few minutes the mixture is back to room temperature. After using, immediately recap, and put back in the freezer. I have kept mixed Crystal Coat for up to six months using this procedure.

FINISHING TECHNIQUES

A good finish really starts with the thread and the actual wrapping. Always store thread in dustproof containers, wrap in a dust-free area, and wash your hands before wrapping.

Color preserver

If you are going to use color preserver, apply a minimum of three coats. If using a thick finish, plan on using more coats. Allow twenty-four hours between the first and second coat, and again after the last coat before applying the wrapping finish. For the "in-between coats," you can tell when it is dry when all odor is gone. The color preserver should be as thin as water. If not, thin at least the first two coats with lacquer thinner.

Apply when or where the humidity is low. If the preserver turns whitish, the humidity was too high. Apply the next coat in low humidity, and it will melt into the first coat, eliminating the white cast. As you apply the color preserver pay particular attention to the area around the guide feet. An empty space or tunnel exists along each side of a guide foot where the thread bridges from the top of the guide foot to the side of the blank. The threads forming this tunnel must be completely saturated with color preserver, and the open end near the guide ring must be completely sealed off. If not, wrapping finish may enter the tunnel and cause blushing, or mottled spots in the final finish. Incidentally, another cause of blushing is from not allowing adequate drying time between coats of color perserver—especially the last one before the wrapping finish.

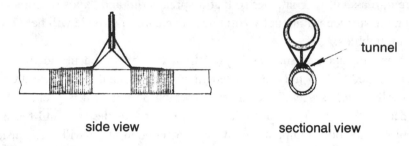

side view   sectional view

Color preserver must fill tunnel along guide feet.

Applying the finish

A dust-free area is an absolute necessity for a perfect finish. If your work area has an unpainted cement floor, it must be vacuumed periodically to remove the fine powdery residue that forms on the cement. Don't apply finish in a basement when there is traffic on the floor above, or fine dust will filter down. Wait until family activity on the first floor has subsided for the night. A great deal of dust or fine lint is carried on your clothing and readily transferred to a rod being finished. Wear a long nylon lab coat, or a thin nylon windbreaker—you'll be surprised at the difference it makes. If possible, use a separate room for finishing rods—one where there is generally little traffic and where dust can be kept under control. Mixing utensils and brushes should be stored in dustproof containers.

High humidity can cause problems with any finish. Epoxy and varnish will dry too slowly, while polymers will set up too quickly. Temperatures over 75° will accelerate the setup of all finishes, so work at a temperature around 70°.

Before applying the finish, *very lightly* wipe the wraps with a tack rag to remove dust and lint. Never wipe a blank briskly with a plain cloth. This creates a static electric charge which attracts and holds dust and lint. To prolong the life of your tack rag, store it in a capped, wide-mouth jar, such as a peanut-butter jar.

Varnish is best applied with your fingertip, which lessens the chance of bubbles. Epoxy will flow best from a soft brush. Hold the brush at 90° to the wrap and rotate the rod. Do not apply such a thick coating that runs and sags develop.

Polymer finishes are applied most easily with a slightly stiff bristle brush. Use brush strokes along the axis of the blank and across the winds of thread. Extra effort is required to brush out the bubbles. After about five minutes, check the wraps for bubbles and brush again if necessary.

The finish should extend about ⅛ inch past the end of the thread wraps for proper protection. On thin finishes this is easily done, and the edge of the finish line kept straight. On all thick finishes it may help to place a band of masking tape around the blank ⅛ inch beyond the wrap. Brush the finish over the wraps and the edge of the tape. As soon as all the wraps are finished, carefully peel off the tape bands.

The inscription above the butt wrap is covered with an extension of the finish applied to the thread. Brush the first coat along the axis of the rod to thin the coating progressively toward the tip. Make sure you cover not only the inscription, but any of the blank's finish that had been dulled by steel wool. Try to feather the upper edge of the finish into the original factory-applied blank finish. Repeat the procedure for the second coat, but feather the coat at a point not as far up on the blank. Any additional coats of finish given the butt wrap should end about ⅛ inch past the thread.

After the finish is applied, move around as little as possible to keep down dust. It is best to clean mixing utensils in another room, or as far away from the wrapped rod as possible. I even tiptoe from the room and carefully close the door!

The time required between the first and second coats, and subsequent coats if desired, depends upon the finish. Carefully check directions on the container. Some modern varnishes dry fast enough that two or even three coats can be applied within a twenty-four-hour period. The older formulas should be allowed to dry a full twenty-four hours between coats. Thin epoxies such as Crystal Coat can have a second full coat applied about thirty to forty-five minutes after the first. The initial coat will not be dry, but a second wet coat can be flowed on. Let both of these coats dry overnight before adding a third coat where necessary. This kind of finish can be built as thick as desired on butt wraps, etc., but can be kept thin on the smaller-diameter tip section.

If more than forty-eight hours elapses between coats of epoxy, the finish will have cured to the point where another coat will not adhere as well as it should. In that case, lightly break the surface of the finish with steel wool or very fine sandpaper before applying another coat.

Polymers require at least thirty-six hours between coats for good adhesion. On those thicker polymers that do not have good abrasion resistance, a coat of thin epoxy can be applied on top. Lightly dull the cured polymer with steel wool first, then apply the epoxy. This technique is useful where a thick coating is desired on a decorative butt wrap. From experience, I know that Crystal Coat will not cause any ambering when used in this manner.

If, despite your best efforts, specks of dust and lint did find their way into the finish, you can save the wrap. After the finish is cured, sand it lightly to remove the rough spots caused by dust—or bubbles. Wipe clean with a tack rag and apply a thin epoxy finish. This time try to be more careful about eliminating dust and lint in the finishing area.

When thick finishes, or multiple heavy coats of thin finish, are used on a rod, or just on the butt wrap, it is advisable to rotate the rod slowly while the finish cures. If this is not done, there is a high probability of runs and sags. Any low-rpm motor can be used, and a barbecue-spit motor is ideal. The rod will have to be supported on rod rollers, and the height of the rollers and the motor shaft adjusted so both are the same. You can either shim the support of the motor or use adjustable-height ball-bearing lathe supports.

There are as many ways to attach the butt of the rod to the motor shaft as there are rod builders. On casting rods, the butt ferrule can be clamped into an old chuck from a casting handle. With a little creative modification the chuck can be attached to the motor shaft. Very little torque or resistance is present, so the rig does not have to be very strong.

RodCrafter Joy Dunlap attaches his heavy offshore trolling rods with a homemade rig. He uses about a 6-inch length of keystock which is driven into an empty 1-ounce thread spool. The spool is turned down on the end to accept a length of automobile heater hose. He has made up several sizes to fit various-diameter rod butts. A hose clamp is slipped over the hose to hold it to the butt.

Personally, I have found that if the motor and rollers are the same height, I can use just strips of masking tape. I center the butt on the center of the motor shaft, using the adjustable-height lathe supports. Then I spiral a few lengths of tape around the motor shaft and the butt, alternating directions of the spiral. The tape is bent around the parts as necessary, then pushed, even crumpled, tightly in place.

Mild heat applied to the rotating rod will speed the cure a bit. You can use heat lamps or photoflood lamps. Be careful not to place the heat source too close, or blistering of the finish will occur. The temperature at the rod should never exceed 150° and, to be safe, try to keep it a bit lower.

NINE

Tools

Very few people who try custom rod building make only one rod. They find the endeavor so fascinating and the end product so much better than a factory rod that they just naturally build more rods. As they do, many discover needs for various tools to simplify a particular function or to enable better control of quality. The ingenuity of rod builders in this regard is amazing, especially when we consider that custom rod makers come from all walks of life with widely differing backgrounds.

Every issue of the *RodCrafters Journal* has had at least one article on tools designed by rod makers. Some, such as George Fish's thread tool and James R. Youmans's adjustable-height ball-bearing lathe supports, have had such broad application that we have had them manufactured for sale in our supply business. One is quite simple, the other more complex, yet either can be made by the reader.

Because of space limitations it is impossible to list here all of the many excellent tools designed by RodCrafters. We have tried to select a broad enough variety to show different aspects of construction and different ways of solving a common problem. The way to use this chapter, then, is to find those ideas and designs that best fit your needs, shop facilities, and available materials. No doubt you can then add your own personal design twists and come up with a tool ideally suited to you and your needs.

TOOLS FOR CORK WORK

As cork rings are glued to the blank it helps to have a tool to push each firmly against the previous one. A good tool for this purpose consists of a board with various-size holes drilled in the center. These holes should be slightly larger than the butt diameters of the blanks you normally work with. After the cork is glued in place the board is slipped over the blank. By grasping the ends of the board you can push the corks firmly together. If you are using thin contact cement on the faces of the rings combined with epoxy on the blank, the tool is excellent. Slip the board in place and tap on it with a hammer for a solid contact-cement joint.

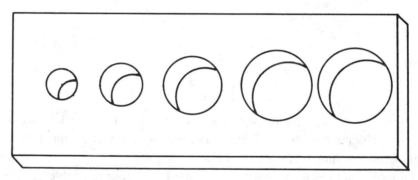

Pushboard with various-sized holes for seating cork rings and pushing resilient grips along blank.

When the glue being used calls for clamping, or when it is felt that mild clamping of cork rings will help, a number of tools can be used. For example, short lengths of rings can be clamped with a standard caulking gun. This is a simple way to make short lengths of cork cylinders from which grips can be fabricated. For clamping rings glued to the blank. RodCrafter James L. Merlock modified a regular adjustable pipe clamp. He had a U-shaped metal plate welded onto the adjustable end. This slips around the blank, but retains the cork rings. On a spinning rod, for example, he first glues and clamps the butt grip. When it is dry he fits, then clamps, the reel seat and foregrip.

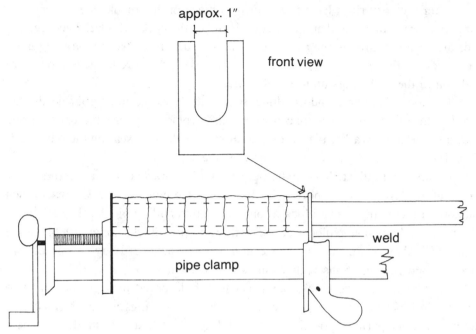

Jim Merlock's modified pipe clamp.

A different approach is used by RodCrafter Earl C. Davidson for gluing cork rings onto a blank. His jig consists of two large washers $1/8 \times {}^{15}/16 \times 2¼$ inches O.D. In addition to the center hole, each washer has two smaller $3/16$-inch holes drilled near the rim and 180° apart. Other parts of the jig include two $3/16 \times 10$-inch threaded rods, two nuts, and two wing nuts to fit on the threaded rods.

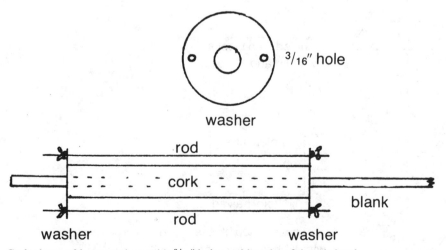

Cork clamp of large washers with $3/16''$ holes and lengths of threaded rod.

After the cork rings have been glued in place on the blank, the washers are slipped over the blank so that one is at each end of the cork cylinder. The threaded rods are inserted through the rim holes, and the nuts, followed by the wing nuts, are placed on the ends of the rods. The nuts and wing nuts are tightened to square and clamp the cork rings until the glue dries.

The tool is versatile and the dimensions can be varied to fit your needs. On a rod with a fixed reel seat, one washer can be placed against the cork on one end, and the other washer placed on the far side of the reel seat on the other end. This draws the cork tightly against the reel seat.

A more complicated but extremely versatile cork clamp was designed by RodCrafter Clifford G. Webb. Basically, the device consists of a ½×4×32-inch backboard (A) with a fixed block at one end, three sliding blocks (B), and a set of cut-out and holed stop blocks (C). The three sliding blocks are adjustable along a ¼×28-inch groove, cut into the center of the backboard, by means of two ¼×1½-inch carriage bolts with washers and wing nuts.

Each of the sliding blocks has a 1¾-inch hole bored through the center to permit the blocks to pass over any cork project using rings up to 1½ inches in diameter. This permits positioning the sliding blocks, as required, anywhere along the backboard. Thus, the jig can be used on any type handle, including gluing both parts of a split-grip surf handle at the same time.

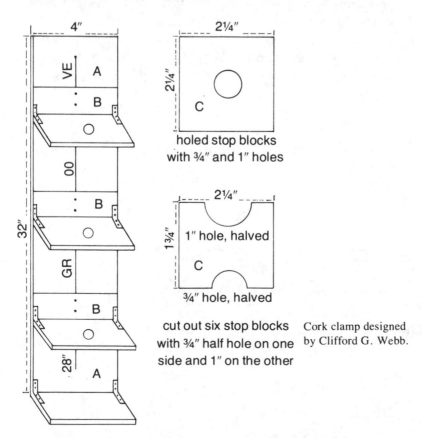

holed stop blocks
with ¾" and 1" holes

cut out six stop blocks
with ¾" half hole on one
side and 1" on the other

Cork clamp designed by Clifford G. Webb.

The cut-out blocks are used along with the sliding blocks. They prevent the cork rings from passing through the large hole in the sliding block when it is positioned against the cork rings being glued. One of the holed stop blocks has a ¾-inch-diameter hole and the other has a 1-inch hole. These holes are center-bored, enabling the stop blocks to be passed over the rod tip or handle shaft and placed against the project being glued. On some projects, only a holed stop block is necessary, and on others, the cut-out stop blocks are required as well. When using the cut-out stop blocks, it is necessary to use two of the blocks at each sliding block position.

In use, a stop block is placed against the cork with a sliding block behind it. The wing nuts are tightened firmly and the top of the sliding block is tapped very lightly with a hammer. *Caution:* Do not force the blocks too tightly against the cork rings. To do so will distort the rings and cause them to pull away from the blank. Only light pressure, sufficient to keep the rings pushed securely together, is required.

The tool is quite versatile and adaptable to all kinds of handles. For example, the entire handle of a one-piece surf rod can be clamped. Use one sliding block and one holed stop block at the foregrip and place the butt of the rod against the fixed block at the end. Dimensions can be varied to fit requirements. A smaller version using only one sliding block may fill your needs adequately.

Shaping tools

To shape cork grips, we usually think of using sandpaper. Some other tools that can be used effectively are Stanley Surform Files and Red Devil Company's Dragon Skin. Both remove cork rapidly and should be used only for rough shaping. Another material which comes in grades from coarse to fine is Carborundum screen. This material looks a lot like wire or plastic window screening. The screening has been coated with Carborundum cutting grit, and the open pattern allows the cork dust to rapidly fall away. Available in square sheets, it is easily cut with scissors into narrow strips.

HOSEL AND TRIM RING CLAMP

The method explained in *Fiberglass Rod Making* for fabricating hosels and trim rings of wood, plastic, or combinations thereof is based on using a hole saw. Most of these utilize a ¼-inch drill bit in the center. The resulting ¼-inch center hole must usually be enlarged to fit the diameter of the blank. RodCrafter Ken

Wiebe designed a clamp for holding these pieces without marring them when enlarging the center hole. This otherwise can be a problem with tapered hosels and butt caps.

The clamp consists of two plates of flat iron ¼ inch thick by 1½ inches wide by 3½ inches long. Holes are drilled and tapped to accept two 2×⅜-inch Nat. Course Std. bolts, one on each end of the clamp. Holes of the desired diameter to match the blank are also drilled in the center of the plates. In use, the tapered hosel is slipped between the two plates and aligned with the center holes. The bolts are then tightened, and the entire assembly held in a vise for drilling out the center of the hosel (see diagram).

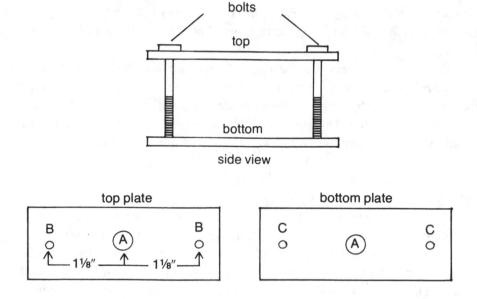

Hosel and trim-ring clamp.

To make the clamp, use a center punch to mark the top plate for the ''A'' center hole and the two ''B'' holes (see figure). Clamp the top and bottom plates together and use a ⅛-inch drill bit to drill through both plates for all three holes. Separate the plates and use a ⅜-inch drill bit to enlarge the ''B'' holes only, on the top plate. Next, take the bottom plate and use a $5/16$-inch drill bit to enlarge the ''C'' holes only. After drilling the ''C'' holes, tap them with a ⅜×16 N.C.S. tap to provide threads for the two bolts. The center ''A'' holes can be drilled to whatever size required for the diameter of the blank.

THREAD TOOL

I have already referred to this clever little tool so many times in the chapter on wrapping that you probably expect some kind of magic wand that will make the wraps for you. Obviously, it won't. But it will do all the things mentioned, and I'm so sold on it that I think every custom rod builder should have two of them. RodCrafter George Fish designed it and kindly sent me a couple. Now, I don't know how I ever got along without them. I still keep finding new uses.

Its beauty lies in its simplicity and utility. Take a piece of $3/32$-inch-diameter stainless-steel drill rod. A length of 4 or 4½ inches works just fine. Round one end on a grinding wheel. At the other end, grind about one-third of the length to a level taper, but do not bring it to a real fine point. Next, flatten the taper on three or four sides.

You now have the desired shape, but all edges must be heavily buffed to completely smooth and polish the entire tool. Use a buffing wheel and plenty of rouge. Make sure the flattened sides and the point are all polished slightly round. The point should be soft enough that it will not scratch anything. The whole tool must be smooth enough that it will never snag wrapping thread. Test it on a piece of woman's nylon stocking.

I won't try to list all the uses, just the main three functions. The round sides make an excellent burnisher. The soft point enables you to position individual threads on intricate butt wraps. And the flattened edges work beautifully for packing threads tightly together.

FOUR-THREAD WRAPPING TOOL

If you make many cross wraps in which you wind bands of up to four threads wide, and have difficulty in keeping the threads from twisting, you might want to consider making this tool. I first saw it in use at a National RodCrafter Seminar by its designer, Don Dewey. Neglecting to get a photograph, I may have changed the original design somewhat. However, as in building any tool or jig, we all do some redesigning and adjusting. The basic principle is what is important.

What is required is a board on which four vertical pegs are mounted to hold the thread spools, a device to adjust tension, and a method of keeping the threads separate and untangled. Any arrangement of parts which will accomplish this is fine. The unit could be built on a wood base that could be either clamped or screwed to the workbench. An alternate for stability would be weighting the base with lead.

317

A simple arrangement would have the pegs (dowels) on the rear of the base. From there the individual threads could pass through a common hair comb mounted vertically. The comb could be set between two low pieces of wood glued to the base, and the comb held between them with nonflowing epoxy such as PC-7. Next, the threads would pass through a thread tension device that would keep the threads separated. This could be a pair of boards mounted on bolts from beneath the base. The bottom board could be glued to the base while the top board floated on the two bolts. A number of layers of paper could be glued to the face of each board to prevent raising fuzz on the thread as it passed through under tension. Alternative facing of the boards could be sheets of smooth Plexiglas with the edges rounded. Two wing nuts and washers would top the bolts and be tightened to provide tension on the thread. Just in front of the tension device, and along the front edge of the unit's base, another comb could be mounted.

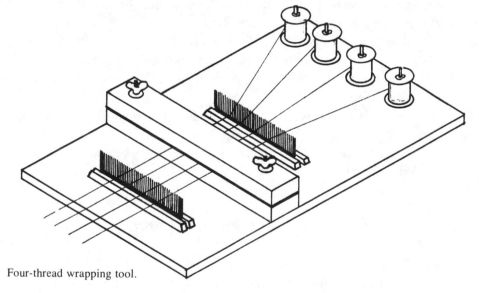

Four-thread wrapping tool.

To use the unit, the wing nuts are turned to open the space between the tension boards. The threads are then passed through the teeth of the first comb, between the tension boards, and then through the teeth of the second comb. The wing nuts are tightened for the desired thread tension. The ends of the thread are brought together in front of the unit and a piece of masking tape is placed across the band of thread. This keeps the thread from becoming twisted after it leaves the last comb. The thread is then taped in place on the rod and the band wound on. At the end of the wrap for that band of thread it is taped in place on the rod. Before it is cut with scissors, a piece of tape is again placed across the band of thread to keep it from twisting.

WRAPPING JIGS

If you are going to wrap more than an occasional rod, you will find it worth your while to build some kind of wrapping jig. Basically this consists of a support on which to rest and rotate the rod, and a device for applying easily adjustable thread tension. We are talking here of an entirely hand-powered jig, as distinguished from a power wrapping tool. Some of the tools, however, can also be pressed into service for an occasional use with power for various operations.

When designing and building a wrapping jig you should give some thought to where it will be placed. The working height must be comfortable *for you*, and it must fit into your available space. Perhaps it also will have to be collapsible for storage, or portable. Consider also the direction from which you prefer the thread to come. Some like it to feed from behind the blank, others from beneath and in front. The jig also will have to be long enough to provide steady support for the longest rod you are likely to build. Long one-piece rods will require three supports instead of two. Of necessity, you will have to take into account your skill and working familiarity with various materials, their availability, and the shop resources at your disposal.

Casters

Perhaps the most commonly used supports for rod wrapping are furniture casters. These are available in various diameters and in two styles of mountings. One style comes on a small metal plate which attaches with four wood screws. The other style is on a metal rod which fits inside a hole in the bottom of furniture legs. Either style can be used; it's a matter of which you find the most convenient to mount.

When mounting casters they must be close enough so that the fine-diameter tip section of rods will not slip between them. Ideally, they should just touch each other so that when one rotates it causes the other to rotate. However, plastic casters of this type are not always perfectly round. If one of them has a high side, it may bind if mounted too close. You will have to check this when mounting any pair of casters, and adjust the distance between them so they rotate freely.

Most of these casters are also made to swivel, many being mounted with ball-bearing raceways. For use as a rod support, you do not want them to move from alignment with each other. So, plan to immobilize the swivel mechanism by any convenient means. A hole can be drilled and a pin inserted, or nonflowing epoxy, such as PC-7, can be molded around the base to prevent swiveling.

If your workbench is of about the height that you find comfortable, the casters can be mounted on blocks made of pieces of 2×4 lumber. These can be notched on the bottom to slide along a rail mounted on your workbench. The rail can be attached to the bench top with two countersunk screws, one at each end. When not in use, the rails can thus be removed and the wrapping supports stored.

Casters also cradle the rod on RodCrafter Donald B. Doggett's wrapping jig. His tool permits adjusting the position of the caster blocks so they will not move, yet the entire rod support can be slid to any position desired. This is possible by a sliding bar which holds the caster blocks. The bar is a 4½-foot length of 2×4, sanded smooth on all sides. The bar slides freely between two guide strips of 1×2 lumber. These rails are mounted to the workbench by a $^3/_{16}$×4-inch bolt and wing nut on each end for easy removal.

Bar and casters slide to one side for positioning of rod.

The sliding bar has ½-inch-diameter holes drilled ¾ inch deep and 3 inches apart along the center line of the bar. These holes accept ½-inch-diameter by ⅞-inch-long dowels which are glued to the bottom of the caster blocks as shown in the photo. (A broom handle makes a good-sized dowel for this purpose.) This method of construction enables the rod builder to quickly position the roller blocks where desired. The entire rod support can then be slid to the right or left without actually moving the rod on the rod rollers.

Don uses three roller blocks. When working on one end of a rod, such as

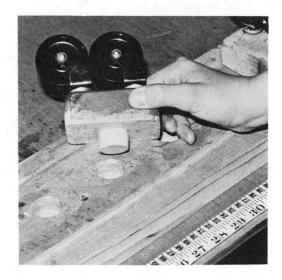

Pieces of dowel on bottom of castor blocks fit into holes in sliding bar.

the tip, he slides the bar to one side and places a roller block on one end of the bar and two on the other end. The rod is thus perfectly supported. The sliding feature enables constant alignment with his thread holder, and is a definite asset when applying wrapping finish. He can then slide the entire unit without risk of smearing the finish at any guide.

A different type of rod-wrapping jig utilizing casters is used by RodCrafter James C. Reigle. His system may be applicable for you if you want to raise the height of your rod supports, or if your workbench is low. It also feeds the thread from below the blank rather than from behind it.

Rod-wrapping jig by James C. Reigle. Thread holder and upright marked by arrows are adjustable along slot in base.

He uses two upright sections, each topped by a pair of rollers on which the rod is placed. The casters are mounted on blocks which are glued to the vertical boards. One upright is permanently attached to the end of a horizontal bed or base made of a wide board. This base board has a slot along its center. The other upright slides in this slot, and is attached with a wing nut. This enables easy adjustment for different length blanks.

The thread holder is mounted on the base beneath the rollers. Its position is also adjustable along the slot and is similarly attached with a wing nut. The thread holder consists of a center mounted upright on a base. Through the upright are mounted two lengths of ¼-inch threaded rod, secured on both sides by a nut and washer. Over each protruding section of threaded rod is mounted a small spring for tension, the spool of thread, a washer, and finally a wing nut for tension adjustment. There are two eyelets mounted on the baseboard. The thread runs from the spool, through the eyelets, and up to the blank at an angle. This arrangement permits seeing the thread as it comes off the spool.

Along with many other rod builders, I had to get into the act and design a rod-wrapping jig. Since it was to be for sale in our supply business, one of my objectives was versatility to accommodate different wrapping styles and various lengths of rods. I chose Philippine Mahogany which is sturdy and holds up well unfinished.

The 32-inch-long bed consists of three ⅝-inch boards plus a 33-inch sliding board which holds a felt-lined U support. This makes the overall working length 65 inches, long enough to support surf rods. The height of the U support is adjustable to accommodate handles and large butt diameter blanks. The board on which it is mounted has an aluminum plate which slides in dado cuts the length of the baseboards.

There are two uprights holding 1⅛-inch nylon rollers. These each slide the length of the bed and can be locked in any position. Each contains two fixed position rollers and a third roller on a swinging arm. This third roller can be lowered on the blank and locked, or simply pushed out of the way. When locked on top of the blank they securely hold even the longest blank. They also eliminate whipping if the rod is revolved under power for wraps or simple cork shaping.

An extremely efficient and versatile thread tension system consists of an adjustable arm on the end of which are four highly polished hard-chrome cupped disks with a spring and thumb screw. This swinging arm is mounted on a baseboard with a blind groove permitting it to be slid forward or backward. The rod builder can therefore position and lock the tension device so that the thread comes from above and behind the blank or below and in front of the blank—or anywhere in between.

Wrapping jig of my design uses three castors on each adjustable upright and felt-lined support, which can be extended. Thread-tension disks can be positioned above or below rod.

On the rear of the tension base plate there is a 2½-inch high steel post which will hold 50-yard, 1-ounce, or 4-ounce spools of thread. There is also an optional chrome bracket that can be screwed to the wood base plate consisting of two additional steel posts. These can be used for convenient thread storage or two or three thread wraps. You may want to incorporate some or all of the ideas to build your own compact and versatile wrapping jig.

Another method of mounting casters for use as rod rollers is on horizontal boards that project out in front of the workbench. This has the advantage of allowing room beneath for one's legs. The boards that hold the rollers need only be as wide as the mounting brackets on the bottom of the casters. They can be permanently attached to the workbench, or designed so they are removable.

RodCrafter Lee Call incorporated this method in his portable rod-building jig. He spends his winters in Aransas Pass, Texas, but makes his home in Kansas. The idea of a portable shop has many applications. For someone with limited space for a rod-building jig, such as in an apartment or a mobile home, it could be ideal. Let's look further at Lee's equipment, which he designed and built mostly of scrap lumber.

The rod-winding rack is 6 feet long and there are four sets of horizontally mounted rollers. A small shelf is built between the center two roller supports, and serves to hold incidentals while at work. The legs at each end are attached with hinges to permit folding.

The horizontal bed of the bench is built so that the thread spool holder slides the complete length, from one end to the other. This enables Lee to move it from point to point along the rod as he wraps each guide. It is always parallel to the rod blank, maintaining the wrapping thread at a consistent right angle to the rod.

Portable shop by Lee Call uses horizontally mounted rollers.

The thread holder is pictured separately. The parallel boards at the bottom slip over the bed of the winding rack. Each of the two bolts that hold the spools of thread has a spring for adjustable thread tension. The bolts are sufficiently long to hold 50-yard, 1-ounce, and 4-ounce spools. The thread passes from each spool through a series of screw eyes to deliver, when desired, both threads together at the rod. Lee uses this arrangement, since his favorite wraps are two-thread wraps.

Thread holder slides on parallel boards and uses screw eyes to route thread.

Going back to the first photo, the white boxlike unit in the rear is a rod-drying rack. Two short legs raise the open end slightly, placing the unit on an angle to the horizontal. The opposite end is closed and has circular slots on the bottom to hold the ends of the rods. In the middle is a crosspiece which has circular slots cut from the top. In use, a rod handle is placed over the middle piece and the butt is slipped under the closed end. The weight of the rods holds the handles in position and the slots keep the rods from accidentally touching each other.

Cork rings, guides, thread, butt caps and other components and tools are stored in two tackle boxes and a homemade wood cabinet. The swing-out trays with the usual dividers for lures are ideal for keeping parts sorted. Shelves to hold plastic trays of various sizes serve the same purpose in the cabinet. A clever "guillotine" door always closes itself when not in use, and the cabinet has a convenient carrying handle on top.

Portable shop folded for storage or transport.

Rod rollers made of casters are occasionally used for other purposes besides cradling the rod while it is hand wrapped. One common use is for supports when rotating a rod with a barbecue-spit motor while a heavy finish cures on a decorative butt wrap. Of less frequent use, due to whipping of the rod, is to support it when power underwraps are made. In all probability, the height of the motor and the power supply (such as a sewing-machine motor) is different in each case. Unless one wants to mount each of these power sources on a bracket so that they will all be of the same height, or to make a set of separate rollers of a height for each application, the obvious answer is make the height of the rod rollers adjustable. RodCrafter Earl Davidson shared some solutions in the *RodCrafters Journal* that could be helpful, here, to the reader.

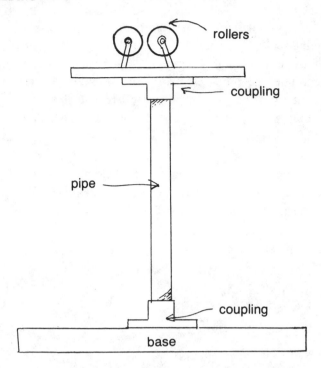

Height of rod rollers is adjustable
by using different lengths of pipe.

A pair of rollers can be mounted on a plate. On the underside of the plate a common, threaded female coupling is either epoxied or screwed. A heavier base plate with an identical threaded coupling, mounted on top, serves as a base or stand. Between the two plates a length of pipe with threads to fit the couplings is inserted. Different lengths of pipe to provide the exact height for each piece of equipment is all that is needed to adapt your supports to the specific job at hand. A variation would be that instead of threaded couplings and threaded pipe, smooth bore couplings with a hole and set screw be used with matching size un-threaded lengths of pipe.

V-blocks

Departing from the use of casters, another approach to rod supports can be used. These consist of wood uprights with V-shaped cradles at the top. Earl Davidson also detailed how this form of rod support could be made adjustable for height.

Onto a sturdy block base is mounted a vertical board with a slot in the center running most of its upper length. A matching vertical board with the center slot on the lower end is attached with a bolt and wing nut to the first. By loosening the wing nut, the height can be adjusted as needed, and then tightened securely in place. If rollers are preferred, a wood block is mounted on top of the second board, and the rollers attached to it.

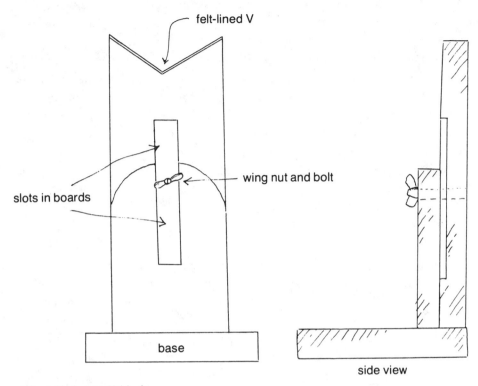

Adjustable-height V-blocks.

Now that we have broached the subject of V-blocks for rod-wrapping supports, let's take a closer look. They can be used in most any jig that would use casters for rod rollers. They are most usually made of upright boards, which should not be too thick to keep down friction. Most commonly they are lined with strips of felt glued to the wood. RodCrafter Sid Sloan feels he has found a better material that is easier to apply. Available at most drugstores, it is Dr. Scholl's Kurotex, and comes in rolls 7 inches wide and 2½ feet long. It has an adhesive back that sticks to any clean surface. It can be applied not only to V-blocks, but to the surface of nylon casters for a soft touch. To reduce friction, RodCrafter Erv Svetz lines his V-blocks with strips of teflon.

Rod-wrapping jigs can be made from most any available and familiar material. A good example of this is the tool made by RodCrafter Larry Landy and built on a base of plywood. The horizontal sliding base supports are made of square metal tubing obtained as scraps from a welding shop. A piece of smaller tubing is bolted to the base with a flat washer underneath. This provides clearance for the two pieces of larger-diameter tubing, holding the rod, to slide. The upright supports are welded in place. On top of each is glued a V-block made from scrap PVC plastic tubing. This was heated in the oven and rolled flat, then the V was cut out.

The thread-spool holder is simply a round disk with pegs of wood dowel in it. A center bolt and wing nut permit it to be rotated to bring the desired color of thread to the front. The thread-tension device consists of a piece of flat iron bent at a right angle for mounting on the plywood base. To it is soldered a polished rod bent to serve as a thread guide. Also welded to the flat iron is a ¼ × 1¼-inch bolt. Over the bolt are slipped two highly polished convex metal disks, a spring, and a wing nut. The thread passes under the unit, between the disks, and up over the thread guide. Tension is adjusted by tightening the wing nut.

Custom rollers

"Ball-bearing rod rollers with tires" is what RodCrafter Carl Reinisch calls his rod supports. To make a pair of rollers he used ball-bearing aircraft pulleys with a groove for ¹/₁₆-to-⅛-inch cable. One pulley is 3 inches in diameter and its mate 1¼ inches in diameter. The larger pulley is arranged to be closer to the thread tension unit. Used this way, the blank will not climb over the large pulley as easily as when both are the same diameter. The "tires" are O-rings to fit the grooves. If O-rings of the proper size cannot be found, larger ones can be used. Just cut them as required, join the butts together, and glue them in place. When cutting O-rings, do not stretch them, since they have a memory and will subsequently contract.

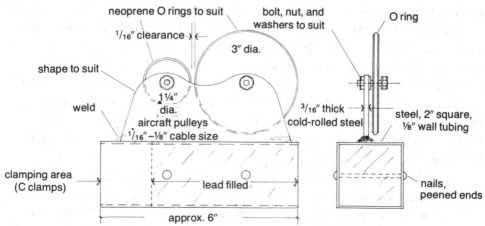

Rod rollers of aircraft pulleys with rubber O-rings, designed by Carl Reinisch.

Three aircraft pulleys with rubber
O-rings used as rod rollers by Al Clark.

Rollers of this type can be supported in any one of the previously described ways. Carl used a section of 2-inch-square steel tubing and some $^3/_{16}$-inch-thick steel plate. The plate is shaped to match the pulleys. The tubing forming the base was drilled to accept a few nails whose ends were peened over. The tube was then filled three-quarters with lead to provide weight and stability. Two such roller units are used.

If you are a machinist, or have a friend who is, you may want to consider the very handsome, functional rod rollers and combination thread holder and tension machine built by RodCrafter Beryl Ross. I secured one of these from Beryl

Rollers of hard rubber with hand rests, built by Beryl Ross.

329

a few years ago (he will make them for sale on a custom-order basis), and can vouch for their quality and efficiency. Beryl was a farmer and machinist before he retired to his rod-building business, and still has his own basement machine shop. Just about all the parts on his equipment are made entirely of solid aluminum bar stock—and beautifully machined.

The bases of the rollers are 5 inches in diameter by ⅞-inch thick with ⅛-inch-thick plastic foam on the bottom. The upright is an integral part of the base and is tapped and threaded to accept a bolt welded on the bottom of the roller housing. The large roller is 2⅞ inches in diameter and the smaller one is 1⅞ inches in diameter. Both are of hard rubber, ½ inch thick. A $1/16$-inch-thick aluminum plate is contoured to fit the rollers and bent over the top to form two hand rests. I have found these rests to be extremely helpful while wrapping. A third roller without hand rests is used for long one-piece rods.

The thread holder and tension machine are attached to a $5¼ \times 10¾ \times ⅞$-inch solid aluminum base. This also has ⅛-inch plastic foam on the bottom. Slightly to the rear of center is mounted the thread holder with four 3-inch rods. These are threaded on the end to accept a wing nut in addition to a spring and washer, thus permitting individual spool tension adjustment. To accommodate small 50-yard spools, ½-inch spacers are first slipped over the rods. These spacers are stored on four corner posts. On the thread holder there are also two tip-tops. The entire thread holder rotates and can be locked in any position with a wing nut on top.

Along the front of the base is mounted a sewing-machine adjustable thread

Thread holder and tension machine by Beryl Ross.

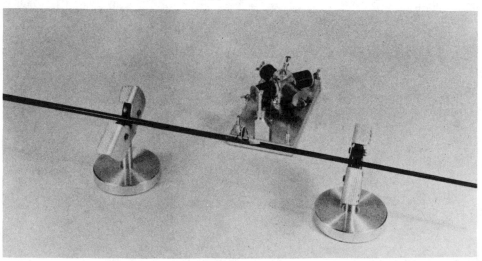

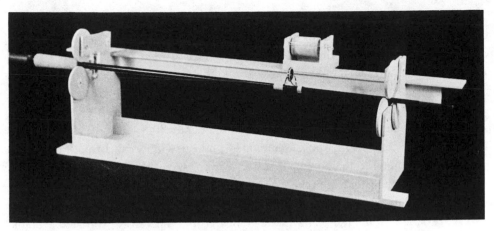

Wrapping jig built of sheet cycolac plastic, by Gene Blocchi.

tension device. Between it and the thread holder there is a tall spring-steel rod with a tip-top on the end. This serves as a visual indicator of the tension on the thread. The thread goes from the spool to a tip-top on the thread holder, through the tension device, to the tension indicator, and then to the rod. A dust cover of ⅛-inch-thick clear plastic fits over the entire thread-holder unit when it is not in use.

Plastic wrapping jig

Working with familiar materials is important when making your equipment, and that is exactly what RodCrafter Gene Blocchi did. All the parts on Gene's tool, except some necessary metal hardware, are made of ³/₁₆-inch sheet cycolac plastic. They were cut to shape and either cemented or riveted together.

The wrapping jig will hold any rod, from long one-piece surf to small ultralight. It is relatively small, lightweight, and easily portable for storage. A unique feature is that it maintains its own tension on the blank, so you can stop to answer the phone or handle any interruption. The boxlike design of the base provides a handy enclosed tray for holding the small implements of our craft.

Dimensions on this or any of the jigs discussed are not critical and can easily be adapted to your own needs. We are listing them merely so you can get an idea of the proportions used by the designer. The base on Gene's tool is 27 inches long by 7 inches deep. The front and back of the base box are made of panels 1¾ inches high. The end pieces each hold a pair of rollers or "wheels." These wheels are mounted, one on each side of the end piece, and are positioned so that they overlap a bit front to back. This forms a V which cradles the blank.

The 2½-inch-diameter "wheels" or rollers are cut from the same ³/₁₆-inch cycolac by using a circle cutter on a drill press. After they are cut out, the edges are beveled slightly and sanded smooth. A hole is drilled in the center so they rotate easily on a rivet (they could also be mounted on bolts and nuts). A washer serves as a spacer between the wheel and the end piece of the frame.

The end pieces are shaped so that there is a 1½-inch-deep post at the rear, which extends about 2¾ inches higher than the center line of the two previously mentioned wheels. On this post is mounted an arm with a third rotating wheel. The arm is attached to the post so that it is free to swivel on the connecting rivet. A coil spring extends between the swivel arm and the side piece holding the other two wheels. This pulls the top wheel (on the swivel arm) down between the other two wheels, and holds the blank under light tension. Therefore, to place a blank in the jig for wrapping, the two swivel arms must be lifted. Once in the machine it will not roll of its own accord from thread tension, but is easily rotated by hand for wrapping.

A third assembly, identical to the end pieces on the boxlike frame, contains the same three-wheel arrangement. It has a small, flat base so that it can be used inside the box between the end pieces, or clamped to the workbench at any distance needed to support a long rod.

A thread-tension device slides along a 2-inch-wide horizontal panel on the back of the machine. The panel is 32 inches long, so it extends beyond the end plates. This arrangement, incidentally, is ideal for wrapping tip-tops. The thread-tension device is a small box on which one end moves on a threaded bolt. The spool of thread is held on a plastic rod which simply drops into slots cut on each end piece. In addition to the spool, it contains a spring and two washers. A wing nut on the outside of the fixed end piece draws the opposite, moveable end piece against the spring, and provides the thread tension.

POWER WRAPPING TOOL

Let's immediately differentiate between a rod lathe and a power wrapping tool. A rod lathe must be more powerful in order to turn grips, hosels, etc. It needs a much stronger connection between motor and rod, and must revolve absolutely true on its axis with no vibration. By contrast, a rod-wrapping tool needs only enough power to turn the rod against thread tension. A light-duty connection is all that is required, and it is not necessary for the rod to rotate precisely true and vibration-free. It is used for making underwraps, and if you get good enough, guide wraps.

Ideally a wrapping tool should be able to be rotated easily by hand to facilitate the starting and ending of wraps. This precludes pulleys and gears as speed reducers, or the turning resistance of a powerful motor. Most frequently power is provided by a sewing-machine motor with a variable-speed foot pedal. Sewing-machine motors turn at 5000 rpm, which proves a bit fast for many rod builders. An educated foot is required to depress the pedal to a minimum. One solution is an electronic speed-reducing control which varies motor speed from zero to full with no loss of power.

Other approaches to motors include an old fan motor. This is used by Rod-Crafter "Boots" Voigt with a small chuck to hold the rod by the tip. The motor does not revolve at nearly as high a speed as a sewing-machine motor. The slight weight of the handle also keeps the rod from whipping on caster rod rollers. Rod-Crafter L. W. Cannon uses a small 40 rpm motor whose speed he finds ideal for wrapping.

For attaching the rod to the motor shaft any of the devices listed later for use on rod lathes can be employed. However, only a light-duty connection is required. A common method is to use a variety of sizes of rubber crutch tips and/or butt caps. A hole is drilled in the center and a washer and bolt inserted from the inside. Another washer and a nut are placed over the protruding bolt. The bolt is slipped into a small, keyless chuck or a simple sleeve, that locks over the motor shaft and bolt. The crutch tip or butt cap is slipped on the rod (minus butt cap). If a tighter fit is needed, a bit of masking tape is wrapped on the end of the rod grip.

To support the rod during rotation, rod rollers or padded V-blocks can be used. It is preferable if the height of the motor on the supports is slightly adjustable. This allows mounting the rod with just the least bit of pressure against the supports in order to help reduce whipping.

ROD LATHES

In the earlier chapters on grips and handle assemblies there were many references to using a rod lathe. A lathe is not only the most accurate but the easiest way of shaping handles of cork or resilient grips, fitting hosels, custom butt caps, trim rings, winding checks, scoring reel seats, and a host of other rod-building jobs. While not specifically designed for it, many rod lathes can be used as a power wrapping tool, especially for underwraps. They will also hold a small grinding wheel for dressing guide feet, or a buffing wheel for polishing. Just as a wood or metal lathe is one of the most versatile machines in a general shop, a rod-building lathe is a boon to the custom maker. Once you have one you will wonder how you ever did without it.

A woodworking lathe will not fill the bill as a rod lathe for several reasons. It does not have a long enough bed between power head and tail stock to accommodate even one section of a typical two-piece rod. Neither does it have a center support. Unlike a rigid piece of a solid wood or metal, a fishing rod is designed to flex. At even moderate rotation speeds a blank starts to whip, or flex, in the midsection between the two end supports. At that point it is no longer revolving on its axis, and shaping a round handle becomes impossible. Rather than trying to modify a wood lathe it is easier, and better, to either buy or build a lathe designed solely for rod building.

There are three primary components to a rod lathe. Starting with the power source, the motor need not be as powerful as that of a regular wood lathe. It does, however, have to be arranged so that it has sufficient torque for shaping all kinds of grips and cutting small wood and plastic parts. The power source must also be stable and vibration-free. Second, there has to be a convenient but strong means of attaching the rod to the power source. Third is the system of supports for the rotating rod. They must eliminate whip and be as friction-free as possible. A fourth optional component is a bed of some type as an aid in aligning the power source and the rod supports.

Power sources

A quality, heavy-duty sewing-machine motor is capable of delivering the required power if it is used with a system of pulleys in a gear ratio of about 8:1. This converts speed to power and reduces the 5000 rpm to a workable 625 rpm. Use a motor that has a shaft at both ends. You can then select the direction of rotation (clockwise or counterclockwise) to your preference for the job at hand. A good heavy-duty motor will also come with full mounting brackets on each side for easy, sturdy installation.

The best, and also the easiest, way to mount a sewing-machine motor and the required pulleys is with a "polishing head." This is a housing commonly used to mount polishing wheels and grinding wheels. When mounted on a board, or directly on a workbench, it provides just about the right height for the rod over the work surface. Sleeve bearings are fine for the speeds used; just keep them well oiled. An on-off switch can be used, but a variable-speed foot pedal will add great versatility and a better degree of control.

A power source which you may already have is an electric drill. The ⅜-inch size is adequate, but the larger chuck on a ½-inch drill is more versatile. A variable-speed model which can be locked at any speed is preferable. The drill can be mounted quickly in one of the commercially available stands, or you can make your own.

Another source of power may be an electric motor from an otherwise worn-out appliance. Any such motor of $1/5$ hp to $1/2$ hp can be used. These usually are 1600-1750-rpm motors which, although a bit fast, can be used as direct drive. Better, more controllable results will be obtained if you reduce the speed with pulleys. You can even use multiple pulleys for more than one fixed speed, similar to the arrangement common on wood lathes. Instead of pulleys with a motor of this type you might want to consider an electronic motor speed control. The simpler direct-drive arrangement can be used, yet by turning a dial you control the speed of the motor from 0 to full rpm—without any loss of motor power. With it you can still use a variable-speed foot pedal.

Attachment to rod

The easiest method of attachment is a chuck. However, if we want a chuck with enough capacity to hold the large butt diameters of some finished rods, we need a heavy, expensive piece of equipment. There is a small, lightweight chuck available, called a Super Chuck. With jaws reversed, it has a large 2¼-inch capacity. The depth of the jaws is not great, but it is adequate for rod work. It is light enough to be powered by a sewing-machine motor with pulleys as described above. Its only drawbacks are that it is not inexpensive and it requires a specially threaded shaft.

Rod lathe using polishing head, pulleys, sewing-machine motor, Super Chuck, and adjustable-height ball-bearing lathe support.

335

If you are using an electric drill for a power source, you already have a chuck. It will be limited to the size drill used, either ⅜ or ½ inch. This will hold smaller blanks if you leave the last cork off, or trim ½ inch or less from the butt of the blank. On a fly rod using a closed-end fly-reel seat, the seat would have to be mounted last, after the handle and any other turning work was completed. There are, however, a number of mandrels and techniques that can be used with a small chuck and a large-diameter blank. These are discussed below.

A rod lathe using a polishing head has a shaft in the head. This is threaded and a ½-inch keyed chuck similar to those on drills can be used. Or, a keyless chuck can usually be found with matching threads. This type of chuck can be tightened by hand with enough gripping force for most rod work, and is less expensive than a keyed chuck.

For a direct-drive installation, a work arbor and threaded mandrel to hold a chuck can be employed. If you use the "Crusenberry mandrels" or "Terrell mandrels" discussed below, you will not need a chuck. Without a chuck you do lose some of the versatility for operations other than turning a blank. The Crusenberry mandrels can be used with or without a chuck.

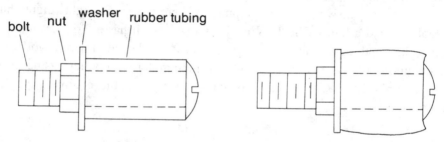

Mandrels to grip blank from the inside expand by tightening nut.

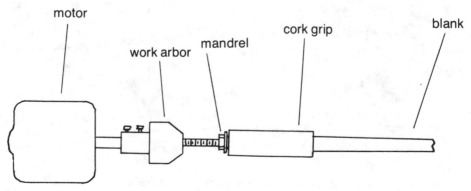

Direct drive lathe with appliance motor, work arbor, and "Crusenberry Mandrel."

The mandrels designed by RodCrafter Harry Crusenberry are simple to make and work very well. I have often used them myself ever since Harry told me about them. As noted, they can be used with a work arbor, available at hardware stores to fit most motor shafts (see drawing).

"Crusenberry mandrels" of assorted sizes.

Harry's mandrel is made from a bolt and rubber tubing, held together with a washer and a hex nut. By tightening the hex nut against the washer, pressure is applied to the tubing, which causes the tubing to expand. If you use a piece of tubing that is closely sized to the inside diameter of the blank, the expansion causes the tubing to grip the inside of the blank securely. Since the tubing expands uniformly, there is no wobble as the blank turns. It is automatically centered on the arbor.

The inside diameter of the tubing is important to the effectiveness of the mandrel. The tubing should fit snugly over the bolt. Therefore, to get different sizes for different blanks, use larger or smaller bolts and tubing to fit them. Rubber and synthetic tubing of various sizes is available at auto supply stores and hardware stores. Use the tubing sold for windshield washers, windshield-wiper vacuums, and gas lines, to suggest a few. The diameter of the round head on the bolt must be smaller than the tubing. On very large sizes this may mean grinding down the diameter of the bolt head, as well as turning down the portion of the bolt shank that fits in the chuck.

The mandrels designed by RodCrafter Jamison Terrell are for use directly on a motor shaft. A friend with access to a metal lathe can make up a variety of sizes for you, or it should not be too expensive to have them made by a local machine shop. The basic design of the mandrel is a series of ½-inch-long steps in solid steel rod. Each step is $1/16$ inch smaller in diameter than the previous step. The surfaces of the steps are knurled. A blind hole is bored in the large-diameter end so that the mandrel can be slipped over your motor shaft. A hole is drilled and tapped in the side to accept a set screw so that it is held securely on the motor shaft (see drawing). To use the mandrel, slip the blank over the end to the point where the widest knurled section fits inside the blank. If necessary, a knurled section can be filled out with a few wraps of masking tape. Use a hose clamp over the butt of the blank to anchor it. Do not tighten the clamp too much or you could split the blank.

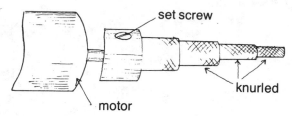

Mandrel designed by Jamison Terrell for use directly on appliance motor shaft.

For blanks up to ½ inch in inside diameter, a mandrel made from a *very straight* rat-tail file can be used. This system is utilized by RodCrafter Elwood E. Banks. A file with a taper from about ½ to ¼ inch will handle blanks in that size range. For smaller-diameter blanks, simply use a smaller-size file. To prepare the files, cut off all but 1 inch of the tang (pointed handle end) with a hacksaw. The 1 inch remaining will serve as a shank to fit into a ½-inch chuck. For a smaller chuck, have the shank turned down. In use, the blank is slipped over the file. The directional rotation of the teeth on the file grips the inside of the blank in such a manner that it tends to pull the blank tighter.

Effective tapered hardwood mandrels can also be used. Again, a variety of sizes can be made. RodCrafter L. W. Cannon makes them to press-fit directly onto the motor shaft (see drawing). This is done by making the end large enough

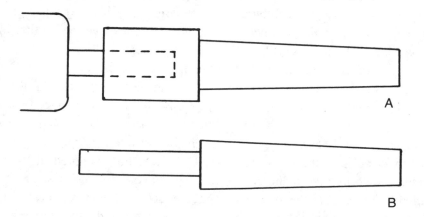

Tapered wood mandrels. A: Press-fit onto motor shaft. B: For use in chuck.

and drilling the correct-size blind hole. A hole in the side with a set screw will make an even stronger connection. If you use a chuck on your lathe, turn the untapered ends to a level outside diameter that will just fit into your chuck. In use, the diameter of the tapered mandrel can be built up with masking tape when needed. If slippage occurs, a layer of double-stick tape, or carpet tape, can be added.

With all of the mandrels discussed that fit inside the blank, it is necessary to leave the butt cap off the rod until all shaping is completed. The recess for the butt cap can be shaped, and when the rod is removed from the lathe the butt cap is glued in place. Any final dressing of the cork to blend perfectly with the outside diameter of the butt cap is easily done by hand with sandpaper or an emery board. On fly rods using reel seats with closed end caps, all fitting is done for the reel seat beforehand, but it is not installed until after the turning operations are complete. It is thus glued on last.

So, there is an assortment of power sources and systems for attaching a rod. From among them you should be able to find a method or combination of methods to enable you to build a very effective rod lathe. You may presently be using a better system or have suggested improvements. By all means let me encourage you to become associated with RodCrafters and to share and learn so that, together, we may all advance the craft.

Rod supports

The most critical part of a rod lathe is the support system used to keep the rod revolving true in a straight line on its axis. As noted earlier, a blank is designed to flex and will therefore whip when it is rotated at even moderate speeds. A rod lathe must employ a support system to completely eliminate that whipping action. Otherwise, it will be impossible to turn grips or any part perfectly round.

Hand wrapping jigs frequently use rod rollers, and the tapered blank is merely laid across them. When we make a rod lathe we attach the blank with a strong connection at a fixed height. The center line of the chuck can be the same height as the center line of the rollers, but that will not solve the problem because *blanks are tapered*, and we build rods on *different size blanks*. We would have to use adjustable-height rollers such as described earlier, or shim each set of rollers to the exact height for the portion of the blank it is to support. Even if we did this we would find it unsatisfactory. At speeds high enough for efficient shaping, the blank starts to vibrate and whip, bouncing up and down on the rollers. So we are back to whip control again. Also, suppose we wanted to shape a wood or plastic hosel directly on the blank. We would then be applying pressure at a right angle to the blank. This will definitely cause it to move or whip on the rollers.

Without belaboring the problems further, what is needed is a rod-support system that (1) can be adjusted precisely to any desired height, (2) will clamp the blank firmly on all sides, making it revolve true, (3) will be practically friction-free to prevent damage to the blank and allow use of relatively low-power motors without strain, (4) can be moved to any position along any length blank, and (5) is itself stable, once in position.

I have been exposed to, examined, and used a wide assortment of rod-lathe support systems. Beyond a doubt, I feel the best and most versatile is the one designed by RodCrafter James R. Youmans. My feelings on this were so strong that we requested he make these so that we could sell them through our rod-building-supply business. It takes Jim about ten hours to make a unit, and he simply did not have the time. We therefore entered an arrangement to have them manufactured for us. However, you can make one yourself, and full directions and working drawings are given below.

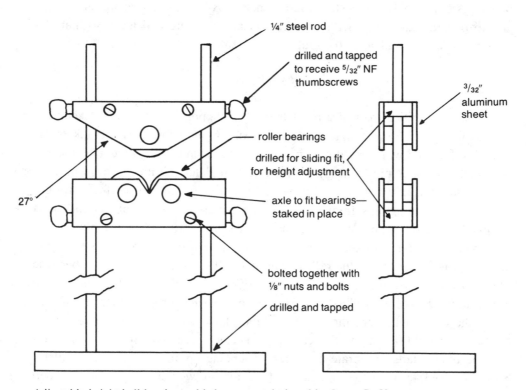

Adjustable-height ball-bearing rod lathe support designed by James R. Youmans.

The heart of the unit consists of three ball bearings, one on the sliding top plate, and two on the sliding bottom plate. These are ⅞ inch O.D., $5/16$ inch bore, and $11/32$ inch wide, NICE No. 1603 DC. They are small so that the cross-section triangle where the bearings meet will accept small-diameter rod tips.

The general dimensions of the unit can be altered to fit your needs. For framing the sliding plates housing the bearings, use $3/32$-inch aluminum sheet cut to shape and held together with short bolts. The base plate needs to be large enough and sturdy enough to support the unit. If necessary, in use it can be clamped to the work surface. Half-inch aluminum plate works very well.

The two upright rods, on which each plate with the bearings slides, can be $7/32$ or ¼ inch. On the sides of each plate to lock it in place on the vertical rods, $5/32$-inch bolts with wing nuts are used.

To use the unit, temporarily slide the top plate up near the top, and adjust the height of the bottom plate to just below the center of your chuck. Place the blank into the chuck of your power head. Determine where the blank will rest on the ball bearings, and put a few winds of masking tape around the blank at that point. (This will prevent marring, and help make a good fit of the blank against the bearings.) Adjust the height of the bottom plate so that when the blank rests on the bearings it is perfectly level. Lock the bottom plate in place. Now, lower the top plate so that the single ball bearing is right against the blank, and lock that plate in position. The blank is now held securely in place on all sides, but will revolve with little or no friction because of the ball bearings.

When shaping a handle, locate the unit near the middle of the blank. Best stability is achieved, especially on longer or lighter blanks, by using two units. Then one is placed relatively near the handle and the other at the opposite end of the blank. If you do any bamboo-rod repair work, these units are perfect for truing and sizing the rod for ferrule installation. In this situation you would place a support near the end of the rod section where the ferrule is to be fit. The other would be placed in the middle of the rod section. Some wraps of masking tape around the rod convert the five- or six-sided profile to a round shape for easy rotation on the ball bearings.

The units are light in weight and easily portable. They therefore can be used in conjunction with other tools, or for other purposes. If you have a powered wrapping jig, they are excellent rod supports. You will find wrapping is easier since the blank is stable, revolving precisely on its axis. Many rod builders rotate their rods at low rpm while the wrapping finish dries, particularly where a heavy coat of finish has been applied on a butt wrap. A barbecue-spit motor, or other low-rpm motor, is an ideal combination with the rod lathe supports. Since the rod is clamped between ball bearings, there is no danger that it will fall off the rollers and ruin the finish. With the top plate removed they can even be used as rod rollers for regular hand wrapping. You will undoubtedly find other uses.

It was mentioned earlier that some rod makers prefer some sort of lathe bed to keep the lathe components easily aligned. If you make the base of each ball-bearing rod-lathe support square with the corners just slightly rounded, an alignment bed is easily made. Parallel wood rails can be screwed to the workbench. The distance between the rails is such that the lathe-support bases will fit, and slide, between them. The rails can have straight sides, or they can be notched along the bottom. The dimensions of the notch are made to fit the thickness of the lathe-support bases. The lathe supports are then slid into the open end of the rails and moved to any desired position.

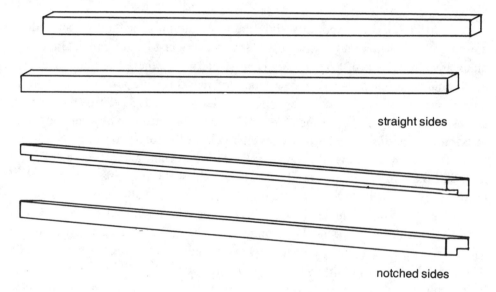

straight sides

notched sides

Parallel wood rails can be used as an alignment bed for lathe with Youmans's supports. Rails can be straight-sided or notched to fit base plate.

It is a good idea to mount your lathe power souce on a square sheet of plywood. A sheet ¾ inch thick is ideal. Any screws or bolts that must be inserted all the way through the board can be inserted from the bottom through countersunk holes, keeping the bottom smooth and flat. To keep this base board from sliding in use, the entire underside, or portions along the sides, can be covered with Stays-Put. This is a nonslip cushioned rubber with adhesive backing which has similar applications on many rod-building tools. When mounting the power source make sure the driveshaft is aligned at 90° to one side. Then the base board can be placed against the bed rails for perfect alignment.

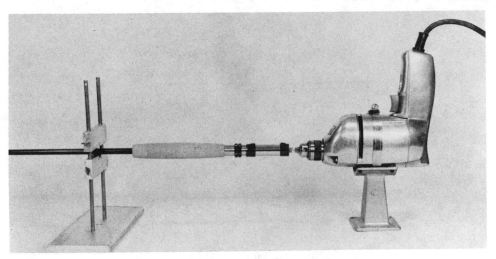

Rod lathe of electric drill, Crusenberry mandrel, and ball-bearing lathe support.

In the chapter on grips, a cork-shaping tool, or jig, was discussed for repeat-edly turning out the same shape grips on handles. One end of a board was cut to the desired shape and coated with cutting grit imbedded in epoxy. This was fed horizontally into the revolving cylinder of cork rings. To keep the cutting board aligned with the center line of the revolving blank, the jig in which it slides is constructed to the appropriate height for your rod lathe. Minor height adjust-ments, if needed, can be made by placing boards as shims beneath the power-source base board, and the ball-bearing lathe supports adjusted accordingly. The same can be done for the jig discussed below.

RodCrafter L. W. Cannon uses a cork-shaping jig that is built much like a wood miter box. His has two long parallel sides with low end pieces or spreaders. It could just as easily be built with a bottom piece to which the two long sides were screwed and glued. The jig is set beneath the revolving cork cylinder on the blank. The top edges of the box are of a height so that they project above the center line of the blank by one-half the diameter of the desired grip. They are contoured to the shape of the grip and therefore should be sawed to shape at the same time before assembly (see drawings). To shape the cork a ½-¾-inch-thick wood sanding block is slid along the top edges of the parallel sides. This block must be long enough to extend over the edges of the contoured boards, and one edge is covered with sandpaper or cutting grit. Finish sanding is done with the jig removed. Incidentally, if you build a lathe bed of notched rails, small strips can be glued along the sides at the bottom to fit into the notches. This will serve to hold the jig in position so that it does not tip.

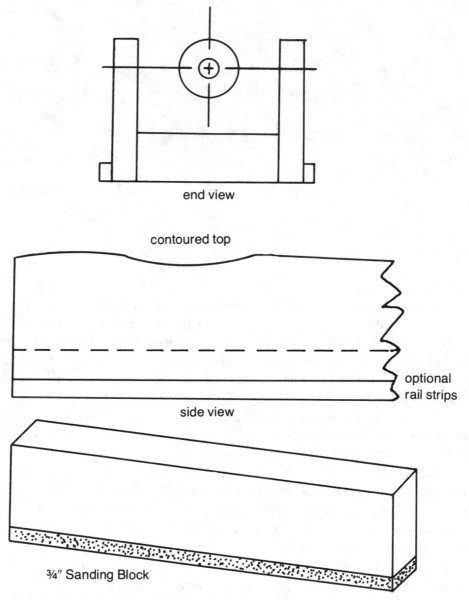

end view

contoured top

optional
rail strips

side view

¾″ Sanding Block

Cork-shaping jig for making duplicate grips. Sanding block is slid across contoured top.

STATIC-DEFLECTION-TEST STAND

As we noted before, a static deflection test can be helpful at times. This is where a blank or rod is mounted in a horizontal position along a wall and a weight

344

is suspended from the tip. We can then see the pattern of the arc described by the blank. The block can also be rotated to determine the high side. It must be remembered that this is a static picture of deflection and does not necessarily indicate the dynamic aspects of a blank in motion.

A very simple way to mount a blank is by the use of two pegs placed in the wall so that the one at the butt is on top while the other, a few inches forward, is underneath the blank. RodCrafter Beryl Ross uses a static deflection test to match the action of a customer's favorite bass casting rod. To do this he made a bracket that will hold up to four rods or blanks at one time and allows for perfect horizontal alignment. The bracket is mounted in the corner, a few inches from the adjacent viewing wall.

The bracket is made from a length of aluminum I-beam bolted along the bottom to an 18-inch-long aluminum plate. On the front edge of the I-beam are cut four U-shaped notches. Just below each notch and on the bottom plate are threaded holes for adjusting screws. Each screw (really a bolt) has a plastic cap on the end so it will not mar the blank. On the back edge of the I-beam are four holes into which the butts of the blanks can be slipped (see photo).

Bracket to hold blanks or rods for static deflection tests.

In use, the blanks are slipped into the rear holes and rested in the U-shaped notches. The adjusting screws are then used to get the tip ends of each blank perfectly level. A weight (Beryl uses 8 ounces for bass casting rods) is then suspended from the tip. To keep the weight from sliding off a blank without a tiptop, a rubber band is wrapped repeatedly around the tip section until it is quite tight and slipproof. Using blanks from his stock, Beryl can then match the favorite rod. To do so he may have to use a longer blank and trim either or both ends.

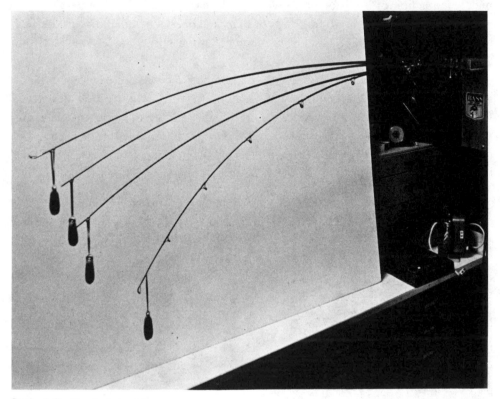

Static-deflection-test stand in use.

SIZE CONVERSION CHART

Fiberglass Rod Making contained a size conversion chart, but the following is more complete and includes the metric scale. My thanks to RodCrafter Joy Dunlap, who made the chart.

SIZE CONVERSION CHART

64ths Inch Tackle Size	Metric	Fraction	Decimal
	0.42 mm	1/64″	.0156″
	0.50 mm		.0312″
		1/32″	.0312″
	0.80 mm		.0315″
	1.00 mm		.03937″
3		3/64″	.0468″
3-1/2		7/128″	.0546
4		1/16″ (4/64)	.0625
4-1/2		9/128″	.0703
5	7	5/64″	.0781
	2.0 mm		.07874
5-1/2		11/128″	.0859
6		3/32″ (6/64)	.0937
6-1/2		13/128″	.1015
7		7/64″	.1093
7-1/2		15/128″	.1171
	3		.11811
8		1/8″ (8/64)	.125
9		9/64″	.1406
10		5/32″ (10/64)	.1562
	4		.15748
11		11/64″	.1718
12		3/16″ (12/64)	.1875
	5		.19685
13		13/64″	.2031
14		7/32″ (14/64)	.2187
15		15/64″	.2343
	6		.23622
16		1/4″ (16/64)	.25
17		17/64″	.2656
	7		.27559
18		9/32″ (18/64)	.2812
19		19/64″	.2968
20		5/16″ (20/64)	.3125
21	8	21/64″	.3261
22		11/32″ (22/64)	.3437
	9		.35433
23		23/64″	.3593
24		3/8″ (24/64)	.375
25	10.0 mm	25/64″	.3906
26	10.5 mm	13/32″ (26/64)	.4062
27	11.0 mm	27/64″	.4218
28		7/16″ (28/64)	.4375
29	11.5 mm	29/64″	.4531
30	12.0 mm	15/32″ (30/64)	.4687
31		31/64″	.4843
	12.5 mm	63/128″	
32		1/2″ (32/64)	.5
	13.0 mm		
33		33/64″	.5156

SIZE CONVERSION CHART

64ths Inch Tackle Size	Metric	Fraction	Decimal
34	13.5 mm	17/32" (34/64)	.5312
35		35/64"	.5468
	14.0 mm		
36		9/16" (36/64)	.5625
37		37/64"	.5781
	14.5 mm		
38		19/32" (38/64)	.5937
	15.0 mm		
39		39/64"	.6093
40		5/8" (40/64)	.625
41	16.0 mm	41/64"	.6406
42		21/32" (42/64)	.6562
43		43/64"	.6718
44		11/16" (44/64)	.6875
45		45/64"	.7031
46		23/32" (46/64)	.7187
	18.0 mm		
47		47/64"	.7343
48		3/4" (48/64)	.75
49		49/64"	.7656
50		25/32" (50/64)	.7812
51	20.0 mm	51/64"	.7968
52		13/16" (52/64)	.8125
53		53/64"	.8281
54		27/32" (54/64)	.8437
55		55/65"	.8593
56		7/8" (56/64)	.875
57		57/64"	.8906
58		29/32" (58/64)	.9062
59		59/64"	.9218
60		15/16" (60/64)	.9375
61	24.0 mm	61/64"	.9531
62		31/32" (62/64)	.9685
63		63/64"	.9843
64	25.7 mm	1"	1.00
		1-3/16"	
	30.0 mm		1.1811
		1-17/64"	
	32.0 mm		1.25984
		1-27/64"	
	36.0 mm		1.41732
		1-37/64"	
	40.0 mm		1.5748
		1-57/64"	
	48.0 mm		1.88976
		1-63/64"	
	50.0 mm		1.9685
		2-24/64"	
	60.0 mm		2.3622

INDEX

Roman Letter Symbols

$\circledA$ area bounded by center line of the perimeter of a thin tube

A area, area of cross section

c distance from neutral axis or from center of twist to extreme fiber

E modulus of elasticity in tension or compression

F force

f frequency, flexibility coefficient

G modulus of elasticity in shear

I moment of inertia of cross-sectional area

I_p polar moment of inertia of circular cross-sectional area

K stress concentration factor, effective length factor for columns

k spring constant, constant; k = kilopound = kip = 1000 lb.

L length; $L_e = KL$ effective column length

M moment, bending moment, mass

M_p plastic moment

m mass, moment caused by virtual unit force

P force, concentrated load

p pressure intensity, axial force due to unit force

Q first or statical moment of area A_{fghj} around neutral axis

q distributed load intensity, shear flow

R reaction, radius

r radius, radius of gyration

S elastic section-modulus ($S = I/c$)

T torque, temperature

t thickness, width, tangential deviation

U strain energy

u internal force caused by virtual unit load, axial or radial displacement

V shear force (often vertical), volume

v deflection of beam, velocity

W total weight, work

w weight or load per unit of length

Z Plastic section modulus

AE Axial rigidity; EI Flexural rigidity; GI_p Torsional rigidity

Greek Letter Symbols

α (alpha)   Coefficient of thermal expansion, general angle

γ (gamma)   shear strain, weight per unit volume

Δ (delta)   total deformation or deflection, change of any designated function

ε (epsilon)   normal strain

θ (theta)   slope angle for elastic curve, angle of inclination of line on body

κ (kappa)   curvature

λ (lambda)   eigenvalue in column buckling problems

ν (nu)   Poisson's ratio

ρ (rho)   radius, radius of curvature

σ (sigma)   tensile or compressive stress (i.e., normal stress)

τ (tau)   shear stress

ϕ (phi)   total angle of twist, general angle

Engineering Mechanics of
SOLIDS

Second Edition

Egor P. Popov

Professor in the Graduate School
University of California–Berkeley

In collaboration with

Toader A. Balan

Professor of Structural Engineering
Technical University of Moldova, Chisinau

Prentice Hall
Upper Saddle River, New Jersey 07458

Library of Congress Cataloging-in-Publication Data

Popov, E. P. (Egor Paul)
    Engineering mechanics of solids / Egor P. Popov, -- 2nd ed.
      p. cm.
    Includes bibliographical references and index.
    ISBN 0-13-726159-4
    1. Strength of materials.   I. Title.
  TA405.P677   1998
  620.1'12—dc21   98–15677
                                      CIP

Acquisitions Editor: Eric Svendsen
Editorial/Production Supervision: Rose Kernan
Editor-in-Chief: Marcia Horton
Managing Editor: Eileen Clark
Copy Editing: Patricia Daly
Cover Designer: Bruce Kenselaar
Assistant Vice-President of Production and Manufacturing: David W. Riccardi
Manufacturing Buyer: Pat Brown
Editorial Assistant: Griffin Cable

Printed in the United States of America

10   9   8   7   6   5   4   3   2

ISBN 0-13-726159-4

Prentice-Hall International (UK) Limited, *London*
Prentice-Hall of Australia Pty, Limited, *Sydney*
Prentice-Hall Canada Inc., *Toronto*
Prentice-Hall Hispanoamericana, S.A., *Mexico*
Prentice-Hall of India Private Limited, *New Delhi*
Prentice-Hall of Japan, Inc., *Tokyo*
Pearson Education Asia Pte. Ltd., *Singapore*
Editora Prentice-Hall do Brasil, Ltda., *Rio de Janeiro*
Prentice-Hall, *Upper Saddle River, NJ*

On the Cover: Fragments of the ancient Paris Louvre palace in the background, and the new pyramidal addition in the foreground.

To the memory of my dear
Irene

Contents

3 Axial Deformation of Bars: Statically Determinate Systems,   91

4 Axial Deformation of Bars: Statically Indeterminate Systems,   131

Preface

The Second Edition of *The Engineering Mechanics of Solids* has been significantly modified yet it retains its character as a complete traditional text on mechanics of solids with advance overtones. For permitting a greater flexibility in the selection of assignments, the text has been subdivided into a larger number of chapters. In this manner it is convenient for the instructor to carefully omit unwanted material without losing continuity.

In the new revision a number of avant-garde topics are considered. An advanced analytical expression for cyclic loading has been provided, and a novel failure surface for *brittle* material has been introduced. The latter item complements the famous van Mises yield surface for *ductile* materials. The fundamentals of the probabilistic basis for structural design are included, whereas the more specialized topics on this subject have been deleted from this edition. The chapter on the mechanical properties of materials has been substantially expanded. There is a more extensive treatment of the true stress-strain diagrams, and there are new sections on fatigue and viscoelastic behavior.

The text is written with a bias toward the SI system of units, especially on the problems for the solution by the students. Numerical tables provide a choice between the SI and the US customary units.

By virtue of the topics chosen, it is believed the text is sufficiently general to be useful to civil, mechanical, and aeronautical engineers.

The new edition benefited from enthusiastic support of Dr. Toader A. Balan, who was very helpful in offering useful suggestions throughout the text. Specifically, he greatly contributed to the chapter on the mechanical properties of materials, suggested introducing an elegant analytical formulation for cyclic behavior of inelastic materials, and deduced a novel expression for the failure surface of brittle materials.

I am indebted to Professors Keith Hjelmstad of the University of Illinois-Urbana and Vassilis Panoskaltsis of the Case Western Reserve University for meticulously examining the manuscript and offering meaningful suggestions. Special gratitude is sincerely acknowledged to the many colleagues at the University of California, Berkeley in the Department of Civil and Environmental Engineering, who over the years greatly influenced the development and growth of this book. Among these, it is a particular pleasure to thank Professors A. C. Scordelis, R. W. Clough,

R. L Taylor, E. L. Wilson, and the late Professors H. D. Eberhart and R. Seban from Mechanical Engineering.

It is also a pleasure to acknowledge the assistance of Professor A. der Kiureghian of UC Berkeley who offered useful suggestions with the section on probabilistic basis for structural design, Professor J. L. Meek of the University of Queensland, Australia, who influenced the development of the section on virtual work of discrete systems, and Dr. S. Nagarajan, a Research Scientist at the Lockheed Missiles & Space Company, who contributed to the formulation of the displacement method in Chapter 19. Rose Kernan of the Prentice Hall editorial staff offered competent help in getting this book out in great shape.

Egor P. Popov
Berkeley

1

Stress

1-1. Introduction

In all engineering construction, the component parts of a structure or a machine must be assigned definite physical sizes. Such parts must be properly proportioned to resist the actual or probable forces that may be imposed upon them. Thus, the walls of a pressure vessel must be of adequate strength to withstand the internal pressure; the floors of a building must be sufficiently strong for their intended purpose; the shaft of a machine must be of adequate size to carry the required torque; a wing of an airplane must safely withstand the aerodynamic loads that may come upon it in takeoff, flight, and landing. Likewise, the parts of a composite structure must be rigid enough so as not to deflect or "sag" excessively when in operation under the imposed loads. A floor of a building may be strong enough but yet may deflect excessively, which in some instances may cause misalignment of manufacturing equipment, or in other cases result in the cracking of a plaster ceiling attached underneath. Also a member may be so thin or slender that, upon being subjected to compressive loading, it will collapse through buckling (i.e., the initial configuration of a member may become unstable). The ability to determine the maximum load that a slender column can carry before buckling occurs or the safe level of vacuum that can be maintained by a vessel is of great practical importance.

In engineering practice, such requirements must be met with the minimum expenditure of a given material. Aside from cost, at times—as in the design of satellites—the feasibility and success of the whole mission may depend on the weight of a package. The subject of *mechanics of materials,* or the *strength of materials,* as it has been traditionally called, involves analytical methods for determining the **strength, stiffness** (deformation characteristics), and **stability** of the various load-carrying members. Alternately, the subject may be called the *mechanics of solid deformable bodies,* or simply *mechanics of solids.*

Mechanics of solids is a fairly old subject, generally dated from the work of Galileo in the early part of the seventeenth century. Prior to his investigations into the behavior of solid bodies under loads, constructors followed precedents and empirical rules. Galileo was the first to attempt to explain the behavior of some of the members under load on a rational basis. He studied members in tension and compression, and notably beams used in the construction of hulls of ships for the Italian navy. Of course, much progress has been made since that time, but it must be noted in passing that much is owed in the development of this subject to the French investigators, among whom a group of outstanding men such as Coulomb, Poisson, Navier, St. Venant, and Cauchy, who worked at the break of the nineteenth century, have left an indelible impression on this subject.

The subject of mechanics of solids cuts broadly across all branches of the engineering profession with remarkably many applications. Its methods are needed by designers of offshore structures; by civil engineers in the design of bridges and buildings; by mining engineers and architectural engineers, each of whom is interested in structures; by nuclear engineers in the design of reactor components; by mechanical and chemical engineers, who rely upon the methods of this subject for the design of machinery and pressure vessels; by metallurgists, who need the fundamental concepts of this subject in order to understand how to improve existing materials further; and finally by electrical engineers, who need the methods of this subject because of the importance of the mechanical engineering phases of many portions of electrical equipment. Engineering mechanics of solids, contrasted with the mathematical theory of continuum mechanics, has characteristic methods all its own, although the two approaches overlap. It is a definite discipline and one of the most fundamental subjects of an engineering curriculum, standing alongside such other basic subjects as fluid mechanics, thermodynamics, as well as electrical theory.

The behavior of a member subjected to forces depends not only on the fundamental laws of Newtonian mechanics that govern the equilibrium of the forces, but also on the mechanical *characteristics* of the materials of which the member is fabricated. The necessary information regarding the latter comes from the laboratory, where materials are subjected to the action of accurately known forces and the behavior of test specimens is observed with particular regard to such phenomena as the occurrence of breaks, deformations, etc. Determination of such phenomena is a vital part of the subject, but this branch is left to other books.[1] Here the end results of such investigations are of interest, and this book is concerned with the analytical or mathematical part of the subject in contradistinction to experimentation. For these reasons, it is seen that mechanics of solids is a blended science of experiment and Newtonian postulates of analytical mechanics. It is presumed that the reader has some familiarity with both of these areas. In the development of this subject, statics plays a particularly dominant role.

This text will be limited to the simpler topics of the subject. In spite of the relative simplicity of the methods employed here, the resulting techniques are unusually useful as they apply to a vast number of technically important problems.

The subject matter can be mastered best by solving numerous problems. The number of basic formulas necessary for the analysis and design of structural and machine members by the methods of engineering mechanics of solids is relatively small; however, throughout this study, the reader must develop an ability to *visualize* a problem and the nature of the quantities being computed. *Complete, carefully drawn diagrammatic sketches of problems to be solved will pay large dividends in a quicker and more complete mastery of this subject.*

There are three major parts in this chapter. The general concepts of stress are treated first. This is followed with a particular case of stress distribution in axially loaded members. Strength design criteria based on stress are discussed in the last part of the chapter.

Part A   GENERAL CONCEPTS: STRESS

1-2. Method of Sections

One of the main problems of engineering mechanics of solids is the investigation of the internal resistance of a body; that is, *the nature of forces set up within a body to balance the effect of the externally applied forces.* For this purpose, a uniform method of approach is employed. A complete diagrammatic sketch of the member to be investigated is prepared, on which *all* of the external forces acting on a body are shown at their respective points of application. Such a sketch is called a *free-body* diagram. All forces acting on

---

[1]W. D. Callister, *Materials Science and Engineering* (New York: Wiley, 1985). J. F. Shackelford, *Introduction to Materials Science for Engineers* (New York: Macmillan, 1985). L. H. Van Vlack, *Materials Science for Engineers,* 5th ed. (Reading, MA: Addison-Wesley, 1985).

a body, including the reactive forces caused by the supports and the weight[2] of the body itself due to its mass, are considered external forces. Moreover, since a stable body at rest is in equilibrium, the forces acting on it satisfy the equations of static equilibrium. Thus, if the forces acting on a body such as shown in Fig. 1-1(a) satisfy the equations of static equilibrium and are all shown acting on it, the sketch represents a free-body diagram. Next, since a determination of the internal forces caused by the external ones is one of the principal concerns of this subject, an arbitrary section is passed through the body, completely separating it into two parts. The result of such a process can be seen in Figs. 1-1(b) and (c), where an arbitrary plane *ABCD* separates the original solid body of Fig. 1-1(a) into two *distinct* parts. This process will be referred to as the *method of sections*. Then, if the body as a whole is in equilibrium, *any part* of it must also be in equilibrium. For such parts of a body, however, some of the forces necessary to maintain equilibrium must act at the cut section. These considerations lead to the following fundamental conclusion: *The externally applied forces to one side of an arbitrary cut must be balanced by the internal forces developed at the cut,* or, briefly, the external forces are balanced by the internal forces. Later it will be seen that the cutting planes will be oriented in particular directions to fit special requirements. However, the method of sections will be relied upon as a first step in solving *all* problems where internal forces are being investigated.

In discussing the method of sections, it is significant to note that some moving bodies, although not in static equilibrium, are in dynamic equilibrium. These problems can be reduced to problems of static equilibrium. First, the acceleration *a* of the part in question is computed; then it is multiplied by the mass *m* of the body, giving a force $F = ma$. If the force so computed is applied to the body at its mass center in a direction opposite to the acceleration, the dynamic problem is reduced to one of statics. This is the so-called *d'Alembert principle*. With this point of view, all bodies can be thought of as being instantaneously in a state of static equilibrium. Hence, for any body, whether in static or dynamic equilibrium, a free-body diagram can be prepared on which the necessary forces to maintain the body as a whole in equilibrium can be shown. From then on, the problem is the same as discussed before.

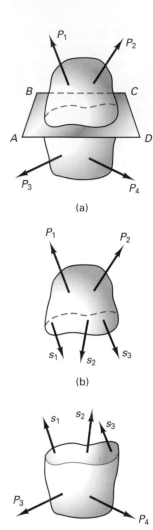

Fig. 1-1   Sectioning of a body.

1-3. Definition of Stress

In general, the internal forces acting on infinitesimal areas of a cut are of varying magnitudes and directions, as was shown earlier in Figs. 1-1(b) and (c), and as is again shown in Fig. 1-2(a). These forces are vectorial in nature and they maintain the externally applied forces in equilibrium. In

[2]Strictly speaking, the weight of the body, or, more generally, the inertial forces due to acceleration, etc., are "body forces" and act throughout the body in a manner associated with the units of volume of the body. However, in most instances, these body forces can be considered as external loads acting through the body's center of mass.

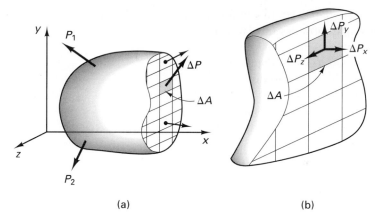

Fig. 1-2 Sectioned body: (a) free body with some internal forces, (b) enlarged view with components of $\Delta\boldsymbol{P}$.

mechanics of solids it is particularly significant to determine the intensity of these forces on the various portions of a section as resistance to deformation and to forces depends on these intensities. In general, they vary from point to point and are inclined with respect to the plane of the section. It is advantageous to resolve these intensities perpendicular and parallel to the section investigated. As an example, the components of a force vector $\Delta\boldsymbol{P}$ acting on an area ΔA are shown in Fig. 1-2(b). In this particular diagram, the section through the body is perpendicular to the x axis, and the directions of ΔP_x and of the normal to ΔA coincide. The component parallel to the section is further resolved into components along the y and z axes. In this text since the directions of force vectors and their components are generally known, their scalar representation employing italicized rather than bold-faced letters is commonly used.

Since the components of the intensity of force per unit area—that is, of *stress*—hold true only at a point, the mathematical definition[3] of stress is

$$\tau_{xx} = \lim_{\Delta A \to 0} \frac{\Delta P_x}{\Delta A} \quad \tau_{xy} = \lim_{\Delta A \to 0} \frac{\Delta P_y}{\Delta A} \quad \text{and} \quad \tau_{xz} = \lim_{\Delta A \to 0} \frac{\Delta P_z}{\Delta A}$$

where, in all three cases, the first subscript of τ (tau) indicates that the plane perpendicular to the x axis is considered, and the second designates the direction of the stress component. In the next section, all possible combinations of subscripts for stress will be considered.

The intensity of the force perpendicular to or normal to the section is called the *normal stress* at a point. It is customary to refer to normal stresses that cause traction or tension on the surface of a section as *tensile stresses*. On the other hand, those that are pushing against it are *compressive stresses*.

---

[3] As $\Delta A \to 0$, some question from the atomic point of view exists in defining stress in this manner. However, a homogeneous (uniform) model for nonhomogeneous matter appears to have worked well.

In this book, normal stresses will usually be designated by the letter σ (sigma) instead of by a double subscript on τ. A single subscript then suffices to designate the direction of the axis. The other components of the intensity of force act parallel to the plane of the elementary area. These components are called *shear* or *shearing stresses*. Shear stresses will be always designated by τ.

The reader should form a clear mental picture of the stresses called normal and those called shearing. To repeat, normal stresses result from force components perpendicular to the plane of the cut, and shear stresses result from components tangential to the plane of the cut.

It is seen from the definitions that since they represent the intensity of force on an area, stresses are measured in units of force divided by units of area. In the U.S. customary system, units for stress are pounds per square inch, abbreviated *psi*. In many cases, it will be found convenient to use as a unit of force the coined word *kip*, meaning kilopound, or 1000 lb. The stress in kips per square inch is abbreviated *ksi*. It should be noted that the unit pound referred to here implies a pound-force, not a pound-mass. Such ambiguities are avoided in the modernized version of the metric system referred to as the International System of Units or SI units.[4] SI units are being increasingly adopted and will largely be used in this text along with the U.S. customary system of units . The base units in SI are *meter*[5] (m) for length, *kilogram* (kg) for mass, and *second* (s) for time. The derived unit for area is a *square meter* (m^2), and for acceleration, a *meter per second squared* (m/s^2). The unit of force is defined as a unit mass subjected to a unit acceleration—that is, *kilogram-meter per second squared* ($kg \cdot m/s^2$)— and is designated a *newton* (N). The unit of stress is the *newton per square meter* (N/m^2), also designated a *pascal* (Pa). Multiple and submultiple prefixes representing steps of 1000 are recommended. For example, force can be shown in *millinewtons* (1 mN = 0.001 N), *newtons,* or *kilonewtons* (1 kN = 1000 N), length in *millimeters* (1 mm = 0.001 m), *meters,* or *kilometers* (1 km = 1000 m), and stress in *kilopascals* (1 kPa = 10^3 Pa), *megapascals* (1 MPa = 10^6 Pa), or *gigapascals* (1 GPa = 10^9 Pa), etc.[6]

The stress expressed numerically in units of N/m^2 may appear to be unusually small to those familiar with the U.S. customary system of units. This is because the force of 1 newton is small in relation to a pound-force, and 1 square meter is associated with a much larger area than 1 square inch. Therefore, it is often more convenient in most applications to think in terms of a force of 1 newton acting on 1 square millimeter. The units for such a quantity are N/mm^2, which corresponds to *megapascals* (MPa).

[4]From the French, Systéme International d'Unités.

[5]Also spelled *metre*.

[6]A detailed discussion of SI units, including conversion factors, rules for SI style, and usage, can be found in a comprehensive guide published by the American Society for Testing and Materials as ASTM *Standard for Metric Practice* E-380-86. For convenience, a short table of conversion factors is included on the inside back cover.

Some conversion factors from U.S. customary to SI units are given on the inside of the back cover. It may be useful to note that approximately 1 in $\approx$ 25 mm, 1 pound-force $\approx$ 4.4 newtons, 1 psi $\approx$ 7000 Pa, or 1 ksi $\approx$ 7 MPa.

It should be emphasized that *stresses multiplied by the respective areas on which they act give forces.* At an *imaginary* section, a vector sum of these forces, called *stress resultants, keeps a body in equilibrium.* In engineering mechanics of solid, the stress resultants at a selected section are generally determined first, and then, using established formulas, stresses are determined.

1-4. Stress Tensor

If, in addition to the section implied in the free body of Fig. 1-2, another plane an infinitesimal distance away and parallel to the first were passed through the body, an elementary slice would be isolated. Then, if an additional two pairs of planes were passed normal to the first pair, a cube of infinitesimal dimensions would be isolated from the body. Such a cube is shown in Fig. 1-3(a). All stresses acting on this cube are identified on the diagram. As noted earlier, the first subscripts on the τ's associate the stress with a plane perpendicular to a given axis; the second subscripts designate the direction of the stress. On the *near faces* of the cube (i.e., on the faces away from the origin), the directions of stress are positive if they coincide with the positive directions of the axes. On the faces of the cube toward the origin, from the action–reaction equilibrium concept, positive stresses act in the direction opposite to the positive directions of the axes. (Note that for normal stresses, by changing the symbol for the normal stress from τ

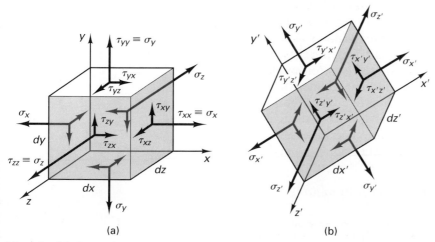

(a)   (b)

Fig. 1-3 (a) General state of stress acting on an infinitesimal element in the initial coordinate system. (b) General state of stress acting on an infinitesimal element defined in a rotated system of coordinate axes. All stresses have positive sense.

to σ, a single subscript on σ suffices to define this quantity without ambiguity.) The designations for stresses shown in Fig. 1-3(a) are widely used in the mathematical theories of elasticity and plasticity.

If at a point in question a different set of axes are chosen, the corresponding stresses are as shown in Fig. 1-3(b). These stresses are related, but are not generally equal, to those shown in Fig. 1-3(a). The process of changing stresses from one set of coordinate axes to another is termed *stress transformation*. The state of stress at a point that can be defined by three components on each of the three mutually perpendicular (orthogonal) axes in mathematical terminology is called a *tensor*. Precise mathematical processes apply for transforming tensors, including stresses, from one set of axes to another. A more complete discussion of this problem is given in Chapter 11.

An examination of the stress symbols in Fig. 1-3(a) shows that there are three normal stresses: $\tau_{xx} \equiv \sigma_x, \tau_{yy} \equiv \sigma_y, \tau_{zz} \equiv \sigma_z$; and six shearing stresses: τ_{xy}, $\tau_{yx}, \tau_{yz}, \tau_{zy}, \tau_{zx}, \tau_{xz}$. By contrast, a force vector P has only three components: P_x, P_y, and P_z. These can be written in an orderly manner as a column vector:

$$\begin{pmatrix} P_x \\ P_y \\ P_z \end{pmatrix} \tag{1-1a}$$

Analogously, the stress components can be assembled as follows:

$$\begin{pmatrix} \tau_{xx} & \tau_{xy} & \tau_{xz} \\ \tau_{yx} & \tau_{yy} & \tau_{yz} \\ \tau_{zx} & \tau_{zy} & \tau_{zz} \end{pmatrix} \equiv \begin{pmatrix} \sigma_x & \tau_{xy} & \tau_{xz} \\ \tau_{yx} & \sigma_y & \tau_{yz} \\ \tau_{zx} & \tau_{zy} & \sigma_z \end{pmatrix} \tag{1-1b}$$

This is a matrix representation of the *stress tensor*. It is a second-rank tensor requiring two indices to identify its elements or components. A vector is a first-rank tensor, and a scalar is a zero-rank tensor. Sometimes, for brevity, a stress tensor is written in indicial notation as τ_{ij}, where it is understood that i and j can assume designations x, y, and z as noted in Eq. 1-1b.

Next, it will be shown that the stress tensor is symmetric (i.e., $\tau_{ij} = \tau_{ji}$). This follows directly from the equilibrium requirements for an element. For this purpose, let the dimensions of the infinitesimal element be dx, dy, and dz, and sum the moments of forces about an axis such as the z axis in Fig. 1-4. Only the stresses entering the problem are shown in the figure. By neglecting the infinitesimals of higher order,[7] this process is equivalent to taking the moment about the z axis in Fig. 1-4(a) or about point C in its two-dimensional representation in Fig. 1-4(b). Thus,

$$M_C = 0 \curvearrowright + \qquad + (\tau_{yx})(dx\,dz)(dy) - (\tau_{xy})(dy\,dz)(dx) = 0$$

[7]The possibility of an infinitesimal change in stress from one face of the cube to another and the possibility of the presence of body (inertial) forces exist. By first considering an element $\Delta x\,\Delta y\,\Delta z$ and proceeding to the limit, it can be shown rigorously that these quantities are of higher order and therefore negligible.

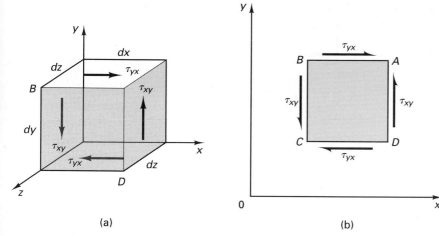

Fig. 1-4   Elements in pure shear.

where the expressions in parentheses correspond respectively to stress, area, and moment arm. Simplifying,

$$\tau_{yx} = \tau_{xy}$$

(1-2)

Similarly, it can be shown that $\tau_{xz} = \tau_x$ and $\tau_{yz} = \tau_{zy}$. Hence, the subscripts for the shear stresses are commutative (i.e., their order may be interchanged), and the stress tensor is symmetric.

The implication of Eq. 1-2 is very important. The fact that subscripts are commutative signifies that shear stresses on mutually perpendicular planes of an infinitesimal element are numerically equal, and $\Sigma M_z = 0$ is not satisfied by a single pair of shear stresses. On diagrams, as in Fig. 1-4(b), the arrowheads of the shear stresses must meet at diametrically opposite corners of an element to satisfy equilibrium conditions.

In most subsequent situations considered in this text, more than two pairs of shear stresses will seldom act on an element simultaneously. Hence, the subscripts used before to identify the planes and the directions of the shear stresses become superfluous. In such cases, shear stresses will be designated by τ without any subscripts. However, one must remember that shear stresses always occur in two pairs.

This notation simplification can be used to advantage for the state of stress shown in Fig. 1-5. The two-dimensional stress shown in the figure is referred to as *plane stress*. In matrix representation such a stress can be written as

$$\begin{pmatrix} \sigma_x & \tau & 0 \\ \tau & \sigma_y & 0 \\ 0 & 0 & 0 \end{pmatrix}$$

(1-3)

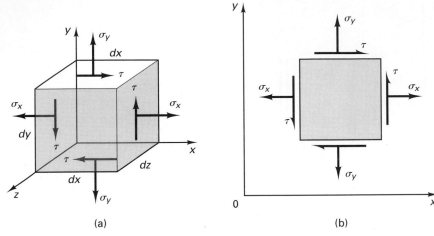

Fig. 1-5   Elements in plane stress.

It should be noted that the initially selected system of axes may not yield the most significant information about the stress at a point. Therefore, by using the procedures of stress transformation, the stresses are examined on other planes. Using such procedures, it will be shown later that a particular set of coordinates exists that diagonalize the stress tensor to read

$$
\begin{pmatrix}
\sigma_1 & 0 & 0 \\
0 & \sigma_2 & 0 \\
0 & 0 & \sigma_3
\end{pmatrix}
\tag{1-4}
$$

Note the absence of shear stresses. For the three-dimensional case, the stresses are said to be *triaxial,* since three stresses are necessary to describe the state of stress completely.

For plane stress $\sigma_3 = 0$ and the state of stress is *biaxial.* Such stresses occur, for example, in thin sheets stressed in two mutually perpendicular directions. For axially loaded members, discussed in the next section, only one element of the stress tensor survives; such a state of stress is referred to as *uniaxial.* In Chapter 11, an inverse problem[8] will be discussed: how this one term can be resolved to yield four or more elements of a stress tensor.

1-5. Differential Equations of Equilibrium

An infinitesimal element of a body must be in equilibrium. For the two-dimensional case, the system of stresses acting on an infinitesimal element $(dx)(dy)(1)$ is shown in Fig. 1-6. In this derivation, the element is of unit thick-

---

[8]Some readers may prefer at this time to study the first several sections in Chapter 11.

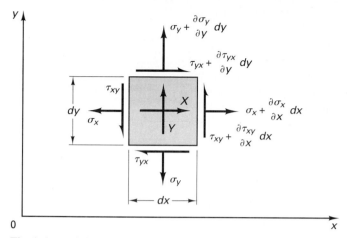

Fig. 1-6   Infinitesimal element with stresses and body forces.

ness in the direction perpendicular to the plane of the paper. Note that the possibility of an increment in stresses from one face of the element to another is accounted for. For example, since the rate of change of σ_x in the x direction is $\partial\sigma_x/\partial x$ and a step of dx is made, the increment is $(\partial\sigma_x/\partial x)\,dx$. The partial derivative notation has to be used to differentiate between the directions.

The inertial or body forces, such as those caused by the weight or the magnetic effect, are designated X and Y and are associated with the unit volume of the material. With these notations,

$$\Sigma\,F_x = 0 \rightarrow +\,, \qquad \left(\sigma_x + \frac{\partial\sigma_x}{\partial x}\,dx\right)(dy \times 1) - \sigma_x(dy \times 1)$$

$$+ \left(\tau_{yx} + \frac{\partial\tau_{yx}}{\partial y}\,dy\right)(dx \times 1) - \tau_{yx}(dx \times 1) + X(dx\,dy \times 1) = 0$$

Simplifying and recalling that $\tau_{xy} = \tau_{yx}$ holds true, one obtains the basic equilibrium equation for the x direction. This equation, together with an analogous one for the y direction, reads

$$\frac{\partial\sigma_x}{\partial x} + \frac{\partial\tau_{yx}}{\partial y} + X = 0$$

$$\frac{\partial\tau_{xy}}{\partial x} + \frac{\partial\sigma_y}{\partial y} + Y = 0$$

(1-5)

The moment equilibrium of the element requiring $\Sigma\,M_z = 0$ is assured by having $\tau_{xy} = \tau_{yx}$.

It can be shown that for the three-dimensional case, a typical equation from a set of three is

$$\frac{\partial\sigma_x}{\partial x} + \frac{\partial\tau_{yx}}{\partial y} + \frac{\partial\tau_{zx}}{\partial z} + X = 0$$

Note that in deriving the previous equations, mechanical properties of the material have not been used. This means that these equations are applicable whether a material is elastic, plastic, or viscoelastic. Also it is very important to note that there are not enough equations of equilibrium to solve for the unknown stresses. In the two-dimensional case, given by Eq. 1-5, there are three unknown stresses, σ_x, σ_y, and τ_{xy}, and only two equations. For the three-dimensional case, there are six stresses, but only three equations. Thus, all problems in stress analysis are internally statically intractable or *indeterminate*. A simple example as to how a *static equilibrium* equation is supplemented by *kinematic* requirements and *mechanical properties of a material* for the solution of a problem is given in Section 5-14. In engineering mechanics of solids, such as that presented in this text, this indeterminacy is eliminated by introducing appropriate assumptions, which is equivalent to having additional equations.

A *numerical procedure* that involves discretizing a body into a large number of *small finite elements,* instead of the infinitesimal ones as before, is now often used in complex problems. Such finite element analyses rely on high-speed electronic computers for solving large systems of simultaneous equations. In the finite element method, just as in the mathematical approach, the equations of statics are supplemented by the kinematic relations and mechanical properties of a material. A few examples given later in this book show comparisons among the "exact" solutions of the mathematical theory of elasticity and those found using the finite element technique and/or conventional solutions based on the methods of engineering mechanics of solids.

Part B   Stress Analysis of Axially Loaded Bars

1-6. Maximum Normal Stress in Axially Loaded Bars

In most practical situations with axially loaded bars, it is expedient to determine directly the maximum normal stress. These stresses develop *on sections perpendicular to the bar axis.* For such sections, the cross-sectional area of a bar is a minimum and the applied force component is a maximum, resulting in a maximum normal stress. The procedure for determining this stress is shown in Fig. 1-7.

Here, as shown in Fig. 1-7(a), the axial force P is applied to the prismatic bar on the right. For equilibrium, an equal but opposite force P must act on the left end. To distinguish between the applied force and the reaction, a

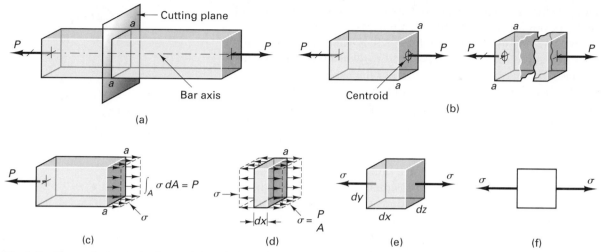

Fig. 1-7 Successive steps in determining the largest normal stress in an axially loaded bar.

slash is drawn across the reaction force vector P. This form of identification will be used frequently in this text. Finding the reactions is usually the first essential step in solving a problem.

To determine the stresses, a free-body diagram is prepared either for the left or the right part of the bar, divided by the cutting plane, as in Fig. 1-7(b). At any section, the force vector P passes through the bar's *centroid*. As shown in Fig. 1-7(c), the reaction on the left end is equilibrated at section *a–a* by a *uniformly distributed normal stress* σ. The sum of these stresses multiplied by their respective areas generate a stress resultant that is *statically equivalent* to the force P. A thin slice of the bar with equal uniformly distributed normal stresses of opposite sense on the two parallel sections is shown in Fig. 1-7(d). This *uniaxial* state of stress may be represented on an infinitesimal cube, as shown in Fig. 1-7(e). However, a simplified diagram such as shown in Fig. 1-7(f) is commonly used.

The basic equation for determining directly the maximum normal stress in an axially loaded bar is given here in customary form without any subscript on σ. Subscripts, however, are frequently added to indicate the direction of the bar axis. This equation gives the largest normal stress at a section taken perpendicular to the axis of a member. Thus,

$$\sigma = \frac{\text{force}}{\text{area}} = \frac{P}{A} \quad \left[\frac{N}{m^2}\right] \text{ or } \left[\frac{lb}{in^2}\right] \qquad (1\text{-}6)$$

where P is the applied axial force, and A is the cross-sectional area of the member. In calculations, it is usually convenient to use $N/mm^2 = MPa$ in the SI system of units and *ksi* in the U.S. customary system.

It is instructive to note that the normal stress σ given by Eq. 1-6, and schematically represented in Fig. 1-7(e), is a complete description of the state of stress in an axially loaded bar. Only one diagonal term, σ_x, remains in the matrix representation of the stress tensor given by Eq. 1-1b. This remaining term is associated with the direction of the bar axis.

Equation 1-6 strictly applies only to *prismatic* bars (i.e., to bars having a constant cross-sectional area). However, the equation is reasonably accurate for slightly tapered members.[9] For a discussion of situations where an abrupt change in the cross-sectional area occurs, causing severe perturbation in stress, see Section 3-3.

As noted before, the stress resultant for a uniformly distributed stress acts through the centroid of a cross-sectional area and assures the equilibrium of an axially loaded member. If the loading is more complex, such as that for the machine part shown in Fig. 1-8, the stress distribution is nonuniform. Here, at section a–a, in addition to the axial force P, a bending couple, or moment, M must also be developed. Such problems will be treated in Chapter 8.

Similar reasoning applies to axially loaded compression members and Eq. 1-6 can be used. However, one must exercise additional care when compression members are investigated. These may be so slender that they may not behave in the fashion considered. For example, an ordinary fishing rod under a rather small axial compression force has a tendency to buckle sideways and could collapse. The consideration of such *instability* of compression members is deferred until Chapter 16. *Equation 1-6 is applicable only for axially loaded compression members that are rather chunky* (i.e., to short blocks). As will be shown in Chapter 16, a block whose *least* dimension is approximately one-tenth of its length may usually be considered a short block. For example, a 50×100 mm wooden piece may be 500 mm long and still be considered a short block.

Sometimes compressive stresses arise where one body is supported by another. If the resultant of the applied forces coincides with the centroid of the contact area between the two bodies, the intensity of force, or stress, between the two bodies can again be determined from Eq. 1-6. It is customary to refer to this normal stress as a *bearing stress*. Figure 1-9, where a short block bears on a concrete pier and the latter bears on the soil, illustrates such a stress. Numerous similar situations arise in mechanical problems under washers used for distributing concentrated forces. These bearing stresses can be approximated by dividing the applied force P by the corresponding contact area giving a useful *nominal bearing stress.*

In accepting Eq. 1-6, it must be kept in mind that the material's behavior is *idealized.* Each and every particle of a body is assumed to contribute equally to the resistance of the force. A perfect *homogeneity* of the material

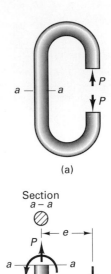

(a)

Section a–a

$M = Pe$

(b)

Fig. 1-8   A member with a nonuniform stress distribution at section a–a.

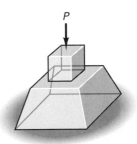

Fig. 1-9   Bearing stresses occur between the block and pier, as well as between the pier and soil.

[9]For accurate solutions for tapered bars, see S. P. Timoshenko and J. N. Goodier, *Theory of Elasticity,* 3rd ed. (New York: McGraw-Hill, 1970), 109.

is implied by such an assumption. Real materials, such as metals, consist of a great many grains, whereas wood is fibrous. In real materials, some particles will contribute more to the resistance of a force than others. Ideal stress distributions such as shown in Figs. 1-7(d) and (e) actually do not exist if the scale chosen is sufficiently small. The true stress distribution varies in each particular case and is a highly irregular, jagged affair somewhat, as shown in Fig. 1-10(a). However, on the average, statistically speaking, computations based on Eq. 1-6 are correct, and, hence, the computed average stress represents a highly significant quantity.

It is also important to note that the basic equations for determining stresses, such as given by Eq. 1-6, *assume initially stress-free material.* However, in reality, as materials are being manufactured, they are often rolled, extruded, forged, welded, peened, and hammered. In castings, materials cool unevenly. These processes can set up high internal stresses called *residual stresses.* For example, hot steel plates during a rolling operation are pulled between rollers, as shown schematically in Fig. 1-10(b). This process causes the development of larger normal stresses near the outer surfaces than in the middle of a plate. These stresses are equivalent to an average normal stress σ_{av} that may be considered to generate a force that propels a plate through the rolls. On leaving the rolls, the plate shown in Fig. 1-10(c) is relieved of this force, and as per Eq. 1-6, the σ_{av} is subtracted from the stresses that existed during rolling. The stress pattern of the residual normal stresses is shown in Fig. 1-10(c). These residual stresses are self-equilibrating (i.e., they are in equilibrium without any externally applied forces). In real problems, such residual stresses may be large and should be carefully investigated and then added to the calculated stresses for the initially stress-free material.

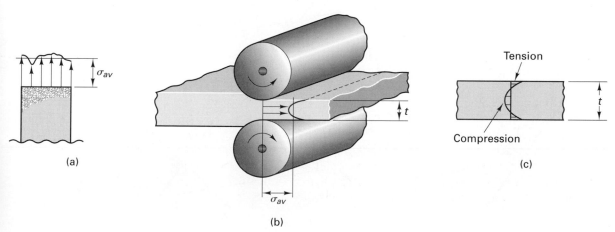

Fig. 1-10   (a) Schematic illustration of stress irregularity in material due to lack of homogeneity, (b) variation of tensile stress across a plate during a rolling operation, and (c) residual stress in a rolled plate.

1.7. Stresses on Inclined Sections in Axially Loaded Bars

The traditional approach of engineering mechanics of solids will be used for determining the internal stresses on arbitrarily inclined sections in axially loaded bars. The first steps in this procedure are illustrated in Fig. 1-11. Here, since an axial force *P* is applied on the right end of a prismatic bar, for equilibrium, an equal but opposite force *P* must act on the left end.

In the problem at hand, after the reactive force *P* is determined, free-body diagrams for the bar segments, isolated by sections such as *a–a* or *b–b*, are prepared. In both cases, the force *P* required for equilibrium is shown at the sections. However, in order to obtain the conventional stresses, which are the most convenient ones in stress analysis, the force *P* is replaced by its components along the selected axes. A wavy line through the vectors *P* indicates their replacement by components. For illustrative purposes, little is gained by considering the case shown in Fig. 1-11(b) requiring three force components. The analysis simply becomes more cumbersome. Instead, the case shown in Fig. 1-11(c), having only two components of *P* in the plane of symmetry of the bar cross section, is considered in detail. One of these components is normal to the section; the other is in the plane of the section.

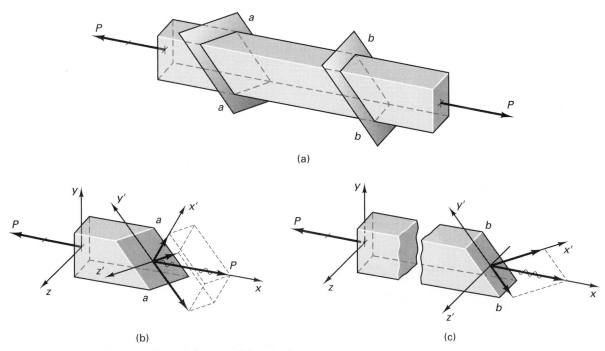

Fig. 1-11   Sectioning of a prismatic bar on arbitrary planes.

As an example of a detailed analysis of stresses in a bar on inclined planes, consider two sections 90 degrees apart perpendicular to the bar sides, as shown in Fig. 1-12(a). The section a–a is at an angle θ with the vertical. An isolated part of the bar to the left of this section is shown in Fig. 1-12(b). Note that the normal to the section coinciding with the x axis also forms an angle θ with the x axis. *The applied force, the reaction, as well as the equilibrating force P at the section all act through the centroid of the bar section.* As shown in Fig. 1-12(b), the equilibrating force P is resolved into two components: the normal force component, $P \cos \theta$, and the shear component, $P \sin \theta$. The area of the inclined cross section is $A / \cos \theta$. Therefore, the normal stress σ_θ and the shear stress τ_θ, shown in Figs. 1-12(c) and (d), are given by the following two equations:

$$\sigma_\theta = \frac{\text{force}}{\text{area}} = \frac{P \cos \theta}{A / \cos \theta} = \frac{P}{A} \cos^2 \theta \qquad (1\text{-}7a)$$

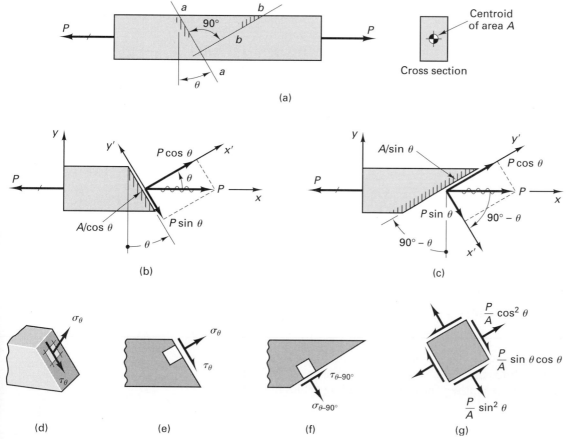

Fig. 1-12   Sectioning of a prismatic bar on mutually perpendicular planes.

and

$$\tau_\theta = -\frac{P\sin\theta}{A/\cos\theta} = \frac{P}{A}\sin\theta\cos\theta \qquad (1\text{-}7b)$$

The negative sign in Eq. 1-7b is used to conform to the sign convention for shear stresses introduced earlier. See, for example Fig. 1-11. The need for a negative sign is evident by noting that the shear force $P\sin\theta$ acts in the direction opposite to that of the y' axis.

It is important to note that the basic procedure of engineering mechanics of solids used here gives the *average* or *mean* stress at a section. These stresses are determined from the axial forces necessary for equilibrium at a section. Therefore, they *always* satisfy *statics*. However, based on the additional requirements of *kinematics* (geometric deformations) and *mechanical properties of a material,* large *local* stresses are known to arise in the proximity of concentrated forces. This also occurs at abrupt changes in cross-sectional areas. The average stresses at a section are accurate at a distance about equal to the depth of the member from the concentrated forces or abrupt changes in cross-sectional area. The use of this simplified procedure will be rationalized in Section 3-3 as *Saint Venant's principle.*

Equations 1-7a and 1-7b show that the normal and shear stresses vary with the angle θ. The sense of these stresses is shown in Figs. 1-12(d) and (e). The normal stress σ_θ reaches its maximum value for $\theta = 0°$ (i.e., when the section is perpendicular to the axis of the rod). The corresponding shear stress is zero. This leads to the conclusion that the maximum normal stress σ_{max} in an axially loaded bar can be simply determined from the following equation:

$$\sigma_{max} = \sigma_x = \frac{P}{A} \qquad (1\text{-}8)$$

where P is the applied force, and A is the cross-sectional area of the bar. This precisely corresponds to Eq. 1-6 established earlier on a more intuitive basis.

Equations 1-7(a) and 1-7(b) also show that for $\theta = \pm 90°$, both the normal and the shear stresses vanish. This is as it should be, since no stresses act along the top and bottom free boundaries (surfaces) of the bar.

To find the maximum shear stress acting in a bar, one must differentiate Eq. 1-7(b) with respect to θ, and set the derivative equal to zero. On carrying out this operation and simplifying the results, one obtains

$$\tan\theta = \pm 1 \qquad (1\text{-}9)$$

leading to the conclusion that τ_{max} occurs on planes of either $+45°$ or $-45°$ with the axis of the bar. Since the sense in which a shear stress acts is usually immaterial, on substituting either one of the preceding values of θ into Eq. 1-7(b), one finds

$$\tau_{max} = \frac{P}{2A} = \frac{\sigma_x}{2} \qquad (1\text{-}10)$$

Therefore, the maximum shear stress in an axially loaded bar is only half as large as the maximum normal stress.

Following the same procedure, the normal and shear stresses can be found on the section b–b. On noting that the angle locating this plane from the vertical is best measured clockwise instead of counterclockwise, as in the former case, this angle should be treated as a negative quantity in Eq. 1-7b. Hence, the subscript $-(90° - \theta) = \theta - 90°$ will be used in designating the stresses. From Fig. 1-12(e), one obtains

$$\sigma_{\theta-90°} = \frac{P\sin\theta}{A/\sin\theta} = \frac{P}{A}\sin^2\theta \qquad (1\text{-}11)$$

and

$$\tau_{\theta-90°} = \frac{P\cos\theta}{A/\sin\theta} = \frac{P}{A}\sin\theta\,\cos\theta \qquad (1\text{-}12)$$

Note that in this case, since the direction of the shear force and the y' axis have the same sense, the expression in Eq. 1-12 is positive. Equation 1-12 can be obtained from Eq. 1-7b by substituting the angle $\theta - 90°$. The sense of $\sigma_{\theta-90°}$ and $\tau_{\theta-90°}$ is shown in Fig. 1-12(f).

The combined results of the analysis for sections a–a and b–b are shown on an infinitesimal element in Fig. 1-12(g). Note that the normal stresses on the adjoining element faces are not equal, whereas the shear stresses are. The latter finding is in complete agreement with the earlier general conclusion reached in Section 1-4, showing that shear stresses on mutually perpendicular planes must be equal.

1-8. Shear Stresses

Some engineering materials (for example, low-carbon steel) are weaker in shear than in tension, and, at large loads, slip develops along the planes of maximum shear stress. According to Eqs. 1-9 and 1-10, these *glide or slip planes* in a tensile specimen form 45° angles with the axis of a bar, where the maximum shear stress $\tau_{max} = P/2A$ occurs. On the polished surface of a specimen, these lines can be readily observed and are called *Lüders lines*.[10] This kind of material behavior exhibits a *ductile failure*.

In many routine engineering applications, large shear stresses may develop at critical locations. To determine such stresses precisely is often difficult. However, by *assuming* that in the plane of a section a *uniformly distributed shear stress* develops, a solution can readily be found. By using this approach, the average shear stress τ_{av} is determined by dividing the shear force V in the plane of the section by the corresponding area A.

---

[10]Also know and *Piobert lines*. Named in honor, respectively, of German and French nineteenth-century investigators.

$$\boxed{\tau_{av} = \frac{\text{force}}{\text{area}} = \frac{V}{A}} \quad \left[\frac{N}{m^2} \right] \text{ or } \left[\frac{lb}{in^2} \right] \qquad (1\text{-}13)$$

Some examples as to where Eq. 1-13 can be used to advantage are shown in Fig. 1-13. In Fig. 1-13(a), a small block is shown glued to a larger one. By separating the upper block from the lower one by an imaginary section, the equilibrium diagram shown in Fig. 1-13(b) is obtained. The small applied couple Pe, causing small normal stresses acting perpendicular to the section a–a, is commonly neglected. On this basis τ_{av}, shown in Fig. 1-13(c), can be found using Eq. 1-13 by dividing P by the area A of the section a–a. A similar procedure is used for determining τ_{av} for the problem shown in Fig. 1-13(d). However, in this case, *two* glued surfaces are available for transferring the applied force P. The same approach, employing imaginary sections, is applicable to solid members.

Examples of two bolted connections are shown in Figs. 1-14(a) and (e). These connections can be analyzed in two different ways. In one approach, it is assumed that a tightened bolt develops a sufficiently large clamping force, so that the friction developed between the faying (contacting) surfaces prevents a joint from slipping. For such designs, high-strength bolts are commonly employed. An alternative widely used approach assumes enough slippage occurs, such that the applied force is transferred first to a bolt and then from the bolt to the connecting plate, as illustrated in Figs. 1-14(b) and (f). To determine τ_{av} in these bolts, one simply uses the cross-sectional area A of a bolt instead of the area of the joint contact surface to compute the average shear stress. The bolt shown in Fig. 1-14(a) is said to be in *single* shear, whereas the one in Fig. 1-14(e) is in *double* shear.

In bolted connections, another aspect of the problem requires consideration. In cases such as those in Figs. 1-14(a) and (e), as the force P is applied, a highly irregular pressure develops between a bolt and the plates. The *average* nominal intensity of this pressure is obtained by dividing the force transmitted by the projected area of the bolt onto the plate. This is referred to as the *bearing stress*. The bearing stress in Fig. 1-14(a) is $\sigma_b = P/td$, where t is the thickness of the plate and d is the diameter of the bolt. For the case in Fig. 1-14(e), the bearing stresses for the middle plate and the outer plates are $\sigma_1 = P/t_1 d$ and $\sigma_2 = P/2t_2 d$, respectively.

The same procedure is also applicable for riveted assemblies.

In the previous design approach, the frictional resistance between the faying surfaces at the connectors has been neglected. However, if the clamping force developed by a connector is both sufficiently large and reliable, the capacity of a joint can be determined on the basis of the friction force between the faying surfaces. This condition is illustrated in Fig.1-15. With the use of high-strength bolts with yield strength on the order of 100 ksi (700 MPa), this is an acceptable method in structural steel design. The required tightening of such bolts is usually specified to be about 70% of their tensile strength. For the purposes of simplified

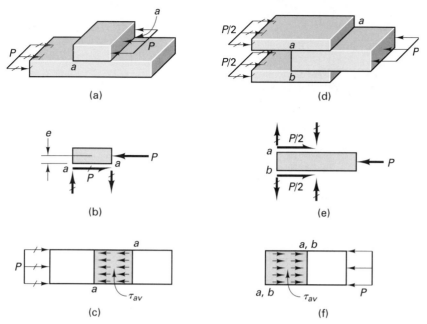

Fig. 1-13   Loading conditions causing shear stresses between interfaces of glued blocks.

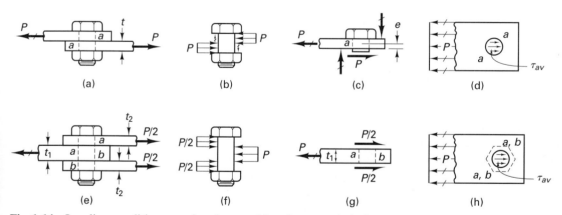

Fig. 1-14   Loading conditions causing shear and bearing stress in bolts.

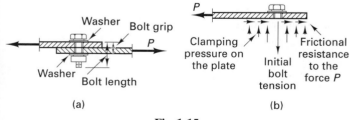

Fig. 1-15

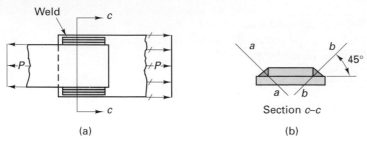

Fig. 1-16   Loading condition causing critical shear in two planes of fillet welds.

analysis, an allowable shear stress based on the nominal area of a bolt is specified. These stresses are based on experiments. This enables the design of connections using high-strength bolts to be carried out in the same manner as that for ordinary bolts or rivets.

For another manner of joining members together is welding. An example of a connection with fillet welds is shown in Fig. 1-16. The maximum shear stress occurs in the planes a–a and b–b, as shown in Fig. 1-16(b). The capacity of such welds is usually given in units of force per unit length of weld.

1-9. Analysis for Normal and Shear Stresses

Once the axial force P or the shear force V, as well as the area A, are determined in a given problem, Eqs. 1-6 and 1-13 for normal and shear stresses can be readily applied. These equations giving, respectively, the maximum magnitudes of normal and shear stress are particularly important as they appraise the greatest demand on the strength of a material. These greatest stresses occur at a section of *minimum* cross-sectional area and/or the greatest axial force. Such sections are called *critical sections*. In the simpler problems, the critical section for the particular arrangement being analyzed can usually be found by inspection. In others, this may require an extensive analysis, which now often is done with the aid of a computer. To determine the force P or V that acts through a member is usually a more difficult task. In the majority of problems treated in this text, the latter information is obtained from statics.

For the equilibrium of a body in space, the equations of statics require the fulfillment of the following conditions:

$$
\begin{aligned}
\Sigma F_x &= 0 & \Sigma M_x &= 0 \\
\Sigma F_y &= 0 & \Sigma M_y &= 0 \\
\Sigma F_z &= 0 & \Sigma M_z &= 0
\end{aligned}
\qquad (1\text{-}14)
$$

The first column of Eq. 1-14 states that the sum of *all* forces acting on a body in any (x, y, z) direction must be zero. The second column notes that the summation of moments of *all* forces around *any* axis parallel to any (x, y, z) direction must also be zero for equilibrium. In a *planar* problem (i.e., all members and forces lie in a single plane, such as the x-y plane), relations $\Sigma F_z = 0, \Sigma M_x = 0$, and $\Sigma M_y = 0$, while still valid, are trivial.

These equations of statics are directly applicable to deformable solid bodies. The deformations tolerated in engineering structures are usually negligible in comparison with the overall dimensions of structures. Therefore, *for the purposes of obtaining the forces in members, the initial undeformed dimensions of members are used in computations.*

If the equations of statics suffice for determining the external reactions as well as the internal stress resultants, a structural system is *statically determinate.* An example is shown in Fig. 1-17(a). However, if for the same beam and loading conditions, additional supports are provided, as in Figs. 1-17(b) and (c), the number of *independent* equations of statics is insufficient to solve for the reactions. In Fig. 1-17(b), any one of the vertical reactions can be removed and the structural system remains stable and tractable. Similarly, any two reactions can be dispensed with for the beam in Fig. 1-17(c). Both of these beams are statically *indeterminate.* The reactions that can be removed leaving a stable system statically determinate are superfluous or *redundant.* Such redundancies can also arise within the internal system of forces. Depending on the number of the redundant internal forces or reactions, the system is said to be indeterminate to the *first degree,* as in Fig. 1-17(b), to the *second degree,* as in Fig. 1-17(c), etc. Multiple degrees of statical indeterminacy frequently arise in practice, and one of the important objectives of this subject is to provide an introduction to the methods of solution for such problems. Procedures for solving such problems will be introduced gradually.

Equations 1-14 should already be familiar to the reader. However, several examples where they are applied will now be given, emphasizing solution techniques generally used in engineering mechanics of solids. These statically determinate examples will serve as an informal review of some of the principles of statics and will show applications of Eqs. 1-6 and 1-13.

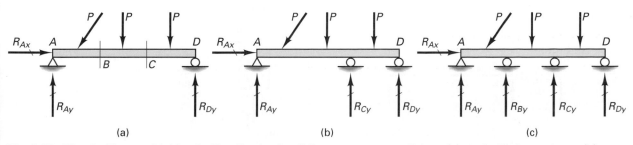

Fig. 1-17   Identical beam with identical loading having different support conditions: (a) statically determinate, (b) statically indeterminate to the first degree, (c) statically indeterminate to the second degree.

Example 1-1

The beam *BE* in Fig. 1-18(a) is used for hoisting machinery. It is anchored by two bolts at *B,* and at *C* it rests on a parapet wall. The essential details are given in the figure. Note that the bolts are threaded, as shown in Fig. 1-18(d), with $d = 16$ mm at the root of the threads. If this hoist can be subjected to a force of 10 kN, determine the stress in bolts *BD* and the bearing stress at *C*. Assume that the weight of the beam is negligible in comparison with the loads handled.

SOLUTION

To solve this problem, the actual situation is idealized and a free-body diagram is made on which all known and unknown forces are indicated. This is shown in Fig. 1-18(b). The vertical reactions of *B* and *C* are unknown. They are indicated, respectively, as R_{By} and R_{Cy}, where the first subscript identifies the location, and the second the line of action of the unknown force. As the long bolts *BD* are not effective in resisting the horizontal force, only an unknown horizontal reaction at *C* is assumed and marked as R_{Cx}. The

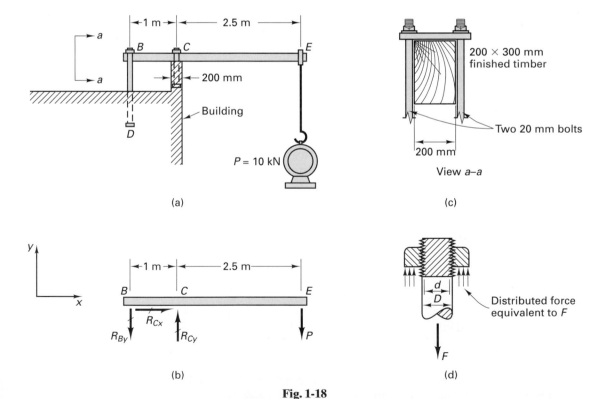

Fig. 1-18

applied known force P is shown in its proper location. After a free-body diagram is prepared, the equations of statics are applied and solved for the unknown forces.

$$\Sigma F_x = 0 \qquad\qquad\qquad\qquad\qquad R_{Cx} = 0$$

$$\Sigma M_B = 0 \curvearrowright + \qquad 10(2.5 + 1) - R_{Cy} \times 1 = 0 \qquad R_{Cy} = 35 \text{ kN} \uparrow$$

$$\Sigma M_c = 0 \curvearrowright + \qquad 10 \times 2.5 - R_{By} \times 1 = 0 \qquad R_{By} = 25 \text{ kN} \uparrow$$

$$Check: \ \Sigma F_y = 0 \uparrow + \qquad -25 + 35 - 10 = 0$$

These steps complete and check the work of determining the forces. The various areas of the material that resist these forces are determined next, and Eq. 1-6 is applied.

Cross-sectional area of one 20-mm bolt: $A = \pi 10^2 = 314 \text{ mm}^2$. This is not the minimum area of a bolt; threads reduce it.

The cross-sectional area of one 20-mm bolt at the root of the threads is

$$A_{net} = \pi \, 8^2 = 201 \text{ mm}^2$$

Maximum normal tensile stress[11] in each of the two bolts BD:

$$\sigma_{max} = \frac{R_{By}}{2A} = \frac{25 \times 10^3}{2 \times 201} = 62 \text{ N/mm}^2 = 62 \text{ MPa}$$

Tensile stress in the shank of the bolts BD:

$$\sigma = \frac{25 \times 10^3}{2 \times 314} = 39.8 \text{ N/mm}^2 = 39.8 \text{ MPa}$$

Contact area at C:

$$A = 200 \times 200 = 40 \times 10^3 \text{ mm}^2$$

Bearing stress at C:

$$\sigma_b = \frac{R_{Cy}}{A} = \frac{35 \times 10^3}{40 \times 10^3} = 0.875 \text{ N/mm}^2 = 0.875 \text{ MPa}$$

The calculated stress for the bolt shank can be represented in the manner of Eq. 1-1b as

$$\begin{pmatrix} 0 & 0 & 0 \\ 0 & +39.8 & 0 \\ 0 & 0 & 0 \end{pmatrix} \text{MPa}$$

where the y axis is taken in the direction of the applied load. In ordinary problems, the complete result is implied but is seldom written down in such detail.

---

[11]See also discussion on stress concentrations, Section 3-3.

Example 1-2

The concrete pier shown in Fig. 1-19(a) is loaded at the top with a uniformly distributed load of 20 kN/m². Investigate the state of stress at a
level 1 m above the base. Concrete weighs approximately 25 kN/m³.

SOLUTION
In this problem, the weight of the structure itself is appreciable and must
be included in the calculations.
  Weight of the whole pier:

$$W = [(0.5 + 1.5)/2] \times 0.5 \times 2 \times 25 = 25 \text{ kN}$$

Total applied force:

$$P = 20 \times 0.5 \times 0.5 = 5 \text{ kN}$$

From $\Sigma F_y = 0$, reaction at the base:

$$R = W + P = 30 \text{ kN}$$

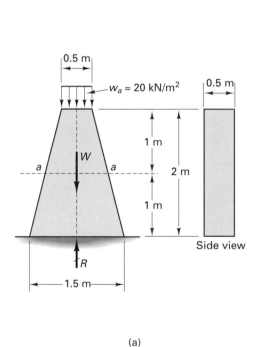

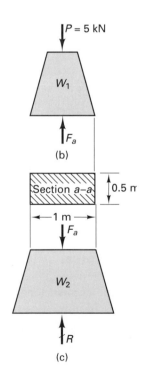

(a)

(b)

(c)

Fig. 1-19

These forces are shown schematically in the diagrams as concentrated forces acting through their respective centroids. Then, to determine the stress at the desired level, the body is cut into two separate parts. A free-body diagram for either part is sufficient to solve the problem. For comparison, the problem is solved both ways.

Using the upper part of the pier as a free body, Fig. 1-19(b), the weight of the pier above the section:

$$W_1 = (0.5 + 1) \times 0.5 \times 1 \times 25/2 = 9.4 \text{ kN}$$

From $\Sigma F_y = 0$, the force at the section:

$$F_a = P + W_1 = 14.4 \text{ kN}$$

Hence, using Eq. 1-6, the normal stress at the level $a-a$ is

$$\sigma_a = \frac{F_a}{A} = \frac{14.4}{0.5 \times 1} = 28.8 \text{ kN/m}^2$$

This stress is compressive as F_a acts on the section.

Using the lower part of the pier as a free body, Fig. 1-19(c), the weight of the pier below the section:

$$W_2 = (1 + 1.5) \times 0.5 \times 1 \times 25/2 = 15.6 \text{ kN}$$

From $\Sigma F_y = 0$, the force at the section:

$$F_a = R - W_2 = 14.4 \text{ kN}$$

The remainder of the problem is the same as before. The pier considered here has a vertical axis of symmetry, making the application of Eq. 1-6 possible.[12]

Example 1-3

A bracket of negligible weight shown in Fig. 1-20(a) is loaded with a vertical force P of 3 kips. For interconnection purposes, the bar ends are clevised (forked). Pertinent dimensions are shown in the figure. Find the axial stresses in members AB and BC and the bearing and shear stresses for pin C. All pins are 0.375 in in diameter.

SOLUTION

First, an idealized free-body diagram consisting of the two bars pinned at the ends is prepared; see Fig. 1-20(b). As there are no intermediate forces acting on the bars and the applied force acts through the joint at B, the forces in the

[12]Strictly speaking, the solution obtained is not exact, as the sides of the pier are sloping. If the included angle between these sides is large, this solution is inadequate. For further details, see S. Timoshenko and J. N. Goodier, *Theory of Elasticity*, 3rd ed. (New York: McGraw-Hill, 1970), 110.

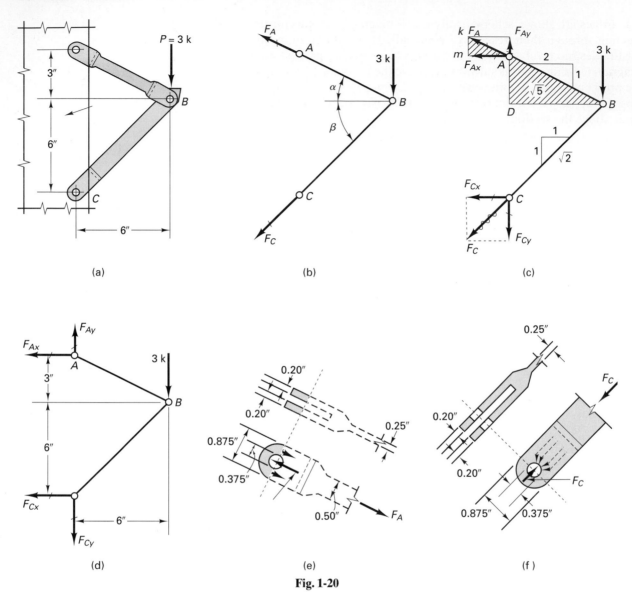

(a)

(b)

(c)

(d)

(e)

(f)

Fig. 1-20

bars are directed along the lines AB and BC, and the bars AB and BC are loaded axially. The magnitudes of the forces are unknown and are labeled F_A and F_C in the diagram.[13] These forces can be determined graphically by completing a triangle of forces FA, FC, and P. These forces may also be found analytically from two simultaneous equations $\Sigma F_y = 0$ and $\Sigma F_x = 0$, written in terms of the unknowns F_A and F_C, a known force P, and two known

---

[13]In frameworks it is convenient to assume that all unknown forces are tensile. A negative answer in the solution then indicates that the bar is in compression.

angles α and β. Both these procedures are possible. However, in this book, it will usually be found advantageous to proceed in a different way. Instead of treating forces F_A and F_C directly, their components are used; and instead of $\Sigma F = 0$, $\Sigma M = 0$ becomes the main tool.

Any force can be resolved into components. For example, F_A can be resolved into F_{Ax} and F_{Ay}, as in Fig. 1-20(c). Conversely, if any one of the components of a directed force is known, the force itself can be determined. This follows from similarity of dimensions and force triangles. In Fig. 1-20(c), the triangles Akm and BAD are similar triangles (both are shaded in the diagram). Hence, if F_{Ax} is known,

$$F_A = (AB/DB)F_{Ax}$$

Similarly, $F_{Ay} = (AD/DB)F_{Ax}$. Note further that AB/DB or AD/DB are ratios; hence, relative dimensions of members can be used. Such relative dimensions are shown by a little triangle on member AB and again on BC. In the problem at hand,

$$F_A = (\sqrt{5}/2)F_{Ax} \quad \text{and} \quad F_{Ay} = F_{Ax}/2$$

Adopting the procedure of resolving forces, a revised free-body diagram, Fig. 1-20(d), is prepared. Two components of force are necessary at the pin joints. After the forces are determined by statics, Eq. 1-6 is applied several times, thinking in terms of a free body of an individual member:

$$\Sigma M_C = 0 \curvearrowleft + \qquad + F_{Ax}(3 + 6) - 3(6) = 0 \qquad F_{Ax} = +2 \text{ k}$$

$$F_{Ay} = F_{Ax}/2 = 2/2 = +1 \text{ k}$$

$$F_A = 2(\sqrt{5}/2) = +2.23 \text{ k}$$

$$\Sigma M_A = 0 \curvearrowleft + \qquad + 3(6) + F_{Cx}(9) = 0, \qquad F_{Cx} = -2 \text{ k}$$

$$F_{Cy} = F_{Cx} = -2 \text{ k}$$

$$F_C = \sqrt{2}(-2) = -2.83 \text{ k}$$

$$\text{Check } \Sigma F_x = 0 \qquad F_{Ax} + F_{Cx} = 2 - 2 = 0$$

$$\Sigma F_y = 0 \qquad F_{Ay} - F_{Cy} - P = 1 - (-2) - 3 = 0$$

Tensile stress in main bar AB:

$$\sigma_{AB} = \frac{F_A}{A} = \frac{2.23}{0.25 \times 0.50} = 17.8 \text{ ksi}$$

Tensile stress in clevis of bar AB, Fig. 1-20(e):

$$(\sigma_{AB})_{\text{clevis}} = \frac{F_A}{A_{\text{net}}} = \frac{2.23}{2 \times 0.20 \times (0.875 - 0.375)} = 11.2 \text{ ksi}$$

Compressive stress in main bar BC:

$$\sigma_{BC} = \frac{F_C}{A} = \frac{2.83}{0.875 \times 0.25} = 12.9 \text{ ksi}$$

In the compression member, the net section at the clevis need not be investigated; see Fig. 1-20(f) for the transfer of forces. The bearing stress at the pin is more critical. Bearing between pin C and the clevis:

$$\sigma_b = \frac{F_C}{A_{\text{bearing}}} = \frac{2.83}{0.375 \times 0.20 \times 2} = 18.8 \text{ ksi}$$

Bearing between the pin C and the main plate:

$$\sigma_b = \frac{F_C}{A} = \frac{2.83}{0.375 \times 0.25} = 30.2 \text{ ksi}$$

Double shear in pin C:

$$\tau = \frac{F_C}{A} = \frac{2.83}{2\pi (0.375/2)^2} = 12.9 \text{ ksi}$$

For a complete analysis of this bracket, other pins should be investigated. However, it can be seen by inspection that the other pins in this case are stressed either the same amount as computed or less.

The advantages of the method used in the last example for finding forces in members should now be apparent. It can also be applied with success in a problem such as the one shown in Fig. 1-21. The force F_A transmitted by the curved member AB acts through points A and B, since the forces applied at A and B must be collinear. By resolving this force at A', the same procedure can be followed. Wavy lines through F_A and F_C indicate that these forces are replaced by the two components shown. Alternatively, the force F_A can be resolved at A, and since $F_{Ay} = (y/x)F_{Ax}$, the application of $\Sigma M_C = 0$ yields F_{Ax}.

In frames, where the applied forces do not act through a joint, proceed as before as far as possible. Then isolate an individual member and, using its free-body diagram, complete the determination of forces. If inclined forces are acting on the structure, resolve them into convenient components.

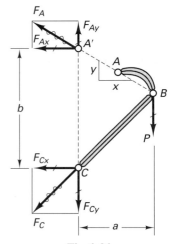

Fig. 1-21

Example 1-4

Consider the idealized system shown in Fig. 1-22, where a 5-kg mass is to be spun on a frictionless plane at 10 Hz. If a light rod CD is attached at C, and its stress can reach 200 MPa, what is the required size of the rod? Neglect the weight of the rod and assume that the rod is enlarged at the ends to compensate for the threads.

SOLUTION

The rod angular velocity ω is 20π rad/s. The acceleration a of the mass toward the center of rotation is $\omega^2 R$, where R is the distance CD. By multiplying the mass m by the acceleration, the force F acting on the rod is

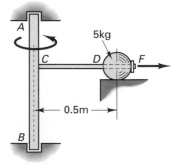

Fig. 1-22

obtained. As shown in the figure, according to the d'Alembert principle, this force acts in the opposite direction to that of the acceleration. Therefore,

$$F = ma = m\omega^2 R = 5 \times (20\pi)^2 \times 0.500 = 9870 \text{ kg} \cdot \text{m/s}^2 = 9870 \text{ N}$$

$$A_{\text{net}} = \frac{9870}{200} = 49.3 \text{ mm}^2$$

An 8-mm round rod having an area $A = 50.3 \text{ mm}^2$ would be satisfactory.

The additional pull at C caused by the mass of the rod, which was not considered, is

$$F_1 = \int_0^R (m_1 \, dr) \, \omega^2 r$$

where m_1 is the mass of the rod per unit length, and $(m_1 \, dr)$ is its infinitesimal mass at a variable distance r from the vertical rod AB. The total pull at C caused by the rod and the mass of 5-kg at the end is $F + F_1$.

1-10. Member Strength as a Design Criterion

The purpose for calculating stresses in members of a structural system is to compare them with the experimentally determined material strengths in order to assure desired performance. Physical testing of materials in a laboratory provides information regarding a material's resistance to stress. In a laboratory, specimens of known material, manufacturing process, and heat treatment are carefully prepared to desired dimensions. Then these specimens are subjected to successively increasing known forces. In the most widely used test, a round rod or a rectangular bar is subjected to tension and the specimen is loaded until it finally ruptures. The force necessary to cause rupture is called the *ultimate* load. By dividing this ultimate load by the *original* cross-sectional area of the specimen, the *ultimate strength* (stress) of a material is obtained. The tensile test is used most widely. However, compression, bending, torsion, and shearing tests are also employed.[14] Tables 1A and B of the Appendix give ultimate strengths and other physical properties for a few materials.

For applications where a force comes on and off the structure a number of times, the materials cannot withstand the ultimate stress of a static test. In such cases, the "ultimate strength" depends on the number of times the force is applied as the material works at a particular stress level. Such experimental points indicate the number of cycles required to break the

[14]ASTM (American Society for Testing and Materials, 1916 Race Str. Philadelphia, PA 19103) issues an *Annual Book of ASTM Standards* now consisting of 66 volumes, divided into 16 sections, giving classification of materials, ASTM standard specifications, and detailed test methods. ASTM material designation such as A36 steel is frequently used in this book.

specimen at a particular stress under the application of a fluctuating load. Such tests are called "fatigue tests," and the corresponding curves are termed *S-N* (stress-number) diagrams. This behavior is discussed in Section 2-10 of the next chapter.

Stress-dependent deformations may also play a key role in selecting the permissible or allowable stress for a given material, since some materials deform an unpermissible amount prior to fracture. Some materials deform plastically under a sustained load, a phenomenon called *creep*. Experience with turbines, tightened bolts in mechanical equipment, and wooden or reinforced concrete beams indicate some of the examples where creep may be a problem. In some instances, the rate of load application has a major effect, as some materials become considerably stronger at very rapidly applied loads. Likewise, the effect of temperature usually has a very important effect on the endurance limit. Some of these issues are discussed further in Section 2-8 and 2-9. At the design level, most of these problems can be controlled by reducing design stresses.

The aforementioned facts, coupled with the impossibility of determining stresses accurately in complicated structures and machines, necessitate a substantial reduction of stress compared to the ultimate strength of a material in a static test. For example, ordinary steel will withstand an ultimate stress in tension of 500 MPa (70 ksi) and more. However, it deforms rather suddenly and severely at the stress level of about 350 MPa (50 ksi), and it is customary in the United States to use an allowable stress of around 200 MPa (30 ksi) for structural work. This allowable stress is even further reduced to about 100 MPa (15 ksi) for parts that are subjected to alternating loads because of the fatigue characteristics of the material. *Fatigue properties of materials are of utmost importance in mechanical equipment.*

The decision process in choosing an appropriate allowable stress is further complicated since there is *great uncertainty in the magnitudes of the applied loads.* During the life of a machine or a structure, occasional overloads are almost a certainty, but their magnitudes can only be estimated at best.

These difficult problems are now resolved using two alternative approaches. In the traditional approach, in the spirit of classical mechanics, *unique magnitudes* are assigned to the applied forces as well as to the *allowable stresses.* In this manner, these two principal parameters are precisely known (i.e., determinate) in the design process. This *deterministic* approach is commonly used in current practice and will be largely adhered to in this text. However, as the complexity of engineering hardware systems increases, less reliance can be placed on past experience and a limited number of experiments. Instead, after identification of the main parameters in a given stress-analysis problem, their statistical variability is assessed, leading to the *probabilistic* method of estimating structural safety. This approach has found favor in the design of advanced aircraft and offshore structures and is emerging in structural design of buildings and bridges. A brief discussion of the probabilistic approach to structural design is given in Section 1-12. The traditional deterministic approach is discussed next.

1-11. Deterministic Design of Members: Axially Loaded Bars

In the deterministic design of members, a stress resultant is determined at the highest stressed section using conventional mechanics. For axially loaded bars, it means determining the largest internal axial force P at a minimum cross section. Then, for the selected material, an allowable stress σ_{allow} must be chosen.

Professional engineering groups, large companies, as well as city, state, and federal authorities prescribe or recommend[15] allowable stresses for different materials, depending on the application. Often such stresses are called the allowable *fiber*[16] stresses.

Since, according to Eq. 1-6, stress times area is equal to a force, the allowable and ultimate stresses may be converted into the allowable and ultimate forces or "loads," respectively, that a member can resist. Also a significant ratio may be formed:

$$\frac{\text{ultimate load for a member}}{\text{allowable load for a member}}$$

This is the basic definition of the *factor of safety*, F.S. This ratio must always be greater than unity. Traditionally this factor is recast in terms of stresses as

$$\text{F.S.} = \frac{\text{maximum useful material strength (stress)}}{\text{allowable stress}}$$

and is widely used not only for axially loaded members, but also for any type of member and loading conditions. As will become apparent from subsequent reading, whereas this definition of F.S. in terms of elastic stresses is satisfactory for some cases, it can be misleading in others.

In the aircraft industry, the term *factor of safety* is replaced by another, defined as

$$\frac{\text{ultimate load}}{\text{design load}} - 1$$

---

[15]For example, see the American Institute of Steel Construction *Manual,* Building Construction Code of any large city, ANC-5 *Strength of Aircraft Elements* issued by the Army-Navy Civil Committee on Aircraft Design Criteria, etc.

[16]The adjective *fiber* in this sense is used for two reasons. Many original experiments were made on wood, which is fibrous in character. Also in several derivations that follow, the concept of a continuous filament or fiber in a member is a convenient device for visualizing its action.

and is known as the *margin of safety*. In the past, this ratio was usually recast to read

$$\frac{\text{ultimate stress}}{\text{maximum stress caused by the design load}} - 1$$

The newer analytical methods, some of which will be pointed out in the text as they occur, can provide reasonable estimates of the ultimate loads for complex systems and should be used in the basic definition of F.S. as well as of margin of safety. For example, for static loadings, instead of designing members at working loads using allowable stress, an alternative approach consisting of selecting member sizes for their *ultimate* or *limit load* is becoming widely adopted. In such cases, the ultimate load is usually obtained by multiplying the working loads by a suitably chosen *load factors*. For bars in simple tension or compression, this leads to the same results. Significantly different results may be obtained in many other cases where inelastic behavior is more complex. In this text, however, the customary *allowable stress design* (ASD) approach will largely be followed.

The application of the ASD approach for axially loaded members is both simple and direct. From Eq. 1-6, it follows that the required net area A of a member is

$$A = \frac{P}{\sigma_{\text{allow}}} \tag{1-15}$$

where P is the applied axial force and σ_{allow} is the allowable stress. Equation 1-15 is generally applicable to tension members and short compression blocks. *For slender compression members, the question of their stability arises and the methods discussed in Chapter 16 must be used.*

The simplicity of Eq. 1-15 is unrelated to its importance. A large number of problems requiring its use occurs in practice. The following problems illustrate some application of Eq. 1-15 as well as provide additional review in statics.

Example 1-5

Reduce the size of bar AB in Example 1-3 by using a better material such as chrome-vanadium steel. The ultimate strength of this steel is approximately 120 ksi. Use a factor of safety of 2.5.

SOLUTION

$\sigma_{\text{allow}} = 120/2.5 = 48$ ksi. From Example 1-3, the force in the bar AB: $F_A = +2.23$ kips. Required area: $A_{\text{net}} = 2.23/48 = 0.0464$ in^2. Adopt: 0.20-in by 0.25-in bar. This provides an area of $(0.20)(0.25) = 0.050$ in^2, which is slightly in excess of the required area. Many other proportions of the bar are possible.

With the cross-sectional area selected, the actual or working stress is somewhat below the allowable stress: $\sigma_{actual} = 2.23/(0.050) = 44.6$ ksi. The actual factor of safety is $120/(44.6) = 2.69$, and the actual margin of safety is 1.69.

In a complete redesign, clevis and pins should also be reviewed and, if possible, decreased in dimensions.

Example 1-6

Select members *FC* and *CB* in the truss of Fig. 1-23(a) to carry an inclined force *P* of 650 kN. Set the allowable tensile stress at 140 MPa.

SOLUTION

If all members of the truss were to be designed, forces in all members would have to be found. In practice, this is now done by employing computer programs developed on the basis of matrix structural analysis[17] or by directly analyzing the truss by the method of joints. However, if only a few members are to be designed or checked, the method of sections illustrated here is quicker.

It is generally understood that a planar truss, such as shown in the figure, is stable in the direction perpendicular to the plane of the paper. Practically, this is accomplished by introducing braces at right angles to the plane of the truss. In this example, the design of compression members is avoided, as this will be treated in the chapter on columns.

To determine the forces in the members to be designed, the reactions for the whole structure are computed first. This is done by completely disregarding the interior framing. Only reaction and force components definitely located at their points of application are indicated on a free-body diagram of the whole structure; see Fig. 1-23(b). After the reactions are determined, free-body diagrams of a part of the structure are used to determine the forces in the members considered; see Figs. 1-23(c) and (d).

Using the free-body diagram in Fig. 1-23(b),

$$\Sigma F_x = 0 \qquad R_{Dx} - 520 = 0 \qquad R_{Dx} = 520 \text{ kN}$$

$$\Sigma M_E = 0 \curvearrowright + \qquad R_{Dy} \times 3 - 390 \times 0.5 - 520 \times 1.5 = 0$$

$$R_{Dy} = 325 \text{ kN}$$

$$\Sigma M_D = 0 \curvearrowright + \qquad R_E \times 3 + 520 \times 1.5 - 390 \times 2.5 = 0$$

$$R_E = 65 \text{ kN}$$

[17]See, for example, O. C. Zienkiewicz and R. L. Taylor, *The Finite Element Method,* Vol. 1, 4th ed. (London: McGraw-Hill, 1989).

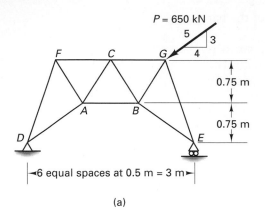

(a)

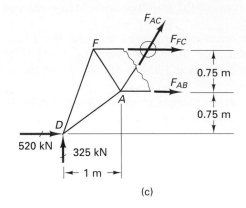

(c)

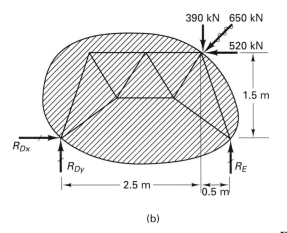

(b)

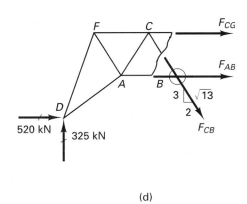

(d)

Fig. 1-23

Check: $\Sigma F_y = 0 \quad 325 - 390 + 65 = 0$

Using the free-body diagram in Fig. 1-23(c),

$$\Sigma M_A = 0 \curvearrowright + \qquad F_{FC} \times 0.75 + 325 \times 1 - 520 \times 0.75 = 0$$

$$F_{FC} = +86.7 \text{ kN}$$

$$A_{FC} = Ff_{FC}/\sigma_{\text{allow}} = 86.7 \times 10^3/140 = 620 \text{ mm}^2$$

$$(\text{use } 12.5 \times 50\text{-mm bar})$$

Using the free-body diagram in Fig. 1-23(d),

$$\Sigma F_y = 0 \qquad -(F_{CB})_y + 325 = 0 \qquad (F_{CB})_y = +325 \text{ kN}$$

$$F_{CB} = \sqrt{13}(F_{CB})_y/3 = +391 \text{ kN}$$

$$A_{CB} = F_{CB}/\sigma_{\text{allow}} = 391 \times 10^3/140 = 2790 \text{ mm}^2$$

(use two bars 30×50 mm)

1-12. Probabilistic Basis for Structural Design

In the conventional (deterministic) design of members, the possibility of failure is reduced to acceptably small levels by factors of safety based on judgment derived from past successful and unsuccessful performances. By contrast, in the probabilistic approach, variability in material properties, fabrication-size tolerances, as well as uncertainties in loading and even design approximations can be appraised on a statistical basis. As far as possible, the proposed criteria are calibrated against well-established cases, as disregard of past successful applications is out of the question. The probabilistic approach has the advantage of consistency in the factors of safety, not only for individual members, but also for complex structural assemblies. Important risk analyses of complete engineering systems are based on the same premises.

Theoretical Basis   In statistical terminology, the data set of test results X_1, X_2, ..., X_n is termed *sample population,* where each X_i is called a *sample* (numerical observation). In the analysis of such data sets, several quantities of major importance are generally computed. One of these is the *sample mean* (average), $\overline{X}$; another is the *sample variance,* S^2. For n samples, these quantities are defined as

$$\overline{X} = \frac{1}{n} \sum_{i=1}^{n} X_i \tag{1-16}$$

and

$$S^2 = \frac{1}{n} \sum_{i=1}^{n} (X_i - \overline{X})^2 \tag{1-17}$$

A positive square root of the sample variance (i.e., S) is called the *sample standard deviation.* Dividing S by $\overline{X}$, one obtains the *coefficient of variance, V*:

$$V = S/\overline{X} \tag{1-18}$$

Quantities $\overline{X}$, S (or S^2), and V play dominant roles in the theory of probability. The mean $\overline{X}$, is the *expected sample value;* the standard deviation, S, is a *measure of dispersion* (scatter) of the data; and the coefficient variation, V, is a dimensionless measure of the amount of variability relative to the value of the mean.

A *frequency distribution* provides a compact summary of a data set. The first step in constructing a frequency distribution is to divide the relevant measurement axis into a collection of non-overlapping intervals such that each observation in the data set is contained in one of these intervals. Each of the resulting intervals is called a *class interval*, or simply a class.

A graphical representation of a frequency distribution can be obtained by constructing a *histogram*, for which the boundaries of adjacent class intervals are marked on the horizontal axis and the frequency distributions are marked on the vertical axis.

The term *probability* can be explained using classical probability concept, according to which one can say that *if there are* n *equally likely possibilities, of which one must occur and* s *are regarded as favorable, or as* "success," *then the probability of a* "success" *is given by* s/n.

For approximating the dispersion of observed data the *probability density functions* (PDFs) are used, which are integrated to obtain probabilities. In applied probability the most widely used PDFs are based on *normal* or *Gaussian*[18] distribution. The analytical form of such PDF of a random variable Z—that is, $f_z(z)$—is given as

$$f_z(z) = \frac{1}{\sqrt{2\pi}\,\sigma_z} \exp\left[-\frac{1}{2}\left(\frac{z-\mu_z}{\sigma_z}\right)^2\right] \tag{1-19}$$

where

$$\mu_z = \int_{-\infty}^{+\infty} z f_z(z)\,dz \tag{1-20}$$

and

$$\sigma_z^2 = \int_{-\infty}^{+\infty} (z-\mu_z)^2 f_z(z)\,dz \tag{1-21}$$

The constant $1/\sqrt{2\pi}$ in Eq. 1-19 is selected so that the normalized frequency diagram encloses a unit area; that is,

$$F_z(z) = \int_{-\infty}^{+\infty} f_z(z)\,dz = 1 \tag{1-22}$$

which means that the occurrence of Z within its entire range is a certainty.

In the previous equations μ_z is referred to as the *mean* and σ_z is the *standard deviation* of the probability densities. A typical PDF of Z with normal distribution is shown in Fig. 1-24. It should be noted that in applications, the theoretical model is usually selected by setting $\mu_z = \overline{X}$, and $\sigma_z = S$.

Some interesting properties of $f_z(z)$ are illustrated in Fig. 1-25. Thus, from Fig. 1-25(a), it can be seen that the probability of the occurrence of an outcome between one standard deviation on either side of the mean is 88.27%. As shown in Fig. 1-25(b), between two standard deviations on either side of the mean, this value becomes 95.45%. The areas enclosed under the curve tails that are three standard deviations from the mean are only 0.135% of

---

[18]So named in honor of the great German mathematician Karl Friedrich Gauss (1777–1855), who first introduced this function based on theoretical considerations.

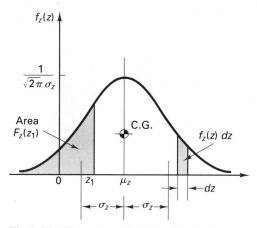

Fig. 1-24   Normal probability density function (PDF) of Z.

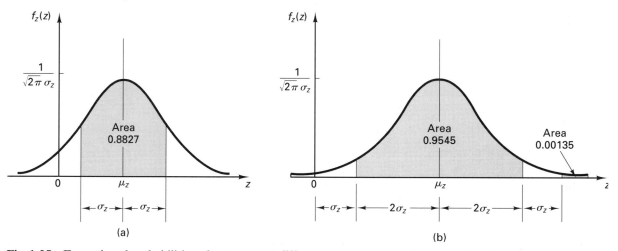

Fig. 1-25   Examples of probabilities of outcomes at different amounts of standard deviation from the mean.

the total outcomes. As will become apparent later, the small number of outcomes likely to take place under $f_z(z)$ several standard deviations away from the mean is of the utmost importance in appraising structural safety.

Experimental Evidence   As an example of the probabilistic approach based on statistics, consider the behavior of specimens for three sets of similar experiments. For one set, experimental results of several compression tests for identical short wooden blocks are plotted in Fig. 1-26(a).[19] Similar

[19]See J. M. Illston, J. M. Dinwoodie, and A. A. Smith, *Concrete, Timber, and Metals* (New York: Van Nostrand Reinhold, 1979), Fig. 14.3, p. 439, Crown Copyright, ©Building Research Establishment, U.K.

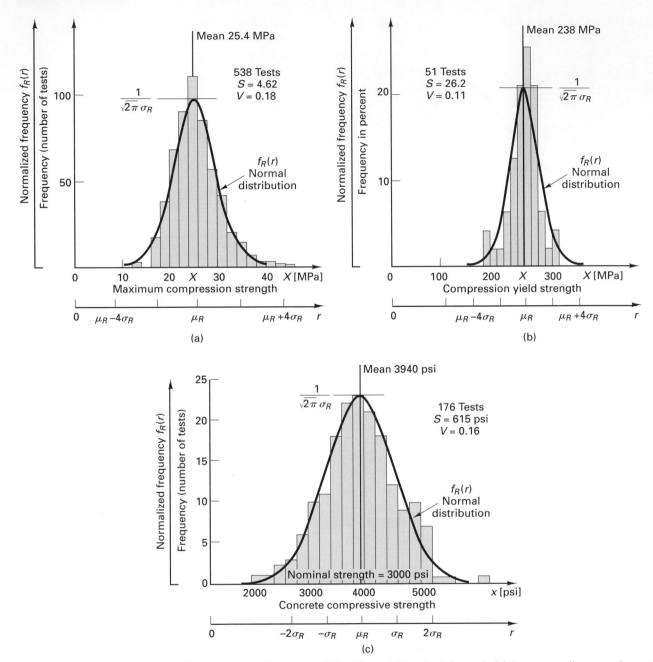

Fig. 1-26   (a) Histogram of maximum compression strength for Western Hemlock (wood); (b) frequency diagram of compression yield strength of ASTM grades A7 and A36 steels; (c) concrete.

results are shown for steel stub columns in Fig. 1-26(b)[20] and for concrete in Fig. 1-26(c).[21] The bar widths in these histograms correspond to a narrow range of compression stress for which a given number of specimens were either crushed (wood and concrete) or have yielded (steel). In these diagrams, the inner scales apply to direct experimental results.

In Fig. 1-26 in addition to the histograms, theoretical curves for the three cases are also shown. The bell-shaped curves are the PDFs of material resistance R.

Practical Formulations
For a probabilistic appraisal of the structural safety of a member or a structure, one must have a statistically determined resistance PDF $f_R(r)$, such as discussed before, and a corresponding load effect PDF. Again statistical studies show that since the loads are susceptible to variations, their effect on a member or a structure can be expressed in probabilistic form. Such load effects, resembling $f_R(r)$, will be designated as $f_Q(q)$. For a given member or a structure, these functions define the behavior of the same critical parameter such as a force, stress, or deflection. Two such functions probabilistically defining the load effect $f_Q(q)$ *and the resistance* $f_R(r)$ for a force acting on a member are shown in Fig. 1-27. For purposes of illustration, it is assumed that the load effect $f_Q(q)$ has a larger standard deviation (i.e., larger dispersion of the load) than that for the member resistance.

In conventional (deterministic) design, the load magnitudes are usually set above the observed mean. This condition is represented by Q_n in Fig. 1-27. On the other hand, in order to avoid possible rejections, a supplier will typically provide a material with an average strength slightly greater than specified. For this reason, calculated nominal member resistance R_n would be below the mean. On this basis, the conventional factor of safety is simply defined as R_n/Q_n.

In reality, both *Q and R are uncertain quantities and there is no unique answer to the safety problem.* To illustrate the interaction between the two main variables in Fig. 1-28, $f_R(r)$ is shown along the horizontal axis and $f_Q(q)$ is plotted along the vertical axis. For the ensemble of an infinite number of possible outcomes, a line at 45° corresponding to $R = Q$ divides the graph into two regions. For $R > Q$, no failure can occur. For example, for the range of small and large outcomes Q_1, Q_2, Q_3, the resistance outcomes, respectively, R_1, R_2, R_3 suffice to preserve the integrity of a member. However, for outcomes Q_3 and R_1 with a common point at D and falling in the region where $R < Q$, a failure would take place.

While enlightening, the preceding process is difficult to apply in practice. Fortunately, however, it can be mathematically demonstrated that for

---

[20]See T. V. Galambos and M. K. Ravindra, "Tentative load and resistance design criteria for steel buildings," *Research Report No. 18,* Structural Division, Washington University, 1973.

[21]See J. G. Macgregor, *Reinforced Concrete, Mechanics and Design,* 3rd ed. (Upper Saddle River, NJ: Prentice Hall, 1996).

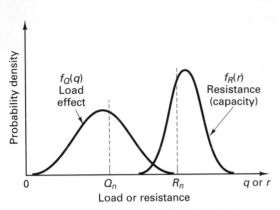

Fig. 1-27 Probability density functions for the two main random variables (load and resistance).

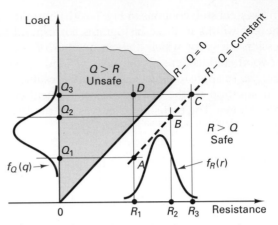

Fig. 1-28 Probabilistic definition of safe and unsafe structural regions.

normal distribution of R and Q their difference (i.e., $R - Q$) is also a normal distribution. In this manner, the information implied in Fig. 1-28 can be compressed into a single normal PDF such as that shown in Fig. 1-29. In this diagram the *probability of failure*, p_f, is given by the area under the tail of the curve to the left of the origin. A possible magnitude of a p_f may be surmised from Fig. 1-25(b). A member would survive in all instances to the right of the origin.

In addition to the failure limit states emphasized before, the probabilistic approach is suitable for other situation. Important among these are the serviceability limit states. Control of maximum deflections or limitations on undesirable vibrations can also be treated in probabilistic terms.

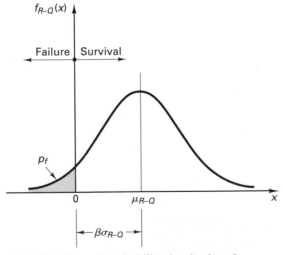

Fig. 1-29 Normal probability density function.

PROBLEMS

Section 1-5

1-1. Verify equilibrium Eq. 1-5 for the x direction with the aid of a sketch, similar to Fig. 1-6, where the stress increments for three-dimensional stresses are shown.

1-2. Show that the differential equations of equilibrium for a two-dimensional plane stress problem in polar coordinates are

$$\frac{\partial \sigma_r}{\partial r} + \frac{1}{r} \frac{\partial \tau_{r\theta}}{\partial \theta} + \frac{\sigma_r - \sigma_\theta}{r} = 0$$

$$\frac{\partial \tau_{r\theta}}{\partial r} + \frac{1}{r} \frac{\partial \sigma_\theta}{\partial \theta} + \frac{2\tau_{r\theta}}{r} = 0$$

The symbols are defined in the figure. Body forces are neglected in this formulation.

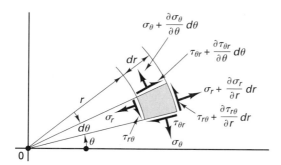

Fig. P1-2

Section 1-6

1-3. If an axial tensile force of 110 kips is applied to a member made of a W 8 × 24 section, what will the tensile stress be? What will the stress be if the member is a C 12 × 20.7 section? For designation and cross-sectional areas of these members, see Tables 4A and 5 in the Appendix.

1-4. In California a common concrete foundation block in residential construction is similar to that shown in Fig. 1-9. If the floor construction and the applied loads (called live loads) are estimated to be 50 lb/sq ft and the pier supports 40 sq ft of floor, what is the magnitude of the applied force P? If the Douglas Fir wooden post is $5\frac{1}{2} \times 5\frac{1}{2}$ in in cross section (size for 6 × 6 in), what is the axial stress in the post and the bearing stress on the concrete block? If the concrete foundation block is 16 × 16 in square at the base, what is the bearing stress on the soil in lb/sq ft? Neglect the weight of the pier.

1-5. An axially loaded connecting link having a T cross section in the figure is subjected to a uniform tensile stress of 150 MPa. Determine the magnitude of the applied force and the location of stress resultant. All dimensions are in mm.

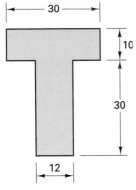

Fig. P1-5

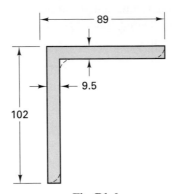

Fig. P1-6

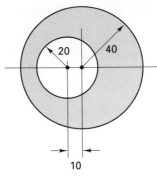

Fig. P1-7

1-6. A short $102 \times 89 \times 9.5$ mm steel angle is subjected to a compressive force causing uniformly distributed stress of 16 ksi. Idealize the cross section as shown in figure and compare it with the handbook value of $A = 1720$ mm^2, where the refinement in rounding the corners is considered. Determine the location of the stress resultant. Compare with the handbook values of 24.3 mm and 30.8 mm.

1-7 and 1-8. Short aluminum alloy members have the cross-sectional dimensions shown in the figures. If they are subjected to axial compressive forces of 100 kN each, find the points of application for these forces to cause no bending. All dimensions are in mm.

1-9. A bar of variable cross section, held on the left, is subjected to two concentrated forces, P_1 and P_2, as shown in the figure. (a) Find the maximum axial stress if $P_1 = 50$ kN and $P_2 = 40$ kN, $A_1 = 60$ mm^2 and $A_2 = 30$ mm^2. (b) On two separate diagrams, plot the axial force and the axial stress along the length of the bar.

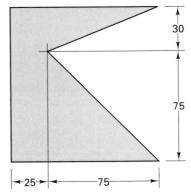

Fig. P1-8

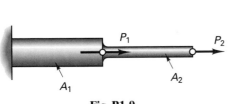

Fig. P1-9

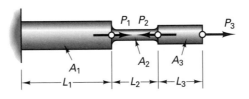

Fig. P1-10

1-10. A bar of variable cross section, held on the left, is subjected to three forces, $P_1 = 4$ kN, $P_2 = -2$ kN, and $P_3 = 3$ kN, as shown in the figure. On two separate diagrams, plot the axial force and the axial stress along the length of the bar. Let $A_1 = 200$ mm^2, $A_2 = 100$ mm^2, and $A_3 = 150$ mm^2.

1-11. Rework Problem 1-10 by reversing the direction of the force P_2.

1-12. Determine the bearing stresses caused by the applied force at A, B, and C for the wooden structure shown in the figure. All member sizes shown are nominal. See Table 9 in the Appendix for U.S. standard sizes of lumber.

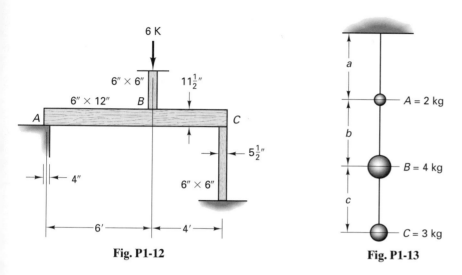

Fig. P1-12   Fig. P1-13

1-13. Three metal balls are suspended by three wires of equal length arranged in sequence as shown in Fig. P1-13. The masses of the balls, starting at the top, are 2 kg, 4 kg, and 3 kg. In the same order, beginning at the top, the wires have the following diameters: 2 mm, 1.5 mm, and 1 mm, respectively. (a) Determine the highest stressed wire, (b) by changing the location of the balls optimize mass locations to achieve a system with minimum stresses.

Sections 1-6 and 1-7

1-14. On the same graph, plot the normal stress σ_θ and the shear stress τ_θ as functions of the angle θ defined in Fig. 1-12. Angle θ should range from $0°$ to $360°$ on the abscissa. Identify the maxima and minima for these functions.

1-15. In Fig. 1-12(a), determine the angles θ where the magnitudes of σ_θ and τ_θ are equal.

1-16. Using polar coordinate axes, on the same graph, plot σ_θ and τ_θ as functions of angle θ defined in Fig. 1-12. Identify the maxima and minima for these functions.

1-17. A 10-mm square bar is subjected to a tensile force $P = 20$ kN, as shown in Fig. 1-12(a). (a) Using statics, determine the normal and shear stresses acting on sections a–a and b–b for $\theta = 30°$. (b) Verify the results using Eqs. 1-7a and 1-7b. (c) Show the results as in Fig. 1-12(g).

1-18. Repeat Problem 1-17 for a 1/2-in square bar if $P = 5$ kips and $\theta = 20°$.

1-19. A glued lap splice is to be made in a 10 × 20 mm rectangular member at α = 20°, as shown in the figure. Assuming that the shear strength of the glued joint controls the design, what axial force *P* can be applied to the member? Assume the shear strength of the glued joint to be 10 MPa.

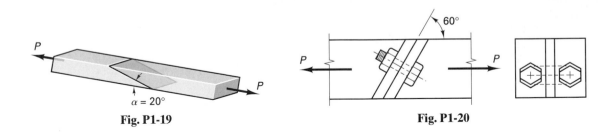

Fig. P1-19   **Fig. P1-20**

1-20. The steel tees are bolted by two 19-mm bolts as shown in the figure. Determine the average normal and shear bolt stresses along the 60° plane of contact between the tees. The applied axial force *P* = 100 kN.

Section 1-8

1-21. A 40 × 80 mm wooden plank is glued to two 20 × 80 mm planks, as shown in Fig. 1-13(d). If each of the two glued surfaces is 40 × 80 mm and the applied force *P* = 20 kN, what is the average shear stress in the joints?

1-22. Two 10-mm thick steel plates are fastened together, as shown in the figure, by means of two 20-mm bolts that fit tightly into the holes. If the joint transmits a tensile force of 45 kN, determine (a) the average normal stress in the plates at a section where no holes occur; (b) the average normal stress at the critical section; (c) the average shearing stress in the bolts; and (d) the average bearing stress between the bolts and the plates.

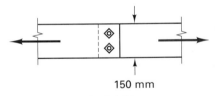

150 mm

Fig. P1-22

1-23. An exploded view of a bolted connection resembling that shown in Figs. 1-14(e), (f), (g), and (h) is shown in Fig. P1-23.[1] The width of the plates is 60 mm; their thicknesses are *t* = 10 mm. The snugly fitting bolt is 20 mm in diameter. Calculate the maximum normal stress in the plates at the critical section due to an applied tensile force *P* = 70 kN. For the same condition calculate in the bearing and shear stresses in the bolt.

1-24. The power between two parallel shafts is transferred by means of a roller chain mounted on sprockets (Fig. P1-24). If the force developed by the chain at the driver sprocket *C* and *P* = 10 kN, what is the shear stress in the keys? The keys for both sprockets are the same. Note that by knowing the magnitude of the force *P* and the pitch diameter of a sprocket, the applied torque to the shaft becomes known. Find the force acting on 6 (wide) × 4 × 10 mm keys.

---

[1] After G. Dreyer, *Festigkeislehre and Elastizitàtslehre* (Leipzig, Germany: Janecke, 1938).

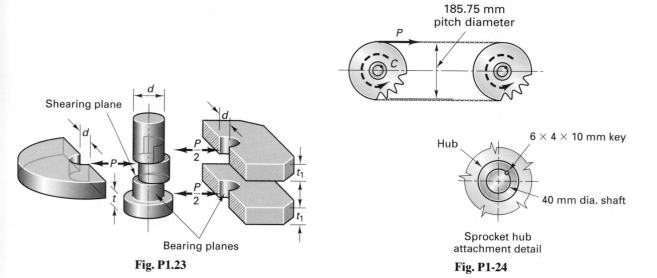

185.75 mm
pitch diameter

P

C

Hub

6 × 4 × 10 mm key

40 mm dia. shaft

Sprocket hub
attachment detail

Fig. P1-24

Shearing plane

d

d

d

$\frac{P}{2}$

$\frac{P}{2}$

P

t

t_1

t_1

Bearing planes

Fig. P1.23

1-25. Per American Institute of Steel Construction, for bolts to transfer a shear force without slipping, the bolts must be thoroughly tightened. For example, for a 1-in, high-strength steel bolt of A490 grade, the minimum tension is 64 k, resulting in an allowable shear force of 16.5 k. The hardened steel washers used with such bolts are 2 in outside diameter. With these data, estimate the pressure developed under washer. Further, assuming that the effective material 0.5 in below the plate surface is 3 in in diameter, determine the average pressure for this condition. (See Fig. 1-15.)

1-26. Consider the fillet welds shown in Fig. P1-26. Noting that the critical stress occurs in a 45° weld throat such as *ab*, derive an equation expressing the allowable force *Q* per inch of weld. Let the allowable shear stress through the throat be 21 ksi.

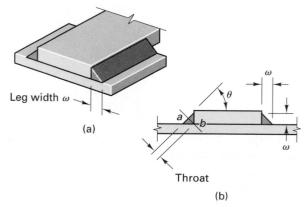

Leg width *ω*

(a)

θ

ω

a

b

ω

Throat

(b)

Fig. P1-26

1-27.   Rework Example 1-3 in SI units given in the figure.

1-28.   A 2-mm-thick hollow circular tube of 30 mm outside diameter is subjected on the outside surface to a constant shear of 10 Pa in the axial direction, as shown in the figure. If the tube is 400 mm long, what is the maximum axial stress? Plot the variation of the axial stress along the tube.

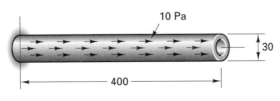

10 Pa

30

400

Fig. P1-28

1-29.   A short compression member is made up of two standard steel pipes, as shown in the figure. If the allowable stress in compression is 100 MPa, (a) what is the allowable axial load P_1 if the axial load $P_2 = 200$ kN; (b) what is the allowable load P_1 if load $P_2 = 65$ kN? See Table 7 in the Appendix for cross-sectional areas of U.S. standard pipes.

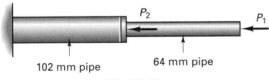

P_2

P_1

64 mm pipe

102 mm pipe

Fig. P1-29

1-30.   A rod of variable cross section built in at one end is subjected to three axial forces as shown in the figure. Find the maximum normal stress.

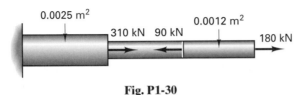

0.0025 m²

0.0012 m²

310 kN   90 kN

180 kN

Fig. P1-30

1-31.   Rework the preceding problem, assuming that the (axial) end force, instead of being 180 kN, is to be such as to cause the same maximum normal stresses in the two sizes of the rod. The 90 kN and the 310 kN axial forces remain applied, and the maximum normal stress for the smaller part of the rod may be either between these two forces or nearer to the free end. Investigate both conditions.

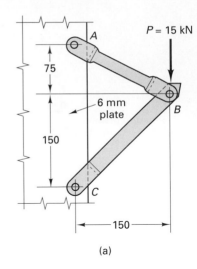

(a)

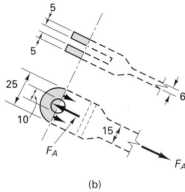

(b)

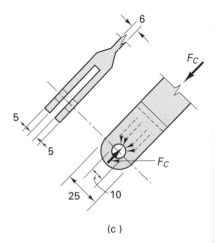

(c)

(All dimensions in mm)

Fig. P1-27

1-32. What is the shear stress in bolt A caused by the applied load shown in the figure? The bolt is 6 mm in diameter, and it acts in double shear. All dimensions are in mm.

1-33. A control pedal for actuating a spring mechanism is shown in the figure. Calculate the shear stress in pins A and B due to force P when it causes a stress of 75 MPa in rod AB. Both pins are in double shear.

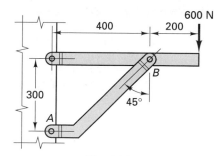

Fig. P1-32

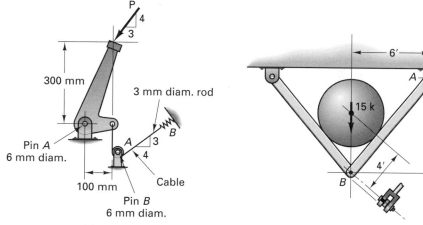

Fig. P1-33

Fig. P1-34

1-34. A 6-ft-diameter cylindrical tank is to be supported at each end of a hanger arranged as shown in the figure. The total weight supported by the two hangers is 15 ksi. Determine the shear stresses in the 1-in-diameter pins at points A and B due to the weight of the tank. Neglect the weight of the hangers and assume that contact between the tank and the hangers is frictionless.

1-35. Two steel wires with well-designed attachments and a joint are subjected to an external force of 800 N, as shown in the figure. The diameter of wire AB is 2.68 mm and that of wire BC is 2.52 mm. (a) Determine the stresses in the wires caused by the applied vertical force. (b) Are the wire sizes well chosen?

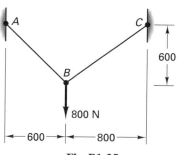

Fig. P1-35

1-36. A force of 800 kN is propped up by two pin-joined 102-mm nomical diameter standard steel pipes as shown in the figure (see Table 7 in the Appendix for structural properties). Determine the axial stresses in each of the two pipes caused by the applied force. All forces lay in a plan.

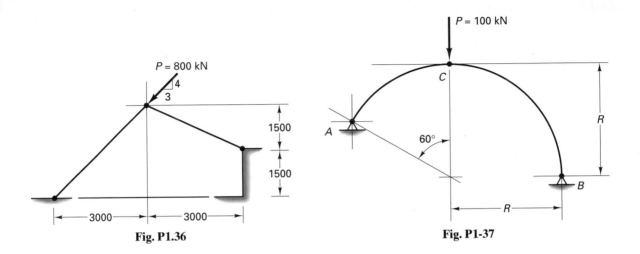

Fig. P1.36

Fig. P1-37

1-37. A planar circular three-hinge arch consists of two segments as shown in the figure. Determine the reactions *A* and *B* caused by the application of a vertical force *P* = 100 kN at *C* hinge. If the hinge pins at *A* and *B* are 20 mm in diameter and each pin acts in double shear, what shear stresses develop in the pins due to *P*?

1-38. A braced structural frame is designed to resist the lateral forces shown in the figure. Neglecting the frame weight, determine the axial stresses in members *BD*, *FG*, and *DE*; the respective areas for these members are 160, 400, and 130 mm².

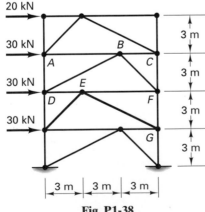

Fig. P1-38

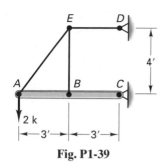

Fig. P1-39

1-39. A planar system consists of a rectangular beam *AC* supported by steel members *AE* and *BE* and a pin at *C*, as shown in the figure. Member *AE* is made up of two 6 by 25 mm parallel flat bars, and pin *C*, acting in double shear, is 19 mm in diameter. Determine the axial stress in bars *AE* and the shear in pin *C*.

1-40. By means of numerous vertical hangers, the cable shown in the figure is designed to support a continuously distributed load. This load, together with the cable and hangers, can be approximated as a uniformly distributed load of 2 kN/m. Determine the cross section required for the cable if the yield strength of the material is 1000 MPa and the required factor of safety is 2. (*Hint:* The cable assumes the shape of a parabola and develops only a horizontal force *H* at its lowest point. The larger resultant at a support is equal to the largest force in the cable.)

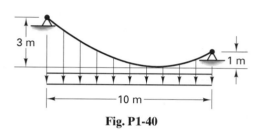

Fig. P1-40

1-41. Three equal 0.5-kg masses are attached to a 10-mm-diameter wire, as shown in the figure, and are rotated around a vertical axis, as shown in Fig. P1-41, on a frictionless plane at 4 Hz. Determine the axial stresses in the three segments of the wire and plot the results on a diagram as a function of *r*. Consider the masses to be concentrated as points.

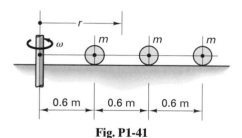

Fig. P1-41

1-42. A bar of constant cross-sectional area *A* is rotated around one of its ends in a horizontal plane with a constant angular velocity ω, as in the figure. The unit weight of the material is γ. Determine the variation of the stress σ along the bar and plot the result on a diagram as a function of *r*.

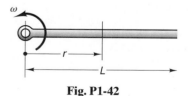

Fig. P1-42

1-43. A small bulldozer is to be designed to horizontally push with a force of 36 kN while a vertical downward force of 18 kN can develop on the blade, as shown in the figure. Two symmetrically patched pins A are to resist the applied forces. What size pins should be used if the allowable shear stress is 20 MPa?

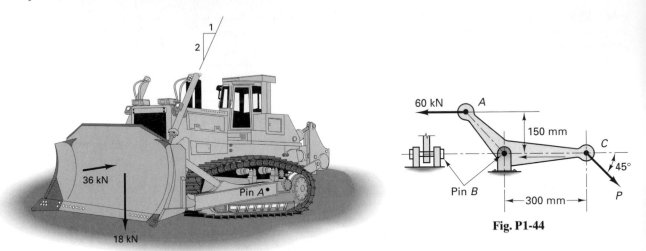

Fig. P1-43

Fig. P1-44

1-44. What is the required diameter of pin B for the bell crank mechanism shown in the figure if an applied force of 60 kN at A is resisted by a force P at C? The allowable shear stress is 100 MPa.

1-45. A joint for transmitting a tensile force is to be made by means of a pin, as shown in the figure. If the diameter of the rods being connected is D, what should be the diameter d of the pin? Assume that the allowable shear stress in the pin is one-half the maximum tensile stress in the rods. (In Section 12-16, it will be shown that this ratio for the allowable stresses is an excellent assumption for many materials.)

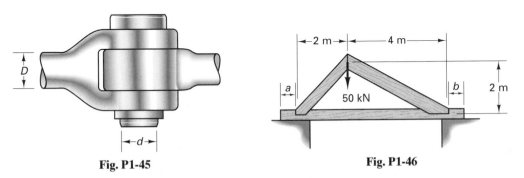

Fig. P1-45

Fig. P1-46

1-46. What minimum distances a and b are required beyond the notches in the horizontal member of the truss shown in the figure? All members are nominally 200×200 mm in cross section. (See Table 9 in the Appendix for the actual size.) Assume the ultimate strength of wood in shear parallel to the grain to be 3.5 MPa. Use a factor of safety of 5. (This detail is not recommended.)

1-47. For the structure shown in the figure, calculate the size of the bolt and area of the bearing plates required if the allowable stresses are 18,000 psi in tension and 500 psi in bearing. Neglect the weight of the beams.

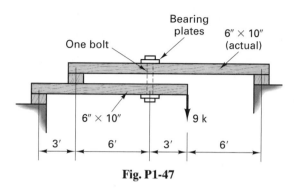

Fig. P1-47

1-48. Find the required cross-sectional areas for all tension members in Example 1-6. The allowable stress is 140 MPa.

1-49. Rework Example 1-6 after revising the data as follows: The total height of the truss is 2.5 m, the total width is 5 m, the applied force P is 600 kN. Let the allowable tensile stress be 140 MPa.

1-50. Two high-strength steel rods of different diameters are attached at A and C and support a mass M at B, as shown in the figure. What mass M can be supported? The ultimate strength of the rods is 800 MPa, and the factor of safety is to be 2. Rod AB has $A = 200$ mm²; rod BC has $A = 400$ mm². (The ends of the rods in such applications require special attachments.)

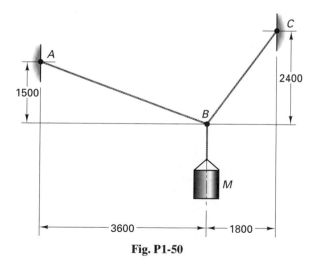

Fig. P1-50

1-51.   A 30-kg mass is hung by means of a pulley as shown in the figure. The pulley is supported by the frame *ABC*. Find the required cross-sectional areas for members *AC* and *BC* if the allowable stress in tension is 140 MPa and in compression, determined by the method of Chapter 16, is 96 MPa.

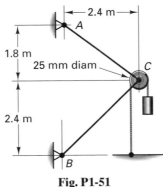

Fig. P1-51

1-52.   A beam with a force of 500 kN at one end is supported by a strutted cable as shown in the figure. Find the horizontal and vertical components of the reactions at *A, B,* and *D*. If the allowable tensile stress is 140 MPa and the allowable compressive stress is 100 MPa, what is the required cross-sectional area of members *AC, BC,* and *CE*? (*Hint:* Isolate the beam *DF* first.)

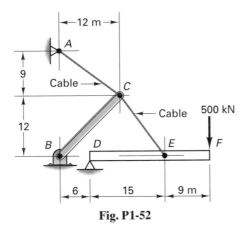

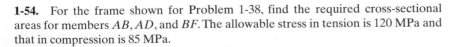

Fig. P1-52

1-53.   A tower used for a highline is shown in the figure. If it is subjected to a horizontal force of 600 kN and the allowable stresses are 100 MPa in compression and 140 MPa in tension, what is the required cross-sectional area of each member? All members are pin connected.

1-54.   For the frame shown for Problem 1-38, find the required cross-sectional areas for members *AB, AD,* and *BF*. The allowable stress in tension is 120 MPa and that in compression is 85 MPa.

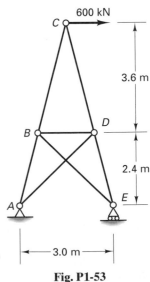

Fig. P1-53

1-55. A planar truss system has the dimensions shown in the figure. Member AE is continuous and can resist bending. All joints are pinned. Determine the diameter required for tension member AB to carry the applied force at A. The allowable stress is 40 ksi.

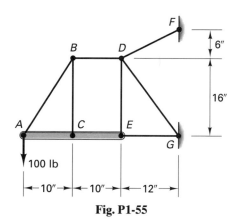

Fig. P1-55

1-56. A planar frame has the dimensions shown in the figure. Members AC and DF are continuous and can resist bending. All joints are pinned. Determine the diameter required of a high-strength steel rod for member CD. Assume that the ultimate strength for the rod is 1250 MPa and that the efficiency of the end attachments is 80%. The safety factor for the rod is 1.5.

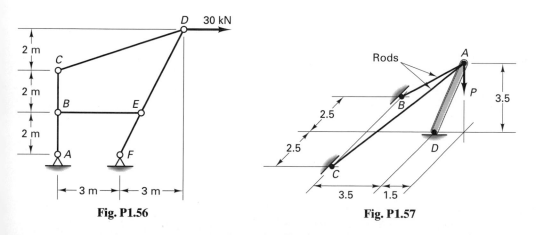

Fig. P1.56　　　　　　**Fig. P1.57**

1-57. To support a load $P = 200$ kN, determine the necessary diameter for rods AB and AC for the tripod shown in the figure. Neglect the weight of the structure and assume that the joints are pin connected. No allowance has to be made for threads. The allowable tensile strength is 120 MPa. All dimensions are in meters.

1-58. A pin-connected frame for supporting a force P is shown in the figure. Stress σ in both members AB and BC is to be the same. Determine the angle α necessary to achieve the minimum weight of construction. Members AB and BC have a constant cross section.

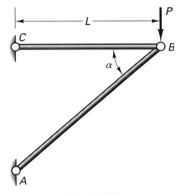

Fig. P1-58

Section 1-11

1-59. By integrating the probability function or using a table (state source), verify the areas contained within one and two standard deviations from the mean shown in Fig. 1-25.

1-60. By direct algebra verify the standard deviations from the mean for the example in Fig. 1-26(c).

2

Strain

2-1. Introduction

This chapter will show how stress can be related to deformation per unit length, or strain, of a specimen using experimental means for establishing a *stress-strain relation* for a specific material. This relation is called the *constitutive model* of a material and conveys the most important mechanical properties of a material during a loading process. The constitutive model of a material is based on results from *experiments* performed under very simple loading conditions. When a constitutive relation is combined with the equilibrium and compatibility equations, general structural behavior can be predicted.

2-2. The Tension Test and the Normal Strain

The mechanical properties of materials used in engineering are determined by experiments performed on small specimens. These experiments are conducted in laboratories equipped with testing machines, like the one

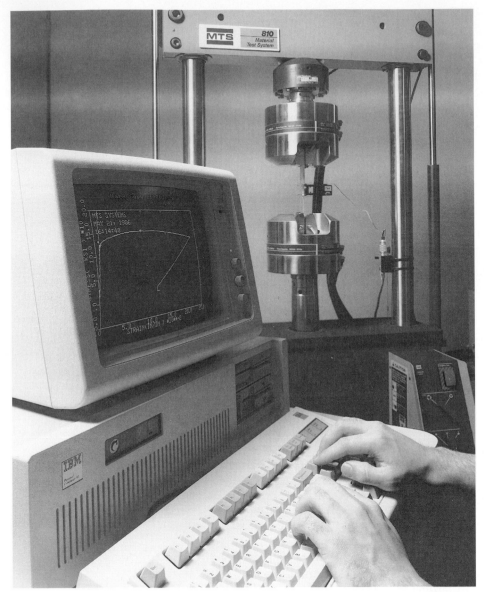

Fig. 2-1   Universal testing machine (courtesy of MTS System Corporation).

shown in Fig. 2-1, capable of loading in tension or compression. Several types of tests have been developed to evaluate material properties under different load conditions, such as short-duration static and cyclic, and there are tests of extended duration and impulsive loading. Over the years, each one of these tests become standardized so that the results obtained from different laboratories can be compared. In the United States the American Society for Testing and Materials (ASTM) has published guidelines for performing such tests and provides limits for which the use of a particular material is considered acceptable.

One of the most important experiments to perform is the *tension or compression test,* in which an increasing axial force P is applied to a cylindrical specimen such as shown in Fig. 2-2. The original cross-sectional area A_0 of the central portion of the specimen is accurately determined and two gage marks are inscribed at a distance L_0 apart. The distance L_0 is called a *gage length* of the specimen. In an experiment, the change in the length of this distance is measured using a device called an *extensometer.* In tension tests, instead of a cylindrical specimen, flat rectangular bars are frequently used.

During an experiment, the change in gage length is recorded as a function of the applied force. With the same load and longer gage length, a larger deformation is observed than when the gage length is small. Therefore, it is more fundamental to refer to the observed deformation per unit of length of the gage (i.e., to the intensity of deformation).

If L_0 is the initial gage length and L is the observed length under a given load, the gage elongation $\Delta L = L - L_0$. The elongation (contraction) ε per unit of the initial gage length is given as

$$\varepsilon = \frac{\Delta L}{L_0} \qquad (2\text{-}1)$$

This expression defines the *tension (compression) strain.* Since this strain is associated with the normal stress, it is usually called the *normal strain.* It is a dimensionless quantity, but it is customary to refer to it as a having the dimension of *mm/mm, in/in, m/m,* or $\mu m/m$ (microstrain). Sometimes strain is given as a percentage of the original length. The quantity ε generally is very small. In most engineering applications of the type considered in this text, it is of the order of magnitude of 0.1%.

Since the strains generally encountered are very small, it is possible to employ a highly versatile means for measuring them using expendable *electric strain gages.* These are made of very fine wire or foil that is glued to the member being investigated. As the forces are applied to the member, elongation or contraction of the wires or foil takes place concurrent with similar changes in the material. These changes in length alter the electrical resistance of the gage, which can be measured and calibrated to indicate the strain taking place. Such gages, suitable for different environmental conditions, are available in a range of lengths, varying from 4 to 140 mm. A schematic diagram of wire gage is shown in Fig. 2-3, and an enlarged photograph of a typical small foil gage is shown in Fig. 2-4.[1]

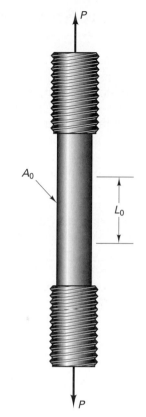

Fig. 2-2   Cylindrical test specimen.

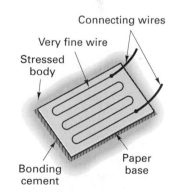

Fig. 2-3   Wire strain gage (protective cover not shown).

---

[1]See Society for Experimental Mechanics (SEM), A. S. Kobayashi, ed., *Handbook on Experimental Mechanics* (Englewood Cliffs, NJ: Prentice Hall, 1987).

2-3. Stress-Strain Relationships

In solid mechanics, the mechanical behavior of real materials under load is of primary importance. Experiments, mainly tension or compression tests, provide basic information on this behavior. In these experiments, the macroscopic (overall) response of specimens to the applied loads is observed in order to determine empirical force-deformation relationships. Researchers in material science attempt to provide reasons for the observed behavior.

It should be apparent from the previous discussion that for general purposes, it is more fundamental to report the strain of a member in tension or compression than to report the elongation of its gage. Similarly, stress is a more significant parameter than force since the effect on a material of an applied force P depends primarily on the cross-sectional area of the member. As a consequence, in the experimental study of the mechanical properties of materials, it is customary to plot diagrams of the relationship between stress and strain in a particular test. These curves are called the *stress-strain diagrams.*[2] Such diagrams, for most practical purposes, are assumed to be independent of the size of the specimen and of its gage length. There are two ways in which these diagrams can be described. Both of them are discussed in this section.

Engineering Stress-Strain Diagrams   Assuming that the stress is constant over the cross section of the central portion of the specimen and along the gage length, the *nominal* or *engineering stress,* σ, can be determined. Thus, dividing the applied force P by the specimen's original cross-sectional area A_0,

$$\sigma = \frac{P}{A_0} \qquad (2\text{-}2)$$

Likewise, the *nominal* or *engineering strain,* ε, is found directly from the strain gage reading or by dividing the change in the gage length ΔL by the specimen's original gage length L_0 and applying Eq. 2-1. Here the strain is assumed to be constant throughout the gage length.

If the computed values of σ and corresponding ε are plotted on a graph, for which the ordinate is the stress and the abscissa is the strain, the resulting curve is called the *engineering stress-strain diagram.* This diagram is very important in engineering since it provides the means for obtaining various mechanical properties of a material without regard to its physical size or shape. As an example, the characteristics of the engineering stress-

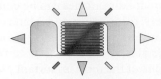

Fig. 2-4   Typical single-element metal-foil electrical-resistance strain gage (courtesy of Micro-Measurements Division, Measurement Group, Inc., Raleigh, North Carolina).

---

[2]Stress-strain diagrams were originated by Jacob Bernoulli (1654–1705) and J. V. Poncelet (1788–1867). See S. P. Timoshenko, *History of Strength of Materials* (New York: Dover Publications, Inc., 1983).

strain diagram for ductile steel, a commonly used material for making structural members and mechanical elements, will be discussed.

The general shape of the stress-strain diagram for a ductile steel specimen loaded in tension to failure for a monotonically increasing load is well known from numerous tests. A plot of the normal stress σ versus engineering strain ε, shown in Fig. 2-5, can be subdivided into four well-defined regions:

1. The linear elastic region
2. The yield plateau
3. The strain-hardening region
4. The postultimate stress or strain-softening region.

The linear elastic region $0 \leq \varepsilon_s \leq \varepsilon_y$ of the stress-strain curve, where ε_y is the yield strain, is a straight line (see Fig. 2-5).

In the yield plateau region $\varepsilon_y < \varepsilon_s < \varepsilon_{sh}$, where ε_{sh} is the strain at initiation of hardening strain, which begins at the point $A(\varepsilon_y, \sigma_y)$, the steel behaves plastically. This specific region of the stress-strain curve is shown in the inset of Fig. 2-5 and is assumed to be horizontal. The yield stress, σ_y, corresponding to the idealized yield plateau must therefore be taken as an arbitrary average value within the range of this plateau.

The point at which the yield plateau ends and strain hardening begins is not obvious. Before strain hardening initiates, a dip generally occurs in the yield plateau, followed by a steep increase that suddenly changes slope into the relatively smooth strain-hardening region. The strain-hardening region (see Fig. 2-5) ranges from the idealized point $B(\varepsilon_{sh}, \sigma_y)$, at which

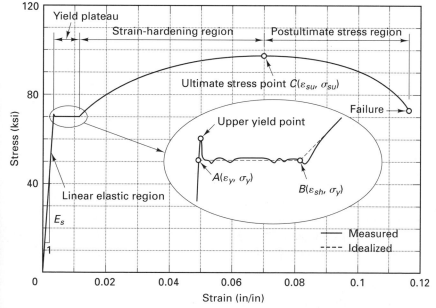

Fig. 2-5   Stress-strain diagram for ductile steel. (After Ref. 11.)

strain hardening begins, to the ultimate point $C(\varepsilon_{su}, \sigma_{su})$, that corresponds to the moment at which the maximum tensile stress is resisted and the process of *necking* begins. Necking is displayed by contraction of the specimen, as shown in Fig. 2-6.

In the postultimate region $\varepsilon_s \geq \varepsilon_{su}$, the shape of stress-strain curve is related to the location and gage length over which experimental data are collected. Therefore, it is assumed that the ultimate point $C(\varepsilon_{su}, \sigma_{su})$ marks the end of useful region of the stress-strain curve.

In the past it was generally assumed that the monotonic stress-strain curve of ductile steel subjected to compression is equal and opposite to the tension curve. However, the experimental data from monotonic tests show that the tension and compression engineering stress-strain curves are practically coincident only when the strain is small. The differences between the two diagrams, shown *exaggerated* in Fig. 2-7, begin to appear in the strain-hardening region, where the extent of the strain becomes more pronounced, when necking/barreling develops in the tensile/compression test.

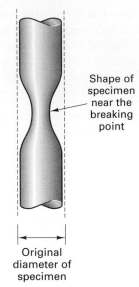

Shape of specimen near the breaking point

Original diameter of specimen

Fig. 2-6   Necking of ductile steel specimen.

True Stress-Strain Diagrams   In some engineering applications (for example, in metal forming), the strains may be large. For such purposes the total strain is defined as the sum of incremental strains $\Delta\bar{\varepsilon}$; thus

$$\bar{\varepsilon} = \sum \Delta\bar{\varepsilon} = \sum \frac{\Delta L}{L} \tag{2-3}$$

where L is the *current gage length* of the specimen when the increment of elongation (contraction) ΔL occurs. If L_0 is the initial gage length of the specimen, then in the limit as $\Delta L \to 0$ the strain $\bar{\varepsilon}$ corresponding to the gage length L_f can be defined by the following integral:

$$\bar{\varepsilon} = \int_{L_0}^{L_f} \frac{dL}{L} = \ln\left(\frac{L_f}{L_0}\right) \tag{2-4}$$

This strain, obtained by adding up the increments of strains, which are based on the current dimensions of a specimen, is called a *natural*[3] or *true strain*. Sometimes the true strain is called *logarithmic strain* because of the form of Eq. 2-4.

For small strains, the true strain $\bar{\varepsilon}$ defined by Eq. 2-4 essentially coincides with the engineering strain ε. If, under the integral, the length L is set equal to L_0, the strain definition given by Eq. 2-1 is obtained.

During plastic strain of a uniform specimen subjected to axial tension (compression), the cross-sectional area gets smaller (larger) as the specimen elongates (shortens). A more accurate description of the actual stress experienced by the specimen can be given by the *true stress* concept.[4] The

---

[3]Natural strains were introduced by P. Ludwik in 1909, a renowned German engineer.

[4]See J. Marin, *Mechanical Behavior of Engineering Materials* (Englewood Cliffs, NJ: Prentice Hall, 1962).

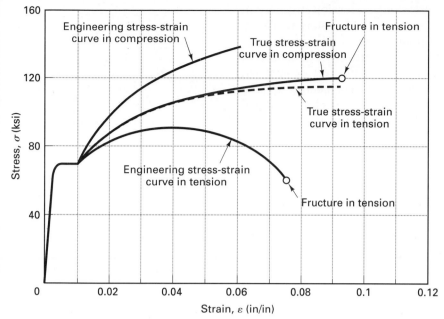

Fig. 2-7   Comparison of tension and compression monotonic stress-strain diagrams. (After Ref. 11).

true stress, $\bar{\sigma}$, is related to the instantaneous cross-sectional area, A, and the applied force F as

$$\bar{\sigma} = \frac{F}{A} \qquad (2\text{-}5)$$

Since plastic strain involves no volume change—that is, $A_0 L_0 = AL$ and $L = L_0 (1 + \varepsilon)$—

$$\frac{A_0}{A} = \frac{L}{L_0} = (1 + \varepsilon) \qquad (2\text{-}6)$$

which, using Eq. 2-2 and noting that $F = P$, allows to relate the true stress and engineering stress as follows:

$$\boxed{\bar{\sigma} = \frac{F}{A} = \frac{F}{A_0}(1 + \varepsilon) = \sigma(1 + \varepsilon)} \qquad (2\text{-}7)$$

If the value of the $\bar{\sigma}$ is so defined and the corresponding $\bar{\varepsilon}$ are plotted on a graph, for which the ordinate is the true stress and the abscissa is the true strain, the resulting curve is called the *true stress-strain diagram.* The true stress-strain diagrams for ductile materials (such as a ductile steel), the compression, and the tension true stress-strain diagrams practically coincide, whereas the two engineering stress-strain diagrams drift apart.

In Fig. 2-7, in the same quadrant, compression and tension stress-strain diagrams are illustrated for a monotonic test of a ductile steel specimen plotted in the true and engineering coordinate systems. As can be seen, both compression and tension true stress-strain diagrams are similar until the effect of buckling becomes noticeable at a strain level of approximately 6% in the compression test. Comparison of the engineering and the true stress-strain diagrams shows that in tension, since the cross-sectional area decreases as the specimen elongates, the true stress is greater than engineering stress, whereas in compression as the specimen shortens, the cross-sectional area increases and thus the true stress is less than the corresponding engineering stress.

It is important to recognize that experimentally determined stress-strain diagrams differ widely for different materials. Even for the same material they differ since the test results depend on such variables as the material's composition, microscopic imperfections, the manner of fabrication, the speed of loading, and the temperature at which the test is conducted. The *engineering* stress-strain diagrams for a few representative materials are illustrated in Figs. 2-8 and 2-9. These are shown to a larger scale for strain in Fig. 2-9. Since for most engineering applications deformations must be

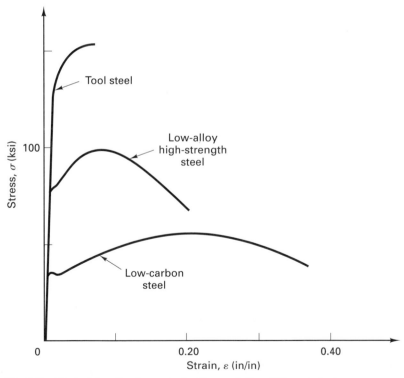

Fig. 2-8   Typical tensile stress-strain diagrams for different steels.

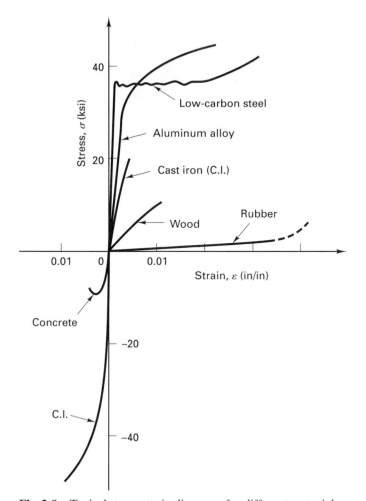

Fig. 2-9   Typical stress-strain diagrams for different materials.

limited, the lower range of strains is particularly important. The large deformations of materials of great importance in the analysis of such operations
as forging, forming, and drawing are not pursued.

   In calculating *engineering* stress using Eq. 2-2, the original cross-sectional
A_0 is generally designated by A.

   Illustrations of fractured tension specimens after monotonic tension
tests (i.e., where the loads were gradually applied in one direction) are
shown in Fig. 2-10. Steel and aluminum alloy specimens exhibit ductile
behavior, and a fracture occurs only after a considerable amount of deformation. This behavior is clearly exemplified in their respective stress-strain
diagrams (see Fig. 2-9).

   The failures of steel and aluminum occur primarily due to shear strain
along the planes forming approximately 45° angles with the axis of the rod
(see Sections 1-7 and 1-8). A typical "cup and cone" fracture may be

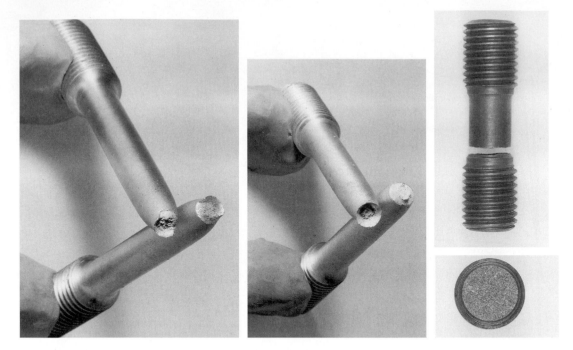

Fig. 2-10   Ductile fractures for (a) A572 steel specimen and (b) 6061-T6 aluminum alloy. Brittle fracture for (c) cast iron. (Numbers refer to the ASTM designation for steel and that of the Aluminum Association for aluminum alloy.)

detected in the photographs of steel and aluminum specimens. By contrast, the failure of a cast-iron specimen typically occurs very suddenly, exhibiting a square fracture across the cross section. Such cleavage or separation fractures are typical of brittle materials.

2-4. Hooke's Law

For a limited range from the origin, the experimental values of stress versus strain lie essentially on a straight line. This holds true almost without reservations for the entire range for glass at room temperature. It is true for mild steel up to some point, such as A in Fig. 2-5. It holds nearly true up to very close to the failure point for many high-grade alloy steels. On the other hand, the straight part of the curve hardly exists in concrete, soil, annealed copper, aluminum, or cast iron. Nevertheless, for all practical purposes, up to some such point, such as A in Fig. 2-11, *the relationship between stress and strain may be said to be linear for all materials.* This

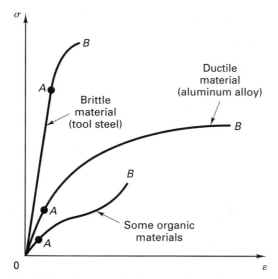

Fig. 2-11   Stress-strain diagrams for various materials.

sweeping idealization and generalization applicable to all materials is known as *Hooke's law*.[5] Symbolically, this law can be expressed by the equation

$$\sigma = E\varepsilon \tag{2-8}$$

which simply means that stress is directly proportional to strain, where the constant of proportionality is E. This constant E is called the *elastic modulus,* modulus of elasticity, or Young's modulus.[6] As ε is dimensionless, E has the units of stress in this relation. In the U.S. customary systems of units, it is usually measured in pounds per square inch, and in the SI units it is measured in newtons per square meter (or Pa, which stands for pascals).

Graphically, E is interpreted as the slope of a straight line from the origin to the rather vague point A on a uniaxial stress-strain diagram. The stress corresponding to the latter point is termed the *proportional or elastic limit* of the material. Physically, the elastic modulus represents the stiffness

---

[5]Actually, Robert Hooke, an English scientist, worked with springs and not with rods. In 1676, he announced an anagram "c e i i n o s s s t t u v," which in Latin is *Ut Tensio sic Vis* (the force varies as the stretch).

[6]Young's modulus is so called in honor of Thomas Young, the English scientist. His *Lectures on Natural Philosophy,* published in 1807, contain a definition of the modulus of elasticity.

of the material to an imposed load. *The value of the elastic modulus is a definite property of a material.* From experiments, it is known that ε is *always a very small quantity;* hence, E must be large. Its approximate values are tabulated for a few materials in Tables 1A and B of the Appendix. For all steels, E at room temperature is between 29 and 30×10^6 psi, or 200 and 207 GPa.

It follows from the foregoing discussion that *Hooke's law applies only up to the proportional limit of the material.* This is highly significant because in most of the subsequent treatment, the derived formulas are based on this law. Clearly, then, such formulas are limited to the material's behavior in the lower range of stresses.

Some materials—notably single crystals and wood—possess different elastic moduli in different directions. Such materials, having different physical properties in different directions, are called *anisotropic.* A consideration of such materials is excluded from this text. The vast majority of engineering materials consist of a large number of randomly oriented crystals. Because of this random orientation, properties of materials become essentially alike in any direction.[7] Such materials are called *isotropic.* With some exceptions, such as wood, in this text, *complete homogeneity* (sameness from point to point) and *isotropy of materials are generally assumed.*

2-5. Further Remarks on Stress-Strain Relationships

In addition to the proportional limit defined in Section 2-4, several other interesting points can be observed on the stress-strain diagrams. For instance, the highest point (see the ultimate stress point C in Fig. 2-5) corresponds to the *ultimate strength* of a material. Stress associated with the yield plateau of the stress-strain curve (see the inset of Fig. 2-5) is called the *yield strength* of a material. As will be brought out later, this remarkable property of mild steel, in common with other ductile materials, is significant in stress analysis. For the present, note that at essentially constant stress, strains 15 to 20 times those that take place up to the proportional limit occur during yielding. At the yield stress, a large amount of deformation takes place at constant stress. The yielding phenomenon is absent in most materials.

A study of stress-strain diagrams shows that the yield strength (stress) is so near the proportional limit that, for most purposes, the two may be taken to be the same. However, it is much easier to locate the former. For materials that do not possess a well-defined yield strength, one is sometimes "invented" by the use of the so-called offset method. This is illus-

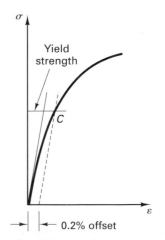

Fig. 2-12   Offset method of determining the yield strength of a material.

---

[7]Rolling operations produce preferential orientation of crystalline grains in some materials.

trated in Fig. 2-12, where a line offset an arbitrary amount of 0.2% of strain is drawn parallel to the straight-line portion of the stress-strain diagram. Point *C* is taken as the yield strength of the material at 0.2% offset.

That a material is elastic usually implies that stress is directly proportional to strain, as in Hooke's law. Such materials are called *linearly elastic* or Hookean. A material responding in a nonlinear manner and yet, when unloaded, returning back along the loading path to its initial stress-free state of deformation is also an elastic material. Such materials are called *nonlinear elastic*. The difference between the two types of elastic materials is highlighted in Figs. 2-13(a) and (b). If in stressing a material its elastic limit is exceed, on unloading it usually responds approximately in a linearly elastic manner, as shown in Fig. 2-13(c), and a permanent deformation, or set, develops at no external load. As will become apparent after the study in Section 3-5, the area enclosed by the loop corresponds to dissipated energy released through heat. Ideal materials are considered not to dissipate any energy under monotonic or cyclic loading.

For ductile materials, stress-strain diagrams obtained for short compression blocks are reasonably close to those found in tension. Brittle materials, such as cast iron and concrete, are very weak in tension but not in compression. For these materials, the diagrams differ considerably, depending on the sense of the applied force.

It is well to note that in some of the subsequent analyses, it will be advantageous to refer to elastic bodies and systems as springs. Sketches such as shown in Figs. 2-14 are frequently used in practice for interpreting the physical behavior of mechanical systems.

(a)

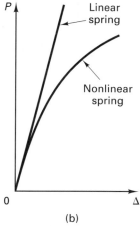

(b)

Fig. 2-14   Stress-strain response of a spring: (a) linear elastic (Hookean), (b) nonlinear elastic.

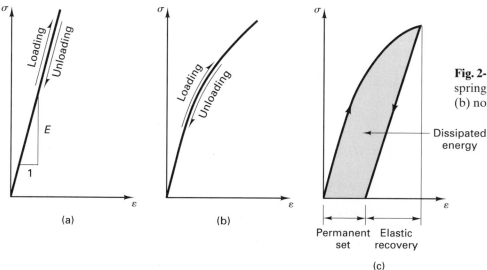

(a)   (b)

(c)

Fig. 2-13   Stress-strain diagrams: (a) linear elastic material, (b) nonlinear elastic material, (c) inelastic or plastic material.

2-6. Poisson's Ratio

In addition to the deformation of materials in the direction of the applied force, another remarkable property can be observed in all solid materials—namely, that at right angles to the applied uniaxial force, a certain amount of lateral (transverse) expansion or contraction takes place. This phenomenon is illustrated in Fig. 2-15 where the deformations are *greatly exaggerated.* For clarity, this physical fact may be restated thus: If a solid body is subjected to an axial tension, it contracts laterally; on the other hand, if it is compressed, the material "squashes out" sideways. With this in mind, directions of lateral deformations are easily determined, depending on the sense of the applied force.

For a general theory, it is preferable to refer to these lateral deformations on the basis of deformations per *unit* of length of the transverse dimension. Thus, the lateral *deformations* on a *relative* basis can be expressed in in/in or m/m. These relative unit lateral deformations are termed *lateral strains.* Moreover, it is known from experiments that lateral strains bear a *constant* relationship to the longitudinal or axial strains caused by an axial force, provided a material remains *elastic* and is homogeneous and isotropic. This constant is a definite property of a material, just like the elastic modulus E, and is called *Poisson's ratio.*[8] It will be denoted by ν (nu) and is defined as follows:

$$\nu = \left| \frac{\text{lateral strain}}{\text{axial strain}} \right| = -\frac{\text{lateral strain}}{\text{axial strain}} \qquad (2\text{-}9)$$

where the axial strains are caused by uniaxial stress only (i.e., by simple tension or compression). The second, alternative form of Eq. 2-9 is true because the lateral and axial strains are always of opposite sign for uniaxial stress.

The value of ν fluctuates for different materials over a relatively narrow range. Generally, it is on the order of 0.25 to 0.35. In extreme cases, values as low as 0.1 (some concretes) and as high as 0.5 (rubber) occur. The latter value is the *largest possible.* It is normally attained by materials during plastic flow and signifies constancy of volume.[9] In this text, Poisson's ratio will be used only when materials behave elastically.

In conclusion, note that the Poisson effect exhibited by materials causes *no additonal stresses* other than those considered earlier *unless the transverse deformation is inhibited or prevented.*

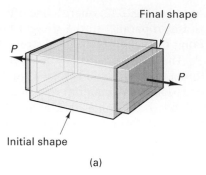

(a)

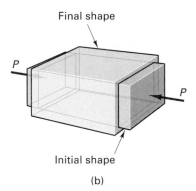

(b)

Fig. 2-15 (a) Lateral contraction and (b) lateral expansion of solid bodies subjected to axial forces (Poisson's effect).

Example 2-1

Consider a carefully conducted experiment where an aluminum bar of 50-mm diameter is stressed in a testing machine, as shown in Fig. 2-16. At a certain instant the applied force P is 100 kN, while the measured elongation

[8]Named after S. D. Poisson, a French scientist who formulated this concept in 1828.

[9]A. Nadai, *Theory of Flow and Fracture of Solids,* Vol. 1 (New York: McGraw-Hill, 1950).

of the rod is 0.219 mm in a 300-mm gage length, and the diameter's dimension is decreased by 0.01215 mm. Calculate the constant v of the material.

SOLUTION
Transverse or lateral strain:

$$\varepsilon_t = \frac{\Delta_t}{D} = -\frac{0.01215}{50} = -0.000243 \text{ mm/mm}$$

In this case, the lateral strain ε_t is negative, since the diameter of the bar *decreases* by Δ_t.

Axial strain:

$$\varepsilon_a = \frac{\Delta}{L} = +\frac{0.219}{300} = 0.00073 \text{ mm/mm}$$

Poisson's ratio:

$$v = -\frac{\varepsilon_t}{\varepsilon_a} = -\frac{(-0.000243)}{0.00073} = 0.333$$

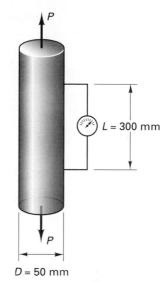

$L = 300$ mm

$D = 50$ mm

Fig. 2-16

In practice, when a study of physical quantities, such as v, is being made, it is best to work with the corresponding stress-strain diagram to be assured that the quantities determined are associated with the elastic range of the material behavior.

2-7. Thermal Strain and Deformation

With changes in temperature, solid bodies change their dimensions. If the temperature increases, generally a body expands, whereas if the temperature decreases, a solid body will contract. Ordinarily, over a limited range of temperature change this expansion or contraction is linearly related to the temperature increase or decrease that occurs. If the body material is homogeneous and isotropic, it has been found that the thermal strain ε_T caused by a change in temperature ΔT, measured in degrees Celsius (°C) or Fahrenheit (°F), can be expressed as

$$\boxed{\varepsilon_T = \alpha \, \Delta T} \qquad (2\text{-}10)$$

where α is a property of the material, referred to as the *coefficient of linear thermal expansion*. The units of α measure strain per degree of temperature. They are 1/°F in the U.S. customary system of units, and 1/°C in the SI system. Typical values of parameter α are given in Tables 1A and 1B in the Appendix.

Equal thermal strains develop in every direction for unconstrained homogeneous isotropic materials. For a specimen of length L_0 subjected to a uniform temperature, the extensional deformation Δ_T due to a change in temperature of ΔT is

$$\Delta_T = \alpha \, \Delta T \, L_0 \qquad (2\text{-}11)$$

For a decrease in temperature, ΔT assumes negative values.

   An illustration of the thermal effect on deformation of a square and round specimen, due to an increase of temperature is shown in Fig. 2-17.

2-8. Other Idealizations of Constitutive Relations

In an increasingly larger number of technical problems, stress analyses based on the assumption of linearly elastic behavior are insufficient. For this reason, several additional stress-strain relations or *constitutive relations*, are now in general use. The three idealized stress-strain relations shown in Fig. 2-18 are encountered particularly often. The two shown in Figs. 2-18(a) and (b) will be used in this text; the one in Fig. 2-18(c) is often more realistic, but its use is considerably more complicated and generally will be avoided because of the introductory nature of this book.

   The idealized $\sigma - \varepsilon$ relationship shown in Fig. 2-18(a) is applicable to problems in which the elastic strains can be neglected in relation to the plastic ones. This occurs if plastic (inelastic) strains are dominant. Perfectly (ideally) plastic behavior means that a large amount of unbounded deformation can take place at a constant stress. The idealization shown in

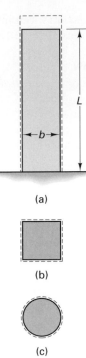

Fig. 2-17   Thermal expansions of bars resting on frictionless surface.

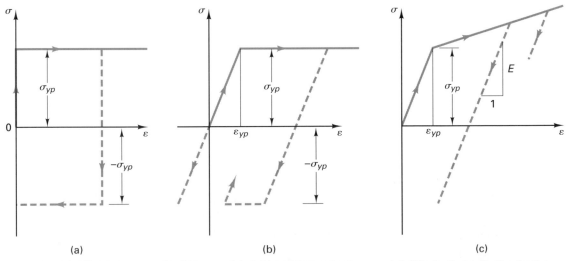

Fig. 2-18   Idealized stress-strain diagrams: (a) rigid perfectly plastic material, (b) elastic perfectly plastic material, and (c) elastic linearly hardening material.

Fig. 2-18(b) is particularly useful if both the elastic and plastic strains have to be included. This situation frequently arises in analysis. Both of these idealizations are patterned after monotonical loading of ductile steel (see Fig. 2-5), where at the yield stress σ_y, a substantial yield plateau in the stress-strain diagram is observed. In both instances, since the deformations are generally small, it is assumed that the mechanical properties of the material are the same in tension and compression. It is also assumed that during unloading, the material behaves elastically. For the case shown in Fig. 2-18(b), a stress can range and terminate anywhere between $+\sigma_y$ and $-\sigma_y$. For moderate amounts of plastic straining, this assumption is in good agreement with experimental observations.

The $\sigma - \varepsilon$ idealization shown in Fig. 2-18(c) provides a reasonable approximation for many materials and is more accurate than the previous two models over a wider range of strain. Beyond the elastic range, on an increase in strain, many materials resist additional stress (i.e., they *strain harden*), as illustrated in Fig. 2-5 for mild steel.

In some refined analyses, the stress-strain idealization shown in Fig. 2-18 may not be sufficiently accurate. Fortunately, with the use of computers, much better modeling of real behavior of materials is possible. For completeness, one such well-known analytical formulation follows. Implementation of this formulation requires a considerable amount of computer programming, and this approach is not intended for general use in this text.

A model capable of representing a wide range of stress-strain curves has been developed by Ramberg and Osgood.[10] This model is defined by the following equation:

$$\varepsilon \frac{\sigma}{E} + K\left(\frac{\sigma}{E}\right)^n \tag{2-12}$$

where E, K, and n are the characteristic parameters for a given material. The shape of the curve represented by the Eq. 2-12 is determined by the parameters K and n.

In most applications, it is advantageous to work with the inverse of Eq. 2-12 (i.e., to express stress as a function of strain). An accurate simulation of cyclic stress-strain response of a material can be obtained using the following equation[11]:

$$\sigma_s = {}^k\sigma_y \frac{(1-\rho)}{2}\left[1 + \frac{(1+\rho)}{(1-\rho)}\frac{\varepsilon_s - {}^k\varepsilon_r}{{}^k\varepsilon_y} - \sqrt{\left(\frac{\varepsilon_s - {}^k\varepsilon_r}{{}^k\varepsilon_y} - 1\right)^2 + {}^k\delta}\right]$$

$$(k = 0, 1, \ldots, n) \tag{2-13}$$

[10]W. Ramberg and W. R. Osgood, "Description of stress-strain curves by three parameters," *NACA Rep. TN-902* (Washington, DC: National Advisory Committee on Aeronautics, 1943).

[11]T. A. Balan, F. C. Filippou, and E. P. Popov, "Hysteretic model of ordinary and high strength reinforcing steel," *J. Eng. Struct.*, ASCE, No. 3 Mar. 1998, Vol. 124.

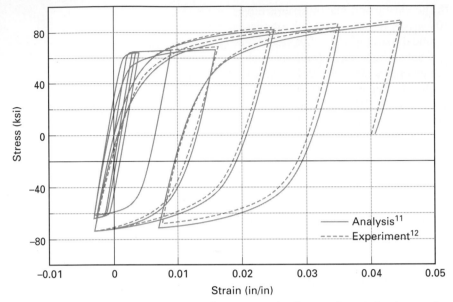

Fig. 2-19   Computer simulation of cyclic stress-strain diagram for reinforcing steel.

where E_h is the strain-hardening modulus; E_s is the modulus of material; $\rho = E_h/E_s$ is the hardening ratio of the material; ${}^k\sigma_y$ and ${}^k\varepsilon_y$ are the current yield stress and strain, respectively, after the kth reversal; σ_s and ε_s are the current stress and strain, respectively; ${}^k\varepsilon_r$ is the current strain at the kth reversal point; and ${}^k\delta$ is the strength degradation parameter after the kth reversal.

The computer simulation of cyclic stress-strain diagram for the reinforcing steel specimen[12] shown in Fig. 2-19 is in excellent agreement with experimental results. In this diagram, a series of characteristic loops, referred to as *hysteretic loops*, are associated with the dissipated energy (see Section 3-5).

Under rapid or impact loading, two additional material parameters have relevance: *resilience* and *toughness*. Resilience defines the ability of material to absorb energy without suffering plastic strain. The area in the elastic region under a stress-strain diagram, as will be shown in Section 3-5, represents the density of strain energy that can be absorbed without any permanent damage to the material. This area is called the *modulus of resilience U_R* and is equivalent to the shaded triangular area shown in Fig. 2-20(a).

Toughness defines the ability of material to absorb energy prior to fracture. It can be shown (see Section 3-5) that the area under the stress-strain

[12]S-Y. M. Ma, V. V. Bertero, and E. P. Popov, "Experimental and analytical studies on the hysteretic behavior of reinforced concrete rectangular and T-beams," *EERC Rep. 76-02*, Earthquake Engineering Research Center, Berkeley, CA, 1976.

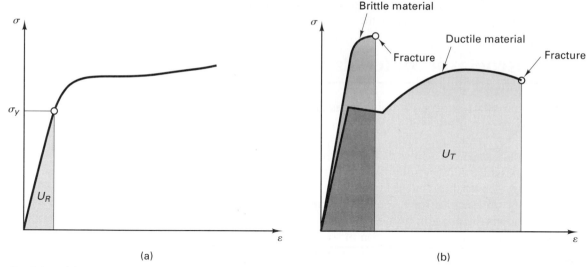

Fig. 2-20   (a) Modulus of resilience U_R, (b) modulus of toughness U_T.

diagram represents the density of strain energy absorbed by material prior to fracture. The area under the complete monotonic stress-strain diagram is called *the modulus of toughness U_T*. Figure 2-20(b) illustrates the modulus of toughness for brittle and ductile materials. The figure shows that a brittle material, even of greater ultimate strength, generally absorbs much less energy from impact loading than a ductile material.

Another aspect of material behavior may occur when a structural member is subjected to loading that must be sustained over long periods of time. Under such loading at certain temperatures, a material can exhibit a property called *creep*. Creep is defined as a time-dependent permanent deformation of material under stress, maintained at a constant value. Large plastic strains and, finally, rupture can result from creep. The time for creep rupture varies from hours to years for different materials, depending on stress level and temperature. For some materials, however, such as polymers and composites—including wood and concrete—temperature is not an important factor, and creep can occur strictly from long-term load application.

For practical purposes, when creep becomes important, a material should be designed to resist a specified creep strain for a given period of time. In this case, an important mechanical property that is used for the design of members subjected to creep is *creep strength* of the material. This parameter represents the highest initial stress the material can withstand during a specified time without causing a given amount of creep strain.

In connection with creep effect, another important time-dependent phenomenon may occur. The prestress in bolts of mechanical assemblies operating at high temperatures, as well as prestress in steel tendons in reinforced concrete, tends to decrease gradually with time. This phenomenon is referred to as *stress relaxation*. Some basic analytical aspects of both creep and stress relaxation are considered in the next section.

2-9. Linearly Viscoelastic Materials

In the preceding discussion of stress-strain relations, it is tacitly assumed that the materials are inviscid (i.e., they exhibit no time-dependent flow or creep phenomena). However, asphalt pavements, solid propellant in rocket motors, high-polymer plastics, and concrete, as well as machine elements at elevated temperatures, gradually deform under stress, and such deformations are usually not fully recoverable. A few elementary notions of this problem are considered in this section for the uniaxial state of stress. A more complete investigation is the concern of rheology.[13]

For elastic materials stress is said to be a function of strain only. On the other hand, for viscous materials stress depends not only on strain but also on the rate at which the strain is applied. This may be clarified by examining the conceptual models in Fig. 2-21. For the linearly elastic spring the stress is proportional to the strain. For an element with a viscous liquid in the dashpot, the higher the strain rate, the higher the stress necessary to maintain the motion of the applied force. For brevity, the strain rate—the derivative of the strain with respect to time—will be designated by an ε with a dot over it.

In the preceding terms, for an elastic material $\sigma = \sigma(\varepsilon)$; but for a viscoelastic material, since the stress is a function of both the strain and the strain rate, $\sigma = \sigma(\varepsilon, \dot{\varepsilon})$. The simplest relation among these quantities can be stated as

$$\sigma = E\varepsilon + \eta\dot{\varepsilon} \tag{2-14}$$

where the constant η (eta) is the coefficient of viscosity. The last term linearly relates the stress to the strain rate, as shown in Fig. 2-21(b). If this term is zero, one obtains an ordinary Hooke's law. The material behavior described by Eq. 2-14 is associated with the names of Voigt and Kelvin,[14] who first used it in the analysis of viscoelastic materials. For this reason the idealized material of Eq. 2-14 is referred to as the *Voigt-Kelvin solid*.

Although certainly not fundamental, it is convenient to introduce a conceptual model to clarify the meaning of Eq. 2-14. Such a model is obtained by placing a spring and a dashpot in parallel as in Fig. 2-21(c). As the stress σ is applied, the same strain is induced in the spring and in the dashpot; that is, $\varepsilon_d = \varepsilon_s = \varepsilon$, where the subscripts designate the dashpot (*d*) and the spring (*s*), respectively. The total stress (force) σ is the sum of the stress σ_d and σ_s (i.e., $\sigma = \sigma_d + \sigma_s$). By using Hooke's law and a linear

---

[13]See, for example, F. R. Eirich, ed., *Rheology* (New York: Academic Press, Inc., 1956).

[14]W. Voigt (1850–1919), a theoretical physicist, taught at Gottingen University, Germany. Lord Kelvin (William Thomson) (1824–1907) was a British physicist.

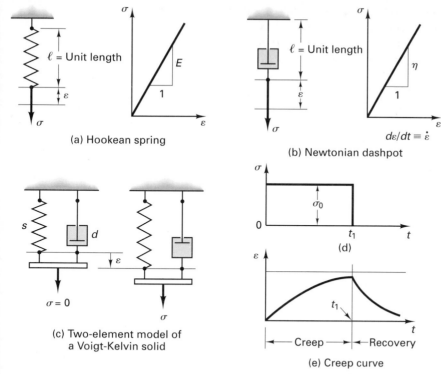

Fig. 2-21   Models of material response.

stress-strain rate relationship for the Newtonian liquid, one obtains Eq. 2-14, which may be written as

$$\dot{\varepsilon} + (E/\eta)\varepsilon = \sigma/\eta \qquad (2\text{-}15)$$

Example 2-2

Determine the creep of a Voigt-Kelvin solid subjected to a constant stress σ_0. Initially the model is unstrained.

SOLUTION

Noting that the stress $\sigma = \sigma_0$ is constant, one can show that the homogeneous and the particular solutions of Eq. 2-15 give

$$\varepsilon = Ae^{-(E/\eta)t} + \sigma_0/E$$

where A is a constant that can be found from the condition that $\varepsilon(0) = 0 = A + \sigma_0/E$ (i.e., $A = -\sigma_0/E$). Therefore,

$$\varepsilon = (1 - e^{-(E/\eta)t})(\sigma_0/E)$$

As time increases, the strain asymptotically approaches the maximum strain associated with the elastic spring until, finally, all the applied stress is carried by the spring, and the dashpot becomes inactive. If the stress is removed at an earlier time, as in Fig. 2-21(d), an asymptotic recovery of the strain takes place [Fig. 2-21(e)].

The preceding solution shows that the Voigt-Kelvin material exhibits a delayed elastic response; for this reason it is termed an *anelastic* material. Its behavior can be likened to that of an elastic sponge filled with a viscous fluid in which ultimately all the applied load is carried by the elastic core. Based on experimental evidence, it is known that such behavior is not typical of most materials. Another linear combination of stress, stress rate, and strain rate can be formulated that is more representative.

By endowing a body with an instantaneous elastic response together with a time-dependent displacement, one can obtain a reasonable approximation of the behavior of many viscoelastic materials. The simplest model having such properties can be visualized as a combination in series of a linear spring and a linear dashpot, as in Fig. 2-22. Material of this type is

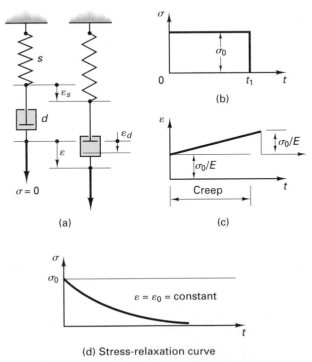

(d) Stress-relaxation curve

Fig. 2-22   Two-element model of a Maxwell solid.

called a *Maxwell solid.*[15] In the model in Fig. 2-22(a), if a stress σ is applied, the stress (force) through the dashpot (d) is the same as that through the spring (s) (i.e., $\sigma_d = \sigma_s = \sigma$). However, since each element of the model contributes to the total strain, $\varepsilon = \varepsilon_s + \varepsilon_d$, where the subscripts, as before, designate the spring (s) and the dashpot (d), respectively. The strain relation must be differentiated with respect to time since for viscous materials only the connection between the stress and the strain rate is known. On the other hand, for elastic materials with E constant, on differentiating Hooke's law with respect to time, one has $\dot{\varepsilon} = \dot{\sigma}/E$. Then, upon adding the strain rates for the two elements and simplifying, one obtains the basic differential equation for the response of the Maxwell solid:

$$\dot{\varepsilon} = \dot{\varepsilon}_s + \dot{\varepsilon}_d = \dot{\sigma}/E + \sigma/\eta \quad \text{or} \quad \dot{\sigma} + (E/\eta)\sigma = E\dot{\varepsilon} \quad (2\text{-}16)$$

For the Maxwell solid in pure shear an analogous expression applies:

$$\dot{\gamma} = \dot{\tau}/G + \tau/\bar{\eta} \quad (2\text{-}17)$$

where, as before, dots over the quantities represent their derivatives with respect to time, and $\bar{\eta}$ is the coefficient of viscosity in shear.

Example 2-3

A Maxwell solid is subjected to a step loading as shown in Fig. 2-22(b) (i.e., a constant stress σ_0 acts during a time interval $0 (< t < t_1)$. Determine the strain response.

SOLUTION

In this case the applied stress σ does not change with time; hence $\dot{\sigma} = 0$. At time $t = 0$ an instantaneous elastic strain $\varepsilon_0 = \sigma_0/E$ occurs, which is the initial constant of integration. Upon release of the stress, this strain is completely recovered. On this basis, using Eq. 2-16,

$$\frac{d\varepsilon}{dt} = \frac{\sigma_0}{\eta} \quad \text{or} \quad \varepsilon = \frac{\sigma_0}{\eta}t + C_1 \quad \text{and} \quad \varepsilon = \frac{\sigma_0}{E} + \frac{\sigma_0}{\eta}t$$

This relation applies in the interval $0 < t < t_1$. At $t = t_1$ strain of σ_0/E is recovered, and $(\sigma_0/\eta)t_1$ is the *permanent* or *residual strain*. These results are indicated in Fig. 2-22(c). The solution exemplifies an elementary creep problem.

---

[15]James Clerk Maxwell (1831–1879), a renowned British physicist, made a number of important contributions to the mechanics of solids.

Example 2-4

If a Maxwell solid is initially strained an amount ε_0 causing an initial stress of σ_0, and the strain ε_0 is maintained, how does the stress vary with time?

SOLUTION

Here the strain rate $\dot{\varepsilon} = 0$ since no change in strain is permitted. This fact simplifies Eq. 2-16. To determine the constant of integration, one notes that at $t = 0$ the stress is σ_0. Therefore, the governing differential equation is

$$\frac{d\sigma}{dt} + \frac{E}{\eta}\sigma = 0$$

Solving this equation with a constant of integration A,

$$\sigma = Ae^{-(E/\eta)t}, \qquad \text{and, since} \qquad \sigma(0) = \sigma_0, \qquad \sigma = \sigma_0 e^{-(E/\eta)t}$$

This result is plotted in Fig. 2-22(d). It is interesting to note how with time the stress gradually decreases, tending asymptotically toward zero. This situation is characteristic of an initially stressed bolt at high temperature that clamps rigid flanges of a machine or of a tendon in a prestressed concrete beam. As the material creeps, stress relaxation takes place. For this reason a Maxwell material sometimes is referred to as a *relaxing material.* This problem is of great practical importance in many applications.

The foregoing procedures can be generalized to many more materials. A combination in series of the Maxwell and the Voigt-Kelvin models establishes the basic model, the Standard Solid, for studying linearly viscoelastic materials. Other combinations of springs and dashpots with different constants have been used effectively for representing high polymers, fibers, concrete, etc. Extensions to three-dimensional problems have also been achieved.[16] The extension of the theory to nonlinear viscoelastic materials is being actively pursued.

From a phenomenological point of view, for real materials the relaxation and creep curves must be considered fundamental properties of a given material and must be determined experimentally. In a relaxation experiment a constant strain ε_0 is maintained and the corresponding stress $\sigma(t)$ is determined. By dividing $\sigma(t)$ by ε_0 the *relaxation modulus E(t)* is obtained. A qualitative curve for such an experiment is shown in Fig. 2-23(a). If data from several relaxation experiments done at different constant strains ε_0 give the same relaxation modulus $E(t)$, the material is *linearly viscoelastic.*

In a creep experiment a constant stress σ_0 is maintained and the corresponding strain $\varepsilon(t)$. is obtained. By dividing $\varepsilon(t)$ by σ_0, one finds the *creep*

[16]D. R. Bland, *The Theory of Linear Viscoelasticity* (Long Island City, NY: Pergamon Press, Inc., 1960), 19.

compliance $J_c(t)$. A typical function of $J_c(t)$ is shown in Fig. 2-23(b). Again, if the creep-compliance curves for several experiments performed at different stress levels coincide, the viscoelastic material is linear. Stated another way, for linear, viscoelastic materials at any constant stress σ_0 or strain ε_0, one has

$$\varepsilon(t) = \sigma_0 J_c(t) \qquad \text{and} \qquad \sigma(t) = \varepsilon_0 E(t) \qquad (2\text{-}18)$$

For application of the preceding equations, it is important to note the Boltzmann[17] superposition principle, which is valid for a number of materials. This principle asserts that the strain at a given time is the sum of the strains caused by the loads applied independently for their respective durations of time. For example, if, as shown in Fig. 2-23(c), a stress σ_0 is applied at $t = 0$, the strain at any time $t > 0$ is $\sigma_0 J_c(t)$. Then, if at time t_1 another stress σ_1 is added, for $t > t_1$ the additional strain is $\sigma_1 J_c(t - t_1)$. For the second load application the same creep-compliance function applies, but its origin is moved to t_1. In general,

$$\varepsilon(t) = \sigma_0 J_c(t) + \sigma_1 J_c(t - t_1)$$
$$+ \sigma_2 J_c(t - t_2) + \cdots \qquad (2\text{-}19)$$

Boltzmann's principle also applies if a succession of strains is applied to a material. For such a case the relation analogous to Eq. 2-19 is[18]

$$\sigma(t) = \varepsilon_0 E(t) + \varepsilon_1 E(t - t_1) + \varepsilon_2 E(t - t_2) + \cdots \qquad (2\text{-}20)$$

Analogous relations to Eqs. 2-19 and 2-10 can be written for linear viscoelastic materials in pure shear.

The material constants for creep and relaxation are strongly affected by temperature. In this regard it is instructive to examine the experimentally determined stress-strain diagrams[19] for aluminum in Fig. 2-24. (The numbers in parentheses refer to the strain rates measured in inches per inch per second.) Here the pronounced effects of strain rates and temperature on the mechanical behavior of this material can be clearly seen.

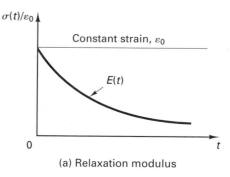

(a) Relaxation modulus

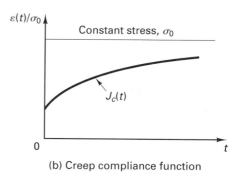

(b) Creep compliance function

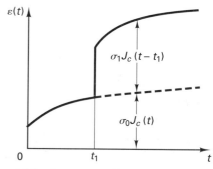

(c) Strain superposition according to Boltzmann's principle

Fig. 2-23   Typical behavior of viscoelastic materials.

[17]L. Boltzmann (1844–1906) was a distinguished physicist particularly known for his research on the kinetic theory of gases and in quantum mechanics and statistical mechanics. He taught at Graz and Vienna, Austria, and at Leipzig and Munich, Germany.

[18]If a continuous change in $\varepsilon(t)$ occurs, Eq. 2-20 can be written in the form of a Duhamel integral as

$$\sigma(t) = \int_{-\infty}^{t} E(t - t') \frac{d\varepsilon}{dt'} dt'$$

An analogous expression also applies to $\varepsilon(t)$:

$$\varepsilon(t) = \int_{-\infty}^{t} J_c(t - t') \frac{d\sigma}{dt'} dt'$$

[19]K. G. Hoge, "Influence of strain rate on mechanical properties of 6061-T6 aluminum under uniaxial and biaxial states of stress," *Experimental Mechanics,* **6,** no. 10 (April 1966), 204.

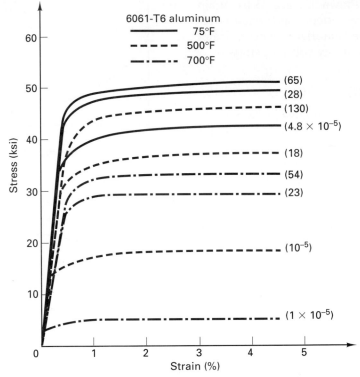

Fig. 2-24   Effect of strain rate and temperature on stress-strain curves for 6061-T6 aluminum. ($\dot{\varepsilon}$ are in in/in per sec.)

Conclusions for viscoelastic materials based on short-duration tests at one temperature can be grossly misleading.

2-10 Cyclic Loading: Fatigue

In previous sections, the stress-strain diagrams have implied monotonically increasing or decreasing loading. However, actually the vast majority of structural and mechanical elements are subjected to repeated loading for many cycles, termed *cyclic loading*. Examples of members and/or structures subjected to cyclic loading are numerous: buildings and bridges under earthquake- and wind-induced forces, aircraft, ships, steam or gas turbine blades, offshore platforms, and many others.

As shown by experimental studies,[20] the loads that do not cause fracture in a single application can result in fracture when applied repeatedly.

---

[20]See, for example, J. A. Collins, *Failure of Materials in Mechanical Design* (New York: John Wiley & Sons, 1981).

The phenomenon of fracture under cyclic loading is referred to as *fatigue*. During the cyclic loading fracture of material may occur after a few cycles (referred to as *low-cycle fatigue*) or after millions of cycles (referred to as *high-cycle fatigue*).

The mechanisms of fatigue failure are complex and beyond the scope of this text. From an engineering viewpoint, however, this failure apparently results from the fact that there are regions, usually on the surface of a member, where the localized stress (or strain) is much greater than the average stress (or strain) acting over the cross section. As this higher stress (or strain) is cycled, it leads to the initiation of *fatigue cracks*. Once a fatigue crack is initiated, additional cycles of loading cause a further propagation of that crack into the material. Eventually the cross-sectional area of the member is reduced to some critical size, when the load can no longer be sustained, and as a result sudden fracture occurs.

The number of cycles required to initiate a fatigue crack is called the *fatigue-initiation life*. The period of fatigue-crack growth from initiation to failure is called the *fatigue-propagation life*. Thus, the *total fatigue life* is defined as the sum of two lives. For a given member the total fatigue life is strongly influenced by the quality of the surface finish, the possible residual stress within the member, the presence of fabrication imperfections such as cracks and defects, the presence of stress concentrations, the chemical nature of the environment, and the material itself. For example, a preexisting crack in a member, such as a weld crack, reduces the fatigue-initiation life essentially to zero, and as a result the total fatigue life is equal to the propagation life.

The mechanical properties of materials under cyclic loading are determined by testing small specimens of the material. Generally the specimens are simple bars, beams, etc., similar to the specimens used in tension tests (see Fig. 2-1). These tests are called *fatigue tests* and are conducted to obtain information on either initiation life or the total fatigue life. The two most common types of cyclic loadings used in fatigue tests are the so-called *constant-amplitude* and *variable-amplitude* loading.

Constant-Amplitude Cycling   In *constant-amplitude cyclic loading*, the stress range $\Delta\sigma = \sigma_{max} - \sigma_{min}$ is constant throughout the entire loading history, as shown in Fig. 2-25. During the loading the applied stress is varied from σ_{max} to σ_{min}, and the stress amplitude $\sigma_{amp} = (\sigma_{max} - \sigma_{min})/2$ remains constant.

Constant-amplitude fatigue tests are performed on a series of identical machined specimens. Each specimen is subjected to a specified stress range at constant amplitude and cycled until a fatigue crack is initiated. The test results are plotted as a graph representing the stress amplitude S (or $\Delta\sigma$) as the ordinate and the number of cycles to failure N as abscissa. This graph is called the *S-N* or *stress-fatigue life diagram,* and is most often plotted on a semilogarithmic scale.

Examples of *S-N* diagrams for two common engineering metals (structural steel and aluminum) are shown in Fig. 2-26. For the particular material

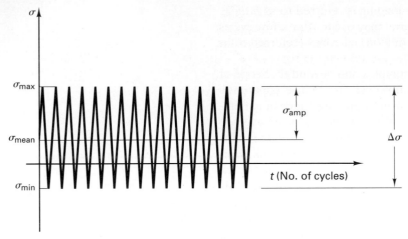

Fig. 2-25   Constant-amplitude cyclic loading.

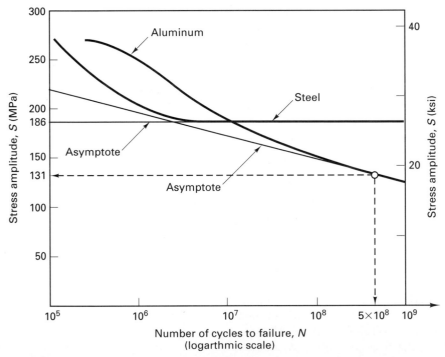

Fig. 2-26   *S-N* diagrams for structural steel and an aluminum alloy (after Collins, *Failure of Materials*).

tested, these diagrams can be used to estimate the fatigue life for the specified stress range. It can be seen that for large values of N, the S-N diagrams approach asymptotes. A point on the S-N diagram, corresponding to the stress on an asymptote, determines the *fatigue strength* or the *endurance limit* S_{el} of the material. More generally, the endurance limit is defined as the maximum stress range that can be applied repeatedly for an infinite life without fracturing the material. As can be seen from Fig. 2-26, the particular structural steel tested has a value of $S_{el} = 186$ MPa, whereas for the particular aluminum alloy tested, for the stress range having a life of 500 million cycles, $S_{el} = 131$ MPa can be specified. Typical values of the endurance limit for various engineering materials are available in technical literature.

It is important to note that the constant-amplitude high-cyclic fatigue generally occurs in machinery parts subjected to reciprocal long-term loads. However, even for other types of types of members, constant-amplitude loading is the most common type studied experimentally.

Variable-Amplitude Cycling: Cumulative Damage For many structures, fatigue loadings are not of constant amplitude but rather of variable or random amplitude, as shown in Fig. 2-27(a). Examples of this type of fatigue loading are numerous: truck traffic on bridges, wind loading on aircraft, and wave loadings on ships. Such *variable-* or *random-amplitude cyclic loadings* make the direct use of the conventional S-N diagrams inapplicable since such diagrams are developed for constant stress amplitude tests.

To analyze the fatigue behavior of a member subjected to random-amplitude cyclic loading, a procedure for some means of characterizing these random stress fluctuations is necessary. The most desirable approach of determining the fatigue behavior of members subjected to the variable-amplitude loading is to use test results performed under identical loading histories. For some critical situations this is actually done. However, a more frequent approach is to use constant-amplitude test results in conjunction with a *cumulative damage* model to predict fatigue behavior of members subjected to variable loading conditions. The basic postulate adopted in cumulative damage concept is that cycling at any given stress amplitude produces *fatigue damage*.

One of the most widely used approaches, and historically the oldest, is the *Palmgren-Miner hypothesis* or *linear damage rule*.[21] In this approach, the failure of material is said to occur when

$$\sum_{i=1}^{k} D_i \geq 1 \qquad \left(D_i = \frac{n_i}{N_{fi}} \right) \qquad (2\text{-}21)$$

[21]Proposed by Palmgren in 1924 and later developed by Miner in 1945. See M. A. Miner, "Cumulative damage in fatigue," *Trans. ASME, J. Applied Mech.*, 67, Series A, (1945), 159–164. Similar empirical rules have also been proposed by Soderberg as well as Goodman. See A. P. Boresi and O. M. Sidebottom, *Advanced Mechanics of Materials*, 4th ed. (New York: John Wiley & Sons, 1985).

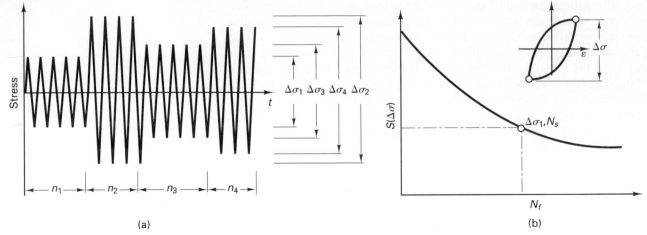

Fig. 2-27 (a) Variable-amplitude loading. (b) Typical *S-N* diagram.

where k = number of loading sequences at a particular stress amplitude, D_i = damage produced by a stress amplitude of $\Delta\sigma_i$, n_i = number of applied cycles at a constant amplitude of $\Delta\sigma_i$ [see Fig. 2-27(a)], and N_{fi} = fatigue life at a constant amplitude of $\Delta\sigma_i$ [see Fig. 2-27(b)].

Low-Cycle Fatigue   The *S-N* diagrams shown in Fig. 2-26 for a constant stress amplitude are generally for tests below the elastic limit of the material; that is, when the maximum applied stress amplitudes in developing the *S-N* diagrams are in the linear elastic region of the monotonic stress-strain diagram (see Fig. 2-5). However, there are situations in which structural members are subjected to relatively high cyclic loads (for example, members subjected to thermal loading, piping subjected to large cyclic deformations, structures during an earthquake, nuclear pressure-vessel components). In these cases significant amounts of plastic strain are induced during each cycle, and short lives resulting in a small numbers of cycles exhibit failure if these relatively large loads are repeatedly applied. This type of cyclic behavior is termed *low-cycle fatigue.*

In low-cycle fatigue, the *strain amplitude* rather than the stress amplitude becomes the controlling parameter, since there can be large variations in strain amplitude accompanied by small changes in stress amplitude. The usual method of displaying the results of low-cycle fatigue tests is to plot a graph representing the *strain amplitude* as the ordinate and the number of cycles (or reversals) to failure as the abscissa. This graph is called the *strain-fatigue life diagram.* An example of a strain-fatigue life diagram for nickel-steel alloy[22] is shown in Fig. 2-28.

[22]See R. W. Landgraf, "The resistance of metal to cyclic deformation," *Achievement on High Fatigue Resistance in Metal and Alloys, STP-467, ASTM,* Philadelphia, PA, 1970.

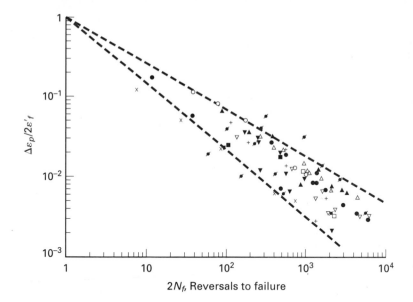

Fig. 2-28   Low cycle fatigue plot of plastic strain amplitude $\Delta\,\varepsilon_p/2\epsilon'_f$ versus number of reversals to failure for an array of hardened nickel-alloy steels. The normalizing parameter $\mathbf{2\varepsilon'_f}$ refers to 0.2% offset yield strength (after Landgraf, "Resistance of metal").

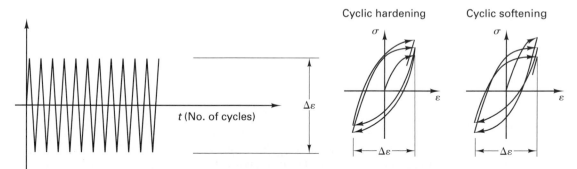

Fig. 2-29   Strain hardening and strain softening phenomenona under strain cycling.

The stress-strain behavior of materials under strain cycling is typically nonlinear and history dependent. It has been observed that the stress-strain response of most materials changes significantly with cyclic straining into the plastic range. Some materials exhibit cyclic strain hardening and others exhibit strain softening, as illustrated in Fig. 2-29.

As a general rule, materials that are initially hard and strong (heat treated) will cyclically strain soften, whereas initially soft materials will strain harden. Cyclic material models rather than monotonic stress-strain diagrams should then be used to predict the behavior of these materials. The determination of cyclic material models is described in advanced treatises on fatigue.

PROBLEMS

Section 2-2 through 2-4

2-1.   A standard steel specimen of 13 mm diameter elongated 0.22 mm in a 200 mm gage length when it was subjected to a tensile force of 29.5 kN. If the specimen was known to be in the elastic range, what is the elastic modulus of the steel?

2-2.   A steel rod 10 m long used in a control mechanism must transmit a tensile force of 5 kN without stretching more than 3 mm, nor exceeding an allowable stress of 150 MN/m². What must the diameter of the rod be? Give the answer to the nearest millimeter. $E = 200$ GPa.

2-3.   A solid cylinder of 50 mm diameter and 900 mm length is subjected to a tensile force of 120 kN. One part of this cylinder, L_1 long, is of steel; the other part, fastened to steel, is aluminum and is L_2 long. (a) Determine the lengths L_1 and L_2 so that the two materials elongate an equal amount. (b) What is the total elongation of the cylinder? $E_{St} = 200$ GPa; $E_{Al} = 70$ GPa.

2-4.   In one of the California oil fields, a very long steel drill pipe got stuck in hard clay (see figure). It was necessary to determine at what depth this occurred. The engineer on the job ordered the pipe subjected to a large upward tensile force. As a result of this operation the pipe came up elastically 600 mm. At the same time the pipe elongated 0.035 mm in a 200 mm gage length. Approximately where was the pipe stuck? Assume that the cross-sectional area of the pipe was constant and that the media surrounding the pipe hindered elastic deformation of the pipe in a static test very little.

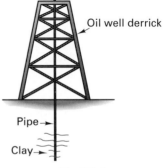

Oil well derrick

Pipe→

Clay→

Fig. P2-4

2-5.   By scaling the ordinates on the engineering stress-strain diagram in Fig. 2-7, obtain the approximate values of stress at 0.1, 0.2, 1.0, 2.0, and 4.0% of strain. Then, for these values of strain using Eq. 2-7, determine the true stresses in tension and compression and exhibit the results on a plot without exaggeration. For the same conditions make a study in the change in the cross-sectional area. (These issues become very important in drawing on metals.)

2-6.   A hard-drawn copper wire is stretched between points A and B 50 m apart at $-35°C$ developing a sag of 300 mm in the middle of the span (see Fig. P2-6). What would the maximum sag of the wire be if the temperature changed to $+35°C$? Assume the linear coefficient thermal expansion for the copper wire to be $16 \times 10^{-6}/°C$. Approximate the shape of defected wire either by a catenary or a parabola; let the wire length $ds \approx dx$.

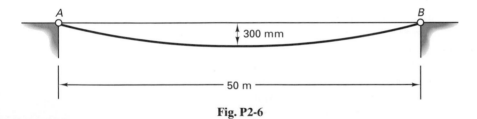

A B

↕ 300 mm

50 m

Fig. P2-6

Section 2-6 and 2-7

2-7. A cast brass rod 60 mm in diameter and 150 mm long is compressed axially by a uniformly distributed force of 200 kN. Determine the increase in diameter caused by the applied force. $E = 85$ GPa; $v = 0.30$.

2-8. Suppose that in an apparatus it is necessary to maintain precisely the cross section of a 20 mm circular nickel steel bar. If this bar is heated to 200°C, what tensile force should be applied to the bar to maintain its cross-sectional dimension? What should be the applied axial force if the rod were made of aluminum? Assume for stainless steel that $E = 200$ GPa, and $\alpha = 11.7 \times 10^{-6}$ per °C, and for 6061-T4 aluminum $E = 70$ GPa, and $\alpha = 23.4 \times 10^{-6}$ per °C.

2-9. A 5 kg mass moves in a horizontal circle at the end of a 1.5 m steel wire with such an angular velocity that the wire makes an angle of 30° with the vertical. What is the proper diameter for the wire if the allowable tensile stress for high-strength steel is 300 MPa? How much will the wire extend during whirling? Let $E = 200$ GPa.

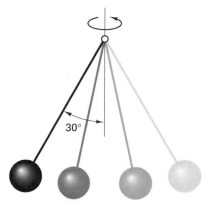

30°

Fig. P2-9

Section 2-8

2-10. Determine the approximate toughness moduli for three grades of steel, shown in Fig. 2-8.

Section 2-9

2-11. Suppose that a series of tension tests is performed on several identical specimens of Maxwell material. In each experiment the strain rate is held constant. (a) Sketch a family of stress-strain curves that would result from this series of tests. (b) In each case, what is the elastic modulus E at $t = 0$? (c) Discuss the implication of the results.

2-12. A Standard Solid for a viscoelastic material is obtained by placing in series a Maxwell and a Kelvin unit, as shown in figure (a). This model is capable of representing most of the essential features of viscoelastic behavior. Sketch the strain-time relationship that results from the stress-time input shown in figure (b).

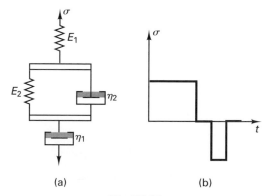

(a)   (b)

Fig. P2-12

2-13.   Consider a pipe of a linearly viscoelastic material that spans horizontally across a distance L. This pipe is empty for 16 hr a day, and is filled 8 hr. The ratio of the weight of the filled pipe to its empty weight is 5. (a) Assuming that the material is Maxwellian, sketch a diagram showing the center deflection as a function of time for two typical days. (b) For the same conditions of input, sketch another diagram for a material having the properties of a Standard Solid (see Prob. 2-12).

2-14.   For many materials the assumption of linear viscoelasticity is not satisfactory. To treat such cases a number of empirical relations for steady-state creep have been proposed. One such widely used relation is $\dot{\varepsilon} = B\sigma^n$, where B is a constant and the experimentally determined exponent $n > 1$. Show that, using this relation, the maximum stress in a rectangular beam is $\sigma_{max} = (Mc/I)[(2n + 1)/(3n)]$ and that at a distance y from the centroidal axis $\sigma = (y/c)^{1/n}\sigma_{max}$. Sketch the resulting stress distribution for an $n = 6$.

Section 2-10

2-15.   A machine part such as shown in Fig. P2-15 is subjected to a constant-amplitude cyclic loading having equal maximum amplitudes in tension and compression. If the part is made of either steel or of an aluminum alloy and is intended for service of 10^8 cycles, what ultimate stress may be allowed for each of the materials? The ends of the specimen are properly tapered. Make the estimate using Fig. 2-26.

Diameter D

Fig. P2-15

2-16.   By applying the Palmgren-Miner rule, Eq. 2-21, make a study of the permissible stress for two ranges of stress for aluminum-alloy and steel. (a) For both materials in the high range of stress, let the number of cycles by 2×10^6 at 200 MPa and 4×10^5 at 250 MPa. (b) For the low range of stress, let the number of cycles be 5×10^6 at 175 MPa and 4×10^8 cycles at 130 MPa. Make an estimate using Fig. 2-26.

3

Axial Deformation of Bars: Statically Determinate Systems

3-1. Introduction

This chapter is devoted to the problem of determining deformation in axially loaded bars in statically determinate cases. This implies that the axial forces in the member can be determined by the equations of statics alone. In addition to straight bars, hinged two-bar systems are also considered. All of the illustrative examples are developed for linearly elastic material. A case of thermal deformation of a two-bar system is included. Examples for nonlinear materials are left as exercises for the reader.

Important information pertaining to significant increases in stress at changes in member cross sections is provided in Section 3-3, which discusses Saint-Venant's principle. The chapter is concluded with a discussion of elastic strain energy, deflection by the energy method, and impact loads pertaining to uniaxial stresses.

3-2. Deformation of Axially Loaded Bars

When the deflection of an axially loaded member is a design parameter, it is necessary to determine the deformations. Axial deformations are also required in the analysis of statically indeterminate bars. The deflection characteristics of bars also provide necessary information for determining the stiffness of systems in mechanical vibration analysis.

Consider the axially loaded bar shown in Fig. 3-1(a) for deriving a relation for axial bar deformation. The applied forces P_1, P_2, and P_3 are held in equilibrium by the force P_4. The cross-sectional area A of the bar is permitted to change gradually. The change in length that takes place in the bar between points B and D due to the applied force is to be determined.

In order to formulate the relation, Eq. 2-1 for the normal strain is recast for a differential element dx. Thus the normal strain ε_x in the x direction is

$$\varepsilon_x = \frac{du}{dx} \tag{3-1}$$

where, due to the applied forces, u is the absolute displacement of a point on a bar from an initial fixed position in space, and du is the axial deformation of the infinitesimal element. This is the governing differential equation for axially loaded bars.

It is to be noted that the deformations considered in this text are generally *very small* (infinitesimal). This should become apparent from numerical examples throughout this text. Therefore, in calculations the *initial*

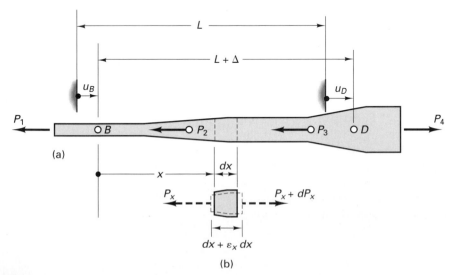

Fig. 3-1   An axially loaded bar.

(undeformed) dimensions of members can be used for calculating deformations. In the following derivation this permits the use of the initial length L, between points such as B and D in Fig. 3-1, rather than its deformed length.

Rearranging Eq. 3-1 as $du = \varepsilon_x \, dx$, assuming the origin of x at B, and integrating,

$$\int_0^L du = u(L) - u(0) = \int_0^L \varepsilon_x \, dx$$

where $u(L) = u_D$ and $u(0) = u_B$ are the absolute or global displacements of points D and B, respectively. As can be seen from the figure, $u(0)$ is a *rigid-body axial translation* of the bar. The difference between these displacements is the change in length Δ between points D and B. Hence

$$\Delta = \int_0^L \varepsilon_x \, dx \qquad (3\text{-}2)$$

Any appropriate constitutive relations can be used to define ε_x.

For linearly elastic materials, according to Hooke's law, $\varepsilon_x = \sigma_x / E$, Eq. 2-8, where $\sigma_x = P_x / A_x$, Eq. 1-6 or 1-8. By substituting these relations into Eq. 3-2 and simplifying,

$$\Delta = \int_0^L \frac{P_x \, dx}{A_x E_x} \qquad (3\text{-}3)$$

where Δ is the change in length of a *linearly elastic* bar of length L, and the force $P_x = P(x)$, the cross-sectional area $A_x = A(x)$, and the elastic modulus $E_x = E(x)$ can vary along the length of a bar. If these conditions do not apply, a different constitive relation must be used for determining ε_x in Eq. 3-2.

PROCEDURE SUMMARY

It should be emphasized that the central theme in engineering mechanics of solids consists of repeatedly applying *three basic concepts*. In developing the theory for axially loaded bars, these basic concepts can be summarized as follows:

1. *Equilibrium conditions* are used for determining the internal resisting forces at a section, first introduced in Chapter 1. As shown in the next chapter, this may require solution of a statically indeterminate problem.

2. *Geometry of deformation* is used in deriving the change in length of a bar due to axial forces by assuming that sections initially

perpendicular to the axis of a bar remain perpendicular after straining; see Fig. 3-1(b).

3. *Material properties* (constitutive relations) are used in relating axial normal stresses to axial normal strain and permit calculation of axial deformations between sections.

Solutions based on this theory assume an *average* stress at a section (see Section 1-6). However, at concentrated forces and abrupt changes in cross section, irregular *local* stresses (and strains) arise. Only at distances about equal to the depth of the member from such disturbances are the stresses and strains in agreement with the developed theory. Therefore, solutions based on the concepts of engineering mechanics of solids are best suited for relatively slender members. The use of this simplified procedure is rationalized in Section 3-3 as *Saint-Venant's principle.*

Several examples showing application of Eq. 3-3 follow.

Example 3-1

Consider bar *BC* of constant cross-sectional area *A* and of length *L* shown in Fig. 3-2(a). Determine the deflection of the free end, caused by the application of a concentrated force *P*. The elastic modulus of the material is *E*.

SOLUTION
The deformed bar is shown in Fig. 3-2(b). **Conceptually, it is often convenient to think of such elastic systems as springs;** see Fig. 3-2(e).

A free-body diagram for an isolated part of the loaded bar to the left of an arbitrary section *a–a* is shown in Fig. 3-2(c). From this diagram, it can be concluded that the axial force P_x is the same everywhere along the bar and is equal to *P*. It is given that $A_x = A$, a constant. By applying Eq. 3-3,

$$\Delta = \int_A^B \frac{P_x \, dx}{A_x E} = \frac{P}{AE} \int_0^L dx = \frac{P}{AE} \, x \, \Big|_0^L = \frac{PL}{AE}$$

Hence

$$\boxed{\Delta = \frac{PL}{AE}} \tag{3-4}$$

A graphic interpretation of the solution is shown in Figs. 3-2(f)–(h). The constant axial bar strain follows by dividing the constant axial force *P* by *AE*. Since the axial strain is constant, the displacements of the points on the bar increase directly with the distance from the origin of *x* at a constant rate. No displacement is possible at the left end.

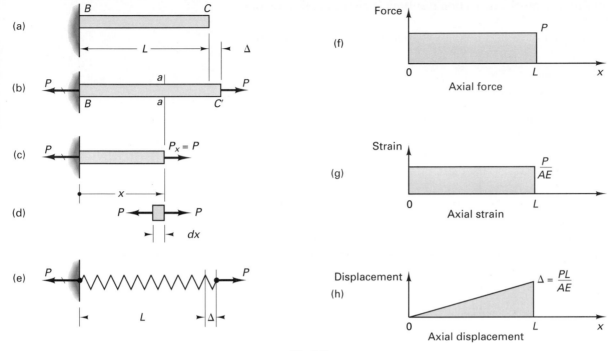

Fig. 3-2

It is seen from Eq. 3-4 that the deflection of the rod is directly proportional to the applied force and the length and is inversely proportional to A and E.

Since Eq. 3-4 frequently occurs in practice, it is meaningful to recast it into the following form:

$$P = (AE/L)\Delta \qquad (3\text{-}5)$$

This equation is related to the familiar definition for the *spring constant* or *stiffness k* reading

$$k = P/\Delta \quad [\text{lb/in}] \text{ or } [\text{N/m}] \qquad (3\text{-}6)$$

This constant represents the force required to produce a unit deflection (i.e., $\Delta = 1$). Therefore, for an axially loaded ith bar or bar segment of length L_i and constant cross section,

$$k_i = \frac{A_i E_i}{L_i} \qquad (3\text{-}7)$$

and the analogy between such a bar and a spring shown in Fig. 3-2(e) is evident. The reciprocal of k defines the *flexibility f*; that is,

$$f = 1/k = \Delta/P \quad [\text{in/lb}] \text{ or } [\text{m/N}] \qquad (3\text{-}8)$$

The constant f represents the deflection resulting from the application of a unit force (i.e., $P = 1$).

For the particular case of an axially loaded ith bar of constant cross section,

$$f_i = \frac{L_i}{A_i E_i} \qquad (3\text{-}9)$$

The concepts of structural stiffness and flexibility are widely used in structural analysis, including mechanical-vibration problems. For more complex structural systems, the expressions for k and f become more involved.

Example 3-2

Determine the relative displacement of point D from O for the elastic steel bar of variable cross section shown in Fig. 3-3(a) caused by the application of concentrated forces $P_1 = 100$ kN and $P_3 = 200$ kN acting to the left, and $P_2 = 250$ kN and $P_4 = 50$ kN acting to the right. The respective areas for bar segments OB, BC, and CD are 1000, 2000, and 1000 mm². Let $E = 200$ GPa.

SOLUTION

By inspection, it can be seen that the bar is in equilibrium. *Such a check must always be made before starting a problem.* The variation in P_x along the length of the bar is determined by taking three sections, a–a, b–b, and c–c, in Fig. 3-3(a) and determining the necessary forces for equilibrium in the free-body diagrams in Figs. 3-3(b)–(d). This leads to the conclusion that *within each bar segment,* the forces are *constant,* resulting in the axial force diagram shown in Fig. 3-3(e). Therefore, the solution of the deformation problem consists of adding algebraically the individual deformations for the three segments. Equation 3-4 is applicable for *each* segment. Hence, the total axial deformation for the bar can be written as

$$\Delta = \sum_i \frac{P_i L_i}{A_i E} = \frac{P_{OB} L_{OB}}{A_{OB} E} + \frac{P_{BC} L_{BC}}{A_{BC} E} + \frac{P_{CD} L_{CD}}{A_{CD} E}$$

where the subscripts identify the segments.

Using this relation, the relative displacement between O and D is

$$\Delta = + \frac{100 \times 10^3 \times 2000}{1000 \times 200 \times 10^3} - \frac{150 \times 10^3 \times 1000}{2000 \times 200 \times 10^3} + \frac{50 \times 10^3 \times 1500}{1000 \times 200 \times 10^3}$$

$$= +1.000 - 0.375 + 0.375 = +1.000 \text{ mm}$$

Note that in spite of large stresses in the bar, the elongation is very small.

A graphic interpretation of the solution is shown in Figs. 3-3(f) and (g). By dividing the axial forces in the bar segments by the corresponding AE, the axial strains along the bar are obtained. These strains are constant

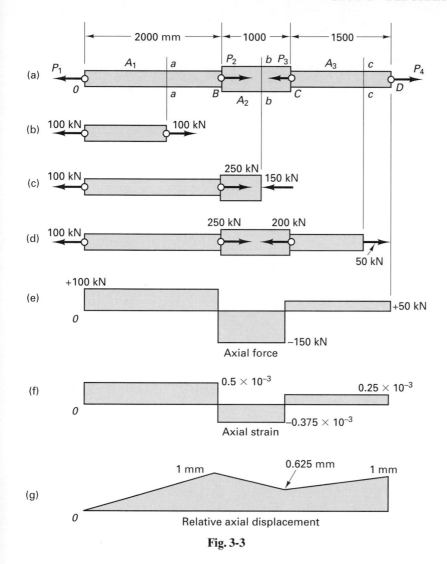

Fig. 3-3

within each bar segment. The area of the strain diagram for each segment of the bar gives the change in length for that segment. These values correspond to those displayed numerically before.

Example 3-3

Determine the deflection of free end B of elastic bar OB caused by its own weight w lb/in; see Fig. 3-4. The constant cross-sectional area is A. Assume that the constant E is given.

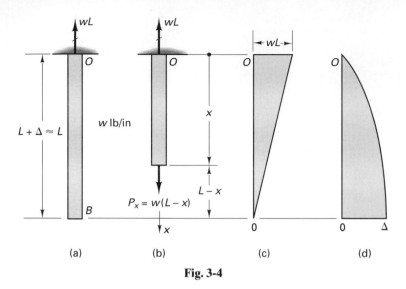

Fig. 3-4

SOLUTION

The free-body diagrams of the bar and its truncated segment are shown, respectively, in Figs. 3-4(a) and (b). These two steps are essential in the solution of such problems. The graph for the axial force $P_x = w(L - x)$ is in Fig. 3-4(c). By applying Eq. 3-3, the change in bar length $\Delta(x)$ at a generic point x,

$$\Delta(x) = \int_0^x \frac{P_x\,dx}{A_x E} = \frac{1}{AE}\int w(L - x)\,dx = \frac{w}{AE}\left(Lx - \frac{x^2}{2}\right)$$

A plot of this function is shown in Fig. 3-4(d), with its maximum as B.

The deflection of B is

$$\Delta = \Delta(L) = \frac{w}{AE}\left(L^2 - \frac{L^2}{2}\right) = \frac{wL^2}{2AE} = \frac{WL}{2AE}$$

where $W = wL$ is the *total* weight of the bar.

If a concentrated force P, in *addition* to the bar's own weight, were acting on bar OB at end B, the total deflection due to the *two causes* would be obtained by *superposition* as

$$\Delta = \frac{PL}{AE} + \frac{WL}{2AE} = \frac{[P + (W/2)]L}{AE}$$

In problems where the area of a rod is variable, a proper *function* for it must be substituted into Eq. 3-3 to determine deflections. In practice, it is sometimes sufficiently accurate to analyze such problems by approximating the shape of a rod by a *finite number* of elements, as shown in Fig. 3-5. The deflections for each one of these elements are added to obtain the

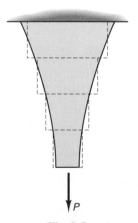

Fig. 3-5

total deflection. Because of the rapid variation in the cross section shown, the solution would be approximate.

Example 3-4

For the bracket analyzed for stresses in Example 1-3, determine the deflection of point B caused by the applied vertical force $P = 3$ kips. Also determine the vertical stiffness of the bracket at B. Assume that the members are made of 2024-T4 aluminum alloy and that they have constant cross-sectional areas (i.e., neglect the enlargements at the connections). See the idealization in Fig. 3-6(a).

SOLUTION

As found in Example 1-3, the axial stresses in the bars of the bracket are $\sigma_{AB} = 17.8$ ksi and $\sigma_{BC} = 12.9$ ksi. The length of member AB is 6.71 in and that of BC is 8.49 in. Per Table 1A in the Appendix, for the specified material, $E = 10.6 \times 10^3$ ksi. Therefore, according to Eq. 3-4, the individual member length changes are

$$\Delta_{AB} = \left[\frac{PL}{AE} \right]_{AB} = \left[\sigma \frac{L}{E} \right]_{AB} = \frac{17.8 \times 6.71}{10.6 \times 10^3} = 11.3 \times 10^{-3} \text{ in}$$

(elongation)

$$\Delta_{BC} = -\frac{12.9 \times 8.29}{10.6 \times 10^3} = -10.3 \times 10^{-3} \text{ in} \qquad \text{(contraction)}$$

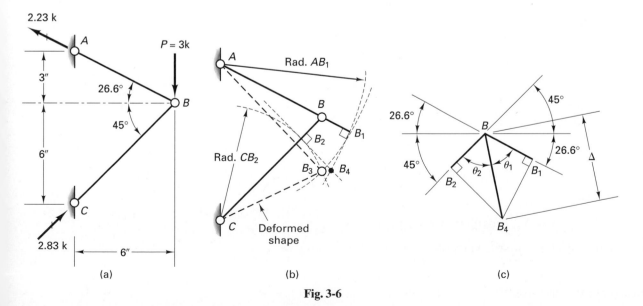

(a) (b) (c)

Fig. 3-6

These length changes, as BB_1 and BB_2, are shown to a greatly exaggerated scale in relation to the bar lengths in Fig. 3-6(b). The indicated locations of points B_1 and B_2 are incompatible with the physical requirements of the problem. Therefore, elongated bar AB_1 and shortened bar CB_2 must be rotated around their respective support points A and C such that points B_1 and B_2 meet at common point B_3. This is shown schematically in Fig. 3-6(b). However, since in classical solid mechanics one deals with small (infinitesimal) deformations, an approximation can be introduced. In such analyses, it is customary to assume that short arcs of large circles can be approximated by normals to the members along which the bar ends move to achieve compatibility at the joints. This construction[1] is indicated in Fig. 3-6(b), locating point B_4. An enlarged detail of the changes in bar lengths and this approach for locating point B_4 is shown in Fig. 3-6(c). The required numerical results can be obtained either graphically or by using trigonometry. Here the latter procedure is followed.

If Δ is the deflection or displacement of point B to position B_4, Fig. 3-6(c), and changes in bar lengths $\Delta_{BC} = BB_2$ and $\Delta_{AB} = BB_1$,

$$\Delta_{BC} = \Delta\cos\theta_2 \quad \text{and} \quad \Delta_{AB} = \Delta\cos\theta_1$$

On forming equal ratios for both sides of these equations, substituting the numerical values for Δ_{BC} and Δ_{AB} found earlier, and simplifying, one obtains

$$\frac{\cos\theta_2}{\cos\theta_1} = \frac{\Delta_{BC}}{\Delta_{AB}} = \frac{10.3 \times 10^{-3}}{11.3 \times 10^{-3}} = 0.912$$

However, since

$$\theta_2 = 180° - 45° - 26.6° - \theta_1 = 108.4° - \theta_1$$

it follows that

$$\cos\theta_2 = \cos 108.4° \cos\theta_1 + \sin 108.4° \sin\theta_1$$

and

$$\frac{\cos\theta_2}{\cos\theta_1} = \cos 108.4° + \sin 108.4° \tan\theta_1 = 0.912$$

Therefore,

$$\tan\theta_1 = 1.29 \quad \text{and} \quad \theta_1 = 52.2°$$

Based on this result,

$$\Delta = \Delta_{AB}/\cos\theta_1 = 18.4 \times 10^{-3} \text{ in}$$

forming an angle of $11.2°$ with the vertical.

---

[1]First introduced by M. Williot in 1877.

Since $\Delta_{\text{vert}} = \Delta \cos 11.2° = 18.0 \times 10^{-3}$ in, the vertical stiffness of the bracket is given by the spring constant

$$k = \frac{P}{\Delta_{\text{vert}}} = \frac{3}{18.0 \times 10^{-3}} = 167 \text{ kips/in}$$

This problem contains geometric nonlinearity in displacement, which has been neglected; therefore, the solution is accurate only for small deformations, a common practice for many engineering problems.

Example 3-5

Determine the displacement of point B in Example 3-4 caused by an increase in temperature of 100°F. See Fig. 3-7(a).

SOLUTION

Determining the deflection at point B due to an increase in temperature is similar to the solution of Example 3-4 for finding the deflection of the same point caused by stress. Per Table 1A in the Appendix, the coefficient of thermal expansion for 2024-T4 aluminum alloy is 12.9×10^{-6} per °F. Hence, from Eq. 2-11, and using the lengths of members given in Example 3-4,

$$\Delta_{AB} = 12.9 \times 10^{-6} \times 100 \times 6.71 = 8.656 \times 10^{-3} \text{ in}$$

$$\Delta_{BC} = 12.9 \times 10^{-6} \times 100 \times 8.49 = 10.95 \times 10^{-3} \text{ in}$$

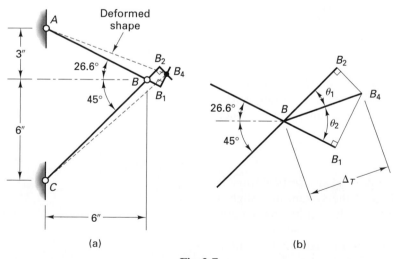

(a)　　　　　　　　　(b)

Fig. 3-7

Here the displacement Δ_T of point B to position B_4, Fig. 3-7(b), caused by a change in temperature, is related to the bar elongations in the following manner:

$$\Delta_T \cos \theta_2 = \Delta_{AB} \quad \text{and} \quad \Delta_T \cos \theta_1 = \Delta_{BC}$$

Forming equal ratios for both sides of these equations, substituting numerical values for Δ_{AB} and Δ_{BC}, and simplifying leads to the following result:

$$\frac{\cos \theta_2}{\cos \theta_1} = \frac{\Delta_{AB}}{\Delta_{BC}} = \frac{8.656 \times 10^{-3}}{10.95 \times 10^{-3}} = 0.7905$$

Here, however, $\theta_2 = 45° + 26.6° - \theta_1 = 71.6° - \theta_1$; therefore,

$$\cos \theta_2 = \cos 71.6° \cos \theta_1 + \sin 71.6° \sin \theta_1$$

and

$$\frac{\cos \theta_2}{\cos \theta_1} = \cos 71.6° + \sin 71.6° \tan \theta_1 = 0.7905$$

Hence,

$$\tan \theta_1 = 0.500 \quad \text{and} \quad \theta_1 = 26.6°$$

Based on this result,

$$\Delta_T = \Delta_{BC} / \cos \theta_1 = 12.2 \times 10^{-3} \text{ in}$$

forming an angle of $45° - \theta_1 = 18.4°$ with the horizontal.

It is interesting to note that the small displacement Δ_T is of comparable order of magnitude to that found due to the applied vertical force P in Example 3-4.

Example 3-6

Two hinge-ended elastic bars of equal lengths and cross-sectional areas attached to immovable supports are joined in the middle by a pin, as shown in Fig. 3-8(a). Initially, points A, B, and C are on a straight line. Determine the vertical deflection Δ of point C as a function of applied force P. Consider small deflections only.

SOLUTION

The given structural system is incapable of supporting any vertical force in its initial configuration. Therefore, equilibrium of the system in a slightly deflected condition must be examined, Fig. 3-8(b), where initial bar lengths L become L^*. For this position of the bars, one can write an equation of equilibrium for joint C' and express elongations of the bars via two different paths. One such relation for elongation of each bar follows from Eq. 3-4

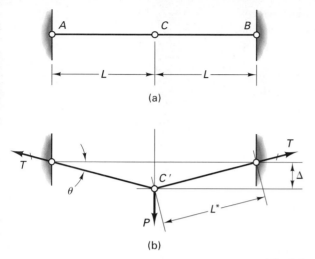

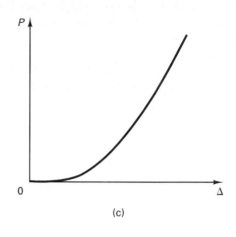

Fig. 3-8

and the other from purely geometric considerations. On these bases, from equilibrium,

$$P = 2T \sin \theta$$

and

$$\frac{TL^*}{AE} = L^* - L = L^* - L^* \cos \theta$$

Hence,

$$T = AE(1 - \cos \theta)$$

On substituting this expression for T into the first equation,

$$P = 2AE(1 - \cos \theta) \sin \theta$$

Further, by expanding $\cos \theta$ and $\sin \theta$ into Taylor's series,

$$P = 2AE\left(\frac{\theta^2}{2!} - \frac{\theta^4}{4!} + \cdots \right)\left(\theta - \frac{\theta^3}{3!} + \cdots \right)$$

On retaining only one term in each series,

$$P \approx AE\theta^3$$

However, since the analysis is being made for small deflections, angle $\theta \approx \Delta/L$. Therefore,

$$P \approx \frac{AE}{L^3}\Delta^3 \quad \text{or} \quad \Delta = L\sqrt[3]{\frac{P}{AE}} \tag{3-10}$$

This result, shown qualitatively in Fig. 3-8(c), clearly exhibits the highly nonlinear relationship between P and Δ. By contrast, most of the problems that will be encountered in this text will lead to linear relationships between loads and displacements. The more accurate solutions of this problem show that the approximate solution just obtained gives good results for Δ/L, on the order 0.3.

In this problem, the effect of geometry change on equilibrium was considered, whereas in Example 3-4, it was neglected because the displacement was very small.

3-3. Saint-Venant's Principle and Stress Concentrations

The analysis of axially loaded bars based on engineering mechanics of solids is very accurate for bars of constant cross section when transmitting uniformly distributed end forces. For such ideal conditions stresses and strains are uniform everywhere. In reality, however, applied forces often approximate concentrated forces, and the cross sections of members can change abruptly. This causes stress and strain disturbances in the proximity of such forces and changes in cross sections. In the past these situations were studied analytically using the *mathematical theory of elasticity*. In such an approach, the behavior of two- or three-dimensional *infinitesimal elements* is formulated and the conditions of equilibrium, deformation, and mechanical properties of material[2] are satisfied subject to the prescribed boundary conditions. More recently a powerful numerical procedure has been developed, where a body is subdivided into a *discrete number* of finite elements, such as squares or cubes, and the analysis is carried out with a computer. This is called the *finite element method* of analysis. The end results of analyses by either one of these two methods can be used very effectively to supplement solutions in engineering mechanics of solids. An example showing the more accurate solutions by these two advanced methods for the nature of stress distribution at concentrated force follows. These solutions provide comparison with those found by applying the method of engineering mechanics of solids.

A short block is shown in Fig. 3-9(a) acted upon by concentrated forces at its ends. Analyzing this block for stresses as a two-dimensional problem using the methods of the theory of elasticity gives the results shown in Figs. 3-9(b), (c), and (d).[3] The *average* stress σ_{av} as given by Eq. 1-6 is also shown on these diagrams. From these it can be noted that at a section a distance $b/4$ from an end, Fig. 3-9(b), the maximum normal stress greatly

---

[2]These are the same basic concepts as used in engineering mechanics of solids.

[3]S. Timoshenko and J. N. Goodier, *Theory of Elasticity,* 3rd. ed. (New York: McGraw-Hill, 1970), 60. Fig. 3-9 is adapted from this source.

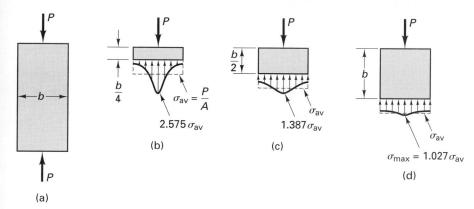

Fig. 3-9   Stress distribution near a concentrated force in a rectangular elastic plate.

exceeds the average. For a purely elastic material the maximum stress theoretically becomes infinite right under the concentrated force, since a finite force acts on a zero area. In real situations, however, a truly concentrated force is not possible and virtually all materials exhibit some plastic behavior; therefore the attainment of an infinite stress is impossible.

It is important to note two basic aspects from this solution. First, the *average* stress for all cases, being based on conditions of equilibrium, is always correct. Second, the normal stresses at a distance equal to the width of the member are essentially uniform.

The second observation illustrates the famed *Saint-Venant's principle,* which was enunciated by the great French elastician in 1855. In common engineering terms it simply means that the manner of force application on stresses is important only in the vicinity of the region where the force is applied. This also holds true for the disturbances caused by changes in cross section. Consciously or unconsciously this principle is nearly always applied in idealized load-carrying systems.

Using the finite element method,[4] the results of a solution for the same problem are shown in Fig. 3-10. The initial undeformed mesh into which the planar block is arbitrarily subdivided and the *greatly exaggerated deformed mesh* caused by the applied force are shown in Fig. 3-10(a). By placing the mesh on rollers as shown, only the upper half of the block needed to be analyzed because of symmetry around the midsection. The calculated stress contours in Fig. 3-10(b) clearly show the development of large stresses in the vicinity of the concentrated force. Unlike the solution based on mathematical elasticity, in the finite element model the stresses at the applied force are very large, but finite, because of finite mesh size. As to

[4]For this subject see, for example, O. C. Zienkiewicz and R. L. Taylor, *The Finite Element Method,* Vol. 1, 4th ed. (London: McGraw-Hill Ltd., 1989); K. J. Bathe and E. L. Wilson, *Numerical Methods in Finite Element Analysis* (Englewood Cliffs, NJ: Prentice Hall, 1976); R. H. Gallagher, *Finite Element Fundamentals* (Englewood Cliffs, NJ: Prentice Hall, 1975).

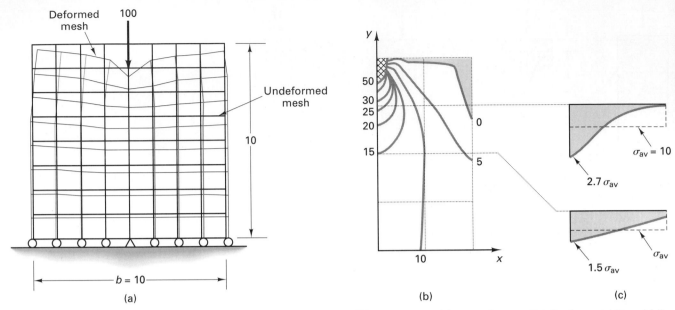

Fig. 3-10   (a) Undeformed and deformed mesh of an elastic plate; (b) σ_y contours; (c) normal stress distributions at $b/4$ and $b/2$ below top.

be expected, the corners carry no stress. The stress distribution at $b/4$ and $b/2$ below the top, shown in Fig. 3-10(c), are in reasonable agreement with the more accurate results given in Figs. 3-9(b) and (c). Better agreement can be achieved by using a finer mesh. However, no matter how fine a mesh is chosen, the finite element procedure cannot provide a solution *at a point load.* In Fig. 3-10(b) this is identified by a cross-hatched element. The same is true in the classical mathematical theory of elasticity, and one has to resort to the procedures of *fracture mechanics to obtain insight into such problems.*

The versatile method of finite elements can be applied to bodies of any shape and for any load distribution. Its use in accurate stress analysis problems is gaining an ever wider use. However, because of the simplicity of the procedures discussed in this text, at least for preliminary design, they remain indispensable.

The example just cited is extreme, since theoretically infinite stresses appear to be possible at the concentrated force. There are numerous situations, however, such as at bolt holes or changes in cross section, where the *maximum* normal stresses are finite. These maximum stresses, in relation to the *average* stress as given by Eq. 1-6 for linearly elastic materials, depend *only* on the *geometrical proportions* of a member. The ratio of the maximum to the average stress is called the *stress-concentration factor,* desig-

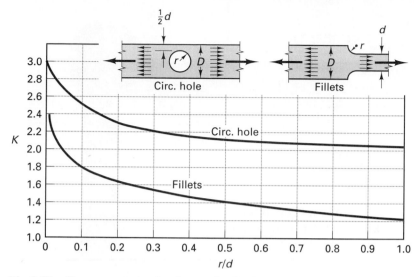

Fig. 3-11   Stress-concentration factors for flat bars in tension.

nated in this text as K. Many such factors are available in technical literature[5] as functions of the geometrical parameters of members. For the
example given before, at a depth below the top equal to one-quarter width,
$K = 2.575$. Hence $\sigma_{max} = 2.575\ \sigma_{av}$. Generalizing this scheme, the maximum normal stress at a section is

$$\sigma_{max} = K\sigma_{av} = K\frac{P}{A} \tag{3-11}$$

where K is an appropriate stress-concentration factor, and P/A is the average stress per Eq. 1-6.

Two particularly significant stress-concentration factors for *flat* axially
loaded bars are shown in Fig. 3-11.[6] The Ks that may be read from the graphs
give the *ratio* of the maximum normal stress to the average stress on the net
section as shown in Fig. 3-12. A considerable stress concentration also occurs
at the root of threads. This depends to a large degree on the sharpness of the
cut. For ordinary threads, the stress-concentration factor is on the order of 2
to 3. The application of Eq. 3-11 presents no difficulties, provided proper
graphs or tables of K are available. In the past many such factors have been
determined using the methods of photoelasticity (see Section 13-4).

[5]R. J. Roark and W. C. Young, *Formulas for Stress and Strain,* 5th ed. (New York:
McGraw-Hill, 1975).

[6]This figure is adapted from M. M. Frocht, "Factors of stress concentration photoelastically determined," *Trans. ASME,* **57,** (1935), A-67.

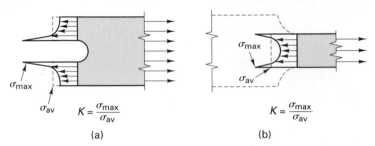

$$K = \frac{\sigma_{max}}{\sigma_{av}} \qquad \qquad K = \frac{\sigma_{max}}{\sigma_{av}}$$

(a)   (b)

Fig. 3-12   Measuring of the stress-concentration factor K.

Fig. 3-13   Low-cycle tensile fatigue fracture of 7/8 in A325 steel bolt.

An example of low-cycle fatigue fracture in tension of a high-strength bolt with a minimum specified strength of 120 ksi (830 MPa) is shown in Fig. 3-13. Note that the fracture occurred at the root of the threads.

Example 3-7

Find the maximum stress in member AB in the forked end A in Example 1-3.

SOLUTION
Geometrical proportions:

$$\frac{\text{radius of the hole}}{\text{net width}} = \frac{3/16}{1/2} = 0.375$$

From Fig. 3-11:[7] $K \approx 2.15$ for $r/d = 0.375$.
Average stress from Example 1-3: $\sigma_{av} = P/A_{net} = 11.2$ ksi.
Maximum stress, Eq. 3.11: $\sigma_{max} = K\sigma_{av} = 2.15 \times 11.2 = 24.1$ ksi.

This answer indicates that a large local increase in stress occurs at this hole, a fact that may be highly significant.

In considering stress-concentration factors in design, it must be remembered that their theoretical or photoelastic determination is based on the use of Hooke's law. If members are *gradually* stressed beyond the proportional limit of a *ductile* material, these factors lose their significance. For example, consider a flat bar of *mild steel,* of the proportions shown in Fig. 3-14, that is subjected to a gradually increasing force P. The stress distribution will be geometrically similar to that shown in Fig. 3-12 until σ_{max} reaches the yield point of the material. This is illustrated in the top diagram in Fig. 3-14.

---

[7]Actually, the stress concentration depends on the condition of the hole, whether it is empty or filled with a bolt or pin.

However, with a further increase in the applied force, σ_{max} remains the same, as a great deal of deformation can take place while the material yields. Therefore, the stress at A remains virtually frozen at the same value. Nevertheless, for equilibrium, stresses acting over the net area must be high enough to resist the increased P. This condition is shown in the middle diagram of Fig. 3-14. Finally, for ideally plastic material, stress becomes uniform across the entire net section. Hence, for ductile materials prior to rupture, the local stress concentration is practically eliminated, and a nearly uniform distribution of stress across the net section occurs prior to necking.

The previous argument is not quite as true for materials less ductile than mild steel. Nevertheless, the tendency is in that direction unless the material is unusually brittle, like glass. The argument presented applies to situations where the force is gradually applied or is static in character. *It is not applicable for fluctuating loads, as found in some machine parts.* For fatigue loadings, the working stress level that is actually reached *locally* determines the fatigue behavior of the member. The maximum permissible stress is set from an *S-N* diagram (Section 2-10). *Failure of most machine parts can be traced to progressive cracking that originates at points of high stress.* In machine design, then, stress concentrations are of paramount importance, although some machine designers feel that the theoretical stress concentration factors are somewhat high. Apparently, some tendency is present to smooth out the stress peaks, even in members subjected to cyclic loads.

From the previous discussion and accompanying charts, it should be apparent why a competent machine designer tries to "streamline" the junctures and transitions of elements that make up a structure.

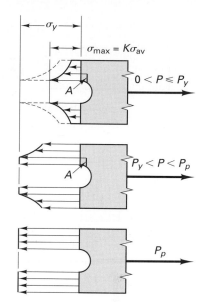

Fig. 3-14   Stress distribution at a hole in an elastic, ideally plastic flat bar with progressively increasing applied force P.

3-4. The Tension Test Revisited

In Sections 2-2 and 2-3 the conventional tension test was described. Now that you have been introduced to the concept of stress concentrations, it is appropriate to point out the dramatic consequences of the presence of stress risers in a tension test. For this purpose consider a sequence of test specimens made from the same mild steel circular bar with different size machined grooves, as shown in Fig. 3-15(a).[8] The smallest width of the circular groove for Bar 12 is 0.5 in (12.72 mm), the one for Bar 13 is 0.75 in (19.05 mm), and the largest for Bar 16 is 8 in (203.2 mm). The shank of a circular specimen such as shown in Fig. 3-15(a) is usually 0.505 in (12.8 mm) in diameter and 15 in (381 mm) long.

The load-displacement diagrams for the preceding array of specimens made from the same material, as shown in Fig. 3-15(b), are entirely different. The material with the small groove in Bar 12 is so thoroughly laterally

---

[8]See C. W. McGregor, "Yield point of mild steel," *Trans. ASME,* **53,** APM-53-15, 187–200. This work was suggested by S. Timoshenko.

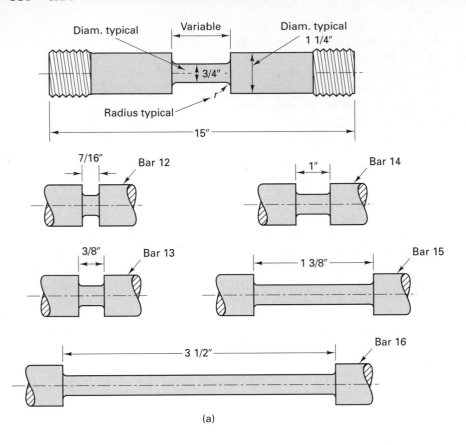

(a)

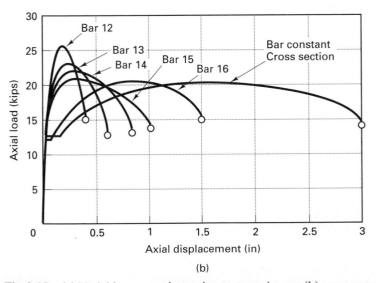

(b)

Fig. 3-15 (a) Variable grooves in tension test specimens; (b) corresponding load-displacement diagrams (adapted from McGregor).

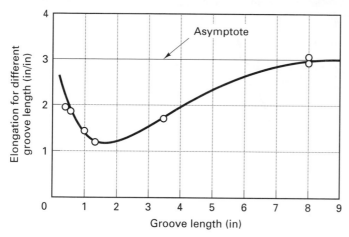

Fig. 3-16   Elongation as function of groove length.

restrained by the low-stressed material in the bar of larger cross section above and below the groove that it cannot deform plastically, and the material strength is mobilized to resist the axial stress. The specimen shows dangerously small ductility, although its axial strength is large. Bar 13, with a slightly longer groove, while decreasing in axial strength, exhibits more ductility. Bars 14 and 15 show further decrease in axial strength but demonstrate a better ductility. A more ductile behavior is further accentuated by Bar 15, and the results from Bar 16 approach the test from a standard-length specimen.

It is instructive to note the percent elongation in bars with different length grooves (Fig. 3-16). Here it can be seen that as the groove width increases, the percent of elongation approaches asymptotically a constant value. This explains the reason for a standard length of a test bar to be relatively long.

The dramatically different behavior of material at notches and grooves is clearly brought out by Fig. 3-16. The actual stress distribution in and near a groove now can be carefully examined by the finite element method using a very fine mesh. The problem is very important in critical applications.

3-5. Elastic Strain Energy for Uniaxial Stress

In mechanics, energy is defined as the capacity to do work, and work is the product of a force times the distance in the direction that the force moves. In solid deformable bodies, stresses multiplied by their respective areas are forces, and deformations are distances. The product of these two quantities is the *internal work* done in a body by externally applied forces. This internal work is stored in an elastic body as the *internal elastic energy of*

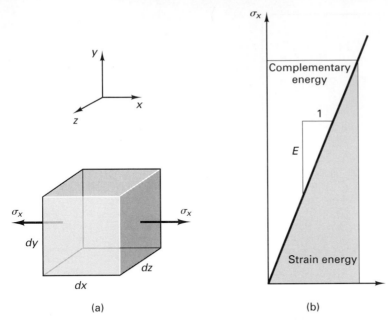

Fig. 3-17   (a) An element in uniaxial tension and (b) a Hookean stress-strain diagram.

deformation, or the *elastic strain energy.* A procedure for computing the internal energy in axially loaded bars is discussed next.

Consider an infinitesimal element, such as shown in Fig. 3-17(a), subjected to a normal stress σ_x. The force acting on the right or the left face of this element is $\sigma_x \, dy \, dz$, where $dy \, dz$ is an infinitesimal area of the element. Because of this force, the element elongates an amount $\varepsilon_x \, dx$, where ε_x is normal strain in the x direction. If the element is made of a linearly elastic material, stress is proportional to strain; Fig. 3-17(b). Therefore, if the element is initially free of stress, the force that finally acts on the element increases linearly from zero until it attains its full value. The average force acting on the element while deformation is taking place is $\frac{1}{2}\sigma_x \, dy \, dz$. This average force multiplied by the distance through which it acts is the work done on the element. For a perfectly elastic body, no energy is dissipated and the work done on the element is stored as recoverable internal strain energy. Thus, the internal elastic strain energy U for an infinitesimal element subjected to uniaxial stress is

$$dU = \underbrace{\underbrace{\tfrac{1}{2}\sigma_x \, dy \, dz}_{\substack{\text{average} \\ \text{force}}} \times \underbrace{\varepsilon_x \, dx}_{\text{distance}}}_{\text{work}} = \tfrac{1}{2}\sigma_x \varepsilon_x \, dx \, dy \, dz = \tfrac{1}{2}\sigma_x \varepsilon_x \, dV \qquad (3\text{-}12)$$

where dV is the volume of the element.

By recasting Eq. 3-12, one obtains the strain energy stored in an elastic body per *unit volume* of the material, or its *strain-energy density U_o*. Thus,

$$U_o = \frac{dU}{dV} = \frac{\sigma_x \varepsilon_x}{2} \tag{3-13}$$

This expression may be graphically interpreted as an area under the inclined line on the stress-strain diagram; Fig. 3-17(b). The corresponding area enclosed by the inclined line and the vertical axis is called the *complementary energy*, a concept to be used in Chapter 18. For linearly elastic materials, the two areas are equal. Expressions analogous to Eq. 3-13 apply to the normal stresses σ_y and σ_z and to the corresponding normal strains ε_y and ε_z.

Since in the elastic range Hooke's law applies, $\sigma_x = E\varepsilon_x$, Eq. 3-13 may be written as

$$U_o = \frac{dU}{dV} = \frac{E\varepsilon_x^2}{2} = \frac{\sigma_x^2}{2E} \tag{3-14}$$

or

$$U = \int_{\text{vol}} \frac{\sigma_x^2}{2E} \, dV \tag{3-15}$$

These forms of the equation for the elastic strain energy are convenient in applications, although they mask the dependence of the energy expression on force and distance.

For a particular material, substitution into Eq. 3-14 of the value of the stress at the proportional limit gives an index of the material's ability to store or absorb energy without permanent deformation. The quantity so found is called the *modulus of resilience* and is used to differentiate materials for applications where energy must be absorbed by members. For example, a steel with a proportional limit of 200 MPa and an E of 200 GPa has a modulus of resilience of $\sigma^2/2E = 200^2/2 \times 200 \times 10^3 = 0.10$ N-mm/mm^3, whereas a good grade of Douglas fir, having a proportional limit of 40 MPa and an E of 12 GPa has a comparable modulus of resilience of 0.07 N · mm/mm^3. (See Fig. 2-20.)

By analogous reasoning, the area under a complete stress-strain diagram, Fig. 3-18, gives a measure of a material's ability to absorb energy up to fracture and is called its *toughness*. The larger the total area under the stress-strain diagram, the tougher the material. In the inelastic range, only a small part of the energy absorbed by a material is recoverable. Most of the energy is *dissipated* in permanently deforming the material and is lost in heat. The energy that may be recovered when a specimen has been stressed to some such point as A in Fig. 3-18(b) is represented by the triangle ABC. Line AB of this triangle is parallel to line OD, since all materials essentially behave elastically upon the release of stress.

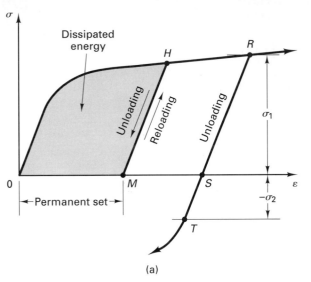

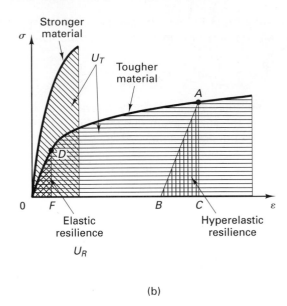

(a)

(b)

Fig. 3-18   Some typical properties of materials.

Example 3-8

Two elastic bars, whose proportions are shown in Fig. 3-19, are to absorb the same amount of energy delivered by axial forces at the free end. Neglecting stress concentrations, compare the stresses in the two bars. The cross-sectional area of the left bar is A, and that of the right bar is A and $2A$ as shown.

SOLUTION

The bar shown in Fig. 3-19(a) is of uniform cross-sectional area; therefore, the normal stress σ_1 is constant throughout. Using Eq. 3-15 and integrating over the volume V of the bar, one can write the total energy for the bar as

$$U_1 = \int_V \frac{\sigma_1^2}{2E}\, dV = \frac{\sigma_2^2}{2E} \int_V dV = \frac{\sigma_1^2}{2E}(AL)$$

where A is the cross-sectional area of the bar and L is its length.

The bar shown in Fig. 3-19(b) is of variable cross section. Therefore, if the stress σ_2 acts in the lower part of the bar, the stress in the upper part is $\frac{1}{2}\sigma_2$. Again, by using Eq. 3-15 and integrating over the volume of the bar, it

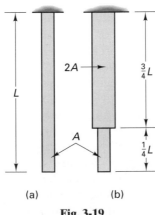

(a)   (b)

Fig. 3-19

is found that the total energy that this bar will absorb in terms of the stress σ_2 is

$$U_2 = \int_V \frac{\sigma^2}{2E} dV = \frac{\sigma_2^2}{2E} \int_{\text{lower part}} dV + \frac{(\sigma_2/2)^2}{2E} \int_{\text{upper part}} dV$$

$$= \frac{\sigma_2^2}{2E}\left(\frac{AL}{4}\right) + \frac{(\sigma_2/2)^2}{2E}\left(2A\,\frac{3L}{4}\right) = \frac{\sigma_2^2}{2E}\left(\frac{5}{8}AL\right)$$

If both bars are to absorb the same amount of energy, $U_1 = U_2$ and

$$\frac{\sigma_1^2}{2E}(AL) = \frac{\sigma_2^2}{2E}\left(\frac{5}{8}AL\right) \quad \text{or} \quad \sigma_2 = 1.265\sigma_1$$

Hence, for the same energy load, the stress in the "reinforced" bar is 26.5% higher than in the plain bar. The enlargement of the cross-sectional area over a part of the bar is actually detrimental. This situation is not found in the design of members for static loads.

3-6. Deflections by the Energy Method

The principle of conservation of energy may be used very effectively for finding deflections of elastic members due to applied forces. General methods for accomplishing this will be discussed in Chapters 17 and 18. Here a more limited objective, determining the deflection caused by the application of a single axial force, is considered. For such a purpose, the internal strain energy U for a member is that simply equated to the external work W_e due to the applied force. That is,

$$\boxed{U = W_e} \tag{3-16}$$

In this treatment, it is assumed that the external force is gradually applied. This means that, as it is being applied, its full effect on a member is reached in a manner similar to that shown in Fig. 3-17(b) for stress. Therefore, the external work W_e is equal to one-half of the total force multiplied by the deflection in the direction of the force action. In the next section, this approach will be generalized for dynamic loads.

Example 3-9

Find the deflection of the free end of an elastic rod of constant cross-sectional area A and length L due to axial force P applied at the free end.

SOLUTION

If force P is gradually applied to the rod, external work, $W_e = \frac{1}{2}P\Delta$, where Δ is the deflection of the end of the rod. The expression for the internal strain energy U of the rod was found in Example 3-8, and since $\sigma_1 = P/A$, it is

$$U = \frac{\sigma_1^2}{2E}AL = \frac{P^2L}{2AE}$$

Then, from $W_e = U$,

$$\frac{P\Delta}{2} = \frac{P^2L}{2AE} \quad \text{and} \quad \Delta = \frac{PL}{AE}$$

which is the same as Eq. 3-4.

The use of Eq. 3-16 can be extended to bar systems consisting of several members. Since internal strain energy is a positive *scalar* quantity, the energies for the several members can be simply added arithmetically. This total strain energy U can then be equated to the external work W_e caused by one force for finding the deflection in the direction of that force. To illustrate, for the bracket shown in Fig. 3-6 for Example 3-4,

$$U = \frac{1}{2}\frac{P_{AB}^2 L_{AB}}{A_{AB}E} + \frac{1}{2}\frac{P_{BC}^2 L_{BC}}{A_{BC}E} = \frac{1}{2}P\Delta$$

where the subscripts refer to members. A solution of this equation gives deflection Δ of force P.

This method is extended in Chapter 18 to solution of problems with any number of applied forces for finding the deflections at any point in any direction.

3-7. Dynamic and Impact Loads

A freely falling weight, or a moving body, that strikes a structure delivers what is called a *dynamic* or *impact* load or force. Problems involving such forces may be analyzed rather simply on the basis of the following idealizing assumptions:

1. Materials behave elastically, and no dissipation of energy takes place at the point of impact or at the supports due to local inelastic deformation of materials.
2. The inertia of a system resisting an impact may be neglected.
3. The deflection of a system is directly proportional to the magnitude of the applied force whether a force is dynamically or statically applied.

Then, using the principle of conservation of energy, it may be further assumed that at the *instant* a moving body is stopped, its kinetic energy is completely transformed into the internal strain energy of the resisting system. At this instant, the maximum deflection of a resisting system occurs and vibrations begin. However, since only maximum stresses and deflections are of primary interest, this subject will not be pursued.

As an example of a dynamic force applied to an elastic system, consider a falling weight striking a spring. This situation is illustrated in Fig. 3-20(a), where a weight W falls from a height h above the free length of a spring. *This system represents a very general case, since conceptually, every elastic system may be treated as an equivalent spring.* Using the spring constant k, the static deflection Δ_{st} of the spring due to the weight W is $\Delta_{st} = W/k$. Similarly, the maximum dynamic deflection $\Delta_{max} = P_{dyn}/k$, where P_{dyn} is the maximum dynamic force experienced by the spring. Therefore, the dynamic force in terms of the weight W and the deflections of the spring is

$$P_{dyn} = \frac{\Delta_{max}}{\Delta_{st}} W \qquad (3\text{-}17)$$

This relationship is shown in Fig. 3-20(b).

At the instant the spring deflects its maximum amount, all energy of the falling weight is transformed into the strain energy of the spring. Therefore, an equation representing the equality of external work to internal strain energy may be written as

$$W(h + \Delta_{max}) = \frac{1}{2} P_{dyn}\Delta_{max} \qquad (3\text{-}18)$$

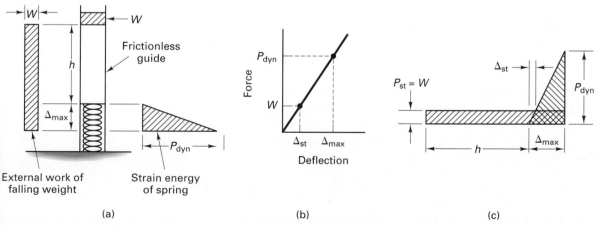

External work of
falling weight

Strain energy
of spring

(a)

(b)

(c)

Fig. 3-20 Behavior of an elastic system under an impact force.

A graphical interpretation of this equation is shown in Fig. 3-20(c). Note that a factor of one-half appears in front of the strain-energy expression, since the spring takes on the load *gradually*. Then, from Eq. 3-17,

$$W(h + \Delta_{max}) = \frac{1}{2} \frac{(\Delta_{max})^2}{\Delta_{st}} W$$

or

$$(\Delta_{max})^2 - 2\Delta_{st}\Delta_{max} - 2h\Delta_{st} = 0$$

Hence

$$\Delta_{max} = \Delta_{st} + \sqrt{(\Delta_{st})^2 + 2h\Delta_{st}}$$

or

$$\Delta_{max} = \Delta_{st}\left(1 + \sqrt{1 + \frac{2h}{\Delta_{st}}}\right) \qquad (3\text{-}19)$$

and, again using Eq. 3-17,

$$\boxed{P_{dyn} = W\left(1 + \sqrt{1 + \frac{2h}{\Delta_{st}}}\right)} \qquad (3\text{-}20)$$

Equation 3-19 gives the maximum deflection occurring in a spring struck by a weight W falling from a height h, and Eq. 3-20 gives the maximum force experienced by the spring for the same condition. To apply these equations, the static deflection Δ_{st} caused by the gradually applied known weight W is computed by the formulas derived earlier.

After the effective dynamic force P_{dyn} is found, it may be used in computations as a static force. The magnification effect of a static force when dynamically applied is termed the *impact factor* and is given by the expression in parentheses appearing in Eqs. 3-19 and 3-20. The impact factor is surprisingly large in most cases. For example, if a force is applied to an elastic system *suddenly* (i.e., $h = 0$), it is equivalent to *twice* the same force *gradually* applied. If h is large compared to Δ_{st}, the impact factor is approximately equal to $\sqrt{2h/\Delta_{st}}$.

Similar equations may be derived for the case where a weight W is moving horizontally with a velocity v and is suddenly stopped by an elastic body. For this purpose, it is necessary to replace the external work done by the falling weight in the preceding derivation by the kinetic energy of a moving body, *using a consistent system of units*. Therefore, since the kinetic energy of a moving body is $Wv^2/2g$, where g is the acceleration of gravity, it can be shown that

$$P_{dyn} = W\sqrt{\frac{v^2}{g\Delta_{st}}} \quad \text{and} \quad \Delta_{max} = \Delta_{st}\sqrt{\frac{v^2}{g\Delta_{st}}} \qquad (3\text{-}21)$$

where Δ_{st} is the static deflection caused by W acting in the horizontal direction. In Eq. 3-21, W is in U.S. customary units.

Example 3-10

Determine the maximum stress in the steel rod shown in Fig. 3-21 caused by a mass of 4 kg falling freely through a distance of 1 m. Consider two cases: one as shown in the figure, and another when the rubber washer is removed. For the steel rod, assume $E = 200$ GPa, and for the washer, take $k = 4.5$ N/mm.

SOLUTION

The 4-kg mass applies a static force $P = ma = 4 \times 9.81 = 39.2$ N. The rod area $A = \pi \times 15^2/4 = 177$ mm². Note that the rod length is 1500 mm.

Solution for rod with washer:

$$\Delta_{st} = \frac{PL}{AE} + \frac{P}{k} = \frac{39.2 \times 1500}{177 \times 200 \times 10^3} + \frac{39.2}{4.5}$$

$$= 1.66 \times 10^{-3} + 8.71 = 8.71 \text{ mm}$$

$$\sigma_{max-dyn} = \frac{P_{dyn}}{A} = \frac{39.2}{177}\left(1 + \sqrt{1 + \frac{2 \times 1}{8.71 \times 10^{-3}}}\right) = 3.58 \text{ MPa}$$

Solution for rod without washer:

$$\sigma_{max-dyn} = \frac{39.2}{177}\left(1 + \sqrt{1 + \frac{2 \times 1}{1.66 \times 10^{-6}}}\right) = 243 \text{ MPa}$$

The large difference in the stresses for the two solutions suggests the need for flexible systems for resisting dynamic loads. A further study of this problem, and taking into account the results obtained in Example 3-8, leads to the conclusion that for obtaining the smallest dynamic stresses for the same system, one should

1. select a material with a small elastic modulus;
2. make the total volume of the member large;
3. stress the material uniformly, and avoid stress concentrations.

Several cases can be cited as illustrations of practical situations where these principles are used. Wood is used in railroad ties since its E is low, and the cost per unit volume of the material is small. In pneumatic cylinders and jackhammers, Fig. 3-22, very long bolts are used to attach the ends to the tube. Long bolts provide a large volume of material, which, in operation, is uniformly stressed in tension. In the early stages of the development of this equipment, short bolts were used, and frequent failures occurred.

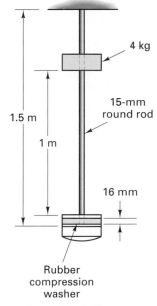

Fig. 3-21

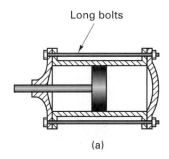

Long bolts

(a)

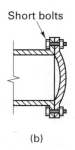

Short bolts

(b)

Fig. 3-22   (a) Good design and (b) bad design of a pneumatic cylinder.

PROBLEMS

Section 3-2

3-1. A cast magnesium alloy bar 500 mm long is to resist an axial tensile force of 10 kN. What should the diameter of the bar be so not to exceed the axial stress of 100 MPa or elongation of 0.1%?

3-2. A steel rod 10 m long used in a control mechanism must transmit a tensile force of 5 kN without stretching more than 4 mm or exceeding an allowable stress of 150 MPa. (a) What is the diameter of the rod? Give the answer to the nearest millimeter. $E = 210$ GPa. Does strength or stiffness of the rod control the design? (b) Find the spring constant for the rod.

3-3. Revise the data in Example 3-2 to read as follows: $P_1 = 10$ kips, $P_3 = 100$ kips, and $P_4 = 50$ kips; the bar segments AB, BC, and CD are, respectively, 4, 2, and 3ft long. Then find (a) the force P_2 necessary for equilibrium and (b) the total elongation of rod AD. The cross-sectional area of the rod from A to B is 1 in², from B to C is 4 in², and from C to D is 2 in². Let $E = 30 \times 10^3$ ksi. (c) Plot the axial displacement diagram along the bar. (d) Find the axial spring constant of the bar.

3-4. A mass $m = 2$ kg is attached to a 20-mm-diameter nickel alloy rod 400 mm long. Determine the frequency of vibration. Consider mass concentrated at a point, and neglect the weight of the rod. For the rod, let $E = 180$ GPa. The natural frequency of vibration is given as $f = \sqrt{g/\Delta}/(2\pi)$ Hz, where g is the gravitational acceleration and Δ is the statical deflection of the system.

3-5. Consider the three metal balls problem described in Problem P1-13 and develop a solution with masses located for minimum stresses in the wires. Then (a) plot the axial forces distribution in the three wires, (b) plot the axial strain in the wires, and (c) plot displacement diagram for the balls. Assume that the relevant deformations occur in the wires only (i.e., consider the balls rigid). All wires are of equal length (1000 mm) and, beginning at the top, have the following diameters: 2 mm, 1.5 mm, and 1 mm, respectively. The wires are made of high-strength steel having an $E = 200$ GPa and ultimate strength $\sigma_{ult} = 1200$ MPa.

3-6. In Example 3-2, Fig. 3-3, assume that point O is fixed. Reverse the direction of force P_4, and determine its magnitude such that the point D would not move. Plot the axial force, axial strain, and displacement diagrams for the bar with the revised conditions.

3-7. Assume that segments L_1, L_2, and L_3 of the round member of variable cross section in Problem 1-10 are, respectively, 600, 500, and 400 mm long. Plot the axial force, the axial strain, and the axial displacement diagrams along the bar length $E = 200$ GPa. Find the axial spring constant for the system.

3-8. A solid bar 50 mm in diameter and 2000 mm long consists of a steel and an aluminum part fastened together, as shown in the figure. When axial force P is applied to the system, a strain gage attached to the aluminum indicates an axial strain of 873 μm/m. (a) Determine the magnitude of applied force P. (b) If the sys-

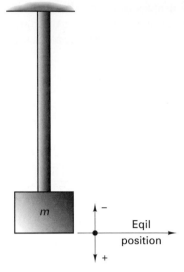

Fig. P3-4

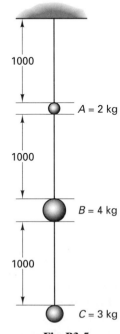

1000

$A = 2$ kg

1000

$B = 4$ kg

1000

$C = 3$ kg

Fig. P3-5

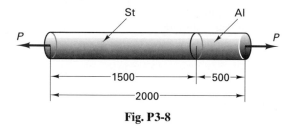

Fig. P3-8

tem behaves elastically, find the total elongation of the bar. Let $E_{St} = 200$ GPa, and $E_{Al} = 70$ GPa.

3-9. An AE42X1 die cast magnesium alloy bar 600 mm long with a cross-sectional area of 200 mm² is axially loaded by a force P. The stress-strain diagram for the material can be idealized as shown in the figure. If this bar is strained five times the 0.2% offset tensile strength, what force does the bar carry? If the applied force is released, what remains as the permanent set in the bar?

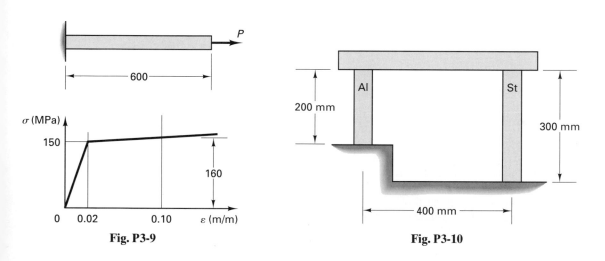

Fig. P3-9   **Fig. P3-10**

3-10. A rigid bar rests on aluminum-alloy and steel uprights, as shown in the figure. (a) Determine the inclination of the horizontal bar after a raise in temperature of 100°C. Assume the coefficients of thermal expansion for aluminum alloy and steel to be, respectively, $23.2 \times 10^{-6}/°C$ and $11.7 \times 10^{-6}/°C$. To a greatly exaggerated scale, sketch the position of the bar after the raise in temperature. (b) What stresses would develop in the upright members if their tops were prevented from expanding? Let the elastic moduli for aluminum alloy and steel be, respectively, 75 GPa and 200 GPa. Compare the obtained stresses with those given in Table 1 of the Appendix. (*Hint:* The tendency for thermal expansion is counteracted by elastic contraction.)

3-11.   A steel bar 2 in wide and 0.5 in thick is 25 in long, as shown in the figure. On application of force P, the bar width becomes narrower by 0.3×10^{-3} in. Estimate the magnitude of applied force P and the axial elongation of the bar. Assume elastic behavior and take $E = 30 \times 10^3$ ksi and $v = 0.25$.

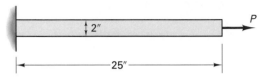

Fig. P3-11

3-12.   A 10-mm-thick, low-alloy-steel plate 180 mm wide and 2000 mm long is subjected to a set of uniformly distributed frictional forces along its two edges, as shown in the figure. If the total decrease in the transverse 180-mm dimension at section a–a due to the applied forces is 16×10^{-3} mm, what is the total elongation of the bar in the longitudinal direction? Let $E = 200$ GPa and $v = 0.25$. Assume that the steel behaves as a linearly elastic material.

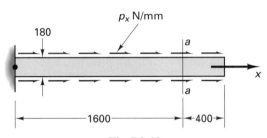

Fig. P3-12

3-13.   A uniform timber pile, which has been driven to a depth L in clay, carries an applied load of F at the top. This load is resisted entirely by friction f along the pile, which varies in the parabolic manner shown in the figure. (a) Determine the total shortening of the pile in terms of F, L, A, and E. (b) If $P = 400$ kN, $L = 10$ m, $A = 64{,}000$ mm^2, and $E = 10$ GPa, how much does such a pile shorten? (*Hint:* From the equilibrium requirement, first determine the constant k.)

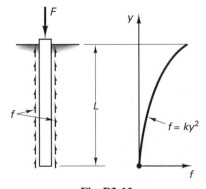

Fig. P3-13

3-14.   Two wires are connected to a rigid bar, as shown in the figure. The wire on the left is of copper alloy having $A = 0.10$ in^2 and $E = 20 \times 10^6$ psi. The aluminum-alloy wire on the right has $A = 0.20$ in^2 and $E = 10 \times 10^6$ psi. (a) If a weight $W = 2000$ lb is applied as shown, how much will it deflect due to the stretch in the wires? (b) Where should the weight be located such that the bar would remain horizontal?

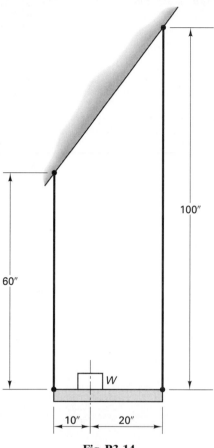

100"

60"

W

10"   20"

Fig. P3-14

3-15.   In Example 3-3, Fig. 3-4, determine the magnitude of an upward force that would have to be applied at the free end to cause no displacement of the end B. Plot the axial force and the displacement diagrams for the revised problem.

3-16.   In Example 3-3, Fig. 3-4, subdivide the bar length L into four segments similar to that shown in Fig. 3-5, and at the bottom of each segment apply a vertical downward force $W/4$. Determine the deflection of point B using this approximation, and compare it with $\Delta = WL/(2AE)$. Repeat the solution by subdividing the length of the bar into 10 segments applying $W/10$ forces at the nodes, and note the improvement in the results. Try subdividing the bar into 20 segments.

3-17. A wall bracket is constructed as shown in the figure. All joints may be considered pin connected. Steel rod AB has a cross-sectional area of 5 mm². Member BC is a rigid beam. If a 1000-mm-diameter frictionless drum weighing 500 kg is placed in the position shown, what will be the elongation of rod AB? Let $E = 200$ GN/m².

3-18. Determine the shortening of steel tubular spreader bar AB due to application of tensile forces at C and D. The cross-sectional area of the tube is 100 mm². Let $E = 200$ GPa.

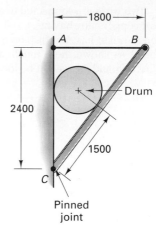

Fig. P3-17

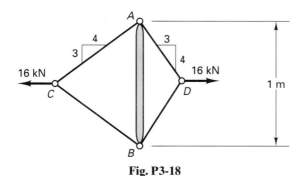

Fig. P3-18

3-19. A planar mechanical system consists of two rigid bars, BD and EG, and three rods, AB, CF, and EH, as shown in the figure. On application of force P at G the stress in all rods is 15 ksi. Each rod is 20 in long. (a) Determine the vertical deflection of points B, D, E, and G caused by the application of force $P = 300$ lb. (Since vertical displacements are small, the horizontal displacements are negligibly small.) (b) Show the deflected shape for the system, greatly exaggerating the vertical displacements. Let $E = 30 \times 10^3$ ksi.

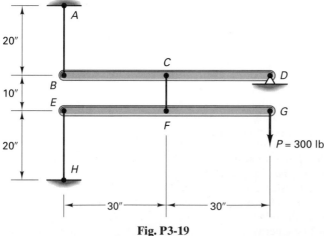

Fig. P3-19

3-20. If in Example 3-3, the rod is a 1-in^2 aluminum bar weighing 1.17 lb/ft, what should its length be for the free end to elongate 0.250 in under its own weight? $E = 10 \times 10^6$ psi.

3-21. What will be the deflection of the free end of the rod in Example 3-3 if, instead of Hooke's law, the stress-strain relationship is $\sigma = E\varepsilon^n$, where n is a number dependent on the properties of the material?

3-22. A rod of two different cross-sectional areas is made of soft copper and is subjected to a tensile load as shown in the figure. (a) Determine the elongation of the rod caused by the application of force $P = 5$ kips. Assume that the axial stress-strain relationship is

$$\varepsilon = \sigma/16{,}000 + (\sigma/165)^3$$

where σ is in ksi. (b) Find the residual bar elongation upon removal of force P. Assume that during unloading, copper behaves as a linearly elastic material with an E equal to the tangent to the virgin σ-ε curve at the origin.

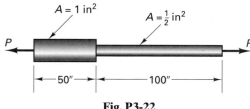

Fig. P3-22

3-23. A two-bar system has the configuration shown in the figure. The cross-sectional area for bar AB is 130 mm^2 and for bar BC is 100 mm^2. If the stress-strain diagram for the rods is bilinear as shown, how much would each wire elongate due to the application of vertical force $P = 20$ kN?

3-24. The small tapered symmetric piece shown in the figure is cut from a 4-mm-thick plate. Determine the increase in length of this piece caused by its own weight when hung from the top. The mass per unit volume for this material is γ and the elastic modulus is E.

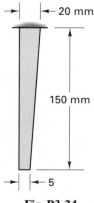

Fig. P3-24

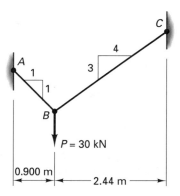

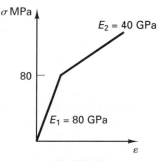

Fig. P3-23

3-25.   Two bars are to be cut from a 1-in-thick metal plate so that both bars have a constant thickness of 1 in. Bar A is to have a constant width of 2 in throughout its entire length. Bar B is to be 3 in wide at the top and 1 in wide at the bottom. Each bar is to be subjected to the same load P. Determine the ratio L_A/L_B so that both bars will stretch the same amount. Neglect the weight of the bar.

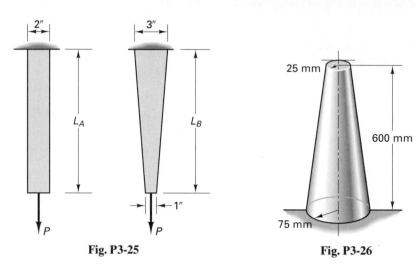

Fig. P3-25   **Fig. P3-26**

3-26.   The dimensions of a frustum of a right circular cone supported at the large end on a rigid base are shown in the figure. Determine the deflection of the top due to the weight of the body. The unit weight of material is γ; the elastic modulus is E. (*Hint:* Consider the origin of the coordinate axes at the vertex of the extended cone.)

3-27.   Find the total elongation Δ of a slender elastic bar of constant cross-sectional area A, such as shown in the figure, if it is rotated in a horizontal plane with an angular velocity of ω radians per second. The unit weight of the material is γ. Neglect the small amount of extra material by the pin. (*Hint:* First find the stress at a section a distance r from the pin by integrating the effect of the inertial forces between r and L. See Example 1-4.)

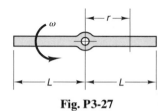

Fig. P3-27

3-28.   An elastic rod having a cross-sectional area A is bonded to the surrounding material, which has a thickness a, as shown in the figure. Determine the change in the length of the rod due to the application of force P. Assume that the support provided for the rod by the surrounding material varies linearly as shown. Express the answer in terms of $P, A, a,$ and E, where E is the elastic modulus of the rod.

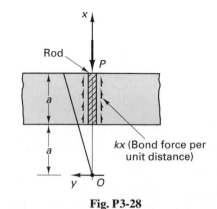

Fig. P3-28

3-29.   For the same frame as in Example 3-4, Fig. 3-6, find the horizontal and vertical deflections at point B caused by applying a horizontal force of 3 kips at B. Assume linearly elastic behavior of the material.

3-30.   Determine the horizontal and vertical elastic displacements of load point B for the two-bar system having the dimensions shown in the figure. Assume that for each bar, $AE = 10^4$ kips.

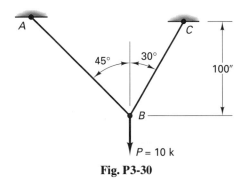

Fig. P3-30

3-31.   For the data given in Problem 3-20, assuming linearly elastic behavior, find the horizontal and vertical displacements of load point B. Let $E = 80$ GPa.

3-32.   Rework Example 3-5, Fig. 3-7, assuming that only the bar AB experiences an increase in temperature.

3-33.   A jib crane has the dimensions shown in the figure. Rod AB has a cross-sectional area of 300 mm^2 and tube BC, 320 mm^2. (a) Find the vertical stiffness of the crane at point B. (b) Determine the vertical deflection caused by the application of force $P = 16$ kN. Let $E = 200$ GPa.

3-34.   Assume that in Problem 3-33 the force P is replaced by a mass of 2000 kg attached at B. Determine the natural frequency of vibration in the vertical direction for this system. The fundamental frequency of vibration is given by $f = \sqrt{g/\Delta}/(2\pi)$ Hz, where g is the gravitational acceleration and Δ is the statical deflection.

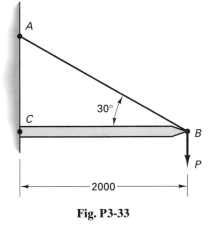

Fig. P3-33

3-35.   For the data given in Problem 3-23, find the vertical and horizontal displacement of point B caused by a rise in temperature of 100°F in the rod. Assume elastic behavior and use α and E given in Table 1B of the Appendix for 6061-T6 aluminum alloy.

3-36.   For the data given in Problem 3-33, find the vertical and horizontal displacements of point B caused by a rise in temperature of 80°C only in the rod. Let $\alpha = 11.7 \times 10^{-6}/°C$.

Section 3-3

3-37.   A 6- by 75-mm plate 600 mm long has a circular hole of 25 mm diameter located in its center. Find the axial tensile force that can be applied to this plate in the longitudinal direction without exceeding an allowable stress of 220 MPa.

3-38. Determine the extent by which a machined flat tensile bar used in a mechanical application is weakened by having an enlarged section, as shown in the figure. Since the bar is to be loaded cyclically, consider stress concentrations.

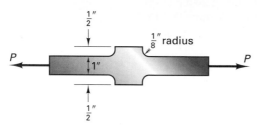

Fig. P3-38

3-39. A machine part 10 mm thick, having the dimensions shown in the figure, is to be subjected to cyclic loading. If the maximum stress is limited to 60 MPa, determine allowable force P. Approximate the stress concentration factors from Fig. 3-11. Where might a potential fracture occur?

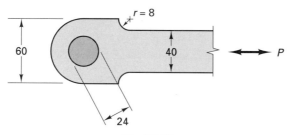

Fig. P3-39

3-40. A machine part of constant thickness for transmitting cyclical axial loading should have the dimensions shown in the figure. (a) Select the thickness needed in the member for transmitting an axial force of 12 kN in order to limit the maximum stress to 80 MPa. Approximate the stress concentration factors from Fig. 3-11. (b) Where might a potential fracture occur?

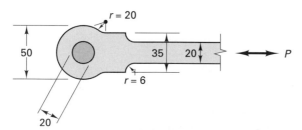

Fig. P3-40

3-41.   One end of a 10-mm-square steel bar for cyclic load application is shown in the figure. Assuming that it is intended for service of 10×10^6 constant-amplitude cyclic loading with a safety factor of 2, determine the strength of this attachment. Use Figs. 2-25 and 3-11 for estimating the allowable stress.

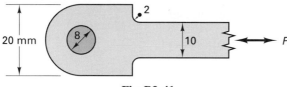

Fig. P3-41

3-42.   A long slot is made from a 10- by 60-mm alloy steel bar 240 mm long, as shown in the figure. (a) Find the maximum stress if axial force $P = 300$ kN is applied to the bar. Assume that the upper curve in Fig. 3-11 is applicable. (b) For the same case, determine the total elongation of the rod. Neglect local effects of stress concentrations and assume that the reduced cross-sectional area extends for 120 mm. (c) Estimate the elongation of the same rod if $P = 350$ kN. Assume that steel yields 0.020 mm/mm at a stress of 1000 MPa. (d) On removal of the load in part (c), what is the residual deflection? Let $E = 200$ GPa.

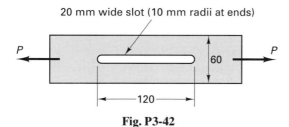

Fig. P3-42

Section 3-4

3-43.   Compare elastic resiliences at yield points, and hyperelastic resiliences just short of the ultimate tensile strength, for three materials: 2024-T4 aluminum alloy, AM100A magnesium alloy, and 0.2% carbon steel. Use Table 1A for physical properties of the material.

3-44.   Using the data in Figs. 3-15(a) and (b), make an estimate of the modulus of toughness for the three bars: No. 12, No. 15, and a bar of constant cross section. Note that the curves are shown with axial loads and axial displacements. As given, they are not stress-strain diagrams. What conclusions can be drawn for practical applications?

Sections 3-5 and 3-6

3-45.   Verify the vertical deflection of point B caused by applied force $P = 3$ kips in Example 3-4 using Eq. 3-16.

3-46.   By applying Eq. 3-16, find the deflection of point G in Problem 3-16.

3-47. Find the vertical deflection of point B caused by the applied load in Problem 3-26 using Eq. 3-16.

3-48. Find the vertical deflection of point B caused by the applied force P in Problem 3-28 using Eq. 3-16.

3-49. A mechanical system consisting of a steel spreader bar AB and four high-strength steel rods, AC, CB, AD, and DB, is subjected to forces at C and D, as shown in the figure. Determine the increase in distance CD that would occur on applying the two 8-kN forces. Both bars AC and CB have a cross-sectional area of 20 mm², and both bars AD and DB, 40 mm². The cross-sectional area of the spreader bar is 100 mm². Let $E = 200$ GPa.

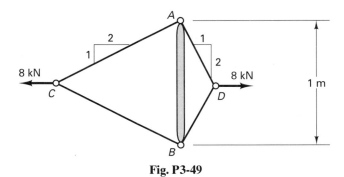

Fig. P3-49

Section 3-7

3-50. Compare the dynamic stresses in the three steel bars of different diameters shown in the figure in their response to 1.5-kg masses falling freely through a distance of 1 m. Let $E = 200$ GPa. Assume no energy is dissipated through plastic deformation of the impact surfaces or at points of high local stresses occurring at supports.

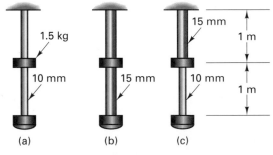

Fig. P3-50

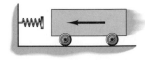

Fig. P3-51

3-51. Determine the stiffness required in the spring, for the system shown in the figure, for stopping a mass of 2 kg moving at a velocity of 3 m/s such that, during impact, the spring deflection would not exceed 20 mm. Neglect frictional effects.

4

Axial Deformation of Bars: Statically Indeterminate Systems

4-1. Introduction

The preceding chapter considered axial deformation of statically determinate bars due to various causes. This chapter extends this topic to the treatment of a much broader class of statically indeterminate systems. The mere fact that both ends of a bar are restrained from movement or rigidly held requires a supplementary investigation of the deformation of such bar systems to satisfy the geometric boundary conditions. Both linearly elastic and inelastic cases are considered, and several different approaches for the solution of such problems are advanced.

4-2. General Considerations

As pointed in Section 1-9, for some structural systems, the equations for static equilibrium are insufficient for determining reactions. In such cases, some of the reactions are superfluous or redundant for maintaining equilibrium. In some other situations, redundancy may also result if some of the internal forces cannot be determined using the equations of statics alone. In both cases such statical indeterminacy can arise in axially loaded systems. Two simple idealized examples are shown in Fig. 4-1. For the system shown in Fig. 4-1(a), reactions R_1 and R_2 cannot be determined using equations of statics alone. However, for the system shown in Fig. 4-1(b), whereas the reaction can be readily found, the distribution of forces between the two springs requires additional consideration. In both instances, the deformation characteristics of the system components must be considered.

There are various procedures for resolving structural indeterminacy in order to reduce a problem to statical determinacy such that the internal forces can readily be found. Common to all of these procedures, the same three basic concepts encountered before are applied and must be satisfied:

1. *Equilibrium conditions* for the system must be assured both in the local and global sense.
2. *Geometric compatibility* among the deformed parts of a body and at the boundaries must be satisfied.
3. *Constitutive relations* (stress-strain relations) for the materials of the system must be complied with.

Two general methods for solving simpler problems will be presented. The approach in one of these methods consists of first removing and then restoring a redundant reaction such that the compatibility condition at the boundaries is satisfied. This is the *force method* of analysis, since solution is obtained directly for the unknown reaction forces. Alternatively, the compatibility of displacements of adjoining members and at the boundaries is maintained throughout the loading process, and solutions for displacements are obtained from equilibrium equations. This is the *displacement method* of analysis.

It is important to reiterate that in either one of these methods, the fundamental problem consists of fulfilling the three basic requirements: *equilibrium, compatibility,* and *conformity with constitutive relations.* The sequence in which they are applied is immaterial.

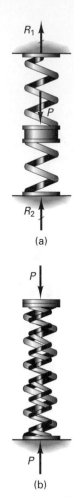

Fig. 4-1 Examples of (a) external statical indeterminacy, and (b) internal statical indeterminancy.

4-3. Force Method of Analysis

As an example of the force method of analysis, consider the linearly elastic axially loaded bar system shown in Fig. 4-2. The initially undeformed bars are shown in Fig. 4-2(a) with zig-zag lines as a reminder that they can be treated as springs. On applying force P at B, reactions R_1 and R_2 develop at the ends and the system deforms, as shown in Fig. 4-2(b). Since only one nontrivial equation of statics is available for determining the two reactions, this system is statically indeterminate to the first degree. Here the upward direction of the applied force P, as well as that assumed for R_1 and R_2, coincides

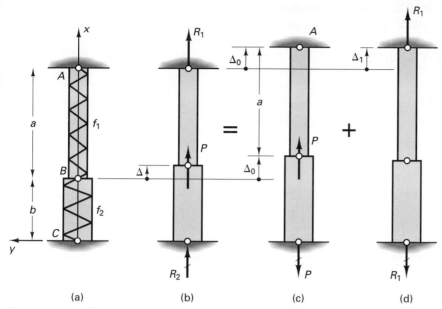

Fig. 4-2   Force (flexibility) method of elastic analysis for a statically indeterminate axially loaded bar. Deformations are greatly exaggerated.

with the positive direction of the x axis. For this reason, these quantities will be treated as positive. With this sign convention, if an applied force acts downward, it would be taken as negative. A calculated reaction with a negative sign signifies that it acts in the opposite direction from the assumed. Adherence to this sign convention is desirable, although in axially loaded bar problems, it is not essential since the directions of deflections and reactions usually can be seen by inspection. However, for computer solutions, as well as for the more complex problems discussed in Chapter 17 and 18, a strict adherence to a selected sign convention becomes necessary.

In applying the force method to axially loaded bars, one of the reactions is temporarily removed, making the system statically determinate. Here an arbitrary choice is made to remove the upper reaction R_1, permitting the system of two bar segments to deform, as shown in Fig. 4-2(c). Such a simplified structural system is referred to as the *primary system,* since, from the point of view of statics, it can, by itself, carry the applied load. (However, from the point of view of strength, the redundant reaction may be necessary and, thus, in the actual field situation, cannot be removed.) Note that only the bottom bar segment is stressed here. Therefore, the same axial deformation Δ_0 occurs at A, at the top of bar, as at point B. Then if the flexibility of the lower elastic bar is f_2, the deflection

$$\Delta_0 = f_2 P \qquad (4\text{-}1)$$

This result, shown in Fig. 4-2(c), violates the geometric boundary condition at A. In order to comply, the deflection Δ_1 caused by R_1 acting on the *unloaded* bar ABC is found next; see Fig. 4-2(d). This deflection is caused by the stretching of both bars. Therefore, if the flexibilities of these bars are f_1 and f_2, Fig. 4-2(a), the deflection

$$\Delta_1 = (f_1 + f_2)R_1 \qquad (4\text{-}2)$$

The compatibility of deformations at A is then achieved by requiring that

$$\boxed{\Delta_0 + \Delta_1 = 0} \qquad (4\text{-}3)$$

By substituting Eqs. 4-1 and 4-2 into Eq. 4-3 and solving for R_1, one has

$$R_1 = -\frac{f_2}{f_1 + f_2}P \qquad (4\text{-}4)$$

The negative sign of the result indicates that R_1 acts in the opposite direction from the assumed. As to be expected, according to Eq. 4-2, this also holds true for Δ_1.

The complete solution of this statically indeterminate problem is the algebraic sum of the solutions shown in Figs. 4-2(c) and (d). After the reactions become known, the previously discussed procedures for determining the internal forces and deflections apply.

Inasmuch as member flexibilities are particularly useful in formulating solutions by the force method, this approach is also known as the *flexibility method* of analysis.

The algebraic sum of the two solutions, as before, is an application of the *principle of superposition* and will be encountered frequently in this text. This principle is based upon the premise that the resultant stress or strain in a system due to several forces is the algebraic sum of their effects when separately applied. *This assumption is true only if each effect is linearly related to the force causing it.* It is only approximately true when the deflections or deformations due to one force cause an abnormal change in the effect of another force. Fortunately, the magnitudes of deflections are relatively small in most engineering structures. In that regard, it is important to note that the deformation shown in Figs. 4-2(b) to (d) are *greatly exaggerated.* Moreover, since the deformations are very small, the *undeformed* (i.e., the initial) *bar lengths are used in calculating throughout.*

An illustration of force-deformation relationships for linear and nonlinear systems is shown in Fig. 4-3. For the linear systems considered, here doubling a displacement, say from Δ_1 to Δ_2, also doubles the load. This is not so for a nonlinear system. Therefore, for linear systems experiencing small deformations, the sequence or number of loads is immaterial.

The procedure just described is very general for linear systems, and any number of axial loads, bar cross sections, different material properties, as well as thermal effects on the length of a bar system can be included in the

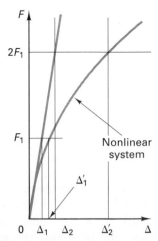

Fig. 4-3   Comparison of force-displacement relationships between linear and nonlinear systems.

analysis. However, the force method is not favored in practice because a systemic selection of the redundants for *large* problems is difficult.

Three examples follow that illustrate applications of the force method to axially loaded elastic bar systems.

Example 4-1

An elastic bar fixed at both ends is loaded as shown in Fig. 4-4. The known flexibility coefficients f and $2f$ for each of the three bar segments are shown in the figure. Determine the reactions and plot the axial force and the axial displacement diagrams for the bar.

SOLUTION

Remove the lower support to obtain the free-body diagram shown in Fig. 4-4(b) and calculate Δ_0. Since the applied forces act downward, because of the sign convention adopted in Fig. 4-2(b), they carry negative signs. The deflection caused by R_2 on an unloaded system is calculated next. Then, on solving Eq. 4-3, the reaction R_2 is determined. The remainder of the solution follows the same procedure as that described in Example 3-2.

$$\Delta_0 = \sum_i f_i P_i = -2fP - f(2P + P) = -5fP$$

and

$$\Delta_1 = (2f + f + f)R_2 = 4fR_2$$

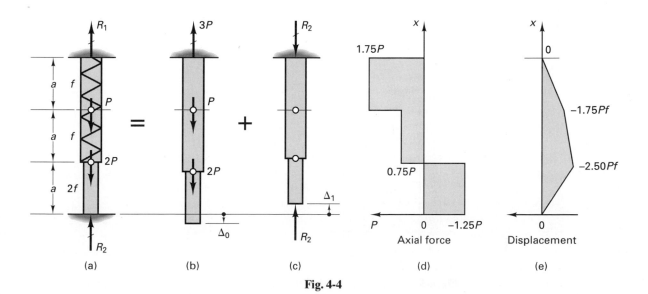

Fig. 4-4

Since

$$\Delta_1 + \Delta_2 = 0, \qquad R_2 = 1.25P$$

Note that the applied forces are supported by a compressive reaction at the bottom and a tensile reaction at the top. In problems where the bar lengths and the cross-sectional areas, together with the elastic moduli I for the materials, are given, the flexibilities are determined using Eq. 3-9.

The axial force diagram is plotted in Fig. 4-4(d). The compressive force in the bottom third of the bar causes a *downward* deflection of $1.25P \times 2f = 2.5Pf$. The tensile forces stretch the remainder of the bar $0.75Pf + 1.75Pf$ such that displacement at the top is zero. In this manner, the kinematic boundary conditions are satisfied at both ends of the bar.

Example 4-2

An elastic bar is held at both ends, as shown in Fig. 4-5. If the bar temperature increases by ΔT, what axial force develops in the bar? AE for the bar is constant.

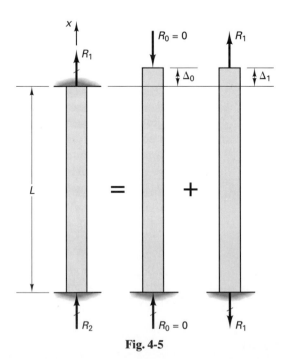

Fig. 4-5

SOLUTION

First, the upper support is removed and Δ_0 is determined using Eq. 2-11. The raising of the temperature causes no axial force in the bar. Thus, by using Eq. 3-8, Δ_1 is calculated. By applying Eq. 4-3, the axial force in the bar, R_1, caused by the rise in temperature is found.

$$\Delta_0 = \alpha \, \Delta T \, L_0$$

and

$$\Delta_1 = R_1 f = \frac{R_1 L}{AE}$$

Since

$$\Delta_0 + \Delta_1 = 0, \qquad R_1 = -\alpha \, \Delta T \, AE$$

Example 4-3

For the planar system of the three elastic bars shown in Fig. 4-6(a), determine the forces in the bars caused by applied force P. The cross-sectional area A of each bar is the same, and their elastic modulus is E.

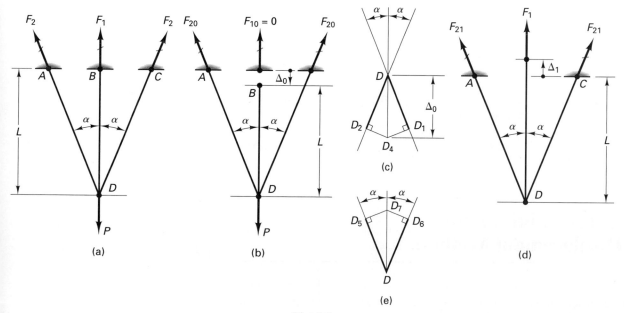

Fig. 4-6

SOLUTION

A free-body diagram of the assumed primary system with the support from the middle bar removed by cutting it at point B is shown in Fig. 4-6(b). Then, by using statics, the forces in the bars are determined, and the deflection of point D is calculated using the procedure illustrated in Example 3-4. Since bar BD carries no force, deflection Δ_0 at point B is the same as it is at point D. Recognizing symmetry,

$$F_{10} = 0 \qquad \text{and} \qquad 2F_{20}\cos\alpha = P$$

Therefore,

$$F_{20} = \frac{P}{2\cos\alpha}$$

Since

$$L_{AD}\cos\alpha = L, \qquad L_{AD} = L/\cos\alpha$$

Hence, per Eq. 3-4, the stretch of bar AD in the primary system is

$$(\Delta_{AD})_0 = \frac{PL}{2AE\cos^2\alpha}$$

However, since Δ_0 equals DD_4 in Fig. 4-6(c),

$$\Delta_0 \cos\alpha = (\Delta_{AD})_0 \qquad \text{and} \qquad \Delta_0 = -\frac{PL}{2AE\cos^3\alpha}$$

where the negative sign signifies that the deflection is downward.

The same kind of relationship applies to the upward deflection of Point D caused by the force F_1; see Figs. 4-6(d) and (e). However, the deflection of point B is increased by the stretch of the bar BD. The latter quantity is calculated using Eq. 3-4 again. On this basis,

$$\Delta_1 = \frac{F_1 L}{AE} + \frac{F_1 L}{2AE\cos^3\alpha}$$

By applying Eq. 4-3 (i.e., $\Delta_0 + \Delta_1 = 0$) and noting from statics that $F_1 + 2F_2\cos\alpha = P$, on simplification,

$$F_1 = \frac{P}{2\cos^3\alpha + 1} \qquad \text{and} \qquad F_2 = \frac{P}{2\cos^3\alpha + 1}\cos^2\alpha \qquad (4\text{-}5)$$

4-4. Introduction to the Displacement Method

Another well-organized procedure for analyzing statically indeterminate problems is based on determining the displacements at selected points and providing information for finding the reactions and internal forces. As an

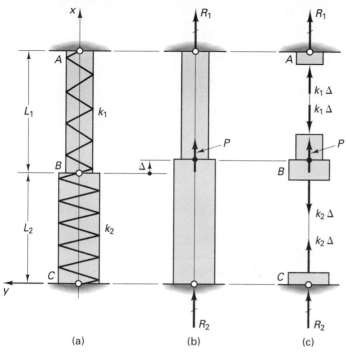

Fig. 4-7   Displacement (stiffness) method of analysis for a statically indeterminate axially loaded bar.

example of this *displacement method* of analysis, consider the elastic axially loaded bar system shown in Fig. 4-7. The stiffnesses, $k_i = A_i E_i / L_i$, Eq. 3-7, for the bar segments are indicated in the figure as k_1 and k_2. An applied force P at point B causes reactions R_1 and R_2. These forces and the displacement Δ at B are considered positive when they act in the positive direction of the x axis. This problem is statically indeterminate to the first degree.

The main objective in this method of analysis is to determine the displacement Δ, the principal parameter of the problem. In this example, there is only one such quantity and therefore the problem is said to have *one degree of kinematic indeterminacy,* or *one degree of freedom.* This is the only class of problems that is discussed in this section. More complex cases with several axial loads and changes in the cross sections of the bars, giving rise to several degrees of freedom, are considered in the next section.

In this illustrative problem, it can be seen that the displacement Δ at B causes compression in the upper bar AB and tension in the lower bar BC. Therefor, if k_1 and k_2 are the respective stiffnesses for the bars, the respective internal forces are $k_1 \Delta$ and $k_2 \Delta$. These *internal* forces and reactions are shown on isolated free-bodies at points A, B, and C in Fig. 4-7(c). These points are referred to as the node points. The sense of the internal forces is known since the upper bar is in compression and the lower one is in tension. By writing an equilibrium equation for the free body at node B, one has

$$-k_1\Delta - k_2\Delta + P = 0 \tag{4-6}$$

and

$$\Delta = \frac{P}{k_1 + k_2} \tag{4-7}$$

The equilibrium equations for the free bodies at nodes A and C are

$$R_1 = -k_1\Delta \quad \text{and} \quad R_2 = -k_2\Delta \tag{4-8}$$

Hence, with the aid of Eq. 4-7,

$$R_1 = -\frac{k_1}{k_1 + k_2}P \quad \text{and} \quad R_2 = -\frac{k_2}{k_1 + k_2}P \tag{4-9}$$

The negative signs in Eq. 4-9 indicate that the reactions act in the opposite direction from the assumed.

Since in this solution bar stiffnesses are employed, this procedure is often called the *stiffness method*.

Example 4-4

An elastic stepped bar is loaded as shown in Fig. 4-8. Using the displacement method, find the reactions. The bar segment stiffnesses k_1 and k_2, their areas A_1 and A_2, and E are given.

SOLUTION
According to Eq. 3-7, the stiffnesses k's for the upper and lower bar segments, respectively, are

$$k_1 = A_1E/a \quad \text{and} \quad k_2 = A_2E/b$$

Therefore, per Eq. 4-7, the deflection Δ at B due to *downward* force P_1 is

$$\Delta = -\frac{P_1}{k_1 + k_2} = -\frac{P_1}{A_1E/a + A_2E/b}$$

According to Eqs. 4-8, $R_1 = -k_1\Delta$ and $R_2 = -k_2\Delta$. By substituting the preceding expressions for Δ, k_1, and k_2, one obtains

$$R_1 = \frac{P_1}{1 + aA_2/bA_1} \quad \text{and} \quad R_2 = \frac{P_1}{1 + bA_1/aA_2} \tag{4-10}$$

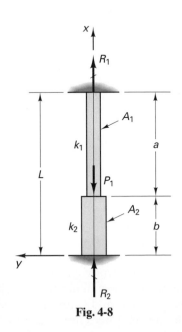

Fig. 4-8

4-5. Displacement Method with Several Degrees of Freedom

In this section the displacement method is extended for axially loaded bars to include several degrees of freedom (d.o.f.). This method is the most widely used approach for solving both linear and nonlinear problems. However, the discussion will be limited to linearly elastic problems. As already noted in the previous section, solution of nonlinear problems using this method is beyond the scope of this text.

The displacement method is perfectly general and can be used for the analysis of statically determinate as well as indeterminate problems. With this in mind, consider a bar system consisting of three segments of variable stiffness defined by their respective spring constants k_i's, as shown in Fig. 4-9(a). Each one of these segments terminates at a node point, some of which are common to the two adjoining bar segments. Each node, marked in the figure from 1 to 4, is permitted to displace vertically in either direction. Therefore, this bar system has four degrees of freedom (i.e., one d.o.f. per node).

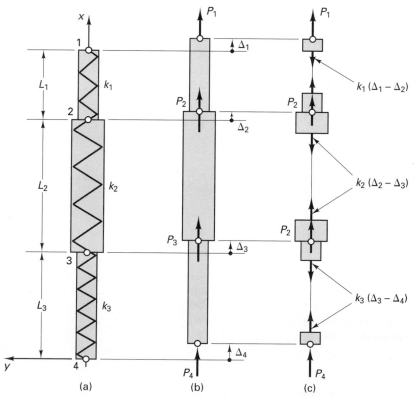

Fig. 4-9   Axially loaded bar with four degrees of freedom.

An application of forces at the nodes causes the bar system to displace in a geometrically compatible manner, as shown in Fig 4-9(b). Here both the applied forces and the node displacements are shown, with the positive sense coinciding with the positive direction of the x axis. Possible displacements at the nodes give rise to several special cases. With no deflection at the ends, one has a statically indeterminate problem. If, however, only one node point is held and forces or displacements are applied at the other nodes, the problem is statically determinate. However, if a displacement is specified at a node, it is not possible also to specify an applied force and vice versa.

With imposition of the applied forces and/or displacements, internal forces develop in the bar system. The magnitude and sense of these forces can be arrived at in the following manner. With the adopted sign convention, the bar segment extension[1] between the ith and the $(i + 1)$th nodes is $\Delta_i - \Delta_{i+1}$. By multiplying this stretch by the spring constant for the bar segment, the internal tensile force $(\Delta_i - \Delta_{i+1})k_i$ is determined. Free-body diagrams for isolated nodes showing these internal as well as applied node forces are shown in Fig. 4-9(c).

The problem is resolved by writing equilibrium equation $\Sigma F_x = 0$ for each node. Thus, beginning with node 1, the following set of equations is obtained:

$$
\begin{aligned}
P_1 - k_1(\Delta_1 - \Delta_2) &= 0 \\
P_2 + k_1(\Delta_1 - \Delta_2) - k_2(\Delta_2 - \Delta_3) &= 0 \\
P_3 \qquad\qquad + k_2(\Delta_2 - \Delta_3) - k_3(\Delta_3 - \Delta_4) &= 0 \\
P_4 \qquad\qquad\qquad\qquad\qquad + k_3(\Delta_3 - \Delta_4) &= 0
\end{aligned}
\tag{4-11}
$$

It is to customary recast these equations in the following form:

$$
\begin{aligned}
k_1\Delta_1 \quad - k_1\Delta_2 &= P_1 \\
-k_1\Delta_1 + (k_1 + k_2)\Delta_2 \quad - k_2\Delta_3 &= P_2 \\
-k_2\Delta_2 + (k_2 + k_3)\Delta_3 - k_3\Delta_4 &= P_3 \\
- k_3\Delta_3 + k_3\Delta_4 &= P_4
\end{aligned}
\tag{4-12}
$$

In most problems, the applied forces P_i's are known, and the remaining P_i's occurring at nodes of zero displacement are reactions. However, these equations can be applied to a broader range of problems by specifying displacements instead of applied forces. In such cases, at least one node must have a known (often zero) displacement where a reaction would develop. As noted earlier, at any one node, one can specify either an applied force or a displacement, but not both. These equations are solved simultaneously for the unknown quantities.

[1]This can be clarified by noting the effect on a bar segment of node displacements taken one at a time.

In typical applications of the displacement method, either the deflection Δ_i's or reactions P_i's are the unknowns, and for clarity it is customary to recast Eq. 4-12 in the following matrix form:

$$
\begin{bmatrix}
k_1 & -k_1 & 0 & 0 \\
-k_1 & k_1 + k_2 & -k_2 & 0 \\
0 & -k_2 & k_2 + k_3 & -k_3 \\
0 & 0 & -k_3 & k_3
\end{bmatrix}
\begin{Bmatrix}
\Delta_1 \\ \Delta_2 \\ \Delta_3 \\ \Delta_4
\end{Bmatrix}
=
\begin{Bmatrix}
P_1 \\ P_2 \\ P_3 \\ P_4
\end{Bmatrix}
\qquad (4\text{-}13)
$$

This equation shows how the system *symmetric stiffness matrix* is built up from the member stiffnesses. The pattern of this matrix repeats for any number of node points. This formulation more clearly than the earlier case of single d.o.f. system shows why this approach is often referred to as the *stiffness method*. Excellent computer programs are available for solving these equations simultaneously.[2] In Eq. 4-13, to eliminate rigid-body displacement at least one of the Δ's must be zero and its P free.

The displacement method is used extensively in practice in the analysis of large, complex problems with the aid of computers. Two simple examples follow.

Example 4-5

For the elastic weightless bar held at both ends, as shown in Fig. 4-10, determine the node displacement and the reactions using the displacement method. The cross section of the bar is constant throughout.

SOLUTION

Here only Δ_2 and Δ_3 have to be found as $\Delta_1 = \Delta_4 = 0$. Therefore, the system has two degrees of kinematic freedom. The stiffness coefficient k is the same for each segment of the bar. Applying Eqs. 4-12 and setting $\Delta_1 = \Delta_4 = 0$, one obtains

$$
\begin{aligned}
-k\,\Delta_2 &= R_1 \\
2k\,\Delta_2 - k\,\Delta_3 &= -P \\
-k\,\Delta_2 + 2k\,\Delta_3 &= -P \\
-k\,\Delta_3 &= R_2
\end{aligned}
$$

By solving the second and third equations simultaneously, $\Delta_2 = \Delta_3 = -P/k$, and then from the first and the last equations, $R_1 = R_2 = P$. This result, which could be anticipated, means that, in effect, the upper load is hung from

[2]E. L. Wilson, CAL-86, *Computer Assisted Learning of Structural Analysis and the CAL/SAP Development System,* Report No. UCB/SESM-86/05, Department of Civil Engineering, University of California, Berkeley, California, 1986.

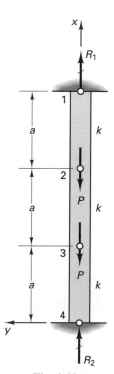

Fig. 4-10

the top and the bottom one is supported at the base. The middle segment of the bar does not distort and deflects as a rigid body through a distance of $\Delta_2 = \Delta_3$.

In this problem, the force method would be simpler to apply than the displacement method since there is only one degree of static indeterminacy.

Example 4-6

(a) Consider the same loaded bar as in Example 4-5 supported only at the top and free at the bottom; see Fig. 4-11. Determine the node displacements and the reaction. For this case, $R_2 = 0$. (b) Rework part (a) if the free end is displaced $3P/k$ upward.

SOLUTION

(a) Here $\Delta_1 = 0$, and three nodal displacements, Δ_2, Δ_3, and Δ_4, must be determined. Therefore, this statically determinate problem has three degrees of freedom. Applying Eqs. 4-12 one has

$$-k\,\Delta_2 \qquad\qquad = R_1$$
$$2k\,\Delta_2 \; -k\,\Delta_3 \qquad = -P$$
$$-k\,\Delta_2 + 2k\,\Delta_3 - k\,\Delta_4 \; = -P$$
$$-k\,\Delta_3 + k\,\Delta_4 = 0$$

By solving the last three equations simultaneously, $\Delta_2 = 2P/k$, $\Delta_3 = \Delta_4 = -3P/k$ and then from the first equation, $R_1 = 2P$. These results can be easily checked by the procedures discussed in Chapter 3.

(b) In this case, a force R_2 of unknown magnitude must be applied at the free end to cause the specified displacement $\Delta_4 = 3P/k$. As before, $\Delta_1 = 0$. Therefore, whereas the first three equations established for part (a) apply, the fourth equation must be revised to read

$$-k\,\Delta_3 + k\,\Delta_4 = R_2$$

After substituting the given value for Δ_4 and solving the four applicable equations simultaneously, $\Delta_2 = 0$, $\Delta_3 = P/k$, and $R_1 = 0$.

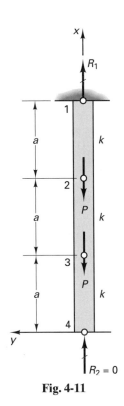

Fig. 4-11

4-6. Statically Indeterminate Nonlinear Problems

The procedures discussed in the preceding three sections are very effective for solution of *linearly elastic* statically indeterminate axially loaded bar problems. By limiting the problems to one degree of kinematic indeterminacy, the procedures can be extended to include cases of inelastic material behavior. In this approach, the stepped bar in Fig.4-12 or the symmetric bars in Fig. 4-6 can be analyzed regardless of the mechanical properties in each part of a two-part system. On the other hand, the bar in Fig. 4-4(a), having two degrees of kinematic indeterminacy and three distinctly differently stressed segments, is not susceptible to this kind of analysis.

In this extended approach, the forces remain the unknowns and are related at the juncture of the two systems by a compatibility condition. In such problems, a global *equilibrium* equation can always be written for a system. For example, for the bar in Fig. 4-12, such an equation is

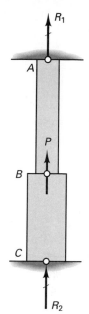

$$R_1 + R_2 + P = 0 \qquad (4\text{-}14)$$

Then, to assure *compatibility* at the juncture of the two bar segments, the deflections at B are determined using two different paths. Therefore, since ends A and C are held, the deflection of bar AB at B is Δ_{AB} and that for bar BC is Δ_{BC}; and it follows that

$$\Delta_{AB} = \Delta_{BC} \qquad (4\text{-}15)$$

Fig. 4-12   A bar of nonlinear material.

In calculating these quantities, it is usually convenient to visualize the bars cut and separated at B, and to determine Δ's for each part of the system maintained in equilibrium by the forces at the cut.

Any appropriate constitutive laws, including thermal effects and movement of supports, can be included in formulating the last equation. If the bar behavior is *linearly elastic*, with the aid of Eq. 3-4, the specialized equation becomes

$$\frac{R_1 L_1}{A_1 E_1} = \frac{R_2 L_2}{A_2 E_2} \qquad (4\text{-}16)$$

Since no restrictions are placed on the constitutive relations for calculating deflections in Eq. 4-15, numerous nonlinear problems are tractable. Problems with internal statical indeterminacy can be solved in a similar manner. It must be emphasized, however, that, except for continuous members of linearly elastic material, *superposition cannot be used with the described procedure*. Several examples using the just-described procedure, as well as some other variations, follow.

Example 4-7

A stepped bar is held at both ends at immovable supports; see Fig. 4-13(a). The upper part of the bar has a cross-sectional area A_1; the area of the lower part is A_2. (a) If the material of the bar is elastic with an elastic modulus E,

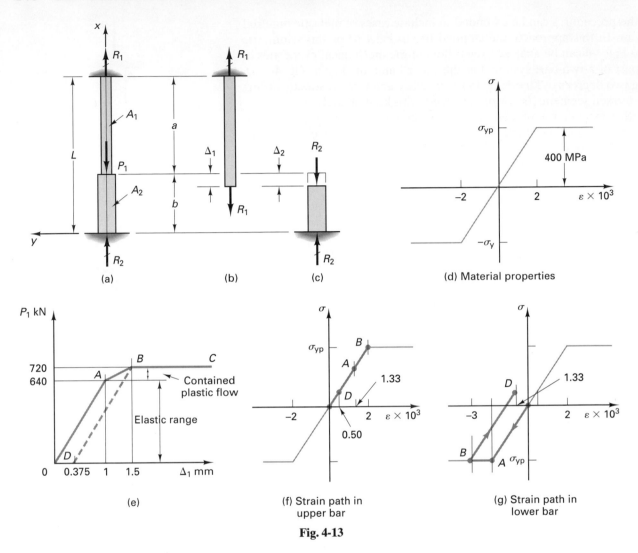

(a)   (b)   (c)   (d) Material properties

(e)

(f) Strain path in
upper bar

(g) Strain path in
lower bar

Fig. 4-13

what are the reactions R_1 and R_2 caused by the application of an axial force P_1 at the point of discontinuity of the section? Use Eqs. 4-14 and 4-16. (b) If $A_1 = 600$ mm², $A_2 = 1200$ mm², $a = 750$ mm, $b = 500$ mm, and the material is linearly elastic–perfectly plastic, as shown in Fig. 4-13(d), determine the displacement Δ_1 of the step as a function of the applied force P_1. Let $E = 200$ Gpa. (c) Assuming that at the instant of impending yield in the whole bar, the applied force P_1 is removed, determine the residual force in the bar and the residual deflection at the bar step. (d) Using a stress-strain diagram for the material, show the strain history for each of the two bar parts during application and removal of force P_1.

SOLUTION

(a) In this approach, it is convenient to visualize the bar as divided in two, as shown in Figs. 4-13(b) and (c). The upper part is subjected throughout its length to a tensile force R_1 and elongates an amount Δ_1. The lower part contracts an amount Δ_2 under the action of a compressive force R_2. These deflections must be equal. Therefore, using Eqs. 4-14 and 4-15 or their equivalent, Eq. 4-16, one has the following:

From statics:

$$R_1 + R_2 = P_1$$

From compatibility:

$$\Delta_1 = \Delta_2 \quad \text{or} \quad \frac{R_1 a}{A_1 E} = \frac{R_2 b}{A_2 E}$$

By solving these two equations simultaneously,

$$R_1 = \frac{P_1}{1 + aA_2/bA_1} \quad \text{and} \quad R_2 = \frac{P_1}{1 + bA_1/aA_2} \quad \text{(4-10)}$$

yielding the same result as found in Example 4-4.

(b) By direct substitution of data into Eqs. 4-10,

$$R_1 = \frac{P_1}{1 + 750 \times 1200/(500 \times 600)} = \frac{P_1}{4} \quad \text{and} \quad R_2 = \frac{3P_1}{4}$$

Hence, the normal stresses are

$$\sigma_1 = R_1/A_1 = P/2400 \quad \text{and} \quad \sigma_2 = R_2/A_2 = -P/1600$$

As $|\sigma_2| > \sigma_1$, the load at impending yield is found by setting $\sigma_2 = -400$ MPa. At this load, the lower part of the bar just reaches yield, and the strain attains the magnitude of $\varepsilon_{yp} = \sigma_{yp}/E = 2 \times 10^{-3}$. Therefore, from the previous relationship between σ_2 and P,

$$P_{yp} = 1600\sigma_{yp} = 640 \times 10^3 \text{ N} = 640 \text{ kN}$$

and

$$\Delta_2 = \Delta_1 = \varepsilon_{yp} b = 2 \times 10^{-3} \times 500 = 1 \text{ mm}$$

These quantities locate point A in Fig. 4-13(e).

On increasing P_1 above 640 kN, the lower part of the bar continues to yield, carrying a compressive force $R_2 = \sigma_{yp} A_2 = 480$ kN. At the point of impending yield for the whole bar, the upper part just reaches yield. This occurs when $R_1 = \sigma_{yp} A_1 = 240$ kN and the strain in the upper part just reaches $\varepsilon_{yp} = \sigma_{yp}/E$. Therefore,

$$P_1 = R_1 + R_2 = 720 \text{ kN}$$

and

$$\Delta_1 = \varepsilon_{yp} a = 2 \times 10^{-3} \times 750 = 1.5 \text{ mm}$$

These quantities locate point B in Fig. 4-13(e). Beyond this point, the plastic flow is uncontained and $P_1 = 720$ kN is the *ultimate* or *limit* load of the rod.

Note the simplicity of calculating the limit load, which, however, provides no information on the deflection characteristics of the system. In general, plastic limit analysis is simpler than elastic analysis, which in turn is simpler than tracing the elastic-plastic load-deflection relationship.

(c) According to the solution in part (b), when the applied force P_1 just reaches 720 kN and deflects 1.5 mm, point B in Fig. 4-13(e), the whole bar becomes plastic. At this instant, $R_1 = 240$ kN and $R_2 = 480$ kN. On removing this force, the bar rebounds elastically (see Section 2-8). In the elastic equations, such a force must be treated with an opposite sign from that of the initially applied force. Therefore, per the solution found for part (b) based on Eqs. 4-10, the upper and lower reactions caused by the removal of the force P_1 are, respectively, $-P_1/4$ and $-3P_1/4$.

The residual force R_{res} in the bar is equal to the initial force in either one of the bar parts, less the reduction in these forces caused by the removal of the applied force. Hence, for the upper part of the bar,

$$R_{res} = R_1 - P_1/4 = 240 - 720/4 = 60 \text{ kN}$$

Likewise, for the lower part of the bar,

$$R_{res} = R_2 - 3P_1/4 = 480 - 3 \times 720/4 = 60 \text{ kN}$$

Both results are the same, as they should be, as no applied force remains at the bar discontinuity.

The residual deflection at the bar discontinuity can be determined using either part of the bar. For example, since the upper part loses $P_1/4 = 180$ kN of the tensile force, based on Eq. 3-4, it contracts $aP_1/(4A_1E) = 1.125$ mm. Hence, the residual deflection is $1.5 - 1.125 = 0.375$ mm, as shown in Fig. 4-13(e). The elastic rebound shown in this figure by the dashed line BD is parallel to OA.

(d) The strain histories for the two parts of the bar are given in Figs. 4-13(f) and (g). As shown in part (b), the lower segment begins to yield first. At that instant, $\Delta_1 = 1$ mm and the strain in the lower bar is $\Delta_1/b = 2 \times 10^{-3}$, whereas in the upper bar it is $\Delta_1/a = 1.33 \times 10^{-3}$. These results are identified by points A in the figures. The instant when the upper bar begins to yield occurs at $\Delta_1 = 1.5$ mm. Therefore, the strains in both parts of the bar have increased by a factor of 1.5 and are so shown in the figures by their respective points B. No increase in the stress can occur in the lower bar during this time, as it is in a state of pure plastic deformation. When the applied load is completely removed, the residual deflection $\Delta_1 = 0.375$ mm. Hence the corresponding residual strains Δ_1/a and Δ_1/b are, respectively

0.50×10^{-3} and 0.75×10^{-3} m/m. The corresponding points are identified by points D in Figs. 4-13(f) and (g).

Example 4-8

A 30-in-long aluminum rod is enclosed within a steel-alloy tube; see Figs. 4-14(a) and (b). The two materials are bonded together. If the stress-strain diagrams for the two materials can be idealized as shown, respectively, in Fig. 4-14(d), what end deflection will occur for $P_1 = 80$ kips and for $P_2 = 125$ kips? The cross-sectional areas of steel A_s and of aluminum A_a are the same and equal to 0.5 in².

SOLUTION

This problem is internally statically indeterminate since the manner in which the resistance to the force P is distributed between the two materials is unknown. However, the total axial force at an arbitrary section can be determined easily; see Fig. 4-14(c). For an internal statically indeterminate problem, the requirements of equilibrium remain valid, but an additional condition is necessary to solve the problem. This auxiliary condition comes from the requirements of compatibility of deformations. However, since

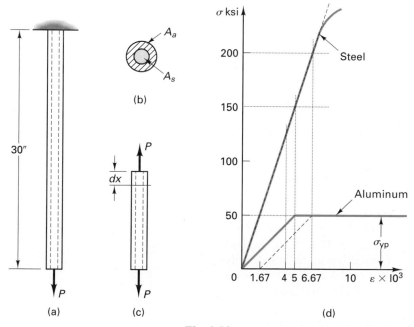

Fig. 4-14

the requirements of statics involve forces and deformations involve displacements, a connecting condition based on the property of materials must be added.

Let subscripts a and s on P, ε, and σ identify these quantities as being for aluminum and steel, respectively. Then, noting that the applied force is supported by a force developed in steel and aluminum and that at every section the displacement or the strain of the two materials is the same, and tentatively assuming elastic response of both materials, one has the following:

From equilibrium:

$$P_a + P_s = P_1 \text{ or } P_2$$

From compatibility:

$$\Delta_a = \Delta_s \qquad \text{or} \qquad \varepsilon_a = \varepsilon_s$$

From material properties:

$$\varepsilon_a = \sigma_a / E_a \qquad \text{and} \qquad \varepsilon_s = \sigma_s / E_s$$

By noting that $\sigma_a = P_a / A_a$ and $\sigma_s = P_s / A_s$, one can solve the three equations. From the diagram the elastic moduli are $E_s = 30 \times 10^6$ psi and $E_a = 10 \times 10^6$ psi. Thus,

$$\varepsilon_a = \varepsilon_s = \frac{\sigma_a}{E_a} = \frac{\sigma_s}{E_s} = \frac{P_a}{A_a E_a} = \frac{P_s}{A_s E_s}$$

Hence, $P_s = [A_s E_s / (A_a E_a)] P_a = 3 P_a$, and $P_a + 3 P_a = P_1 = 80$ k; therefore, $P_a = 20$ k, and $P_s = 60$ k.

By applying Eq. 3-4 to either material, the tip deflection for 80 kips will be

$$\Delta = \frac{P_s L}{A_s E_s} = \frac{P_a L}{A_a E_a} = \frac{20 \times 10^3 \times 30}{0.5 \times 10 \times 10^6} = 0.120 \text{ in}$$

This corresponds to a strain of $0.120/30 = 4 \times 10^{-3}$ in/in. In this range, both materials respond elastically, which satisfies the material-property assumption made at the beginning of this solution. In fact, as may be seen from Fig. 4-14(d), since for the linearly elastic response the strain can reach 5×10^{-3} in/in for both materials, by direct proportion, the applied force P can be as large as 100 kips.

At $P = 100$ kips, the stress in aluminum reaches 50 ksi. According to the idealized stress-strain diagram, no higher stress can be resisted by this material, although the strains may continue to increase. Therefore, beyond $P = 100$ kips, the aluminum rod can be counted upon to resist only $P_a = A_a \sigma_{yp} = 0.5 \times 50 = 25$ kips. The remainder of the applied load must be carried by the steel tube. Therefore for $P_2 = 125$ kips, 100 kips must be carried by the steel tube. Hence, $\sigma_s = 100/0.5 = 200$ ksi. At this stress level, $\varepsilon_s = 200/(30 \times 10^3) = 6.67 \times 10^{-3}$ in/in. Therefore, the tip deflection

$$\Delta = \varepsilon_s L = 6.67 \times 10^{-3} \times 30 = 0.200 \text{ in}$$

Note that it is not possible to determine Δ from the strain in aluminum, since no unique strain corresponds to the stress beyond 50 ksi, which is all that the aluminum rod can carry. However, in this case, the elastic steel tube constrains the plastic flow. Therefore, since the strains in both materials are the same—that is, $\varepsilon_s = \varepsilon_a = 6.67 \times 10^{-3}$ in/in; see Fig. 4-14(d).

If the applied force $P_2 = 125$ kips were removed, both materials in the rod would rebound elastically. Thus, if one imagines the bond between the two materials broken, the steel tube would return to its initial shape. But a permanent set (stretch) of $(6.67 - 5) \times 10^{-3} = 1.67 \times 10^{-3}$ in/in would occur in the aluminum rod. This incompatibility of strain cannot develop if the two materials are bonded together. Instead, residual stresses develop, which maintain the same axial deformation in both materials. In this case, the aluminum rod remains slightly compressed and the steel tube is slightly stretched. The procedure for the solution of this kind of problem is illustrated in the next example.

Example 4-9

A steel rod with a cross-sectional area of 2 in³ and a length of 15.0025 in is loosely inserted into a copper tube, as shown in Fig. 4-15. The copper tube has a cross-sectional area of 3 in² and is 15.0000 in long. If an axial force $P = 25$ kips is applied through a rigid cap, what stresses will develop in the two materials? Assume that the elastic moduli of steel and copper are $E_s = 30 \times 10^6$ psi and $E_{cu} = 17 \times 10^6$ psi, respectively.

SOLUTION
If the applied force P is sufficiently large to close the small gap, a force P_s will be developed in the steel rod and a force P_{cu} in the copper tube. Moreover, upon loading, the steel rod will compress axially Δ_s, which is as

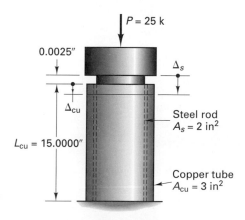

Fig. 4-15

much as the axial deformation Δ_{cu} of the copper tube plus the initial gap. Hence,

From statics:

$$P_s + P_{cu} = 25,000 \text{ lb}$$

From compatibility:

$$\Delta_s = \Delta_{cu} + 0.0025$$

By applying Eq. 3-4, $\Delta = PL/AE$, substituting, and simplifying,

$$\frac{P_s L_s}{A_s E_s} = \frac{P_{cu} L_{cu}}{A_{cu} E_{cu}} + 0.0025$$

$$\frac{15.0025}{2 \times 30 \times 10^6} P_s - \frac{15}{3 \times 17 \times 10^6} P_{cu} = 0.0025$$

$$P_s - 1.176 P_{cu} = 10,000 \text{ lb}$$

Solving the two equations simultaneously,

$$P_{cu} = 6900 \text{ lb} \qquad \text{and} \qquad P_s = 18,100 \text{ lb}$$

and dividing these forces by the respective cross-sectional areas gives

$$\sigma_{cu} = 6900/3 = 2300 \text{ psi} \qquad \text{and} \qquad \sigma_s = 18,100/2 = 9050 \text{ psi}$$

If either of these stresses were above the proportional limit of its material or if the applied force were too small to close the gap, the preceding solution would not be valid. Also note that since the deformations considered are small, it is sufficiently accurate to use $L_s = L_{cu}$.

ALTERNATIVE SOLUTION

The force F necessary to close the gap may be found first, using Eq. 3-4. In developing this force, the rod acts as a "spring" and resists a part of the applied force. The remaining force P' causes equal deflections Δ_s' and Δ_{cu}' in the two materials.

$$F = \frac{\Delta A_s E_s}{L_s} = \frac{0.0025 \times 2 \times 30 \times 10^6}{15.0025} = 10,000 \text{ lb} = 10 \text{ kips}$$

$$P' = P - F = 25 - 10 = 15 \text{ kips}$$

Then if P_s' is the force resisted by the steel rod, in addition to the force F, and P_{cu}' is the force carried by the copper tube,

From statics:

$$P_s' + P_{cu}' = P' = 15$$

From compatibility:

$$\Delta_s' = \Delta_{cu}' \qquad \text{or} \qquad \frac{P_s' L_s}{A_s E_s} = \frac{P_{cu}' L_{cu}}{A_{cu} E_{cu}}$$

$$\frac{15}{2 \times 30 \times 10^6} P_s' = \frac{15}{3 \times 17 \times 10^6} P_{cu}' \qquad P_{cu}' = \frac{17}{20} P_s'$$

By solving the two appropriate equations simultaneously, it is found that $P_{cu}' = 6.9$ kips and $P_s' = 8.1$ kips, or $P_s = P_s' + F = 18.1$ kips.

If $(\sigma_{yp})_s = 40$ ksi and $(\sigma_{yp})_{cu} = 10$ ksi, the limit load for this assembly can be determined as follows:

$$P_{ult} = (\sigma_{yp})_s A_s + (\sigma_{yp})_{cu} A_{cu} = 110 \text{ kips}$$

At the ultimate load, both materials yield; therefore, the small discrepancy in the initial lengths of the parts is of no consequence.

Example 4-10

A copper tube 12 in long and having a cross-sectional area of 3 in² is placed between two very rigid caps made of Invar[3]; see Fig. 4-16(a). Four $\frac{3}{4}$-in steel bolts are symmetrically arranged parallel to the axis of the tube and are lightly tightened. Find the stress in the tube if the temperature of the assembly is raised from 60°F to 160°F. Let $E_{cu} = 17 \times 10^6$ psi, $E_s = 30 \times 10^6$ psi, $\alpha_{cu} = 9.1 \times 10^{-6}$ per °F, and $\alpha_s = 6.5 \times 10^{-6}$ per °F.

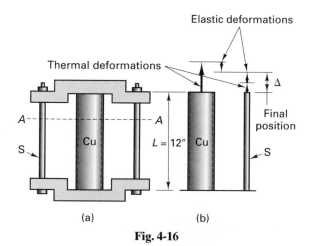

(a)   (b)

Fig. 4-16

[3]Invar is a steel alloy that at ordinary temperatures has an $\alpha \approx 0$ and for this reason is used in the best grades of surveyor's tapes and watch springs.

SOLUTION

If the copper tube and the steel bolts were free to expand, the axial thermal elongations shown in Fig. 4-16(b) would take place. However, since the axial deformation of the tube must be the same as that of the bolts, the copper tube will be pushed back and the bolts will be pulled out so that the net deformations will be the same. Moreover, as can be established by considering a free body of the assembly above some arbitrary section such as A–A in Fig. 4-16(a), the compressive force P_{cu} in the copper tube and the tensile force P_s in the steel bolts are equal. Hence,

From statics:

$$P_{cu} = P_s = P$$

From compatibility:

$$\Delta_{cu} = \Delta_s = \Delta$$

This kinematic relation, on the basis of Fig. 4-16(b) with the aid of Eqs. 2-11 and 3-4, becomes

$$\alpha_{cu}\,\Delta T\,L_{cu} - \frac{P_{cu}L_{cu}}{A_{cu}E_{cu}} = \alpha_s\,\Delta T\,L_s + \frac{P_sL_s}{A_sE_s}$$

or, since $L_{cu} = L_s$, $\Delta T = 100°F$ and 0.442 in^2 is the cross section of one bolt:

$$9.1 \times 10^{-6} \times 100 - \frac{P_{cu}}{3 \times 17 \times 10^6}$$

$$= 6.5 \times 10^{-6} \times 100 + \frac{P_s}{4 \times 0.442 \times 30 \times 10^6}$$

By solving the two equations simultaneously, $P = 6750$ lb. Therefore, the stress in the copper tube is $\sigma_{cu} = 6750/3 = 2250$ psi.

The kinematic expression just used may also be set up on the basis of the following statement: The differential expansion of the two materials due to the change in temperature is accommodated by or is equal to the elastic deformations that take place in the two materials.

Example 4-11

A steel bolt having a cross-sectional area $A_1 = 600$ mm^2 is used to grip two steel washers of total thickness L, each having the cross-sectional area $A_2 = 5400$ mm^2; see Fig. 4-17(a). If the bolt in this assembly is tightened initially so that its stress is 150 MPa, what will be the final stress in this bolt after a force $P = 75$ kN is applied to the assembly?

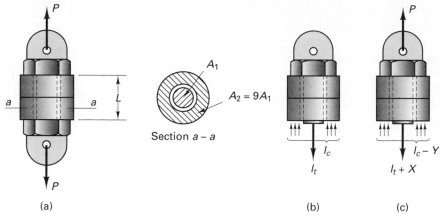

Fig. 4-17

SOLUTION

A free body corresponding to the initial conditions of the assembly is in Fig. 4-17(b), where I_t is the initial tensile force in the bolt and I_c is the initial compressive force in the washers. From statics, $I_t = I_c$. A free body of the assembly after the force P is applied is shown in Fig. 4-17(c), where X designates the increase in the tensile force in the bolt and Y is the decrease in the compressive force on the washers due to P. As a result of these forces, X and Y, if the adjacent parts remain in contact, the bolt elongates the same amount as the washers expand elastically. Hence, the final conditions are as follows:

From statics:

$$P + (I_c - Y) = (I_t + X)$$

or, since $I_c = I_t$,

$$X + Y = P$$

From compatibility:

$$\Delta_{\text{bolt}} = \Delta_{\text{washers}}$$

By applying Eq. 3-4,

$$\frac{XL}{A_1 E} = \frac{YL}{A_2 E} \quad \text{i.e.,} \quad Y = \frac{A_2}{A_1} X$$

By solving the two equations simultaneously,

$$X = \frac{P}{1 + A_2/A_1} = \frac{P}{1 + 9} = 0.1P = 7.5 \text{ kN}$$

Therefore, the increase of the stress in the bolt is $X/A_1 = 12.5$ MPa, and the stress in the bolt after the application of the force P becomes 162.5 MPa.

This remarkable result indicates that most of the applied force is carried by decreasing the initial compressive force on the assembled washers since $Y = 0.9P$.

The solution is not valid if one of the materials ceases to behave elastically or if the applied force is such that the initial precompression of the assembled parts is destroyed.

Situations approximating the preceding idealized problem are found in many practical applications. A hot rivet used in the assembly of plates, upon cooling, develops within it enormous tensile stresses. Thoroughly tightened bolts, as in the head of an automobile engine or in the flange of a pressure vessel, have high initial tensile stresses; so do the steel tendons in a prestressed concrete beam. It is crucial that on applying the working loads, only a small increase occurs in the initial tensile stresses.

Example 4-12

Extend the solution of Example 4-3 for the frame shown in Fig. 4-18(a) into the plastic range of material behavior and plot a force-displacement diagram. The cross-sectional area A of each bar is the same. Assume ideal elastic-plastic behavior with the material yielding at σ_{yp}.

SOLUTION
The *equilibrium equation* for forces at joint C, Fig. 4-18(c), recognizing symmetry, is

$$F_1 + 2F_2 \cos \alpha = P$$

The *compatibility equation* at joint C, Fig. 4-18(a), relating the elongations in bars AC' and DC' with that of bar BC' is

$$\Delta_2 = \Delta_1 \cos \alpha$$

In both of these equations, it is assumed that the deformations are small. However, these equations hold true whether the bar material behaves elastically or plastically.

By noting that the inclined bars are $L/(\cos \alpha)$ long, using Eq. 3-4 and the established compatibility equation,

$$\frac{F_2[L/\cos\alpha]}{AE} = \frac{F_1 L}{AE} \cos\alpha \quad \text{or} \quad F_2 = F_1 \cos^2\alpha$$

Substituting the last expression into the equilibrium equation at joint C and simplifying leads to the same results as found in Example 4-3:

$$F_1 = \frac{P}{1 + 2\cos^3\alpha} \quad \text{and} \quad F_2 = \frac{P}{1 + 2\cos^3\alpha}\cos^2\alpha \quad (4\text{-}5)$$

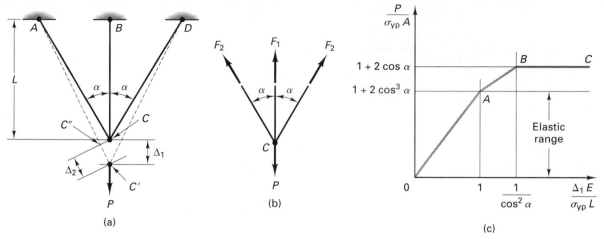

Fig. 4-18

It is seen from this solution that the maximum force occurs in the vertical bar. At the impending yield $F_1 = \sigma_{yp}A$, and, per Eq. 3-4, $\Delta_1 = \sigma_{yp}L/E$. By substituting $F_1 = \sigma_{yp}A$ into the left side of Eq. 4-5, the force $P = \sigma_{yp}A(1 + 2\cos^3\alpha)$ at the limit of elastic behavior is obtained. This value of P occurring at $\Delta_1 = \sigma_{yp}L/E$ is identified by point A in Fig. 4-18(c).

By increasing force P above the first yield in the vertical bar, force $F_1 = \sigma_{yp}A$ remains constant, and the equation of statics at joint C is sufficient for determining force F_2 until the stress in the inclined bars reaches σ_{yp}. This occurs when $F_2 = \sigma_{yp}A$. At the impending yield in the inclined bars, with the vertical bar already yielding, the joint C equilibrium equation gives $P = \sigma_{yp}A(1 + 2\cos\alpha)$. This condition corresponds to the *plastic limit load* for the system. Note that the procedure for finding this load is rather simple, as the system is statically determinate when the limit load is reached. In Chapter 20, such a limit load is associated with the concept of the *collapse mechanism.*

At the impending yield in the inclined bars, per Eq. 3-4, $\Delta_2 = (\sigma_{yp}/E)[L/\cos\alpha]$ and $\Delta_1 = \Delta_2/\cos\alpha = \sigma_{yp}L/(E\cos^2\alpha)$. This value of Δ_1 locates the abscissa for point B in Fig. 4-18(c). Beyond this point, all bars continue to yield without bound based on ideal plasticity.

4-7. Differential Equation Approach for Deflections

In Section 3-2, the axial deflection u of a bar was, in essence, determined by solving a first-order differential $\varepsilon_x = du/dx$, Eq. 3-1. It is instructive to reformulate this problem as a second-order equation. Such an equation for

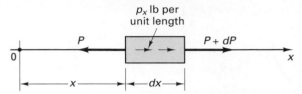

Fig. 4-19   Infinitesimal element of an axially loaded bar.

linearly elastic materials follows from two observations. First, since, in general, $du/dx = \varepsilon = \sigma/E = P/AE$, one has

$$P = AE \frac{du}{dx} \qquad (4\text{-}17)$$

Another relation is based on the equilibrium requirements for an infinitesimal element of an axially loaded bar. For this purpose, consider a typical element such as that in Fig. 4-19, where all forces are shown with a positive sense according to the previously adopted sign convention. Since $\Sigma F_x = 0$ or $dP + p_x\,dx = 0$,

$$\frac{dP}{dx} = -p_x \qquad \left[\frac{\text{lb}}{\text{in}}\right]\left[\frac{\text{N}}{\text{m}}\right] \qquad (4\text{-}18)$$

This equation states that the rate of change with x of the internal axial force P is equal to the negative of the applied force p_x. On this basis, assuming AE constant,

$$\frac{d}{dx}\left(\frac{du}{dx}\right) = \frac{1}{AE}\frac{dP}{dx} \qquad \text{or} \qquad AE\frac{d^2u}{dx^2} = -p_x \qquad (4\text{-}19)$$

It is important to note that the three basic concepts of engineering mechanics of solids are included in deriving this governing differential equation. The requirements of *statics* are satisfied by making use of Eq. 4-18, and those of *kinematics* through the use of Eq. 3-1. The *constitutive relation* is defined by Eq. 2-8. A solution of Eq. 4-19 *subject to the prescribed boundary conditions constitutes a solution of any given axially loaded elastic bar problem.* Equation 4-19 is equally applicable to statically determinate *and* statically indeterminate problems. However, for ease of solution, p_x/AE should be a continuous function. When the function is discontinuous, several alternatives are available. One of them consists of obtaining solutions for each segment of a bar and enforcing continuity conditions at the junctures.[4] This

---

[4]This requires the displacements of the abutting bar segments at a discontinuity to be equal, and that the axial forces acting on an isolated infinitesimal element at the discontinuity be in equilibrium. [See, for example, the element at B in Fig. 4-7(c), where at a discontinuity the force P may also be zero.]

is related to the statically determinate procedure discussed in Section 3-2 and to the statically indeterminate procedure considered in Sections 4-4 and 4-5. For concentrated forces, singularity functions, discussed in Section 7-14, can be used to advantage. However, direct use of Eq. 4-19 for bars where several axial loads are applied and/or cross sections change becomes cumbersome. Therefore, the procedures discussed earlier, including the scheme for dividing problems into statically determinate and indeterminate ones, are more useful in practical applications.

The example that follows illustrates the procedure when p_x is a continuous function.

Example 4-13

(a) Consider a bar of uniform cross section held between two rigid supports spun in a centrifuge such that an approximately uniformly distributed axial force p_o N/m develops in the bar, as shown in Fig. 4-20(a). Determine the reactions at the ends. (b) If the same bar is supported only at one end, Fig. 4-20(b), what will the displacements $u(x)$ be along the bar?

SOLUTION

(a) Using Eq. 4-19 and noting Eq. 4-17, on integrating twice,

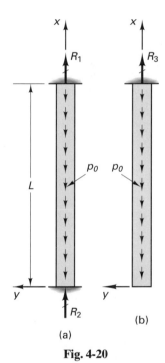

$$AE\frac{d^2u}{dx^2} = -(-p_o) = p_o$$

$$AE\frac{du}{dx} = p_o x + C_1 = P$$

$$AEu = \frac{p_o x^2}{2} + C_1 x + C_2$$

The constants of integration C_1 and C_2 can be found by noting that the deflection u is zero at both ends; that is, $u(0) = 0$ and $u(L) = 0$. Hence, from the last equation,

$$AEu(0) = 0 \quad\text{and}\quad C_2 = 0$$

$$AEu(L) = p_o L^2/2 + C_1 L = 0 \quad\text{and}\quad C_1 = -p_o L/2$$

Since $u'(x) = du/dx$, from Eq. 4-17,

$$R_2 = P(0) = AE\,u'(0) = -p_o L/2$$

The negative sign shows that this force is generated by compressive stresses. Similarly,

$$R_1 = P(L) = AE\,u'(L) = p_o L/2$$

These results indicate that the applied forces are shared equally by the two supports.

(a)

Fig. 4-20

(b)

(b) The general solution for the problem found in (a) remains applicable. However, different constants of integration must be determined from the two boundary conditions. These are $P(0) = 0$ and $u(L) = 0$; hence, $AE\, u'(0) = 0$ and $C_1 = 0$. Similarly,

$$AEu(L) = p_o L^2/2 + C_2 = 0 \qquad \text{and} \qquad C_2 = -p_o L^2/2$$

Therefore,

$$AEu = -\frac{p_o}{2}\left(L^2 - x^2\right)$$

As is to be expected,

$$R_3 = AE\, u'(L) = p_o L$$

PROBLEMS

Section 4-3

4-1. Consider the bar given in Example 3-2 and assume that ends O and D are held and that $P_2 = 390$ kN and $P_3 = 200$ kN act in the directions shown. (a) Determine the reactions. (b) Plot the axial force, axial strain, and axial displacement diagrams.

4-2. If in Problem 4-1, in addition to the applied forces, there is a drop in temperature of 50°C, what reactions would develop at the supports? Let $\alpha = 25 \times 10^{-6}/°C$.

4-3. For the 2-in^2 constant cross-sectional elastic bar shown in the figure, (a) determine the reactions, and (b) plot the axial-force, axial-strain, and axial-displacement diagrams. Let $E = 10 \times 10^3$ ksi.

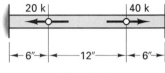

Fig. P4-3

4-4. An aluminum bar with enlarged ends in order to minimize stress concentrations is to be designed to carry a completely reversing 7.5-kN load for 5×10^8 cycles. Determine the required cross section of the bar having a safety factor of 1.8. Use the data in Fig. 2-26, and assume that the bar has a constant cross section.

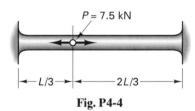

Fig. P4-4

4-5. An elastic bar of variable cross section, held at both ends, is loaded as shown in the figure. The flexibilities of the bar segments are $f/2, f$, and f. Determine the reactions, and plot the axial-force and axial-displacement diagrams.

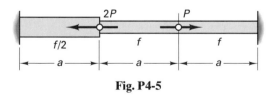

Fig. P4-5

4-6. Consider the same elastic bar of variable cross-sectional area shown in the two alternative figures. Determine deflections Δ_{ab} at a caused by the application of a unit force at b, and show that it is equal to Δ_{ba}, the deflection at b due to the application of a unit force at a. Let $A_1 = 2A_2$. (In Section 19-4 it is shown that this relationship is true in general for elastic systems. It is widely used in analysis. This conclusion can be reached by inspection for statically determinate bars.)

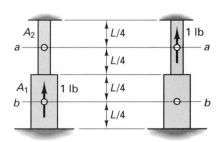

Fig. P4-6

4-7. If a load of 1 kip is applied to a rigid bar suspended by three wires as shown in the figure, what force will be resisted by each wire? The outside wires are aluminum ($E = 10^7$ psi). The inside wire is steel ($E = 30 \times 10^6$ psi). Initially, there is no slack in the wire.

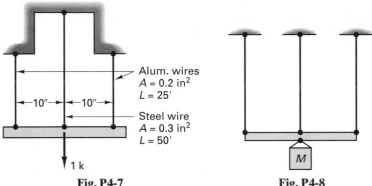

Alum. wires
A = 0.2 in^2
L = 25'

Steel wire
A = 0.3 in^2
L = 50'

10" 10"

1 k

Fig. P4-7

Fig. P4-8

4-8. Three identical, equally spaced steel wires attached to a rigid bar support a mass M developing a downward force of 6 kN, as shown in the figure. Initially, this force is equally distributed among the three wires. The stresses in the wires are well within the linearly elastic range of material behavior. (a) Determine the forces in the wires caused by a temperature drop of 60°C in the right wire. Properties of the wires: $A = 10$ mm^2, $L = 2000$ mm, $E = 200$ GPa, $\alpha = 12.5 \times 10^{-6}/°C$. (b) At what change in temperature would there be a slack in the middle wire?

4-9. If, in the system shown in Fig. P4-7, the applied force of 1 k is replaced by a mass of 500 lb attached to the beam, what would be the natural vertical frequency of vibration? The frequency of vibration is given as $f = \sqrt{g/\Delta}/2$ Hz, where g is the gravitational acceleration and Δ is the statical deflection of the system at the middle.

4-10. Initially, on applying a 3-kN force to a rigid bar hung by three parallel steel wires, all three wires become taut. What additional forces would develop in the wires if the left wire slips out 3 mm from its support? Each of the wires has a cross-sectional area of 10 mm^2 and an elastic modulus of 200 GPa.

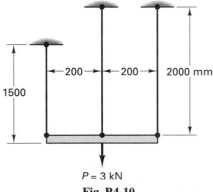

200 200 2000 mm

1500

P = 3 kN

Fig. P4-10

4-11. Rework Example 4-3 by changing the bar inclination angles α to $30°$ and taking the cross-sectional area of bar BD as 2A. The cross sections of bars AD and DC remain equal to A.

4-12. Rework Example 4-3 by assuming that the middle steel bar and the exterior 6061-T6 aluminum alloy bars increase in temperature 50°C. Let $\alpha = 30°, P = 2$ kN, and $L = 2000$ mm; all bars have an $A = 40$ mm². Use Table 1B in the Appendix for physical properties of the materials.

Section 4-4

4-13. An elastic bar held at both ends is loaded by an axial force P, as shown in the figure. Cross section A of the bar is constant. (a) Determine the reactions and interpret the results in relation to the position of the applied force. (b) Plot the axial displacement diagram, assuming that E is known.

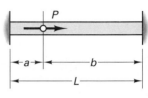

Fig. P4-13

4-14. For symmetrically arranged springs in parallel, the combined spring constant $k = \Sigma_n k_i$; see figure (a). Justify that for the springs in series, as in figure (b), the system spring constant k follows from $1/k = \Sigma_n 1/k_i$, or, alternatively, $f = \Sigma_n f_i$, where f is system flexibility and f_i the flexibility of an ith spring.

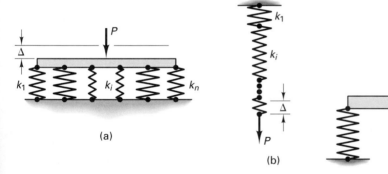

(a)

(b)

Fig. P4-14

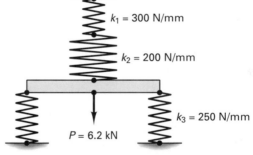

Fig. P4-15

4-15. A symmetrical arrangement of springs is attached to a rigid bar and carries an applied force P, as shown in the figure. (a) Find the reactions. (*Hint:* Use the relationships given in Problem 4-14.) (b) How is the total deflection distributed between the upper two springs?

4-16. Determine the spring constant for the system of two parallel springs shown in Fig. P4-16. (*Hint:* Find the distribution of forces between the springs by applying the unit force shown.)

4-17. Rework Problem 4-7 using the displacement method.

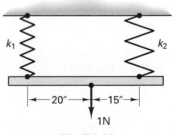

Fig. P4-16

4-18. An elastic bar of variable cross section and held at both ends is axially loaded, as shown in the figure. The cross-sectional area of the small part is A and of the larger, $2A$. (a) Using the displacement method, find the reactions. (b) Plot a qualitative axial-displacement diagram. (*Hint:* Use the relationship given in Problem 4-14 for determining the combined stiffness of the bar segments to the left of P.)

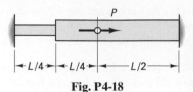

Fig. P4-18

4-19. A bar of constant thickness and held at both ends has the geometry shown in the figure. Determine the reactions caused by the axially applied force P. (*Hint:* First find the stiffness for the tapered part of the bar.)

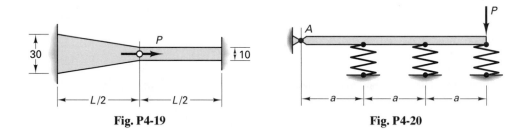

Fig. P4-19   Fig. P4-20

4-20. A rigid bar is hinged at end A and, in addition, is supported on three identical springs, each having stiffness k. (a) What is the degree of statical indeterminacy of this system? (b) How many degrees of freedom are there? (c) Find the forces acting on the springs.

4-21. A rigid bar is supported by a pin at A and two linearly elastic wires at B and C, as shown in the figure. The area of the wire at B is 80 mm² and for the one at C is 100 mm². Determine the reactions at A, B, and C caused by the applied force $P = 6$ kN.

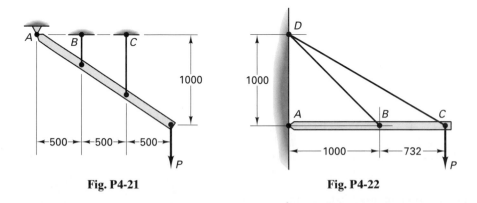

Fig. P4-21   Fig. P4-22

4-22. A rigid bar is supported by a pin at A and two inclined linearly elastic identical wires at B and C. Determine the forces in the wires caused by the applied force $P = 8$ kN.

4-23.   Five steel rods, each having a cross-sectional area of 500 mm², are assembled in a symmetrical manner, as shown in the figure. Assume that the steel behaves as a linearly elastic material with $E = 200$ GPa. Determine the deflection of joint A due to downward force $P = 2$ MN. Assume that, initially, the rods are taut.

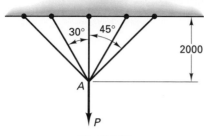

30°   45°

2000

A

P

Fig. P4-23

Section 4-5

4-24.   An elastic bar of variable cross section and held at both ends is axially loaded at several points, as shown in the figure. The cross section for the larger area is $2A$, and for the smaller, A. (a) Compare the degrees of kinematic and static indeterminacies. (b) Determine the reactions if $P_1 = 3P$, $P_2 = 2P$, and $P_3 = P$. (c) Plot the axial-force diagram.

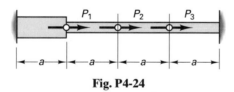

P_1 P_2 P_3

a a a a

Fig. P4-24

4-25.   Rework Problem 4-24 after removing force P_1. (*Hint:* The degree of kinematic indeterminacy can be reduced by using a relationship given in Problem 4-14.)

Section 4-6

4-26.   A material possesses a nonlinear stress-strain relationship given as $\sigma = K\varepsilon^n$, where K and n are material constants. If a rod made of this material and of constant area A is initially fixed at both ends and is then loaded as shown in the figure, how much of applied force P is carried by the left support?

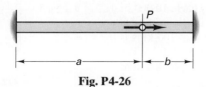

P

a b

Fig. P4-26

4-27. A rod is fixed at A and loaded with an axial force P, as shown in the figure. The material is elastic-perfectly plastic, with $E = 200$ Gpa and a yield stress of 200 MPa. Prior to loading, a gap of 3 mm exists between the end of the rod and fixed support C. (a) Plot the load-displacement diagram for the load point, assuming that P increases from zero to its ultimate value for the rod. The cross section from A to B is 200 mm² and that from B to C is 100 mm². (b) What will be the residual displacement of point B upon release of the applied force?

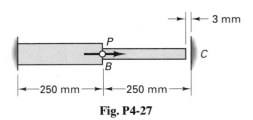

Fig. P4-27

4-28. The cross section of a short, reinforced concrete column is as shown in the figure. Four 1-in round bars serve as reinforcement. (a) Determine the instantaneous elastic strength of the column based on allowable stresses. (b) Estimate the ultimate (plastic) strength of the column. Assume that both materials are elastic-perfectly plastic. For steel, let $\sigma_{allow} = 24$ ksi, $\sigma_{yp} = 60$ ksi, and $E = 30 \times 10^6$ psi, and for concrete, $\sigma_{allow} = 2000$ psi, $\sigma_{yp} = 4600$ psi, and $E = 2 \times 10^6$ psi. (It has been shown experimentally that when steel yields, the concrete "yield" strength is approximately $0.85\sigma_{ult}$, where σ_{ult} is the ultimate compressive strength of an unreinforced cylindrical specimen of the same material, age, and curing conditions. In order to achieve ductile behavior of columns, the use of lateral ties or spiral reinforcement is essential.)

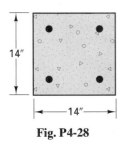

Fig. P4-28

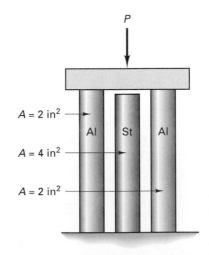

Fig. P4-29

4-29. A rigid platform rests on two aluminum bars ($E = 10^7$ psi) each. 10.000 in long. A third bar made of steel ($E = 30 \times 10^6$ psi) and standing in the middle is 9.995 in long. (a) What will be the stress in the steel bar if a force P of 100 kips is applied on the platform? (b) How much do the aluminum bars shorten? (c) What will be the ultimate (plastic) strength for the system if $(\sigma_{yp})_{A1} = 40$ ksi and $(\sigma_{yp})_{St} = 60$ ksi?

4-30. A force $P = 1$ kN is applied to a rigid bar suspended by three wires, as shown in the figure. All wires are of equal size and the same material. For each wire, $A = 80$ mm^2, $E = 200$ GPa, and $L = 4$ m. If, initially, there were no slack in the wires, how will the applied load distribute between the wires?

4-31. An aluminum rod 7 in long, having two different cross-sectional areas, is inserted into a steel link, as shown in the figure. If at 50°F no axial force exists in the aluminum rod, what will be the magnitude of this force when the temperature rises to 160°F? $E_{Al} = 10^7$ psi and $\alpha_{Al} = 12.0 \times 10^{-6}/°F$; $E_{St} = 30 \times 10^6$ psi and $\alpha_{St} = 6.5 \times 10^{-6}/°F$.

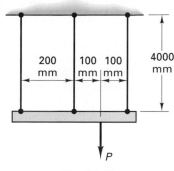

Fig. P4-30

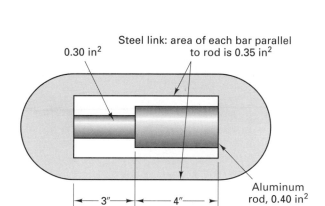

Fig. P4-31

4-32. An aluminum tube is axially compressed between the two heavy nuts of a steel bolt, as shown in the figure. If it is known that the axial stress in the sleeve at 60°C is 20 MPa, at what temperature does this prestress become zero? For the aluminum tube, $A = 1000$ mm^2, $E = 70 \times 10^3$ MPa, and $\alpha = 23.2 \times 10^{-6}$ per °C. For the steel bolt, $A = 500$ mm^2, $E = 200 \times 10^3$ MPa, and $\alpha = 11.7 \times 10^{-6}$ per °C.

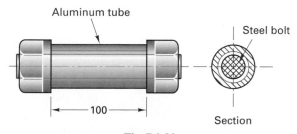

Fig. P4-32

4-33. Rework Example 4-12 after assuming that the elastic modulus E_1 for the middle bar is three times smaller than that for the outside bars (i.e., $E_2 = E_3 = 3E_1$).

4-34. Plot the load-deflection diagram for joint A in Problem 4-23 caused by the applied force P, assuming that the yield stress for the material $\sigma_{yp} = 250$ MPa.

4-35. A creep study of concrete was initiated at the University of California in 1930. One series of the experiments was completed in 1957. The typical arrangement used was as shown in the figure, and initially a compressive stress of 800 psi was applied to the concrete cylinders by tightening the three steel rods. The spring constant of the large spring $k = 6900$ lb per inch; the area of each rod $A = 0.20$ in^2; the effective length of each rod $L = 24$ in; the elastic modulus of the rods $E = 30 \times 10^6$ psi, and E of concrete was approximately 4×10^6 psi. If the change in deformation Δ due to shrinkage and creep in one of the concrete specimens after 27 years was found to be 0.0308 in, what change in stress occurred in the concrete? How well was the constant stress maintained? How does the total deformation in concrete compare with the elastic one? In your calculations include the change of stress in steel rods, but neglect the deformation of the end plates.

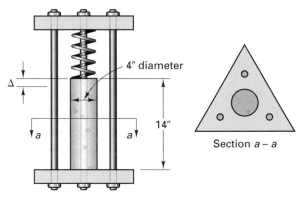

4″ diameter

14″

Section $a-a$

Fig. P4-35

Section 4-7

4-36. Rework Problem 3-27 using Eq. 4-19.

4-37. Rework Problem 3-26 using Eq. 4-19.

4-38. Rework Problem 4-13 using Eq. 4-19 and continuity conditions or singularity functions.

5

Generalized Hooke's Law, Pressure Vessels

5-1. Introduction

In addition to the normal strain discussed in the previous chapter in connection with axially loaded bars, in general, a body may also be subjected to shear strains. For the purposes of deformation analysis, such strains must be related to the applied shear stress. This topic is discussed in Part A of this chapter. In Part B, general mathematical definitions for normal and shear strains are given. Then, by employing the method of superposition, the generalized Hooke's law is synthesized, relating stresses and strains for a three-dimensional state of stress. Next, in Part C, thin-walled pressure vessels and shells of revolution are considered. The generalized Hooke's law is employed for the deformation analysis of these important elements of construction. In the concluding part, Part D, a solution for thick-walled cylinders is developed. This illustrates a solution of a typical boundary-value problem in the mathematical theory of elasticity, and, at the same time, provides bounds on the applicability of the equations established for thin-walled pressure vessels using engineering solid mechanics.

Part A   CONSTITUTIVE RELATIONSHIPS FOR SHEAR

5-2. Stress-Strain Relationships for Shear

In addition to the normal strains related to the axial strains in bars discussed in Chapters 3 and 4, a body may be subjected to shear stresses that cause shear deformations. An example of such deformations is shown in Fig. 5-1. The change in the initial right angle between any two imaginary planes in a body defines *shear strain* γ (gamma). For infinitesimal elements, these small angles are measured in *radians*. The γ subscripts shown in Fig. 5-1 associate a particular shear strain with a pair of coordinate axes. Transformation of shear strain to any other mutually perpendicular set of planes will be discussed in Section 11-13.

For the purposes of deformation analysis, it is essential to establish a relationship between shear strain and shear stress based on experiments. As will become apparent in the next chapter, such experiments are most conveniently performed on thin-walled circular tubes in torsion. The elements of such tubes are essentially in a state of pure shear stress. Illustrations of the conditions prevailing in a tube wall are shown in Fig. 5-2. The corresponding shear strains can be determined from the appropriate geometric measurements.

Note that per Section 1-4, the shear stresses on mutually perpendicular planes are equal; see Fig. 5-2(a). Moreover, since in this discussion, the stresses and strains are limited to a planar case, the subscripts for both can be omitted; see Fig. 5-2(b). By using experiments with thin-walled tubes, the generated shear stress-strain diagrams, except for their scale,

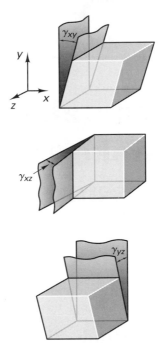

Fig. 5-1   Possible shear deformations of an element.

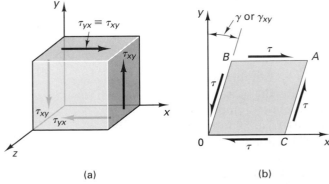

(a)   (b)

Fig. 5-2   Element in pure shear.

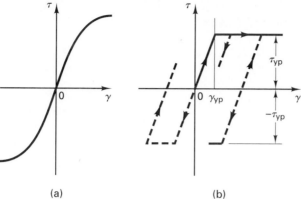

Fig. 5-3   Shear stress-strain diagrams; (a) typical and (b) idealized for a ductile material.

Fig. 5-4   Linear or Hookean relation between pure shear stress and strain.

greatly resemble those usually found for tension specimens (See Figs. 2-5, 2-9, and 2-12).

Two τ–γ diagrams are shown in Fig. 5-3. In the idealized diagram of elastic perfectly plastic behavior, Fig. 5-3(b), τ_{yp} and γ_{yp} designate, respectively, the shear yield stress and the shear yield strain.

In numerous technical problems, the shear stresses do not exceed the yield strength of the material. For most materials in this range of stress, just as for axially loaded bars, a *linear* relationship between pure shear stress and the angle γ it causes can be postulated. Therefore, mathematically, extension of Hooke's law for shear stress and strain reads

$$\tau = G\gamma \tag{5-1}$$

where G is a constant of proportionality called the *shear modulus of elasticity,* or the *modulus of rigidity.* Like E, G is a constant for a given material. For emphasis, the relationship given by Eq. 5-1 is shown in Fig. 5-4.

Example 5-1

One of the shear mountings for a small piece of vibrating mechanical equipment has the dimensions shown in Fig. 5-5. The 8-mm-thick pad of Grade 50 rubber[1] has $G = 0.64\ \text{N/mm}^2$. Determine the shear spring constant k_s for this mounting. Neglect the stiffness of the outer metal plates to which the rubber is bonded.

[1]P. B. Lindley, *Engineering Design with Natural Rubber* (Hertford, England: Malaysian Rubber Producers' Research Association, 1978).

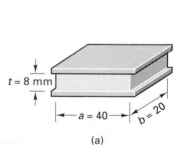

$t = 8\ \text{mm}$

$a = 40$ $b = 20$

(a)

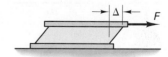

Δ F

Fig. 5-5

SOLUTION

Here $\gamma \approx \dfrac{\Delta}{t}$; hence from Eq. 5-1,

$$\tau = G\gamma = \frac{G\,\Delta}{t}$$

Further,

$$F = \tau ab = \frac{G\,\Delta ab}{t}$$

Therefore,

$$k_s = \frac{F}{\Delta} = \frac{Gab}{t} = \frac{0.64 \times 20 \times 40}{8} = 64 \text{ N/mm}$$

This solution neglects small local effects at the ends since no shear stresses act at the two boundaries.

5-3. Elastic Strain Energy for Shear Stresses

An expression for the elastic strain energy for an infinitesimal element in pure shear may be established in a manner analogous to that for one in uniaxial stress. Thus, consider an element in a state of shear, as shown in Fig. 5-6(a). The deformed shape of this element is shown in Fig. 5-6(b), where it is assumed that the bottom plane of the element is fixed in

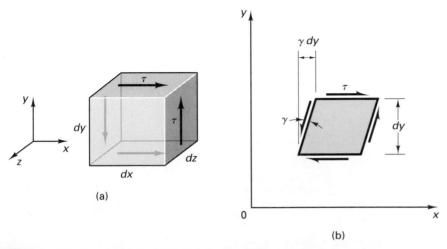

(a)

(b)

Fig. 5-6   An element for deriving strain energy due to pure shear stresses.

position.[2] As this element is deformed, the force on the top plane reaches a final value of $\tau\,dx\,dz$. The total displacement of this force for a small deformation of the element is $\gamma\,dy;$ see Fig. 5-6(b). Therefore, since the external work done on the element is equal to the internal recoverable elastic strain energy,

$$dU_{\text{shear}} = \underbrace{\frac{1}{2}\tau\,dx\,dz}_{\text{average force}} \times \underbrace{\gamma\,dy}_{\text{distance}} = \frac{1}{2}\tau\gamma\,dx\,dy\,dz = \frac{1}{2}\tau\gamma\,dV \tag{5-2}$$

where dV is the volume of the infinitesimal element.

By recasting Eq. 5-2, the strain-energy density for shear becomes

$$(U_o)_{\text{shear}} = \left(\frac{dU}{dV}\right)_{\text{shear}} = \frac{\tau\gamma}{2} \tag{5-3}$$

By using Hooke's law for shear stresses, $\tau = G\gamma$, Eq. 5-3 may be recast as

$$(U_o)_{\text{shear}} = \left(\frac{dU}{dV}\right)_{\text{shear}} = \frac{\tau^2}{2G} \tag{5-4}$$

or

$$U_{\text{shear}} = \int_{\text{vol}} \frac{\tau^2}{2G}\,dV \tag{5-5}$$

Note the similarity of Eqs. 5-2–5-5 to Eqs. 3-12–3-15 for elements in a state of uniaxial stress.

Applications of these equations are given in Chapters 6, 14, and 18.

Part B   GENERALIZED CONCEPTS OF STRAIN AND HOOKE'S LAW

5-4. Mathematical Definition of Strain[3]

Since strains generally vary from point to point, the definitions of strain must relate to an infinitesimal element. With this in mind, consider an extensional strain taking place in one direction, as shown in Fig. 5-7(a). Some points like A and B move to A' and B', respectively. During straining, point A experiences a displacement u. The displacement of point B is

---

[2]This assumption does not make the expression less general.

[3]This and the next section can be omitted without loss of continuity in the text.

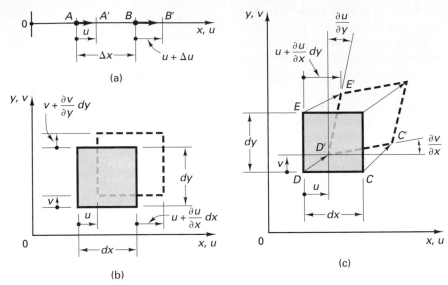

Fig. 5-7   One- and two-dimensional strained elements in intial and final positions.

$u + \Delta u$, since in addition to the rigid-body displacement u, common to the whole element Δx, a stretch Δu takes place within the element. On this basis, the definition of the extensional or normal strain is[4]

$$\varepsilon = \lim_{\Delta x \to 0} \frac{\Delta u}{\Delta x} = \frac{du}{dx} \qquad (5\text{-}6)$$

If a body is strained in orthogonal directions, as shown for a two-dimensional case in Fig. 5-7(b), subscripts must be attached to ϵ to differentiate between the directions of the strains. For the same reason, it is also necessary to change the ordinary derivatives to partial ones. Therefore, if at a point of a body, u, v, and w are the three displacement components occurring, respectively, in the x, y, and z directions of the coordinate axes, the basic definitions of *normal strain* become

$$\varepsilon_x = \frac{\partial u}{\partial x} \qquad \varepsilon_y = \frac{\partial v}{\partial y} \qquad \varepsilon_z = \frac{\partial w}{\partial z} \qquad (5\text{-}7)$$

[4]A more fundamental definition of extensional strain, more amenable to the more general concepts of *stretching* or *extending,* can be expressed, using Fig. 5-7(c), as

$$\varepsilon_x = \lim_{\Delta x \to 0} \frac{D'C' - DC}{DC} \qquad (5\text{-}6a)$$

where the vectorial displacements of points C and D are $\mathbf{u}_C = CC'$ and $\mathbf{u}_D = DD'$. For the small deformations considered here, Eq. 5-6a reduces to Eq. 5-6. Also see Sections 11-11 and 11-12.

Note that double subscripts, analogously to those of stress, can be used for these strains. Thus,

$$\varepsilon_x \equiv \varepsilon_{xx} \quad \varepsilon_y \equiv \varepsilon_{yy} \quad \varepsilon_z \equiv \varepsilon_{zz} \tag{5-8}$$

where one of the subscripts designates the direction of the line element, and the other the direction of the displacement. Positive signs apply to elongations.

In addition to normal strains, an element can also experience a shear strain, as shown in the x-y plane in Fig. 5-7(c). This inclines the sides of the deformed element in relation to the x and the y axes. Since v is the displacement in the y direction, as one moves in the x direction, $\partial v/\partial x$ is the slope of the initially horizontal side of the infinitesimal element. Similarly, the vertical side tilts through an angle $\partial u/\partial y$. On this basis, the initially right angle CDE is reduced by the amount $\partial v/\partial x + \partial u/\partial y$. Therefore, for small angle changes, the definition of the *shear strain* associated with the xy coordinates is

$$\gamma_{xy} = \gamma_{yx} = \frac{\partial v}{\partial x} + \frac{\partial u}{\partial y} \tag{5-9}$$

To arrive at this expression, it is assumed that tangents of small angles are equal to the angles themselves in radian measure. A positive sign for the shear strain applies when the element is deformed, as shown in Fig. 5-7(c). (This deformation corresponds to the positive directions of the shear stresses; see Fig. 1-4.)

The definitions for the shear strains for the xz and yz planes are similar to Eq. 5-9:

$$\gamma_{xz} = \gamma_{zx} = \frac{\partial w}{\partial x} + \frac{\partial u}{\partial z} \qquad \gamma_{yz} = \gamma_{zy} = \frac{\partial w}{\partial y} + \frac{\partial v}{\partial z} \tag{5-10}$$

In Eqs. 5-9 and 5-10, the subscripts on γ can be permuted. This is permissible since no meaningful distinction can be made between the two sequences of each alternative subscript.

In examining Eqs. 5-7, 5-9, and 5-10, note that these six strain-displacement equations depend only on three displacement components u, v, and w. Therefore, these equations cannot be independent. Three independent equations can be developed showing the interrelationships among ε_{xx}, ε_{yy}, ε_{zz}, γ_{xy}, γ_{yz}, and γ_{zx}. The number of such equations reduces to one for a two-dimensional case. The derivation and application of these equations, known as the *equations of compatibility*, are given in texts on the theory of elasticity.

5-5. Strain Tensor

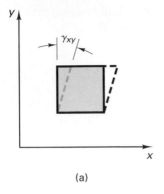

(a)

The normal and the shear strains defined in the preceding section together express the strain tensor, which is highly analogous to the stress tensor already discussed. It is necessary, however, to modify the relations for the shear strains in order to have a tensor, an entity that must obey certain laws of transformation.[5] Thus, the physically attractive definition of the shear strain as the change in angle γ is not acceptable when the shear strain is a component of a tensor. Heuristically, this may be attributed to the following. In Fig. 5-8(a), positive γ_{xy} is measured from the vertical direction. The same positive γ_{xy} is measured from the horizontal direction in Fig. 5-8(b). In Fig. 5-8(c), the same amount of shear deformation is shown to consist of two $\gamma_{xy}/2$'s. The deformed elements in Figs. 5-8(a) and (b) can be obtained by rotating the element in 5-8(c) as a rigid body through an angle of $\gamma_{xy}/2$. The scheme shown in Fig. 5-8(c) is the correct one for defining the shear-strain component as an element of a tensor. Since in this definition the element is not rotated as a rigid body, the strain is said to be *pure* or *irrotational.* Following this approach, one redefines the shear strains as

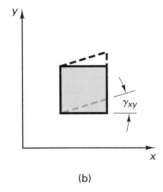

(b)

$$\varepsilon_{xy} = \varepsilon_{yx} = \frac{\gamma_{xy}}{2} = \frac{\gamma_{yx}}{2}$$

$$\varepsilon_{yz} = \varepsilon_{zy} = \frac{\gamma_{yz}}{2} = \frac{\gamma_{zy}}{2} \qquad (5\text{-}11)$$

$$\varepsilon_{zx} = \varepsilon_{xz} = \frac{\gamma_{zx}}{2} = \frac{\gamma_{xz}}{2}$$

From these equations, the strain tensor in matrix representation can be assembled as follows:

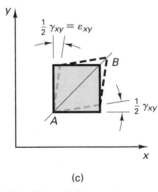

(c)

Fig. 5-8   Shear deformations.

$$\begin{pmatrix} \varepsilon_x & \dfrac{\gamma_{xy}}{2} & \dfrac{\gamma_{xz}}{2} \\ \dfrac{\gamma_{yx}}{2} & \varepsilon_y & \dfrac{\gamma_{yz}}{2} \\ \dfrac{\gamma_{zx}}{2} & \dfrac{\gamma_{zx}}{2} & \varepsilon_z \end{pmatrix} \equiv \begin{pmatrix} \varepsilon_{xx} & \varepsilon_{xy} & \varepsilon_{xz} \\ \varepsilon_{yx} & \varepsilon_{yy} & \varepsilon_{yz} \\ \varepsilon_{zx} & \varepsilon_{zy} & \varepsilon_{zz} \end{pmatrix} \qquad (5\text{-}12)$$

The strain tensor is symmetric. Mathematically, the notation employed in the last expression is particularly attractive and has wide acceptance in continuum mechanics (elasticity, plasticity, rheology, etc.). Just as for the stress tensor, using indicial notation, one can write ε_{ij} for the strain tensor.

---

[5]Rigorous discussion of this question is beyond the scope of this text. A better appreciation of it will develop, however, after study of Chapter 11, where strain transformation for a two-dimensional case is considered.

Analogous to the stress tensor, the strain tensor can be diagonalized, having only ε_1, ε_2, and ε_3 as the surviving components. For a two-dimensional problem, $\epsilon_3 = 0$; and one has the case of *plane strain*. The tensor for this situation is

$$\begin{pmatrix} \varepsilon_{xx} & \varepsilon_{xy} & 0 \\ \varepsilon_{yx} & \varepsilon_{yy} & 0 \\ 0 & 0 & 0 \end{pmatrix} \quad \text{or} \quad \begin{pmatrix} \varepsilon_1 & 0 & 0 \\ 0 & \varepsilon_2 & 0 \\ 0 & 0 & 0 \end{pmatrix} \quad \text{or} \quad \begin{pmatrix} \varepsilon_1 & 0 \\ 0 & \varepsilon_2 \end{pmatrix} \quad (5\text{-}13)$$

The transformation of strain suggested by Eq. 5-13 will be considered in Chapter 11.

The similarities and differences between plane strain and plane stress, defined in Section 1-4, will be discussed in the next section after introduction of the generalized Hooke's law.

The reader should note that in discussing the concept of strain, the mechanical properties of the material were not involved. The equations are applicable whatever the mechanical behavior of the material. However, only small strains are defined by the presented equations. Also, strains give only the relative displacement of points; rigid-body displacements do not affect the strains.

5-6. Generalized Hooke's Law for Isotropic Materials

In this section, six basic relationships between a general state of stress and strain are synthesized using the principle of superposition from the previously established simpler stress-strain equations. This set of equations is referred to as the *generalized Hooke's law*. These equations are applicable only to homogeneous *isotropic materials* (i.e., materials having the same properties in all directions). Hooke's law becomes more complex for anisotropic materials. For example, wood has decidedly different properties in the longitudinal, radial, and transverse directions (i.e., in the three orthogonal directions). Such materials, referred to as *orthotropic,* have nine independent material constants, whereas, as it will be shown in the next section, isotropic materials have only two. For fully *anisotropic* crystalline materials the number of independent material constants can be as large as 21.[6] In this book consideration is basically limited to isotropic materials, although by properly selecting the directions of axes, the developed procedures can be applied to orthotropic problems.

[6]A. P. Boresi and O. M. Sidebottom, *Advanced Mechanics of Materials,* 4th ed. (New York: Wiley, 1985); I. S. Sokolnikoff, *Mathematical Theory of Elasticity* (New York: McGraw-Hill, 1956); L. E. Malvern, *Introduction to the Mechanics of a Continuous Medium* (Englewood Cliffs, NJ: Prentice Hall, 1969).

Notable examples of these are wood and synthetic materials, such as cor-rugated sheets or filament-reinforced plastics.

According to the basic concept of Hooke's law, a linear relationship exists between the applied stress and the resulting strain, such as shown in Fig. 5-9. During this process, a lateral contraction or expansion of a body takes place, depending on whether a body is being stretched or com-pressed. The extent of the lateral deformation is analytically formulated using Poisson's ratio (see Section 2-6). Qualitative illustrations of deforma-tions caused by stresses applied along the coordinate axes are shown in Fig. 5-10.

Consider first that the element shown in Fig. 5-10(a) is subjected only to a tensile stress σ_x, as shown in Fig. 5-10(b). For this case, from $\sigma = E\epsilon$, Eq. 2-8, one has $\varepsilon_x' = \sigma_x/E$, where ε_x' is the strain in the x direction. The corresponding lateral strains ε_y' and ε_z' along the y and z axes, respectively, follow, using Poisson's ratio, Eq. 2-9, and are $\varepsilon_y' = \varepsilon_x' = -\nu\sigma_x/E$. Similar expressions for strains ε_x'', ε_y'', and ε_z'' apply when the element is stressed, as shown in Fig. 5-10(c), and again for strains ε_x''', ε_y''', and ε_z''', when stressed, as shown in Fig. 5-10(d). By *superposing* these strains, complete expressions for normal strains ε_x, ε_y, and ε_z are obtained.

Since shear strains for the Cartesian axes can be treated as illustrated in Fig. 5-1, for the general problem only, the introduction of the appropri-ate subscripts into Eq. 5-1 are needed.

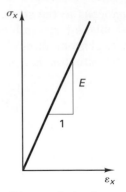

Fig. 5-9   Linear relation between uni-axial stress and extensional strain.

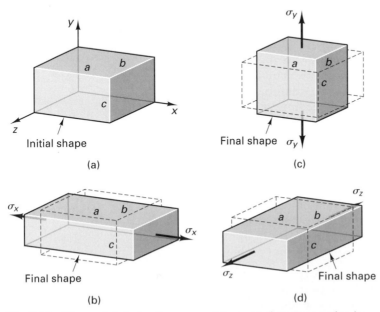

Fig. 5-10   Element deformations caused by normal stresses acting in directions of coordinate axes.

Based on the foregoing, six equations for the generalized Hooke's law for *isotropic linearly elastic materials* for use with Cartesian coordinates can be written as follows:

$$
\begin{aligned}
\varepsilon_x &= \frac{\sigma_x}{E} - \nu\frac{\sigma_y}{3} - \nu\frac{\sigma_z}{E} & \gamma_{xy} &= \frac{\tau_{xy}}{G} \\
\varepsilon_y &= -\nu\frac{\sigma_x}{E} + \frac{\sigma_y}{E} - \nu\frac{\sigma_z}{E} & \gamma_{yz} &= \frac{\tau_{yz}}{G} \\
\varepsilon_z &= -\nu\frac{\sigma_x}{E} - \nu\frac{\sigma_y}{E} + \frac{\sigma_z}{E} & \gamma_{zx} &= \frac{\tau_{zx}}{G}
\end{aligned}
\tag{5-14}
$$

By solving these equations simultaneously for the stress,

$$
\begin{aligned}
\sigma_x &= \lambda(\varepsilon_x + \varepsilon_y + \varepsilon_z) + \mu\varepsilon_x & \tau_{xy} &= G\gamma_{xy} \\
\sigma_y &= \lambda(\varepsilon_x + \varepsilon_y + \varepsilon_z) + \mu\varepsilon_y & \tau_{yz} &= G\gamma_{yz} \\
\sigma_z &= \lambda(\varepsilon_x + \varepsilon_y + \varepsilon_z) + \mu\varepsilon_z & \tau_{zx} &= G\gamma_{zx}
\end{aligned}
\tag{5-15}
$$

where λ and μ are the Lame[7] parameters, which are related to the Young's modulus E and Poisson's ratio ν, as follows:

$$
\lambda = \frac{\nu E}{(1 + \nu)(1 - 2\nu)} \quad \text{and} \quad \mu = \frac{E}{(1 + \nu)}
$$

If the normal stresses are compressive, the signs of the corresponding terms change in Eq. 5-14 for the normal strains. The positive sense of the shear strains corresponding to the positive direction of the shear stresses (Fig. 1-3) is shown Figs. 5-1 and 5-2. In the next section, it will be shown that in Eqs. 5-14 and 5-15, the three elastic constants, E, ν, and G are not independent of each other, and that for *isotropic* materials, there are only two constants.

If a body made of linear-elastic isotropic material is subjected to temperature change ΔT along with the stresses, normal strain expressions in Eq. 5-14 should be modified by adding to each the expression of the thermal strain given by Eq. 2-10. Thus, the total strain in such a body due to both the stresses and temperature change are

$$
\begin{aligned}
\varepsilon_x &= \frac{\sigma_x}{E} - \nu\frac{\sigma_y}{E} - \nu\frac{\sigma_z}{E} + \alpha\,\Delta T \\
\varepsilon_y &= -\nu\frac{\sigma_x}{E} + \frac{\sigma_y}{E} - \nu\frac{\sigma_z}{E} + \alpha\,\Delta T \\
\varepsilon_z &= -\nu\frac{\sigma_x}{E} - \nu\frac{\sigma_y}{E} + \frac{\sigma_z}{E} + \alpha\,\Delta T
\end{aligned}
\tag{5-16}
$$

[7]Named in honor of the great French scientist M. G. Lame (1795–1870).

where α is the coefficient of linear thermal expansion discussed in Section 2-7. No changes in shear strains due to a change in temperature take place in isotropic materials since such materials have the same properties in all directions.

It should be clearly understood that Eq. 5-14 gives strains (i.e., *deformations per unit length*). If the strain is constant along the length of a member, in order to determine the deformation of such a member, the strain must be multiplied by the member's length. For example, the normal deformation Δ_x in the x direction is given as

$$\Delta_x = \varepsilon_x L_x \qquad (5\text{-}17)$$

where L_x is the member's length in the x direction. Similar relations apply for Δ_y and Δ_z. An integration process is used when strains vary along for length.

From the generalized Hooke's law equations, some useful comments can be made to clarify the distinction between *plane stress* and *plane strain* problems. An examination of Eq. 1-3 for the plane stress problem shows that σ_x and σ_y may exist. If either one or both of these stresses are present, according to the third Eq. 5-14, a normal strain ε_z will develop. Conversely, in the plane strain problem, defined by Eq. 5-13, the normal strain ε_z must be zero. Therefore, in this case, if either σ_x and/or σ_y are present, it can be concluded from the third Eq. 5-14 that σ_z should not be zero. The similarity and the difference between the two kinds of problems can be further clarified using the following table, where the stresses and strains are shown in matrix form.

	Plane Stress				*Plane Strain*	

$$\begin{pmatrix} \sigma_x & \tau & 0 \\ \tau & \sigma_y & 0 \\ 0 & 0 & 0 \end{pmatrix} \qquad \begin{pmatrix} \varepsilon_x & \gamma/2 & 0 \\ \gamma/2 & \varepsilon_y & 0 \\ 0 & 0 & 0 \end{pmatrix}$$

$$\begin{pmatrix} \varepsilon_x & \gamma/2 & 0 \\ \gamma/2 & \varepsilon_y & 0 \\ 0 & 0 & \varepsilon_z \end{pmatrix} \qquad \begin{pmatrix} \sigma_x & \tau & 0 \\ \tau & \sigma_y & 0 \\ 0 & 0 & \sigma_z \end{pmatrix}$$

Example 5-2

A 50-mm cube of steel is subjected to a uniform pressure of 200 MPa acting on all faces. Determine the change in dimension between two parallel faces of the cube. Let $E = 200$ GPa and $v = 0.25$.

SOLUTION

Using the first expression in Eq. 5-14 and Eq. 5-17, and noting that pressure is a compressive stress,

$$\varepsilon_x = \frac{(-200)}{200 \times 10^3} - \left(\frac{1}{4}\right)\frac{(-200)}{200 \times 10^3} - \left(\frac{1}{4}\right)\frac{(-200)}{200 \times 10^3}$$

$$= -5 \times 10^{-4} \text{ mm/mm}$$

$$\Delta_x = \varepsilon_x L_x = -5 \times 10^{-4} \times 50 = -0.025 \text{ mm (contraction)}$$

In this case $\Delta_x = \Delta_y = \Delta_z$.

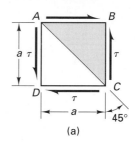

(a)

5-7. *E, G,* and ν **Relationships**

In order to demonstrate the relationship among E, G, and ν, first it must be shown that a state of pure shear, such as shown in Fig. 5-11(a), can be *transformed* into an *equivalent system of normal stresses.* This can be shown in the following manner.

Bisect square element *ABCD* by diagonal *AC* and isolate a triangular element, as shown in Fig. 5-11(b). If this element is dz thick, then each area associated with sides *AB* or *BC* is dA, and that associated with the diagonal *AC* is $\sqrt{2}\, dA$. Since the shear stress acting on the areas dA is τ, the **forces** acting on these areas are $\tau\, dA$. The components of these forces acting *toward* diagonal *BD* are in equilibrium. On the other hand, the *components* parallel to diagonal *BD* develop a resultant $\tau\sqrt{2}\, dA$ acting normal to *AC*. This **force** is equilibrated by the normal stresses σ_1 acting on area $\sqrt{2}\, dA$ associated with diagonal *AC*. This gives rise to a **force** $\sigma_1\sqrt{2}\, dA$ shown in the figure. Since the shear stress resultant and this force must be equal, it follows that $\sigma_1 = \tau$. These *stresses* are shown in Fig. 5-11(c) and **cannont** be treated as forces.

By isolating an element with a side *BD*, as shown in Fig. 3-11(d), and proceeding in the same manner as before, a conclusion is reached that $\sigma_2 = -\tau$. The results of the two analyses are displayed in Fig. 5-11(e). This representation of stress is completely *equivalent* to that shown in Fig. 5-11(a). Therefore, *a pure shear stress at a point can be alternatively represented by the normal stresses at 45° with the directions of the shear stresses,* as shown in Fig. 5-11(e), and numerically,

$$\sigma_1 = -\sigma_2 = \tau \tag{5-18}$$

This important stress transformation enables one to proceed in establishing the relationship among E, G, and ν. For this purpose, consider the deformed element shown in Fig. 5-12, and determine the strain in diagonal *DB* on two different bases. In one approach, determine strain from shear stresses; in the other, from the equivalent normal stresses.

Considering only infinitesimal deformations, and letting $\sin \gamma \approx \tan \gamma \approx \gamma$ and $\cos \gamma \approx 1$, it follows that displacement *BB′* due to shear is $a\gamma$. The projection of this displacement onto diagonal *DB′*, which, to the order of the approximation adopted, is equal to the stretch of *DB*, is $a\gamma/\sqrt{2}$.

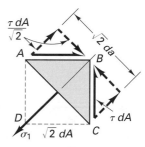

(b) Force diagram

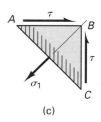

(c)

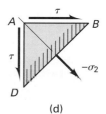

(d)

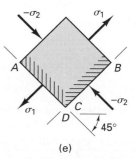

(e)

Fig. 5-11 Transformation of pure shear stress into equivalent normal stresses.

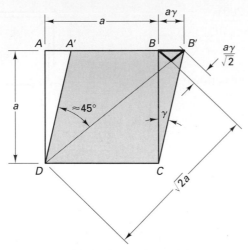

Fig. 5-12   Kinematics of element deformation for establishing a relationship between shear and extensional strains.

Therefore, since the length of DB is $\sqrt{2}a$, its normal strain $\varepsilon_{45°}$ is $\gamma/2$. Hence, recalling that $\tau = G\gamma$, Eq. 5-1, one has

$$\varepsilon_{45°} = \frac{\tau}{2G} \qquad (5\text{-}19)$$

However, the shear stresses causing the deformation shown in Fig. 5-12 are equivalent to the normal stresses represented in Fig. 5-11(e). Therefore, if the x axis is directed along diagonal DB, the first Eq. 5-14 can be applied by taking $\sigma_x = \sigma_1, \sigma_y = -\sigma_2$, and $\sigma_z = 0$. In this manner an alternative expression for the normal strain in diagonal DB is found.

$$\varepsilon_{45°} = \frac{\sigma_1}{E} - v\frac{\sigma_2}{E} = \frac{\tau}{E}(1 + v) \qquad (5\text{-}20)$$

Equating the two alternative relations for the strain along the shear diagonal and simplifying,

$$\boxed{G = \frac{E}{2(1 + v)}} \qquad (5\text{-}21)$$

This is the basic relation between E, G, and v; it shows that these quantities are not independent of one another. If any two of these are determined experimentally, the third can be computed. Note that the shear modulus G

is always less than the elastic modulus E, since the Poisson ratio v is a positive quantity. For most materials, v is in the neighborhood of 0.25.

5.8. Dilatation and Bulk Modulus

By extending some of the established concepts, one can derive an equation for volumetric changes in elastic materials subjected to stress. In the process of doing this, two new terms are introduced and defined.

The sides dx, dy, and dz of an infinitesimal element after straining become $(1 + \varepsilon_x) \, dx$, $(1 + \varepsilon_y) \, dy$, and $(1 + \varepsilon_z) \, dz$, respectively. After subtracting the initial volume from the volume of the strained element, the change in volume is determined. This is

$$(1 + \varepsilon_x) \, dx \, (1 + \varepsilon_y) \, dy \, (1 + \varepsilon_z) \, dz - dx \, dy \, dz \approx (\varepsilon_x + \varepsilon_y + \varepsilon_z) \, dx \, dy \, dz$$

where the products of strain $\varepsilon_x\varepsilon_y + \varepsilon_y\varepsilon_z + \varepsilon_z + \varepsilon_x + \varepsilon_x\varepsilon_y\varepsilon_z$, being small, are neglected. Therefore, in the infinitesimal (small) strain theory, e, the change in volume per unit volume, often referred to as *dilatation*, is defined as

$$\boxed{e = \varepsilon_x + \varepsilon_y + \varepsilon_z} \qquad (5\text{-}22)$$

The shear strains cause no change in volume.

Based on the generalized Hooke's law, the dilatation can be found in terms of stresses and material constants. For this purpose, the first three Eqs. 5-14 must be added together. This yields

$$e = \varepsilon_x + \varepsilon_y + \varepsilon_z = \frac{1 - 2v}{E} (\sigma_x + \sigma_y + \sigma_z) \qquad (5\text{-}23)$$

which means that dilatation is proportional to the algebraic sum of all normal stresses.

If an elastic body is subjected to hydrostatic pressure of uniform intensity p, so that $\sigma_x = \sigma_y = \sigma_z = -p$, then from Eq. 5-23,

$$e = -\frac{3(1 - 2v)}{E} p \qquad \text{or} \qquad \boxed{\frac{-p}{e} = k = \frac{E}{3(1 - 2v)}} \qquad (5\text{-}24)$$

The quantity k represents the ratio of the hydrostatic compressive stress to the decrease in volume and is called the *modulus of compression*, or *bulk modulus*.

Part C   THIN-WALLED PRESSURE VESSELS

5-9. Cylindrical and Spherical Pressure Vessels

In this section, attention is directed toward two types of thin-walled pressure vessels: cylindrical and spherical. Both of these types of vessels are very widely used in industry; hence, this topic is of great practical importance. In analyzing such vessels for elastic deformations, an application of the generalized Hooke's law is required.

The walls of an ideal thin-walled pressure vessel act as a membrane (i.e., the walls resist bending). A sphere is an ideal shape for a closed pressure vessel is the contents are of negligible weight; a cylindrical vessel is also good with the exception of the junctures with the ends, a matter to be commented on in more detail in the next section.

The analysis of pressure vessels will begin by considering a cylindrical pressure vessel such as a boiler, as shown in Fig. 5-13(a). A segment is iso-

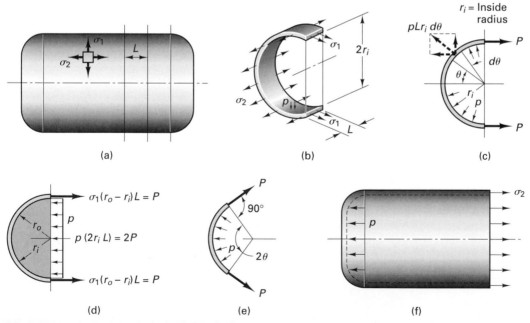

Fig. 5-13 Diagrams for analysis of thin-walled cylindrical pressure vessels.

lated from this vessel by passing two planes perpendicular to the axis of the cylinder and one additional longitudinal plane *through* the same axis, shown in Fig. 5-13(b). The conditions of symmetry exclude the presence of any shear stresses in the planes of the sections, as shear stresses would cause an incompatible distortion of the cylinder. Along the sections of the cylindrical free body there can be only normal stresses. The two that occur are the *circumferential* or *hoop stresses* σ_h and the *longitudinal stresses* σ_{ll}, identified in Fig. 5-13(b) as $\sigma_1 = \sigma_h$ and $\sigma_2 = \sigma_l$. These stresses multiplied by their respective areas maintain the cylindrical element in equilibrium with the internal pressure. On this basis, by making reference to Fig. 5-13(d), the internal pressure p multiplied by the projected area $2r_iL$, where r_i is the inside radius, generates the force acting on the cylindrical element. This force is balanced by the two forces P developed by the hoop stresses $\sigma_h = \sigma_1$ multiplied by their respective areas $L(r_o - r_i)$. In this relation r_o is the outside radius of the cylinder. Equating the opposing forces, Fig. 5-13(d), to assure equilibrium of the horizontal forces, one has

$$p(2r_iL) = 2\sigma_l(r_o - r_i)L \qquad (5\text{-}25)$$

and since $(r_o - r_i) = t$, the thickness of the cylinder, the basic expression for determining, the *circumferential or hoop stress* in a cylinder is

$$\boxed{\sigma_1 = \frac{pr_i}{t}} \qquad (5\text{-}26)$$

This equation is valid only for thin-walled cylinders, as it gives the *average* stress in the hoop. However, as is shown in Example 5-6, the wall thickness can reach one-tenth of the internal radius and the error in applying Eq. 5-25 will still be small. Since this equation is used primarily for *thin-walled* vessels, where $r_i \approx r_o$, the subscript for the radius is usually omitted.

Equation 5-25 can also be derived by passing two longitudinal sections, as shown in Fig. 5-13(e). Because of the assumed membrane action, the forces P in the hoop must be considered acting tangentially to the cylinder. The horizontal components of the forces P maintain the horizontal component of the internal pressure in a state of static equilibrium.

The other normal stress σ_2 acting in a cylindrical pressure vessel acts *longitudinally,* Fig. 5-13(b), and it is determined by solving a simple axial-force problem. By passing a section through the vessel perpendicular to its axis, a free body as shown in Fig. 5-13(f) is obtained. The force developed by the internal pressure is $p\pi r_i^2$, and the force developed by the longitudinal stress σ_2 in the walls is $\sigma_2(\pi r_o^2 - \pi r_i^2)$. Equating these two forces and solving for σ_2,

$$p\pi r_i^2 = \sigma_2(\pi r_P^2 - \pi r_i^2)$$

$$\sigma_2 = \frac{pr_i^2}{r_o^2 - r_i^2} = \frac{pr_i^2}{(r_o + r_i)(r_o - r_i)}$$

However, as pointed out earlier, $r_o - r_i = t$, the thickness of the cylindrical wall, and since this development is restricted to *thin-walled* vessels, $r_o \approx r_i \approx r$; hence,

$$\sigma_2 = \frac{pr}{2t} \qquad (5\text{-}27)$$

Note that for *thin-walled cylindrical* pressure vessels, $\sigma_2 \approx \sigma_1/2$.

An analogous method of analysis can be used to derive an expression for *thin-walled* spherical pressure vessels. By passing a section through the center of the sphere of Fig. 5-14(a), a hemisphere shown in Fig. 5-14(b) is isolated. By using the same notation as before, an equation identical to Eq. 5-27 can be derived. However, for a sphere, *any section that passes through the center of the sphere yields the same result* whatever the inclination of the element's side; see Fig. 5-14(c). Hence, the maximum membrane stresses for thin-walled *spherical pressure vessels* are

$$\sigma_1 = \sigma_2 = \frac{pr}{2t} \qquad (5\text{-}28)$$

Infinitesimal elements for the vessels analyzed showing the normal stresses σ_1 and σ_2 viewed from the outside are indicated in Figs. 5-14(a), (b), and (c). According to Eq. 1-10, the maximum shear stresses associated with these normal stresses are half as large. The planes on which these shear stresses act may be identified on elements viewed toward a section through the wall of a vessel. Such a section is shown in Fig. 5-15. The stress σ_2 acts perpendicularly to the plane of the figure.

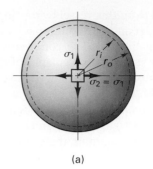

(a)

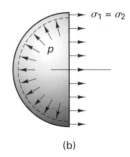

(b)

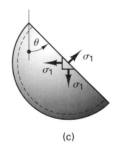

(c)

Fig. 5-14 Thin-walled spherical pressure vessel.

Example 5-3

Consider a closed cylindrical steel pressure vessel, as shown in Fig. 5-13(a). The radius of the cylinder is 1000 mm and its wall thickness is 10 mm. (a) Determine the hoop and the longitudinal stresses in the cylindrical wall caused by an internal pressure of 0.80 MPa. (b) Calculate the change in diameter of the cylinder caused by pressurization. Let $E = 200$ GPa and $v = 0.25$. Assume that $r_i \approx r_o \approx r$.

SOLUTION
The stresses follow by direct application of Eqs. 5-26 and 5-27:

$$\sigma_1 = \frac{pr}{t} = \frac{0.8 \times 1}{10 \times 10^{-3}} = 80 \text{ MPa}$$

and

$$\sigma_2 = \frac{pr}{2t} = \frac{0.8 \times 1}{2 \times 10 \times 10^{-3}} = 40 \text{ MPa}$$

The stress perpendicular to the cylinder wall, $\sigma_3 = p = 0.80$ MPa, on the inside decreases to zero on the outside. Being small, it can be neglected. Hence, on setting $\sigma_x = \sigma_1$, $\sigma_y = \sigma_2$, and $\sigma_z = 0$ in the first expression in Eq. 5-14, one obtains the hoop strain ε_1:

$$\varepsilon_1 = \frac{\sigma_1}{E} - \nu\frac{\sigma_2}{E} = \frac{80}{200 \times 10^3} - \frac{40}{4 \times 200 \times 10^3}$$

$$= 0.35 \times 10^{-3} \text{ mm/mm}$$

On pressurizing the cylinder, the radius r increases by an amount Δ. For this condition, the hoop strain ε_1 can be found by calculating the difference in the strained and the unstrained hoop circumferences and dividing this quantity by the initial hoop length. Therefore,

$$\varepsilon_1 = \frac{2\pi(r + \Delta) - 2\pi r}{2\pi r} = \frac{\Delta}{r} \tag{5-29}$$

By recasting this expression and substituting the numerical value for ε_1 found earlier,

$$\Delta = \varepsilon_1 r = 0.35 \times 10^{-3} \times 10^3 = 0.35 \text{ mm}$$

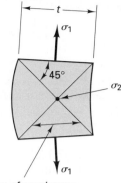

Planes of maximum shear stresses

Fig. 5-15   In yielded steel pressure vessels shear slip planes at 45° can be observed on etched specimens.

Example 5-4

Consider a steel spherical pressure vessel of radius 1000 mm having a wall thickness of 10 mm. (a) Determine the maximum membrane stresses caused by an internal pressure of 0.80 MPa. (b) Calculate the change in diameter in the sphere caused by pressurization. Let $E = 200$ GPa and $\nu = 0.25$. Assume that $r_i \approx r_o \approx r$.

SOLUTION
The maximum membrane normal stresses follow directly from Eq. 5-28.

$$\sigma_1 = \sigma_2 = \frac{pr}{2t} = \frac{0.80 \times 1}{2 \times 10 \times 10^{-3}} = 40 \text{ MPa}$$

The same procedure as in the previous example can be used for finding the expansion of the sphere due to pressurization. Hence, if Δ is the increase in the radius r due to this cause, $\Delta = \varepsilon_1 r$, where ε_1 is the membrane strain on the great circle. From the first expression in Eq. 5-14, one has

$$\epsilon_1 = \frac{\sigma_1}{E} - \nu\frac{\sigma_2}{E} = \frac{40}{200 \times 10^3} - \frac{40}{4 \times 200 \times 10^3}$$

$$= 0.15 \times 10^{-3} \text{ mm/mm}$$

Hence,

$$\Delta = \varepsilon_1 r = 0.15 \times 10^{-3} \times 10^3 = 0.15 \text{ mm}$$

Example 5-5

For an industrial laboratory a pilot unit is to employ a pressure vessel of the dimensions shown in Fig. 5-16. The vessel will operate at an internal pressure of 0.7 MPa. If for this unit 20 bolts are to be used on a 650-mm bolt circle diameter, what is the required bolt diameter at the root of the threads? Set the allowable stress in tension for the bolts at 125 MPa; however, assume that at the root of the bolt threads the stress concentration factor is 2.

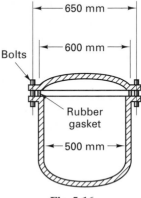

Fig. 5-16

SOLUTION
The vertical force F acting on the cover is caused by the internal pressure p of 0.7 MPa acting on the horizontal projected area within the self-sealing rubber gasket; that is,

$$F = 0.7 \times 10^6 \times \pi(600/2)^2 = 198 \times 10^9 \text{ N}$$

Assuming that this force is equally distributed among the 20 bolts, the force P per bolt is $198 \times 10^9/20 = 9.90 \times 10^9$ N. Using the given stress-concentration factor $K = 2$ and applying Eq. 3-11, the required bolt area A at the root of the threads

$$A = K\frac{P}{\sigma_{\text{allow}}} = \frac{2 \times 9.90 \times 10^9}{125 \times 10^6} = 158 \text{ mm}^2$$

Hence the required bolt diameter d at the root of the threads $d = 2\sqrt{A/\pi} = 14.2$ mm. Note from Example 4-11 that initial tightening of the bolts results in a relatively small increase in total bolt stress when the vessel is pressurized.

5-10. Remarks on Thin-Walled Pressure Vessels

It is instructive to note that for comparable size and wall thickness, the maximum normal stress in a spherical pressure vessel is only about one-half as large as that in a cylindrical one. The reason for this can be clarified by making reference to Figs. 5-17 and 5-18. In a cylindrical pressure vessel,

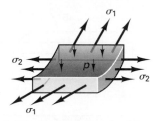

Fig. 5-17   An element of a thin-walled cylindrical pressure vessel.

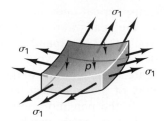

Fig. 5-18   An element of a thin-walled spherical pressure vessel.

the longitudinal stresses, σ_2, parallel to the vessel's axis do not contribute to maintaining the equilibrium of the internal pressure p acting on the curved surface; whereas in a spherical vessel, a system of equal stresses resists the applied internal pressure. These stresses, given by Eqs. 5-26 and 5-28, are treated as biaxial, although the internal pressure p acting on the wall causes local compressive stresses on the inside equal to this pressure. As already pointed out in Example 5-3, such stresses are small in comparison with the membrane stresses σ_1 and σ_2 and are generally ignored for thin-walled pressure vessels. A more complete discussion of this problem is given in Section 5-13 and Example 5-6. A much more important problem arises at geometrical changes in the shape of a vessel due to pressurization. These can cause a disturbance in the membrane action. An illustration of this condition is given in Fig. 5-19 using the numerical results found in Examples 5-3 and 5-4.

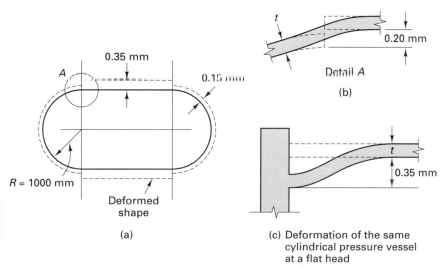

Fig. 5-19   Exaggerated deformations of pressure vessels at discontinuities.

If a cylindrical pressure vessel has hemispherical ends, as shown in Fig. 5-19(a), and if initially the cylinder and the heads were independent of each other, under pressurization they would tend to expand, as shown by the dashed lines. In general, the cylinder and the ends would expand by different amounts and would tend to create a discontinuity in the wall, as shown at A. However, physical continuity of the wall must be maintained by local bending and shear stresses in the neighborhood of the juncture, as shown in Fig. 5-19(b). If, instead of relatively flexible hemispherical ends, thick end plates are used, the local bending and shear stresses increase considerably; see Fig. 5-19(c). For this reason, the ends (heads) of pressure vessels must by designed very carefully.[8] Flat ends are very undesirable.

A majority of pressure vessels are manufactured from curved sheets that are joined together by means of welding. Examples of welds used in pressure vessels are shown in Fig. 5-20, with preference given to the different types of butt joints.

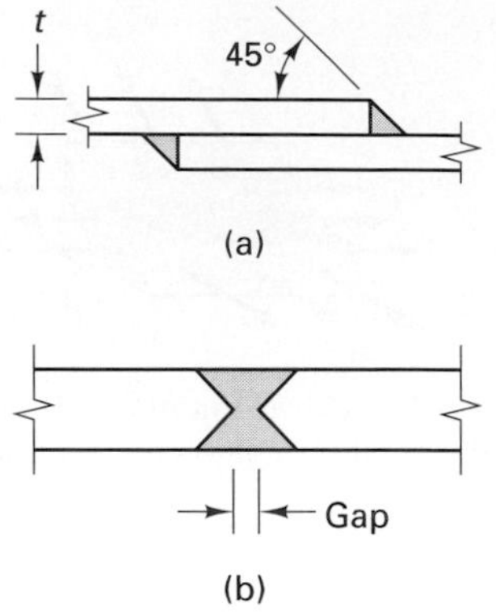

In conclusion, it must be emphasized that the formulas derived for thin-walled pressure vessels in the preceding section should be used only for cases of *internal pressure.* If a vessel is to be designed for external pressure, as in the case of a vacuum tank or a submarine, *instability* (buckling) of the walls may occur, and stress calculations based on the previous formulas can be meaningless.

Fig. 5-20   Examples of welds used in pressure vessels. (a) Double-fillet lap joint, and (b) double-welded butt joint with V grooves.

Part D   THICK-WALLED CYLINDERS

5-11. Introduction

Analysis of thick-walled cylinders under internal and external pressure is discussed in this part. This problem is related to the thin-walled cylindrical pressure vessel problem treated earlier. In order to solve the posed problem, a characteristic method of the *mathematical theory of elasticity* is employed. This consists of assuring equilibrium for each infinitesimal element and, through the use of geometric relations, allowing only their compatible (possible) deformations. The equilibrium conditions are related to those of deformation using the generalized Hooke's law. Then the governing differential equation established on the preceding bases is solved *sub-*

---

[8]The American Society of Mechanical Engineers (ASME) Unfired Pressure Vessel Code gives practical information on the design of ends; the necessary theory is beyond the scope of this text. In spite of this limitation, the elementary formulas for thin-walled cylinders developed here are suitable in the majority of cases.

ject to the prescribed boundary conditions. This approach differs from that used in engineering mechanics of solids, where the internal statical indeterminancy is resolved by means of a plausible kinematic assumption in each particular case. Occasionally, in engineering mechanics of solids, it becomes necessary to draw upon the solutions obtained using the methods of the mathematical theory of elasticity. This, for example, was already resorted to in treating stress concentrations at discontinuities in axially loaded bars. Solutions of two- and three-dimensional problems using the finite element approach, philosophically, are in many respects similar to the methods of the mathematical theory of elasticity. In both cases, one seeks solutions to *boundary-value problems.*

Mathematically, the problem of thick-walled cylinders is rather simple, yet it clearly displays the characteristic method used in elasticity. Here the solution is carried further by including inelastic behavior of thick-walled cylinders. Both the elastic-plastic and the plastic states are examined.

The solution of the problem of thick-walled cylinders under internal pressure provides bounds on the applicability of the equations developed earlier for thin-walled cylinders. This solution is also useful for the design of extrusion molds and other mechanical equipment.

5-12. Solution of the General Problem

Consider a long cylinder with axially restrained ends whose cross section has the dimensions shown in Fig. 5-21(a).[9] The inside radius of this cylinder is r_i; the outside radius is r_o. Let the internal pressure in the cylinder be p_i and the outside, or external, pressure by p_o. Stresses in the wall of the cylinder caused by these pressures are sought.

This problem can be conveniently solved by using cylindrical coordinates. Since the cylinder is long, every ring of unit thickness measured perpendicular to the plane of the paper is stressed alike. A typical infinitesimal element of unit thickness is defined by two radii, r and $r + dr$, and an angle $d\phi$, as shown in Fig. 5-21(b).

If the normal radial stress acting on the infinitesimal element at a distance r from the center of the cylinder is σ_r, this variable stress at a distance $r + dr$ will be $\sigma_r + (d\sigma_r/dr)\, dr$. Both normal *tangential* stresses acting on the other two faces of the element are σ_r. These stresses, analogous to the hoop stresses in a thin cylinder, are equal. Moreover, since from the condition of symmetry every element at the same radial distance from the center must be stressed alike, *no shear stresses act on the element shown.* Further, the axial stresses σ_x on the two faces of the element are equal and opposite normal to the plane of the paper.

---

[9]This problem was originally solved by Lamé, a French engineer, in 1833 and is sometimes referred to as the Lamé problem.

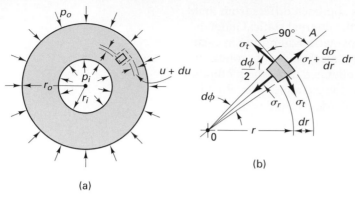

(a)

(b)

Fig. 5-21   Thick-walled cylinder.

The nature of the stresses acting on an infinitesimal element having been formulated, a characteristic elasticity solution proceeds along the following pattern of reasoning.

Static Equilibrium   The element chosen must be in static equilibrium. To express this mathematically requires the evaluation of *forces* acting on the element. These forces are obtained by multiplying stresses by their respective areas. The area on which σ_r acts is $1 \times r\,d\phi$; that on which $\sigma_r + d\sigma_r$ acts is $1 \times (r + dr)\,d\phi$; and each area on which σ_t acts is $1 \times dr$. The weight of the element itself is neglected. Since the angle included between the sides of the element is $d\phi$, both tangential stresses are inclined $\frac{1}{2}\,d\phi$ to the line perpendicular to OA. Then, summing the forces along a radial line, $\sum F_r = 0$,

$$\sigma_r r\,d\phi + 2\sigma_t\,dr\left(\frac{d\phi}{2}\right) - \left(\sigma_r + \frac{d\sigma_r}{dr}\,dr\right)(r + dr)\,d\phi = 0$$

Simplifying, and neglecting the infinitesimals of higher order,

$$\sigma_t - \sigma_r - r\frac{d\sigma_r}{dr} = 0 \quad \text{or} \quad \frac{d\sigma_r}{dr} + \frac{\sigma_r - \sigma_t}{r} = 0 \quad (5\text{-}30)$$

This one equation has two unknown stresses, σ_t and σ_r. Intermediate steps are required to express this equation in terms of one unknown so that it can be solved. This is done by introducing the geometry of deformations and properties of materials into the problem.

Geometric Compatibility   The deformation of an element is described by its strains in the radial and tangential directions. If u represents the *radial displacement* or *movement* of a cylindrical surface of radius r, Fig. 5-21(a), $u + (du/dr) \, dr$ is the radial displacement or movement of the adjacent surface of radius $r + dr$. Hence, the strain ε_r of an element in the radial direction is

$$\varepsilon_r = \frac{\left(u + \dfrac{du}{dr} \, dr\right) - u}{dr} = \frac{du}{dr} \tag{5-31}$$

The strain ε_t in the tangential direction follows by subtracting from the length of the circumference of the deformed cylindrical surface of radius $r + u$ the circumference of the unstrained cylinder of radius r and dividing the difference by the latter length. Hence,

$$\varepsilon_t = \frac{2\pi(r + u) - 2\pi r}{2\pi r} = \frac{u}{r} \tag{5-32}$$

Note that Eqs. 5-31 and 5-32 give strains expressed in terms of *one* unknown variable u.

Properties of Material   The generalized Hooke's law relating strains to stresses is given by Eq. 5-14 and can be restated here in the form[10]

$$\varepsilon_r = \frac{1}{E}(\sigma_r - v\sigma_t - v\sigma_x) \tag{5-33}$$

$$\varepsilon_t = \frac{1}{E}(-v\sigma_r + \sigma_t - v\sigma_x) \tag{5-34}$$

$$\varepsilon_x = \frac{1}{E}(-v\sigma_r - v\sigma_t + \sigma_x) \tag{5-35}$$

However, in the case of the thick-walled cylinder with axially restrained deformation, the problem is one of *plane strain* (i.e., $\epsilon_x = 0$). The last equation then leads to a relation for the axial stress as

$$\sigma_x = v(\sigma_r + \sigma_t) \tag{5-36}$$

Introducing this result into Eqs. 5-33 and 5-34 and solving them simultaneously gives expressions for stresses σ_r and σ_t in terms of strains:

$$\sigma_r = \frac{E}{(1 + v)(1 - 2v)} [(1 - v)\varepsilon_r + v\varepsilon_t] \tag{5-37}$$

$$\sigma_t = \frac{E}{(1 + v)(1 - 2v)} [v\varepsilon_r + (1 - v)\varepsilon_t] \tag{5-38}$$

These equations bring the plane strain condition into the problem for elastic material.

---

[10]Since an infinitesimal cylindrical element includes an *infinitesimal* angle between two of its sides, it can be treated as if it were an element in a Cartesian coordinate system.

Formation of the Differential Equation   Now the equilibrium equation, Eq. 5-30 can be expressed in terms of one variable u. Thus, one eliminates the strains ϵ_r and ϵ_t from Eqs. 5-37 and 5-38 by expressing them in terms of the displacement u, as given by Eqs. 5-31 and 5-32; then the radial and tangential stresses are

$$\sigma_r = \frac{E}{(1 + v)(1 - 2v)}\left[(1 - v)\frac{du}{dr} + v\frac{u}{r}\right]$$

and   (5-39)

$$\sigma_t = \frac{E}{(1 - v)(1 - 2v)}\left[v\frac{du}{dr} + (1 - v)\frac{u}{r}\right]$$

and, by substituting these values into Eq. 5-30 and simplifying, the desired governing differential equation is obtained:

$$\frac{d^2u}{dr^2} + \frac{1}{r}\frac{du}{dr} - \frac{u}{r^2} = 0$$ (5-40)

Solution of the Differential Equation   As can be verified by substitution, the general solution of Eq. 5-30 which gives the radial displacement u of any point on the cylinder, is

$$u = A_1r + A_2/r$$ (5-41)

where the constants A_1 and A_2 must be determined from the conditions at the *boundaries* of the body.

Unfortunately, for the determination of the constants A_1 and A_2, the displacement u is not known at either the inner or the outer boundary of the cylinder's wall. However, the known pressures are equal to the radial stresses acting on the elements at the respective radii. Hence,

$$\sigma_r(r_i) = -p_i \quad \text{and} \quad \sigma_r(r_o) = -p_o$$ (5-42)

where the minus signs are used to indicate compressive stresses. Moreover, since u as given by Eq. 5-41 and $du/dr = A_1 - A_2/r^2$ can be substituted into the expression for σ_r given by Eq. 5-39, the boundary conditions given by Eqs. 5-39 become

$$\sigma_r(r_i) = -p_i = \frac{E}{(1 + v)(1 - 2v)}\left[A_1 - (1 - 2v)\frac{A_2}{r_i^2}\right]$$

(5-43)

$$\sigma_r(r_o) = -p_o = \frac{E}{(1 + v)(1 - 2v)}\left[A_1 - (1 - 2v)\frac{A_2}{r_o^2}\right]$$

Solving these equations simultaneously for A_1 and A_2 yields

$$A_1 = \frac{(1 + v)(1 - 2v)}{E} \frac{p_i r_i^2 - p_o r_o^2}{r_o^2 - r_i^2}$$

$$A_2 = \frac{1 + v}{E} \frac{(p_i - p_o) r_i^2 r_o^2}{r_o^2 - r_i^2} \qquad (5\text{-}44)$$

These constants, when used in Eq. 5-41, permit determination of the radial displacement of any point on the elastic cylinder subjected to the specified pressures. Thus, displacements of the inner and outer boundaries of the cylinder can be computed.

If Eq. 5-41 and its derivative, together with the constants given by Eqs. 5-44, are substituted into Eqs. 5-39, and the results are simplified, general equations for the radial and tangential stresses at any point of an elastic cylinder are obtained. These are

$$\sigma_r = C_1 - \frac{C_2}{r^2} \qquad \text{and} \qquad \sigma_t = C_1 + \frac{C_2}{r^2} \qquad (5\text{-}45)$$

where

$$C_1 = \frac{p_i r_i^2 - p_o r_o^2}{r_o^2 - r_i^2} \qquad \text{and} \qquad C_2 = \frac{(p_i - p_o) r_i^2 r_o^2}{r_o^2 - r_i^2}$$

Note that $\sigma_r + \sigma_t$ is constant over the whole cross-sectional area of the cylinder. This means that the axial stress σ_x as given by Eq. 5-36 is also constant over the entire cross-sectional area of the thick-walled cylinder.

Remarks on the Thin-Disc Problem

The stress-strain relations used for a thick-walled cylinder corresponded to a *plane strain* condition. If, on the other hand, an annular thin disc were to be considered, the *plane stress* condition [i.e., $\sigma_x = 0$ and $\varepsilon_x = -v(\sigma_x + \sigma_y)/E$] governs. (See the discussion at the end of Section 5-6.) For this case, the stress-strain Eqs. 5-33 and 5-34 reduce to

$$\varepsilon_r = \frac{1}{E}(\sigma_r - v\sigma_t) \qquad \text{and} \qquad \varepsilon_t = \frac{1}{E}(-v\sigma_r + \sigma_t) \qquad (5\text{-}46)$$

and, by solving these equations simultaneously,

$$\sigma_r = \frac{E}{1 - v^2}(\varepsilon_r + v\varepsilon_t) \qquad \text{and} \qquad \sigma_t = \frac{E}{1 - v^2}(\varepsilon_t + v\varepsilon_r) \qquad (5\text{-}47)$$

It is these stress-strain relations that must be used in the solution process. However, the resulting differential equation remains the same as Eq. 5-40, and the radial and tangential stresses are also identical to those in the thick-walled cylinder and are given by Eq. 5-45. The only difference is that a different constant A_1 must be used in Eq. 5-41 for determining the radial displacement u. The constant A_2 remains the same as in Eq. 5-44, whereas A_1 becomes

$$A_1 = \frac{1 - \nu}{E} \frac{p_i r_i^2 - p_o r_o^2}{r_o^2 - r_i^2} \tag{5-48}$$

5-13. Special Cases

Internal pressure only (i.e., $p_i \neq 0$ and $p_o = 0$), Fig. 5-22. For this case, Eqs. 5-45 simplify to

$$\sigma_r = \frac{p_i r_i^2}{r_o^2 - r_i^2}\left(1 - \frac{r_0^2}{r^2}\right)$$

$$\sigma_t = \frac{p_i r_i^2}{r_o^2 - r_i^2}\left(1 + \frac{r_o^2}{r^2}\right) \tag{5-49}$$

Since $r_o^2/r^2 \geq 1$, σ_r is always a compressive stress and is maximum at $r = r_i$. Similarly, σ_t is always a tensile stress, and its maximum also occurs at $r = r_i$.

For brittle materials, the second Eq. 5-49 generally governs the design. However, for ductile materials, such as mild steel, it is more appropriate to adopt the criterion for the initiation of yielding due to shear rather than the material's capacity for resisting normal stress. This issue does not arise for thin-walled cylinders. In such problems, the maximum radial stress, equal to p_i, is negligible in comparison with σ_1. Therefore, according to Eq. 1-10, the relationship between the maximum normal and shear stresses is simple and direct, being $\tau_{max} = \sigma_1/2$, and either the normal or shear yield can be used as a criterion. However, for thick-walled cylinders, the radial stress σ_r may be of the same order of magnitude as σ_t. For such a case, the maximum shear stress must be found by superposing the effects from both of the large normal stresses[11] in the manner shown in Fig. 5-23. Both of these stresses reach their maximum values at the inner surface of the cylinder. The maximum shear stress found in this manner should be compared with the maximum shear stress that a material can attain. Such a value can be taken as $\sigma_{yp}/2$, where σ_{yp} is the normal yield stress in uniaxial tension. On this basis,

$$\tau_{max} = \frac{(\sigma_t)_{max} - (\sigma_r)_{max}}{2} = \frac{p_i r_o^2}{r_o^2 - r_i^2} = \frac{\sigma_{yp}}{2} \tag{5-50}$$

and

$$p_i = p_{yp} = \frac{\sigma_{yp}(r_o^2 - r_i^2)}{2r_o^2} \tag{5-51}$$

[11]The axial stress σ_z given by Eq. 5-36 does not enter the problem, since for $0 < \nu \leq 0.5$, this stress has an intermediate value between σ_t and σ_r.

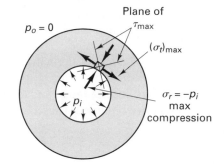

Fig. 5-22   An element in which τ_{max} occurs.

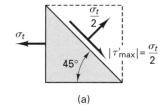

(a)

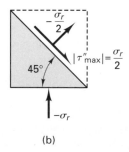

(b)

Fig. 5-23   Stress transformations for obtaining maximum shear stresses.

External pressure only (i.e., $p_i = 0$ and $p_o \neq 0$). For this case, Eqs. 5-45 simplify to

$$\sigma_r = -\frac{p_o r_o^2}{r_o^2 - r_i^2}\left(1 - \frac{r_i^2}{r^2}\right)$$

$$\sigma_t = -\frac{p_o r_o^2}{r_o^2 - r_i^2}\left(1 + \frac{r_i^2}{r^2}\right)$$

(5-52)

Since $r_i^2/r^2 \leq 1$, both stresses are always compressive. The maximum compressive stress is σ_t and occurs at $r = r_i$.

Equations 5-52 must not be used for very thin-walled cylinders. Buckling of the walls may occur and strength formulas give misleading results.

Example 5-6

Make a comparison of the tangential stress distribution caused by the internal pressure p_i as given by the Lamé formula in Section 5-12 with the distribution given by the approximate formula for thin-walled cylinders of Section 5-9 if (a) $r_o = 1.1r_i$, and (b) $r_o = 4r_i$; see Fig. 5-24.

SOLUTION
(a) Using Eq. 5-49b for σ_t,

$$(\sigma_t)_{r=r_i} = (\sigma_t)_{max} = \frac{p_i r_i^2}{(1.1r_i)^2 - r_i^2}\left[1 + \frac{(1.1r_i)^2}{r_i^2}\right] = 10.5p_i$$

$$(\sigma_t)_{r=r_o} = (\sigma_t)_{min} = \frac{p_i r_i^2}{(1.1r_i)^2 - r_i^2}\left[1 + \left(\frac{1.1r_i}{1.1r_i}\right)^2\right] = 9.5p_i$$

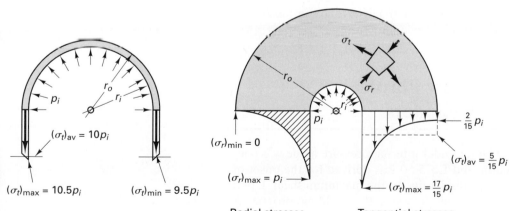

Radial stresses   Tangential stresses

Fig. 5-24

while, since the wall thickness $t = 0.1r_i$, the *average* hoop stress given by Eq. 5-26 is

$$(\sigma_t)_{\text{avg}} = \frac{p_i r_i}{t} = \frac{p_i r_i}{0.1 r_i} = 10 p_i$$

These results are shown in Fig. 5-24(a). Note particularly that in using Eq. 5-26, no appreciable error is involved.

(b) By using Eq. 5-49b for σ_t, the tangential stresses are obtained as before. These are

$$(\sigma_t)_{r=r_i} = (\sigma_t)_{\text{max}} = \frac{p_i r_i^2}{(4r_i)^2 - r_i^2}\left[1 + \frac{(4r_i)^2}{r_i^2}\right] = \frac{17}{15} p_i$$

$$(\sigma_t)_{r=r_o} = (\sigma_t)_{\text{min}} = \frac{p_i r_i^2}{(4r_i)^2 - r_i^2}\left[1 + \left(\frac{4r_i}{4r_i}\right)^2\right] = \frac{2}{15} p_i$$

The tangential stress is plotted in Fig. 5-24(b). A striking variation of the tangential stress can be observed from this figure. The average tangential stress given by Eq. 5-26, using $t = 3r_i$, is

$$(\sigma_t)_{\text{av}} = \frac{p_i r_i}{t} = \frac{5}{15} p_i = \frac{1}{3} p_i$$

The stress is nowhere near the true maximum stress.

The radial stresses were also computed by using Eq. 5-49a for σ_r, and the results are shown by the shaded area in Fig. 5-24(b).

It is interesting to note that no matter how thick a cylinder is made to resist internal pressure, the maximum tangential stress will not be smaller than p_i. In practice, this necessitates special techniques to reduce the maximum stress. For example, in gun manufacture, instead of using a single cylinder, another cylinder is shrunk onto the smaller one, which sets up initial *compressive stresses* in the inner cylinder and tensile stresses in the outer one. In operation, the compressive stress in the inner cylinder is released first, and only then does this cylinder begin to act in tension. A greater range of operating pressures is obtained thereby.

5-14. Behavior of Ideally Plastic Thick-Walled Cylinders

The case of a thick-walled cylinder under internal pressure alone was considered in the previous section, and Eq. 5-50 was derived for the onset of yield at the inner surface of the cylinder due to the maximum shear. Upon subsequent increase in the internal pressure, the yielding progresses toward the outer surface, and an elastic-plastic state prevails in the cylinder with a limiting radius c beyond which the cross section remains elastic. As the pressure increases, the radius c also increases until, eventually, the entire cross section becomes fully plastic at the ultimate load.

In the following discussion, as before, the maximum shear criterion for ideally plastic material will be assumed as

$$\tau_{max} = \frac{\sigma_t - \sigma_r}{2} = \frac{\sigma_{yp}}{2} \tag{5-53}$$

As noted earlier, this implies that σ_x has an intermediate value between σ_t and σ_r. A reexamination of Eqs. 5-36 and 5-49 shows this to be true in the elastic range, provided that $0 < v < 0.5$, but in the plastic range, this applies only if the ratio of outer to inner radius, r_o/r_i, is less than a certain value.[12] For $v = 0.3$, this ratio can be established to be 5.75; hence, the solutions to be obtained in this section will be valid only as long as $r_o < 5.75r_i$ (with $v = 0.3$). The task of finding the stress distribution is more complicated when this condition is not satisfied and is beyond the scope of this book.

Plastic Behavior of Thick-Walled Cylinders
The equations of static equilibrium are applicable, regardless of whether the elastic or plastic state is considered. Hence, Eq. 5-30 is applicable but must be supplemented by a yield condition.

Static equilibrium, Eq. 5-30:

$$\frac{d\sigma_r}{dr} + \frac{\sigma_r - \sigma_t}{r} = 0$$

Yield condition, Eq. 5-53:

$$\frac{\sigma_r - \sigma_r}{2} = \frac{\sigma_{yp}}{2}$$

By combining these two equations, the basic differential equation becomes

$$\frac{d\sigma_r}{dr} - \frac{\sigma_{yp}}{r} = 0 \quad \text{or} \quad d\sigma_r = \frac{\sigma_{yp}}{r} dr \tag{5-54}$$

The solution of this can be written as

$$\sigma_r = \sigma_{yp} \ln r + C \tag{5-55}$$

For a cylinder with inner radius a and outer radius b, the boundary condition (zero external pressure) can be expressed as

$$\sigma_r(b) = 0 = \sigma_{yp} \ln b + C \tag{5-56}$$

Hence, the integration constant C is given as

$$C = -\sigma_{yp} \ln b$$

---

[12]See W. T. Koiter, "On Partially Plastic Thick-Walled Tubes," *Biezeno Anniversary Volume on Applied Mechanics* (Haarlem, Holland: H. Stam, 1953), 233–251.

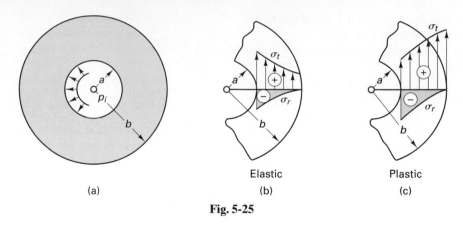

Elastic (b)

Plastic (c)

(a)

Fig. 5-25

The radial and tangential stresses are then obtained, using Eqs. 5-55 and 5-53, respectively. Thus,

$$\sigma_r = \sigma_{yp}(\ln r - \ln b) = \sigma_{yp} \ln r/b \qquad (5\text{-}57)$$

$$\sigma_t = \sigma_{yp} + \sigma_r = \sigma_{yp}(1 + \ln r/b) \qquad (5\text{-}58)$$

The stress distributions given by Eqs. 5-57 and 5-58 are shown in Fig. 5-25(c), whereas Fig. 5-25(b) shows the elastic stress distributions. Since the fully plastic state represents the ultimate collapse of the thick-walled cylinder, the ultimate internal pressure, using Eq. 5-57, is given as

$$p_{ult} = \sigma_r(a) = \sigma_{yp} \ln a/b \qquad (5\text{-}59)$$

Elastic-Plastic Behavior of Thick-Walled Cylinders   For any value of p_i that is intermediate to the yield and ultimate values given by Eqs. 5-51 and 5-59, respectively (i.e., $p_{yp} < p_i < p_{ult}$), the cross section of the cylinder between the inner radius a and an intermediate radius c is fully plastic, whereas that between c and the outer radius b is in the elastic domain, Fig. 5-26. At the elastic-plastic interface, the yield condition is just satisfied, and the corresponding radial stress X can be computed using Eq. 5-51 with $r_i = c$ and $r_o = b$; hence,

$$X = \frac{\sigma_{yp}}{2} \frac{b^2 - c^2}{b^2} \qquad (5\text{-}60)$$

This stress becomes the boundary condition to be used in conjunction with Eq. 5-55 for a fully plastic segment with inner radius a and outer radius c. Hence,

$$\sigma_r(c) = -X = -\frac{\sigma_{yp}}{2} \frac{b^2 - c^2}{b^2} = \sigma_{yp} \ln c + C \qquad (5\text{-}61)$$

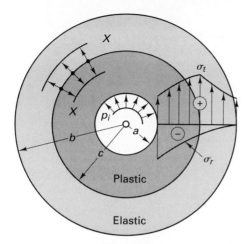

Fig. 5-26

and

$$C = -\frac{\sigma_{yp}}{2}\frac{b^2 - c^2}{b^2} - \sigma_{yp}\ln c \qquad (5\text{-}62)$$

By substituting this value of C into Eq. 5-57, the radial stress in the plastic region is obtained as

$$\sigma_r = \sigma_{yp}\ln\frac{r}{c} - \frac{\sigma_{yp}}{2}\frac{b^2 - c^2}{b^2} \qquad (5\text{-}63)$$

and, by using Eq. 5-53, the tangential stress in the plastic zone becomes

$$\sigma_t = \sigma_{yp} + \sigma_r = \sigma_{yp}\left(1 + \ln\frac{r}{c}\right) - \frac{\sigma_{yp}}{2}\frac{b^2 - c^2}{b^2} \qquad (5\text{-}64)$$

The internal pressure p_i at which the plastic zone extends from a to c can be obtained, using Eq. 5-63, simply as $p_i = \sigma_r(a)$. Equations 5-49, with $r_i = c$ and $r_o = b$, provide the necessary relations for calculating the stress distributions in the elastic zone.

PROBLEMS

Section 5-2

5-1. Redesign the shear mounting in Example 5-1 to retain the same shear spring constant k_s, but changing its dimensions to a square pad with 10-mm-thick rubber.

5-2. Determine the spring constant k_s for a shear pad made from polyurethane elastomer 20 mm square and 6 mm thick. The pad is similar to that shown in Fig. 5-5. The material constants are $G = 10$ kPa and $\gamma = 0.50$.

Section 5-3

5-3. Calculate the elastic shear energy at shear yield strength and hyperelastic resilience just short of the ultimate shear strength for 2024-T4 aluminum alloy and 0.2% carbon steel. Base the physical properties on the data given in Table 1A or 1B in the Appendix.

Section 5-6

5-4. Consider a 4-in square steel bar subjected to transverse biaxial tensile stresses of 20 ksi in the x direction and 10 ksi in the y direction. (a) Assuming the bar to be in a state of plane stress, determine the strain in the z direction and the elongations of the plate in the x and y directions. (b) Assuming the bar to be in a state of plane strain, determine the stress in the z direction and the elongations of the bar in the x and y directions. Let $E = 30 \times 10^3$ ksi and $v = 0.25$.

5-5. A rectangular copper alloy block such as shown in Fig. 5-10(a) has the following dimensions: $a = 200$ mm, $b = 120$ mm, and $c = 100$ mm. This block is subjected to a triaxial loading in equilibrium having the following magnitude: $P_x = -4.80$ MPa, $P_y = +2.40$ MPa, and $P_z = +2.00$ MPa. Assuming that the applied forces are uniformly distributed on the respective faces, determine the size changes that take place along a, b, and c. Let $E = 140$ GPa and $v = 0.35$.

5-6. Rework the preceding problem by changing the applied forces such that $P_x = +2.40$ MPa, $P_y = -1.20$ MPa, and $P_z = -2.00$ MPa. What should be the magnitude of P_x acting alone to cause the same deformation along a as the other three forces?

5-7. A piece of 50 by 250 by 10-mm steel plate is subjected to uniformly distributed stresses along its edges (see the figure). (a) If $P_x = 100$ kN and $P_y = 200$ kN, what change in thickness occurs due to the application of these forces? (b) To cause the same change in thickness as in part (a) by P_x alone, what must be its magnitude? Let $E = 200$ GPa and $v = 0.25$.

5-8. A rectangular titanium plate similar to that shown in Fig. 5-10(a) has the following dimensions. $a = 20$ mm, $b = 15$ mm, and $c = 5$ mm. Uniformly distributed tensile forces of 7.50 kN act in the z direction. Determine the strains in the x, y, and z directions. Let $E = 120$ GPa, and $v = 0.35$.

5-9. Assuming for steel an $E = 200$ GPa and a $v = 0.25$, calculate the Lamé parameters.

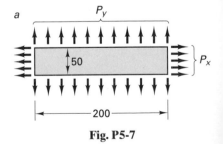

Fig. P5-7

Sections 5-7 and 5-8

5-10. If a nickel alloy has an $E = 180$ MPa and it is estimated that $\nu = 0.25$, what is its shear modulus?

5-11. If for a lead $E = 16$ MPa and it is estimated that $\nu = 0.45$, what is its shear modulus G and bulk modulus k?

5-12. Using the values for E and G given in Table 1A of the Appendix, calculate Poisson's ratios for 2024-T4 aluminum alloy and steel.

5-13. Using Table 1A of the Appendix, calculate the bulk moduli for 6061-T6 aluminum alloy and steel in U.S. customary units.

5-14. What are the values of G and bulk modulus k for glass if $E = 65$ MPa and $\nu = 0.22$, for steel if $E = 200$ MPa and $\nu = 0.25$, and for lead if $E = 16$ MPa and $\nu = 0.45$?

Section 5-9

5-15. A stainless-steel cylindrical shell has a 30-in inside diameter and is 0.5 in thick. If the tensile strength of the material is 80 ksi and the factor of safety is 5, what is the allowable working pressure? Assume that appropriate hemispherical ends are provided. Also estimate the bursting pressure.

5-16. A "penstock" (i.e., a pipe for conveying water to a hydroelectric turbine) operates at a head of 80 m. If the diameter of the penstock is 0.75 m and the allowable stress 60 MPa, what wall thickness is required?

5-17. A tank of butt-welded construction for the storage of gasoline is to be 12 m in diameter and 5 m high. (a) Select the plate thickness for the bottom row of plates. Allow 160 MPa for steel in tension and assume the efficiency of welds at 80%. Add approximately 3 mm to the computed wall thickness to compensate for corrosion. Neglect local stresses at the juncture of the vertical walls with the bottom. (Specific gravity of the gasoline to be stored is 0.721.) (b) Assuming that the bottom of the tank does not restrain the displacement of the tank walls, what increase in diameter would occur at the bottom? $E = 200$ GPa and $\nu = 0.25$.

5-18. A cylindrical vessel is used for storing ammonia (NH_3) at the maximum temperature of 50°C. The vapor pressure of NH_3 at 50°C is 20 atm. The thickness of the vessel material is limited to 20 mm with a tensile strength of 400 MPa. (a) If the factor of safety is 5, assuming that all welds will be inspected with X-rays, what can be the maximum diameter of the vessel? (b) For the selected wall thickness, calculate the change in diameter that would occur with ammonia at 50°C.

5-19. An air chamber for a pump, the sectional side view of which is shown in mm in the figure, consists of two pieces. Compute the number of 19-mm bolts (*net* area 195 mm²) required to attach the chamber to the cylinder at plane A–A. The allowable tensile stress in the bolts is 50 MPa, and the water and air pressure is 1.5 MPa.

5-20. A water tank made of wood staves is 6 m in diameter and 4 m high. Specify the spacing of 30-by-6-mm steel hoops if the allowable tensile stress for steel is set at 90 MPa. Use uniform hoop spacing within each meter of the tank's height.

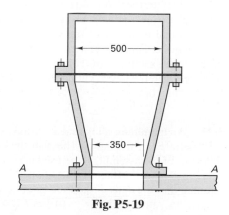

Fig. P5-19

5-21. A cylindrical pressure vessel of 120 in *outside* diameter, used for processing rubber, is 36 ft long. If the cylindrical portion of the vessel is made from 1-in-thick steel plate and the vessel operates at 120 psi internal pressure, determine the total elongation of the circumference and the increase in the diameter's dimension caused by the operating pressure. $E = 29 \times 10^6$ psi and $\nu = 0.25$.

5-22. A thin ring is heated in oil 150°C above room temperature. In this condition, the ring just slips on a solid cylinder, as shown in the figure. Assuming the cylinder to be completely rigid, (a) determine the hoop stress that develops in the ring upon cooling, and (b) determine what bearing develops between the ring and the cylinder. Let $\alpha = 20 \times 10^{-6}/°C$ and $E = 70$ GPa.

5-23. A copper alloy wire is stretched taut across the diameter of a cylindrical pressure vessel, as shown in the figure. For the wire: $A = 0.060$ mm^2, $E = 140$ GPa, and $\alpha = 18 \times 10^{-6}/°C$. The diameter of the steel pressure vessel is 2000 mm and the wall thickness is 10 mm. (In calculations, do not differentiate between the inside and mean diameters of the cylinder.) For steel, let $E = 200$ GPa, $\alpha_{St} = 12 \times 10^{-6}/°C$, and Poisson's ratio $\nu = 0.30$. If this vessel is pressurized to 1 MPa and, at the same time, the temperature drops 50°C, what stress would develop in the wire? Assume that the temperature of the wire as well as that of the cylinder simultaneously becomes lower and that the deformation of the cylinder caused by the pull of the wire can be neglected.

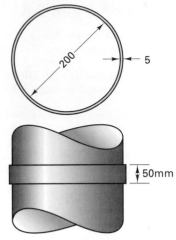

Fig. P5-22

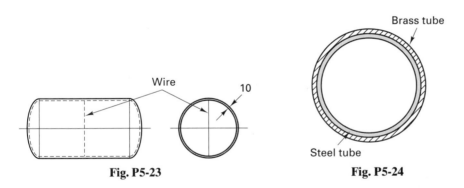

Fig. P5-23   **Fig. P5-24**

5-24. A cylindrical pressure vessel shown in the figure is made by shrinking a brass tube over a mild steel tube. Both cylinders have a wall thickness of 0.25 in. The nominal diameter of the vessel is 20 in and is to be used in all calculations involving the diameter. When the brass cylinder is heated 100°F above room temperature, it exactly fits over the steel cylinder, which is at room temperature. What is the stress in the brass cylinder when the composite vessels cool to room temperature? For brass: $E_{Br} = 16 \times 16^6$ psi and $\alpha_{Br} = 10.7 \times 10^{-6}/°F$. For steel: $E_{St} = 30 \times 10^6$ psi and $\alpha_{St} = 6.7 \times 10^{-6}/°F$.

5-25. An aluminum-alloy tube is shrunk onto a steel tube to form the pressure vessel illustrated in the figure. The wall thickness of each tube is 4 mm. The average diameter of the assembly to be used in calculations is 400 mm. If the composite tube is pressurized at 2 MPa, what additional hoop stress develops in the aluminum tube? Assume that the ends of the tube can freely expand, preventing the development of longitudinal stresses (i.e., $\sigma_x = 0$). Let $E_{Al} = 70 \times 10^3$ MPa and $E_{St} = 200 \times 10^3$ MPa.

(*Hint:* The interface pressure, say $\bar{p}$, between the two materials acts to cause hoop tension in the outer tube and hoop compression in the inner tube.)

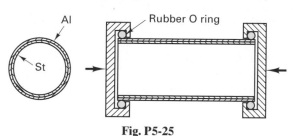

Fig. P5-25

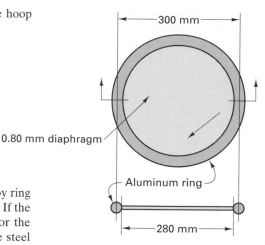

Fig. P5-26

5-26. A steel diaphragm 0.80 mm thick is stretched inside an aluminum-alloy ring as shown in the figure. The ring is made from a round rod of 20-mm diameter. If the temperature is raised 40°C, what stresses are induced in the diaphragm? For the aluminum alloy $E_a = 70$ GPa, $G_a = 26$ GPa, and $\alpha_a = 23 \times 10^{-6}/°C$. For the steel diaphragm $E_s = 200$ GPa, $G_s = 83$ GPa, and $\alpha_s = 1.2 \times 10^{-6}/°C$.

5-27. Exceptionally light-weight pressure vessels have been developed by employing glass filaments for resisting the tensile forces and using epoxy resin as a binder. A diagram of a filament-wound cylinder is shown in the figure. If the winding is needed to resist only hoop stresses, the helix angle $\alpha = 90°$. If, however, the cylinder is closed, both hoop and longitudinal forces develop, and the required helix angle of the filaments $\alpha \approx 55°$ ($\tan^2 \alpha = 2$). Verify this result. (*Hint:* Isolate an element of unit width and a developed length of $\tan \alpha$ as in the figure. For such an element, the same number of filaments is cut by each section. Therefore, if F is a force in a filament and n is the number of filaments at a section, $P_y = Fn \sin \alpha$. Force P_x can be found similarly. An equation based on the known ratio between the longitudinal and the hoop stress leads to the required result.)

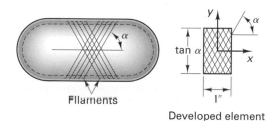

Fig. P5-27

Sections 5-12 and 5-13

5-28. Verify the solution of Eq. 5-30.

5-29. Show that the ratio of the maximum tangential stress to the average tangential stress for a thick-walled cylinder subjected only to internal pressure is $(1 + \beta^2)/(1 + \beta)$, where $\beta = r_o/r_i$.

5-30. Show that no matter how large the outside diameter of a cylinder, subjected only to internal pressure, is made, the maximum tangential stress is not less than p_i. (*Hint:* Let $r_o \to \infty$.)

5-31.   An alloy-steel cylinder has a 150 mm ID (inside diameter) and a 450-mm OD. If it is subjected to an internal pressure of $p_i = 150$ MPa ($p_o = 0$), (a) determine the radial and tangential stress distributions and show the results on a plot. (b) Determine the maximum (principal) shear stress. (c) Determine the change in external and internal diameters. $E = 200$ GPa and $v = 0.25$.

5-32.   An alloy-steel cylinder has a 200-mm ID and a 400-mm OD. If it is subjected to an internal pressure of $p_i = 120$ MPa ($p_o = 0$), (a) determine the radial and tangential stress distributions and show the results on a plot. (b) Determine the maximum (principal) shear stress. (c) Determine the changes in external and internal diameters. $E = 200$ GPa and $v = 0.25$.

5-33.   Rework Problem 5-32 with $p_i = 0$ and $p_o = 80$ MPa.

5-34.   Rework Problem 5-32 with $p_i = 160$ MPa and $p_o = 80$ MPa.

5-35.   Isolate one-half of the cylinder of Problem 5-34 by passing a plane through the axis of the cylinder. Then, by integrating the tangential stresses over the respective areas, show that the isolated free body is in equilibrium.

5-36.   Design a thick-walled cylinder of a 4-in internal diameter for an internal pressure of 8000 psi such as to provide (a) a factor of safety of 2 against any yielding in the cylinder and (b) a factor of safety of 3 against ultimate collapse. The yield stress of steel in tension is 40 ksi.

5-37.   A 16-in OD steel cylinder with approximately a 10-in bore (ID) is shrunk onto another steel cylinder of 10-in OD with a 6-in ID. Initially, the internal diameter of the outer cylinder was 0.01 in smaller than the external diameter of the inner cylinder. The assembly was accomplished by heating the larger cylinder in oil. For both cylinders, $E = 30 \times 10^6$ psi and $v = 0.25$. (a) Determine the pressure at the boundaries between the two cylinders. (*Hint:* The elastic increase in the diameter of the outer cylinder with the elastic decrease in the diameter of the inner cylinder accommodates the initial interference between the two cylinders.) (b) Determine the tangential and radial stresses caused by the pressure found in part (a). Show the results on a plot. (c) Determine the internal pressure to which the composite cylinder may be subjected without exceeding a tangential stress of 20,000 psi in the inner cylinder. (*Hint:* After assembly, the cylinders act as one unit. The initial compressive stress in the inner cylinder is released first.) (d) Superpose the tangential stresses found in part (b) with the tangential stresses resulting from the internal pressure found in part (c). Show the results on a plot.

5-38.   Set up the differential equation for a thin disc rotating with an angular velocity of ω rad/s. The unit weight of the material is γ. [*Hint:* Consider an element as in Fig. 5-21(b) and add an inertia term.]

Section 5-14

5-39.   For a thick-walled cylinder of inner radius a and outer radius $b = 2a$, (a) calculate the internal pressure at which the elastic-plastic boundary is at $r = 1.5\,a$, (b) determine the radial and tangential stress distributions due to the internal pressure found in part (a) and show them on a plot, and (c) calculate the ultimate collapse load. Assume the material to be elastic perfectly plastic, with a yield stress of 350 MPa.

6

Torsion

6-1. Introduction

Detailed methods of analysis for determining stresses and deformations in axially loaded bars were presented in the first four chapters. Analogous relations for members subjected to torques about their longitudinal axes are developed in this chapter. The constitutive relations for shear discussed in the preceding chapter will be employed for this purpose. *The investigations are confined to the effect of a single type of action (i.e., of a torque causing a twist or torsion in a member).* Members subjected simultaneously to torque and bending, frequently occurring in practice, are treated in Chapter 13.

By far, the major part of this chapter is devoted to the consideration of members having circular cross sections, either solid or tubular. Solution of such elastic and inelastic problems can be obtained using the procedures of engineering mechanics of solids. For the solution of torsion problems having noncircular cross sections, methods of the mathematical theory of elasticity (or finite elements) must be employed. This topic is briefly discussed in order to make the reader aware of the differences in such solutions from that for circular members. Further, to lend emphasis to the difference in the solutions discussed, this chapter is subdivided into four distinct parts. It should be noted, however, that in practice, members for transmitting torque, such as shafts for motors, torque tubes for power equipment, etc., are predominantly circular or tubular in cross section. Therefore, numerous applications fall within the scope of the formulas derived in this chapter.

6-2. Application of the Method of Sections

In engineering solid mechanics, in analyzing members for torque, regardless of the type of cross section, the basic method of sections (Section 1-2) is employed. For the torsion problems discussed here, there is *only one* relevant equation of statics. Thus, if the x axis is directed along a member, such an equation is $\Sigma\, M_x = 0$. Therefore, for statically determinate systems, there can only be one reactive torque. After determining this torque, an analysis begins by separating a member of a *section perpendicular to the axis of a member.* Then either side of a member can be isolated and the *internal* torque found. This internal torque must *balance* the externally applied torques (i.e., *the external and the internal torques are equal*) but have opposite sense. In statically determinate problems, the formal calculation of a reaction may be bypassed by isolating a bar segment with the unsupported end. Nevertheless, an equilibrium of the whole system must always be assured. In statically indeterminate problems, the reactions must always be found before one can calculate the internal torques. Some guidance on calculating reactions in statically indeterminate problems is provided in Section 6-9 of this chapter.

For simplicity, the members treated in this chapter will be assumed "weightless" or supported at frequent enough intervals to make the effect of bending negligible. Axial forces that may also act simultaneously on the bars are excluded for the present.

Example 6.1

Find the internal torque at section *K–K* for the shaft shown in Fig. 6-1(a) and acted upon by the three torques indicated.

SOLUTION
The 30 N · m torque at *C* is balanced by the two torques of 20 and 10 N · m at *A* and *B*, respectively. Therefore, the body as a whole is in equilibrium. Next, by passing a section *K–K* perpendicular to the axis of the rod *anywhere* between *A* and *B*, a free body of a part of the shaft, shown in Fig. 6-1(b), is obtained. Whereupon, from $\Sigma\, M_x = 0$, or

$$\text{externally applied torque} = \text{internal torque}$$

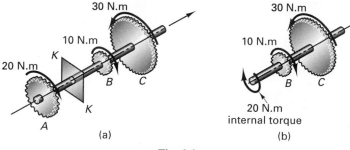

Fig. 6-1

the conclusion is reached that the internal or resisting torque developed in the shaft between *A* and *B* is 20 N · m. Similar considerations lead to the conclusion that the internal torque resisted by the shaft between *B* and *C* is 30 N · m.

It may be seen intuitively that for a member of constant cross section, the maximum internal torque causes the maximum stress and imposes the most severe condition on the material. Hence, in investigating a torsion member, several sections may have to be examined to determine the largest internal torque. A section where the largest internal torque is developed is the *critical section*. In example 6-1, the critical section is anywhere between points *B* and *C*. If the torsion member varies in size, it is more difficult to decide where the material is critically stressed. Several sections may have to be investigated and *stresses computed* to determine the critical section. These situations are analogous to the case of an axially loaded rod, and means must be developed to determine stresses as a function of the internal torque and the size of the member. In the next several sections, the necessary formulas are derived.

Instead of curved arrows as in Fig. 6-1, double-headed vectors following the right-hand screw rule sign convention will also be used in this text; see Fig. 6-2. The torque **T** is a vector, similar to the force vector **P** encountered in Section 1-4. Since the direction of **T** is known a priori, for simplicity its scalar representation as *T* is used.

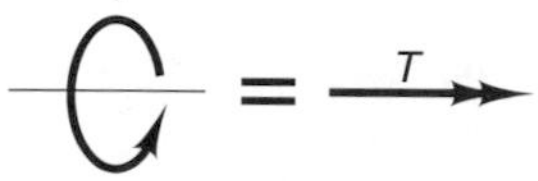

Fig. 6-2   Alternative representations of torque.

Part A   TORSION OF CIRCULAR ELASTIC BARS

6-3. Basic Assumptions for Circular Members

To establish a relation between the internal torque and the stresses it sets up in members with *circular solid and tubular cross sections,* it is necessary to make two assumptions, the validity of which will be justified later. These, in addition to the homogeneity of the material, are as follows:

1. A plane section of material perpendicular to the axis of a circular member remains *plane* after the torques are applied (i.e., no *warpage* or distortion of parallel planes normal to the axis of a member takes place).[1]

2. In a circular member subjected to torque, *shear strains* γ *vary linearly from the central axis,* reaching γ_{max} at the periphery. This assumption is illustrated in Fig. 6-3 and means that an imaginary plane such as DO_1O_3C moves to $D'O_1O_3C$ when the torque is applied. Alternatively, if an imaginary radius O_3C is considered fixed in direction, similar radii initially at O_2B and O_1D rotate to the respective new positions O_2B' and O_1D'. These radii remain straight.

    It must be emphasized that these assumptions *hold only for circular solid and tubular members.* For this class of members, these assumptions work so well that they *apply beyond the limit of the elastic behavior of a material.* These assumptions will be used again in Section 6-13, where stress distribution beyond the proportional limit is discussed.

3. If attention is confined to the linearly *elastic* material, Hooke's law applies, and it follows that shear stress is proportional to shear strain. For this case complete agreement between experimentally determined and computed quantities is found with the derived stress and deformation formulas based on these assumptions. Moreover, their validity can be rigorously demonstrated by the methods of the mathematical theory of elasticity.

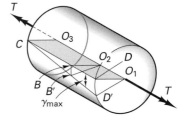

Fig. 6-3 Variation of strain in circular member subjected to torque.

---

[1]For small deformations it is assumed that parallel planes perpendicular to the axis *remain a constant* distance apart. This is not true if deformations are large. However, since the usual deformations are very small, stresses not considered here are negligible. For details, see S. Timoshenko, *Strength of Materials,* 3rd. ed., Part II, *Advanced Theory and Problems* (New York: Van Nostrand, 1956), Chapter VI.

6-4. The Torsion Formula

In the *elastic* case, on the basis of the previous assumptions, since stress is proportional to strain, and the latter varies linearly from the center, *stresses vary linearly from the central axis of a circular member.* The stresses induced by the assumed distortions are *shear* stresses and lie in the plane parallel to the section taken normal to the axis of a rod. The variation of the shear stress follows directly from the shear-strain assumption and the use of Hooke's law for shear, Eq. 5-1. This is illustrated in Fig. 6-4. Unlike the case of an axially loaded rod, this stress is *not* of uniform intensity. The maximum shear stress occurs at points most remote from the center O and is designated τ_{max}. These points, such as points C and D in Figs. 6-3 and 6-4, lie at the periphery of a section at a distance c from the center. For linear shear stress variation, at *any* arbitrary point at a distance ρ from O, the shear stress is $(\rho/c)\tau_{max}$.

The resisting torque can be expressed in terms of stress once the stress distribution at a section is established. For equilibrium this internal resisting torque must equal the externally applied torque T. Hence,

$$\underbrace{\underbrace{\frac{\rho}{c}\,\tau_{max}}_{\text{Stress}}\;\underbrace{dA}_{\text{area}}}_{\text{force}}\quad \underbrace{\rho}_{\text{arm}} = T$$
$$\underbrace{}_{\text{torque}}$$

where the integral sums up all torques developed on the cut by the infinitesimal forces acting at a distance ρ from a member's axis, O in Fig. 6-4, over the whole area A of the cross section, and where T is the resisting torque.

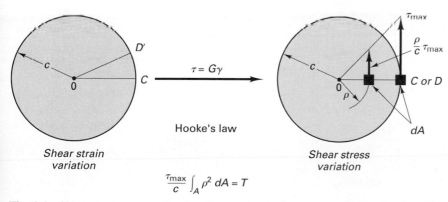

Shear strain variation

$\tau = G\gamma$

Hooke's law

Shear stress variation

$$\frac{\tau_{max}}{c}\int_A \rho^2\, dA = T$$

Fig. 6-4   Shear strain assumption leading to elastic shear stress distribution in a circular member.

At any given section, τ_{max} and c are constant; hence, the previous relation can be written as

$$\frac{\tau_{max}}{c} \int_A \rho^2 \, dA = T \qquad (6\text{-}1)$$

However, $\int_A \rho^2 \, dA$, *the polar moment of inertia* of a cross-sectional area, is also a constant for a particular cross-sectional area. It will be designated by I_p in this text. For a circular section, $dA = 2\pi\rho \, d\rho$, where $2\pi\rho$ is the circumference of an annulus[2] with a radius ρ of width $d\rho$. Hence,

$$I_P = \int_A \rho^2 \, dA = \int_0^c 2\pi\rho^3 \, d\rho = 2\pi \left.\frac{\rho^4}{4}\right|_0^c = \frac{\pi c^4}{2} = \frac{\pi d^4}{32} \qquad (6\text{-}2)$$

That is,

$$\boxed{I_p = \frac{\pi c^4}{2} = \frac{\pi d^4}{32}} \qquad (6\text{-}2)$$

where d is the diameter of a solid circular shaft. If c or d is measured in millimeters, I_p has the units of mm^4; if in inches, the units become in^4.

By using the symbol I_p for the polar moment of inertia of a circular area, Eq. 6-1 may be written more compactly as

$$\boxed{\tau_{max} = \frac{Tc}{I_p}} \qquad (6\text{-}3)$$

This equation is the well-known *torsion formula*[3] for circular shafts that expresses the maximum shear stress in terms of the resisting torque and the dimensions of a member. In applying this formula, the internal torque T can be expressed in newton-meters, $N \cdot m$, or inch-pounds, c in meters or inches, and I_p in m^4 or in ^{4}. Such usage makes the units of the torsional shear stress

$$\frac{[N \cdot m][m]}{[m^4]} = \left[\frac{N}{m^2}\right]$$

or *pascals* (Pa) in SI units, or

$$\frac{[in\text{-}lb][in]}{[in^4]} = \left[\frac{lb}{in^2}\right]$$

or *psi* in the U.S. customary units.

---

[2]An annulus is an area contained between two concentric circles.

[3]It was developed by Coulomb, a French engineer, in about 1775 in connection with his work on electric instruments. His name has been immortalized by its use for a practical unit of quantity in electricity.

A more general relation that Eq. 6-3 for a shear stress, τ, at *any* point a distance ρ from the center of a section is

$$\tau = \frac{\rho}{c}\,\tau_{max} = \frac{T\rho}{I_p} \qquad (6\text{-}4)$$

Equations 6-3 and 6-4 *are applicable* with equal rigor *to circular tubes*, since the same assumptions as used in the previous derivation apply. It is necessary, however, to modify I_p. For a tube, as may be seen from Fig. 6-5, the limits of integration for Eq. 6-2 extend from b to c. Hence, for a *circular tube,*

$$I_p = \int_A \rho^2\, dA = \int_b^c 2\pi\rho^3\, d\rho = \frac{\pi c^4}{2} - \frac{\pi b^4}{2} \qquad (6\text{-}5)$$

or, stated otherwise, I_p for a circular tube equals $+I_p$ for a solid shaft using the outer diameter and $-I_p$ for a solid shaft using the inner diameter.

For very *thin* tubes, if b is nearly equal to c, and $c - b = t$, the thickness of the tube, I_p reduces to a simple approximate expression:

$$I_p \approx 2\pi R_{av}^3 t \qquad (6\text{-}6)$$

where $R_{av} = (b + c)/2$, which is sufficiently accurate in some applications.

If a circular bar is made from two different materials bonded together, as shown in Fig. 6-6(a), the same *strain* assumption applies as for a solid member. For such a case, through Hooke's law, the shear *stress* distribution becomes, as in Fig. 6-6(b). If the shear modulus for the outer stiffer tube is G_1 and that of the inner softer core is G_2, the ratio of the respective shear stresses on a ring of radius OB is G_1/G_2.

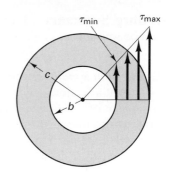

Fig. 6-5 Variation of stress in an elastic circular tube.

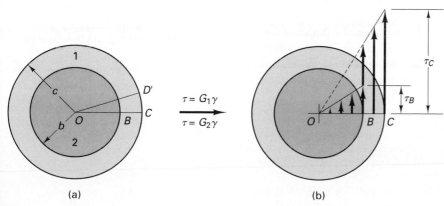

Fig. 6-6 Elastic behavior of a circular member in torsion having an inner core of soft material.

Procedure Summary   For the torsion problem of circular shafts the *three basic concepts* of engineering mechanics of solids as used previously may be summarized in the following manner:

1. *Equilibrium conditions* are used for determining the internal resisting torques at a section.
2. *Geometry of deformation* (kinematics) is postulated such that shear strain varies linearly from the axis of a shaft.
3. *Material properties* (constitutive relations) are used to relate shear strains to shear stresses and permit calculation of shear stresses at a section.

Only a linear elastic case using Hooke's law is considered in the preceding discussion. This is extended to nonlinear material behavior in Section 6-13.

These basic concepts are used for determining both stresses and angles of twist of circular shafts. However, similar to the case for axially loaded bars, large *local* stresses arise at points of application of concentrated torques or changes in cross section. According to *Saint-Venant's principle,* the stresses and strains are accurately described by the developed theory only beyond a distance about equal to the diameter of a shaft from these locations. Typically local stresses are determined by using stress-concentration factors.

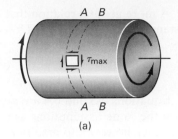

(a)

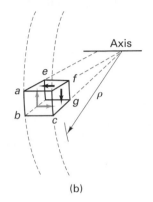

(b)

6-5. Remarks on the Torsion Formula

So far the shear stresses as given by Eqs. 6-3 and 6-4 have been thought of as acting only in the plane of a cut perpendicular to the axis of the shaft. There indeed they are acting to form a couple resisting the externally applied torques. However, to understand the problem further, an infinitesimal cylindrical element[4] shown in Fig. 6-7(b), is isolated.

The shear stresses acting in the planes perpendicular to the axis of the rod are known from Eq. 6-4. *Their directions coincide with the direction of the internal torque.* (This should be clearly visualized by the reader.) On adjoining parallel planes of a disc-like element, these stresses act in opposite directions. However, these shear stresses acting in the plane of the cuts taken normal to the axis of a rod *cannot exist alone,* as was shown in Section 1-4. Numerically, equal shear stresses must act on the axial planes [such as the planes *aef* and *bcg* in Fig. 6-7(b)] to fulfill the requirements of static equilibrium for an element.[5]

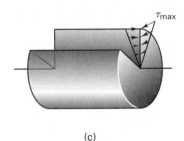

(c)

Fig. 6-7   Existence of shear stresses on mutually perpendicular planes in a circular shaft subjected to torque.

---

[4]Two planes perpendicular to the axis of the rod, two planes through the axis, and two surfaces at different radii are used to isolate this element. Properties of such an element are expressible mathematically in cylindrical coordinates.

[5]Note that the maximum shear stresses, as shown diagrammatically in Fig. 6-7(a), actually act on planes perpendicular to the axis of the rod and on planes passing through the axis of the rod. The representation shown is purely schematic. The free *surface* of a shaft is *free* of all stresses.

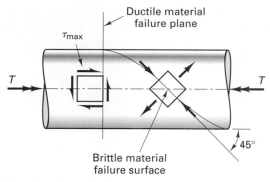

Fig. 6-8   Potential torsional failure surfaces in ductile and brittle materials.

Shear stresses acting in the axial planes follow the same variation in intensity as do the shear stresses in the planes perpendicular to the axis of the rod. This variation of shear stresses on the mutually perpendicular planes is shown in Fig. 6-7(c), where a portion of the shaft has been removed for the purposes of illustration.

According to Section 5-7, such *shear* stresses can be *transformed* into an *equivalent* system of *normal* stresses acting at angles of 45° with the shear stresses (see Fig. 5-11). Numerically, these stresses are related to each other in the following manner: $\tau = \sigma_1 = -\sigma_2$. Therefore, if the shear strength of a material is less than its strength in tension, a shear failure takes place on a plane perpendicular to the axis of a bar; see Fig. 6-8. This kind of failure occurs gradually and exhibits *ductile* behavior. Alternatively, if the converse is true (i.e., $\sigma_1 < \tau$), a brittle fracture is caused by the tensile stresses along a helix forming an angle of 45° with the bar axis[6]; see Fig. 6-8. A photograph of a ductile fracture of a steel specimen is shown in Fig. 6-9, and that of a brittle fracture for cast iron in Fig. 6-10. Another example of a brittle fracture, for sandstone, is shown in Fig. 6-11.

The stress transformation brought into the previous discussion, since it does not depend on material properties, is also applicable to anisotropic materials. For example, wood exhibits drastically different properties of strength in different directions. The shearing strength of wood on planes parallel to the grain is much less than on planes perpendicular to the grain. Hence, although equal intensities of the shear stress exist on mutually perpendicular planes, wooden shafts of inadequate size fail longitudinally along axial planes. Such shafts are occasionally used in the process industries.

Fig. 6-9   Fractured torsion specimen of A322 steel.

---

[6]Ordinary chalk behaves similarly. This may be demonstrated in the classroom by twisting a piece of chalk to failure.

Fig. 6-10   Fractured cast iron specimen in torsion. The photograph on the right shows the specimen more widely separated.

Fig. 6-11   Part of fractured sandstone core specimen in torsion. (Experiment by D. Pirtz.)

Example 6-2

Find the maximum torsional shear stress in shaft AC shown in Fig. 6-1(a). Assume the shaft from A to C is 10 mm in diameter.

SOLUTION
From Example 6-1, the maximum internal torque resisted by this shaft is known to be 30 N · m. Hence, $T = 30$ N · m, and $c = d/2 = 5$ mm. From Eq. 6-2,

$$I_p = \frac{\pi d^4}{32} = \frac{\pi \times 10^4}{32} = 982 \text{ mm}^4$$

and from Eq. 6-3,

$$\tau_{\text{max}} = \frac{Tc}{I_p} = \frac{30 \times 10^3 \times 5}{982} = 153 \text{ MPa}$$

This maximum shear stress at 5 mm from the axis of the rod acts in the plane of a cut perpendicular to the axis of the rod *and* along the longitudinal planes passing through the axis of the rod [Fig. 6-7(c)]. Just as for a Cartesian element, the shear stresses on mutually perpendicular planes for a cylindrical element are equal. It is instructive to note that the results of this solution can be represented in matrix form by two elements in a stress tensor as

$$\begin{pmatrix} 0 & \tau_{max} & 0 \\ \tau_{max} & 0 & 0 \\ 0 & 0 & 0 \end{pmatrix} = \begin{pmatrix} 0 & 153 & 0 \\ 153 & 0 & 0 \\ 0 & 0 & 0 \end{pmatrix} \text{MPa} \qquad (6\text{-}7)$$

This is to be contrasted with the fully populated stress tensor given by Eq. 1-1b.

Example 6-3

Consider a long tube of 20 mm outside diameter, d_0, and of 16 mm inside diameter, d_i, twisted about its longitudinal axis with a torque T of 40 N · m. Determine the shear stresses at the outside and the inside of the tube; see Fig. 6-12.

SOLUTION
From Eq. 6-5,

$$I_p = \frac{\pi(c^4 - b^4)}{2} = \frac{\pi(d_o^4 - d_i^4)}{32} = \frac{\pi(20^4 - 16^4)}{32} = 9270 \text{ mm}^4$$

and from Eq. 6-3,

$$\tau_{max} = \frac{Tc}{I_p} = \frac{40 \times 10^3 \times 10}{9270} = 43.1 \text{ MPa}$$

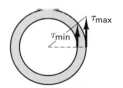

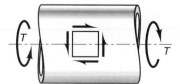

Fig. 6-12

Similarly, from Eq. 6-4,

$$\tau_{min} = \frac{T\rho}{I_p} = \frac{40 \times 10^3 \times 8}{9270} = 34.5 \text{ MPa}$$

In a thin-walled tube, all of the material works at approximately the same stress level. Therefore, thin-walled tubes are more efficient in transmitting torque than solid shafts. Such tubes are also useful for creating an essentially uniform "field" of pure shear stress needed for establishing τ–γ relationships (Section 5-2). To avoid local buckling, however, the wall thickness cannot be excessively thin.

6-6. Design of Circular Members in Torsion for Strength

In designing members for strength, allowable shear stresses must be selected. These depend on the information available from experiments and on the intended application. Accurate information on the capacity of materials to resist shear stresses comes from tests on thin-walled tubes. Solid shafting is employed in routine tests. Moreover, as torsion members are so often used in power equipment, many fatigue experiments are done. Typically, the shear strength of ductile materials is only about half as large as their tensile strength. The ASME (American Society of Mechanical Engineers) code of recommended practice for transmission shafting gives an allowable value in shear stress of 8000 psi for unspecified steel and 0.3 of yield, or 0.18 of ultimate, shear strength, whichever is smaller.[7] In practical designs, suddenly applied and shock loads warrant special considerations. (See Section 6-11.)

After the torque to be transmitted by a shaft is determined and the maximum allowable shear stress is selected, according to Eq. 6-3, the proportions of a member are given as

$$\boxed{\frac{I_p}{c} = \frac{T}{\tau_{max}}} \tag{6-8}$$

where I_p/c is the *parameter* on which the elastic strength of a shaft depends. For an axially loaded rod, such a parameter is the cross-sectional area of a member. For a *solid shaft*, $I_p/c = \pi c^3/2$, where c is the outside radius. By using this expression and Eq. 6-8, the required radius of a shaft can be determined. Any number of *tubular* shafts can be chosen to satisfy Eq. 6-8

---

[7]Recommendations for other materials may be found in machine design books. For example, see J. E. Shigley, *Mechanical Engineering Design,* 3rd ed. (New York: McGraw-Hill, 1977) or R. C. Juvinal, *Stress, Strain, and Strength* (New York: McGraw-Hill, 1967).

by varying the ratio of the outer radius to the inner radius, c/b, to provide the required value of I_p/c.

The reader should carefully note that large local stresses generally develop at changes in cross sections and at splines and keyways, where the torque is actually transmitted. These questions, of critical importance in the design of rotating shafts, are briefly discussed in the next section.

Members subjected to torque are very widely used as rotating shafts for transmitting power. For future reference, a formula is derived for the conversion of horsepower, the conventional unit used in the industry, into torque acting through the shaft. By definition, 1 hp does the work of 745.7 N · m/s. One N · m/s is conveniently referred to as a watt (W) in the SI units. Thus, 1 hp can be converted into 745.7 W. Likewise, it will be recalled from dynamics that power is equal to torque multiplied by the angle, measured in radians, through which the shaft rotates per unit of time. For a shaft rotating with a frequency of f Hz,[8] the angle is $2\pi f$ rad/s. Hence, if a shaft were transmitting a constant torque T measured in N · m, it would do $2\pi fT$ N · m of work per second. Equating this to the horsepower supplied,

$$\text{hp} \times 745.7 = 2\pi fT \quad [\text{N} \cdot \text{m/s}]$$

or

$$T = \frac{119 \times \text{hp}}{f} \quad [\text{N} \cdot \text{m}] \qquad (6\text{-}9)$$

or

$$T = \frac{159 \times \text{kW}}{f} \quad [\text{N} \cdot \text{m}] \qquad (6\text{-}10)$$

where f is the frequency in hertz of the shaft transmitting the horsepower, hp, or kilowatts, kW. These equations convert the applied power into applied torque.

In the U.S. customary system of units, 1 hp does work of 550 ft-lb per second, or $550 \times 12 \times 60$ in-lb per minute. If the shaft rotates at N rpm (revolutions per minute), an equation similar to those just given can be obtained:

$$T = \frac{63,000 \times \text{hp}}{N} \quad [\text{in-lb}] \qquad (6\text{-}11)$$

Example 6-4

Select a solid shaft for a 10-hp motor operating at 30 Hz. The maximum shear stress is limited to 55 MPa.

[8] 1 hertz (Hz) = 1 cycle per second (cps).

SOLUTION

From Eq. 6-9,

$$T = \frac{119 \times \text{hp}}{f} = \frac{119 \times 10}{30} = 39.7 \text{ N} \cdot \text{m}$$

and from Eq. 6-8,

$$\frac{I_p}{c} = \frac{T}{\tau_{max}} = \frac{39.7 \times 10^3}{55} = 722 \text{ mm}^3$$

$$\frac{I_p}{c} = \frac{\pi c^3}{2} \quad \text{or} \quad c^3 = \frac{2 I_p}{\pi c} = \frac{2 \times 722}{\pi} = 460 \text{ mm}^3$$

Hence, $c = 7.72$ mm or $d = 2c = 15.4$ mm.

For practical purposes, a 16-mm shaft would probably be selected.

Example 6-5

Select solid shafts to transmit 150 kW each without exceeding a shear stress of 70 MPa. One of these shafts operates at a frequency of 0.30 Hz and the other at a frequency of 300 Hz.

SOLUTION

Subscript 1 applies to the low-speed shaft and 2 to the high-speed shaft. From Eq. 6-10,

$$T_1 = \frac{159 \times \text{kW}}{f_1} = \frac{159 \times 150}{0.30} = 79{,}500 \text{ N} \cdot \text{m}$$

Similarly,

$$T_2 = 79.5 \text{ N} \cdot \text{m}$$

From Eq. 6-8,

$$\frac{I_{p1}}{c} = \frac{T_1}{\tau_{max}} = \frac{79{,}500}{70} = 1.14 \times 10^6 \text{ mm}^3$$

$$\frac{I_{p1}}{c} = \frac{\pi d_1^3}{16} \quad \text{or} \quad d_1^3 = \frac{16}{\pi}(1.14 \times 10^6) = 5.81 \times 10^6 \text{ mm}^3$$

Hence,

$$d_1 = 180 \text{ mm} \quad \text{and} \quad d_2 = 18 \text{ mm}$$

This example illustrates the reason for the modern tendency to use high-speed machines in mechanical equipment. The difference in size of the two shafts is striking. Further savings in the weight of the material can be effected by using hollow tubes.

6-7. Stress Concentrations

Equation 6-3, 6-4, and 6-8 apply only to solid and tubular circular shafts while the material behaves elastically. Moreover, the cross-sectional areas along the shaft should remain reasonably constant. If a *gradual* variation in the diameter takes place, the previous equations give satisfactory solutions. On the other hand, for stepped shafts where the diameters of the adjoining portions change abruptly, large perturbations of shear stresses take place. High *local* shear stresses occur at points away from the center of the shaft. Methods of determining these local concentrations of stress are beyond the scope of this text. However, by forming a ratio of the true maximum shear stress to the maximum stress given by Eq. 6-3, a torsional stress-concentration factor can be obtained. An analogous method was used for obtaining the stress-concentration factors in axially loaded members. (Section 3-3). These factors depend only on the geometry of a member. Stress-concentration factors for various proportions of stepped round shafts are shown in Fig. 6-13.[9]

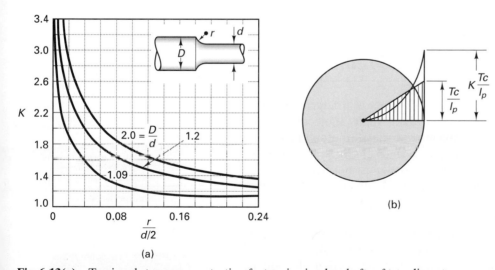

Fig. 6-13(a)   Torsional stress-concentration factors in circular shafts of two diameters. (b) Stress increase at a fillet.

[9]This figure is adapted from a paper by L. S. Jacobsen, "Torsional-Stress Concentrations in Shafts of Circular and Variable Diameter," *Trans. ASME,* **47** (1925), 632.

To obtain the actual stress at a geometrical discontinuity of a stepped shaft, a curve for a particular D/d is selected in Fig. 6-13. Then, corresponding to the given $r/(d/2)$ ratio, the stress-concentration factor K is read from the curve. Lastly, from the definition of K, the actual maximum shear stress is obtained from the modified Eq. 6-3:

$$\tau_{max} = K\frac{Tc}{I_p} \qquad (6\text{-}12)$$

where the shear stress Tc/I_p is determined for the smaller shaft.

A study of stress-concentration factors shown in Fig. 6-13 emphasizes the need for a generous fillet radius r at all sections where a transition in the shaft diameter is made.

Considerable stress increases also occur in shafts at oil holes and at keyways for attaching pulleys and gears to the shaft. A shaft prepared for a key, Fig. 6-14, is no longer a circular member. However, according to the procedures suggested by the ASME, in ordinary design, computations for shafts with keyways may be made using Eq. 6-3 or 6-8, but the allowable shear stress must be *reduced* by 25%. This presumably compensates for the stress concentration, reduction in cross-sectional area, and cyclic loading.

Fig. 6-14   Circular shaft with a keyway.

Because of some inelastic or nonlinear response in real materials, for reasons analogous to those pointed out in Section 3-3, the theoretical stress concentrations based on the behavior of linearly elastic material tend to be somewhat high.

6-8. Angle of Twist of Circular Members

In this section, attention will be directed to a method for determining the angle of twist for solid and tubular circular *elastic* shafts subjected to torsional loading. The interest in this problem is at least threefold. First, it is important to predict the twist of a shaft per se since at times it is not sufficient to design it only to be strong enough: It also must not deform excessively. Then, magnitudes of angular rotations of shafts are needed in the torsional vibration analysis of machinery. Finally, the angular twist of members is needed in dealing with statically indeterminate torsional problems.

According to assumption 1 stated in Section 6-3, planes perpendicular to the axis of a circular rod do not warp. The elements of a shaft undergo deformation of the type shown in Fig. 6-15(b). The shaded element is shown in its undistorted form in Fig. 6-15(a). From such a shaft, a typical element of length dx is shown isolated in Fig. 6-16 similar to Fig. 6-3.

In the element shown, a line on its surface such as CD is initially parallel to the axis of the shaft. After the torque is applied, it assumes a new position CD'. At the same time, by virtue of assumption 2, Section 6-3,

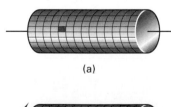

(a)

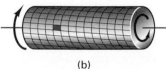

(b)

Fig. 6-15   Circular shaft (a) before and (b) after torque is applied.

radius OD remains straight and rotates through a small angle $d\phi$ to a new position OD'.

Denoting the small angle DCD' by γ_{max}, from geometry, one has two alternative expressions for the arc DD':

$$\text{arc } DD' = \gamma_{max}\, dx \qquad \text{or} \qquad \text{arc } DD' = d\phi\, c$$

where both angles are small and are measured in radians. Hence,

$$\gamma_{max}\, dx = d\phi\, c \qquad (6\text{-}13)$$

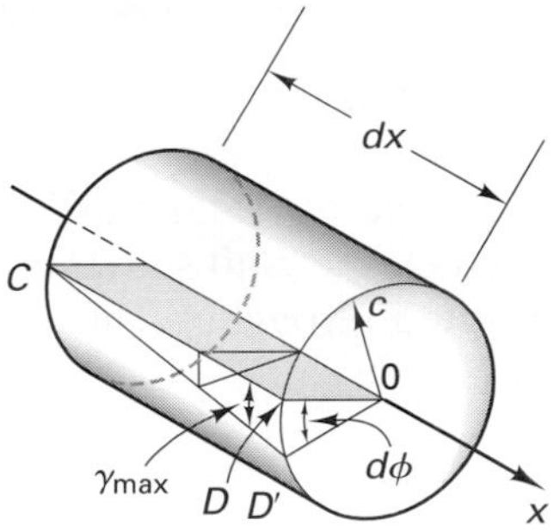

The γ_{max} applies only in the zone of an infinitesimal "tube" of constant maximum shear stress τ_{max}. Limiting attention to linearly elastic response makes Hooke's law applicable. Therefore, according to Eq. 5-1, the angle γ_{max} is proportional to τ_{max} (i.e., $\gamma_{max} = \tau_{max}/G$). Moreover, by Eq. 6-3, $\tau_{max} = Tc/I_p$. Hence, $\gamma_{max} = Tc/(I_p G)$.[10] By substituting the latter expression into Eq. 6-13 and simplifying, the governing differential equation for the angle of twist is obtained:

$$\frac{d\phi}{dx} = \frac{T}{I_p G} \qquad \text{or} \qquad d\phi = \frac{T\, dx}{I_p G} \qquad (6\text{-}14)$$

This gives the relative angle of twist of two adjoining sections of infinitesimal distance dx apart. To find the total angle of twist ϕ between any two sections A and B on a shaft a finite distance apart, the rotations of all elements must be summed. Hence, a general expression for the angle of twist between any two sections of a shaft of a linearly elastic material is

$$\phi = \phi_B - \phi_A = \int_A^B d\phi = \int_A^B \frac{T_x\, dx}{I_{px} G} \qquad (6\text{-}15)$$

where ϕ_B and ϕ_A are, respectively, the global shaft rotations at ends B and A. The rotation at A may not necessarily be zero. In this equation, the internal torque T_x, the polar moment of inertia I_{px}, as well as G, may vary along the length of a shaft. In such cases, $T_x = T(x)$, $I_{px} = I_p(x)$, and $G = G(x)$. The direction of the angle of twist ϕ coincides with the direction of the applied torque T.

Equation 6-15 is valid for both solid and hollow circular shafts, which follows from the assumptions used in the derivation. The angle ϕ is measured in radians. Note the great similarity of this relation to Eq. 3-3 for the deformation of axially loaded rods. The following three examples illustrate applications of these concepts.

Fig. 6-16 Deformation of a circular bar element due to torque.

---

[10] The foregoing argument can be carried out in terms of any γ, which progressively becomes smaller as the axis of the rod is approached. The only difference in derivation consists in taking an arc corresponding to DD' an arbitrary distance ρ from the center of the shaft and using $T\rho/I_p$ instead of Tc/I_p for τ.

Example 6-6

Find the relative rotation of section B–B with respect to section A–A of the solid elastic shaft shown in Fig. 6-17 when a constant torque T is being transmitted through it. The polar moment of inertia of the cross-sectional area I_p is constant.

SOLUTION

In this case, $T_x = T$ and I_p is constant; hence, from Eq. 6-15,

$$\phi = \int_A^B \frac{T_x \, dx}{I_p G} = \int_O^L \frac{T \, dx}{I_p G} = \frac{T}{I_p G} \int_O^L dx = \frac{TL}{I_p G}$$

That is,

$$\boxed{\phi = \frac{TL}{I_p G}} \tag{6-16}$$

In applying Eq. 6-16, note particularly that the angle ϕ is expressed in *radians*. Also observe the great similarity of this relation to Eq. 3-4, $\Delta = PL/AE$, for axially loaded bars. Here $\phi \Leftrightarrow \Delta$, $T \Leftrightarrow P$, $I_p \Leftrightarrow A$, and $G \Leftrightarrow E$. Analogous to Eq. 3-4, Eq. 6-16 can be recast to express the *torsional spring constant*, or *torsional stiffness, k_t* as

$$\boxed{k_t = \frac{T}{\phi} = \frac{I_p G}{L}} \left[\frac{\text{in-lb}}{\text{rad}} \right] \quad \text{or} \quad \left[\frac{\text{N} \cdot \text{m}}{\text{rad}} \right] \tag{6-17}$$

This constant represents the torque required to cause a rotation of 1 radian (i.e., $\phi = 1$). It depends only on the material properties and size of the member. As for axially loaded bars, one can visualize torsion members as springs; see Fig. 6-18.

The reciprocal of k_t defines the *torsional flexibility f_t*. Hence, for a circular solid or hollow shaft,

$$f_t = \frac{1}{k_t} = \frac{L}{I_p G} \left[\frac{\text{rad}}{\text{in-lb}} \right] \quad \text{or} \quad \left[\frac{\text{rad}}{\text{N} \cdot \text{m}} \right] \tag{6-18}$$

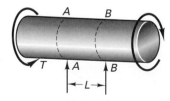

Fig. 6-17

Fig. 6-18 Schematic representation of a torsion spring.

This constant defines the rotation resulting from application of a unit torque (i.e., $T = 1$). On multiplying by the torque T, one obtains Eq. 6-16.

If, in the analysis, a shaft must be subdivided into a number of regions, appropriate identifying subscripts should be attached to the definitions given by Eqs. 6-17 and 6-18. For example, for the ith segment of a bar, one can write $(k_t)_i = I_p G_i / L_i$ and $(f_t)_i = L_i / I_p G_i$.

The previous equations are widely used in mechanical vibration analyses of transmission shafts, including crank shafts.[11] These equations are also useful for solving statically indeterminate problems, considered in the next section. These equations are required in the design of members for torsional stiffness when it is essential to limit the amount of twist. For such applications, note that I_p rather than the I_p/c used in strength calculations, is the governing parameter. In axially loaded bar problems, the cross-sectional area A serves both purposes.

Lastly, it should be noted that since in a torsion test ϕ, T, L, and I_p can be measured or calculated from the dimensions of a specimen, the shear modulus of elasticity for a specimen can be determined from Eq. 6-16 since $G = TL / I_p \phi$.

Example 6-7

Consider the stepped shaft shown in Fig. 6-19(a) rigidly attached to a wall at E, and determine the angle of twist of the end A when the two torques at B and at D are applied. Assume the shear modulus G to be 80 GPa, a typical value for steels.

SOLUTION

Except for the difference in parameters, the solution of this problem is very similar to that of Example 3-2 for an axially loaded bar. First, the torque of E is determined to assure equilibrium. Then internal torques at arbitrary sections, isolating the *left* segment of a shaft, such as shown in Fig. 6-19(b), are examined. If the direction of the torque vector T coincides with that of the positive x axis, it is taken as positive, or vice versa. This leads to the conclusion that between A and B there is no torque, whereas between B and D the torque is $+ 150$ Nm. The torque between D and E is $+1150$ Nm. The torque diagram is drawn in Fig. 6-19(c). The internal torques, identified by subscripts for the various shaft segments, are

$$T_{AB} = 0, \; T_{BD} = T_{BC} = T_{CD} = 150 \; \text{N} \cdot \text{m, and} \; T_{DE} = 1150 \; \text{N} \cdot \text{m}$$

---

[11]According to S. P. Timoshenko, *Vibration Problems in Engineering,* 2nd ed. (New York: Van Nostrand, 1937), in 1902, H. Frahm, a German engineer, was the first to recognize and study this important problem.

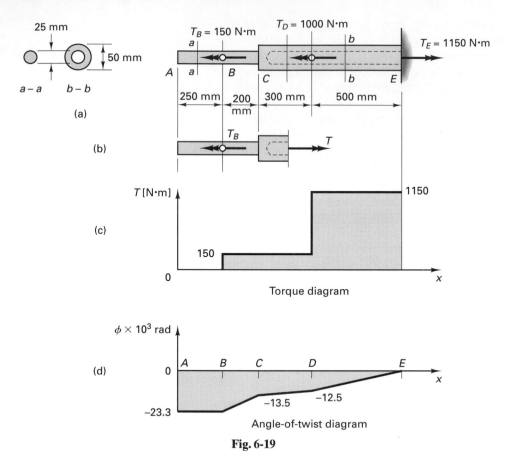

Fig. 6-19

The polar moments of inertia for the two kinds of cross sections occurring in this problem are found using Eq. 6-2 and 6-5; giving

$$(I_p)_{AB} = (I_p)_{BC} = \frac{\pi d^4}{32} = \frac{\pi \times 25^4}{32} = 38.3 \times 10^3 \text{ mm}^4$$

$$(I_p)_{CD} = (I_p)_{DE} = \frac{\pi}{32}(d_0^4 - d_i^4) = \frac{\pi}{32}(50^4 - 25^4) = 575 \times 10^3 \text{ mm}^4$$

To find the angle of twist of the end A, Eq. 6-15 is applied for each segment and the results summed. The limits of integration for the segments occur at points where the values of T or I_p change abruptly.

$$\phi = \int_A^E \frac{T_x\, dx}{I_{px}G} = \int_A^B \frac{T_{AB}\, dx}{(I_p)_{AB}G} + \int_B^C \frac{T_{BC}\, dx}{(I_p)_{BC}G} + \int_C^D \frac{T_{CD}\, dx}{(I_p)_{CD}G} + \int_D^E \frac{T_{DE}\, dx}{(I_p)_{DE}G}$$

In the last group of integrals, T's and I_p's are constant between the limits considered, so each integral reverts to a known solution, Eq. 6-16. Hence,

$$\phi = \sum_i \frac{T_i L_i}{(I_p)_i G_i} = \frac{T_{AB} L_{AB}}{(I_p)_{AB} G} + \frac{T_{BC} L_{BC}}{(I_p)_{BC} G} + \frac{T_{CD} L_{CD}}{(I_p)_{CD} G} + \frac{T_{DE} L_{DE}}{(I_p)_{DE} G}$$

$$= 0 + \frac{150 \times 10^3 \times 200}{38.3 \times 10^3 \times 80 \times 10^3} + \frac{150 \times 10^3 \times 300}{575 \times 10^3 \times 80 \times 10^3}$$

$$+ \frac{1150 \times 10^3 \times 500}{575 \times 10^3 \times 80 \times 10^3}$$

$$= 0 + 9.8 \times 10^{-3} + 1.0 \times 10^{-3} + 12.5 \times 10^{-3} = 23.3 \times 10^{-3} \, \text{rad}$$

As can be noted from the preceding equations, the angles of twist for the four shaft segments starting from the left end are 0 rad, 9.8×10^{-3} rad, 1.0×10^{-3} rad, and 12.5×10^{-3} rad. Summing these quantities beginning from A, in order to obtain the function for the angle of twist along the shaft, gives the broken line from A to E, shown in Fig. 6-19(d). Since no shaft twist can occur at the built-in end, this function must be zero at E, as required by the boundary condition. Therefore, according to the adopted sign convention, the angle of twist at A is -23.3×10^{-3} rad occurring in the direction of applied torques.

No doubt local disturbances in stresses and strains occur at the applied concentrated torques and the change in the shaft size, as well as at the built-in end. However, these are local effects having limited influence on the overall behavior of the shaft.

Example 6-8

Determine the torsional stiffness k_τ for the rubber bushing shown in Fig. 6-20. Assume that the rubber is bonded to the steel shaft and the outer steel tube, which is attached to a machine housing. The shear modulus for the rubber is G. Neglect deformations in the metal parts of the assembly.

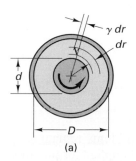

(a)

SOLUTION

Due to the axial symmetry of the problem, on every imaginary cylindrical surface of rubber of radius r, the applied torque T is resisted by constant shear stresses τ. The area of the imaginary surface is $2\pi rL$. On this basis, the equilibrium equation for the applied torque T and the resisting torque developed by the shear stresses τ acting at a radius r is

$$T = (2\pi rL)\tau r \qquad [\text{area} \times \text{stress} \times \text{arm}]$$

From this relation, $\tau = T/2\pi r^2 L$. Hence, by using the Hooke's law given by Eq. 5-1, the shear strain γ can be determined for an infinitesimal tube of radius r and thickness dr, Fig. 6-20(a), from the following relations:

$$\gamma = \frac{\tau}{G} = \frac{T}{2\pi L G r^2}$$

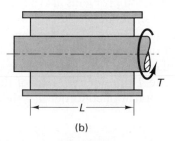

(b)

Fig. 6-20

This shear strain in an infinitesimal tube permits the shaft to rotate through an infinitesimal angle $d\phi$. Since in the limit $r + dr$ is equal to r, the magnitude of this angle is

$$d\phi = \frac{\gamma \, dr}{r}$$

The total rotation ϕ of the shaft is an integral, over the rubber bushings, of these infinitesimal rotations; that is,

$$\phi = \int d\phi = \frac{T}{2\pi LG} \int_{d/2}^{D/2} \frac{dr}{r^3} = \frac{T}{\pi LG}\left(\frac{1}{d^2} - \frac{1}{D^2}\right)$$

from which

$$k_t = \frac{T}{\phi} = \frac{\pi LG}{1/d^2 - 1/D^2} \tag{6-19}$$

6-9. Statically Indeterminate Problems

The analysis of statically indeterminate members subjected to twist parallels the procedures discussed earlier in Chapter 3 in connection with axially loaded bars. In considering *linearly elastic* problems with *one* degree of *external* indeterminacy (i.e., cases where there are two reactions), the *force* (flexibility) method is particularly advantageous. Such problems are reduced to statical determinacy by removing one of the redundant reactions and calculating the rotation ϕ_0 at the released support. The required boundary conditions are then restored by twisting the member at the released end through an angle ϕ_1 such that

$$\phi_0 + \phi_1 = 0 \tag{6-20}$$

Such problems remain simple to analyze regardless of the number and kinds of applied torques or variations in the shaft size or material.

Torsion problems also occur with *internal* statical indeterminacy in composite shafts built up from two or more tubes or materials, such as shown in Fig. 6-6. In such cases, the angle of twist ϕ is the same for each constituent part of the member. Therefore, the *displacement* (stiffness) method is particularly simple to apply to linearly elastic problems. In such problems, the torque T_i for each ith part of the shafts is $T_i = (k_t)_i \phi_i$, Eqs. 6-16 and 6-17. The total applied torque T is then the sum of n parts; that is,

$$T = \sum_{i=1}^{n} T_i = \sum_{i=1}^{n} (k_t)_i \phi_i \tag{6-21}$$

For complex *externally* statically indeterminate elastic problems with several kinematic degrees of freedom, the general displacement method similar to that given in Section 4-6 can be used. Here, however, the discussion is limited to the case of *one d.o.f.* Such cases can be analyzed using the procedure described in Section 4-6. Applying this approach to the shaft in Fig. 6-21, one can write the following two basic equations:

For global equilibrium:

$$T_1 + T_2 + T = 0 \tag{6-22}$$

For geometric compatibility:

$$\phi_{AB} = \phi_{BC} \tag{6-23}$$

where ϕ_{AB} and ϕ_{BC} are, respectively, the twists at B of the bar segments AB and BC, assuming that ends A and C are fixed.

According to Eq. 6-16, for linearly *elastic* behavior, Eq. 6-23 becomes

$$\frac{T_1 L_1}{(I_p)_1 G_1} = \frac{T_2 L_2}{(I_p)_2 G_2} \tag{6-24}$$

where the shear moduli are given as G_1 and G_2 to provide for the possibility of different materials in the two parts of the shaft.

Solutions for one d.o.f. statically indeterminate *inelastic* problems closely follow the procedure given in Example 4-7 for axially loaded bars.

The previous procedures can be applied to the analysis of statically indeterminate bars having cross sections other than circular, such as discussed in Sections 6-14 and 6-16.

An example of an application of the force method for a statically indeterminate elastic problem follows.

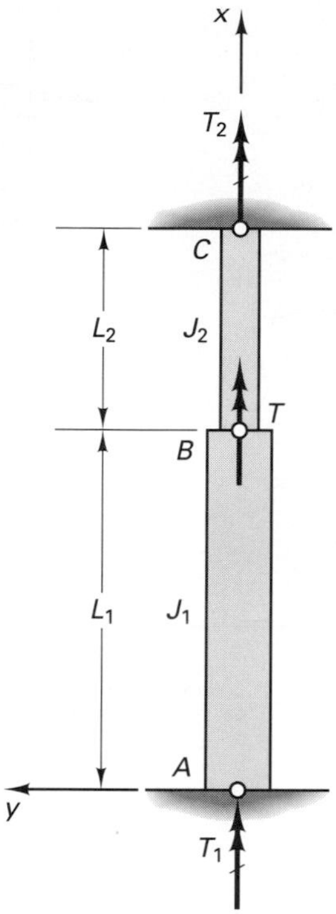

Fig. 6-21 Externally statically indeterminate bar in torsion.

Example 6-9

Assume that the stepped shaft of Example 6-7, while loaded in the same manner is now built-in at both ends, as shown in Fig. 6-22. Determine the end reactions and plot the torque diagram for the shaft. Apply the force method.

SOLUTION

There are two unknown reactions, T_A and T_E. One of them can be considered as redundant, and, arbitrarily, reaction T_A is removed. This results in the free-body diagram shown in Fig. 6-22(b). The solution to Example 6-7 gives the end rotation $\phi_0 = 23.3 \times 10^{-3}$ rad.

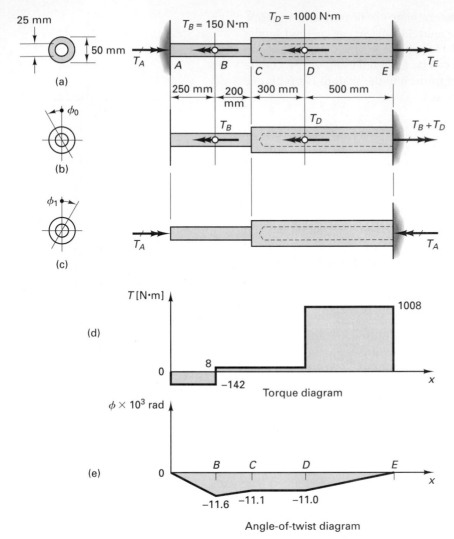

Fig. 6-22

From Example 6-7, $(I_p)_{AC} = 38.3 \times 10^3 \text{ mm}^2$ and $(I_p)_{CE} = 575 \times 10^3 \text{ mm}^2$. By applying T_A to the *unloaded* bar, as shown in Fig. 6-22(c), end rotation ϕ_1 at end A is found using Eq. 6-16.

$$\phi_1 = \sum_i \frac{T_i L_i}{(I_p)_i G_i}$$

$$= T_A \times 10^3 \left(\frac{450}{38.3 \times 10^3 \times 80 \times 10^3} + \frac{800}{575 \times 10^3 \times 80 \times 10^3} \right)$$

$$= (147 \times 10^{-6} + 17 \times 10^{-6}) T_A = 164 \times 10^{-6} T_A \text{ rad}$$

where T_A has the units of N · m.

Using Eq. 6-20 and defining rotation in the direction T_A as positive, one has

$$-23.3 \times 10^{-3} + 164 \times 10^{-6} T_A = 0$$

Hence,

$$T_A = 142 \text{ N} \cdot \text{m} \quad \text{and} \quad T_B = 1150 - 142 = 1008 \text{ N} \cdot \text{m}$$

The torque diagram for the shaft is shown in Fig. 6-22(d). As in Fig. 6-19(c) of Example 6-7, if the direction of the internal torque vector T on the *left* part of an isolated shaft segment coincides with that of the positive x axis, it is taken as positive. Note that most of the applied torque is resisted at the end E. Since the shaft from A to C is more flexible than from C to E, only a small torque develops at A.

Calculating the angles of twist for the four segments of the shafts, as in Example 6-7, the angle of twist diagram along the shaft, Fig. 6-22(e), can be obtained. (Verification of this diagram is left as an exercise for the reader.) The angle of twist at A and E must be zero from the prescribed boundary conditions. As to be expected, the shaft twists in the direction of the applied torques.

Whereas this problem is indeterminate only to the first degree, it has three kinematic degrees of freedom. Two of these are associated with the applied torques and one with the change in the shaft size. Therefore, an application of the displacement method would be more cumbersome, requiring three simultaneous equations.

6-10. Alternative Differential Equation Approach for Torsion Problems

For constant $I_p G$, Eq. 6-14 can be recast into a second-order differential equation. Preliminary to this step, consider an element, shown in Fig. 6-23, subjected to the end torques T and $T + dT$ and to an applied distributed torque t_x having the units of in-lb/in or $\text{N} \cdot \text{m/m}$. By using the right-hand screw rule for the torques, all these quantities are shown in the figure as having a positive sense. For equilibrium of this infinitesimal element,

$$t_x \, dx + dT = 0 \quad \text{or} \quad \frac{dT}{dx} = -t_x \qquad (6\text{-}25)$$

On differentiating Eq. 6-14 with respect to x,

$$I_p G \frac{d^2\phi}{dx^2} = \frac{dT}{dx} = -t_x \qquad (6\text{-}26)$$

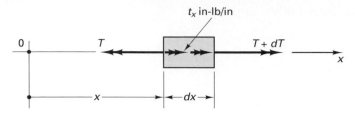

Fig. 6-23   Infinitesimal element of a circular bar subjected to torque.

The constants appearing in the solution of this differential equation are determined from the boundary conditions at the ends of a shaft, and either the rotation ϕ or the torque T must be specified. The rotation boundary conditions for ϕ should be evident from the problem, whereas those for the torque T follow from Eq. 4-14 since $T = I_p G \, d\phi/dx$.

Equation 6-26 can be used for solution of statically determinate and indeterminate problems. By making use of singularity functions, discussed in Section 6-16, this equation can be employed for problems with concentrated moments.

The following example illustrates the application of Eq. 6-26 when the applied torque is a continuous function.

Example 6-10

Consider an elastic circular bar having a constant $I_p G$ subjected to a uniformly varying torque t_x, as shown in Fig. 6-24. Determine the rotation of the bar along its length and the reactions at ends A and B for two cases: (a) Assume that end A is free and that end B is built-in, (b) assume that both ends of the bar are fixed.

SOLUTION
(a) By integrating Eq. 6-26 twice and determining the constants of integration C_1 and C_2 from the boundary conditions, the required solution is determined.

$$I_p G \frac{d^2\phi}{dx^2} = -t_x = \frac{x}{L} t_o$$

$$I_p G \frac{d\phi}{dx} = T = \frac{-t_o x^2}{2L} + C_1$$

$$T_A = T(0) = 0 \qquad \text{hence, } C_1 = 0$$

$$T_B = T(L) = -\frac{t_o L}{2}$$

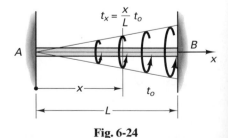

Fig. 6-24

$$I_p G \phi = -\frac{t_o x^3}{6L} + C_2$$

$$\phi_B = \phi(L) = 0 \qquad \text{hence, } C_2 = \frac{t_o L^2}{6}$$

$$I_p G \phi = \frac{t_o L^2}{6} - \frac{t_o x^3}{6L}$$

The negative sign for T_B means that the torque vector acts in the direction opposite to that of the positive x axis.

(b) Except for the change in the boundary conditions, the solution procedure is the same as in part (a).

$$I_p G \frac{d^2\phi}{dx^2} = -t_x = -\frac{x}{L} t_o$$

$$I_p G \frac{d\phi}{dx} = T = -\frac{t_o x^2}{2L} + C_1$$

$$I_p G \phi = -\frac{t_o x^3}{6L} + C_1 x + C_2$$

$$\phi_A = \phi(0) = 0 \qquad \text{hence, } C_2 = 0$$

$$\phi_B = \phi(L) = 0 \qquad \text{hence, } C_1 = \frac{t_o L}{6}$$

$$I_p G \phi = \frac{t_o L x}{6} - \frac{t_o x^3}{6L}$$

$$T_A = T(0) = \frac{t_o L}{6}$$

$$T_B = T(L) = -\frac{t_o L}{2} + \frac{t_o L}{6} = -\frac{t_o L}{3}$$

6-11. Energy and Impact Loads

The concepts of elastic strain energy and impact loads discussed in Sections 3-5 and 3-6 for axially loaded members, as well as those in Section 5-3 for pure shear, transfer directly to the torsion problem. For example, the deflection of a member can be determined by equating the internal shear strain energy U_{sh} for a member of the external work W_e due to the applied force, Eq. 3-16. This concept can be applied to static problems (Example 3-9), as well as to elementary solutions of dynamic problems.

Example 6-11

(a) Find the energy absorbed by an elastic circular shaft subjected to a constant torque in terms of maximum shear stress and the volume of material; see Fig. 6-25. (b) Find the rotation of the end of an elastic circular shaft with respect to the built-in end when a torque T is applied at the free end.

SOLUTION
(a) The shear stress in an elastic circular shaft subjected to a torque varies linearly from the longitudinal axis. Hence, the shear stress acting on an element at a distance ρ from the center of the cross section is $\tau_{max}\rho/c$. Then, using Eq. 5-5 and integrating over the volume V of the rod of L in length, one obtains

$$U_{sh} = \int_V \frac{\tau^2}{2G}\,dV = \int_V \frac{\tau_{max}^2 \rho^2}{2Gc^2}\,2\pi\rho\,d\rho\,L$$

$$= \frac{\tau_{max}^2}{2G}\frac{2\pi L}{c^2}\int_0^c \rho^3\,d\rho = \frac{\tau_{max}^2}{2G}\frac{2\pi L}{c^2}\frac{c^4}{4}$$

$$= \frac{\tau_{max}^2}{2G}\left(\frac{1}{2}\,\text{vol}\right)$$

If there were uniform shear stress throughout the member, a more efficient arrangement for absorbing energy would be obtained. Rubber bushings (Example 6-8) with their small G values provide an excellent device for absorbing shock torques from a shaft.

(b) If torque T is gradually applied to the shaft, the external work $W_e = \frac{1}{2}T\phi$, where ϕ is the angular rotation of the free end in radians. The expression for the internal train energy U_{sh}, which was found in part (a), may be written in a

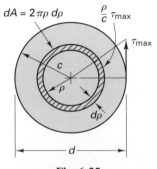

$dA = 2\pi\rho\,d\rho$ $\frac{\rho}{c}\tau_{max}$

τ_{max}

c

ρ

$d\rho$

d

Fig. 6-25

more convenient form by noting that $\tau_{max} = Tc/I_p$, the volume of the rod $\pi c^2 L$, and $I_p = \pi c^4/2$. Thus,

$$U_{sh} = \frac{\tau_{max}^2}{2G}\left(\frac{1}{2}\,\text{vol}\right) = \frac{T^2 c^2}{2I_p^2 G}\frac{1}{2}\,\pi c^2 L = \frac{T^2 L}{2I_p G}$$

Then, from $W_e = U_{sh}$,

$$\frac{T\phi}{2} = \frac{T^2 L}{2I_p G} \qquad \text{and} \qquad \phi = \frac{TL}{I_p G}$$

which is the same as Eq. 6-16.

6-12. Shaft Couplings

Frequently, situations arise where the available lengths of shafting are not long enough. Likewise, for maintenance or assembly reasons, it is often desirable to make up a long shaft from several pieces. To join the pieces of a shaft together, the so-called flanged shaft couplings of the type shown in Fig. 6-26 are used. When bolted together, such couplings are termed *rigid*, to differentiate them from another called *flexible* that provides for mis-alignment of adjoining shafts. The latter type is almost universally used to join the shaft of a motor to the driven equipment. Here only rigid-type couplings are considered. The reader is referred to machine-design texts and manufacturer's catalogs for the other type.

For rigid couplings, it is customary to assume that shear strains in the bolts vary directly (linearly) as their distance from the axis of the shaft. Friction between the flanges is neglected. Therefore, analogous to the tor-sion problem of circular shafts, if the bolts are of the same material, elastic shear *stresses* in the bolts also vary linearly as their respective distances from the center of a coupling. The shear stress in any one bolt is assumed to be *uniform* and is governed by the distance from its center to the center

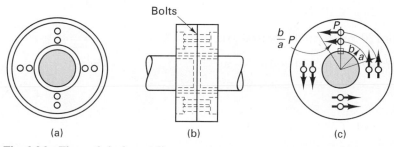

(a)   (b)   (c)

Fig. 6-26   Flanged shaft coupling.

of the coupling. Then, if the shear stress in a bolt is multiplied by its cross-sectional area, the force in a bolt is found. On this basis, for example, for bolts of *equal size* in two "bolt circles," the forces on the bolts located by the respective radii a and b are as shown in Fig. 6-26(c). The moment of the forces developed by the bolts around the axis of a shaft gives the torque capacity of a coupling.

The previous reasoning is the same as that used in deriving the torsion formula for circular shafts, except that, instead of a continuous cross section, a discrete number of points is considered. This analysis is crude, since stress concentrations are undoubtedly present at the points of contact of the bolts with the flanges of a coupling.

The outlined method of analysis is valid only for the case of a coupling in which the bolts act primarily in shear. However, in some couplings, the bolts are tightened so much that the coupling acts in a different fashion. The initial tension in the bolts is great enough to cause the entire coupling to act in friction. Under these circumstances, the suggested analysis is not valid, or is valid only as a measure of the ultimate strength of the coupling should the stresses in the bolts be reduced. However, if high tensile strength bolts are used, there is little danger of this happening, and the strength of the coupling may be greater than it would be if the bolts had to act in shear.[12]

Example 6-12

Estimate the torque-carrying capacity of a steel coupling forged integrally with the shaft, shown in Fig. 6-27, as controlled by an allowable shear stress of 40 MPa in the eight bolts. The bolt circle is diameter 240 mm.

SOLUTION
Area of one bolt:

$$A = (1/4)\pi(30)^2 = 706 \text{ mm}^2$$

Allowable force for one bolt:

$$P_{\text{allow}} = A\tau_{\text{allow}} = 706 \times 40 = 28.2 \times 10^3 \text{ N}$$

Since eight bolts are available at a distance of 120 mm from the central axis,

$$T_{\text{allow}} = 28.2 \times 10^3 \times 120 \times 8 = 27.1 \times 10^6 \text{ N} \cdot \text{mm} = 27.1 \times 10^3 \text{ N} \cdot \text{m}$$

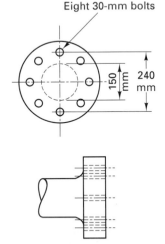

Eight 30-mm bolts

150 mm

240 mm

Fig. 6-27

---

[12]See "Symposium on High-Strength Bolts," Part I, by L. T. Wyly, and Part II by E. J. Ruble, *Proc. AISC* (1950). Also see section 1-8.

Part B   TORSION OF INELASTIC CIRCULAR BARS

6-13. Shear Stresses and Deformations in Circular Shafts in the Inelastic Range

The torsion formula for circular sections previously derived is based on Hooke's law. Therefore, it applies only up to the point where the proportional limit of a material in shear is reached in the outer annulus of a shaft. Now the solution will be extended to include inelastic behavior of a material. As before, the equilibrium requirements at a section must be met. The deformation assumption of linear strain variation from the axis remains applicable. Only the difference in material properties affects the solution.

A section through a shaft is shown in Fig. 6-28(a). The linear strain variation is shown schematically in the same figure. Some possible mechanical properties of materials in shear, obtained, for example, in experiments with thin tubes in torsion, are shown in Figs. 6-28(b), (c), and (d). The corresponding shear stress distribution is shown to the right in each case. The stresses are determined from the strain. For example, if the shear strain is a at an interior annulus, Fig. 6-28(a), the corresponding stress is found from the stress-strain diagram. This procedure is appliable to solid shafts as well as to integral shafts made of concentric tubes of different materials, provided that the corresponding stress-strain diagrams are used. The derivation for a linearly elastic material is simply a special case of this approach.

After the stress distribution is known, torque T carried by these stresses is found as before; that is,

$$T = \int_A (\tau \, dA)\rho \qquad (6\text{-}27)$$

This integral must be evaluated over the cross-sectional area of the shaft.

Although the shear stress distribution after the elastic limit is exceeded is nonlinear and the elastic torsion formula, Eq. 6-3, does not apply, it is sometimes used to calculate a fictitious stress for the ultimate torque. The computed stress is called the *modulus of rupture*; see the largest ordinates of the dashed lines in Figs. 6-28(f) and (g). It serves as a rough index of the ultimate strength of a material in torsion. For a thin-walled tube, the stress distribution is very nearly the same regardless of the mechanical properties of the material; see Fig. 6-29. For this reason, experiments with thin-walled tubes are widely used in establishing the shear stress-strain τ-γ diagrams.

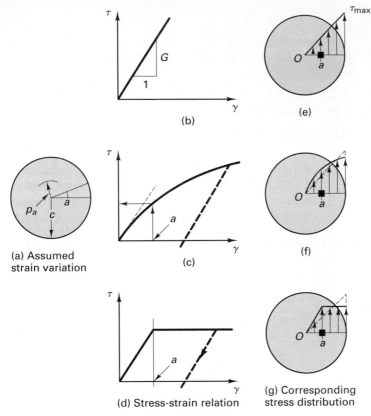

(a) Assumed
strain variation

(b)

(c)

(d) Stress-strain relation

(e)

(f)

(g) Corresponding
stress distribution

Fig. 6-28   Stresses in circular members due to torque.

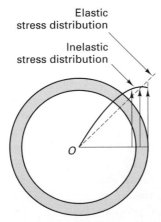

Elastic
stress distribution

Inelastic
stress distribution

Fig. 6-29   For thin-walled tubes the
difference between elastic and inelastic stresses is small.

If a shaft is strained into the inelastic range and the applied torque is then removed, every "imaginary" annulus rebounds elastically. Because of the differences in the strain paths, which cause permanent set in the material, residual stresses develop. This process will be illustrated in one of the examples that follow.

For determining the rate of twist of a circular shaft or tube, Eq. 6-13 can be used in the following form:

$$\frac{d\phi}{dx} = \frac{\gamma_{max}}{c} = \frac{\gamma_a}{\rho_a} \qquad (6\text{-}28)$$

Here either the maximum shear strain at c or the strain at ρ_a determined from the stress-strain diagram must be used.

Example 6-13

A solid steel shaft of 24 mm diameter is so severely twisted that only an 8-mm-diameter elastic core remains on the inside, Fig. 6-30(a). If the material properties can be idealized, as shown in Fig. 6-30(b), what residual stresses and residual rotation will remain upon release of the applied torque? Let $G = 80$ GPa.

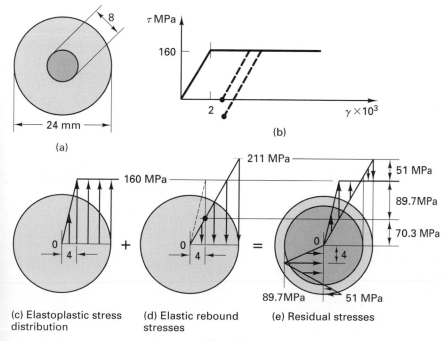

(a)

(b)

(c) Elastoplastic stress distribution

(d) Elastic rebound stresses

(e) Residual stresses

Fig. 6-30

SOLUTION

To begin, the magnitude of the initially applied torque and the corresponding angle of twist must be determined. The stress distribution corresponding
to the given condition is shown in Fig. 6-30(c). The stresses vary linearly
from 0 to 160 MPa when $0 \leq \rho \leq 4$ mm; the stress is a constant 160 MPa for
$\rho > 4$ mm. Equation 6-27 can be used to determine the applied torque T.
The release of torque T causes elastic stresses, and Eq. 6-3 applies; see
Fig. 6-30(d). The difference between the two stress distributions, corresponding to no external torque, gives the residual stresses.

$$
T = \int_A \tau \rho \, dA = \int_0^c 2\pi \tau \rho^2 \, d\rho = \int_0^4 \left(\frac{\rho}{4} 160 \right) 2\pi \rho^2 \, d\rho
$$

$$
+ \int_4^{12} (160) 2\pi \rho^2 \, d\rho
$$

$$
= (16 + 558) \times 10^3 \, \text{N} \cdot \text{mm} = 574 \times 10^3 \, \text{N} \cdot \text{mm}
$$

Note the small contribution to the total of the first integral.

$$
\tau_{max} = \frac{Tc}{I_p} = \frac{574 \times 10^3 \times 12}{(\pi/32) \times 24^4} = 211 \, \text{MPa}
$$

At $\rho = 12$ mm, $\tau_{residual} = 211 - 160 = 51$ MPa.

Two alternative residual stress diagrams are shown in Fig. 6-30(e). For
clarity, the initial results are replotted from the vertical line. In the entire
shaded portion of the diagram, the residual torque is clockwise; an exactly
equal residual torque acts in the opposite direction in the inner portion of
the shaft.

The initial rotation is best determined by calculating the twist of the
elastic core. At $\rho = 4$ mm, $\gamma = 2 \times 10^{-3}$. The elastic rebound of the shaft is
given by Eq. 6-16. The difference between the inelastic and the elastic
twists gives the residual rotation per unit length of shaft. If the initial
torque is reapplied in the same direction, the shaft responds elastically.

Inelastic:

$$
\frac{d\phi}{dx} = \frac{\gamma_a}{\rho_a} = \frac{2 \times 10^{-3}}{4 \times 10^{-3}} = 0.50 \, \text{rad/m}
$$

Elastic:

$$
\frac{d\phi}{dx} = \frac{T}{I_p G} = \frac{574 \times 10^3 \times 10^3}{(\pi/32) \times 24^4 \times 80 \times 10^3} = 0.22 \, \text{rad/m}
$$

Residual:

$$
\frac{d\phi}{dx} = 0.50 - 0.22 = 0.28 \, \text{rad/m}
$$

Example 6-14

Determine the ultimate torque carried by a solid circular shaft of mild steel when shear stresses above the proportional limit are reached essentially everywhere. For mild steel, the shear stress-strain diagram can be idealized to that shown in Fig. 6-31(a). The shear yield-point stress, τ_{yp}, is to be taken as being the same as the proportional limit in shear, τ_{pl}.

SOLUTION

If a very large torque is imposed on a member, large strains take place everywhere, except near the center. Corresponding to the large strains for the idealized material considered, the yield-point shear stress will be reached everywhere except near the center. However, the resistance to the applied torque offered by the material located near the center of the shaft is negligible as the corresponding ρ's are small, Fig. 6-31(b). (See the contribution to torque T by the elastic action in Example 6-13.) Hence, it can be assumed with a sufficient degree of accuracy that a constant shear stress τ_{yp} is acting everywhere on the section considered. The torque corresponding to this condition may be considered the *ultimate limit* torque. [Figure 6-31(c) gives a firmer basis for this statement.] Thus,

$$T_{ult} = \int_A (\tau_{yp}\, dA)\rho = \int_0^c 2\pi\rho^2\tau_{yp}\, d\rho = \frac{2\pi c^3}{3}\tau_{yp} \qquad (6\text{-}29)$$

$$= \frac{4}{3}\frac{\tau_{yp}}{c}\frac{\pi c^4}{2} = \frac{4}{3}\frac{\tau_{yp}I_p}{c}$$

Since the maximum elastic torque capacity of a solid shaft is $T_{yp} = \tau_{yp}I_p/c$, Eq. 6-3, and T_{ult} is $\frac{4}{3}$ times this value, the remaining torque capacity after yield is $\frac{1}{3}$ of that at yield. A plot of torque T versus θ, the angle of twist per unit distance, as full plasticity develops is shown in Figure 6-31(c). Point A corresponds to the results found in the preceding example, line AB is the elastic rebound, and point B is the residual θ for the same problem.

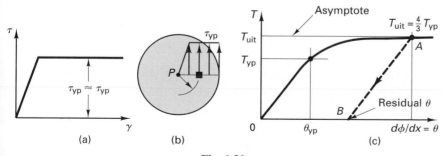

Fig. 6-31

It should be noted that in machine members, because of the fatigue properties of materials, the ultimate static capacity of the shafts as evaluated here is often of minor importance.

Part C   TORSION OF SOLID NONCIRCULAR MEMBERS

6-14. Solid Bars of Any Cross Section

The analytical treatment of solid noncircular members in torsion is beyond the scope of this book. Mathematically, the problem is complex.[13] The first two assumptions stated in Section 6-3 do not apply for noncircular members. Sections perpendicular to the axis of a member warp when a torque is applied. The nature of the distortions that take place in a rectangular section can be surmised from Fig. 6-32.[14] For a rectangular member, the corner elements do not distort at all. Therefore, shear stresses at the corners are zero; they are maximum at the midpoints of the long sides. Figure 6-33 shows the shear stress distribution along three radial lines emanating from the center. Note particularly the difference in this stress distribution compared with that of a circular section. For the latter, the stress is a maximum at the most remote point, but for the former, the stress is zero at the most remote point. This situation can be clarified by considering a corner element, as shown in Fig. 6-34. If a shear stress τ existed at the corner, it could be resolved into two components parallel to the edges of the bar. However, as shears always occur in pairs acting on mutually perpendicular planes, these components would have to be met by shears lying in the planes of the outside surfaces. The latter situation is impossible as outside surfaces are free of all stresses. Hence, τ must be zero. Similar considerations can be applied to other points on the boundary. All shear stresses in the plane of a cut near the boundaries act parallel to them.

Analytical solutions for torsion of rectangular, elastic members have been obtained.[15] The methods used are beyond the scope of this book. The

---

[13]This problem remained unsolved until the famous French elastician B. de Saint Venant developed a solution for such problems in 1853. The general torsion problem is sometimes referred to as the St. Venant problem.

[14]An experiment with a rubber eraser on which a rectangular grating is ruled demonstrates this type of distortion.

[15]S. Timoshenko and J. N. Goodier, *Theory of Elasticity,* 3rd ed. (New York: McGraw-Hill, 1970), 312. The table of coefficients that follows is adapted from this source.

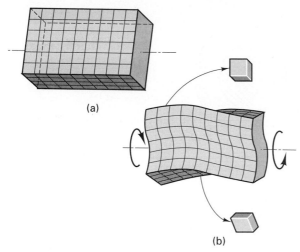

Fig. 6-32   Rectangular bar (a) before and (b) after a torque is applied.

final results of such analysis, however, are of interest. For the maximum shear stress (see Fig. 6-33) and the angle of twist, these results can be put into the following form:

$$\tau_{max} = \frac{T}{\alpha b t^2} \quad \text{and} \quad \phi = \frac{TL}{\beta b t^3 G} \tag{6-30}$$

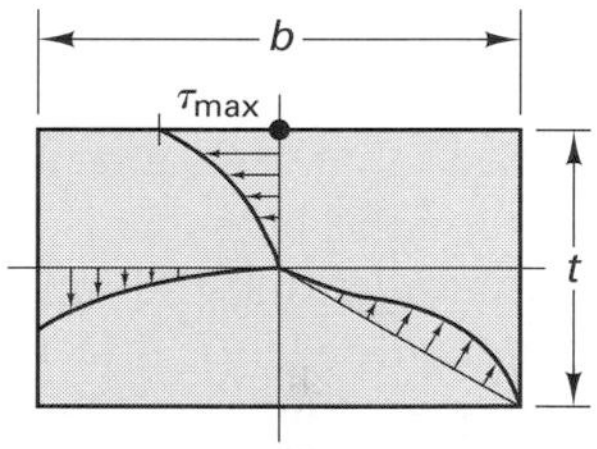

where T, as before, is the applied torque, b is the length of the long side, and t is the thickness or width of the short side of a rectangular section. The values of parameters α and β depend upon the ration b/t. A few of these values are recorded in the following table. For thin sections, where b is much greater than t, the values of α and β approach 1/3.

Fig. 6-33   Shear stress distribution in a rectangular shaft subjected to a torque.

Table of Coefficients for Rectangular Bars

b/t	1.00	1.50	2.00	3.00	6.00	10.0	∞
α	0.208	0.231	0.246	0.267	0.299	0.312	0.333
β	0.141	0.196	0.229	0.263	0.299	0.312	0.333

It is useful to recast the second Eq. 6-30 to express the torsional stiffness k_t for a rectangular section, giving

$$k_t = \frac{T}{\phi} = \beta b t^3 \frac{G}{L} \tag{6-31}$$

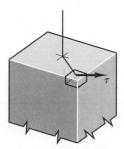

Fig. 6-34   The shear stress shown cannot exist.

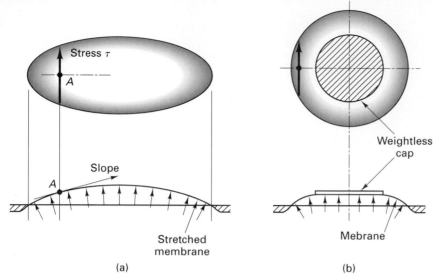

Fig. 6-35   Membrane analogy: (a) simply connected region, and (b) multiply connected (tubular) region.

Formulas such as these are available for many other types of cross-sectional areas in more advanced books.[16]

For cases that cannot be conveniently solved mathematically, a remarkable method has been devised.[17] It happens that the solution of the partial differential equation that must be solved in the elastic torsion problem is mathematically identical to that for a thin membrane, such as a soap film, lightly stretched over a hole. This hole must be geometrically similar to the cross section of the shaft being studied. Light air pressure must be kept on one side of the membrane. Then the following can be shown to be true:

1. The shear stress at any point is proportional to the slope of the stretched membrane at the same point, Fig. 6-35(a).
2. The direction of a particular shear stress at a point is at right angles to the slope of the membrane at the same point, Fig. 6-35(a).
3. Twice the volume enclosed by the membrane is proportional to the torque carried by the section.

The foregoing analogy is called the *membrane analogy*. In addition to its value in experimental applications, it is a very useful mental aid for visu-

---

[16]R. J. Roark and W. C. Young, *Formulas for Stress and Strain,* 5th ed. (New York: McGraw-Hill, 1975). Finite element analyses for solid bars of arbitrary cross section are also available. See, for example, L. R. Herrmann, "Elastic torsional analysis of irregular shapes," *J. Eng. Mech. Div., ASCE* (December 1965), 91 EMD, 11–19.

[17]This analogy was introduced by the German engineering scientist L. Prandtl in 1903.

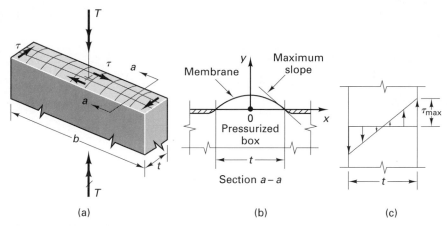

Fig. 6-36   Illustration of the membrane analogy for a rectangular bar in torsion.

alizing stresses and torque capacities of members. For example, consider a narrow rectangular bar subjected to torque T, as shown in Fig. 6-36. A stretched membrane for this member is shown in Fig. 6-36(a). If such a membrane is lightly stretched by internal pressure, a section through the membrane is a parabola, Fig. 6-36(b). For this surface, the maximum slope, hence maximum shear stress, occurs along the edges, Fig. 6-36(c). *No shear stress develops along a line bisecting the bar thickness t.* The maximum shear stresses along the short sides are small. The volume enclosed by the membrane is directly proportional to the torque the member can carry at a given maximum stress. For this reason, the sections shown in Fig. 6-37 can carry approximately the same torque at the same maximum shear stress (same maximum slope of the membrane) since the volume enclosed by the membranes would be approximately the same in all cases. (For all these shapes, $b = L$ and the t's are equal.) However, use of a little imagination will convince the reader that the contour lines of a soap film will "pile up" at points a of reentrant corners. Hence, high local stresses will occur at those points. An inscribed circle within the cross-sectional area of a section is tangent to the maximum stress at a boundary.

Another analogy, the *sand-heap analogy,* has been developed for plastic torsion.[18] Dry sand is poured onto a raised flat surface having the shape of the cross section of the member. The surface of the sand heap so formed assumes a constant slope. For example, a cone is formed on a circular disc, or a pyramid on a square base. The constant maximum slope of the sand corresponds to the limiting surface of the membrane in the previous analogy. The volume of the sand heap, hence its weight, is proportional to the fully plastic

[18]A. Nadai, *Theory of Flow and Fracture of Solids,* Vol. 1, 2nd ed. (New York: McGraw-Hill, 1950).

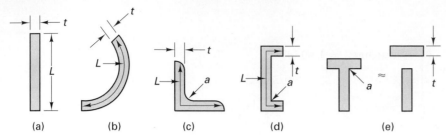

Fig. 6-37   Members of equal cross-sectional areas of the same thickness carrying the same torque.

torque carried by a section. The other items in connection with the sand surface have the same interpretation as those in the membrane analogy.

Statically indeterminate bars having any cross section are susceptible to the analysis procedures discussed in Section 6-9.

Example 6-15

By using the membrane analogy, determine an approximate value for the torsion constant $(I_p)_{\text{equiv}}$ for a W12 × 65 steel beam; see Fig. 6-38. Compare the calculated value with the 2.18 in^4 given in the *AISC Manual of Steel Construction.* (see Table 4A in the Appendix).

SOLUTION
By comparing the equations given for ϕ for a circular section, Eq. 6-16, with that for a rectangular bar, Eq. 6-30, it can be concluded that $(I_p)_{\text{equiv}} = \beta bt^3$. Further, a W12 × 65 section can be approximated, as implied in Fig. 6-37(e), by three separate narrow bars: two flanges and a

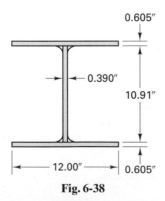

0.605"

0.390"

10.91"

12.00"

0.605"

Fig. 6-38

web. Since b/t for the flanges is $12/0.605 = 19.8$ and that for the web is $10.91/0.390 = 28.0$, from the table for both cases, $\beta \approx \frac{1}{3}$. Hence,

$$(I_p)_{\text{equiv}} = \tfrac{1}{3}(2 \times 12 \times 0.605^3 + 10.91 \times 0.390^3) = 1.99 \text{ in}^4$$

The value given in the *AISC Manual* is larger (2.18 in⁴). The discrepancy can be attributed to neglecting the fillets at the four inside corners.

This problem can be solved from a different point of view using Eq. 6-21. The numerical work is identical.

6-15. Warpage of Thin-Walled Open Sections[19]

The solution of the general elastic torsion problem discussed in the preceding section is associated with the name of Saint-Venant. Solutions based on this rigorous approach (which includes membrane analogy) for thin-walled open sections[20] may result in significant inaccuracies in some engineering applications. As pointed out in connection with the twist of a narrow rectangular bar, Fig. 6-36, no shear stresses develop along a line bisecting thickness t. This means that *no in-plane deformation can take place along the entire width and length of the bar's middle surface.* The same holds true for middle surfaces of curved bars, as well as for an assembly of bars. In this sense, an I section, shown in Fig. 6-39, consists of three flat bars, and, during twisting, the *three* middle surfaces of these bars *do not develop in-plane deformations.*

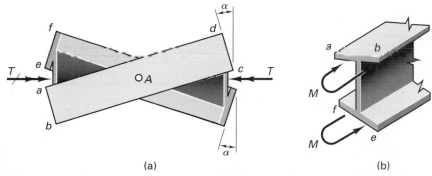

(a)   (b)

Fig. 6-39   Cross-sectional warpage due to applied torque.

---

[19]This section presents only a qualitative discussion of this important topic.

[20]In mathematics, the boundaries of such sections are referred to as simply connected (i.e., such sections are neither tubular nor hollow).

By virtue of symmetry, this *I* section twists around its centroidal axis, which in this case is also the center of twist. During twisting, as the beam flanges displace laterally, the *undeformed* middle surface *abcd* rotates about point *A*, Fig. 6-39(a). Similar behavior is exhibited by the middle surface of the other flange. In this manner, plane sections of an *I* beam warp (i.e., cease to be plane) during twisting. By contrast, for circular members, the sections perpendicular to the axis remain plane during twisting (see Section 6-3, assumption 1). Although warpage of the cross section does take place for other *thick* sections, including rectangular bars, this effect is negligible. On the other hand, for *thin-walled* torsion members, commonly employed in aircraft, automobiles, ships, bridges, etc., the cross-sectional warpage, or its restraint, may have an important effect[21] on member strength and, particularly, on its stiffness.

Warpage of cross sections in torsion is restrained in many engineering applications. For example, by welding an end of a steel *I* beam to a rigid support, the attached cross section cannot warp. To maintain required compatibility of deformations, in-plane flange moments *M*, shown in Fig. 6-39(b),[22] must develop. Such an enforced restraint effectively stiffens a beam and reduces its twist. This effect is local in character and, at some distance from the support, becomes unimportant. Nevertheless, for short beams, cutouts, etc., the warpage-restraint effect is dominant. This important topic is beyond the scope of this text.[23]

Part D   TORSION OF THIN-WALLED TUBULAR MEMBERS

6-16. Thin-Walled Hollow Members

Unlike solid noncircular members, *thin-walled* tubes of any shape can be rather simply analyzed for the magnitude of the shear stresses and the angle of twist caused by a torque applied to the tube. Thus, consider a tube of an arbitrary shape with varying wall thickness, such as shown in

---

[21]V. Z. Vlasov, in a series of 1940 papers, made basic contributions to this subject. See his book, *Thin-walled Elastic Beams,* 2nd ed. (Washington, DC: Israel Translations, Office of Technical Services, 1961).

[22]Shears that occur in the flanges and efficiently carry part of the applied torque are not shown in the diagram.

[23]For details, see, for example, J. T. Oden and E. A. Ripperger, *Mechanics of Elastic Structures,* 2nd ed. (New York: McGraw-Hill, 1981).

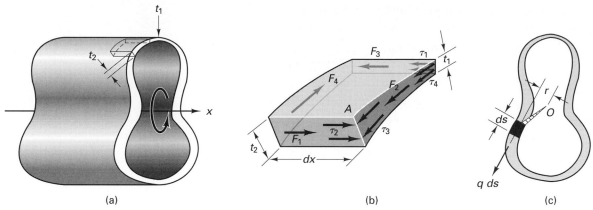

Fig. 6-40   Thin-walled tubular member of variable thickness.

Fig. 6-40(a), F_1, F_2, F_3, and F_4. These forces are equal to the shear stresses acting on the cut planes multiplied by the respective areas.

From $\Sigma F_x = 0$, $F_1 = F_3$, but $F_1 = \tau_2 t_2 \, dx$, and $F_3 = \tau_1 t_1 \, dx$, where τ_2 and τ_1 are shear stresses acting on the respective areas $t_2 \, dx$ and $t_1 \, dx$. Hence, $\tau_2 t_2 \, dx = \tau_1 t_1 \, dx$, or $\tau_1 t_1 = \tau_2 t_2$. However, since the longitudinal sections were taken an arbitrary distance apart, it follows from the previous relations that the product of the shear stress and the wall thickness is the same (i.e., constant) on any such planes. This constant will be denoted by q, which is measured in the units of force per unit distance along the perimeter. Therefore, its units are either N/m or lb/in.

In Section 1-4, Eq. 1-2, it was established that shear stresses on mutually perpendicular planes are equal at a corner of an element. Hence, at a corner such as A in Fig. 6-40(b), $\tau_2 = \tau_3$; similarly, $\tau_1 = \tau_4$. Therefore, $\tau_4 t_1 = \tau_3 t_2$, or, in general, q is constant in the plane of a section perpendicular to the axis of a member. On this basis, an analogy can be formulated. The inner and outer boundaries of the wall can be thought of as being the boundaries of a channel. Then one can imagine a constant quantity of water steadily circulating in this channel. In this arrangement, the quantity of water flowing through a plane across the channel is constant. Because of this analogy, the quantity q has been termed *shear flow*.

Next consider the cross section of the tube as shown in Fig. 6-40(c). The force per unit distance of the perimeter of this tube, by virtue of the previous argument, is constant and is the shear flow q. This shear flow multiplied by the length ds of the perimeter gives a force $q \, ds$ per differential length. The product of this infinitesimal force $q \, ds$ and r around some convenient point such as O, Fig. 6-40(c), gives the contribution of an element to the resistance of applied torque T. Adding or integrating this,

$$T = \oint rq \, ds \qquad (6\text{-}32)$$

where the integration process is carried around the tube along the center line of the perimeter. Since for a tube, q is a constant, this equation may be written as

$$T = q \oint r \, ds \qquad (6\text{-}33)$$

Instead of carrying out the actual integration, a simple interpretation of the integral is available. It can be seen from Fig. 6-40(c) that $r \, ds$ is twice the value of the shaded area of an infinitesimal triangle of altitude r and base ds. Hence the complete integral is twice the whole area bounded by the center line of the perimeter of the tube. Defining this area by a special symbol $\circledA$, one obtains

$$T = 2\circledA q \qquad \text{or} \qquad q = \frac{T}{2\circledA} \qquad (6\text{-}34)$$

This equation[24] applies only to *thin-walled* tubes. The area $\circledA$ is approximately an average of the two areas enclosed by the inside and the outside surfaces of a tube, or, as noted, it is an area enclosed by the center line of the wall's contour. Equation 6-34 is not applicable at all if the tube is slit, when Eqs. 6-30 should be used.

Since for any tube, the shear flow q given in Eq. 6-34 is constant, from the definition of shear flow, the shear stress at any point of a tube where the wall thickness is t is

$$\boxed{\tau = \frac{q}{t}} \qquad (6\text{-}35)$$

In the elastic range, Eqs. 6-34 and 6-35 are applicable to any shape of tube. For inelastic behavior, Eq. 6-35 applies only if thickness t is constant. The analysis of tubes of more than one cell is beyond the scope of this book.[25]

For linearly *elastic* materials, the angle of twist for a hollow tube can be found by applying the principle of conservation of energy, Eq. 3-16. In this derivation, it is convenient to introduce the angle of twist per unit length of the tube defined as $\theta = d\phi/dx$. The elastic shear strain energy for the tube should also be per unit length of the tube. Hence, Eq. 5-5 for the elastic strain energy here reduces to $U_{sh} = \int_{vol}(\tau^2/2G) \, dV$, where $dV = 1 \times t \, ds$. By substituting Eq. 6-35 and then Eq. 6-34 into this relation and simplifying,

$$\overline{U}_{sh} = \oint \frac{T^2}{8\circledA^2 Gt} \, ds = \frac{T^2}{8\circledA^2 G} \oint \frac{ds}{t} \qquad (6\text{-}36)$$

where, in the last expression, the constants are taken outside the integral.

[24]Equation 6-34 is sometimes called Bredt's formula in honor of the German engineer who developed it.

[25]J. T. Oden and E. A. Ripperger, *Mechanics and Elastic Structures,* 2nd ed. (New York: McGraw-Hill, 1981).

Equating this relation to the external work per unit length of member expressed as $\overline{W}_e = T\theta/2$, the governing differential equation becomes

$$\theta = \frac{d\phi}{dx} = \frac{T}{4\textcircled{A}^2 G}\oint \frac{ds}{t} \tag{6-37}$$

Here again it is useful to recast Eq. 6-37 to express the torsional stiffness k_t for a thin-walled hollow tube. Since for a prismatic tube subjected to a constant torque, $\phi = \theta L$,

$$k_t = \frac{T}{\phi} = \frac{4\textcircled{A}^2}{\displaystyle\oint ds/t}\frac{G}{L} \tag{6-38}$$

The cross-sectional warpage discussed in Section 6-15 is not very important for tubular members. Analysis of statically indeterminate tubular members follows the procedures discussed earlier.

Example 6-16

Rework Example 6-3 using Eqs. 6-34 and 6-35. The tube has outside and inside radii of 10 and 8 mm, respectively, and the applied torque is 40 N · m.

SOLUTION
The mean radius of the tube is 9 mm and the wall thickness is 2 mm. Hence,

$$\tau = \frac{q}{t} = \frac{T}{2\textcircled{A}t} = \frac{40 \times 10^3}{2\pi \times 9^2 \times 2} = 39.3 \text{ MPa}$$

Note that by using Eqs. 6-34 and 6-35, only one shear stress is obtained and that it is just about the average of the two stresses computed in Example 6-3. The thinner the walls, the more accurate the answer, or vice versa.

It is interesting to note that a rectangular tube, shown in Fig. 6-41, with a wall thickness of 2 mm, for the same torque will have nearly the same shear stress as that of the circular tube. This is so because its enclosed area is about the same as the $\textcircled{A}$ of the circular tube. However, some local stress concentrations will be present at the inside (reentrant) corners of the square tube.

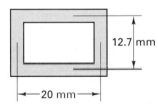

12.7 mm

20 mm

Fig. 6-41

Example 6-17

An aluminum extrusion has the cross section shown in Fig. 6-42. If torque $T = 300$ N · m is applied, (a) determine the maximum shear stresses that would develop in the three different parts of the member, and (b) find the torsional stiffness of the member. Neglect stress concentrations.

SOLUTION

The cross section consists essentially of three parts: a circular knob ①, a rectangular bar ②, and a rectangular hollow box with variable wall thickness ③. During application of torque T, each one of these elements rotates through the same angle ϕ, and therefore each element resists a torque $(k_t)_i\phi$. Hence, according to Eq. 6-21, the total torque resisted by the member is the sum of these quantities for the three parts. The expressions for $(k_t)_i$'s for the parts are given, respectively, by Eqs. 6-17, 6-31, and 6-38. These constants are

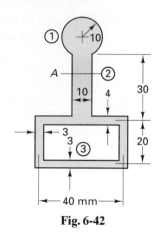

Fig. 6-42

$$(k_t)_1 = I_p \frac{G}{L} = \frac{\pi \times 10^4}{2} \frac{G}{L} = 1.57 \times 10^4 \frac{G}{L}$$

$$(k_t)_2 = \beta b t^3 \frac{G}{L} = 0.263 \times 30 \times 10^3 \frac{G}{L} = 0.789 \times 10^4 \frac{G}{L}$$

$$(k_t)_3 = \frac{4\textcircled{A}^2}{\oint ds/t} \frac{G}{L} = \frac{4 \times (40 \times 20)^2}{(40 + 2 \times 20)/3 + 40/4} \frac{G}{L} = 6.98 \times 10^4 \frac{G}{L}$$

where all numerical values are in mm. In evaluating the integral in the last equation, it is assumed that the 4-mm thickness of the box extends for 40 mm.

By adding the stiffnesses for the parts, the member torsional stiffness $\Sigma (k_t)_i = 9.34 \times 10^4 G/L$

The applied torque is distributed among the three parts in a ratio of $(k_t)_i/\Sigma (k_t)_i$. On this basis, the torques are $300 \times (1.57 \times 10^4 G/L)$ $(9.34 \times 10^4 G/L) = 50.4$ N·m for the knob, 25.3 N·m for the bar, and 224 N·m for the box. The maximum stresses in each of the parts are determined using, respectively, Eqs. 6-3, 6-30, and 6-34.

$$\tau_{1\text{-max}} = \frac{Tc}{I_p} = \frac{50.4 \times 10^3 \times 10}{\pi \times 10^4/2} = 32.1 \ \text{MPa}$$

$$\tau_{2\text{-max}} = \frac{T}{\alpha b t^2} = \frac{25.3 \times 10^3}{0.267 \times 30 \times 10^2} = 31.6 \ \text{MPa}$$

$$\tau_{3\text{-max}} = \frac{T}{2\textcircled{A}t} = \frac{224 \times 10^3}{2 \times 40 \times 20 \times 3} = 46.7 \ \text{MPa}$$

Stress $\tau_{1\text{-max}}$ occurs along the perimeter of the knob, $\tau_{2\text{-max}}$ at the midheight of the bar, and $\tau_{3\text{-max}}$ in the 3-mm walls of the tube. Due to the approximations made, these stresses cannot be considered precise. In mechanical applications, stress concentrations may be particularly important. Membrane analogy can be used to great advantage to determine the location of stress concentrations. Generous fillets at reentrant corners can be a remedy.

Member torsional stiffness found in this manner, such as needed for vibration analysis and for the solution of statically indeterminate elastic problems, would be sufficiently accurate since local effects such as stress concentrations play a minor role.

PROBLEMS

Sections 6-2

6-1. The solid cylindrical shaft of variable size, as shown in mm on the figure, is acted upon by the torques indicated. What is the maximum torsional stress in the shaft, and between what two pulleys does it occur?

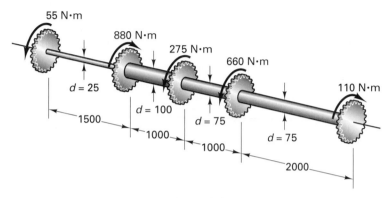

Fig. P6-1

Sections 6-4 and 6-5

6-2. A 100-mm-diameter core of 50 mm radius is bored out from a 200-mm-diameter solid circular shaft. What percentage of the torsional strength is lost by this operation?

6-3. A solid circular shaft of 40 mm diameter is to be replaced by a hollow circular tube. If the outside diameter of the tube is limited to 60 mm, what must be the thickness of the tube for the same linearly elastic material working at the same maximum stress? Determine the ratio of weights for the two shafts.

6-4. A 20-mm round shaft 500 mm long is built in at one end subjected to a torque T at the free end, as shown in the figure. If a linear gage placed on the surface at 45° with the horizontal reads a strain of 4×10^{-3} mm/mm when the torque is applied, what would be the angle of twist of the shaft? Let $E = 180$ GPa and $G = 70$ GPa. (*Hint:* Note the information given in Fig. 6-8.)

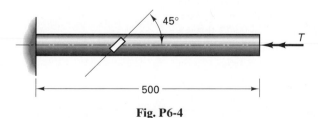

Fig. P6-4

Section 6-6

6-5. A 100-mm-diameter solid-steel shaft transmits 400 kW at 2 Hz. (a) Determine the maximum shear stress. (b) What would be the required shaft diameter to operate at 4 Hz at the same maximum stress?

6-6. A motor, through a set of gears, drives a line shaft, as shown in the figure, at 630 rpm. Thirty horsepower (hp) are delivered to a machine on the right; 90 hp on the left. Select a solid round shaft of the same size throughout. The allowable shear stress is 5750 psi.

6-7. On a lathe, one of the gear trains is made as shown in the figure. The small driving spur gear powered by a 2-kW motor mounted on a 12-mm shaft has 28 teeth. The driven gear has 90 teeth. This effectively reduces the speed of the large gear by a factor of 28/90. What should be the size of the shaft for the large gear if made of the same material as the small gear?

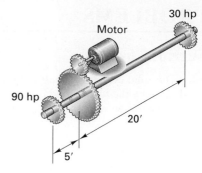

Fig. P6-6

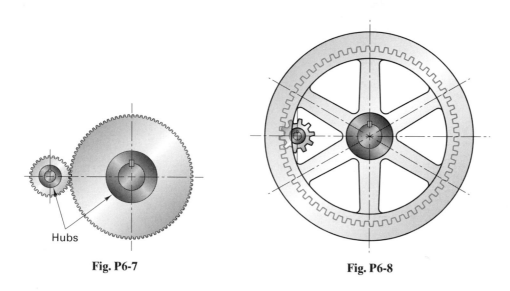

Fig. P6-7   **Fig. P6-8**

6-8. The small gear of an internal gear train shown in the figure is powered by a 500-kW motor at 30 Hz. Whereas this small gear has 10 teeth, the large gear it drives has 30. Hence the large gear rotates at 10 Hz. If the allowable shear stress is 60 MPa, what are required sizes of the shafts?

6-9. A 40-mm-diameter aluminum alloy shaft for constant-amplitude cyclic loading is to sustain service of 5×10^8 cycles with a safety factor of 1.8. Use data in Fig. 2-26, and divide the normal stress given in this figure by 2. As shown in Chapter 12, this is a good conservative assumption (i.e., $\tau = \sigma/2$). Find the torque that may be applied to this shaft.

6-10. (a) Design a hollow steel shaft to transmit 300 hp at 75 rpm without exceeding a shear stress of 8000 psi. Use 1.2:1 as the ratio of the outside diameter to the inside diameter. (b) What solid shaft could be used instead?

6-11. A 100-hp motor is driving a line shaft through gear A at 26.3 rpm. Bevel gears at B and C drive rubber-cement mixers. If the power requirement of the mixer driven by gear B is 25 hp and that of C is 75 hp, what are the required shaft diameters? The allowable shear stress in the shaft is 6000 psi. A sufficient number of bearings is provided to avoid bending.

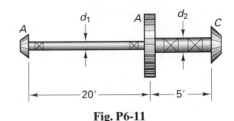

Fig. P6-11

Section 6-7

6-12. A solid circular shaft of 150 mm diameter is machined down to a diameter of 75 mm along a part of the shaft. If, at the transition point of the two diameters, the fillet radius is 12 mm, what maximum shear stress is developed when a torque of 2700 N · m is applied to the shaft? What will the maximum shear stress be if the fillet radius is reduced to 3 mm?

6-13. Find the required fillet radius for the juncture of a 6-in-diameter shaft with a 4-in-diameter segment if the shaft transmits 110 hp at 100 rpm and the maximum shear stress is limited to 8000 psi.

6-14. Two stepped shafts of different proportions are made from the same nickel steel. In the one, the larger 40-mm-diameter shaft is machined down a 20-mm shaft. At the transition between the two shaft sizes, a semicircular fillet having a radius of 1 mm is introduced (see the figure). The second shaft, similarly machined, has the larger part 30 mm in diameter and the other 18 mm. A fillet at the transition has a radius of 2 mm. Which shaft assembly is more advantageous from the stress point of view?

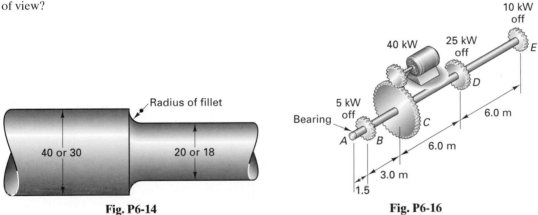

Fig. P6-14   **Fig. P6-16**

Section 6-8

6-15. What must be the length of a 6-mm-diameter aluminum wire so that it could be twisted through one complete revolution without exceeding a shear stress of 42 MPa? $G = 27$ GPa.

6-16. The solid 50-mm-diameter steel line shaft shown in the figure is driven by a 40-kW motor at 3 Hz. (a) Find the maximum torsional stresses in sections AB, BC, CD, and DE of the shaft. (b) Determine the total angle of twist between A and E. Let $G = 84$ GPa.

6-17. A hollow steel rod 6 in long is used as a torsional spring. The ratio of inside to outside diameters is 0.5. The required stiffness for this spring is 0.10 of a degree per 1 in-lb of torque. (a) Determine the outside diameter of this rod. $G = 12 \times 10^6$ psi. (b) What is the torsional spring constant for this rod?

6-18. A solid aluminum-alloy shaft 60 mm in diameter and 1000 mm long is to be replaced by a tubular steel shaft of the same outer diameter such that the new shaft would neither exceed twice the maximum shear stress nor the angle of twist of the aluminum shaft. (a) What should be the inner radius of the tubular steel shaft? Let $G_{Al} = 28$ GPa and $G_{St} = 84$ GPa. (b) Which of the two criteria governs?

6-19. Two gears are attached to two 60-mm-diameter steel shafts, as shown in the figure. The gear at B has a 200-mm pitch diameter; the gear at C, a 400-mm pitch diameter. Through what angle will end A turn if at A a torque of 600 N · m is applied and end D of the second shaft is prevented from rotating? $G = 84$ GPa.

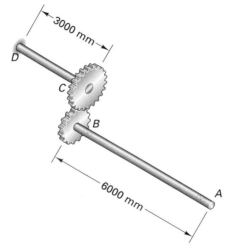

Fig. P6-19

6-20. A circular steel shaft of the dimensions shown in the figure is subjected to three torques: $T_1 = 28$ k-in, $T_2 = -8$ k-in, and $T_3 = 10$ k-in. (a) What is the angle of twist of the right end due to the applied torques? (b) Plot the angle-of-twist diagram along the shaft. Let $G = 12 \times 10^6$ psi.

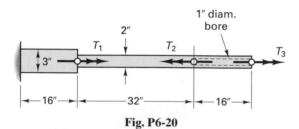

Fig. P6-20

6-21. A dynamometer is employed to calibrate the required power input to operate an exhaust fan at 20 Hz. The dynamometer consists of a 12-mm-diameter solid shaft and two discs attached to the shaft 300 mm apart, as shown in the figure. One disc is fastened through a tube at the input end; the other is near the output end. The relative displacement of these two discs as viewed in stroboscopic light was found to be 6° 0′. Compute the power input in hp required to operate the fan at the given speed. Let $G = 84$ GPa.

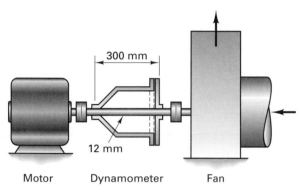

300 mm

12 mm

Motor   Dynamometer   Fan

Fig. P6-21

6-22. A nickel alloy tube has a 30-mm outside diameter and a 20-mm inside diameter. The material's $G = 70$ MPa. Determine the torsional flexibility for a tube 1 m long.

6-23. A thin circular disc with a mass m = 2 kg is attached to a 500-mm-long vertical shaft extending from a fixed end at the top, as shown in the figure. (a) If the shaft is made of steel ($G = 83$ MPa) and is 24 mm in diameter, what is the frequency of torsional vibration of the system? The equation for the fundamental frequency of vibration $f_n = (1/2\pi)\sqrt{k_t/I_{mz}}$, where the mass moment of inertia of the disc about the z axis $I_{mz} = m R^2/2$. (b) What would be the required diameter of the shaft to develop the same frequency of vibration if the it were made from an aluminum alloy ($G = 26$ GPa)?

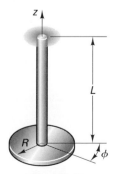

z

L

R

ϕ

Fig. P6-23

6-24. A solid tapered steel shaft is rigidly fastened to a fixed support at one end and is subjected to a torque T at the other end (see the figure). Find the angular rotation of the free end if $d_1 = 150$ mm, $d_2 = 50$ mm, $L = 500$ mm, and $T = 3$ kN $\cdot$ m. Assume that the usual assumptions of strain in prismatic circular shafts subjected to torque apply, and let $G = 200$ GPa. (b) Determine the torsional flexibility of the shaft.

Fig. P6-24

6-25. A thin-walled elastic frustum of a cone has the dimensions shown in the figure. (a) Determine the torsional stiffness of this member (i.e., the magnitude of torque per unit angle of twist). The shearing modulus for the material is G. (b) What is the torsional flexibility of this member?

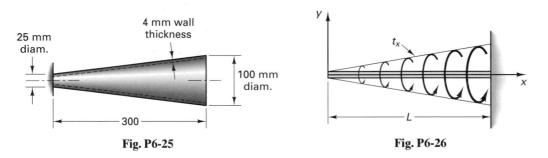

Fig. P6-25   **Fig. P6-26**

6-26. The loading on a control torque tube for an aileron of an airplane may be idealized by a uniformly varying torque $t_x = kx$ in-lb/in, where k is a constant (see the figure). Determine the angle of twist of the free end. Assume $I_p G$ to be constant.

6-27. A torque applied to a circular shaft is idealized as uniformly varying from the built-in end; see the figure. Determine the angle of twist of the right end. The torsional rigidity $I_p G$ of the shaft is constant.

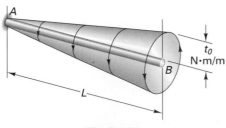

Fig. P6-27

6-28. A 2000-mm-long circular shaft attached at one end and free at the other is subjected to a linearly varying distributed torque along its length, as shown in the figure. The torsional rigidity I_pG of the shaft is constant. Determine the angle of twist at the free end caused by the applied torque.

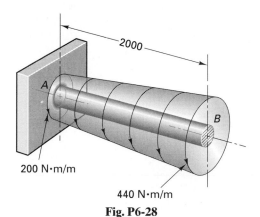

200 N·m/m

440 N·m/m

Fig. P6-28

Section 6-9

6-29. An aluminum-alloy tube is shrunk onto a steel rod, forming a shaft that acts as a unit. This shaft is 1 m long and has the cross section shown in the figure. Assume elastic behavior and let $E_{st} = 3E_{Al} = 210$ GPa. (a) What stresses would be caused by applying a torque $T = 20$ kN · m? Show the shear stress distribution on a graph. (b) Determine the torsional stiffness and flexibility of the shaft.

6-30. A tube of 50 mm outside diameter and 2 mm thickness is attached at the ends by means of rigid flanges to a solid shaft of 25 mm diameter, as shown in the figure. If both the tube and the shaft are made of the same linearly elastic material, what part of the applied torque T is carried by the tube?

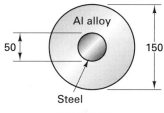

Al alloy

Steel

Fig. P6-29

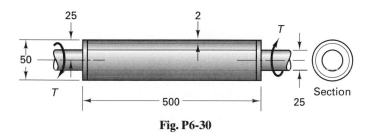

Fig. P6-30

6-31. Assume that in Problem 6-30, prior to welding the rigid end plates, the shaft is subjected to a torque of 200 N · m and maintained in this condition during the welding process. What residual torque will remain in the shaft upon release of the applied torque?

6-32. Using the displacement method, determine the reactions for the shaft shown in Fig. 6-21 for the following data: $T = 40$ k-in, $L_1 = 15$ in, $L_2 = 10$ in, $(I_p)_1 = 2\pi$ in^4, $(I_p)_2 = \pi/2$ in^4, and $G_1 = G_2 = G = 12 \times 10^3$ ksi. Also plot the angle of twist diagram for the shaft along its length.

6-33. Consider the same elastic stepped circular shaft shown in the two alternative figures. Using the force method, determine the angle of twist ϕ_{ab} at a caused by the application of a unit of torque at b, and show that it is equal to ϕ_{ba}, the angle of twist at b due to the application of a unit of torque at a. Let $(I_p)_1 = 3(I_p)_2$. (See Problem 4-6.)

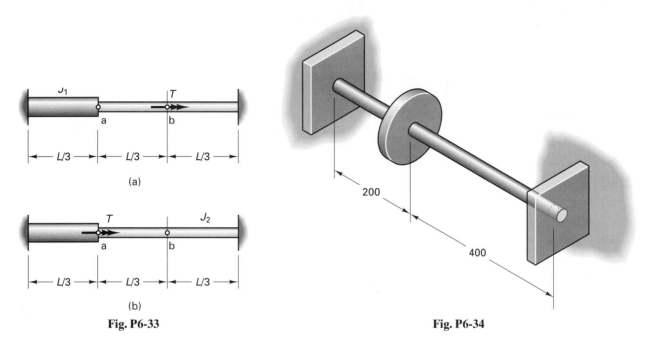

(a)

(b)

Fig. P6-33

Fig. P6-34

6-34. A circular disc with a mass of 50 kb is attached at a third point of a 600-mm-long solid steel shaft built in at both ends, as shown in the figure. The shaft is 40 mm in diameter. Determine the fundamental torsional frequency of the system. Neglect the weight of the shaft. For the frequency formula, see Problem 6-23.

6-35. (a) Using the force method, determine the reactions for the circular stepped shaft shown in the figure. The applied torques are $T_1 = 600$ lb-in $T_2 = 500$ lb-in, and $T_3 = 200$ lb-in. The shaft diameters are $d_1 = 2.83$ in and $d_2 = 2.38$ in. (b) Plot the angle-of-twist diagram for the shaft along its length. Let $E = 10 \times 10^3$ ksi, and $v = \frac{1}{3}$.

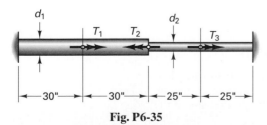

Fig. P6-35

6-36.   An elastic circular shaft attached at both ends is subjected to a uniformly distributed torque t_o per unit length along one-half of its length, as shown in the figure. (a) Using the force method, find the reactions. (b) Determine the angle of maximum twist and plot the angle of twist diagram along the shaft length. The torsional rigidity I_pG of the shaft is constant.

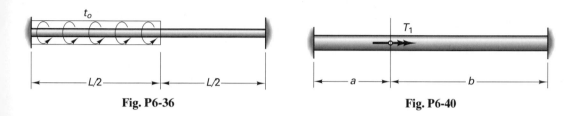

Fig. P6-36   Fig. P6-40

6-37.   Assume that the shaft in Problem 6-27 is attached at both ends. (a) Using the force method, determine the reactions. (b) Find the angle of maximum twist and plot the angle-of-twist diagram along the shaft length.

Section 6-10

6-38.   Rework Problem 6-27 using Eq. 6-26.

6-39.   Rework Problem 6-28 using Eq. 6-26.

6-40.   Using Eq. 6-26 and continuity conditions (see Section 4-7) or singularity functions, determine the reactions at the built-in ends caused by the application of torque T_1; see the figure. Plot the torque $T(x)$ and the angle-of-twist $\varphi(x)$ diagrams.

6-41.   Using Eq. 6-26 and continuity conditions (see Section 4-7) or singularity functions, determine the reactions caused by a uniformly distributed torque t_o along one-half of the shaft length, as shown in the figure for Problem 6-36. Sketch the angle-of-twist diagram along the shaft length.

Section 6-11

6-42.   A circular stepped shaft has the dimensions shown in the figure. (a) Using an energy method, determine the angle of twist at the loaded end. G is given. (b) Check the result using Eq. 6-16.

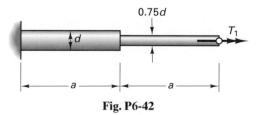

Fig. P6-42

Section 6-12

6-43. A coupling is made with eight $\frac{3}{4}$-in-diameter high-strength bolts located on a 10-in-diameter bolt circle. (a) Calculate the torque that can be transmitted by this coupling if the allowable shear stress in the bolts is 10.5 ksi. (b) Find the hp that can be transmitted when the shaft and couplings are rotating at 300 rpm.

6-44. A flange coupling has six bolts having a cross-sectional area of 0.2 in^2 each in a 8-in-diameter bolt circle, and six bolts having a cross-sectional area of 0.5 in^2 each in a 5-in-diameter bolt circle. If the allowable shear stress in the bolt is 16 ksi, what is the torque capacity of this coupling?

Section 6-13

6-45. A specimen of an SAE 1060 steel bar of 20 mm diameter and 450 mm length failed at a torque of 800 N · m What is the modulus of rupture of this steel in torsion?

6-46. A solid steel shaft of 20 mm diameter and 1000 mm long is twisted such that a 16-mm-diameter core remains elastic; see the figure. (a) Determine the torque applied to cause the yield state. (b) Find the residual stress distribution that would occur on removing the torque. Draw the residual-stress pattern with the critical values. Assume the idealized mechanical properties for the material given in Fig. 6-30(b) of Example 6-13.

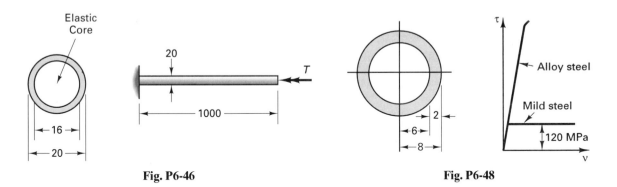

Fig. P6-46   Fig. P6-48

6-47. If the shaft in Problem 6-46 is twisted at the free end through an angle $\phi = 25$ rad and then released, what will be the residual angle ϕ? Also find the residual shear stresses. Draw the residual-stress pattern with the critical values.

6-48. A thin tube of nickel-alloy steel is shrunk onto a solid circular rod of mild steel. The cross-sectional dimensions of the composite shaft are shown in mm on the figure. Determine the torque developed by this shaft if the maximum shear stress measured on the surface is 480 MPa. For either steel, $G = 120$ GPa. However, the mild steel yields in shear at 120 MPa, whereas the alloy steel remains essentially linearly elastic into the 600-MPa range. Idealized τ-γ diagrams for the two materials are illustrated in the figure.

6-49. If in Problem 6-48 the applied torque is released, (a) what will be the residual stress pattern? Draw the results with the critical values. (b) Determine the residual angle of twist per unit length of shaft.

Section 6-14

6-50. Compare the maximum shear stress and angle of twist for members of equal length and cross-sectional areas for a square section, a rectangular section, and a circular section. All members are subjected to the same torque. The circular section is 100 mm in diameter and the rectangular section is 25 mm wide.

6-51. Compare the torsional strength and stiffness of thin-walled tubes of circular cross section of linearly elastic material with and without a longitudinal slot (see the figure).

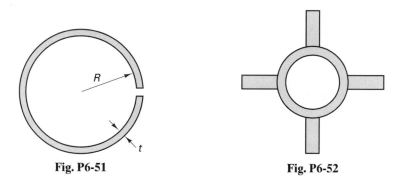

Fig. P6-51   **Fig. P6-52**

6-52. An agitator shaft acting as a torsional member is made by welding four rectangular bars to a circular pipe, as shown in the figure. The pipe is of 4 in outside diameter and is $\frac{1}{2}$ in thick; each of the rectangular bars is one by 2 in. If the maximum elastic shear stress, neglecting the stress concentrations, is limited to 10 ksi, what torque T can be applied to this member?

6-53. Using the sand-heap analogy, determine the ultimate torsional moment of resistance for a rectangular section of a by $2a$. (*Hint:* First, using the analogy, verify Eq. 6-29 for a solid circular shaft, where the height of the heap is $c\tau_{yp}$. Twice the volume included by the heap yields the required results.)

6-54. A torsion member has the cross section shown in the figure. Estimate the torsion constant $I_{p\,equiv}$.

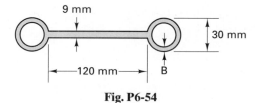

Fig. P6-54

6-55. Consider three cross sections: a circle, an ellipse, and equilateral triangle with the dimensions shown. (a) Apply membrane analogy and locate the points of maximum stress. (b) Determine τ_{max} and ϕ for the sections. Let $T = 1000\,\text{N} \cdot \text{m}$. The formulas for the elliptic section are $\tau_{max} = 2T/(\pi ab^2)$ and $\phi = TL/KG$, where $K = \pi a^3 b^3/(a^2 + b^2)$; for the equilateral triangular section $\tau_{max} = 20T/a^3$ and $K = a^4\sqrt{3}/80$; for both cases, $\phi = TL/KG$. (After R. J. Roark in *Formulas for Stress and Strain,* New York: McGraw-Hill, 1943.) Let $a = 20\,\text{mm}, b = r = 15\,\text{mm}$.

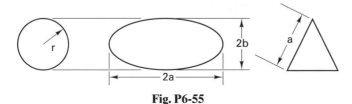

Fig. P6-55

6-56. Let each of the three cross-sectional areas of the members in Problem 6-55 be equal to 1200 mm². Determine τ_{max} for each case. Recall that the cross-sectional area of an ellipse is $A = \pi ab$.

6-57. Determine the relative sizes of the cross sections in Problem 6-55 to have the same torsional rigidity. Recall, as in the preceding problem, that $A = \pi ab$ for an ellipse.

Section 6-16

6-58. For a member having the cross section shown in the figure, find the maximum shear stresses and the angle of twist per unit length due to an applied torque of 1000 in-lb. Neglect stress concentration. Comment on the advantage gained by the increase in the wall thickness over part of the cross section.

6-59. A thin-walled cross section in the form of a simplified airfoil is shown in the figure. Determine the torque it would carry at a maximum shear stress of 20 MPa. Neglect the effect of stress concentrations. Is there any advantage to thicken the inclined plates? Use centerline dimensions.

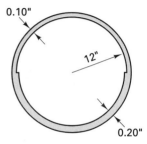

Fig. P6-58

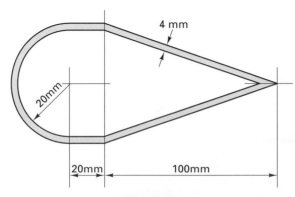

Fig. P6-59

6-60.   A shaft having the cross section shown in the figure is subjected to a torque $T = 150$ N $\cdot$ m. (a) Estimate the percentage of torque carried by each of the two cross-sectional components, and calculate maximum shear stresses in each part, neglecting stress concentrations. (b) Find the angle of twist per unit length caused by the applied torque. Let $G = 25 \times 10^3$ GPa.

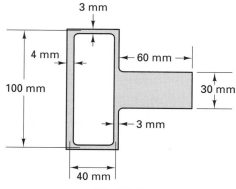

Fig. P6-60

6-61.   An aluminum alloy extrusion is made in the form of a rectangular box. Determine the elastic torsional strength of this member if the stress in shear is limited to 120 MPa. What is the torsional flexibility of a box 400 mm long?

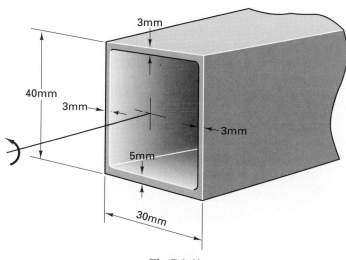

Fig. P6-61

6-62. A shaft built in at both ends is made of a 20-mm solid square bar and a 30-mm square tube welded at the juncture of the two sections to a plate that forms a pointer projecting in the horizontal direction; see the figure. The square tube has a wall thickness of 1.5 mm. Determine the vertical displacement of the tip of the pointer that would be caused by the application of the two torques T_1 and $2T_1$ when the maximum shearing stress in the shaft is 40 MPa. Neglect stress concentrations and let $G = 200$ GPa.

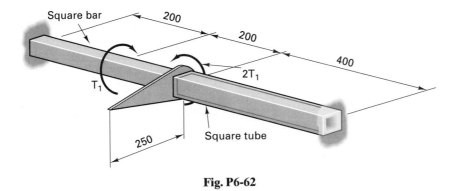

Fig. P6-62

7

Beam Statics

7-1. Introduction

In many instances in structural and machine design, members must resist forces applied laterally or transversely to their axes. Such members are called *beams*. The main members supporting floors of buildings are beams, just as an axle of a car is a beam. Many shafts of machinery act simultaneously as torsion members and as beams. With modern materials, the beam is a dominant member of construction. The determination of the system of internal forces necessary for equilibrium of any beam segment will be the main objective of this chapter.

For a beam with all forces in the same plane (i.e., a *planar* beam problem), a system of *three* internal force components can develop at a section. These are the axial force, the shear, and the bending moment. Determining these quantities is the focus of this chapter.

The chapter is divided into four parts. In Part A, methods for calculating reactions are reviewed; in Parts B and C, two different procedures for calculating the internal shear, V, and bending moment, M, and their graphic representations along a beam are discussed. In Part D, an optional topic on singularity functions for solving such problems is introduced.

Attention will be largely confined to consideration of single beams, which, for convenience, will be shown in the horizontal position. Some discussion of related problems of planar frames resisting axial forces, shears, and bending moments is also given. Only statically determinate systems will be fully analyzed for these quantities. Special procedures to be developed in subsequent chapters are required for determining reactions in statically indeterminate problems for complete solutions. Extension to members in three-dimensional systems, where there are *six* possible internal force components, will be introduced in later chapters as needed and will rely on the reader's knowledge of statics. In such problems at a section of a member there can be an axial force, two shear components, two bending moment components, and a torque.

Part A   CALCULATION OF REACTIONS

7-2. Diagrammatic Conventions for Supports and Loads[1]

In studying planar structures, it is essential to adopt diagrammatic conventions for their supports and loadings inasmuch as several kinds of supports and a great variety of loads are possible. Adherence to such conventions avoids confusion and minimizes the chances of making mistakes. These conventions form the pictorial language of engineers.

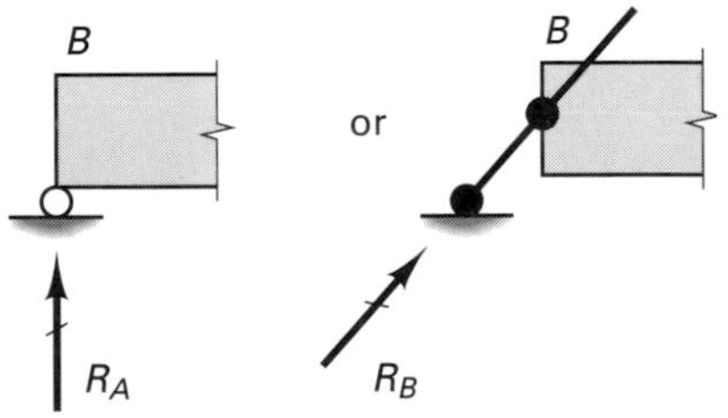

Three basic types of supports are recognized for planar structures. These are identified by the kind of resistance they offer to the acting forces. One type of support is physically realized by a *roller* or a *link*. It is capable of resisting a force in only one *specific direction* coincident with the *line of action,* as shown in Fig. 7-1. A link must be provided if the reaction acts away from the beam (i.e., a beam is not permitted to lift off from the support). In such cases it may be helpful to show the roller on top of the beam for clarity. This practice usually will be followed in this text.

Occasionally a roller support, as in Fig. 7-2, is used that can resist only a force that acts perpendicular to the plane *CD*.

Another type of support is a *pin*, shown diagrammatically in Fig. 7-3. A pinned support is capable of resisting a force acting in *any direction* of the plane. Hence, in general, the reaction at such a support may have two components, one in the horizontal and one in the vertical direction. Unlike the

Fig. 7-1   Roller or link support.

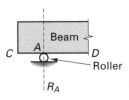

Fig. 7-2   Alternative type of roller support.

---

[1]This and the next section are an informal review of statics.

ratio applying to the roller or link support, that between the reaction components for the pinned support is *not fixed.* To determine these two components, two equations of statics must be used.

The third type of support is able to resist a force in any direction *and is also capable of resisting a moment or a couple.* Physically, such a support is obtained by building a beam into a wall, casting it into concrete, or welding the end of a member to the main structure. A system of *three* forces can exist at such a support, two components of force and a moment. Such a support is called a *fixed support* (i.e., the built-in end is fixed or prevented from rotating). The standard convention for indicating it is shown in Fig. 7-4.

To differentiate fixed supports from the roller and pin supports, which are not capable of resisting moment, the latter two are termed *simple supports.* In practice, engineers usually use their judgment and assume the supports to be of one of the three types, although in actual construction, supports for beams do not always clearly fall into these classifications.

The applied loads generally considered in this chapter consist of concentrated forces shown on diagrams by vectors and distributed forces indicated by a sequence of vectors. An example of uniformly varying load is illustrated in Fig. 7-5, where it is assumed that the vertical beam is 1 m wide and γ (N/m^3) is the unit weight of the liquid. For this type of loading, it should be noted that the maximum intensity of the load of q_0 (N/m) is applicable only at the bottom. It is twice as large as the average intensity of pressure. Hence, the total force exerted by this loading on the beam wall is $(q_0 h/2)$ N, and its resultant acts at a distance $h/3$ above the vessel's bottom. Horizontal bottoms of vessels containing liquid are loaded uniformly. Various aerodynamic loadings are of distributed type.

In passing, it should be noted that in both machine design and structural problems, numerous situations arise where, in a global sense, concentrated moments are applied to flexural members. An example is illustrated in Fig. 7-6. Note that by adding to the system a cantilever CE on the left with an upward force P, the axial force in the member AB is eliminated, and effectively only a concentrated moment is applied at C.

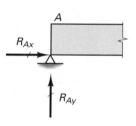

Fig. 7-3   Pinned support.

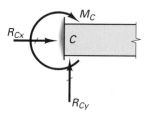

Fig. 7-4   Fixed support.

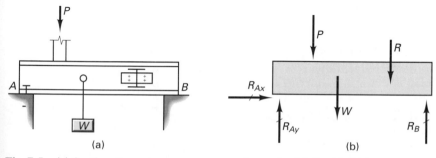

(a)   (b)

Fig. 7-5   (a) Section through narrow rectangular tank with liquid, (b) hydrostatic loading on a vertical wall of a tank.

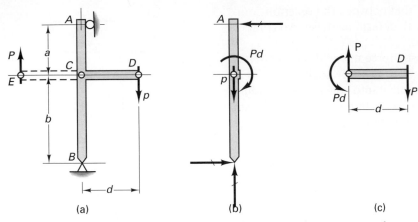

(a)   (b)   (c)

Fig. 7-6   Loaded cantilever *CD* applies an axial force and a concentrated moment to the vertical member.

It is to be noted that for reasons given in Section 1-4 for *P*, and in Section 6-2 for *M*, scalar representation for force vectors is adopted in this chapter.

7-3. Calculations of Beam Reactions

All subsequent work with beams in this chapter will begin with determination of the reactions. When all of the forces are applied in one plane, three equations of static equilibrium are available for the analysis. These are $\Sigma F_x = 0$, $\Sigma F_y = 0$, and $\Sigma M_z = 0$, and they were discussed in Chapter 1. For straight beams in the horizontal position, the *x* axis will be taken in a horizontal direction, the *y* axis in the upward vertical direction, and the *z* axis normal the plane of paper. The application of these equations to several beam problems is illustrated in the following examples and is intended to serve as a review of this important procedure. The deformation of beams, being small, is neglected when the equations of statics are applied. For stable beams, the small amount of deformation that does take place changes the points of application of the forces imperceptibly.

Example 7-1

Find the reaction at the supports for a simple beam loaded as shown in Fig. 7-7(a). Neglect the weight of the beam.

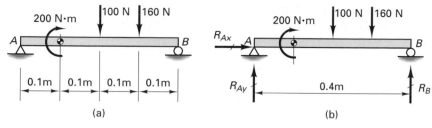

Fig. 7-7

SOLUTION

The loading of the beam is already given in diagramatic form. The nature of the supports is examined next, and the unknown components of these reactions are clearly indicated on the diagram. The beam, with the unknown reaction components and all the applied forces, is redrawn in Fig. 7-7(b) to emphasize this important step in constructing a free-body diagram. In order to differentiate among the applied forces and reactions, following the suggestion made in Section 1-5, slashes are drawn across the reaction force vectors.

At A, *two* unknown reaction components may exist, since the end is pinned. The reaction at B can act only in a vertical direction since the end is on a roller. The points of application of all forces are carefully noted. After a free-body diagram of the beam is made, the equations of statics are applied to obtain the solution.

$$\Sigma F_x = 0 \qquad\qquad\qquad R_{Ax} = 0$$

$$\Sigma M_A = 0 \curvearrowright + \quad 200 + 100 \times 0.2 + 160 \quad \times 0.3 - R_B \times 0.4 = 0$$

$$R_B = +670 \text{ N} \uparrow$$

$$\Sigma M_B = 0 \curvearrowright + \quad R_{Ay} \times 0.4 + 200 - 100 \quad \times 0.2 - 160 \times 0.1 = 0$$

$$R_{Ay} = -410 \text{ N} \downarrow$$

Check: $\Sigma F_y = 0 \uparrow +$ $\qquad\qquad -410 - 100 - 160 + 670 = 0$

Note that $\Sigma F_x = 0$ uses one of the three independent equations of statics; thus, only two additional reaction components can be determined from statics. If more unknown reaction components or moments exist at the support, the problem becomes statically indeterminate.

Note that the concentrated moment applied at C enters only into the expressions for the summation of moments. The positive sign of R_B indicates that its direction has been correctly assumed in Fig. 7-7(b). The opposite is the case of R_{Ay}, and the vertical reaction of A acts downward. A check on the arithmetical work is available if the calculations are made as shown.

Example 7-2

Find the reactions for the partially loaded beam with a uniformly varying load shown in Fig. 7-8(a). Neglect the weight of the beam.

SOLUTION

An examination of the supporting conditions indicates that there are three unknown reaction components; hence, the beam is statically determinate. These and the applied load are shown in Fig. 7-8(b). Note particularly that the configuration of the member is not important for computing the reactions. A crudely shaped outline, bearing no resemblance to the actual beam, is indicated to emphasize this point. However, this new body is supported at points A and B in the same manner as the original beam.

For calculating the reactions, the distributed load is replaced by an equivalent concentrated force P. It acts through the centroid of the distributed forces. These pertinent quantities are marked on the working sketch, Fig. 7-8(b). After a free-body diagram is prepared, the solution follows by applying the equations of static equilibrium.

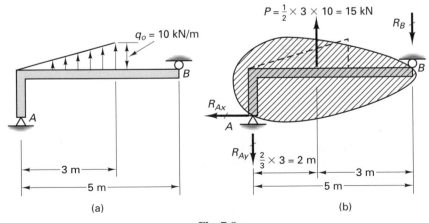

(a)   (b)

Fig. 7-8

$\Sigma F_x = 0$ $R_{Ax} = 0$

$\Sigma M_A = 0 \curvearrowleft +$ $+ 15 \times 2 - R_B \times 5 = 0$ $R_B = 6\,\text{kN} \downarrow$

$\Sigma M_B = 0 \curvearrowright +$ $- R_{Ay} \times 5 + 15 \times 3 = 0$ $R_{Ay} = 9\,\text{kN} \downarrow$

Check: $\Sigma F_y = 0 \uparrow +$ $-9 + 15 - 6 = 0$

Example 7-3

Determine the reactions at A and B for the beam shown in Fig. 7-9(a) due to the applied force.

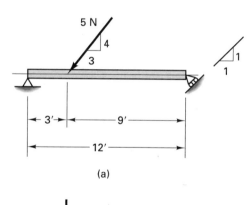

(a)

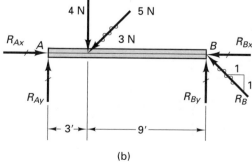

(b)

Fig. 7-9

SOLUTION

A free-body diagram is shown in Fig. 7-9(b). At A, there are two unknown reaction components, R_{Ax} and R_{Ay}. At B, the reaction R_B acts normal to the supporting plane and constitutes a single unknown. It is expedient to replace this force by the two components R_{By} and R_{Bx}, which in this particular problem are numerically equal. Similarly, it is best to replace the inclined force with the two components shown. These steps reduce the problem to one where all forces are either horizontal or vertical. This is of great convenience in applying the equations of static equilibrium.

$$\Sigma M_A = 0 \curvearrowright + \qquad 4 \times 3 - R_{By} \times 12 = 0 \qquad R_{By} = 1\,\mathrm{k}\uparrow \; = |R_{Bx}|$$

$$\Sigma M_B = 0 \curvearrowright + \qquad R_{Ay} \times 12 - 4 \times 9 = 0 \qquad R_{Ay} = 3\,\mathrm{k}\uparrow$$

$$\Sigma F_x = 0 \rightarrow + \qquad R_{Ax} - 3 - 1 \quad = 0 \qquad R_{Ax} = 4\,\mathrm{k}\rightarrow$$

$$R_A = \sqrt{4^2 + 3^2} = 5\mathrm{k}$$

$$R_B = \sqrt{1^2 + 1^2} = \sqrt{2}\mathrm{k}$$

$$\textit{Check: } \Sigma F_y = 0 \uparrow + \qquad\qquad +3 - 4 + 1 = 0$$

Occasionally, *hinges* or *pinned joints* are introduced into beams and frames. A hinge is capable of transmitting only horizontal and vertical forces. *No moment can be transmitted at a hinged joint.* Therefore, the point where a hinge occurs is a particularly convenient location for "separation" of the structure into parts for purposes of computing the reactions. This process is illustrated in Fig. 7-10. Each part of the beam so separated is

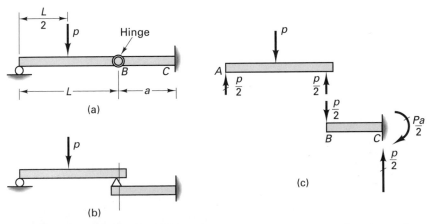

Fig. 7-10 Structures "separated" at hinges to determine the reactions by statics.

treated independently. Each hinge provides an extra axis around which moments may be taken to determine reactions. The introduction of a hinge or hinges into a continuous beam in many cases makes the system statically determinate. The introduction of a hinge into a determinate beam results in a beam that is not stable. Note that the reaction at the hinge for one beam acts in an *opposite direction* on the other beam.

Part B   DIRECT APPROACH FOR P, V, AND M

7-4. Application of the Method of Sections

The main objective of this chapter is to establish procedures for determining the forces that exist at a section of a beam or a frame. To obtain these forces, the method of sections, the basic approach of solid mechanics, will be applied. This procedure is referred to here as a direct approach.

The analysis of any beam or frame for determining the *internal forces* begins with the preparation of a free-body diagram showing both the applied and the reactive forces. The reactions can always be computed using the equations of equilibrium provided the system is statically determinate. If the system is statically indeterminate, the reactions are appropriately labeled and shown on the free body. In this manner, for either case, the complete force system is identified. In the subsequent steps of analysis, *no distinction has to be made between the applied and reactive forces.* The method of sections can then be applied at any section of a structure by employing the previously used concept that if a *whole body* is in equilibrium, *any part* of it is likewise in equilibrium.

To be specific, consider a beam, such as shown in Fig. 7-11(a), with certain concentrated and distributed forces acting on it. The reactions are also presumed to be known, since they may be computed as in the examples considered earlier in Section 7-3. The externally applied forces and the reactions at the support keep the *whole body* in equilibrium. Now consider an imaginary cut *X–X normal* to the axis of the beam, which separates the beam into two segments, as shown in Figs. 7-11(b) and (c). Note particularly that the imaginary section goes through the distributed load and separates it too. Each of these beam segments is a free body that must be in equilibrium. These conditions of equilibrium require the existence of a system of internal forces at the cut section of the beam. In general, at a section of such a member, a vertical force, a horizontal force, and a

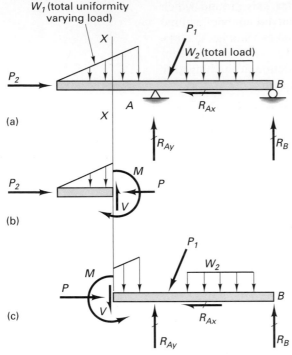

Fig. 7-11 An application of the method of sections to a statically determinate beam.

moment are necessary to maintain the isolated part in equilibrium. These quantities take on a special significance in beams and therefore will be discussed separately.

7-5. Axial Force in Beams

A horizontal force such as P, shown in Fig. 7-11(b) or (c), may be necessary at a section of a beam to satisfy the conditions of equilibrium. The magnitude and sense of this force follows from a particular solution of the equation $\Sigma F_x = 0$. If the horizontal force P acts toward the section, it is called a *thrust;* if away, it is called *axial tension.* In referring to either of these forces, the term *axial force* is used. The effect of an axial force on a section of a member has already been discussed in Chapters 1 and 2. It was shown that it is imperative to apply this force through the *centroid* of the cross-sectional area of a member to avoid bending. Similarly, here *the line of action of the axial force will always be directed through the centroid of the beam's cross-sectional area.*

Any section along a beam may be examined for the magnitude of the axial force in the previous manner. The tensile force at a section is customarily taken positive. The axial force (thrust) at section X–X in Figs. 7-11(b) and (c) is equal to the horizontal force P_2.

7-6. Shear in Beams

In general, to maintain a segment of a beam, such as that shown in Fig. 7-11(b), in equilibrium, there must be an internal vertical force at V at the cut to satisfy the equation $\Sigma F_y = 0$. This internal force V, acting *at right angles* to the axis of the beam, is called the *shear,* or *shear force. The shear is numerically equal to the algebraic sum of* **all** *the vertical components of the external forces acting on the isolated segment,* but it is opposite in direction. Given the qualitative data shown in Fig. 7-11(b), V is opposite in direction to the downward load to the left of the section. This shear may also be computed by considering the right-hand segment shown in Fig. 7-11(c). It is then equal numerically and is opposite in direction to the sum of all the vertical forces, including the vertical reaction components, to the right of the section. Whether the right-hand segment or the left is used to determine the shear at a section is immaterial—arithmetical simplicity governs. Shears at *any other section* may be computed similarly.

At this time, a significant observation must be made. The *same* shear shown in Figs. 7-11(b) and (c) at the section X–X is opposite in direction in the two diagrams. For that *part* of the downward load W_1 to the left of section X–X, the beam at the section provides an upward support to maintain vertical forces in equilibrium. Conversely, the loaded portion of the beam exerts a downward force *on* the beam, as shown in Fig. 7-11(c). At a section, "two directions" of shear must be differentiated, depending upon *which segment* of the beam is considered. This follows from the familiar action-reaction concept of statics and has occurred earlier in the case of an axially loaded rod, and again in the torsion problem.

The direction of the shear at section X–X would be reversed in *both* diagrams if the distributed load W_1 were acting upward. Frequently, a similar reversal in the direction of shear takes place at one section or another along a beam. Therefore, the adoption of a sign convention is necessary to differentiate between the two possible directions of shear. The definition of positive shear is illustrated in Fig. 7-12. A *downward* internal force V acting at a section on an isolated *left segment* of the beam, as in Fig. 7-12(a), or an *upward* force V acting at the same section on the *right segment* of the beam, as in Fig. 7-12(b), corresponds to positive shear. Positive shears are shown in Fig. 7-12(c) for an element isolated from a beam by two sections, and again in Fig. 7-12(d). The shear at section X–X of Fig. 7-11(a) is a negative shear. Note that in addition to specifying the direction of a shear V, it is essential to associate it with a particular side of a section, Fig. 7-12(c). This is also true with stresses. (See discussion in Sections 1-3 and 1-4.)

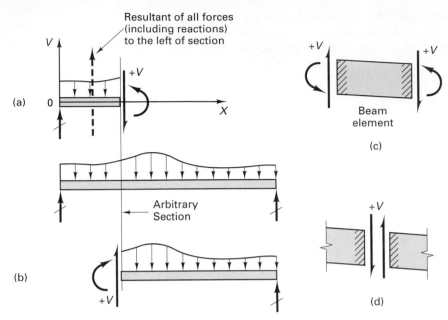

Fig. 7-12   Definition of positive shear.

The selected sign convention for shear in this book is the one generally used. Historically, it appears to be based on directing the coordinate axes, as shown in Fig. 7-13(a). A few books[2] reverse the direction of positive shear to be consistent with the direction of axes in Fig. 7-13(b).

7-7. Bending Moment in Beams

The internal shear and axial forces at a section of a beam satisfy only two equations of equilibrium: $\Sigma F_x = 0$ and $\Sigma F_y = 0$. The remaining condition of static equilibrium for a planar problem is $\Sigma M_z = 0$. This, in general, can be satisfied only by developing a couple or an *internal resisting moment* within the cross-sectional area of the cut to counteract the moment caused by the external forces. The internal resisting moment must act in a direction opposite to the external moment to satisfy the governing equation $\Sigma M_z = 0$. It follows from the same equation that *the magnitude of the internal resisting moment equals the external moment.* These moments tend to bend a beam in the plane of the loads and are usually referred as *bending moments.*

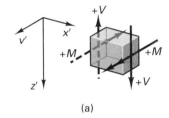

(a)

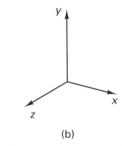

(b)

Fig. 7-13   Positive sense of shear and bending moment defined in (a) is used in this text with coordinates shown in (b).

[2]S. H. Crandall, N. C. Dahl and T. J. Lardner, *An Introduction to the Mechanics of Solids,* 2nd ed. (New York: McGraw-Hill, 1978); J. L. Meriam, *Statics,* 2nd ed. (New York: Wiley, 1971); E. P. Popov, *Introduction to Mechanics of Solids* (Englewood Cliffs, NJ: Prentice Hall, 1968).

To determine an internal bending moment maintaining a beam segment in equilibrium, either the left- or the right-hand part of a beam free body can be used, as shown in Figs. 7-11(b) and (c). The magnitude of the bending moment is found by the summation of the moments caused by all forces multiplied by their respective arms. The internal forces V and P, as well as the applied couples, must be included in the sum. In order to exclude the moments caused by V and P, it is advantageous to *select the point of intersection of these two internal forces as the point around which the moments are summed.* This point lies on the *centroidal axis* of the beam cross section. In Figs. 7-11(b) and (c), the internal bending moment may be physically interpreted as a pull on the top fibers of the beam and a push on the lower ones.

If the load W_1 in Fig. 7-11(a) were acting in the opposite direction, the resisting moments in Figs. 7-11(b) *and* (c) would reverse. This and similar situations require the adoption of a sign convention for the bending moments. This convention is associated with a definite physical action of the beam. For example, in Figs. 7-11(b) and (c), the internal moments shown cause tension in the upper part of the beam and compression in the lower. This tends to increase the length of the top surface of the beam and to contract the lower surface. A continuous occurrence of such moments along the beam makes the beam deform convex upward (i.e., "shed water"). Such bending moments are assigned a *negative sign.* Conversely, a positive moment is defined as one that produces compression in the top part and tension in the lower part of a beam's cross section. Under such circumstances, the beam assumes a shape that "retains water." For example, a simple beam supporting a group of downward forces deflects down as shown in *exaggerated* form in Fig. 7-14(a), a fact suggested by physical intuition. Definitions for positive and negative bending moments are shown in Figs. 7-14(b) and (c). Note that, as for shears V, in addition to the sense of M, it is also *essential to associate the moment for a particular side of a section.*

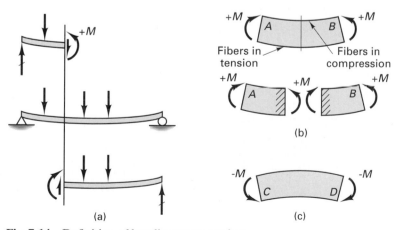

Fig. 7-14   Definition of bending moment signs.

Example 7-4

Consider earlier Example 7-2 and determine the internal system of forces at sections a–a and b–b; see Fig. 7-15(a).

SOLUTION

A free body for the member, including reactions, is shown in Fig. 7-15(a). A free body to the left of section a–a in Fig. 7-15(b) shows the maximum ordinate for the isolated part of the applied load. From equilibrium conditions,

$$V_a = -9 + \frac{1}{2} \times 2 \times \frac{2}{3} \times 10 = -2.33 \text{ kN}$$

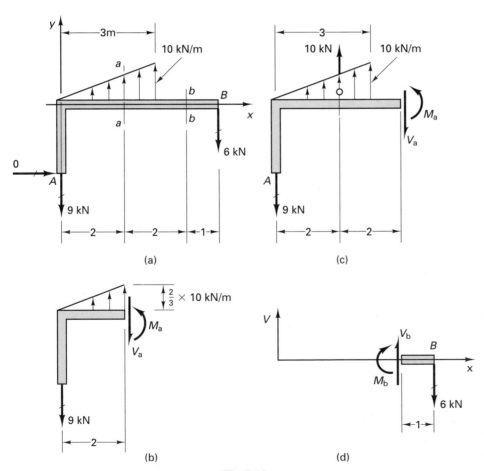

Fig. 7-15

and

$$M_a = -9 \times 2 + \frac{1}{2} \times 2 \times \frac{2}{3} \times 10 \times \frac{1}{3} \times 2 = -13.6 \text{ kN} \cdot \text{m}$$

These forces have opposite senses from those shown in the figure.

A free body to the left of section b–b is shown in Fig. 7-15(c), and to the right in Fig. 7-15(d). It is evident that the second free body is simpler for calculations, giving directly

$$V_b = +6 \text{ kN}$$

and

$$M_b = -6 \times 1 = -6 \text{ kN} \cdot \text{m}$$

The same procedure can be used for frames consisting of several members rigidly joined together as well as for curved bars. In all such cases, the sections must be perpendicular to the axis of a member.

7-8. *P, V*, and *M* Diagrams

By the methods discussed before, the magnitude and sense of axial forces, shears, and bending moments may be obtained at many sections of a beam. Moreover, with the sign conventions adopted for these quantities, a plot of their values may be made on *separate* diagrams. On such diagrams, ordinates may be laid off equal to the computed quantities from a base line representing the length of a beam. When these ordinate points are plotted and interconnected by lines, graphical representations of the functions are obtained. These diagrams, corresponding to the kind of quantities they depict, are called, respectively, *the axial-force diagram, the shear diagram, or the bending-moment diagram*. With the aid of such diagrams, the magnitudes and locations of the various quantities become immediately apparent. It is convenient to make these plots directly below the free-body diagram of the beam, using the same horizontal scale for the length of the beam. Draftsmanlike precision in making such diagrams is usually unnecessary, although the significant ordinates are generally marked with their numerical value.

The axial-force diagrams are not as commonly used as the shear and the bending-moment diagrams. This is so because the majority of beams investigated in practice are loaded by forces that act perpendicular to the axis of the beam. For such loadings of a beam, there are no axial forces at any section.

Shear and moment diagrams are exceedingly important. From them, a designer sees at a glance the kind of performance that is desired from a beam at every section. The procedure of sectioning a beam or a frame and finding the system of forces at the section is the most fundamental approach. It will be used in the following illustrative examples. In some of these examples, algebraic expressions for these functions along a beam will be given.

A systematic method for rapidly constructing shear and moment diagrams will be discussed in the next part of this chapter.

Example 7-5

Construct axial-force, shear, and bending-moment diagrams for the beam shown in Fig. 7-16(a) due to the inclined force $P = 5$ k.

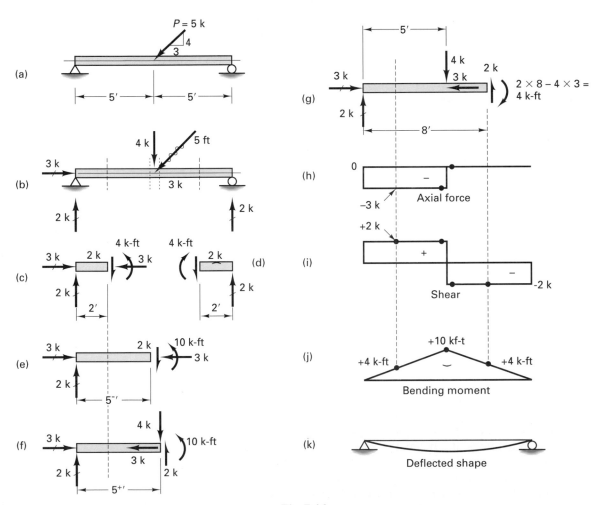

Fig. 7-16

SOLUTION

A free-body diagram of the beam is shown in Fig. 7-16(b). Reactions follow from inspection after the applied force is resolved into the two components. Then several sections through the beam are investigated, as shown in Figs. 7-16(c)–(g). In every case, the same question is posed: *What are the necessary internal forces to keep the segment of the beam in equilibrium?* The corresponding quantities are recorded on the respective free-body diagrams of the beam segment. The ordinates for these quantities are indicated by heavy dots in Figs. 7-16(h)–(j), with due attention paid to their signs.

Note that the free bodies shown in Figs. 7-16(d) and (g) are alternates, as they furnish the same information, and normally both would not be made. Note that a section *just to the left* of the applied force has one sign of shear, Fig. 7-16(e), whereas *just to the right,* Fig. 7-16(f), it has another. This indicates the importance of determining shears on either side of a concentrated force. For the condition shown, the beam *does not resist* a shear that is equal to the whole force. The bending moment in both cases is the same.

In this particular case, after a few individual points have been established on the three diagrams in Figs. 7-16(h)–(j), the behavior of the respective quantities across the whole length of the beam may be reasoned out. Thus, although the segment of the beam shown in Fig. 7-16(c) is 2 ft long, it may vary in length anywhere from zero to *just to the left* of the applied force, and *no change in the shear and the axial force occurs.* Hence, the ordinates in Figs. 7-16(h) and (i) *remain* constant for this segment of the beam. On the other hand, the bending moment depends directly on the distance from the support; hence, it varies linearly, as shown in Fig. 7-16(j). Similar reasoning applies to the segment shown in Fig. 7-16(d), enabling one to complete the three diagrams on the right-hand side. The use of the free body of Fig. 7-16(g) for completing the diagram to the right of center yields the same result.

The sign of a bending moment, per Figs. 7-14(b) and (c), defines the sense in which a beam bends. Since, in this problem, throughout the beam length, the moments are positive, the beam curves to "retain water." In order to emphasize this physical behavior, some analysts find it advantageous to draw a short curved line directly below the moment diagram, as shown in Fig. 7-16(k), to indicate the manner in which a beam or a beam segment curves.

Sometimes, in addition to or instead of the shear or moment diagrams, analytical expressions for these functions are necessary. For the origin of x at the left end of the beam, the following relations apply:

$$V = +2 \text{ k} \qquad\qquad \text{for } 0 < x < 5$$
$$V = -2 \text{ k} \qquad\qquad \text{for } 5 < x < 10$$
$$M = +2x \text{ k-ft} \qquad\qquad \text{for } 0 \leq x \leq 5$$
$$M = +2x - 4(x - 5) = +20 - 2x \text{ k-ft} \qquad \text{for } 5 \leq x \leq 10$$

These expressions can be easily established by mentally replacing the distances of 2 ft and 8 ft, respectively, in Figs. 7-16(c) and (g) by an x.

Example 7-6

Determine axial-force, shear, and bending-moment diagrams for the cantilever loaded with an inclined force at the end; see Fig. 7-17(a).

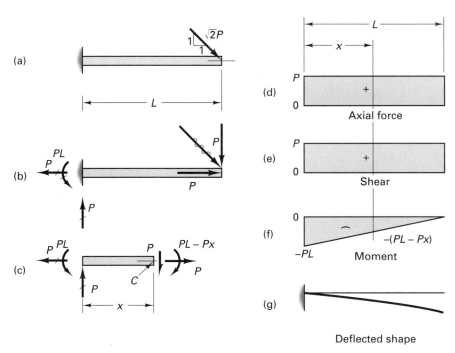

Fig. 7-17

SOLUTION

First, the inclined force is replaced by the two components shown in Fig. 7-17(b) and the reactions are determined. The *three* unknowns at the support follow from the familiar equations of statics. This completes the free-body diagram shown in Fig. 7-17(b). *Completeness in indicating all of these forces is of the utmost importance.*

A segment of the beam is shown in Fig. 7-17(c); from this segment, it may be seen that the axial force and the shear force remain the same regardless of the distance x. On the other hand, the bending moment is a variable quantity. A summation of moments around C gives $PL - Px$ acting in the direction shown. This represents a *negative* moment. The moment at the support is likewise a *negative* bending moment as it tends to pull on the *upper* fibers of the beam. The three diagrams are plotted in Figs. 7-17(d)–(f).

Example 7-7

Construct shear and bending-moment diagrams for the beam loaded with the forces shown in Fig. 7-18(a).

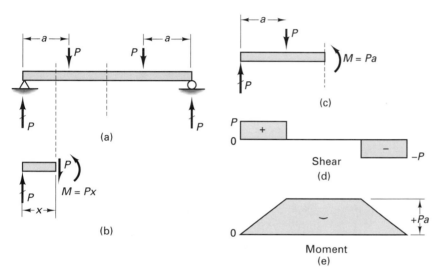

Fig. 7-18

SOLUTION

An arbitrary section at a distance x from the left support isolates the beam segment shown in Fig. 7-18(b). This section is applicable for any value of x just to the left of the applied force P. The shear, regardless of the distance from the support, remains constant and is $+P$. The bending moment varies linearly from the support, reaching a maximum of $+Pa$.

An arbitrary section applicable anywhere *between* the two applied forces is shown in Fig. 7-18(c). No shear force is necessary to maintain equilibrium of a segment in this part of the beam. Only a constant bending moment of $+Pa$ must be resisted by the beam in this zone. Such a state of bending or flexure is called *pure* bending.

Shear and bending-moment diagrams for this loading condition are shown in Figs. 7-18(d) and (e). No axial-force diagram is necessary, as there is no axial force at any section of the beam.

Example 7-8

Plot shear and a bending-moment diagram for a simple beam with a uniformly distributed load; see Fig. 7-19.

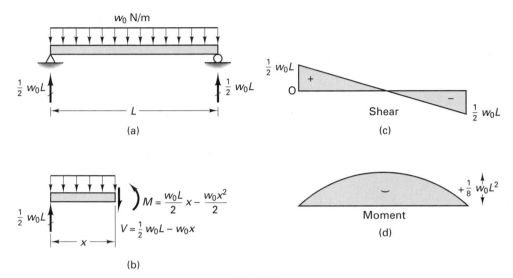

Fig. 7-19

SOLUTION

The best way of solving this problem is to write algebraic expressions for the quantities sought. For this purpose, an arbitrary section taken at a distance x from the left support is used to isolate the segment shown in Fig. 7-19(b). Since the applied load is continuously distributed along the beam, this section is typical and applies to *any section* along the length of the beam.

The shear V is equal to the left upward reaction *less* the load to the left of the section. The internal bending moment M resists the moment caused by the reaction on the left *less* the moment caused by the forces to the left of the same section. The summation of moments is performed around an axis *at the section*. Although it is customary to isolate the left-hand segment, similar expressions may be obtained by considering the right-hand segment of the beam, with due attention paid to sign conventions. The plot of the V and M functions is shown in Figs. 7-19(c) and (d).

Example 7-9

For the beam in Example 7-4, shown in Fig. 7-20(a), express the shear V and the bending moment M as a function of x along the horizontal member.

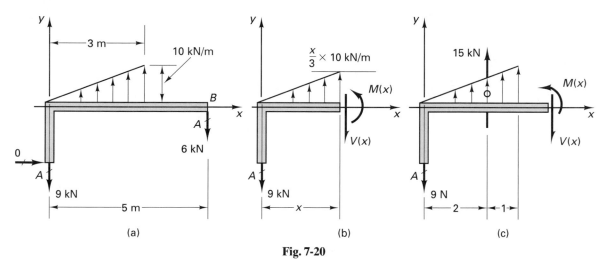

Fig. 7-20

SOLUTION

Unlike the preceding example, in this case, a load discontinuity occurs at $x = 3$ m. Therefore, the solution is determined in two parts for each of which the functions V and M are continuous. A free-body diagram for the beam segment under the load is shown in Fig. 7-20(b), and for the remainder in Fig. 7-20(c). The required expressions for $0 < x < 3$ are

$$V(x) = -9 + \frac{1}{2}x\left(\frac{x}{3} \times 10\right) = -9 + \frac{5}{3}x^2 \text{ kN}$$

$$M(x) = -9x + \frac{1}{2}x\left(\frac{x}{3} \times 10\right)\left(\frac{x}{3}\right) = -9x + \frac{5}{9}x^3 \text{ kN} \cdot \text{m}$$

For $3 < x < 5$,

$$V(x) = -9 + 15 = +6 \text{ kN}$$

$$M(x) = -9x + 15(x - 2) = 6x - 30 \text{ kN} \cdot \text{m}$$

To obtain the last expression, it would have been a little simpler to use a free-body diagram similar to Fig. 7-15(d).

This problem can also be solved using the singularity functions discussed in Section 7-16.

Example 7-10

Write analytic expressions for V and M for the beam shown in Fig. 7-21.

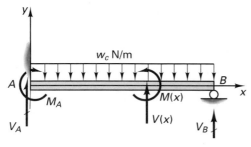

Fig. 7-21

SOLUTION

Unlike the preceding cases, this is a statically indeterminate problem to the first degree having one redundant reaction. There is no horizontal reaction at A. Except for carefully identifying the unknown reactions as V_A, V_B, and M_A, the procedure is the same as before, although numerical results cannot be obtained until the reactions are determined. On this basis, at a distance x away from the origin,

$$V(x) = V_A - w_o x$$

and

$$M(x) = M_A + V_A x - (w_o x)x/2$$
$$= M_A + V_A x - w_o x^2/2$$

Sometimes, it will be necessary to use such expressions in the process of solving for unknown reactions in Chapters 14 and 17.

Example 7-11

Consider a structural system of three interconnected straight bars, as shown in Fig. 7-22(a). At arbitrary sections, determine the internal forces P, V, and M in the members caused by the application of a vertical force P_1 at D.

SOLUTION

The frame is conveniently analyzed by isolating the three straight members, as shown in Fig. 7-22(b). For each case, a different coordinate system

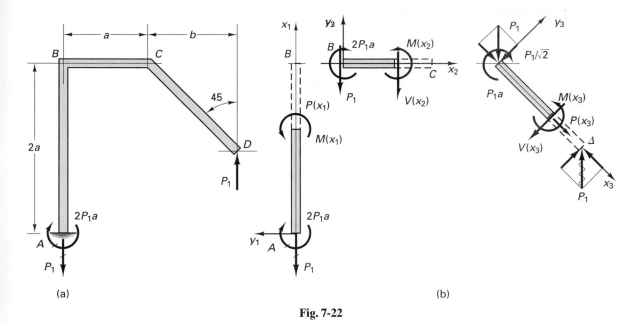

Fig. 7-22

is indicated, and sections through the members are shown at arbitrary distances from the origins.

The solution begins by calculating the reaction at A, which is then shown on beam segment AB. At an arbitrary section through this beam, the internal forces are seen to be

$$P(x_1) = +P_1, \; V(x_1) = 0 \quad \text{and} \quad M(x_1) = +2P_1a$$

These forces are constant throughout the length of the vertical bar and become the reactions at B for the beam segment BC. It is important to note that the axial force in member AB acts as shear in BC. After the reactions at B for BC are known, the usual procedure gives the following internal forces:

$$P(x_2) = 0, \; V(x_2) = -P_1, \quad \text{and} \quad M(x_2) = +2P_1a - P_1x_2$$

For member CD, except for the need for resolving the force P_1 at C, the procedure for determining the internal forces is the same as before, giving

$$P(x_3) = -P_1/\sqrt{2}, \; V(x_3) = -P_1/\sqrt{2}, \quad \text{and} \quad M(x_3) = +P_1a - P_1x_3/\sqrt{2}$$

By substituting $x_3 = \sqrt{2}a$ into the last expression, it can be verified that the bending moment at D is zero, as it should be.

Shear and bending-moment diagrams for this structural system can be plotted directly on the outline of the frame.

Example 7-12

Consider a curved beam whose centroidal axis is bent into a semicircle of 0.2 m radius, as shown in Fig. 7-23(a). If this member is being pulled by the 1000-N forces shown, find the axial force, the shear, and the bending moment at section A–A, $\alpha = 45°$. The centroidal axis and the applied forces all lie in the same plane.

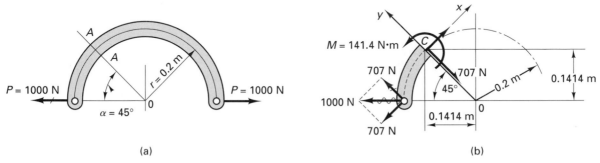

(a)   (b)

Fig. 7-23

SOLUTION

There is no essential difference in the method of attack in this problem compared with that in a straight-beam problem. The body as a whole is examined for conditions of equilibrium. From the conditions of the problem here, such is already the case. Next, a segment of the beam is isolated; see Fig. 7-23(b). *Section A–A is taken perpendicular to the axis of the beam.* Before determining the quantities wanted at the cut, the applied force P is resolved into components parallel and perpendicular to the cut. These directions are taken, respectively, as the y and x axes. This resolution replaces P by the components shown in Fig. 7-23(b). From $\Sigma F_x = 0$, the axial force at the cut is $+707$ N. From $\Sigma F_y = 0$, the shear is 707 N in the direction shown. The bending moment at the cut can be determined in several different ways. For example, if $\Sigma M_O = 0$ is used, note that the lines of action of the applied force P and the shear at the section pass through O. Therefore, only the axial force at the centroid of the cut times the radius has to be considered, and the *resisting* bending moment is $707(0.2) = 141.4$ N $\cdot$ m, acting in the direction shown. An alternative solution may be obtained by applying $\Sigma M_C = 0$. At C, a point lying on the centroid, the axial force and the shear intersect. The bending moment is then the product of the applied force P and the 0.1414-m arm. In both of these methods of determining bending moment, use of the components of the force P is avoided as this is more involved arithmetically.

It is suggested that the reader complete this problem in terms of a general angle α. Several interesting observations may be made from such a general solution. The moments at the ends will vanish for $\alpha = 0°$ and $\alpha = 180°$. For $\alpha = 90°$, the shear vanishes and the axial force becomes equal to the applied force P. Likewise, the maximum bending moment is associated with $\alpha = 90°$.

Part C   V AND M BY INTEGRATION

7-9. Differential Equations of Equilibrium for a Beam Element

Instead of the direct approach of cutting a beam and determining shear and moment at a section by statics, an efficient alternative procedure can be used. For this purpose, certain fundamental differential relations must be derived. These can be used for the construction of shear and moment diagrams as well as for the calculation of reactions.

Consider a beam element Δx long, isolated by two adjoining sections taken perpendicular to its axis. Fig. 7-24(b). Such an element is shown as a free body in Fig. 7-24(c). All the forces shown acting on this element have positive sense. The positive sense of the distributed external force q is taken to coincide with the direction of the positive y axis. As the shear and the moment may each change from one section to the next, note that on the right side of the element, these quantities are, respectively, designated $V + \Delta V$ and $M + \Delta M$.

From the condition for equilibrium of vertical forces, one obtains[3]

$$\sum F_y = 0 \uparrow + \quad V + q\Delta x - (V + \Delta V) = 0$$

or

$$\frac{\Delta V}{\Delta x} = q \qquad (7\text{-}1)$$

For equilibrium, the summation of moments around A also must be zero. So, upon noting that from point A the arm of the distributed force is $\Delta x/2$, one has

$$\sum M_A = 0 \curvearrowleft + \quad (M + \Delta M) - V\Delta x - M - (q\Delta x)(\Delta x/2) = 0$$

---

[3]No variation of $q(x)$ within Δx need be considered since, in the limit as $\Delta x \to 0$, the change in q becomes negligibly small. This simplification is not an approximation.

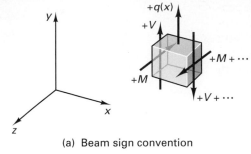

(a) Beam sign convention

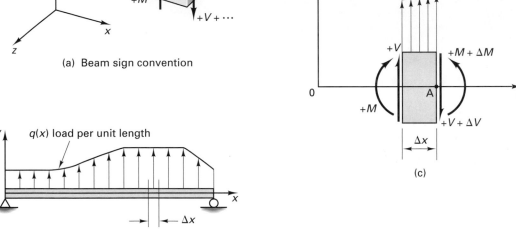

(c)

q(x) load per unit length

(b)

Fig. 7-24   Beam and beam elements between adjoining sections.

or

$$\frac{\Delta M}{\Delta x} = V + \frac{q\Delta x}{2} \qquad (7\text{-}2)$$

Equations 7-1 and 7-2 in the limit as $\Delta x \to 0$ yield the following two basic differential equations:

$$\boxed{\frac{dV}{dx} = q} \qquad (7\text{-}3)$$

and

$$\boxed{\frac{dM}{dx} = V} \qquad (7\text{-}4)$$

By substituting Eq. 7-4 into Eq. 7-3, another useful reaction is obtained:

$$\frac{d}{dx}\left(\frac{dM}{dx}\right) = \frac{d^2M}{dx^2} = q \qquad (7\text{-}5)$$

This differential equation can be used for determining reactions of statically determinate beams from the boundary conditions, whereas Eqs. 7-3 and 7-4 are very convenient for construction of shear and moment diagrams. These applications will be discussed next.

7-10.   Shear Diagrams by Integration of the Load

Transposing and integrating Eq. 7-3 gives the shear V:

$$V = \int_0^x q \, dx + C_1 \qquad (7\text{-}6)$$

By assigning definite limits to this integral, it is seen that the shear at a section is simply an integral (i.e., a sum) of the vertical forces along the beam from the left end of the beam *to the section in question* plus a constant of integration C_1. This constant is equal to the shear on the left-hand end. Between any two definite sections of a beam, the shear changes by the amount of the vertical force included *between* these sections. If no force occurs between any two sections, no change in shear takes place. If a concentrated force comes into the summation, a discontinuity, or a "jump," in the value of the shear occurs. The continuous summation process remains valid nevertheless, since a concentrated force may be thought of as being a distributed force extending for an infinitesimal distance along the beam.

On the basis of the preceding reasoning, a shear diagram can be established by the summation process. For this purpose, *the reactions must always be determined first.* Then the vertical components of forces *and reactions* are successively summed *from the left end* of the beam to preserve the mathematical sign convention for shear adopted in Fig. 7-12. The shear at a section is simply equal to the sum of *all* vertical forces to the left of the section.

When the shear diagram is constructed from the load diagram by the summation process, two important observations can be made regarding its shape. First, the sense of the applied load determines the sign of the slope of the shear diagram. If the applied load acts upward, the slope of the shear diagram is positive, and vice versa. Second, this slope is equal to the corresponding applied load intensity. For example, consider a segment of a beam with a uniformly distributed downward load w_o and known shears at both ends, as shown in Fig. 7-25(a). Since here the applied load intensity w_o is *negative* and *uniformly distributed* (i.e., $q = -w_o = $ constant), the slope of the shear diagram exhibits the same characteristics. Alternatively, the linearly varying load intensity acting upward on a beam segment with known shears at the ends, shown in Fig. 7-25(b), gives rise to a differently shaped shear diagram. Near the left end of this segment, the locally applied *upward* load q_1 is *smaller* than the

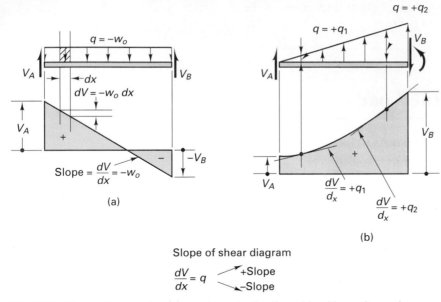

Fig. 7-25 Shear diagrams for (a) a uniformly distributed load intensity, and (b) a uniformly increasing load intensity.

corresponding one q_2 near the right end. Therefore, the *positive* slope of the shear diagram on the left is *smaller* than it is on the right, and the shear diagram is concave upward.

Do not fail to note that *a mere systematic consecutive summation of the vertical components of the forces is all that is necessary to obtain the shear diagram.* When the consecutive summation process is used, the diagram must end up with the previously calculated shear (reaction) at the right end of a beam. No shear acts through the beam just beyond the last vertical force or reaction. *The fact that the diagram closes in this manner offers an important check on the arithmetical calculations.* This check should never be ignored. It permits one to obtain solutions independently with almost complete assurance of being correct. The semigraphical procedure of integration outlined before is very convenient in practical problems. It is the basis for sketching qualitative shear diagrams rapidly.

From the physical point of view, the shear sign convention is not completely consistent. Whenever beams are analyzed, a shear diagram drawn from one side of the beam is opposite in sign to a diagram constructed by looking at the same beam from the other side. The reader should verify this statement on some simple cases, such as a cantilever with a concentrated force at the end and a simply supported beam with a concentrated force in the middle. For design purposes, the sign of the shear is usually unimportant.

7-11.   Moment Diagrams by Integration of the Shear

Transposing and integrating Eq. 7-4 gives the bending moment

$$M + \int_0^x V\, dx\ + C_2 \qquad\qquad (7\text{-}7)$$

where C_2 is a constant of integration corresponding to boundary conditions at $x = 0$. This equation is analogous to Eq. 7-6 developed for the construction of shear diagrams. The meaning of the term $V\, dx$ is shown
graphically by the hatched areas of the shear diagrams in Fig. 7-26. The
summation of these areas between definite sections through a beam corresponds to an evaluation of the definite integral. If the ends of a beam are
on rollers, pin-ended, or free, the starting and the terminal moments are
zero. If the end is built-in (fixed against rotation), in statically determinate

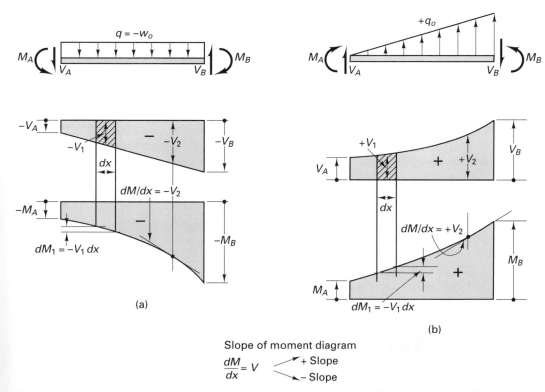

Fig. 7-26   Shear and moment diagrams for (a) a uniformly distributed load intensity, and (b) a uniformly increasing load intensity.

beams, the end moment is known from the reaction calculations. If the fixed end of a beam is on the left, this moment with the proper[4] sign is the *initial constant of integration* C_2.

By proceeding *continuously along the beam from the left-hand end* and summing up the areas of the shear diagram with due regard to their sign, the moment diagram is obtained. This process of obtaining the moment diagram from the shear diagram by summation is exactly the same as that employed earlier to go from loading to shear diagrams. *The change in moment in a given segment of a beam is equal to the area of the corresponding shear diagram.* Qualitatively, the shape of a moment diagram can be easily established from the slopes at some selected points along the beam. These slopes have the same sign and magnitude as the corresponding shears on the shear diagram, since according to Eq. 7-4, $dM/dx = V$. Alternatively, the change of moment $dM = V\, dx$ can be studied along the beam. Examples are shown in Fig. 7-26. According to these principles, variable shears cause nonlinear variation of the moment. A constant shear produces a uniform change in the bending moment, resulting in a straight line in the moment diagram. If no shear occurs along a certain portion of a beam, *no change in moment* takes place.

Since $dM/dx = V$, according to the fundamental theorem of calculus, the *maximum or minimum moment occurs where the shear is zero.*

In a bending-moment diagram obtained by summation, *at the right-hand end* of the beam, an invaluable check on the work is available again. *The terminal conditions for the moment must be satisfied.* If the end is free or pinned, the computed sum must equal zero. If the end is built-in, the end moment computed by summation equals the one calculated initially for the reaction. These are the boundary conditions and must always be satisfied.

Example 7-13

Construct shear and moment diagrams for the symmetrically loaded beam shown in Fig. 7-27(a) by the integration process.

SOLUTION

The reactions are each equal to P. To obtain the shear diagram, Fig. 7-27(b), the summation of forces is started from the left end. The left reaction acts *up,* so an ordinate on the shear diagram at this force equal to P is plotted *up.* Since there are no other forces until the quarter point, *no change in the magnitude of the shear ordinate is made until that point.* Then a downward

---

[4]Bending moments carry signs according to the convention adopted in Fig. 7-14. Moments that cause *compression* in the top fibers of the beam are positive.

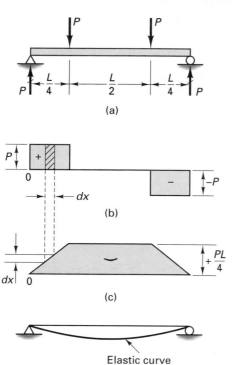

Fig. 7-27

force P brings the ordinate back to the base line, and this zero ordinate remains until the next downward force P is reached where the shear changes to $-P$. At the right end, the upward reaction closes the diagram and provides a check on the work. This shear diagram is *antisymmetrical*.

The moment diagram, Fig. 7-27(c), is obtained by summing up the area of the shear diagram. As the beam is simply supported, the moment at the left end is zero. The sum of the positive portion of the shear diagram *increases at a constant rate* along the beam until the quarter point, where the moment reaches a magnitude of $+PL/4$. This moment remains constant in the middle half of the beam. *No change in the moment can be made in this zone* as there is no corresponding shear area.

Beyond the second force, the moment decreases by $-P\,dx$ in *every dx*. Hence, the moment diagram in this zone has a constant, negative slope. Since the positive and the negative areas of the shear diagram are equal, at the right end, the moment is zero. This is as it should be, since the right end is on a roller. Thus, a check on the work is obtained. This moment diagram is *symmetrical*.

Example 7-14

Consider a simple beam with a uniformly increasing load intensity from an end, as shown in Fig. 7-28(a). The total applied load is W. (a) Construct shear and moment diagrams with the aid of the integration process. (b) Derive expressions for V and M using Eq. 7-5.

SOLUTION

(a) Since the total load $W = kL^2/2$, $k = 2W/L^2$. For the given load distribution, the downward reactions are $W/3$ and $2W/3$, as shown in Fig. 7-28(a). Therefore, the shear diagram given in Fig. 7-28(b) begins and ends as shown. Since the rate of applied load is smaller on the left end than on the right, the shear diagram is concave upward. The point of zero shear occurs where the reaction on the left is balanced by the applied load; that is,

$$\frac{W}{3} = \frac{1}{2}x_1\frac{2W}{L^2}x_1 \quad \text{hence,} \ x_1 = \frac{L}{\sqrt{3}}$$

At x_1, the bending moment is maximum; therefore,

$$M_{\max} = M\left(\frac{L}{\sqrt{3}}\right) = -\frac{W}{3}\frac{L}{\sqrt{3}} + \frac{1}{2}\frac{L}{\sqrt{3}}\frac{2W}{L^2}\frac{L}{\sqrt{3}}\left(\frac{1}{3}\frac{L}{\sqrt{3}}\right) = \frac{2WL}{9\sqrt{3}}$$

By following the rules given in Fig. 7-26, the moment diagram has the shape shown in Fig. 7-28(c).

Although the shear and bending moment diagrams could be sketched qualitatively, it was necessary to supplement the results analytically for determining the critical values.

(b) Applying Eq. 7-5 and integrating it twice, one has

$$\frac{d^2M}{dx^2} = q = +kx = +\frac{2W}{L^2}x$$

$$\frac{dM}{dx} = \frac{kx^2}{2} + C_1 \quad \text{and} \quad M = \frac{kx^3}{6} + C_1x + C_2$$

However, the boundary conditions require that the moments at $x = 0$ and $x = L$ be zero; that is, $M(0) = 0$ and $M(L) = 0$. Therefore, since

$$M(0) = 0 \quad C_2 = 0$$

and, similarly, since $M(L) = 0$,

$$\frac{kL^3}{6} + C_1L = 0 \quad \text{or} \quad C_1 = -\frac{kL^2}{6}$$

With these constants,

$$V = \frac{dM}{dx} = \frac{kx^2}{2} - \frac{kL^2}{6} = \frac{Wx^2}{L^2} - \frac{W}{3}$$

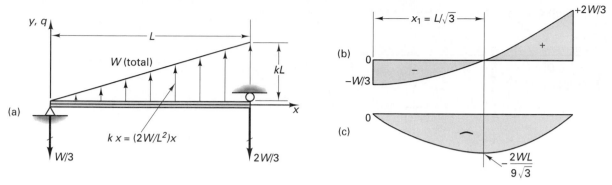

Fig. 7-28

and

$$M = \frac{kx^2}{6} - \frac{kL^2x}{6} = \frac{Wx^3}{3L^2} - \frac{Wx}{3}$$

These results agree with those found earlier.

The attractive features of the boundary-value approach used in this example for solving differential equations can be extended to situations of discontinuous loads using the singularity functions discussed in Section 7-14.

Example 7-15

Construct shear and bending-moment diagrams for loaded beam shown in Fig. 7-29(a) with the aid of the integration process.

SOLUTION

Reactions must be calculated first, and, before proceeding further, the inclined force is resolved into its horizontal and vertical components. The horizontal reaction at A is 120 kN and acts to the right. From $\Sigma M_A = 0$, the vertical reaction at B is found to be 125 kN (check this). Similarly, the reaction at A is 165 kN. The sum of the vertical reaction components is 290 kN and equals the sum of the vertical forces.

The diagram for the axial force is shown in Fig. 7-29(b). This compressive force only acts in the segment AD of the beam.

With reactions known, the summation of forces is begun from the left end of the beam to obtain the shear diagram, Fig. 7-29(c). At first, the downward-distributed load accumulates at a slow rate. Then, as the load intensity increases, for an equal increment of distance along the beam, a larger change in shear occurs. Hence, the shear diagram in zone CA is a

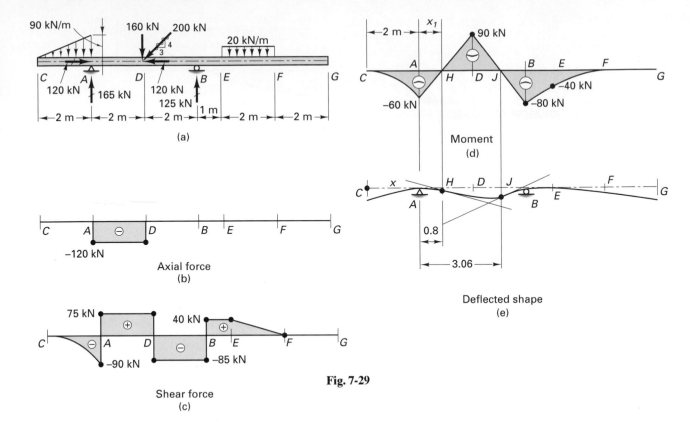

(a)

Axial force
(b)

Shear force
(c)

Moment
(d)

Deflected shape
(e)

Fig. 7-29

curved line that is concave down. This is in accord with Eq. 7-3, illustrated in Fig. 7-25. Since $dV/dx = q = -w_o$, the negative slope of this shear diagram is smaller on the left and increases toward A. The total downward force from C to A is 90 kN, and this is the negative ordinate of the shear diagram, *just to the left of the support A*. At A, the upward reaction of 165 kN moves the ordinate of shear diagram to +75 kN. This value of shear applies to a section through the beam *just to the right* of the support A. The abrupt *change* in the shear at A is equal to the reaction, but this total does not represent the shear through the beam.

No forces are applied to the beam between A and D; hence, there is no change in the value of the shear. At D, the 160 kN downward component of the concentrated force drops the value of the shear to -85 kN. Similarly, the value of the shear raised to $+40$ kN at B. Since between E and F, the uniformly distributed load acts downward, according to Eq. 7-3 and as shown in Fig. 7-25, a decrease in shear takes place at a constant rate of 20 kN/m. Thus at F the shear is zero, which serves as the final check.

To construct the moment diagram shown in Fig. 7-29(d) by the summation method, areas of the shear diagram in Fig. 7-29(c) must be continuously summed from the left end. In the segment CA, at first, less area is contributed to the sum in the moment diagram. This is in accord with Eq. 7-4, $dM/dx = V$, as illustrated in Fig. 7-26. Here V, defining the slope of the moment diagram, is negative and progressively becomes larger to the right. The moment at A is equal to the area of the shear diagram in the segment CA. This area is enclosed by a curved line, and it may be determined by integration,[5] since the shear along this segment may be expressed analytically.

This procedure often is cumbersome, and instead the bending moment at A may be obtained from the fundamental definition of a moment at a section. By passing a section through A and isolating the segment CA, the moment at A is found. The other areas of the shear diagram in this example are easily determined. Due attention must be paid to the signs of these areas. It is convenient to arrange the work in tabular form. At the right end of the beam, the customary check is obtained.

$$
\begin{array}{lll}
M_A & (-2 \times 90/2)(2/3)\ =\ -60\ \text{kN}\cdot\text{m} & \text{(moment around } A) \\
& \underline{+75 \times 2 = +150} & \text{(shear area } A \text{ to } D) \\
M_D & +90\ \text{kN}\cdot\text{m} & \\
& \underline{-85 \times 2 = -170} & \text{(shear area } D \text{ to } B) \\
M_B & -80\ \text{kN}\cdot\text{m} & \\
& \underline{+40 \times 1 = +40} & \text{(shear area } B \text{ to } E) \\
M_E & -40\ \text{kN}\cdot\text{m} & \\
& \underline{+2 \times 40/2 = +40} & \text{(shear area } E \text{ to } F) \\
M_F & -0\ \text{kN}\cdot\text{m} & \text{(check)}
\end{array}
$$

7-12. Effect of Concentrated Moment on Moment Diagrams

In the derivation for moment diagrams by summation of shear-diagram areas, no *external concentrated moment* acting on the infinitesimal element was included, yet such a moment may actually be applied. Hence, the summation process derived applies only up to the point of application of an

[5]In this case, the shear curve is a second-degree parabola whose vertex is on a vertical line through A. For areas enclosed by various curves, see Table 2 of the Appendix.

external moment. *At a section just beyond an externally applied moment, a different bending moment is required to maintain the segment of a beam in equilibrium.* For example, in Fig. 7-30 an external clockwise moment M_A is acting on the element of the beam at A. Then, if the internal clockwise moment on the left is M_O, for equilibrium of the element, the resisting counterclockwise moment on the right must be $M_O + M_A$. At the point of the externally applied moment, a discontinuity, or a "jump," equal to the concentrated moment appears in the moment diagram. Hence, in applying the summation process, due regard must be given the concentrated moments as their effect is not apparent in the shear diagram. The conventional summation process may be applied up to the point of application of a concentrated moment. At this point, a vertical "jump" equal to the external moment must be made in the diagram. The direction of this vertical "jump" in the diagram depends upon the sense of the concentrated moment and is best determined with the aid of a sketch analogous to Fig. 7-30. After the discontinuity in the moment diagram is passed, the summation process of the shear-diagram areas may be continued over the remainder of the beam.

Fig. 7-30   An external concentrated moment acting on an element of a beam.

Example 7-16

Construct the bending-moment diagram for the horizontal beam loaded as shown in Fig. 7-31(a).

SOLUTION

By taking moments about either end of the beam, the vertical reactions are found to be $P/6$. At A, the reaction acts down; at C, it acts up. From $\Sigma F_x = 0$, it is known that at A, a horizontal reaction equal to P acts to the

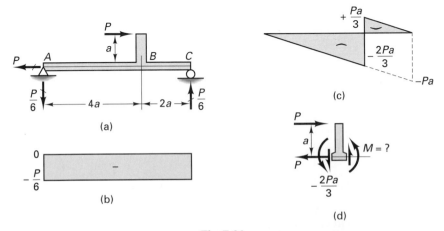

Fig. 7-31

left. The shear diagram is drawn next; see Fig. 7-31(b). It has a constant negative ordinate for the *whole* length of the beam. After this, by using the summation process, the moment diagram shown in Fig. 7-31(c) is constructed. The moment at the left end of the beam is zero, since the support is pinned. The total change in moment from A to B is given by the area of the shear diagram between these sections and equals $-2Pa/3$. The moment diagram in zone AB has a constant negative slope. For further analysis, an element is isolated from the beam, as shown in Fig. 7-31(d). The moment on the left-hand side of this element is *known to be* $-2Pa/3$, and the concentrated moment caused by the applied force P about the neutral axis of the beam is Pa; hence, for equilibrium, the moment on the right side of the element must be $+Pa/3$. At B, an upward "jump" of $+Pa$ is made in the moment diagram, and just to the right of B, the ordinate is $+Pa/3$. Beyond point B, the summation of the shear diagram area is continued. The area between B and C is equal to $-Pa/3$. This value *closes* the moment diagram at the right end of the beam, and thus the boundary conditions are satisfied. Note that the lines in the moment diagram that are inclined downward to the right are parallel. This follows because the shear everywhere along the beam is negative and constant.

Example 7-17

Construct shear and moment diagrams for the member shown in Fig. 7-32(a). All dimensions are shown in mm. Neglect the weight of the beam.

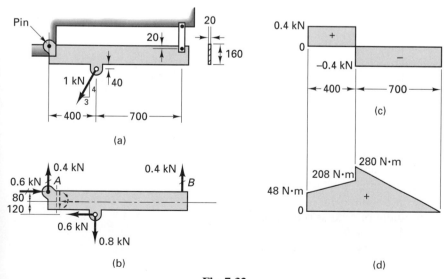

(a)

(b)

(c)

(d)

Fig. 7-32

SOLUTION

In this case, unlike all cases considered so far, definite dimensions are assigned for the *depth* of the beam. The beam, for simplicity, is assumed to be rectangular in its cross-sectional area; consequently, the *centroidal axis* lies 80 mm below the top of the beam. Note carefully that this beam is not supported at the centroidal axis.

A free-body diagram of the beam with the applied force resolved into components is shown in Fig. 7-32(b). Reactions are computed in the usual manner. Moreover, since the shear diagram is concerned only with the vertical forces, it is easily constructed and is shown in Fig. 7-32(c).

In constructing the moment diagram shown in Fig. 7-32(d), particular care must be exercised. As was emphasized earlier, the bending moments may always be determined by considering a segment of a beam, and they are most conveniently computed by taking moments of external forces *around a point on the centroidal axis of the beam.* Thus, by passing a section just to the right of A and considering the left-hand segment, it can be seen that a positive moment of 48 N · m is resisted by the beam at this end. Hence, the plot of the moment diagram must *start* with an ordinate of $+48$ N · m. The other point on the beam where a concentrated moment occurs is C. Here the horizontal component of the applied force induces a clockwise moment of $0.6 \times 120 = 72$ N · m around the neutral axis. Just to the right of C, this moment must be resisted by an additional positive moment. This causes a discontinuity in the moment diagram. The summation process of the shear-diagram areas applies for the segments of the beam where no external moments are applied. The necessary calculations are carried out in tabular form.

$$M_A \qquad\qquad\qquad +0.6 \times 800 = +48 \text{ N} \cdot \text{m}$$

$$+0.4 \times 400 = \underline{+160} \qquad \text{(shear area } A \text{ to } C)$$

$$\text{Moment just to left} \quad \text{of } C \qquad\quad = +208 \text{ N} \cdot \text{m}$$

$$+0.6 \times 120 = \underline{+72} \qquad \text{(external moment at } C)$$

$$\text{Moment just to right of } C \qquad = +280 \text{ kN} \cdot \text{m}$$

$$-0.4 \times 700 = \underline{-280} \qquad \text{(shear area } C \text{ to } B)$$

$$M_B \qquad\qquad\qquad\qquad\quad = 0 \qquad\qquad \text{(check)}$$

Note that in solving this problem, the forces were considered *wherever they actually act on the beam.* The investigation for shear and moments at a section of a beam determines what the beam is actually experiencing. At times, this differs from the procedure of determining reactions, where the actual framing or configuration of a member is not important.

Again, it must be emphasized that if a moment or a shear is needed at a *particular* section through any member, *the basic method of sections may always be used.* For inclined members, the shear acts *normal to the axis of the beam.*

7-13.   Moment Diagrams and the Elastic Curve

As defined in Section 7-7, a positive moment causes a beam to deform concave upward or to "retain water," and vice versa. Hence, the shape of the deflected axis of a beam can be *definitely* established from the *sign* of the moment diagram. The trace of this axis of a loaded elastic beam in a deflected position is known as the *elastic curve*. It is customary to show the elastic curve on a sketch, where the actual small deflections tolerated in practice are greatly *exaggerated*. A sketch of the elastic curve clarifies the physical action of a beam. It also provides a useful basis for quantitative calculations of beam deflections, to be discussed in Sections 15-2 and 15-3. Some of the preceding examples for which bending-moment diagrams were constructed will be used to illustrate the physical action of a beam.

An inspection of Fig. 7-27(c) shows that the bending moment throughout the length of the beam is *positive*. Accordingly, the elastic curve shown in Fig. 7-27(d) is *concave up at every point*. Correct representation of convexity or concavity of the elastic curve is important. In this case, the ends of the beam rest on supports.

In a more complex moment diagram, Fig. 7-29(e), zones of positive and negative moment occur. Corresponding to the zones of negative moment, a *definite* curvature of the elastic curve that is concave down takes place; see Fig. 7-29(e). On the other hand, for the zone *HJ*, where the positive moment occurs, the concavity of the elastic curve is upward. Where curves join, as at *H* and *J*, there are lines that are *tangent* to the two joining curves since the beam is physically *continuous*. Also note that the free end *FG* of the beam is tangent to the elastic curve at *F*. There is no curvature in *FG*, since the moment is zero in that segment of the beam.

If the suggestion made in Example 7-5, indicating the curvature of beam segments by means of short curved lines on the moment diagram, is followed, as in Fig. 7-29(d), the elastic curve is simply an assembly of such curves drawn to a proper scale.

The point of transition on the elastic curve into reverse curvature is called the *point of inflection* or contraflexure. At this point, the moment changes its sign, and the beam is not called upon to resist any moment. This fact often makes these points a desirable place for a field connection of large members, and their location is calculated. A procedure for determining points of inflection will be illustrated in the next example.

Example 7-18

Find the location of the inflection points for the beam analyzed in Example 7-15; see Fig. 7-29(a).

SOLUTION

By definition, an inflection point corresponds to a point on a beam where the bending moment is zero. Hence, an inflection point can be located by setting up an algebraic expression for the moment in a beam for the segment where such a point is anticipated and solving this relation equated to zero. By measuring x from end C of the beam, Fig. 7-29(e), the bending moment for segment AD of the beam is $M = -(2 \times 90/2)(x - 2 \times 2/3) + 165 \times (x - 2)$. By simplifying and setting this expression equal to zero, a solution is obtained:

$$M = 75x - 210 = 0 \quad x = 2.80 \text{ m}$$

Therefore, the inflection point occurring in segment AD of the beam is $2.80 - 2.00 = 0.80$ m from the support A.

Similarly, by writing an algebraic expression for the bending moment for segment DB and setting it equal to zero, the location of inflection point J is found:

$$M = -(2 \times 90/2)(x - 2 \times 2/3) + 165 \times (x - 2) - 160 \times (x - 4) = 0$$

where $x = 5.06$ m; hence the distance $AJ = 3.06$ m.

Often a more convenient method for finding the inflection points is to utilize the known relations between the shear and moment diagrams. Thus, since the moment at A is -60 kN, the point of zero moment occurs when the positive portion of the shear-diagram area from A to H equals this moment (i.e., $-60 + 75 \times x_1 = 0$). Hence, distance $AH = 60/75 = 0.8$ m as before.

Similarly, by beginning with a known positive moment of $+90$ kN · m, the second inflection point is known to occur when a portion of the negative shear-diagram area between D and J reduces this values to zero. Hence, distance $DJ = 90/85 = 1.06$ m, or distance $AJ = 2 + 1.06 = 3.06$ m.

Just as any infinitesimal beam element must be in equilibrium, so must also any corner element in a frame with rigid joints. Therefore, the bending moments at a corner can act only either as shown in Fig. 7-33(a) or 7-33(b). The associated parts of elastic curve are shown in these figures.

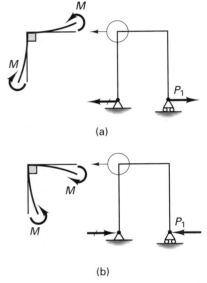

(a)

(b)

Fig. 7-33   Elastic curves at corners of planar rigid frames.

Part D   V AND M BY SINGULARITY FUNCTIONS

7-14. Applications of Singularity Functions

As was pointed out earlier, analytical expressions for the shear $V(x)$ and the moment $M(x)$ of a given beam may be needed in an analysis. If the loading $q(x)$ is a continuous function between the supports, solution of the differential equation $d^2M/dx^2 = q(x)$ is a convenient approach for determining $V(x)$ and $M(x)$ (see Example 7-14). Here this will be extended to situations in which the loading function is discontinuous. For this purpose, the notation of operational calculus will be used. The functions $q(x)$ considered here are polynomials with integral powers of x. The treatment of other functions is beyond the scope of this text. For the functions considered, however, the method is perfectly general. Further applications of this approach will be given in Chapter 14 for calculating deflections of beams. The singularity functions presented here are not suitable for beams having variable cross section.

Consider a beam loaded as in Fig. 7-34. Since the applied loads are point (concentrated) forces, four distinct regions exist to which different bending moment expressions apply. These are

$$M = R_1 x \qquad\qquad \text{when } 0 \le x \le d$$

$$M = R_1 x - P_1(x - d) \qquad\qquad \text{when } d \le x < b$$

$$M = R_1 x - P_1(x - d) + M_b \qquad \text{when } b < x \le c$$

$$M = R_1 x - P_1(x - d) + M_b + P_2(x - c) \quad \text{when } c \le x \le L$$

All four equations can be written as one, providing one defines the following symbolic function:

$$\langle x - a \rangle^n = \begin{cases} 0 & \text{for } 0 < x < a \\ (x - a)^n & \text{for } a < x < \infty \end{cases} \qquad (7\text{-}8)$$

where $n \ge 0$ $(n = 0, 1, 2, \ldots)$.

The expression enclosed by the pointed brackets does not exist until x reaches a. For x beyond a, the expression becomes an ordinary binomial. For $n = 0$ and for $x > a$, the function is unity. On this basis, the four separate functions for $M(x)$ given for the beam of Fig. 7-34 can be combined into one expression that is applicable across the whole span:[6]

$$M = R_1 \langle x - 0 \rangle^1 - P_1 \langle x - d \rangle^1 + M_b \langle x - b \rangle^0 + P_2 \langle x - c \rangle^1$$

Here the values of a are $0, d, b$, and c, respectively.

To work with this function further, it is convenient to introduce two additional symbolic functions. One is for the concentrated force, treating it as a degenerate case of a distributed load. The other is for the concentrated moment, treating it similarly. Rules for integrating all these functions must also be established. In this discussion, the heuristic (nonrigorous) approach will be followed.

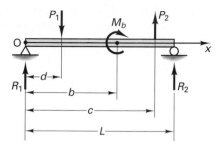

Fig. 7-34 A loaded beam.

---

[6]This approach was first introduced by A. Clebsch in 1862. O. Heavside, in his *Electromagnetic Theory*, initiated and greatly extended the methods of operational calculus. In 1919, W. H. Macauly specifically suggested the use of special brackets for beam problems. The reader interested in further and/or more rigorous development of this topic should cosult texts on methematics treating Laplace transforms.

A concentrated (point) force may be considered as an enormously strong distributed load acting over a small interval ε, Fig. 7-35(a). By treating ϵ as a constant, the following is true:

$$\lim_{\varepsilon \to 0} \int_{a-\varepsilon/2}^{a+\varepsilon/2} \frac{P}{\varepsilon}\, dx = P \qquad (7\text{-}9)$$

Here it can be noted that P/ε has the dimensions of force per unit distance such as N/mm and corresponds to the distributed load $q(x)$ in the earlier treatment. Therefore, as $\langle x - a \rangle^1 \to 0$, by an analogy of $\langle x - a \rangle^1$ to ε, for a concentrated force at $x = a$.

$$q = P\langle x - a \rangle_*^{-1} \qquad (7\text{-}10)$$

For q, this expression is dimensionally correct, although $\langle x - a \rangle_*^{-1}$ at $x = a$ becomes infinite and by definition is zero everywhere else. Thus, it is a *singular function*. In Eq. 7-10, the asterisk subscript of the bracket is a reminder that according to Eq. 7-9, the integral of this expression extending over the range ε remains bounded and, upon integration, yields the point force itself. Therefore, a special symbolic rule of integration must be adopted:

$$\int_0^x P\langle x - a \rangle_*^{-1}\, dx = P\langle x - a \rangle^0 \qquad (7\text{-}11)$$

The coefficient P in the previous functions is known as the *strength* of singularity. For P equal to unity, the *unit point load function* $\langle x - a \rangle_*^{-1}$ is also called the *Dirac delta* or the *unit impulse function*.

By analogous reasoning, see Fig. 7-35(b), the loading function q for concentrated moment at $x = a$ is

$$q = M_a\langle x - a \rangle_*^{-2} \qquad (7\text{-}12)$$

This function, in being integrated twice, defines two symbolic rules of integration. The second integral, except for the exchange of P by M, has already been stated as Eq. 7-11.

$$\int_0^x M_a\langle x - a \rangle_*^{-2}\, dx = M_a\langle x - a \rangle_*^{-1} \qquad (7\text{-}13)$$

$$\int_0^x M_a\langle x - a \rangle_*^{-1}\, dx = M_a\langle x - a \rangle^0 \qquad (7\text{-}14)$$

In Eq. 7-12, the expression is correct dimensionally since q has the units of M/mm. For M_a equal to unity, one obtains the *unit point moment function*,

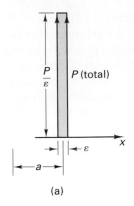

(a)

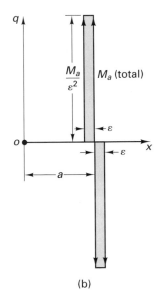

(b)

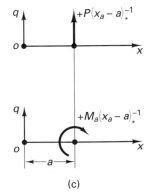

(c)

Fig. 7-35   Concentrated force P and moment $_a$: (a) and (b) considered as distributed load, and (c) symbolic notation for P and M at a.

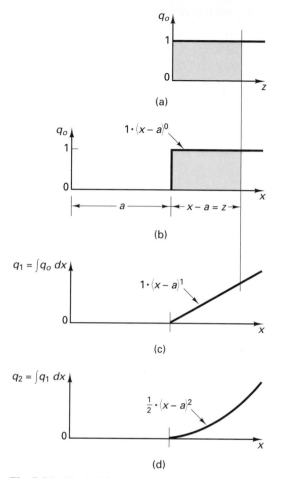

Fig. 7-36 Typical integrations.

$\langle x - a \rangle_*^{-2}$, which is also called the *doublet* or *dipole.*. This function is also singular, being infinite at $x = a$ and zero elsewhere. However, after integrating twice, a bounded result is obtained. Equations 7-10, 7-12, and 7-13 are symbolic in character. The relation of these equations to the given point loads is clearly evident from Eqs. 7-11 and 7-14.

The integral of binomial functions in pointed brackets for $n \geq 0$ is given by the following rule:

$$\int_0^x \langle x - a \rangle_n \, dx = \frac{\langle x - a \rangle^{n+1}}{n+1} \qquad \text{for } n \geq 0 \qquad (7\text{-}15)$$

This integration process is shown in Fig. 7-36. If the distance a is set equal to zero, one obtains conventional integrals.

Example 7-19

Using symbolic functional notation, determine $V(x)$ and $M(x)$ caused by the loading in Fig. 7-37(a).

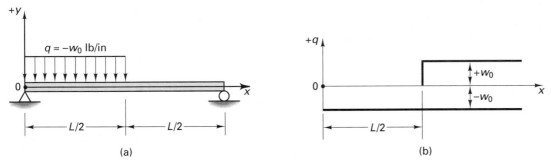

(a)   (b)

Fig. 7-37

SOLUTION

To solve this problem, Eq. 7-5 can be used. The applied load $q(x)$ acts downward and begins at $x = 0$. Therefore, a term $q = -w_0$ or $w_0\langle x - 0\rangle^0$, which means the same, must exist. This function, however, propagates across the whole span; see Fig. 7-37(b). To terminate the distributed load at $x = L/2$ as required in this problem, another function $+w_o\langle x - L/2\rangle^0$ must be added. The two expressions together represent correctly the applied load.

For this simply supported beam, the known boundary conditions are $M(0) = 0$ and $M(L) = 0$. These are used to determine the reactions:

$$\frac{d^2M}{dx^2} = q = -w_o\langle x - 0\rangle^0 + w_o\langle x - L/2\rangle^0$$

$$\frac{dM}{dx} = V = -w_o\langle x - 0\rangle^1 + w_o\langle x - L/2\rangle^1 + C_1$$

$$M(x) = -\tfrac{1}{2}w_o\langle x - 0\rangle^2 + \tfrac{1}{2}w_o\langle x - L/2\rangle^2 + C_1x + C_2$$

$$M(0) = C_2 = 0$$

$$M(L) = -\tfrac{1}{2}w_oL^2 + \tfrac{1}{2}w_o(L/2)^2 + C_1L = 0$$

Hence,

$$C_1 = +\tfrac{3}{8}p_oL$$

and

$$V(x) = -w_0\langle x - 0\rangle^1 + w_o\langle x - L/2\rangle^1 + \tfrac{3}{8}w_oL$$

$$M(x) = -\tfrac{1}{2}w_0\langle x - 0\rangle^2 + \tfrac{1}{2}w_o\langle x - L/2\rangle^2 + \tfrac{3}{8}w_oLx$$

After the solution is obtained, these relations are more easily read by rewriting them in conventional form:

$$\left.\begin{array}{l} V = +\frac{3}{8}w_0L - w_ox \\ M = +\frac{3}{8}w_oLx - \frac{1}{2}w_ox^2 \end{array}\right\} \quad \text{when } 0 < x \le L/2$$

$$\left.\begin{array}{l} V = +\frac{3}{8}w_oL - \frac{1}{2}W_oL = -\frac{1}{8}w_oL \\ M = +\frac{1}{8}w_oL^2 - \frac{1}{8}w_oLx \end{array}\right\} \quad \text{when } L/2 \le x < L$$

The reactions can be checked by conventional statics. By setting $V = 0$, the location of maximum moment can be found. A plot of these functions is left for the reader to complete.

Example 7-20

Find $V(x)$ and $M(x)$ for a beam loaded as shown in Fig. 7-38. Use singularity functions and treat it as a boundary-value problem.

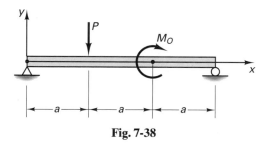

Fig. 7-38

SOLUTION

By making direct use of Eqs. 7-10 and 7-12, the function $q(x)$ can be written in symbolic form. From the conditions $M(0) = 0$ and $M(L) = 0$, with $L = 3a$, the constants of integration can be found.

$$d^2M/dx^2 = q = -P\langle x - a\rangle_*^{-1} + Pa\langle x - 2a\rangle_*^{-2}$$

$$dM/dx = V = -P\langle x - a\rangle^0 + Pa\langle x - 2a\rangle_*^{-1} + C_1$$

$$M = -P\langle x - a\rangle^1 + Pa\langle x - 2a\rangle^0 + C_1x + C_2$$

$$M(0) = C_2 = 0$$

and

$$M(3a) = -2Pa + Pa + 3C_1a = 0$$

Hence,

$$C_1 = +\tfrac{1}{3}P = \tfrac{1}{3}P\langle x - 0\rangle^0$$

and

$$V(x) = +\tfrac{1}{3}P\langle x - 0\rangle^0 - P\langle x - a\rangle^0 + Pa\langle x - 2a\rangle_*^{-1}$$

$$M(x) = +\tfrac{1}{3}P\langle x - 0\rangle^1 - P\langle x - a\rangle^1 + Pa\langle x - 2a\rangle^0$$

In the final expression for $V(x)$, the last term has no value if the expression is written in conventional form. Such terms are used only as tracers during the integration process.

It is suggested that the reader check the reactions by conventional statics, write out $V(x)$ and $M(x)$ for the three ranges of the beam within which these functions are continuous, and compare these with a plot of the shear and moment diagrams constructed by the summation procedure.

A suggestion of the manner of representing a uniformly varying load, Fig. 7-39(a), acting on a part of a beam is indicated in Fig. 7-39(b). Three separate functions are needed to define the given load completely.

In the previous discussion, it has been tacitly assumed that the reactions are at the ends of the beams. If such is not the case, the unknown constants C_1 and C_2 must be introduced into Eq. 7-5 as point loads; that is, as

$$C_1\langle x - a\rangle_*^{-1} \quad \text{and} \quad C_2\langle x - b\rangle_*^{-1}$$

This is the condition shown in Fig. 7-39(c). No additional constants of integration are necessary in a solution obtained in this manner.

Singularity functions can be used to advantage in statically indeterminate problems for axially loaded bars, as well as for torsion members and beams. However, the solutions are *limited to prismatic members*. If the cross section varies along the length of a member, the procedure for using singularity functions becomes impractical.

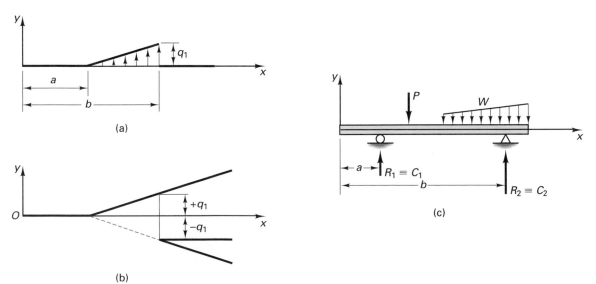

Fig. 7-39   Illustration for formulating singularity functions for reactions.

PROBLEMS

Section 7-3

7-1 through 7-4. Determine the reaction components caused by the applied loads for the planar framing shown in the figures. *Correctly drawn free-body diagrams are essential parts of solutions.* (*Hint for Prob. 7-1:* The effect on a structure of two cable forces acting over a frictionless pulley is the same as that of the same two forces applied at the center of the axle. Prove before using.)

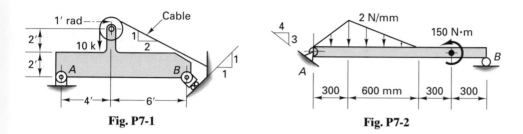

Fig. P7-1   Fig. P7-2

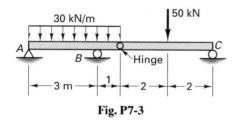

Fig. P7-3

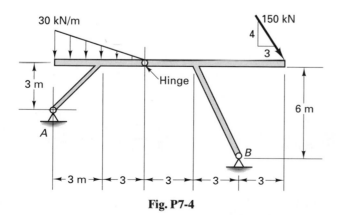

Fig. P7-4

Sections 7-5 through 7-7

7-5 through 7-19. For the planar structures shown in the figures , find the reactions and determine the axial forces P, the shears V, and the bending moments M caused by the applied loads at sections a–a, b–b, etc., as specified. Magnitude and sense of calculated quantities should be shown on separate free-body diagrams. For simplicity, assume that members can be represented by lines. When sections such as a–a and b–b are shown close together, one section is just to the left of a given dimension and the other is just to the right.

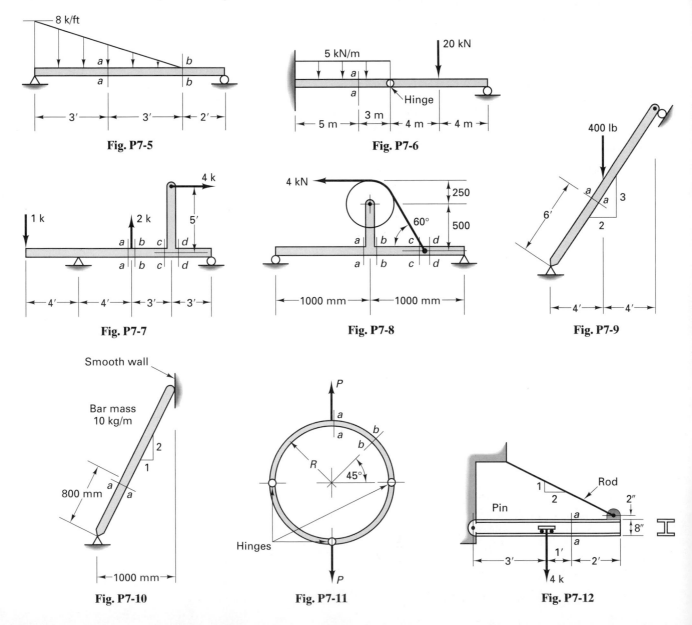

Fig. P7-5

Fig. P7-6

Fig. P7-7

Fig. P7-8

Fig. P7-9

Fig. P7-10

Fig. P7-11

Fig. P7-12

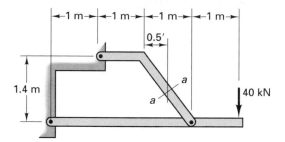

Fig. P7-13

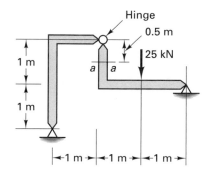

Fig. P7-14

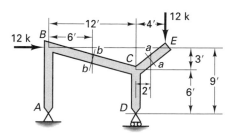

Fig. P7-15

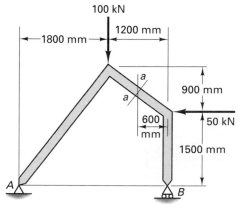

Fig. P7-16

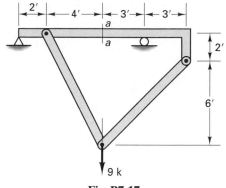

Fig. P7-17

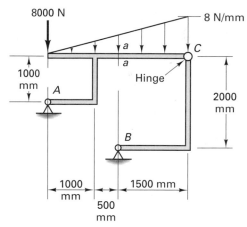

Fig. P7-18

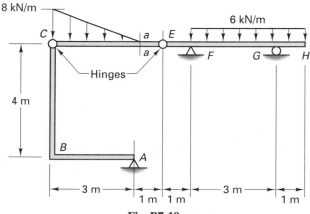

Fig. P7-19

Section 7-8

7-20 through 7-24. Plot shear and moment diagrams for the beams shown in the figures.

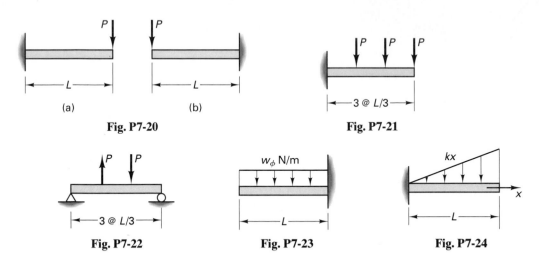

(a)　　　　　　　　(b)

Fig. P7-20　　　　　　　　**Fig. P7-21**

Fig. P7-22　　　**Fig. P7-23**　　　**Fig. P7-24**

7-25. Plot shear and moment diagrams for the beam shown in fig. 7-15.

7-26 through 7-28. For the beams loaded as shown in the figures, write explicit expressions for $M(x)$'s along the spans. Assume the origins of x at A. Since the applied loads are discontinuous, different functions apply for regions AC and CB.

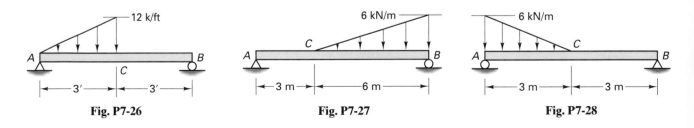

Fig. P7-26　　　**Fig. P7-27**　　　**Fig. P7-28**

7-29 through 7-31. Write explicit expressions for $M(x)$ along the spans for the statically indeterminate beams loaded as shown in the figures . Assume the origins of x at A. Consider the reactions on the left as unknowns. Take advantage of symmetry in Prob. 7-29.

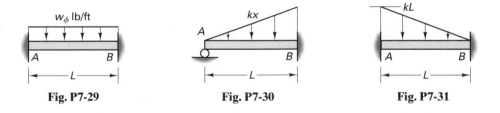

Fig. P7-29　　　**Fig. P7-30**　　　**Fig. P7-31**

7-32. Establish general expressions for the axial force $P(\theta)$, shear $V(\theta)$, and moment $M(\theta)$ for the curved bar in Example 7-12, Fig. 7-23. Angle θ is measured counterclockwise from the positive x axis.

7-33. Establish general expressions for the axial force $P(\theta)$, shear $V(\theta)$, and moment $M(\theta)$ for the ring with three hinges of Prob. 7-11. Angle θ is measured counterclockwise from the positive x axis.

7-34. A rectangular bar bent into a semicircle is built in at one end and is subjected to a radial pressure of p lb per unit length (see figure). Write the general expressions for $P(\theta)$, $V(\theta)$, and $M(\theta)$, and plot results on a polar diagram. Show positive directions assumed for P, V, and M on a free-body diagram.

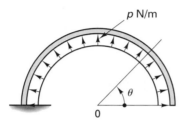

p N/m

0

Bar radius = R

Fig. P7-34

7-35. A bar in the shape of a right angle, as shown in the figure , is fixed at one of its ends. (a) Write the general expressions for V, M, and T (torque) caused by the application of a force F normal to the plane of the bent bar. Plot the results. (b) If, in addition to the applied force F, the weight of the bar w lb per unit length is also to be considered, what system of internal force components develops at the fixed end?

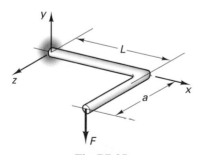

Fig. P7-35

Section 7-9

7-36. Using the differential equation, Eq. 7-5, determine $V(x)$ and $M(x)$ for the beam loaded as shown in Prob. 7-24. Verify the reactions using conventional statics. [*Hint:* The constants of integration can be found from the boundary conditions $V(L) = 0$ and $M(L) = 0$.]

7-37 through 7-39.   Using Eq. 7-5 for the statically determinate beams shown in the figures, find $V(x)$ and $M(x)$ and the reactions at the supports. Plot the shear and moment diagrams. (*Hint:* The constants of integration are found from the boundary conditions for V and M. This approach cannot be extended to statically indeterminate beams, which require the use of a higher order differential equation, discussed in Chapter 10.)

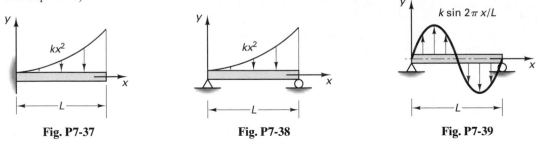

Fig. P7-37   Fig. P7-38   Fig. P7-39

Sections 7-10 and 7-11

Problems 7-20 through 7-31 can also be assigned for solution using the methods developed in these two sections.

7-40 through 7-66.   Plot shear and moment diagrams for the beams shown in the figures using the methods of Section 7-10 and 7-11. It is also suggested to draw the deflected shapes of the beams using the criteria given in Fig. 7-14. (A more detailed discussion for drawing such shapes is given in Section 7-13.)

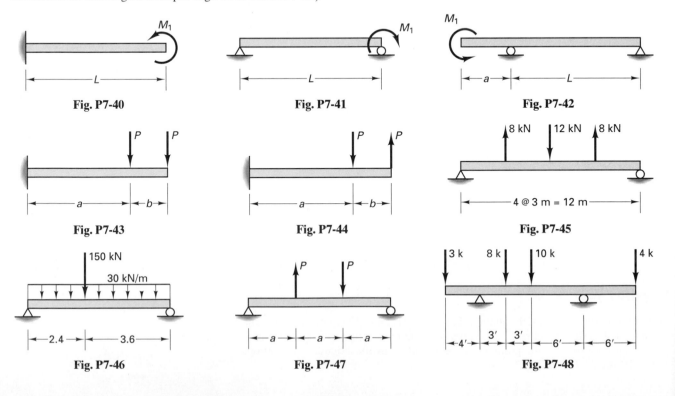

Fig. P7-40   Fig. P7-41   Fig. P7-42

Fig. P7-43   Fig. P7-44   Fig. P7-45

Fig. P7-46   Fig. P7-47   Fig. P7-48

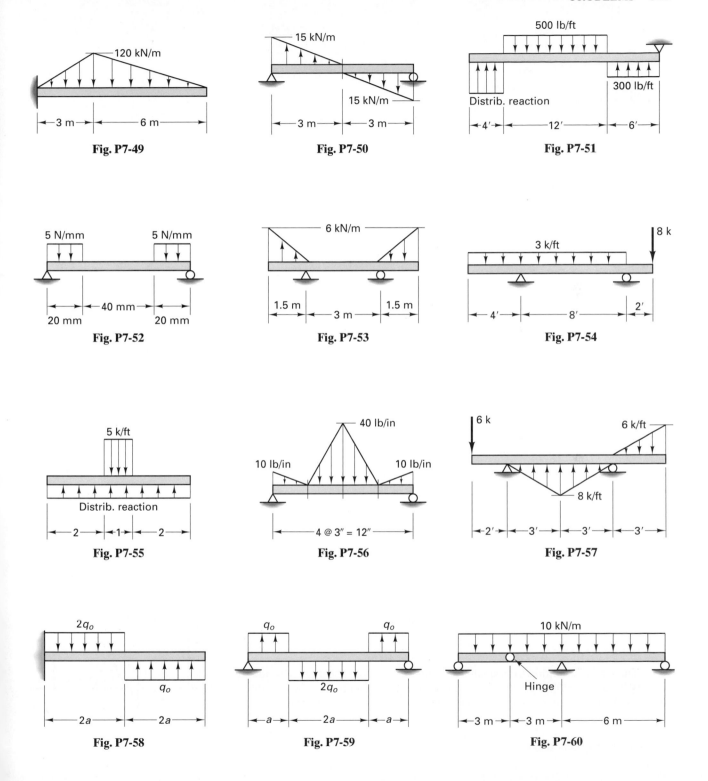

Fig. P7-49

Fig. P7-50

Fig. P7-51

Fig. P7-52

Fig. P7-53

Fig. P7-54

Fig. P7-55

Fig. P7-56

Fig. P7-57

Fig. P7-58

Fig. P7-59

Fig. P7-60

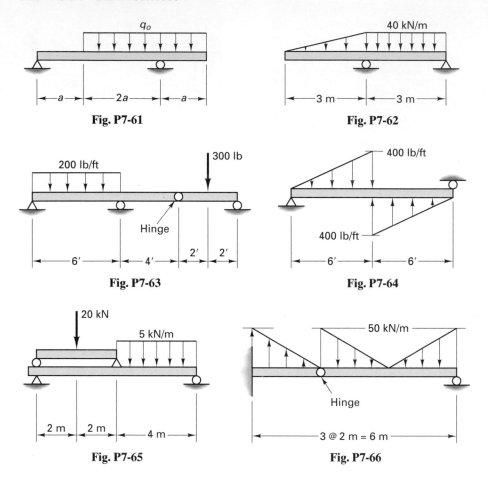

Fig. P7-61

Fig. P7-62

Fig. P7-63

Fig. P7-64

Fig. P7-65

Fig. P7-66

7-67. A small narrow barge is loaded as shown in the figure. Plot shear and moment diagrams for the applied loading.

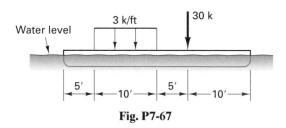

Fig. P7-67

7-68. The load distribution for a small single-engine airplane in flight may be idealized as shown in the figure. In this diagram, vector A represents the weight of the engine; B, the uniformly distributed cabin weight; C, the weight of the aft fuselage; and D, the forces from the tail control surfaces. The upward forces E are developed by the two longerons from the wings. Using this data, construct plausible, qualitative shear and moment diagrams for the fuselage.

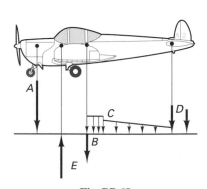

Fig. P7-68

7-69.   The moment diagram for a beam supported at A and B is shown in the figure. How is the beam loaded?

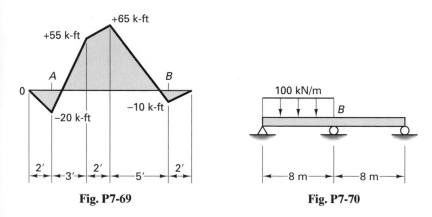

Fig. P7-69   Fig. P7-70

7-70.   The redundant moment over support B for the beam shown in the figure can be shown to be -400 kN $\cdot$ m by the methods discussed in Chapter 14. Plot the shear and moment diagrams for this beam.

7-71 through 7-73.   For the structural systems shown in the figures, plot the axial force P, shear V, and moment M diagrams. Note that the axial force and shear contribute to the equilibrium of forces at a joint in bent members (see Fig. 7-22).

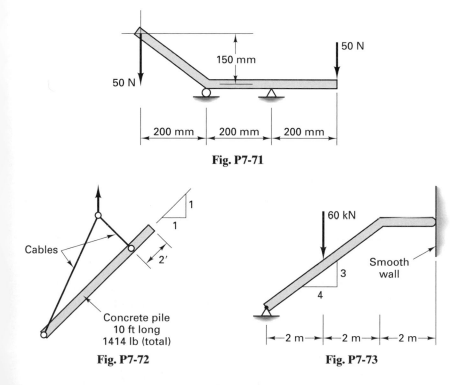

Fig. P7-71

Fig. P7-72   Fig. P7-73

7-74. For member DF of the frame in Problem 1-56, plot the axial force, shear, and moment diagrams caused by the applied force.

7-75 and 7-76. It is customary to idealize the support forces as concentrated at a point. In some cases the distributed forces are also treated as concentrated forces. These are simplifications of complex problems. In these two problems, (a) determine the reactions according to the load pattern shown, (b) plot shear and moment diagrams for these cases, (c) treat reactions in Problem 7-75 and the distributed force in Problem 7-76 as concentrated forces and plot the corresponding shear and moment diagrams, and (d) state in percentage the discrepancy in the maximum moments between the two solutions. Consider whether the clear span or center to center of reaction forces gives a more accurate result.

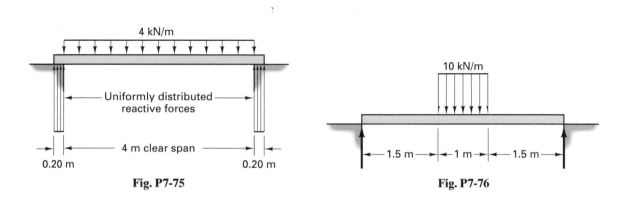

Fig. P7-75   Fig. P7-76

Sections 7-12 and 7-13

7-77 through 7-83. For the structural systems shown in the figures , plot the axial force P, shear V, and moment M diagrams due to the applied loads. These diagrams are to be confined only to the main horizontal members. Note that the beams in the last four problems have finite depth.

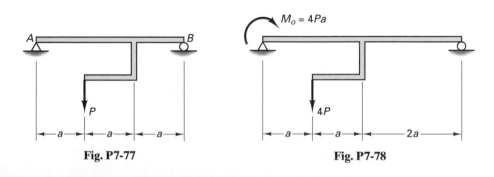

Fig. P7-77   Fig. P7-78

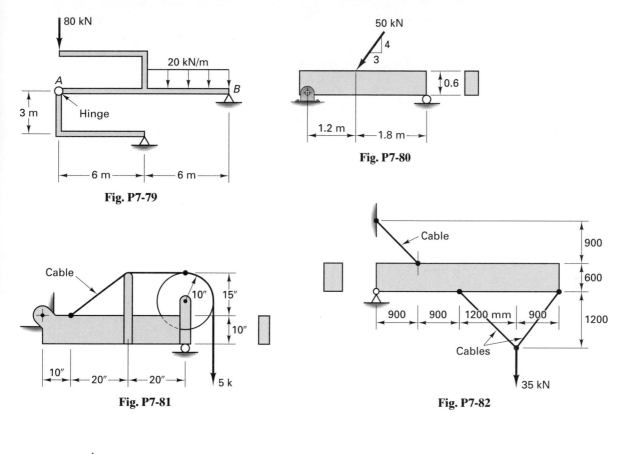

Fig. P7-79

Fig. P7-80

Fig. P7-81

Fig. P7-82

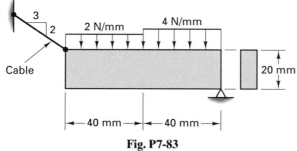

Fig. P7-83

7-84. Sketch the elastic curve for the beam loaded as shown in Problem 7-42.

7-85. Sketch the elastic curve for the beam loaded as shown in Problem 7-54.

7-86. Sketch the elastic curve for the beam loaded as shown in Problem 7-60.

7-87. Sketch the elastic curve for the beam loaded as shown in Problem 7-73.

Section 7-14

7-88 through 7-93.   For the beams loaded as shown in the figures, using singularity functions and Eq. 7-5, (a) find $V(x)$ and $M(x)$. Check reactions by conventional statics. (b) Plot shear and moment diagrams.

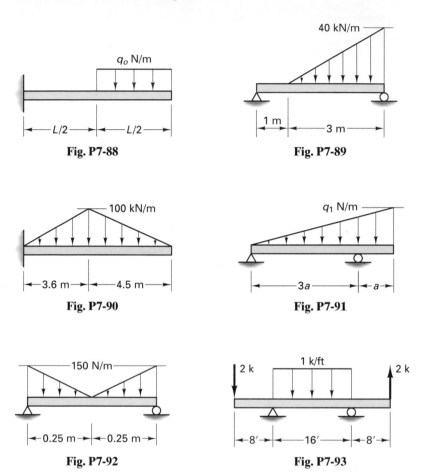

q_o N/m

L/2   L/2

Fig. P7-88

40 kN/m

1 m   3 m

Fig. P7-89

100 kN/m

3.6 m   4.5 m

Fig. P7-90

q_1 N/m

3a   a

Fig. P7-91

150 N/m

0.25 m   0.25 m

Fig. P7-92

2 k   1 k/ft   2 k

8′   16′   8′

Fig. P7-93

8

Symmetric Beam Bending

8-1. Introduction

In the previous chapter, it was shown that a system of internal forces consisting of an axial force, a shear force, and a bending moment may develop in planar frames and beams. The stresses caused by an axial force were already discussed in Chapters 1 and 3. In this chapter, the stresses due to bending of members having *symmetric* cross sections and subjected to bending in the plane of symmetry are considered. Both elastic and inelastic stress distributions caused by bending are discussed. Stress distribution in curved bars is also included. In the next chapter, the problem is generalized to include *unsymmetric* bending of members with symmetric cross sections as well as bending of members of arbitrary cross section. Consideration is also given to problems where bending occurs in the presence of axial forces.

For simplicity, members will generally be shown as beams in a horizontal position. When a segment of a beam is in equilibrium under the action of bending moments alone, such a condition is referred to as *pure bending,* or *flexure.* A cantilever loaded with a concentrated moment at the end, or a segment of a beam between the concentrated forces, as shown in Fig. 7-18, are examples of pure bending. Studies in subsequent chapters will show that usually the *bending stresses* in slender beams are dominant. Therefore, the formulas derived in this chapter for pure bending are directly applicable in numerous design situations.

It is important to note that some beams, by virtue of their slenderness or lack of lateral support, may become unstable under an applied load and may buckle laterally and collapse. Such beams do not come within the scope of this chapter. A better appreciation of the instability phenomenon will result after the study of column buckling in Chapter 16.

8-2. Basic Kinematic Assumption

In the simplified engineering theory of bending, to establish the relation among the applied bending moment, the cross-sectional properties of a member, and the internal stresses and deformations, the approach applied earlier in the torsion problem is again employed. This requires, first, that a plausible deformation assumption reduce the internally statically indeterminate problem to a determinate one; second, that the deformations causing strains be related to stresses through the appropriate stress-strain relations; and, finally, that the equilibrium requirements of external and internal forces be met. The key kinematic assumption for the deformation of a beam as used in the simplified theory is discussed in this section. A generalization of this assumption forms the basis for the theories of plates and shells.

For present purposes, consider a horizontal prismatic beam having a cross section with a vertical axis of symmetry; see Fig. 8-1(a). A horizontal line through the centroid of the cross section will be referred to as the axis of a beam. Next, consider a typical element of the beam between two planes perpendicular to the beam axis. In side view, such an element is identified in the figure as *abcd*. When such a beam is subjected to equal end moments M_z acting around the z axis, Fig. 8-1(b), this beam bends in the plane of symmetry, and the planes initially perpendicular to the beam axis slightly tilt. Nevertheless, the lines such as *ad* and *bc* becoming *a'd'* and *b'c'* remain straight.[1] This observation forms the basis for the fundamental hypothesis[2] of the flexure theory. It may be stated thus: *Plane sections through a beam taken normal to its axis remain plane after the beam is subjected to bending.*

---

[1] This can be demonstrated by using a rubber model with a ruled grating drawn on it. Alternatively, thin vertical rods passing through the rubber block can be used. In the immediate vicinity of the applied moments, the deformation is more complex. However, in accord with the Saint-Venant's principle (Section 3-3), this is only a local phenomenon that rapidly dissipates.

[2] This hypothesis with an inaccuracy was first introduced by Jacob Bernoulli (1645–1705), a Swiss mathematician. At a later date a great Swiss mathematician, Leonard Euler (1707–1783), who largely worked in Russia and Germany, made important use of this concept. This assumption is often referred to as the Benoulli-Euler hypothesis. In the correct final form, it dates back to the writings of the French engineering educator M. Navier (1785–1836).

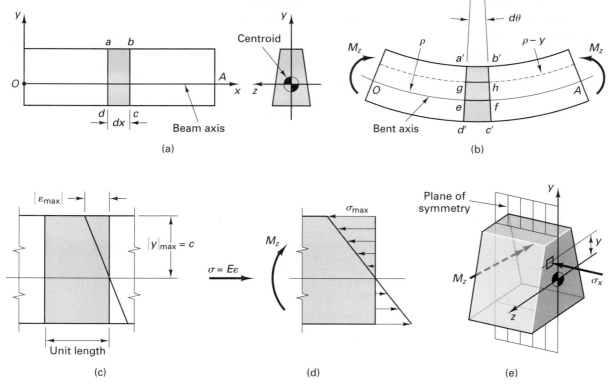

Figure 8-1   Assumed behavior of elastic beam in bending.

As demonstrated in texts on the theory of elasticity, this assumption is completely true for elastic, rectangular members in pure bending. If shears also exist, a small error is introduced.[3] Practically, however, this assumption is generally applicable with a high degree of accuracy whether the material behaves elastically or plastically, providing the depth of the beam is small in relation to its span. In this chapter, the stress analysis of all beams is based on this assumption.

In pure bending of a prismatic beam, the beam axis deforms into a part of a circle of radius ρ, (rho) as shown in Fig. 8-1(b). For an element defined by an infinitesimal angle $d\theta$, the fiber length ef of the beam axis is given as $ds = \rho\, d\theta$. Hence,

$$\boxed{\frac{d\theta}{ds} = \frac{1}{\rho} = \kappa} \qquad (8\text{-}1)$$

where the reciprocal of ρ defines the axis *curvature* κ (kappa). In pure bending of prismatic beams, both ρ and κ are constant.

[3]See the discussion in Section 10-5.

The fiber length gh located on a radius $\rho - y$ can be found similarly. Therefore, the difference between fiber lengths gh and ef identified here as $d\hat{u}$ can be expressed as follows:

$$d\hat{u} = (\rho - y)\, d\theta - \rho\, d\theta = -y\, d\theta \qquad (8\text{-}2)$$

By dividing by ds and using Eq. 8-1, the last term becomes κ. Moreover, since the deflection and rotations of the beam axis are very small, the cosines of the angles involved in making the projections of $d\hat{u}$ and ds onto the horizontal axis are very nearly unity. Therefore, in the development of the simplified beam theory, it is possible to replace $d\hat{u}$ by du, the axial fiber deformation, and ds by dx.[4] Hence, by dividing Eq. 8-2 by ds and approximating $d\hat{u}/ds$ by du/dx, which, according to Eq. 3-1, is the normal strain ε_x, one has

$$\boxed{\varepsilon_x = -\kappa y} \qquad (8\text{-}3)$$

This equation establishes the expression for the basic kinematic hypothesis for the flexure theory. However, although it is clear that the strain in a bent beam varies along the beam depth linearly with y, information is lacking for locating the origin of the y axis. With the aid of Hooke's law and an equation of equilibrium, this problem is resolved in the next section.

8-3. The Elastic Flexure Formula

By using Hooke's law, the expression for the normal strain given by Eq. 8-3 can be recast into a relation for the normal longitudinal stress σ_x:

$$\boxed{\sigma_x = E\varepsilon_x = -E\kappa y} \qquad (8\text{-}4)$$

In this equation, the variable y can assume both positive and negative values.

Two nontrivial equations of equilibrium are available to solve the beam flexure problem. One of these determines the origin for y; the second completes the solution for the flexure formula. Using the first one of these equations, requiring that in pure bending, the sum of all forces at a section in the x direction must vanish, one has

$$\Sigma F_x = 0 \qquad \int_A \sigma_x\, dA = 0 \qquad (8\text{-}5)$$

[4]A further discussion of the approximations involved is found in Section 14-3.

where the subscript A indicates that the summation of the infinitesimal forces must be carried out over the entire cross-sectional area A of the beam. This equation with the aid of Eq. 8-4 can be rewritten as

$$\int_A -E\kappa y \, dA = -E\kappa \int_A y \, dA = 0 \qquad (8\text{-}6)$$

where the constants E and κ are taken outside the second integral. By definition, this integral $\int y \, dA = \bar{y}A$, where $\bar{y}$ is the distance from the origin to the centroid of an area A. Since here this integral equals zero and area A is not zero, distance $\bar{y}$ must be set equal to zero. Therefore, the z axis must pass through the *centroid* of a section. According to Eqs. 8-3 and 8-4, this means that along the z axis so chosen, both the normal strain ε_x and the normal stress σ_x are zero. In bending theory, this axis is referred to as the *neutral axis* of a beam. The neutral axis for any *elastic* beam of homogenous material can be easily determined by finding the centroid of a cross-sectional area.

Based on this result, linear variation in strain is schematically shown in Fig. 8-1(c). The corresponding *elastic* stress distribution in accordance with Eq. 8-4 is shown in Fig. 8-1(d). Both the absolute maximum strain ε_x and the absolute maximum stress σ_{max} occur at the *largest* value of y.

Alternative representations of the elastic bending stress distribution in a beam are illustrated in Fig. 8-2. Note the need for awareness that the problem is *three dimensional,* although for simplicity two-dimensional representations are generally used. The locus of a neutral axis along a length of a beam defines the *neutral surface,* as noted in Fig. 8-3.

To complete the derivation of the elastic flexure formula, the second relevant equation of equilibrium must be brought in: The sum of the externally

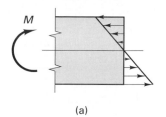

(a)

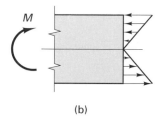

(b)

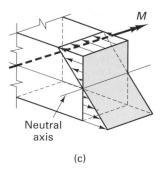

Neutral axis

(c)

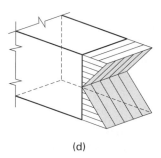

(d)

Figure 8-2 Alternative representations of bending moment.

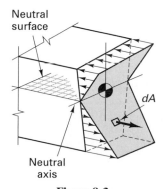

Neutral surface

dA

Neutral axis

Figure 8-3

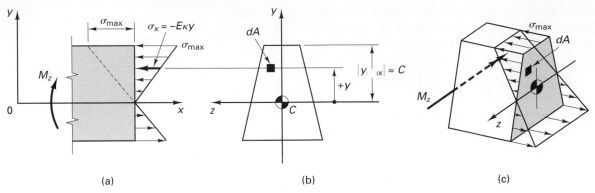

Figure 8-4   Segment of a beam in pure flexure.

applied and the internal resisting moments must vanish (i.e., be in equilibrium). For the beam segment in Fig. 8-4(a), this yields

$$\Sigma M_O = 0 \curvearrowright + \qquad M_z - \underbrace{\int_A \underbrace{E\kappa y}_{\text{stress}} \quad \underbrace{dA}_{\text{area}}}_{\text{force}} \qquad \underbrace{y}_{\text{arm}} = 0 \qquad (8\text{-}7)$$

A negative sign in front of the integral is necessary because the *compressive* stresses σ_x develop a counterclockwise moment around the z axis. The
tensile stresses below the neutral axis, where y's have a negative sign, contribute to this moment in the same manner. This sign also follows directly
from Eq. 8-4. From a slightly different point of view, Eq. 8-7 states that the
clockwise external moment M_z is balanced by the counterclockwise
moment developed by the internal stresses at a section. Recasting Eq. 8-7
into this form, and recognizing that E and κ are constants,

$$M_z = E\kappa \int_A y^2 \, dA \qquad (8\text{-}8)$$

In mechanics, the last integral, depending only on the geometrical properties of a cross-sectional area, is called the rectangular *moment of inertia* or
second moment of the area A and will be designated in this text by I. It must
be found with respect to the cross section's neutral (centroidal) axis. Since
I must always be determined with respect to a particular axis, it is often
meaningful to identify it with a subscript corresponding to such an axis. For
the case considered, this subscript is z; that is,

$$\boxed{I_z = \int_A y^2 \, dA} \qquad (8\text{-}9)$$

With this notation, Eq. 8-8 yields the following result:

$$\kappa = \frac{M_z}{EI_z} \tag{8-10}$$

This is the basic relation giving the curvature of an elastic beam subjected to a specified moment.

By substituting Eq. 8-10 into Eq. 8-4, the elastic *flexure formula*[5] for beams is obtained:

$$\sigma_x = -\frac{M_z}{I_z} y \tag{8-11}$$

The derivation of this formula was carried out with the coordinate axes shown in Fig. 8-5(a). If the derivation for a member having a doubly symmetric cross section were done with the coordinates shown in Fig. 8-5(b), the expression for the longitudinal stress σ_x would read

$$\sigma_x = +\frac{M_y}{I_y} z \tag{8-12}$$

The sign reversal in relation to Eq. 8-11 is necessary because a positive M_y causes tensile stresses for positive z's.

Application of these equations to biaxial bending as well as an extension of the bending theory for beams with unsymmetric cross sections is considered in Sections 9-2 and 9-5. In this chapter, attention is confined to beams having symmetric cross sections bent in the plane of symmetry. For such applications, it is customary to recast the flexure formula to give the *maximum* normal stress σ_{max} directly and to designate the value of $|y|_{max}$ by c. It is also common practice to dispense with the sign, as in Eq. 8-11, as well as with subscripts on M and I. Since the normal stresses must develop a couple statically equivalent to the internal bending moment, their sense can be determined by inspection. On this basis, the flexure formula becomes

$$\sigma_{max} = \frac{Mc}{I} \tag{8-13}$$

[5]It took nearly two centuries to develop this seemingly simple expression. The first attempts to solve the flexure problem were made by Galileo in the seventeenth century. In the form in which it is used today, the problem was solved in the early part of the nineteenth century. Generally, Navier is credited for this accomplishment. However, some maintain that credit should go to Coulomb, who also derived the torsion formula.

In conformity with the preceding practice, in dealing with bending of *symmetric* beam sections, the simplified notation of leaving out z subscripts in Eq. 8-11 on M and I will be employed often in this text.

The flexure formula and its variations discussed before are of unusually great importance in applications to structural and machine design. In applying these formulas, the internal bending moment can be expressed in newton-meters (N · m) or inch-pounds (in-lb), c in meters [m] or inches [in], and I in m^4 or in^4. The use of consistent units as indicated makes the units of σ: $(N \cdot M)(m)/(m^4) = N/m^2 = Pa$, or $[in\text{-}lb][in]/[in^4] = [lb/in^2] = psi$, as to be expected.

It should be noted that σ_x, as given by Eqs. 8-11 and 8-12, is the only stress that results from pure bending of a beam. Therefore, in the matrix representation of the stress tensor, one has

$$\begin{pmatrix} \sigma_x & 0 & 0 \\ 0 & 0 & 0 \\ 0 & 0 & 0 \end{pmatrix}$$

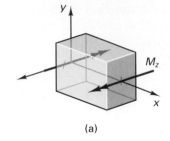

(a)

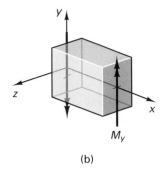

(b)

Figure 8-5   Definitions of positive moments.

As will be pointed out in Chapter 11, this stress may be transformed or resolved into stresses acting along different sets of coordinate axes.

In concluding this discussion, it is interesting to note that due to Poisson's ratio, the compressed zone of a beam expands laterally;[6] the tensile zone contracts. The strains in the y and z directions are $\varepsilon_y = \varepsilon_z = \nu\varepsilon_x$, where $\varepsilon_x = \sigma_x/E$ and σ_x is given by Eq. 8-11. This is in complete agreement with the rigorous solution. Poisson's effect, as may be shown by the methods of elasticity, deforms the neutral axis into a curve of large radius; and the neutral surface becomes curved in two opposite directions; see Fig. 8-6. In the previous treatment, the neutral surface was assumed to be curved in one direction only. These interesting details are not significant in most practical problems.

Procedure Summary and Extensions

The same *three basic concepts* of engineering mechanics of solids that were used in developing the theories are axially loaded bars and circular shafts in torsion are used in the preceding derivation of flexure formulas. These may be summarized as follows:

1. *Equilibrium conditions* (statics) are used for determining the internal resisting bending moment at a section.
2. *Geometry of deformation* (kinematics) is used by assuming that plane sections through a beam remain plane after deformation. This leads to the conclusion that normal strains along a beam section vary linearly from the neutral axis.

---

[6]An experiment with an ordinary rubber eraser is recommended!

3. *Properties of materials* (constitutive relations) in the form of Hooke's law are assumed to apply to the longitudinal normal strains. The Poisson effect of transverse contraction and expansion is neglected.

In extending this approach to bending of beams of two and more materials (Section 8-9), as well as to inelastic bending of beams (Section 8-8), the first two of the enumerated concepts remain fully applicable. Only the third, dealing with the mechanical properties of materials, must be modified. As an example of a change necessary for such cases, consider the beam having the cross section shown in Fig. 8-7(a). This beam is made up of two materials, 1 and 2, bonded together at their interface. The elastic moduli for the two materials are E_1 and E_2, where the subscripts identify the material. For the purposes of discussion assume that $E_2 > E_1$.

When such a composite beam is bent, as for a beam of one material, the strains vary linearly, as shown in Fig. 8-7(b). However, the longitudinal stresses depend on the elastic moduli and are shown in Fig. 8-7(c). At the interface between the two materials, whereas the strain for both materials is the same, the stresses are different and depend on the magnitudes of E_1 and E_2. The remaining issue in such problems consists of locating the neutral axis or surface. This can be easily done for beams having cross sections with symmetry around the vertical axes.

For beams of several different materials, the elastic moduli for each material must be identified. Let E_i be such an elastic modulus for the ith material in a composite cross section. Then Eq. 8-4 can be generalized to read

$$\sigma_x = E_i \varepsilon_x = -E_i \kappa y \qquad (8\text{-}14)$$

where, from Fig. 8-7(a), $y = y_b - \bar{y}_b$. In this relation y_b is arbitrarily measured from the bottom of the section, and $\bar{y}_b$ locates the neutral axis as shown.

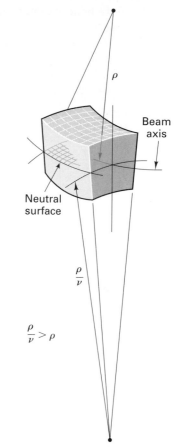

Figure 8-6   Segment of a bent beam.

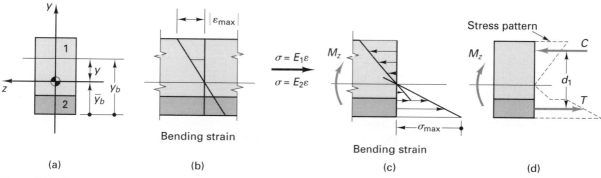

Figure 8-7   Beam of two elastic materials in bending where $E_2 > E_1$.

Since for pure bending the force F_x at a section in the x direction must vanish, following the same procedure as before, and substituting Eq. 8-14 into Eq. 8-5,

$$F_x = \int_A \sigma_x \, dA = -\kappa \int_A E_i y \, dA = 0 \qquad (8\text{-}15)$$

The last expression differs from Eq. 8-6 only by not placing E_i outside of the integral. By substituting $y = y_b - \bar{y}_b$ into Eq. 8-15, and recognizing that $\bar{y}_b$ is constant,

$$-\kappa \int_A E_i y_b \, dA + \kappa \bar{y}_b \int_A E_i \, dA = 0$$

and

$$\bar{y}_b = \frac{\displaystyle\int_A E_i y_b \, dA}{\displaystyle\int_A E_i \, dA} \qquad (8\text{-}16)$$

where the integration must be carried out with appropriate E_i's, for each material. This equation defines the *modulus-weighted centroid* and locates the neutral axis.

Essentially the same process is used for inelastic bending analysis of beams by changing the stress-strain relations. The first two of the enumerated basic concepts remain applicable.

The developed theory for elastic beams of *one* material is in complete agreement with the mathematically exact solution[7] based on the theory of elasticity for pure bending of an elastic rectangular bar. However, even for this limited case, the boundary conditions at the ends require the surface stresses σ_x to be distributed over the ends as given by Eq. 8-11. For this case plane sections through a beam remain precisely plane after bending. However, in usual applications, per *Saint-Venant's principle,* it is generally assumed that the stresses, at a distance about equal to the depth of a member away from the applied moment, are essentially uniform and are given by Eq. 8-11. The local stresses at points of force application or change in cross section are calculated using stress concentration factors. In applications the theory discussed is routinely applied to any kind of cross section, whether a material is elastic or plastic.

In conclusion it should be noted that, in all cases in pure bending, the stresses acting on the area above the neutral axis develop a force of one sense, whereas those below the neutral axis develop a force acting in the

[7]S. Timoshenko and J. N. Goodier, *Theory of Elasticity,* 3rd ed. (New York: McGraw-Hill, 1970), 284.

opposite direction. An example is shown in Fig. 8-7(d), where the tension T is equal to the compression C, and the $T - C$ couple is equal to the moment M_z. This method of reducing stresses to forces and a couple can be used to advantage in some problems.

8-4. Computation of the Moment of Inertia

In applying the flexure formula, the rectangular moment of inertia I of the cross-sectional area about the neutral axis must be determined. Its value is defined by the integral of $y^2\,dA$ over the entire cross-sectional area of a member, and it must be emphasized that for the flexure formula, the moment of inertia must be computed around the neutral axis. This axis passes through the centroid of the cross-sectional area. It is shown in Sections 9-6 and 9-7 that for symmetric cross sections, the neutral axis is perpendicular to the axis of symmetry. The moment of inertia around such an axis is either a maximum or a minimum, and for that reason, this axis is one of the *principal* axes for an area. The procedures for determining centroids and moments of inertia of areas are generally thoroughly discussed in texts on statics.[8] However, for completeness, they are reviewed in what follows.

The first step in evaluating I for an area is to find its centroid. An integration of $y^2\,dA$ is then performed with respect to the horizontal axis passing through the area's centroid. In applications of the flexure formula, the actual integration over areas is necessary for only a few elementary shapes, such as rectangles and triangles. Values of moments of inertia for some simple shapes may be found in texts on statics as well as in any standard civil or mechanical engineering handbook (also see Table 2 of the Appendix). Most cross-sectional areas used may be divided into a combination of these simple shapes. To find I for an area composed of several simple shapes, the *parallel-axis theorem* (sometimes called the *transfer formula*) is necessary; its development follows.

Consider that the area A shown in Fig. 8-8 is a *part* of a complex area of a cross section of a beam in flexure. The centroidal axis z_c for *this* area is at a distance d_z from the centroidal z axis for the *whole* cross-sectional area. Then, by definition, the moment of inertia I_{z_c} of the area A around its z_c axis is

$$I_{z_c} = \int_A y_c^2\,dA \qquad (8\text{-}17)$$

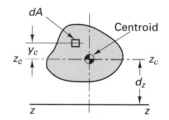

Figure 8-8   Area for deriving the parallel-axis theorem.

[8]For example, see J. L. Meriam and L. G. Kraige, *Engineering Mechanics,* Vol. 1, Statics, 2nd ed. (New York: Wiley, 1986).

On the other hand, the moment of inertia $_z$ of the *same* area A around the z axis is

$$I_z = \int_A (y_c + d_z)^2\, dA$$

By squaring the quantities in the parentheses and placing the constants outside the integrals,

$$I_z = \int_A y_c^2\, dA + 2d_z \int_A y_c\, dA + d_z^2 \int_A dA$$

Here the first integral according to Eq. 8-17 is equal to I_{z_c}, the second integral vanishes as y_c passes through the centroid of A, and the last integral reduces to Ad_z^2. Hence,

$$\boxed{I_z = I_{z_c} + Ad_z^2} \tag{8-18}$$

This is the *parallel-axis theorem.* It can be stated as follows: The moment of inertia of an area around any axis is equal to the moment of inertia of the same area around a parallel axis passing through the area's centroid, plus the product of the same area and the square of the distance between the two axes.

In calculations, Eq. 8-18 must be applied to *each* part into which a cross-sectional area has been subdivided and the results summed to obtain I_z for the whole section; that is,

$$I_z \text{ (whole section)} = \Sigma(I_{z_c} + Ad_z^2) \tag{8-18a}$$

After this process is completed, the z subscript may be dropped in treating bending of *symmetric* cross sections.

The following examples illustrate the method of computing I directly by integration for two simple areas. Then an application of the parallel-axis theorem to a composite area is given. Values for I for commercially fabricated steel beams, angles, and pipes are given in Tables 3 to 8 of the Appendix.

Example 8-1

Find the moment of inertia around the horizontal axis passing through the centroid for the rectangular area shown in Fig. 8-9.

SOLUTION
The centroid of this section lies at the intersection of the two axes of symmetry. Here it is convenient to take dA as $b\, dy$. Hence,

$$I_z = I_o = \int_A y^2\, dA = \int_{-h/2}^{+h/2} y^2 b\, dy = b\left.\frac{y^3}{3}\right|_{-h/2}^{+h/2} = \frac{bh^3}{12}$$

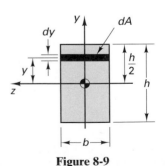

Figure 8-9

Hence,

$$I_z = \frac{bh^3}{12} \quad \text{and} \quad I_y = \frac{b^3h}{12} \quad (8\text{-}19)$$

These expressions are used frequently, as rectangular beams are common.

Example 8-2

Find the moment of inertia about a diameter for a circular area of radius c; see Fig. 8-10.

SOLUTION

To find I for a circle, first note that $\rho^2 = z^2 + y^2$, as may be seen from the figure. Then using the definition of I_p, noting the symmetry around both axes, and using Eq. 6-2,

$$I_p = \int_A \rho^2 \, dA = \int_A (y^2 + z^2) \, dA = \int_A y^2 \, dA + \int_A z^2 \, dA$$

$$= I_z + I_y = 2I_z$$

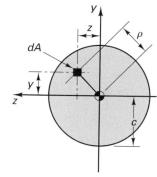

Figure 8-10

$$I_z = I_y = \frac{I_p}{2} = \frac{\pi c^4}{4} \quad (8\text{-}20)$$

In mechanical applications, circular shafts often act as beams; hence, Eq. 8-20 will be found useful. For a tubular shaft, the moment of inertia of the hollow interior must be subtracted from the last expression.

Example 8-3

Determine the moment of inertia I around the horizontal axis for the area shown in mm in Fig. 8-11 for use in the flexure formula.

SOLUTION

As the moment of inertia is for use in the flexure formula, it must be obtained around the axis through the centroid of the area. Hence, the centroid of the area must be found first. This is most easily done by treating the entire outer section and deducting the hollow interior from it. For convenience, the work is carried out in tabular form. Then the parallel-axis theorem is used to obtain I.

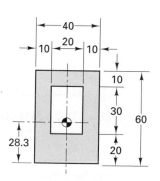

Figure 8-11

Area	A (mm^2)	y (mm) (from bottom)	Ay
Entire area	$40 \times 60 = 2400$	30	72 000
Hollow interior	$-20 \times 30 = -600$	35	$-21\,000$
	$\Sigma A = 1800$ mm^2		$\Sigma Ay = 51\,000$ mm^3

$$\bar{y} = \frac{\Sigma Ay}{\Sigma A} = \frac{51\,000}{1800} = 28.3 \text{ mm from bottom}$$

For the entire area:

$$I_{z_c} = \frac{bh^3}{12} = \frac{40 \times 60^3}{12} = 72 \times 10^4 \text{ mm}^4$$

$$Ad^2 = 2400(30 - 28.3)^2 = \underline{0.69 \times 10^4 \text{mm}^4}$$

$$I_z = 72.69 \times 10^4 \text{ mm}^4$$

For the hollow interior:

$$I_z = \frac{bh^3}{12} = \frac{20 \times 30^3}{12} = 4.50 \times 10^4 \text{ mm}^4$$

$$Ad^2 = 600(35 - 28.3)^2 = \underline{2.69 \times 10^4 \text{ mm}^4}$$

$$I_z = 7.19 \times 10^4 \text{ mm}^4$$

For the composite section:

$$I_z = (72.69 - 7.19)10^4 = 65.50 \times 10^4 \text{ mm}^4$$

Note particularly that in applying the parallel-axis theorem, each element of the composite area contributes two terms to the total I. One term is the moment of inertia of an area around its own centroidal axis, and the other term is due to the transfer to its axis to the centroid of the whole area. Methodical work is the prime requisite in solving such problems correctly.

8-5.   Applications for the Elastic Flexure Formula

The largest stress at a section of a beam is given by Eq. 8-13, $\sigma_{max} = Mc/I$, and in most practical problems, it is this maximum stress that has to be determined. Therefore, it is desirable to make the process of determining

σ_{max} as simple as possible. This can be accomplished by noting that both I and c are constants for a given section of a beam. Hence, I/c is a constant. Moreover, since this ratio is only a function of the cross-sectional dimensions of a beam, it can be uniquely determined for any cross-sectional area. This ratio is called the *elastic section modulus* of a section and will be designated by S. With this notation, Eq. 8-13 becomes

$$\sigma_{max} = \frac{Mc}{I} = \frac{M}{I/c} = \frac{M}{S} \tag{8-21}$$

or, stated otherwise,

$$\text{maximum bending stress} = \frac{\text{bending moment}}{\text{elastic section modulus}}$$

If the moment of inertia I is measured in in^4 (or m^4) and c in in (or m), S is measured in in^3 (or m^3). Likewise, if M is measured in in-lb or (N · m), the units of stress, as before, become psi (or N/m^2). It bears repeating that the distance c as used here is measured from the neutral axis to the most remote fiber of the beam. This makes $I/c = S$ a minimum, and consequently M/S gives the maximum stress. The efficient sections for resisting elastic bending have as large an S as possible for a given amount of material. This is accomplished by locating as much of the material as possible far from the neutral axis.

The use of the *elastic section modulus* in Eq. 8-21 corresponds somewhat to the use of the area term A in Eq. 1-5 ($\sigma = P/A$). However, only the maximum flexural stress on a section is obtained from Eq. 8-21, whereas the stress computed from Eq. 1-5 holds true across the whole section of the member.

Equation 8-21 is widely used in practice because of its simplicity. To facilitate its use, section moduli for many manufactured cross sections are tabulated in handbooks. Values for a few steel sections are given in Tables 3 to 9 in the Appendix. Equation 8-21 is particularly convenient for the design of beams. Once the maximum bending moment for a beam is determined and an allowable stress is decided upon, Eq. 8-21 may be solved for the required section modulus. This information is sufficient to select a beam. However, a detailed consideration of beam design will be delayed until Chapter 13. This is necessary inasmuch as a shear force, which in turn causes stresses, usually also acts at a beam section. The interaction of the various kinds of stresses must be considered first to gain complete insight into the problem.

The following two examples illustrate calculations for bending stresses at specified sections, where, in addition to bending moments, shears are also required for equilibrium. As shown in the next chapter, the presence of small or moderate shears does not significantly affect the bending stresses in slender beams. Both moment and shear frequently occur at the same selection simultaneously.

Example 8-4

A 300-by-400-mm wooden cantilever beam weighing 0.75 kN/m carries an upward concentrated force of 20 kN at the end, as shown in Fig. 8-12(a). Determine the maximum bending stresses at a section 2 m from the free end.

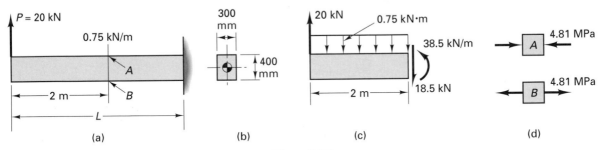

Figure 8-12

SOLUTION

A free-body diagram for a 2-m segment of the beam is shown in Fig. 8-12(c). To keep this segment in equilibrium requires a shear of $20 - (0.75 \times 2) = 18.5$ kN and a bending moment of $(20 \times 2) - (0.75 \times 2 \times 1) = 38.5$ kN·m at the section. Both of these quantities are shown with their proper sense in Fig. 8-12(c). The distance from the neutral axis to the extreme fibers $c = 200$ mm. This is applicable to both the tension and the compression fibers.

From Eq. 8-19,

$$I_z = \frac{bh^3}{12} = \frac{300 \times 400^3}{12} = 16 \times 10^8 \text{ mm}$$

From Eq. 8-13,

$$\sigma_{max} = \frac{Mc}{I} = \frac{38.5 \times 10^6 \times 200}{16 \times 10^8} = \pm 4.81 \text{ MPa}$$

From the sense of the bending moment shown in Fig. 8-12(c), the top fibers of the beam are seen to be in compression and the bottom ones in tension. In the answer given, the positive sign applies to the tensile stress and the negative sign applies to the compressive stress. Both of these stresses decrease at a linear rate toward the neutral axis, where the bending stress is zero. The normal stresses acting on infinitesimal elements at A and B are shown in Fig. 8-12(d). It is important to learn to make such a representation of an element as it will be frequently used in Chapters 11 and 13.

ALTERNATIVE SOLUTION

If only the maximum stress is desired, the equation involving the section modulus may be used. The section modulus for a rectangular section in algebraic form is

$$S = \frac{I}{c} = \frac{bh^3}{12} \frac{2}{h} = \frac{bh^2}{6} \tag{8-22}$$

In this problem, $S = 300 \times 400^2/6 = 8 \times 10^6 \text{ mm}^3$, and by Eq. 6-21,

$$\sigma_{max} = \frac{M}{S} = \frac{38.5 \times 10^6}{8 \times 10^6} = 4.81 \text{ MPa}$$

Both solutions lead to identical results.

Example 8-5

Find the maximum tensile and compressive stresses acting normal to section A—A of the machine bracket shown in Fig. 8-13(a) caused by the applied force of 8 kips.

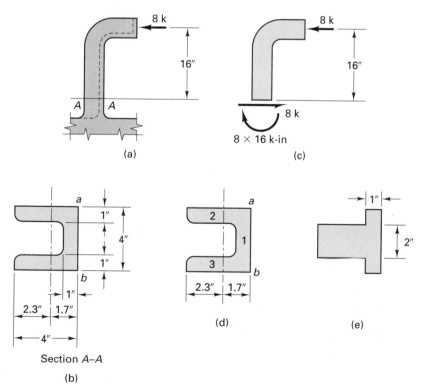

Figure 8-13

SOLUTION

The shear and bending moment of proper magnitude and sense to maintain the segment of the member in equilibrium are shown in Fig. 8-13(c). Next, the neutral axis of the beam must be located. This is done by locating the centroid of the area shown in Fig. 8-13(b); see also Fig. 8-13(d). Then the moment of inertia about the neutral axis is computed. In both these calculations, the legs of the cross section are assumed to be rectangular, neglecting fillets. Then, keeping in mind the sense of the resisting bending moment and applying Eq. 8-13, one obtains the desired values.

Area Number	$A(\text{in}^2)$	y (in) (from ab)	Ay
1	4.0	0.5	2.0
2	3.0	2.5	7.5
3	3.0	2.5	7.5
	$\Sigma A = 10.0 \text{ in}^2$		$\Sigma Ay = 17.0 \text{ in}^3$

$$\bar{y} = \frac{\Sigma Ay}{\Sigma A} = \frac{17.0}{10.0} = 1.70 \text{ in} \quad \text{from line } ab$$

$$I = \Sigma (I_o + Ad^2) = \frac{4 \times 1^3}{12} + 4 \times 1.2^2$$

$$+ \frac{2 \times 1 \times 3^3}{12} + 2 \times 3 \times 0.8^2 = 14.43 \text{ in}^4$$

$$\sigma_{max} = \frac{Mc}{I} = \frac{8 \times 16 \times 2.3}{14.43} = 20.4 \text{ ksi} \quad \text{(compression)}$$

$$\sigma_{max} = \frac{Mc}{I} = \frac{8 \times 16 \times 1.7}{14.43} = 15.1 \text{ ksi} \quad \text{(tension)}$$

These stresses vary linearly toward the neutral axis and vanish there. The results obtained would be the same if the cross-sectional area of the bracket were made T-shaped, as shown in Fig. 8-13(e). The properties of this section about the significant axis are the same as those of the channel. Both these sections have an axis of symmetry.

The previous example shows that members resisting flexure may be proportioned so as to have a different maximum stress in tension than in compression. This is significant for materials having different strengths in tension and compression. For example, cast iron is strong in compression and weak in tension. Thus, the proportions of a cast-iron member may be so set as to have a low maximum tensile stress. The potential capacity of the material may thus be better utilized.

Example 8-6

Consider a rectangular beam of two materials bonded together as shown in Fig. 8-14(a). The upper 150-by-250-mm part is wood, $E_w = 10$ GPa; the lower 10-by-150-mm strap is steel, $E_s = 200$ GPa. If this beam is subjected to a bending moment of 30 kN · m around a horizontal axis, using the approach shown in Fig. 8-7, determine the maximum stresses in the wood and steel.

SOLUTION

By applying Eq. 8-16, the location of the neutral axis above the bottom is found:

$$\bar{y}_b = \frac{\displaystyle\int_0^{10} E_s y_b b \, dy_b + \int_{10}^{260} E_w y_b b \, dy_b}{\displaystyle\int_0^{10} E_s b \, dy_b + \int_{10}^{260} E_w b \, dy_b}$$

$$= \frac{200 \times 10^2/2 + 10 \times (260^2 - 10^2)/2}{200 \times 10 + 10 \times 250} = 77.2 \text{ mm}$$

As the beam width cancels out, the remainder of the calculations are carried out for a unit width of the beam. Bypassing the beam strain diagram, as it is the same as that shown in Fig. 8-7(b), the elastic bending stress distribution is shown in Fig. 8-14(b). The location of the neutral surface is indentified by the dimensions 77.2 mm and 182.8 mm. Then, by designating the maximum compressive stress in wood by σ_w^c, several auxiliary qualities are calculated:

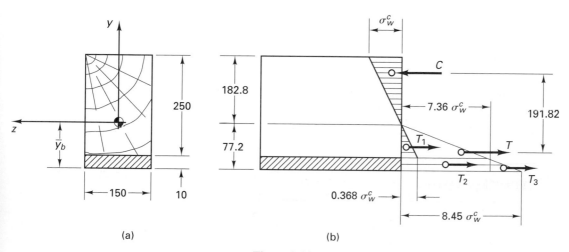

(a) (b)

Figure 8-14

Maximum tensile stress in wood:

$$\sigma_w^t = \sigma_w^c \times (77.2 - 10)/182.8 = 0.368\sigma_w^c$$

On noting that $E_s = 20 \times E_w$, the maximum tensile stress in steel:

$$\sigma_s^t = 20(77.2/182.8) \times \sigma_w^c = 8.45\sigma_w^c$$

Stress in steel at contact surface with wood:

$$\sigma_s = (67.2/77.2) \times \sigma_s^t = 7.36\sigma_w^c$$

Based on these stress quantities, the tensile forces T_1, T_2, T_3 and the compressive force C [see Fig. 8-14(b)] are determined:

$$T_1 = \frac{1}{2} \times 67.2 \times 0.368 \times \sigma_w^c = 12.36\sigma_w^c$$

$$T_2 = 10 \times 7.36 \times \sigma_w^c = 73.6\sigma_w^c$$

$$T_3 = \frac{1}{2} \times 10 \times (8.45 - 7.36) \times \sigma_w^c = 5.45\sigma_w^c$$

Hence, $T = T_1 + T_2 + T_3 = 91.4\sigma_w^c$, and $C = \frac{1}{2} \times 182.8 \times \sigma_w^c = 91.4\sigma_w^c$. Therefore, $T = |C|$, as it should be.

It can be shown that the tensile force resultant T is 7.25 mm from the beam bottom, and the compressive force resultant C is $182.8/3 = 60.93$ mm from the beam top. Therefore, the distance T and C is $260 - 7.25 - 60.93 = 191.82$ mm.

On dividing the applied moment by the width of the beam, the applied moment per unit width of the beam is obtained (i.e., $30 \times 10^6/150 = 200 \times 10^3$ N · mm/mm). Then, dividing this moment by the distance between T and C,

$$T = |C| = 200 \times 10^3/191.82 = 1040 \text{ N/mm}$$

The maximum compressive stress in the wood follows from

$$C = \frac{1}{2} 182.8\sigma_w^c = 1040 \text{ N/mm}$$

Hence, $\sigma_w^c = 11.38$ Mpa, and the maximum tensile stress in steel $\sigma_s^t = 8.45 \times \sigma_w^c = 96.2$ MPa.

8-6. Stress Concentrations

The flexure theory developed in the preceding sections applies only to beams of constant cross section (i.e., *prismatic* beams). If the cross-sectional area of the beam varies gradually, no significant deviation from

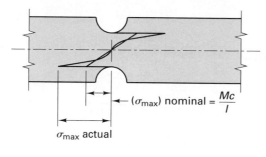

$$K = \frac{(\sigma_{max})\ actual}{(\sigma_{max})\ nominal}$$

Figure 8-15 Meaning of stress-concentration factor in bending.

the stress pattern discussed earlier takes place. However, if notches, grooves, bolt holes, or an abrupt change in the cross-sectional area of the beam occur, high *local* stresses arise. This situation is analogous to the ones discussed earlier for axial and torsion members. Again, it is very difficult to obtain analytical expressions for the actual stress. In the past, most of the information regarding the actual stress distribution came from accurate photoelastic experiments. Numerical methods employing finite elements are now extensively used for the same purpose.

Fortunately, as in the other cases discussed, only the geometric proportions of the member affect the local stress pattern. Moreover, since interest generally is in the maximum stress, stress-concentrations factors may be used to an advantage. The ratio K of the actual maximum stress to the nominal maximum stress in the *minimum* section, as given by Eq. 8-13, is defined as the stress-concentration factor in bending. This concept is illustrated in Fig. 8-15. Hence, in general,

$$(\sigma_{max})_{actual} = K \frac{Mc}{I} \qquad (8\text{-}23)$$

In this equation Mc/I is for the small width of a bar.

Figures 8-16 and 8-17 are plots of stress-concentration factors for two representative cases.[9] The factor K, depending on the proportions of the member, may be obtained from these diagrams. A study of these graphs indicates the desirability of generous fillets and the elimination of sharp notches to reduce local stress concentrations. These remedies are highly desirable in machine design. For ductile materials, where the applied forces are static, stress concentrations are less important.

---

[9] These figures are adapted from a paper by M. M. Frocht, "Factors of stress concentration photoelastically determined," *Trans. ASME*, **57** (1935), A-67.

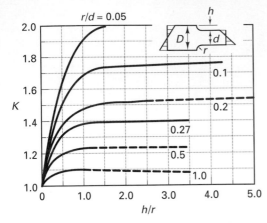

Figure 8-16 Stress-concentration factors in pure bending for flat bars with various fillets.

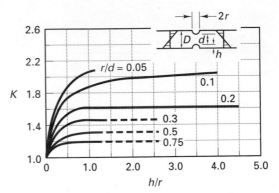

Figure 8-17 Stress-concentration factors in bending for grooved flat bars.

Stress concentrations become particularly significant if the cross-sectional area has reentrant angles. For example, high localized stresses may occur at the point where the flange[10] and the web of an I beam meet. To minimize these, commercially rolled or extruded shapes have a generous fillet at all such points.

In addition to stress concentrations caused by changes in the cross-sectional area of a beam, another effect is significant. Forces often are applied over a limited area of a beam. Moreover, the reactions act only locally on a beam at the points of support. In the previous treatment, all such forces were idealized as concentrated forces. In practice, the average bearing pressure between the member delivering such a force and the beam are computed at the point of contact of such forces with the beam. This bearing pressure, or stress, acts normal to the neutral surface of a beam and is at *right angles to the bending stresses discussed in this chapter*. A more detailed study of the effect of such forces shows that they cause a disturbance of all stresses on a local scale, and the bearing pressure as normally computed is a crude approximation. The stresses at right angles to the flexural stresses behave more nearly as shown in Fig. 3-9.

The reader must remember that the stress-concentration factors apply only while the material behaves elastically. Inelastic behavior of material tends to reduce these factors.

---

[10]The *web* is a thin vertical part of a beam. Thin horizontal parts of a beam are called *flanges.*

8-7. Elastic Strain Energy in Pure Bending

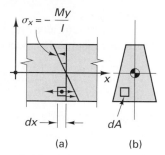

In Section 3-5, the elastic strain energy for an infinitesimal element subjected to a normal stress was formulated. Using this as a basis, the elastic strain energy for beams in pure bending can be found. For this case, the normal stress varies linearly from the neutral axis, as shown in Fig. 8-18, and, according to Eq. 8-11, in simplified notation, this stress $\sigma = -My/I$. The volume of a typical infinitesimal beam element is $dx\,dA$, where dx is its length and dA is its cross-sectional area. By substituting these expressions into Eq. 3-15 and integrating over the volume V of the beam, the expression for the elastic strain energy U in a beam in pure bending is obtained:

$$U = \int_V \frac{\sigma_x^2}{2E}\,dV = \int_V \frac{1}{2E}\left(-\frac{My}{I}\right)^2 dx\,dA$$

Figure 8-18 A beam segment for deriving strain energy in bending.

Rearranging terms and remembering that M at a section of a beam is constant and that the order of performing the integration is arbitrary,

$$U = \int_{\text{length}} \frac{M^2}{2EI^2}\,dx \int_{\text{area}} y^2\,dA = \int_0^L \frac{M^2\,dx}{2EI} \tag{8-24}$$

where the last simplification is possible since, by definition, $I = \int y^2\,dA$. Equation 8-24 reduces the volume integral for the elastic energy of prismatic beams in pure flexure to a single integral taken over the length L of a beam.

Alternatively, Eq. 8-24 can be derived from a different point of view, by considering an elementary segment of a beam dx long, as is shown in Fig. 8-19. Before the application of bending moments M, the two planes perpendicular to the axis of the beam are parallel. After the application of the bending moments, extensions of the same two planes, which remain planes, intersect at O, and the angle included between these two planes is $d\theta$. Moreover, since the full value of the moment M is attained *gradually,* the *average* moment acting through an angle $d\theta$ is $\frac{1}{2}M\,d\theta$. Hence, the external work W_e done on a segment of a beam is $dW_e = \frac{1}{2}M\,d\theta$. Further, since for small deflections $dx \approx \rho\,d\theta$, where ρ is the radius of curvature of the elastic curve, per Eq. 8-10 $1/\rho = M/EI$. Hence, from the principle of conservation of energy, the internal strain energy of an element of a beam is

$$dU = dW_e = \frac{1}{2}M\,d\theta = \frac{1}{2}M\frac{dx}{\rho} = \frac{M^2\,dx}{2EI}$$

which has the same meaning as Eq. 8-24.

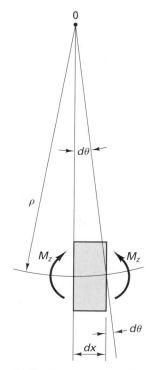

Figure 8-19 Beam segment for alternative derivation of strain energy in bending.

Example 8-7

Find the elastic strain energy stored in a rectangular cantilever beam due to a bending moment M applied at the end; see Fig. 8-20.

SOLUTION

The bending moment at every section of this beam, as well as the flexural rigidity EI, is constant. By direct application of Eq. 8-24,

$$U = \int_0^L \frac{M^2 \, dx}{2EI} = \frac{M^2}{2EI} \int_0^L dx = \frac{M^2 L}{2EI}$$

It is instructive to write this result in another form. Thus, since $\sigma_{max} = Mc/I$, $M = \sigma_{max} I/c = 2\sigma_{max} I/h$, and $I = bh^3/12$,

$$U = \frac{(2\sigma_{max} I/h)^2 L}{2EI} = \frac{\sigma_{max}^2}{2E}\left(\frac{bh\,L}{3}\right) = \frac{\sigma_{max}^2}{2E}\left(\frac{1}{3}\,vol\right)$$

For a given maximum stress, the volume of the material in this beam is only one-third as effective for absorbing energy as it would be in a uniformly stressed bar, where $U = (\sigma^2/2E)(vol)$. This results from *variable* stresses in a beam. If the bending moment also varies along a prismatic beam, the volume of the material becomes even less effective.

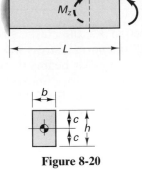

Figure 8-20

8-8. Inelastic Bending of Beams

For reasons of economy, it is becoming increasingly important to determine member strengths beyond the elastic limit. In this section the inelastic bending of beams in the postelastic range of material behavior is considered. Here, as in the elastic case, the discussion is limited to pure bending of beams around an axis perpendicular to the axis of symmetry of the beam cross section. In the next chapter, the elastic bending of beams with unsymmetric cross sections is considered.

The elastic bending theory for beams can be readily extended to inelastic bending by introducing a uniaxial nonlinear stress-strain relationship for the material. The basic requirements of statics and kinematics of deformation remain the same as for the elastic case.

To illustrate the analysis procedure, consider a beam having a cross section such as shown in Fig. 8-21(a). By assuming, as before, that plane sections remain plane after deformation, the longitudinal normal strains vary linearly, as in Fig. 8-21(b). For the several selected strains $\varepsilon_1, \varepsilon_2, \ldots, \varepsilon_5$ in this diagram, the corresponding stresses $\sigma_1, \sigma_2, \ldots, \sigma_5$ are defined on the given stress-strain diagram in Fig. 8-21(c). A plot of these stresses along a section establishes a possible stress distribution in the beam along the curved line AB, as illustrated in Fig. 8-21(d). (Except for vertical scale, this line precisely corresponds to the curved line in the stress-strain diagram.) These stresses, acting on the corresponding area of the cross section, develop a compressive force C above the neutral axis and a tensile force T

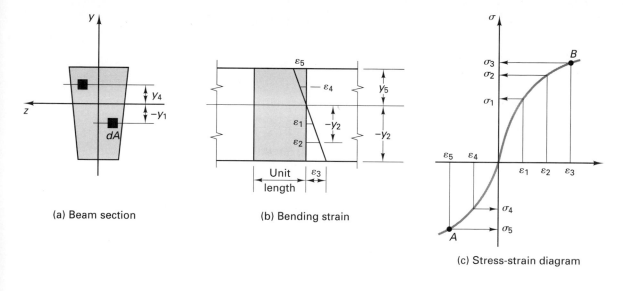

(a) Beam section

(b) Bending strain

(c) Stress-strain diagram

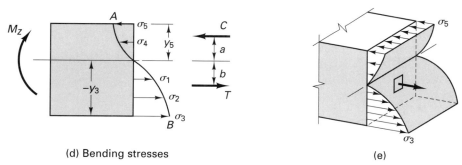

(d) Bending stresses

(e)

Figure 8-21   Inelastic bending of a beam.

below it. When $T = C$, a correct location of the neutral axis is found. This condition is equivalent to the statement that at a section

$$\int_A \sigma \, dA = 0 \qquad (8\text{-}25)$$

where σ is the normal bending stress acting on a section.

Finding the location of the neutral axis such that $T = C$ may require a trial-and-error process, although direct procedures have been devised for some cross sections.[11] After the neutral axis is correctly located, the resisting bending moment M_z at the same section is known to be

[11]A. Nadai, *Theory of Flow and Fracture of Solids,* vol. I (New York: McGraw-Hill, 1950), 356.

$C(a + b)$ or $T(a + b)$, see Fig. 8-21(d). Alternatively, in the form of a general equation,

$$M_z = -\int \sigma y \, dA \qquad (8\text{-}26)$$

The problem is greatly simplified if the beam cross section is symmetric around the horizontal axis and material properties are the same in tension and compression. For these conditions it is known a priori that the neutral axis passes through the centroid of the section, and Eq. 8-26 can be directly applied. The behavior of such a beam in bending is shown qualitatively in Fig. 8-22. A sequence of progressively increasing strains associated with plane sections is shown in Fig. 8-22(b). These maximum strains define the maximum stresses in the outer fibers of the beam, Fig. 8-22(c), resulting in progressively increasing bending stresses.

As can be seen from Figs. 8-22(a) and (c), the maximum attainable stress is σ_3. The instantaneous stress distribution in the beam associated with σ_3, for this brittle material, is given by the curved line AB in Fig. 8-22(c). However, in routine experiments, the *nominal stress* in the extreme fibers is often computed by applying the elastic flexure formula, Eq. 8-13, using the experimentally determined ultimate bending moment. The stress so found is called the *rupture modulus* of the material in bending. This stress is associated with the line CD in Fig. 8-22(c) and is larger than the stress actually attained.

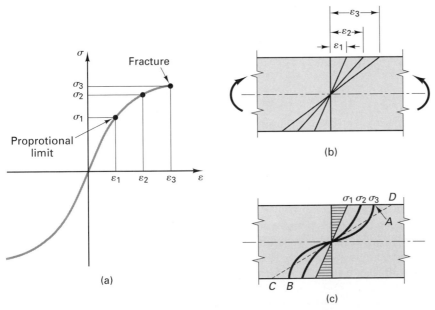

Figure 8-22 Rectangular beam in bending exceeding of the proportional limit of the material.

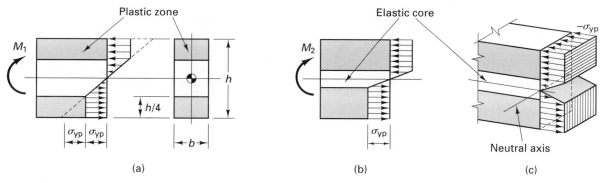

Figure 8-23   Elastic-plastic beam at large levels of training.

The elastic perfectly plastic idealization [Fig. 2-18(b)], for reasons of simplicity, is very frequently used for beams of ductile materials in determining their behavior in bending, and as an important example of inelastic bending. Consider a rectangular beam of elastic-plastic material; see Fig. 8-23. In such an idealization of material behavior, a sharp separation of the member into distinct elastic and plastic zones is possible. For example, if the strain in the extreme fibers is double that at the beginning of yielding, only the middle half of the beam remains elastic; see Fig. 8-23(a). In this case, the outer quarters of the beam yield. The magnitude of moment M_1 corresponding to this condition can be readily computed (see Example 8-10). At higher strains, the elastic zone, or core, diminishes. Stress distribution corresponding to this situation is shown in Figs. 8-23(b) and (c).

Example 8-8

Determine the ultimate plastic capacity in flexure of a mild steel beam of rectangular cross section. Consider the material to be ideally elastic-plastic.

SOLUTION

The idealized stress-strain diagram is shown in Fig. 8-24(a). It is assumed that the material has the same properties in tension and compression. The strains that can take place in steel during yielding are much greater than the maximum elastic strain (15 to 20 times the latter quantity). Since unacceptably large deformations of a beam would occur at larger strains, the plastic moment may be taken as the ultimate moment.

The stress distribution shown in Fig. 8-24(b) applies after a large amount of deformation takes place. In computing the resisting moment, the stresses corresponding to triangular areas *abc* and *bde* may be neglected without unduly impairing the accuracy. They contribute little resistance to the applied bending moment because of their short moment arms. Hence, the

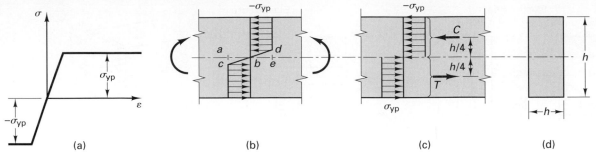

Figure 8-24

idealization of the stress distribution to that shown in Fig. 8-24(c) is permissible and has a simple physical meaning. The whole upper half of the beam is subjected to a *uniform compressive* stress $-\sigma_{yp}$, whereas the lower half is all under a *uniform tension* σ_{yp}. That the beam is divided evenly into a tension and a compression zone follows from symmetry. Numerically,

$$C = T = \sigma_{yp}(bh/2) \quad \text{i.e., stress} \times \text{area}$$

Each one of these forces acts at a distance $h/4$ from the neutral axis. Hence, the *plastic*, or ultimate resisting, moment of the beam is

$$M_p \equiv M_{ult} = C\left(\frac{h}{4} + \frac{h}{4}\right) = \sigma_{yp}\frac{bh^2}{4}$$

where b is the breadth of the beam and h is its height.

The same solution may be obtained by directly applying Eqs. 8-25 and 8-26. Noting the sign of stresses, one can conclude the Eq. 8-25 is satisfied by taking the neutral axis through the middle of the beam. By taking $dA = b\,dy$ and noting the symmetry around the neutral axis, one changes Eq. 8-26 to

$$M_p \equiv M_{ult} = -2\int_0^{h/2} (-\sigma_{yp})yb\,dy = \sigma_{yp}bh^2/4 \qquad (8\text{-}27)$$

The resisting bending moment of a beam of rectangular section when the outer fibers just reach σ_{yp}, as given by the elastic flexure formula, is

$$M_{yp} = \sigma_{yp}I/c = \sigma_{yp}(bh^2/6); \quad \text{therefore, } M_p/M_{yp} = 1.50$$

The ratio M_p/M_{yp} depends only on the cross-sectional properties of a member and is called the *shape factor*. The shape factor just given for the rectangular beam shows that M_{yp} may be exceeded by 50% before the ultimate plastic capacity of a rectangular beam is reached.

For static loads such as occur in buildings, ultimate capacities can be approximately determined using plastic moments. The procedures based on such concepts are referred to as *the plastic method of analysis* or *design*. For such work, *plastic section modulus* Z is defined as follows:

$$M_p = \sigma_{yp}Z \qquad (8\text{-}28)$$

For the rectangular beam just analyzed, $Z = bh^2/4$.

The *Steel Construction Manual*[12] provides a table of plastic section moduli for many common steel shapes. An abridged list of these moduli for steel sections is given in Table 8 of the Appendix. For a given M_p and σ_{yp}, the solution of Eq. 8-28 for Z is very simple.

The method of limit or plastic analysis is unacceptable in machine design in situations where fatigue properties of the material are important.

Example 8-9

Find the residual stresses in a rectangular beam upon removal of the ultimate plastic bending moment.

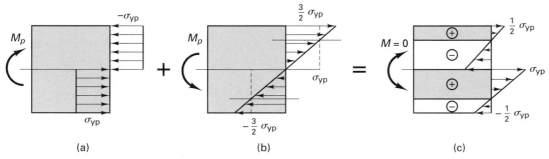

Figure 8-25   Residual stress distribution in a rectangular bar.

SOLUTION

The stress distribution associated with an ultimate plastic moment is shown in Fig. 8-25(a). The magnitude of this moment has been determined in the preceding example and is $M_p = \sigma_{yp}bh^2/4$. Upon release of this plastic moment M_p, every fiber in the beam can rebound elastically. The material elastic range during the unloading is double that which could take place initially (see Fig. 2-18). Therefore, since $M_{yp} = \sigma_{yp}bh^2/6$ and the moment being released is $\sigma_{yp}(bh^2/4)$ or 1.5 M_{yp}, the maximum stress calculated on the basis of elastic action is $\frac{3}{2}\sigma_{yp}$, as shown in Fig. 8-25(b). Superimposing the initial stresses at M_p with the elastic rebound stresses due to the release of M_p, one finds the residual stresses; see Fig. 8-25(c). Both tensile and compressive longitudinal residual stresses remain in the beam. The tensile zones are colored in the figure. If such a beam were machined by gradually reducing its depth, the release of the residual stresses would cause undesirable deformations of the bar.

[12]American Institute of Steel Construction, *AISC Steel Construction Manual*, 2nd ed. (Chicago: AISC, 1994).

Example 8-10

Determine the moment resisting capacity of an elastic-plastic rectangular beam.

SOLUTION

To make the problem more definite, consider a cantilever loaded as shown in Fig. 8-26(a). If the beam is made of ideal elastic-plastic material and the applied force P is large enough to cause yielding, plastic zones will be formed (shown shaded in the figure). At an arbitrary section a–a, the corresponding stress distribution will be shown in Fig. 8-26(c). The elastic zone extends over the depth of $2y_o$. Noting that within the elastic zone the stresses vary linearly and that everywhere in the plastic zone the longitudinal stress is σ_{yp}, the resisting moment M is

$$M = -2\int_0^{y_o}\left(-\frac{y}{y_o}\sigma_{yp}\right)(b\,dy)y - 2\int_{y_o}^{h/2}(-\sigma_{yp})(b\,dy)y \quad (8\text{-}29)$$

$$= \sigma_{yp}\frac{bh^2}{4} - \sigma_{yp}\frac{by_o^2}{3} = M_p - \sigma_{yp}\frac{by_o^2}{3}$$

where the last simplification is done in accordance with Eq. 8-27. In this general equation, if $y_o = 0$, the moment capacity becomes equal to the ultimate plastic moment. However, if $y_o = h/2$, the moment reverts to the limiting elastic case, where $M = \sigma_{yp}bh^2/6$. When the applied bending moment along the span is known, the elastic-plastic boundary can be determined by solving Eq. 8-29 for y_o. As long as an elastic zone or core remains, the plastic deformations cannot progress without a limit. This is a case of contained plastic flow.

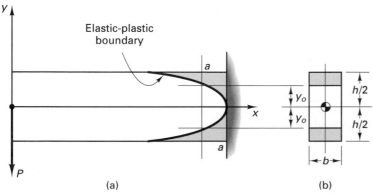
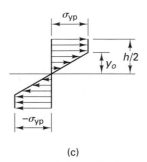

Figure 8-26   Elastic-plastic cantilever beam.

After the applied force P is released, along the length of the beam where plastic deformations occurred, residual stresses will remain. A typical residual stress distribution for this region is shown in Fig. 8-27. This is a more realistic stress distribution pattern than the one shown in Fig. 8-25(c), where the idealization of sharply dividing the tension and compression zones in the beam at the neutral axis in reality is impossible to attain. That pattern of stress distribution represents the limiting case of the stress distribution pattern given in Fig. 8-27. Many inelastic materials tend to have a stress-strain relationship such as shown in Fig. 8-22(a). The residual stress pattern for such materials would resemble the stress difference between curved line AB and straight line CD of Fig. 8-22(c).

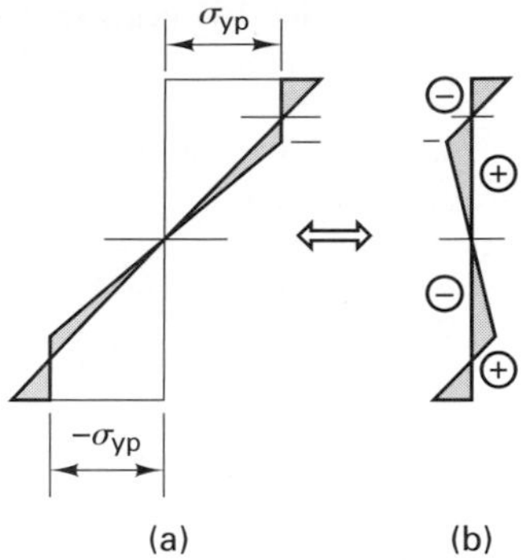

Figure 8-27   Residual stress distribution in the beam.

Example 8-11

Determine the plastic moment strength for the reinforced concrete beam in Example 8-13. Assume that the steel reinforcement yields at 40,000 psi and that the ultimate strength of concrete $f'_c = 2500$ psi..

SOLUTION
When the reinforcing steel begins to yield, large deformations commence. This is taken to be the ultimate capacity of steel; hence, $T_{ult} = A_s\sigma_{yp}$.

At the ultimate of plastic moment, experimental evidence indicates that the compressive stresses in concrete can be approximated by the rectangular stress block shown in Fig. 8-28.[13] It is customary to assume the

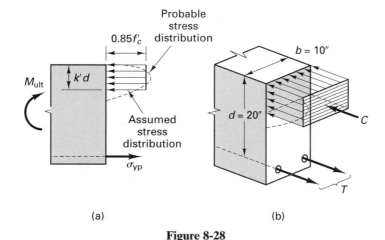

Figure 8-28

[13]For further details, see P. M. Ferguson, J. E. Breen, and J. O. Jirsa, *Reinforced Concrete Fundamentals,* 5th ed. (New York: Wiley, 1988); or R. Park and T. Paulay, *Reinforced Concrete Structures* (New York: Wiley, 1975).

average stress in this compressive stress block to be $0.85 f_c'$. On this basis, keeping in mind that $T_{ult} = C_{ult}$, one has

$$T_{ult} = \sigma_{yp} A_s = 40{,}000 \times 2 = 80{,}000 \text{ lb} = C_{ult}$$

$$k'd = \frac{C_{ult}}{0.85 f_c' b} = \frac{80{,}000}{0.85 \times 2500 \times 10} = 3.77 \text{ in}$$

$$M_{ult} = T_{ult}(d - k'd/2) = 80{,}000(20 - 3.77/2)/12 = 121{,}000 \text{ ft-lb}$$

8-9. Beams of Composite Cross Section

Important uses of beams made of different materials occur in practice. Wooden beams are sometimes reinforced by metal straps, plastics are reinforced with fibers, and reinforced concrete is concrete with steel reinforcing bars. The elastic bending theory discussed before can be readily extended to include such beams of composite cross section.

Consider an elastic beam of several materials bonded together with a vertical axis of symmetry, as shown in Fig. 8-29(a). The elastic moduli E_i for the different materials are given. As for a homogeneous material, the longitudinal extensional strains ε_x are assumed to vary linearly, as shown in Fig. 8-29(b). The neutral axis for this section, passing through the *modulus-weighted* centroid, is located by the distance $\bar{y}_b$ and can be calculated using Eq. 8-16. The stresses shown in Fig. 8-29(c) follow from Eq. 8-14. At the interfaces between two materials, depending on the relative values of their E_i's, a sharp discontinuity in stress magnitudes arises.

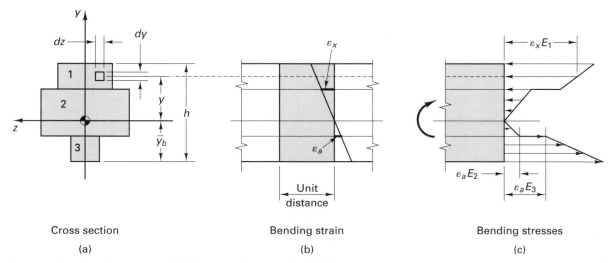

Cross section	Bending strain	Bending stresses
(a)	(b)	(c)

Figure 8-29 Elastic beam composite cross section in bending.

Following the same procedures as in Eq. 8-7, the resisting bending moment

$$M_z = \kappa \int_A E_i y^2 \, dA = \kappa(EI)* \qquad (8\text{-}30)$$

where the curvature κ, being constant for the section, is taken outside the integral, and $(EI)*$ defines symbolically the value of the integral in the middle expression. Hence,

$$\kappa = \frac{M_z}{(EI)*} \qquad (8\text{-}31)$$

and, by substituting this relation into Eqs. 8-3 and 8-14,

$$\varepsilon_x = -\frac{M_z}{(EI)*} y \quad \text{and} \quad \sigma_x = E_i \frac{M_z}{(EI)*} y \qquad (8\text{-}32)$$

where the last expression is an analogue to Eq. 8-11 and can be immediately specialized for a homogeneous beam.

In calculations of bending of composite cross sections, sometimes it is useful to introduce the concept of an *equivalent* or *transformed cross-sectional area* in *one* material. This requires arbitrary selection of a *reference* E_i, defined here as E_{ref}. Using this notation, the integral in Eq. 8-15, for constant curvature κ, can be recast as follows:

$$\boxed{\int_A E_i y \, dA = E_{\text{ref}} \int_a y \frac{E_i}{E_{\text{ref}}} \, dA = E_{\text{ref}} \int_A y(n_i \, dA) = 0} \qquad (8\text{-}33)$$

where $n_i \, dA = (E_i/E_{\text{ref}}) \, dA$. Therefore, a beam of composite cross section can be considered to have the mechanical properties of the *reference material,* provided the differential areas dA are multiplied by n_i, the ratio of E_i to E_{ref}. After transforming a cross section in this manner, conventional elastic analysis is applicable. In transformed sections the stresses *vary linearly* from the neural axis in *all* materials. The actual stresses are obtained for the reference material, whereas the stresses in the other materials must be multiplied by n_i.

This procedure is illustrated in the two examples that follow.

Example 8-12

Consider a composite beam of the cross-sectional dimensoins shown in Fig. 8-30(a). The upper 150-by-250-mm part is wood, $E_w = 10$ GPa; the lower 10-by-150-mm strap is steel, $E_s = 200$ GPa. If this beam is subjected to a bending moment of 30 kN · m around a horizontal axis, what are the maximum stresses in the steel and wood?

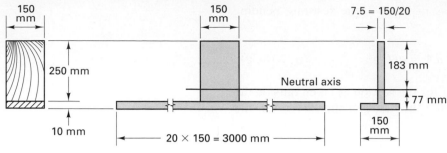

Figure 8-30

SOLUTION

Select E_w as E_{ref}. Then $n_s = E_s/E_w = 20$. Hence, the transformed cross section is as in Fig. 8-30(b) with the equivalent width of steel equal to $150 \times 20 = 3000$ mm. The centroid and moment of inertia around the centroidal axis for this transformed section are, respectively,

$$\bar{y} = \frac{150 \times 250 \times 125 + 10 \times 3000 \times 255}{150 \times 250 + 10 \times 3000} = 183 \text{ mm} \quad \text{(from the top)}$$

$$I_z = \frac{150 \times 250^3}{12} + 150 \times 250 \times 58^2 + \frac{3000 \times 10^3}{12} + 10 \times 3000 \times 72^2$$

$$= 478 \times 10^6 \text{ mm}^4$$

The maximum stress in the wood is

$$(\sigma_w)_{max} = \frac{Mc}{I} = \frac{0.03 \times 10^9 \times 183}{478 \times 10^6} = 11.5 \text{ MPa}$$

The maximum stress in the steel is

$$(\sigma_s)_{max} = n\sigma_w = 20 \times \frac{0.03 \times 10^9 \times 77}{478 \times 10^6} = 96.7 \text{ MPa}$$

ALTERNATIVE SOLUTION

Select E_s as E_{ref}. Then $n_w = E_w/E_s = 1/20$, and the transformed section is as in Fig. 8-30(c).

$$\bar{y} = \frac{7.5 \times 250 \times 135 + 150 \times 10 \times 5}{7.5 \times 250 + 150 \times 10}$$

$$= 77 \text{ mm} \quad \text{(from the bottom)}$$

$$I_z = \frac{7.5 \times 250^3}{12} + 7.5 \times 250 \times 58^2 + \frac{150 \times 10^3}{12}$$

$$+ 150 \times 10 \times 72^2 = 23.9 \times 10^6 \text{ mm}^4$$

$$(\sigma_s)_{\text{max}} = \frac{0.03 \times 10^9 \times 77}{23.9 \times 10^6} = 96.7 \text{ Mpa}$$

$$(\sigma_w)_{\text{max}} = \frac{\sigma_s}{n} = \frac{1}{20} \times \frac{0.03 \times 10^9 \times 183}{23.9 \times 10^6} = 11.5 \text{ MPa}$$

Note that if the transformed section is an equivalent wooden section, the stresses in the actual wooden piece are obtained directly. Conversely, if the equivalent section is steel, stresses in steel are obtained directly. The stress in a material stiffer than the material of the transformed section is increased, since, to cause the same unit strain, a higher stress is required.

Example 8-13

Determine the maximum stress in the concrete and the steel for a rein-forced-concrete beam with the section shown in Fig. 8-31(a) if it is sub-jected to a positive bending moment of 50,000 ft-lb. The reinforcement consists to two #9 steel bars. (These bars are $1\frac{1}{8}$ in in diameter and have a cross-sectional area of 1 in².) Assume the ratio of E for steel to that of con-crete to be 15 (i.e., $n = 15$).

SOLUTION
Plane sections are assumed to remain plane in an elastic reinforced-concrete beam. Strains vary linearly from the neutral axis, as shown in Fig. 8-31(b) by the line ab. A transformed section in terms of concrete is used to solve this problem. However, concrete is so weak in tension that there is no assurance that minute cracks will not occur in the tension zone

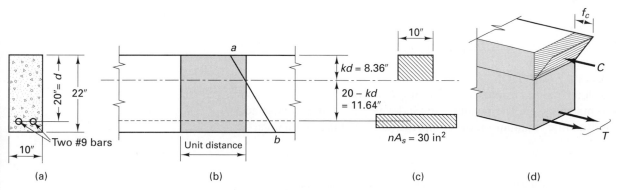

Figure 8-31

of the beam. For this reason, no credit is given to concrete for resisting tension. On the basis of this assumption, concrete in the tension zone of a beam only holds the reinforcing steel in place.[14] Hence, in this analysis, it virtually does not exist at all, and the transformed section assumes the form shown in Fig. 8-31(c). The cross section of concrete has the beam shape above the neutral axis; below it, no concrete is shown. Steel, of course, can resist tension, so it is shown as the transformed concrete area. For computation purposes, the steel is located by a single dimension from the neutral axis to its centroid. There is a negligible difference between this distance and the true distances to the various steel fibers.

So far, the idea of the neutral axis has been used, but its location is unknown. However, it is known that this axis coincides with the axis through the centroid of the transformed section. It is further known that the first (or statical) moment of the area on one side of a centroidal axis is equal to the first moment of the area on the other side. Thus, let kd be the distance from the top of the beam to the centroidal axis, as shown in Fig. 8-31(c), where k is the unknown ratio[15] and d is the distance from the top of the beam to the center of the steel. An algebraic restatement of the foregoing locates the neutral axis, about which I is computed and stresses are determined as in the preceding example.

$$\underbrace{10(kd)}_{\substack{\text{concrete} \\ \text{area}}} \quad \underbrace{(kd/2)}_{\text{arm}} = \underbrace{30}_{\substack{\text{transformed} \\ \text{steel area}}} \quad \underbrace{(20 - kd)}_{\text{arm}}$$

$$5(kd)^2 = 600 - 30(kd)$$

$$(kd)^2 + 6(kd) - 120 = 0$$

Hence,

$$kd = 8.36 \text{ in} \quad \text{and} \quad 20 - kd = 11.64 \text{ in}$$

$$I = \frac{10(8.36)^3}{12} + 10(8.36)\left(\frac{8.36}{2}\right)^2 + 0 + 30(11.64)^2 = 6020 \text{ in}^4$$

$$(\sigma_c)_{max} = \frac{Mc}{I} = \frac{50,000 \times 12 \times 8.36}{6020} = 833 \text{ psi}$$

$$\sigma_s = n\frac{Mc}{I} = \frac{15 \times 50,000 \times 12 \times 11.64}{6020} = 17,400 \text{ psi}$$

ALTERNATIVE SOLUTION

After kd is determined, instead of computing I, a procedure evident from Fig. 8-31(d) may be used. The resultant force developed by the stresses acting in a "hydrostatic" manner on the compression side of the beam must be

---

[14]Actually, it is used to resist shear and provide fireproofing for the steel.

[15]This conforms to the usual notation used in books on reinforced concrete. In this text, h is generally used to represent the height or depth of the beam.

located $kd/3$ below the top of the beam. Moreover, if b is the width of the beam, this resultant force $C = \frac{1}{2}(\sigma_c)_{max}b(kd)$ (average stress times area). The resultant tensile force T acts at the center of the steel and is equal to $A_s\sigma_s$, where A_s is the cross-sectional area of the steel. Then, if jd is the distance between T and C, and since $T = C$, the applied moment M is resisted by a couple equal to Tjd or Cjd.

$$jd = d - kd/3 = 20 - (8.36/3) = 17.21 \text{ in}$$

$$M = Cjd = \frac{1}{2}b(kd)(\sigma_c)_{max}(jd)$$

$$(\sigma_c)_{max} = \frac{2M}{b(kd)(jd)} = \frac{2 \times 50,000 \times 12}{10 \times 8.36 \times 17.21} = 833 \text{ psi}$$

$$M = Tjd = A_s\sigma_s jd$$

$$\sigma_s = \frac{M}{A_s(jd)} = \frac{50,000 \times 12}{2 \times 17.21} = 17,400 \text{ psi}$$

Both methods naturally give the same answer. The second method is more convenient in practical applications. Since steel and concrete have different allowable stresses, the beam is said to have balanced reinforcement when it is designed so that the respective stresses are at their allowable level simultaneously. Note that the beam shown would have become virtually worthless if the bending moments were applied in the opposite direction.

8-10. Curved Bars

The flexure theory for curved bars is developed in this section. Attention is confined to bars having an axis symmetry of the cross section, with this axis lying in one plane along the length of the bar. Only the elastic case is treated,[16] with the usual proviso that the elastic modulus is the same in tension and compression.

Consider a curved member such as shown in Figs. 8-32(a) and (b). The outer fibers are at a distance of r_o from the center of curvature O. The inner fibers are at a distance of r_i. The distance from 0 to the centroidal axis is $\bar{r}$. The solution[17] of this problem is again based on the familiar assumption: Sections perpendicular to the axis of the beam remain plane after a

---

[16]For plastic analysis of curved bars, see, for example, H. D. Conway, "Elastic-plastic bending of curved bars of constant and variable thickness," *J. Appl. Mech.* 27/no. 4 (December 1960), 733–734.

[17]This approximate solution was developed by E. Winkler in 1858. The exact solution of the same problem by the methods of the mathematical theory of elasticity is due to M. Golovin, who solved it in 1881.

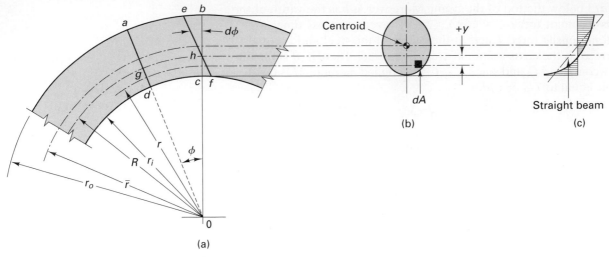

Figure 8-32   Curved bar in pure bending.

bending moment M is applied. This is diagrammatically represented by the line *ef* in relation to an element of the beam *abcd*. The element is defined by the central angle ϕ.

Although the basic deformation assumption is the same as for straight beams, and, from Hooke's law, the normal stress $\sigma = E\varepsilon$, a difficulty is encountered. The initial length of a beam fiber such as *gh* depends upon the distance r from the center of curvature. Thus, although the total deformation of beam fibers (described by the small angle $d\phi$) follows a linear law, strains do not. The elongation of a generic fiber *gh* is $(R - r) d\phi$, where R is the distance from 0 to the neutral surface (not yet known), and its initial length is $r\phi$. The strain ε of any arbitrary fiber is $(R - r)(d\phi)/r\phi$, and the normal stress σ on an element dA of the cross-sectional area is

$$\sigma = E\varepsilon = E\frac{(R - r)\, d\phi}{r\phi} \qquad (8\text{-}34)$$

For future use, note also that

$$\frac{\sigma r}{R - r} = \frac{E\, d\phi}{\phi} \qquad (8\text{-}35)$$

Equation 8-34 gives the normal stress acting on an element of area of the cross section of a curved beam. The location of the neutral axis follows from the condition that the summation of the forces acting perpendicular to the section must be equal to zero; that is,

$$\Sigma F_n = 0 \qquad \int_A \sigma\, dA = \int_A \frac{E(R - r)\, d\phi}{r\phi}\, dA = 0$$

However, since E, R, ϕ and $d\phi$ are constant at any one section of a stressed bar, they may be taken outside the integral sign and a solution for R obtained. Thus,

$$\frac{E\,d\phi}{\phi}\int_A \frac{R - r}{r}\,dA = \frac{E\,d\phi}{\phi}\left(R\int_A \frac{dA}{r} - \int_A dA\right) = 0$$

$$R = \frac{A}{\displaystyle\int_A dA/r} \tag{8-36}$$

where A is the cross-sectional area of the beam and R locates the neutral axis. Note that the neutral axis so found does not coincide with the centroidal axis. This differs from the situation found to be true for straight elastic beams.

Now that the location of the neutral axis is known, the equation for the stress distribution is obtained by equating the external moment to the internal resisting moment built up by the stresses given by Eq. 8-34. The summation of moments is made around the z axis, which is normal to the plane of the figure at O in Fig. 8-32(a).

$$\sum M_z = 0 \qquad M = \int_A \underset{\text{force}}{\sigma\,dA}\ \underset{\text{arm}}{(R - r)} = \int_A \frac{E(R - r)^2\,d\phi}{r\phi}\,dA$$

Again, remembering that E, R, ϕ, and $d\phi$ are constant at a section, using Eq. 8-35, and performing the algebraic steps indicated, the following is obtained:

$$M = \frac{E\,d\phi}{\phi}\int_A \frac{(R - r)^2}{r}\,dA = \frac{\sigma r}{R - r}\int_A \frac{(R - r)^2}{r}\,dA$$

$$= \frac{\sigma r}{R - r}\int_A \frac{R^2 - Rr - Rr + r^2}{r}\,dA$$

$$= \frac{\sigma r}{R - r}\left(R^2\int_A \frac{dA}{r} - R\int_A dA - R\int_A dA + \int_A r\,dA\right)$$

Here, since R is a constant, the first two integrals vanish, as may be seen from the expression in parentheses appearing just before Eq. 8-36. The third integral is A, and the last integral, by definition, is $\bar{r}A$, where $\bar{r}$ is the radius of the centroidal axis. Hence,

$$M = \frac{\sigma r}{R - r}(\bar{r}A - RA)$$

from where the normal stress acting on a curved beam at a distance r from the center of curvature is

$$\sigma = \frac{M(R - r)}{rA(\bar{r} - R)} \tag{8-37}$$

If positive y is measured toward the center of curvature from the neutral axis, and $\bar{r} - R = e$, Eq. 8-37 may be written in a form that more closely resembles the flexure formula for straight beams:

$$\sigma = \frac{My}{Ae(R - y)} \qquad (8\text{-}38)$$

These equations indicate that the stress distribution in a curved bar follows a hyperbolic pattern. A comparison of this result with the one that follows from the formula for straight bars is shown in Fig. 8-32(c). Note particularly that in the curved bar, the neutral axis is pulled toward the center of the curvature of the beam. This results from the higher stresses developed below the neutral axis. The theory developed applies, of course, only to elastic stress distribution and only to beams in pure bending. For a consideration of situations where an axial force is also present at a section, see Example 9-3.

Example 8-14

Compare stresses in a 50-by-50-mm rectangular bar subjected to end moments of 2083 N · m in three special cases: (a) straight beam, (b) beam curved to a radius of 250 mm along the centroidal axis (i.e., $\bar{r} = 250$ mm), Fig. 8-33(a), and (c) beam curved to $\bar{r} = 75$ mm.

SOLUTION
(a) This follows directly by applying Eqs. 8-21 and 8-22:

$$S = bh^2/6 = 50 \times 50^2/6 = 20.83 \times 10^3 \text{ mm}^3$$

$$\sigma_{\text{max}} = \frac{M}{S} = \frac{2083 \times 10^3}{20.83 \times 10^3} = \pm 100 \text{ MPa}$$

This result is shown in Fig. 8-33(c). $\bar{r} = \infty$ since a straight bar has an infinite radius of curvature.

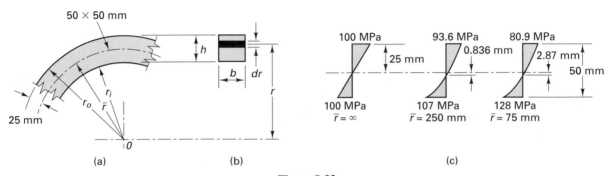

Figure 8-33

To solve parts (b) and (c), the neutral axes must be located first. This is found in general terms by integrating Eq. 8-36. For the rectangular section, the elementary area is taken as $b\,dr$, Fig. 8-33(b). The integration is carried out between the limits r_i and r_o, the inner and outer radii, respectively. We have

$$R = \frac{A}{\int_A dA/r} = \frac{bh}{\int_{r_i}^{r_o} b\,dr/r} = \frac{h}{\int_{r_i}^{r_o} dr/r}$$

$$= \frac{h}{|\ln r|_{r_i}^{r_o}} = \frac{h}{\ln (r_o/r_i)} = \frac{h}{2.3026 \log (r_o/r_i)} \tag{8-39}$$

where h is the depth of the section, ln is the natural logarithm, and log is a logarithm with a base of 10 (common logarithm).

(b) For this case, $h = 50$ mm, $\bar{r} = 250$ mm, $r_i = 225$ mm, and $r_o = 275$ mm. The solution is obtained by evaluating Eqs. 8-39 and 8-37. Subscript i refers to the normal stress σ of the inside fibers; o of the outside fibers.

$$R = \frac{50}{(\ln 275/225)} = 249.164 \text{ mm}$$

$$e = \bar{r} - R = 250 - 249.164 = 0.836 \text{ mm}$$

$$\sigma_i = \frac{M(R - r_i)}{r_i A(\bar{r} - R)} = \frac{2083 \times 10^3 \times (249.164 - 225)}{225 \times 50^2 \times 0.836}$$

$$= 107 \text{ MPa}$$

$$\sigma_o = \frac{M(R - r_o)}{r_o A(\bar{r} - R)} = \frac{2083 \times 10^3 \times (249.164 - 275)}{275 \times 50^2 \times 0.836}$$

$$= -93.6 \text{ MPa}$$

The negative sign of σ_o indicates a compressive stress. These quantities and the corresponding stress distribution are shown in Fig. 8-33(c); $\bar{r} = 250$ mm.

(c) This case is computed in the same way. Here $h = 50$ mm, $\bar{r} = 75$ mm $r_i = 50$ mm and $r_o = 100$. Results of the computation as shown in Fig. 8-33(c).

$$R = \frac{50}{\ln (100/50)} = \frac{50}{\ln 2} = 72.13 \text{ mm}$$

$$e = \bar{r} - R = 75 - 73.13 = 2.87 \text{ mm}$$

$$\sigma_i = \frac{2083 \times 10^3 \times (72.13 - 50)}{50 \times 50^2 \times 2.87} = 128 \text{ MPa}$$

$$\sigma_o = \frac{2083 \times 10^3 \times (72.13 - 100)}{100 \times 50^2 \times 2.87} = -80.9 \text{ MPa}$$

Several important conclusions, generally true, may be reached from the preceding example. First, *the usual flexure formula is reasonably good for beams of large radii.* Only 7% error in the maximum stress occurs in part (b) for $\bar{r}/h = 5$, an error tolerable for most applications. For great ratios of $\bar{r}/h$, this error diminishes. As the curvature of the beam increases, the stress on the concave side rapidly increases over the one given by the usual flexure formula. When $\bar{r}/h = 1.5$, a 28% error occurs. Second, the evaluation of the integral for R over the cross-sectional area may become very complex. Finally, calculations of R must be very accurate since differences between R and numerically comparable quantities are used in the stress formula.

The last two difficulties prompted the development of other methods of solution. One such method consists of expanding certain terms of the solution into a series,[18] another of building up a solution on the basis of a special transformed section. Yet another approach consists of working "in reverse." Curved beams of various cross sections, curvatures, and applied moments are analyzed for stress; then these quantities are divided by a flexural stress that would exist for the same beam *if it were straight.* These ratios are then tabulated.[19] Hence, conversely, if stress in a curved beam is wanted, it is given as

$$\sigma = K\frac{Mc}{I} \qquad (8\text{-}40)$$

where the coefficient K is obtained from a table or a graph and Mc/I is computed as in the usual flexure formula.

An expression for the distance from the center of curvature to the neutral axis of a curved beam of circular cross-sectional area is now given for future reference:

$$R = \frac{\bar{r} + \sqrt{\bar{r}^2 - c^2}}{2} \qquad (8\text{-}41)$$

where $\bar{r}$ is the distance from the center of curvature to the centroid and c is the radius of the circular cross-sectional area.

[18] S. Timoshenko, *Strength of Materials,* 3rd ed., Part I (Princeton: NJ: Van Nostrand, 1955), 369 and 373.

[19] R. J. Roark and W. C. Young, *Formulas for Stress and Strain,* 5th ed. (New York: McGraw-Hill, 1975).

PROBLEMS

Sections 8-3 through 8-8

8-1 through 8-8. Determine the bending moment capacities around the horizontal axes for the cross-sectional areas with the dimensions shown in the figures. The allowable elastic stress is either 165 MPa or 24 ksi. For properties of W steel shapes, channels, and angles, see Tables 3, 4, 5, and 6, respectively, in the Appendix.

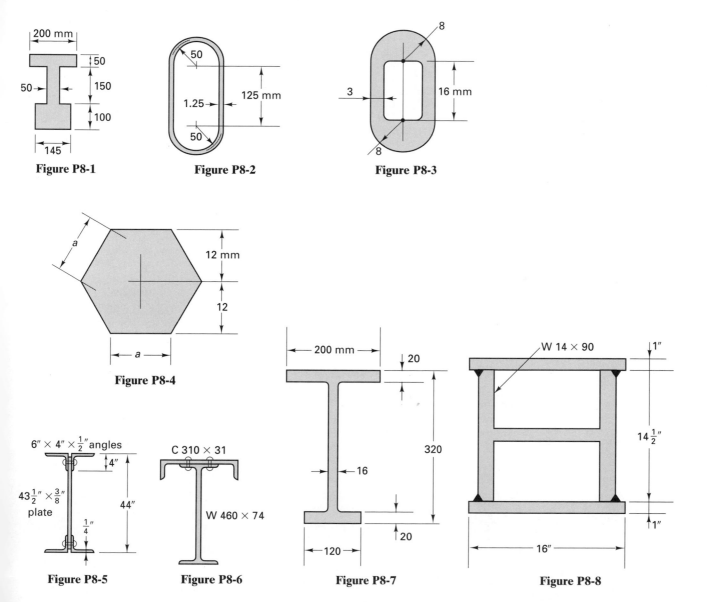

Figure P8-1

Figure P8-2

Figure P8-3

Figure P8-4

Figure P8-5

Figure P8-6

Figure P8-7

Figure P8-8

8-9. For the three cross sections shown in the figure, the same amount of material is employed in each case. Calculate the moments of inertia I and the elastic section moduli I/c for these sections. The first parameter determines stiffness (see Chapter 14) and the second determines the strength of a cross section, Eq. 8-21.

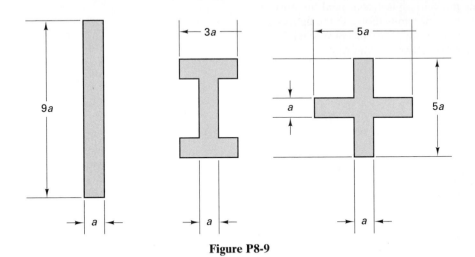

Figure P8-9

8-10. Verify the section moduli given in the Appendix tables for S 310×74, W 360×134, and C 380×50.

8-11. A W 460×74 steel beam is supported at A and B as shown in the figure. What is the magnitude of the uniformly distributed load if a strain gage attached to the top of the upper flange measures 0.0002 mm/mm when the load is applied? $E = 200$ GPa.

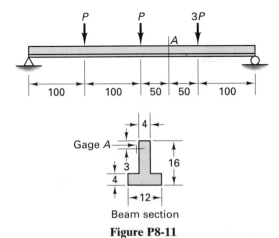

Beam section

Figure P8-11

8-12. A small steel T beam is used in an inverted position to span 400 mm. If, due to the application of the three forces shown in the figure, the longitudinal gage at A registers a compressive strain of 50×10^{-5}, how large are the applied forces? $E = 200$ GPa.

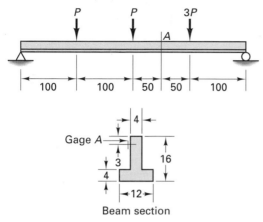

Beam section

Figure P8-12

8-13 and 8-14. Determine *elastic* positive bending-moment capacities around the horizontal axes for beams having the cross sections shown in the figures. The maximum elastic stress in tension for Problem 8-13 is 10 ksi and, in compression, 15 ksi; the corresponding stresses for Problem 8-14 are 100 MPa and 150 MPa.

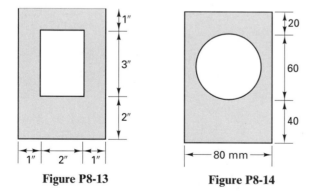

Figure P8-13   **Figure P8-14**

8-15. A beam having a solid rectangular cross section with the dimensions shown in the figure is subjected to a positive bending moment of 16 kN · m acting around the horizontal axis. (a) Find the compressive force acting on the shaded area of the cross section developed by the bending stresses. (b) Find the tensile force acting on the cross-hatched area of the cross section.

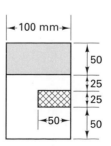

Figure P8-15

8-16.   Consider a linearly elastic beam subjected to a bending moment M around its principal axis z for which the moment of inertia of the cross-sectional area is I. Show that for such a beam, the normal force F acting on any part of the cross-sectional area A_1 is

$$F = MQ/I$$

where

$$Q = \int_{A_1} y \, dA = \bar{y} A_1$$

and $\bar{y}$ is the distance from the neutral axis of the cross section to the centroid of the area A_1, as shown in the figure.

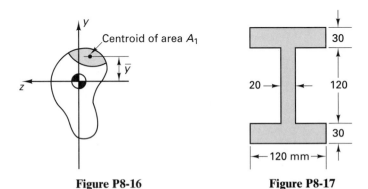

Figure P8-16   **Figure P8-17**

8-17.   Determine the magnitude and position of the total tensile force T acting on this section when a positive moment of 80 kN · m is applied. Since the magnitude of this tensile force T equals the compressive force C acting on the section, verify that the T–C couple is equal to the applied moment.

8-18.   Two 2×6 in full-sized wooden planks are glued together to form a T section, as shown in the figure.

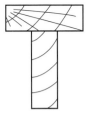

Figure P8-18

If a positive bending moment of 2270 ft-lb is applied to such a beam acting around a horizontal axis, (a) find the stresses at the extreme fibers, (b) calculate the total compressive force developed by the normal stresses above the neutral axis because of the bending of the beam, and (c) find the total force due to the tensile bending stresses at a section, and compare it with the result found in (b).

8-19. By integration, determine the force developed by the bending stresses and its position acting on the shaded area of the cross section of the beam shown in the figure if the beam is subjected to a negative bending moment of 3500 N · m acting around the horizontal axis.

Figure P8-19　　　　**Figure P8-20**

8-20. A beam has the cross section of an isosceles triangle, as shown in the figure, and is subjected to a negative bending moment of 4000 N · m around the horizontal axis. (a) Show by integration that $I_o = bh^3/36$. (b) Determine the location and magnitude of the resultant tensile and compressive forces acting on a section if $b = h = 150$ mm.

8-21. For a linearly elastic material, at the same maximum stress for a square member in the two different positions shown in the figure, determine the ratio of the bending moments. Bending takes place around the horizontal axis.

8-22. Show that the elastic stress in a rectangular beam bent around its diagonal can be reduced by removing the small triangular areas, as shown in the figure. This is referred to as the Emerson paradox.[1] [*Hint:* Let the sides of the removed triangular areas be ka, where k is constant. In calculating I for the section, treat it as consisting of two rectangles, the large one having sides $(1 - k)a$, and the small one having the width $ka\sqrt{2}$.]

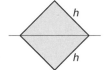

Figure P8-21

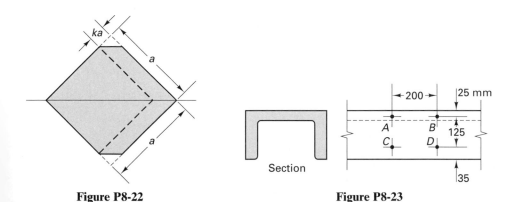

Figure P8-22　　　　**Figure P8-23**

8-23 A channel-shaped member shown in the figure acts as a horizontal beam in a machine. When vertical forces are applied to this member, the distance AB increases by 0.025 mm and the distance CD decreases by 0.230 mm. What is the sense of the applied moment, and what normal stresses occur in the extreme fibers? $E = 200$ MPa.

---

[1]In 1864, in Saint-Venant's additions to Navier's book he calls the removed fibers useless. However, he, as well as Emerson, recognized that the *elastic* failure of these fibers does not indicate that the truncated section possesses greater static strength than the complete section. However, in machine design, for members subjected to fatigue, the removal of sharp corners may be advantageous. See I. Todhunter and K. Pearson, *A History of the Theory of Elasticity and of the Strength of Materials* (New York: Dover, 1960). Vol II, Part I, p. 109.

8-24.   A solid steel beam having the cross-sectional dimensions partially shown in the figure was loaded in the laboratory in pure bending. Bending took place around a horizontal neutral axis. Strain measurements showed that the top fibers contracted 0.0003 m/m longitudinally; the bottom fibers elongated 0.0006 m/m longitudinally. Determine the total normal force that acted on the shaded area indicated in the figure at the time the strain measurements were made. $E = 200$ GPa. All dimensions are in mm.

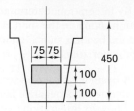

Figure P8-24

8-25.   As the screw of a large steel C clamp, such as shown in the figure, is tightened upon an object, the strain in the horizontal direction due to bending only is being measured by a strain gage at point B. If a strain of 900×10^{-6} in/in is noted, what is the force on the screw corresponding to the value of the observed strain? $E = 30 \times 10^6$ psi.

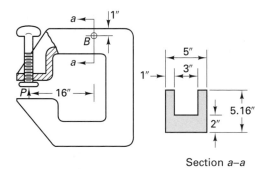

Section *a–a*

Figure P8-25

8-26.   A T beam shown in the figure is made of a material the behavior of which may be idealized as having a tensile proportional limit of 20 MPa and a compressive proportional limit of 40 MPa. With a factor of safety of $1\frac{1}{2}$ on the initiation of yielding, find the magnitude of the largest force F that may be applied to this beam in a downward direction as well as in an upward direction. Base answers only on the consideration of the maximum bending stresses caused by F.

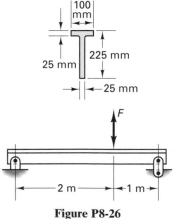

Figure P8-26

8-27. A 150×300 mm rectangular section is subjected to a positive bending moment of $240\,000$ N · m around the "strong" axis. The material of the beam is non-isotropic and is such that the modulus of elasticity in tensions is $1\frac{1}{2}$ times as great as in compression; see the figure. If the stresses do not exceed the proportional limit, find the maximum tensile and compressive stresses in the beam.

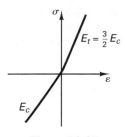

Figure P8-27

8-28 through 8-30. Using the procedure shown in Example 8-6, consider the beam cross sections shown in the figures. In Problems 8-28 and 8-29, the upper and side plates, respectively, as well as the upper piece in Problem 8-30 are brass, with an $E_b = 86$ GPa. The other pieces bonded to the brass are steel, with an $E_s = 200$ GPa. Determine the flexural strength for the cross sections around the horizontal axis such that the stresses would not exceed 40 MPa.

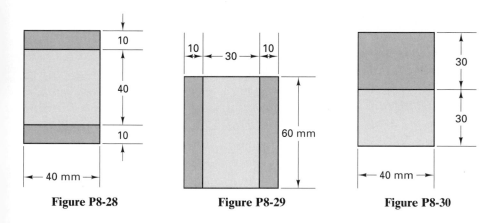

Figure P8-28	**Figure P8-29**	**Figure P8-30**

8-31. A composite beam of two different materials has the cross section shown in Fig. 8-7(a). For the upper 50×80 mm bar, the elastic modulus $E_1 = 15$ GPa, and the lower 50×20 mm bar, $E_2 = 40$ GPa. Find the maximum bending stresses in both materials caused by an applied positive moment of 12 kN · m acting around the z axis.

Section 8-6

8-32. A small beam, shown in the figure, is to carry a cyclically applied load of 80 N/mm. The beam is 12-mm thick and spans 160 mm. Determine the maximum stress at midspan and at depth transition points. Assume that the factors given in Fig. 8-16 are sufficiently accurate. Do not consider the stress concentrations at the supports.

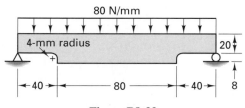

Figure P8-32

8-33.   Considering the beam of a 160-mm span and the loading conditions given in the preceding problem, determine the distances from the supports such that the stresses at midspan and at the depth transition points are the same.

Figure P8-33

8-34.   Suppose that a flat nickel steel bar serves as a machine part subjected to cyclic force P as shown in the figure. Determine the allowable magnitude of this force if for the imposed requirement the allowable stress is 500 MPa.

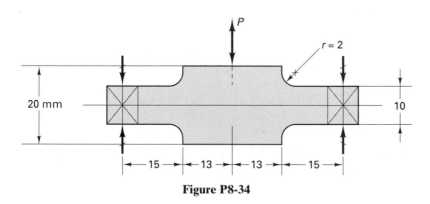

Figure P8-34

Section 8-7

8-35.   Show the elastic strain energy due to bending for a simple uniformly loaded beam of rectangular cross section is $(\sigma_{max}^2/2E)(\frac{8}{45}AL)$, where σ_{max} is the maximum bending stress, A is the cross-sectional area, and L is the length of the beam.

8-36.   Show that $U_{bending} = (\sigma_{max}^2/2E)(\text{Vol}/9)$ for a cantilever of rectangular cross section supporting a concentrated load P at the end.

Section 8-8

8-37 through 8-41.   Find the ratios M_{ult}/M_{yp} for beams having the cross sections shown in the figures. Bending occurs around the horizontal axes. Assume idealized elastic-plastic behavior, as in Example 8-8.

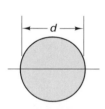

Figure P8-37

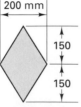

Figure P8-38

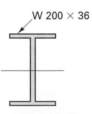

Figure P8-39

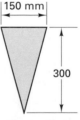

Figure P8-40

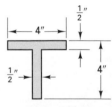

Figure P8-41

8-42. Find the ultimate moment capacity for a beam having the cross section shown for Problem 8-1. Assume that the material yields in tension and in compression at 200 MPa.

8-43. A steel I beam subjected to pure bending develops a longitudinal strain of -1.6×10^{-3} in the top flange in the location shown on the figure. (a) What bending moment causes this strain? Assume ideal elastic-plastic material behavior with $E = 200$ GPa and $\sigma_{yp} = 240$ MPa. (b) What residual strain would remain in the gage upon release of the applied load? (c) Draw the residual stress pattern.

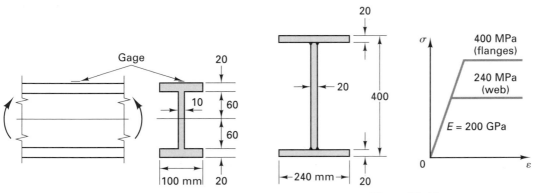

Figure P8-43   **Figure P8-44**

8-44. An I beam is made up from three steel plates welded together as shown in the figure. The flanges are of stronger steel than the web. (a) What bending moment would the section develop when the largest stresses in the flanges just reach yield? The stress-strain properties of the two steels can be idealized as shown on the diagram. (b) Draw the residual stress pattern.

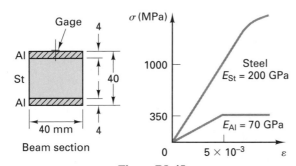

Figure P8-45

8-45. A small sandwich beam spanning 400 mm is made up by bonding two aluminum alloy strips to an alloy steel bar, as shown in the figure. The idealized stress-strain diagrams are shown in the figure. What is the magnitude of the applied bending moment if it causes -7.5×10^{-3} longitudinal strain in the gage glued to the top of the aluminum alloy strip?

8-46. On applying a bending moment around the horizontal axis to the T beam having the dimensions shown in the figure, the measured longitudinal strain at gage A is -2×10^{-3}. Determine the magnitude of the applied bending moment if the stress-strain relation for the material can be idealized as shown on the diagram.

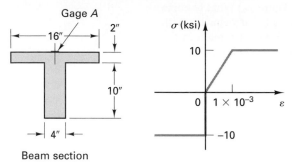

Figure P8-46

8-47. A 100×180 mm rectangular beam is of a material with the stress-strain characteristics shown in the figure. (a) Find the largest moment for which the entire cross section remains elastic. (b) Determine the ultimate moment capacity, and draw the resulting stress distribution. (c) What is the residual stress distribution after a release of the ultimate bending moment? (d) Show that the residual stresses are self-equilibrating.

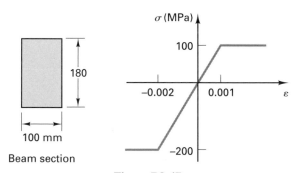

Figure P8-47

Section 8-9

Problems 8-28 through 8-30 can be assigned for solution using transformed sections, and vice versa, for Problems 8-48 through 8-50.

8-48. Consider a composite beam whose cross section is made from three different materials bonded together, as shown in Fig. 8-29(a). Bar 1 is 40×20 mm and has an elastic modulus $E_1 = 15$ GPa; bar 2 is 60×40 mm with $E_2 = 10$ GPa; and bar 3 is 20×20 mm with $E_3 = 30$ GPa. Determine the maximum bending stresses in each of the three materials caused by an applied moment of 10 kN · m acting around the z axis. Do not use the method of transformed sections; use the method shown in Example 8-6.

8-49 through 8-51. Using transformed sections, determine the maximum bending stresses in each of the two materials for the composite beams shown in the figures when subjected to positive bending moments of 80 kN · m each. E_{St} = 210 GPa and E_{Al} = 70 GPa. (*Hint for Problem 8-50:* For an ellipse with semiaxes a and b, $I = \pi a b^3/4$ around the major centroidal axis.)

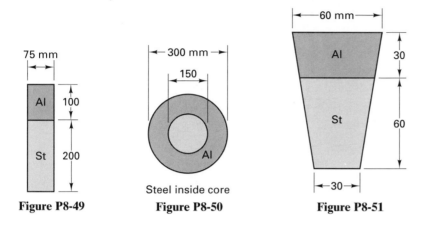

Figure P8-49   Figure P8-50   Figure P8-51

8-52 and 8-53. Determine the allowable bending moment around horizontal neutral axes for the composite beams of wood and steel plates having the cross-sectional dimensions shown in the figures. Materials are fastened so that they act as a unit. E_{St} = 30 × 10⁶ psi and E_w = 1.2 × 10⁶ psi. The allowable bending stresses are σ_{St} = 20 ksi and σ_w = 1.2 ksi.

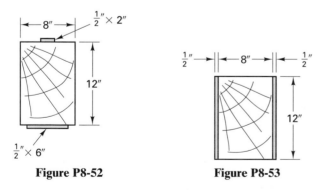

Figure P8-52   Figure P8-53

8-54. A 150-mm-thick concrete slab is longitudinally reinforced with steel bars, as shown in the figure. Determine the allowable bending moment per 1-m width of this slab. Assume n = 12 and the allowable stresses for steel and concrete as 150 MN/m² and 8 MN/m², respectively.

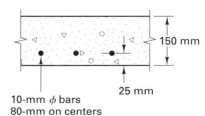

10-mm ϕ bars
80-mm on centers

Figure P8-54

8-55. A beam has the cross section shown in the figure and is subjected to a positive bending moment that causes a tensile stress in the steel of 20 ksi. If $n = 12$, what is the value of the bending moment?

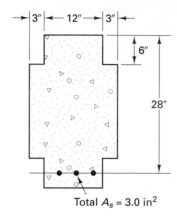

Total $A_s = 3.0$ in^2

Figure P8-55

Section 8-10

8-56. Reword Example 8-14 by changing h to 100 mm.

8-57. Derive Eq. 8-41.

8-58. What is the largest bending moment that may be applied to a curved bar, such as shown in Fig. 8-32(a), with $\bar{r} = 3$ in, if it has a circular cross-sectional area of 2 in diameter and the allowable stress is 12 ksi?

9

Unsymmetric (Skew) Beam Bending

9-1. Introduction

In this chapter, stress analysis of beam bending (discussed in the preceding chapter) is extended to more general cases. First, elastic unsymmetric (skew) bending of prismatic beams with doubly symmetric cross sections is considered. Then, employing the method of superposition, elastic bending with axial forces is treated. Inelastic bending with axial forces of doubly symmetric sections is considered next. This is followed by a discussion of bending of prismatic beams with arbitrary cross section. In order to treat this topic, basic equations for the area moments and products of inertia are established, followed by equations for the principal axes of inertia. Using these equations, the general equations for determining linear elastic bending stresses in beams with arbitrary cross section are established.

Part A   DOUBLY SYMMETRIC CROSS SECTIONS

9-2. Bending about Both Principal Axes

As a simple example of **skew** or unsymmetrical pure bending, consider the rectangular beam shown in Fig. 9-1. The applied moments M act in the plane *abcd*. By using the vector representation for **M** shown in Fig. 9-1(b), this vector forms an angle α with the z axis and can be resolved into the two components, M_y and M_z. Since the cross section of this beam has symmetry about both axes, the formulas derived in Section 8-3 are directly applicable. Because of symmetry, the product of inertia for this section is zero, and the orthogonal axes shown are the *principal* axes for the cross section. This also holds true for the centroidal axes of singly symmetric areas. (For details see Section 9-6 and 9-7.)

By assuming *elastic* behavior of the material, a superposition of the stresses caused by M_y and M_z is the solution to the problem. Hence, using Eqs. 8-11 and 8-12,

$$\sigma_x = -\frac{M_z y}{I_z} + \frac{M_y z}{I_y} \tag{9-1}$$

where all terms have the previously defined meanings.

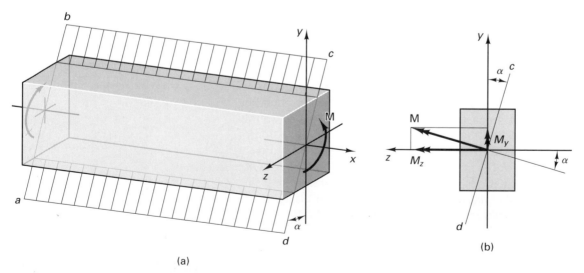

(a)

(b)

Fig. 9-1   Unsymmetric (skew) bending of a beam with doubly symmetric cross section.

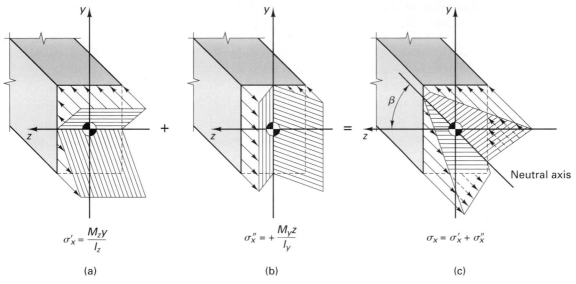

$$\sigma'_x = \frac{M_z y}{I_z}$$

$$\sigma''_x = +\frac{M_y z}{I_y}$$

$$\sigma_x = \sigma'_x + \sigma''_x$$

(a)   (b)   (c)

Fig. 9-2   Superposition of elastic bending stresses.

A graphical illustration of superposition is given in Fig. 9-2. Note that a line of zero stress (i.e., a neutral axis) forms at an angle β with the z axis. Analytically, such an axis can be determined by setting the stress given by Eq. 9-1 to zero; that is,

$$-\frac{M_z y}{I_z} + \frac{M_y z}{I_y} = 0 \quad \text{or} \quad \tan \beta = \frac{y}{z} = \frac{M_y I_z}{M_z I_y} \qquad (9\text{-}2)$$

Since, in general, $M_y = M \sin \alpha$ and $M_z = M \cos \alpha$, this equation reduces to

$$\tan \beta = \frac{I_z}{I_y} \tan \alpha \qquad (9\text{-}3)$$

This equation shows that unless $I_z = I_y$, or α is either $0°$ or $90°$, the angles α and β are not equal. Therefore, in general, the neutral axis and the normal to a plane in which the applied moment acts do not coincide.

The results just given can be generalized to apply to beams having cross sections of any shape provided the *principal* axes are employed. To justify this statement, consider a beam with the arbitrary cross section shown in Fig. 9-3. Let such an elastic beam be bent about the *principal z* axis and assume that the stress distribution is given as $\sigma_x = -M_z y/I_z$, Eq. 8-11. If this stress distribution causes no bending moment M_y around the y axis, this is the correct solution of the problem. Forming such an expression gives

$$M_y = \int_A -\frac{M_z}{I_z} yz\, dA = -\frac{M_z}{I} \int_A yz\, dA = 0 \qquad (9\text{-}4)$$

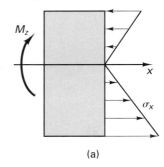

(a)

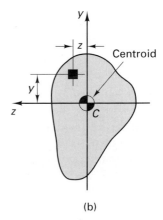

(b)

Fig. 9-3   Pure bending around a principal axis.

where the constants are placed in front of the second integral, which is equal to zero because, by definition, a product of inertia for a principal axis vanishes.

By virtue of the foregoing, the restriction placed on the elastic flexure formula at the beginning of the chapter limiting it to applications for symmetric cross sections can be removed. However, in the application of Eq. 9-1, *the principal axes for a cross section must be used.* A procedure for bypassing this requirement is given in Section 9-8.

Example 9-1

The 100-by-150-mm wooden beam shown in Fig. 9-4(a) is used to support a uniformly distributed load of 4 kN (total) on a simple span of 3 m. The applied load acts in a plane making an angle of 30° with the vertical, as shown in Fig. 9-4(b) and again in Fig. 9-4(c). Calculate the maximum bending stress at midspan, and, for the same section, locate the neutral axis. Neglect the weight of the beam.

SOLUTION

The maximum bending *in the plane of the applied load* occurs at midspan, and, according to Example 7-8, it is equal to $w_oL^2/8$ or $WL/8$, where W is the total load on span L. Hence,

$$M = \frac{WL}{8} = \frac{4 \times 3}{8} = 1.5 \text{ kN} \cdot \text{m}$$

Next, this moment is resolved into components acting around the respective axes, and I_z and I_y are calculated:

$$M_z = M \cos \alpha = 1.5 \times \sqrt{3}/2 = 1.3 \text{ kN} \cdot \text{m}$$

$$M_y = M \sin \alpha = 1.5 \times 0.5 = 0.75 \text{ kN} \cdot \text{m}$$

$$I_z = 100 \times 150^3/12 = 28.1 \times 10^6 \text{ mm}^4$$

$$I_y = 150 \times 100^3/12 = 12.5 \times 10^6 \text{ mm}^4$$

By considering the sense of the moment components, it can be concluded that the maximum tensile stress occurs at A. Similar reasoning applies when considering the other corner points. Alternatively, the values for the coordinate points can be substituted directly into Eq. 9-1. On either basis,

$$\sigma_A = -\frac{M_z(-c_1)}{I_z} + \frac{M_yc_2}{I_y} = \frac{1.3 \times 10^6 \times 75}{28.1 \times 10^6} + \frac{0.75 \times 10^6 \times 50}{12.5 \times 10^6}$$

$$= +3.47 + 3.00 = +6.47 \text{ MPa}$$

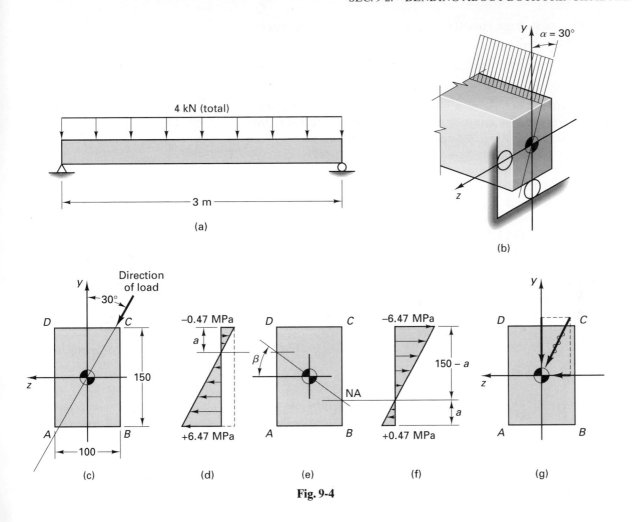

Fig. 9-4

$$\sigma_B = +3.47 - 3.00 = +0.47 \text{ MPa}$$

$$\sigma_C = -3.47 - 3.00 = -6.47 \text{ MPa}$$

$$\sigma_D = -3.47 + 3.00 = -0.47 \text{ MPa}$$

Note that the stress magnitudes on diametrically opposite corners are numerically equal.

The neutral axis is located by the angle β, using Eq. 9-3:

$$\tan \beta = \frac{28.1 \times 10^6}{12.5 \times 10^6} \tan 30° = 1.30 \quad \text{or} \quad \beta = 52.4°$$

Alternatively, it can be found from the stress distribution, which varies linearly between any two points. For example, from similar triangles, $a/(150 - a) = 0.47/6.47$, giving $a = 10.2$ mm. This locates the neutral axis shown in Fig. 9-4(e) as it must pass through the section centroid. These results lead to the same β.

When unsymmetrical bending of a beam is caused by applied transverse forces, another procedure equivalent to that just given *is often more convenient.* The applied forces are first resolved into components that act parallel to the principal axes of the cross-sectional area. Then the bending moments caused by these components around the respective axes are computed for use in the flexure formula. In Example 9-1, such components of the applied load are shown in Fig. 9-4(g). To avoid *torsional stresses,* the applied transverse forces must act through the *shear center,* a concept discussed in the next chapter. For bilaterally symmetrical sections (e.g., a rectangle, a circle, an I beam, etc.), the *shear center coincides with the geometric center (centroid) of the cross section.* For other cross sections, such as a channel, the shear center lies elsewhere, as at *S* shown in Fig. 9-5, and it is at this point that the transverse force must be applied to prevent occurrence of torsional stresses. Single angles acting as beams must be treated similarly (see Fig. 10-24). For analysis of unsymmetrical bending, the applied forces must be resolved *at* the shear center parallel to the principal axes of the cross section.

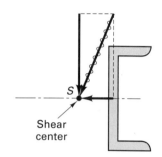

Fig. 9-5 Lateral force through shear center *S* causes no torsion.

9-3. Elastic Bending with Axial Loads

A solution for pure bending around both principal axes of a member can be extended to include the effect of axial loads by employing *superposition.* Such an approach is applicable only in the range of *elastic* behavior of members. Further, if an applied axial force causes compression, a member must be stocky, lest a buckling problem of the type considered in Chapter 16 arise. With these reservations, Eq. 9-1 can be generalized to read

$$\sigma_x = \frac{P}{A} - \frac{M_z y}{I_z} + \frac{M_y z}{I_y} \qquad (9\text{-}5)$$

where P is taken positive for axial tensile forces, and bending takes place around the two *principal y* and *z* axes.

For the particular case of an eccentrically applied force, consider the case shown in Fig. 9-6(a). By applying two equal but opposite forces P at centroid C, as shown in Fig. 9-6(b), an *equivalent* problem is obtained. In this formulation, the applied axial force P acting at C gives rise to the term P/A in Eq. 9-5; whereas a couple Pd developed by the opposed forces P a distance d apart causes unsymmetrical bending. The moment Pd applied by this couple can be resolved into two components along the principal

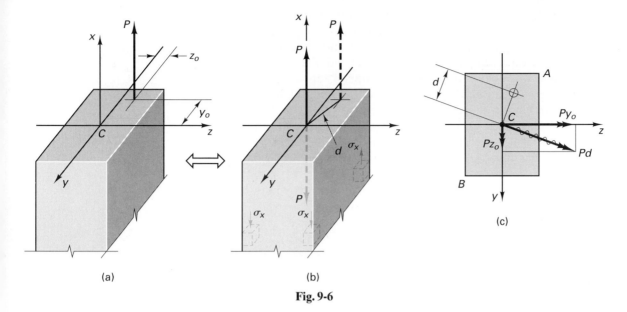

(a)   (b)

Fig. 9-6

(c)

axes, as shown in Fig. 9-6(c). These components are $M_y = Pz_o$ and $M_z = Py_o$. Since the sense of these moments coincides with the positive directions of the y and z axes, these moments in Eq. 9-6 are positive.

Provided the principal axes are used, Eq. 9-5 can be applied to members of any cross section. In some instances, however, it may be more advantageous to use an arbitrary set of orthogonal axes and to determine the bending stresses using Eq. 9-33 given in Section 9-8. To complete a solution, the normal stress caused by axial force must be superposed.

It is instructive to note that in calculus, the equation of a plane is given as

$$Ax + By + Cz + D = 0 \qquad (9\text{-}6)$$

where A, B, C, and D are constants. By setting $A = 1$, $x = \sigma_x$, $B = M_z/I_z$, $C = -M_y/I_y$, and $D = -P/A$, it can be recognized that Eq. 9-5 defines a plane. Similarly, since $\varepsilon = \sigma/E$, Eq. 9-5 can be recast in terms of strain to read

$$\varepsilon_x = x = -(by + cz + d) \qquad (9\text{-}7)$$

where $a = 1$, and b, c, and d are constants. Since this equation also defines a plane, the basic strain assumption of the simplified engineering theory of flexure is verified. However, because of the presence of axial strain due to P, the "plane sections" not only rotate, but also translate an amount P/AE.

Based on the preceding discussion, it can be concluded that the longitudinal strain magnitudes in members subjected to bending and axial forces can be represented by distances from a reference plane to an inclined plane. The same is true for *elastic* stresses. These inclined planes intersect the reference plane in a line. This line of *zero stress* or *strain* is analogous to the neutral axis occurring in pure bending. Unlike the former case, however, when $P \neq 0$, this line does not pass through the centroid of a section. For large axial forces and small bending moments, the line of zero stress or strain may lie outside a cross section. The significance of this line is that the normal stresses or strains vary from it linearly.

It should be noted that in many instances, the bending moment in a member is caused by transverse forces rather than by an eccentrically applied axial force, such as illustrated in Fig. 9-6. In such cases, Eq. 9-5 remains applicable.

Several illustrative examples follow, beginning with situations where bending takes place only around one of the principal axes.

Example 9-2

A 50-by-75-mm, 1.5-m-long elastic bar of negligible weight is loaded as shown in mm in Fig. 9-7(a). Determine the maximum tensile and compressive stresses acting normal to the section through the beam.

SOLUTION

To emphasize the method of superposition, this problem is solved by dividing it into two parts. In Fig. 9-7(b), the bar is shown subjected only to the axial force, and in Fig. 9-7(c) the same bar is shown subjected only to the transverse force. For the axial force, the normal stress throughout the length of the bar is

$$\sigma = \frac{P}{A} = \frac{25 \times 10^3}{50 \times 75} = 6.67 \text{ MPa} \quad \text{(tension)}$$

This result is indicated in Fig. 9-7(d). The normal stresses due to the transverse force depend on the magnitude of the bending moment, and the maximum bending moment occurs at the applied force. As the left reaction is 2.7 kN, $M_{max} = 2.7 \times 10^3 \times 375 = 1.013 \times 10^6$ N · mm. From the flexure formula, the maximum stresses at the extreme fibers caused by this moment are

$$\sigma = \frac{Mc}{I} = \frac{6M}{bh^2} = \frac{61 \times 1.013 \times 10^6}{50 \times 75^2} = \pm 21.6 \text{ MPa}$$

These stresses act normal to the section of the beam and decrease linearly toward the neutral axis, as in Fig. 9-7(e). Then, to obtain the compound stress for any particular element, bending stresses must be added algebraically to the direct tensile stress. Thus, as may be seen from Fig. 9-7(f), at point A, the resultant normal stress is 14.9 MPa compression, and at B, it is

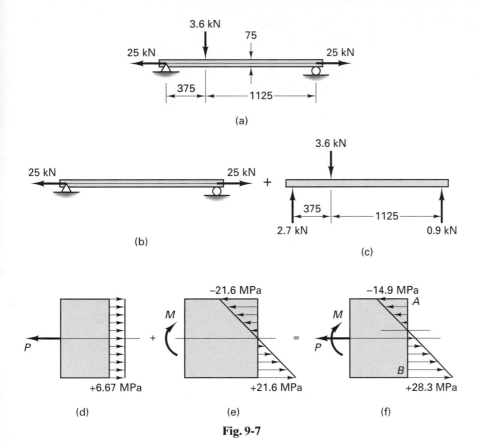

Fig. 9-7

28.3 MPa tension. Side views of the stress vectors as commonly drawn are shown in the figure.

Although in this problem the given axial force is larger than the transverse force, bending causes higher stresses. However, the reader is cautioned not to regard slender compression members in the same light.

Note that in the final result, the line of zero stress, which is located at the centroid of the section for flexure, moves upward. Also note that the local stresses, caused by the concentrated force, which act normal to the top surface of the beam, were not considered. Generally, these stresses are treated independently as local bearing stresses.

The stress distribution shown in Fig. 9-7(f) would change if instead of the axial tensile forces applied at the ends, compressive forces of the same magnitude were acting on the member. The maximum tensile stress would be reduced to 14.9 MPa from 28.3 MPa, which would be desirable in a beam made of a material weak in tension and carrying a transverse load. This idea is utilized in prestressed construction. Tendons made of high-strength steel rods or cable passing through a beam with anchorages at the ends are used to precompress concrete beams. Such artificially applied forces inhibit the development of tensile stresses. Prestressing also has been used in racing-car frames.

Example 9-3

A 50-by-50-mm elastic bar bent into a ∪ shape, as in Fig. 9-8(a), is acted upon by two opposing forces P of 8.33 kN each. Determine the maximum normal stress occurring at section A–B.

SOLUTION
The section to be investigated is in the curved region of the bar, but this makes no essential difference in the procedure. First, a segment of the bar is taken as a free body, as shown in Fig. 9-8(b). At section A–B, the axial force, applied at the centroid of the section, and the bending moment necessary to maintain equilibrium are determined. Then, each element of the force system is considered separately. The stress caused by the axial forces is

$$\sigma = \frac{P}{A} = \frac{8.33 \times 10^3}{50 \times 50} = 3.33 \text{ MPa} \quad \text{(compression)}$$

and is shown in the first diagram of Fig. 9-8(c). The normal stresses caused by the bending moment may be obtained by using Eq. 8-37. However, for this bar, bent to a 75-mm radius, the solution is already known from Example 8-14. The stress distribution corresponding to this case is shown in the second diagram of Fig. 9-8(c). By superposing the results of these two solutions, the compound stress distribution is obtained. This is shown in the

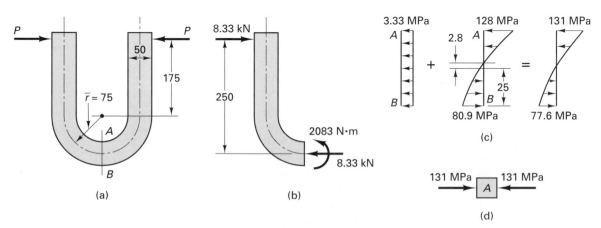

Fig. 9-8

third diagram of Fig. 9-8(c). The maximum compressive stress occurs at A and is 131 MPa. An isolated element for point A is shown in Fig. 9-8(d). Shear stresses are absent at section $A-B$ as no shear force is necessary to maintain equilibrium of the segment shown in Fig. 9-8(b). The relative insignificance of the stress caused by the axial force is striking.

Problems similar to the preceding commonly occur in machine design. Hooks, C clamps, frames of punch presses, etc. illustrate the variety of situations to which the foregoing methods of analysis must be applied.

Example 9-4

Consider a tapered block having a rectangular cross section at the base, as shown in Figs. 9-9(a) and (b). Determine the maximum eccentricity e such that the stress at B caused by the applied force P is zero.

SOLUTION
In order to maintain applied force P in equilibrium, there must be an axial compressive force P and a moment Pe at the base having the senses shown. The stress caused by the axial force is $\sigma = -P/A = -P/bh$, whereas the largest tensile stress caused by bending is $\sigma_{\max} = Mc/I = M/S = 6Pe/bh^2$, where $bh^2/6$ is the elastic section modulus of the rectangular cross section. To satisfy the condition for having stress at B equal to zero, it follows that

$$\sigma_B = -\frac{P}{bh} + \frac{6Pe}{bh^2} = 0 \quad \text{or} \quad e = \frac{h}{6}$$

which means that if force P is applied at a distance of $h/6$ from the centroidal axis of the cross section, the stress at B is just zero. Stress distributions across the base corresponding, respectively, to the axial force and bending moment are shown in Figs. 9-9(c) and (d), and their algebraic sum in Fig. 9-9(e).

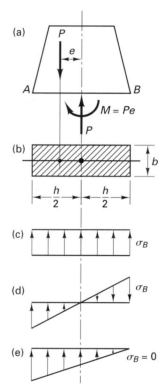

Fig. 9-9   Location of force P causing zero stress at B.

In the preceding problem, if force P were applied closer to the centroid of the section, a smaller bending moment would be developed at a section $A-B$, and there would be some compression stress at B. The same argument may be repeated for the force acting to the right of the centroidal axis. Hence, a practical rule, much used by the early designers of masonry structures, may be formulated thus: *If the resultant of all vertical forces acts within the middle third of the rectangular cross section, there is no tension in the material at that section.* It is understood that the resultant acts in a vertical plane containing one of the axes of symmetry of the rectangular cross-sectional area.

The foregoing discussion may be generalized in order to apply to any planar system of forces acting on a member. The resultant of these forces may be made to intersect the plane of the cross section, as is shown in Fig. 9-10. At the point of intersection of this resultant with the section, it may be resolved into horizontal and vertical components. If the vertical component of the resultant fulfills the conditions of the former problem, no tension will be developed at point B, as the horizontal component causes only shear stresses. Hence, a more general "middle-third" rule may be stated thus: There will be no tension at a section of a member of a *rectangular* cross section if the resultant of the forces above this section *intersects* one of the axes of symmetry of the section within the middle third.

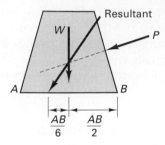

Fig. 9-10   Resultant causing no tension at B.

Example 9-5

Find the stress distribution at section $ABCD$ for the block shown in mm in Fig. 9-11(a) if $P = 64$ kN. At the same section, locate the line of zero stress. Neglect the weight of the block.

SOLUTION

In this problem, it is somewhat simpler to recast Eq. 9-5 with the aid of Eq. 8-22, defining the elastic section modulus $S = I/c$ as $bh^2/6$. The normal stress at any Ith corner of the block can be found directly from such a transformed equation. This equation reads

$$\sigma_1 = \frac{P}{A} - \frac{M_z}{S_z} + \frac{M_y}{S_y} \tag{9-8}$$

where $S_z = bh^2/6$ and $S_y = hb^2/6$.

The forces acting on section $ABCD$, Fig. 9-11(c), are $P = -64 \times 10^3$ N, $M_y = -64 \times 10^3 \times 150 = -9.6 \times 10^6$ N · mm, and $M_z = -64 \times 10^3 \times (75 + 75) = -9.6 \times 10^6$ N · mm. The cross-sectional area has the following properties: $A = 150 \times 300 = 45 \times 10^3$ mm^2, $S_z = 300 \times 150^2/6 = 1.125 \times 10^6$ mm^3, and $S_y = 150 \times 300^2/6 = 2.25 \times 10^6$ mm^3.

The normal stresses at the corners are found using Eq. 9-8, assigning signs for the stresses caused by moments by inspection. For example, from Fig. 9-11(c), it can be seen that due to M_y, the stresses at corners A and D are compressive. Other cases are treated similarly. Using this approach,

$$\sigma_A = -\frac{64 \times 10^3}{45 \times 10^3} - \frac{9.6 \times 10^6}{1.125 \times 10^6} - \frac{9.6 \times 10^6}{2.25 \times 10^6}$$

$$= -1.42 - 8.53 - 4.27 = -14.2 \text{ MPa}$$

$$\sigma_B = -1.42 - 8.53 + 4.27 = -5.7 \text{ MPa}$$

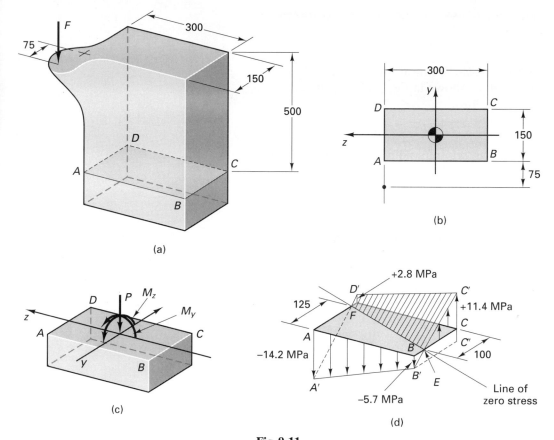

Fig. 9-11

$$\sigma_C = -1.42 + 8.53 + 4.27 = +11.4 \text{ MPa}$$

$$\sigma_D = -1.42 + 8.53 - 4.27 = +2.8 \text{ MPa}$$

These stresses are shown in Fig. 9-11(d). The ends of these four stress vectors at A', B', C', and D' lie in the plane $A'B'C'D'$. The vertical distance between planes $ABCD$ and $A'B'C'D'$ defines the total stress on any point on the cross section. The intersection of plane $A'B'C'D'$ with plane $ABCD$ locates the line of zero stress FE.

By drawing a line $B'C''$ parallel to BC, similar triangles $C'B'C''$ and $C'EC$ are obtained; thus, the distance $CE = [11.4/(11.4 + 5.7)]150 = 100$ mm. Similarly, distance AF is found to be 125 mm. Points E and F locate the line of zero stress. If the weight of the block is neglected, the stress distribution on any other section parallel to $ABCD$ is the same.

Example 9-6

Find the zone over which the vertical downward force P_o may be applied to the rectangular weightless block shown in Fig. 9-12(a) without causing any tensile stresses at the section A–B.

SOLUTION

The force $P = -P_o$ is placed at an arbitrary point in the first quadrant of the yz coordinate system shown. Then the same reasoning used in the preceding example shows that with this position of the force, the greatest tendency for a tensile stress exists at A. With $P = -P_o$, $M_z = +P_o y$, and $M_y = -P_o z$, setting the stress at A equal to zero fulfills the limiting condition of the problem. Using Eq. 9-5 allows the stress at A to be expressed as

$$\sigma_A = 0 = \frac{-P_o}{A} - \frac{(P_o y)(-b/2)}{I_{zz}} + \frac{(-P_o z)(-h/2)}{I_{yy}}$$

or

$$-\frac{P_o}{A} + \frac{P_o y}{b^2 h/6} + \frac{P_o z}{bh^2/6} = 0$$

Simplifying,

$$\frac{z}{h/6} + \frac{y}{b/6} = 1$$

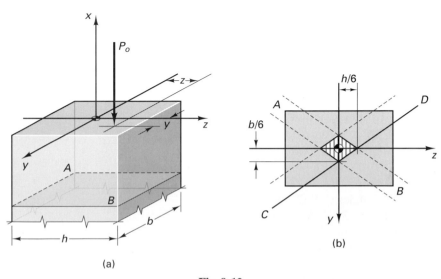

(a)

(b)

Fig. 9-12

which is an equation of a straight line. It shows that when $z = 0$, $y = b/6$; and when $y = 0$, $z = h/6$. Hence, this line may be represented by line CD in Fig. 9-12(b). A vertical force may be applied to the block anywhere on this line and the stress at A will be zero. Similar lines may be established for the other three corners of the section; these are shown in Fig. 9-12(b). If force P is applied on any one of these lines or on any line parallel to such a line toward the centroid of the section, there will be no tensile stress at the corresponding corner. Hence, force P may be applied anywhere within the ruled area in Fig. 9-12(b) without causing tensile stress at any of the four corners or anywhere else. This zone of the cross-sectional area is called the *kern* of a section. By limiting the possible location of the force to the lines of symmetry of the rectangular cross section, the results found in this example verify the "middle-third" rule discussed in Example 9-4.

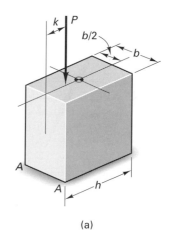

(a)

Example 9-7

Consider a "weightless" rigid block resting on a linearly elastic foundation not capable of transmitting any tensile stresses, as shown in Fig. 9-13(a). Determine the stress distribution in the foundation when applied force P is so placed that a part of the block lifts off.

SOLUTION

Assume that only a portion AB of the foundation of length x and width b is effective in resisting applied force P. This corresponds to the shaded area in Fig. 9-13(c). The stress along line B–B is zero by definition. Hence, the following equation for the stress at B may be written:

$$\sigma_B = -\frac{P}{xb} + P\left(\frac{x}{2} - k\right)\frac{6}{bx^2} = 0$$

where $x/2 - k$ is the eccentricity of the applied force with respect to the centroidal axis of the shaded contact area, and $bx^2/6$ is its section modulus. By solving for x, it is found that $x = 3k$ and the pressure distribution will be "triangular," as shown in Fig. 9-13(b) (why?). As k decreases, the intensity of pressure on line A–A increases; when k is zero, the block becomes unstable.

Problems such as this arise, for example, in the design of foundations for chimneys, as no tensile stresses can develop at the contact surface of a concrete pad with soil. Similar problems arise in foundations for heavy machinery. Similar reasoning can be applied where a number of forces are acting on a member and the contact area is of any shape.

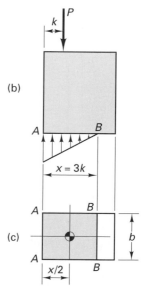

Fig. 9-13   Stresses between two contacting surfaces that do not transmit tensile forces.

9-4. Inelastic Bending with Axial Loads

In Section 8-8, it is pointed out that the basic kinematic assumption that plane sections through a beam taken normal to its axis remain plane after a beam is bent remains valid even if the material behaves inelastically. Similarly, plane sections perpendicular to a beam axis move along it parallel to themselves when an inelastic member is loaded axially. For small deformations, the *normal strains* corresponding to these actions can be *superposed*. As a result of such superposition, a plane defined by Eq. 9-14 can be formulated. Such general analysis of inelastic beams is rather cumbersome and is not considered in this text.[1] Here attention is confined to a planar case.

The superposition of strains for a planar member simultaneously subjected to an axial force P and a bending moment M is shown schematically in Fig. 9-14. For clarity, the strains are greatly exaggerated. Superposition of strains due to P and M moves a plane section axially and rotates it as shown. If axial force P causes strain larger than any strain of opposite sign that is caused by M, the combined strains will not change their sign within a section.

By supplementing these basic kinematic assumptions with the stress-strain relations and conditions of equilibrium, one can solve either elastic or inelastic problems. It is important to note, however, that *superposition of stresses is applicable only in elastic problems where deformations are small.*

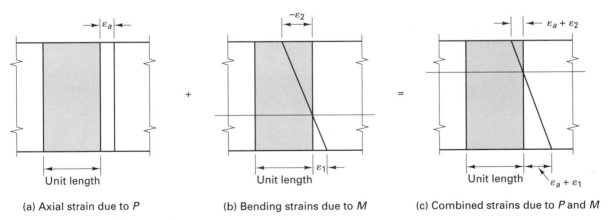

(a) Axial strain due to P (b) Bending strains due to M (c) Combined strains due to P and M

Fig. 9-14   Superposition of strains.

[1]M. S. Aghbabian and E. P. Popov, "Unsymmetrical bending of rectangular beams beyond the elastic limit," *Proceedings, First U.S. National Congress of Applied Mechanics* (Michigan: Edwards Bros., 1951), 579–584.

An example follows illustrating an elastic as well as an inelastic solution for a member simultaneously subjected to bending and axial forces.

Example 9-8

Consider a rectangular elastic-plastic beam bent around the horizontal axis and simultaneously subjected to an axial tensile force. Determine the magnitudes of the axial forces and moments associated with the stress distributions shown in Figs. 9-15(a), (b), and (e).

SOLUTION

The stress distribution shown in Fig. 9-15(a) corresponds to the limiting elastic case, where the maximum stress is at the point of impending yielding. For this case, the stress-superposition approach can be used. Hence,

$$\sigma_{max} = \sigma_{yp} = \frac{P_1}{A} + \frac{M_1 c}{I} \qquad (9\text{-}9)$$

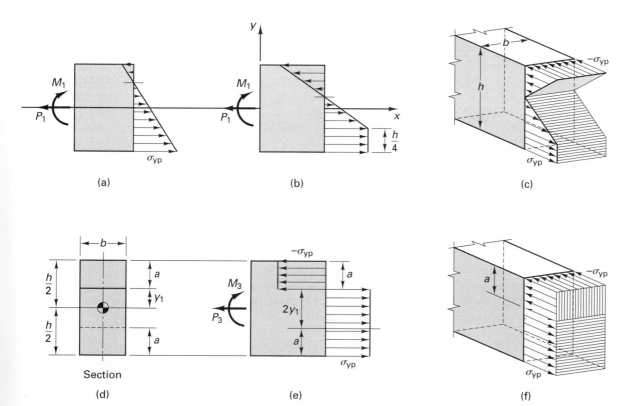

Fig. 9-15 Combined axial and bending stresses: (a) elastic stress distribution, (b) and (c) elastic-plastic stress distribution, and (e) and (f) fully plastic stress distribution.

Force P at yield can be defined as $P_{yp} = A\sigma_{yp}$; from Eq. 8-21, the moment at yield is $M_{yp} = (I/c)\sigma_{yp}$. Dividing Eq. 9-9 by σ_{yp} and substituting the relations for P_{yp} and M_{yp}, after simplification,

$$\frac{P_1}{P_{yp}} + \frac{M_1}{M_{yp}} = 1 \qquad (9\text{-}10)$$

This establishes a relationship between P_1 and M_1 so that the maximum stress just equals σ_{yp}. A plot of this equation corresponding to the case of impending yield is represented by a straight line in Fig. 9-16. Plots of such relations are called *interaction curves* or *diagrams*.

The stress distribution shown in Figs. 9-15(b) and (c) occurs after yielding has taken place in the lower quarter of the beam. With this stress distribution given, one can determine directly the magnitudes of P and M from the conditions of equilibrium. If, on the other hand, P and M were given, since superposition does not apply, a cumbersome process would be necessary to determine the stress distribution.

For the stresses given in Figs. 9-15(b) and (c), one simply applies Eqs. 8-25 and 8-26 developed for inelastic bending of beams, except that in Eq. 8-25, the sum of the normal stresses must equal axial force P. Noting that in the elastic zone, the stress can be expressed algebraically as $\sigma = \sigma_{yp}/3 - \sigma_{yp}y/(3h/8)$ and that in the plastic zone $\sigma = \sigma_{yp}$, one has

$$P_2 = \int_A \sigma\,dA = \int_{-h/4}^{+h/2} \frac{\sigma_{yp}}{3}\left(1 - \frac{8y}{h}\right)b\,dy + \int_{-h/2}^{-h/4} \sigma_{yp}b\,dy = \sigma_{yp}\frac{bh}{4}$$

$$M_2 = -\int_A \sigma y\,dA = -\int_{-h/4}^{+h/2} \frac{\sigma_{yp}}{3}\left(1 - \frac{8y}{h}\right)yb\,dy - \int_{-h/2}^{-h/4} \sigma_{yp}yb\,dy$$

$$= \frac{3}{16}\sigma_{yp}bh^2$$

Note that the axial force just found exactly equals the force acting on the plastic area of the section. Moment M_2 is greater than $M_{yp} = \sigma_{yp}bh^2/6$ and less than $M_{ult} = M_p = \sigma_{yp}bh^2/4$; see Eq. 8-27.

The axial force and moment corresponding to the fully plastic case shown in Figs. 9-15(e) and (f) are simple to determine. As may be seen from Fig. 9-15(e), the axial force is developed by σ_{yp} acting on the area $2y_1b$. Because of symmetry, these stresses make no contribution to the moment. Forces acting on the top and the bottom areas $ab = [(h/2) - y_1]b$, Fig. 9-15(d), form a couple with a moment arm of $h - a = h/2 + y_1$. Therefore,

$$P_3 = 2y_1b\sigma_{yp} \qquad \text{or} \qquad y_1 = P_3/2b\sigma_{yp}$$

and

$$M_3 = ab\sigma_{yp}(h - a) = \sigma_{yp}b(h^2/4 - y_1^2) = M_p - \sigma_{yp}by_1^2$$

$$= \frac{3M_{yp}}{2} - \frac{P_3^2}{4b\sigma_{yp}}$$

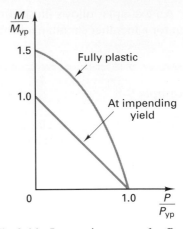

Fig. 9-16   Interaction curves for P and M for a rectangular member.

Then, dividing by $M_p = 3M_{yp}/2 = \sigma_{yp}bh^2/4$ and simplifying, one obtains

$$\frac{2M_3}{3M_{yp}} + \left(\frac{P_3}{P_{yp}}\right)^2 = 1 \qquad (9\text{-}11)$$

This is a general equation for the interaction curve for P and M necessary to achieve the fully plastic condition in a rectangular member (see Fig. 9-16). Unlike the equation for the elastic case, the relation is nonlinear.

Part B BEAMS WITH ARBITRARY CROSS SECTION

9-5. Preliminary Remarks

As noted in the introduction, analytical treatment of prismatic beams having arbitrary cross section requires the basic equations for area moments and products of inertia, as well as the corresponding transfer-of-axes formulas. Further, for bending analysis of such beams, the general flexure formula must be established. The derived formulas can be used either with an arbitrary set of orthogonal axes in the plane of the cross section or with the principal axes of inertia.

9-6. Area Moments and Products of Inertia

Moments of inertia, or second moments of area around the z axis, were already encountered in connection with symmetric cross sections. Here this concept is generalized for two orthogonal axes for any cross-sectional shape. With the yz coordinates chosen as shown in Fig. 9-17, by definition, the moments and products of inertia of an area are given as

$$I_z = \int y^2\, dA \quad I_y = \int z^2\, dA \quad \text{and} \quad I_{yz} = \int yz\, dA \quad (9\text{-}12)$$

Note that these axes are chosen to pass through the centroid C of the area. The use of such *centroidal* axes is essential in the solution of bending problems. It is also important to note that the product of inertia vanishes either for *doubly* or *singly symmetric* areas; see Fig. 9-18. This can be seen by referring to Fig. 9-18(b), where, due to symmetry, for each $y(+z)\, dA$, there is a $y(-z)\, dA$, and their sum vanishes.

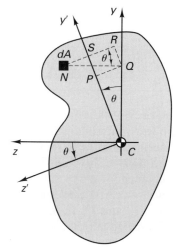

Fig. 9-17 Rotation of coordinate axes.

In Section 8-4, it was shown that in calculating moments of inertia for symmetric cross sections having complex areas, it is advantageous to subdivide such areas into simple parts for which the moments of inertia are available in formulas. Then, by applying the parallel-axis theorem to each part and adding, Eq. 8-18a, the moment of inertia for the whole section is obtained. By making reference to the general case shown in Fig. 9-19, it can be concluded that the previously developed formula, Eq. 8-18, for the transfer of a moment of inertia for an area from the z_c to the z axis remains applicable. Moreover, except for a change in notation, a similar formula applies for transferring a moment of inertia from the y_c to the y axis. Therefore, the following two formulas for the transfer of axes are available for the moments of inertia:

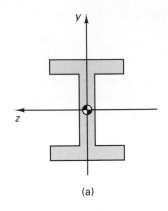

(a)

$$I_z = I_{z_c} + Ad_z^2 \tag{9-13}$$

and

$$I_y = I_{y_c} + Ad_y^2 \tag{9-14}$$

where I_{z_c} and I_{y_c} are, respectively, moments of inertia around the z_c and y_c axes, A is the area considered, and d_z and d_y are, respectively, the distances from C to the axes z and y.

By starting with the definition for the product of inertia, Eq. 9-12, and following the same procedure as before for I_z and I_y, the transfer-of-axis formula for the product of inertia, after simplifications, becomes

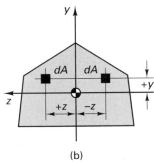

(b)

Fig. 9-18 (a) Doubly and (b) singly symmetric cross sections.

$$I_{yz} = \int (y_c + d_z)(z_c + d_y)\, dA = I_{y_c z_c} + Ad_y d_z \tag{9-15}$$

where $I_{y_c z_c}$ is the product of inertia of the area A around the centroidal y_c and z_c axes.

As noted earlier, the respective expressions given by Eqs. 8-18, 9-14, and 9-15 for all parts of a complex area should be summed to obtain I_y, I_z, and I_{yz} for the whole cross section.

9-7. Principal Axes of Inertia

In the previous discussion, the yz centroidal axes for an area of a general shape were chosen arbitrarily. Therefore, it is important to investigate how the moments and product of inertia change if these orthogonal axes are rotated. This is shown in Fig. 9-17, where the axes are rotated through an angle θ, forming a new set of $y'z'$ coordinates. Generally, the moments and product of inertia corresponding to these axes are different from the values of I_y, I_z, and I_{yz}. In order to transform these quantities from one set of coordinates to another, one notes that

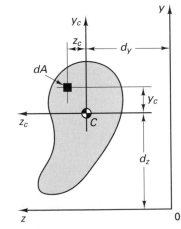

Fig. 9-19 Parallel transfer of axes.

$$y' = CP + PS = y \cos\theta + z \sin\theta$$

$$z' = NR - RS = z \cos\theta - y \sin\theta$$

Then, based on the definitions for moments and product of inertia given in Eqs. 9-12,

$$I_{z'} = \int (y')^2 dA = \int (y \cos\theta + z \sin\theta)^2 dA$$

$$= \cos^2\theta \int y^2\, dA + \sin^2\theta \int z^2\, dA + 2\sin\theta \cos\theta \int yz\, d\theta$$

$$= I_z \cos^2\theta + I_y \sin^2\theta + 2I_{yz} \sin\theta \cos\theta$$

$$= I_z \frac{1 + \cos 2\theta}{2} + I_y \frac{1 - \cos 2\theta}{2} + I_{yz} \sin 2\theta$$

Hence, on using trigonometric identities,

$$I_{z'} = \frac{I_z + I_y}{2} + \frac{I_z - I_y}{2} \cos 2\theta + I_{yz} \sin 2\theta \tag{9-16}$$

Similarly,

$$I_{y'} = \frac{I_z + I_y}{2} - \frac{I_z - I_y}{2} \cos 2\theta - I_{yz} \sin 2\theta \tag{9-17}$$

and

$$I_{y'z'} = -\frac{I_z - I_y}{2} \sin 2\theta + I_{yz} \cos 2\theta \tag{9-18}$$

These equations relate the moments and the product of inertia of an area (second moments) in the new $y'z'$ coordinates to the initial ones in the yz coordinates through the angle θ. Note that $I_{y'} + I_{z'} = I_y + I_z$ (i.e., the sum of the moments of inertia around two mutually perpendicular axes) remains the same (i.e., *invariant*) regardless of the angle θ. As noted earlier, the product of inertia I_{yz} vanishes for doubly and singly symmetric sections.

A maximum or a minimum value of $I_{z'}$ or $I_{y'}$ can be found by differentiating either Eq. 9-16 or 9-17 with respect to θ and setting the derivative equal to zero. That is,

$$\frac{dI_{z'}}{d\theta} = -(I_z - I_y)\sin 2\theta + 2I_{yz} \cos 2\theta = 0$$

Hence,

$$\tan 2\theta_1 = \frac{2I_{yz}}{I_z - I_y} \tag{9-19}$$

This equation gives two roots within 360° that are 180° apart. Since this is for a double angle $2\theta_1$, the roots for θ_1 are 90° apart. One of these roots locates an axis around which the moment of inertia is a maximum; the other locates the conjugate axis for the minimum moment of inertia. These two centroidal axes are known as the *principal axes of inertia*. As can be noted from Eq. 9-18, the same angles define the axes for which the product of inertia is zero. This means that *the product of inertia for the principal axes is zero.*

By defining sines and cosines in terms of the double angle roots of Eq. 9-19 (see Fig. 11-5), substituting these into Eq. 9-16 or Eq. 9-17, and simplifying, expressions for the *principal moments of inertia* are found:

$$I_{\substack{max \\ min}} = I_1 \text{ or } I_2 = \frac{I_z + I_y}{2} \pm \sqrt{\left(\frac{I_z - I_y}{2}\right)^2 + I_{yz}^2} \qquad (9\text{-}20)$$

where, by definition, $I_1 = I_{max}$ and $I_2 = I_{min}$. The axes for which these maximum and minimum moments of inertia apply are defined by Eq. 9-19. By directly substituting one of the roots of this equation into Eq. 9-16, one can determine whether the selected root gives a maximum or a minimum value of the moment of inertia.

Example 9-9

For an angle having the cross section shown in mm in Fig. 9-20, find the principal axes and the principal moments of inertia.

SOLUTION

It can be verified by the procedure discussed earlier that the centroid of the area lies 74.3 mm from the bottom and 24.3 mm from the left side. The moments and product of inertia about the y and z axes can be calculated by dividing the angle into two rectangles and using the transfer-of-axes Eqs. 8-18, 9-14, and 9-15. Due to the symmetry of the two rectangles into which the angle is divided, there are no product of inertia terms for these parts around their own centroidal axes. For rectangles around their centroidal axes, $I = bh^3/12$, Eq. 8-19.

$$I_z = 20 \times 180^3/12 + 20 \times 180 \times (125.7 - 90)^2 + 100 \times 20^3/12$$
$$+ 100 \times 20 \times (-74.3 + 10)^2 = 22.64 \times 10^6 \text{ mm}^4$$

$$I_y = 180 \times 20^3/12 + 180 \times 20 \times (24.3 - 10)^2 + 20 \times 100^3/12$$
$$+ 20 \times 100 \times (-50 + 24.3)^2 = 3.84 \times 10^6 \text{ mm}^4$$

$$I_{yz} = 0 + 20 \times 180 \times (125.7 - 90)(24.3 - 10) + 0 + 100$$
$$\times 20(-74.3 + 10)(-50 + 24.3) = 5.14 \times 10^6 \text{ mm}^4$$

By substituting these values into Eq. 9-20,

$$I_{max} = I_1 = 23.95 \times 10^6 \text{ mm}^4 \text{ and } I_{min} = I_2 = 2.53 \times 10^6 \text{ mm}^4$$

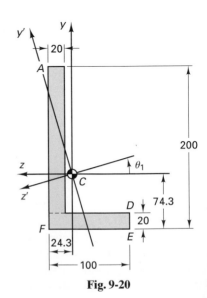

Fig. 9-20

From Eq. 9-19,

$$\tan 2\theta_1 = \frac{2 \times 5.14 \times 10^6}{(22.64 - 3.84) \times 10^6} = 0.547 \quad \text{hence,} \quad \theta_1 = 14.34°$$

From inspection of Fig. 9-20, this angle is seen to define an axis for the maximum moment of inertia. A substitution of this value of θ_1 into Eq. 9-16 can confirm this conclusion. In this case, I_{max} is associated with the z' axis at $\theta_1 = 14.34°$ (i.e., $I_{max} = I_{z'}$); conversely, $I_{min} = I_{y'}$.

9-8. Bending of Beams with Arbitrary Cross Section

A general equation for *pure* bending of *elastic* members of arbitrary cross section whose reference axes are not the principal axes can be formulated using the same approach as for the symmetrical cross sections considered earlier. Again, it is assumed that any plane section through a beam, taken normal to its axis, remains plane after the beam is subjected to bending. Then two basic requirements for equilibrium are enforced: (1) The total axial force on any cross section of a beam must be zero, and (2) the external bending moment at a section must be developed by the internal stresses acting on the cross section. Hooke's law is postulated for uniaxial normal strain.

In order to derive the required equation, consider a beam having an arbitrary cross section such as that shown in Fig. 9-21. The orientation of

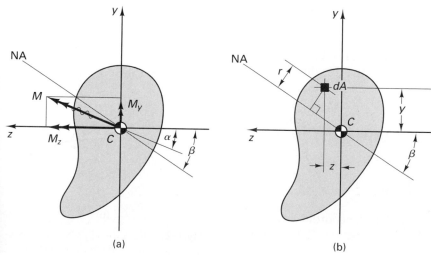

(a)   (b)

Fig. 9-21   Bending of unsymmetric cross section.

the y and z orthogonal axes is chosen arbitrarily. Let this beam be subjected to a pure bending moment M having the components M_y and M_z, respectively, around the y and z axes; see Fig. 9-21(a).

According to the fundamental hypothesis, during bending, a *plane* section through a beam would rotate and intersect the yz plane at an angle β with the z axis, as shown in the figure. A generic infinitesimal area dA in the positive quadrant of the y and z axes is located by the perpendicular distance r from this line. Then, analogous to Eq. 8-3, the longitudinal normal strain ε_x is assumed to be

$$\varepsilon_x = -\kappa r \qquad (9\text{-}21)$$

where, in the chosen coordinates,

$$r = y \cos \beta - z \sin \beta \qquad (9\text{-}22)$$

Then, by analogy to Eq. 8-4, the longitudinal *elastic* stress σ_x acting on the cross section is

$$\sigma_x = E\varepsilon_x = -E\kappa r \qquad (9\text{-}23)$$

and, using Eq. 9-22, this relation becomes

$$\sigma_x = -E\kappa y \cos \beta + E\kappa z \sin \beta \qquad (9\text{-}24)$$

where $\kappa \cos \beta$ is the projected curvature κ_y in the xy plane, as may be seen from the limiting case of setting β equal to zero. Similarly, $\kappa \sin \beta$ is the projected curvature κ_z in the xz plane. By adopting this notation, Eq. 9-24 can be recast to read

$$\sigma_x = -E\kappa_y y + E\kappa_z z \qquad (9\text{-}25)$$

The difference in signs in the two expressions on the right side of the equations arises from the adopted sign convention and can be clarified by making reference to Fig. 9-22. Here it can be noted that a mathematically defined positive curvature, causing an increase in the slope of a bent beam with an increase in the distance from the origin, gives rise to two different cases. In the xy plane, positive curvature and positive bending moments have the same sense. The opposite is true in the xz plane. Hence, the normal stresses σ_x due to these two curvatures must be of opposite sign.

By having an analytic expression for σ_x, Eq. 9-25, the condition that the sum of all forces in the x direction must equal zero (i.e., $\Sigma F_x = 0$) can be written as

$$\int \sigma_x \, dA = -E\kappa_y \int y \, dA + E\kappa_z \int z \, dA = 0 \qquad (9\text{-}26)$$

This equation is identically satisfied provided that the coordinate axes are taken with their origin at the *centroid* of the cross section. This result was anticipated, and the arbitrary orthogonal axes in Fig. 9-21 are shown passing through the centroid C of the cross section.

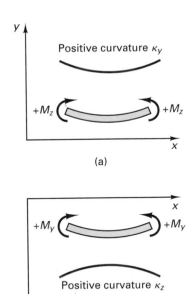

Fig. 9-22 Relationships between positive moments and curvatures in xy and xz planes.

By imposing the conditions of moment equilibrium at a section, two moment component equations can be written requiring that the externally applied moment around either axis is balanced by the internal system of stresses. One of these equations pertains to the moments around the z axis; the other, around the y axis. Hence, as previously defined, if M_z is the known applied moment component around the z axis and M_y is the known applied moment component around the y axis, one has the following two equations (σ_x sign in Eq. 9-28 reversed as in Eq. 8-12):

$$M_z = \int -\sigma_x y \, dA = E\kappa_y \int y^2 \, dA - E\kappa_z \int yz \, dA \qquad (9\text{-}27)$$

and

$$M_y = \int +\sigma_x z \, dA = -E\kappa_y \int yz \, dA + E\kappa_z \int z^2 \, dA \qquad (9\text{-}28)$$

where the constants are taken outside the integrals in the expressions on the right. The meaning of these integrals is discussed in Section 9-6. According to Eq. 9-12, these integrals define the moments and product of inertia for a cross-sectional area as $I_z, I_y,$ and $I_{yz},$ permitting the recasting of the last two equations as

$$EI_z\kappa_y - EI_{yz}\kappa_z = M_z \qquad (9\text{-}29)$$

and

$$-EI_{yz}\kappa_y + EI_y\kappa_z = M_y \qquad (9\text{-}30)$$

Solving these two equations simultaneously gives

$$E\kappa_y = \frac{M_z I_y + M_y I_{yz}}{I_y I_z - I_{yz}^2} \qquad (9\text{-}31)$$

and

$$E\kappa_z = \frac{M_y I_z + M_z I_{yz}}{I_y I_z - I_{yz}^2} \qquad (9\text{-}32)$$

By substituting these constants in Eq. 9-25, the expression for the *elastic* bending stress σ_x for *any* beam cross section with arbitrarily directed orthogonal coordinate axes is

$$\sigma_x = -\frac{M_z I_y + M_y I_{yz}}{I_y I_z - I_{yz}^2} y + \frac{M_y I_z + M_z I_{yz}}{I_y I_z - I_{yz}^2} z \qquad (9\text{-}33)$$

This is the *generalized flexure formula*. If the principal axes for a cross section are used, where I_{yz} is zero, this equation simplifies to Eq. 9-1.

By setting Eq. 9-33 equal to zero, the angle β for locating the neutral axis in the *arbitrary* coordinate system is obtained, giving

$$\tan \beta = \frac{y}{z} = \frac{M_y I_z + M_z I_{yz}}{M_z I_y + M_y I_{yz}} \qquad (9\text{-}34)$$

For the principal axes, this equation reverts to Eq. 9-2.

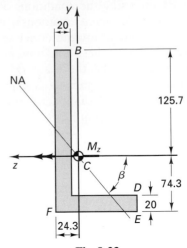

Fig. 9-23

Example 9-10

Using the general equation for elastic bending stress, find the stresses at points B and F for the angle shown in mm in Fig. 9-23. Show that these stresses are, respectively, the minimum and the maximum. The applied moment $M_z = 10$ kN $\cdot$ m.

SOLUTION

In Example 9-9, it is found that $I_z = 22.64 \times 10^6$ mm^4, $I_y = 3.84 \times 10^6$ mm^4, and $I_{yz} = 5.14 \times 10^6$ mm^4. Substituting these values and $M_z = +10$ kN $\cdot$ m into Eq. 9-33 and defining, respectively, the coordinates of points B and F as $(125.7, 4.3)$ and $(-74.3, 24.3)$, one has

$$\sigma_B = -\frac{10 \times 10^6 \times 3.84 \times 10^6}{3.84 \times 22.64 \times 10^{12} - 5.14^2 \times 10^{12}} \times 125.7$$

$$+ \frac{10 \times 10^6 \times 5.14 \times 10^6}{3.84 \times 22.64 \times 10^{12} - 5.14^2 \times 10^{12}} \times 4.3$$

$$= -0.6345 \times 125.7 + 0.8493 \times 4.3 = -76.1 \text{ MPa}$$

and

$$\sigma_F = -0.6345 \times (-74.3) + 0.8943 \times 24.3 = +67.8 \text{ MPa}$$

To show that these stresses are the minimum and maximum, respectively, locate the neutral axis using Eq. 9-34, giving

$$\tan \beta = \frac{10 \times 10^6 \times 5.14 \times 10^6}{10 \times 10^6 \times 3.84 \times 10^6} = 1.34 \quad \text{or} \quad \beta = 53.3°$$

By sketching this line on the given cross section, it is evident by inspection that the farthest distances measured perpendicular to NA are associated with points B and F. Therefore, the largest stresses occur at these points.

Example 9-11

Using the principal axes, determine the maximum tensile and compressive stresses caused by a bending moment of 10 kN $\cdot$ m acting around the horizontal axis for the angle shown in mm in Fig. 9-24.

SOLUTION

It is *incorrect* to solve this problem using the y and z coordinates shown using conventional flexure formulas. The solution can be obtained, however, with such formulas using the *principal axes* for the cross section.

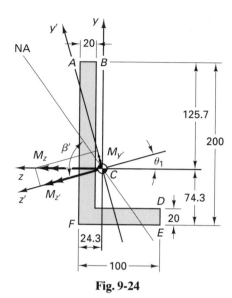

Fig. 9-24

These were determined in Example 9-9, where it was found that the axes must be rotated counterclockwise through an angle $\theta_1 = 14.34°$ to locate such axes. For these principal axes, $I_{max} = I_{z'} = 23.95 \times 10^6$ mm^4 and $I_{min} = I_{y'} = 2.53 \times 10^6$ mm^4. For these axes,

$$M_{z'} = +M_z \cos \theta_1 = 10 \times 10^6 \cos 14.34° = 9.689 \times 10^6 \text{ N} \cdot \text{mm}$$

$$M_{y'} = +M_z \sin \theta_1 = 10 \times 10^6 \sin 14.34° = 2.475 \times 10^6 \text{ N} \cdot \text{mm}$$

The highest stressed points on the cross section lie at points farthest from the neutral axis. To locate this axis, the angle β is given by Eq. 9-3. Hence, using the y' and z' coordinates,

$$\tan \beta' = \frac{I_{z'}}{I_{y'}} \tan \theta_1 = \frac{23.95 \times 10^6}{2.53 \times 10^6} \tan 14.34° = 2.42$$

and $\beta' = 67.5°$. Since this angle is measured from the z' axis, it forms an angle of $67.5° - 14.3° = 53.2°$ with the z axis. Note the large inclination of the neutral axis with respect to the z axis, which is much larger than θ_1.

Having established the neutral axis, by inspection of the sketch, it can be seen that the highest stressed point in compression is at B, whereas that in tension is at F. By locating these points in the $y'z'$ coordinate system of the *principal axes* and applying Eq. 9-1, the required are found:

$$y_B' = z_B \sin \theta_1 + y_B \cos \theta_1 = +4.3 \sin \theta_1 + 125.7 \cos \theta_1 = 122.9 \text{ mm}$$

$$z_B' = z_B \cos \theta_1 - y_B \sin \theta_1 = +4.3 \cos \theta_1 - 125.7 \sin \theta_1 = -26.95 \text{ mm}$$

$$\sigma_B = -\frac{M_{z'} y_B'}{I_{z'}} + \frac{M_{y'} z_B'}{I_{y'}}$$

$$= -\frac{9.689 \times 10^6 \times 122.9}{23.95 \times 10^6} + \frac{2.475 \times 10^6 \times (-26.95)}{2.53 \times 10^6}$$

$$= -76.1 \text{ MPa}$$

Similarly,

$$y_F' = z_F \sin \theta_1 + y_F \cos \theta_1 = 24.3 \sin \theta_1 - 74.3 \cos \theta_1 = -65.97 \text{ mm}$$

$$z_F' = z_F \cos \theta_1 - y_F \sin \theta_1 = 24.3 \cos \theta_1 + 74.3 \sin \theta_1 = +41.93 \text{ mm}$$

$$\sigma_F = -\frac{M_{z'} y_F'}{I_{z'}} + \frac{M_{y'} z_F'}{I_{y'}}$$

$$= -\frac{9.689 \times 10^6 \times (-65.97)}{23.95 \times 10^6} + \frac{2.475 \times 10^6 \times 41.93}{2.53 \times 10^6}$$

$$= +67.7 \text{ MPa}$$

PROBLEMS

Section 9-2

9-1. Rework Example 9-1 by assuming that the span is 6000 mm, the beam is 150 × 200 mm, and α is 20°.

9-2. A 150 × 200 mm beam spanning 6000 mm is loaded in the middle of the span with an inclined force of 5 kN along the diagonal of the cross section, as shown in the figure. Determine the largest bending stresses and locate the neutral axis.

9-3. A box beam made from an extruded aluminum alloy having 5 414mm wall thickness is loaded by an inclined force $P = 100$ N, as shown in the figure. Determine the maximum stress on section $a–b$. For the box beam, use centerline dimensions for finding I. (Note that the stress is far away from the support, where large local stress concentrations are unlikely.)

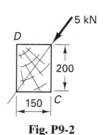

Fig. P9-2

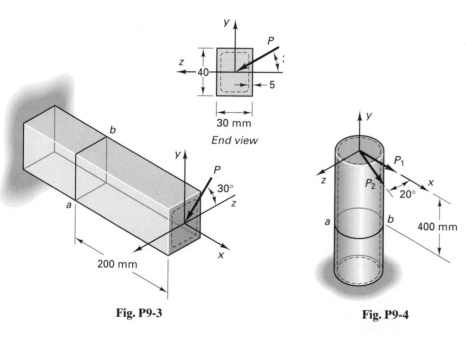

Fig. P9-3   **Fig. P9-4**

9-4. A standard steel pipe with a nominal outside diameter of 310 mm (12 in) is acted upon by two horizontally applied forces $P_1 = 50$ N and $P_2 = 60$ N. Determine the maximum and the minimum stresses acting on section $a–b$. For pipe dimensions, see Appendix 7.

9-5. A standard steel pipe with a nominal outside diameter of 203 mm (8 in) is acted upon by a force $P_1 = 20$ N in the x direction and a force $P_2 = 30$ N in the z direction. Determine the maximum stress acting on section $a–b$. (See Appendix 7 for pipe dimensions.)

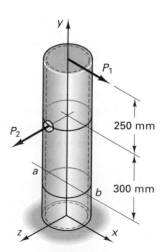

Fig. P9-5

9-6.   A 3-m cantilever made up from the standard steel shape S 310 × 74 has its web in a vertical position, as shown in the figure. Determine the maximum bending stresses 1 m from the support caused by the application of the variously inclined force P acting through the centroid of the section at the free end. Let α be 0°, 1°, and 5°.

9-7.   A beam having the cross-sectional dimensions, in mm, shown in the figure is subjected to a bending moment of 500 N · m around its horizontal axis. Determine the maximum bending stresses.

9-8.   A biaxially symmetric cruciform aluminum extrusion has the cross-sectional dimensions, in mm, shown in the figure. It is used in a tilted position as a cantilever to carry an applied force $P = 100$ N at the end. (a) Determine the maximum flexural tensile stress 150 mm from the loaded end of the cantilever. Assume linearly elastic behavior of the material. (b) Locate a point of zero stress on line AB.

9-9.   Determine the bending stresses at the corners in the cantilever loaded, as shown in the figure, at a section 600 mm from the free end. Also locate the neutral axis.

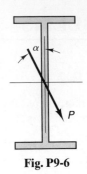

Fig. P9-6

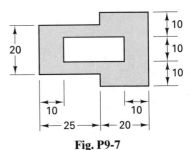

Fig. P9-7

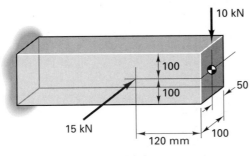

Fig. P9-9

Section 9-3

9-10.   A W 250 × 49 beam 3 m long is subjected to a pull P of 400 kN, as shown in the figure. At the ends, where the pin connections are made, the beam is reinforced with doubler plates. Determine the maximum flange stress in the middle of the member caused by the applied forces P. Qualitatively, briefly discuss the load transfer at the ends. Most likely, where are the highest stressed regions in this member?

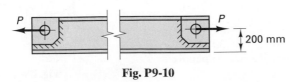

Fig. P9-10

9-11. For the machine link shown in the figure, determine the offset distance *e* such that the tensile and compressive stresses in the T section are equal.

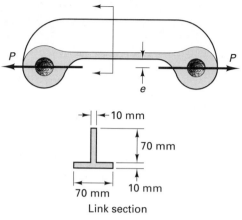

Link section

Fig. P9-11

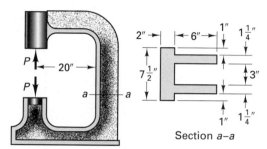

Section *a–a*

Fig. P9-12

9-12. A frame for a punch press has the proportions shown in the figure. What force *P* can be applied to this frame controlled by the stresses in the sections such as *a–a* if the allowable stresses are 4000 psi in tension and 12,000 psi in compression?

9-13. A force of 198 k is applied to bar *BC* at *C*, as shown in the figure. Find the maximum stress acting normal to section *a–a*. Member *BC* is made from a piece of 6-by-6-in steel bar. Neglect the weight of the bar.

9-14. Calculate the maximum compressive stress acting on section *a–a* caused by the applied load for the structure shown in the figure. The cross section at section *a–a* is that of a solid circular bar of 2-in diameter.

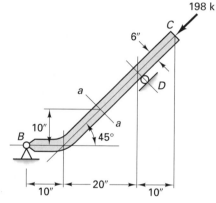

Fig. P9-13

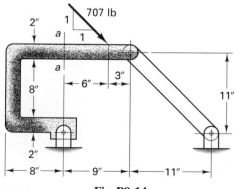

Fig. P9-14

9-15. Compute the maximum compressive stress acting normal to section *a–a* for the structure shown in the figure. Post *AB* has a 12-by-12-in cross section. Neglect the weight of the structure.

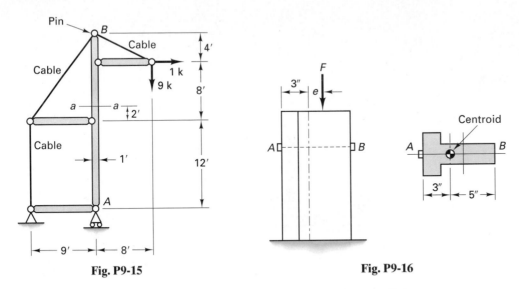

Fig. P9-15   Fig. P9-16

9-16. In order to obtain the magnitude of an eccentric vertical force *F* on a tee-shaped steel column, strain gages are attached at *A* and *B*, as shown in the figure. Determine the force *F* if the longitudinal strain at *A* is -100×10^{-6} in/in and at *B* is -800×10^{-6} in/in. $E = 30 \times 10^{6}$ psi and $G = 12 \times 10^{6}$ psi. The cross-sectional area of the column is 24 in².

9-17. A bar having a 100×80 mm cross section is subjected to a force *F*, as shown in the figure. The longitudinal stresses on the extreme fibers at two sections 200 mm apart are determined experimentally to be $\sigma_A = 0$; $\sigma_B = -30$ MPa; $\sigma_C = -24$ MPa; and $\sigma_D = -6$ MPa. Determine the magnitude of the vertical and horizontal components of force *F*.

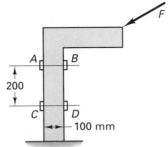

Fig. P9-17

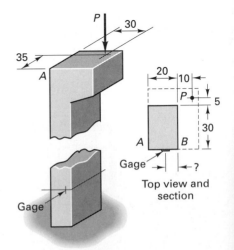

Fig. P9-18

9-18. A rectangular vertical member fixed at the base is loaded as shown in the figure. Find the location for a gage on member face *AB* such that no longitudinal strain would occur due to the application of force $P = 6$ kN. Does the answer depend on the magnitude of force *P*? Assume elastic behavior. All dimensions are given in mm.

9-19. An inclined tensile force F is applied to an aluminum alloy bar such that its line of action goes through the centroid of the bar, as shown in mm in the figure. (The detail of the attachment is not shown.) What is the magnitude of force F if it causes a longitudinal strain of $+20 \times 10^{-6}$ in the gage at A? Assume that the bar behaves as a linearly elastic material and let $E = 70$ GPa.

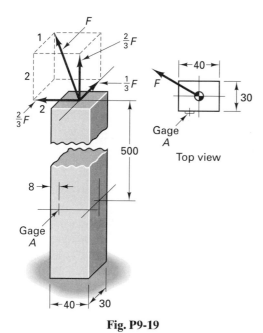

Fig. P9-19

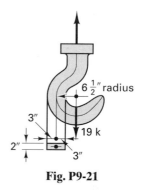

Fig. P9-20   **Fig. P9-21**

9-20. A magnesium alloy bar is bonded to a steel bar of the same size forming a beam having the cross-sectional dimensions in mm shown in the figure. (a) If on application of an eccentric axial force P, the upper longitudinal gage measures a compressive strain of 2×10^{-3}, and the lower one a tensile strain of 2×10^{-3}, what is the magnitude of applied force P? Assume elastic behavior of the materials with $E_{Mg} = 45$ GPa and $E_{St} = 200$ GPa. (b) Where would one have to apply axial force P to cause no bending? (It is interesting to note that this locates the neutral axis for this beam.)

9-21. A steel hook, having the proportions in the figure, is subjected to a downward force of 19 k. The radius of the centroidal curved axis is 6 in. Determine the maximum stress in this hook.

9-22. A steel bar of 4 mm diameter is bent into a nearly complete circular ring of 300 mm outside diameter, as shown in the figure. (a) Calculate the maximum stress in this ring caused by applying two 10-kN forces at the open end. (b) Find the ratio of the maximum stress found in (a) to the largest compressive stress acting normal to the same section.

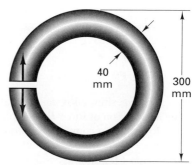

Fig. P9-22

9-23. A short block has cross-sectional dimensions in plan view as shown in the figure. Determine the range along the line A–A over which a downward vertical force could be applied to the top of the block without causing any tension at the base. Neglect the weight of the block.

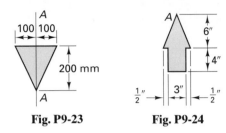

Fig. P9-23   Fig. P9-24

9-24. The cross-sectional area in plan view of a short block is in the shape of an "arrow," as shown in the figure. Find the position of the vertical downward force on the line of symmetry of this section so that the stress at A is just zero.

9-25. Determine the kern for a member having a solid circular cross section.

9-26. What should be the total weight h of the dam shown in the cross-sectional view be so that the foundation pressure at A is just zero? Assume that water weighs 62.5 lb/ft³ and concrete 150 lb/ft³.

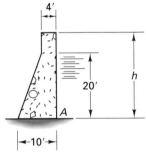

Fig. P9-26

Section 9-4

9-27. A T beam of perfectly elastic plastic material has the dimensions shown in the figure. (a) If the longitudinal strain at the bottom of the flange is $-\varepsilon_{yp}$ and is known to be zero at the juncture of the web and the flange, what axial force P and bending moment M act on the beam? (b) What would the strain reading be after the applied forces causing P and M in (a) are removed? Let $\sigma_{yp} = 200$ MPa.

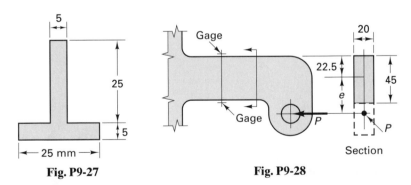

Fig. P9-27   Fig. P9-28

9-28. A magnesium alloy casting has the dimensions given in the figure in mm. During application of force P, the upper gage recorded a tensile strain of 3×10^{-3}, and the lower one a compressive strain of 6×10^{-3}. (a) Estimate the magnitude of applied force P and its eccentricity e assuming idealized behavior for the material. Let $\sigma_{yp} = 135$ MPa and $\varepsilon_{yp} = 3 \times 10^{-3}$. (b) What will be the reading of the gages when the applied force P is released?

Sections 9-6 and 9-7

9-29. (a) Find the product of inertia for the triangular area shown in the figure with respect to the given axes. (b) For the same area, determine the product of inertia with respect to the vertical and horizontal axes through the centroid.

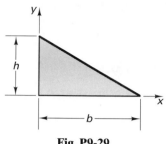

Fig. P9-29

9-30. Idealize the cross section of $102 \times 102 \times 12.7$ equal length angle as shown in the figure (i.e., omit the fillet and rounded corners). (a) Locate the centroid of the section, (b) calculate $I_y, I_z,$ and I_{yz} with respect to the centroidal axes, (c) locate the principal axes and calculate I_{max} and I_{min}, and (d) check the results in (c) by inspection and using Table 6B in the Appendix. (See the hint in Problem 9-31. *Note:* In U.S. customary units, the angle is $4 \times 4 \times 1/2$ in.)

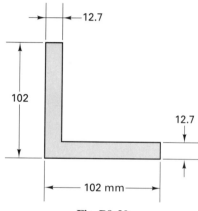

Fig. P9-30

9-31. (a) Find the principal axes and principal moments of inertia for the cross-sectional area of the angle shown in the figure. (b) The given dimensions of the cross section, except for small radii at the ends and a fillet, correspond to the cross-sectional dimensions of an $8 \times 6 \times 1$ in angle listed in Table 7 of the Appendix. Using the information given in that table, calculate the principal moments of inertia and compare with the results found in (a). (*Hint:* Note that per Section 16-6 and Example 16-2, $I_{min} = Ar^2_{min}$. The r listed in Table 7 for the z axis is r_{min}. Further, from the invariance condition, $I_{min} + I_{max} = I_{x'} + I_{y'} = I_x + I_y$; hence one can readily solve for the I_{max}.)

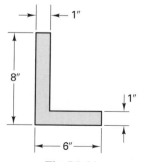

Fig. P9-31

9-32. For the Z cross section shown in the figure, first determine area moments of inertia I_y, I_z, and I_{yz}; then obtain the directions of the principal axes and principal moments of inertia.

Section 9-8

9-33. Rework Example 9-10 for an applied moment $M_y = 4$ kN $\cdot$ m.

9-34. A $102 \times 102 \times 12.7$ equal-legs-angle cantilever 1000 mm long is built in at one end and carries an applied force 200 N at the other end. Determine the largest stresses at a section 800 mm from the applied force. (*Note:* The properties of the angle are analyzed in Problem 9-30. As shown in Fig. 10-24, the applied load causes no twist of the angle.)

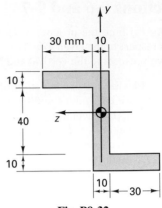

Fig. P9-32

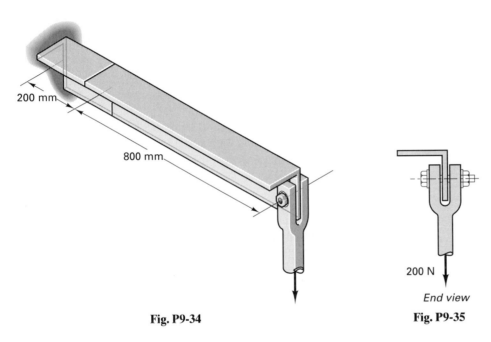

Fig. P9-34   **Fig. P9-35**

9-35. For a similar condition as in the preceding problem, rework the problem using the angle given in Problem 9-31 with the long leg directed vertically downward.

10

Shear Stresses in Beams

10-1. Introduction

This chapter is devoted to a study of shear stresses in beams caused by transverse shear. The related problem of attaching separate longitudinal parts of a beam by means of bolts, gluing, or welding is also considered. *Superposition* of direct shear stresses caused by transverse shear with those caused by torque, as in springs, is also treated. This problem is analogous to that encountered in the previous chapter in the study of beams simultaneously subjected to bending and axial forces.

The discussion in this chapter is largely limited to *elastic* analyses, the most widely used approach in the solution of the type of problems considered.

10-2. Preliminary Remarks

In deriving the torsion and the flexure formulas, the same sequence of reasoning was employed. First, a strain distribution was assumed across the section; next, properties of the material were brought in to relate these strains to stresses; and, finally, the equations of equilibrium were used to establish the desired relations. However, the development of the expression linking the shear force and the cross-sectional area of a beam to the stress follows a different path. The previous procedure cannot be employed, as no simple assumption for the strain distribution due to the shear force can be made. Instead, an indirect approach is used. *The stress distribution caused by flexure, as determined in the preceding two chapters, is assumed, which, together with the equilibrium requirements, resolves the problem of the shear stresses.*

First, it will be necessary to recall that the shear force is *inseparably* linked with a *change* in the bending moment at adjoining sections through a beam. Thus, if a shear and a bending moment are present at one section through a beam, a *different* bending moment will exist at an adjoining section, although the shear may remain constant. This will lead to the establishment of the shear stresses on the imaginary longitudinal planes through the members that are parallel to its axis. Then, since at a point, equal shear stresses exist on the mutually perpendicular planes, the shear stresses whose direction is coincident with the shear force at a section will be determined. Initially, only beams having symmetrical cross sections with applied forces acting in the plane of symmetry will be considered. The related problem of determining interconnection requirements for fastening together several longitudinal elements of built-up or composite beams will also be discussed.

In order to gain some insight into the problem, recall Eq. 7-4. Writing it in two alternative forms, we obtain

$$dM = V\,dx \quad \text{or} \quad \frac{dM}{dx} = V \tag{10-1}$$

Equation 10-1 means that if shear V is acting at a section, there will be a *change* in the bending moment M on an adjoining section. The *difference* between the bending moments on the adjoining sections is equal to $V\,dx$. If no shear is acting, *no change in the bending moment occurs.* Alternatively, the rate of change in moment along a beam is equal to the shear. Therefore, although shear is treated in this chapter as an independent action on a beam, it is *inseparably* linked with the change in the bending moment along the beam's length.

As an example, consider the shear and moment diagrams from Example 7-7, shown in Fig. 10-1. Here at any two sections, such as A and B, taken through the beam anywhere between applied forces P, the bending moment is the same. *No shear* acts at these sections. On the other hand, between any two sections, such as C and D, near the support, a change in the bending moment does take place. Shear forces act at these sections. These shears are shown acting on an element of the beam in Fig. 10-1(d). Note that in this zone of the beam, the *change* in the bending moment in a distance dx is $P\,dx$, as shear V is equal to P. In subsequent discussion, the possibility of equal, as well as of different, bending moments on two adjoining sections through a beam is of great importance.

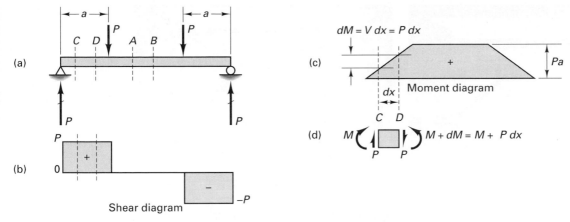

Fig. 10-1   Shear and bending moment diagrams for the loading shown.

Before a detailed analysis is given, a study of a sequence of photographs of a model (Fig. 10-2) may prove helpful. The model represents a segment of an I beam. In Fig. 10-2(a), in addition to the beam itself, blocks simulating stress distribution caused by bending moments may be seen. The moment on the right is assumed to be larger than the one on the left. This system of forces is in equilibrium providing vertical shears V (not seen in this view) also act on the beam segment. By separating the model along the neutral surface, one obtains two separate parts of the beam segment, as shown in Fig. 10-2(b). Again, either one of these parts alone must be in equilibrium.

If the upper and the lower segments of Fig. 10-2(b) are connected by a dowel or a bolt in an actual beam, the axial forces on either the upper or the lower part caused by the bending-moment stresses must be maintained in equilibrium by a force in the dowel. The force that must be resisted can be evaluated by summing the forces in the axial direction caused by bending stresses. In performing such a calculation, either the upper or the lower part of the beam segment can be used. The horizontal force transmitted by the dowel is the force needed to balance the net force caused by the bending stresses acting on the two adjoining sections. Alternatively, by subtracting the same bending stress on both ends of the segment, the same results can be obtained. This is shown schematically in Fig. 10-2(c), where, assuming a zero bending moment on the left, only the normal stresses due to the increment in moment within the segment need be shown acting on the right.

If, initially, the I beam considered is one piece requiring no bolts or dowels, an imaginary longitudinal plane can be used to separate the beam segment into two parts; see Fig. 10-2(d). As before, the net force that must be developed across the cut area to maintain equilibrium can be determined. Dividing this force by the area of the imaginary horizontal cut gives average shear stresses acting in this plane. In the analysis, it is again

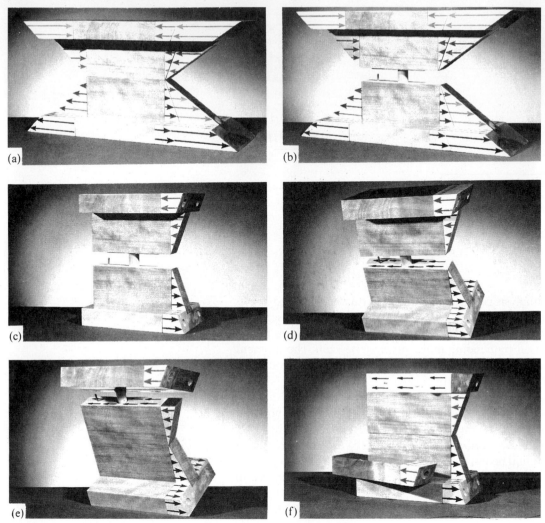

Fig. 10-2   Shear flow model of an I beam. (a) Beam segment with bending stresses simulated by blocks. (b) Shear force transmitted through a dowel. (c) For determining the force on a dowel, only a change in moment is needed. (d) The longitudinal shear force divided by the area of the imaginary cut yields shear stress. (e) Horizontal cut below the flange for determining the shear stress. (f) Vertical cut through the flange for determining the shear stress.

expedient to work with the change in bending moment rather than with the total moments on the end sections.

After the shear stresses on one of the planes are found [i.e., the horizontal one in Fig. 10-2(d)], shear stresses on mutually perpendicular planes of an infinitesimal element also become known since they must be numerically equal; see Eq. 1-2. This approach establishes the shear stresses in the plane of the beam section taken normal to its axis.

The process discussed is quite general; two additional illustrations of separating the segment of the beam are in Figs. 10-2(e) and (f). In Fig. 10-2(e), the imaginary horizontal plane separates the beam just below the flange. Either the upper or the lower part of this beam can be used in calculating the shear stresses in the cut. The imaginary vertical plane cuts off a part of the flange in Fig. 10-2(f). This permits calculation of shear stresses lying in a vertical plane in the figure.

Before finally proceeding with the development of equations for determining the shear stresses in connecting bolts and in beams, an intuitive example is worthy of note. Consider a wooden plank placed on top of another, as shown in Fig. 10-3. If these planks act as a beam and are not interconnected, sliding at the surfaces of their contact will take place. The interconnection of these planks with nails or glue is necessary to make them act as an integral beam. In the next section, an equation will be derived for determining the required interconnection between the component parts of a beam to make them act as a unit. In the following section, this equation will be specialized to yield shear stresses in solid beams.

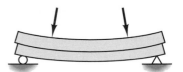

Fig. 10-3   Sliding between planks not fastened together.

10-3. Shear Flow

Consider an elastic beam made from several continuous longitudinal planks whose cross section is shown in Fig. 10-4(a). For simplicity, the beam has a rectangular cross section, but such a limitation is not necessary. To make this beam act as an integral member, it is assumed that the planks are fastened at intervals by vertical bolts. An element of this beam isolated by two parallel sections, both of which are perpendicular to the axis of the beam, is shown in Fig. 10-4(b).

If the element shown in Fig. 10-4(b) is subjected to a bending moment $+M_A$ at end A and to $+M_B$ at end B, bending stresses that act normal to the sections are developed. These bending stresses vary linearly from their respective neutral axes, and at any point at a distance y from the neutral axis are $-M_B y/I$ on the B end and $-M_A y/I$ on the A end.

From the beam element, Fig. 10-4(b), isolate the top plank, as shown in Fig. 10-4(c). The fibers of this plank nearest the neutral axis are located by the distance y_1. Then, since stress times area is equal to force, the forces acting perpendicular to ends A and B of this plank may be determined. At end B, the force acting on an infinitesimal area dA at a distance y from the neutral axis is $(-M_B y/I)\, dA$. The total force acting on the area $fghj$, A_{fghj}, is the sum, or the integral, of these elementary forces over this area. Denoting the total force acting normal to the area $fghj$ by F_B and remembering that, at section B, M_B, and I are constants, one obtains the following relation:

$$F_B = \int_{\substack{\text{area} \\ fghi}} -\frac{M_B y}{I}\, dA = -\frac{M_B}{I} \int_{\substack{\text{area} \\ fghi}} y\, dA = -\frac{M_B Q}{I} \qquad (10\text{-}2)$$

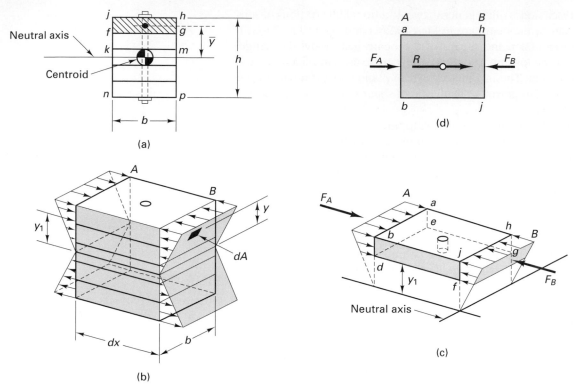

Fig. 10-4   Elements for deriving shear flow in a beam.

where

$$Q = \int_{\substack{\text{area} \\ fghj}} y \, dA = A_{fghj}\,\bar{y} \qquad (10\text{-}3)$$

The integral defining Q is the first, or the statical, moment of area *fghj* around the neutral axis. By definition, $\bar{y}$ is the distance from the neutral axis to the centroid of A_{fghj}.[1] Illustrations of the manner of determining Q are in Fig. 10-5. Equation 10-2 provides a convenient means of calculating the longitudinal force acting normal to any selected part of the cross-sectional area.

Next consider end A of the element in Fig. 10-4(c). One can then express the total force acting normal to the area *abde* as

$$F_A = -\frac{M_A}{I}\int_{\substack{\text{area} \\ \textit{ábde}}} y \, dA = -\frac{M_A Q}{I} \qquad (10\text{-}4)$$

where the meaning of Q is the same as that in Eq. 10-2 since for prismatic beams, an area such as *fghj* is equal to the area *abde*. Hence, if the

---

[1]Area *fgpn* and its $\bar{y}$ may also be used to find $|Q|$.

moments at A and B were equal, it would follow that $F_A = F_B$, and the bolt shown in the figure would perform a nominal function of keeping the planks together and would not be needed to resist any known longitudinal forces.

On the other hand, if M_A is not equal to M_B, which is always the case when shears are present at the adjoining sections, F_A is not equal to F_B. More push (or pull) develops on one end of a "plank" than on the other, as different normal stresses act on the section from the two sides. Thus, if $M_A \neq M_B$, equilibrium of the horizontal forces in Fig. 10-4(c) may be attained only by developing a horizontal resisting force R in the bolt. If $M_B > M_A$, then $|F_B| > |F_A|$, and $|F_A| + R = |F_B|$, as in Fig. 10-4(d). The force $|F_B| - |F_A| = R$ tends to shear the bolt in the plane of the plank $edfg$.[2] If the shear force acting across the bolt at level km, Fig. 10-4(a), were to be investigated, the two upper planks should be considered as one unit.

If $M_A \neq M_B$ and the element of the beam is only dx long, the bending moments on the adjoining sections change by an infinitesimal amount. Thus, if the bending moment at A is M_A, the bending moment at B is $M_B = M_A + dM$. Likewise, in the same distance dx, the longitudinal forces F_A and F_B change by an infinitesimal force dF (i.e., $|F_B| - |F_A| = dF$). By substituting these relations into the expression for F_B and F_A found previously, with areas $fghj$ and $abde$ taken equal, one obtains an expression for the differential longitudinal push (or pull) dF:

$$dF = |F_B| - |F_A| = \left(\frac{M_A + dM}{I} \right)Q - \left(\frac{M_A}{I} \right)Q = \frac{dM}{I}Q$$

In the final expression for dF, the actual bending moments at the adjoining sections are eliminated. Only the difference in the bending moments dM at the adjoining sections remains in the equation.

Instead of working with a force dF, which is developed in a distance dx, it is more significant to obtain a similar force per unit of beam length. This quantity is obtained by dividing dF by dx. Physically, this quantity represents the difference between F_B and F_A for an element of the beam of unit length. The quantity dF/dx will be designated by q and will be referred to as the *shear flow*. Since force is measured in newtons or pounds, shear flow q has units of newtons per meter or pounds per inch. Then, recalling that $dM/dx = V$, one obtains the following expression for the shear flow in beams:

$$q = \frac{dF}{dx} = \frac{dM}{dx}\frac{1}{I}\int_{\substack{\text{area} \\ fghj}} y\, dA = \frac{V A_{fghj}\bar{y}}{I} = \frac{VQ}{I} \qquad (10\text{-}5)$$

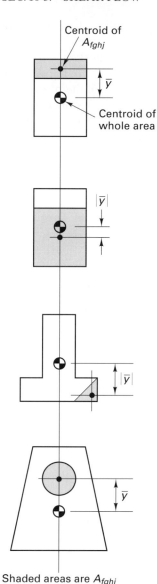

Centroid of A_{fghj}

Centroid of whole area

Shaded areas are A_{fghj}

Fig. 10-5   Procedure for determining $|Q|$.

---

[2] The forces $(|F_B| - |F_A|)$ and R are not collinear, but the element shown in Fig. 10-4(c) is in equilibrium. To avoid ambiguity, shear forces acting in the vertical cuts are omitted from the diagram.

In this equation, *I* is the moment of inertia of the *entire* cross-sectional area around the neutral axis, just as it is in the flexure formula from which it came. The total shear force at the section investigated is represented by *V*, and the integral of *y* *dA* for determining *Q* extends only over the cross-sectional area of the beam to one side of this area at which *q* is investigated.

In retrospect, note carefully that Eq. 10-5 *was derived on the basis of the elastic flexure formula,* but no term for a bending moment appears in the final expressions. This resulted from the fact that only the change in the bending moments at the adjoining sections had to be considered, and the latter quantity is linked with shear *V*. Shear *V* was substituted for dM/dx, and this masks the origin of the established relations. Equation 10-5 is very useful in determining the necessary interconnection between the elements making up a beam. This will be illustrated by examples.

Example 10-1

Two long wooden planks form a T section of a beam, as shown in mm in Fig. 10-6(a). If this beam transmits a constant vertical shear of 3000 N, find the necessary spacing of the nails between the two planks to make the beam act as a unit. Assume that the allowable shear force per nail is 700 N.

SOLUTION

In attacking such problems, the analyst must ask: What part of a beam has a tendency to slide longitudinally from the remainder? Here this occurs in the plane of contact of the two planks; Eq. 10-5 must be applied to determine the shear flow in this plane. To do this, the neutral axis of the whole section and its moment of inertia around the neutral axis must be found. Then, as *V* is known and *Q* is defined as the statical moment of the area of

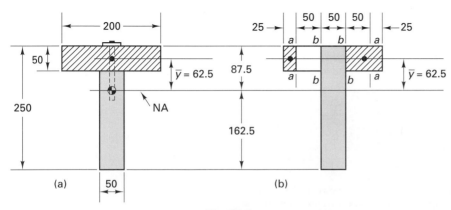

Fig. 10-6

the upper plank around the neutral axis, q may be determined. The distance y_c from the top to the neutral axis is

$$y_c = \frac{50 \times 200 \times 25 + 50 \times 200 \times 150}{50 \times 200 + 50 \times 200} = 87.5 \text{ mm}$$

$$I = \frac{200 \times 50^3}{12} + 50 \times 200 \times 62.5^2 + \frac{50 \times 200^3}{12} + 50 \times 200 \times 62.5^2$$

$$= 113.54 \times 10^6 \text{ mm}^4$$

$$Q = A_{fghj}\bar{y} = 50 \times 200 \times (87.5 - 25) = 625 \times 10^3 \text{ mm}^3$$

$$q = \frac{VQ}{I} = \frac{3000 \times 625 \times 10^3}{113.54 \times 10^6} = 16.5 \text{ N/mm}$$

Thus, a force of 16.5 N/mm must be transferred from one plank to the other along the length of the beam. However, from the data given, each nail is capable of resisting a force of 700 N; hence, one nail is adequate for transmitting shear along $700/16.5 = 42$ mm of the beam length. As shear remains constant at the consecutive sections of the beam, the nails should be spaced throughout at 42-mm intervals.

SOLUTION FOR AN ALTERNATIVE ARRANGEMENT OF PLANKS

If, instead of using the two planks as before, a beam of the same cross section were made from five pieces, shown in Fig. 10-6(b), a different nailing schedule would be required.

To begin, the shear flow between one of the outer 25-by-50-mm planks and the remainder of the beam is found, and although the contact surface a–a is vertical, the procedure is the same. The push or pull on an element is built up in the same manner:

$$Q = A_{fghj}\bar{y} = 25 \times 50 \times 62.5 = 78.1 \times 10^3 \text{ mm}^3$$

$$q = \frac{VQ}{I} = \frac{3000 \times 78.1 \times 10^3}{113.5 \times 10^6} = 2.06 \text{ N/mm}$$

If the same nails as before are used to join the 25-by-50-mm piece to the 50-by-50-mm piece, they may be $700/2.06 = 340$ mm apart. This nailing applies to both sections a–a.

To determine the shear flow between the 50-by-250-mm vertical piece and either one of the 50-by-50-mm pieces, the whole 75-by-50-mm area must be used to determine Q. It is the difference of pushes (or pulls) on this whole area that causes the unbalanced force that must be transferred at the surface b–b:

$$Q = A_{fghj}\bar{y} = 75 \times 50 \times 62.5 = 234 \times 10^3 \text{ mm}^3$$

$$q = \frac{VQ}{I} = \frac{3000 \times 234 \times 10^3}{113.4 \times 10^6} = 6.19 \text{ N/mm}$$

Nails should be spaced at $700/6.19 = 113$ mm intervals along the length of the beam in both sections $b–b$. These nails should be driven in first, then the 25-by-50-mm pieces put on.

Example 10-2

A simple beam on a 6-m span carriers a load of 3 kN/m, including its own weight. The beam's cross section is to be made from several wooden pieces, as is shown in mm in Fig. 10-7(a). Specify the spacing of the 10-mm lag screws shown that is necessary to fasten this beam together. Assume that one 10-mm lag screw, as determined by laboratory tests, is good for 2 kN when transmitting lateral load parallel to the grain of the wood. For the *entire* section, I is equal to 2.36×10^9 mm^2.

SOLUTION

To find the spacing of the lag screws, the shear flow at section $a–a$ must be determined. The loading on the given beam is shown in Fig. 10-7(b), and to show the variation of the shear along the beam, the shear diagram is constructed in Fig. 10-7(c). Next, to apply the shear flow formula,

$$\int_{\substack{area \\ fghj}} y \, dA = Q$$

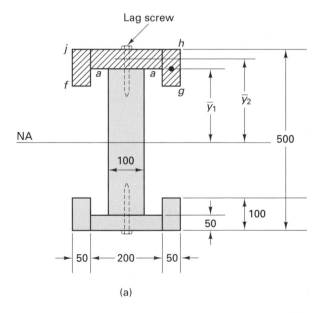

(a)

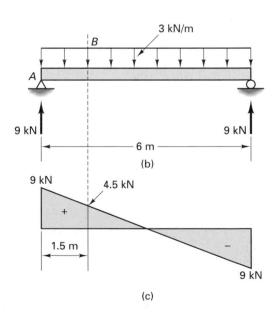

Fig. 10-7

must be determined. This is done by considering the *hatched* area to one side of the cut *a–a* in Fig. 10-7(a). The statical moment of this area is most conveniently computed by multiplying the areas of the *two* 50-by-100-mm pieces by the distances from their centroids to the neutral axis of the beam and adding to this product a similar quantity for the 50-by-200-mm piece. The largest shear flow occurs at the supports, as the largest vertical shears *V* of 9 kN act there:

$$Q = A_{fghj}\bar{y} = 2A_1\bar{y}_1 + A_2\bar{y}_2$$

$$= 2 \times 50 \times 100 \times 200 + 50 \times 200 \times 225 = 4.25 \times 10^6 \text{ mm}^3$$

$$q = \frac{VQ}{I} = \frac{9 \times 4.25 \times 10^9}{2.36 \times 10^9} = 16.2 \text{ N/mm}$$

At the supports, the spacing of the lag screws must be $2 \times 10^3/16.2 = 123$ mm apart. This spacing of the lag screws applies only at a section where shear *V* is equal to 9 kN. Similar calculations for a section where $V = 4.5$ kN give $q = 8.1$ N/mm, and the spacing of the lag screws becomes $2 \times 10^3/8.1 = 246$ mm. Thus, it is proper to specify the use of 10-mm lag screws on 120-mm centers for a distance of 1.5 m nearest both of the supports and 240-mm spacing of the same lag screws for the middle half of the beam. A greater refinement in making the transition from one spacing of fastenings to another may be desirable in some problems. The *same spacing* of lag screws should be used at section *b–b* as at section *a–a*.

In numerous practical applications, beams are made up by bolting or riveting longitudinal pieces, as shown in Fig. 10-8(a), or welding them, as shown in Fig. 10-8(b). Spacing of selected bolts or rivets, as well as sizing of welds, is determined using procedures analogous to those described before. The strength of individual bolts or rivets as well as welds is discussed in Section 1-8. Note that the bolts may be staggered along the length of a beam and that some may act in double shear. The welds may be either continuous or intermittent.

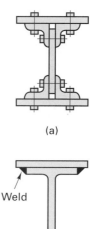

(a)

Weld

(b)

Fig. 10-8   Composite beam sections: (a) plate girder, (b) I beam reinforced with plates.

10-4. The Shear Stress Formula for Beams

The shear stress formula for beams may be obtained by modifying the shear flow formula. Thus, analogous to the earlier procedure, an element of a beam may be isolated between two adjoining sections taken perpendicular to the axis of the beam. Then by passing *another imaginary longitudinal section* through this element parallel to the axis of the beam, a new element is obtained, which corresponds to the element of one "plank" used in the earlier derivations. A side view of such an element is shown in Fig. 10-9(a), where the imaginary longitudinal cut is made at a

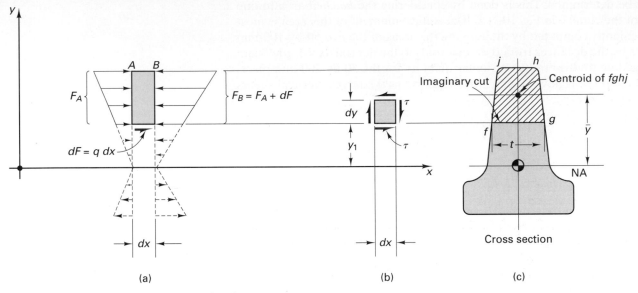

Fig. 10-9   Derivation of shear stresses in a beam.

distance y_1 from the neutral axis. The cross-sectional area of the beam is shown in Fig. 10-9(c).

If shear forces exist at the sections through the beam, a different bending moment acts at section A than at B. Hence, more push or pull is developed on one side of the *partial area fghj* than on the other, and, as before, this *longitudinal* force in a distance dx is

$$dF = \frac{dM}{I} \int_{\substack{\text{area}\\fghj}} y \, dA = \frac{dM}{I} A_{fghj}\bar{y} = \frac{dM}{I} Q$$

In a *solid* beam, the force resisting dF may be developed only *in the plane* of the longitudinal cut taken parallel to the axis of the beam. Therefore, assuming that the shear stress τ is *uniformly distributed*[3] across the section of width t, the shear stress in the *longitudinal plane* may be obtained by dividing dF by the area $t \, dx$. This yields the horizontal shear stress τ. For an *infinitesimal* element, however, numerically equal shear stresses[4] act on the mutually perpendicular planes; see Fig. 10-9(b). Hence,

---

[3]This procedure is best suited to situations where the section sides are parallel and are away from significant changes in the shape of the cross section. For limitations see Section 10-6.

[4]Note that the sense of positive τ agrees with the positive sense for V in beams adopted in Section 7-6.

the same relation gives *simultaneously* the longitudinal shear stress and the shear stress *in the plane of the vertical section at the longitudinal cut:*[5]

$$\tau = \frac{dF}{dx\, t} = \frac{dM}{dx} \frac{A_{fghj}\bar{y}}{It}$$

This equation may be simplified, since according to Eq. 10-1, $dM/dx = V$, and, by Eq. 10-5, $q = VQ/I$. Hence,

$$\tau = \frac{VA_{fghj}\bar{y}}{It} = \frac{VQ}{It} = \frac{q}{t} \qquad (10\text{-}6)$$

Equation 10-6 is the important formula for the shear stresses in a beam.[6] It gives the shear stresses *at* the longitudinal cut. As before, V is the *total* shear force at a section, and I is the moment of inertia of the *whole* cross-sectional area about the neutral axis. Both V and I are constant at a section through a beam. Here Q is the statical moment around the neutral axis of the *partial* area of the cross section to one side of the imaginary longitudinal cut, and $\bar{y}$ is the distance from the neutral axis of the beam to the centroid of the partial area A_{fghj}. Finally, t is the width of the imaginary longitudinal cut, which is usually equal to the thickness or width of the member. The shear stress at different longitudinal cuts through the beam assumes different values as the values of Q and t for such sections differ.

Care must be exercised in making the longitudinal cuts preparatory for use in Eq. 10-6. The proper sectioning of some cross-sectional areas of beams is shown in Figs. 10-10(a), (b), (d), and (e). The use of inclined cutting planes should be avoided *unless* the section is made across a small thickness. When the axis of symmetry of the cross-sectional area of the beam is vertical and in the plane of the applied forces, the longitudinal cuts are usually made horizontally. In such cases, the solution of Eq. 10-6 gives simultaneous values of *horizontal and vertical* shear stresses, as such planes are mutually perpendicular; see Eq. 1-2. The latter stresses act in the plane of the transverse section through the beam. Collectively, these shear stresses resist the shear force at the same section, thus satisfying the relation of statics, $\Sigma F_y = 0$. The validity of this statement for a special case will be proved in Example 10-3.

---

[5]The presence of $\bar{y}$ in this relation may be explained differently. If the shear is present at a section through a beam, the moments at the adjoining sections are M and $M + dM$. The magnitude of M is irrelevant for determining the shear stresses. Hence, alternately, *no* moment need be considered at one section *if at the adjoining section, a bending moment* dM *is assumed to act.* Then on a partial area of the section, such as the shaded area in Fig. 10-9(c), this bending moment dM will cause an *average normal stress* $(dM)\bar{y}/I$, as given by the flexure formula. In the latter relation, $\bar{y}$ locates the fiber that is at an *average* distance from the neutral axis in the *partial* area of a section. Multiplying $(dM)\bar{y}/I$ by the partial area of the section leads to the same expression for dF as before.

[6]This formula was derived by D. I. Jouravsky in 1855. Its development was prompted by observing horizontal cracks in wood ties on several of the railroad bridges between Moscow and St. Petersburg.

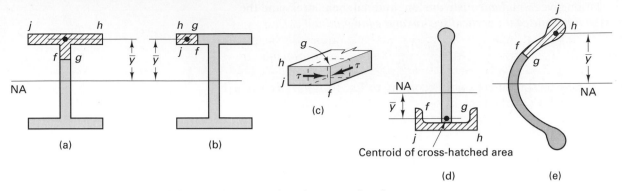

Fig. 10-10   Sectioning for partial areas of cross sections for computing shear stresses.

For thin members only, Eq. 10-6 may be used to determine the shear stresses with a cut such as *f–g* of Fig. 10-10(b). These shear stresses act in a vertical plane and are directed perpendicularly to the plane of the paper. Matching shear stresses act horizontally; see Fig. 10-10(c). These shear stresses act in *entirely different directions* than those obtained by making horizontal cuts, such as *f–g* in Figs. 10-10(a) and (d). As these shear stresses do not contribute directly to the resistance of vertical shear *V*, their significance will be discussed in Section 10-7.

Procedure Summary

The same *three basic concepts* of engineering mechanics of solids as before are used in developing the formula for shear stresses in beams. However, their use is less direct.

1. *Equilibrium conditions* are used,
   (a) for determining the shear at a section
   (b) by using the relationship between the shear and the rate of change in bending moment along a span, and
   (c) by determining the force at a longitudinal section of a beam element for obtaining the average shear stress.
2. *Geometry of deformation,* as in pure bending, is assumed such that plane sections remain plane after deformation, leading to the conclusion that normal strains in a section vary linearly from the neutral axis. Since, due to shear, the cross sections do not remain plane, but warp, this assumption is less accurate than for pure bending. However, for small and moderate magnitudes of shear, and slender members, this assumption is satisfactory.
3. *Material properties* are considered to obey Hooke's law, although extension to other constitutive relations is possible for elementary solutions.

These conditions treat the problem as one dimensional, and the assumed geometry of deformation is insensitive to the effects of concentrated forces and/or changes in the cross-sectional areas of beams. Therefore, again, reliance is largely placed on *Saint-Venant's principle*. In other words, only at distances beyond the member depth from such disturbances are the solutions accurate. Therefore, solutions are best suited for slender members; see Section 10-5. Further, rigorous solutions show that for wide longitudinal sections, solutions are somewhat inaccurate due to complex warpage of their cross sections near the sides.

An application of Eq. 10-6 for determining shear stresses in a rectangular beam is given next. Based on the results obtained in this example, a general discussion follows of the effect of shear on warpage of initially plane sections in beams. Then two additional examples on the application of Eq. 10-6 are provided.

Example 10-3

Derive an expression for the shear stress distribution in a beam of solid rectangular cross section transmitting a vertical shear V.

SOLUTION

The cross-sectional area of the beam is shown in Fig. 10-11(a). A longitudinal cut through the beam at a distance y_1 from the neutral axis isolates the partial area $fghj$ of the cross section. Here $t = b$, and the infinitesimal area of the cross section may be conveniently expressed as $b\ dy$. By applying

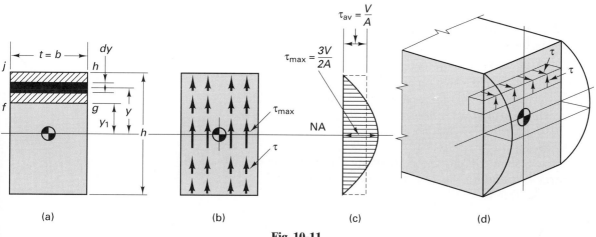

Fig. 10-11

Eq. 10-6, the horizontal shear stress is found *at* level y_1 of the beam. *At* the same cut, numerically equal vertical shear stresses act *in the plane of the cross section;* see Eq. 1-2. So,

$$\tau = \frac{VQ}{It} = \frac{V}{It} \int_{\substack{\text{area} \\ \text{fghj}}} y\, dA = \frac{V}{Ib} \int_{y1}^{h/2} by\, dy$$

(10-7)

$$= \frac{V}{I} \left. \frac{y^2}{2} \right|_{y1}^{h/2} = \frac{V}{2I}\left[\left(\frac{h}{2}\right)^2 - y_1^2 \right]$$

This equation shows that in a beam of rectangular cross section, both the horizontal and the vertical shear stresses vary parabolically. The maximum value of the shear stress is obtained when y_1 is equal to zero. *In the plane of the cross section,* Fig. 10-11(b), this is diagrammatically represented by τ_{max} *at* the neutral axis of the beam. At increasing distances from the neutral axis, the shear stresses gradually diminish. At the upper and lower boundaries of the beam, the shear stresses cease to exist as $y_1 = \pm h/2$. These values of the shear stresses at the various levels of the beam may be represented by the parabola shown in Fig. 10-11(c). An isometric view of the beam with horizontal and vertical shear stresses is shown in Fig. 10-11(d).

To satisfy the condition of statics, $\Sigma F_y = 0$, at a section of the beam, the sum of all the vertical shear stresses τ times their respective areas dA must be equal to the vertical shear V. That this is the case may be shown by integrating $\tau\, dA$ over the *whole* cross-sectional area A of the beam, using the general expression for τ found previously:

$$\int_A \tau\, dA = \frac{V}{2I} \int_{-h/2}^{+h/2} \left[\left(\frac{h}{2}\right)_2^2 - y_1^2 \right] b\, dy_1 = \frac{Vb}{2I}\left[\left(\frac{h}{2}\right)^2 y_1 - \left(\frac{y_1^3}{3}\right) \right]_{-h/2}^{+h/2}$$

$$= \frac{Vb}{2bh^3/12}\left[\left(\frac{h}{2}\right)^2 h - \frac{2}{3}\left(\frac{h}{2}\right)^3 \right] = V$$

As the derivation of Eq. 10-6 was indirect, this proof showing that the shear stresses integrated over the section equal the vertical shear is reassuring. Moreover, since an agreement in signs is found, this result indicates that *the direction of the shear stresses at the section through a beam is the same as that of the shear force* V. This fact may be used to determine the sense of the shear stresses.

As noted before, the maximum shear stress in a rectangular beam occurs at the neutral axis, and for this case, the general expression for τ_{max} may be simplified by setting $y_1 = 0$:

$$\tau_{max} = \frac{Vh^2}{8I} = \frac{Vh^2}{8bh^3/12} = \frac{3}{2}\frac{V}{bh} = \frac{3}{2}\frac{V}{A}$$

(10-8a)

where V is the total shear and A is the *entire* cross-sectional area. The same result may be obtained more directly if it is noted that to make VQ/It a maximum, Q must attain its largest value, as in this case V, I, and t are constants. From the property of the statical moments of areas around a centroidal axis, the maximum value of Q is obtained by considering one-half the cross-sectional area around the neutral axis of the beam. Hence, alternately,

$$\tau_{max} = \frac{VQ}{It} = \frac{V\left(\dfrac{bh}{2}\right)\left(\dfrac{h}{4}\right)}{\left(\dfrac{bh^3}{12}\right)b} = \frac{3}{2}\frac{V}{A} \qquad (10\text{-}8b)$$

Since beams of rectangular cross-sectional area are used frequently in practice, Eq. 10-8b is very useful. It is widely used in the design of wooden beams since the shear strength of wood on planes parallel to the grain is small. Thus, although equal shear stresses exist on mutually perpendicular planes, wooden beams have a tendency to split longitudinally along the neutral axis. Note that the maximum shear stress is $1\frac{1}{2}$ times as great as the *average shear stress* V/A. Nevertheless, in the analysis of bolts and rivets, it is customary to determine the shear strengths by dividing the shear force V by the cross-sectional area A. (See Section 1-8.) Such practice is considered justified since the allowable and ultimate strengths are initially determined in this manner from tests. For beams, on the other hand, Eq. 10-6 is generally applied.

ALTERNATIVE SOLUTION

From the point of view of elasticity, internal stresses and strains in beams are statically indeterminate. However, in the engineering theory discussed here, the introduction of a kinematic hypothesis that plane sections remain plane after bending changes this situation. Here, in Eq. 8-11, it is asserted that in a beam, $\sigma_x = -My/I$. Therefore, from the conditions of no shear stress at the top and the bottom boundaries, $\tau_{yx} = 0$ at $y = \pm h/2$, the constant of integration is found.

From Eq. 1-5a, with $-X = 0$,

$$\frac{\partial\sigma_x}{\partial x} + \frac{\partial\tau_{xy}}{\partial y} = 0$$

But

$$\sigma_x = -\frac{My}{I}$$

Hence,[7]

$$\frac{\partial\sigma_x}{\partial x} = -\frac{\partial M}{\partial x}\frac{y}{I} = \frac{Vy}{I}$$

[7]In the elasticity sign convention used here, positive shear stress acts upward on the right face of an element, as shown in Fig. 1-5. By analogy this requires that $\partial M/\partial x = -V$.

Thus,

$$\frac{Vy}{I} + \frac{d\tau_{xy}}{dy} = 0$$

Upon integrating, we obtain

$$\tau_{xy} = -\frac{Vy^2}{2I} + C_1$$

Since

$$\tau_{xy}(\pm h/2) = 0$$

one has

$$C_1 = \frac{Vh^2}{8I}$$

and

$$\tau_{xy} = \tau_{yx} = \frac{V}{2I}\left[\left(\frac{h}{2}\right)^2 - y^2\right]$$

This agrees with the result found earlier, since here $y = y_1$.

10-5. Warpage of Plane Sections Due to Shear

A solution based on the mathematical theory of elasticity for a rectangular beam subjected simultaneously to bending *and* shear shows that plane sections perpendicular to the beam axis warp (i.e., they do not remain plane). This can also be concluded from Eq. 10-7 derived in the preceding example.

According to Hooke's law, shear strains must be associated with shear stresses. Therefore, the shear stresses given by Eq. 10-7 give rise to shear strains. According to this equation, the maximum shear stress, and hence, maximum shear strain, occurs at $y = 0$; conversely, no shear strain takes place at $y = \pm h/2$. This behavior warps the initially plane sections through a beam, as shown qualitatively in Fig. 10-12, and contradicts the fundamental assumption of the simplified bending theory for pure flexure. However, based on rigorous analysis, warpage of the sections is known to be important only for very short members and is negligibly small for slender members. This can be substantiated by the two-dimensional finite element studies for rectangular cantilevers shown in Figs. 10-13 and 10-14. In both instances, the beams are fixed along lines AB at the nodal points indicated by dots in the figures. To avoid local disturbances of the type shown earlier in Fig. 3-10, in each case applied forces P are distributed parabolically per Eq. 10-7 to the nodal points along lines CD.

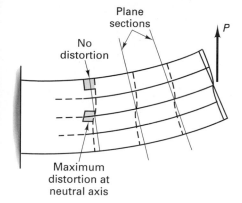

Fig. 10-12   Shear distortions in a beam.

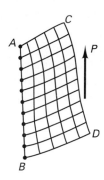

Fig. 10-13   Deformed mesh for a short cantilever from a finite element solution.

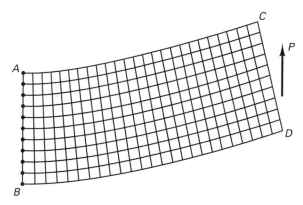

Fig. 10-14   Finite element solution showing deformation of a moderately long cantilever.

The displacements of the nodal points of the elements for both beams shown in the figures are *greatly exaggerated.* For the numerical values used, they are increased by a factor of 3000 compared with the linear dimensions of the members. Considerable warpage of the initially plane sections can be clearly observed for the short cantilever in Fig. 10-13. By contrast, for the longer member in Fig. 10-14, the warpage of the sections is imperceptible. This study, together with an examination of analytical results as well as experimental measurements on beams, suggests that the assumption of "plane sections" is reasonable. It should also be noted that if shear force V along a beam is constant and the boundaries provide no restraint, the warping of all cross sections is the same. Therefore, the strain distribution caused by bending remains the same as in pure bending. Based on these considerations, a far-reaching conclusion can be made that the presence of shear at a section does not invalidate the expressions for bending stresses derived earlier.

It is cautioned, however, that local disturbances of stresses occur at the points of load applications, and the use of the elementary elastic theory for short beams is questionable. (At this time it is recommended to read Section 13-3, in which limitations of the beam theory discussed in this text are pointed out.)

Example 10-4

Using the simplified theory, determine the shear stress distribution due to shear V in the elastic-plastic zone of a rectangular beam.

SOLUTION

This situation occurs, for example, in a cantilever loaded as shown in Fig. 10-15(a). In the elastic-plastic zone, the external bending moment $M = -Px$, whereas, according to Eq. 8-29, the internal resisting moment $M = M_p - \sigma_{yp}by_o^2/3$. Upon noting that y_o varies with x and differentiating the preceding equations, one notes the following equality:

$$\frac{dM}{dx} = -P = -\frac{2by_o\sigma_{yp}}{3}\frac{dy_o}{dx}$$

This relation will be needed later. First, however, proceeding as in the elastic case, consider the equilibrium of a beam element, as shown in Fig. 10-15(b).

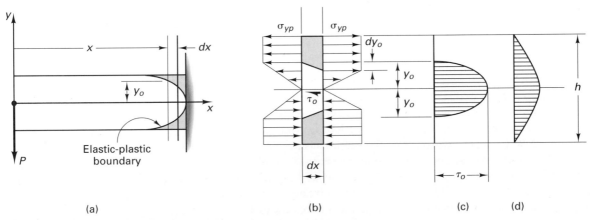

(a)   (b)   (c)   (d)

Fig. 10-15   Shear stress distribution in a rectangular elastic-plastic beam.

Larger longitudinal forces act on the right side of this element than on the left. By separating the beam at the neutral axis and equating the force at the cut to the difference in the longitudinal force, one obtains

$$\tau_o \, dx \, b = \sigma_{yp} \, dy_o \, b/2$$

where b is the width of the beam. After substituting dy_o/dx from the relation found earlier and eliminating b, one finds the maximum horizontal shear stress τ_o to be

$$\tau_o = \frac{\sigma_{yp}}{2} \frac{dy_o}{dx} = \frac{3P}{4by_o} = \frac{3}{2} \frac{P}{A_o} \tag{10-9}$$

where A_o is the cross-sectional area of the elastic part of the cross section. The shear stress distribution for the elastic-plastic case is shown in Fig. 10-15(c). This can be contrasted with that for the elastic case, shown in Fig. 10-15(d). Since equal and opposite normal stresses occur in the plastic zones, no unbalance in longitudinal forces occurs and no shear stresses are developed.

This elementary solution has been refined by using a more carefully formulated criterion of yielding caused by the simultaneous action of normal and shear stresses.[8]

Example 10-5

An I beam is loaded as shown in Fig. 10-16(a). If it has the cross section shown in Fig. 10-16(c), determine the shear stresses at the levels indicated. Neglect the weight of the beam.

SOLUTION

From the free-body diagram of the beam segment in Fig. 10-16(b), it is seen that the vertical shear at all sections is 50 kips. Bending moments do not enter directly into the present problem. The shear flow at the various levels of the beam is computed in the following table using Eq. 10-5. Since $\tau = q/t$, from Eq. 10-6, the shear stresses are obtained by dividing the shear flows by the respective widths of the beam:

$$I = 6 \times 12^3/12 - 5.5 \times 11^3/12 = 254 \text{ in}^4$$

For use in Eq. 10-5, the ratio $V/I = 50,000/254 = 197 \text{ lb/in}^4$. Some results at selected horizontal sections are given in the following table:

---

[8]D. C. Drucker, "The effect of shear on the plastic bending of beams," *J. Appl. Mech.*, **23** (1956), 509–514.

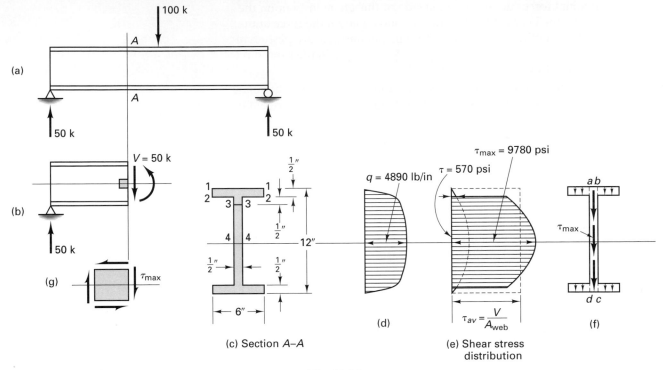

(a)

(b)

$V = 50$ k

(g)

τ_{max}

100 k

50 k

50 k

50 k

(c) Section A–A

12"

6"

$q = 4890$ lb/in

(d)

$\tau = 570$ psi

$\tau_{max} = 9780$ psi

$\tau_{av} = \dfrac{V}{A_{web}}$

(e) Shear stress distribution

τ_{max}

(f)

Fig. 10-16

Level	A_{fghj}[a]	$\bar{y}$[b]	$Q = A_{fghj}\bar{y}$	$q = VQ/I$	t	τ (psi)
1–1	0	6	0	0	6.0	0
					6.0	570
2–2	$0.5 \times 6 = 3.00$	5.75	17.25	3400	0.5	6800
3–3	$\begin{cases} 0.5 \times 6 = 3.00 \\ 0.5 \times 0.5 = 0.25 \end{cases}$	$\begin{matrix} 5.75 \\ 5.25 \end{matrix}$	$\left.\begin{matrix} 17.25 \\ 1.31 \end{matrix}\right\}18.56$	3650	0.5	7300
4–4	$\begin{cases} 0.5 \times 6 = 3.00 \\ 0.5 \times 5.5 = 2.75 \end{cases}$	$\begin{matrix} 5.75 \\ 2.75 \end{matrix}$	$\left.\begin{matrix} 17.25 \\ 7.56 \end{matrix}\right\}24.81$	4890	0.5	9780

[a] A_{fghj} is the partial area of the cross section above a given level in in.^{2}.
[b] $\bar{y}$ is distance in mm from the neutral axis to the centroid of the partial area.

The positive signs of τ show that, for the section considered, the stresses act downward on the right face of the elements. This sense of the shear stresses coincides with the sense of shear force V. For this reason, a strict adherence to the sign convention is often unnecessary. It is always true that $\int_A \tau \, dA$ is equal to V and has the same sense.

Note that at level 2–2, two widths are used to determine the shear stress—one just above the line 2–2, and one just below. A width of 6 in corresponds to the first case, and 0.5 in to the second. This transition point will be discussed in the next section. The results obtained, which by virtue of symmetry are also applicable to the lower half of the section, are plotted in Figs. 10-16(d) and (e). By a method similar to the one used in the preceding example, it may be shown that the curves in Fig. 10-16(e) are parts of a second-degree parabola.

The variation of the shear stress indicated by Fig. 10-16(e) may be interpreted as shown in Fig. 10-16(f). The maximum shear stress occurs at the neutral axis, and the vertical shear stresses throughout the web of the beam are nearly of the same magnitude. The vertical shear stresses occurring in the flanges are very small. For this reason, the maximum shear stress in an I beam is often approximated by dividing the total shear V by the cross-sectional area of the web, with the web height assumed equal to the beam's overall height, area $abcd$ in Fig. 10-16(f). Hence,

$$(\tau_{max})_{approx} = \frac{V}{A_{web}} \tag{10-10}$$

In the example considered, this gives

$$(\tau_{max})_{approx} = \frac{50,000}{0.5 \times 12} = 8330 \text{ psi}$$

This stress differs by about 15% from the one found by the accurate formula. For most cross sections, a much closer approximation to the true maximum shear stress may be obtained by dividing the shear by the web area between the flanges only. For this example, this procedure gives a stress of 9091 psi, which is an error of only about 8%. It should be clear from the foregoing that division of V by the whole cross-sectional area of the beam to obtain the shear stress is not permissible.

An element of the beam at the neutral axis is shown in Fig. 10-16(g). At levels 3–3 and 2–2, bending stresses, in addition to the shear stresses, act on the vertical faces of the elements. No shear stresses and only bending stresses act on the elements at level 1–1.

The sides of cross sections were assumed to be parallel in all the preceding examples. If they are not parallel, both Q and t vary with the section level, and the maximum shear stress may not occur at the neutral axis. However, using Eq. 10-6, the maximum *average* shear stress can always be found. For example, it can be shown that for a symmetric triangular cross section, such a maximum shear stress is midway between the apex and the base. For such cross sections, the stresses vary across a longitudinal section and are particularly inaccurate near the sloping sides; see Fig. 10-18. Similar results may develop at longitudinal sections taken at an angle with the axes.

The same procedures as described before are used for determining longitudinal shear stresses in composite beams at bonded or glued surfaces.

10-6.   Some Limitations of the Shear Stress Formula

The shear stress formula for beams is based on the flexure formula. Hence, all of the limitations imposed on the flexure formula apply. The material is assumed to be elastic with the same elastic modulus in tension as in compression. The theory developed applies only to straight beams. Moreover, there are additional limitations that are not present in the flexure formula. Some of these will be discussed now.

Consider a section through the I beam analyzed in Example 10-5. Some of the results of this analysis are reproduced in Fig. 10-17. The shear stresses computed earlier for level 1–1 apply to the infinitesimal element *a*. The vertical shear stress is zero for this element. Likewise, *no* shear stresses exist *on* the top plane of the beam. This is as it should be, since the top *surface* of the beam is a *free* surface. In mathematical phraseology, this means that the conditions at the boundary are satisfied. For beams of rectangular cross section, the situation at the boundaries is correct.

A different condition is found when the shear stresses determined for the I beam at levels 2–2 are scrutinized. The shear stresses were found to be 570 psi for the elements such as *b* or *c* shown in the figure. This requires matching horizontal shear stresses on the inner surfaces of the flanges. However, the latter surfaces *must be free* of the shear stresses, as they are *free boundaries* of the beam. This leads to a contradiction that cannot be resolved by the methods of engineering mechanics of solids. The more advanced techniques of the mathematical theory of elasticity or three-dimensional finite element analysis must be used to obtain an accurate solution.

Fortunately, the aforementioned defect of the shear stress formula for beams is not serious. The vertical shear stresses in the flanges are small. The large shear stresses occur in the web and, for all practical purposes, are correctly given by Eq. 10-6. *No appreciable error is involved by using the rela-*

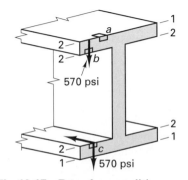

Fig. 10-17   Boundary conditions are not satisfied at the levels 2–2.

tions derived in this chapter for thin-walled members, and the majority of beams belong to this group. Moreover, as stated earlier, the solution for the shear stresses for a beam with a rectangular cross section is correct.

In mechanical applications, circular shafts frequently act as beams. Hence, beams having a solid circular cross section form an important class. These beams are not "thin walled." An examination of the boundary conditions for circular members, Fig. 10-18(a), leads to the conclusion that when shear stresses are present, they must act parallel to the boundary. As no matching shear stress can exist *on* the free surface of a beam, no shear stress component can act normal to the boundary. However, according to Eq. 10-6, *vertical* shear stresses of *equal* intensity act at every level, such as *ac* in Fig. 10-18(b). This is incompatible with the boundary conditions for elements *a* and *c*, and the solution indicated by Eq. 10-6 is inconsistent.[9] Fortunately, the *maximum* shear stresses occurring at the neutral axis satisfy the boundary conditions and are within about 5% of their true value.[10]

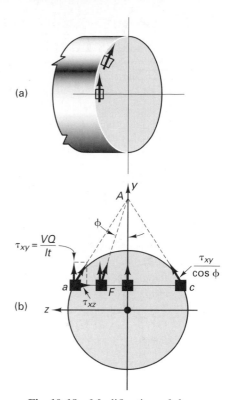

Fig. 10-18 Modification of shear stresses to satisfy the boundary conditions.

10-7. Shear Stress in Beam Flanges

In an I beam, the existence of shear stresses acting in a vertical longitudinal cut, such as *c–c* in Fig. 10-19(a), was indicated in Fig. 10-2(f) and Section 10-4. These shear stresses act perpendicular to the plane of the paper. Their magnitude may be found by applying Eq. 10-6, and their sense follows by considering the bending moments at the adjoining sections through the beam. For example, if, for the beam shown in Fig. 10-19(b), *positive* bending moments increase toward the reader, larger *normal* forces act on the *near* section. For the elements shown, $\tau t \, dx$ or $q \, dx$ must aid the smaller force acting on the partial area of the cross section. This fixes the sense of the shear stresses in the longitudinal cuts. However, numerically equal shear stresses act on the mutually perpendicular planes of an *infinitesimal* element, and the shear stresses on such planes either meet or part with their directional arrowheads at a corner. Hence, the sense of the shear stresses in the plane of the section also becomes known.

The magnitude of the shear stresses varies for the different vertical cuts. For example, if cut *c–c* in Fig. 10-19(a) is at the edge of the beam, the

---

[9]The exact elastic solution of this problem is beyond the scope of this text. However, a better approximation of the true stresses may be obtained rather simply. First, an assumption is made that the shear stress as found by Eq. 10-6 gives a true *component* of the shear stress acting in the *vertical direction*. Then, since at every level the shear stresses at the boundary must act tangent to the boundary, the lines of action of these shear stresses intersect at some point, such as *A* in Fig. 10-18(b). Thus, a second assumption is made that all shear stresses at a given level act in a direction toward a single point, such as *A* in Fig. 10-18(b). Therefore, the shear stress at any point, such as *F*, becomes equal to $\tau_{xy}/\cos \phi$. The stress system found in this manner is consistent.

[10]A. E. H. Love, *Mathematical Theory of Elasticity,* 4th ed. (New York: Dover, 1944), 348.

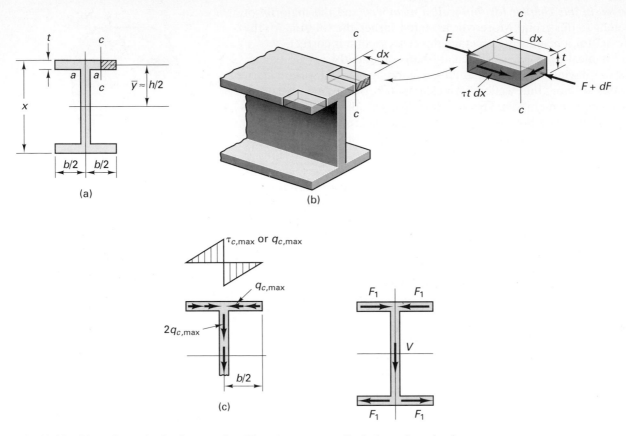

Fig. 10-19   Shear forces in the flanges of an I beam act perpendicularly to the axis of symmetry.

hatched area of the beam's cross section is zero. However, if the thickness of the flange is constant, and cut c–c is made progressively closer to the web, this area increases from zero at a linear rate. Moreover, as $\bar{y}$ remains constant for any such area, Q also increases linearly from zero toward the web. Therefore, since V and I are constant at any section through the beam, shear flow $q_c = VQ/I$ follows the same variation. If the thickness of the flange remains the same, the shear stress $\tau_c = VQ/It$ varies similarly. The same variation of q_c and τ_c applies on both sides of the axis of symmetry of the cross section. However, as may be seen from Fig. 10-19(b), these quantities in the plane of the cross section act in *opposite* directions on the two sides. The variation of these shear stresses or shear flows is represented in Fig. 10-19(c), where, for simplicity, it is assumed that the web has zero thickness.

In common with all stresses, the shear stresses shown in Fig. 10-19(c), when integrated over the area on which they act, are equivalent to a force. The magnitude of the horizontal force F_1 for *one-half* of the flange, shown in Fig. 10-19(d), is equal to the *average* shear stress multiplied by *one-half of the whole area of the flange;* that is,

$$F_1 = \left(\frac{\tau_{c-\max}}{2}\right)\left(\frac{bt}{2}\right) \quad \text{or} \quad F_1 = \left(\frac{q_{c-\max}}{2}\right)\left(\frac{b}{2}\right) \qquad (10\text{-}11)$$

If an I beam transmits a vertical shear, these horizontal forces act in the upper and lower flanges. However, because of the *symmetry* of the cross section, these equal forces occur in pairs and *oppose* each other and cause no apparent external effect.

To determine the shear flow at the juncture of the flange and the web, as in cut *a–a* in Fig. 10-19(a), the *whole* area of the flange times $\bar{y}$ must be used in computing the value of Q. However, since in finding $q_{c,\max}$, *one-half* the flange area times the same $\bar{y}$ has already been used, the *sum* of the *two horizontal shear flows* coming in from opposite sides gives the *vertical* shear flow[11] at cut *a–a*. Hence, figuratively speaking, the horizontal shear flows "turn through 90° and merge to become the vertical shear flow." Thus, the shear flows at the various horizontal cuts through the web may be determined in the manner explained in the preceding sections. Moreover, as the resistance to the vertical shear V in thin-walled I beams is developed mainly in the web, it is so shown in Fig. 10-19(d). The sense of the shear stresses and shear flows *in the web* coincides with the direction of the shear V. Note that the vertical shear flow "splits" upon reaching the lower flange. This is represented in Fig. 10-19(d) by the two forces F_1, which are the result of the horizontal shear flows in the flanges.

The shear forces that act at a section of an I beam are shown in Fig. 10-19(d), and, for equilibrium, *the applied vertical forces must act through the centroid of the cross-sectional area* to be coincident with V. If the forces are so applied, *no torsion* of the member will occur. This is true for all sections having cross-sectional areas with an axis of symmetry. To avoid torsion of such members, the applied forces must act in the plane of symmetry of the cross section and the axis of the beam. A beam with an unsymmetrical section will be discussed next.

10-8. Shear Center

Consider a beam having the cross section of a channel; see Fig. 10-20(a). The walls of this channel are assumed to be sufficiently thin that the computations may be based on *centerline* dimensions. Bending of this channel takes place around the horizontal axis, and although this cross section does not have a vertical axis of symmetry, it will be *assumed* that the bending

---

[11]The same statement *cannot* be made with regard to the shear stresses, as the thickness of the flange may differ from that of the web.

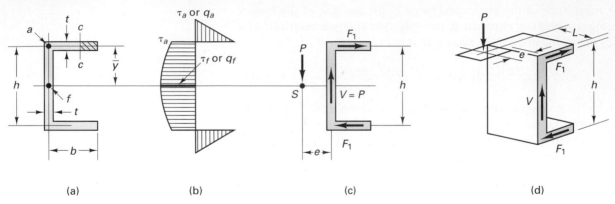

Fig. 10-20   Deriving location of shear center for a channel.

stresses are given by the usual flexure formula. Assuming further that this channel resists a vertical shear, the bending moments will vary from one section through the beam to another.

By taking an arbitrary vertical cut such as c–c in Fig. 10-20(a), q and τ may be found in the usual manner. Along the horizontal legs of the channel, these quantities vary linearly from the free edge, just as they do for one side of the flange in an I beam. The variation of q and τ is parabolic along the web. The variation of these quantities is shown in Fig. 10-20(b), where they are plotted along the centerline of the channel's section.

The *average* shear stress $\tau_a/2$ multiplied by the areas of the flange gives a force $F_1 = (\tau_a/2)bt$, and the sum of the vertical shear stresses over the area of the web is the shear $V = \int_{-h/2}^{+h/2} \tau t \, dy$.[12] These shear forces acting in the plane of the cross section are shown in Fig. 10-20(c) and indicate that a force V *and a couple* F_1h are developed at the section through the channel. Physically, there is a tendency for the channel to twist around some longitudinal axis. To prevent twisting and thus maintain the applicability of the initially assumed bending-stress distribution, the externally applied forces must be applied in such a manner as to *balance the internal couple* F_1h. For example, consider the segment of a cantilever beam of negligible weight, shown in Fig. 10-20(d), to which a vertical force P is applied parallel to the web at a distance e from the web's *centerline*. To maintain this applied force in equilibrium, an *equal and opposite* shear force V must be developed in the web. Likewise, to cause *no twisting of the channel,* couple Pe must *equal* couple F_1h. At the same section through the channel, bending moment PL is resisted by the *usual* flexural stresses (these are not shown in the figure).

---

[12]When the thickness of a channel is variable, it is more convenient to find F_1 and V by using the respective shear flows; that is, $F_1 = (q_a/2)b$ and $V = \int_{-h/2}^{+h/2} q \, dy$. Since the flanges are thin, the vertical shear force carried by them is negligible.

An expression for distance e, locating the plane in which force P must be applied so as to cause *no twist* in the channel, may now be obtained. Thus, remembering that $F_1h = Pe$ and $P = V$,

$$e = \frac{F_1h}{P} = \frac{(1/2)\tau_a bth}{P} = \frac{bth}{2P}\frac{VQ}{It} = \frac{bth}{2P}\frac{Vbt(h/2)}{It} = \frac{b^2h^2t}{4I} \quad (10\text{-}12)$$

Note that distance e is independent of the magnitude of applied force P, as well as of its location along the beam. Distance e is a property of a section and is measured outward from the *center* of the web to the applied force.

A similar investigation may be made to locate the plane in which the horizontal forces must be applied so as to cause no twist in the channel. However, for the channel considered, by virtue of symmetry, it may be seen that this plane coincides with the neutral plane of the former case. The intersection of these two mutually perpendicular planes with the plane of the cross section locates a point that is called the *shear center*.[13] The shear center is designated by the letter S in Fig. 10-20(c). The shear center for any cross section lies on a longitudinal line parallel to the axis of the beam. *Any transverse force applied through the shear center causes no torsion of the beam.* A detailed investigation of this problem shows that when a member of any cross-sectional area *is* twisted, the twist takes place around the shear center, which remains fixed. For this reason, the shear center is sometimes called the *center of twist*.

For cross-sectional areas having one axis of symmetry, the shear center is always located on the axis of symmetry. For those that have two axes of symmetry, the shear center coincides with the centroid of the cross-sectional area. This is the case for the I beam that was considered in the previous section.

The exact location of the shear center for unsymmetrical cross sections of thick materials is difficult to obtain and is known only in a few cases. If the material is *thin,* as has been assumed in the preceding discussion, relatively simple procedures may always be devised to locate the shear center of the cross section. The usual procedure consists of determining the shear forces, as F_1 and V before, at a section, and then finding the location of the external force necessary to keep these forces in equilibrium.

Example 10-6

Find the approximate location of the shear center for a beam with the cross section of the channel shown in Fig. 10-21.

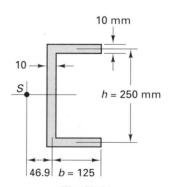

Fig. 10-21

---

[13]It was only in 1921 that A. Eggenschwyler and R. Maillart of Switzerland clarified this concept.

SOLUTION

Instead of using Eq. 10-12 directly, we may make some further simplifications. The moment of inertia of a thin-walled channel around its neutral axis may be found with sufficient accuracy by neglecting the moment of inertia of the flanges *around their own axes* (only!). This expression for I may then be substituted into Eq. 10-12, and, after simplifications, a formula for e of channels is obtained:

$$I \approx I_{web} + (Ad^2)_{flanges} = th^3/12 + 2bt(h/2)^2 = th^3/12 + bth^2/2$$

$$e = \frac{b^2h^2t}{4I} = \frac{b^2h^2t}{4(bth^2/2 + th^3/12)} = \frac{b}{2 + h/3b} \qquad (10\text{-}13)$$

Equation 10-13 shows that when the width of flanges b is very large, e approaches its maximum value of $b/2$. When h is very large, e approaches its minimum value of zero. Otherwise, e assumes an intermediate value between these two limits. For the numerical data given in Fig. 10-21,

$$e = \frac{125}{2 + 250/(3 \times 125)} = 46.9 \text{ mm}$$

Hence, the shear center S is $46.9 - 5.0 = 41.9$ mm from the outside vertical face of the channel.

Example 10-7

Find the approximate location of the shear center for the cross section of the I beam shown in Fig. 10-22(a). Note that the flanges are unequal.

SOLUTION

This cross section has a horizontal axis of symmetry, and the shear center is located on it; where it is located remains to be answered. Applied force P causes significant bending and shear stresses *only in the flanges,* and the contribution of the web to the resistance of applied force P is negligible.

Let the shear force resisted by the left flange of the beam be V_1, and by the right flange V_2. For equilibrium, $V_1 + V_2 = P$. Likewise, to have no twist of the section, from $\Sigma M_A = 0$, $Pe = V_2h$ (or $Pf = V_1h$). Thus, only V_2 remains to be determined to solve the problem. This may be done by noting that the right flange is actually an ordinary rectangular beam. The shear stress (or shear flow) in such a beam is distributed parabolically, as seen in Fig. 10-22(b), and since the area of a parabola is two-thirds of the base times the maximum altitude, $V_2 = \frac{2}{3}b_2(q_2)_{max}$. However, since the total shear $V = P$, by Eq. 10-5, $(q_2)_{max} = VQ/I = PQ/I$, where Q is the statical

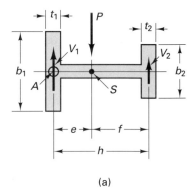

(a)

$q_{2, max}$

Shear flow in
right flange

(b)

Fig. 10-22

moment of the *upper half of the right-hand flange* and I is the moment of inertia of the *whole* section. Hence,

$$Pe = V_2 h = \frac{2}{3} b_2 (q_2)_{max} h = \frac{\frac{2}{3} h b_2 P Q}{I}$$

(10-14)

$$e = \frac{2 h b_2}{3I} Q = \frac{2 h b_2}{3I} \frac{b_2 t_2}{2} \frac{b_2}{4} = \frac{h}{I} \frac{t_2 b_2^3}{12} = \frac{h I_2}{I}$$

where I_2 is the moment of inertia of the *right-hand flange* around the neutral axis. Similarly, it may be shown that $f = h I_1 / I$, where I_1 applies to the *left flange*. If the web of the beam is thin, as originally assumed, $I \approx I_1 + I_2$, and $e + f = h$, as is to be expected.

A similar analysis leads to the conclusion that the shear center for a symmetrical angle is located at the intersection of the centerlines of its legs, as shown in Figs. 10-23(a) and (b). This follows since the shear flow at every section, as c–c, is directed along the centerline of a leg. These shear flows yield two identical forces, F_1, in the legs. The vertical components of these forces equal the vertical shear applied through S. An analogous situation is also found for any angle or T section, as shown in Figs. 10-24(a) and (b). The location of the shear center for various members is particularly important in aircraft applications.[14]

As remarked earlier, in order to prevent torsion of a beam, the applied force must act through the shear center. When such a force forms an angle with the vertical, it is best to resolve it into components along the principal axes of the cross section, as shown in Fig. 9-5. If force P is applied outside

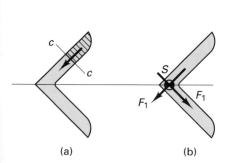

(a)   (b)

Fig. 10-23   Shear center for an equal leg angle is at S.

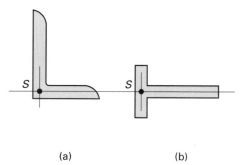

(a)   (b)

Fig. 10-24   Shear center for the sections shown is at S.

---

[14]For further details, see E. F. Bruhn, *Analysis and Design of Flight Vehicle Structures* (Cincinnati: Tri-State, 1965). See also P. Kuhn, *Stresses in Aircraft and Shell Structures* (New York: McGraw-Hill, 1956).

shear center S, as shown in Fig. 10-25, two equal but opposite forces P can be introduced at S without changing the problem. Then, in addition to the stresses caused by P applied at S, the torsional stresses caused by the torque equal to Pd must be considered, as described in Chapter 6.

It is to be noted that generally, in addition to the shear stresses discussed in this chapter, bending stresses usually also act on the elements considered. Transformation of this kind of state of stress is discussed in Chapter 11. In the remainder of this chapter, only superposition of the shear stresses is considered.

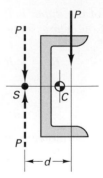

Fig. 10-25   Torsion bending of a channel.

10-9. Combined Direct and Torsional Shear Stresses

The analysis for combined direct and torsional shear stresses consists of two parts that are then superposed. In one of these parts, the direct shear stresses are determined using the procedures described earlier in this chapter; in the second, the shear stresses caused by torques susceptible to the methods of analysis treated in Chapter 6 are used.

The two analyses for combined shear stresses must be determined for the *same elementary area* regardless of cause. Multiplying these stresses by the respective area gives *forces*. Since these forces can be added vectorially, on reversing the process (i.e., on dividing the vector sum by the initial area), one obtains the combined shear stress. Such being the case, the shear stresses acting on the *same plane* of an infinitesimal element can be combined vectorially.[15] Generally, the maximum torsional shear stresses as well as the maximum direct shear stress for beams occur at the boundaries of cross sections and are collinear. Therefore, an algebraic sum of these stresses gives the combined shear stress at a point. However, on the interior of such members, a vectorial sum of the direct and torsional stresses is necessary.

In treating beam problems, as noted earlier, it must be recognized that in addition to the shear stresses discussed before, generally, normal stresses caused by bending also act on the elements considered. Procedures for combining such normal stresses with shear stresses are discussed in the next chapter.

Example 10-8

Find the maximum shear stress due to the applied forces in plane A–B of the 10-mm-diameter high-strength steel shaft shown in Fig. 10-26(a).

---

[15]The inverse problem of resolving a shear stress was considered in connection with Fig. 6-34.

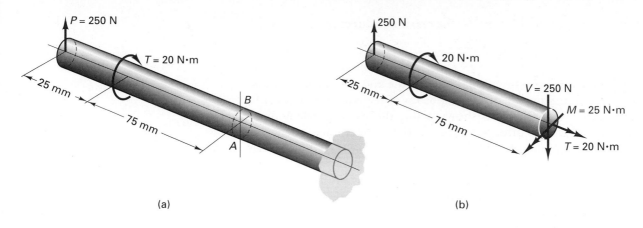

(a)   (b)

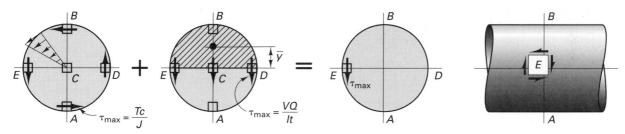

Fig. 10-26

SOLUTION

Since only the stresses due to the applied forces are required, the weight of the shaft need not be considered. The free body of a segment of the shaft is shown in Fig. 10-26(b). The system of forces at the cut necessary to keep this segment in equilibrium consists of a torque, $T = 20$ N · m, a shear, $V = 250$ N, and a bending moment, $M = 25$ N · m.

Due to torque T, the shear stresses in cut A–B vary linearly from the axis of the shaft and reach the maximum value given by Eq. 6-3, $\tau_{max} = Tc/I_p$. These maximum shear stresses, agreeing in sense with the *resisting* torque T, are shown at points A, B, D, and E in Fig. 10-26(c).

The direct shear stresses caused by shear force V may be obtained by using Eq. 10-6, $\tau = VQ/It$. For elements A and B, Fig. 10-26(d), $Q = 0$; hence, $\tau = 0$. The shear stress reaches its maximum value at level ED. For this, Q is equal to the cross-hatched area shown in Fig. 10-26(d) multiplied by the distance from its centroid to the neutral axis. The latter quantity is $\bar{y} = 4c/3\pi$, where c is the radius of the cross-sectional area; see Table 2 in the Appendix. Hence,

$$Q = \frac{\pi c^2}{2} \frac{4c}{3\pi} = \frac{2c^3}{3}$$

Moreover, since $t = 2c$ and $I = \pi c^4/4$, the maximum direct shear stress is

$$\tau_{max} = \frac{VQ}{It} = \frac{V}{2c} \frac{2c^3}{3} \frac{4}{\pi c^4} = \frac{4V}{3\pi c^2} = \frac{4V}{3A} \qquad (10\text{-}15)$$

where A is the *entire* cross-sectional area of the rod. (A similar expression was derived in Example 10-3 for a beam of rectangular section.) In Fig. 10-26(d), this shear stress is shown acting down on the elementary areas at E, C, and D. This direction agrees with the direction of shear V.

To find the maximum combined shear stress in plane A–B, the stresses shown in Figs. 10-26(c) and (d) are superposed. Inspection shows that the maximum shear stress is at E, since in the two diagrams, the shear stresses at E act in the same direction. There are no direct shear stresses at A and B, while at C there is no torsional shear stress. The two shear stresses act in *opposite* directions at D.

The combined shear stresses at the five points, A, B, C, D, and E, unlike most of the interior points, require no formal vectorial addition for determining their magnitudes. Since the torsional shear stresses at the interior points are smaller than those at the boundary, the maximum combined shear occurs at E:

$$I_p = \frac{\pi d^4}{32} = \frac{\pi \times 10^4}{32} = 982 \text{ mm}^4$$

$$I = \frac{I_p}{2} = 491 \text{ mm}^4$$

$$A = \frac{1}{4}\pi d^2 = 78.5 \text{ mm}^2$$

$$(\tau_{max})_{torsion} = \frac{Tc}{I_p} = \frac{20 \times 10^3 \times 5}{982} = 102 \text{ MPa}$$

$$(\tau_{max})_{direct} = \frac{VQ}{It} = \frac{4V}{3A} = \frac{4 \times 250}{3 \times 78.5} = 4 \text{ MPa}$$

$$\tau_E = 102 + 4 = 106 \text{ MPa}$$

A planar representation of the shear stress at E with the matching stresses on the longitudinal planes is shown in Fig. 10-26(f). No normal stress acts on this element, as it is located on the neutral axis.

10-10. Stresses in Closely Coiled Helical Springs[16]

Helical springs, such as the one shown in Fig. 10-27(a), are often used as elements of machines. With certain limitations, these springs may be analyzed for stresses by a method similar to the one used in the preceding

[16]This section is on a specialized topic and is optional.

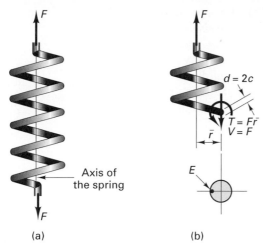

Fig. 10-27   Closely coiled helical spring.

example. The discussion will be limited to springs manufactured from rods or wires of circular cross section.[17] Moreover, *any one coil of such a spring will be assumed to lie in a plane that is nearly perpendicular to the axis of the spring.* This requires that the adjoining coils be close together. With this limitation, a section taken perpendicular to the axis of the spring's rod becomes *nearly vertical.*[18] Hence, to maintain equilibrium of a segment of the spring, only a shear force $V = F$ and a torque $T = F\bar{r}$ are required at *any* section through the rod; see Fig. 10-27(b). Note that $\bar{r}$ is the distance from the axis of the spring to the *centroid of the rod's cross-sectional area.*

Here it should be noted that in previous work, it has been reiterated that if a shear is present at a section, a change in the bending moment must take place along the member. Here a shear acts at every section of the rod, yet neither a bending moment nor a change in it appears to occur. This is so only because the rod is *curved.* Such an element of the rod viewed from the top is shown in Fig. 10-28. At both ends of the element, the torques are equal to $F\bar{r}$ and, using vectorial representation, act in the directions shown. The component of these vectors toward the axis of the spring O, resolved at the point of intersection of the vectors, $2F\bar{r}\, d\phi/2 = F\bar{r}\, d\phi$, opposes the couple developed by the vertical shears $V = F$, which are $\bar{r}\, d\phi$ apart.

The maximum shear stress at an arbitrary section through the rod could be obtained as in the preceding example, by superposing the torsional and the direct shearing stresses. This maximum shear stress occurs at

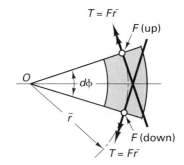

Fig. 10-28

[17]For an extensive discussion on springs, see A. M. Wahl, *Mechanical Springs* (Cleveland: Penton, 1944).

[18]This eliminates the necessity of considering an axial force and a bending moment at the section taken through the spring.

the inside of the coil at point E, as shown in Fig. 10-27(b). However, in the analysis of springs, it has become *customary to assume that the shear stress caused by the direct shear force is uniformly distributed over the cross-sectional area of the rod.* Hence, the nominal direct shear stress for any point on the cross section is $\tau = F/A$. Superposition of this *nominal* direct and the torsional shear stress at E gives the maximum combined shear stress. Thus, since $T = F\bar{r}$, $d = 2c$, and $I_p = \pi d^4/32$,

$$\tau_{max} = \frac{F}{A} + \frac{Tc}{I_p} = \frac{Tc}{I_p}\left(\frac{FI_p}{ATc} + 1\right) = \frac{16F\bar{r}}{\pi d^3}\left(\frac{d}{4\bar{r}} + 1\right) \quad (10\text{-}16)$$

It is seen from this equation that as the diameter of the rod d becomes small in relation to the coil radius $\bar{r}$, the effect of the direct shear stress also becomes small. On the other hand, if the reverse is true, the first term in the parentheses becomes important. However, in the latter case, the results indicated by Eq. 10-16 are considerably in error, and Eq. 10-16 should not be used, as it is based on the torsion formula for *straight rods*. As d becomes numerically comparable to $\bar{r}$, the length of the inside fibers of the coil differs greatly from the length of the outside fibers, and the assumptions of strain used in the torsion formula are not applicable.

The spring problem has been solved exactly[19] by the methods of the mathematical theory of elasticity, and while these results are complicated, for any one spring they may be made to depend on a single parameter $m = 2\bar{r}/d$, which is called the *spring index*. Thus, Eq. 10-16 may be rewritten as

$$\tau_{max} = K\frac{16F\bar{r}}{\pi d^3} \quad (10\text{-}17)$$

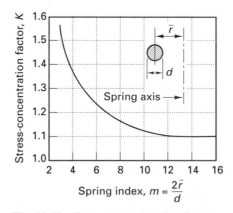

Fig. 10-29 Stress-concentration factors for helical round-wire compression or tension springs.

[19]O. Goehner, "Die Berechnung Zylindrischer Schraubenfedern," *Zeitschrift des Vereins deutscher Ingenieure,* **76,** no. 1 (March 1932), 269.

where K may be interpreted as a stress-concentration factor for closely coiled helical springs made from circular rods. A plot of K versus the spring index is shown[20] in Fig. 10-29. For heavy springs, the spring index is small; hence, the stress-concentration factor K becomes important. For all cases, factor K accounts for the correct amount of direct shear stress. Very high stresses are commonly allowed in springs because high-strength materials are used in their fabrication. For good-quality spring steel, working shear stresses range anywhere from 200 to 700 MPa (30 to 100 ksi).

10-11.   Deflection of Closely Coiled Helical Springs

For completeness, the deflection of closely coiled helical springs will be discussed in this section. Attention will be confined to closely coiled helical springs with a large spring index (i.e., the diameter of the wire will be assumed small in comparison with the radius of the coil). This permits the treatment of an element of a spring between two closely adjoining sections through the wire as a *straight circular bar in torsion*. The effect of direct shear on the deflection of the spring will be ignored. This is usually permissible as the latter effect is small.

Consider a helical spring such as shown in Fig. 10-30. A typical element AB of this spring is subjected throughout its length to a torque $T = F\bar{r}$. This torque causes a relative rotation between the two adjoining planes, A and B, and with sufficient accuracy, the amount of this rotation may be obtained by using Eq. 6-14, $d\phi = T\, dx/I_p G$, for straight circular bars. For this equation, the applied torque $T = F\bar{r}$, dx is the length of the element, G is the shear modulus of elasticity, and I_p is the polar moment of inertia of the *wire's cross-sectional area*.

If the plane A of the wire is imagined as fixed, the rotation of the plane B is given by the foregoing expression. The contribution of this element to the movement of force F at C is equal to distance BC multiplied by angle $d\phi$ (i.e., $CD = BC\, d\phi$). However, since element AB is small, distance CD is also small, and this distance may be considered perpendicular (although it is an arc) to line BC. Moreover, only the vertical component of this deflection is significant, as in a spring consisting of many coils, for any element on one side of the spring, there is a corresponding equivalent element on the other. The diametrically opposite elements of the spring

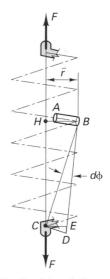

Fig. 10-30   Deriving deflection for a helical spring.

---

[20] An analytical expression that gives the value of K within 1 or 2% of the true value is frequently used. This expression in terms of spring index m is $K_1 = (4m - 1)/(4m - 4) + 0.615/m$. It was derived by A. M. Wahl in the 1940s on the basis of some simplifying assumptions and is known as the *Wahl correction factor* for curvature in helical springs.

balance out the horizontal component of the deflection and permit only the vertical deflection of force F. Therefore, by finding the *vertical* increment ED of the deflection of force F due to an element of spring AB and summing such increments for *all* elements of the spring, the deflection of the whole spring is obtained.

From similar triangles CDE and CBH,

$$\frac{ED}{CD} = \frac{HB}{BC} \quad \text{or} \quad ED = \frac{CD}{BC}HB$$

However, $CD = BC\,d\phi$, $HB = \bar{r}$, and ED may be denoted by $d\Delta$, as it represents an infinitesimal vertical deflection of the spring due to rotation of an element AB. Thus, $d\Delta = \bar{r}\,d\phi$ and

$$\Delta = \int d\Delta = \int \bar{r}\,d\phi = \int_0^L \bar{r}\,\frac{T\,dx}{I_pG} = \frac{TL\bar{r}}{I_pG}$$

However, $T = F\bar{r}$, and for a closely coiled spring, the *length* L *of the wire* may be taken with sufficient accuracy as $2\pi\bar{r}N$, where N is the number of *live* or active coils of the spring. Hence, the deflection Δ of the spring is

$$\Delta = \frac{2\pi F\bar{r}^3N}{I_pG} \tag{10-18a}$$

or, if the value of I_p for the wire is substituted,

$$\Delta = \frac{64F\bar{r}^3N}{Gd^4} \tag{10-18b}$$

Equations 10-18a and 10-18b give the deflection of a closely coiled helical spring along its axis when such a spring is subjected to either a tensile or compressive force F. In these formulas, the effect of the direct shear stress on the deflection is neglected (i.e., they give only the effect of torsional deformations).

The behavior of a spring may be conveniently defined by its *spring constant* k. From Eq. 10-18b, the spring constant for a helical spring made from a wire with a circular cross section is

$$k = \frac{F}{\Delta} = \frac{Gd^4}{64\bar{r}^3N} \quad \left[\frac{N}{m}\right] \quad \text{or} \quad \left[\frac{lb}{in}\right]$$

Example 10-9

Find the maximum stress in the 15-mm-diameter steel rod shown in Fig. 10-31 caused by a 3-kg mass freely falling through 0.5 m. The steel helical spring of 35-mm outside diameter inserted into the system is made of 5 mm of round wire and has 10 live coils. Let $E = 200$ GPa and $G = 80$ GPa.

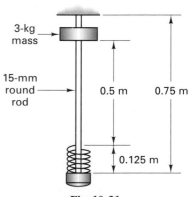

3-kg mass

15-mm round rod

0.5 m   0.75 m

0.125 m

Fig. 10-31

SOLUTION

The static deflection of the 3-kg mass exerting a force of $3g = 29.4$ N on the spring is computed first. It consists of two parts: the deflection of the rod given by Eq. 3-4, and the deflection of the spring given by Eq. 10-18b. For use in Eq. 10-18b, $\bar{r} = 15$ mm. Then, from Eq. 3-20, the dynamic force acting on the spring and the rod is found. This force is used for finding the stress in the rod. Here the rod cross-sectional area $A = \pi \times 15^2/4 = 177$ mm^2.

$$\Delta_{st} = \Delta_{rod} + \Delta_{spr} = \frac{PL}{AE} + \frac{64F\bar{r}^3N}{Gd^4}$$

$$= \frac{29.4 \times 750}{177 \times 200 \times 10^3} + \frac{64 \times 29.4 \times 15^3 \times 10}{80 \times 10^3 \times 5^4} = 1.27 \text{ mm}$$

$$P_{dyn} = W\left(1 + \sqrt{1 + \frac{2h}{\Delta_{st}}}\right) = 29.4\left(1 + \sqrt{1 + \frac{2 \times 500}{1.27}}\right) = 855 \text{ N}$$

$$\sigma_{dyn} = \frac{P_{dyn}}{A} = \frac{855}{177} = 4.8 \text{ MPa}$$

For a free fall of the mass of 0.5 m without the spring, an elastic rod stress would be 210 MPa. For the system with the spring, most of the reduction in stress is due to Δ_{spr}.

PROBLEMS

Section 10-3

10-1. Assuming that a member consists of five 50-by-150-mm full-sized wooden planks bolted together, as shown in the cross-sectional view in Fig. 10-4(a), show that $A_{fghj}\bar{y}_1 = A_{fgpn}\bar{y}_2$, where $\bar{y}_1$ is the distance from the centroid of the whole area to the centroid of area A_{fghj}, and $\bar{y}_2$ the corresponding distance for the area A_{fgpn}.

10-2. The cross section of a beam made up of a full-sized 6×6-in member reinforced with a 2×6-in plank is shown in the figure. What forces are exerted on 20d (20-penny) common nails, spaced 6 in apart and staggered, when force $P = 500$ lb is applied to the middle of the span? Calculate the shear flow two ways: using the cross section of the plank and then using the cross section of the larger member.

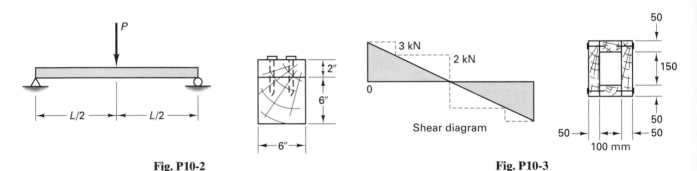

Fig. P10-2   **Fig. P10-3**

10-3. The shear diagram for the box beam supporting a uniformly distributed load is conservatively approximated for design by the stepped diagram shown in the figure. If the beam is nailed together from four pieces, as shown in the cross section, what nail spacing should be used along the span? Assume that each nail is good for 300 N in shear.

10-4. A 10-in square box beam is to be made from four 2-in-thick wood pieces. Two possible designs are considered, as shown in the figure. Moreover, the design shown in (a) can be turned 90° in the application. (a) Select the design requiring the minimum amount of nailing for transmitting shear. (b) If the shear to be transmitted by this member is 800 lb, what is the nail spacing for the best design? The nailing is to be done with 20d (20-penny) common nails that are good for 140 lb each in shear.

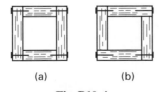

(a)   (b)

Fig. P10-4

10-5. A beam is loaded so that the moment diagram varies, as shown in the figure. For the cross section shown, determine the bolt spacing for the critical region of the span. The bolts are arranged in pairs, and the allowable shear force per high-strength bolt is 120 kN.

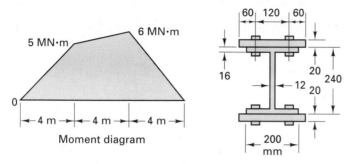

Fig. P10-5

10-6. A 4.5-m wooden beam overhangs 3 m and carries a concentrated force $P = 3945$ N at the end. (See figure.) The beam is made up of full-sized, 50-mm-thick boards nailed together with nails that have a shear resistance of 400 N each. The moment of inertia of the whole cross section is approximately 740×10^6 mm⁴. (a) What should be the longitudinal spacing of the nails connecting board A with boards B and C in the region of high shear? (b) For the same region, what should be the longitudinal spacing of the nails connecting board D with boards B and C? In calculations, neglect the weight of the beam.

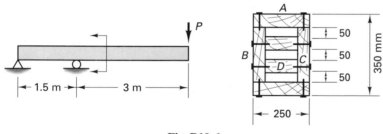

Fig. P10-6

10-7. Two W 200 × 36 beams are arranged as shown in the figure. Determine the bending and shear capacities of this member if the allowable bending stress is 160 MPa and the shear capacity of each bolt is 90 kN. The bolts are arranged in pairs and are spaced 150 mm on center.

Fig. P10-7

10-8. A plate girder is made up from two $14 \times \frac{1}{2}$-in cover plates, four $6 \times 4 \times \frac{1}{2}$-in angles, and a $39\frac{1}{2} \times \frac{3}{8}$-in web plate, as shown in the figure. If at the section considered, a total vertical shear of 150 k is transmitted, what must be the spacing of rivets A and B? For the girder around the neutral axis, I is 14,560 in[4]. Assume $\frac{3}{4}$-in rivets, and note that one rivet is good for 6.63 k in single shear, 13.25 k in double shear, and 11.3 k in bearing on a $\frac{3}{8}$-in plate.

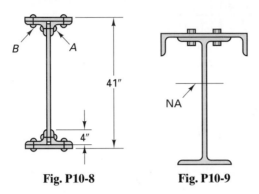

Fig. P10-8   Fig. P10-9

10-9. A simply supported beam has a cross section consisting of a C 310 × 31 and a W 460 × 74 fastened together by 19-mm-diameter bolts spaced longitudinally 150 mm apart in each row, as shown in the figure. If this beam is loaded with a downward-concentrated force of 500 kN in the middle of the span, what is the shear stress in the bolts? Neglect the weight of the beam.

10-10. A T-flange girder is used to support a 900-kN load in the middle of a 7-m simple span. The dimensions of the girder are given in the figure in a cross-sectional view. If the 22-mm-diameter rivets are spaced 125 mm apart longitudinally, what shear stress will be developed in the rivets by the applied loading? The moment of inertia of the girder around the neutral axis is approximately 4300×10^6 mm[4].

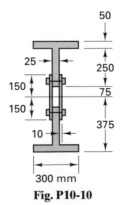

Fig. P10-10

10-11. An aircraft shear-resistant[1] plate girder is made up of four $50 \times 40 \times 3$-mm angles ($A = 270$ mm[2] for each angle) and a 1.63-mm web, as shown in the figure. Neglecting the skin, the moment of inertia of this section is $47.6 \cdot E + 06$ mm[4].

Rivets A are 4.76 mm in diameter and are spaced longitudinally 30 mm apart in each row. These rivets are good for 3.56 kN each in single shear. If 25 kN shear is to be transmitted by this section, what factor of safety, if any, is available for the rivets? In the calculations, make no reduction in areas for the rivet holes.

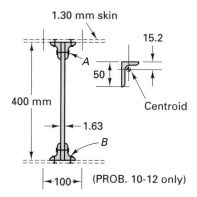

Fig. P10-11 and P10-12

10-12.   Assume that in the preceding problem, 100 mm of the skin may be included at the top and at the bottom in the moment of inertia of the section. Then, assuming 30-mm spacing for rivets A and 50-mm spacing for each row of rivets B, calculate the shear stresses in the rivets due to a shear $V = 25$ kN.

Sections 10-4 and 10-5

10-13.   Show that a formula, analogous to Eq. 10-8a, for beams having a solid circular cross section of area A is $\tau_{max} = \frac{4}{3} V/A$.

10-14.   Show that a formula, analogous to Eq. 10-8a, for thin-walled circular tubes acting as beams having a net cross-sectional area A is $\tau_{max} = 2\ V/A$.

10-15.   A T beam has the cross section shown in the figure. Calculate the shear stresses for the indicated six horizontal sections when the beam transmits a vertical shear of 240 kN. Plot the results as in Fig. 10-16(e).

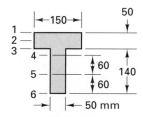

Fig. P10-15

[1]In aircraft design in some plate girders, webs are permitted to wrinkle, resulting in the so-called *semitension field beams*. To differentiate between the beams, if the web does not wrinkle, the term *shear resistant* is used.

10-16. A box beam has the cross section shown in the figure. Calculate shear stresses at several horizontal sections when the beam bending moment changes along the beam at the rate of 500 kN · m/m, and plot the results as in Fig. 10-16(e).

10-17. A thin-walled extrusion has a cross section in the form of an isosceles triangle, as shown in the figure. Using Eq. 10-6, determine the shear stresses at the midheight and centroidal levels of the cross section corresponding to the vertical shear $V = 100$ kN. Calculate the approximate section properties for the member using the *centerline dimensions* shown on the detail. (*Hint:* For a thin inclined rectangular area, $I = bLh^2/12$, where b is its width, L its length, and h its vertical height. Justify before using.)

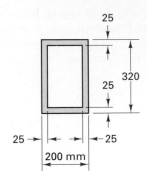

Fig. P10-16

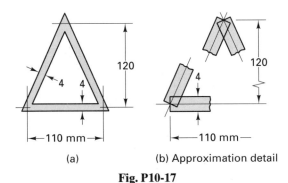

(a)   (b) Approximation detail

Fig. P10-17

10-18. A beam has a cross-sectional area in the form of an isosceles triangle for which the base b is equal to one-half its height h. (a) Using calculus and the conventional stress-analysis formula, determine the location of the maximum shear stress caused by a vertical shear V. Draw the manner in which the shear stress varies across the section. (b) If $b = 25$ mm, $h = 50$ mm, and τ_{max} is limited to 100 MPa, what is the maximum vertical shear V that this section may carry?

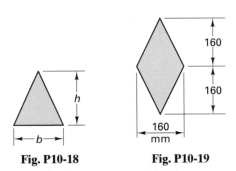

Fig. P10-18   **Fig. P10-19**

10-19. A beam has a rhombic cross section, as shown in the figure. Assume that this beam transmits a vertical shear of 5000 N, and investigate the shear stresses at levels 40 mm apart, beginning with the apex. Report the results on a plot similar to the one shown in Fig. 10-16(e).

10-20. A beam is loaded such that the moment diagram varies as shown in the figure. (a) Find the maximum longitudinal shear force acting on the $\frac{1}{2}$-in-diameter bolts spaced 12 in apart. (b) Find the shear stress in the glued joint.

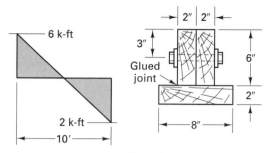

Fig. P10-20

10-21. A beam has the cross-sectional dimensions shown in the figure. If the allowable stresses are 100 MPa in tension, 200 MPa in compression, and 50 MPa in shear, what is the maximum allowable shear and the maximum allowable bending moment for this beam? Consider only the vertical loading of the beam and confine calculations for shear to sections a–a and b–b.

10-22. A wooden I beam is made up with a narrow lower flange because of space limitations, as shown in the figure. The lower flange is fastened to the web with nails spaced longitudinally 6 in apart, and the vertical boards in the lower flange are glued in place. Determine the stress in the glued joints and the force carried by each nail in the nailed joint if the beam is subjected to a vertical shear of 400 lb. The moment of inertia for the whole section around the neutral axis is 2640 in⁴.

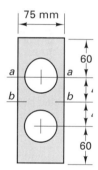

Fig. P10-21

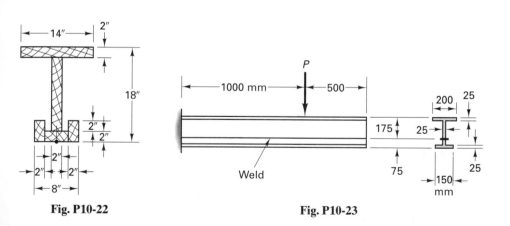

Fig. P10-22   **Fig. P10-23**

10-23. A steel cantilever beam is fabricated from two structural tees welded together, as shown in the figure. Determine the allowable force P that the beam can carry if the allowable stress in bending is 150 MPa; in shear, 100 MPa; and along the weld, 2 MN/m. Neglect the weight of the beam.

10-24. A box beam is fabricated by nailing plywood sides to two longitudinal wooden pieces, as shown in the figure. If the allowable shear stress for plywood is 1.5 MPa and the allowable shear strength per nail is 500 N, determine the maximum allowable vertical shear for this member.

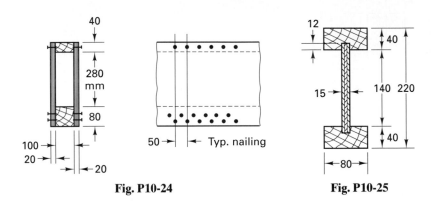

Fig. P10-24   Fig. P10-25

10-25. A wooden joist having the cross-sectional dimensions, in mm, shown in the figure is to be made from Douglas Fir lumber flanges and structural-grade plywood web. If the allowable shear stress on plywood is 2 MPa, what strength glue must be specified for the interfaces between the flanges and the web for a balanced design in shear?

10-26. A beam is made up of four 50×100-mm full-sized Douglas Fir pieces that are glued to a 25×500-mm Douglas Fir plywood web, as shown in the figure. Determine the maximum allowable shear and the maximum allowable bending moment that this section can carry if the allowable bending stress is 10 MPa; the allowable shear stress in plywood is 600 kN/m^2, and the allowable shearing stress in the glued joints is 300 kN/m^2. All dimensions in the figure are in mm.

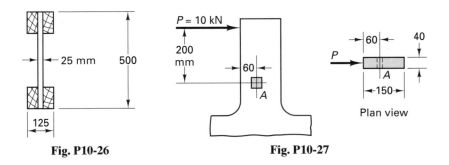

Fig. P10-26   Fig. P10-27

10-27. Calculate the bending and the shear stresses due to the applied force P acting on the element A for the cantilever shown in the figure, and show these stresses acting on an isolated sketch of the element.

10-28.   A W 14 × 90 beam supports a uniformly distributed load of 4 k/ft, including its own weight, as shown in the figure. Determine the bending and the shear stresses acting on elements A and B. Show the magnitude and sense of the computed quantities on infinitesimal elements.

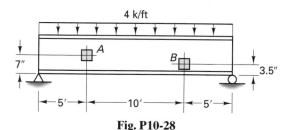

Fig. P10-28

10-29.   Isolate the 100 × 150 × 200-mm shaded element from the rectangular beam having a 200 × 300-mm cross section and loaded as shown in the figure. On a free-body diagram, indicate the location, magnitude, and sense of all resultant forces due to the bending and shear stresses acting on this segment. Neglect the weight of the beam.

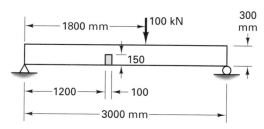

Fig. P10-29

10-30.   Two steel bars are bonded to an aluminum alloy core, making up a sandwich beam having the cross section shown in the figure. If this beam is loaded so that the bending moment changes at the rate of 5 kN · m/m, what maximum shear stress develops in the member? For steel, E_{St} = 210 GPa; for aluminum alloy, E_{Al} = 70 GPa. (*Hint:* The stress distribution pattern can be established, as shown in Fig. 8-7(c), and only the change in bending moment per unit distance along the beam need be considered, as shown in Fig. 10-2(d). Alternatively, a transformed section, discussed in Section 8-9, can be used.)

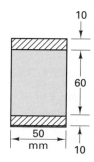

Fig. P10-30

10-31. The cross section of a beam of two different materials has the dimensions shown in the figure. The elastic modulus for the vertical web members is $E_w = 200$ MPa and that for the five pieces for the flange material is $E_f = 100$ MPa. If the vertical shear transmitted by this member is 20 kN, (a) what is the maximum shear stress in the web? (b) What is the largest shear stress between the webs and the flange material? (See the hint in the preceding problem.)

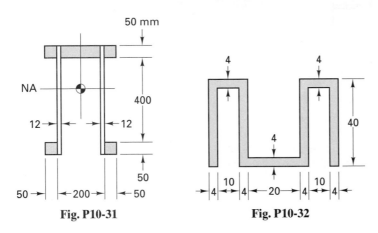

Fig. P10-31   Fig. P10-32

10-32. An aluminum alloy extrusion for use as a beam has the cross-sectional dimensions in mm shown in the figure. Due to a vertical shear $V = 10$ kN, determine the shear stresses in the vertical walls of the member at the horizontal section passing through the section centroid.

10-33. The cross-sectional dimensions of a beam of a synthetic thermoplastic material are given in mm in the figure. The member material is 3-mm thick throughout. (a) Calculate the moment of inertia I for the entire cross-sectional area around the horizontal centroidal axis. Use centerline dimensions as shown in Problem 10-17. (b) Determine the magnitudes of the shear stresses at sections a–a, b–b, and c–c due to the vertical shear $V = 10$ kN.

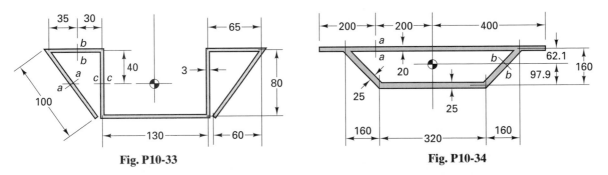

Fig. P10-33   Fig. P10-34

10-34. A metal box beam has the cross section in mm shown in the figure. If V/I is 0.006 N/mm⁴, what shear stresses occur at sections a–a and b–b? The centroid for the cross section is given. Use centerline dimensions for calculating area properties. (See Problem 10-17.) (*Hint:* Take advantage of symmetry.)

10-35. A metal beam is made up of four $30 \times 24 \times 4$-mm angles attached with an adequate number of bolts to a 100×4-mm web plate, as shown in the figure. Determine the shear stresses at section a–a. Let $V/I = 0.01$ N/mm⁴.

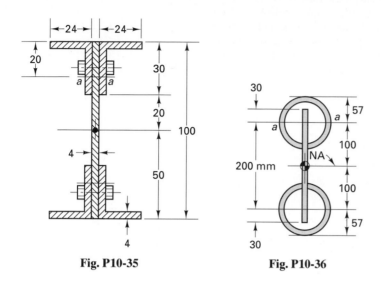

Fig. P10-35   Fig. P10-36

10-36. A beam is fabricated by slotting standard steel pipes of 102-mm nominal diameter longitudinally and then securely welding them to a 260×10-mm web plate, as shown in the figure. If, at a certain section, this beam transmits a vertical shear of 200 kN, determine the shear stress in the pipe and in the web plate at a level 100 mm above the neutral axis.

10-37. A simply supported composite beam carrying a uniform load over a span of 10 m is made up by bolting a 100-mm-by-300-mm timber to the upper flange of a steel beam, as shown in the figure. (All dimensions in the figure are in mm.) Strain gages located at midspan on the inner surfaces of the steel flanges indicate strains as follows: Strain gage A: $\varepsilon = -420 \times 10^{-6}$; strain gage B: $\varepsilon = +700 \times 10^{-6}$. (a) Compute the total force acting on the timber at this section. (b) If the bolts are placed two in a row at 600-mm apart uniformly, what is the average shear force carried by each bolt? Assume that each bolt contributes equally to the resistance of the total force. Let $E_{\text{steel}} = 200$ GPa and $E_{\text{timber}} = 10$ GPa.

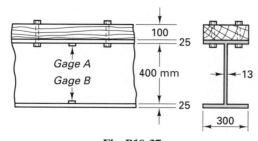

Fig. P10-37

Sections 10-7 and 10-8

10-38.   A beam having a cross section with the dimensions in mm shown in the figure is in a region where there is a constant, positive vertical shear of 100 kN. (a) Calculate the shear flow q acting at each of the four sections indicated in the figure. (b) Assuming a positive bending moment of 27 kN · m at one section and a larger moment at the adjoining section 10 mm away, draw isometric sketches of each segment of the beam isolated by the sections 10 mm apart and the four sections shown in the figure, and on the sketches indicate all forces acting on the segments. Neglect vertical shear stresses in the flanges.

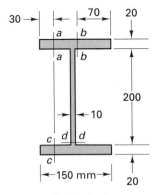

Fig. P10-38

10-39.   A beam having the cross section with the dimensions shown in the figure transmits a vertical shear $V = 7$ k applied through the shear center. (a) Determine the shear stresses at sections a–a, b–b, and c–c. I around the neutral axis is 35.7 in⁴. The thickness of the material is $\frac{1}{2}$ in throughout. (b) Sketch the shear stress distribution along the centerline of the member.

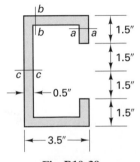

Fig. P10-39

10-40 through 10-44.   Determine the location of the shear center for the beams having the cross-sectional dimensions shown in the figures. All members are to be considered thin walled, and calculations should be based on the centerline dimensions.

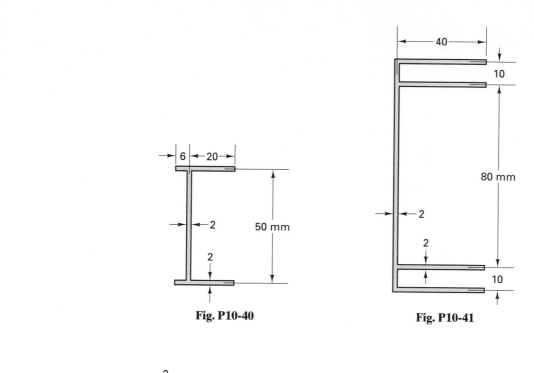

Fig. P10-40

Fig. P10-41

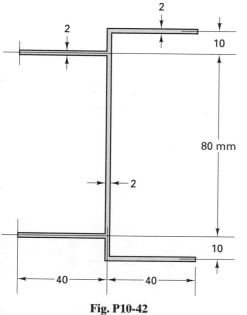

Fig. P10-42

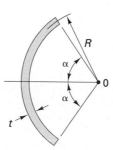

Fig. P10-43

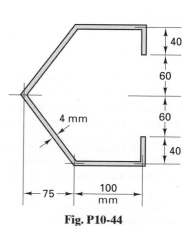

Fig. P10-44

10-45. Show that for the Z cross section shown in part (a) of the figure, the shear center lies on the vertical axis passing through the section's centroid. Demonstrating that the force resultant due to the internal shear flow is zero in each flange constitutes a proof. (*Hint:* Apply vertical shear force V_y shown in the figure. Since the position of the shear center is independent of the magnitude of shear V_y, it can be chosen arbitrarily. Likewise, it is the rate of change in M, as in Fig. 10-2(d), rather than its magnitude, that is of importance. Therefore, let the change in moment ΔM in a unit span distance be $V_y \times 1 = 10$ lb-in. Using this ΔM, calculate the stresses along the centerline of the Z section using the generalized flexure formula, Eq. 9-33. Such calculations should verify the normal stress distribution shown in part (b) of the figure. By integrating these stresses along the section centerline, as in Fig. 10-20(b), the shear flow in the plane of the section is found, shown in part (c) of the figure. The force resultants based on these shears vanish in both flanges.) Note that for the given section, $I_z = 2.133$ in^4, $I_y = 0.533$ in^4, and $I_{yz} = 0.800$ in^4.

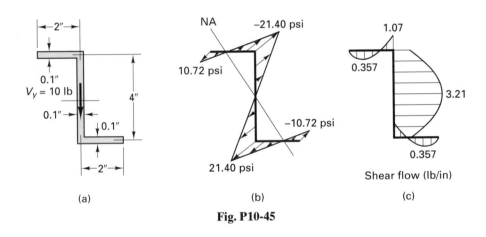

Fig. P10-45

10-46. Show that for the Z cross section in the preceding problem, the shear center lies on the horizontal line passing through the section's centroid. Demonstrating that an applied horizontal force is equally divided between the two flanges constitutes a solution of the problem. (*Hint:* Apply a horizontal force V_z, say equal to 50 N, through the section's centroid, and, as in the preceding problem, calculate the normal stresses and the shear stresses in the plane of the cross section. An auxiliary plot of the shear stresses along the section centerline is useful in the solution. Note that the resultant shear force in the web is zero.)

10-47 and 10-48. Determine the location of the shear center for the beams with idealized cross sections shown in the respective figures. Neglect the areas of the plates connecting the longitudinal stringers, each one of which has an effective area A concentrated at a point for resisting longitudinal forces. There are two such areas in Fig. 10-47 and eight in Fig. 10-48. (This kind of idealization is often used in aircraft design.)

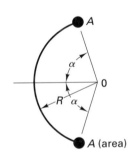

Fig. P10-47

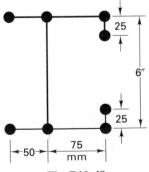

Fig. P10-48

Section 10-9

10-49 through 10-51.   Cantilevers of the kind shown in the figure for Problem 10-49 are subjected to horizontal forces P, causing bending, direct shear, and torsion. Determine the stresses at the surfaces due to these actions at points A and B, and show the results on isolated infinitesimal elements. Elements A should be viewed from the top, and elements B from the left. Use centerline dimensions for the box in calculating the torsional stresses in Problem 10-49. The details for applying forces P are not shown.

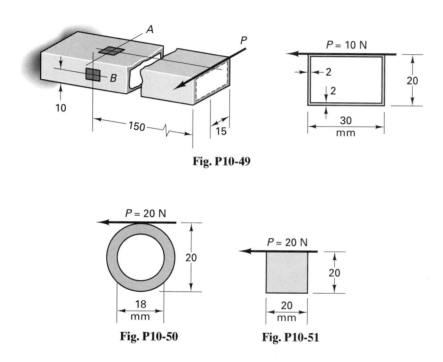

Fig. P10-49

Fig. P10-50   **Fig. P10-51**

Sections 10-10 and 10-11

10-52.   A helical valve spring is made of $\frac{1}{4}$-in-diameter steel wire and has an outside diameter of 2 in. In operation, the compressive force applied to this spring varies from 20 lb minimum to 70 lb maximum. If there are eight active coils, what is the valve lift (or travel), and what is the maximum shear stress in the spring when in operation? $G = 11.6 \times 10^6$ psi.

10-53.   If a helical tension spring consisting of 16 live coils of 6-mm steel wire and of 30-mm outside diameter is attached to the end of another helical tension spring of 18 live coils of 8-mm steel wire and of 40-mm outside diameter, what is the spring constant for this two-spring system? What is the largest force that may be applied to these springs without exceeding a shear stress of 480 MPa? $G = 82$ GN/m².

10-54.   A heavy helical steel spring is made from a 1-in-diameter rod and has an outside diameter of 9 in. As originally manufactured, it has the pitch $p = 3\frac{1}{2}$ in; see the figure. If a force P, of such magnitude that the rod's $\frac{1}{8}$-in-thick outer annulus becomes plastic, is applied to this spring, estimate the reduction of the pitch of the spring on removal of the load. Assume linearly elastic-plastic material with $\tau_{yp} = 50$ ksi, and $G = 12 \times 10^3$ ksi. Neglect the effects of stress concentration and of the direct shear on deflection.

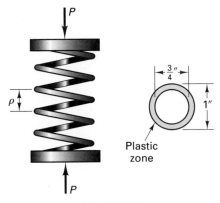

Fig. P10-54

11

Stress and Strain Transformation

11-1. Introduction

In the two parts of this chapter, a formal treatment for changing the components of the state of stress or strain given in one set of coordinate axes to any other set of rotated axes is discussed. This transformation of stress or strain between any two different sets of coordinate axes is a mathematical process and does not necessarily require the use of formulas derived earlier. The connection between the established stress-analysis formulas and stress transformation is considered in Chapter 13. Transformation of stress is discussed in Part A of this chapter; strain transformation in Part B. In both instances, *the discussion is largely confined to problems in two dimensions.* The possibility of transforming a given state of stress involving both normal and shear stresses to any other set of rotated coordinate axes permits an examination of the effect of such stresses on a material. In this manner, criteria for the onset of yield or the occurrence of fracture can be hypothesized. This important topic is treated in the next chapter.

Part A   TRANSFORMATION OF STRESS

11-2. The Basic Problem

In several of the preceding chapters, stresses caused by separate actions causing either normal and/or shear stresses were considered. The superposition of normal stresses acting on the same element, when axial forces and bending occur simultaneously, was discussed in Chapter 9. Similarly, the superposition of shear stresses caused by torque and direct shear was considered in Chapter 10. Moreover, in Chapter 5, Section 5-7, it was demonstrated that a state of pure shear can be transformed into an *equivalent* state of normal stresses (Fig. 5-11). Often in stress analysis, a more general problem arises, such as shown in Fig. 11-1(a). In the illustrated case, element A is subjected to a normal stress σ_x due to axial pull *and* bending, and *simultaneously* experiences a direct shear stress τ_{xy}. The combined normal stress σ_x follows by superposition. However, the combination of the normal stress σ_x with the shear stress τ_{xy} requires special treatment. Essentially, this requires a consideration of stresses on an inclined plane, such as shown in Fig. 11-1(b). Since an inclined plane may be chosen arbitrarily, the state of stress at a point can be described in an *infinite number of ways*, which are all *equivalent*.

Stress has a magnitude and a sense and is *also* associated with an area over which it acts. Such mathematical entities are *tensors* and are of a higher order than vectors.[1] However, the components of the stress on the *same area* are vectors. These stress components can be superposed by *vector addition*. As noted earlier, this was used in Chapters 9 and 10. Therefore, the stresses can be referred to as *stress vectors* or *tractions*, provided they act on the same surface in or on a body. Only a change in the orientation of an area displays the nonvectorial character of the stress as a whole.

In the discussion that follows, direct use of stress vectors is avoided by multiplying stresses by their respective areas to obtain forces, which are vectors, and then adding them vectorially. On obtaining the force components on an inclined plane, the process is reversed by dividing these force components by the inclined area to obtain the stresses on such planes.

This procedure will be first illustrated by a numerical example. Then the developed approach will be generalized to obtain algebraic relations for a stress transformation for finding stresses on any inclined plane from a given state of stress. The methods used in these derivations do not involve

---

[1]*Scalars* are tensors of rank zero, *vectors* are tensors of the first rank, and stresses and strains are second-rank tensors. See Sections 1-4.

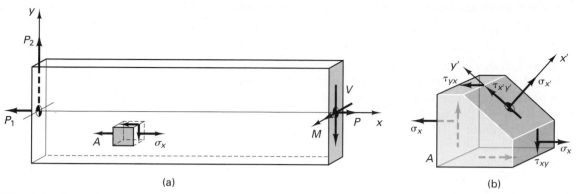

(a)

Fig. 11-1   State of stress at a point on different planes.

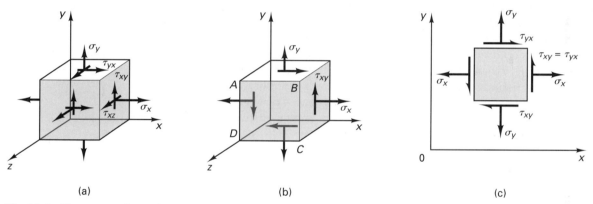

(a)   (b)   (c)

Fig. 11-2   Representations of stresses acting on an element.

properties of a material. Therefore, provided the initial stresses are given, the derived relations are applicable whether the material behaves elastically or plastically or even if it is not a solid. However, the planes on which the normal or the shear stresses reach their *maximum intensity* have a particularly significant effect on materials.

The general state of stress shown in Fig. 11-2(a) will not be considered in deriving the laws of stress transformation at a point. Instead, the two-dimensional stress problem indicated in Fig. 11-2(b) will be studied. In practical applications, this is a particularly important case as it is usually possible to select a critical element at an outer boundary of a member. The outside face of such an element, as *ABCD* in the figure, is generally free of significant surface stresses, whereas the stresses right at the surface acting parallel to it are usually the largest. Planar representation of the stresses, as shown in Fig. 11-2(c), will be used in most derivations and examples.

Example 11-1

Let the state of stress for an element of unit thickness be as shown in Fig. 11-3(a). An alternative representation of the state of stress at the same point may be given on an infinitesimal wedge with an angle of $\alpha = 22\frac{1}{2}°$, as in Fig. 11-3(b). Find the stresses that must act on plane AB of the wedge to keep the element in equilibrium.

SOLUTION

Wedge ABC is part of the element in Fig. 11-3(a); therefore, the stresses on faces AC and BC are known. The unknown normal and shear stresses acting on face AB are designated in the figure by δ_α and τ_α, respectively. Their sense is assumed arbitrarily.

To determine σ_α and τ_α, for convenience only, let the area of the face defined by line AB be unity such as m². Then the area corresponding to line AC is equal to $1 \times \cos \alpha = 0.924$ m² and that to BC is equal to $1 \times \sin \alpha = 0.383$ m². (More rigorously, the area corresponding to line AB should be taken as dA, but this quantity cancels out in the subsequent algebraic expressions.) Forces F_1, F_2, F_3, and F_4, Fig. 11-3(c), can be obtained by multiplying the stresses by their respective areas. The unknown equilibrant forces N and S act, respectively, normal and tangential to plane AB. Then applying the equations of static equilibrium to the forces acting on the wedge given forces N and S.

$$F_1 = 3 \times 0.924 = 2.78 \text{ MN} \quad F_2 = 2 \times 0.924 = 1.85 \text{ MN}$$

$$F_3 = 2 \times 0.383 = 0.766 \text{ MN} \quad F_4 = 1 \times 0.383 = 0.383 \text{ MN}$$

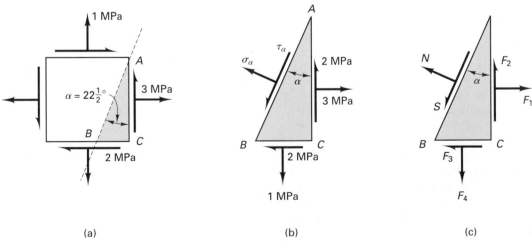

(a)   (b)   (c)

Fig. 11-3

$$\sum F_N = 0 \qquad N = F_1 \cos\alpha - F_2 \sin\alpha - F_3 \cos\alpha + F_4 \sin\alpha$$

$$= 2.78(0.924) - 1.85(0.383) - 0.766(0.924)$$

$$+ 0.383(0.383)$$

$$= 1.29 \text{ MN}$$

$$\sum F_S = 0 \qquad S = F_1 \sin\alpha + F_2 \cos\alpha - F_3 \sin\alpha - F_4 \cos\alpha$$

$$= 2.78(0.383) + 1.85(0.924) - 0.766(0.383)$$

$$- 0.383(0.924)$$

$$= 2.12 \text{ MN}$$

Forces N and S act on the plane defined by AB, which was initially assumed to be 1 m². Their positive signs indicate that their assumed directions were chosen correctly. By dividing these forces by the area on which they act, the stresses acting on plane AB are obtained. Thus, $\sigma_\alpha = 1.29$ MPa and $\tau_\alpha = 2.12$ MPa and act in the direction shown in Fig. 11-3(b).

The foregoing procedure accomplished something remarkable: It transformed the *description* of the state of stress from one set of planes to another. Either system of stresses pertaining to an infinitesimal element describes the state of stress at the same point of a body.

The procedure of isolating a wedge and using the equations of the equilibrium of forces to determine stresses on inclined planes is fundamental. Ordinary sign conventions of statics suffice to solve any problem. The reader is urged to return to this approach whenever questions arise regarding the more advanced procedures developed in the remainder of this chapter.

11-3. Transformation of Stresses in Two-Dimensional Problems

By following the same procedure as in the last example, equations for the normal and shear stresses acting on an inclined plane can be derived in algebraic form. Such expressions are called stress-transformation equations. These equations are based on the initially given stresses acting on an element of known orientation and the plane being investigated defined by a normal to it. The dependence of the stresses on the inclination of the plane is clearly apparent.

Algebraic equations are developed using an element of unit thickness in Fig. 11-4(a) in a state of two-dimensional stress initially referred to the

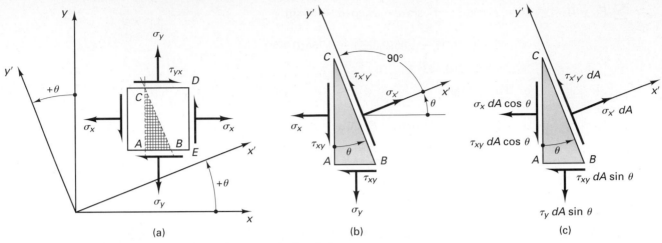

Fig. 11-4   Derivation of stress transformation on an inclined plane.

xy axes. If normal stresses σ_x and σ_y are tensile stresses, they are taken as positive, and are negative if compressive. *Positive shear stress is defined as acting upward in the positive direction of the y axis on the right (positive) face DE of the element.* This sign convention for shear stresses was introduced in Chapter 1 (see Fig. 1-3) and is generally used in continuum mechanics (elasticity, plasticity, rheology). However, it *differs* from the conventional *beam shear sign convention* used in Chapters 7 and 10. Here the stress transformation is sought from the xy coordinate axes to the $x'y'$ axes. The angle θ, which locates the x' axis, is positive when measured from the x axis toward the y axis in a counterclockwise direction.

The *outward normal* to the section forms an angle θ with the x axis. If an area of the wedge isolated by this section is dA, the areas associated with the faces AC and AB are $dA \cos \theta$ and $dA \sin \theta$, respectively. By multiplying the stresses by their respective areas, a diagram with the forces acting on the wedge is constructed. Fig. 11-4(c). Then, by applying the equations of static equilibrium to the forces acting on the wedge, stresses $\sigma_{x'}$ and $\tau_{x'y'}$ are obtained:

$$\sum F_{x'} = 0 \quad \sigma_{x'} dA = \sigma_x \, dA \cos \theta \cos \theta + \sigma_y \, dA \sin \theta \sin \theta$$

$$+ \tau_{xy} \, dA \cos \theta \sin \theta + \tau_{xy} \, dA \sin \theta \cos \theta$$

$$\sigma_{x'} = \sigma_x \cos^2 \theta + \sigma_y \sin^2 \theta + 2\tau_{xy} \sin \theta \cos \theta$$

$$= \sigma_x \frac{1 + \cos 2\theta}{2} + \sigma_y \frac{1 - \cos 2\theta}{2} + \tau_{xy} \sin 2\theta$$

$$\sigma_{x'} = \frac{\sigma_x + \sigma_y}{2} + \frac{\sigma_x - \sigma_y}{2} \cos 2\theta + \tau_{xy} \sin 2\theta \qquad (11\text{-}1)$$

Similarly, from $\Sigma F_{y'} = 0$,

$$\tau_{x'y'} = -\frac{\sigma_x - \sigma_y}{2} \sin 2\theta + \tau_{xy} \cos 2\theta \qquad (11\text{-}2)$$

Equations 11-1 and 11-2 are the general expressions for the normal and the shear stress, respectively, on any plane located by the angle θ and caused by a known system of stresses. These relations are the equations for transformation of stress from one set of coordinate axes to another. Note particularly that σ_x, σ_y, and τ_{xy} are initially known stresses.

Replacing θ in Eq. 11-1 by $\theta + 90°$ gives the normal stress in the direction of the y' axis. This stress can be designated as $\sigma_{y'}$; see Fig. 1-3(b). Hence, on noting that $\cos(2\theta + 180°) = -\cos 2\theta$ and $\sin(2\theta + 180°) = -\sin 2\theta$, one has

$$\sigma_{y'} = \frac{\sigma_x + \sigma_y}{2} - \frac{\sigma_x - \sigma_y}{2} \cos 2\theta - \tau_{xy} \sin 2\theta \qquad (11\text{-}3)$$

By adding Eqs. 11-1 and 11-3,

$$\sigma_{x'} + \sigma_{y'} = \sigma_x + \sigma_y \qquad (11\text{-}4)$$

meaning that the sum of the normal stresses on any two mutually perpendicular planes remains the same[2] (i.e., *invariant*), regardless of the angle θ.

Mathematically analogous equations were found in Section 9-7 in connection with area moments and products of inertia. The transformation equations in both cases are alike.

It is to be noted that in *plane strain* problems for a linearly elastic material, where $\varepsilon_z = \gamma_{zx} = \gamma_{zy} = 0$, a normal stress σ_z can also develop. From Eq. 5-14c, this stress is given as

$$\sigma_z = v(\sigma_x + \sigma_y) \qquad (11\text{-}5)$$

The forces resulting from this stress do not enter the relevant equilibrium equations used in deriving stress-transformation expressions. Moreover, by virtue of Eq. 11-4, the $\sigma_x + \sigma_y$ term in Eq. 11-5 remains constant regardless of θ. Therefore, the derived equations for stress transformation are applicable for problems of *plane stress* as well as *plane strain*.

---

[2]A similar relation for three-dimensional problems is $\sigma_{x'} + \sigma_{y'} + \sigma_{z'} = \sigma_x + \sigma_y + \sigma_z$.

11-4. Principal Stresses in Two-Dimensional Problems

Interest often centers on the determination of the largest possible stress, as given by Eqs. 11-1 and 11-2, and the planes on which such stresses occur are found first. To find the plane for a maximum or a minimum normal stress. Eq. 11-1 is differentiated with respect to θ and the derivative set equal to zero; that is,

$$\frac{d\sigma_{x'}}{d\theta} = -\frac{\sigma_x - \sigma_y}{2} 2 \sin 2\theta + 2\tau_{xy} \cos 2\theta = 0$$

Hence,

$$\tan 2\theta_1 = \frac{\tau_{xy}}{(\sigma_x - \sigma_y)/2} \tag{11-6}$$

where the subscript of the angle θ is used to designate the angle that defines the plane of the maximum or minimum normal stress. Equation 11-6 has two roots, since the value of the tangent of an angle in the diametrically opposite quadrant is the same, as may be seen from Fig. 11-5. These roots are 180° apart, and, as Eq. 11-6 is for a double angle, the roots of θ_1 are 90° apart. One of these roots locates a plane on which the maximum normal stress acts; the other locates the corresponding plane for the minimum normal stress. To distinguish between these two roots, a prime and double prime notation is used.

Before evaluating these stresses, carefully observe that if the location of planes on which no shear stresses act is wanted, Eq. 11-2 must be set equal to zero. This yields the same relation as that in Eq. 11-6. Therefore, an important conclusion is reached: On planes on which maximum or minimum nor-

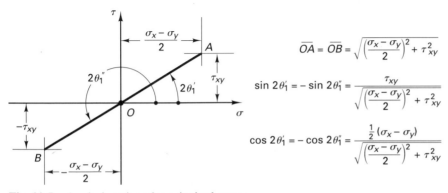

$$\overline{OA} = \overline{OB} = \sqrt{\left(\frac{\sigma_x - \sigma_y}{2}\right)^2 + \tau_{xy}^2}$$

$$\sin 2\theta_1' = -\sin 2\theta_1'' = \frac{\tau_{xy}}{\sqrt{\left(\frac{\sigma_x - \sigma_y}{2}\right)^2 + \tau_{xy}^2}}$$

$$\cos 2\theta_1' = -\cos 2\theta_1'' = \frac{\frac{1}{2}(\sigma_x - \sigma_y)}{\sqrt{\left(\frac{\sigma_x - \sigma_y}{2}\right)^2 + \tau_{xy}^2}}$$

Fig. 11-5   Angle functions for principal stresses.

mal stresses occur, there are no shear stresses. These planes are called the *principal planes* of stress, and the stresses acting on these planes—the maximum and minimum normal stresses—are called the *principal stresses.*

The magnitudes of the principal stresses can be obtained by substituting the values of the sine and cosine functions corresponding to the double angle given by Eq. 11-6 into Eq. 11-1. Then the results are simplified, and the expression for the maximum normal stress (denoted by σ_1) and the minimum normal stress (denoted by σ_2) becomes

$$(\sigma_{x'}) \, {}^{max}_{min} = \sigma_{1 \text{ or } 2} = \frac{\sigma_x + \sigma_y}{2} \pm \sqrt{\left(\frac{\sigma_x - \sigma_y}{2}\right)^2 + \tau_{xy}^2} \qquad (11\text{-}7)$$

where the positive sign in front of the square root must be used to obtain σ_1 and the negative sign to obtain σ_2. The planes on which these stresses act can be determined by using Eq. 11-6. A particular root of Eq. 11-6 substituted into Eq. 11-1 will check the result found from Eq. 11-4 and at the same time will locate the plane on which this principal stress acts.

11.5 Maximum Shear Stresses in Two-Dimensional Problems

If σ_x, σ_y, and τ_{xy} are known for an element, the shear stress on any plane defined by an angle θ is given by Eq. 11-2, and a study similar to the one made before for the normal stresses may be made for the shear stress. Thus, similarly, to locate the planes on which the maximum or the minimum shear stresses act, Eq. 11-2 must be differentiated with respect to θ and the derivative set equal to zero. When this is carried out and the results are simplified,

$$\tan 2\theta_2 = -\frac{(\sigma_x - \sigma_y)/2}{\tau_{xy}} \qquad (11\text{-}8)$$

where the subscript 2 is attached to θ to designate the plane on which the shear stress is a maximum or a minimum. Like Eq. 11-6, Eq. 11-8 has two roots, which again may be distinguished by attaching to θ_2 a prime or a double prime notation. The two planes defined by this equation are mutually perpendicular. Moreover, the value of $\tan 2\theta_2$ given by Eq. 11-8 is a negative reciprocal of the value of $\tan 2\theta_1$ in Eq. 11-6. Hence, the roots for the double angles of Eq. 11-8 are 90° away from the corresponding roots of Eq. 11-6. This means that the angles that locate the planes of maximum or minimum shear stress form angles of 45° with the planes of the principal stresses. A substitution into Eq. 11-2 of the sine and cosine functions corresponding to the double angle given by Eq. 11-8 and determined in a manner analogous to that in Fig. 11-5 gives the maximum and the minimum values of the shear stresses. These, after simplifications, are

$$\tau_{\substack{max \\ min}} = \pm \sqrt{\left(\frac{\sigma_x - \sigma_y}{2}\right)^2 + \tau_{xy}^2} \qquad (11\text{-}9)$$

Thus, the maximum shear stress differs from the minimum shear stress only in sign. Moreover, since the two roots given by Eq. 11-8 locate planes 90° apart, this result also means that the numerical values of the shear stresses on the mutually perpendicular planes are the same. This concept was repeatedly used after being established in Section 1-4. In this derivation, the difference in sign of the two shear stresses arises from the convention for locating the planes on which these stresses act. From the physical point of view, these signs have no meaning, and for this reason, the largest shear stress regardless of sign will often be called the *maximum shear stress*.

The definite sense of the shear stress can always be determined by direct substitution of the particular root of θ_2 into Eq. 11-2. A positive shear stress indicates that it acts in the direction assumed in Fig. 11-4(b), and vice versa. The determination of the maximum shear stress is of utmost importance for materials that are weak in shear strength. This will be discussed further in Chapter 12.

Unlike the principal stresses for which no shear stresses occur on the principal planes, the maximum shear stresses act on planes that are usually not free of normal stresses. Substitution of θ_2 from Eq. 11-8 into Eq. 11-1 shows that the normal stresses that act on the planes of the maximum shear stresses are

$$\sigma' = \frac{\sigma_x + \sigma_y}{2} \qquad (11\text{-}10)$$

Therefore, a normal stress acts simultaneously with the maximum shear stress unless $\sigma_x + \sigma_y$ vanishes.

If σ_x and σ_y in Eq. 11-9 are the principal stress, τ_{xy} is zero and Eq. 11-9 simplifies to

$$\tau_{\substack{max \\ min}} = \pm \frac{\sigma_1 - \sigma_2}{2} \qquad (11\text{-}11)$$

Here it is useful to recall a relationship between pure shear and the principal stresses discussed earlier in connection with Fig. 5-11. The results of this analysis are displayed in Fig. 11-6. Equation 11-6 clearly shows that in the absence of normal stresses, the principal stresses are numerically equal to the shear stress. The sense of the normal stresses follows from Eq. 11-6. The shear stresses act toward the diagonal DF in the direction of the principal tensile stresses; see Fig. 11-6(a).

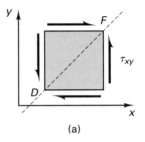

(a)

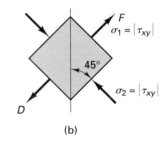

(b)

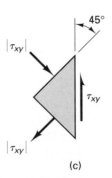

(c)

Fig. 11-6   Equivalent representations for pure shear stress.

Example 11-2

For the state of stress in Example 11-1, reproduced in Fig. 11-7(a), (a) rework the previous problem for $\theta = -22\frac{1}{2}°$, using the general equations for the transformation of stress; (b) find the principal stresses and show their sense on a properly oriented element; and (c) find the maximum shear stresses with the associated normal stresses and show the results on a properly oriented element.

SOLUTION

(a) By directly applying Eqs. 11-1 and 11-2 for $\theta = -22\frac{1}{2}°$, with $\sigma_x = +3$ MPa, $\sigma_y = +1$ MPa, and $\tau_{xy} = +2$ MPa, one has

$$\sigma_{x'} = \frac{3+1}{2} + \frac{3-1}{2}\cos(-45°) + 2\sin(-45°)$$

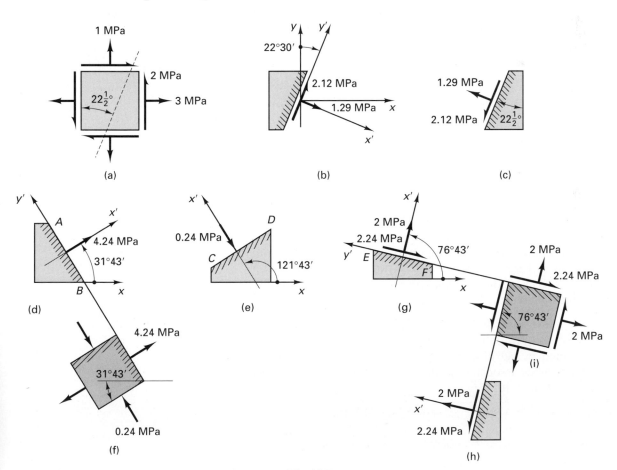

(a)   (b)   (c)

(d)   (e)   (g)

(f)   (h)   (i)

Fig. 11-7

$$= 2 + 1 \times 0.707 - 2 \times 0.707 = +1.29 \text{ MPa}$$

$$\tau_{x'y'} = -\frac{3-1}{2} \sin(-45°) + 2 \cos(-45°)$$

$$= +1 \times 0.707 + 2 \times 0.707 = +2.12 \text{ MPa}$$

The positive sign of $\sigma_{x'}$ indicates tension; whereas the positive sign of $\tau_{x'y'}$ indicates that the shear stress acts in the $+y'$ direction, as shown in Fig. 11-4(b). These results are shown in Fig. 11-7(b) as well as in Fig. 11-7(c).

(b) The principal stresses are obtained by means of Eq. 11-7. The planes on which the principal stresses act are found by using Eq. 11-6.

$$\sigma_{1,2} = \frac{3+1}{2} \pm \sqrt{\left(\frac{3-1}{2}\right)^2 + 2^2} = 2 \pm 2.24$$

$$\sigma_1 = 4.24 \text{ MPa (tension)} \qquad \sigma_2 = 0.24 \text{ MPa (compression)}$$

$$\tan 2\theta_1 = \frac{\tau_{xy}}{(\sigma_x - \sigma_y)/2} = \frac{2}{(3-1)/2} = 2$$

$$2\theta_1 = 63°26' \qquad \text{or} \qquad 63°26' + 180° = 243°26'$$

Hence,

$$\theta_1' = 31°43' \qquad \text{and} \qquad \theta_1'' = 121°43'$$

This locates the two principal planes, AB and CD, Figs. 11-7(d) and (e), on which σ_1 and σ_2 act. On which one of these planes the principal stresses act is unknown. So Eq. 11-1 is solved by using, for example $\theta_1' = 31°43'$. The stress found by this calculation is the stress that acts on plane AB. Then, since $2\theta_1' = 63°26'$,

$$\sigma_{x'} = \frac{3+1}{2} + \frac{3-1}{2} \cos 63°26' + 2 \sin 63°26' = +4.24 \text{ MPa} = \sigma_1$$

This result, besides giving a check on the previous calculations, shows that the maximum principal stress acts on plane AB. The complete state of stress at the given point in terms of the principal stresses is shown in Fig. 11-7(f). Note that the results satisfy Eq. 11-4.

(c) The maximum shear stress is found by using Eq. 11-9. The planes on which these stresses act are defined by Eq. 11-8. The sense of the shear stresses is determined by substituting one of the roots of Eq. 11-8 into Eq. 11-2. Normal stresses associated with the maximum shear stress are determined by using Eq. 11-10.

$$\tau_{max} = \sqrt{[(3-1)/2]^2 + 2^2} = \sqrt{5} = 2.24 \text{ MPa}$$

$$\tan 2\theta_2 = -\frac{(3-1)/2}{2} = -0.500$$

$$2\theta_2 = 153°26' \qquad \text{or} \qquad 153°26' + 180° = 333°26'$$

Hence,

$$\theta_2' = 76°43' \quad \text{and} \quad \theta_2'' = 166°43'$$

These planes are shown in Figs. 11-7(g) and (h). Then, by using $2\theta_2' = 153°26'$ in Eq. 11-2,

$$\tau_{x'y'} = -\frac{3-1}{2}\sin 153°26' + 2\cos 153°26' = -2.24 \text{ MPa}$$

which means that the shear along plane EF has an opposite sense to that of the y' axis. From Eq. 11-11,

$$\sigma' = \frac{3+1}{2} = 2 \text{ MPa}$$

The complete results are shown in Fig. 11-7(i). Note again that Eq. 11-4 is satisfied.

The description of the state of stress can now be exhibited in three alternative forms: as the originally given data, and in terms of the stresses found in parts (b) and (c) of this problem. All these descriptions of the state of stress at the given point are equivalent. In matrix representation, this yields

$$\begin{pmatrix} 3 & 2 \\ 2 & 1 \end{pmatrix} \quad \text{or} \quad \begin{pmatrix} 4.24 & 0 \\ 0 & -0.24 \end{pmatrix} \quad \text{or} \quad \begin{pmatrix} 2 & -2.24 \\ -2.24 & 2 \end{pmatrix} \text{MPa}$$

11-6. Mohr's Circle of Stress for Two-Dimensional Problems

In this section, the basic equations (Eqs. 11-1 and 11-2) for the stress transformation at a point will be reexamined in order to interpret them graphically. In doing this, two objectives will be pursued. First, by graphically interpreting these equations, a greater insight into the general problem of stress transformation will be achieved. This is the main purpose of this section. Second, with the aid of graphical construction, a quicker solution of stress-transformation problems can often be obtained. This will be discussed in the following section.

A careful study of Eqs. 11-1 and 11-2 shows that they represent a circle written in parametric form. That they do represent a circle is made clearer by first rewriting them as

$$\sigma_{x'} - \frac{\sigma_x + \sigma_y}{2} = \frac{\sigma_x - \sigma_y}{2}\cos 2\theta + \tau_{xy}\sin 2\theta \qquad (11\text{-}12)$$

$$\tau_{x'y'} = -\frac{\sigma_x - \sigma_y}{2}\sin 2\theta + \tau_{xy}\cos 2\theta \qquad (11\text{-}13)$$

Then by squaring both these equations, adding, and simplifying,

$$\left(\sigma_{x'} - \frac{\sigma_x + \sigma_y}{2}\right)^2 + \tau_{x'y'}^2 = \left(\frac{\sigma_x - \sigma_y}{2}\right)^2 + \tau_{xy}^2 \qquad (11\text{-}14)$$

In a given problem, σ_x, σ_y, and τ_{xy} are the three known constants, and $\sigma_{x'}$ and $\tau_{x'y'}$ are the variables. Hence, Eq. 11-14 may be written in more compact form as

$$(\sigma_{x'} - a)^2 + \tau_{x'y'}^2 = b^2 \qquad (11\text{-}15)$$

where $a = (\sigma_x + \sigma_y)/2$ and $b^2 = [(\sigma_x - \sigma_y)/2]^2 + \tau_{xy}^2$ are constants.

This equation is the familiar expression of analytical geometry, $(x - a)^2 + y^2 = b^2$, for a circle of radius b with its center at $(+a,0)$. Hence, if a circle satisfying this equation is plotted, the simultaneous values of a point (x, y) on this circle correspond to $\sigma_{x'}$ and $\tau_{x'y'}$ for a particular orientation of an inclined plane. The ordinate of a point on the circle is the shear stress $\tau_{x'y'}$; the abscissa is the normal stress $\sigma_{x'}$. The circle so constructed is called a *circle of stress* or *Mohr's circles of stress*.[3]

By using the previous interpretation, a Mohr's circle for the stresses given in Fig. 11-8(a) is plotted in Fig. 11-8(c) with σ and τ as the coordinate axes. The center C is at (a,O), and the circle radius $R = b$. Hence,

$$a = OC = \frac{\sigma_x + \sigma_y}{2} \qquad (11\text{-}16)$$

and

$$b = R = \sqrt{\left(\frac{\sigma_x - \sigma_y}{2}\right)^2 + \tau_{xy}^2} \qquad (11\text{-}17)$$

The coordinates for point A on the circle correspond to the stresses in Fig. 11-8(a) on the right face of the element. For this face of the element, $\theta = 0°$ (i.e., the xy and the $x'y'$ axes coincide), $\sigma_{x'} = \sigma_x$, and $\tau_{x'y'} = \tau_{xy}$. The positive directions for these stresses coincide with the positive directions of the axes. Since $AD/CD = \tau_{xy}/[(\sigma_x - \sigma_y)/2]$, according to Eq. 11-6, the angle ACD is equal to $2\theta_1$. The coordinates for the conjugate point B correspond to the stresses in Fig. 11-8(a) on the upper face of the element. This follows from Eqs. 11-1 and 11-2 with $\theta = 90°$ or, for σ_y', from Eq. 11-3 with $\theta = 0°$.

The same reasoning applies to any other orientation of an element, such as shown in Fig. 11-8(b). A pair of conjugate points J and K can always be found on the circle to give the corresponding stresses, Fig. 11-8(c). An infinity of possible states of stress dependent on the angle θ are defined by the stress circle. Therefore, the following important observations regarding the state of stress at a point can be made based on the Mohr's circle:

1. The largest possible normal stress is σ_1; the smallest is σ_2. No shear stresses exist together with either one of these principal stresses.

---

[3]It is so named in honor of Otto Mohr of Germany, who in 1895 suggested its use in stress-analysis problems.

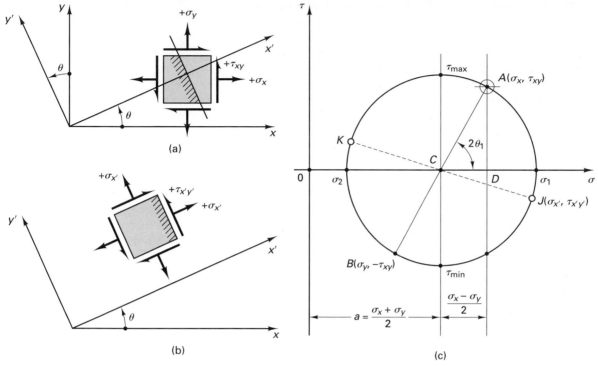

Fig. 11-8 Mohr's circle of stress.

2. The largest shear stress τ_{max} is numerically equal to the radius of the circle, also to $(\sigma_1 - \sigma_2)/2$. A normal stress equal to $(\sigma_1 + \sigma_2)/2$ acts on each of the planes of maximum shear stress.
3. If $\sigma_1 = \sigma_2$, Mohr's circle degenerates into a point, and no shear stresses at all develop in the xy plane.
4. If $\sigma_x + \sigma_y = 0$, the center of Mohr's circle coincides with the origin of the $\sigma\tau$ coordinates, and the state of pure shear exists.
5. The sum of the normal stresses on any two mutually perpendicular planes is invariant; that is,

$$\sigma_x + \sigma_y = \sigma_1 + \sigma_2 = \sigma_{x'} + \sigma_{y'} = \text{constant}$$

11-7. Construction of Mohr's Circles for Stress Transformation

The transformation of two-dimensional states of stress from one set of coordinates to another can always be made by direct application of statics as in Example 11-1, or, using the derived equations in Sections 11-3, 11-4, and 11-5. The latter equations can readily be programmed for a computer. However, the graphical display of stress transformations using a Mohr's circle offers a comprehensive view of a solution and is useful in some applications. Two alternative techniques for achieving such solutions are given in what follows. The physical planes on which the transformed stresses act are clearly displayed in the first method; in the second, the derivation for stress transformation is simpler, although determining the direction of the transformed stress is a little less convenient. The choice of method is a matter of preference.

Method I   The basic problem consists of constructing the circle of stress for given stresses σ_x, σ_y, and τ_{xy}, such as shown in Fig. 11-9(a), and then determining the state of stress on an *arbitrary* plane a–a. A procedure for determining the stresses on any inclined plane requires justification on the basis of the equations derived in Section 11-3.

According to Eq. 11-16, the center C of a Mohr's circle of stress is located on the σ axis at a distance $(\sigma_x + \sigma_y)/2$ from the origin. Point A on the circle has the coordinates (σ_x, τ_{xy}) corresponding to the *stresses acting on the right-hand face of the element* in the positive direction of the coordinate axes, Fig. 11-9(a). Point A will be referred to as the *origin of planes*. This information is sufficient to draw a circle of stress, Fig. 11-9(b).

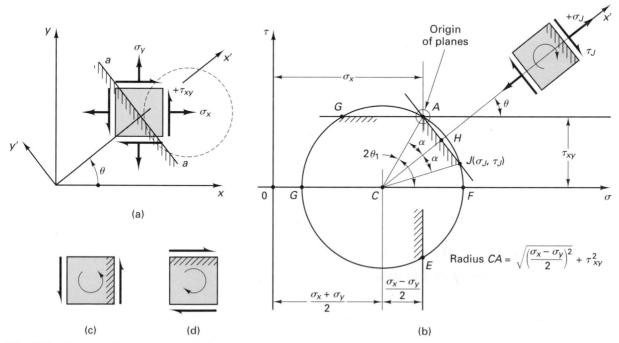

Fig. 11-9   Construction of Mohr's circle for determining stresses on an arbitrary plane.

The next step consists of drawing on the circle of stress a line through A parallel to plane a–a in the physical plane of Fig. 11-9(a). The intersection of this line at J with the stress circle gives the stresses acting on plane a–a. This requires some justification. For this purpose, the indicated geometric construction must be reviewed in detail.

According to the previous derivation shown in Fig. 11-8(c), angle ACF in Fig. 11-9(b) is equal to $2\theta_1$. Further, since line CH is drawn perpendicular to line AJ, angle ACJ is bisected, and $\alpha = 2\theta_1 - \theta$. Hence, angle JCF is $\theta - \alpha = 2\theta - 2\theta_1$, and it remains to be shown that the coordinates of point J define the stresses acting on inclined plane a–a. For this purpose, one notes from Fig. 11-9(b) that if R is the radius of a circle, $R \cos 2\theta_1 = (\sigma_x - \sigma_y)/2$ and $R \sin 2\theta_1 = \tau_{xy}$. Then, forming expressions for the normal and shear stresses at J based on the construction of the circle in Fig. 11-9(b) and making use of trigonometric identities for double angles, one has

$$\sigma_J = \frac{\sigma_x + \sigma_y}{2} + R\cos(2\theta - 2\theta_1)$$

$$= \frac{\sigma_x + \sigma_y}{2} + R\,(\cos 2\theta \cos 2\theta_1 + \sin 2\theta \sin 2\theta_1) \quad (11\text{-}18)$$

$$= \frac{\sigma_x + \sigma_y}{2} + \frac{\sigma_x - \sigma_y}{2}\cos 2\theta + \tau_{xy}\sin 2\theta$$

and

$$\tau_J = R\sin(2\theta - 2\theta_1) = R\sin 2\theta \cos 2\theta_1 - R\cos 2\theta \sin 2\theta_1$$

$$= + \frac{\sigma_x - \sigma_y}{2}\sin 2\theta - \tau_{xy}\cos 2\theta \qquad (11\text{-}19)$$

Except for the sign of τ_J, the last expressions are identical to Eqs. 11-1 and 11-2 and, therefore, define the stresses acting on the element shown in the upper right quadrant of Fig. 11-9(b). The hatched side of this element is parallel to line AJ on the stress circle, which is parallel to line a–a in Fig. 11-9(a). However, since the sign of τ_J is opposite to that in the basic transformation, Eq. 11-2, a special rule for the direction of shear stress has to be introduced.

For this purpose, consider the initial data for the element shown in Fig. 11-9(a), where all stresses are shown with positive sense. By isolating the shear stresses acting on the vertical faces, Fig. 11-9(c), it can be seen that *these stresses alone* cause a *counterclockwise* couple. By considering lines emanating from the origin of planes A, for the first case, Fig. 11-9(c), the circle is intersected at E, whereas for the second case, Fig. 11-9(d), it is intersected at G. This can be generalized into a rule: If the point of intersection of a line emanating from the origin of planes A intersects the circle *above* the σ axis, the shear stresses on the opposite sides of an element cause a *clockwise* couple. Conversely, if the point of intersection lies *below* the σ axis, the shear stresses on the opposite sides cause a *counterclockwise*

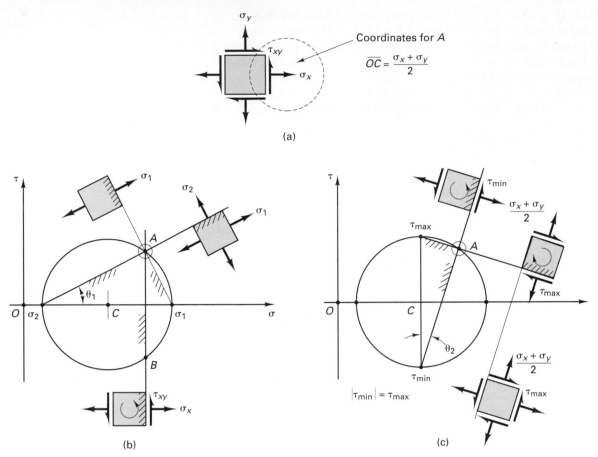

Fig. 11-10 Determining principal normal and maximal shear stresses.

couple. According to this rule, the shear stresses at J in Fig. 11-9(b) act with a clockwise sense.

This general procedure is illustrated for two particularly important cases. For the data given in Fig. 11-10(a), the principal stresses are found in Fig. 11-10(b), and the maximum shear stresses are found in Fig. 11-10(c). For the first case, it is known that the extreme values on the abscissa, σ_1 and σ_2, give the principal stresses. Connecting these points with the origin of planes A locates the planes on which these stresses act. Angle θ_1 can be determined by trigonometry. Either one of the two solutions is sufficient to obtain the complete solution shown on the element on the right.

The magnitudes of the maximum absolute shear stresses are known to be given by the radius of the Mohr's circle. As shown in Fig. 11-10(c), these stresses are located above and below C. Connecting these points with the origin of planes A determines the planes on which these stresses act. The corresponding elements are shown in the upper two diagrams of the elements, where the associated mean normal stresses are also indicated. Either one of these solutions with the aid of equilibrium concepts is sufficient for the complete solution shown on the bottom element in the figure.

Method 2   The state of stress in the xy coordinate system is shown in Fig. 11-11(a). The origin for these coordinates is arbitrarily chosen at the center of the infinitesimal element. The objective is to transform the given stresses to those in the rotated set of $x'y'$ axes as shown in Figs. 11-11(a) and (b) by using Mohr's circle.

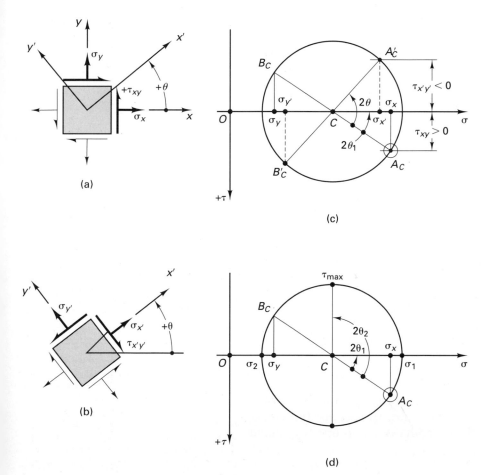

Fig. 11-11   Alternative construction of Mohr's circle of stress. Stresses on arbitrary and principal normal and shear planes are shown in (c) and (d), respectively.

As before, the center C of the Mohr's circle is located at $(\sigma_x + \sigma_y)/2$. Again, the right-hand face of the element defines σ_x and τ_{xy} used to locate a point on the circle. However,

> if $\tau_{xy} > 0$, it is plotted *downward* at σ_x, and
> if $\tau_{xy} < 0$, it is plotted *upward* at σ_x.

This, in effect, amounts to directing the positive τ axis downward, and is so shown in Fig. 11-11(c). The coordinates of σ_x and τ_{xy} locate the governing point A_C on the circle. This point corresponds to point A in the earlier construction; see Fig. 11-8. However, because of the opposite directions of the positive τ axes, whereas points A and A_C are related, they are not the same. Point B_C, conjugate to point A_C, can be located on the circle as shown in Fig. 11-11(c). The double angle 2θ follows from geometry.

Next the diameter $A_C B_C$ is rotated through an angle 2θ in the *same sense* that the x' axis is rotated through the angle θ with respect to the x axis. Then the new point A_C' determines the stresses $\sigma_{x'}$ and $\tau_{x'y'}$ on the right-hand face of the element in Fig. 11-11(b). Note that for the case shown, the shear stress $\tau_{x'y'}$ is negative, since at $\sigma_{x'}$ it is above the σ axis. Similar considerations apply to the conjugate point B_C' defining the stresses on the plane normal to the y' axis.

The expressions for $\sigma_{x'}$ and $\tau_{x'y'}$ can be formulated from the construction of the Mohr's circle shown in Fig. 11-11(c) using Eqs. 11-16 and 11-17. After simplifications, these relations, except for the sign of $\tau_{x'y'}$, reduce to the basic stress transformation relations, Eqs. 11-1 and 11-2. Hence this construction of the Mohr's circle is justified. For proof, modify Eqs. 11-18 and 11-19.

The procedure for determining the principal normal stress is shown in Fig. 11-11(d). After drawing a Mohr's circle, the principal stresses σ_1 and σ_2 are known. The required rotation θ_1 of the axes in the direction of these stresses is obtained by calculating the double angle $2\theta_1$ from the diagram. Similarly, the principal shear stresses are given by the coordinates of the points on a circle at their extreme values on the τ axis. The required rotation θ_2 of these axes is obtained by calculating the double angle $2\theta_2$ from the diagram.

Method 1 is used in the two examples that follow.

Example 11-3

Given the state of stress shown in Fig. 11-12(a), transform it (a) into the principal stresses, and (b) into the maximum shear stresses and the associated normal stresses. Show the results for both cases on properly oriented elements. Use Method I.

SOLUTION
To construct Mohr's circle of stress, the following quantities are required:

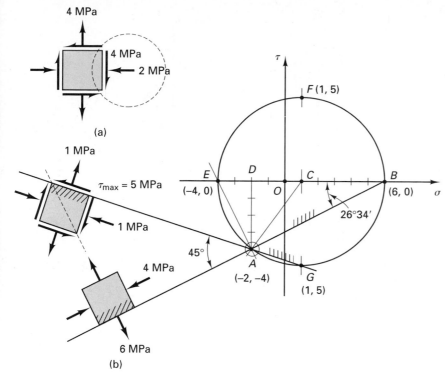

Fig. 11-12

1. Center of circle on the σ axis: $(-2 + 4)/2 = +1$ MPa
2. Origin of planes A from data on the right face of element: $(-2, -4)$ MPa
3. Radius of circle: $CA = \sqrt{CD^2 + DA^2} = 5$ MPa

After drawing the circle, one obtains $\sigma_1 = +6$ MPa, $\sigma_2 = -4$ MPa, and $\tau_{max} = 5$ MPa.

Line AB on the stress circle locates the principal plane for $\sigma_1 = 6$ MPa. The angle θ_1 is $26°34'$, since $\tan \theta_1 = AD/DB = 4/8 = 0.5$. The other principal stress, $\sigma_2 = -4$ MPa, acts at right angle to the aforementioned plane. These results are shown on a properly oriented element.

Line AG on the circle at $45°$ with the principal planes determines the planes for maximum shear, $\tau_{max} = 5$ MPa, and the associated mean normal stress $\sigma' = 1$ MPa. The latter stress corresponds to σ at the circle center. Complete results are shown on a properly oriented element.

It is worthy to note that the directions of the principal stresses can be anticipated and can be used in calculations as a check. A suitable inspection procedure is shown in Fig. 11-13. To begin with, it is known that tensile stresses of equal magnitude to the shear stress develop along a diagonal, as shown in Fig. 11-6. Therefore, the maximum tensile stress σ_1, which is the

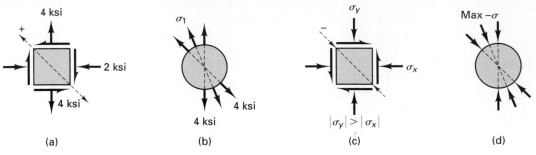

Fig. 11-13   Qualitative estimates of directions for principal stresses.

result of all stresses, must act as shown in Fig. 11-13(b). Situations with compressive stresses can be treated similarly, Fig. 11-13(d).

Example 11-4

Using Mohr's circle, transform the stresses shown in Fig. 11-14(a) into stresses acting on the plane at an angle of $22\frac{1}{2}°$ with the vertical axis. Use Method I.

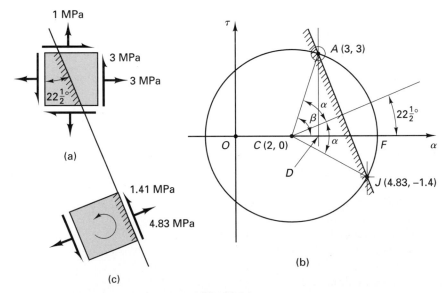

Fig. 11-14

SOLUTION

For this case, the center of the circle is at $(1 + 3)/2 = +2$ MPa on the σ axis. The origin of planes A is at $(3,3)$, and the radius $R = \sqrt{1^2 + 3^2} = 3.16$ MPa . By using these data, a stress circle is plotted in Fig. 11-14(b) on which an inclined line at 22.5° locating point J is drawn.

Angle β is 71.57°, since $\tan \beta = AD/CD = 3$. A normal to AJ forms an angle of 22.5° with the σ axis. Therefore, $\alpha = 71.57° - 22.5° = 49.07°$, and angle FCJ is $\alpha - 22.5° = 26.57°$. This locates J on the circle. Hence, $\sigma_J = 2 + R \cos(-26.57°) = 2 + 3.16(0.894) = 4.83$ MPa, and $\tau_J = R \sin(-26.57°) = 3.16(-0.447) = -1.41$ MPa.

These results are shown on a properly oriented element in Fig. 11-14(c). Since τ_J is negative, the shear stresses are shown acting counterclockwise.

Again it should be remarked that the equations for stress transformation are identical in form to the equations for determining the principal axes and moments of inertia of areas (Section 9-3). Therefore, Mohr's circle can be constructed for finding these equations.[4]

11-8. Principal Stresses for a General State of Stress[5]

Traditionally, in an introductory text on solid mechanics, attention is largely confined to stresses in two dimensions. Since, however, the physical elements studied are always three dimensional, for completeness, it is desirable to consider the consequences of three dimensionality on stress transformations. The concepts developed in this section have an impact on the discussion that follows in this chapter, as well as on some issues considered in the next chapter.

Consider a general state of stress and define an infinitesimal tetrahedron[6] as shown in Fig. 11-15(a). Instead of considering an inclined plane in the xy coordinate system, as before for a wedge, the unknown stresses are sought on an arbitrary oblique plane ABC in the three-dimensional xyz coordinate system. A set of known stresses on the other three faces of the mutually perpendicular planes of the tetrahedron is given. These stresses are the same as shown earlier in Fig. 1-3(a).

A unit normal **n** to the oblique plane defines its orientation. This unit vector is identified by its direction cosines l, m, and n, where $\cos \alpha = l$, $\cos \beta = m$, and $\cos \gamma = n$. The meaning of these quantities is illustrated in

---

[4]See J. L. Meriam and L. G. Kraige, *Statics,* 2nd ed. (New York: Wiley, 1986).

[5]This section is more advanced and can be omitted.

[6]A tetrahedron was first introduced in the study of stress transformations by the great French mathematician A. L. Cauchy in the 1820s.

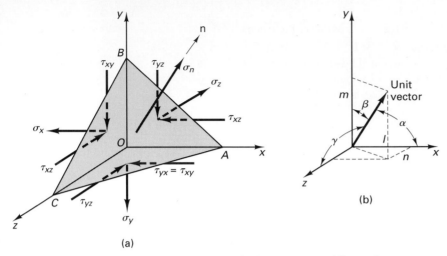

(a)

(b)

Fig. 11-15   Tetrahedron for deriving a principal stress on an oblique plane.

Fig. 11-15(b). From the same figure, it can be noted that since $l^2 + n^2 = d^2$ and $d^2 + m^2 = 1$:

$$l^2 + m^2 + n^2 = 1 \qquad (11\text{-}20)$$

Further, if the infinitesimal area ABC is defined as $dA_{ABC} \equiv dA$, then the three areas of the tetrahedron along the coordinate axes, identified by their subscripts, are $dA_{BOC} = dA\ l$, $dA_{AOC} = dA\ m$, and $dA_{AOB} = dA\ n$.[7]

Force equilibrium equations for the tetrahedron can now be written by multiplying the stresses given in Fig. 11-15(a) by the respective areas established. For simplicity, it will be assumed that only a *normal stress* σ_n (i.e., a *principal stress*) is acting on face ABC. The components of the corresponding normal force ($\sigma_n\, dA$) are obtained by resolving it along the coordinate axes using the direction cosines, Fig. 11-15(b). On this basis,

$$\sum F_x = 0 \qquad (\sigma_n\, dA)l - \sigma_x\, dA\ l - \tau_{xy}\, dA\ m - \tau_{xz} dA\ n = 0$$

$$\sum F_y = 0 \qquad (\sigma_n\, dA)m - \sigma_y\, dA\ m - \tau_{yz}\, dA\ n - \tau_{xy} dA\ l = 0 \quad (11\text{-}21)$$

$$\sum F_z = 0 \qquad (\sigma_n\, dA)n - \sigma_z dA\ n - \tau_{xz}\, dA\ l - \tau_{yz} dA\ m = 0$$

[7]These areas are the projection of dA on the respective coordinate planes. To clarify, consider the two-dimensional wedge shown in Fig. 11-16 and compare the volumes using two different paths. Let the area associated with side AC be A_{AC} and the corresponding wedge height be AB. Then the wedge volume is $A_{AC}AB/2$. On the other hand, if the area for the side CB is A_{CB} and the wedge height is $AB \cos \theta = ABl$, the volume is $A_{CB}AB/2$. By equating the volumes and simplifying, $A_{AC} = A_{CB}l$. By carrying out this procedure in three dimensions, the relations given in the text can be justified.

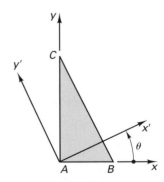

Fig. 11-16

Simplifying, changing signs, and regrouping terms,

$$(\sigma_x - \sigma_n)l + \tau_{xy}m + \tau_{xz}n = 0$$

$$\tau_{xy}l + (\sigma_y - \sigma_n)m + \tau_{yz}n = 0 \qquad (11\text{-}22)$$

$$\tau_{xz}l + \tau_{yz}m + (\sigma_z - \sigma_n)n = 0$$

By virtue of Eq. 11-20, all three direction cosines cannot be zero. However, the system of linear homogeneous equations has a nontrivial solution if and only if the determinant of the coefficients of l, m, and n vanishes. Hence,

$$\begin{vmatrix} \sigma_x - \sigma_n & \tau_{xy} & \tau_{xz} \\ \tau_{xy} & \sigma_y - \sigma_n & \tau_{yz} \\ \tau_{xz} & \tau_{yz} & \sigma_z - \sigma_n \end{vmatrix} = 0 \qquad (11\text{-}23)$$

Expansion of this determinant gives

$$\sigma_n^3 - I_1\sigma_n^2 + I_2\sigma_n - I_3 = 0 \qquad (11\text{-}24)$$

where

$$I_1 = \sigma_1 + \sigma_2 + \sigma_3 \qquad (11\text{-}25)$$

$$I_2 = \sigma_x\sigma_y + \sigma_y\sigma_z + \sigma_z\sigma_x - (\tau_{xy}^2 + \tau_{yz}^2 + \tau_{zx}^2) \qquad (11\text{-}26)$$

$$I_3 = \sigma_x\sigma_y\sigma_z + 2\tau_{xy}\tau_{yz}\tau_{zx} - (\sigma_x\tau_{yz}^2 + \sigma_y\tau_{zx}^2 + \sigma_z\tau_{xy}^2) \qquad (11\text{-}27)$$

Here, if the initial coordinate system is changed (thereby changing the three mutually perpendicular planes of the tetrahedron), the σ_n on the inclined plane must remain the same. Therefore, the constants I_1, I_2, and I_3 in Eq. 11-24 must also remain the same, and hence they are *invariant*. Moreover, since the matrix of Eq. 11-23 is symmetric and all of its elements are real, according to the Descartes rule of signs, in general, Eq. 11-24 has *three real roots.*[8] These roots are the eigenvalues of the determinental Eq. 11-23 and are the *principal normal stresses* at a given point.

Since the cubic Eq. 11-24 has real roots, its solution can be found in trigonometric form. Using the well-known formulas of algebra, the principal normal stresses can be expressed in terms of the invariants of stress deviator:[9]

$$\sigma_1 = \sigma_0 + 2(|J_2/3|)^{\frac{1}{2}} \cos(\theta)$$

$$\sigma_2 = \sigma_0 - 2(|J_2/3|)^{\frac{1}{2}} \cos\left(\theta + \frac{\pi}{3}\right) \qquad (11\text{-}28)$$

$$\sigma_3 = \sigma_0 - 2(|J_2/3|)^{\frac{1}{2}} \cos\left(\theta - \frac{\pi}{3}\right)$$

[8]I. S. Sokolnikoff, *Mathematical Theory of Elasticity*, 2nd ed. (New York: McGraw-Hill, 1950), 47.

[9]V. V. Sokolovskii, *Theory of Plasticity*, 2nd ed. (Moscow: Gostehizdat, 1950) [in Russian].

where angle θ (sometimes called the angle of the type of stress state or Lode angle) is defined as

$$\theta = \frac{1}{3} \arccos\left(-\frac{J_3}{2\left(|J_2/3|\right)^{\frac{3}{2}}}\right) \tag{11-29}$$

and J_2, J_3 are the invariants of stress deviator

$$J_2 = s_x s_y + s_y s_z + s_z s_x - \tau_{xy}^2 - \tau_{yz}^2 - \tau_{zx}^2$$

$$J_3 = -\left(s_x s_y s_z - s_x \tau_{yz}^2 - s_y \tau_{zx}^2 - s_z \tau_{xy}^2\right) \tag{11-30}$$

in which

$$s_x = \sigma_x - \sigma_0, \quad s_y = \sigma_y - \sigma_0, \quad s_z = \sigma_z - \sigma_0$$

$$\sigma_0 = \frac{1}{3}\left(\sigma_x + \sigma_y + \sigma_z\right) \tag{11-31}$$

Analogous to Eq. 11-11, the maximum shear stresses at a given point can be expressed in terms of the principal normal stresses as follows:

$$\tau_1 = \pm\frac{1}{2}(\sigma_2 - \sigma_3), \quad \tau_2 = \pm\frac{1}{2}(\sigma_3 - \sigma_1), \quad \tau_3 = \pm\frac{1}{2}(\sigma_1 - \sigma_2) \tag{11-32}$$

Any one of the roots defined by Eq. 11-28 can be substituted into any two of Eq. 11-22, and together with Eq. 11-20 they form a set of three simultaneous equations. A solution of these equations gives the direction cosines for the selected principal stresses. The three principal directions for the principal stresses are *orthogonal*. The planes normal to the principal directions are the *principal planes of stress*.

The values of the direction cosines of principal stress $\sigma_i (i = 1,2,3)$ can be determined from the following system of equations:

$$(\sigma_x - \sigma_i)l_i + \tau_{xy}m_i + \tau_{zx}n_i = 0$$

$$\tau_{xy}l_i + (\sigma_y - \sigma_i)m_i + \tau_{yz}n_i = 0 \quad (i = 1, 2, 3) \tag{11-33}$$

$$\tau_{zx}l_i + \tau_{yz}m_i + (\sigma_x - \sigma_i)n_i = 0$$

$$l_i^2 + m_i^2 + n_i^2 = 1 \quad (i = 1, 2, 3) \tag{11-34}$$

where, dividing Eqs. 11-33 by, for example, n_i, solving any two of these equations with reference to (l_i/n_i) and (m_i/n_i), and using Eq. 11-34, one obtains the solution:

$$n_i = \frac{1}{\sqrt{\left(\frac{l_i}{n_i}\right)^2 + \left(\frac{m_i}{n_i}\right)^2 + 1}}, \quad l_i = \left(\frac{l_i}{n_i}\right)n_i,$$

$$m_i = \left(\frac{m_i}{n_i}\right)n_i, \quad (i = 1, 2, 3) \tag{11-35}$$

11-9. Mohr's Circle for a General State of Stress

In the preceding section, it was shown that for a general state of stress, there are three orthogonal principal stresses, σ_1, σ_2, and σ_3, provided $\sigma_1 \neq \sigma_2 \neq \sigma_3$. These stresses act along the principal axes. Plane stress problems fall within the scope of the general theory when one of the principal stresses is zero. So do the plane strain problems when one of the principal stresses is given by Eq. 11-5. However, degenerate cases arise requiring special treatment.

If only two of the principal stresses are equal, the remaining principal stress has a unique direction. Any other two orthogonal directions of an orthogonal triad are the principal directions. This case may be referred to as a *cylindrical* or *axisymmetric* state of stress.[10] If all three principal stresses are equal, the state of stress is said to be *spherical*. Any triad of orthogonal axes for this case gives the principal axes.

For the general case, consider the illustration given in Fig. 11-17, where the ordered principal stresses are $\sigma_1 > \sigma_2 > \sigma_3$. Suppose further that, after an appropriate stress transformation, principal axes 1, 2, and 3 and the corresponding principal stresses are oriented as shown on an element in Fig. 11-17(a). By viewing this element along the three principal axes, 3 two-dimensional diagrams, shown in Fig. 11-17(b) are obtained. For each of these diagrams, one can draw a Mohr's circle of stress. This is shown in Fig. 11-17(c) with a cluster of three circles. As far as the stress magnitudes are concerned, the outer circle is the most important one.

Although by definition (Section 11-4) the principal stresses are the maximum and the minimum ones, it is of interest as to where on a plot, such as Fig. 11-17(c), the stresses on all arbitrary oblique planes lie. Such a plane is designated by K in Fig. 11-17(a). The results of this study, considering stresses in three dimensions, show[11] that the coordinate points for all possible planes lie either on one of the three circles or in an area between them, shown hatched in Fig. 11-17(c). A series of circles is defined within this area having their centers on the σ axis by holding any one of the direction cosines constant. Therefore, it is convenient to refer to the three circles drawn as the *principal stress circles*. The largest of these is the *major* principal stress circle.

Inasmuch as all stresses in their various transformations may play a role in causing either yield or breakdown of a material, it is often instructive to plot all three principal circles of stress, as shown in Fig. 11-17(c). Two examples of this kind follow. In making such plots, the degenerate cases, when two or all principal stresses are equal, must be kept in mind. For such cases, a Mohr's circle becomes a point.

[10]O. Hoffman and G. Sachs, *Introduction to the Theory of Plasticity for Engineers* (New York: McGraw-Hill, 1953).

[11]*Ibid.*, 13.

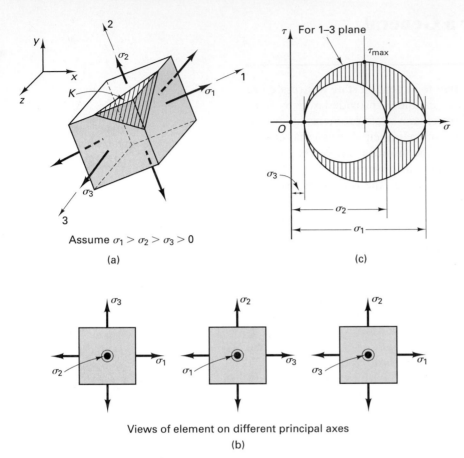

Assume $\sigma_1 > \sigma_2 > \sigma_3 > 0$

(a)

(c)

Views of element on different principal axes

(b)

Fig. 11-17   Triaxial state of stress.

Example 11-5

For the data of Example 11-3, repeated in Fig. 11-18(a), construct three Mohr's principal circles of stress by viewing an element from three principal directions. Assume that this is a plane stress problem.

SOLUTION

The principal stresses for this problem in two dimensions have already been determined in Example 11-3. The results are repeated in Fig. 11-18(b). Since this is a plane stress problem, the stress in the direction normal to the paper is zero. The complete state of stress showing all principal stresses is in Fig. 11-18(c). The 3 two-dimensional diagrams of the element viewed

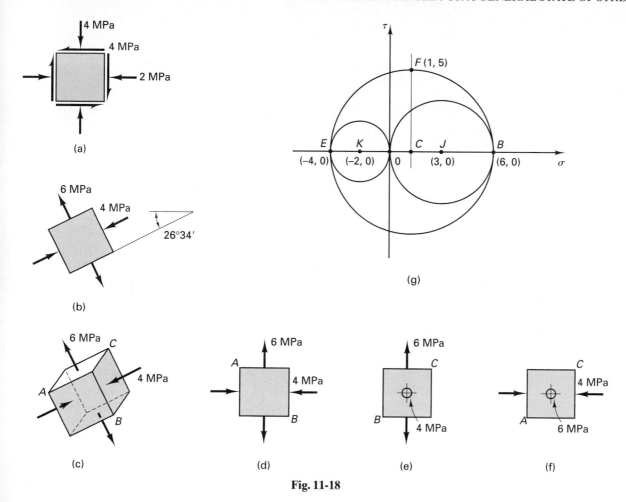

(a)

(b)

(g)

(c)

(d)

(e)

(f)

Fig. 11-18

from different directions are in Figs. 11-18(d)–(f). The cluster of three Mohr's principal circles is shown in Fig. 11-18(g).

If the given stresses were for a *plane strain* problem, the middle principal stress, instead of being zero, per Eq. 11-5, would be $\sigma_2 = \nu(6-4) = +2\nu$, where ν is Poisson's ratio.

Example 11-6

For the plane stress shown in Fig. 11-19(a), draw the three Mohr's principal circle diagrams and determine the state of stress for maximum shear.

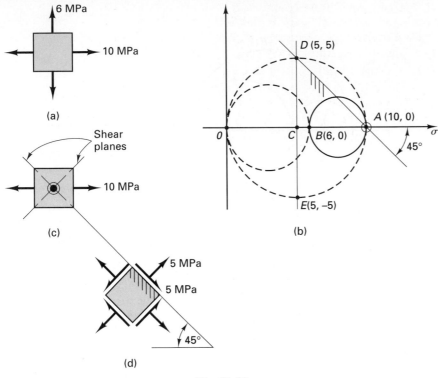

Fig. 11-19

SOLUTION

Two of the principal stresses are given; the third is zero, as this is a plane stress problem. The three principal stress circles are shown in Fig. 11-19(b). The maximum shear stress occurs in the planes shown in Fig. 11-19(c). This stress is associated with point D on the major principal circle, and in physical orientation is given in Fig. 11-19(d).

This type of problem occurs in pressure-vessel analyses, where it is important to recognize that large shear stresses may arise.

Part B   TRANSFORMATION OF STRAIN

11-10. Strains in Two Dimensions

In the following four sections, study is directed toward strain transformation in two dimensions. This includes consideration of plane stress and plain strain problems. It will be shown that the transformation of normal and shear strains from one set of rotated axes to another is completely analogous to the transformation of normal and shear stresses presented earlier. Therefore, after establishing the strain transformation equations, it is possible to introduce Mohr's circle of strain. A procedure of reducing surface strain measurements made by means of strain gages into principal stresses completes this part of the chapter.

In studying the strains at a point, only the relative displacement of the adjoining points is of importance. Translation and rotation of an element as a whole are of no consequence since these displacements are *rigid-body displacements*. For example, if the extensional strain of a diagonal *ds* of the original element in Fig. 11-20(a) is being studied, the element in its deformed condition can be brought back for comparison purposes, as shown in Fig. 11-20(c). It is immaterial whether the horizontal (dashed) or the vertical (dotted) sides of the deformed and the undeformed elements are matched to determine $d\Delta$. For the small strains and rotations considered, the relevant quantity, elongation $d\Delta$ in the direction of the diagonal, is essentially the same regardless of the method of comparison employed. In treating strains in this manner, only kinematic questions have relevance. The mechanical properties of material do not enter the problem.

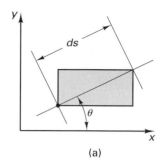

(a)

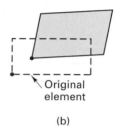

(b)

11-11. Transformation of Strain in Two Dimensions: Geometric Approach

In establishing the equations for the transformation of strain, strict adherence to a sign convention is necessary. The sign convention used here is related to the one chosen for the stresses in Section 11-4. The normal strains ε_x and ε_y corresponding to elongations in the x and y directions, respectively, are taken positive. The shear strain is considered positive if the 90° angle between the x and the y axes becomes smaller. For convenience in deriving the strain transformation equations, the element distorted by positive shear strain will be taken as that shown in Fig. 11-21(a).

Next, suppose that the strains ε_x, ε_y, and γ_{xy} associated with the xy axes are known and extensional strain along some new x' axis is required. The new $x'y'$ system of axes is related to the xy axes, as in Fig. 11-21(b). In these new coordinates, a length OA, which is dx' long, may be thought of as being a diagonal of a rectangular differential element dx by dy in the initial coordinates.

By considering point O fixed, one can compute the displacements of point A caused by the imposed strains on a different basis in the two coordinate systems. The displacement in the x direction is $AA' = \varepsilon_x\,dx$; in the y direction, $A'A'' = \varepsilon_y\,dy$. For the shear strain, assuming it causes the horizontal displacement shown in Fig. 11-21(a), $A''A''' = \gamma_{xy}\,dy$. The order in

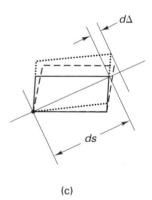

(c)

Fig. 11-20   Strains are determined from relative deformations.

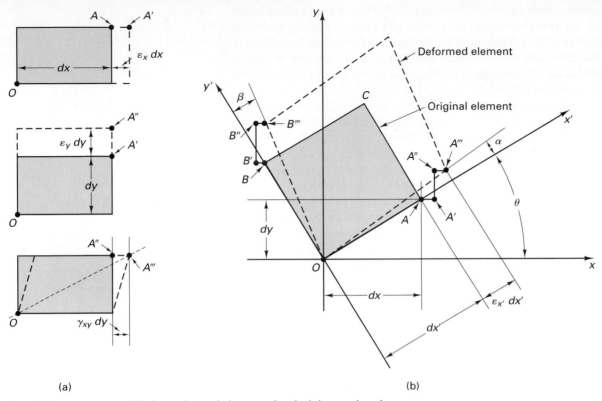

Fig. 11-21 Exaggerated deformations of elements for deriving strains along new axes.

which these displacements occur is arbitrary. In Fig. 11-21(b), displacement AA' is shown first, then $A'AA''$, and finally $A''A''''$. By projecting these displacements onto the x' axis, one finds the displacement of point A along the x' axis. Then, recognizing that by definition, $\varepsilon_{x'}\,dx'$ in the $x'y'$ coordinate system is also the elongation of OA, one has the following equality:

$$\varepsilon_{x'}dx' = AA'\cos\theta + A'A''\sin\theta + A''A'''\cos\theta$$

By substituting the appropriate expressions for the displacements and dividing through by dx', one has

$$\varepsilon_{x'} = \varepsilon_x\frac{dx}{dx'}\cos\theta + \varepsilon_y\frac{dy}{dx'}\sin\theta + \gamma_{xy}\frac{dy}{dx'}\cos\theta$$

Since, however, $dx/dx' = \cos\theta$ and $dy/dx' = \sin\theta$,

$$\boxed{\varepsilon_{x'} = \varepsilon_x\cos^2\theta + \varepsilon_y\sin^2\theta + \gamma_{xy}\sin\theta\cos\theta} \qquad (11\text{-}36)$$

Equation 11-36 is the basic expression for normal strain transformation in a plane in an arbitrary direction defined by the x' axis.[12] In order to apply this equation, ε_x, ε_y, and γ_{xy} must be known. By use of trigonometric identities already encountered in deriving Eq. 11-1, the last equation can also be rewritten as

$$\varepsilon_{x'} = \frac{\varepsilon_x + \varepsilon_y}{2} + \frac{\varepsilon_x - \varepsilon_y}{2}\cos 2\theta + \frac{\gamma_{xy}}{2}\sin 2\theta \qquad (11\text{-}37)$$

To complete the study of strain transformation at a point, shear-strain transformation must also be established. For this purpose, consider an element $OACB$ with sides OA and OB directed along the x' and the y' axes, as shown in Fig. 11-21(b). By definition, the shear strain for this element is the change in angle AOB. From the figure, the change of this angle is $\alpha + \beta$.

For small deformations, the small angle α can be determined by projecting the displacements AA', $A'A''$, and $A''A'''$ onto a normal to OA and dividing this quantity by dx'. In applying this approach, the tangent of the angle is assumed equal to the angle itself. This is acceptable as the strains are small. Thus,

$$\alpha \approx \tan\alpha = \frac{-AA'\sin\theta + A'A''\cos\theta - A''A'''\sin\theta}{dx'}$$

$$= -\varepsilon_x\frac{dx}{dx'}\sin\theta + \varepsilon_y\frac{dy}{dx'}\cos\theta - \gamma_y\frac{dy}{dx'}\sin\theta$$

$$= -(\varepsilon_x - \varepsilon_y)\sin\theta\cos\theta - \gamma_{xy}\sin^2\theta$$

By analogous reasoning,

$$\beta \approx -(\varepsilon_x - \varepsilon_y)\sin\theta\cos\theta + \gamma_{xy}\cos^2\theta$$

Therefore, since the shear strain $\gamma_{x'y'}$ of an angle included between the $x'y'$ axes is $\beta + \alpha$, one has

$$\gamma_{x'y'} = -2(\varepsilon_x - \varepsilon_y)\sin\theta\cos\theta + \gamma_{xy}(\cos^2\theta - \sin^2\theta)$$

or

$$\gamma_{x'y'} = -(\varepsilon_x - \varepsilon_y)\sin 2\theta + y_{xy}\cos 2\theta \qquad (11\text{-}38)$$

---

[12]Using direction cosines l, m, and n (see Section 11-8), Eq. 11-28 can be rewritten as

$$\varepsilon_{x'} = \varepsilon_x l^2 + \varepsilon_y m^2 + \gamma_{xy}lm \qquad (11\text{-}36a)$$

As is shown in books on the theory of elasticity or continuum mechanics, this normal strain transformation in three dimensions becomes

$$\varepsilon_{x'} = \varepsilon_x l^2 + \varepsilon_y m^2 + \varepsilon_z n^2 + \gamma_{xy}lm + \gamma_{yz}mn + \gamma_{zx}ln$$

Therefore, Eq. 11-36 can be applied *only* for strain transformation in two dimensions.

This is the second fundamental expression for the transformation of strain. Note that when $\theta = 0°$, the shear strain associated with the xy axes is recovered.

The basic equations (Eqs. 11-37 and 11-38) for strain transformation in a plane are analogous to Eqs. 11-1 and 11-2 for stress transformation in two dimensions. Fundamentally, this is because both stresses and strains are second-rank tensors and mathematically obey the same laws of transformation. This similarity will be emphasized in discussing Mohr's circle of strain.

11-12. Transformation of Strain in Two Dimensions: Analytic Approach

Situations arise where strains associated with one set of rectangular coordinate axes are transformed to an equivalent set of strains on rotated axes. Such a condition is shown in Fig. 11-22, where the initial xy axes are rotated counterclockwise through angle θ to define angle $x'y'$ coordinate system.

There are several procedures to relate the strains in xy coordinate system to that in the $x'y'$ system. Here an analytical approach is pursued. This requires establishing a relationship between the two coordinate systems. Thus, if an arbitrary point A of a body in the xy coordinate system is at x and y, in the $x'y'$ system the same point is at x' and y'. From Fig. 11-22 it can be seen that (see the heavy lines in the figure)

$$x' = x \cos \theta + y \sin \theta$$
$$y' = -x \sin \theta + y \cos \theta$$

(11-39)

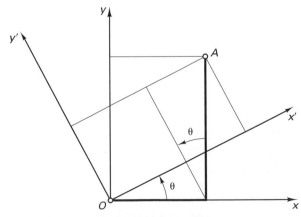

Fig. 11-22   Coordinate transformation.

These two equations can be conveniently written in matrix form as

$$\begin{Bmatrix} x' \\ y' \end{Bmatrix} = \begin{bmatrix} \cos\theta & \sin\theta \\ -\sin\theta & \cos\theta \end{bmatrix} \begin{Bmatrix} x \\ y \end{Bmatrix} \tag{11-40}$$

This matrix equation represents a rotation of the $x'y'$ axes as a function of θ. The determinant of this matrix is unity; hence its transpose is equal to the inverse. Therefore,

$$\begin{Bmatrix} x \\ y \end{Bmatrix} = \begin{bmatrix} \cos\theta & -\sin\theta \\ \sin\theta & \cos\theta \end{bmatrix} \begin{Bmatrix} x' \\ y' \end{Bmatrix} \tag{11-41}$$

or, written in longhand for convenience in subsequent algebraic manipulations,

$$x = x'\cos\theta - y'\sin\theta$$
$$y = x'\sin\theta + y'\cos\theta \tag{11-42}$$

Since the same rules of transformation from one coordinate system to the other apply to the small linear displacements u and v, similar to Eq. 11-39,

$$u' = u\cos\theta + v\sin\theta$$
$$v' = -u\sin\theta + v\cos\theta \tag{11-43}$$

Then, recalling the definition of the *normal strain* (Eq. 5-7), and applying the chain rule of differentiation, the normal strain in the x' direction is

$$\varepsilon_{x'} = \frac{\partial u'}{\partial x'} = \frac{\partial u'}{\partial x}\frac{\partial x}{\partial x'} + \frac{\partial u'}{\partial y}\frac{\partial y}{\partial x'} \tag{11-44}$$

and

$$\varepsilon_{x'} = \frac{\partial}{\partial x}(u\cos\theta + v\sin\theta)\frac{\partial}{\partial x'}(x'\cos\theta - y'\sin\theta)$$

$$+ \frac{\partial}{\partial y}(u\cos\theta + v\sin\theta)\frac{\partial}{\partial x'}(x'\cos\theta + y'\sin\theta)$$

$$= \frac{\partial u}{\partial x}\cos^2\theta + \left(\frac{\partial u}{\partial y} + \frac{\partial v}{\partial x}\right)\sin\theta\cos\theta + \frac{\partial v}{\partial y}\sin^2\theta$$

$$= \varepsilon_x\cos^2\theta + \gamma_{xy}\sin\theta\cos\theta + \varepsilon_y\sin^2\theta$$

Hence the basic equations of transformation as in Section 11-11 are:

$$\boxed{\varepsilon_{x'} = \varepsilon_x\cos^2\theta + \varepsilon_y\sin^2\theta + \gamma_{xy}\sin\theta\cos\theta} \tag{11-36}$$

$$\boxed{\varepsilon_{x'} = \frac{\varepsilon_x + \varepsilon_y}{2} + \frac{\varepsilon_x - \varepsilon_y}{2}\cos 2\theta + \frac{\gamma_{xy}}{2}\sin 2\theta} \tag{11-37}$$

To complete the study of strain transformation at a point using the analytical approach, shear-strain transformation must be established. By following an analogous procedure to the foregoing, one first recalls Eq. 5-9, writing it in the rotated coordinates as

$$\gamma_{x'y'} = \frac{\partial v'}{\partial x'} + \frac{\partial u'}{\partial y'} \tag{11-45}$$

Then, proceeding much the same as earlier, one has

$$\gamma_{x'y'} = -2(\varepsilon_x - \varepsilon_y)\sin\theta\cos\theta + \gamma_{xy}(\cos^2\theta - \sin^2\theta)$$

or

$$\boxed{\gamma_{x'y'} = -(\varepsilon_x - \varepsilon_y)\sin 2\theta + \gamma_{xy}\cos 2\theta} \tag{11-38}$$

11-13. Mohr's Circle for Two-Dimensional Strain

The two basic equations for the transformations of strains in two dimensions derived in the preceding section mathematically resemble the equations for the transformation of stresses derived in Section 11-3. To achieve greater similarity between the appearances of the new equations and those of the earlier ones, Eq. 11-38 after division throughout by 2 is rewritten as Eq. 11-45:

$$\varepsilon_{x'} = \frac{\varepsilon_x + \varepsilon_y}{2} + \frac{\varepsilon_x - \varepsilon_y}{2}\cos 2\theta + \frac{\gamma_{xy}}{2}\sin 2\theta \tag{11-38}$$

$$\boxed{\frac{\gamma_{x'y'}}{2} = -\frac{\varepsilon_x - \varepsilon_y}{2}\sin 2\theta + \frac{\gamma_{xy}}{2}\cos 2\theta} \tag{11-46}$$

Since these strain-transformation equations with the shear strains divided by 2 are mathematically identical to the stress transformation Eqs. 11-1 and 11-2, Mohr's circle of strain can be constructed. In this construction, every point on the circle gives two values: one for the normal strain, the other for the shear strain *divided by 2*. (For further reasons, see Section 5-5.) Strains corresponding to elongation are positive; for contraction, they are negative. For positive shear strains the angle between the x and the y axes becomes smaller; see Fig. 11-23. In plotting the circle, the positive axes are taken *in accordance with the sign convention for Method 1 for Mohr's circle of stress,* upward and to the right. The vertical axis is measured in terms of $\gamma/2$.

As an illustration of Mohr's circle of strain, consider that ε_x, ε_y, and $+\gamma_{xy}$ are given. Then, on the $\varepsilon - \gamma/2$ axes in Fig. 11-23, the center of the cir-

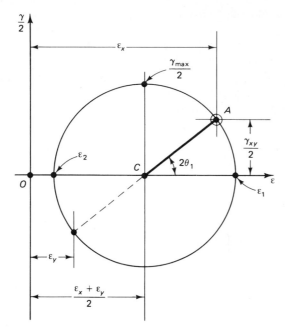

Fig. 11-23   Mohr's circle of strain using sign convention of Method I, Section 11-7.

cle C is at $[(\varepsilon_x + \varepsilon_y/2, 0]$ and, from the given data, the origin of planes A on the circle is at $(\varepsilon_x, \gamma_{xy}/2)$. An examination of this circle leads to conclusions analogous to those reached before for the circle of stress.

1. The maximum normal strain is ε_1; the minimum is ε_2. These are the principal strains, and no shear strains are associated with them. The directions of the normal strains coincide with the directions of the principal stresses. As can be deduced from the circle, the analytical expression for the principal strains is

$$(\varepsilon_{x'})_{\substack{max \\ min}} = \varepsilon_{1 \text{ or } 2} = \frac{\varepsilon_x + \varepsilon_y}{2} \pm \sqrt{\left(\frac{\varepsilon_x - \varepsilon_y}{2}\right)^2 + \left(\frac{\gamma_{xy}}{2}\right)^2} \qquad (11\text{-}47)$$

where the positive sign in front of the square root is to be used for ε_1, the maximum principal strain in the algebraic sense. The negative sign is to be used for ε_2, the minimum principal strain. The planes on which the principal strains act can be defined analytically from Eq. 11-46 by setting it equal to zero. Thus,

$$\tan 2\theta_1 = \frac{\gamma_{xy}}{\varepsilon_x - \varepsilon_y} \qquad (11\text{-}48)$$

Since this equation has two roots, it is completely analogous to Eq. 11-6 and can be treated in the same manner.

2. The largest shear strain γ_{max} is equal to *two times* the radius of the circle. Normal strains of $(\varepsilon_1 + \varepsilon_2)/2$ in two mutually perpendicular directions are associated with the maximum shear strain.

3. The sum of normal strains in any two mutually perpendicular directions is *invariant* (i.e., $\varepsilon_1 + \varepsilon_2 = \varepsilon_x + \varepsilon_y = $ constant). Other properties of strains at a point can be established by studying the circle further.

Mathematically, in every respect, strain transformation is identical to stress transformation. Therefore, in a general three-dimensional strain problem, there are three principal directions in which principal normal strains develop. For *plane strain,* when $\varepsilon_z = \gamma_{zx} = \gamma_{zy} = 0$, besides the two principal strains ε_1 and ε_2, another principal strain $\varepsilon_3 = \varepsilon_z = 0$. By identifying the latter principal strain by a point on the $\varepsilon - \gamma/2$ plot, it is possible to draw a cluster of three principal strain circles just as before for the stress circles. (Figs. 11-17 and 11-18). This procedure is illustrated in the next example. Mohr's strain circles degenerate to a point when two or three principal strains are equal.

For determining strain in the z direction for *plane stress,* one must first form an inverse of the first three of Eqs. 5-14 (i.e., to solve then simultaneously to express stresses in terms of strain). For the stress in the z direction, this gives

$$\sigma_z = \frac{E}{(1 + v)(1 - 2v)}[(1 - v)\varepsilon_z + v(\varepsilon_x + \varepsilon_y)] \qquad (11\text{-}49)$$

Then, since for plane stress $\sigma_z = 0$,

$$\varepsilon_z = -\frac{v}{1 - v}(\varepsilon_x + \varepsilon_y) \qquad (11\text{-}50)$$

Since $(\varepsilon_x + \varepsilon_y)$ is invariant, ε_z remains constant for any planar coordinate transformation. Hence, at a point, either the Mohr's circle of strain or its fundamental equivalent of algebraic transformations for the two-dimensional problem is applicable.

Example 11-7

It is observed that an element of a body in a state of plane strain contracts 500 μm/m along the x axis, elongates 300 μm/m in the y direction, and distorts through an angle[13] of 600 μrad, as shown in Fig. 11-24(a). Using Mohr's circle, determine the in-plane principal strains for the given data

[13]This measurement may be made by scribing a small square on a body, straining the body, and then measuring the change in angle that takes place. Photographic enlargements of grids, or photogrammetric procedures, have been used for this purpose.

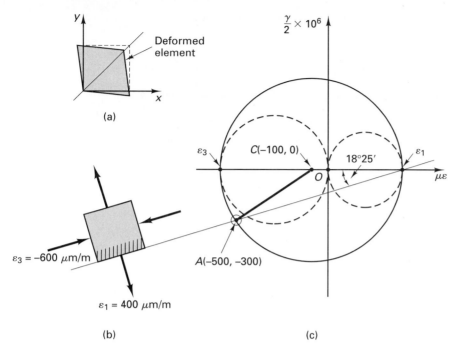

(a)

(b)   (c)

Fig. 11-24 Mohr's circle of strain using sign convention of Method 1, Section 11-7.

and show the direction in which they occur. On the same diagram, draw the remaining two principal strain circles.

SOLUTION

The given data are $\varepsilon_x = -500$ μm/m, $\varepsilon_y = +300$ μm/m, and $\gamma_{xy} = -600$ μm/m. Hence, on the $\varepsilon - \gamma/2$ system of axes, the center C is at $(\varepsilon_x + \varepsilon_y)/2 = -100$ μm/m from O, Fig 11-24(c). The origin of planes A is at $(-500, -300)$. The circle radius AC is 500 μm/m. Hence, $\varepsilon_1 = +400$ μm/m acts in the direction perpendicular to line $A\varepsilon_1$, and $\varepsilon_3 = -600$ μm/m acts in the direction perpendicular to the line $A\varepsilon_3$ (not shown). From geometry, $\theta = \tan^{-1} 300/900 = 18°25'$.

Since this is a *plane strain* problem, another principal strain, $\varepsilon_2 = 0$, is at the origin O of the coordinate axes. Therefore, the two small dashed-line strain circles are shown on the figure to complete the problem.

11-14. Strain Rosettes

Measurements of normal strain are particularly simple to make, and highly reliable techniques have been developed for this purpose. In such work, these strains are measured along several closely clustered gage

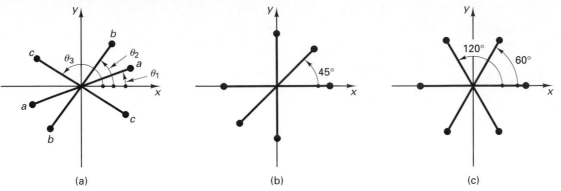

(a)   (b)   (c)

Fig. 11-25   (a) General strain rosette; (b) rectangular or 45° strain rosette; (c) equiangular or delta rosette.

lines, diagrammatically indicated in Fig. 11-25(a) by lines a–a, b–b, and c–c. These gage lines may be located on the member investigated with reference to some coordinate axes (such as x and y) by the respective angles θ_1, θ_2, and θ_3. By comparing the initial distance between any two corresponding gage points with the distance in the stressed member, the elongation in the gage length is obtained. Dividing the elongation by the gage length gives the strain in the θ_1 direction, which will be designated $\varepsilon_{\theta 1}$. By performing the same operation with the other gage lines, $\varepsilon_{\theta 2}$ and $\varepsilon_{\theta 3}$ are obtained. If the distances between the gage points are small, measurements approximating the strains at a point are obtained.

Arrangements of gage lines at a point in a cluster, as shown in Fig. 11-25, are called *strain rosettes*. If three strain measurements are taken at a rosette, the information is sufficient to determine the complete state of plane strain at a point.

As already noted in Section 2-2, a particularly versatile and accurate method for measuring strain employs electric strain gages. These gages, made either of fine wire or foil glued to a member, are very sensitive for measuring the change in electrical resistance due to deformation in a member. An appropriate calibration[14] relates gage resistance to strain. Several types of rosettes are in general use. These usually consist of three single-element gages grouped together, as shown in Fig. 11-26. Metal-foil rosettes of this type are available in a wide range of sizes, with active gage lengths varying from 0.8 to 12 mm.

If angles θ_1, θ_2, and θ_3, together with the corresponding strains $\varepsilon_{\theta 1}$, $\varepsilon_{\theta 2}$, and $\varepsilon_{\theta 3}$, are known from measurements, three simultaneous equations patterned

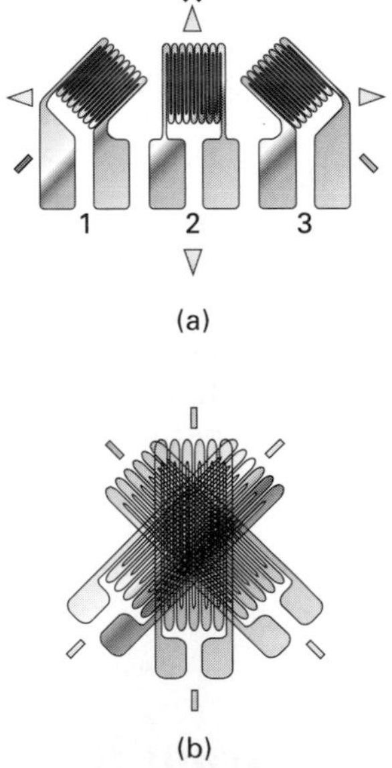

[14]See Society for Experimental Mechanics (SEM), A. S. Kobayashi (ed.), *Handbook on Experimental Mechanics* (Englewood Cliffs, NJ: Prentice Hall, 1987).

(a)

(b)

Fig. 11-26   Three-element metal-foil electrical-resistance strain gages (courtesy of Micro-Measurements Division, Measurements Group, Inc., Raleigh, North Carolina, U.S.A.).

after Eq. 11-36 can be written. In writing these equations, it is convenient to employ the following notation: $\varepsilon_{x'} \equiv \varepsilon_{\theta 1}, \equiv \varepsilon_{\theta 2}$, and $\varepsilon_{x'''} \equiv \varepsilon_{\theta 3}$. Using this symbolism, we obtain

$$\varepsilon_{\theta 1} = \varepsilon_x \cos^2 \theta_1 + \varepsilon_y \sin^2 \theta_1 + \gamma_{xy} \sin \theta_1 \cos \theta_1$$

$$\varepsilon_{\theta 2} = \varepsilon_x \cos^2 \theta_2 + \varepsilon_y \sin^2 \theta_2 + \gamma_{xy} \sin \theta_2 \cos \theta_2 \qquad (11\text{-}51)$$

$$\varepsilon_{\theta 3} = \varepsilon_x \cos^2 \theta_3 + \varepsilon_y \sin^2 \theta_3 + \gamma_{xy} \sin \theta_3 \cos \theta_3$$

This set of equations can be solved for $\varepsilon_{\theta 1}$, $\varepsilon_{\theta 2}$, and γ_{xy}, and the problem reverts to the cases already considered.

To minimize computational work, the gages in a rosette are usually arranged in an orderly manner. For example, in Fig. 11-25(b), $\theta_1 = 0°$, $\theta_2 = 45°$, and $\theta_3 = 90°$. This arrangement of gage lines is known as the *rectangular* or the 45° *strain rosette*. By direct substitution into Eq. 11-51, it is found that for this rosette

$$\varepsilon_x = \varepsilon_{0°} \qquad \varepsilon_y = \varepsilon_{90°} \qquad 2\varepsilon_{45°} = \varepsilon_x + \varepsilon_y + \gamma_{xy}$$

or

$$\boxed{\gamma_{xy} = 2\varepsilon_{45°} - (\varepsilon_{0°} + \varepsilon_{90°})} \qquad (11\text{-}52)$$

Thus, ε_x, ε_y, and γ_{xy} become known. Variations of this arrangement are shown in Fig. 11-26.

Another arrangement of gage lines is shown in Fig. 11-25(c). This is known as the *equiangular,* or the *delta,* or the 60° *rosette.* Again, by substituting into Eq. 11-51 and simplifying.

$$\boxed{\varepsilon_x = \varepsilon_{0°}} \qquad \boxed{\varepsilon_y = (2\varepsilon_{60°} + 2\varepsilon_{120°} - \varepsilon_{0°})/3} \qquad (11\text{-}53a)$$

and

$$\boxed{\gamma_{xy} = 2(\varepsilon_{60°} - \varepsilon_{120°})/\sqrt{3}} \qquad (11\text{-}53b)$$

Other types of rosettes are occasionally used in experiments. The data from all rosettes can be analyzed by applying Eq. 11-51, solving for ε_x, ε_y, and γ_{xy}, and then either applying the strain-transformation equations or constructing Mohr's circle for finding the principal strains.

Sometimes rosettes with more than three lines are used. An additional gage line measurement provides a check on the experimental work. For these rosettes, the invariance of the strains in the mutually perpendicular directions can be used to check the data.

The application of the experimental rosette technique in complicated problems of stress analysis is almost indispensable.

In most problems where strain rosettes are used, it is necessary to determine the principal stresses at the point of strain measurement. In this problem, the surface where the strains are measured is generally free of significant normal surface stresses (i.e., $\sigma_z = 0$). Therefore, this is a *plane stress* problem. Hence, the relevant Eqs. 5-14 written in terms of principal stresses, σ_1 and σ_2, become

$$\varepsilon_1 = \frac{\sigma_1}{E} - v\frac{\sigma_2}{E} \quad \text{and} \quad \varepsilon_2 = \frac{\sigma_2}{E} - v\frac{\sigma_1}{E} \qquad (11\text{-}54)$$

Solving these equations simultaneously for the principal stresses, one obtains the required relations:

$$\boxed{\sigma_1 = \frac{E}{1 - v^2}(\varepsilon_1 + v\varepsilon_2)} \quad \boxed{\sigma_2 = \frac{E}{1 - v^2}(\varepsilon_2 + v\varepsilon_1)} \quad (11\text{-}55)$$

The elastic constants E and v must be determined from some appropriate experiments. With the aid of such experimental work, very complicated problems can be solved successfully.

Example 11-8

At a certain point on a steel machine part, measurements with an electric rectangular rosette indicate that $\varepsilon_{0°} = -500$ μm/m, $\varepsilon_{45°} = +200$ μm/m, and $\varepsilon_{90°} = +300$ μm/m. Assuming that $E = 200$ GPa and $v = 0.3$, find the principal stresses at the point investigated.

SOLUTION
From Eq. 11-52,

$$\gamma_{xy} = 2\varepsilon_{45°} - (\varepsilon_{0°} + \varepsilon_{90°}) = 2 \times 200 - (-500 + 300) = 600 \text{ μm/m}$$

The principal strains for this data were determined in Example 11-7 and are $\varepsilon_1 = 400$ μm/m and $\varepsilon_2 = -600$ μm/m. Hence, using Eqs. 11-55.

$$\sigma_1 = \frac{200 \times 10^3}{1 - 0.3^2}[400 + 0.3 \times (-600)] \times 10^{-6} = +48.4 \text{ MPa}$$

$$\sigma_2 = \frac{200 \times 10^3}{1 - 0.3^2}(-600 + 0.3 \times 400) \times 10^{-6} = 105 \text{ MPa}$$

Tensile stress σ_1 acts in the direction of ε_1; see Fig. 11-24. The compressive stress σ_2 acts in the direction of ε_2.

PROBLEMS

Section 11-2

11-1. Infinitesimal elements A, B, C, D, and E are shown in the figures for two different members. Draw each element separately, and on the isolated element, indicate the stress acting on it. For each stress, clearly show its direction and sense by arrows, and state the formula one would use in its calculation. Neglect the weight of the members.

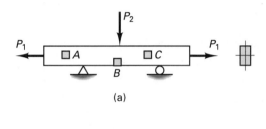

(a)

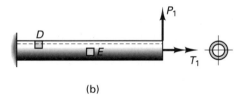

(b)

Fig. P11-1

11-2 through 11-5. For the infinitesimal elements shown in the figures, find the normal and shear stresses acting on the indicated inclined planes. Use the "wedge" method of analysis discussed in Example 11-1.

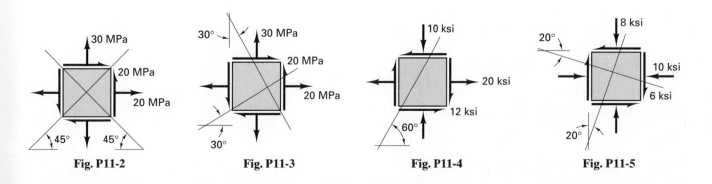

Fig. P11-2   Fig. P11-3   Fig. P11-4   Fig. P11-5

11-6. The magnitudes and sense of the stresses at a point are as shown in the figure. Determine the stresses acting on the vertical and horizontal planes.

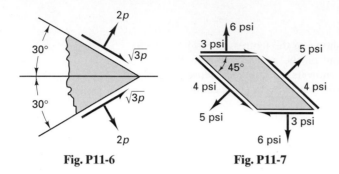

Fig. P11-6   **Fig. P11-7**

11-7. The infinitesimal element shown in the figure is in equilibrium. Determine the normal and shear stresses acting on the vertical plane.

11-8. At a particular point in a wooden member, the state of stress is as shown in the figure. The direction of the grain in the wood makes an angle of $+30°$ with the x axis. The allowable shear stress parallel to the grain is 150 psi for this wood. Is this state of stress permissible? Verify your answer by calculations.

11-9. After the erection of a heavy structure, it is estimated that the state of stress in the rock foundation will be essentially two dimensional and as shown in the figure. If the rock is stratified, the strata making an angle of $30°$ with the vertical, is the anticipated state of stress permissible? Assume that the static coefficient of friction of rock on rock is 0.50, and along the planes of stratification cohesion is 85 kN/m².

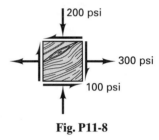

Fig. P11-8

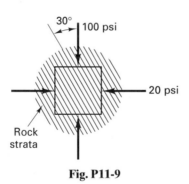

Fig. P11-9

Sections 11-3 through 11-5

11-10. Derive Eq. 11-2.

11-11. Using Eqs. 11-1 and 11-2, rework Problem 11-2.

11-12. Using Eqs. 11-1 and 11-2, rework Problem 11-3.

11-13. Using Eqs. 11-1 and 11-2, rework Problem 11-4.

11-14.   Using Eqs. 11-1 and 11-2, rework Problem 11-5.

11-15.   If at point $\sigma_x = +8$ ksi, $\sigma_y = +2$ ksi, and $\tau = +4$ ksi, what are the principal stresses? Show their magnitude and sense on a properly oriented element.

11-16.   Determine the maximum (principal) shear stresses and the associated normal stresses for the last problem. Show the results on a properly oriented element.

11-17 through 11-20.   For the following data, using the stress-transformation equations, (a) find the principal stresses and show their sense on properly oriented elements; (b) find the maximum (principal) shear stresses with the associated normal stresses and show the results on properly oriented elements; and (c) check the invariance of the normal stresses for solutions in (a) and (b).

11-17. $\sigma_x = -30$ ksi, $\sigma_y = +10$ ksi, and $\tau = -20$ ksi

11-18. $\sigma_x = 0$, $\sigma_y = +20$ ksi, and $\tau = +10$ ksi

11-19. $\sigma_x = -40$ MPA, $\sigma_y = +10$ MPa, and $\tau = +20$ MPa

11-20. $\begin{pmatrix} 20 & -20 \\ -20 & -10 \end{pmatrix}$ MPa

11-21. $\begin{pmatrix} 0 & -30 \\ -30 & -40 \end{pmatrix}$ ksi

Sections 11-6 and 11-7

11-22 through 11-25.   Draw Mohr's circles for the states of stress shown in the figures. (a) Determine the principal stresses and show their sense on properly oriented isolated elements. (b) Find the maximum (principal) shear stresses with the associated normal stresses and show the results on properly oriented elements. For both cases, check the invariance of the normal stresses.

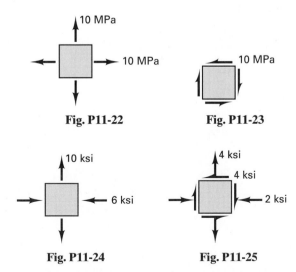

Fig. P11-22   Fig. P11-23

Fig. P11-24   Fig. P11-25

11-26 through 11-32.   For the following data, using Mohr's circles of stress *and trigonometry*, (a) find the principal stresses and show their sense on properly oriented isolated elements; (b) find the maximum (principal) shear stresses with the associated normal stresses and show the results on properly oriented elements. In each case, check the invariance of the normal stresses.

11-26. $\sigma_x = +50$ MPa, $\sigma_y = +30$ MPa, and $\tau = +20$ MPa

11-27. $\sigma_x = +80$ psi, $\sigma_y = +20$ psi, and $\tau = +40$ *psi*

11-28. $\sigma_x = -30$ ksi, $\sigma_y = +10$ ksi, and $\tau = -20$ ksi

11-29. $\sigma_x = -40$ MPa, $\sigma_y = -30$ MPa, and $\tau = +25$ MPa

11-30. $\sigma_x = -15$ MPa, $\sigma_y = +35$ MPa, and $\tau = +60$ MPa

11-31. $\sigma_x = +20$ ksi, $\sigma_y = 0$, and $\tau = -15$ ksi

11-32. $\sigma_x = 0$, $\sigma_y = -20$ ksi, and $\tau = -10$ ksi

11-33 through 11-36.   For the following data, using Mohr's circle of stress, determine the normal and shear stresses acting on the planes defined by the given angle θ. Show the results on isolated elements.

11-33. $\sigma_x = \sigma_1 = 0$, $\sigma_y = \sigma_2 = -20$ ksi, for $\theta = +30°$

11-34.   Rework Problem 11-4 with $\theta = +30°$.

11-35.   Rework Problem 11-2 with $\theta = +45°$.

11-36. $\sigma_x = \sigma_y = 0$, $\tau = -20$ ksi, for $\theta = 20°$

11-37.   For the data shown for Problem 11-6, using Mohr's circle of stress, find the principal stresses and show the results on a properly oriented element.

11-38.   For the data shown for Problem 11-7, using Mohr's circle of stress, find the principal stresses and the orientation of the planes on which these act.

11-39.   Using Mohr's circle, determine the angle between the right-hand face of the element shown in the figure and the plane or planes where the normal stress is zero. Check the result using the "wedge" method. Show the stresses with proper sense on the rotated element(s).

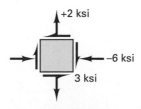

Fig. P11-39

11-40. A clevice transmits a force F to a bracket, as shown in the figure. Stress analysis of this bracket gives the following stress components acting on element A: 1000 psi due to bending, 1500 psi due to axial force, and 600 psi due to shear. (Note that these are stress magnitudes only; their directions and senses must be determined by inspection.) (a) Indicate the resultant stresses on a drawing of the isolated element A. (b) Using Mohr's circle for the state of stress found in (a), determine the principal stresses and the maximum shear stresses with the associated normal stresses. Show the results on properly oriented elements.

11-41. At point A on an unloaded edge of an elastic body, oriented as shown in the figure with respect to the x–y axes, the maximum shear stress is 3500 kN/m^2. (a) Find the principal stresses, and (b) determine the state of stress on an element oriented with its edges parallel to the x–y axes. Show the results on a drawing of the element at A.

11-42. Consider a semi-infinite linearly elastic body with a concentrated line load of P lb per inch. (See figure.) This approximates a long footing on a soil foundation or a knife edge pressing on a large, flat piece of metal (an idealization of roller-bearing reaction on the race). Using the methods of elasticity, one can show[1] that the application of the load causes only radial stresses, which are given by

$$\sigma_r = -\frac{2P}{\pi}\frac{\cos\theta}{r}$$

Since this is the only stress, it is a principal stress. Also, for infinitesimal elements, no distinction need be made between the Cartesian and the polar elements. Transform σ_r into σ_x, σ_y, and τ_{xy} at a constant depth a below the surface.

Fig. P11-40

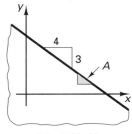

Fig. P11-41

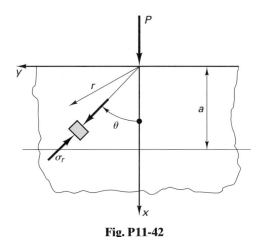

Fig. P11-42

[1]S. Timoshenko and J. N. Goodier, *Theory of Elasticity*, 2nd ed. (New York: McGraw-Hill, 1951), 85.

11-43.   Consider an elastic wedge of unit thickness subjected to a concentrated line load P at the apex, as shown in the figure . According to the elasticity solution[2] this loading causes only radial stress distribution, which is given by

$$\sigma_r = -\frac{P \cos \theta}{r[\alpha + \frac{1}{2}\sin 2\alpha]}$$

Based on this formula, determine the vertical stress distribution on a horizontal section at a distance a below the apex. Compare the maximum stress so found with the one given by Eq. 1-6 for $\alpha = 10°$ and $45°$.

11-44.   An elastic wedge of unit thickness is subjected to a vertical force P, as shown in the figure. For such a wedge the elasticity solution shows that only radial stress distribution exists and is given[3] by

$$\sigma_r = \frac{P \cos \theta}{r[\alpha - \frac{1}{2}\sin 2\alpha]}$$

Determine the normal and the shearing stresses on a vertical section at distance x from the applied force P and compare with the elementary solutions. If $\alpha = 30°$, find the percentage of discrepancy among the maximum stresses in the alternative solutions.

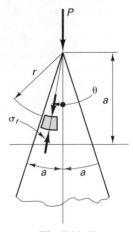

Fig. P11-43

Sections 11-8 and 11-9

11-45.   Determine the principal stresses and their directions for the following stress tensor:

$$\begin{pmatrix} 3 & 0 & 0 \\ 0 & 2 & 2 \\ 0 & 2 & 5 \end{pmatrix} \text{ksi}$$

Use the procedure discussed in Section 11-8. The direction cosines should be normalized. (This problem can also be solved using the equations for stress transformation discussed in Sections 11-4 and 11-7.)

11-46.   For the following stress tensor, determine (a) the stress invariants, (b) the principal stresses, and (c) the direction of the largest principal stress. The direction cosines for this principal stress should be normalized.

$$\begin{pmatrix} 10 & 4 & -6 \\ 4 & -6 & 8 \\ -6 & 8 & 14 \end{pmatrix} \text{MPa}$$

11-47.   For the data in Problem 11-26, determine the principal stresses and draw the three principal circles of stress.

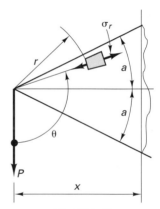

Fig. P11-44

[2]*Ibid.*, 97.
[3]*Ibid.*

11-48.   For the data in Problem 11-28, determine the principal stresses and draw the three principal circles of stress.

11-49.   By applying Eqs. 11-39 and 11-45, determine the principal stresses and their directions for the data given in Example 11-3.

Sections 11-11 and 11-12

11-50.   Rederive Eq. 11-36 by assuming that the shear deformation occurs first, then the deformation in the y-direction, and finally the deformation in the x-direction.

11-51.   With the aid of Fig. 11-20, show that

$$\beta = -(\epsilon_x - \epsilon_y) \sin\theta \cos\theta + \gamma_{xy} \cos^2\theta$$

11-52.   If the unit strains are $\varepsilon_x = -120$ μm/m, $\varepsilon_y = +1120$ μm/m, and $\gamma = -200$ μm/m, what are the principal strains and in which directions do they occur? Use Eqs. 11-47 and 11-48.

11-53.   If the unit strains are $\varepsilon_x = -800$ μm/m, $\varepsilon_y = -200$ μm/m, and $\gamma = +800$ μm/m, what are the principal strains and in which direction do they occur? Use Eqs. 11-47 and 11-48.

11-54.   For the following strain tensor, using the method analogous to that described in Section 11-8 for stress transformation, determine (a) the principal strains, and (b) the directions of the maximum and minimum principal strains.

$$\begin{pmatrix} 70 & -10\sqrt{3} & 0 \\ -10\sqrt{3} & 5 & 0 \\ 0 & 0 & -20 \end{pmatrix} \mu\text{m/m}$$

Section 11-13

11-55.   Rework Problem 11-48 using Mohr's circle of strain.

11-56.   Rework Problem 11-49 using Mohr's circle of strain.

Section 11-14

11-57.   The measured strains for a rectangular rosette, attached to a stressed steel member, are $\varepsilon_{0°} = -220$ μm/m, $\varepsilon_{45°} = +120$ μm/m, and $\varepsilon_{90°} = +220$ μm/m. What are the principal stresses and in which directions do they act? $E = 30 \times 10^6$ psi, and $\nu = 0.3$.

11-58.   The measured strains for an equiangular rosette, attached to a stressed aluminum alloy member, are $\varepsilon_{0°} = +400$ μm/m, $\varepsilon_{60°} = +400$ μm/m, and $\varepsilon_{120°} = -600$ μm/m. What are the principal stresses and in which directions do they act? $E = 70$ GPa, and $\nu = 0.25$.

11-59. The data for a strain rosette with four gage lines attached to a stressed aluminum alloy member are $\varepsilon_{0°} = -120$ μm/m, $\varepsilon_{45°} = +400$ μm/m, $\varepsilon_{90°} = +1120$ μm/m, and $\varepsilon_{135°} = +600$ μm/m. Check the consistency of the data. Then determine the principal stresses and the directions in which they act. Use the values of E and ν given in Problem 11-58.

11-60. At a point in a stressed elastic plate, the following information is known: maximum shear strain $\gamma_{max} = 500$ μm/m, and the sum of the normal stresses on two perpendicular planes passing through the point is 27.5 MPa. The elastic properties of the plate are $E = 200$ GPa, $G = 80$ GPa, and $\nu = 0.25$. Calculate the magnitude of the principal stresses at the point.

12

Yield and Fracture Criteria

12-1. Introduction

From the preceding study of the text, it should be apparent that in numerous technical problems, the state of stress and strain at critical points may be very complex. Idealized mathematical procedures for determining those states, as well as their transformations to different coordinates, are available. However, the precise response of real materials to such stresses and strains defies accurate formulations. A number of questions remain unsettled and are part of an active area of materials research. As yet, no comprehensive theory can provide accurate predictions of material behavior under the multitude of static, dynamic, impact, and cyclic loading, as well as temperature effects. Only the classical idealization of yield and fracture criteria for materials is discussed here. Of necessity, they are used in the majority of structural and machine designs. These strength theories are structured to apply to particular classes of materials. The two most widely accepted criteria for the onset of inelastic behavior (yield) for ductile materials under combined stresses are discussed first. This is followed by presentation of a fracture criterion for brittle materials. It must be

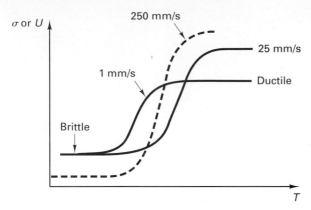

Fig 12-1 Typical transition curves for stress or energy to fracture versus temperature for low-carbon steel (adapted from Manjoine, see footnote 1).

emphasized that, in classifying materials in this manner, one refers to the brittle or ductile state of the material, as this characteristic is greatly affected by temperature as well as by the state of stress itself. For example, some low-carbon steels, below their transition temperatures of about 10°C (+50°F), become brittle, lose their excellent ductile properties,[1] and behave like different materials (Fig. 12-1). Experimental evidence shows that the transition temperature is sensitive to the rate of load application. For the faster rates, the transition temperature tends to occur at a higher temperature.

Most of the information on yielding and fracture of materials under the action of biaxial stresses comes from experiments on thin-walled cylinders. A typical arrangement for such an experiment is shown in Fig. 12-2. The ends of the thin-walled cylinder of the material being investigated are closed by substantial caps. This forms the hollow interior of a cylindrical pressure vessel. By pressurizing the available space until the yielding or bursting occurs, the elements of the wall are subjected to biaxial stresses of a constant ratio $\sigma_1/\sigma_2 = 2$. By applying an additional tensile force P to the caps, the σ_2 stress is increased to any predetermined amount $\sigma_2 + \sigma''$. By applying a comprehensive force, the σ_2 stress can be minimized or eliminated. Actual compressive stress in the longitudinal direction is undesirable, as the tube may buckle. By maintaining a fixed ratio between the principal stresses until the failure point is reached, the desired data on a material are obtained. Analogous experiments with tubes simultaneously subjected to torque, axial force, and pressure are also used. An interpretation of these data, together with all other related experimental evidence,

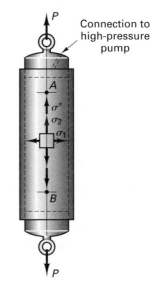

Fig. 12-2 Arrangement for controlled ratios of principal stresses.

---

[1]See M. J. Manjoine, "Influence of rate of strain and temperature on yield stresses of mild steel," *J. Appl. Mech., ASME* (1944), A211–218.

including the simple tension tests, permits a formulation of theories of failure for various materials subjected to combined stresses.

12-2. Maximum Shear-Stress Theory

The maximum shear-stress theory,[2] or simply the maximum shear theory, results from the observation that in a *ductile* material, slip occurs during yielding along critically oriented planes. This suggests that the maximum shear stress plays the key role, and it is assumed that yielding of the material depends only on the maximum shear stress that is attained within an element. Therefore, whenever a certain critical value τ_{cr} is reached, yielding in an element commences.[3] For a given material, this value usually is set equal to the shear stress at yield in simple tension or compression. Hence, according to Eq. 11-9, if $\sigma_x = \pm\sigma_1 \neq 0$ and $\sigma_y = \tau_{xy} = 0$,

$$\tau_{max} \equiv \tau_{cr} = \left| \pm \frac{\sigma_1}{2} \right| = \frac{\sigma_{yp}}{2} \tag{12-1}$$

which means that if σ_{yp} is the yield-point stress found, for example, in a simple tension test, the corresponding maximum shear stress is half as large. This conclusion also follows easily from Mohr's circle of stress.

In applying this criterion to a biaxial plane stress problem, two different cases arise. In one case, the signs of the principal stresses σ_1 and σ_2 are the same. Taking them, for example, to be tensile, as in Fig. 12-3(a), and setting $\sigma_3 = 0$, the resulting Mohr's principal stress circles are as shown in Fig. 12-3(b). Here the maximum shear stress is of the same magnitude as would occur in a simple uniaxial stress, as in Figs. 12-3(a) and (c). Therefore, if $|\sigma_1| > |\sigma_2|$, then according to Eq. 12-1, $|\sigma_1|$ must not exceed σ_{yp}. Similarly, if $|\sigma_2| > |\sigma_1|$, $|\sigma_2|$ must not be greater than σ_{yp}. Therefore, the criteria corresponding to this case are

$$\boxed{|\sigma_1| \le \sigma_{yp}} \quad \text{and} \quad \boxed{|\sigma_2| \le \sigma_{yp}} \tag{12-2}$$

The second case is considered in Fig. 12-3(d)–(f), where the signs of σ_1 and σ_2 are opposite, and $\sigma_3 = 0$. The largest Mohr's circle passes through σ_1 and σ_2, and the maximum shear stress $\tau_{max} = (|\sigma_1| + |\sigma_2|)/2$. The alternative possible slip planes are identified in Fig. 12-3(d) and (f). This maximum

---

[2]This theory appears to have been originally proposed by C. A. Coulomb in 1773. In 1868, H. Tresca presented the results of his work on the flow of metals under great pressures to the French Academy. Now this theory often bears his name.

[3]In single crystals, slip occurs along preferential planes and in preferential directions. In studies of this phenomenon, the effective component of the shear stress causing slip must be carefully determined. Here it is assumed that because of the random orientation of numerous crystals, the material has isotropic properties, and so by determining τ_{max}, one finds the critical shear stress.

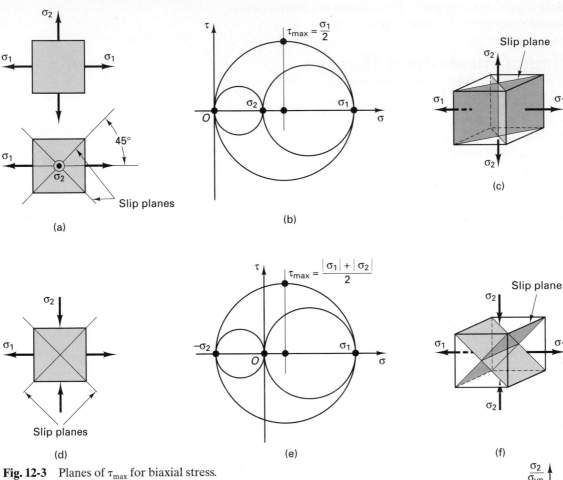

Fig. 12-3   Planes of τ_{max} for biaxial stress.

shear stress cannot exceed the shear yield criterion in simple tension (i.e., $\tau_{max} \leq \sigma_{yp}/2$). Hence,

$$\left| \pm \frac{\sigma_1 - \sigma_2}{2} \right| \leq \frac{\sigma_{yp}}{2} \qquad (12\text{-}3)$$

or, for impending yield,

$$\frac{\sigma_1}{\sigma_{yp}} - \frac{\sigma_2}{\sigma_{yp}} = \pm 1 \qquad (12\text{-}4)$$

A plot of this equation gives the two sloping lines shown in Fig. 12-4. Dividing Eqs. 12-2 by σ_{yp} puts them into the same form as Eq. 12-4. These

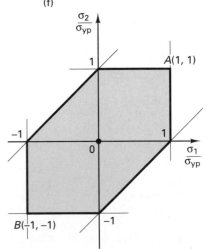

Fig. 12-4   Yield criterion based on maximum shear stress.

modified equations, $\sigma_1/\sigma_{yp} = \pm 1$ and $\sigma_2/\sigma_{yp} = \pm 1$, plot, respectively, in Fig. 12-4 as two vertical and two horizontal lines. Then, by treating σ_1/σ_{yp} and σ_2/σ_{yp} as coordinates of a point in this principal stress space, some important conclusions can be reached.

If a point defined by σ_1/σ_{yp} and σ_2/σ_{yp} falls on the hexagon shown in Fig. 12-4, a material begins and continues to yield. No such stress points can lie outside the hexagon because one of the three yield criteria equations given before for perfectly plastic material would be violated. The stress points falling within the hexagon indicate that a material behaves elastically.

Note that, according to the maximum shear theory, if hydrostatic tensile or compressive stresses are added (i.e., stresses such that $\sigma_1' = \sigma_2' = \sigma_3'$), no change in the material response is predicted. Adding these stresses merely shifts the Mohr's circles of stress along the σ-axis, and τ_{max} remains the same. Also note that since the maximum shear stresses are defined on planes irrespective of material directional properties, it is implicit that the material is *isotropic*.

The derived yield criterion for perfectly plastic material is often referred to as the *Tresca yield condition* and is one of the widely used laws of plasticity.

12-3. Maximum Distortion-energy Theory

Another widely accepted criterion of yielding for *ductile* isotropic materials is based on energy concepts.[4] In this approach, the total elastic energy is divided into two parts: one associated with the volumetric changes of the material, and the other causing shear distortions. By equating the shear distortion energy at yield point in simple tension to that under combined stress, the yield criterion for combined stress is established.

In order to derive the expression giving the yield condition for combined stress, the procedure of resolving the general state of stress must be employed. This is based on the concept of superposition. For example, it is possible to consider the stress tensor of the three principal stresses—σ_1, σ_2, and σ_3—to consist of two additive component tensors. The elements of one component tensor are defined as the mean "hydrostatic" stress:

$$\bar{\sigma} = \frac{\sigma_1 + \sigma_2 + \sigma_3}{3} \qquad (12\text{-}5)$$

---

[4]The first attempt to use the total energy as the criterion of yielding was made by E. Beltrami of Italy in 1885. In its present form, the theory was proposed by M. T. Huber of Poland in 1904 and was further developed and explained by R. von Mises (1913) and H. Hencky (1925), both of Germany and the United States.

The elements of the other tensor are $(\sigma_1 - \bar{\sigma})$, $(\sigma_2 - \bar{\sigma})$, and $(\sigma_3 - \bar{\sigma})$. Writing this in matrix representation, one has

$$
\begin{pmatrix}
\sigma_1 & 0 & 0 \\
0 & \sigma_2 & 0 \\
0 & 0 & \sigma_3
\end{pmatrix}
=
\begin{pmatrix}
\bar{\sigma} & 0 & 0 \\
0 & \bar{\sigma} & 0 \\
0 & 0 & \bar{\sigma}
\end{pmatrix}
+
\begin{pmatrix}
\sigma_1 - \bar{\sigma} & 0 & 0 \\
0 & \sigma_2 - \bar{\sigma} & 0 \\
0 & 0 & \sigma_3 - \bar{\sigma}
\end{pmatrix}
\quad (12\text{-}6)
$$

This resolution of the general state of stress is shown schematically in Fig. 12-5. The special case of resolving the uniaxial state of the stress in the figure has been carried a step further. The sum of the stresses in Fig. 12-5(f) and (g) corresponds to the last tensor of Eq. 12-6.

For the three-dimensional state of stress, the Mohr's circle for the first tensor component of Eq. 12-6 degenerates into a point located at $\bar{\sigma}$ on the σ-axis. Therefore, the stresses associated with this tensor are the same in every possible direction. For this reason, this tensor is called the *spherical stress tensor*. Alternatively, from Eq. 5-23, which states that dilatation of an elastic body is proportional to $\bar{\sigma}$, this tensor is also called the *dilatational stress tensor*.

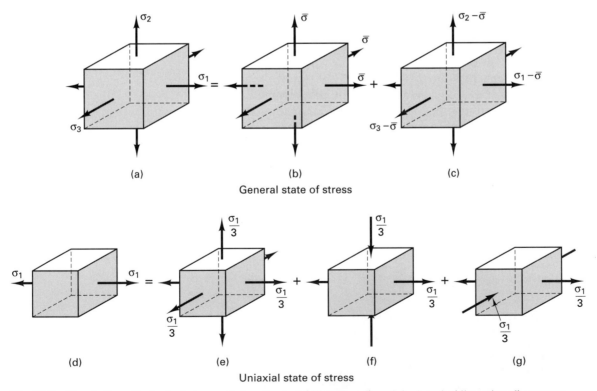

Fig. 12-5 Resolution of principal stresses into spherical (dilatational) and deviatoric (distortional) stresses.

The last tensor of Eq. 12-6 is called the *deviatoric* or *distortional stress tensor.* A good reason for the choice of these terms may be seen from Fig. 12-5(f) and (g). The state of stress consisting of tension and compression on the mutually perpendicular planes is equivalent to pure shear stress. The latter system of stresses is known to cause no volumetric changes in isotropic materials, but instead distorts or deviates the element from its initial cubic shape.

Having established the basis for resolving or decomposing the state of stress into dilatational and distortional components, one may find the strain energy due to distortion. For this purpose, first the strain energy per unit volume (i.e., strain density) for a three-dimensional state of stress must be found. Since this quantity does not depend on the choice of coordinate axes, it is convenient to express it in terms of principal stresses and strains. Thus, generalizing Eq. 3-13 for three dimensions using superposition, one has

$$U_O = U_{\text{total}} = \frac{1}{2}\sigma_1\varepsilon_1 + \frac{1}{2}\sigma_2\varepsilon_2 + \frac{1}{2}\sigma_3\varepsilon_3 \qquad (12\text{-}7)$$

where, by substituting for strains, Eqs. 5-14, expressed in terms of principal stresses, after simplifications, become

$$U_{\text{total}} = \frac{1}{2E}(\sigma_1^2 + \sigma_2^2 + \sigma_3^2) - \frac{\nu}{E}(\sigma_1\sigma_2 + \sigma_2\sigma_3 + \sigma_3\sigma_1) \qquad (12\text{-}8)$$

The strain energy per unit volume due to the dilatational stresses can be determined from this equation by first setting $\sigma_1 = \sigma_2 = \sigma_3 = p$, and then replacing p by $\bar{\sigma} = (\sigma_1 + \sigma_2 + \sigma_3)/3$. Thus,

$$U_{\text{dilatation}} = \frac{3(1 - 2\nu)}{2E}p^2 = \frac{1 - 2\nu}{6E}(\sigma_1 + \sigma_2 + \sigma_3)^2 \qquad (12\text{-}9)$$

By substracting Eq. 12-9 from Eq. 12-8, simplifying, and noting from Eq. 5-21 that $G = E/2(1 + \nu)$, one finds the distortion strain energy for combined stress:

$$U_{\text{distortion}} = \frac{1}{12G}[(\sigma_1 - \sigma_2)^2 + (\sigma_2 - \sigma_3)^2 + (\sigma_3 - \sigma_1)^2] \qquad (12\text{-}10)$$

According to the basic assumption of the distortion-energy theory, the expression of Eq. 12-10 must be equated to the maximum elastic distortion energy in simple tension. The latter condition occurs when one of the principal stresses reaches the yield point, σ_{yp}, of the material. The distortion strain energy for this is $2\sigma_{\text{yp}}^2/12G$. Equating this to Eq. 12-10 after minor simplifications, one obtains the basic law for yielding of an ideally plastic material:

$$\boxed{(\sigma_1 - \sigma_2)^2 + (\sigma_2 - \sigma_3)^2 + (\sigma_3 - \sigma_1)^2 = 2\sigma_{\text{yp}}^2} \qquad (12\text{-}11)$$

For plane stress, $\sigma_3 = 0$, and Eq. 12-11 in dimensionless form becomes

$$\left(\frac{\sigma_1}{\sigma_{yp}}\right)^2 - \left(\frac{\sigma_1}{\sigma_{yp}}\frac{\sigma_2}{\sigma_{yp}}\right) + \left(\frac{\sigma_2}{\sigma_{yp}}\right)^2 = 1 \qquad (12\text{-}12)$$

This is an equation of an ellipse, a plot of which is shown in Fig. 12-6. Any stress falling within the ellipse indicates that the material behaves elastically. Points on the ellipse indicate that the material is yielding. This is the same interpretation as that given earlier for Fig. 12-4. On unloading, the material behaves elastically.

This theory does not predict changes in the material response when hydrostatic tensile or compressive stresses are added. Since only differences of the stresses are involved in Eq. 12-11, adding a constant stress to each does not alter the yield condition. For this reason, in the three-dimensional stress space, the yield surface becomes a cylinder with an axis having all three direction cosines equal to $1/\sqrt{3}$. Such a cylinder is shown in Fig. 12-7(a). The ellipse in Fig. 12-6 is simply the intersection of this cylinder with the σ_1–σ_2 plane. It can also be shown that the yield surface for the maximum shear stress criterion is a hexagon that fits into the tube, shown in Fig. 12-7.

The fundamental relation given by Eq. 12-11 may also be derived by formulating the second invariant, Eq. 11-26, of the deviatoric stresses given by the last matrix in Eq. 12-6. Such an approach is generally favored in the mathematical theory of plasticity. The derivation given before gives greater emphasis to physical behavior. As can be noted from the structure of Eq. 12-11 and the accompanying Figs. 12-6 and 12-7, it is a continuous

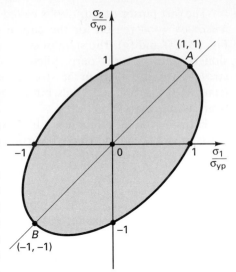

Fig. 12-6   Yield criterion based on maximum distortion energy.

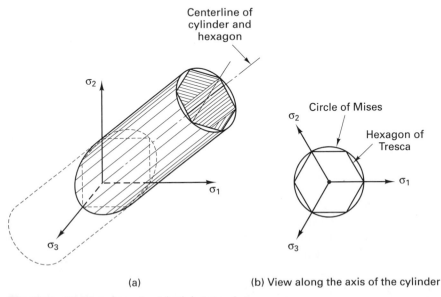

(a)   (b) View along the axis of the cylinder

Fig. 12-7   Yield surfaces for triaxial state of stress.

function, making it attractive in analytical and numerical applications. This widely used constitutive equation for perfectly plastic material is often referred to as the *Huber-Hencky-Mises,* or simply the *von Mises, yield condition.*[5]

Both the maximum shear stress and the distortion-energy yield conditions have been used in the study of viscoelastic phenomena under combined stress. Extension of these ideas to strain-hardening materials is also possible. Such topics, however, are beyond the scope of this text.

12-4. Comparison of Maximum-shear and Distortion-energy Theories for Plane Stress

Plane stress problems occur especially frequently in practice and are largely emphasized in this text. Therefore, it is useful to make a comparison between the two most widely used yield criteria for ductile materials for this case. The maximum shear-stress criterion directs its attention to the maximum shear stress in an element. The distortion-energy criterion does this in a more comprehensive manner by considering in three dimensions the energy caused by shear deformations. Since shear stresses are the main parameters in both approaches, the difference between the two is not large. A comparison between them for plane stress is shown in Fig. 12-8. Here the Tresca hexagon for the maximum shear-stress theory and the von Mises ellipse for the maximum distortion-energy theory have the meanings already described. Either one of the lines gives a criterion for yield for a perfectly plastic material. Yield of a material is said to begin whenever either uniaxial or biaxial stresses reach the bounding lines. If a stress point for the principal stresses σ_1 and σ_2 falls within these curves, a material behaves elastically. Since no strain-hardening behavior (see Fig. 2-18) is included in these mathematical models, no stress points can lie outside the curves, as yielding continued as the stress level given by the curves. More advanced theories are not considered in this text.[6]

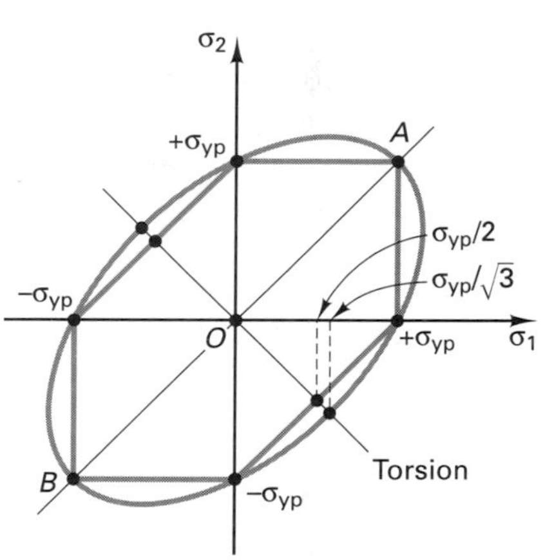

It can be seen from Fig. 12-8 that the discrepancy between the two theories is not very large, the maximum shear-stress theory being in general more conservative. As to be expected, the uniaxial stresses given by both are equal to those corresponding to simple tension or compression. It is assumed that

Fig. 12-8   Comparison of Tresca and von Mises yield criteria.

---

[5]In the past, this condition has also been referred to as the *octahedral shearing stress theory.* See A. Nadai, *Theory of Flow and Fracture of Solids* (New York: McGraw-Hill, 1950), 104, or A. P. Boresi and O. M. Sidebottom, *Advanced Mechanics of Materials,* 4th ed. (New York: Wiley, 1985), 18.

[6]K. Washizu, *Variational Methods in Elasticity and Plasticity,* 2nd ed. (New York: Pergamon, 1975); L. E. Malvern, *Introduction to the Mechanics of a Continuous Medium* (Englewood Cliffs: Prentice Hall, 1969).

these basic stresses are of *equal* magnitude. The yield criteria in the second and fourth quadrant indicate smaller strengths at yield than that for uniaxial stresses. The largest discrepancy occurs when two of the principal stresses are equal but of opposite sign. This condition develops, for example, in torsion of thin-walled tubes. According to the maximum shear-stress theory, when $\pm\sigma_1 = \mp\sigma_2$, these stresses at yield can reach only $\sigma_{yp}/2$. The maximum distortion-energy theory limits this stress to $\sigma_{yp}/\sqrt{3} = 0.577\sigma_{yp}$. Points corresponding to these stresses are identified in Fig. 12-8. These values of yield in shear stress are frequently used in design applications.

12-5. Maximum Normal-stress Theory

The maximum normal-stress theory, or simply the maximum stress theory,[7] asserts that failure or fracture of a material occurs when the maximum normal stress at a point reaches a critical value regardless of the other stresses. Only the largest principal stress must be determined to apply this criterion. The critical value of stress σ_{ult} is usually determined in a tensile experiment, where the failure of a specimen is defined to be either excessively large elongation or fracture. Usually, the latter is implied.

Experimental evidence indicates that this theory applies well to *brittle* materials in all ranges of stresses, providing a tensile principal stress exists. Failure is characterized by the separation, or the cleavage, fracture. This mechanism of failure differs drastically from the ductile fracture, which is accompanied by large deformations due to slip along the planes of maximum shear stress.

The maximum stress theory can be interpreted on graphs, as can the other theories. This is done in Fig. 12-9. Failure occurs if points fall on the surface. Unlike the previous theories, this stress criterion gives a bounded surface of the stress space.

12-6. Comparison of Yield and Fracture Criteria

Comparison of some classical experimental results with the yield and fracture criteria presented before is shown in Fig. 12-10.[8] Note the particularly good agreement between the maximum distortion-energy theory and

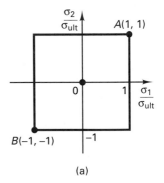

(a)

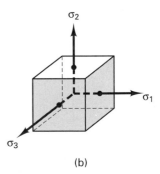

(b)

Fig. 12-9   Fracture envelope based on maximum stress criterion.

---

[7]This theory is generally credited to W. J. M. Rankine, an eminent British educator (1820–1872). An analogous theory based on the maximum strain, rather than stress, being the basic criterion of failure was proposed by the great French elastician, B. de Saint-Venant (1797–1886). Experimental evidence does not corroborate the latter approach.

[8]The experimental points shown on this figure are based on classical experiments by several investigators. The figure is adapted from a compilation made by G. Murphy, *Advanced Mechanics of Materials* (New York: McGraw-Hill, 1964), 83.

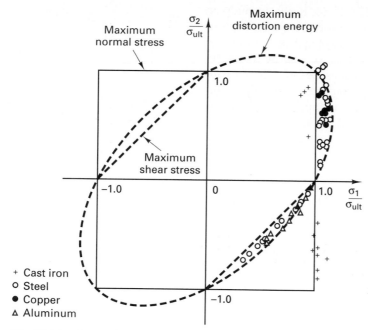

Fig. 12-10   Comparison of yield and fracture criteria with test data.

experimental results for ductile materials. However, the maximum normal-stress theory appears to be best for brittle materials and can be unsafe for ductile materials.

All the theories for uniaxial stress agree since the simple tension test is the standard of comparison. Therefore, if one of the principal stresses at a point is large in comparison with the other, all theories give practically the same results. The discrepancy between the criteria is greatest in the second and fourth quadrants, when both principal stresses are numerically equal.

In the development of the theories discussed before, it has been assumed that the properties of material in tension and compression are alike—the plots shown in several of the preceding figures have two axes of symmetry. On the other hand, it is known that some materials, such as rocks, cast iron, concrete, and soils, have drastically different properties depending on the sense of the applied stress. This is the greatest flaw in applying the classical idealizations to materials having large differences in their mechanical behavior in tension and compression. An early attempt to adopt the maximum shear theory to achieve better agreement with experiments was made by Duguet in 1885.[9] The improved model recognizes the higher strengths of brittle materials in biaxial compression than in tension. Therefore, the region in biaxial tension in the principal stress space is made

[9]A. Nadai, *Theory of Flow and Fracture of Solids* (New York: McGraw-Hill, 1950).

smaller than it is for biaxial compression; see Fig. 12-11. In the second and fourth quadrants, a linear change between the two aforementioned regions is assumed. A. A. Griffith,[10] in a sense, refined the explanation for the previous observations by introducing the idea of surface energy at microscopic cracks and showing the greater seriousness of tensile stresses compared with compressive ones with respect to failure. According to this theory, an existing crack will rapidly propagate if the available elastic strain energy release rate is greater than the increase in the surface energy of the crack. The original Griffith concept has been considerably expanded by G. R. Irwin.[11]

Another important attempt for rationalizing fracture of materials having different properties in tension and compression is due to Mohr.[12] In this approach, several different experiments must be conducted on the same material. For example, if the results of experiments in tension, compression, and shear are available, the results can be represented on the same plot using their respective largest principal stress circles, as shown in Fig. 12-12(a). The points of contact of the *envelopes* with the stress circles define the state of stress at a fracture. For example, if such a point is A (or A'), the stresses and the plane(s) on which they can be found using the established procedure for Mohr's circle of stress (Section 11-7). The corresponding planes for points A or A' are shown in Fig. 12-12(b), and a material such as duraluminum does fracture in tension at a flat angle, as shown. Similarly, by relating the fracture planes to either point B or B', the fracture occurs at a steep angle characteristic of concrete cylinders tested in compression, as in Fig. 12-12(c). Such agreements with experiments support the assumed approach.

The data from Fig. 12-12(a) can be replotted in the principal stress space, as in Fig. 12-12(d). Since in the first quadrant, the *minimum* principal stress $\sigma_3 = 0$, and in the third quadrant, $\sigma_3 = 0$ is the *maximum* principal stress, per Fig. 12-12(a)–(c), in these quadrants the fracture lines in the principal stress space are similar to those of Fig. 12-11. Moreover, if the material strengths in tension and compression are the same, a hexagon identical to that shown in Fig. 12-10 is obtained. However, whereas the hexagon in Fig. 12-10 gives a *yield* condition for *ductile* materials, in the present context it defines a *fracture* criterion for *brittle* materials.

Extrapolation of Mohr envelopes beyond the range of test data is not advisable. In many applications, this may mean that parts of the stress cir-

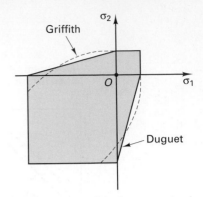

Fig. 12-11   Plausible fracture criteria for brittle materials.

---

[10]A. A. Griffith, "The phenomena of rupture and flow of solids," *Philosophical Transactions of the Royal Society of London,* Series A, **221** (1920), 163–198.

[11]G. R. Irwin, "Fracture mechanics," *Proceedings, First Symposium on Naval Structural Mechanics* (Long Island City, NY: Pergamon, 1958), 557. Also see *A Symposium on Fracture Toughness Testing and Its Applications,* American Society for Testing and Materials Special Technical Publication No. 381 (Philadelphia, PA: American Society for Testing and Materials and Washington, DC: National Aeronautics and Space Administration, 1965).

[12]As noted earlier, Otto Mohr was also principally responsible for the development of the stress circle bearing his name.

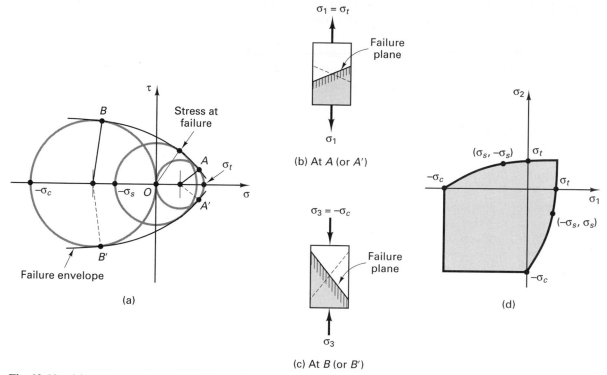

Fig. 12-12 (a) Mohr envelopes, (b) failure planes at A and A', (c) failure planes at B and B', (d) Mohr envelope solution in principal stress space.

cles for tension and compression should be taken as envelope ends. Interpolation along the failure envelopes between these two partial end stress circles is justified, and a stress circle for other conditions can be placed between them. When more extensive data are lacking conservatively, straight-line envelopes can be used.

The use of straight lines for asymptotes has a rational basis and has been found particularly advantageous in soil mechanics. For a loose granular media such as sand, the straight-line Mohr envelopes correspond to the limiting condition of dry friction, $\mu = \tan\phi$; see Fig 12-13. Any circle tangent to the envelope, as at B, gives the state of critical stress. If some cohesion can be developed by the media, the origin O is moved to the right such that at zero stress, the τ intercept is equal to the cohesion. As soils basically cannot transmit tensile stresses, in specialized literature it is customary to direct the compression axis to the right.

Unlike the maximum distortion-energy theory, the fracture theory based on Mohr envelopes, using the largest principal stress circles, neglects dependence on the intermediate principal stress.

Sometimes the yield and fracture criteria discussed before are inconvenient to apply. In such cases, interaction curves such as in Fig. 9-16 can be

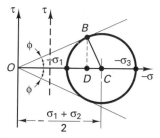

Fig. 12-13 Mohr envelopes for cohesionless granular media.

used to advantage. Experimentally determined curves of this type, unless complicated by a local or buckling phenomenon, are equivalent to the strength criteria discussed here.

In the design of members in the next chapter, departures will be made from strict adherence to the yield and fracture criteria established here, although, unquestionably, these theories provide the rational basis for design.

12-7. Failure Surface for Brittle Materials

The analytical approach applicable to brittle materials has reached significant maturity such that it can be included in a text on engineering mechanics of solids. The available treatment in three-dimensional stress space resembles the yield surface of the von Mises criterion (Fig. 12-7), with a significant difference. The enclosed stress space is capped in the direction of tensile stresses, and the enclosing surface gradually expands. In the limit it becomes a cone, rather than a tube of the Mises criterion.

The surface in stress space, such as shown in Fig. 12-7, that defines the ultimate strength values for any principal stress ratio is usually called the *failure surface,* or *strength model,* of the material. The failure surface of concrete, serving as an illustration for a brittle material, is described here by a modification of the five-parameter surface of William and Warnke.[13] The modified failure surface[14] shown in Fig. 12-14(a) is described by

$$\tau_0(\sigma_0, \theta) = \tau_c \frac{a\eta + b\sqrt{a(\eta^2 - 1) + b^2}}{a\eta^2 + b^2} \qquad (12\text{-}13)$$

where

$$a = \tau_c^2 - \tau_t^2; \quad b = 2\tau_t - \tau_c; \quad \eta = 2\cos\theta \qquad (12\text{-}14)$$

and σ_0 is the hydrostatic stress, defined in Eq. 11-31, and θ is the Lode angle, given by Eq. 11-29.

Equation 12-13 defines the form of the failure surface in the deviatoric plane $\sigma_0 = $ const and describes a smooth convex (elliptical) curve depicted in Fig. 12-14(b). Parameters τ_c and τ_t in Eq. 12-14 are functions of the hydrostatic stress, defined as roots of the quadratic equations

$$\tau_c^2 + A\left(\frac{\tau_c}{\sqrt{2}} + \sigma_0\right) + B = 0 \qquad (12\text{-}15)$$

$$\tau_t^2 + A\left(\frac{\tau_t}{\sqrt{2}}\beta + \sigma_0\right) + B = 0 \qquad (12\text{-}16)$$

[13]See K. J. William and E. P. Warnke, "Constitutive model for the triaxial behavior of concrete," *Int. Association for Bridge and Struct. Engrg. Proc.,* **19**, (1975), 1–30.

[14]See T. A. Balan, F. C. Filippou, and E. P. Popov, "Constitutive model for 3D cyclic analysis of concrete structures," *J. Engrg. Mechanics, ASCE,* **123**, no. 2 (February 1997), 143–153.

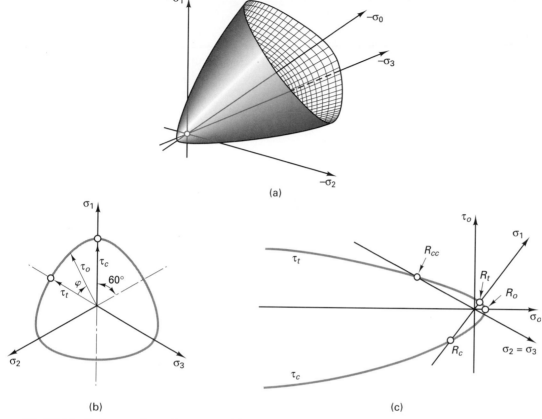

Fig. 12-14   Failure surface of concrete: (a) general view; (b) deviatoric view; (c) meridianal view.

where

$$A = \frac{R_c}{9\alpha}(1 - \alpha^2)(2 + \alpha); \quad B = -\frac{2}{9}R_c^2 \qquad (12\text{-}17)$$

$$\alpha = \frac{R_t}{R_c}; \quad \beta = \frac{4 - \alpha}{2 + \alpha} \qquad (12\text{-}18)$$

and R_c, R_t are the uniaxial compression and tensile strengths, respectively.

It should be noted that Eqs. 12-15 and 12-16 represent the compression ($\theta = 60°$) and the tension ($\theta = 0°$) meridians of the material failure surface. On the plane $\sigma_2 = \sigma_3$ (sometimes called the Rendulic plane), as can be seen in Fig. 12-14(c), the meridianal sections are the parabolic curves, which pass through a set of characteristic points that define the following strength parameters of the material:

R_c, R_t = uniaxial compression and tensile strengths, respectively

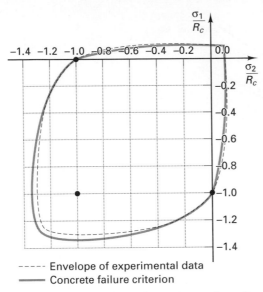

----- Envelope of experimental data
——— Concrete failure criterion

Fig. 12-15   Comparison of experimental results with analytical prediction.

R_{cc} = biaxial compression strengths defined as

$$R_{cc} = \frac{R_c}{4}\left[(1 - \alpha^2) + \sqrt{(1 - \alpha^2)^2 + 16}\right]$$

The meridianal curves intersect the hydrostatic axis at the point of equitriaxial extension (triaxial tensile strength), which can be expressed in terms of uniaxial compression and tensile strength as

$$R_0 = -\frac{B}{A} = \frac{2R_t}{(1 - \alpha^2)(2 + \alpha)}$$

In Fig. 12-15 the material strength predicted by the failure surface is compared with plane stress experimental data.[15] The particular concrete was calibrated by the following strength parameters: R_c = 32.1 MPa (4.66 ksi) and R_t = 3.1 MPa (0.45 ksi). The resulting failure trace of the strength model in plane $\sigma_3 = 0$ provides very close agreement with considered experimental data.

Careful recent experimental research on concrete specimens of different strengths strongly corroborates this approach. This work now has been extended to include strain-hardening effects and has been implemented for use with a computer.[16]

[15]Adopted from H. Kupfer, H. K. Hilsdorf, and H. Rusch, "Behavior of concrete under biaxial stresses," *ACI J.*, **66**, no. 8 (1969), 656–666.

[16]C. Bedard and M. D. Kostovos, "Application of NLFEA to concrete structures," *J. Struct. Div.* ASCE, **111** (ST12) (1985); Z. P. Bažant, ed., *Mechanics of Geomaterials: Rocks, Concrete, Soils* (Chichester: Wiley, 1985).

PROBLEMS

Section 12-2 through 12-5

12-1. Recast the stress tensor given in Problem 11-46 into the spherical and deviatoric stress tensors.

12-2. and 12-3. For the 3×3 stress matrices given, recast them into the spherical and deviatoric stress tensors.

$$\begin{pmatrix} 40 & -30 & 20 \\ -30 & 50 & 10 \\ 20 & 10 & 60 \end{pmatrix} \text{MPa} \quad \text{and} \quad \begin{pmatrix} 50 & -30 & 0 \\ -30 & 70 & -20 \\ 0 & -20 & 60 \end{pmatrix} \text{MPa}$$

12-4. and 12-5. Three cases of plane stress at yield or fracture are shown in the figures. Examine each case and determine what type of failure is likely to occur. Limit the choice of criteria to the maximum normal-stress, distortion-energy, and maximum shear-stress theories. Explain your reasoning.

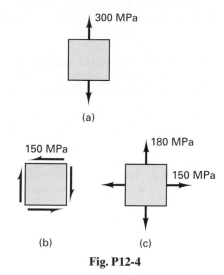

(a)

(b)   (c)

Fig. P12-4

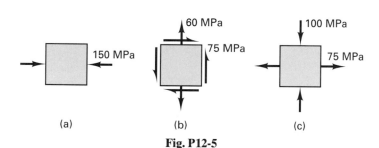

(a)   (b)   (c)

Fig. P12-5

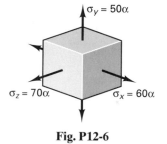

Fig. P12-6

12-6. Assume that a state of triaxial principal stresses develops at a point as shown in the figure. These stresses are directly proportional to a parameter α. If the yield stress $\sigma_{yp} = 250$ MPa, what is α, based on the von Mises yield criterion?

Section 12-6

12-7. In classical experiments on plasticity, a two-dimensional stress field is often obtained by subjecting a thin-walled tube simultaneously to an axial force and a torque. The results of such experiments are reported on σ_x–τ_{xy} plots. If only σ_x and τ_{xy} stresses are studied, how would the theoretical curves based on the Tresca and on the von Mises yield criteria look on such a plot? Derive the two required equations and sketch the results on a diagram.

12-8. Ordinarily, the Tresca and von Mises yield stresses are made to coincide in simple tension. This gives rise to a discrepancy for pure shear. If, instead, the yield condition is assumed to be the same in shear, what discrepancy will result for simple tension and for $\sigma_1 = \sigma_2$?

12-9. A critical element develops the principal stresses, σ_1, σ_2, and σ_3, in the ratio 5:2: -1 (i.e., the stresses are $5p$, $2p$, and $-p$, where p is a parameter). Such loadings are called radial. If this element is subjected to this loading condition, determine the maximum magnitudes the stresses may reach before yielding (a) according to the Tresca yield criterion, and (b) according to the von Mises criterion. Assume that the material yields in tension at 60 ksi.

12-10. A metal bar is being compressed along the x_1-axis between two rigid walls such that $\varepsilon_3 = 0$ and $\sigma_2 = 0$. This process causes an axial stress σ_1 and no shear stresses. Determine the apparent yield value of σ_1 if the material in a conventional compression test exhibits a yield strength σ_{yp} and Poisson's ratio v. Assume that the material is governed by the von Mises yield condition. Find an alternative expression if the Tresca condition is postulated.

13

Elastic Stress Analysis

13-1. Introduction

Formulas for determining the state of stress in elastic members tradition-ally considered in an introductory text on mechanics of solids have been derived in previous chapters. Usually, they give either a normal or a shear stress caused by a single force component acting at a section of a member. For linearly elastic materials, the main formulas are summarized:

1. Normal stresses
   (a) due to an axial force

$$\sigma = \frac{P}{A} \qquad\qquad (1\text{-}6)$$

   (b) due to bending
   • straight members

$$\sigma = -\frac{My}{I} \qquad\qquad (8\text{-}11)$$

- symmetrical curved bars

$$\sigma = \frac{My}{Ae(R - y)} \qquad (8\text{-}38)$$

2. Shear stresses
   (a) due to torque
   - circular shaft

$$\tau = \frac{T\rho}{I_p} \qquad (6\text{-}4)$$

   - rectangular shaft

$$\tau_{max} = \frac{T}{\alpha b t^2} \qquad (6\text{-}30)$$

   - closed thin-walled tube

$$\tau = \frac{T}{2\textcircled{A}t} \qquad (6\text{-}34, 6\text{-}35)$$

   (b) due to shear force in a beam

$$\tau = \frac{VQ}{It} \qquad (10\text{-}6)$$

The superposition of normal stresses caused by axial forces and bending simultaneously using these formulas was discussed in Chapter 9. Likewise, the superposition of shear stresses caused by torque and direct shear acting simultaneously was considered in Chapter 10. In this chapter, the consequences of the simultaneous occurrence of normal *and* shear stresses are examined with the aid of the stress-transformation procedures developed in Chapter 11. This condition commonly occurs in beams and transmission shafts.

In applying the preceding formulas, particularly in the analysis or design of mechanical equipment, stress-concentration factors must be introduced. (See Sections 3-3, 6-7, and 8-6.) Because of the problem of fatigue commonly occurring in such cases, reduced stresses are employed. Special consideration must also be given to dynamic loading. (See Sections 3-7, 6-11, and 8-7.) For such loadings, if occurring in milliseconds, the allowable stresses may be significantly increased.

This chapter is entirely devoted to *elastic* problems, an approach most commonly used at usual working loads. In Part A, the state of stress for some basic cases is discussed from the point of view of stress transformations.

The elastic design of members is considered in Part B. Although the stress-analysis formulas listed before are applicable to both statically determinate and indeterminate problems, discussion will be limited to statically determinate cases. There are at least two reasons for this. First, the more frequently occurring statically indeterminate problems involve beams; these are treated beginning with the next chapter. Second, more significantly, the *design* of statically indeterminate systems in contrast to their stress *analysis* is necessarily complex. As an example, consider an elastic bar of variable cross section, fixed at both ends and subjected to an axial force P, as shown in Fig. 13-1. If the cross-sectional areas of the upper and lower parts of the bar are given, reactions R_1 and R_2 can be found routinely using the procedures discussed in Chapter 3. After either reaction is known, the problem becomes statically determinate, and the bar stresses can be found in the usual manner. However, if this statically indeterminate system were to be *designed,* even this simple problem can become involved. Generally, in a design problem, only the applied force P and the boundary conditions would be known. By varying the two cross-sectional areas of the bar, an infinite number of solutions is possible. Additional constraints in the realm of structural or machine design generally enter the problem. Such problems are, therefore, not considered here.

It is to be emphasized that only the problem of *elastic stresses* is considered in this chapter. Some elastic designs may be governed either by the stiffness or the possible instability of a system. The first requirement commonly arises in deflection control and vibration problems; the second, in lateral instability of members.

The main purpose of this chapter is to provide greater insight into the meaning of stress analysis by solving additional problems. There are an extraordinary number of cases where applications of the basic formulas of engineering mechanics of solids listed before lead to useful results. No new analytical principles are developed in this chapter. However, some simple design procedures for prismatic beams are given.

It is essential to recognize that in all elastic stress-analysis and design problems, the *material is assumed to be initially stress free.* In many engineering materials, significant residual stresses may be present. These may be caused by the manufacturing processes employed: rolling, welding, forging, temperature or hydration shrinkage, etc. (See Fig. 1-10.) *In reality, it is the combination of the residual stresses with those due to the applied forces that cause the initial yield and/or fracture of a member.* In some engineering applications, estimates of residual stresses present a formidable problem.

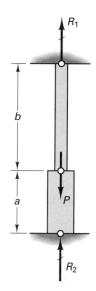

Fig. 13-1   A statically indeterminate problem.

Part A   ELASTIC STRESS ANALYSIS

13-2. State of Stress for Some Basic Cases

The state of stress for four basic cases in the form of examples is considered in this section. By means of Mohr's principal circles of stress, the states of stress at a point are exhibited graphically. From such representations, the critical stresses can be seen readily and related to the yield or fracture criteria discussed in the preceding chapter. The four cases considered pertain to the uniaxial stress, biaxial stress such as ocurs in cylindrical pressure vessels, torsional stresses in circular tubes, and beam stresses caused by bending and shear. Because of the greater complexity of the last problem, some aspects of the solution accuracy are discussed in the next section.

Example 13-1

Consider a state of stress in an axially loaded bar and construct the three principal circles of stress. Relate the critical stresses to yield and fracture criteria.

SOLUTION

The maximum principal stress σ_1 in an axially loaded bar can be found using Eq. 1-8. The remaining two principal stresses are each equal to zero (i.e., $\sigma_2 = \sigma_3 = 0$). The basic infinitesimal element for this case, together with its three planar views, is shown in Fig. 13-2(a). The principal circles of stress are drawn in Fig. 13-2(b). Since σ_1 and σ_2 are equal, Mohr's circle for these stresses degenerates into a point. For clarity, however, it is shown in the diagram by a small circle of zero diameter.

For this case, the maximum shear stress is equal to $\sigma_1/2$, whereas the maximum normal stress is σ_1. Therefore, the manner in which a material fails depends on its relative strengths in these two properties. As already pointed out in Section 2-3 and illustrated in Fig. 2-10, a brittle material

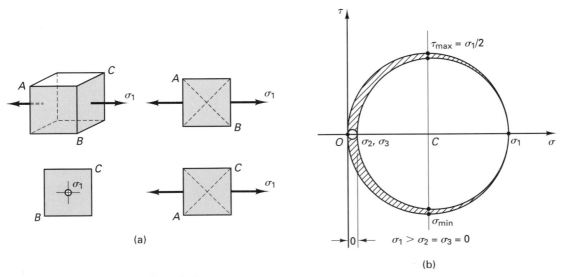

Fig. 13-2   Mohr's circles for a uniaxial state of stress.

(cast iron) fails by a cleavage fracture. This is so because it is weaker in tension than in shear. The reverse is true for a ductile material. The cup and cone fractures shown in Fig. 2-10 for steel and aluminum occur approximately along the planes, forming a 45° angle with the axis of the specimen. These planes are identified by dashed lines in the elements on the right in Fig. 13-2(a). Greater refinements on the mechanism of fracture are possible by considering the behavior of single crystals within a material.

Example 13-2

Consider a state of stress in a thin-walled cylindrical pressure vessel and construct the three principal circles of stress. Relate the results to a yield criterion.

SOLUTION

According to Eqs. 5-26 and 5-27, the ratio of the hoop stress σ_1 to the longitudinal stress σ_2 is approximately 2. These are the principal stresses, as no shear stresses act on the corresponding planes. The third principal stress σ_3 equals the external or internal pressure p, which may be taken as zero since it is small in relation to σ_1 and σ_2. A typical infinitesimal element for the vessel and three planar views shown in Fig. 13-3(a). The principal stress circles are shown in Fig. 13-3(b). The maximum shear stress is found on the *major* stress circle passing through the origin O and σ_1. Its magnitude is $\sigma_1/2$.

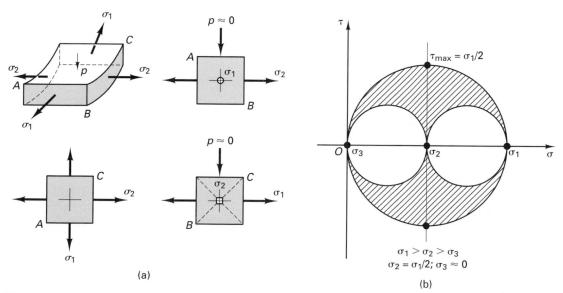

(a)   (b)

Fig. 13-3   Mohr's circles for stresses in a cylindrical wall of a pressure vessel.

The planes on which the maximum shear stresses act are identified by dashed lines in the lower right element. Note that if only the principal stresses σ_1 and σ_2 were considered, the maximum shear stress would only be half as large. In design, the yield criterion based on the maximum distortion theory (see Section 12-4) can also be used.

Construction of pressure vessels from brittle materials is generally avoided, as such materials provide no accommodation or warning of failure through yielding before fracture.

It is interesting to note that for a thin-walled spherical pressure vessel, $\sigma_1 = \sigma_2$, and the corresponding principal stress circle degenerates into a point. Nevertheless, the maximum shear stress is $\sigma_1/2$ since the third principal stress is zero.

Example 13-3

Examine the state of stress in a circular tube subjected to a torque by constructing the three principal circles of stress. Relate the results to yield and fracture criteria.

SOLUTION

The shear stresses for this case can be found using Eq. 6-4. A typical infinitesimal element of the tube and three planar views are shown in Fig. 13-4(a). Here the major principal stress circle has a radius equal to the shear stress τ_0. (See Section 11-7 for rules for constructing Mohr's circle.) Hence, the two principal stresses are σ_1 and σ_3, as shown in Fig. 13-4(b). The middle

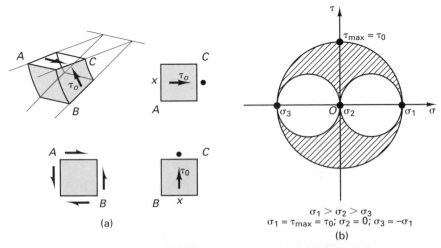

(a)

$$\sigma_1 > \sigma_2 > \sigma_3$$
$$\sigma_1 = \tau_{max} = \tau_0; \ \sigma_2 = 0; \ \sigma_3 = -\sigma_1$$

(b)

Fig. 13-4   Mohr's circles for stresses in a circular tube subjected to torque.

principal stress σ_2 is zero, justifying the drawing of the two small circles shown.

For ductile materials, the strength in shear is smaller than in tension, and, as shown earlier in Fig. 6-9, at failure, a square fracture occurs across a member. If, alternatively, the material is stronger in shear than it is in tension, a characteristic fracture along a helix, shown in Fig. 6-10, is observed.

Example 13-4

A 40 $\times$ 300-mm rectangular elastic beam spans 1000 mm, as shown in Fig. 13-5(a). This beam is braced to prevent lateral buckling. (a) Determine the principal stresses at points K, L, M, L', and K' caused by the application of a concentrated vertical force $P = 80$ kN at midspan to the top of the beam. (b) For the same condition, find the stresses on an inclined plane defined by $\theta = +30°$ for the element L'.

SOLUTION

(a) At section K–K', the shear is 40 kN and the bending moment is 10 kN · m acting in the directions shown in Fig. 13-5(c).

No shear stresses act on element K and K', as they are at the beam boundaries. Therefore, the principal stresses at these points follow directly by applying Eq. 8-21:

$$\sigma_{K\,or\,K'} = \mp \frac{Mc}{I} = \mp \frac{M}{S} = \mp \frac{6M}{bh^2} = \mp \frac{6 \times 10 \times 10^6}{40 \times 300^2} = \mp 16.67 \text{ MPa}$$

The principal stresses acting in the vertical direction are zero. These results are shown in Fig. 13-5(d) and (h).

The normal stresses acting on elements L and L' follow from the previous results by reducing them by a ratio of the distances from the neutral axis to the elements (i.e., by 140/150). The corresponding shear stresses are obtained using Eq. 10-6, for which the cross-hatched area A_{fghj} and the corresponding $\bar{y}$ are shown in Fig. 13-5(b). Hence,

$$\sigma_{L\,or\,L'} = \mp \frac{140}{150} \times \sigma_{K'} = \mp 15.56 \text{ MPa}$$

$$\tau_{L\,or\,L'} = \frac{VA_{fghj}\bar{y}}{It} = \frac{40 \times 10^3 \times 40 \times 10 \times 145}{40 \times 300^3/12 \times 40} = 0.644 \text{ MPa}$$

These results are shown in Fig. 13-5(e) and (g).

Mohr's circle of stress is employed for obtaining the principal stresses at L, as in Fig. 13-5(i), and the results are shown on a rotated element in Fig. 13-5(e). Method 1 of Section 11-7 is used to obtain the results. Note the invariance of the sum of the normal stresses (i.e., $\sigma_x + \sigma_y = \sigma_1 + \sigma_2$ or

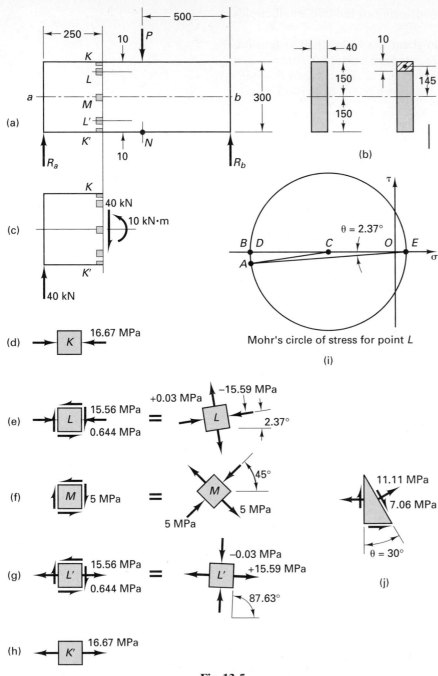

Mohr's circle of stress for point L

(i)

Fig. 13-5

$-15.56 + 0 = -15.59 + 0.03$). A similar solution for the principal stresses at point L' yields the results shown on the rotated element in Fig. 13-5(g).

Point M lies on the neutral axis of the beam; hence, no flexural stress acts on the corresponding element shown in the first sketch of Fig. 13-5(f). The shear stress on the right face of the element at M acts in the same direction as the internal shear at section KK'. Its magnitude can be obtained by applying Eq. 10-6 or directly by using Eq. 10-8a; that is,

$$\tau_{max} = \frac{3}{2}\frac{V}{A} = \frac{1.5 \times 40 \times 10^3}{40 \times 300} = 5 \text{ MPa}$$

The *pure* shear stress transformed into the principal stresses according to Fig. 11-6 is shown on a rotated element in Fig. 13-5(f).

It is significant to further examine qualitatively the results obtained. For this purpose, the computed principal stresses *acting on the corresponding planes* are shown in Figs. 13-6(a) and (b). In Fig 13-6(a), the characteristic behavior of the major (tensile) principal stress at a section of a rectangular beam can be seen. This stress progressively diminishes in magnitude from a maximum value at K' to zero at K. At the same time, the corresponding directions of σ_1 gradually turn through $90°$. A similar observation can be made regarding the minor (compressive) principal stress σ_2 shown in Fig. 13-6(b).

(b) To find the stresses acting on a plane of $\theta = +30°$ through point L', a direct application of Eqs. 11-1 and 11-2 using the stresses shown on the left element in Fig. 13-5(g) and the fact that $2\theta = 60°$ is made:

$$\sigma_\theta = \frac{+15.56}{2} + \frac{+15.56}{2}\cos 60° + (-0.644)\sin 60° = +11.11 \text{ MPa}$$

$$\tau_\theta = \frac{-15.56}{2}\sin 60° + (-0.644)\cos 60° = -7.06 \text{ MPa}$$

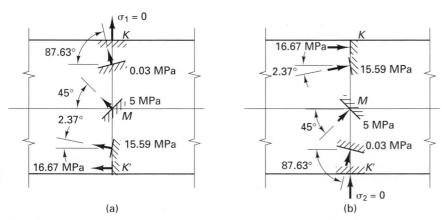

(a)   (b)

Fig. 13-6   (a) Behavior of the major principal stress σ_1. (b) Behavior of the minor principal stress σ_2.

These results are shown in Fig. 13-5(j). The sense of the shearing stress τ_θ is opposite to that shown in Fig. 11-4(b), since the computed quantity is negative. The "wedge technique," explained in Example 11-1, or the Mohr's circle method, discussed in Section 11-7, can be used to obtain the same results.

13.3 Comparative Accuracy of Beam Solutions

The solution in the previous example for a beam considering flexure and shear is based on stresses initially obtained using the conventional formulas of engineering mechanics of solids. These formulas are derived essentially assuming that plane sections in a beam remain plane during bending. Since this basic assumption is not entirely true in all cases, these solutions can be referred to as *elementary*. Therefore, it is instructive to compare the obtained results with a more accurate solution. Such a comparison is made here with a finite element solution, shown in Fig 13-7. Because of the symmetry of the problem, only one-half of the beam was analyzed using 450 finite elements.[1]

The contour lines for the principal stresses are shown in Fig. 13-7(a). Any point lying on a stress contour has a principal stress of the same magnitude and sign. The tensile stresses are identified by the numbers carrying positive signs, and conversely, the compressive stresses have negative signs. The regions where the elementary solutions do not apply are shown in Fig. 13-7(a) with a gray overlay.

Comparisons between the elementary and finite element solutions of the normal stress distribution across section $K–K'$ are shown in Fig. 13-7(b) and that for the shear stress in Fig. 13-7(c). The agreement is seen to be excellent. However, section $K–K'$ is taken midway between the applied concentrated force P and the concentrated reaction R_a. At these points, locally large perturbations in stresses occur, resembling those shown earlier in Figs. 3-9 and 3-10. However, according to the Saint-Venant principle, local stresses rapidly diminish and a regular statically equivalent stress pattern sets in. In practice, large stresses at concentrated forces are reduced by applying them over an area to obtain an acceptable bearing pressure. Theoretically, in an elastic

---

[1]This solution was obtained using the FEAP computer program developed by R. L. Taylor employing isoparametric four-node elements. An automatic mesh-generating technique enables the use of graduated smaller elements at concentrated forces, where the stresses vary more rapidly than elsewhere. Conventional square elements in the FEAP program were used in the previous solutions cited. Since in a two-dimensional plate of finite thickness the in-place stresses vary somewhat across the thickness, in the FEAP formulation, the average values of these stresses through the plate thickness are used. Such stresses are called *generalized plane stresses*.

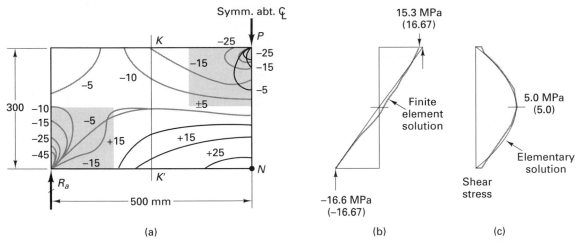

Fig. 13-7   (a) Principal stress contours for Example 13-4 beam determined by finite elements. (b) and (c) Comparisons between elementary and finite element solutions for normal and shear stresses at section K–K'. [Stresses from elementary solutions in (b) and (c) are given in parentheses.] Stress distribution at concentrated forces shown by gray regions is not susceptible to elementary analysis. (See Fig. 3-9 and 3-10.)

body, the stress at a concentrated force is infinite. In reality, some plastic yielding, reducing the stress, takes place in the proximity of the applied force.

It is interesting to note from Fig. 13-7(a) that the ±5 MPa contours coincide for more than half of the span. This condition corresponds to the principal stresses for the middle element M in Fig. 13-5(f), and almost precisely coincides with the neutral axis in the elementary solution. The stress at point N at the bottom of the beam below force P is within 5% of the elementary solution.[2]

The beam is relatively short, having a length-to-depth ratio of 3.33. It is instructive to compare this solution with that for the somewhat longer similar beam having a length-to-depth ratio of 8.33, which is shown in Fig. 13-8. For this beam of 2500-mm span, the applied concentrated force $P = 32$ kN. One-half of this beam was analyzed using 900 finite elements. According to elementary solutions, the maximum bending stress at point N is the same as in the previous case. However, here the shear stress at the neutral axis is 2 MPa. In the figure, the principal stresses of this magnitude define the neutral axis in the elementary solution. In contrast to the earlier case, it is seen that the neutral plane extends essentially across the entire length of the beam. The stress disturbances caused by the concentrated force as well

[2]The Wilson-Stokes analytical and photoelastic solutions developed in the 1890s show that the maximum bending stress caused by a concentrated force in *short* beams is smaller than that given by the elementary flexure theory. The analytical solution shows that it approaches asymptotically the elementary solution with an increasing ratio of the beam length to depth. See M. M. Frocht, *Photoelasticity,* Vol. II (New York: Wiley, 1948), 116.

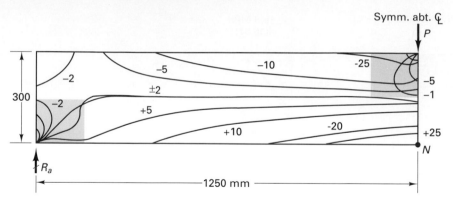

Fig. 13-8 Principal stress contours for left half of a rectangular simply supported beam loaded in the middle.

as reactions are much more localized. Further, the maximum bending stress at point N is within less than 2% of the elementary solution. Since point N is a beam depth away from the applied force P, this solution again provides an example of Saint-Venant's principle, and the elementary formula is sufficiently accurate.

For beams carrying distributed loads, stress perturbations occur primarily at the supports.

For the previous reasons, the elementary formulas of the engineering solid mechanics are generally considered to be sufficiently accurate for the usual design. They are also indispensable for the preliminary design of complex members, where subsequently a member is analyzed by a refined method, such as by finite elements.

Important Observation: A Reiteration It must be emphasized that the elementary formulas of elastic stress analysis are unable to determine the local stress distributions at concentrated loads and abrupt changes in member cross section. This is in accordance with Saint-Venant's principle (Section 3-3), which asserts that at such locations the stresses are perturbed and more advanced methods of analysis must be used. Illustrations of this principle were given for axially loaded blocks (Fig. 3-9), stress concentrations at holes in axially loaded bars (Fig. 3-11), stress concentrations at circular shafts subjected to torque (Fig. 6-13), and the points of concentrated load application and concentrated supports in beams (Figs. 13-7 and 13-8). Note that at distances beyond the beam half-depth, the elementary formulas provide reasonably accurate results (Fig. 13-7(b) and (c)).

The shear distribution in wide-flange beams at supports based on $\tau = VQ/It$, Eq. 10-6, is inaccurate, bringing into question the universally accepted assumption that plane sections remain plane. Adherence to this age-long assumption may not be fully warranted at the connections.

13-4. Experimental Methods of Stress Analysis

In the past, when mathematical procedures became too cumbersome or impossible to apply, the photoelastic method of stress analysis was extensively used to solve practical problems. Many of the stress-concentration factors cited in this text are either drawn or verified by such experimental work. Accurate stresses in an entire specimen can be found using this method.[3]

This traditional area of photoelasticity has been largely taken over by modern numerical techniques. An illustration of such an approach using finite elements has been shown a few times in this text, including the two solutions cited in the preceding section. Nevertheless, photoelastic techniques augmented with computers have now advanced and remain useful in special applications. Moreover, several additional experimental procedures became available. Among these, the Moiré, holographic, and laser speckle interferometries are playing an increasingly important role. These methods are discussed in specialized texts.[4] However, some terminology developed primarily in two-dimensional photoelasticity is in general use and is given for reference.

In the preceding section, the principal stresses of the same algebraic magnitude provided a "map" of *stress contours*. Similarly, the points at which the directions of the minor principal stresses form a *constant angle* with the *x*-axis can be connected. Moreover, since the principal stresses are mutually perpendicular, the direction of the major principal stresses through the same points also forms a constant angle with the *x*-axis. The line so connected is a locus of points along which the principal stresses

Fig. 13-9   Fringe photograph of a rectangular beam. (Photograph by R. W. Clough.)

[3]Figure 13-9 shows regularly spaced and perturbed fringes at concentrated load points. These photoelastic fringes provide a map for the *difference* in principal stresses. They do not directly give contours for selected stresses, as does the finite element method.

[4]See A. S. Kobayashi (ed.), *Handbook on Experimental Mechanics* (Englewood Cliffs, NJ: Prentice Hall, 1987).

have *parallel directions*. This line is called an *isoclinic line*. The adjective *isoclinic* is derived from two Greek words, *isos,* meaning equal, and *klino,* meaning slope or incline. Three isoclinic lines can be found by inspection in a rectangular prismatic beam subjected to transverse load acting normal to its axis. The lines corresponding to the upper and lower boundaries of a beam form two isoclinic lines because, at the boundary, the flexural stresses are the principal stresses and act parallel to the boundaries. The flexural stress is zero at the neutral axis, where only pure shear stresses exist. These pure shear stresses transform into principal stresses, all of which act at an angle of 45° with the axis of the beam. Hence, another iso-clinic line (the 45° isoclinic) is located on the axis of the beam. The other isoclinic lines are curved and are more difficult to determine.

Another set of curves can be drawn for a stressed body for which the magnitude and the sense of the principal stresses are known at a great many points. A curve whose tangent is changing in direction to conform with the direction of the principal stresses is called a *principal stress trajec-tory* or isostatic line. Like the isoclinic lines, the principal stress trajecto-ries *do not* connect the points of equal stresses, but rather, indicate the directions of the principal stresses. Since the principal stresses at any point are mutually perpendicular, the principal stress trajectories for the two principal stresses form a family of orthogonal (mutually perpendicular) curves.[5] An example of idealized stress trajectories for a rectangular beam loaded with a concentrated force at the midspan is shown in Fig. 13-10. The principal stress trajectories corresponding to the tensile stresses are shown in the figure by solid lines; those for the compressive stresses are shown dashed. The trajectory pattern (not shown) is severely disturbed at the supports and at the point of application of load *P*, as can be surmised from Fig. 13-7(a).

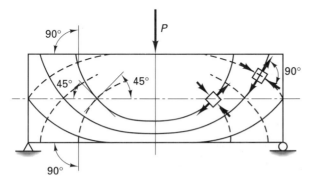

Fig. 13-10   Principal stress trajectories for a rectangu-lar beam.

---

[5]A somewhat analogous situation is found in fluid mechanics, where in "two-dimensional" fluid flow problems, the *streamlines* and the *equipotential lines* form an orthogonal system of curves, the *flow net.*

Part B ELASTIC DESIGN FOR STRENGTH

13-5. Design of Axially Loaded Members

Axially loaded tensile members and short compression members[6] are designed for strength using Eq. 1-15 (i.e., $A = P/\sigma_{\text{allow}}$). The *critical section* for an axially loaded member occurs at a section of minimum cross-sectional area, where the stress is a maximum. This requires the use of *net,* rather than gross, cross-sectional areas. If an abrupt discontinuity in the cross-sectional area is imposed by the design requirements, the use of Eq. 3-11, $\sigma_{\text{max}} = KP/A$, is appropriate. The use of the latter formula is necessary in the design of machine parts to account for the local stress concentrations where fatigue failure may occur. In design of static structures, such as buildings, stress-concentration factors are seldom considered. (See Fig. 3-14.)

Besides the normal stresses, given by the previous equations, shear stresses act on inclined planes. Therefore, if a material is weak in shear strength in comparison to its strength in tension or compression, it will fail along planes approximating the planes of the maximum shear stress, as discussed in Section 12-6. However, regardless of the type of fracture that may actually take place, the allowable stress for design of axially loaded members is customarily based on the *normal* stress. This design procedure is consistent. The maximum normal stress that a material can withstand at failure is directly related to the *ultimate* strength of the material. Hence, although the actual break may occur on an inclined plane, the maximum normal stress can be considered as the ultimate strength.

If in the design it is necessary to consider the deflection or stiffness of an axially loaded member, the use of Eqs. 3-2 and 3-4 is appropriate. *In some situations, these criteria govern the selection of members.*

13-6. Design of Torsion Members

Explicit formulas for elastic design of circular tubular and solid shafts are provided in Section 6-6. Some stress-concentration factors essential in design of such members subjected to cyclic loading are given in Section 6-7. Large local shear stresses can develop at changes in the cross-sectional area. Stress-analysis formulas for some noncircular solid and thin-walled tubular members are given in Sections 6-14 and 6-16. In these sections, the corresponding formulas for calculating the stiffnesses of these members are

---

[6]Slender compression members are discussed in Chapter 15.

also provided. Except for stress-concentration factors, these formulas are suitable for the design of torsion members for many types of cross sections.

Most torsion members are designed by selecting an *allowable shear stress*. This amounts to a direct use of the maximum shear theory of failure. However, it is helpful to bear in mind that a state of pure shear stress, which occurs in torsion, can be transformed into the principal stresses, and, in brittle materials, tensile fractures may be caused by the tensile principal stress.

A similar approach is used in the design of shafts for gear trains in mechanical equipment. However, in such cases, the shafts, in addition to carrying a torque, also act as beams. Therefore, this topic is postponed until Section 13-10.

13-7.   Design Criteria for Prismatic Beams

If a beam is subjected to *pure bending,* its fibers are assumed to be in a state of uniaxial stress. If, further, a beam is prismatic (i.e., of a constant cross-sectional area and shape), the critical section occurs at the section of the greatest bending moment. By assigning an allowable stress, we can determine the section modulus of such a beam using Eq. 8-21, $S = M/\sigma_{max}$. After the required section modulus is known, a beam of correct proportions can be selected. However, if a beam resists shear in addition to bending, its design becomes more involved.

Consider the prismatic rectangular beam of Example 13-4 at a section 250 mm from the left support, where the beam transmits a bending moment *and* a shear; see Fig. 13-11(a). The principal stresses at points K, L, M, L', and K' at this section were found before and are reproduced in Fig. 13-11(b). If this section were the critical section, it is seen that the design of this beam, based on the maximum normal stress theory, would be governed by the stresses *at the extreme fibers,* as no other stresses exceed these stresses. For a prismatic beam, these stresses depend only on the magnitude of the bending moment and are largest at a section where the maximum bending moment occurs. Therefore, in ordinary design it is *not* necessary to perform the combined stress analysis for interior points. In the example considered, the maximum bending moment is at the middle of the span. The foregoing may be generalized into a basic rule for the design of prismatic beams: *A critical section for a prismatic beam carrying transverse forces acting normal to its axis occurs where the bending moment reaches its absolute maximum.*

For cross sections without two axes of symmetry, such as T beams, made from material that has different properties in tension than in compression, the *largest* moments of *both senses* (positive or negative) must be examined. Under some circumstances, a smaller bending moment of one sense may cause a more critical stress than a larger moment of another sense.

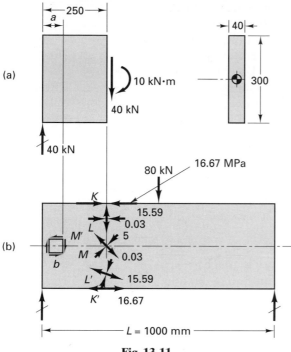

(a)

(b)

Fig. 13-11

The section at which the extreme fiber stress of either sign in relation to the respective allowable stress is highest is the critical section.

The previous criterion for the design of prismatic beams is incomplete, as attention was specifically directed to the stresses caused by the moment. In some cases, the shear stresses caused by the shear at a section may control the design. In the example considered, Fig. 13-11, the magnitude of the shear remains constant at every section through the beam. At a small distance a from the left support, the maximum shear is still 40 kN, whereas the bending moment, $40a$ kN · m, is small. The maximum shear stress at the neutral axis corresponding to $V = 40$ kN is the same at point M' as it is at point M.[7] Therefore, since in a general problem the bending stresses may be small, they may not control the selection of a beam, and *another critical section for any prismatic beam occurs where the shear is a maximum.* In applying this criterion, it is customary to work directly with the maximum shear stress that may be obtained from Eq. 10-6, $\tau = VQ/It$, and not transform τ_{max} so found into the principal stresses. For rectangular and I beams, the maximum shear stress given by Eq. 10-6 reduces to Eqs. 10-8a and 10-10, $\tau_{max} = (3/2)V/A$ and $(\tau_{max})_{approx} = V/A_{web}$, respectively.

---

[7]At point M, the shear stresses are shown transformed into the principal stresses.

Whether the section where the bending moment is a maximum or the section where the shear is a maximum governs the selection of a prismatic beam depends on the loading and the material used. Generally, the allowable shear stress is less than the allowable bending stress. For example, for steel, the ratio between these allowable stresses is about 1/2, whereas for some woods, it may be as low as 1/15.[8] Regardless of these ratios of stresses, *the bending stresses usually control the selection of a beam.* Only in beams spanning a short distance does shear control the design. For small lengths of beams, the applied forces and reactions have small moment arms, and the required resisting bending moments are small. On the other hand, the shear forces may be large if the applied forces are large.

The two criteria for the design of beams are accurate if the two critical sections are in different locations. However, in some instances the maximum bending moment and the maximum shear occur at the *same* section through the beam. In such situations, sometimes higher combined stresses than σ_{max} and τ_{max}, as given by Eqs. 8-21 and 10-6, may exist at the interior points. For example, consider an I beam of negligible weight that carries a force P at the middle of the span, Fig. 13-12(a). The maximum bending moment occurs at midspan. Except for sign, the shear is the same on either side of the applied force. At a section just to the right or just to the left of the applied force, the maximum moment *and* the maximum shear occur simultaneously. A section just to the left of P, with the corresponding system of forces acting on it, is shown in Fig. 13-12(b). For this section, it can be shown that the stresses at the extreme fibers are 2.50 ksi, whereas the principal stresses at the juncture of the web with the flanges, neglecting stress concentrations, are ± 2.81 ksi and ± 0.51 ksi, acting as shown in Fig. 13-12(c) and (d).

It is customary not to consider directly the effect of the local disturbance on longitudinal stresses in the neighborhood of an applied concentrated force. Instead the problem of local stresses is resolved by requiring a sufficiently large contact area for the applied force so as to obtain an acceptable bearing stress. For some materials, such as wood, this may require the use of steel bearing plates in order to spread the effect of the concentrated force.

From this example, it is seen that the maximum normal stress does not always occur at the extreme fibers. Nevertheless, only the maximum normal stresses and the maximum shear stress at the neutral axis are investigated in ordinary design. In design codes, the allowable stresses are presumably set sufficiently low so that an adequate factor of safety remains, even though the higher combined stresses are disregarded. By increasing a span for the same applied concentrated force, the flexural stresses increase linearly with the span length, whereas the shear stresses remain constant. Hence, in most cases, the bending stresses rapidly become dominant. Therefore, generally, it

---

[8]Wood is weak in shear strength *parallel* to its grain.

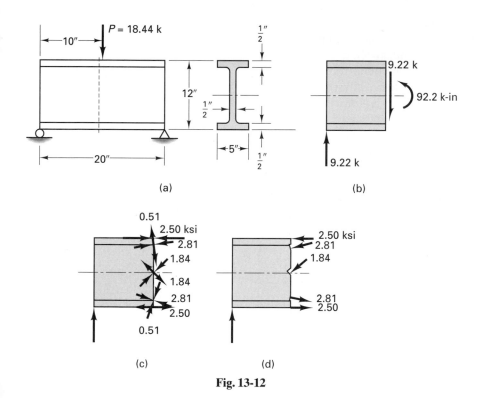

Fig. 13-12

is necessary to perform the combined stress analysis only for very short beams or in unusual arrangements.

From the previous discussion, it is seen that, for the design of prismatic beams, the critical sections must be determined in every problem, as the design is entirely based on the stresses developed at these sections. The critical sections are best located with the aid of shear and bending-moment diagrams. The required values of M_{max} and V_{max} can be determined easily from such diagrams. The construction of these diagrams is discussed in Chapter 7.

13-8. Design of Prismatic Beams

As noted in the preceding section, the customary approach for design of prismatic beams is controlled by the maximum stresses at the *critical sections*. One such critical section usually occurs where the bending moment is a maximum; the other where the shear is a maximum. These sections are conveniently determined with the aid of shear and moment diagrams.[9] In most cases,[10] the *absolute maximum moment* (i.e., whether positive or negative) is used for selecting a member. Likewise, the afore-mentioned maximum shear is critical for the design. For example, con-sider a simple beam with a concentrated force, as shown in Fig. 13-13. The shear diagram, neglecting the weight of the beam, is shown in Fig. 13-13(a) as it is ordinarily constructed by assuming the applied force concen-trated at a point. In Fig. 13-13(b), an allowance is made for the width of the applied force and reactions, assuming them uniformly distributed along the beam. Note that in either case, the design shears are less than the applied force.

The allowable stresses to be used in design are prescribed by various authorities. In most cases, the designer must follow a code, depending on the location of the installation. In different codes, even for the same mater-ial and the same use, the allowable stresses differ.

In elastic design, after the critical values of moment and shear are deter-mined and the allowable stresses are selected, the beam is usually first designed to resist a maximum moment using Eq. 8-13 or 8-21 ($\sigma_{max} = M/S$ or $\sigma_{max} = Mc/I$). Then the beam is *checked* for shear stress. As most beams are governed by flexural stresses, this procedure is convenient. However, in some cases, particularly in timber and concrete design, the shear stress fre-quently controls the dimensions of the cross section.

The method used in computing the shear stress depends on the type of beam cross section. For rectangular sections, the maximum shear stress is 1.5 times the average stress, Eq. 10-8. For wide flange and I beams, the total allowable vertical shear is taken as the area of the *web* multiplied by an allowable shear stress, Eq. 10-10. For other cases, Eq. 10-6, $\tau = VQ/It$, is used.

Usually, there are several types or sizes of commercially available mem-bers that may be used for a given beam. Unless specific size limitations are placed on the beam, the lightest member is used for economy. The proce-dure of selecting a member is a trial-and-error process.

It should also be noted that some beams must be selected on the basis of allowable deflections. This topic is treated in the next chapter.

For beams with statically applied loads, such as occur in buildings, there is an increasing trend to design them on the basis of inelastic (plastic) behavior. This approach is considered in Chapter 21.

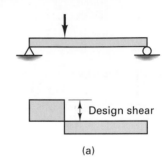

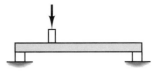

Design shear

(a)

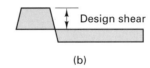

Design shear

(b)

Fig. 13-13   Design shear.

---

[9]With experience, construction of complete diagrams may be avoided. After reactions are computed and a section where $V = 0$ or a change of sign is determined, the maximum moment corresponding to this section may be found directly by using the method of sec-tions. For simple loadings, various handbooks give formulas for the maximum shear and moment.

[10]This is not always true for materials that have different properties in tension and compression.

Example 13-5

Select a Douglas fir beam of rectangular cross section to carry two concentrated forces, as shown in Fig. 13-14(a). The allowable stress in bending is 8 MPa; in shear, 0.7 MPa; and in bearing perpendicular to the grain of the wood, 1.4 MPa.

SOLUTION

Shear and moment diagrams for the applied forces are prepared first and are shown, respectively, in Fig. 13-14(b) and (c). From Fig. 13-14(c), it is seen that $M_{max} = 10$ kN $\cdot$ m. From Eq. 8-21,

$$S = \frac{M}{\sigma_{allow}} = \frac{10 \times 10^6}{8} = 1.25 \times 10^6 \text{ mm}^3$$

By *arbitrarily assuming* that the depth h of the beam is to be two times greater than its width b, from Eq. 8-22,

$$S = \frac{bh^2}{6} = \frac{h^3}{12} = 1.25 \times 10^6$$

Hence, the required $h = 247$ mm and $b = 123$ mm.

Let a *surfaced* beam 140-by-240 mm, having a section modulus $S = 1.34 \times 10^6$ mm^3, be used to fulfill this requirement. For this beam, from Eq. 10-8a,

$$\tau_{max} = \frac{3V}{2A} = \frac{3 \times 8 \times 10^3}{2 \times 140 \times 240} = 0.357 \text{ MPa}$$

This stress is well within the allowable limit. Hence, the beam is satisfactory.

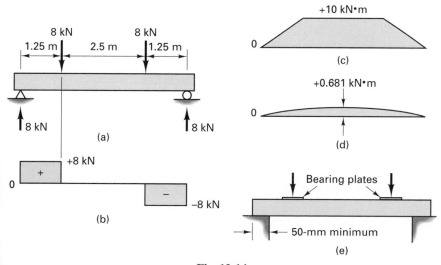

Fig. 13-14

Note that other proportions of the beam can be used, and a more direct method of design is to find a beam of size corresponding to the wanted section modulus directly from a table similar to Table 9 in the Appendix, which gives properties of standard dressed sections in the U.S. conventional units.

The analysis was made without regard for the beam's own weight, which initially is unknown. (Experienced designers often make an allowance for the weight of the beam at the outset.) However, this may be accounted for now. Assuming that wood weighs 6.5 kN/m³, the beam selected weighs 0.218 kN per linear meter. This uniformly distributed load causes a parabolic bending-moment diagram, shown in Fig. 13-14(d), where the maximum ordinate is $w_o L^2/8 = 0.218 \times 5^2/8 = 0.681$ kN·m. (See Fig. 7-19.) This bending-moment diagram should be added to the moment diagram caused by the applied forces. Inspection of these diagrams shows that the maximum bending moment due to both causes is $0.681 + 10 = 10.68$ kN·m. Hence, the required section modulus actually is

$$S = \frac{M}{\sigma_{\text{allow}}} = \frac{10.68 \times 10^6}{8} = 1.34 \times 10^6 \text{ mm}^3$$

The surfaced 140-by-240-mm beam already selected provides the required S.

In order to avoid the crushing of wood at the supports and at applied concentrated forces, adequate bearing areas for these forces must be provided. Neglecting the weight of the beam, such areas A at the four locations, according to Eq. 1-6, should be

$$A = \frac{P}{\sigma_{\text{allow}}} = \frac{8 \times 10^3}{1.4} = 5710 \text{ mm}^2$$

These areas can be provided by conservatively specifying that the beam's ends rest on at least 50-by-140-mm (7000-mm²) supports, whereas at the concentrated forces, 80-by-80-mm (6400-mm²) steel washers be used.

Example 13-6

Select an I beam or a wide-flange steel beam to support the load shown in Fig. 13-15(a). For the beam $\sigma_{\text{allow}} = 24$ ksi and $\tau_{\text{allow}} = 14.5$ ksi.

SOLUTION
The shear and the bending-moment diagrams for the loaded beam are shown in Fig. 13-15(b) and (c), respectively. The maximum moment is 36 k-ft. From Eq. 8-21,

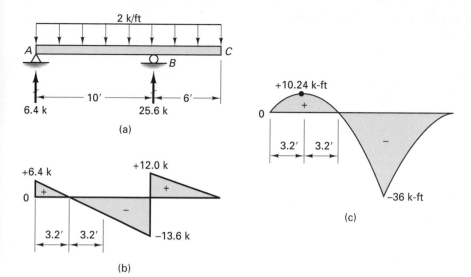

(a)

(b)

(c)

Fig. 13-15

$$S = \frac{36 \times 12}{24} = 18.0 \text{ in}^3$$

Examination of Tables 3 and 4A in the Appendix shows that this requirement for a section modulus is met by a 10-in S section weighing 35 lb/ft ($S = I_x/c = 29.4$ in^3). In a more complete table a lighter section can be found. However, a lighter 8-in wide-flange W section weighing 24 lb/ft ($S = 20.9$ in^3) also is adequate. Therefore, for reasons of economy, the lighter W8 $\times$ 24 section will be used. The beam weight is small in comparison with the applied loads and will be neglected in calculations.

From Fig. 13-15(b), $V_{max} = 13.6$ kips. Hence, from Eq. 7-10,

$$(\tau_{max})_{approx} = \frac{V}{A_{web}} = \frac{13.6}{0.245 \times 7.93} = 7.00 \text{ ksi}$$

This stress is below the allowable value, and the selected beam is satisfactory.

At the supports or concentrated forces, S and wide-flange beams should be checked for crippling of the webs. This phenomenon is illustrated at the bottom of Fig. 13-16(a). Crippling of the webs is more critical for members with thin webs than direct bearing of the flanges, which may be investigated as in the preceding example. To preclude crippling, a design rule is specified by the AISC. It states that the direct stress on area, $(a + k)t$ at the ends and $(a_1 + 2k)t$ at the interior points, must not exceed $0.75\sigma_{yp}$. In these expressions, a and a_1 are the respective lengths of bearing of the applied forces at exterior or interior portions of a beam, Fig. 13-16(b), t is the thickness of the web, and k is the distance from the outer face of a flange to the toe of the web fillet. The values of k and t are tabulated in manufacturers' catalogs.

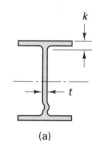

(a)

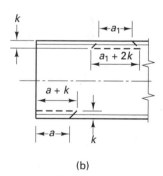

(b)

Fig. 13-16

For this example, assuming $\sigma_{yp} = 36$ ksi, $0.75\sigma_{yp} = 27$ ksi, and the *mini-mum* widths of the supports, according to the rule, are as follows:

At support A:

$$27(a + k)t = 6.4 \quad \text{or} \quad 27(a + 7/8) \times 0.245 = 6.4$$

and

$$a = 0.09 \text{ in}$$

At support B:

$$27(a_1 + 2k)t = 25.6 \quad \text{or} \quad 27(a_1 + 2 \times 7/8) \times 0.245 = 25.6$$

and

$$a_1 = 2.12 \text{ in}$$

These requirements can easily be met in an actual case.

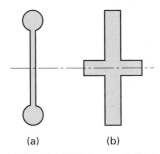

(a)   (b)

Fig. 13-17 (a) Efficient and (b) inefficient sections for flexure.

The preceding two examples illustrate the design of beams whose cross sections have two axes of symmetry. In both cases, the bending moments controlled the design, and, since this is usually true, it is significant to note which members are efficient in flexure. A concentration of as much material as possible away from the neutral axis results in the best sections for resisting flexure, Fig. 13-17(a). Material concentrated near the outside fibers works at a high stress. For this reason, I-type sections, which approximate this requirement, are widely used in practice.

The previous statements apply for materials having nearly equal properties in tension and compression. If this is not the case, a deliberate shift of the neutral axis from the midheight position is desirable. This accounts for the wide use of T and channel sections for such materials (see Example 8-5).

Finally, two other items warrant particular attention in the design of beams. In many cases, the loads for which a beam is designed are transient in character. They may be placed on the beam all at once, piecemeal, or in *different locations*. The loads, which are not a part of the "dead weight" of the structure itself, are called *live loads*. They must be so placed as to cause the highest possible stresses in a beam. In many cases, the placement may be determined by inspection. For example, in a simple beam with a single moving load, the placement of the load at midspan causes the largest bending moment, whereas placing the same load very near to a support causes the greatest shear. For most building work, the live load, which supposedly provides for the most severe expected loading condition, is specified in building codes on the basis of a load per unit floor area. Multiplying this live load by the spacing of parallel beams gives the *uniformly distributed live load* per unit length of the beam. For design purposes, this load is added to the dead weight of construction. Situations where the applied force is delivered to a beam with a shock or impacts are discussed in Section 14-11.

The second item pertains to *lateral instability* of beams. The beam's flanges, if not held laterally, may be so narrow in relation to the span that a beam may buckle sideways and collapse.

13.9. Design of Nonprismatic Beams

It should be apparent from the preceding discussion that the selection of a prismatic beam is based only on the stresses at the critical sections. At all other sections through the beam, the stresses will be below the allowable level. Therefore, the potential capacity of a given material is not fully utilized. This situation may be improved by designing a beam of variable cross section (i.e., by making the beam nonprismatic). Since flexural stresses control the design of most beams, as has been shown, the cross sections may everywhere be made just strong enough to resist the corresponding moment. Such beams are called *beams of constant strength*. Shear governs the design at sections through these beams where the bending moment is small.

Example 13-7

Design a cantilever of constant strength for resisting a concentrated force applied at the end. Neglect the beam's own weight.

SOLUTION

A cantilever with a concentrated force applied at the end is shown in Fig. 13-18(a); the corresponding moment diagram is plotted in Fig. 13-18(b). Basing the design on the bending moment, the required section modulus at an arbitrary section is given by Eq. 8-21:

$$S = \frac{M}{\sigma_{\text{allow}}} = \frac{Px}{\sigma_{\text{allow}}}$$

A great many cross-sectional areas satisfy this requirement; so, first, it will be assumed that the beam will be of rectangular cross section and of *constant height h*. The section modulus for this beam is given by Eq. 8-22 as $bh^2/6 = S$; hence,

$$\frac{bh^2}{6} = \frac{Px}{\sigma_{\text{allow}}} \quad \text{or} \quad b = \left(\frac{6P}{h^2\sigma_{\text{allow}}}\right)x = \frac{b_o}{L}x \qquad (13\text{-}1)$$

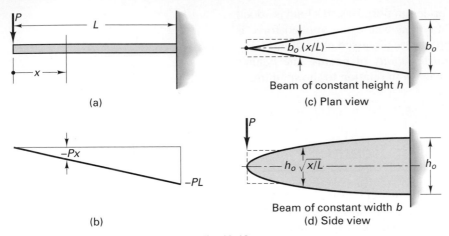

Fig. 13-18

where the expression in parentheses is a constant and is set equal to b_o/L, so that when $x = L$, the width is b_o. A beam of constant strength with a constant depth in a plan view looks like the wedge[11] shown in Fig. 13-18(c). Near the free end, this wedge must be modified to be of adequate strength to resist the shear force $V = P$.

If the width or breadth b *of the beam is constant,*

$$\frac{bh^2}{6} = \frac{Px}{\sigma_{allow}} \quad \text{or} \quad h = \sqrt{\frac{6Px}{b\sigma_{allow}}} = h_o\sqrt{\frac{x}{L}} \qquad (13\text{-}2)$$

This expression indicates that a cantilever of constant width loaded at the end is also of constant strength if its height varies parabolically from the free end, Fig. 13-18(d).

Beams of approximately constant strength are used in leaf springs and in many machine parts that are cast or forged. In structural work, an approximation to a beam of constant strength is frequently made. For example, the moment diagram for the beam loaded as shown in Fig. 13-19(a) is given by lines AB and BC in Fig. 13-19(b). By selecting a beam of flexural capacity equal only to M_1, the middle portion of the beam is overstressed. However, cover plates can be provided near the middle of the beam to boost the flexural capacity of the composite beam to the required value of the maximum moment. For the case shown, the cover plates must extend at least over the length DE of the beam, and in practice they are made somewhat longer. A

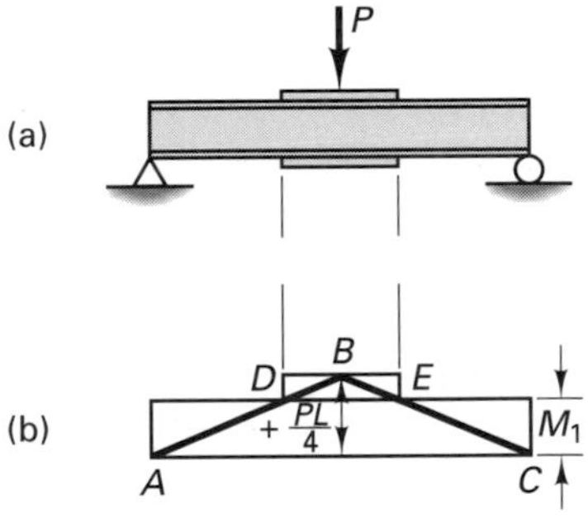

Fig. 13-19   Coverplated I beam.

---

[11]Since this beam is not of constant cross-sectional area, the use of the elementary flexure formula is not entirely correct. When the angle included by the sides of the wedge is small, little error is involved. As this angle becomes large, the error may be considerable. An exact solution shows that when the total included angle is 40°, the solution is in error by nearly 10%.

leaf spring, approximating a beam of constant strength such as in Fig. 13-18(c), is shown in Fig. 13-20.

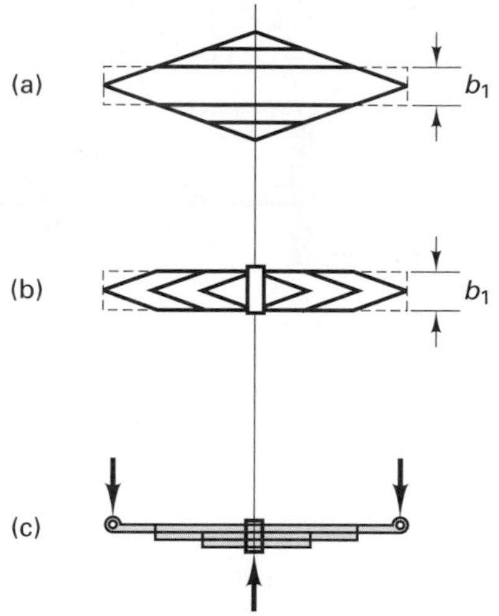

Fig. 13-20 Leaf spring.

13-10. Design of Complex Members

In many instances, the design of complex members cannot be carried out in a routine manner as was done in the preceding simple examples. Sometimes the size of a member must be *assumed* and a complete stress analysis performed at sections where the stresses appear critical. Designs of this type may require several revisions. Finite element analyses with increasing frequency are used in such cases for final design. Alternatively, experimental methods are also resorted to since elementary formulas may not be sufficiently accurate.

As a last example in this chapter, a transmission shaft problems is analyzed. A direct analytical procedure is possible in this problem, which is of great importance in the design of power equipment.

Example 13-8

Select the size of a solid steel shaft to drive the two sprockets shown in Fig. 13-21(a). These sprockets drive $1\frac{3}{4}$-in pitch roller chains,[12] as shown in Fig. 13-21(b) and (c). Pitch diameters of the sprockets shown in the figures are from a manufacturer's catalog. A 20-hp speed-reducer unit is coupled directly to the shaft and drives it at 63 rpm. At each sprocket, 10 hp is taken off. Assume the maximum shear theory of failure, and let $\tau_{allow} = 6$ ksi.

SOLUTION

According to Eq. 6-11, the torque delivered to shaft segment CD is $T = 63,000(\text{hp}/N) = (63,000)20/63 = 20,000$ lb-in $= 20$ k-in. Hence, torques T_1 and T_2 delivered to the sprockets are $T/2 = 10$ k-in *each*. Since the chains are arranged as shown in Fig. 13-21(b) and (c), the pull in the chain at sprocket B is $P_1 = T_1/(D_1/2) = 10/(10.632/2) = 1.88$ k-in. Similarly, $P_2 = 10/(7.313/2) = 2.73$ k. The pull P_1 on the chain *is equivalent to* a torque T_1 and a vertical force at B, as shown in Fig. 13-21(d). At C, force P_2 acts horizontally and exerts a torque T_2. A complete free-body diagram for shaft AD is shown in Fig. 13-21(d).

[12]Similar sprockets and roller chains are commonly used on bicycles.

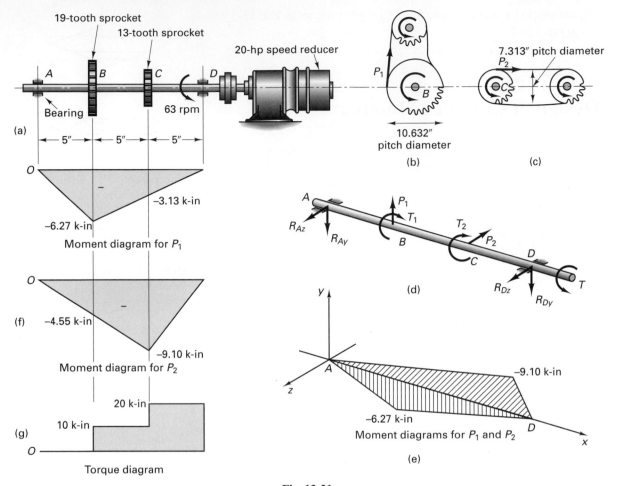

(a)

(b)

(c)

(d)

(e)

(f)

(g)

19-tooth sprocket

13-tooth sprocket

20-hp speed reducer

7.313″ pitch diameter

Bearing

63 rpm

10.632″ pitch diameter

-3.13 k-in

-6.27 k-in

Moment diagram for P_1

-4.55 k-in

-9.10 k-in

Moment diagram for P_2

20 k-in

10 k-in

Torque diagram

-9.10 k-in

-6.27 k-in

Moment diagrams for P_1 and P_2

Fig. 13-21

It is seen from the free-body diagram that this shaft is simultaneously sub-jected to bending and torque. These effects on the member are best studied with the aid of appropriate diagrams, which are shown in Fig. 13-21(e)–(g). Next, note that although bending takes place in two planes, a *vectorial resultant of the moments* may be used in the flexure formula, since the beam has a circular cross section.

By keeping the last statement in mind, the general Eq. 11-9, giving the maximum shear stress, reduces in this problem of bending and torsion to

$$\tau_{\max} = \sqrt{\left(\frac{\sigma_{\text{bending}}}{2}\right)^2 + \tau_{\text{torsion}}{}^2}$$

$$\tau_{\max} = \sqrt{\left(\frac{Mc}{2I}\right)^2 + \left(\frac{Tc}{I_p}\right)^2}$$

However, since for a circular cross section, $I_p = 2I$, Eq. 8-20, $I_p = \pi d^4/32$, Eq. 6-2, and $c = d/2$, the last expression reduces to

$$\tau_{max} = \frac{16}{\pi d^3}\sqrt{M^2 + T^2}$$

By assigning the allowable shear stress to τ_{max}, a design formula, based on the maximum shear theory[13] of failure, for a shaft subjected to bending and torsion is obtained as

$$d = \sqrt[3]{\frac{16}{\pi \tau_{allow}}\sqrt{M^2 + T^2}}$$

This formula may be used to select the diameter of a shaft simultaneously subjected to bending and torque. In the example investigated, a few trials should convince the reader that $\sqrt{M^2 + T^2}$ is largest at sprocket C; hence, the critical section is at C. Thus,

$$M^2 + T^2 = (M_{vert})^2 + (M_{horiz})^2 + T^2$$
$$= (6.27/2)^2 + 9.10^2 + 20^2 = 492. \ k^2\text{-in}^2$$
$$d = \sqrt[3]{\frac{16}{6\pi}\sqrt{492}} = 2.66 \text{ in}$$

A $2\frac{11}{16}$-in diameter shaft, which is a commercial size, should be used.

The effect of shock load on the shaft has been neglected in the foregoing analysis. For some equipment, where the machine operation is jerky, this condition requires special consideration. The initially assumed allowable stress presumably allows for keyways and fatigue of the material.

Although Eq. 13-3 and similar ones based on other failure criteria are widely used in practice, the reader is cautioned in applying them.[14] In many machines, shaft diameters change abruptly, giving rise to stress concentrations. In stress analysis, this requires the use of stress-concentration factors

---

[13]See Problem 13-52 for the formula based on the maximum stress theory of failure.

[14]For further details on mechanical design, see A. H. Burr, *Mechanical Analysis and Design* (New York: Elsevier, 1982); A. D. Deutchman, W. J. Michaels, and C. E. Wilson, *Machine Design, Theory and Practice* (New York: Macmillan, 1975); J. E. Shigley, *Mechanical Engineering Design,* 3rd ed. (New York: McGraw-Hill, 1977); M. F. Spotts, *Design of Machine Elements,* 6th ed. (Englewood Cliffs, NJ: Prentice Hall, 1985).

For design on steel, aluminum alloys, and wood structures, see the references in the relevant sections of Chapter 16, and C. G. Salmon and J. E. Johnson, *Steel Structures,* 3rd ed. (New York: Harper & Row, 1990).

References for design in reinforced concrete are given after Example 8-11, and J. G. Macgregor, *Reinforced concrete, mechanics and design,* 3rd ed. (Upper Saddle River, N J: Prentice Hall, 1996).

in bending, which are usually different from those in torsion. Therefore, the problem should be analyzed by considering the actual stresses at the critical section. (See Fig. 13-22.) Then an appropriate procedure, such as Mohr's circle of stress, should be used to determine the significant stress, depending on the selected fracture criteria.

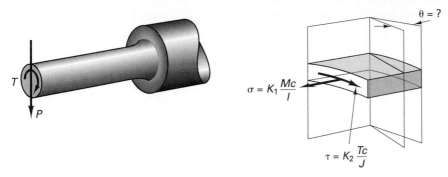

Fig. 13-22   Analysis of a shaft with stress concentrations.

PROBLEMS

Section 13-2. Miscellaneous Stress Analysis Problems

13-1. A concrete cylinder tested in a vertical position failed at a compressive stress of 30 MPa. The failure occurred on a plane of 30° with the vertical. On a clear sketch, show the normal and shear stresses that acted on the plane of failure.

13-2. In a research investigation on the creep of lead, it was necessary to control the state of stress for the element of a tube. In one such case, a long cylindrical tube with closed ends was pressurized and simultaneously subjected to a torque. The tube was 100 mm in outside diameter with 4-mm walls. What were the principal stresses at the outside surface of the wall of the cylinder if the chamber was pressurized to 1.5 MPa and the externally applied torque was 200 N · m?

13-3. A cylindrical thin-walled tank weighing 100 lb/ft is supported as shown in the figure. If, in addition, it is subjected to an internal pressure of 200 psi, what state of stress would develop at points A and B? Show the results on isolated elements. The mean radius of the tank is 10 in, and its thickness is 0.20 in. Comment on the importance of the dead weight of the tank in the total stresses.

13-4. A cylindrical pressure vessel and its contents are lifted by cables, as shown in the figure. The mean diameter of the cylinder is 600 mm, and its wall thickness is 6 mm. Determine the state of stress at points A and B and show the calculated results on isolated elements when the vessel is pressurized to 0.50 MPa and the vessel's mass is 102 kg/m.

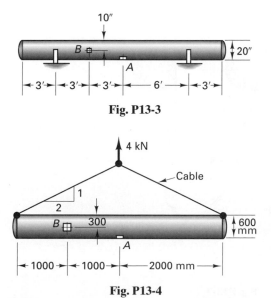

Fig. P13-3

Fig. P13-4

13-5. A cylindrical pressure vessel of 2500-mm diameter with walls 12 mm thick operates at 1.5 MPa internal pressure. If the plates are butt-welded on a 30° helical spiral (see figure), determine the stresses acting normal and tangential to the weld.

13-6. A cylindrical thin-walled pressure vessel with mean radius $r = 300$ mm and thickness $t = 6$ mm is hoisted by two cables into the position shown in the figure. If the vessel is pressurized to 0.50 MPa gage pressure and the vessel weighs 102 kg/m, determine the state of stress at point A. Show the results on a properly oriented isolated element.

13-7. A fractionating column, 45 ft long, is made of a 12-in-inside-diameter standard steel pipe weighing 49.56 lb/ft. (See Table 7 of the Appendix.) This pipe is operating in a vertical position, as indicated on the sketch. If this pipe is internally pressurized to 600 psi and is subjected to a wind load of 40 lb/ft of height, what is the state of stress at point A? Clearly show your calculated stresses on an isolated element; principal stresses need not be found.

13-8. A cylindrical thin-walled pressure vessel with a mean diameter of 20 in and thickness of 0.25 in is rigidly attached to a wall, forming a cantilever, as shown in the figure. (a) If an internal pressure of 250 psi is applied and, in addition, an external eccentric force $P = 31.4$ k acts on the assembly, what stresses are caused at point A? Show the results on a properly oriented element. (b) What maximum shear stress develops in the element? (*Caution:* All three principal Mohr's circles of stress should be examined.)

13-9. A cylindrical thin-walled pressure vessel rigidly attached to a wall, as shown in the figure, is subjected to an internal pressure of p and an externally applied torque T. Due to these combined causes, the stresses on plane $a-a$ are $\sigma_{x'} = 0$ and $\tau_{x'y'} = 10$ MPa. Determine the internal pressure p and the magnitude of the torque T. The mean diameter of the vessel is 400 mm, and the wall thickness is 6 mm.

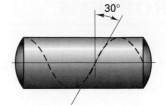

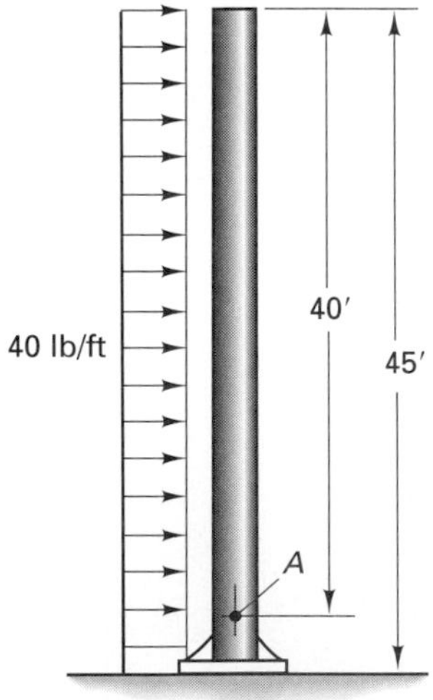

Fig. P13-5

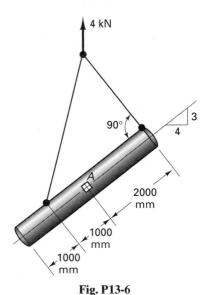

Fig. P13-6

Fig. P13-7

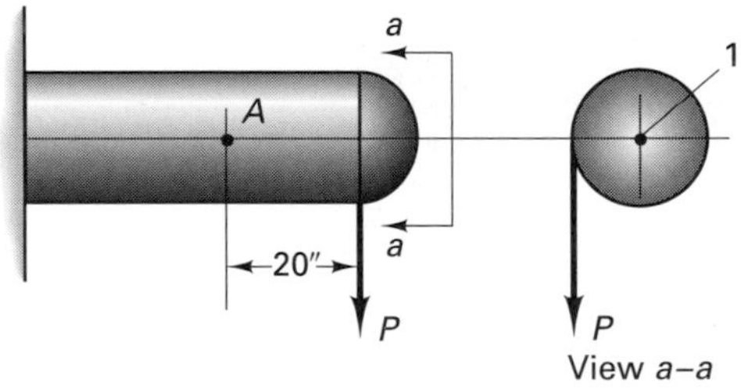

Fig. P13-8

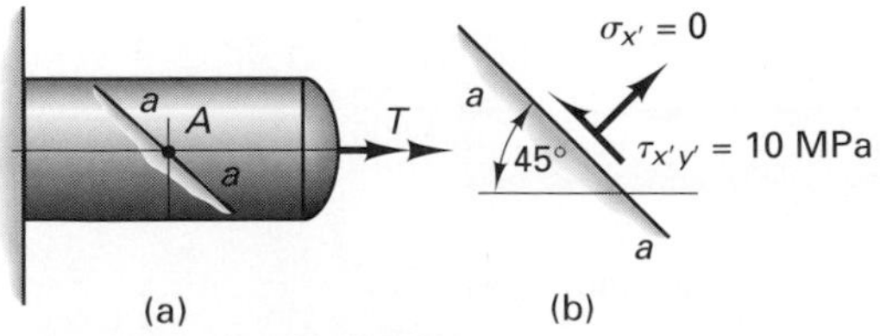

Fig. P13-9

13-10. An assembly of seamless stainless steel tubing forming a part of a piping system is arranged as shown in the figure. A flexible expansion joint is inserted at C, which is capable of resisting hoop stresses, but transmits no longitudinal force. The tubing is 60 mm in outside diameter and is 2 mm thick. If the pipe is pressurized to 2 MPa, determine the state of stress at points A and B. Show the results on infinitesimal elements viewed from the outside. No distinction between the inside and outside dimensions of the tube need be made in the calculations. All dimensions shown on the figure are in mm. No stress transformations are required.[1]

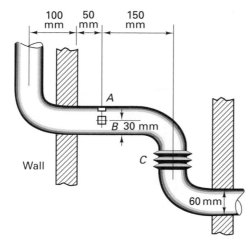

Fig. P13-10

13-11. At point A on the upstream face of a dam, the water pressure is -40 kPa, and a measured tensile stress in the dam parallel to this surface is 20 kPa. Calculate stresses σ_x, σ_y, and τ_{xy} at that point and show them on an isolated element.

13-12. A special hoist supports a 15-k load by means of a cable, as shown in the figure. Determine the principal stresses at point A due to this load.

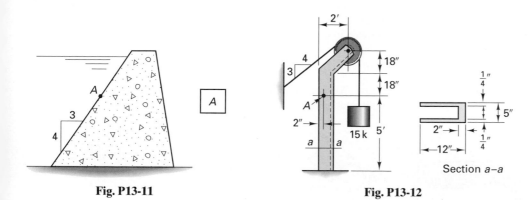

Fig. P13-11   **Fig. P13-12**

[1]Data in the problem are fictitious; however, a major failure occurred at a petrochemical plant due to an oversight of basic behavior of this system of piping. (Courtesy of I. Finnie.)

13-13. By applying a vertical force P, the toggle clamp, as shown in the figure, exerts a force of 1000 lb on a cylindrical object. The movable jaw slides in a guide that prevents its upward movement. (a) Determine the magnitude of the applied vertical force P and the downward force component developed at hinge A; (b) determine the stresses due to axial thrust, transverse shear, and bending moment acting on an element at point C of section a–a; (c) draw an element at point C with sides parallel and perpendicular to the axis of member BA and show the stresses acting on the element; and (d) using Mohr's circle, determine the largest principal stress and the maximum shear stress at C.

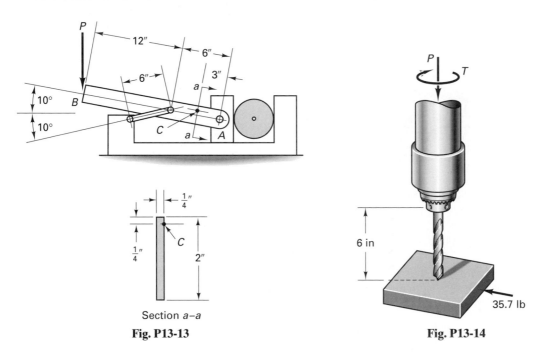

Section a–a

Fig. P13-13

Fig. P13-14

13-14. A $\frac{1}{2}$-in-diameter drill bit is inserted into a chuck, as shown in the figure. During the drilling operation, an axial force $P = 3.92$ k and a torque $T = 10\pi/128$ k-in act on the bit. If a horizontal force of 35.7 lb is accidentally applied to the plate being drilled, what is the magnitude of the largest principal stress that develops at the top of the drill bit? Determine the critically stressed point on the drill by inspection.

13-15. A solid circular shaft is loaded as shown in the figure. At section $ACBD$ the stresses due to the 10-kN force and the weight of the shaft and round drum are

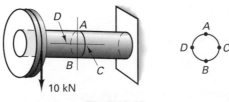

Fig. P13-15

found to be as follows: maximum bending stress is 40 MN/m², maximum torsional stress is 30 MN/m², and maximum shear stress due to V is 6 MN/m². (a) Set up elements at points A, B, C, and D and indicate the magnitudes and directions of the stresses acting on them. In each case, state from which direction the element is observed. (b) Using Mohr's circle, find directions and magnitudes of the principal stresses and of the maximum shear stress at point A.

13-16. A circular bar of 2-in-diameter with a rectangular block attached at its free end is suspended as shown in the figure. Also, a horizontal force is applied eccentrically to the block as shown. Analysis of the stresses at section $ABCD$ gives the following results: Maximum bending stress is 1000 psi, maximum torsional stress is 300 psi, maximum shear stress due to V is 400 psi, and direct axial stress is 200 psi. (a) Set up an element at point A and indicate the magnitudes and directions of the stresses acting on it (the top edge of the element to coincide with section $ABCD$). (b) Using Mohr's circle, find the direction and the magnitude of the maximum (principal) shear stresses and the associated normal stresses at point A.

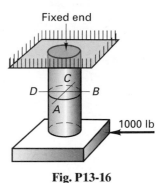

Fig. P13-16

13-17. A bent rectangular bar is subjected to an inclined force of 3000 N, as shown in the figure. The cross section of the bar is 12×12 mm. (a) Determine the state of stress at point A caused by the applied force and show the results on an element. (b) Find the maximum principal stress.

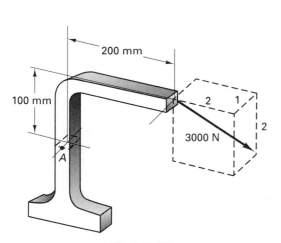

Fig. P13-17

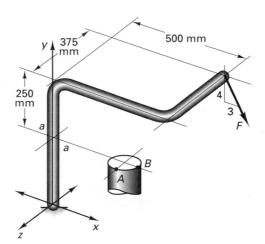

Fig. P13-18

13-18. A 50-mm-diameter rod is subjected at its free end to an inclined force $F = 225\pi$ N, as shown in the figure. (The force F in plan view acts in the direction of the x-axis.) Determine the magnitudes and directions of the stresses due to F on the elements A and B at section a–a. Show the results on elements clearly related to the points on the rod. Principal stresses are not required.

13-19. A horizontal 12×12-mm rectangular bar 100 mm long is attached at one end to a rigid support. Two of the bar's sides form an angle of $30°$ with the vertical, as shown in the figure. By means of an attachment (not shown), a vertical force

$F = 4.45$ N is applied acting through a corner of the bar. (See the figure.) Calculate the stress at points A and B caused by the applied force F. Neglect stress concentrations. Show the results on the elements viewed from the top. Stress transformations to obtain principal stresses are optional.

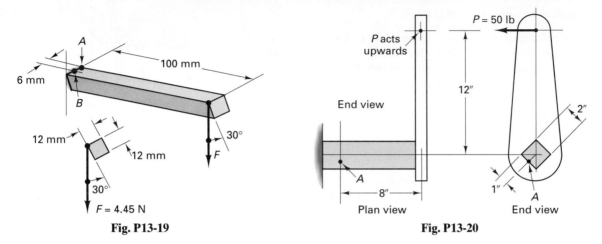

Fig. P13-19   Fig. P13-20

13-20.   A 2×2-in square bar is attached to a rigid support, as shown in the figure. Determine the principal stresses at point A caused by force $P = 50$ lb applied to the crank.

13-21.   A 400-lb sign is supported by a $2\frac{1}{2}$-in standard-weight steel pipe, as shown in the figure. The maximum horizontal wind force acting on this sign is estimated to

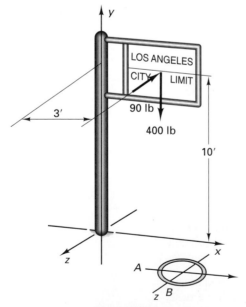

Fig. P13-21

be 90 lb. Determine the state of stress caused by this loading at points A and B at the built-in end. Principal stresses are not required. Indicate results on sketches of elements cut out from the pipe at these points. These elements are to be viewed from outside the pipe.

13-22. For the circular three-hinged arch rib shown in the figure, determine the principal stresses 75 mm above the centroid of the cross section at section a–a due to the applied vertical load on the left half of the structure. Because of the large curvature, the rib at the section investigated can be treated as a straight bar.

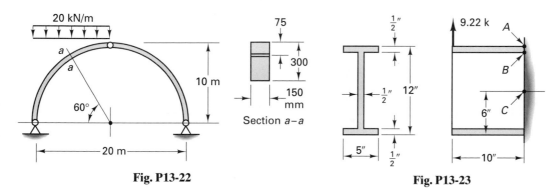

Fig. P13-22   **Fig. P13-23**

13-23. A short I beam cantilever is loaded as shown in the figure. Find the principal stresses and their directions at points A, B, and C. Point B is in the web at the juncture with the flange. Neglect the weight of the beam and ignore the effect of stress concentrations. Use the accurate formula to determine the shear stresses.

13-24. The cantilever shown in the figure is loaded by an inclined force P acting in the plane of symmetry of the cross section. (a) What is the magnitude of applied force P if it causes an axial strain of 200 μm/m at point A? $E = 30 \times 10^6$ psi. (b) What is the maximum principal strain at A?

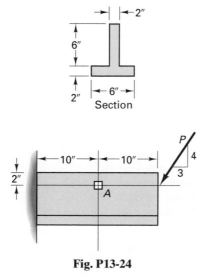

Fig. P13-24

13-25. The principal shear stress at point A caused by application of force P is 120 psi; see the figure. What is the magnitude of P?

13-26. A simple beam 50×120 mm spans 1500 mm and supports a uniformly distributed load of 80 kN/m, including its own weight. Determine the principal stresses and their directions at points A, B, C, D, and E at the section shown in the figure.

13-27. A 100×400-mm rectangular wooden beam supports a 40-kN load, as shown in the figure. The grain of the wood makes an angle of 20° with the axis of the beam. Find the shear stresses at points A and B along the grain of the wood due to the applied concentrated force.

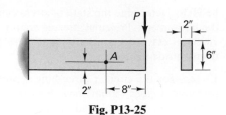

Fig. P13-25

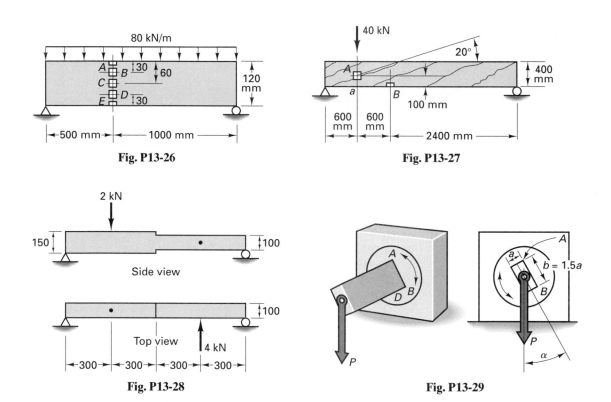

Fig. P13-26

Fig. P13-27

Fig. P13-28

Fig. P13-29

13-28. Find the largest bending stress for the beam shown in the figure due to the applied loads. Neglect stress concentrations. All dimensions in the figure are in mm.

13-29. In a mechanical device, a horizontal rectangular bar of length L is fixed at the rotating end and is loaded by a strap through a bolt with a vertical force P at the free end, as shown in the figure. Find the angle α for which the normal stress at A is maximum and locate the neutral axis for the beam in this position. Neglect stress concentration, which would have to be considered in an actual problem.

13-30. A 50-mm-diameter shaft is simultaneously subjected to a torque and pure bending. At every section of this shaft, the largest principal stress caused by the applied loading is $+160$ MPa, and, simultaneously, the largest longitudinal tensile stress is $+120$ MPa. Determine the applied bending moment and torque.

13-31. Compare the moment-carrying capacity of a $102 \times 102 \times 12.7$-mm steel angle in the two different positions shown in the figure. In both cases, the applied vertical load acts through the shear center. (*Hint:* Table 6B gives the least radius of gyration, r, for the cross section. Hence, per Eq. 16-19a, $I_{min} = Ar^2_{min}$. Alternatively, I_{min} can be calculated directly by considering the angle to consist of two plates.)

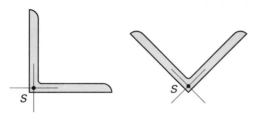

Fig. P13-31

13-32. A fire alarm is set up with a piece of brass wire as the sensitive element, as schematically shown in the figure. If the gap is 2 mm when there is no tension in the wire, find the number of turns that should be taken on the screw to set the alarm so that the contacts will open at a temperature rise of 40°C. For the brass bar, $EI = 20$ N·m², and the spring constant $k = 20$ N/mm. The brass wire is 4.5 m long, has an $A = 6$ mm², an $E = 100$ GPa, and an $\alpha = 20 \times 10^{-6}$ per °C. The adjusting screw has one thread per mm.

13-33. Two metal strips of equal thickness but of different material are bonded together and are attached at one end to act as a cantilever, as shown in the figure. Determine the tip deflection caused by a change in temperature of δT. Let the coefficient of expansion of one bar be α_1, and of the other bar be α_2. Assume that the elastic moduli for both materials are the same. Such bimetallic elements are widely used in temperature-control devices. (*Hint:* Consider that a longitudinal force and a moment exist in each strip. The strains at the joint are the same in the two materials.)

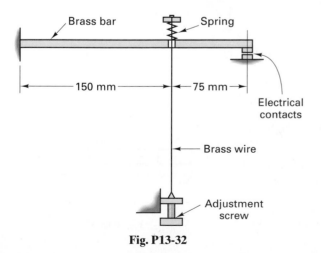

Fig. P13-32

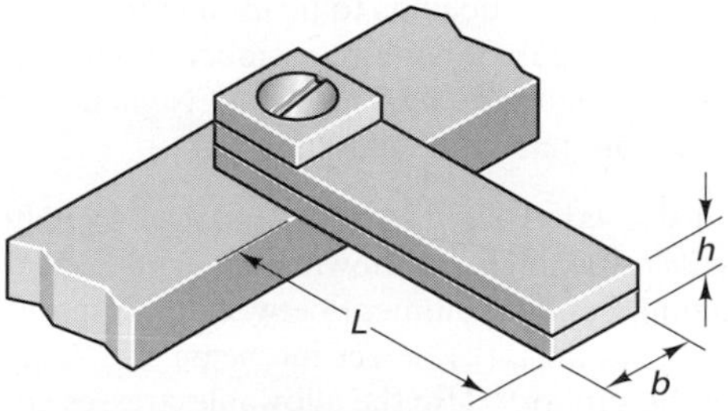

Fig. P13-33

Sections 13-5 and 13-6

13-34. Select the diameter for a solid circular steel shaft to transmit a torque of 6 kN · m and a bending moment of 4 kN · m if the maximum allowable shear stress is 80 MPa.

13-35. For the loading condition and the allowable shear stress given in the preceding problem, determine the diameter of a hollow circular steel shaft such that the ratio of the inside diameter to the outside diameter is 0.80.

Section 13-8

13-36. A Douglas fir wood beam of rectangular cross section is loaded as shown in the figure. What is the required standard dressed size for the member, and what are the minimum sizes of the bearing plates under the concentrated forces and the minimum beam lengths at the supports? In the calculations, consider the weight of the beam. The allowable stress in bending is 1250 psi; in shear, 95 psi; and in compression perpendicular to the grain, 625 psi. Use Table 9 for actual lumber sectional properties.

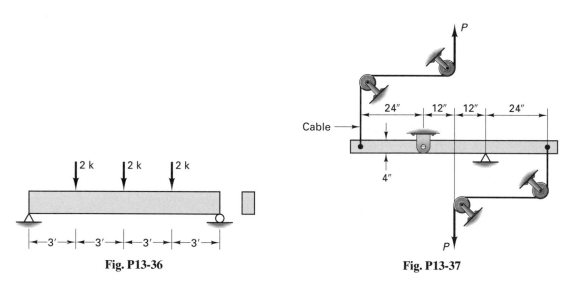

Fig. P13-36   **Fig. P13-37**

13-37. A standard-size wood beam is to be used in the device shown in the figure to transmit a force $P = 250$ lb. What size member should be used if the allowable stresses are as given in the preceding problem? Neglect the weight of the beam. Select a beam of 3-in nominal width; use Table 9.

13-38. A standard-size wood beam 16 ft long is to carry a uniformly distributed load of 2 k/ft, including its own weight, as shown in the figure. (a) Determine the length a such that the maximum bending moment between the supports is numerically equal to that over the right support. (b) Select the beam size required and calculate the minimum length of the supports. Use the allowable stresses given in Problem 13-36.

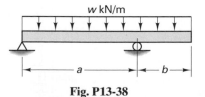

Fig. P13-38

13-39. A 100 × 150-mm (actual size) wooden beam is to be symmetrically loaded with two equal loads P, as shown in the figure. Determine the position of these loads and their magnitudes when a bending stress of 10 MPa and a shearing stress of 2.5 MPa are just reached. Neglect the weight of the beam.

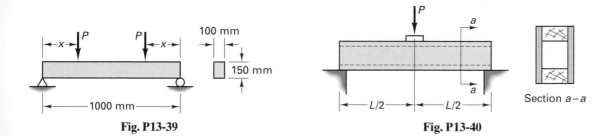

Fig. P13-39   **Fig. P13-40**

13-40. A 300-mm-deep box beam is fabricated by gluing two pieces of 75 × 200-mm plywood to two wood pieces to form the cross section shown in the figure. If the beam is to be used to carry a concentrated force in the middle of a span (see the figure), (a) based on the shear capacity of the section, what may be the magnitude of the applied force P; (b) how long may the span be; and (c) what bearing areas should be provided under the concentrated forces? Neglect the weight of the beam. The allowable stresses are 8 MPa in bending, 800 kPa in shear for plywood, 400 kPa in shear for glued joints, and 4.3 MPa in compression perpendicular to the grain.

13-41. A plastic beam is to be made from two 20 × 60-mm pieces to span 600 mm and to carry an intermittently applied, uniformly distributed load w. The pieces can be arranged in two alternative ways, as shown in the figure. The allowable stresses are 4 MPa in flexure, 600 kPa shear in plastic, and 400 kPa shear in glue. Which arrangement of pieces should be used, and what load w can be applied?

13-42. Consider two alternative beam designs for spanning 24 ft to support a uniformly distributed load of 1 k/ft. Both beams are simply supported. One of the beams is to be of steel, the other of wood. The allowable stresses for steel are 24 ksi in bending and 14.4 ksi in shear; and those for wood, respectively, are 1250 psi and 95 psi. (a) Find the size required for each beam based on the given strength criteria. (In a comprehensive design, beam deflections are also generally determined.) Consider the beam weights in the calculations; see Tables 4B and 9 in the Appendix. (b) What percentage of the total load is due to the weight of the beam in each case?

13-43. Select either an S or a W lightest section for a beam with overhangs for carrying an applied uniformly distributed load of 2 k/ft, as shown in the figure. The specified load includes the beam weight. The allowable stresses are 24 ksi in bending and 14.4 ksi in shear.

13-44. A portion of the floor-framing plan for an office building is shown in the figure. Wooden joists spanning 12 ft are spaced 16 in apart and support a wooden floor above and a plastered ceiling below. Assume that the floor may be loaded by the occupants everywhere by as much as 75 lb per square foot of floor area (live

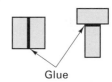

Glue

Fig. P13-41

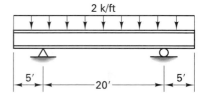

Fig. P13-43

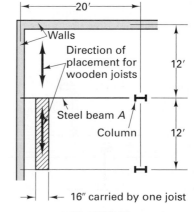

Fig. P13-44

load). Assume further that floor, joists, and ceiling weigh 25 lb per square foot of the floor area (dead load). (a) Determine the depth required for standard commercial joists nominally 2 in wide. For wood, the allowable bending stress is 1200 psi and the shear stress is 100 psi. (b) Select the size required for steel beam A. Since the joists delivering the load to this beam are spaced closely, assume that the beam is loaded by a uniformly distributed load. The allowable stresses for steel are 24 ksi and 14.4 ksi for bending and shear, respectively. Use a W or an S beam, whichever is lighter. Neglect the depth of the column.

13-45. A bay of an apartment house floor is framed as shown in the figure. Determine the required size of minimum weight for steel beam A. Assume that the floor may be loaded everywhere as much as 75 lb/ft² of floor area (live load). Assume further that the weight of the hardwood flooring, structural concrete slab, plastered ceiling below, steel beam being selected, etc., also amounts to approximately 75 lb/ft² of floor area (dead load). Use the allowable stresses given in part (b) of Problem 13-44.

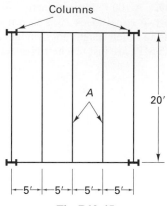

Fig. P13-45

13-46. A four-wheel car running on rails is to be used in light industrial service. When loaded, a force of 10 kN is applied to each bearing. If the bearings are located with respect to the rails, as in the figure, what size round axle should be used? Assume the allowable bending stress to be 80 MPa and the allowable shear stress to be 40 MPa.

13-47. A standard steel beam (S shape) serves as a rail for an overhead traveling crane of 4-ton capacity; see the figure. Determine the required size for the beam and the maximum force on the hanger. Locate the crane so as to cause maximum stresses for each condition. Assume a pinned connection at the wall, and neglect the weight of the beam in calculations. The allowable stress in bending is 16 ksi and that in shear is 9.6 ksi.

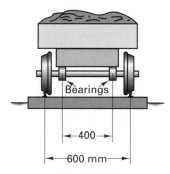

Fig. P13-46

13-48. A glue-laminated wooden beam supports a rail and is loaded by one side of a four-wheel cart, as shown in the figure. The beam is made up from 40 × 100-mm board laminates. (a) Locate the cart so as to cause the maximum bending moment in the beam. (b) Locate the cart to cause the maximum shear in the beam. (c) Determine the number of board laminates required. The allowable stresses are 14 MPa in bending and 1MPa in shear. In calculations, neglect the weight of the beam. (*Hint:* Locate the left wheel of the cart a distance x from the left support and write an expression for the bending moment. Setting the derivative of this expression equal to zero determines the position of the cart for the maximum beam moment.)

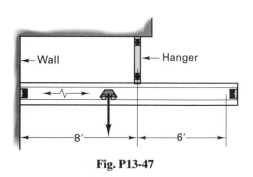

Fig. P13-47

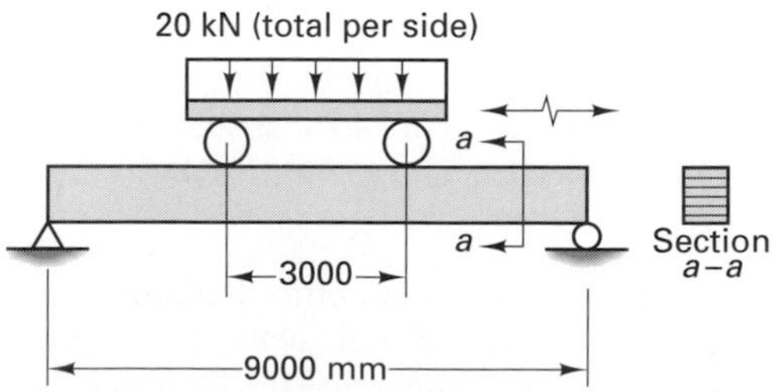

Fig. P13-48

Section 13-9

13-49. Determine the elevation and plan of a cantilever of uniform flexural stress and circular cross section for resisting a concentrated force P applied at the end. Neglect the weight of the member.

13-50. In many engineering design problems, it is very difficult to determine the magnitudes of the loads that will act on a structure or a machine part. Satisfactory performance in an existing installation may provide the basis for extrapolation. With this in mind, suppose that a certain sign, such as shown in the figure, has performed satisfactorily on a 4-in standard steel pipe when its centroid was 10 ft above the ground. What should the size of pipe be if the sign were raised to 30 ft above the ground? Assume that the wind pressure on the sign at the greater height will be 50% greater than it was in the original installation. Vary the size of the pipe along the length as required; however, for ease in fabrication, the successive pipe segments must fit into each other. In arranging the pipe segments, also give some thought to aesthetic considerations. For simplicity in calculations, neglect the weight of the pipes and the wind pressure on the pipes themselves.

13-51. A W 310×97 beam is coverplated with two 200×10-mm plates, as shown in Fig. 13-19(a). If the span is 5 m, (a) what concentrated force P can be applied to the beam, and where can the coverplates be cut off? Neglect the weight of the beam, and assume that the beam section and the coverplates are properly interconnected. Note that coverplates are usually extended a few mm beyond the theoretical cut-off points. (b) Obtain a revised solution if, instead of P, a uniformly distributed load were applied. Assume that the allowable bending stress is 160 MPa in both cases.

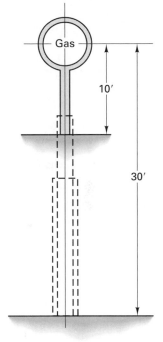

Fig. P13-50

Section 13-10

13-52. (a) Show that the larger principal stress for a circular shaft simultaneously subjected to a torque and a bending moment is

$$\sigma_1 = (c/J)(M + \sqrt{M^2 + T^2})$$

(b) Show that the design formula for shafts, on the basis of the maximum stress theory, is

$$d = \sqrt[3]{\frac{16}{\pi\sigma_{allow}}(M + \sqrt{M^2 + T^2})}$$

13-53. At a critical section, a solid circular shaft transmits a torque of 40 kN · m and a bending moment of 10 kN · m. Determine the size of the shaft required so that the maximum shear stress would not exceed 50 MPa.

13-54. Rework the preceding problem, assuming that $\sigma_{yp} = 100$ MPa and the safety factor is 2 on the von Mises yield criterion given by Eq. 12-12.

13-55. The head shaft of an inclined bucket elevator is arranged as shown in the figure. It is driven at A at 11 rpm and requires 45 kW for steady operation. Assuming that one-half of the delivered horsepower is used at each sprocket, determine the size of shaft required so that the maximum shear stress would not exceed 40 MPa. The assigned stress allows for keyways.

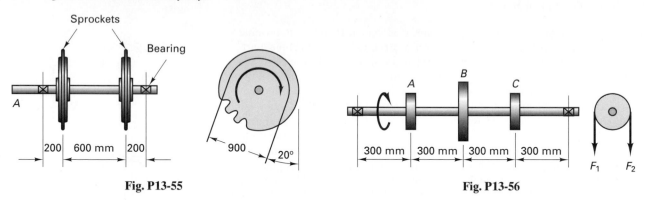

Fig. P13-55   **Fig. P13-56**

13-56. A shaft is fitted with pulleys, as shown in the figure. The end bearings are self-aligning (i.e., they do not introduce moment into the shaft at the supports). Pulley B is the driving pulley. Pulleys A and C are the driven pulleys and take off 900 kN · mm and 300 kN · mm of torque, respectively. The resultant of the pulls at each pulley is 1.80 kN acting downward. Determine the size of the shaft required so that the principal shear stress would not exceed 40 MPa.

13-57. Two pulleys of 4π-in radius are attached to a 2-in-diameter solid shaft, which is supported by bearings, as shown in the figure. If the maximum principal shear stress is limited to 6 ksi, what is the largest magnitude that the forces F can assume? The direct shear stress caused by V need not be considered.

13-58. A low-speed shaft is acted upon by an eccentrically applied load P caused by a force developed between the gears. Determine the allowable magnitude of force P on the basis of the maximum shear-stress theory if $\tau_{allow} = 45$ MPa. The small diameter of the overhung shaft is 75 mm. Consider the critical section to be where the shaft changes diameter, and that $M = 0.3P$ N · m and $T = 0.6P$ N · m.

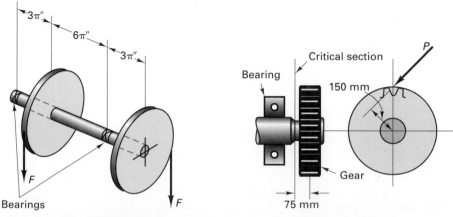

Fig. P13-57   **Fig. P13-58**

Note that since the diameter size changes abruptly, the following stress-concentration factors must be considered: $K_1 = 1.6$ in bending and $K_2 = 1.2$ in torsion.

13-59. A drive shaft for two pulleys is arranged as shown in the figure. The belt tensions are known. Determine the required size of the shaft. Assume that $\tau_{\text{allow}} = 6000$ psi for shafts with keyways. Since the shaft will operate under conditions of suddenly applied load, multiply the given loads by a shock factor of $1\frac{1}{2}$.

13-60. A machine for impregnating fabric with rubber, as for the manufacture of tires, is accomplished by pressing hot rubber into the fabric between powerful rotating cylinders. This process is referred to as calendering. A typical cylinder with approximate dimensions is shown in the figure. The ends of the cylinders are supported in self-aligning roller bearings. (a) Estimate the pressure that can be allowed to develop between the cylinders as a line load p during the passage of the fabric. In calculations, neglect the effect of the reduced size of the cylinders at the ends, and assign an allowable stress for steel using the S–N curve in Fig. 2-26 for 10^7 cycles with a factor of safety of 2.5. Treat supports as applying concentrated forces. (b) Based on (a), design the reduced size of the ends, including the selection of the shoulder fillet at the size transition in the roller. If necessary, assume shear stress $\tau_{\text{allow}} = \sigma_{\text{allow}}/2$. (*Note:* In actual design, deflection of the cylinders under load must be considered.)

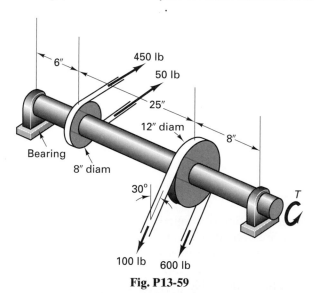

Fig. P13-59

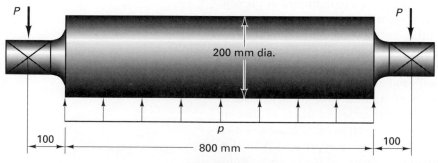

Fig. P13-60

14

Beam Deflections
by Direct Integration

14-1. Introduction

The axis of a beam deflects from its initial position under action of applied forces. Accurate values for these beam deflections are sought in many practical cases: Elements of machines must be sufficiently rigid to prevent misalignment and to maintain dimensional accuracy under load; in buildings, floor beams cannot deflect excessively to avoid the undesirable psychological effect of flexible floors on occupants and to minimize or prevent distress in brittle-finish materials; likewise, information on deformation characteristics of members is essential in the study of vibrations of machines as well as of stationary and flight structures. Deflections are also used in analyses of statically indeterminate problems.

In this chapter, the governing differential equation for the deflection of beams is derived, and the different types of boundary conditions are identified. Several illustrative examples follow for different kinds of loading and boundary conditions, including statically indeterminate beams (which present no special difficulties using this mathematical approach). A section on the application of singularity functions is provided for symbolic solutions for differential equations having discontinuous loading functions along a span. Methods for solving problems by superposition as well as calculation of deflections for unsymmetrical bending are also presented.

An energy method for calculating beam deflections and the effect of impact loads are briefly introduced. The chapter concludes with a discussion of the inelastic deflection of beams. These results are essential for treating the plastic collapse limit states considered in Chapter 20.

14-2. Moment-Curvature Relation

Beam deflections due to bending are determined from deformations taking place along a span. These are based on the kinematic hypothesis that during bending, plane sections through a beam remain plane. This hypothesis was first introduced in Section 8-2 in deriving the flexure formula for beams having symmetric cross sections, and extended in Section 9-8 to beams of arbitrary cross section for bending about either or both principal axes. For the present, it will be assumed that bending takes place only about one of the principal axes of the cross section. Such a case is illustrated in Fig. 14-1, where it is further assumed that the radius of curvature ρ of the *elastic curve* can change along the span. *Except for a slightly greater generality, the derivation that follows leads to the same results as found earlier in Section 8-2.* Deflections due to shear are not considered in this development; some consideration of this problem is given in Section 14-11, Example 14-12.

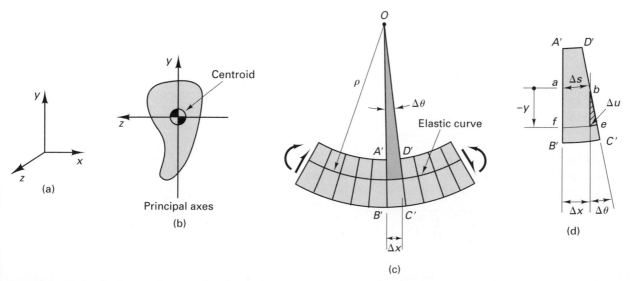

Fig. 14-1   Deformation of a beam in bending.

The center of curvature O for the elastic curve for any element can be found by extending to intersection any two adjoining sections, such as $A'B'$ and $D'C'$. In the enlarged view of element $A'B'C'D'$ in Fig. 14-1(d), it can be seen that in a bent beam, the included angle between two adjoining sections is $\Delta\theta$. If distance y from the neutral surface to the strained fibers is measured in the usual manner as being positive upward, the deformation Δu of any fiber can be expressed as

$$\Delta u = -y \, \Delta\theta \tag{14-1}$$

For negative y's, this yields elongation, which is consistent with the deformation shown in the figure.

The fibers lying in the curved neutral surface of the deformed beam, characterized in Fig 14-1(d) by fiber ab, are not strained at all. Therefore, arc length Δs corresponds to the initial length of all fibers between sections $A'B'$ and $D'C'$. Bearing this in mind, upon dividing Eq. 14-1 by Δs, one can form the following relations:

$$\lim_{\Delta s \to 0} \frac{\Delta u}{\Delta s} = -y \lim_{\Delta s \to 0} \frac{\Delta\theta}{\Delta s} \quad \text{or} \quad \frac{du}{ds} = -y \frac{d\theta}{ds} \tag{14-2}$$

One can recognize that du/ds is the normal strain in a beam fiber at a distance y from the neutral axis. Hence,

$$\frac{du}{ds} = \varepsilon \tag{14-3}$$

The term $d\theta/ds$ in Eq. 14-2 has a clear geometrical meaning. With the aid of Fig 14-1(c), it is seen that, since $\Delta s = \rho\Delta\theta$,

$$\lim_{\Delta s \to 0} \frac{\Delta\theta}{\Delta s} = \frac{d\theta}{ds} = \frac{1}{\rho} = \kappa \tag{14-4}$$

which is the definition of *curvature*[1] κ (kappa) introduced before in Eq. 8-1.

On this basis, upon substituting Eqs. 14-3 and 14-4 into Eq. 14-2, one may express the fundamental relation between curvature of the elastic curve and the normal strain as

$$\boxed{\frac{1}{\rho} = \kappa = -\frac{\varepsilon}{y}} \tag{14-5}$$

It is important to note that as no material properties were used in deriving Eq. 14-5, *this relation can be used for inelastic as well as for elastic problems.* For the *elastic* case, since $\varepsilon = \varepsilon_x = \sigma_x/E$ and $\sigma_x = -My/I$,

$$\boxed{\frac{1}{\rho} = \frac{M}{EI}} \tag{14-6}$$

[1]Note that both θ and s must increase in the same direction.

This equation relates bending moment M at a given section of an elastic beam having a moment of inertia I around the neutral axis to the curvature $1/\rho$ of the elastic curve.

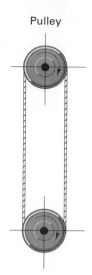

Pulley

Fig. 14-2

Example 14-1

For cutting metal, a band saw 15 mm wide and 0.60 mm thick runs over two pulleys of 400 mm diameter, as shown in Fig. 14-2. What maximum bending stress is developed in the saw as it goes over a pulley? Let $E = 200$ GPa.

SOLUTION

In this application, the material must behave elastically. As the thin saw blade goes over the pulley, it conforms to the radius of the pulley; hence, $\rho \approx 200$ mm.

By using Eq. 8-11, $\sigma = -My/I$, together with Eq. 14-6, after some minor simplifications, a generally useful relation follows:

$$\sigma = -\frac{Ey}{\rho} \qquad (14\text{-}7)$$

With $y = \pm c$, the maximum bending stress in the saw is determined:

$$\sigma_{max} = \frac{Ec}{\rho} = \frac{200 \times 10^3 \times 0.30}{200} = 300 \text{ MPa}$$

The high stress developed in the band saw necessitates superior materials for this application.

14-3. Governing Differential Equation

In texts on analytic geometry, it is shown that in Cartesian coordinates, the curvature of a line is defined as

$$\frac{1}{\rho} = \frac{\dfrac{d^2v}{dx^2}}{\left[1 + \left(\dfrac{dv}{dx}\right)^2\right]^{3/2}} = \frac{v''}{[1 + (v')^2]^{3/2}} \qquad (14\text{-}8)$$

where x and v are the coordinates of a point on a curve. For the problem at hand, distance x locates a point on the elastic curve of a deflected beam, and v gives the deflection of the same point from its initial position.

If Eq. 14-8 were substituted into Eq. 14-6, the exact differential equation for the elastic curve would result. In general, the solution of such an equation is very difficult to achieve. However, since the deflections tolerated in the vast majority of engineering structures are very small, slope dv/dx of the elastic curve is also very small. Therefore, the square of slope v' is a negligible quantity in comparison with unity, and Eq. 14-8 simplifies to

$$\frac{1}{\rho} \approx \frac{d^2v}{dx^2} \qquad (14\text{-}9)$$

This simplification eliminates the *geometric nonlinearity* from the problem, and the governing differential equation for small deflections of elastic beams[2] using Eq. 14-6 is

$$\boxed{\frac{d^2v}{dx^2} = \frac{M}{EI}} \qquad (14\text{-}10)$$

where it is understood that $M = M_z$ and $I = I_z$.

Note that in Eq. 14-10, the xyz coordinate system is employed to locate the material points in a beam for calculating the moment of inertia I. On the other hand, in the planar problem, it is the xv system of axes that is used to locate points on the elastic curve.

The positive direction of the v axis is taken to have the same sense as that of the positive y axis and the positive direction of the applied load q, Fig. 14-3. Note especially that if the positive slope dv/dx of the elastic curve becomes larger as x increases, curvature $1/\rho \approx d^2v/dx^2$ is positive. This sense of curvature agrees with the induced curvature caused by the applied positive moments M. For this reason, the signs are positive on both sides of Eq. 14-10.[3]

---

[2]In some texts, the positive direction for deflection v is taken downward with the x axis directed to the right. For such a choice of coordinates, the positive curvature is concave downward, Fig. 9-19(b). However, if the usual sense for positive moments is retained, Fig. 9-19(a), the corresponding curvature of the bent beam is concave upward. Therefore, since the curvature induced by positive moments M is opposite to that associated with the positive curvature of the elastic curve, one has

$$\frac{d^2v}{dx^2} = -\frac{M}{EI} \qquad (14\text{-}10a)$$

Some texts analyze basic beam deflection problems in the xz plane, as shown in Fig. 9-19(b), and define downward deflection w as positive. In this setting, the governing equation also has a negative sign:

$$\frac{d^2w}{dx^2} = -\frac{M}{EI} \qquad (14\text{-}10b)$$

This notation is particularly favored in the treatment of plates and shells.

[3]The equation of the elastic curve was formulated by James Bernoulli, a Swiss mathematician, in 1694. Leonhard Euler (1707–1783) greatly extended its application.

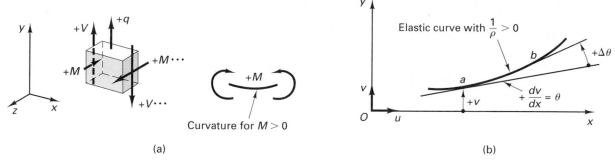

Fig. 14-3   Moment and its relation to curvature.

Generally, only Eq. 14-10 is used in this text, and if biaxial bending occurs, the deflection directions are determined by inspection.

It is important to note that for the elastic curve, at the level of accuracy of Eq. 14-10, one has $ds = dx$. This follows from the fact that, as before, the square of the slope dv/dx is negligibly small compared with unity, and

$$ds = \sqrt{dx^2 + dv^2} = \sqrt{1 + (v')^2}\, dx \approx dx \qquad (14\text{-}11)$$

Thus, in the small-deflection theory, no difference in length is said to exist between the initial length of the beam axis and the arc of the elastic curve. State alternatively, there is no horizontal displacement of the points lying on the neutral surface (i.e., at $y = 0$).

The beam theory discussed here is limited to deflections that are small in relation to span length. However, it is remarkably accurate when compared to exact solutions based on Eq. 14-8. An idea of the accuracy involved may be gained by noting, for example, that there is approximately a 1% error from the exact solution if deflections of a simple span are on the order of one-twentieth of its length. By increasing the deflection to one-tenth of the span length, which ordinarily would be considered an intolerably large deflection, the error is raised to approximately 4%. As stiff flexural members are require in most engineering applications, this limitation of the theory is not serious. For clarity, however, the deflections of beams will be shown greatly exaggerated on all diagrams.

14-4. Alternative Derivation of the Governing Equation

In the classical theories of plates and shells that deal with small deflections, equations analogous to Eq. 14-10 are established. The characteristic approach can be illustrated on the beam problem.

In a deformed condition, point A' on the axis of an unloaded beam, Fig. 14-4, according to Eq. 14-11, is directly above its initial position A. The tangent to the elastic curve at the same point rotates through an angle dv/dx. A plane section with the centroid at A' also rotates through the same angle dv/dx since during bending sections remain normal to the bent axis of a beam. Therefore, the displacement u of a material point at a distance[4] y from the elastic curve is

$$u = -y\frac{dv}{dx} \qquad (14\text{-}12)$$

where the negative sign shows that for positive y and v', the displacement u is toward the origin. For $y = 0$, there is no displacement u, as required by Eq. 14-11.

Next, recall Eq. 3-1, which states that $\varepsilon_x = du/dx$. Therefore, from Eq. 14-12, $\varepsilon_x = -y\,d^2v/dx^2$ since v is a function of x only.

The same normal strain also can be found from Eqs. 5-14 and 8-11, yielding $\varepsilon_x = -My/EI$. On equating the two alternative expressions for ε_x and eliminating y from both sides of the equation,

$$\frac{d^2v}{dx^2} = \frac{M}{EI}$$

which is the previously derived Eq. 14-10.

14-5. Alternative Forms of the Governing Equation

The differential relations among the applied loads, shear, and moment, Eqs. 7-3 and 7-4, can be combined with Eq. 14-10 to yield the following useful sequence of equations:

$$v = \text{deflections of the elastic curve}$$

$$\theta = \frac{dv}{dx} = v' = \text{slope of the elastic curve}$$

$$M = EI\frac{d^2v}{dx^2} = EIv'' \qquad (14\text{-}13)$$

$$V = \frac{dM}{dx} = \frac{d}{dx}\left(EI\frac{d^2v}{dx^2}\right) = (EIv'')'$$

$$q = \frac{dV}{dx} = \frac{d^2}{dx^2}\left(EI\frac{d^2v}{dx^2}\right) = (EIv'')''$$

---

[4]Since angle dv/dx is small, its cosine can be taken as unity.

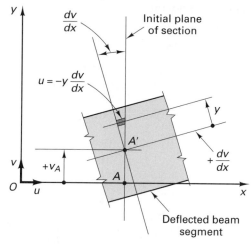

Fig. 14-4   Longitudinal displacements in a beam due to rotation of a plane section.

In applying these relations, the sign convention shown in Fig. 14-3 must be adhered to strictly. For beams with *constant* flexural rigidity EI, Eq. 14-13 simplifies into three alternative governing equations for determining the deflection of a loaded beam:

$$EI\frac{d^2v}{dx^2} = M(x) \qquad \text{(14-14a)}$$

$$EI\frac{d^3v}{dx^3} = V(x) \qquad \text{(14-14b)}$$

$$EI\frac{d^4v}{dx^4} = q(x) \qquad \text{(14-14c)}$$

The choice of one of these equations for determining v depends on the ease with which an expression for load, shear, or moment can be formulated. Fewer constants of integration are needed in the lower-order equations. Equation 14-14b is seldom used, since it is more convenient to begin a solution either with the load function $q(x)$ or the moment function $M(x)$.

14-6. Boundary Conditions

For the solution of beam-deflection problems, in addition to the differential equations, boundary conditions must be prescribed. Several types of homogeneous boundary conditions are as follows:

1. *Clamped or fixed support:* In this case, the displacement v and the slope dv/dx must vanish. Hence, at the end considered, where $x = a$,

$$v(a) = 0 \qquad v'(a) = 0 \tag{14-15a}$$

2. *Roller or pinned support:* At the end considered, no deflection v nor moment M can exist. Hence,

$$v(a) = 0 \qquad M(a) = EIv''(a) = 0 \tag{14-15b}$$

Here the physically evident condition for M is related to the derivative of v with respect to x from Eq. 14-14.

3. *Free end:* Such an end is free of moment and shear. Hence,

$$M(a) = EIv''(a) = 0 \qquad V(a) = (EIv'')'_{x=a} = 0 \tag{14-15c}$$

4. *Guided support:* In this case, free vertical movement is permitted, but the rotation of the end is prevented. The support is not capable of resisting any shear. Therefore,

$$v'(a) = 0 \qquad V(a) = (EIv'')'_{x=a} = 0 \tag{14-15d}$$

The same boundary conditions for beams with *constant EI* are summarized in Fig. 14-5. Note the two basically different types of boundary conditions. Some pertain to the force quantities and are said to be *static boundary conditions*. Others describe geometrical or deformational behavior of an end; these are *kinematic boundary conditions*.

Nonhomogeneous boundary conditions, where a given shear, moment, rotation, or displacement is prescribed at the boundary, also occur in applications. In such cases, the zeros in the appropriate Eqs. 14-15a through 14-15d are replaced by the specified quantity.

These boundary conditions apply both to statically determinate and indeterminate beams. As examples of statically indeterminate single-span beams, consider the three cases shown in Fig. 14-6. The beam in 14-6(a) is indeterminate to the first degree, as any one of the reactions can be removed and the beam will remain stable. In this example, there are no horizontal forces. The boundary conditions shown in Fig. 14-5(a) apply for end A, and those in Fig. 14-5(b), for end B.

The vertical reactions for the beam in 14-6(b) can be found directly from statics. Since the pinned supports cannot move horizontally, there is a tendency for developing horizontal reactions at the supports due to the beam deflection. However, for small beam deflections, according to Eq. 14-11, $ds \approx dx$ and no significant axial strain can develop in transversely loaded beams.[5] Therefore, the horizontal components of the reactions in beams with immovable supports are negligible. On the same basis, no horizontal reactions need be considered for the beam shown in Fig. 14-6(c). Therefore, the beam shown is indeterminate to the second

[5]The horizontal force becomes important in thin plates. See S. Timoshenko and S. Woinowsky-Krieger, *Theory of Plates and Shells,* 2nd ed. (New York: McGraw-Hill, 1959), 6.

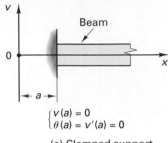

$$\begin{cases} v(a) = 0 \\ \theta(a) = v'(a) = 0 \end{cases}$$

(a) Clamped support

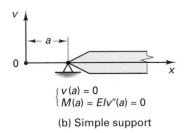

$$\begin{cases} v(a) = 0 \\ M(a) = EIv''(a) = 0 \end{cases}$$

(b) Simple support

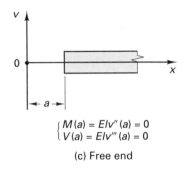

$$\begin{cases} M(a) = EIv''(a) = 0 \\ V(a) = EIv'''(a) = 0 \end{cases}$$

(c) Free end

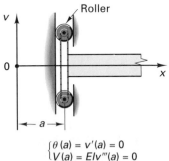

$$\begin{cases} \theta(a) = v'(a) = 0 \\ V(a) = EIv'''(a) = 0 \end{cases}$$

(d) Guided support

Fig. 14-5   Homogeneous boundary conditions for beams with constant EI. In (a) both conditions are *kinematic;* in (c) both are *static;* in (b) and (d), conditions are mixed.

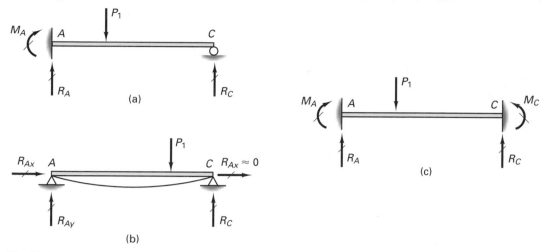

(a)

(b)

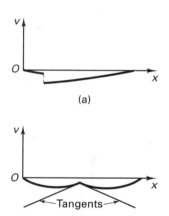

(c)

Fig. 14-6   The beam in (a) is indeterminate to the first degree. If it is assumed that the horizontal reaction component is negligible, the beam in (b) is determinate and in (c) indeterminate to the second degree.

degree. In this case, any two reactive forces can be removed and the beam would remain in equilibrium.

In some problems, discontinuities in the mathematical functions for either load or member stiffness arise along a given span length. Such discontinuities, for example, occur at concentrated forces or moments and at abrupt changes in cross-sectional areas affecting EI. In such cases, the boundary conditions must be supplemented by the physical requirements of *continuity of the elastic curve.* This means that at any juncture of the two zones of a beam where a discontinuity occurs, the deflection and the tangent to the elastic curve must be the same regardless of the direction from which the common point is approached. Unacceptable geometry of elastic curves is illustrated in Fig. 14-7.

By using the singularity functions discussed in Section 14-8, the continuity conditions of the elastic curve are identically satisfied.

(a)

(b)

Fig. 14-7   Unacceptable geometric conditions in a continuous elastic curve.

14-7. Direct Integration Solutions

As a general example of calculating beam deflection, consider Eq. 14-14c, $EIv^{iv} = q(x)$. By successively integrating this expression four times, the formal solution for v is obtained. Thus,

$$EIv^{iv} = EI\frac{d^4v}{dx^4} = EI\frac{d}{dx}(v''') = q(x) \qquad 14\text{-}16a$$

$$EIv''' = \int_0^x q\,dx + C_1$$

$$EIv'' = \int_0^x dx \int_0^x q\, dx + C_1 x + C_2$$

$$EIv' = \int_0^x dx \int_0^x dx \int_0^x q\, dx + C_1 x^2/2 + C_2 x + C_3 \qquad (14\text{-}16b)$$

$$EIv = \int_0^x dx \int_0^x dx \int_0^x dx \int_0^x q\, dx + C_1 x^3/3! + C_2 x^2/2! + C_3 x + C_4$$

In these equations the constants C_1, C_2, C_3, and C_4 have a special physical meaning. Since, per Eq. 14-14b, $EIv''' = V$, by substituting this relation into the second of Eqs. 14-16 and simplifying, Eq. 7-6 is reproduced; that is,

$$V = \int_0^x q\, dx + C_1 \qquad (7\text{-}6)$$

By substituting this relation into Eq. 7-7 and integrating, a different form of Eq. 7-7 is obtained.

$$M = \int_0^x dx \int_0^x q\, dx + C_1 x + C_2 \qquad (14\text{-}17)$$

The right side of this equation is identical to the third of Eqs. 14-16.

These results unequivocally show that the constants C_1 and C_2 are a part of the equilibrium equations and are the *static boundary conditions*. At this point, no kinematics nor material properties enter the problem. However, next, by dividing M by EI for substitution into Eq. 14-10, these properties are brought in, limiting the solutions to the *elastic* behavior of *prismatic* beams. Thus, rewriting Eq. 14-10, for clarity, in several different forms,

$$\frac{d^2v}{dx^2} = \frac{d}{dx}\left(\frac{dv}{dx}\right) = \frac{dv'}{dx} = \frac{M}{EI} \qquad (14\text{-}18)$$

Then, using Eq. 14-17 and integrating twice, the last two relations in Eqs. 14-16 are reproduced. These two equations, and the associated new constants of integration C_3 and C_4, define slope and deflection of the elastic curve (i.e., they describe the kinematics of a laterally loaded beam). These constants are the *kinematic boundary conditions*.

If, instead of Eq. 14-14c, one starts with Eq. 14-14a, $EIv'' = M(x)$, after two integrations the solution is

$$EIv = \int_0^x dx \int_0^x M\, dx + C_3 x + C_4 \qquad (14\text{-}19)$$

In both equations, constants C_1, C_2, C_3, and C_4 must be determined from the conditions at the boundaries. In Eq. 14-19, constants C_1 and C_2 are incorporated into the expression of M. Constants C_1, C_2, C_3/EI, and C_4/EI, respectively, are usually[6] the initial values of V, M, θ, and v at the origin.

The first term on the right-hand side of the last part of Eq. 14-16 and the corresponding one in Eq. 14-19 are the particular solutions of the respective differential equations. The one in Eq. 14-16 is especially interesting as it depends only on the loading condition of the beam. This term remains the same regardless of the prescribed boundary conditions, whereas the *constants* are determined from the boundary conditions.

If the loading, shear, and moment functions are continuous and the flexural rigidity EI is constant, the evaluation of the particular integrals is very direct. When discontinuities occur, solutions can be found for each segment of a beam in which the functions are continuous; the complete solution is then achieved by enforcing continuity conditions at the common boundaries of the beam segments. Alternatively, graphical or numerical procedures[7] of successive integrations can be used very effectively in the solution of practical problems.

Any one of Eqs. 14-14 or 14-16 can be used for finding beam deflection. The choice depends entirely on the initial data and the amount of work necessary for solving a problem. If one begins with the applied load, all four integrations must be performed. On the other hand, if the bending-moment function is written, the number of required integrations is reduced to two.

Procedure Summary   The same *three basic concepts* of engineering mechanics of solids repeatedly applied before are used in developing the elastic deflection theory of beams. These may be summarized as follows:

1. *Equilibrium conditions* (statics) are used for a beam element to establish the relationships between the applied load and shear, Eq. 7-3, as well as between the shear and bending moment, Eq. 7-4.
2. *Geometry of deformation* (kinematics) is used by assuming that plane sections through a beam element remain plane after deformation. Such planes intersect and define beam strains and the radius of curvature for an element. Although in the aforementioned sense the expression for curvature, Eq. 14-4, is exact, the theory is limited to small deflections, since $\sin \theta$ is approximated by θ, Eq. 14-9. No warpage due to shear of sections is accounted for in the formulation.
3. *Properties of materials* (constitutive relations) in the form of Hooke's law, Eq. 2-8, are assumed to apply only to longitudinal normal stresses and strains. Poisson's effect is neglected.

---

[6]In certain cases where transcendental functions are used, these constants do not have this meaning. Basically, the whole function, which includes the constants of integration, must satisfy the conditions at the boundary.

[7]Such procedures are useful in complicated problems. For example, see N. M. Newmark, "Numerical procedure for computing deflections, moments, and buckling loads," *Trans. ASCE*, **108** (1943), 1161. Finite element solutions of such problems are now widely used in practice.

A solution of any one of Eqs. 14-14a, 14-14b, or 14-14c,[8] *subject to the prescribed boundary conditions,* constitutes a solution of a given transversely loaded elastic beam problem. These equations are equally applicable to statically determinate *and* statically indeterminate beam problems.[9] However, the solutions are simpler if the functions $q(x)$ and $I(x)$ are continuous across a span. When discontinuities in either $q(x)$ or $I(x)$ occur, continuity of the elastic curve at such points must be maintained. If I is constant, singularity functions for describing the loads can be effectively used.

It is to be noted that although at load and cross-section discontinuities large local perturbations in strain and stresses develop, beam deflections are less sensitive to these effects. Deflections are determined using integration, a process tending to smooth out the function.

Several illustrative examples of statically determinate and statically indeterminate beam problems follow. The applications of singularity functions for elastic beam deflections is given in the next section.

Example 14-2

A bending moment M_1 is applied at the free end of a cantilever of length L and of constant flexural rigidity EI, Fig. 14-8(a). Find the equation of the elastic curve.

SOLUTION

The boundary conditions are recorded near the figure from *inspection* of the conditions at the ends. At $x = L$, $M(L) = +M_1$, a nonhomogeneous condition.

From a free-body diagram of Fig. 14-8(b), it can be observed that the bending moment is $+M_1$ throughout the beam. By applying Eq. 14-14a, integrating successively, and making use of the boundary conditions, one obtains the solution for v:

$$EI\frac{d^2v}{dx^2} = M = M_1$$

$$EI\frac{dv}{dx} = M_1x + C_3$$

But $\theta(0) = 0$; hence, at $x = 0$, one has $EIv'(0) = C_3 = 0$ and

$$EI\frac{dv}{dx} = M_1x$$

---

[8] The adopted sign convention for applied loads and shear results in all Eqs. 14-13 and 14-14 having positive signs, an advantage in hand calculations.

[9] This is analogous to the axially loaded bar problems discussed in Section 4-7.

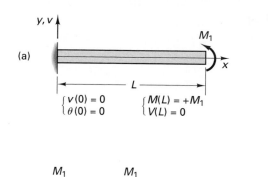

(a)

$$\begin{cases} v(0) = 0 \\ \theta(0) = 0 \end{cases} \qquad \begin{cases} M(L) = +M_1 \\ V(L) = 0 \end{cases}$$

(b)

(c)

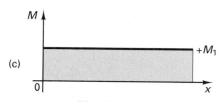

Fig. 14-8

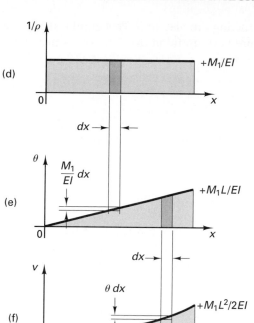

(d)

(e)

(f)

$$EIv = \frac{1}{2} M_1 x^2 + C_4$$

But $v(0) = 0$; hence, $EIv(0) = C_4 = 0$ and

$$v = \frac{M_1 x^2}{2EI} \qquad (14\text{-}20)$$

The positive sign of the result indicates that the deflection due to M_1 is upward. The largest value of v occurs at $x = L$. The slope of the elastic curve at the free end is $+M_1 L/EI$ radians.

Equation 14-20 shows that the elastic curve is a parabola. However, every element of the beam experiences equal moments and deforms alike. Therefore, the elastic curve should be a part of a circle. The inconsistency results from the use of an approximate relation for the curvature $1/\rho$. It can be shown that the error committed is in the ratio of $(\rho - v)^3$ to ρ^3. As the deflection v is much smaller than ρ, the error is very small.

It is important to associate the foregoing successive integration procedure with a graphical solution or interpretation. This is shown in the sequence of Figs. 14-8(c) through (f). First, the conventional moment diagram is shown. Then, using Eqs. 14-9 and 14-10, $1/\rho \approx d^2v/dx^2 = M/EI$, the curvature diagram is plotted in Fig. 14-8(d). For the elastic case, this is simply a plot of M/EI. By integrating the curvature diagram, one obtains the θ diagram. In the next integration, the elastic curve is obtained. In this example, since the beam is fixed at the origin, the conditions $\theta(0) = 0$ and

$v(0) = 0$ are used in constructing the diagrams. This graphical approach or its numerical equivalents are very useful in the solution of problems with variable EI.

Example 14-3

A simple beam supports a uniformly distributed downward load w_o. The flexural rigidity EI is constant. Find the elastic curve by the following three methods: (a) Use the second-order differential equation to obtain the deflection of the beam. (b) Use the fourth-order equation instead of the one in part (a). (c) Illustrate a graphical solution of the problem.

SOLUTION

(a) A diagram of the beam together with the given boundary conditions is shown in Fig. 14-9(a). The expression for M for use in the second-order differential equation has been found in Example 7-8. From Fig. 7-19,

$$M = \frac{w_o L x}{2} - \frac{w_o x^2}{2}$$

Substituting this relation into Eq. 14-14a, integrating it twice, and using the boundary conditions, one finds the equation of the elastic curve:

$$EI \frac{d^2 v}{dx^2} = M = \frac{w_o L x}{2} - \frac{w_o x^2}{2}$$

$$EI \frac{dv}{dx} = \frac{w_o L x^2}{4} - \frac{w_o x^3}{6} + C_3$$

$$EIv = \frac{w_o L x^3}{12} - \frac{w_o x^4}{24} + C_3 x + C_4$$

But $v(0) = 0$; hence, $EIv(0) = 0 = C_4$; and, since $v(L) = 0$,

$$EIv(L) = 0 = \frac{w_o L^4}{24} + C_3 L \quad \text{and} \quad C_3 = -\frac{w_o L^3}{24}$$

(14-21)

$$v = -\frac{w_o x}{24EI}(L^3 - 2Lx^2 + x^3)$$

Because of symmetry, the largest deflection occurs at $x = L/2$. On substituting this value of x into Eq. 14-21, one obtains

$$|v|_{max} = \frac{5 w_o L^4}{384 EI}$$

(14-22)

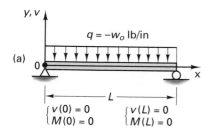

(a)

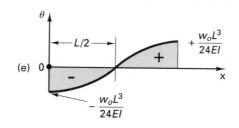

(e)

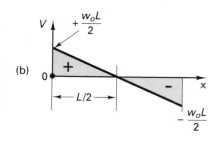

(b)

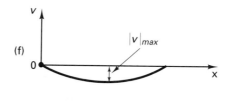

(f)

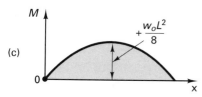

(c)

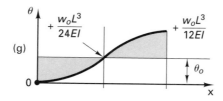

(g)

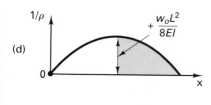

(d)

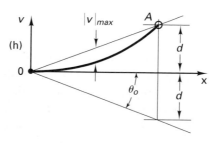

(h)

Fig. 14-9

The condition of symmetry could also have been used to determine constant C_3. Since it is known that $v'(L/2) = 0$, one has

$$EIv'(L/2) = \frac{w_oL(L/2)^2}{4} - \frac{w_o(L/2)^3}{6} + C_3 = 0$$

and, as before, $C_3 = -w_oL^3/24$.

(b) Application of Eq. 14-14c to the solution of this problem is direct. The constants are found from the boundary conditions.

$$EI\frac{d^4v}{dx^4} = q(x) = -w_o$$

$$EI\frac{d^3v}{dx^3} = -w_o x + C_1$$

$$EI\frac{d^2v}{dx^2} = -\frac{w_o x^2}{2} + C_1 x + C_2$$

But $M(0) = 0$; hence, $EIv'''(0) = 0 = C_2$; and, since $M(L) = 0$,

$$EIv''(L) = 0 = -\frac{w_o L^2}{2} + C_1 L \qquad \text{or} \qquad C_1 = \frac{w_o L}{2}$$

hence,

$$EI\frac{d^2v}{dx^2} = \frac{w_o Lx}{2} - \frac{w_o x^2}{2}$$

The remainder of the problem is the same as in part (a). In this approach, no preliminary calculation of reactions is required. As will be shown later, this is advantageous in some statically indeterminate problems.

(c) The steps needed for a graphical solution of the complete problem are in Figs. 14-9(b) through (f). In Figs. 14-9(b) and (c), the conventional shear and moment diagrams are shown. The curvature diagram is obtained by plotting M/EI, as in Fig. 14-9(d).

Since, by virtue of symmetry, the slope to the elastic curve at $x = L/2$ is horizontal, $\theta(L/2) = 0$. Therefore, the construction of the θ diagram can be begun from the center. In this procedure, the right ordinate in Fig. 14-9(e) must equal the shaded area of Fig. 14-4(d), and vice versa. By summing the θ diagram, one finds the elastic deflection v. The shaded area of Fig. 14-9(e) is equal numerically to the maximum deflection. In the foregoing, the condition of symmetry was employed. A generally applicable procedure follows.

After the curvature diagram is established as in Fig. 14-9(d), the θ diagram can be constructed with an assumed initial value of θ at the origin. For example, let $\theta(0) = 0$ and sum the curvature diagram to obtain the θ diagram, Fig. 14-9(g). Note that the shape of the curve so found is identical to that of Fig. 14-9(e). Summing the area of the θ diagram gives the elastic curve. In Fig. 14-9(h), this curve extends from 0 to A. This violates the boundary condition at A, where the deflection must be zero. Correct deflections are given, however, by measuring them vertically from a straight line passing through 0 and A. This inclined line corrects the deflection ordinates caused by the incorrectly assumed $\theta(0)$. In fact, after constructing Fig. 14-9(h), one knows that $\theta(0) = -d/L = -w_o L^3/24EI$. When this value of $\theta(0)$ is used, the problem reverts to the preceding solution, Figs. 14-9(e) and (f). In Fig. 14-9(h), inclined measurements have no meaning. The procedure described is applicable for beams with overhangs. In such cases, the base line for measuring deflections must pass through the support points.

Example 14-4

A beam fixed at both ends supports a uniformly distributed downward load w_o, Fig 14-10(a). The EI for the beam is constant. (a) Find the expression for the elastic curve using the fourth-order governing differential equation. (b) Verify the results found using the second-order differential equation.

SOLUTION

(a) As discussed in connection with Fig. 14-6(c), this beam is statically inde-terminate to the second degree since horizontal reactions are assumed to be zero. The solution is obtained by four successive integrations of Eq. 14-14c in a manner shown in Eqs. 14-16. Then the constants of integration are found from the boundary conditions.

$$EI\frac{d^4v}{dx^4} = q(x) = -w_o$$

$$EI\frac{d^3v}{dx^3} = -w_ox + C_1$$

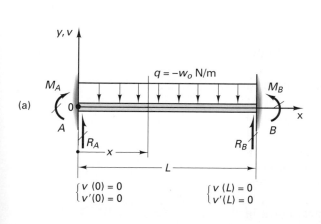

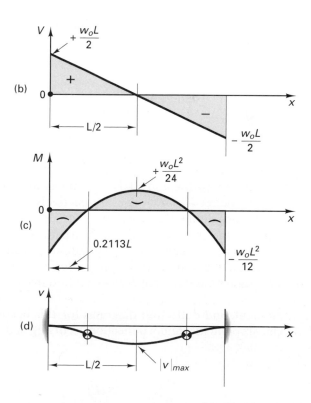

Fig. 14-10

$$EI\frac{d^2v}{dx^2} = -\frac{w_o x^2}{2} + C_1 x + C_2$$

$$EI\frac{dv}{dx} = -\frac{w_o x^3}{6} + C_1\frac{x^2}{2} + C_2 x + C_3$$

$$EIv = -\frac{w_o x^4}{24} + C_1\frac{x^3}{6} + C_2\frac{x^2}{2} + C_3 x + C_4$$

Four kinematic boundary conditions are available for determining the constants of integration:

$$EIv(0) = EIv_A = 0 = C_4$$

$$EIv'(0) = EIv'_A = 0 = C_3$$

$$EIv(L) = EIv_B = 0 = -\frac{w_o L^4}{24} + C_1\frac{L^3}{6} + C_2\frac{L^2}{2}$$

$$EIv'(L) = EIv'_B = 0 = -\frac{w_o L^3}{6} + C_1\frac{L^2}{2} + C_2 L$$

Constants C_3 and C_4 do not enter the last two equations since they are zero. By solving the last two equations simultaneously.

$$C_1 = \frac{w_o L}{2} \quad \text{and} \quad C_2 = -\frac{w_o L^2}{12}$$

By substituting these constants into the equation for the elastic curve, after algebraic simplifications,

$$v = -\frac{w_o x^2}{24EI}(L - x)^2 \tag{14-23}$$

According to Eqs. 14-14a and 14-14b, EI times the second and third derivatives of the deflection $v(x)$ gives, respectively, $M(x)$ and $V(x)$. At $x = 0$, these relations define the reactions at A. Hence, C_1 is the vertical reaction and C_2 is the moment at this support. In this case, because of symmetry, the vertical reactions can be found directly from statics. However, this is not necessary in this typical solution of a *boundary-value problem*. The moment and shear at B can be found from the same expressions at $x = L$.

Shear, moment, and deflection diagrams for this beam are shown in Fig. 14-10. The absolute maximum deflection occurring in the middle of the span is

$$|v|_{\text{max}} = \frac{w_o L^4}{384EI} \tag{14-24}$$

(b) This solution is found using Eq. 14-14a, and, although the vertical reaction at A can be determined directly from statics, it will be treated as an unknown. On this basis,

$$EI\frac{d^2v}{dx^2} = M(x) = M_A + R_A x - \frac{w_o x^2}{2}$$

Integrating twice,

$$EI\frac{dv}{dx} = M_A x + R_A\frac{x^2}{2} - \frac{w_o x^3}{6} + C_3$$

$$EIv = M_A\frac{x^2}{2} + R_A\frac{x^3}{6} - \frac{w_o x^4}{24} + C_3 x + C_4$$

Constants C_3 and C_4 *as well as* R_A and M_A are found from the four kinematic boundary conditions:

$$EIv(0) = EIv_A = 0 = C_4$$

$$EIv'(0) = EIv'^A = 0 = C_3$$

$$EIv(L) = EIv_B = 0 = M_A\frac{L^2}{2} + R_A\frac{L^3}{6} - \frac{w_o L^4}{24}$$

$$EIv'(L) = EIv'_B = 0 = M_A L + R_A\frac{L^2}{2} - \frac{w_o L^4}{6}$$

Solving the last two equations simultaneously,

$$R_A = \frac{w_o L}{2} \qquad \text{and} \qquad M_A = -\frac{w_o L^2}{12}$$

Substituting these expressions into the equation for deflection *with* $C_3 = C_4 = 0$, Eq. 14-23 is again obtained.

Example 14-5

Determine the equation of the elastic curve for the uniformly loaded continuous beam shown in Fig. 14-11(a). Use the second-order differential equation. *EI* is constant.

SOLUTION

Because of symmetry, the solution can be confined to determining the deflection for either span. Also, because of symmetry, it can be concluded that at the middle support, not only is the deflection zero, but since the elastic curve cannot rotate in either direction, its slope is also zero. In this

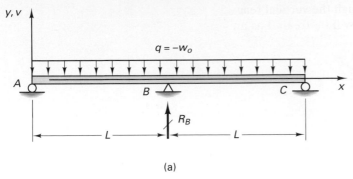

(a)

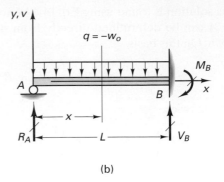

(b)

Fig. 14-11

manner, the problem can be reduced to the one-degree statically indeterminate problem shown in Fig. 14-11(b) with known boundary conditions.

By using Eq. 14-14a, the solution proceeds in the usual manner. First, an expression for $M(x)$ is formulated and two successive integrations of the differential equation are performed. Boundary conditions provide the necessary information for determining the constants of integration *and* an unknown reaction R_A.

Second-order differential-equation solution:

$$EI\frac{d^2v}{dx^2} = M(x) = R_A x - \frac{w_o x^2}{2}$$

$$EI\frac{dv}{dx} = R_A\frac{x^2}{2} - \frac{w_o x^3}{6} + C_3$$

$$EIv = R_A\frac{x^3}{6} - \frac{w_o x^4}{24} + C_3 x + C_4$$

Boundary conditions:

$$EIv(0) = EIv_A = 0 = C_4$$

$$EIv'(L) = EIv'_B = 0 = R_A\frac{L^2}{2} - \frac{w_o L^3}{6} + C_3$$

$$EIv(L) = EIv_B = 0 = R_A\frac{L^3}{6} - \frac{w_o L^4}{24} + C_3 L$$

By solving the last two equations simultaneously,

$$R_A = \frac{3w_o L}{8} \qquad \text{and} \qquad C_3 = -\frac{w_o L^3}{48}$$

which, upon substitution into the equation for the elastic curve, leads to

$$v = -\frac{w_o x}{48EI}(L^3 - 3Lx^2 + 2x^3) \tag{14-25}$$

From symmetry, the reactions at A and C are equal, and, by using statics, the reaction at B is

$$R_B = \frac{5w_oL}{4} \qquad (14\text{-}26)$$

This reaction is also numerically equal to $2V_B$.

Example 14-6

A simple beam supports a concentrated downward force P at a distance a from the left support, Fig. 14-12(a). The flexural rigidity EI is constant. Find the equation of the elastic curve by successive integration.

SOLUTION
The solution will be obtained using the second-order differential equation. The reactions and boundary conditions are noted in Fig. 14-12(a). The moment diagram plotted in Fig. 14-12(b) clearly shows a discontinuity in $M(x)$ at $x = a$, requiring two different functions. At first, the solution proceeds independently for each segment of the beam.

For segment AD

$$\frac{d^2v}{dx^2} = \frac{M}{EI} = \frac{Pb}{EIL}x$$

For segment DB

$$\frac{d^2v}{dx^2} = \frac{M}{EI} = \frac{Pa}{EI} - \frac{Pa}{EIL}x$$

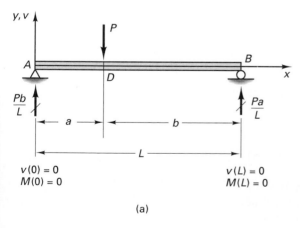

$v(0) = 0$

$M(0) = 0$

$v(L) = 0$

$M(L) = 0$

(a)

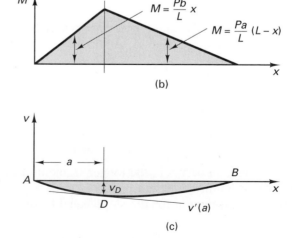

$M = \frac{Pb}{L}x$

$M = \frac{Pa}{L}(L-x)$

(b)

(c)

Fig. 14-12

$$\frac{dv}{dx} = \frac{Pb}{EIL} \frac{x^2}{2} + A_1 \qquad\qquad \frac{dv}{dx} = \frac{Pa}{EI} x - \frac{Pa}{EIL} \frac{x^2}{2} + B_1$$

$$v = \frac{Pb}{EIL} \frac{x^3}{6} + A_1 x + A_2 \qquad\qquad v = \frac{Pa}{EI} \frac{x^3}{2} - \frac{Pa}{EIL} \frac{x^3}{6} + B_1 x + B_2$$

To determine the four constants $A_1, A_2, B_1,$ and $B_2,$ two boundary and two continuity conditions must be used.

For segment AD:

$$v(0) = 0 = A_2$$

For segment DB:

$$v(L) = 0 = \frac{PaL^2}{3EI} + B_1 L + B_2$$

Equating deflections for both segments at $x = a,$

$$v_D = v(a) = \frac{Pa^3 b}{6EIL} + A_1 a = \frac{Pa^3}{2EI} - \frac{Pa^4}{6EIL} + B_1 a + B_2$$

Equating slopes for both segments at $x = a,$

$$\theta_D = v(a) = \frac{Pa^2 b}{2EIL} + A_1 = \frac{Pa^2}{EI} - \frac{Pa^3}{2EIL} + B_1$$

Upon solving the four equations simultaneously, one finds

$$A_1 = -\frac{Pb}{6EIL}(L^2 - b^2) \qquad A_2 = 0$$

$$B_1 = -\frac{Pa}{6EIL}(2L^2 + a^2) \qquad B_2 = \frac{Pa^3}{6EI}$$

With these constants, for example, the elastic curve for segment AD of the beam, after algebraic simplification, becomes

$$v = -\frac{Pbx}{6EIL}(L^2 - b^2 - x^2) \qquad\qquad (14\text{-}27)$$

Deflection v_D at applied force P is

$$v_D = v(a) = -\frac{Pa^2 b^2}{3EIL} \qquad\qquad (14\text{-}28)$$

The largest deflection occurs in the longer segment of the beam. If $a > b,$ the point of maximum deflection is at $x = \sqrt{a(a + 2b)/3},$ which follows from setting the expression for the slope equal to zero. The deflection at this point is

$$|v|_{max} = \frac{Pb(L^2 - b^2)^{3/2}}{9\sqrt{3}\ EIL} \qquad\qquad (14\text{-}29)$$

Usually, the deflection at the center of the span is very nearly equal to the numerically largest deflection. Such a deflection is much simpler to determine, which recommends its use. If force P is applied at the middle of the span, when $a = b = L/2$, by direct substitution into Eq. 14-28 or 14-29.

$$|v|_{\text{max}} = \frac{PL^3}{48EI} \qquad (14\text{-}30)$$

Here it is helpful to recall the definition of the *spring constant,* or *stiffness, k* given by Eq. 3-6. In the present context, for a force P placed at an arbitrary distance a from a support,

$$k = \frac{P}{v_B} = \frac{3EIL}{a^2b^2} \qquad (14\text{-}31)$$

For a particular case, when $a = b = L/2$, this equation reduces to

$$k_o = \frac{48EI}{L^3} \qquad (14\text{-}32)$$

This expression also follows directly from Eq. 14-30.

The previous equations are useful in static and dynamic analyses and are essential in vibration analysis.

The solution of deflection problems having discontinuous load functions is greatly facilitated with the use of singularity functions, discussed in the next section.

Example 14-7

A simply supported beam 5 m long is loaded with a 20-N downward force at a point 4 m from the left support, Fig. 14-13(a). The moment of inertia of the cross section of the beam is $4I_1$ for segment AB and I_1 for the remainder of the beam. Determine the elastic curve.

SOLUTION

A similar problem was solved in the preceding example. Another useful technique will be illustrated here that is convenient in some complicated problems where different M/EI expressions are applicable to several segments of the beam. This method consists of selecting an origin at one end of the beam and carrying out successive integrations until expressions for θ and v are obtained for the first segment. The values of θ and v are then determined at the end of the first segment. Due to continuity conditions, these become the initial constants in the integrations carried out for the next segment. This process is repeated until the far end of the beam is reached; then the boundary conditions are imposed to determine the remaining unknown

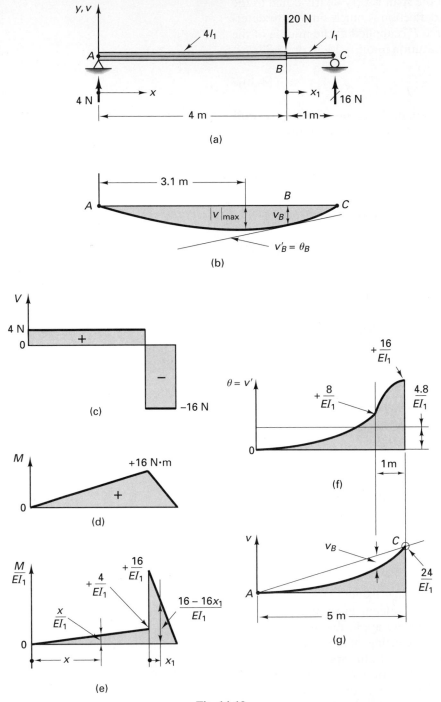

Fig. 14-13

constants. A new origin is used at every juncture of the segments, and all x's are taken to be positive in the same direction.

For segment AB, $0 < x < 4$:

$$M = 4x \quad \text{and} \quad EI = 4EI_1$$

$$\frac{d^2v}{dx^2} = \frac{M}{EI} = \frac{x}{EI_1}$$

$$\theta = \frac{dv}{dx} = \frac{x^2}{2EI_1} + A_1$$

$$v = \frac{x^3}{6EI_1} + A_1x + A_2$$

At $x = 0$, $v(0) = v_A = 0$ and $\theta(0) = \theta_A$. Hence, $A_1 = \theta_A$ and $A_2 = 0$.

At the end of segment AB:

$$\theta(4) = \theta_B = \frac{8}{EI_1} + \theta_A \quad \text{and} \quad v(4) = v_B = \frac{32}{3EI_1} + 4\theta_A$$

For segment BC, $0 < x_1 < 1$:

$$M = 4(4 + x_1) - 20x_1 = 16 - 16x_1 \quad \text{and} \quad EI = EI_1$$

$$\frac{d^2v}{dx_1^2} = \frac{16}{EI_1} - \frac{16x_1}{EI_1}$$

$$\theta = \frac{dv}{dx_1} = \frac{16x_1}{EI_1} - \frac{8x_1^2}{EI_1} + A_3$$

$$v = \frac{8x_1^2}{EI_1} - \frac{8x_1^3}{3EI_1} + A_3x_1 + A_4$$

At $x_1 = 0$, $v(0) = v_B$ and $\theta(0) = \theta_B$. Hence, from the solution before, $A_4 = v_B = 32/3EI_1 + 4\theta_A$, and $A_3 = \theta_B = 8/EI_1 + \theta_A$. The expressions for θ and v in segment BC are then obtained as

$$\theta = \frac{16x_1}{EI_1} - \frac{8x_1^2}{EI_1} + \frac{8}{EI_1} + \theta_A$$

$$v = \frac{8x_1^2}{EI_1} - \frac{8x_1^3}{3EI_1} + \frac{8x_1}{EI_1} + \theta_Ax_1 + \frac{32}{3EI_1} + 4\theta_A$$

Finally, the boundary condition at C is applied to determine the value of θ_A. At $x_1 = 1$, $v(1) = v_c = 0$; therefore,

$$0 = \frac{8}{EI_1} - \frac{8}{3EI_1} + \frac{8}{EI_1} + \theta_A + \frac{32}{3EI_1} + 4\theta_A \quad \text{and} \quad \theta_A = -\frac{4.8}{EI_1}$$

Substituting this value of θ_A into the respective expressions for θ and v, equations for these quantities can be obtained for either segment. For example, the equation for the slope in segment AB is $\theta = x^2/2EI_1 - 24/5EI_1$. Upon setting this quantity equal to zero, x is found to be 3.1 m. The maximum deflection occurs at this value of x, and $|v|_{max} = 9.95/EI_1$. Characteristically, the deflection at the center of the span (at $x = 2.5$ m) is nearly the same, being $9.4/EI_1$.

A self-explanatory graphical procedure is shown in Figs. 14-13(d) through (g). Variations in I cause virtually no complications in the graphical solution, a great advantage in complex problems. Multiple origins can be used as shown in Fig. 14-14 to simplify the numerical work, as in the present example.

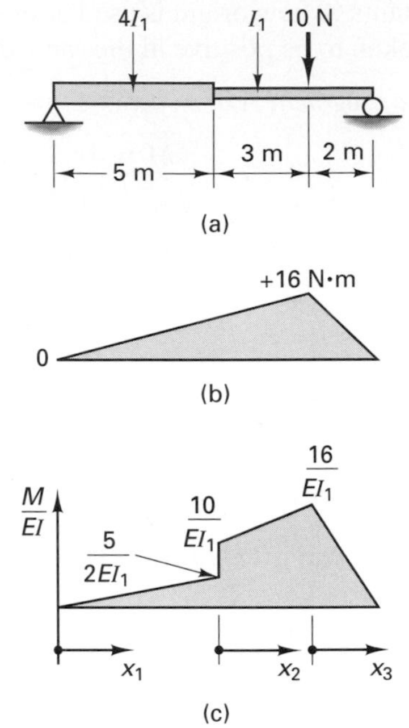

Fig. 14-14   Multiple origins of x.

14-8. Singularity Functions for Beams

The possibility of writing symbolic mathematical expressions for discontinuous functions of load, shear, and moment along a beam using singularity functions was introduced in Section 7-14. These functions can be used very effectively for the solution of statically determinate and indeterminate beam deflection problems. However, it is best to limit their applications to *prismatic beams of constant EI*. Otherwise, considerable complexities arise.

Besides the convenience of solving with singularity function beams of single spans, these functions can also be applied for beams on several supports. In either case, a single symbolic mathematical function for the forces acting on a beam, together with Eq. 14-14c, upon successive integrations gives the solution for a deflection in a problem.[10]

Two illustrative examples follow.

Example 14-8

Rework Example 14-6 using singularity functions.

SOLUTIONS
First, the singularity function for the concerned downward force P is written for the right side of Eq. 14-16. This is followed by successive integrations determining the constants of integrations as convenient.

$$EI\frac{d^4v}{dx^4} = q(x) = -P\langle x - a\rangle_*^{-1}$$

---

[10]Singularity functions can also be used for constructing influence lines for prismatic beams. The required special functions for such problems are given in E. P. Popov, *Introduction to Mechanics of Solids* (Englewood Cliffs, NJ: Prentice Hall, 1968), 403–405.

$$EI\frac{d^3v}{dx_3} = -P\langle x - a\rangle^0 + C_1$$

$$EI\frac{d^2v}{dx^2} = -P\langle x - a\rangle^1 + C_1x + C_2$$

But $M(L) = 0$; hence, $EIv''(0) = 0 = C_2$; and also since $M(L) = 0$,

$$EIv''(L) = -Pb + C_1L = 0 \qquad \text{or} \qquad C_1 = Pb/L$$

$$EI\frac{dv}{dx} = -\frac{P}{2}\langle x - a\rangle^2 + \frac{Pb}{2L}x^2 + C_3$$

$$EIv = -\frac{P}{6}\langle x - a\rangle^3 + \frac{Pb}{6L}x^3 + C_3x + C_4$$

But $v(0) = 0$; hence, $EIv(0) = 0 = C_4$. Similarly, from $v(L) = 0$,

$$EIv(L) = 0 = -\frac{Pb^3}{6} + \frac{PbL^2}{6} + C_3L \qquad \text{or} \qquad C_3 = -\frac{Pb}{6L}(L^2 - b^2)$$

$$v = \frac{Pb}{6EIL}\left[x^3 - (L^2 - b^2)x - \frac{L}{b}\langle x - a\rangle^3\right] \qquad (14\text{-}33)$$

This equation applies to the entire span. For $0 < x < a$, the last term must be omitted. This reduced expression agrees with Eq. 14-27 found earlier.

Example 14-9

Rework Example 14-5 using a singularity function.

SOLUTION

In applying Eq. 14-14c using a singularity function, the whole continuous span for this beam is considered. The unknown reaction R_B is treated as a concentrated upward force. Here, besides the four boundary conditions, it should be noted that the deflection at B is zero. This is a general approach as symmetry in the problem is not utilized.

$$EI\frac{d^4v}{dx^4} = q(x) = -w_o + R_B\langle x - L\rangle_*^{-1}$$

$$EI\frac{d^3v}{dx^3} = -w_ox + R_B\langle x - L\rangle^0 + C_1$$

$$EI\frac{d^2v}{dx^2} = -\frac{w_ox^2}{2} + R_B\langle x - L\rangle^1 + C_1x + C_2$$

$$EI\frac{dv}{dx} = -\frac{w_o x^3}{6} + R_B\frac{\langle x - L\rangle^2}{2} + C_1\frac{x^2}{2} + C_2 x + C_3$$

$$EIv = -\frac{w_o x^4}{24} + R_B\frac{\langle x - L\rangle^3}{6} + C_1\frac{x^3}{6} + C_2\frac{x^2}{2} + C_3 x + C_4$$

Static and kinematic conditions at A, B, and C provide information for determining the constants of integration:

$$EIv''(0) = 0: \qquad\qquad\qquad\qquad\qquad\qquad C_2 = 0$$

$$EIv(0) = 0: \qquad\qquad\qquad\qquad\qquad\qquad C_4 = 0$$

$$EIv(L) = 0: \qquad\qquad -\frac{w_o L^4}{24} + C_1\frac{L^3}{6} + C_3 L = 0$$

$$EIv(2L) = 0: \quad -\frac{2w_o L^4}{3} + R_B\frac{L^3}{6} + C_1\frac{4L^3}{3} + 2C_3 L = 0$$

$$EIv''(2L) = 0: \qquad\qquad -2w_o L^2 + R_B L + 2C_1 L = 0$$

Solving the last three equations simultaneously,

$$C_1 = \frac{3}{8}w_o L \qquad C_3 = -\frac{w_o L^3}{48} \qquad \text{and} \qquad R_B = \frac{5}{4}w_o L$$

Substituting these constants into the equation for beam deflection,

$$v = -\frac{w_o}{48EI}\left(2x^4 - 3Lx^3 + L^3 x - 10L\langle x - L\rangle^3\right)$$

The first three terms in the parentheses agree with those found in Example 14-5. The last term in this equation applies only for $x > L$ when it becomes $10L(x - L)^3$.

14-9. Deflections by Superposition

The integration procedures discussed before for obtaining the elastic deflections of loaded beams are generally applicable. The reader must realize, however, that numerous problems with different loadings have been solved and are readily available.[11] Nearly all the tabulated solutions are made for simple loading conditions. Therefore, in practice, the deflections of beams subjected to several or complicated loading conditions are usually synthesized from the simpler loadings, using the *principle of superposition*. For example, the problem in Fig. 14-15 can be separated into three different cases as shown. The algebraic sum of the three separate solutions gives the total deflection.

[11]See any civil or mechanical engineering handbook.

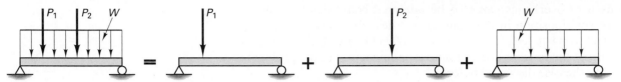

Fig. 14-15 Resolution of a complex problem into several simpler problems.

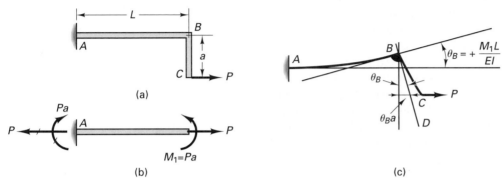

Fig. 14-16 A method of analyzing deflections of frames.

The superposition procedure for determining elastic deflection of beams can be extended to structural systems consisting of several flexural members. For example, consider the simple frame shown in Fig. 14-16(a), for which the deflection of point C due to applied force P is sought. The deflection of vertical leg BC alone can be found by treating it as a cantilever fixed at B. However, due to the applied load, joint B deflects and rotates. This is determined by studying the behavior of member AB.

A free-body diagram for member AB is shown in Fig. 14-16(b). This member is seen to resist axial force P and a moment $M_1 = Pa$. Usually, the effect of axial force P on deflections due to bending can be neglected.[12] The axial elongation of a member usually is also very small in comparison with the bending deflections. Therefore, the problem here can be reduced to that of determining the deflection and rotation of B caused by an end moment M_1. This solution was obtained in Example 14-2, giving the angle θ_B shown in Fig. 14-16(c). By multiplying angle θ_B by length a of the vertical member, the deflection of point C due to rotation of joint B is determined. Then the cantilever deflection of member BC treated alone is increased by $\theta_B a$. The vertical deflection of C is equal to the vertical deflection of point B.

In interpreting the shape of deformed structures, such as shown in Fig. 14-16(c), it must be kept clearly in mind that the deformations are greatly exaggerated. In the small deformation theory discussed here, the cosines of all small angles such as θ_B are taken to equal unity. Both the deflections and the rotations of the elastic curve are small.

[12]See Section 16-9 on beam columns.

Beams with overhangs can also be analyzed conveniently using the concept of superposition in the manner just described. For example, the portion of a beam between the supports, as AB in Fig. 14-17(a), is isolated[13] and rotation of the tangent at B is found. The remainder of the problem is analogous to the case discussed before.

Approximations similar to those just discussed are also made in composite structures. In Fig. 14-8(a), for example, a simple beam rests on a rigid support at one end and on a yielding support with a spring constant k at the other end. If R_B is the reaction at B, support B settles $\Delta = R_B/k$, Fig. 14-18(b). A rigid beam would assume the alignment of line AB', making an angle $\theta_1 = \tan^{-1}(\Delta/L) \approx \Delta/L$ radians with the horizontal line. For an elastic beam, the elastic curve between A and B' may be found in the usual manner. However, since the ordinates, such as ab, Fig. 14-18(b), make a very small angle θ with the vertical, $ab \approx cb$. Hence, the deflection of a point such as b is very nearly $\theta_1 x + cb$. Deflections of beams in situations where hinges are introduced, Fig. 14-18(c), are treated similarly. For these, the tangent to the adjoining elastic curves is *not continuous* across a hinge.

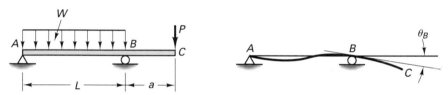

Fig. 14-17   A method of analyzing deflections of an overhang.

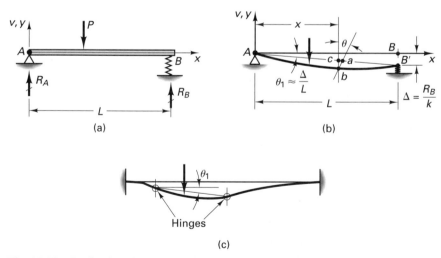

Fig. 14-18   Deflections in a composite structure.

[13] The effect of the overhang on beam segment AB must be included by introducing bending moment $-Pa$ at support B.

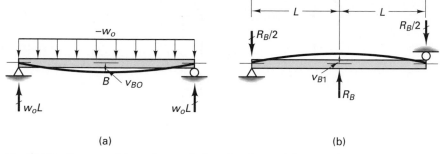

Fig. 14-19   Superposition of two solutions for determining reactions.

The method of superposition can be used effectively for determining deflections or reactions for statically indeterminate beams. As an illustration, consider the continuous beam analyzed in Example 14-5. By removing support R_B, the beam would deflect at the middle, as shown in Fig. 14-19(a). By applying force R_B in an upward direction, the required condition of no displacement at B can be restored. The respective expressions for these deflections are given by Eqs. 14-22 and 14-30. By equating them, R_B is found to be $5w_oL/4$, agreeing with the previous result (see Example 14-5).

Example 14-10

Two cantilever beams AD and BF of equal flexural rigidity $EI = 24 \times 10^{12}\,N \cdot mm^2$, shown in Fig. 14-20(a), are interconnected by a taut steel rod DC ($E = 200$ GPa). Rod DC is 5000 mm long and has a cross section of 300 mm². Find the deflection of cantilever AD at D due to a force $P = 50$ kN applied at F.

SOLUTION

By separating the structure at D, the two free-body diagrams in Figs. 14-20(b) and (c) are obtained. In both diagrams, the same unknown force X is shown acting (a condition of statics). The deflection of point D is the same, whether beam AD at D or the top of rod DC is considered. Deflection Δ_1 of point D in Fig. 14-20(b) is caused by X. Deflection Δ_2 of point D on the rod is equal to the deflection v_c of beam BF caused by forces P *and* X less the elastic stretch of rod DC.

From statics:

$$X_{\text{pull on } AD} = X_{\text{pull on } DC} = X$$

From geometry:

$$\Delta_1 = \Delta_2 \quad \text{or} \quad |v_D| = |v_C| - \Delta_{\text{rod}}$$

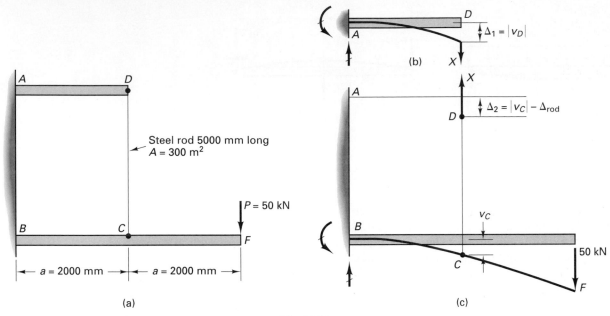

Fig. 14-20

Beam deflections can be found using the methods discussed earlier in this chapter. Alternatively, from Table 10 of the Appendix, in terms of the notation of this problem, one has

$$v_D = -\frac{Xa^3}{3EI} = -\frac{X \times 2^3 \times 10^9}{3 \times 24 \times 10^{12}} = -1.11 \times 10^{-4}X \text{ mm}$$

$$v_{C \text{ due to } X} = +1.11 \times 10^{-4}X \text{ mm}$$

$$v_{C \text{ due to } P} = -\frac{P}{6EI}[2(2a)^3 - 3(2a)^2a + a^3] = -13.9 \text{ mm}$$

and, using Eq. 3-4

$$\Delta_{\text{rod}} = \frac{XL_{CD}}{A_{CD}E} = \frac{X \times 5000}{300 \times 200 \times 10^3} = 0.833 \times 10^{-4}X \text{ mm}$$

Then, equating deflections and treating the downward deflections as negative,

$$-1.11 \times 10^{-4}X = -13.9 + 1.11 \times 10^{-4}X + 0.833 \times 10^{-4}X$$

Hence,

$$X = 45.5 \times 10^3 \text{ N}$$

and

$$v_D = -1.11 \times 10^{-4} \times 45.5 \times 10^3 = -5.05 \text{ mm}$$

Note particularly that in these calculations, the deflection of point C is determined by superposing the effects of applied force P at the end of the cantilever *and* the unknown force X at C.

14-10. Deflections in Unsymmetric Bending

In the preceding discussion, it was assumed that deflections were caused by a beam bending around one of the principal axes. However, if unsymmetric bending takes place, deflections are calculated in each of the principal planes and the deflections so found are *added vectorially*. An example is shown in Fig. 14-21 for a Z section. Here the y and z axes are the principal axes passing through the centroid as well as the shear center of the cross section. A positive deflection v_1 is shown for the beam deflection taking place in the xy plane, and, similarly, w_1 corresponds to the deflection in the xz plane. Their vectorial sum, AA', is the total beam deflection.

In order to prevent torsion, the applied forces must act through the shear center for the cross section. If not, torsional stresses and deformations, treated in Chapter 6, must also be considered.

Beams having significantly different magnitudes of moments of inertia about the two principal axes of a cross section are very sensitive to load alignment. As is shown in the next example, even a small inclination of the applied force from the vertical causes large lateral displacements (and high stresses).

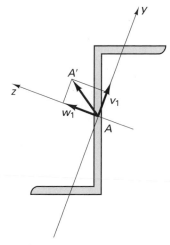

Fig. 14-21   Deflection of a beam subjected to unsymmetric bending.

Example 14-11

A C 380 × 50 steel channel cantilever 2540 mm long is subjected to an inclined force P of 9 kN through the shear center, as shown in Figs. 14-22(a) and (b). Determine the tip deflection at the applied force. Let $E = 200$ GPa.

SOLUTION

The properties for this channel are given in Table 5 in the Appendix: $I_z = 131 \times 10^6$ mm^4 and $I_y = 3.38 \times 10^6$ mm^4. Maximum deflection of a cantilever bent around either principal axis is given in Table 10 of the Appendix: $v_{max} = PL^3/3EI$. Hence, identifying by subscripts H the horizontal

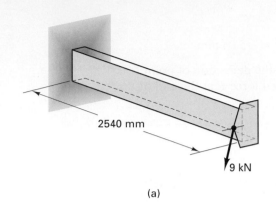

(a)

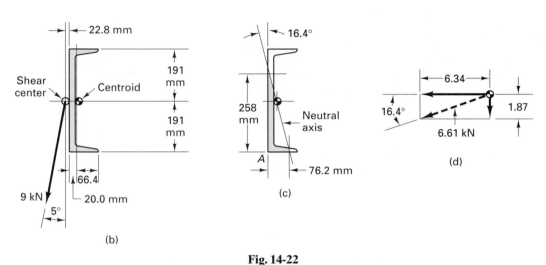

(b)

(c)

(d)

Fig. 14-22

and by V the vertical components of tip deflection Δ and applied force P, one has

$$\Delta_H = \frac{P_H L^3}{3EI_y} = \frac{(9 \times 10^3 \sin 5°) \times 2540^3}{3 \times 200 \times 10^3 \times 3.38 \times 10^6} = 6.34 \text{ mm}$$

$$\Delta_V = \frac{P_V L^3}{3EI_z} = \frac{(9 \times 10^3 \cos 5°) \times 2540^3}{3 \times 200 \times 10^3 \times 131 \times 10^6} = 1.87 \text{ mm}$$

These deflections and their vector sum of 6.61 mm, making an angle of 16.4° with the horizontal, are shown in Fig. 14-22(d).

It is instructive to note that, as to be expected, the *maximum deflection occurs in the direction normal to the neutral axis.* This axis may be located by performing a stress analysis and finding the points of zero stress. One such point is 258 mm above A and the other is 76.2 mm in to the right of A, as shown in Fig. 14-22(c). Alternatively, the neutral axis can be located using Eq. 9-3. Using this approach,

$$\tan\beta = \frac{I_z}{I_y}\tan\alpha = \frac{131 \times 10^6}{3.38 \times 10^6}\tan 5° = 3.39 \qquad \text{and} \qquad \beta = 73.6°$$

and $90° - \beta = 16.4°$ agrees with the angle shown in Fig. 14-22(d).

14-11. Energy Method for Deflections and Impact

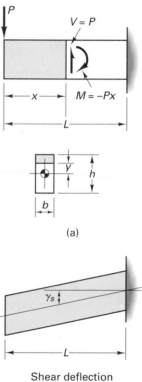

(a)

Shear deflection

(b)

Fig. 14-23

A comprehensive treatment of the energy method for finding beam deflections is given in Chapter 19. Without establishing the necessary theorem, it is possible to solve only a very limited class of problems. Unless special conditions such as symmetry are at hand, direct solutions based on the principle of conservation of energy must be limited to the action of a single force or moment. This limited approach has been found useful in the axial force, torsion, and pure bending problems in Chapters 3, 6, and 8. In beams, one can go a step further and include, if needed, both the bending and the shear strain energies. The procedure based on equating the internal strain energy U to the external work W_e remains the same.

This method permits an assessment of deflections caused by bending in relation to that caused by shear. The following example is concerned with such a problem, where in the solution it is assumed that the force is *gradually applied*. By contrast, in the second example, an impact on a beam caused by a falling mass is considered; in this example, the effect of shear deformation is neglected.

Example 14-12

Find the maximum deflection due to force P applied at the end of a cantilever having a rectangular cross section, Fig. 14-23. Consider the effect of the flexural and shear deformations.

SOLUTION

If force P is gradually applied to the beam, the external work $W_e = \frac{1}{2}P\Delta$, where Δ is the total deflection of the end of the beam. The internal strain energy consists of two parts. One part is due to the bending stresses; the other is caused by the shear stresses. These strain energies may be directly superposed.

The strain energy in pure bending is obtained from Eq. 8-24, $U_{bending} = \int M^2 \, dx/2EI$, by noting that $M = -Px$. The strain energy in shear is found from Eq. 5-5, $U_{shear} = \int (\tau^2/2G) \, dV$. In this particular case, the shear at every section is equal to applied force P, and the shear stress τ, according to Eq. 10-7, is distributed parabolically as

$$\tau = \frac{P}{2I}\left[\left(\frac{h}{2}\right)^2 - y^2\right]$$

At any one level y, this shear stress does not vary across breadth b and length L of the beam. Therefore, the infinitesimal volume dV in the shear energy expression is taken as $Lb \, dy$. By equating the sum of these two internal strain energies to the external work, the total deflection is obtained:

$$U_{bending} = \int_0^L \frac{M^2 dx}{2EI} = \int_0^L \frac{(-Px)^2 \, dx}{2EI} = \frac{P^2 L^3}{6EI}$$

$$U_{shear} = \int_{vol} \frac{\tau^2}{2G} dV = \frac{1}{2G}\int_{-h/2}^{+h/2}\left\{\frac{P}{2I}\left[\left(\frac{h}{2}\right)^2 - y^2\right]\right\}^2 Lb \, dy \qquad (14\text{-}34)$$

$$= \frac{P^2 Lb}{8GI^2}\frac{h^5}{30} = \frac{P^2 Lbh^5}{240G}\left(\frac{12}{bh^3}\right)^2 = \frac{3P^2 L}{5AG}$$

where $A = bh$ is the cross section of the beam. Then

$$W_e = U = U_{bending} + U_{shear}$$

$$\frac{P\Delta}{2} = \frac{P^2 L^3}{6EI} + \frac{3P^2 L}{5AG} \qquad \text{or} \qquad \Delta = \frac{PL^3}{3EI} + \frac{6PL}{5AG}$$

The first term in this answer, $PL^3/3EI$, is the deflection of the beam due to flexure. The second term is the deflection due to shear, assuming no warping restraint at the built-in end. The factor $\alpha = 6/5$ varies for different shapes of the cross section, since it depends on the nature of the shear stress distribution.

It is instructive to recast the expression for the total deflection Δ as

$$\boxed{\Delta = \frac{PL^3}{3EI}\left(1 + \frac{3E}{10G}\frac{h^2}{L^2}\right)} \qquad (14\text{-}35)$$

where, as before, the last term gives the deflection due to shear.

To gain further insight into this problem, in the last expression, replace the ratio E/G by 2.5, a typical value for steels. Then

$$\Delta = (1 + 0.75h^2/L^2)\Delta_{bending} \qquad (14\text{-}35a)$$

From this equation, it can be seen that for a short beam (for example, one with $L = h$), the total deflection is 1.75 times that due to bending alone. Hence, shear deflection is very important in comparable cases. On the other hand, if $L = 10h$, the deflection due to shear is less than 1%. Small deflections due to shear are typical for ordinary slender beams. This fact can be noted further from the original equation for Δ. There, the deflection due to bending increases as the cube of the span length, whereas the deflection due to shear increases directly. Hence, as beam length increases, the bending deflection quickly becomes dominant. For this reason, it is usually possible to neglect the deflection due to shear.

Example 14-13

Find the instantaneous maximum deflections and bending stresses for the 50×50 mm steel beam shown in Fig. 14-24 when struck by a 15.3-kg mass falling from a height 75 mm above the top of the beam, if (a) the beam is on rigid supports, and (b) the beam is supported at each end on springs. Constant k for each spring is 300 N/mm. Let $E = 200$ GPa.

SOLUTION

The deflection of the system due to a statically applied force of 15.3 g $= 15.3 \times 9.81 = 150$ N is computed first. In the first case, this deflection is that of the beam only; see Table 10 of the Appendix. In the second case, the static deflection of the beam is augmented by the deflection of the springs subjected to a 75-N force each. The impact factors are then computed from Eq. 3-19 or 3-20. Static deflections and stresses are multiplied by the impact factors to obtain the answers.

(a)

$$\Delta_{st} = \frac{PL^3}{48EI} = \frac{150 \times 1000^3}{48 \times 200 \times 10^3 \times 50^4/12} = 0.030 \text{ mm}$$

$$\text{impact factor} = 1 + \sqrt{1 + \frac{2h}{\Delta_{st}}}$$

$$= 1 + \sqrt{1 + \frac{2 \times 75}{0.030}} = 71.7$$

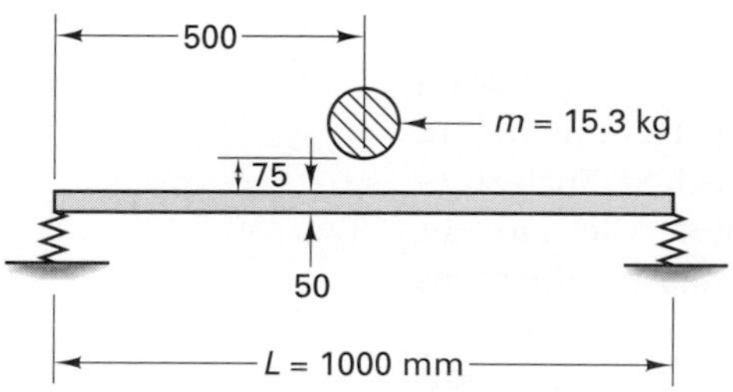

Fig. 14-24

(b)

$$\Delta_{st} = \Delta_{beam} + \Delta_{spr} = 0.030 + \frac{75}{300} = 0.280 \text{ mm}$$

$$\text{impact factor} = 1 + \sqrt{1 + \frac{2 \times 75}{0.280}} = 24.2$$

For either case, the maximum bending stress in the beam due to a static application of P is

$$(\sigma_{max})_{st} = \frac{M}{S} = \frac{PL}{4S} = \frac{150 \times 1000}{4 \times 50^3/6} = 1.800 \text{ MPa}$$

Multiplying the static deflections and stress by the respective impact factors gives the required results

	Static		*Dynamic*	
	With Springs	*No Springs*	*With Springs*	*No Springs*
Δ_{max}, mm	0.280	0.030	6.78	2.15
σ_{max}, MPa	1.80	1.80	43.6	129

It is apparent from this table that large deflections and stresses are caused by a dynamically applied load. The stress for the condition with no springs is particularly large; however, due to the flexibility of the beam, it is not excessive.

14-12. Inelastic Deflection of Beams

All the preceding solutions for beam deflections apply only if the material behaves elastically. This limitation is the result of introducing Hooke's law into the strain-curvature relation, Eq. 14-5, to yield the moment-curvature equation, Eq. 14-6. The subsequence procedures for approximating the curvatures as d^2v/dx^2 and the integration schemes do not depend on the material properties.

Superposition does not apply to inelastic problems, since deflections are not linearly related to the applied forces. As a consequence, in some cases piecewise linear solutions for small load or displacement increments are made until the desired level of load or displacement is reached. Such step-wise linear calculations are made with the aid of a computer. Alternatively, time-consuming trial-and-error solutions are used to calculate deflections in indeterminate beams. However, it is possible to develop simple solutions for *ultimate strengths* of statically determinate and indeterminate beams and frames *assuming ideal plastic behavior of material.* For such a method, a relationship between the bending moment and curvature at a section of a beam must be developed. An illustration defining such a relationship is given in the next example. Essentially, it is this approach that is relied upon in Chapter 20 for plastic limit state analyses of statically determinate and indeterminate beams and simple frames.

The second example that follows discusses the deflection analysis of a statically determinate elastic-plastic beam. The solution demonstrates that as long as at least a part of a beam's cross section remains elastic, the deflections remain bounded (i.e., finite) and can be calculated.

Example 14-14

Determine and plot the moment-curvature relationship for an elastic, ideally plastic rectangular beam.

SOLUTION

In a rectangular elastic-plastic beam at y_o, where the juncture of the elastic and plastic zones occurs, the linear strain $\varepsilon_x = \pm \varepsilon_{yp}$; see Fig. 8-26. Therefore, according to Eq. 14-5, with the curvature $1/\rho = \kappa$,

$$\frac{1}{\rho} = \kappa = -\frac{\varepsilon_{yp}}{y_o} \quad \text{and} \quad \kappa_{yp} = -\frac{\varepsilon_{yp}}{h/2}$$

where the last expression gives the curvature of the member at impending yielding when $y_o = h/2$. From these relations,

$$\frac{y_o}{h/2} = \frac{\kappa_{yp}}{\kappa}$$

By substituting this expression into Eq. 8-29, one obtains the required moment-curvature relationship:

$$M = M_p \left[1 - \frac{1}{3}\left(\frac{y_o}{h/2}\right)^2 \right] = \frac{3}{2} M_{yp} \left[1 - \frac{1}{3}\left(\frac{\kappa_{yp}}{\kappa}\right)^2 \right] \qquad (14\text{-}36)$$

This function is plotted in Fig. 14-25. Note how rapidly it approaches the asymptote. At curvature just double that of the impending yielding, eleven-twelfths, or 91.6%, of the ultimate plastic moment M_p is already reached. At this point, the middle half of the beam remains elastic.

On releasing an applied moment, the beam rebounds elastically, as shown in the figure. On this basis, residual curvature can be determined.

The reader should recall that the ratio of M_p to M_{yp} varies for different cross sections. For example, for a typical steel wide-flange beam, M_p/M_{yp} is about 1.14. Establishing the asymptotes for plastic moments gives a practical

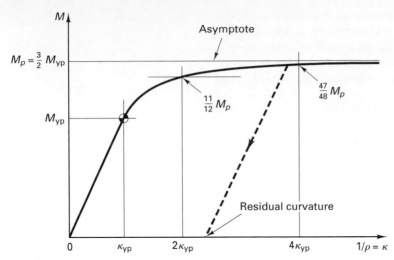

Fig. 14-25   Moment-curvature relation for an elastic-plastic rectangular beam.

basis for finding the ultimate plastic limit state for beams and frames discussed in Chapter 20.

Example 14-15

A 3-in-wide mild-steel cantilever beam has the dimensions shown in Fig. 14-26(a). Determine the tip deflection caused by applying two loads of 5 kips each. Assume $E = 30 \times 10^3$ ksi and $\sigma_{yp} = \pm 40$ ksi.

SOLUTION

The moment diagram is shown in Fig. 14-26(b). From $\sigma_{max} = Mc/I$, it is found that the largest stress in beam segment ab is 24.4 ksi, which indicates elastic behavior. An analogous calculation for the shallow section of the beam gives a stress of 55 ksi, which is not possible as the material yields at 40 ksi.

A check of the ultimate capacity for the 2-in-deep section based on Eq. 8-27 gives

$$M_p = M_{ult} = \sigma_{yp} \frac{bh^2}{4} = \frac{40 \times 3 \times 2^2}{4} = 120 \text{ k-in}$$

This calculation shows that although the beam yields partially, it can carry the applied moment. The applied moment is $\frac{11}{12}M_p$. According to the results found in the preceding example, this means that the curvature in the 2-in-deep

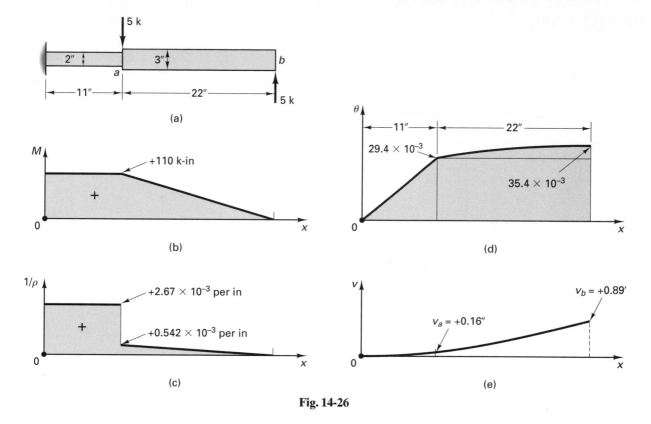

Fig. 14-26

section of the beam is twice that at the beginning of yielding. Therefore, the curvature in the 11-in segment of the beam adjoining the support is

$$\frac{1}{\rho} = 2\kappa_{yp} = 2\frac{\varepsilon_{yp}}{h/2} = 2\frac{\sigma_{yp}}{Eh/2} = \frac{2 \times 40}{30 \times 10^3 \times 1} = 2.67 \times 10^{-3} \text{ per in}$$

The maximum curvature for segment ab is

$$\frac{1}{\rho} = \frac{M_{\max}}{EI} = \frac{\sigma_{\max}}{Ec} = \frac{24.4}{3 \times 10^3 \times 1.5} = 0.542 \times 10^{-3} \text{ per in}$$

These data on curvatures are plotted in Fig. 14-26(c). On integrating this twice with $\theta(0) = 0$ and $v(0) = 0$, the deflected curve, Fig. 14-26(e), is obtained. The tip deflection is 0.89 in upward.

If the applied loads were released, the beam would rebound elastically. As can be verified by elastic analysis, this would cause a tip deflection of 0.64 in. Hence, a residual tip deflection of 0.25 in would remain. The residual curvature would be confined to the 2-in-deep segment of beam.

If the end load were applied alone, the 165 k-in moment at the left end would exceed the plastic moment capacity of 120 k-in and the beam would collapse. Superposition cannot be used to solve this problem.

PROBLEMS

Section 14-2

14-1. A 2×6 mm steel strip 3142 mm long is clamped at one end, as shown in the figure. What is the required end moment to force the strip to touch the wall? What would be the maximum stress when the strip is in the bent condition? $E = 200$ GPa.

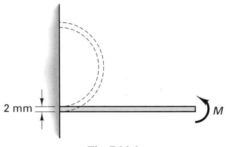

2 mm

M

Fig. P14-1

14-2. A round aluminum bar of 6 mm diameter is bent into a circular ring having a mean diameter of 3 m. What is the maximum stress in the bar? $E = 70$ GPa.

14-3. What will be the radius of curvature of a W 8×18 beam bent around the $X-X$ axis if the stress in the extreme fibers is 36 ksi? $E = 29 \times 10^6$ psi.

14-4. Assume that a straight rectangular bar after severe cold working has a residual stress distribution such as was found in Example 8-9; see Fig. 8-25. (a) If one-sixth of the thickness of this bar is machined off on the top and on the bottom, reducing the bar to two-thirds of its original thickness, what will be the curvature ρ of the machined bar? Assign the necessary parameters to solve this problem in general terms. (b) For the previous conditions, if the bar is 24 mm square by 1000 mm long, what will be the deflection of the bar at the center from the chord through the end? Let $\sigma_{yp} = 400$ MPa and $E = 200$ GPa. Note that for small deflections, the maximum deflection from a chord L long of a curve bent into a circle of radius R is approximately[1] $L^2/(8R)$. (*Hint:* The machining operation removes the internal microresidual stresses.)

Section 14-7

14-5. If the equation of the elastic curve for a simply supported beam of length L having a constant EI is $v = (k/360EI)(-3x^5 + 10x^3L^2 - 7xL^4)$, how is the beam loaded?

---

[1]This follows by retaining the first term of the expansion of $R(1 - \cos \theta)$, where θ is one-half the included angle.

14-6. An elastic beam of constant EI and of length L has the deflected shape $EIv(x) = M_o(x^3 - x^2L)/4L$. (a) Determine the loading and support conditions. (b) Plot the shear and moment diagrams for the beam and sketch the deflected shape.

14-7. Rework Example 14-2 by taking the origin of the coordinate system at the free end.

14-8. Using the exact differential equation, Eq. 14-8, show that the equation of the elastic curve in Example 14-2 is $x^2 + (v - \rho)^2 = \rho^2$, where ρ is a constant. (*Hint:* Let $dv/dx = \tan \theta$ and integrate.)

14-9 through 14-29. (a) Determine the equations of the elastic curves for the beams shown in the figures due to the applied loading for the given boundary conditions. Unless directed otherwise, use Eq. 14-14a or 14-14c, whichever is simpler to apply. For all cases, EI is constant, except that in Problem 14-20, EI varies. Wherever

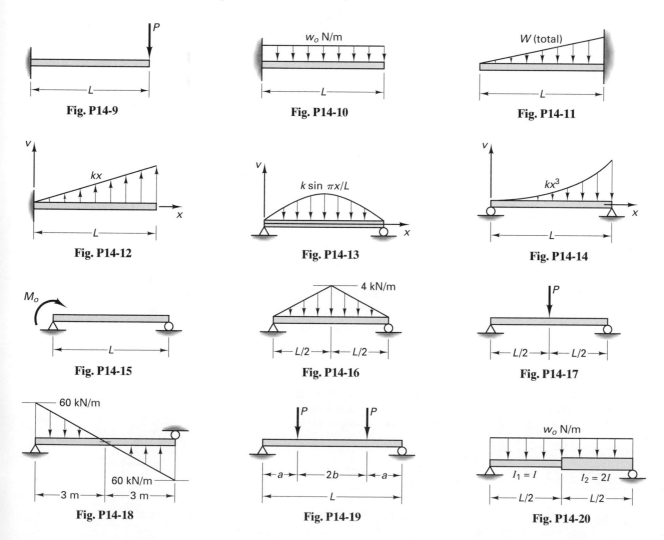

Fig. P14-9

Fig. P14-10

Fig. P14-11

Fig. P14-12

Fig. P14-13

Fig. P14-14

Fig. P14-15

Fig. P14-16

Fig. P14-17

Fig. P14-18

Fig. P14-19

Fig. P14-20

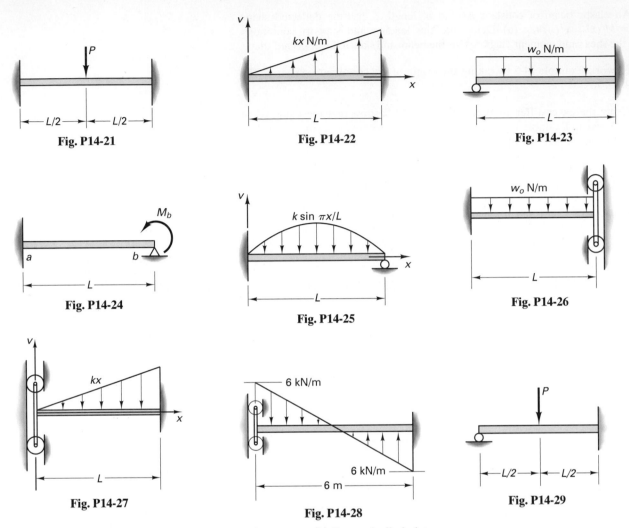

Fig. P14-21

Fig. P14-22

Fig. P14-23

Fig. P14-24

Fig. P14-25

Fig. P14-26

Fig. P14-27

Fig. P14-28

Fig. P14-29

applicable, take advantage of symmetry or antisymmetry. (b) For statically indeterminate cases only, plot shear and moment diagrams, giving all critical ordinates.

Note: In Problems 14-9, 14-10, and 14-15, it is simpler to take the origin on the right and to direct the *x* axis to the left.

14-30 through 14-32. (a) Determine equations for the elastic curves due to an imposed small vertical displacement Δ of the end for the beams of length L and of constant EI shown in the figures . (b) Plot shear and moment diagrams.

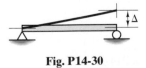

Fig. P14-30

Fig. P14-31

Fig. P14-32

14-33. If in Problem 14-17 the cross-sectional area of the beam is constant and the left half of the span is made of steel ($E = 200$ GPa) and the right half is made of an aluminum alloy ($E = 70$ GPa), determine the equation of the elastic curve.

14-34. What is the equation of the elastic curve for the cantilever of constant width and flexural strength loaded at the end by a concentrated force P? See Figs. 13-18(a) and (d). Neglect the effect of the required increase in beam depth at the end for shear.

14-35. An overhanging beam of constant flexural rigidity EI is loaded as shown in the figure. For portion AB of the beam, (a) find the equation of the elastic curve due to the applied load of $2w_o$ N/m, and (b) determine the maximum deflection between the supports and the deflection midway between the supports.

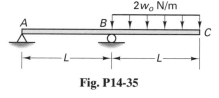

Fig. P14-35

14-36. A beam with an overhang of constant flexural rigidity EI is loaded as shown in the figure. (a) Determine the length a of the overhang such that the elastic curve would be horizontal over support B. (b) Determine the maximum deflection between the supports.

14-37. Using a semigraphical procedure, such as shown in Figs. 14-9 and 14-13, find the deflection of the beam at the point of the applied load; see the figure. Let $I_1 = 400$ in^4, $I_2 = 300$ in^4, and $E = 30 \times 10^6$ psi.

14-38. Using a semigraphical procedure, such as shown in Figs. 14-9 and 14-13, find the deflection at the center of the span for the beam loaded as shown in the figure. Neglect the effect of the axial force on deflection. EI for the beam is constant.

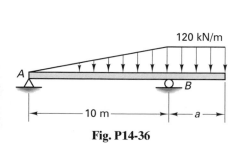

Fig. P14-36

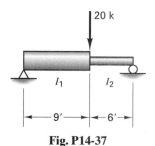

Fig. P14-37

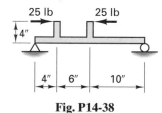

Fig. P14-38

14-39. A steel beam is to span 30 ft and support a 1.2 k/ft uniformly distributed load, including its own weight. Select the required W section of minimum weight, using the abridged Table 4 in the Appendix, for bending around its strong axis. The allowable bending stress is 24 ksi and that for shear is 14.4 ksi. It is also required that the maximum deflection does not exceed 1 in. This requirement corresponds to 1/360th of the span length and is often used to limit deflection due to the applied load in building design. $E = 29 \times 10^3$ ksi.

14-40. A wooden beam is to span 24 ft and to support a 1.2 k/ft uniformly distributed load, including its own weight. Select the size required from Table 9 in the Appendix. The allowable bending stress is 2000 psi and that in shear is 100 psi. The deflection is limited to 1/360th of the span length.

14-41.   The maximum deflection for a simple beam spanning 24 ft and carrying a uniformly distributed load of 40 k total, including its own weight, is limited to 0.5 in. (a) Specify the required steel I beam. Let $E = 30 \times 10^6$ psi. (b) What size aluminum-alloy beam would be needed for the same requirements? Let $E = 10 \times 10^6$ psi, and use Table 3 in the Appendix for section properties. (c) Determine the maximum stresses in both cases.

14-42.   A uniformly loaded 6×12 in (nominal size) wooden beam spans 10 ft and is considered to have satisfactory deflection characteristics. Select an aluminum-alloy I beam, a steel I beam, and a polyester-plastic I beam having the same deflection characteristics. In selecting the beam selections, neglect the differences in their own weights. Let $E = 1.5 \times 10^6$ psi for wood and polyester plastic, $E = 10 \times 10^6$ psi for aluminum, and $E = 30 \times 10^6$ psi for steel. For section properties of all I beams, use Table 4 in the Appendix.

Section 14-8

14-43.   Using singularity functions, rework Problem 14-19.

14-44.   Using singularity functions, rework Problem 14-29.

14-45 through 14-50.   Using singularity functions, obtain equations for the elastic curves for the beams loaded as shown in the figures. EI is constant for all beams.

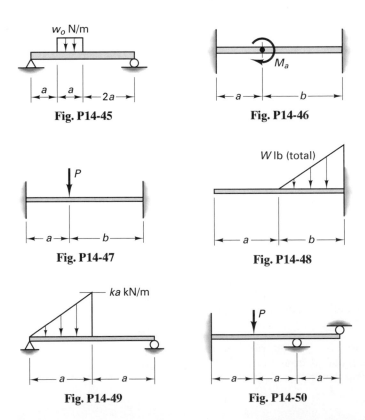

Fig. P14-45

Fig. P14-46

Fig. P14-47

Fig. P14-48

Fig. P14-49

Fig. P14-50

Section 14-9 Use the deflection equations in Examples 14-2 through 14-6 and Table 10 in the Appendix

14-51. (a) From the solution given in Table 10 in the Appendix for a cantilever loaded by a concentrated force P at the end, show that the free-end deflection at A for the cantilever shown in the figure is

$$v_A = \frac{Pb^2}{6EI}(3L - b)$$

(b) Show that the deflection at A due to force P at B is equal to the deflection at B due to force P at A. (See Section 19-4 on Maxwell's theorem of reciprocal deflections.)

14-52. The data for a beam loaded as shown in Fig. 14-17 are $w_o = 30$ kN/m, $P = 25$ kN, $L = 3$ m, and $a = 1.2$ m. If the beam is made from a W 200 $\times$ 36 section ($I = 34.4 \times 10^6$ mm^4), what is the deflection of the free end C caused by the applied loads? $E = 200$ GPa.

14-53. A W 8 $\times$ 40 steel beam is loaded as shown in the figure. Calculate the deflection at the center of the span. $E = 29 \times 10^3$ ksi.

14-54. Using the results found in Example 14-6 for deflection of a beam due to a concentrated force P, determine the deflection at the center of the beam caused by a uniformly distributed downward load w_o. (Treat $w_o\, dx$ as an infinitesimal concentrated force, and integrate.) This method of *influence coefficients* (so named by Maxwell) can be effectively used for many distributed-load problems.

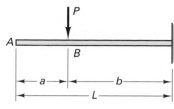

Fig. P14-51

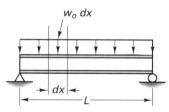

Fig. P14-53

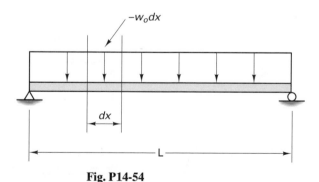

Fig. P14-54

14-55. Using the method outlined in the preceding problem, determine the deflection at the center of the beam for the loading given in Problem 14-49.

14-56. An elastic prismatic beam with an overhang is loaded with a concentrated end moment M_o. Determine the deflection of the free end. The spring constant $k = 48EI/L^3$.

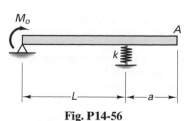

Fig. P14-56

14-57. An L-shaped member, such as shown in Fig. 14-16(a), is made up from a bar of constant cross section. Determine the horizontal and vertical deflections of point C caused by applied force P. Let $a = L/4$. Neglect the effect on deflection of the axial force in the horizontal member and of the shear in the vertical member. Express the results in terms of $P, L, E,$ and I.

14-58. A vertical rod with a concentrated mass at its free end is attached to a rotating plane, as shown in the figure. (a) At what angular velocity ω will the maximum bending stress in the rod just reach yield? (b) For the condition in (a), determine the deflection of the mass. The rod is 5 mm in diameter and its mass is 150×10^{-6} kg/mm. The mass at the top of the rod is 60×10^{-3} kg and can be considered to be concentrated at a point. $\sigma_{yp} = 1$ GPa and $E = 200$ GPa.

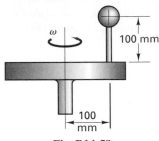

Fig. P14-58

14-59. Two identical, horizontal, simply supported beams span 3.6 m each. The beams cross each other at right angles at their respective midspans. When erected, there is a 6-mm gap between the two beams. If a concentrated downward force of 50 kN is applied at midspan to the upper beam, how much will the lower beam carry? EI for each beam is 6000 kN · m^2.

14-60. The midpoint of a cantilever beam 6 m long rests on the midspan of a simply supported beam 8 m long. Determine the deflection of point A, where the beams meet, which results from the application of a 40-kN force at the end of the cantilever beam. State the answer in terms of EI, which is the same and is constant for both beams.

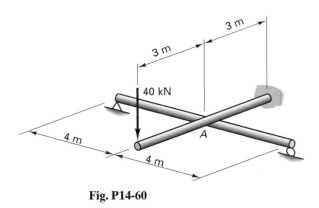

Fig. P14-60

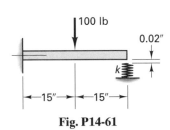

Fig. P14-61

14-61. A 30-in cantilever of constant flexural rigidity, $EI = 10^7$ lb-in^2, initially has a gap of 0.02 in between its end and the spring. The spring constant $k = 10$ k/in. If a force of 100 lb is applied to the cantilever, as shown in the figure, how much of this force will be carried by the spring? (*Hint:* See Problem 14-51.)

14-62. A steel wire 5 m in length with a cross-sectional area equal to 160 mm^2 is stretched tightly between the midpoint of the simple beam and the free end of the cantilever, as shown in the figure. Determine the deflection of the end of the cantilever as a result of a temperature drop of 50°C. For steel wire: $E = 200$ GPa, $\alpha = 12 \times 10^{-6}$ per °C. For both beams: $I = 10 \times 10^6$ mm^4 and $E = 10$ GPa.

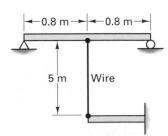

Fig. P14-62

14-63. One end of a W 18 × 50 beam is cast into concrete. It was intended to support the other end with a 1-in^2 steel rod 12 ft long, as shown in the figure. During the installation, however, the nut on the rod was poorly tightened and in the unloaded condition there is a $\frac{1}{2}$-in gap between the top of the nut and the bottom of

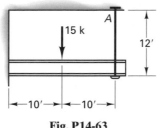

Fig. P14-63

the beam. What tensile force will develop in the rod because a force of 15 kips is applied at the middle of the beam? $E = 30 \times 10^6$ psi. (*Hint:* See Problem 14-51.)

14-64. A steel piano wire 30 in long is stretched from the middle of an aluminum beam *AB* to a rigid support at *C*, as shown in the figure. What is the increase in stress in the wire if the temperature drops 100°F? The cross-sectional area of the wire is 0.0001 in^2 and $E = 30 \times 10^6$ psi. For the aluminum beam, $EI = 1040$ lb-in^2. Let $\alpha_{St} = 6.5 \times 10^{-6}$ per °F, $\alpha_{Al} = 12.9 \times 10^{-6}$ per °F.

14-65. A flexible steel bar is suspended by three steel rods, as shown in the figure, with the dimensions given in mm. If, initially, the rods are taut, what additional forces will develop in the rods due to the application of the force $F = 1500$ N and a drop in temperature of 50°C in the right rod? The cross-sectional area of each rod is 10 mm^2, and $\alpha = 12 \times 10^{-6}$ per °C. For the bar, $I = 2 \times 10^4$ mm^4, and for steel, $E = 200 \times 10^3$ N/mm^2.

14-66. An L-shaped steel rod of 2.125 in diameter is built in at one end to a rigid wall and is simply supported at the other end, as shown in the figure. In the plan the bend is 90°. What bending moment will be developed at the built-in end due to the

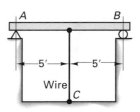

Fig. P14-64

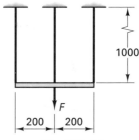

Fig. P14-65

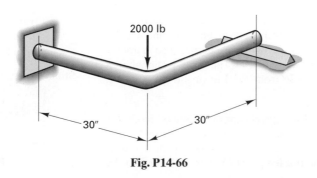

Fig. P14-66

application of a 2000-lb force at the corner of the rod? Assume $E = 30 \times 10^6$ psi, $G = 12 \times 10^6$ psi, and, for simplicity, let $I = 1.00$ in^4 and $I_p = 2.00$ in^4.

14-67. Two parallel circular steel shafts of the same length are fixed at one end and are interconnected at the other end by means of a taut vertical wire, as shown in the figure. The shafts are 40 mm in diameter; the radius of the rigid pulley keyed to the upper shaft is 100 mm. The cross-sectional area of the interconnecting wire is 5 mm^2. If a vertical pull P of 100 N is applied to the lower shaft, how much of the applied force will be carried by the upper shaft? $E = 200$ GPa and $G = 80$ GPa.

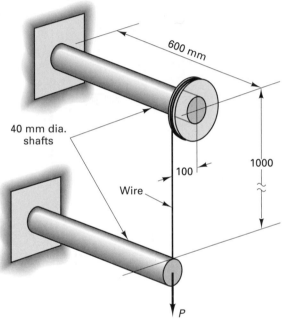

40 mm dia. shafts

Wire

Fig. P14-67

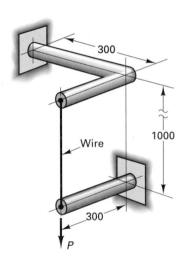

Fig. P14-68

14-68. A horizontal L-shaped rod is connected by a taut wire to a cantilever, as shown in the figure. If a drop in temperature of 100°C takes place and a downward force $P = 250$ N is applied at the end of the cantilever, what maximum bending stress will this cause at the cantilever support? Assume elastic behavior and neglect stress concentrations. All dimensions shown in the figure are in mm. The diameter of the bent rod, as well as that of the cantilever, is 20 mm. The cross-sectional area of the wire is 0.40 mm^2. The assembly is made from steel having $E = 200$ GPA, $\nu = 0.25$, G = 80 GPa, and $\alpha = 11.7 \times 10^{-6}$ per °C.

14-69. The temperature in a furnace is measured by means of a stainless-steel wire placed in it. The wire is fastened to the end of a cantilever beam outside the furnace. The strain measured by the strain gage glued to the outside of the beam is a measure of the temperature. Assuming that the full length of the wire is heated to the

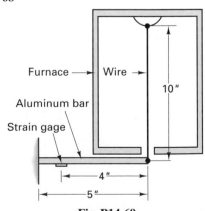

Fig. P14-69

furnace temperature, what is the change in furnace temperature if the gage records a change in strain of -100×10^{-6} in/in? Assume that the wire has sufficient initial tension to perform as intended. The mechanical properties of the materials are as follows: $\alpha_{SS} = 9.5 \times 10^{-6}$ per °F, $\alpha_{Al} = 12 \times 10^{-6}$ per °F, $E_{SS} = 30 \times 10^{6}$ psi, $E_{Al} = 10 \times 10^{6}$ psi, $A_{wire} = 5 \times 10^{-4}$ in², $I_{beam} = 6.5 \times 10^{-4}$ in⁴. The depth of the small beam is 0.25 in.

14-70. With the aid of the first two solutions given in Table 10 of the Appendix, (a) find the reaction at A, and (b) plot the shear and moment diagrams and show the deflected shape of the beam.

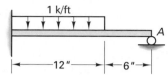

Fig. P14-70

Section 14-10

14-71. A 5-ft-long cantilever is loaded at the end with a force $P = 1000$ lb, forming an angle α with the vertical. The member is an S 8 × 18.4 steel beam. Determine the total tip deflection for $\alpha = 0°$, 10°, 45°, and 90° caused by the applied force. $E = 29 \times 10^{6}$ psi. (b) Verify that deflections are normal to the neutral axes.

Fig. P14-71

14-72. Determine the maximum deflection for the wooden beam in Example 9-1, Fig. 9-4. $E = 12$ GPa for the wood. Verify that the maximum deflection is normal to the neutral axis.

14-73. Consider an aluminum-alloy Z section having the dimensions given in Problem 10-45. If a 100-in horizontal cantilever employing this section is fixed at one end and is subjected to a vertical downward 20-lb force at the centroid of the other end, what is the maximum deflection? How does the direction of this force relate to the neutral axis? $E = 10 \times 10^{3}$ ksi.

Section 14-11

14-74. Consider a W 18 × 35 short steel cantilever fixed at one end and loaded at the free end, as shown in Fig. 14-23. Determine the length of this cantilever such that the deflection due to flexure is the same as that due to shear. The steel yields at 36 ksi in tension or compression and at 21 ksi in shear. Note that unlike a rectangular beam, it can be assumed that only the web yields uniformly in shear. (Although this solution is not exact, the results are representative of actual conditions.)

14-75. A heavy object weighing 4000 lb is dropped in the middle of a 20-ft simple span through a distance of 1 in. If the supporting beam is a W 10 × 33 steel beam, what is the impact factor? Assume elastic behavior. $E = 29 \times 10^{6}$ psi.

Section 14-12

14-76. A 24-mm square bar of a linearly elastic-plastic material is to be wrapped around a round mandrel, as shown in the figure. (a) What mandrel diameter D is required so that the outer thirds of the cross sections become plastic (i.e., the elastic

Fig. P14-76

core is 8 mm deep by 24 mm wide)? Assume the material to be initially stress free with $\sigma_{yp} = 250$ MPa. Let $E = 200$ GPa. The pitch of the helix angle is so small that only the bending of the bar in a plane need be considered. (b) What will be the diameter of the coil after the release of the forces used in forming it? Stated alternatively, determine the coil diameter after the elastic springback.

14-77. A rectangular, weightless, simple beam of linearly elastic-plastic material is loaded in the middle by force P, as shown in the figure. (a) Determine the magnitude of force P that would cause the plastic zone to penetrate one-fourth of the beam depth from each side. (b) For the previous loading condition, sketch the moment-curvature diagram, clearly showing it for the plastic zone.

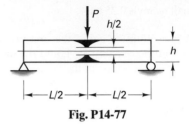

Fig. P14-77

15

Beam Deflections by the Moment-Area Method

15-1. General Remarks

This chapter is devoted to the discussion of deflections for statically determined and indeterminate beams using the *moment-area method,* also called the *area-moment method.* This specialized procedure is particularly convenient if the deflection of only a few points on a beam or a frame are required. For this reason, it can be used to advantage in the solution of statically indeterminate problems and for deflection check. An excellent insight into the kinematics of deformations is obtained by using this method.

This approach was particularly popular in the precomputer era. However, in current usage it provides a quick semigraphical approach for estimating deflections or rotations of beams at selected points.

A deflection analysis of slender beams in the presence of axial compressive forces in some instances may cause a profound increase in deflections, which in turn causes member instability. This topic is considered in the next chapter.

15-2. Introduction to the Moment-Area Method

In numerous engineering applications, where deflections of beams must be determined, the loading is complex and the cross-sectional areas of beams vary. This is the usual situation in machine shafts, where gradual or stepwise variations in the shaft diameter are made to accommodate rotors, bearings, collars, retainers, etc. Likewise, haunched or tapered beams are frequently employed in aircraft as well as in bridge construction. By interpreting semi-graphically the mathematical operations of solving the governing differential equation, an effective procedure for obtaining deflections in complicated situations has been developed. Using this alternative procedure, one finds that problems with load discontinuities and arbitrary variations of inertia of the cross-sectional area of a beam cause no complications and require only a little more arithmetical work for this solution. The solution of such problems is the objective in the following sections on the moment-area method.[1]

The method to be developed is generally used to obtain only the displacement and rotation at a single point on a beam. It may be used to determine the equation of the elastic curve, but no advantage is gained in comparison with the direct solution of the differential equation. Often, however, it is the deflection and/or the angular rotation of the elastic curve, or both, at a particular point of a beam that are of greatest interest in the solution of practical problems.

The method of moment areas is just an alternative method for solving the deflection problem. It possesses the same approximations and limitations discussed earlier in connection with the solution of the differential equation of the elastic curve. By applying it, one determines only the deflection due to the flexure of the beam; deflection due to shear is neglected. Application of the method will be developed for statically determinate and indeterminate beams.

15-3. Moment-Area Theorems

The necessary theorems are based on the geometry of the elastic curve and the associated M/EI diagram. Boundary conditions do not enter into the derivation of the theorems since the theorems are based only on the interpretation of definite integrals. As will be shown later, further geometrical considerations are necessary to solve a complete problem.

---

[1]The development of the moment-area method for finding deflections of beams is due to Charles E. Greene, of the University of Michigan, who taught it to his classes in 1873. Somewhat earlier, in 1868, Otto Mohr, of Dresden, Germany, developed a similar method that appears to have been unknown to Professor Greene.

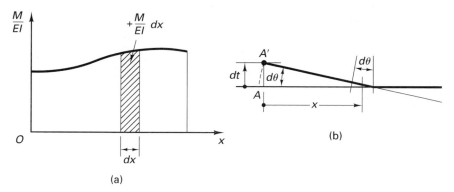

Fig. 15-1 Interpretation of a small angle change in an element.

For deriving the theorems, Eq. 14-10a, $d^2v/dx^2 = M/EI$, can be rewritten in the following alternative forms:

$$\frac{d^2v}{dx^2} = \frac{d}{dx}\left(\frac{dv}{dx}\right) = \frac{d\theta}{dx} = \frac{M}{EI} \quad \text{or} \quad d\theta = \frac{M}{EI}dx \quad (15\text{-}1)$$

From Fig. 15-1(a), quantity $(M/EI)\,dx$ corresponds to an infinitesimal area of the M/EI diagram. According to Eq. 15-1, this area is equal to the change in angle between two adjoining tangents. The contribution of an angle change in one element to the deformation of the elastic curve is shown in Fig. 15-1(b).

If the small angle change $d\theta$ for an element is multiplied by a distance x from an arbitrary origin to the same element, a vertical distance dt is obtained; see Fig. 15-1(b). As only small deflections are considered, no distinction between arc AA' and vertical distance dt need be made. Based on this geometrical reasoning, one has

$$dt = x\,d\theta = \frac{M}{EI}x\,dx \quad (15\text{-}2)$$

Formally integrating Eqs. 15-1 and 15-2 between any two points, such as A and B on a beam (see Fig. 15-2), yields the two moment-area theorems. The **first moment-area theorem** is

$$\int_A^B d\theta = \theta_B - \theta_A = \Delta\theta_{B/A} = \int_A^B \frac{M}{EI}dx \quad (15\text{-}3)$$

where $\Delta\theta_{B/A}$ is the *angle change between B and A*. This change in angle measured in radians between any two tangents at points A and B on the elastic curve is equal to the M/EI area bounded by the ordinates through A and B. Further, if slope θ_A of the elastic curve at A is known, slope θ_B at B is given as

$$\theta_B = \theta_A + \Delta\theta_{B/A} \quad (15\text{-}4)$$

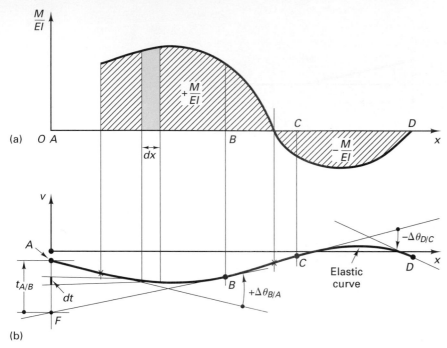

Fig. 15-2   Relationship between the M/EI diagram and the elastic curve.

The first theorem shows that a numerical evaluation of the M/EI area bounded between the ordinates through any two points on the elastic curve gives the angular rotation between the corresponding tangents. In performing this summation, areas corresponding to the positive bending moments are taken positive and those corresponding to the negative moments are taken negative. If the sum of the areas between any two points such as A and B is positive, the tangent on the right rotates in a counterclockwise direction; if negative, the tangent on the right rotates in a clockwise direction; see Fig. 15-2(b). If the net area is zero, the two tangents are parallel.

The quantity dt in Fig. 15-2(b) is due to the effect of curvature of an element. By summing this effect for all elements from A to B, vertical distance AF is obtained. Geometrically, this distance represents the displacement or deviation of a point A from a tangent to the elastic curve at B. Henceforth, it will be termed the *tangential deviation* of a point A from a tangent at B and will be designated $t_{A/B}$. The foregoing, in mathematical form, gives the **second moment-area theorem**:

$$t_{A/B} = \int_A^B d\theta\, x = \int_A^B \frac{M}{EI} x\, dx \qquad (15\text{-}5)$$

This states that the tangential deviation of a point A on the elastic curve from a tangent through another point B also on the elastic curve is equal to the statical (or first) moment of the bounded section of the M/EI diagram around a vertical line through A. In most cases, the tangential deviation is not in itself the desired deflection of a beam.

Using the definition of the center of gravity of an area, one may, for convenience, restate Eq. 15-5 for numerical applications in a simpler form as

$$ t_{A/B} = \Phi\bar{x} \tag{15-6} $$

where Φ is the total area of the M/EI diagram between the two points considered and $\bar{x}$ is the horizontal distance to the centroid of this area *from A*.

By analogous reasoning, the *deviation of a point B from a tangent at A* is

$$ t_{B/A} = \Phi\bar{x}_1 \tag{15-7} $$

where the same M/EI area is used, but $\bar{x}_1$ is measured from the vertical line through point B; see Fig. 15-3. Note carefully the order of the subscript letters for t in these two equations. The point whose deviation is being determined is written first.

In the previous equations, distances $\bar{x}$ and $\bar{x}_1$ are always taken positive; E and I intrinsically are also positive quantities, so the sign of the tangential deviation depends on the sign of the bending moments. A positive value for the tangential deviation indicates that a given point lies above a tangent to the elastic curve drawn through the other point, and vice versa; see Fig. 15-3.

The previous two theorems are applicable between any two points on a *continuous* elastic curve of any beam for any loading. They apply between and beyond the reactions for overhanging and continuous beams. However, it must be emphasized that only relative rotation of the tangents and only tangential deviations are obtained directly. A further consideration of the geometry of the elastic curve at the supports to include the

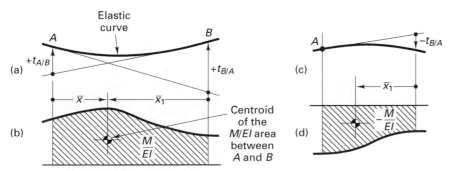

Fig. 15-3   Interpretation of signs for tangential deviation.

boundary conditions is necessary in every case to determine deflections. This will be illustrated in the examples that follow.

In applying the moment-area method, a carefully prepared sketch of the elastic curve is essential. Since no deflection is possible at a pinned or a roller support, the elastic curve is drawn passing through such supports. At a fixed support, neither displacement nor rotation of the tangent to the elastic curve is permitted, so the elastic curve must be drawn tangent to the direction of the unloaded axis of the beam. In preparing a sketch of the elastic curve in the preceding manner, it is customary to exaggerate the anticipated deflections. On such a sketch the deflection of a point on a beam is usually referred to as being above or below its initial position, without emphasis on the signs. To aid in the application of the method, useful properties of areas enclosed by curves and centroids are assembled in Table 2 of the Appendix.

Example 15-1

Consider an aluminum cantilever beam 1600 mm long with a 10-kN force applied 400 mm from the free end, as shown in Fig. 15-4(a). For a distance of 600 mm from the fixed end, the beam is of greater depth than it is beyond, having $I_1 = 50 \times 10^6$ mm^4. For the remaining 1000 mm of the beam, $I_2 = 10 \times 10^6$ mm^4. Find the deflection and the angular rotation of

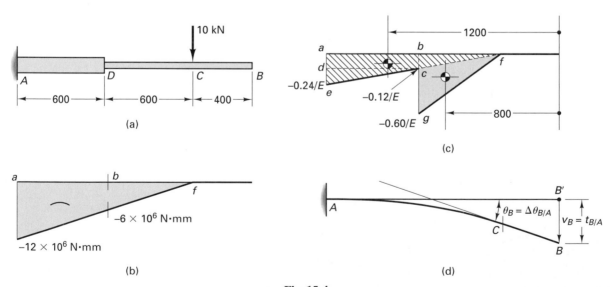

Fig. 15-4

the free end. Neglect the weight of the beam, and assume E for aluminum at 70 GPa.

SOLUTION

The bending-moment diagram is in Fig. 15-4(b). By dividing all ordinates of the M diagram by EI, the M/EI diagram in Fig. 15-4(c) is obtained. Two ordinates appear at point D. One, $-0.12/E$, is applicable just to the left of D; the other, $-0.60/E$, applies just to the right of D. Since the bending moment is negative from A to C, the elastic curve throughout this distance is concave down; see Fig. 15-4(d). At fixed support A, the elastic curve must start out tangent to the initial direction AB' of the unloaded beam. The unloaded straight segment CB of the beam is tangent to the elastic curve at C.

After the foregoing preparatory steps, from the geometry of the sketch of the elastic curve, it may be seen that distance BB' represents the desired deflection of the free end. However, BB' is *also* the tangential deviation of point B from the tangent at A. Therefore, the second moment-area theorem may be used to obtain $t_{B/A}$, which in this special case represents the deflection of the free end. Also, from the geometry of the elastic curve, it is seen that the angle included between lines BC and AB' is the angular rotation of segment CB. This angle is the same as the one included between the tangents to the elastic curve at points A and B, and the first moment-area theorem may be used to compute this quantity.

It is convenient to extend line ec in Fig. 15-4(c) to point f for computing the area of the M/EI diagram. This gives two triangles, the areas of which are easily calculated.

The area of triangle afe:

$$\Phi_1 = -\frac{1200 \times 0.24}{2E} = -\frac{144}{E}$$

The area of triangle feg:

$$\Phi_2 = -\frac{600 \times 0.48}{2E} = -\frac{144}{E}$$

$$\theta_B = \Delta\theta_{B/A} = \int_A^B \frac{M}{EI}dx = \Phi_1 + \Phi_2 = -\frac{288}{70 \times 10^3} = -4.11 \times 10^{-3} \text{ rad}$$

$$v_B = t_{B/A} = \Phi_1\bar{x}_1 + \Phi_2\bar{x}_2$$

$$= \left(-\frac{144}{E}\right) \times 1200 + \left(-\frac{144}{E}\right) \times 800 = -4.11 \text{ mm}$$

The negative sign of $\Delta\theta$ indicates clockwise rotation of the tangent at B in relation to the tangent at A. The negative sign of $t_{B/A}$ means that point B is below a tangent through A.

Example 15-2

Find the deflection due to the concentrated force P applied as shown in Fig. 15.5(a) at the center of a simply supported beam. The flexural rigidity EI is constant.

SOLUTION

The bending-moment diagram is in Fig. 15-5(b). Since EI is constant, the M/EI diagram need not be made, as the areas of the bending-moment diagram divided by EI give the necessary quantities for use in the moment-area theorems. The elastic curve is in Fig. 15-5(c). It is concave upward throughout its length as the bending moments are positive. This curve must pass through the points of the support at A and B.

It is apparent from the diagram of the elastic curve that the desired quantity is represented by distance CC'. Moreover, from purely geometrical or kinematic considerations, $CC' = C'C'' - C''C$, where distance $C''C$ is measured from a tangent to the elastic curve passing through the point of

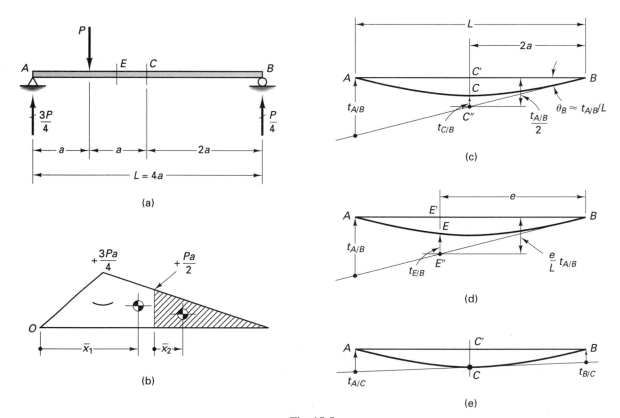

(a)

(b)

(c)

(d)

(e)

Fig. 15-5

support B. However, since the deviation of a support point from a tangent to the elastic curve at the other support may always be computed by the second moment-area theorem, a distance such as $C'C''$ may be found by proportion from the geometry of the figure. In this case, $t_{A/B}$ follows by taking the whole M/EI area between A and B and multiplying it[2] by its $\bar{x}$ measured from a vertical through A; hence, $C'C'' = \frac{1}{2}t_{A/B}$. By another application of the second theorem, $t_{C/B}$, which is equal to $C''C$, is determined. For this case, the M/EI area is hatched in Fig. 15-5(b), and, for it, $\bar{x}$ is measured from C. Since the right reaction is P/4 and the distance $CB = 2a$, the maximum ordinate for the shaded triangle is $+ Pa/2$.

$$v_c = C'C'' - C''C = t_{A/B}/2 - t_{C/B}$$

$$t_{A/B} = \Phi_1\bar{x}_1 = \frac{1}{EI}\left(\frac{4a}{2}\frac{3Pa}{4}\right)\frac{a + 4a}{3} = +\frac{5Pa^3}{2EI}$$

$$t_{C/B} = \Phi_2\bar{x}_2 = \frac{1}{EI}\left(\frac{2a}{2}\frac{Pa}{2}\right)\frac{2a}{3} = +\frac{Pa^3}{3EI}$$

$$v_C = \frac{t_{A/B}}{2} - t_{C/B} = \frac{5Pa^3}{4EI} - \frac{Pa^3}{3EI} = \frac{11Pa^3}{12EI}$$

The positive signs of $t_{A/B}$ and $t_{C/B}$ indicate that points A and C lie above the tangent through B. As may be seen from Fig. 15-5(c), the deflection at the center of the bcam is in a downward direction.

The slope of the elastic curve at C can be found from the slope of one of the ends and from Eq. 15-4. For point B on the right,

$$\theta_B = \theta_C + \Delta\theta_{B/C} \quad \text{or} \quad \theta_C = \theta_B - \Delta\theta_{B/C}$$

$$\theta_C = \frac{t_{A/B}}{L} - \Phi_2 = \frac{5Pa^2}{8EI} - \frac{Pa^2}{2EI} = \frac{Pa^2}{8EI} \quad \text{(counterclockwise)}$$

The previous procedure for finding the deflection of a point on the elastic curve is generally applicable. For example, if the deflection of point E, Fig. 15-5(d), at a distance e from B is wanted, the solution may be formulated as

$$v_E = E'E'' - E'E = (e/L)t_{A/B} - t_{E/B}$$

By locating point E at a variable distance x from one of the supports, the equation of the elastic curve can be obtained.

To simplify the arithmetical work, some care in selecting the tangent at a support must be exercised. Thus, although $v_c = t_{B/A}/2 - t_{C/A}$ (not shown in the diagram), this solution would involve the use of the unshaded portion of the bending-moment diagram to obtain $t_{C/A}$, which is more tedious.

---

[2]See Table 2 of the Appendix for the centroid of the whole triangular area. Alternatively, by treating the whole M/EI area as two triangles,

$$t_{A/B} = \frac{1}{EI}\left(\frac{a}{2}\frac{3Pa}{4}\right)\frac{2a}{3} + \frac{1}{EI}\left(\frac{3a}{2}\frac{3Pa}{4}\right)\left(a + \frac{3a}{3}\right) = +\frac{5Pa^3}{2EI}$$

ALTERNATIVE SOLUTION

The solution of the foregoing problem may be based on a different geo-metrical concept. This is illustrated in Fig. 15-5(e), where a tangent to the elastic curve is drawn at C. Then, since distances AC and CB are equal,

$$v_C = CC' = (t_{A/C} + t_{B/C})/2$$

That is, distance CC' is an average of $t_{A/C}$ and $t_{B/C}$. The tangential deviation $t_{A/C}$ is obtained by taking the first moment of the unshaded M/EI area in Fig. 15-5(b) about A, and $t_{B/C}$ is given by the first moment of the shaded M/EI area about B. The numerical details of this solution are left for com-pletion by the reader. This procedure is usually longer than the first.

Note particularly that if the elastic curve is not symmetrical, the tan-gent at the center of the beam is *not horizontal*.

Example 15-3

For a prismatic beam loaded as in the preceding example, find the maxi-mum deflection caused by applied force P; see Fig. 15-6(a).

SOLUTION

The bending-moment diagram and the elastic curve are shown in Figs. 15-6(b) and (c), respectively. The elastic curve is concave up throughout its length, and the maximum deflection occurs where the tangent to the elastic curve is horizontal. This point of tangency is designated in the figure by D and is located by the unknown horizontal distance d measured from the right support B. Then, by drawing a tangent to the elastic curve through point B at the support, one sees that $\Delta\theta_{B/D} = \theta_B$ since the line passing through the supports is horizontal. However, the slope θ_B of the elastic curve at B may be determined by obtaining $t_{A/B}$ and dividing it by the length of the span. On the other hand, by using the first moment-area theorem, $\Delta\theta_{B/D}$ may be expressed in terms of the shaded area in Fig. 15-6(b). Equating $\Delta\theta_{B/D}$ to θ_B and solving for d locates the horizontal tangent at D. Then, again from geo-metrical considerations, it is seen that the maximum deflection represented by DD' is equal to the tangential deviation of B from a horizontal tangent through D (i.e., $t_{B/D}$).

$$t_{A/B} = \Phi_1 \bar{x}_1 = + \frac{5Pa^3}{2EI} \qquad \text{(see Example 15-2)}$$

$$\theta_B = \frac{t_{A/B}}{L} = \frac{t_{A/B}}{4a} = \frac{5Pa^2}{8EI}$$

$$\Delta\theta_{B/D} = \frac{1}{EI}\left(\frac{d}{2}\frac{Pd}{4}\right) = \frac{Pd^2}{8EI} \quad \text{(area between } D \text{ and } B)$$

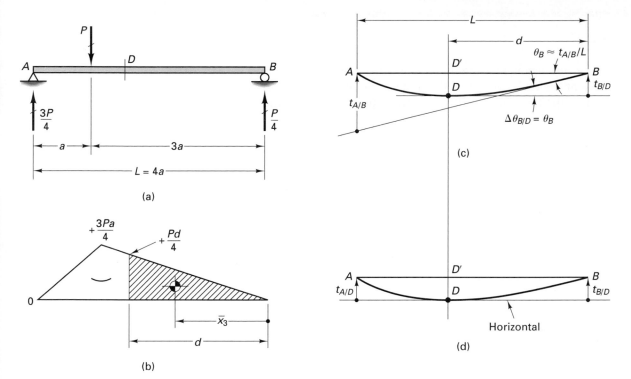

Fig. 15-6

Since $\theta_B = \theta_D + \Delta\theta_{B/D}$ and it is required that $\theta_D = 0$,

$$\Delta\theta_{B/D} = \theta_B \qquad \frac{Pd^2}{8EI} = \frac{5Pa^2}{8EI} \quad \text{hence, } d = \sqrt{5}a$$

$$v_{\max} = v_D = DD' = t_{B/D} = \Phi_3 \bar{x}_3$$

$$= \frac{1}{EI}\left(\frac{d}{2}\frac{Pd}{4}\right)\frac{2d}{3} = \frac{5\sqrt{5}Pa^3}{12EI} = \frac{11.2Pa^3}{12EI}$$

After distance d is found, the maximum deflection may also be obtained as $v_{\max} = t_{A/D}$, or $v_{\max} = (d/L)t_{A/B} - t_{D/B}$ (not shown). Also note that using the condition $t_{A/D} = t_{B/D}$, Fig. 15-6(d), an equation may be set up for d.

It should be apparent from this solution that it is easier to calculate the deflection at the center of the beam, which was illustrated in Example 15-2, than to determine the maximum deflections yet, by examining the end results, one sees that, numerically, the two deflections differ little: $v_{\text{center}} = 11Pa^3/12EI$ as opposed to $v_{\max} = 11.2Pa^3/12EI$. For this reason, in many practical problems of simply supported beams, where all the applied forces act in the same direction, it is often sufficiently accurate to calculate the deflection at the center instead of attempting to obtain the true maximum.

Example 15-4

In a simply supported beam, find the maximum deflection and rotation of the elastic curve at the ends caused by the application of a uniformly distributed load of w_o lb/ft; see Fig. 15-7(a). Flexural rigidity EI is constant.

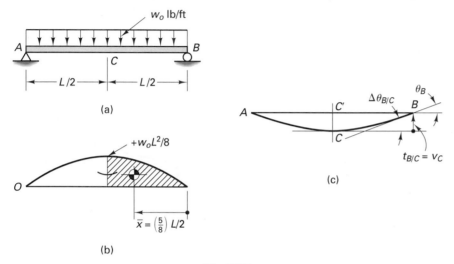

Fig. 15-7

SOLUTION

The bending-moment diagram is shown in Fig. 15-7(b). As established in Example 7-8, it is a second-degree parabola with a maximum value at the vertex of $w_o L^2/8$. The elastic curve passing through the points of supports A and B is shown in Fig. 15-7(c).

In this case, the M/EI diagram is symmetrical about a vertical line passing through the center. Therefore, the elastic curve must be symmetrical, and the tangent to this curve at the center of the beam is horizontal. From the figure, it is seen that $\Delta\theta_{B/C}$ is equal to θ_B, and the rotation of B is equal to one-half the area[3] of the whole M/EI diagram. Distance CC' is the desired deflection, and from the geometry of the figure, it is seen to be equal to $t_{B/C}$ (or $t_{A/C}$, not shown).

$$\Phi = \frac{1}{EI}\left(\frac{2}{3}\frac{L}{2}\frac{w_o L^2}{8}\right) = \frac{w_o L^3}{24EI}$$

[3]See Table 2 of the Appendix for a formula giving an area enclosed by a parabola as well as for $\bar{x}$.

$$\theta_B = \Delta\theta_{B/C} = \Phi = +\frac{w_oL^3}{24EI}$$

$$v_C = v_{max} = t_{B/C} = \Phi\bar{x} = \frac{w_oL^3}{24EI}\frac{5L}{16} = \frac{5w_oL^4}{384EI}$$

The value of the deflection agrees with Eq. 14-22, which expresses the same quantity derived by the integration method. Since point B is above the tangent through C, the sign of v_c is positive.

Example 15-5

Find the deflection of the free end A of the beam shown in Fig. 15-8(a) caused by the applied forces. EI is constant.

SOLUTION

The bending-moment diagram for the applied forces is shown in Fig. 15-8(b). The bending moment changes sign at $a/2$ from the left support. At this point, an inflection in the elastic curve occurs. Corresponding to the positive moment, the curve is concave up, and vice versa. The elastic curve is so drawn and passes over the supports at B and C, Fig. 15-8(c). To begin, the inclination of the tangent to the elastic curve at support B is determined by finding $t_{C/B}$ as the statical moment of the areas with the proper signs of the M/EI diagram between the verticals through C and B about C.

$$t_{C/B} = \Phi_1\bar{x}_1 + \Phi_2\bar{x}_2 + \Phi_3\bar{x}_3$$

$$= \frac{1}{EI}\left[\frac{a}{2}(+Pa)\frac{2a}{3} + \frac{1}{2}\frac{a}{2}(+Pa)\left(a + \frac{1}{3}\frac{a}{2}\right)\right.$$

$$\left. + \frac{1}{2}\frac{a}{2}(-Pa)\left(\frac{3a}{2} + \frac{2}{3}\frac{a}{2}\right)\right]$$

$$= +\frac{Pa^3}{6EI}$$

The positive sign of $t_{C/B}$ indicates that point C is *above the tangent at B*. Hence, a corrected diagram of the elastic curve is made, Fig. 15-8(d), where it is seen that the deflection sought is given by distance AA' and is equal to $AA'' - A'A''$. Further, since triangles $A'A''B$ and $CC'B$ are similar, distance $A'A'' = t_{C/B}/2$. On the other hand, distance AA'' is the deviation of point A from the tangent to the elastic curve at support B. Hence,

$$v_A = AA' = AA'' - A'A'' = t_{C/B}/2$$

$$t_{A/B} = \frac{1}{EI}(\Phi_4\bar{x}_4) = \frac{1}{EI}\left[\frac{a}{2}(-Pa)\frac{2a}{3}\right] = -\frac{Pa^3}{3EI}$$

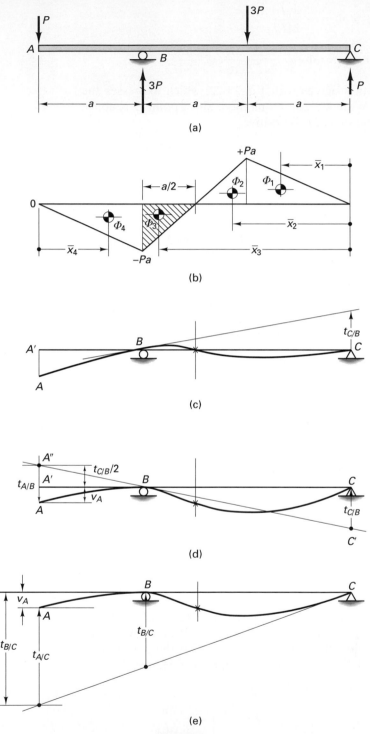

Fig. 15-8

where the negative sign means that point A is below the tangent through B. This sign is not used henceforth, as the geometry of the elastic curve indicates the direction of the actual displacements. Thus, the deflection of point A *below the line passing through the supports is*

$$v_A = \frac{Pa^3}{3EI} - \frac{1}{2}\frac{Pa^3}{6EI} = \frac{Pa^3}{4EI}$$

This example illustrates the necessity of watching the signs of the quantities computed in the applications of the moment-area method, although usually less difficulty is encountered than in this example. For instance, if the deflection of end A is established by first finding the rotation of the elastic curve at C, no ambiguity in the direction of tangents occurs. This scheme of analysis is shown in Fig. 15-8(e), where $v_A = \frac{3}{2}t_{B/C} - t_{A/C}$.

Example 15-6

A simple beam supports two equal and opposite forces P at the quarter points; see Fig. 15.9(a). Find the deflection of the beam at the middle of the span. EI is constant.

SOLUTION

The bending-moment diagram and elastic curve with a tangent at C are shown in Figs. 15-9(b) and (c), respectively. Then, since the statical moments of the positive and negative areas of the bending-moment diagram around A and B, respectively, are numerically equal (i.e., $|t_{A/C}| = |t_{B/C}|$), the deflection of the beam at the center of the span is *zero*. The elastic curve in

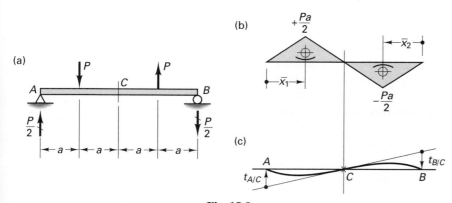

Fig. 15-9

this case is *anti*symmetrical. Noting this, much work may be avoided in obtaining the deflections at the *center of the span*. The deflection of *any other point on the elastic curve can be found in the usual manner*.

The foregoing examples illustrate the manner in which the moment-area method can be used to obtain the deflection of any statically determinate beam. No matter how complex the M/EI diagrams may become, the previous procedures are applicable. In practice, any M/EI diagram whatsoever may be approximated by a number of rectangles and triangles. It is also possible to introduce concentrated angle changes at hinges to account for discontinuities in the direction of the tangents at such points. The magnitudes of the concentrations can be found from kinematic requirements.[4]

For complicated loading conditions, deflections of elastic beams determined by the moment-area method are often best found by superposition. In this manner, the areas of the separate M/EI diagrams may become simple geometrical shapes. In the next section, superposition is used in solving statically indeterminate problems.

The method described here can be used very effectively in determining the inelastic deflection of beams, provided the M/EI diagrams are replaced by the curvature diagrams, such as in Fig. 14-26(c).

15-4. Statically Indeterminate Beams

Statically indeterminate beams can readily be solved for unknown reactions using the moment-area method by employing superposition. After the redundant reactions are determined, the beam deflections and rotations can be found in the usual manner, again often employing superposition. Two different procedures for finding the redundant reactions are considered in this section. In the more widely used procedure, it is recognized that restrained[5] and continuous beams differ from simply supported beams mainly by the presence of redundant moments at the supports. Therefore, bending-moment diagrams for these beams may be considered to consist of two independent parts—one part for the moment caused by all of the applied loading on a beam assumed to be simply supported, the other part for the redundant end moments. Thus, the effect of redundant end moments is superposed on a beam assumed to be simply supported. Physically, this notion can be clarified by imagining an indeterminate beam cut through at the supports while the vertical reactions are maintained.

---

[4]For a systematic treatment of more complex problems, see, for example, A. C. Scordelis and C. M. Smith, "An analytical procedure for calculating truss displacements," *Proc. ASCE,* **732** (July 1955), 732-1−732-17.

[5]Indeterminate beams with one or more fixed ends are called *restrained beams*.

The continuity of the elastic curve of the beam is preserved by the redundant moments.

Although the critical ordinates of the bending-moment diagrams caused by the redundant moments are not known, their shape is known. Application of a redundant moment at an end of a simple beam results in a triangular-shaped moment diagram, with a maximum at the applied moment and a zero ordinate at the other end. Likewise, when end moments are present at both ends of a simple beam, two triangular moment diagrams superpose into a trapezoidal-shaped diagram.

The known and the unknown parts of the bending-moment diagram together give a complete bending-moment diagram. This whole diagram can then be used in applying the moment-area theorems to the continuous elastic curve of a beam. The geometrical conditions of a problem, such as the continuity of the elastic curve at the support or the tangents at built-in ends that cannot rotate, permit a rapid formulation of equations for the unknown values of the redundant moments at the supports.

An alternative method for determining the redundant reactions employs a procedure of plotting the bending-moment diagrams by parts. In applying this method, only one of the existing fixed supports is left in place, creating a cantilever. Then separate bending-moment diagrams for *each one* of the applied forces as well as for the unknown reactions at the unsupported beam end are drawn. The sum of *all* of these moment diagrams for the *cantilever* make up the *complete* bending-moment diagram then used in the usual manner.

In either method, for beams of variable flexural rigidity, the moment diagrams must be divided by the corresponding EI's.

Both methods of solving for the redundant reactions are illustrated in the following examples.

Example 15-7

Find the maximum downward deflection of the small aluminum beam shown in Fig. 15-10(a) due to an applied force $P = 100$ N. The beam's constant flexural rigidity $EI = 60$ N $\cdot$ m^2.

SOLUTION

The solution of this problem consists of two parts. First, a redundant reaction must be determined to establish the numerical values for the bending-moment diagram; then the usual moment-area procedure is applied to find the deflection.

By assuming the beam is released from the redundant end moment, a simple beam-moment diagram is constructed above the base line in Fig. 15-10(b). The moment diagram of known shape due to the unknown

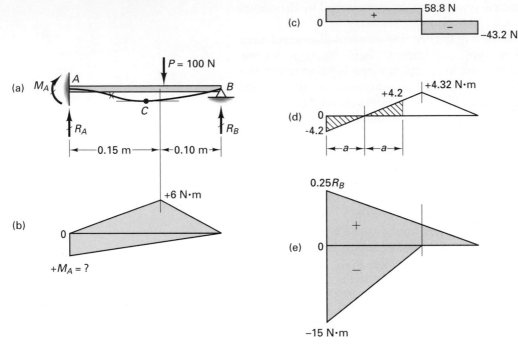

Fig. 15-10

redundant moment M_A is shown on the same diagram below the base line. One assumes M_A to be positive, since in this manner, its correct sign is obtained automatically according to the beam sign convention. The composite diagram represents a *complete* bending-moment diagram.

The tangent at the built-in end remains horizontal after the application of force P. Hence, the geometrical condition is $t_{B/A} = 0$. An equation formulated on this basis yields a solution for M_A.[6] The equations of static equilibrium are used to compute the reactions. The final bending-moment diagram, Fig. 15-10(d), is obtained in the usual manner after the reactions are known. Thus, since $t_{B/A} = 0$,

$$\frac{1}{EI}\left[\frac{1}{2}(0.25)(6)\frac{1}{3}(0.25 + 0.10) + \frac{1}{2}(0.25)M_A\frac{2}{3}(0.25)\right] = 0$$

Hence, $M_A = -4.2$ N · m. Since, initially, M_A was assumed to be positive, and is so shown in Figs. 15-10(a) and (b), this result indicates that actually M_A has an *opposite* sense. The correct sense for M_A must be used in the

---

[6]See Table 2 of the Appendix for the centroidal distance of a whole triangle.

equations of statics that follow and is reflected in the shear and moment diagrams constructed in Figs. 15-10(c) and (d), respectively.

$$\sum M_A = 0 \curvearrowright + 100(0.15) - R_B(0.25) - 4.2 = 0 \quad R_B = 43.2 \text{ N}$$

$$\sum M_B = 0 \curvearrowleft + 100(0.10 + 4.2 - R_A(0.25) = 0 \quad R_A = 56.8 \text{ N}$$

Check: $\sum F_y = 0 \uparrow + \quad 43.2 + 56.8 - 100 \quad = 0$

The maximum deflection occurs where the tangent to the elastic curve is horizontal, point C in Fig. 15-10(a). Hence, by noting that the tangent at A is also horizontal and using the first moment-area theorem, point C is located. This occurs when the hatched areas in Fig. 15-10(d) having opposite signs are equal; that is, at a distance $2a = 2(4.2/56.8) = 0.148$ m from A. The tangential deviation $t_{A/C}$ (or $t_{C/A}$) gives the deflection of point C.

$$v_{\max} = v_C = t_{A/C}$$

$$= \frac{1}{EI}\left[\frac{1}{2} \times 0.074(+4.2)\left(0.074 + \frac{2}{3} \times 0.074\right) \right.$$

$$\left. + \frac{1}{2} \times 0.074(-4.2)\frac{1}{3} \times 0.074 \right]$$

$$= (15.36)10^{-3}/EI = 0.256 \text{ mm} \quad \text{(down)}$$

ALTERNATIVE SOLUTION

A rapid solution can also be obtained by plotting the moment diagram by cantilever parts. This is shown in Fig. 15-10(e). Note that one of the ordinates is in terms of the redundant reaction R_B. Again, using the geometrical condition $t_{B/A} = 0$, one obtains an equation yielding R_B. Other reactions follow by statics. From $t_{B/A} = 0$,

$$\frac{1}{EI}\left[\frac{1}{2}(0.25)(+0.25R_B)\frac{2}{3}(0.25) + \frac{1}{2}(0.15)(-15)\left(0.1 + \frac{2}{3} \times 0.15\right)\right] = 0$$

Hence, $R_B = 43.2$ N, acting up as assumed.

$$\sum M_A = 0 \curvearrowleft + M_A + 43.2(0.25) - 100(0.15) = 0 \quad M_A = 4.2 \text{ N} \cdot \text{m}$$

Here M_A, within the equation of statics for the summation of moments, is considered positive since it is assumed to act in a *counterclockwise* direction. However, in the *beam sign convention,* such an end moment at A is negative.

After the combined moment diagram is constructed, Fig. 15-10(d), the remainder of the work is the same as in the preceding solution.

Example 15-8

Find the moments at the supports for a fixed-end beam loaded with a uniformly distributed load of w_o N/m; see Fig. 15-11(a).

SOLUTION

The moments at the supports are called fixed-end moments, and their determination is of great importance in structural theory. Due to symmetry in this problem, the fixed-end moments are equal, as are the vertical reactions, which are $w_o L/2$ each. The moment diagram for this beam, considered to be simply supported, is a parabola, as shown in Fig. 15-11(b), while the assumed positive fixed-end moments give the rectangular diagram shown in the same figure.

Although this beam is statically indeterminate to the second degree, because of symmetry, a single equation based on a geometrical condition is sufficient to yield the redundant moments. From the geometry of the elastic curve, any one of the following conditions may be used: $\Delta\theta_{A/B} = 0$,[7] $t_{B/A} = 0$, or $t_{A/B} = 0$. From the first condition, $\Delta\theta_{A/B} = 0$,

$$\frac{1}{EI}\left[\frac{2}{3}L\left(+\frac{w_o L^2}{8}\right) + L(+M_A)\right] = 0$$

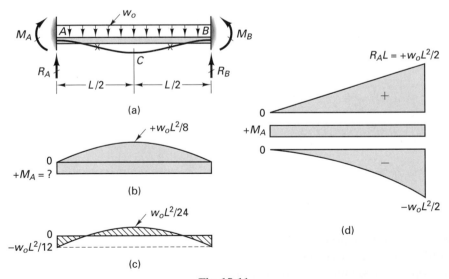

(a)

(b)

(c)

(d)

Fig. 15-11

---

[7]Also, since the tangent at the center of the span is horizontal, $\Delta\theta_{A/C} = 0$ and $\Delta\theta_{C/B} = 0$.

Then

$$M_A = M_B = -\frac{w_o L^2}{12} \qquad (15\text{-}8)$$

The negative sign for these moments indicates that their sense is opposite from that assumed in Figs. 15-11(a) and (b).

The composite moment diagram is shown in Fig. 15-11(c). In comparison with the maximum bending moment of a simple beam, a considerable reduction in the magnitude of the critical moments occurs.

ALTERNATIVE SOLUTION

The moment diagram by cantilever parts is shown in Fig. 15-11(d). Noting that $R_A = R_B = w_o L/2$, and using the same geometrical condition as above, $\Delta\theta_{A/B} = 0$, one can verify the former solution as follows:

$$\frac{1}{EI}\left[\frac{1}{2}L\left(+\frac{w_o L^2}{2} \right) + L(+M_A) + \frac{1}{3}L\left(-\frac{w_o L^2}{2} \right) \right] = 0$$

and

$$M_A = -\frac{w_o L^2}{12}$$

Example 15-9

A beam fixed at both ends carries a concentrated force P, as shown in Fig. 15-12. Find the fixed-end moments. EI is constant.

SOLUTION

By treating beam AB as a simple beam, the moment diagram due to P is shown above the base line in Fig. 15-12(b). The assumed positive fixed-end moments are *not equal* and result in the trapezoidal diagram. Three geometrical conditions for the elastic curve are available to solve this problem, which is indeterminate to the second degree:

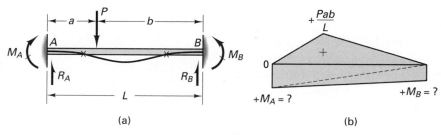

(a)   (b)

Fig. 15-12

(a) $\Delta\theta_{A/B} = 0$, since the change in angle between the tangents at A and B is zero.

(b) $t_{B/A} = 0$, since support B does not deviate from a fixed tangent at A.

(c) Similarly, $t_{A/B} = 0$.

Any two of these conditions may be used; arithmetical simplicity of the resulting equations governs the choice. Thus, by using condition (a), which is always the simplest, and condition (b), the two equations are[8]

$$\Delta\theta_{A/B} = \frac{1}{EI}\left(\frac{1}{2}L\frac{Pab}{L} + \frac{1}{2}LM_A + \frac{1}{2}LM_B\right) = 0$$

or

$$M_A + M_B = -\frac{Pab}{L}$$

$$t_{B/A} = \frac{1}{EI}\left[\frac{1}{2}L\frac{Pab}{L}\frac{1}{3}(L+b) + \frac{1}{2}LM_A\frac{2}{3}L + \frac{1}{2}LM_B\frac{1}{3}L\right] = 0$$

or

$$2M_A + M_B = -\frac{Pab}{L^2}(L+b)$$

Solving the two reduced equations simultaneously gives

$$M_A = -\frac{Pab^2}{L^2}\quad\text{and}\quad M_B = -\frac{Pa^2b}{L^2}$$

These negative moments have an opposite sense from that initially assumed and shown in Figs. 15-12(a) and (b).

Example 15-10

Plot moment and shear diagrams for a continuous beam loaded as shown in Fig. 15-13(a). *EI* is constant for the whole beam.

SOLUTION

This beam is statically indeterminate to the second degree. By treating each span as a simple beam with the redundant moments assumed positive, the moment diagram of Fig. 15-13(c) is obtained. For each span, these diagrams

---

[8]See Table 2 of the Appendix for the centroidal distance of a whole triangle.

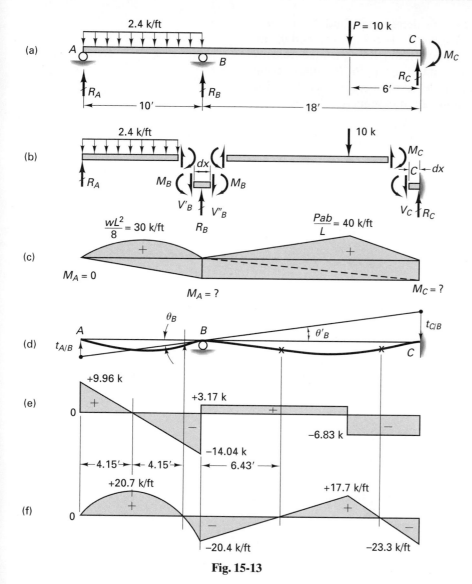

Fig. 15-13

are similar to the ones shown earlier in Figs. 15-10(b) and 15-12(b). No end moments exist at A as this end is on a roller. The clue to the solution is contained in two geometrical conditions for the elastic curve for the whole beam, Fig. 15-13(d):

(a) $\theta_B = \theta'_B$. Since the beam is physically continuous, there is a line at support B that is tangent to the elastic curve in *either* span.

(b) $t_{B/C} = 0$, since support B does not deviate from a fixed tangent at C.

To apply condition (a), $t_{A/B}$ and $t_{C/B}$ are determined, and, by *dividing these quantities by the respective span lengths,* the two angles θ_B and θ'_B are obtained. These angles are equal. However, although $t_{C/B}$ is algebraically expressed as a positive quantity, the tangent through point B is *above* point C. Therefore, this deviation must be considered negative. Hence, by using condition (a), one equation with the redundant moments is obtained.

$$t_{A/B} = \frac{1}{EI}\left[\frac{2}{3}10(+30)\frac{1}{2}10 + \frac{1}{2}10(+M_B)\frac{2}{3}10\right]$$

$$= \frac{1}{EI}\left(1000 + \frac{1}{3}100M_B\right)$$

$$t_{C/B} = \frac{1}{EI}\left[\frac{1}{2}18(+40)\frac{1}{3}(18+6) + \frac{1}{2}18(+M_B)\frac{2}{3}18 + \frac{1}{2}18(+M_c)\frac{1}{3}18\right]$$

$$= \frac{1}{EI}(2880 + 108M_B + 54M_C)$$

Since

$$\theta_B = \theta'_B \quad \text{or} \quad \frac{t_{A/B}}{L_{AB}} = -\frac{t_{C/B}}{L_{CB}}$$

$$\frac{1}{EI}\left(\frac{1000 + 100M_B/3}{10}\right) = -\frac{1}{EI}\left(\frac{2880 + 108M_B + 54M_C}{18}\right)$$

or

$$28M_B/3 + 3M_C = -260$$

Using condition (b) for span BC provides another equation, $t_{B/C} = 0$, or

$$\frac{1}{EI}\left[\frac{1}{2}18(+40)\frac{1}{3}(18+12) + \frac{1}{2}18(+M_B)\frac{1}{3}18 + \frac{1}{2}18(+M_C)\frac{2}{3}18\right] = 0$$

or

$$3M_B + 6M_C = -200$$

Solving the two reduced equations simultaneously,

$$M_B = -20.4 \text{ ft-lb} \quad \text{and} \quad M_C = -23.3 \text{ ft-lb}$$

where the signs agree with the convention of signs used for beams. These moments with their proper sense are shown in Fig. 15-13(b).

After the redundant moments M_A and M_B are found, no new techniques are necessary to construct the moment and shear diagrams. *However, particular care must be exercised to include the moments at the supports while computing shears and reactions.* Usually, isolated beams, as shown in Fig. 15-13(b), are the most convenient freebodies for determining shears. Reactions follow by adding the shears on the adjoining beams.

For free body AB:

$$\sum M_B = 0 \curvearrowright + 2.4(10)5 - 20.4 - 10R_A = 0 \quad R_A = 9.96 \text{ k} \uparrow$$

$$\sum M_A = 0 \curvearrowright + 2.4(10)5 + 20.4 - 10V_B' = 0 \quad V_B' = 14.04 \text{ k} \uparrow$$

For free body BC:

$$\sum M_C = 0 \curvearrowright + 10(6) + 20.4 - 23.3 - 18V_B'' = 0$$

$$V_B'' = 3.17 \text{ k} \uparrow$$

$$\sum M_B = 0 \curvearrowright + 10(12) - 20.4 + 23.3 - 18V_C = 0$$

$$V_C = R_C = 6.83 \text{ k} \uparrow$$

Check:$R_A + V_B' = 24 \text{ k} \uparrow \qquad \text{and} \qquad V_B'' + R_C = 10 \text{ k} \uparrow$

Thus, $R_B = V_B' + V_B'' = 17.21 \text{ kips} \uparrow$.

The complete shear and moment diagrams are shown in Figs. 15-13(e) and (f), respectively.

Generalizing the procedure used in the preceding example, a recurrence formula (i.e., an equation that may be repeatedly applied for every two adjoining spans) may be derived for continuous beams. For any n number of spans, $n - 1$ such equations may be written. This gives enough simultaneous equations for the solution of redundant moments over the supports. This recurrence formula is called the *three-moment equation* because three unknown moments appear in it.[9]

---

[9]For discussion of this procedure, see, for example, E. P. Popov, *Mechanics of Materials,* 2nd ed. (Englewood Cliffs, NJ: Prentice Hall, 1976), 435–440.

PROBLEMS

Section 15-3. Beam deflections for specified points in many of the problems for sections 15-7 and 15-8 can be assigned for solution by the moment-area method.

15-1 through 15-12. Using the moment-area method, determine the deflection and the slope of the elastic curves at points A due to the applied loads for the beams, as shown in the figures. Specify the direction of deflection and of rotation for the calculated quantities. If neither the size of a beam nor its moment of inertia are given, EI is constant. Wherever needed, let $E = 29 \times 10^3$ ksi or 200 GPa. In all cases, a well-prepared sketch of the elastic curve, showing the inflection points, should be made.

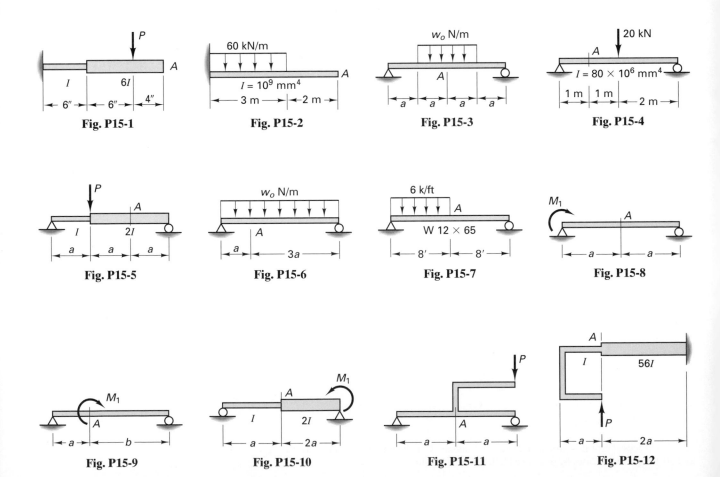

Fig. P15-1   Fig. P15-2   Fig. P15-3   Fig. P15-4

Fig. P15-5   Fig. P15-6   Fig. P15-7   Fig. P15-8

Fig. P15-9   Fig. P15-10   Fig. P15-11   Fig. P15-12

15-13. Determine the deflection at the midspan of a simple beam, loaded as shown in the figure, by solving the two separate problems indicated and superimposing the results. Use the moment-area method. *EI* is constant. (*Note:* Solution of complex problems by subdividing them into a symmetrical part and an unsymmetrical part is often very advantageous because it reduces the numerical work.)

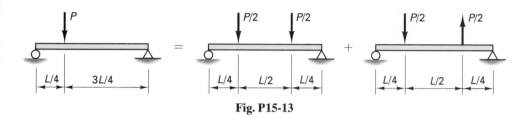

Fig. P15-13

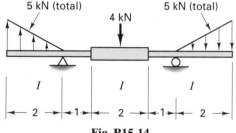

Fig. P15-14

15-14. Determine the elastic deflection at the center of the span for the beam loaded as shown in the figure if $I_1 = 10 \times 10^6$ mm^4, $I_2 = 20 \times 10^6$ mm^4, and $E = 70$ GPa. All given dimensions are in meters.

15-15. Using the moment-area method, establish the equation of the elastic curve for the beam in Problem 14-9.

15-16. Using the moment-area method, establish the equation of the elastic curve for the beam in Problem 15-6.

15-17. Using the moment-area method, determine the maximum deflection for the beam in Problem 15-8.

15-18. Using the moment-area method, determine the maximum deflection for the beam in Problem 15-9.

15-19. Using the moment-area method, determine the maximum deflection for the beam in Problem 15-5.

15-20. Using the moment-area method, determine the maximum deflection for the beam in Problem 15-10.

15-21. Using the moment-area method, rework Problem 14-38, and, in addition, determine the maximum deflection.

15-22. For the beam loaded as shown in the figure, determine (a) the deflection at the center of the span, (b) the deflection at the point of inflection of the elastic curve, and (c) the maximum deflection, $EI = 1800$ lb-in².

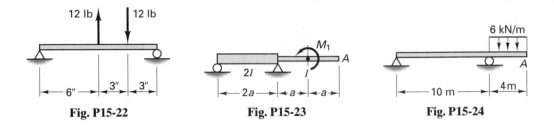

Fig. P15-22   Fig. P15-23   Fig. P15-24

15-23 and 15-24. Using the moment-area method, determine the deflection and slope of the overhang at point A for the beams loaded as shown in the figures. EI in the second problem is constant.

15-25. Determine the maximum *upward* deflection for the overhang of a beam loaded as shown in the figure. E and I are constant.

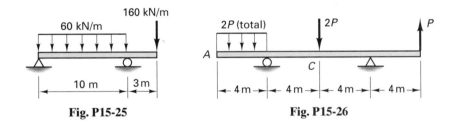

Fig. P15-25   Fig. P15-26

15-26. For the elastic beam of constant flexural rigidity EI, loaded as shown in the figure, find the deflection and the slope at points A and C.

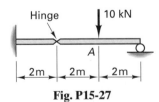

Fig. P15-27

15-27. A structure is formed by joining a simple beam to a cantilever with a hinge, as shown in the figure. If a 10-kN force is applied at the center of the simple span, determine the deflection at A caused by this force. EI is constant over the entire structure.

15-28. A hinged beam system is loaded as shown in the figure. Determine the deflection and slope of the elastic curve at point A.

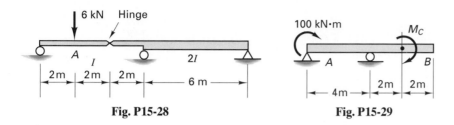

Fig. P15-28   Fig. P15-29

15-29. Beam AB is subjected to an end moment at A and an unknown concentrated moment M_C, as shown in the figure. Using the moment-area method, determine the magnitude of the bending moment M_C so that the deflection at point B will be equal to zero. EI is constant.

15-30. The beam shown in the figure has a constant $EI = 3600 \times 10^6$ lb-in^2. Determine the distance a such that the deflection at A would be 0.25 in if the end were subjected to a concentrated moment $M_A = 15$ k-ft.

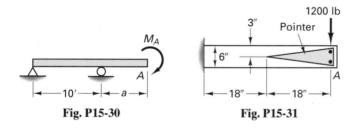

Fig. P15-30   Fig. P15-31

15-31. A light pointer is attached only at A to a 6×6 in (actual) wooden beam, as shown in the figure. Determine the position of the end of the pointer after a concentrated force of 1200 lb is applied. $E = 1.2 \times 10^6$ psi.

15-32. Beam $ABCD$ is initially horizontal. Load P is then applied at C, as shown in the figure. It is desired to place a vertical force at B to bring the position of the beam at B back to the original level $ABCD$. What force is required at B?

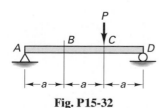

Fig. P15-32

Section 15-4

15-33 and 15-34.   For the beams loaded as shown in the figures, using the moment-area method, determine the redundant reactions and plot shear and moment diagrams. In both problems, EI is constant.

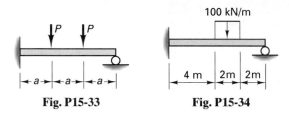

Fig. P15-33   Fig. P15-34

15-35.   For the beam loaded as shown in the figure, (a) determine the ratio of the moment at the fixed end to the applied moment M_A; (b) determine the rotation of the end A. EI is constant.

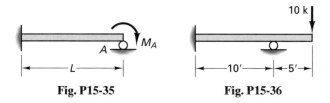

Fig. P15-35   Fig. P15-36

15-36.   (a) Using the moment-area method, determine the redundant moment at the fixed end for the beam shown in the figure, and plot the shear and moment diagrams. Neglect the weight of the beam. (b) Select a W beam using an allowable bending stress of 18,000 psi and a shearing stress of 12,000 psi. (c) Determine the maximum deflection of the beam between the supports and the maximum deflection of the overhang. $E = 29 \times 10^6$ psi.

15-37.   (a) Using the moment-area method, determine the redundant moment at the fixed end for the beam shown in the figure and plot the shear and moment diagrams. Neglect the weight of the beam. (b) Select the depth for a 200-mm-wide wooden beam using an allowable bending stress of 8000 kN/m^2 and a shear stress of 1000 kN/M^2.

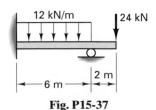

Fig. P15-37

15-38. For the beam of constant flexural rigidity EI and loaded as shown in the figure, (a) determine the reaction and the deflection at point A. The spring constant $k = 3EI/a^3$. (b) Plot the shear and moment diagrams. Show the deflected shape of the beam.

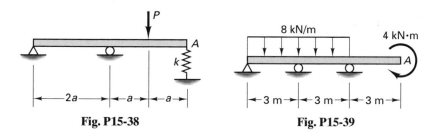

Fig. P15-38   Fig. P15-39

15-39. For the beam loaded as shown in the figure, (a) plot the shear and bending moment diagrams, (b) sketch the shape of the elastic curve showing the point of inflection, and (c) determine the rotation of end A.

15-40. For the beam loaded as shown in the figure, (a) determine the ratio of the moment at the fixed end to the applied moment M_A; (b) determine the rotation of end A.

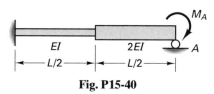

Fig. P15-40

15-41. Using the moment-area method, show that the maximum deflection of a beam fixed at both ends and carrying a uniformly distributed load is one-fifth the maximum deflection of the same beam simply supported. EI is constant.

15-42 and 15-43. For the beams of constant EI shown in the figures, using the moment-area method, (a) determine the fixed-end moments due to the applied loads and plot shear and bending-moment diagrams. (b) Find the maximum deflections.

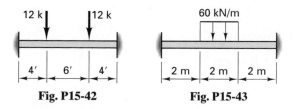

Fig. P15-42   Fig. P15-43

15-44 through 15-47. For the beams of constant flexural rigidity shown in the figures, plot the shear and bending-moment diagrams. Locate points of inflection and sketch the elastic curves.

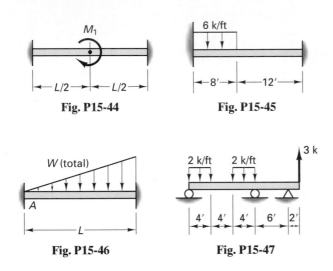

Fig. P15-44   Fig. P15-45

Fig. P15-46   Fig. P15-47

15-48. A beam of constant flexural rigidity EI is fixed at both its ends, a distance L apart. If one of the supports settles vertically downward an amount Δ relative to the other support (without causing any rotation), what moments will be induced at the ends?

15-49 and 15-50. Plot the shear and bending-moment diagrams for the beams of variable flexural rigidities shown in the figures. Locate points of inflection and sketch the elastic curves.

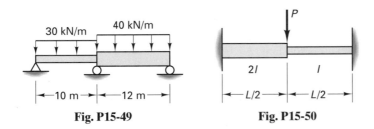

Fig. P15-49   Fig. P15-50

15-51. Rework Example 15-10 after assuming that right support C is pinned.

15-52. After assuming that the left support is fixed, rework Problem 15-47.

15-53. Assuming that both supports A and C are fixed, rework Example 15-10.

16

Columns

16-1. Introduction

The selection of structural and machine elements is based on three characteristics: **strength, stiffness,** and **stability.** The procedures of stress and deformation analyses in a state of *stable* equilibrium were discussed in some detail in the preceding chapters. But not all structural systems are necessarily stable. For example, consider a metal rod with square ends of 10 mm in diameter. If such a rod were made 20 mm long to act as an axially compressed member, no question of instability would enter, and a considerable force could be applied. On the other hand, if another rod of the same material were made 1000 mm long to act in compression, then, at a much smaller load than the short piece could carry, the long rod would buckle laterally and could collapse. A slender measuring stick, if subjected to an axial compression, could fail in the same manner. The consideration of material strength alone is not sufficient to predict the behavior of such members. Stability considerations are primary in some structural systems.

The phenomenon of structural instability occurs in numerous situations where compressive stresses are present. Thin sheets, although fully capable

Fig. 16-1   Typical buckling patterns for thin-walled cylinders (a) in compression and (b) in torsion for a pressurized cylinder. (Courtesy L. A. Harris of North American Aviation, Inc.)

of sustaining tensile loadings, are very poor in transmitting compression. Narrow beams, unbraced laterally, can turn sidewise and collapse under an applied load. Vacuum tanks, as well as submarine hulls, unless properly designed, can severely distort under external pressure and can assume shapes that differ drastically from their original geometry. A thin-walled tube can wrinkle like tissue paper when subjected either to axial compression or a torque; see Fig. 16-1.[1] During some stages of firing, the thin casings of rockets are critically loaded in compression. These are crucially important problems for engineering design. Moreover, often the buckling or wrinkling phenomena observed in loaded members occur rather suddenly. For this reason, many structural instability failures are spectacular and very dangerous.

[1]Figures are adapted from L. A. Harris, H. W. Suer, and W. T. Skene, "Model investigations of unstiffened and stiffened circular shells," *Experimental Mechanics* (July 1961), 3 and 5.

A vast number of the structural instability problems suggested by the preceding listing of problems are beyond the scope of this text.[2] Essentially, only the column problem will be considered here.

For convenience, this chapter is divided into two parts. Part A is devoted to the theory of column buckling, and Part B deals with design applications. First, however, examples of possible instabilities that may occur in straight prismatic members with different cross sections will be discussed. This will be followed by establishing the stability criteria for static equilibrium. The purpose of the next two introductory sections is to clarify for the reader the aspects of column instability considered in the remainder of the chapter.

16-2. Examples of Instability

Analysis of the general instabilty problem of even straight *prismatic* columns discussed in this chapter is rather complex, and it is important to be aware, at least in a *qualitative* way, of the complexities involved to understand the limitations of the subsequently derived equations. Buckling of straight columns is strongly influenced by the type of cross section, and some considerations of this problem follow.

In numerous engineering applications, compression members have tubular cross sections. If the wall thickness is thin, the platelike elements of such members can buckle locally. An example of this behavior is illustrated in Fig. 16-2(a) for a square thin-walled tube. At a sufficiently large axial load, the side walls tend to subdivide into a sequence of alternating inward and outward buckles. As a consequence, the plates carry a smaller axial stress in the regions of large amount of buckling displacement away from corners; see Fig. 16-2(b). For such cases, it is customary to approximate the complex stress distribution by a constant allowable stress acting over an *effective width w* next to the corners or stiffeners.[3] In this text, except for the design of aluminum-alloy columns, it will be assumed that the thicknesses of a column plate element are sufficiently large to exclude the need for considering this local buckling phenomenon.

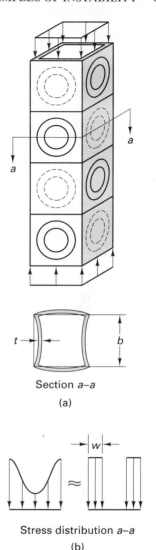

Section *a–a*

(a)

Stress distribution *a–a*

(b)

Fig. 16-2 Schematic of buckled thin-walled square tube.

[2] F. Bleich, *Buckling Strength of Metal Structures* (New York: McGraw-Hill, 1952); D. O. Brush and B. O. Almroth, *Buckling of Bars, Plates, and Shells* (New York: McGraw-Hill, 1975); A. Chajes, *Principles of Structural Stability* (Englewood Cliffs, NJ. Prentice Hall, 1974); G. Gerard et al., *Handbook of Structural Stability*, Parts I–VI, NACA TN, 3781–3786 (Washington, DC: NASA, 1957–1958); B. G. Johnston (ed.), *Design Criteria for Metal Compression Members*, 4th ed. (New York: Wiley, 1988); S. P. Timoshenko and J. M. Gere, *Theory of Elastic Stability*, 2nd ed. (New York: McGraw-Hill, 1961); A. S. Volmire, *Flexible Plates and Shells*, Air Force Flight Dynamics Laboratory (trans.), Technical Report No. 66-216, Wright-Patterson Air Force Base, 1967.

[3] T. von Karman, E. E. Sechler, and L. H. Donnell, "The strength of thin plates in compression," *Trans. ASME, 54,* APM-54-5 (1932), 53–57. See also references given in the last footnote.

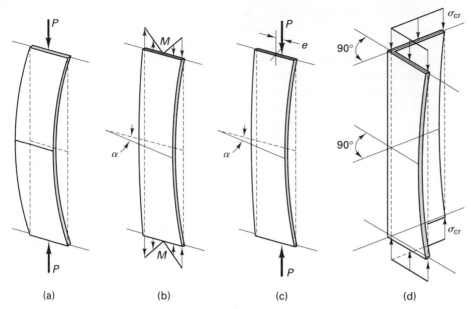

Fig. 16-3   Column buckling modes: (a) pure flexural, (b) and (c) torsional-flexural, and (d) pure torsional.

Some aspects requiring attention in a general column instability problem are illustrated in Fig. 16-3. Here the emphasis is placed on the kind of buckling that is possible in prismatic members. A plank of limited flexural but adequate torsional stiffness subjected to an axial compressive force is shown to buckle in a bending mode; see Fig. 16-3(a). If the same plank is subjected to end moments, Fig. 16-3(b), in addition to a flexural buckling mode, the cross sections also have a tendency to twist. This is a torsion-bending mode of buckling, and the same kind of buckling may occur for the eccentric force P, as shown in Fig. 16-3(c). Lastly, a pure torsional buckling mode is illustrated in Fig. 16-3(d). This occurs when the torsional stiffness of a member is small. As can be recalled from Section 6-14, thin-walled *open sections* are generally poor in torsional stiffness. In contrast, thin-walled *tubular* members are excellent for resisting torques and are torsionally stiff. Therefore, a tubular member, such as shown in Fig. 16-2, generally will not exhibit torsional buckling. A number of the open thin-walled sections in Fig. 16-4 are next examined for their susceptibility to torsional buckling.

Two sections having biaxial symmetry, where centroids C and shear centers S coincide, are shown in Fig. 16-4(a). Compression members having such cross sections buckle either in pure flexure, Fig. 16-3(a), or twist around S, Fig. 16-3(d). For *thin-walled* members, when the torsional stiffness (Section 6-14) is smaller than the flexural stiffness, a column may twist

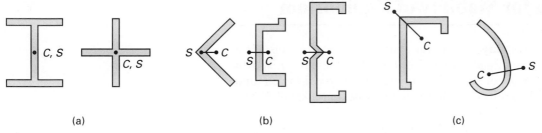

Fig. 16-4 Column sections exhibiting different buckling modes.

before exhibiting flexural buckling. Generally, this is more likely to occur in columns with cruciform cross sections than in I-shaped sections. However, the torsional mode of buckling generally does not control the design, since the usual rolled or extruded metal cross sections are relatively thick.

The cross sections shown in Figs. 16-4(b) and (c) have their centroids C and shear centers S in different locations. Flexural buckling would occur for the sections in Fig. 16-4(b) if the smallest flexural stiffness around the major principal axis is less than the torsional stiffness. Otherwise, simultaneous flexural and torsional buckling would develop, with the member twisting around S. For the sections in Fig. 16-4(c), buckling always occurs in the latter mode. In the subsequent derivations, it will be assumed that the wall thicknesses of members are sufficiently large to exclude the possibility of torsional or torsional-flexural buckling. Compression members having cross sections of the type shown in Fig. 16-4(c) are not considered.

The following interesting cases of possible buckling of straight members are also excluded from consideration in this text. One of these is shown in Fig. 16-5, where two bars with pinned joints at the ends form a very small angle with the horizontal. In this case, it is possible that applied force P can reach a magnitude such that the deformed compressed bars become horizontal. Then, on a slightly further increase in P, the bars *snap through* to a new equilibrium position. This kind of instability is of great importance in shallow thin-walled shells and curved plates. Another possible buckling problem is shown in Fig. 16-6, where a slender circular bar is subjected to torque T. When applied torque T reaches a critical value, the bar snaps into a helical spatial curve.[4] This problem is of importance in the design of long, slender transmission shafts.

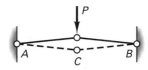

Fig. 16-5 Snap-through of compression bars.

Fig. 16-6 Spiral spatial twist-buckling of a slender shaft.

---

[4]A. G. Greenhill, "On the strength of shafting when exposed both to torsion and to end thrust. Appendix: Theoretical investigation of the stability of shafting under given forces," *Proceedings* (London: Institution of Mechanical Engineers, 1883), 190–209.

16-3. Criteria for Stability of Equilibrium

In order to clarify the stability criteria for static equilibrium,[5] consider a rigid vertical bar with a torsional spring of stiffness k at the base, as shown in Fig. 16-7(a). The behavior of such a bar subjected to vertical force P and horizontal force F is shown in Fig. 16-7(b) for a large and a small F. The question then arises: How will this system behave if $F = 0$?

To answer this question analytically, the system must be *deliberately displaced* a small (infinitesimal) amount consistent with the boundary conditions. Then, if the restoring forces are greater than the forces tending to upset the system, the system is stable, and if the restoring forces are smaller, then the system is unstable.

The rigid bar shown in Fig. 16-7(a) can only rotate. Therefore, it has only one degree of freedom. For an assumed small rotation angle θ, the *restoring moment* is $k\theta$, and, with $F = 0$, the *upsetting moment* is $PL \sin \theta \approx PL\theta$. Therefore, if

$$k\theta > PL\theta \qquad \text{the system is } \textit{stable} \qquad\qquad (16\text{-}1)$$

and

$$k\theta < PL\theta \qquad \text{the system is } \textit{unstable} \qquad\qquad (16\text{-}2)$$

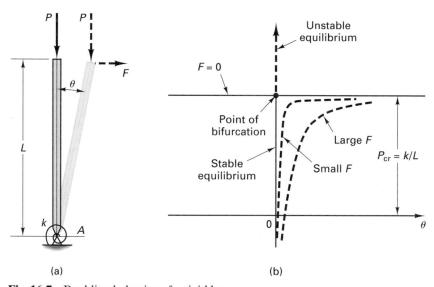

Fig. 16-7   Buckling behavior of a rigid bar.

[5]Some readers may find it advantageous to study Sections 16-9 and 16-10 first, where columns subjected to axial and transverse loads acting simultaneously are considered. Column buckling is the limiting (degenerate) case in such problems.

Right at the transition point, $k\theta = PL\theta$, and the equilibrium is neither stable nor unstable, but is *neutral*. The force associated with this condition is the *critical*, or *buckling, load*, which will be designated P_{cr}. For the bar system considered,

$$P_{cr} = k/L \qquad (16\text{-}3)$$

In the presence of horizontal force F, the $P - \theta$ curves are as shown by the dashed lines in Fig. 16-7(b) becoming asymptotic to the horizontal line at P_{cr}. Similar curves would result by placing the vertical force P eccentrically with respect to the axis of the bar. In either case, even for unstable systems, θ cannot become infinitely large, as there is always a point of equilibrium at θ somewhat less than π. The apparent discrepancy in the graph is caused by assuming in Eqs. 16-1 and 16-2 that θ is small and that $\sin \theta \approx \theta$ and $\cos \theta \approx 1$. The condition found for neutral equilibrium when $F = 0$ can be further elaborated upon by referring to Fig. 16-8.

It is convenient to relate the process for determining the kind of stability to a ball resting on differently shaped frictionless surfaces; see Fig. 16-8. In this figure, in all three cases, the balls in position 1 are in equilibrium. In order to determine the kind of equilibrium, it is necessary to displace the balls an infinitesimal distance $\delta\theta$ to either side. In the first case, Fig. 16-8(a), the ball would roll back to its initial position, and the equilibrium is *stable*. In the second case, Fig. 16-8(b), the ball once displaced will not return to its initial position, and the equilibrium is *unstable*. In the last case, Fig. 16-8(c), the ball can remain in its displaced position, where it is again in equilibrium. Such an equilibrium is *neutral*. Therefore, by analogy, a structural system is in a state of neutral equilibrium when it has at least *two neighboring equilibrium positions* an infinitesimal distance apart. This criterion for neutral equilibrium is applicable only for *infinitesimal* displacements, as at large displacements, different conditions may prevail (Fig. 16-7).

Based on the previous reasoning, the horizontal line for $F = 0$ shown in Fig. 16-7(b) is purely schematic for defining P_{cr}. Theoretically, it has meaning only within an infinitesimal distance from the vertical axis.

To demonstrate this again, consider the rigid vertical bar shown in Fig. 16-7(a) and set $F = 0$. Then, in order to determine *neutral* equilibrium, *displace* the bar in either direction through an angle $\delta\theta$ (*not* through the angle θ shown in the figure) and formulate the equation of equilibrium:

$$PL\,\delta\theta - k\,\delta\theta = 0 \qquad \text{or} \qquad \boxed{(PL - k)\,\delta\theta = 0} \qquad (16\text{-}4)$$

This equation has *two* distinct solutions: first, when $\delta\theta = 0$ and P is arbitrary, Fig. 16-7(b), and, second, when the expression in parentheses vanishes. This second solution yields $P_{cr} = k/L$. For this value of the axial force, $\delta\theta$ is arbitrary. Therefore, there are *two* equilibrium positions at P_{cr}. One of these is for a straight bar, and the other for a bar inclined at an

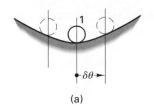

(a)

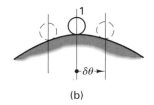

(b)

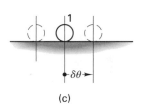

(c)

Fig. 16-8 (a) Stable, (b) unstable, and (c) neutral equilibrium.

angle $\delta\theta$. Since at P_{cr} there are these two branches of the solution, such a point is called the *bifurcation (branch) point*.[6]

In the previous illustration, the rigid bar has only one degree of freedom, since for an arbitrary infinitesimal displacement, the system is completely described by angle $\delta\theta$. A problem with two degrees of freedom is analyzed in the following example.

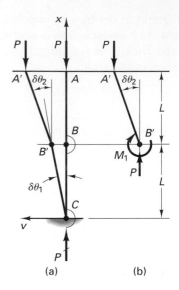

Example 16-1

Two rigid bars, each of length L, forming a straight vertical member as shown in Fig. 16-9(a), have torsional springs of stiffness k at ideal pinned joints B and C. Determine the critical vertical force P_{cr} and the shape of the buckled member.

SOLUTION

In order to determine the critical buckling force P_{cr}, the system must be given a displacement compatible with the boundary conditions. Such a displacement with positive sense is shown as $A'B'C$ in Fig. 16-9(a). Bar BC rotates through an angle $\delta\theta_1$, and bar AB independently rotates through an angle $\delta\theta_2$. Therefore, this system has *two* degrees of freedom. Free-body diagrams for members AB and BC in deflected positions are drawn in Figs. 16-9(b) and (c). Then, assuming that the member rotations are infinitesimal, equations of equilibrium are written for each member. In writing these equations, it should be noted that $M_1 = k(\delta\theta_2 - \delta\theta_1)$, where the terms in parentheses constitute the infinitesimal rotation angle *between* the two bars. On this basis,

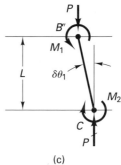

$$\sum M_{B'} = 0: \qquad PL\,\delta\theta_2 - k(\delta\theta_2 - \delta\theta_1) = 0$$

and

$$\sum M_C = 0: \quad PL\,\delta\theta_1 + k(\delta\theta_2 - \delta\theta_1) - k\,\delta\theta_1 = 0$$

Rearranging,

$$k\,\delta\theta_1 - (k - PL)\,\delta\theta_2 = 0$$

$$-(2k - PL)\,\delta\theta_1 + k\,\delta\theta_2 = 0$$

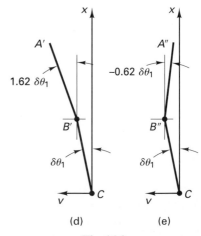

Fig. 16-9

---

[6]The static criterion for neutral equilibrium is not applicable to nonconservative systems where bifurcation does not occur and dynamic criteria must be used. Such cases arise, for example, when applied force P remains tangent to the axis of the deflected bar at the point of application. This problem was extensively studied by H. Ziegler. See his book *Principles of Structural Stability* (Waltham, MA: Blaisdell, 1968).

These two homogeneous linear equations possess a trivial solution, $\delta\theta_1 = \delta\theta_2 = 0$, as well as a nonzero solution[7] if the determinant of the coefficients is zero; that is,

$$\begin{vmatrix} k & -(k - PL) \\ -(2k - PL) & k \end{vmatrix} = 0$$

On expanding this determinant, one obtains the *characteristic equation*

$$P^2 - 3\frac{k}{L}P + \frac{k^2}{L^2} = 0$$

The roots of such an equation are called *eigenvalues,* the *smallest* of which is the critical buckling load. In this case, there are two roots:

$$P_1 = \frac{3 - \sqrt{5}}{2}\frac{k}{L} \qquad \text{and} \qquad P_2 = \frac{3 + \sqrt{5}}{2}\frac{k}{L}$$

and $P_{cr} = P_1$.

Substituting the roots into either one of the simultaneous equations determines the ratios between the rotations of the bars. Thus, for P_1, $\delta\theta_2/\delta\theta_1 = 1.62$, and for P_2, $\delta\theta_2/\delta\theta_1 = -0.62$. The corresponding deflected modes are shown in Figs. 16-9(d) and (e). The one in Fig. 16-9(d) corresponds to P_{cr}. These mode shapes are called *eigenvectors* and are often written in matrix form as

$$\begin{Bmatrix} \delta\theta_1 \\ \delta\theta_2 \end{Bmatrix} = \begin{Bmatrix} 1 \\ 1.62 \end{Bmatrix}\delta\theta_1 \qquad \text{and} \qquad \begin{Bmatrix} \delta\theta_1 \\ \delta\theta_2 \end{Bmatrix} = \begin{Bmatrix} 1 \\ -0.62 \end{Bmatrix}\delta\theta_1$$

where $\delta\theta_1$ is an arbitrary constant.

As can be readily surmised, by increasing the number of hinged bars with springs to represent a column, the degrees of freedom increase. In the limit, a continuous elastic column has an infinite number of degrees of freedom. However, unlike vibration problems, in buckling analysis, only the smallest root is important. The buckling loads for elastic columns with different boundary conditions will be derived in the sections that follow.

Before proceeding with the derivation for critical column loads based on the concept of neutral equilibrium, it is significant to examine the meaning

[7]Heuristically, this can be demonstrated in the following manner. Let two homogeneous linear equations be

$$Ax + By = 0 \qquad \text{and} \qquad Cx + Dy = 0$$

The first one of these equations requires that $y/x = -A/B$, whereas the second that $y/x = -C/D$. For the two equations to be consistent, $A/B = C/D$, or $AD - CB = 0$, which is the value of the expanded determinant for the coefficients in the simultaneous equations. There also is a trivial solution for $x = y = 0$.

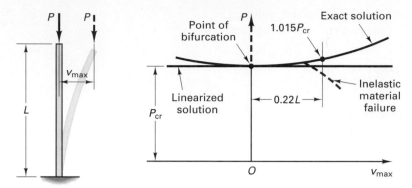

Fig. 16-10   Behavior of an ideal elastic column.

of such analyses. Critical loads do not describe the postbuckling process. However, by using the exact (nonlinear) differential equations for curvature, it can be shown[8] that for *elastic* columns, one can find equilibrium positions *above* P_{cr}. The results of such an analysis are illustrated in Fig. 16-10. Note, especially, that increasing P_{cr} by a mere 1.5% causes a maximum sideways deflection of 22% of the column length.[9] For practical reasons, such enormous deflections can seldom be tolerated. Moreover, the material usually cannot resist the induced bending stresses. Therefore, failure of real columns would be inelastic. Generally, there is little additional postbuckling strength for real columns, and the use of P_{cr} for column capacity is acceptable. This contrasts with the behavior of plates and shells, where significant postbuckling strength may develop.

Another illustration of the meaning of P_{cr} in relation to the behavior of elastic[10] and elastic-plastic[11] columns based on nonlinear analyses is shown in Fig. 16-11. In these plots, columns that are initially bowed into sinusoidal shapes with a maximum center deflection of Δ_o are considered. The paths of equilibrium for these cases vary, depending on the extent of the initial curvature. However, regardless of the magnitude of Δ_o, critical load P_{cr} serves as an asymptote for columns with a small amount of curvature, which are commonly encountered in engineering problems; see Fig. 16-11(b). It is to

[8]J. L. Lagrange, "On the shapes of columns," *Oeuvres de Lagrange,* Vol. 1 (Paris, 1867).

[9]The fact that an elastic column continues to carry a load beyond the buckling stage can be demonstrated by applying a force in excess of the buckling load to a flexible bar or plate, such as a carpenter's saw.

[10]Discussion of elastic deflection of columns, referred to as *Lagrange Elastica,* may be found in S. P. Timoshenko and J. M. Gere, *Theory of Elastic Stability,* 2nd ed. (New York: McGraw-Hill, 1961).

[11]T. von Karman, "Untersuchungen Ueber Knickfestigkeit," *Collected Works of Theodore von Karman*, Volume I, 1902–1913 (London: Butterworth Scientific Publications, 1956), 90–140. See also the previous footnote.

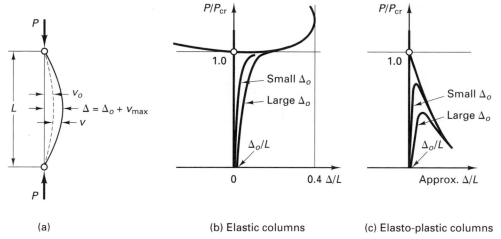

(a)   (b) Elastic columns   (c) Elasto-plastic columns

Fig. 16-11   Behavior of straight and initially curved columns where $(v_o)_{max} = \Delta_o$.

be noted that a *perfectly elastic* initially straight long column with pinned ends, upon buckling into approximately a complete "circle," attains the intolerable deflection of 0.4 of the column length. Behavior of elastic-plastic columns is entirely different; see Fig. 16-11(c). Only a perfectly straight column can reach P_{cr} and thereafter drop precipitously in its carrying capacity. Column imperfections such as crookedness drastically reduce the carrying capacity. Nevertheless, in either case, P_{cr} provides the essential parameter for determining column capacity. With appropriate safeguards, design procedures can be devised employing this key parameter.

Part A   COLUMN BUCKLING THEORY

16-4.   Euler Load for Columns with Pinned Ends

At the critical load, a column that is circular or tubular in its cross-sectional area may buckle sideways in any direction. In the more general case, a compression member does not possess equal flexural rigidity in all directions. The moment of inertia is a maximum around one centroidal axis of the cross-sectional area and a minimum around the other; see Fig. 16-12. The significant flexural rigidity EI of a column depends on the *minimum I*, and at the critical load a column buckles either to one side or the other in

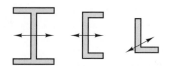

Fig. 16-12   Flexural column buckling occurs in plane of major axis.

the plane of the major axis. The use of a minimum I in the derivation that follows is understood.

Consider the ideal perfectly straight column with pinned supports at both ends; see Fig. 16-13(a). The *least* force at which a buckled mode is possible is the *critical* or *Euler buckling load*.

In order to determine the critical load for this column, the compressed column is *displaced* as shown in Fig. 16-13(b). In this position, the bending moment according to the beam sign convention[12] is $-Pv$. By substituting this value of moment into Eq. 14-10, the differential equation for the elastic curve for the initially straight column becomes

$$\frac{d^2v}{dx^2} = \frac{M}{EI} = -\frac{P}{EI}v \qquad (16\text{-}5)$$

Letting $\lambda^2 = P/EI$ and transposing gives

$$\boxed{\frac{d^2v}{dx^2} + \lambda^2 v = 0} \qquad (16\text{-}6)$$

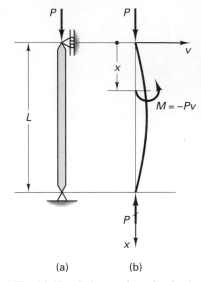

Fig. 16-13   Column pinned at both ends.

This is an equation of the same form as the one for simple harmonic motion, and its solution is

$$v = A \sin \lambda x + B \cos \lambda x \qquad (16\text{-}7)$$

where A and B are arbitrary constants that must be determined from the boundary conditions. These conditions are

$$v(0) = 0 \qquad \text{and} \qquad v(L) = 0$$

Hence,

$$v(0) = 0 = A \sin 0 + B \cos 0 \qquad \text{or} \qquad B = 0$$

and

$$v(L) = 0 = A \sin \lambda L \qquad (16\text{-}8)$$

This equation can be satisfied by taking $A = 0$. However, with AB each equal to zero, as can be seen from Eq. 16-7, is a solution for a straight column and is usually referred to as a trivial solution. An alternative solution is obtained by requiring the sine term in Eq. 16-8 to vanish. This occurs when λn equals $n\pi$, where n is an integer. Therefore, since λ was defined as $\sqrt{P/EI}$, the nth critical force P_n that makes the deflected shape of the column possible follows from setting $\sqrt{P/EI}\, L = n\pi$. Hence,

$$P_n = \frac{n^2 \pi^2 EI}{L^2} \qquad (16\text{-}9)$$

---

[12]For the positive direction of the deflection v shown, the bending moment is negative. If the column were deflected in the opposite direction, the moment would be positive. However, v would be negative. Hence, to make Pv positive, it must likewise be treated as a negative quantity.

These P_n's are the *eigenvalues* for this problem. However, since in stability problems only the *least value* of P_n is of importance, n must be taken as unity, and the *critical* or *Euler load*[13] P_{cr} for an initially *perfectly straight elastic* column with pinned ends becomes

$$P_{cr} = \frac{\pi^2 EI}{L^2} \qquad (16\text{-}10)$$

where E is the elastic modulus of the material, I is the *least* moment of inertia of the constant cross-sectional area of a column, and L is its length. This case of a column pinned at both ends is often referred to as the *fundamental case.*

According to Eq. 16-7, at the critical load, since $B = 0$, the equation of the buckled elastic curve is

$$v = A \sin \lambda x \qquad (16\text{-}11)$$

This is the characteristic, or *eigenfunction,* of this problem, and, since $\lambda = n\pi/L$, n can assume any integer value. There is an infinite number of such functions. In this linearized solution, amplitude A of the buckling mode remains indeterminate. For the fundamental case $n = 1$, the elastic curve is a half-wave sine curve. This shape and the modes corresponding to $n = 2$ and 3 are shown in Fig. 16-14. The higher modes have no physical significance in buckling problems, since the least critical buckling load occurs at $n = 1$.

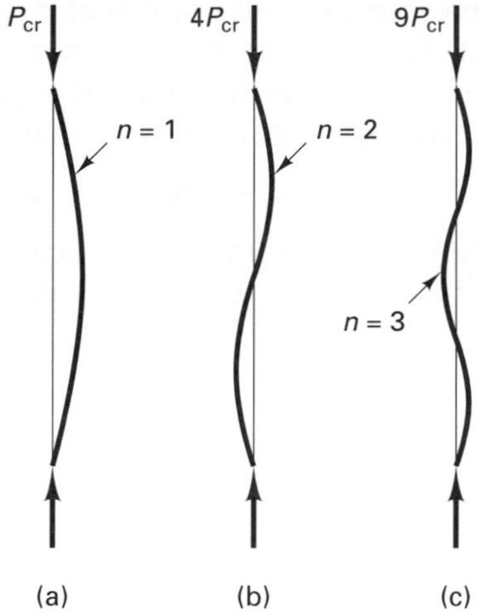

16-5. Euler Loads for Columns with Different End Restraints

The same procedure as that discussed before can be used to determine the critical axial loads for columns with different boundary conditions. The solutions of these problems are very sensitive to the end restraints. Consider, for example, a column with one end fixed and the other pinned, as shown in Fig. 16-15, where the buckled column is drawn in a *deflected* position. Here the effect of unknown end moment M_o and the reactions must be considered in setting up the differential equation for the elastic curve at the critical load:

$$\frac{d^2v}{dx^2} = \frac{M}{EI} = \frac{-Pv + M_o(1 - x/L)}{EI} \qquad (16\text{-}12)$$

Letting $\lambda^2 = P/EI$ as before, and transposing, gives

$$\frac{d^2v}{dx^2} + \lambda^2 v = \frac{\lambda^2 M_o}{P}\left(1 - \frac{x}{L}\right) \qquad (16\text{-}13)$$

[13]This formula was derived by the great mathematician Leonhard Euler in 1757.

Fig. 16-14 First three buckling modes for a column pinned at both ends.

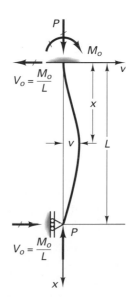

Fig. 16-15 Column fixed at one end and pinned at the other.

The *homogeneous solution* of this differential equation (i.e., when the right side is zero) is the same as that given by Eq. 16-7. The *particular solution,* due to the nonzero right side, is given by dividing the term on that side by λ^2. The complete solution then becomes

$$v = A \sin \lambda x + B \cos \lambda x + (M_o/P)(1 - x/L) \qquad (16\text{-}14)$$

where A and B are arbitrary constants and M_o is the unknown moment at the fixed end. The three kinematic boundary conditions are

$$v(0) = 0 \qquad v(L) = 0 \qquad \text{and } v'(0) = 0$$

Hence,

$$v(0) = 0 = B + M_o/P$$

$$v(L) = 0 = A \sin \lambda L + B \cos \lambda L$$

and

$$v'(0) = 0 = A\lambda - M_o/PL$$

Solving these equations simultaneously, one obtains the following transcendental equation:

$$\lambda L = \tan \lambda L \qquad (16\text{-}15)$$

which must be satisfied for a nontrivial equilibrium shape of the column at the critical load. The smallest root of Eq. 16-15 is

$$\lambda L = 4.493$$

from which the corresponding least eigenvalue or critical load for a *column fixed at one end and pinned at the other* is

$$P_{cr} = \frac{20.19EI}{L^2} = \frac{2.05\pi^2 EI}{L^2} \qquad (16\text{-}16)$$

It can be shown that in the case of a *column fixed at both ends,* Fig. 16-16(d), the critical load is

$$P_{cr} = \frac{4\pi^2 EI}{L^2} \qquad (16\text{-}17a)$$

The last two equations show that by restraining the ends, the critical loads are substantially larger than those in the fundamental case, Eq. 16-10. On the other hand, the critical load for a *free-standing column,*[14] Fig. 16-16(b), with a load at the top is

$$P_{cr} = \frac{\pi^2 EI}{4L^2} \qquad (16\text{-}17b)$$

---

[14]A telephone pole having no external braces and with a heavy transformer at the top is an example.

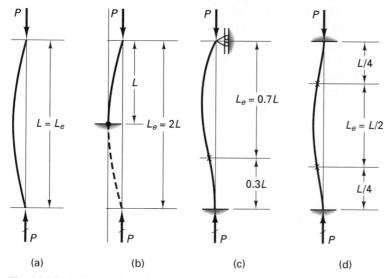

Fig. 16-16 Effective lengths of columns with different restraints.

In this extreme case, the critical load is only one-fourth of that for the fundamental case.

All the previous formulas can be made to resemble the fundamental case, provided that the *effective column length* is used instead of the actual column length. This length turns out to be the distance between the inflection points on the elastic curves. The effective column length L_e for the fundamental case is L, but for the cases discussed it is $0.7L$, $0.5L$, and $2L$, respectively. For a general case, $L_e = KL$, where K is the effective length factor, which depends on the end restraints. Hence, a more general form of the Euler formula, incorporating the concept of the *effective column length* L_e, can be written as

$$P_{cr} = \frac{\pi^2 EI}{(KL)^2} = \frac{\pi^2 EI}{L_e^2} \qquad (16\text{-}18)$$

In contrast to the classical cases shown in Fig. 16-16, actual compression members are seldom truly pinned or completely fixed against rotation at the ends. Because of the uncertainty regarding the fixity of the ends, columns are often assumed to be pin-ended. With the exception of the case shown in Fig. 16-16(b), where it cannot be used, this procedure is conservative.

Procedure Summary Column buckling loads in this and the preceding section are found using the same curvature-moment relation that was derived for the deflection of beams, Eqs. 14-10. However, the bending moments are written for axially loaded columns in slightly *deflected* positions. Mathematically this results in an entirely different kind of second-order differential equation than that for beam flexure. The solution of this equation shows that, for the *same load,* two neighboring equilibrium configurations are possible for a column. One of these configurations corresponds to a straight column, the other to a slightly bent column. The axial force associated simultaneously with the bent and the straight shape of the column is the critical buckling load. This occurs at the *bifurcation* (branching) point of the solution.

In the developed formulation, the columns are assumed to be linearly *elastic* and to have the same cross section throughout the column length. Only the flexural deformations of a column are considered.

For the second-order differential equations considered in this treatment, the same *kinematic* boundary conditions are applicable as for beams in flexure, Fig. 14-5.

Elastic buckling load formulas are truly remarkable. Although they *do not depend on the strength of a material,* they determine the carrying capacity of columns. The only material property involved is the elastic modulus E, which physically represents the stiffness characteristic of a material.

The previous equations *do not apply* if the axial column stress exceeds the proportional limit of the material. This problem is discussed in the next section.

16-6. Limitations of the Euler Formulas

The elastic modulus E was used in the derivation of the Euler formulas for columns; therefore, all the reasoning presented earlier is applicable *while the material behavior remains linearly elastic.* To bring out this significant limitation, Eq. 16-10 is rewritten in a different form. By definition, $I = Ar^2$, where A is the cross-sectional area and r is its *radius of gyration.* Substitution of this relation into Eq. 16-10 gives

$$P_{cr} = \frac{\pi^2 EI}{L_e^2} = \frac{\pi^2 E A r^2}{L_e^2}$$

or

$$\sigma_{cr} = \frac{P_{cr}}{A} = \frac{\pi^2 E}{(L_e/r)^2} \tag{16-19a}$$

where the *critical stress* σ_{cr} for a column is defined as P_{cr}/A (i.e., as an *average* stress over the cross-sectional area A of a column at the critical load P_{cr}). The length of the column is L_e, and r is the *least* radius of gyration of the cross-sectional area, since the original Euler formula is in terms of the minimum I. By using the effective length L_e, the expression becomes general. The ratio L_e/r of the column length to the *least* radius of gyration is

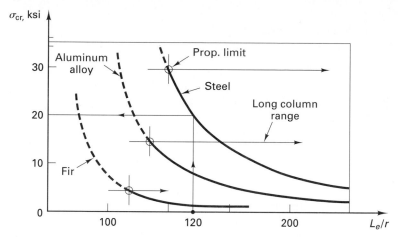

Fig. 16-17   Variation of critical column stress with slenderness ratio for three different materials.

called the column *slenderness ratio. No factor of safety is included in the last equation.*

A graphical interpretation of Eq. 16-19a is shown in Fig. 16-17, where the critical column stress is plotted versus the slenderness ratio for three different materials. For each material, E is constant, and the resulting curve is a hyperbola. However, since Eq. 16-19a is based on the elastic behavior of a material, σ_{cr} determined by this equation cannot exceed the proportional limit of a material. Therefore, the hyperbolas shown in Fig. 16-17 are drawn dashed beyond the individual material's proportional limit, and these portions of the curves *cannot be used.* The necessary modifications of Eq. 16-19a to include inelastic material response will be discussed in the next section.

The useful portions of the hyperbolas do not represent the behavior of one column, but rather the behavior of an infinite number of ideal columns. For example, a particular steel column, say, with an $L_e/r = 120$ may at the most carry a load of $\sigma_1 A$, where $t_1 = t_{cr} = 20$ ksi. Note that σ_{cr} *always decreases with increasing ratios of L/r.* Moreover, note that a precise definition of a long column is now possible with the aid of these diagrams. Thus, a column is said to be long if the elastic Euler formula applies. The beginning of the long-column range is shown for three materials in Fig. 16-17.

Example 16-2

Find the shortest length L for a steel column with pinned ends having a cross-sectional area of 60 by 100 mm, for which the elastic Euler formula applies. Let $E = 200$ GPa and assume the proportional limit to be 250 MPa.

SOLUTION

The minimum moment of inertia of the cross-sectional area $I_{min} = 100 \times 60^3/12 = 1.8 \times 10^6$ mm^4. Hence, the *least radius of gyration r is given* as

$$\boxed{r = r_{min} = \sqrt{\frac{I_{min}}{A}}} \qquad (16\text{-}19b)$$

and

$$r_{min} = \sqrt{\frac{1.8 \times 10^6}{60 \times 100}} = \sqrt{3} \times 10 \text{ mm}$$

Then, using Eq. 16-19a and noting that for a column with pinned ends $L_e = L$, $\sigma_{cr} = \pi^2 E/(L/r)^2$. Solving for the slenderness ratio L/r at the proportional limit,

$$\left(\frac{L}{r}\right)^2 = \frac{\pi^2 E}{\sigma_{cr}} = \frac{\pi^2 \times 200 \times 10^3}{250} = 800\pi^2$$

or

$$\frac{L}{r} = 88.9 \qquad \text{and} \qquad L = 88.9\sqrt{3} \times 10 = 1540 \text{ mm}$$

Therefore, if this column is 1.54 m or more in length, it will buckle elastically because, for such dimensions of the column, the critical stress at buckling will not exceed the proportional limit for the material.

16-7. Generalized Euler Buckling-load Formulas

A typical compression stress-strain diagram for a specimen that is prevented from buckling is shown in Fig. 16-18(a). In the stress range from O to A, the material behaves elastically. If the stress in a column at buckling does not exceed this range, the column buckles elastically. The hyperbola expressed by Eq. 16-19a with an elastic E, is applicable in such a case. This portion of the curve is shown as ST in Fig. 16-18(b). It is important to recall that this curve does not represent the behavior of one column, but rather the behavior of an infinite number of ideal columns of different lengths. The hyperbola beyond the useful range is shown in the figure by dashed lines.

A column with an L_e/r ratio corresponding to point S in Fig. 16-18(b) is the shortest column of a given material and size that will buckle elastically. A shorter column, having a still smaller L_e/r ratio, will not buckle at the proportional limit of the material. On the compression stress-strain diagram, Fig. 16-18(a), this means that the stress level in the column has

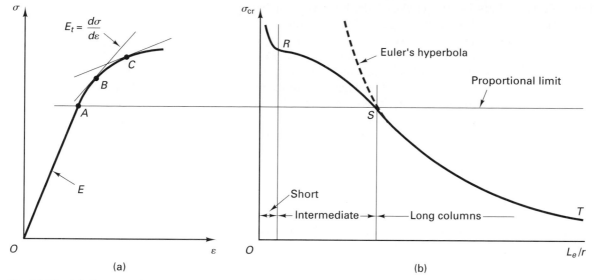

Fig. 16-18   (a) Compression stress-strain diagram, and (b) critical stress in columns versus slenderness ratio.

passed point A and has reached some point B perhaps. At this higher stress level, it may be said that a column of different material has been created, since the stiffness of the material is no longer represented by the elastic modulus. At this point, the material stiffness is given instantaneously by the tangent to the stress-strain curve [i.e., by the *tangent modulus E_t*; see Fig. 16-18(a)]. The column remains stable if its new flexural rigidity $E_t I$ at B is sufficiently large, and it can carry a higher load. As the load is increased, the stress level rises, whereas the tangent modulus decreases. A column of ever "less stiff material" is acting under an increasing load. Substitution of the tangent modulus E_t for the elastic modulus E is then the only modification necessary to make the elastic buckling formulas applicable in the inelastic range. Hence, the *generalized Euler buckling-load formula,* or the *tangent modulus formula,* becomes

$$\sigma_{cr} = \frac{\pi^2 E_t}{(L_e/r)^2} \tag{16-20}$$

Since stresses corresponding to the tangent moduli can be obtained from the compression stress-strain diagram, the L_e/r ratio at which a column will buckle with these values can be obtained from Eq. 16-20. A plot representing this behavior for low and intermediate ratios of L_e/r is shown in Fig. 16-18(b) by the curve from R to S. Tests on individual columns verify this curve with remarkable accuracy.

The tangent modulus formula gives the carrying capacity of a column at the *instant it tends to buckle.* As a column deforms further, the stiffness of the fibers on the concave side continues to exhibit approximately the tangent modulus E_t. The fibers on the convex side, however, on being relieved of some stress, rebound with the original elastic modulus E, as shown in Fig. 16-19 at point C. Inasmuch as two moduli, E_t and E, are used in developing this theory,[15] it is referred to as either the *double-modulus* or the *reduced-modulus theory* of column buckling. For the same column slenderness ratio, this theory always gives a slightly higher column buckling capacity than the tangent-modulus theory. The discrepancy between the two solutions is not very large. The reason for this discrepancy was explained by Shanley.[16] According to his concept, buckling proceeds *simultaneously* with the increasing axial load. The applied load given by the tangent-modulus theory increases asymptotically to that given by the double-modulus theory; see Fig. 16-20. However, prior to reaching the load given by the double-modulus theory, one can anticipate a material yield or failure, making the tangent modulus an attractive choice. It is convenient that in the tangent-modulus theory the mechanical properties for the whole cross section are the same, whereas they vary differently for different cross sections in the double-modulus theory.

The maximum load lying between the tangent-modulus load and the double-modulus load for any time-independent elastic-plastic material and cross section was accurately determined by Lin.[17] Duberg and Wilder[18] have further concluded that for materials whose stress-strain curves change gradually in the inelastic range, the maximum column load can be appreciably above the tangent-modulus load. If, however, the material in the inelastic range tends rapidly to exhibit plastic behavior, the maximum load is only slightly higher than the tangent-modulus load.

As mentioned earlier, columns that buckle elastically are generally referred to as *long columns*. Columns having small L_e/r ratios exhibiting no buckling phenomena are called *short columns*. The remaining columns are of *intermediate length*. At small L_e/r ratios, ductile materials "squash out" and can carry very large loads.

Since length L_e in Eq. 16-20 is treated as the effective length of a column, different end conditions can be analyzed. Following this procedure for comparative purposes, plots of critical stress σ_{cr} versus the slenderness ratio L_e/r for fixed-ended columns and pin-ended ones are shown in Fig. 16-21. It is important to note that the carrying capacity for these two cases per Eqs. 16-10 and 16-17 is in a ratio of 4 to 1 only for columns having the slenderness ratio $(L_e/r)_1$ or greater. For smaller L_e/r ratios, progressively less benefit is derived from restraining the ends. At small L_e/r ratios, the curves merge. It makes little difference whether a "short block" is pinned or fixed at the ends, as strength rather than buckling determines the behavior.

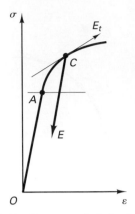

Fig. 16-19 Stress-strain behavior in buckled column.

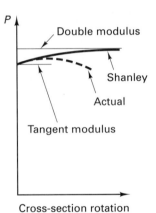

Fig. 16-20 Inelastic buckling loads by different theories.

[15]F. Bleich, *Buckling Strength of Metal Structures* (New York: McGraw-Hill, 1952).

[16]F. R. Shanley, "Inelastic column theory," *J. Aero. Sci.*, **14,** no. 5 (May 1947), 261–267.

[17]T. H. Lin, "Inelastic column buckling," *J. Aeron. Sci.*, **17,** no. 3 (1950), 159–172.

[18]J. E. Duberg and T. W. Wilder, "Column behavior in the plastic stress range," *J. Aeron. Sci.*, **17,** no. 6 (1950), 323–327.

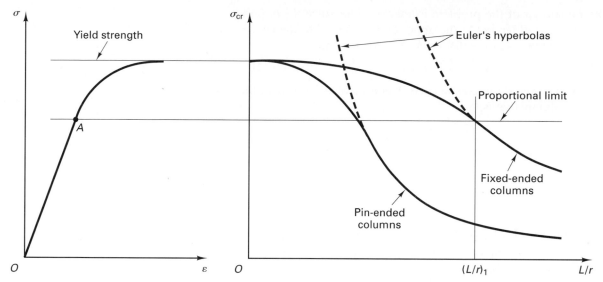

Fig. 16-21   Comparison of the behavior of columns with different end conditions.

16-8.   Eccentric Loads and the Secant Formula

A different method of analysis may be used to determine the capacity of a column than was discussed before. Since no column is perfectly straight nor are the applied forces perfectly concentric, the behavior of real columns may be studied with some statistically determined imperfections or possible misalignments of the applied loads. Then, for the design of an actual column, which is termed "straight," a probable crookedness or an effective load eccentricity may be assigned. Also, there are many columns where an eccentric load is deliberately applied. Thus, an eccentrically loaded column can be studied and its capacity determined on the basis of an allowable elastic stress. *This does not determine the ultimate capacity of a column.*

To analyze the behavior of an eccentrically loaded column, consider the column shown in Fig. 16-22. If the origin of the coordinate axes is taken at the upper force P, the bending moment at any section is $-Pv$, and the differential equation for the elastic curve is the same as for a concentrically loaded column; that is,

$$\frac{d^2v}{dx^2} = \frac{M}{EI} = -\frac{P}{EI}v \qquad (16\text{-}5)$$

where, by again letting $\lambda = \sqrt{P/EI}$, the general solution is as before:

$$v = A\sin\lambda x + B\cos\lambda x \qquad (16\text{-}7)$$

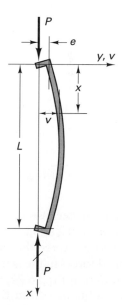

Fig. 16-22   Eccentrically loaded column.

However, the remainder of the problem is not the same, since *the boundary conditions are now different.* At the upper end, v is equal to the eccentricity of the applied load; that is, $v(0) = e$. Hence, $B = e$, and

$$v = A \sin \lambda x + e \cos \lambda x \qquad (16\text{-}21)$$

Next, because of symmetry, the elastic curve has a vertical tangent at the midheight of the column; that is,

$$v'(L/2) = 0$$

Therefore, by setting the derivative of Eq. 16-21 equal to zero at $x = L/2$, it is found that

$$A = e \frac{\sin \lambda L/2}{\cos \lambda L/2}$$

Hence, the equation for the elastic curve is

$$v = e\left(\frac{\sin \lambda L/2}{\cos \lambda L/2} \sin \lambda x + \cos \lambda x \right) \qquad (16\text{-}22)$$

No indeterminancy of any constants appears in this equation, and the maximum deflection v_{max} can be found from it. This maximum deflection occurs at $L/2$, since at this point, the derivative of Eq. 16-22 is equal to zero. Hence,

$$v(L/2) = v_{max} = e\left(\frac{\sin^2 \lambda L/2}{\cos \lambda L/2} + \cos \frac{\lambda L}{2} \right) = e \sec \frac{\lambda L}{2} \qquad (16\text{-}23)$$

For the column shown in Fig. 16-20, the largest bending moment M is developed at the point of maximum deflection and numerically is equal to Pv_{max}. Therefore, since the direct force and the largest bending moment are now known, the *maximum* compressive stress occurring in the column (contrast this with the *average stress* P/A acting on the column) can be computed by the usual formula as

$$\sigma_{max} = \frac{P}{A} + \frac{Mc}{I} = \frac{P}{A} + \frac{Pv_{max}\, c}{Ar^2} = \frac{P}{A}\left(1 + \frac{ec}{r^2} \sec \frac{\lambda L}{2} \right)$$

But $\lambda = \sqrt{P/EI} = \sqrt{P/EAr^2}$; hence,

$$\boxed{\sigma_{max} = \frac{P}{A}\left(1 + \frac{ec}{r^2} \sec \frac{L}{r} \sqrt{\frac{P}{4EA}} \right)} \qquad (16\text{-}24)$$

This equation, because of the secant term, is known as *the secant formula for columns,* and it applies to columns of any length, provided the maximum stress does not exceed the elastic limit. A condition of equal eccentricities of the applied forces in the same direction causes the largest deflection.

Note that in Eq. 16-24, the radius of gyration r *may not be minimum,* since it is obtained from the value of I associated with the axis around which bending occurs. In some cases, a more critical condition for buckling can exist in the direction of no definite eccentricity. Also note that in

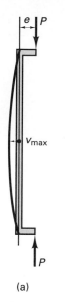

(a)

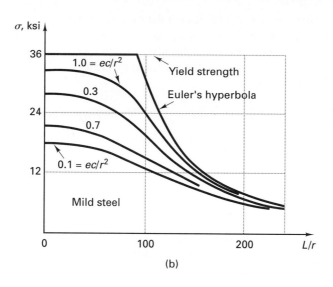

(b)

Fig. 16-23   Results of analyses for different columns by the secant formula with curve ordinates for nPa/A.

Eq. 16-24, *the relation between* σ_{max} *and P is not linear;* σ_{max} *increases faster than P. Therefore, the solutions for maximum stresses in columns caused by different axial forces cannot be superposed;* instead, the forces must be superposed first, and then the stresses can be calculated.

For an allowable force P_a on a column, where n is the factor of safety, nP_a must be substituted for P in Eq. 16-24, and σ_{max} must be set at the yield point of a material; that is,

$$\sigma_{max} = \sigma_{yp} = \frac{nP_a}{A}\left(1 + \frac{ec}{r^2}\sec\frac{L}{r}\sqrt{\frac{nP_a}{4EA}}\right) \qquad (16\text{-}25)$$

This procedure assures a correct factor of safety for the applied force, since such a force can be increased n times before a critical stress is reached. Note the term nP_a appearing under the radical.

Application of Eqs. 16-24 and 16-25 is cumbersome, requiring a trial-and-error procedure. Alternatively, they can be studied graphically, as shown in Fig. 16-23.[19] From this plot, note the large effect that load eccentricity has on short columns and the negligible one on very slender columns. Graphs of this kind form a suitable aid in practical design. The secant equation covers the whole range of column lengths. The greatest

[19]This figure is adapted from D. H. Young, "Rational design of steel columns," *Trans. ASCE,* **101** (1936), 431.

handicap in using this formula is that some eccentricity e must be assumed even for supposedly straight columns, and this is a difficult task.[20]

The secant formula for *short* columns reverts to a familiar expression when L/r approaches zero. For this case, the value of the secant approaches unity; hence, in the limit, Eq. 16-24 becomes

$$\sigma_{\max} = \frac{P}{A} + \frac{Pec}{Ar^2} = \frac{P}{A} + \frac{Mc}{I} \qquad (16\text{-}26)$$

a relation normally used for short blocks.

16-9. Beam-Columns

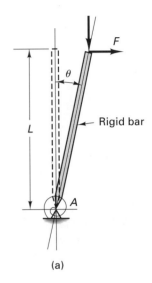

(a)

In the preceding section, the problem of an axially loaded column subjected to equal end moments was considered. This is a special case of a member acted upon simultaneously by an axial force and transverse forces or moments causing bending. Such members are referred to as *beam-columns*. The behavior of beam-columns and the linearized solutions that are generally employed for their analysis can be clarified by the simple example of the rigid bar shown in Fig. 16-24(a). This bar of length L is initially held in a vertical position by a spring at A having a torsional spring constant k. When vertical force P and horizontal force F are applied to the top of the bar, it rotates and the equilibrium equation must be written for the *deformed state,* a form similar to that used in stability analysis. Bearing in mind that $k\theta$ is the resisting moment developed by the spring at A, one obtains

$$\sum M_A = 0 \curvearrowright + \qquad PL\sin\theta + FL\cos\theta - k\theta = 0$$

or

$$P = \frac{k\theta - FL\cos\theta}{L\sin\theta} \qquad (16\text{-}27)$$

The qualitative features of this result are shown in Fig. 16-24(b), and the corresponding curve is labeled as the *exact solution.* It is interesting to note that as $\theta \to \pi$, provided the spring continues to function, a very large force P can be supported by the system. For a force P applied in an upward direction, plotted downward in the figure, angle θ decreases as P increases.

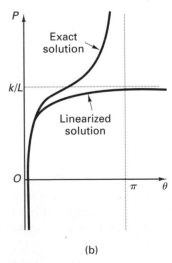

(b)

Fig. 16-24   Rigid bar with one degree of freedom.

[20]Moreover, there is some question as to the philosophical correctness of the secant formula. The fact that the stress reaches a certain value does not mean that the column buckles (i.e., stress is not a measure of buckling load in every case). It can be shown that an additional axial load can be resisted beyond the point where the maximum stress at the critical section is reached. See F. Bleich, *Buckling Strength of Metal Structures* (New York: McGraw-Hill, 1952), Chapter 1.

The solution expressed by Eq. 16-27 is for arbitrarily large deformations. In complex problems, it is difficult to achieve solutions of such generality. Moreover, in the majority of applications, large deformations cannot be tolerated. Therefore, it is usually possible to limit the investigation of the behavior of systems to small and moderately large deformations. In this problem, this can be done by setting $\sin \theta \approx \theta$ and $\cos \theta \approx 1$. In this manner, Eq. 16-27 simplifies to

$$P = \frac{k\theta - FL}{L\theta} \qquad \text{or} \qquad \theta = \frac{FL}{k - PL} \qquad (16\text{-}28)$$

For small finite values of θ, this solution is quite acceptable. On the other hand, as θ increases, the discrepancy between this linearized solution and the exact one becomes very large and loses its physical meaning.

Analogous to this, for the analysis of elastic beam-columns, where the deflections are small to moderate, it is generally sufficiently accurate to employ the usual linear differential equation for elastic deflection of beams. However, in applying this equation, the bending moments caused by the transverse loads as well as the axial forces *must be written for a deflected member*. Such a procedure is illustrated in the next example.

Example 16-3

A beam column is subjected to an axial force P and an upward transverse force F at its midspan; see Fig. 16-25(a). Determine the equation of the elastic curve and the critical axial force P_{cr}. EI is constant.

SOLUTION
The free-body diagram for the *deflected* beam column is shown in Fig. 16-25(b). This diagram assists with formulation of the total bending moment M, which includes the effect of the axial force P multiplied by the deflection v. Thus, using the relation $M = EIv''$, Eq. 14-10, and noting that for the left side of the span, $M = -(F/2)x - Pv$, one has

$$EIv'' = M = -Pv - (F/2)x \qquad 0 \le x \le L/2$$

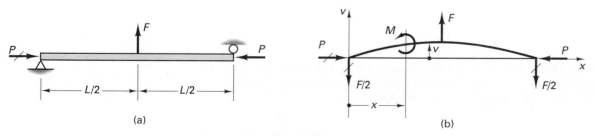

(a)   (b)

Fig. 16-25

or

$$EIv'' + Pv = -(F/2)x$$

By dividing through by EI and letting $\lambda^2 = P/EI$, after some simplification, the governing differential equation becomes

$$\frac{d^2v}{dx^2} + \lambda^2 v = -\frac{\lambda^2 F}{2P}x \qquad 0 \le x \le L/2 \qquad (16\text{-}29)$$

The homogeneous solution of this differential equation is the same as that of Eq. 16-6, and the particular solution equals the right-hand term divided by λ^2. Therefore, the complete solution is

$$v = C_1 \sin \lambda x + C_2 \cos \lambda x - (F/2P)x \qquad (16\text{-}30)$$

Constants C_1 and C_2 follow from the boundary condition, $v(0) = 0$, and from a condition of symmetry, $v'(L/2) = 0$. The first condition gives

$$v(0) = C_2 = 0$$

Since

$$v' = C_1 \lambda \cos \lambda x - C_2 \lambda \sin \lambda x - F/2P$$

with C_2 already known to be zero, the second condition gives

$$v'(L/2) = C_1 \lambda \cos \lambda L/2 - F/2P = 0$$

or

$$C_1 = F/[2P\lambda \cos (\lambda L/2)]$$

On substituting this constant into Eq. 16-30,

$$v = \frac{F}{2P\lambda} \frac{\sin \lambda x}{\cos \lambda L/2} - \frac{F}{2P}x = \frac{F}{2P\lambda}\left(\frac{\sin \lambda x}{\cos \bar{u}} - \lambda x\right) \qquad (16\text{-}31)$$

where the last relationship is obtained by setting

$$\lambda L/2 = \bar{u} \qquad (16\text{-}32)$$

Since the maximum deflection occurs at $x = L/2$, after some simplifications,

$$v_{max} = \frac{F}{2P\lambda}(\tan \bar{u} - \bar{u}) \qquad (16\text{-}33)$$

and the absolute maximum bending moment occurring at midspan is

$$M_{max} = \left| -\frac{FL}{4} - Pv_{max} \right| = \frac{F}{2\lambda} \tan \bar{u} \qquad (16\text{-}34)$$

Equations 16-31, 16-33, and 16-34 become infinite when $\bar{u}$ is a multiple of $\pi/2$ and any odd integer, since then $\cos \bar{u}$ is equal to zero and $\tan \bar{u}$ is infinite. Therefore, for an nth mode, where n is an odd integer,

$$\bar{u} = \frac{\lambda L}{2} = \sqrt{\frac{P_n}{EI}}\frac{L}{2} = \frac{n\pi}{2} \qquad (16\text{-}35)$$

Solving the last two expressions for P_n, and setting $n = 1$, the critical buckling load is obtained:

$$P_n = \frac{n^2 \pi^2 EI}{L^2} \Rightarrow P_{cr} = \frac{\pi^2 EI}{L^2} \qquad (16\text{-}36)$$

This procedure shows that a solution of the *linearized* differential equation yields the *Euler buckling load*, causing infinite deflections and moments. For tensile forces, on the other hand, the deflections are reduced. These trends are similar to those shown in Fig. 16-24(b).

Next it is of considerable practical importance to obtain an approximate solution to this problem that can then be generalized for a great many beam-column problems for finding deflections and maximum moments. For this purpose, expand $\tan \bar{u}$ into the Maclaurin (Taylor) series and substitute the result into Eq. 16-33, making note of Eq. 16-35:

$$\tan \bar{u} = \bar{u} + \frac{1}{3} \bar{u}^3 + \frac{2}{15} \bar{u}^5 + \frac{17}{315} \bar{u}^7 + \frac{62}{2835} \bar{u}^9 + \cdots \quad (16\text{-}37)$$

$$v_{max} = \frac{F}{2P\lambda} \frac{1}{3} \left(\frac{\lambda L}{2} \right)^3 \left(1 + \frac{2}{5} \bar{u}^2 + \frac{17}{105} \bar{u}^4 + \frac{62}{945} \bar{u}^6 + \cdots \right) (16\text{-}38)$$

However, in view of Eqs. 16-35 and 16-36,

$$\bar{u}^2 = \frac{\lambda^2 L^2}{4} = \frac{PL^2}{4EI} = 2.4674 \frac{P}{P_{cr}} \qquad (16\text{-}39)$$

By substituting the last equation into Eq. 16-38 and simplifying,

$$v_{max} = \frac{FL^3}{48EI} \left[1 + 0.9870 \left(\frac{P}{P_{cr}} \right) + 0.9857 \left(\frac{P}{P_{cr}} \right)^2 \right.$$

$$\left. + 0.9855 \left(\frac{P}{P_{cr}} \right)^3 + \cdots \right] \qquad (16\text{-}40)$$

By approximating the coefficients[21] in the bracketed expression by unity and recalling that the sum of the resulting power series[22] can be written in a compact form, one has

$$v_{max} \approx \frac{FL^3}{48EI} \left(\frac{1}{1 - P/P_{cr}} \right) \qquad (16\text{-}41)$$

In this expression, it can be recognized (see Table 10 in the Appendix) that the coefficient in front of the bracket is the beam center deflection *without* the axial force. The bracketed expression gives the *deflection magnification factor* caused by the applied axial force P. When this force reaches P_{cr}, the

---

[21] A. Chajes, *Principles of Structural Stability* (Englewood Cliffs, NJ: Prentice Hall, 1974). For a discussion of elastic-plastic beam-columns, see K. Jezek, "Die Tragfaehigkeit axial gedrueckter und auf Biegung beanspruchter Stahlstaebe," *Der Stahlbau*, 9 (1936), 12, 22, and 39.

[22] This can be verified by dividing unity by the denominator.

deflection becomes infinite. This magnification factor can be used with virtually any kind of transverse loadings as long as they are applied in the same direction, and the results are remarkably accurate for small and moderate deflections.

After the approximate maximum deflection is obtained using Eq. 16-41, the maximum bending moment follows from statics as

$$M_{max} = \left| -\frac{FL}{4} - Pv_{max} \right| \tag{16-42}$$

where the first term is due to transverse loading, and the second to the axial force in a deflected member. For stocky beam-columns, the last term becomes unimportant.

It is important to note that the differential equations, such as Eq. 16-29, for beam-columns are of a different kind than those used for beams loaded transversely only. For this reason, the singularity functions previously presented cannot be applied in these problems.

16-10. Alternative Differential Equations for Beam-Columns

For some solutions of beam-column problems, it is convenient to recast the governing differential equations into different forms from that discussed in the previous section. In order to derive such equations, consider the beam-column element shown in Fig. 16-26, and make the following small-deflection approximations:

$$dv/dx = \tan\theta \approx \sin\theta \approx \theta \qquad \cos\theta \approx 1 \qquad \text{and} \qquad ds \approx dx$$

On this basis, the two equilibrium equations are

$$\sum F_y = 0 \uparrow + \qquad q\,dx + V - (V + dV) = 0$$

$$\sum M_A = 0 \curvearrowright + \qquad M - P\,dv + V\,dx + q\,dx\,dx/2 - (M + dM) = 0$$

The first one of these equations yields

$$\frac{dV}{dx} = q \tag{16-43}$$

which is identical to Eq. 7-3. The second, on neglecting the infinitesimals of higher order, gives

$$V = \frac{dM}{dx} + P\frac{dv}{dx} \tag{16-44}$$

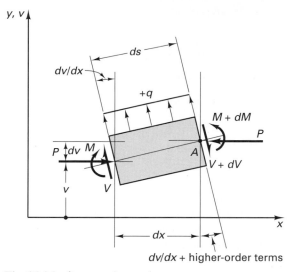

Fig. 16-26 Beam-column element.

Therefore, for beam-columns, shear V, in addition to depending on the rate of change in moment M as in beams, now also depends on the *magnitude of the axial force and the slope of the elastic curve.* The latter term is the component of P along the inclined sections shown in Fig. 16-24.

On substituting Eq. 16-44 into Eq. 16-43 and using the usual beam curvature-moment relation $d^2v/dx^2 = M/EI$, one obtains the two alternative governing differential equations for beam-columns:

$$\frac{d^2M}{dx^2} + \lambda^2 M = q \qquad (16\text{-}45)$$

or

$$\frac{d^4v}{dx^4} + \lambda^2 \frac{d^2v}{dx^2} = \frac{q}{EI} \qquad (16\text{-}46)$$

where, for simplicity, EI is assumed to be constant, and, as before, $\lambda^2 = P/EI$. The boundary conditions for these equations are the same as for beams in flexure (see Fig. 14-5), *except for shear,* where Eq. 16-44 applies. By again making use of the beam curvature-moment relation, Eq. 16-44 in more appropriate alternative form can be written as

$$V = EI \frac{d^3v}{dx^3} + P \frac{dv}{dx} \qquad (16\text{-}44a)$$

If $P = 0$, Eqs. 16-44a, 16-45, and 16-46 revert, respectively, to Eqs. 14-14b, 7-5, and 14-14c for transversely loaded beams.

For future reference, the homogeneous solutions of Eq. 16-46 and several of its derivatives are

$$v = C_1 \sin \lambda x + C_2 \cos \lambda x + C_3 x + C_4 \qquad (16\text{-}47a)$$

$$v' = C_1 \lambda \cos \lambda x - C_2 \lambda \sin \lambda x + C_3 \qquad (16\text{-}47b)$$

$$v'' = -C_1 \lambda^2 \sin \lambda x - C_2 \lambda^2 \cos \lambda x \qquad (16\text{-}47c)$$

$$v''' = -C_1 \lambda^3 \cos \lambda x + C_2 \lambda^3 \sin \lambda x \qquad (16\text{-}47d)$$

These relations are useful for expressing the boundary conditions in evaluating constant $C_1, C_2, C_3,$ and C_4. The use of Eq. 16-44a rather than Eq. 14-14b is essential when shear at a boundary must be considered.

Solutions of homogeneous Eqs. 16-45 and 16-46 for particular boundary conditions lead to critical buckling loads for elastic *prismatic* columns. These solutions have the same meaning as discussed earlier in connection with the equivalent solutions of the second-order differential equations in Sections 16-4 and 16-5.

Example 16-4

A slender bar of constant EI is simultaneously subjected to end moments M_o and axial force P, as shown in Fig. 16-27(a). Determine the maximum deflection and the largest bending moment.

SOLUTION

Within the span, there is no transverse load. Therefore, the right-hand term of Eq. 16-46 is zero, and the homogeneous solution of this equation given by Eq. 16-47a is the complete solution. The boundary conditions are

$$v(0) = 0 \qquad v(L) = 0 \qquad M(0) = -M_o \qquad \text{and} \qquad M(L) = -M_o$$

Since $M = EIv''$, with the aid of Eqs. 16-47a and 16-47c, these conditions yield

$$v(0) = \qquad\qquad + C_2 \qquad\qquad\qquad + C_4 = 0$$

$$v(L) = +C_1 \sin \lambda L + C_2 \cos \lambda L + C_3 L + C_4 = 0$$

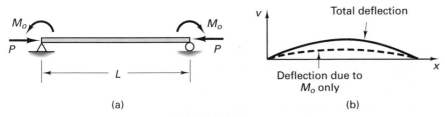

(a)

Total deflection

Deflection due to
M_o only

(b)

Fig. 16-27

$$M(0) = \qquad\qquad -C_2 EI\lambda^2 \qquad\qquad\qquad = -M_o$$

$$M(L) = -C_1 EI\lambda^2 \sin \lambda L - C_2 EI\lambda^2 \cos \lambda L \qquad\qquad = -M_o$$

Solving these four equations simultaneously,

$$C_1 = \frac{M_o}{P}\frac{1 - \cos \lambda L}{\sin \lambda L} \qquad C_2 = -C_4 = \frac{M_o}{P} \qquad \text{and} \qquad C_3 = 0$$

Therefore, the equation of the elastic curve is

$$v = \frac{M_o}{P}\left(\frac{1 - \cos \lambda L}{\sin \lambda L} \sin \lambda x + \cos \lambda x - 1 \right) \qquad (16\text{-}48)$$

The maximum deflection occurs at $x = L/2$. After some simplifications, it is found to be

$$v_{\max} = \frac{M_o}{P}\left(\frac{\sin^2 \lambda L/2}{\cos \lambda L/2} + \cos \frac{\lambda L}{2} - 1 \right) = \frac{M_o}{P}\left(\sec \frac{\lambda L}{2} - 1 \right) \ (16\text{-}49)$$

The largest bending moment also occurs at $x = L/2$. Its absolute maximum is

$$M_{\max} = |-M_o - Pv_{\max}| = M_o \sec \lambda L/2 \qquad (16\text{-}50)$$

This solution is directly comparable to that given in Section 16-8 for an eccentrically loaded column. Two differences in the details of the solutions, however, should be noted. The end moments $M_o = Pe$ of the earlier solution and the x axis of the eccentrically loaded column are at a distance e away from the column axis. Then, with the use of some trigonometric identities, it can be shown that Eqs. 16-22 and 16-48 lead to the same results.

The results again show that in slender members, bending moments can be substantially increased in the presence of axial compressive forces. Similar to the condition encountered in Example 16-3, when $\lambda L/2 = \pi/2$, axial force $P = P_{cr}$ and $v_{\max}$ and $M_{\max}$ become infinite.

If the applied forces are tensile instead of compressive, the sign of P changes and so does the character of Eqs. 16-45 and 16-46. For such cases, the deflections are reduced with increasing axial force P.

Next, Eq. 16-49 is recast into an approximate form in the same manner as has been done in Example 16-3. For this purpose, sec $\lambda L/2 = \sec u$ is expanded into the Maclaurin (Taylor) series and, after substituting into Eq. 16-49, is simplified using Eq. 16-39. Thus,

$$\sec \bar{u} = 1 + \frac{1}{2}\bar{u}^2 + \frac{5}{24}\bar{u}^4 + \frac{61}{720}\bar{u}^6 + \cdots \qquad (16\text{-}51)$$

and

$$v_{\max} = \frac{M_o}{P}\frac{1}{2}\left(\frac{\lambda L}{2}\right)^2 \left[1 + 1.028\left(\frac{P}{P_{cr}}\right) + 1.032\left(\frac{P}{P_{cr}}\right)^2 + \cdots \right] \ (16\text{-}52)$$

Again, all the coefficients in the bracketed expression can be approximated by unity and the power series summed, giving

$$v_{max} \approx \frac{M_o L^2}{8EI} \left(\frac{1}{1 - P/P_{cr}} \right) \tag{16-53}$$

The coefficient in front of the bracketed expression is the deflection at the middle of the span due to the end moments M_o (see Table 11 in the Appendix). The deflection magnification factor due to the axial force P in the brackets is identical to that found earlier in Example 16-3. When force P reaches the Euler buckling load, the deflection becomes infinite according to this *linear small-deflection theory*.

The maximum bending moment at the center of the beam follows from statics:

$$M_{max} = |-M_o - P v_{max}| \tag{16-54}$$

Example 16-5

By using Eq. 16-46 in homogeneous form, determine the Euler buckling load for a column with pinned ends.

SOLUTION
For this purpose, Eq. 16-46 can be written as

$$\frac{d^4 v}{dx^4} + \lambda^2 \frac{d^2 v}{dx^2} = 0 \tag{16-55}$$

The solution of this equation and several of its derivatives is given by Eqs. 16-47. For a pin-ended column, the boundary conditions are

$$v(0) = 0 \qquad v(L) = 0 \qquad M(0) = EIv''(0) = 0$$

and

$$M(L) = EIv''(L) = 0$$

Using these conditions with Eqs. 16-47a and 16-47c, one obtains

$$C_2 \qquad\qquad + C_4 = 0$$

$$C_1 \sin \lambda L \quad + C_2 \cos \lambda L + C_3 L + C_4 = 0$$

$$- C_2 \lambda^2 EI \qquad\qquad = 0$$

$$-C_1 \lambda^2 EI \sin \lambda L - C_2 \lambda^2 EI \cos \lambda L \qquad = 0$$

To obtain a nontrivial solution requires that the determinant of the coefficients for this set of homogeneous algebraic equations be equal to zero (see Example 16-1). Therefore, with $\lambda^2 EI = P$,

$$\begin{vmatrix} 0 & 1 & 0 & 1 \\ \sin \lambda L & \cos\lambda L & L & 1 \\ 0 & -P & 0 & 0 \\ -P \sin \lambda L & -P \cos\lambda L & 0 & 0 \end{vmatrix} = 0$$

The evaluation of this determinant leads to $\sin \lambda L = 0$, which is precisely the same condition as given by Eq. 16-8.

   This approach is advantageous in problems with different boundary conditions, where the axial force and EI remains constant throughout the length of the column. The method cannot be applied directly if the axial force extends over only a part of a member.

Part B   DESIGN OF COLUMNS

16-11. General Considerations

For other than short columns and blocks, the buckling theory for columns shows that their cross-sectional areas should have the largest possible least radius of gyration r. Such a provision for columns assures the smallest possible slenderness ratio, L_e/r, permitting the use of higher stresses. However, as discussed in Section 16-2, limitations must be placed on the minimum thickness of the material to prevent local plate buckling. Since conventional rolled shapes generally have wall-thickness ratios sufficiently large to prevent such buckling, only a brief treatment of this problem as it applies to aluminum-alloy compression members will be given here. Torsional buckling modes that may control the capacity of columns made from thin plate elements and open, unsymmetrical cross sections are excluded from consideration (see Section 16-2).

   Since tubular members have a large radius of gyration in relation to the amount of material in a cross section, they are excellent for use as columns. Wide flange sections (sometimes referred to as H sections) are also very suitable for use as columns and are superior to I sections, which have narrow flanges, resulting in larger ratios of L_e/r. In order to obtain a large radius of gyration, columns are often built up from rolled or extruded shapes, and the individual pieces are spread out to obtain the desired effect. Cross sections for typical bridge compression members are shown in Figs. 16-28(a) and (b), for a derrick boom or a radio tower in Fig. 16-28(c), and for an ordinary truss in Fig. 16-28(d). The angles in the latter case are separated by spacers. The main longitudinal shapes in the other members are separated by plates or are laced (latticed) together by light bars, as shown in Figs. 16-28(e) and (f). Local instability must be carefully guarded against to prevent failures in lacing bars, as shown in Fig. 16-29. Such topics are beyond the scope of this text.[23]

Unavoidable imperfections must be recognized in the practical design of columns. Therefore, specifications usually stipulate not only the quality of material, but also fabrication tolerances for permissible out-of-straightness. The residual stresses caused by the manufacturing process must also be considered. For example, steel wide-flange sections, because of uneven cooling during a hot rolling operation, develop residual stress patterns of the type shown in Fig. 16-30. The maximum residual compressive stresses may be on the order of $0.3\sigma_{yp}$ in such members. Welds in aluminum-alloy members reduce the mechanical properties of the material in the heat-affected zone. For these reasons, experimental results on column buckling have a large scatter.

After initially acceptance of the Euler buckling-load formula beyond its range of applicability, a chaotic situation existed for many years with regard to column-design formulas. Now that the column-buckling phenomenon is more clearly understood, only a few column formula types are in common use. For steel, it is now customary to specify two formulas. One of these is for use for short and intermediate-length columns; the other, for slender columns, Fig. 16-31(a). For the lower range of column length, usually a parabola (and, in a few instances, an inclined straight line) is speci-

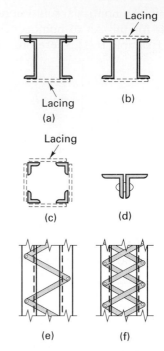

Fig. 16-28 Typical built-up column cross sections.

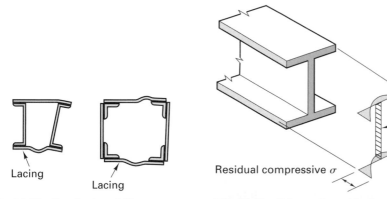

Fig. 16-29 Lattice instability.

Fig. 16-30 Schematic residual stress pattern.

[23]B. G. Johnson (ed.), *Stability Design Criteria for Metal Structures,* 4th ed. (New York: Wiley, 1988).

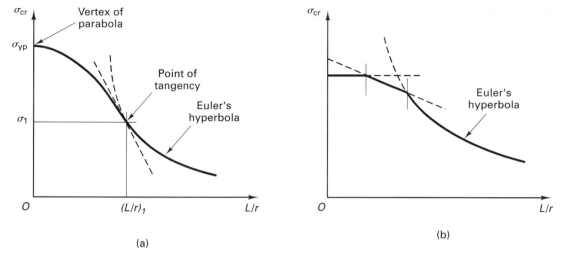

Fig. 16-31   Typical column-buckling curves for design.

fied. In this manner, the basic compressive strength of the material, residual stresses, and fabrication tolerances are accounted for. For slender (long) columns, the Euler elastic buckling load provides the basis for the critical stress. In this range of column lengths, the residual stresses play a relatively minor role. The dominant parameters are the material stiffness, E, and geometric fabrication imperfections. Often the two specified complementary equations have a common tangent at a selected value of L/r. Such a condition cannot be fulfilled if a straight line is used instead of a parabola. In a few specifications, the more conservative approach of using the elastic formula and an allowable stress is made by assuming an accidental eccentricity based on manufacturing tolerances.

For some materials, a sequence of three different equations is specified for the design of columns, Fig. 16-31(b). One of these equations for short columns defines the basic compressive strength of a material. Another equation, specifically applicable for the long column range, is based on the Euler buckling load. An empirical relation, such as an inclined straight line shown in the figure, or a parabola, is specified for columns of intermediate lengths. Such a type of formula is generally given for aluminum alloys and wood.

In applying the design formulas, it is important to observe the following items:

1. The material and fabrication tolerances for which the formula is written.
2. Whether the formula gives the working load (or stress) or whether it estimates the ultimate carrying capacity of a member. If the formula is of the latter type, a safety factor must be introduced.
3. The range of applicability of the formula. Some empirical formulas can lead to unsafe design if used beyond the specified range.

16-12. Concentrically Loaded Columns

As examples of column-design formulas for nominally concentric loading, representative formulas for structural steel, an aluminum alloy, and wood follow. Formulas for eccentrically loaded columns are considered in the next section.

Column Formulas for Structural Steel   The American Institute of Steel Construction (AISC) provides two sets of column formulas with two formulas in each set. One of these sets is for use in the *allowable stress design* (ASD) and the other for the *load and resistance factor design* (LRFD).[24] In the second approach, an implicit probabilistic determination of the reliability of column capacity based on load and resistance factors is made (see Section 1-12). These two sets of formulas follow. Since steels of several different yield strengths are manufactured, the formulas are stated in terms of σ_{yp}, which varies for different steels. The elastic modulus E for all steels is approximately the same and is taken to be 29×10^3 ksi (200 MPa).

AISC ASD Formulas for Columns.   The AISC formula for *allowable* stress, σ_{allow}, for *slender* columns is based on the Euler elastic buckling load with a safety factor of $23/12 = 1.92$. Slender columns are defined as having the slenderness ratio $(L_e/r)_1 = C_c = \sqrt{2\pi^2 E/\sigma_{yp}}$ or greater. Constant C_c corresponds to the critical stress σ_{cr} at the Euler load equal to one-half the steel yield stress σ_{yp}.

The formula for long columns when $(L_e/r) > C_c$ is

$$\sigma_{allow} = \frac{12\pi^2 E}{23(L_e/r)^2} \tag{16-56}$$

where L_e is the effective column length and r is the least radius of gyration for the cross-sectional area. No columns are permitted to exceed an L_e/r of 200.

For an L_e/r ratio less than C_c, AISC specifies a parabolic formula:

$$\sigma_{allow} = \frac{[1 - (L_e/r)^2/2C_c^2]\sigma_{yp}}{\text{F.S.}} \tag{16-57}$$

where F.S., the factor of safety, is defined as

$$\text{F.S.} = \frac{5}{3} + \frac{3(L_e/r)}{8C_c} - \frac{(L_e/r)^3}{8C_c^3}$$

---

[24]For ASD formulas, see *AISC Manual of Steel Construction,* 9th ed. (Chicago: AISC, 1989). For LRFD formulas, see *AISC LRFD Manual of Steel Construction* (Chicago: AISC, 1986). See also B. J. Johnston, F. J. Lin, and T. V. Galambos, *Basic Steel Design,* 3rd ed. (Englewood Cliffs, NJ: Prentice Hall, 1986); C. G. Salmon and J. E. Johnson, *Steel Structures,* 2nd ed. (New York: Harper and Row, 1980); and W-W. Yu, *Cold-formed Steel Design* (New York: Wiley, 1985).

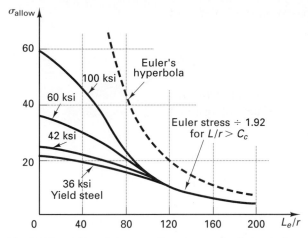

Fig. 16-32   Allowable stress for concentrically loaded columns per AISC specifications.

Note that F.S. varies, being more conservative for the larger ratios of L_e/r. The equation chosen for F.S. approximates a quarter sine curve, with the value of 1.67 at zero L_e/r and 1.92 at C_c. An allowable stress-versus-slenderness ratio for axially loaded columns of several kinds of structural steels is shown in Fig. 16-32.

Since, in practical applications, the ideal restraint of the column ends, assumed in Section 16-5, cannot always be relied upon, conservatively, AISC specifies modification of the effective lengths as follows:

For columns built in at both ends: $L_e = 0.65L$
For columns built in at one end and pinned at the other: $L_e = 0.80L$
For columns built in at one end and free to translate and rotate at the other: $L_e = 2.10L$

No modification need be made for columns pinned at both ends, where $L_e = L$. For other end restraints, see AISC Specifications.

AISC LRFD Formulas for Columns.   Here, again, there are two equations governing column strength, one for elastic and the other for inelastic buckling. The boundary between the inelastic and elastic instability is at $\lambda_c = 1.5$, where the *column slenderness parameter* λ_c is defined as

$$\lambda_c = \frac{L_e}{r\pi} \sqrt{\frac{\sigma_{yp}}{E}} \tag{16-58}$$

This expression results from normalizing the slenderness ratio L_e/r with respect to the slenderness ratio for the Euler elastic critical stress, assuming $\sigma_{cr} = \sigma_{yp}$.

For $\lambda_c > 1.5$, the *critical* buckling stress σ_{cr} is based on the Euler load and is given as

$$\sigma_{cr} = \left[\frac{0.877}{\lambda_c^2} \right] \sigma_{yp} \tag{16-59}$$

where the factor 0.877 is introduced to account for the initial out-of-straightness of the column, see Fig. 16-11(c), and the effects of residual stresses.

For $\lambda_c = 1.5$, an empirical relationship based on extensive experimental and probabilistic studies is given as

$$\sigma_{cr} = (0.658^{\lambda_c^2}) \sigma_{yp} \tag{16-60}$$

This equation includes the effects of residual stresses and initial out-of-straightness.

Both of the previous formulas give the nominal axial strength (capacity) of columns and must be used in conjunction with factored loads and a resistance factor ϕ_c of 0.85. The effective slenderness ratios L_e/r are determined as for the ASD.

Column Formulas for Aluminum Alloys

A large number of aluminum alloys are available for engineering applications. The yield and the ultimate strengths of such alloys vary over a wide range. The elastic modulus for the alloys, however, is reasonably constant. The Aluminum Association (AA)[25] provides a large number of column design formulas for different aluminum alloys. In all of these formulas, the allowable stress varies with the column slenderness ratio, as shown in Fig. 16-32. A representative set of three equations is given here for 6061-T6 alloy. As identified by the first number, the major alloying elements in this aluminum alloy are magnesium and silicon. T6 designates that this alloy has been thermally treated to produce stable temper. This alloy finds its greatest use for heavy-duty structures requiring good corrosion resistance, as in trucks, pipelines, buildings, etc. Alloys such as 2024 and 7075 in their various tempers are used in aircraft, where similar formulas are employed.

The three basic column formulas for 6061-T6 alloy are

$$\sigma_{allow} = 19 \text{ ksi} \qquad\qquad 0 \leq L/r \leq 9.5 \tag{16-61a}$$

$$\sigma_{allow} = 20.2 - 0.126 L/r \text{ ksi} \qquad 9.5 \leq L/r \leq 66 \tag{16-61b}$$

$$\sigma_{allow} = \frac{51{,}000}{(L/r)^2} \text{ ksi} \qquad\qquad 66 \leq L/r \tag{16-61c}$$

[25]*Aluminum Construction Manual,* Section 1, "Specifications for aluminum structures," 5th ed., April 1982; Section 2, "Illustrative examples of design," April 1978; and "Engineering data for aluminum structures," 5th ed., November 1981 (Washington, DC: The Aluminum Association, Inc.).

For aluminum-alloy compression members, the effective lengths are approximated in the same manner as recommended by the AISC. The stresses in Eqs. 16-61a and 16-61b are reduced to 12 ksi within 1 in of a weld.

In designing aluminum-alloy columns, it is also recommended to check local buckling of the column components. Therefore, formulas are also given by the Aluminum Association for the allowable stresses for outstanding flanges or legs and column webs (i.e., flat plates with supported legs). These formulas, in groups of three, are similar to Eqs. 16-61, except that in place of the slenderness ratios L/r, the ratios b/t are used, where b is the width of a plate and t is its thickness. The allowable stresses given by such formulas may govern the design if such stresses are smaller than those required in Eqs. 16-61. Two basic groups of formulas for determining local buckling for 6061-T6 alloy are as follows:

For outstanding legs or flanges:

$$\sigma_{\text{allow}} = 19 \text{ ksi} \qquad\qquad 0 \le b/t \le 5.2 \qquad (16\text{-}62a)$$

$$\sigma_{\text{allow}} = 23.1 - 0.79b/t \text{ ksi} \qquad 5.2 \le b/t \le 12 \qquad (16\text{-}62b)$$

$$\sigma_{\text{allow}} = 1970/(b/t)^2 \text{ ksi} \qquad 12 \le b/t \qquad (16\text{-}62c)$$

For edge-supported plates:[26]

$$\sigma_{\text{allow}} = 19 \text{ ksi} \qquad\qquad 0 \le b/t \le 16 \qquad (16\text{-}63a)$$

$$\sigma_{\text{allow}} = 23.1 - 0.25b/t \text{ ksi} \qquad 16 \le b/t \le 33 \qquad (16\text{-}63b)$$

$$\sigma_{\text{allow}} = 490/(b/t) \text{ ksi} \qquad 33 \le b/t \qquad (16\text{-}63c)$$

Since all three groups of these formulas are given for the *allowable* stresses on gross sections, they include factors of safety for the intended usage.

Column Formulas for Wood

The National Forest Products Association (NFPA)[27] provides the necessary information for the design of wood columns. Here attention will be limited to solid *rectangular* columns. In treating such columns, it is convenient to recast the design formulas in terms of the slenderness ratio L_e/d, where L_e is the effective column length and d is the *least* dimension of the cross section; see Fig. 16-33. On this basis,

$$r_{\min} = \sqrt{\frac{I_{\min}}{A}} = \sqrt{\frac{bd^3}{12}\frac{1}{bd}} = \frac{d}{\sqrt{12}} \qquad (16\text{-}64)$$

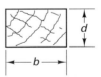

Fig. 16-33 Cross section of a wooden column.

[26]Such as column webs.

[27]See *National Design Specifications for Wood Construction* and *Design Values for Wood Construction, NDS Supplement* (Washington, DC: National Forest Products Association. 1987) Table compiled by National Forest Products Association, See also D. E. Breyer, *Design of Wood Structures,* 2nd ed. (New York: McGraw-Hill, 1988).

Substituting this relation into Eq. 16-19a and dividing the critical stress by the recommended factor of safety of 2.74,

$$\sigma_{allow} = \frac{\pi^2 E}{2.74(L_e/r)^2} = \frac{\pi^2 E}{2.74 \times 12(L_e/d)^2} = \frac{0.30E}{(L_e/d)^2} \quad (16\text{-}65)$$

Since this stress is deduced from the *elastic* Euler formula, a limitation on its use must be placed for the smaller values of L_e/d. In the NFPA *design specifications,* this is achieved by requiring that at a slenderness ratio L_e/d, designated as K, the allowable stress not exceed two-thirds of the design stress F_c for a short wood block in compression parallel to the grain. In the form of an equation, using Eq. 16-65, this means that

$$\frac{2}{3} F_c = \frac{0.3E}{(L_e/d)^2_{min}} = \frac{0.3E}{K^2}$$

Hence,

$$K = \sqrt{\frac{0.45E}{F_c}} = 0.671 \sqrt{\frac{E}{F_c}} \quad (16\text{-}66)$$

The value of K provides the boundary for the least slender column for use in Eq. 16-65. Note that since E and F_c for different woods vary, K assumes different values.

A qualitative graphical representation for the allowable stresses for columns over the permissible range of column slenderness ratios L_e/d is shown in Fig. 16-34. Note that for short columns, a constant stress is specified; for the intermediate and long slenderness ratios, a curve with an inflection point at K is shown. There is a small discontinuity at $L_e/d = 11$.

The allowable stresses in axially loaded wooden rectangular columns are

$$\sigma_{allow} = F_c \qquad\qquad 0 \le L_e/d \le 11 \quad (16\text{-}67a)$$

$$\sigma_{allow} = F_c\left[1 - \frac{1}{3}\left(\frac{L_e/d}{K}\right)^4\right] \qquad 11 < L_e/d \le K \quad (16\text{-}67b)$$

$$\sigma_{allow} = \frac{0.30E}{(L_e/d)^2} \qquad\qquad K \le L_e/d \le 50 \quad (16\text{-}67c)$$

where F_c is the allowable design stress for a short block in compression parallel to grain, E is the modulus of elasticity, and K is defined by Eq. 16-66. Note that the maximum allowable slenderness ratio L_e/d is 50.

It must be recognized that F_c and E for wood are highly variable quantities, depending on species, grading rules, moisture, service conditions, temperature, duration of load, etc. Therefore, in actual applications, the reader should consult texts dealing with such problems in more detail.

The effective lengths are approximated in the same manner as recommended by the AISC.

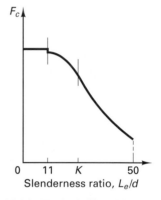

Fig. 16-34 Typical allowable stress for concentrically loaded wood columns per NFPA specifications.

The following examples illustrate some applications of the design formulas for axially loaded columns.

Example 16-6

(a) Determine the allowable axial loads for two 15-ft W 14 × 159 steel columns using AISC ASD formulas when one of the columns has pinned ends and the other has one end fixed and the other pinned. (b) Repeat the solution for two 40-ft W 14 × 159 columns. For the given section, $A = 46.7$ in^2 and $r_{min} = 4.00$ in. Assume A36 steel having $\sigma_{yp} = 36$ ksi.

SOLUTION

For both cases, it is necessary to calculate C_c to determine whether Eq. 16-56 or 16-57 is applicable:

$$C_c = \sqrt{2\pi^2 E/\sigma_{yp}} = \sqrt{2\pi^2 \times 29 \times 10^3/36} = 126.1$$

(a) For the W 14 × 159 shape, the *minimum* $r = 4.00$ in. Hence, for the 15-ft column with pinned ends, $L_e/r = 15 \times 12/4 = 45 < C_c$, and Eq. 16-57 applies. Hence,

$$\sigma_{allow} = \frac{[1 - 45^2/(2 \times 126.1^2)]36}{5/3 + 3 \times 45/(8 \times 126.1) - 45^3/(8 \times 126.1^3)} = 18.78 \text{ ksi}$$

and

$$P_{allow} = A\sigma_{allow} = 46.7 \times 18.78 = 877 \text{ kips}$$

For the column with one end fixed and the other pinned, according to the AISC, the effective length $L_e = 0.8L = 12$ ft. Hence, $L_e/r = 12 \times 12/4 = 36$, and again applying Eq. 16-57, $\sigma_{allow} = 19.50$ ksi and $P_{allow} = A\sigma_{allow} = 46.7 \times 19.50 = 911$ kips.

Here the allowable axial force is increased by 3.9% by fixing one of the column ends.

(b) For a 40-ft column with pinned ends, $L_e/r = 40 \times 12/4 = 120 < C_c$. Hence, using Eq. 16-57 again, it can be determined that $\sigma_{allow} = 10.28$ ksi and $P_{allow} = A\sigma_{allow} = 46.7 \times 10.28 = 480$ kips. Similarly, since for a column fixed at one end and pinned at the other, $L_e/r = 0.8 \times 120 = 96$, Eq. 16-57 gives $\sigma_{allow} = 13.48$ ksi and $P_{allow} = A\sigma_{allow} = 46.7 \times 13.48 = 630$ kips.

For this case, the allowable axial force is increased 31.2% by fixing one of the column ends. This contrasts with the 3.9% found earlier for the shorter columns. This finding is in complete agreement with the generalized Euler theory for columns, Section 16-7. As can be noted from Fig. 16-21, by restraining the ends of *long* columns, a large increase in their strength is obtained at large values of L_e/r. Restraining the ends of short columns results only in a modest increase in their strength.

Example 16-7

Using the AISC ASD column formulas, select a 15-ft-long pin-ended column to carry a concentric load of 200 kips. The structural steel is to be A572, having $\sigma_{yp} = 50$ ksi.

SOLUTION

The required size of the column can be found directly from the tables in the *AISC Steel Construction Manual*. However, this example provides an opportunity to demonstrate the trial-and-error procedure that is so often necessary in design, and the solution presented follows from using this method.

First try: Let $L/r = 0$ (a poor assumption for a column 15 ft long). Then, from Eq. 16-57, since F.S. = 5/3, $\sigma_{allow} = 50/$F.S. = 30 ksi and $A = P/\sigma_{allow} = 200/30 = 6.67$ in². From Table 4A in the Appendix, this requires a W 8 × 24 section, whose $r_{min} = 1.61$ in. Hence, $L/r = 15(12)/1.61 = 112$. With this L/r, the allowable stress is found using Eq. 16-56 or Eq. 16-57, whichever is applicable depending on C_c:

$$C_c = \sqrt{2\pi^2 E/\sigma_{yp}} = \sqrt{2\pi^2 \times 29 \times 10^3/50} = 107 < L/r = 112$$

Hence, using Eq. 16-56,

$$\sigma_{allow} = \frac{12\pi^2 \times 29 \times 10^3}{23 \times 112^2} = 11.9 \text{ ksi}$$

This is much smaller than the initially assumed stress of 30 ksi, and another section must be selected.

Second try: Let $\sigma_{allow} = 11.9$ ksi, as found before. Then $A = 200/11.9 = 16.8$ in², requiring a W 8 × 58 section having $r_{min} = 2.10$ in. Now $L/r = 15(12)/2.10 = 85.7$, which is less than C_c found before. Therefore, Eq. 16-57 applies, and

$$\text{F.S.} = 5/3 + 3(85.7)/(8 \times 107) - (85.7)^3/(8 \times 107^3) = 1.90$$

and

$$\sigma_{allow} = [1 - (85.7)^2/(2 \times 107^2)]50/1.90 = 17.9 \text{ ksi}$$

This stress requires $A = 200/17.9 = 11.2$ in², which is met by a W 8 × 40 section with $r_{min} = 2.04$ in. A calculation of the capacity for this section shows that the allowable axial load for it is 204 kips, which meets the requirements of the problem.

Example 16-8

Determine the design compressive strength P_u for a 15-ft W 14×159 steel column pinned at both ends based on the AISC LRFD provisions. For this section, $A = 46.7$ in^2 and $r_{min} = 4.00$ in. Assume A36 steel having $\sigma_{allow} = 36$ ksi.

SOLUTION

The column slenderness parameter as defined by Eq. 16-58 is

$$\lambda_c = \frac{15 \times 12}{4\pi} \sqrt{\frac{36}{29 \times 10^3}} = 0.5047$$

Since λ_c is less than 1.5, Eq. 16-60 applies for determining the critical stress and

$$\sigma_{cr} = (0.658^{0.5047^2})36 = 32.36 \text{ ksi}$$

Hence, for this column, the *nominal* compressive strength

$$P_n = A\sigma_{cr} = 46.7 \times 32.36 = 1510 \text{ kips}$$

and since the resistance factor $\phi_c = 0.85$, the column-design compressive strength

$$P_u = \phi_c P_n = 0.85 \times 1510 = 1289 \text{ kips}$$

By dividing P_u by $P_{allow} = 877$ kips for a comparable column analyzed in Example 16-6, one obtains 1.46. This load factor gives an indication of the relationship between the ASD and the LRFD for this case.

Example 16-9

Determine the allowable axial loads for two compression members made from 6061-T6 aluminum alloy having a 5 in $\times$ 5 in $\times$ 5.366 lb/ft wide-flange section with the dimensions shown in Fig. 16-35. One of the members is 20 in long and the other is 60 in. Assume each strut to be pinned at both ends. For the given section, $A = 4.563$ in^2 and the minimum radius of gyration $r_{min} = 1.188$ in.

SOLUTION

Regardless of the column length, for aluminum alloys, it is necessary to investigate *local buckling*. For the given section, two calculations must be made, one for the outstanding legs of the flanges and the other for the web.

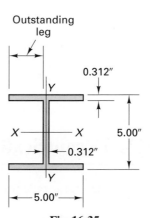

Fig. 16-35

In both instances, b/t values determine the allowable compressive stress. For the flanges,

$$\frac{b_f}{t} = \frac{5 - 0.312}{2 \times 0.312} = 7.51$$

This ratio requires the use of Eq. 16-62b; hence,

$$(\sigma_{\text{allow}})_{\text{flanges}} = 23.1 - 0.79 \times 7.51 = 17.2 \text{ ksi}$$

The web width-thickness ratio is

$$\frac{b_w}{t} = \frac{5 - 2 \times 0.312}{0.312} = 14.0$$

Since this ratio is less than 16, according to Eq. 16-63a,

$$(\sigma_{\text{allow}})_{\text{web}} = 19 \text{ ksi}$$

Overall buckling is investigated using Eqs. 16-47, which depend on L/r, and for a 20-in strut is

$$\frac{L}{r} = \frac{20}{1.188} = 16.8$$

Hence, using Eq. 16-61b,

$$\sigma_{\text{allow}} = 20.2 - 0.126 \times 16.8 = 18.1 \text{ ksi}$$

For this case of a well-balanced design, the allowable stress for local flange buckling controls. Therefore,

$$P_{\text{allow}} = 4.563 \times 17.2 = 78.5 \text{ kips}$$

The slenderness ratio for the 60-in strut is

$$\frac{L}{r} = \frac{60}{1.188} = 50.5$$

Hence, again using Eq. 16-61b,

$$\sigma_{\text{allow}} = 20.2 - 0.126 \times 50.5 = 13.8 \text{ ksi}$$

This stress is smaller than those for local buckling; hence,

$$P_{\text{allow}} = 4.563 \times 13.8 = 63.0 \text{ kips}$$

16-13. Eccentrically Loaded Columns

In the past, the secant-type formulas discussed in Section 16-8 were used as a rational method for the design of eccentrically loaded columns. Two other methods that have found a wide use follow.

Allowable Stress Method   A procedure for designing eccentrically loaded columns is obtained by adapting the elastic solution for short blocks subjected to bending with axial loads, Eq. 9-5, and setting the maximum compressive stress equal to or less than for an axially loaded column. For a planar case, this becomes

$$\sigma_x = \frac{P}{A} + \frac{Mc}{I} \leq \sigma_{\text{allow}} \qquad (16\text{-}68)$$

The compressive stresses in the last equation are treated as positive quantities. If only an eccentric force P is applied, the bending moment $M = Pe$, where e is the load eccentricity; see Fig. 16-36. The allowable stress σ_{allow} is determined from an appropriate formula, such as that given in the preceding section for axially loaded columns of different materials. Usually, the solution of Eq. 16-68 requires a trial-and-error procedure.

For short and intermediate-length columns, the previous procedure is usually conservative, since σ_{allow} for compressive stresses is generally less than the allowable bending stress. On the other hand, this procedure may become unconservative for slender columns, where the deflections are magnified due to the axial force. For such cases, it is appropriate to determine the extent of bending moment magnification caused by column deflection using the approximate deflection magnification factor derived in Example 16-3 or 16-4.

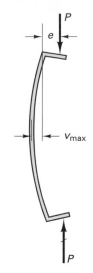

Fig. 16-36 Eccentrically loaded column.

Interaction Method   In an eccentrically loaded column, much of the total stress may result from the applied moment. However, *the allowable stress in flexure is usually higher than the allowable axial stress.* Hence, for a particular column, it is desirable to accomplish some balance between the two stresses, depending on the relative magnitudes of the bending moment and the axial force. Thus, since in bending $\sigma = Mc/I = Mc/Ar_1^2$, where r_1 is the radius of gyration *in the plane of bending,* in effect, area A_b required by bending moment M is

$$A_b = \frac{Mc}{\sigma_{ab}r_1^2}$$

where σ_{ab} is the allowable *maximum stress in bending.* Similarly, area A_a required for axial force P is

$$A_a = \frac{P}{\sigma_{aa}}$$

where σ_{aa} is the *allowable axial stress for the member acting as a column,* which depends on the L/r ratio. Therefore, the *total* area A required for a column subjected to an axial force and a bending moment is

$$A = A_a + A_b = \frac{P}{\sigma_{aa}} + \frac{Mc}{\sigma_{ab}r_1^2} \qquad (16\text{-}69)$$

By dividing by A,

$$\frac{P/A}{\sigma_{aa}} + \frac{Mc/Ar_1^2}{\sigma_{ab}} = 1 \qquad \text{or} \qquad \frac{\sigma_a}{\sigma_{aa}} + \frac{\sigma_b}{\sigma_{ab}} = 1 \qquad (16\text{-}70)$$

where σ_a is the axial stress caused by the applied vertical loads and σ_b is the bending stress caused by the applied moment. If a column is carrying only an axial load and the applied moment is zero, the formula indicates that the column is designed for the stress σ_{aa}. On the other hand, the allowable stress becomes the flexural stress σ_{ab} if there is no direct compressive force acting on the column. Between these two extreme cases, Eq. 16-70 measures the relative importance of the two kinds of action and specifies the nature of their interaction. Hence, it is often referred to as an *interaction formula* and serves as the basis for the specifications in the AISC ASD manual, where it is stated that the sum of these two stress ratios must not exceed unity. The same philosophy has found favor in applications other than those pertaining to structural steel. The Aluminum Association suggests a similar relation. The National Forest Products Association developed a series of formulas to serve the same purpose.

In terms of the notations used by the AISC, Eq. 16-70 is rewritten as

$$\frac{f_a}{F_a} + \frac{f_b}{F_b} \leq 1.0 \qquad (16\text{-}71)$$

In practice, the eccentricity of the load on a column may be such as to cause bending moments about both axes of the cross section. Equation 16-71 is then modified to

$$\frac{f_a}{F_a} + \frac{f_{bx}}{F_{bx}} + \frac{f_{by}}{F_{by}} \leq 1.0 \qquad (16\text{-}72)$$

Subscripts x and y, combined with subscript b, indicate the axis of bending about which a particular stress applies, and

$F_a = $ allowable axial stress if the axial force alone existed

$F_b = $ allowable compressive bending stress if the bending moment alone existed

$f_a = $ computed axial stress

$f_b = $ computed bending stress

At points that are braced in the plane of bending, F_a is equal to 60% of F_y, the yield stress of the material, and

$$\frac{f_a}{0.6F_y} + \frac{f_{bx}}{F_{bx}} + \frac{f_{by}}{F_{by}} \leq 1.0 \qquad (16\text{-}73)$$

At intermediate points in the length of a compression member, the secondary bending moments due to deflection (see Fig. 16-34) can contribute significantly to the combined stress. Following the AISC specifications, this contribution is neglected in cases where f_a/F_a is less than 0.15 (i.e., the axial stress is small in relation to the allowable axial stress), and Eq. 16-73 can still be used. When f_a/F_a is greater than 0.15, the effect of the additional secondary bending moments may be approximated by multiplying both f_{bx} and f_{by} by an *amplification factor*, $C_m/(1 - f_a/F_e')$, which takes into account the slenderness ratio in the plane of bending and also the nature of the end moments. The term in the denominator of the amplification factor brings in the effect of the slenderness ratio through the use of F_e' , the Euler buckling stress (using L_e/r in the plane of bending) divided by 23/12, or 1.92, which is the AISC factor of safety for a very long column with L_e/r greater than C_c. (See Section 16-12 for a definition of C_c.) It can be noted that the amplification factor increases as f_a increases and *blows up* as f_a approaches F_e'. The term C_m in the numerator is a correction factor that takes into account the ratio of the end moments as well as their relative sense of direction. The term C_m is larger if the end moments are such that they cause a single curvature of the member and smaller if they cause a reverse curvature. The formula for $f_a/F_a > 0.15$ then becomes

$$\frac{f_a}{F_a} + \frac{C_{mx}f_{bx}}{(1 - f_a/F_{ex}')F_{bx}} + \frac{C_{my}f_{by}}{(1 - f_a/F_{ey}')F_{by}} \le 1.0 \qquad (16\text{-}74)$$

According to the AISC specifications,[28] the value of C_m shall be taken as follows:

1. For compression members in frames subject to joint translation (side-sway), $C_m = 0.85$.

2. For restrained compression members in frames braced against joint translation and not subject to transverse loading between their supports in the plane of bending,

$$C_m = 0.6 - 0.4M_1/M_2$$

(but not less than 0.4), where M_1/M_2 is the ratio of the smaller to larger moments at the ends of that portion of the member unbraced in the plane of bending under consideration. M_1/M_2 is positive when the member is bent in reverse curvature and negative when it is bent in single curvature.

3. For compression members in frames braced against joint translation in the plane of loading and subjected to transverse loading between their supports, the value of C_m can be determined by rational analysis. However, in lieu of such analysis, the following values may be used: (a) for members whose ends are restrained, $C_m = 0.85$; (b) for members whose ends are unrestrained, $C_m = 1.0$.

---

[28]*AISC Steel Construction Manual,* 9th ed. (Chicago: AISC, 1989), 5–27.

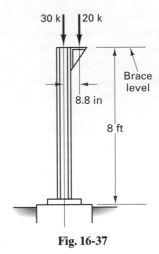

Fig. 16-37

Example 16-10

Select a 6061-T6 aluminum-alloy column for the loading shown in Fig. 16-37 using the allowable stress method. Assume the column to be pinned and laterally supported at both ends.

SOLUTION

In this problem, Eq. 16-68 must be satisfied with σ_{allow} given by one of Eqs. 16-61. By assuming that the column length is in the intermediate range, Eq. 16-61b applies, and the following relation can be written:

$$\frac{30 + 20}{A} + \frac{20 \times 8.8}{S} = \frac{50}{A} + \frac{176}{S} \leq 20.2 - 0.126\frac{L}{r}$$

where A, S, and r depend on the selected column cross section. Note that S applicable to the plane of bending must be used. A trial-and-error procedure is used to solve the problem.

First try: It is convenient to recast the last equation into the following form:

$$\frac{50}{A} + \frac{176}{A}\left(\frac{A}{S}\right) \leq 20.2 - 0.126\frac{L}{r}$$

where $A/S = B$ defines a *bending factor*.[29] These factors are reasonably constant for a whole class of cross sections. Therefore, the solution can begin by selecting a plausible size for a member, which then provides data for A/S, and the preceding equation can be solved for a trial value of A. Following this procedure, *assume* here an 8 in $\times$ 8.5 in $\times$ 8.32 lb/ft aluminum-alloy wide-flange section. The *Aluminum Association Construction Manual* gives the following data for this section: $A = 7.08$ in^2, $S_x = 21.04$ in^3, and $r_{\text{min}} = 1.61$ in. (Geometrically, this cross section is very similar to the W 8 $\times$ 24 steel section given in Table 4A of the Appendix. The corresponding values given there are $A = 7.08$ in^2, $S_x = 20.9$ in^3, and $r_{\text{min}} = 1.61$ in.) Based on these data, $B = A/S_x = 7.08/21.04 = 0.337$. Hence, the basic design equation becomes

$$\frac{50}{A} + \frac{176}{A} \times 0.337 = \frac{109.3}{A} = 20.2 - 0.126 \times \frac{8 \times 12}{1.61} = 12.69$$

The solution of this equation gives $A = 8.61$ in^2, which is larger than that provided by the assumed section and requires another trial.

Second try: Select 8 in $\times$ 8 in $\times$ 10.72 lb/ft, the next larger available section, with $A = 9.12$ in^2, $S_x = 27.41$ in^3, and $r_{\text{min}} = 2.01$ in. (A W 8 $\times$ 31 steel

---

[29]Bending factors are tabulated for many cross sections in the *AISC Manual of Steel Construction* or may be calculated for an assumed section when A and S are known.

section has approximately the same properties.) Substituting these quantities into the first equation approximately formulated before shows that

$$\frac{50}{9.12} + \frac{176}{27.41} = 11.9 \le 20.2 - 0.126 \times \frac{8 \times 12}{2.01} = 14.2 \text{ ksi}$$

Therefore, this section is satisfactory. For a complete solution of this problem, local buckling of flanges and webs should also be checked, as was done in Example 16-9. Such a solution, not given here, shows that the local buckling stresses are larger than the allowable axial stress and do not control the design.

Example 16-11

Select a steel column for the loading shown in Fig. 16-38 using the AISC ASD interaction method. Assume the column to be pinned and laterally braced at both ends. Let $F_y = 50$ ksi and $F_b = 30$ ksi.

SOLUTION

In this problem, the interaction formula, Eq. 16-72 or Eq. 16-73, must be satisfied, depending upon whether f_a/F_a is less than or greater than 0.15. The solution is obtained by trial-and-error process, as is outlined.

First try: Let $L_e/r = 0$, although it is a poor assumption for a 15-ft column. Corresponding to this value of the slenderness ratio, F_a can be calculated, using Eq. 16-57, as $F_a = 50/(5/3) = 30$ ksi. The required area of the section can then be computed using Eq. 16-72:

$$1.0 \ge \frac{f_a}{F_a} + \frac{f_b}{F_b} \qquad \text{or} \qquad A \ge \frac{Af_a}{F_a} + \frac{Af_b}{F_b}$$

Since

$$f_b = \frac{M}{S_x} = \frac{M}{A}\frac{A}{S_x} = \frac{M}{A}B_x \qquad \text{and} \qquad f_a = \frac{P}{A}$$

$$A \ge \frac{P}{F_a} + \frac{M}{F_b}B_x$$

For any one depth of section, the bending factor B_x does not vary a great deal. Therefore, if a W 10 section is to be chosen, a typical value of B_x, established from more extensive tables, is about 0.264. Then

$$A = \frac{200}{30} + \frac{800 \times 0.264}{30} = 13.7 \text{ in}^2$$

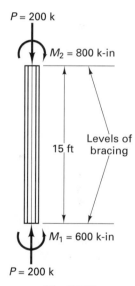

$P = 200$ k

$M_2 = 800$ k-in

15 ft

Levels of bracing

$M_1 = 600$ k-in

$P = 200$ k

Fig. 16-38

Select a W 10×49 section with $A = 14.4$ in^2, $r_{min} = 2.54$ in, $r_x = 4.35$ in, and $B_x = 0.264$, and carry out the necessary calculations to determine whether the interaction Eq. 16-72 or Eq. 16-74 governs:

$$f_a = \frac{P}{A} = \frac{200}{14.4} = 13.9 \text{ ksi} \quad f_b = \frac{MB_x}{A} = \frac{800 \times 0.264}{14.4} = 14.7 \text{ ksi}$$

$$\frac{L_e}{r_{min}} = \frac{15 \times 12}{2.54} = 70.9 < C_c \quad C_c = \sqrt{2\pi^2 E/F_y} = 107$$

Using Eq. 16-57, $F_a = 19.3$ ksi and $f_a/F_a = 13.9/19.3 = 0.72 > 0.15$; hence, the interaction formula of Eq. 16-74 must be checked. For this purpose, using L_e/r_x in the plane of bending, one determines

$$F'_e = \frac{12\pi^2 E}{23(L_e/r_x)^2} = \frac{149 \times 10^3}{(15 \times 12/4.35)^2} = \frac{149 \times 10^3}{(41.4)^2} = 86.9 \text{ ksi}$$

Then, since the end moments subject the column to a single curvature, $M_1/M_2 = -600/800 = -0.75$, and

$$C_m = 0.6 - 0.4M_1/M_2 = 0.6 - (0.4)(-0.75) = 0.9$$

With bending taking place in one plane only, Eq. 16-74 reduces to

$$\frac{f_a}{F_a} + \frac{C_m f_b}{(1 - f_a/F'_e)F_b} \le 1.0$$

On substituting the appropriate quantities into this relation,

$$\frac{13.9}{19.3} + \frac{0.9 \times 14.7}{(1 - 13.9/86.9)30} = 0.72 + 0.52 = 1.24 > 1.0$$

Since Eq. 16-74 is violated, a larger section must be used.

Second try: As an aid in choosing a larger section, assume $F_a = 19.3$ ksi, which is the value computed for the section in the previous trial. Also, using $B_x = 0.264$ for W 10 sections,

$$A \ge \frac{P}{F_a} + \frac{MB_x}{F_b} = \frac{200}{19.3} + \frac{800 \times 0.264}{30} = 17.4 \text{ in}^2$$

Now select a W 10×60 section with $A = 17.6$ in^2, $r_{min} = 2.57$ in, $r_x = 4.39$ in, and $B_x = 0.264$, and proceed as in the first trial to check the interaction formula:

$$f_a = \frac{P}{A} = \frac{200}{17.6} = 11.4 \text{ ksi} \quad f_b = \frac{MB_x}{A} = \frac{800 \times 0.264}{17.6} = 12.0 \text{ ksi}$$

$$\frac{L_e}{r_{min}} = \frac{15 \times 12}{2.57} = 70.0 < C_c$$

Using Eq. 16-57, $F_a = 19.4$ ksi and $f_a/F_a = 11.4/19.4 = 0.59 > 0.15$; hence, Eq. 16-74 must be checked:

$$F_e' = \frac{149 \times 10^3}{(L_e/r_x)^2} = \frac{149 \times 10^3}{(15 \times 12/4.39)^2} = 88.6 \text{ ksi}$$

Again, using Eq. 16-74 for bending in one plane and substituting into it the appropriate quantities, one has

$$\frac{11.4}{19.4} + \frac{0.9 \times 12.0}{(1 - 11.4/88.6)30} = 0.59 + 0.41 = 1.00$$

Since this relation satisfies Eq. 16-74, the W 10×60 section is satisfactory.

16-14. Lateral Stability of Beams

The strength and deflection theory of beams developed in this text applies only if such beams are in *stable equilibrium*. Narrow or slender beams that do not have occasional lateral supports may buckle sideways and thus become unstable; see Fig. 16-39. Theoretical and experimental studies of this problem show that, within limits, reduced bending stresses can be used to maintain the stability of such beams. The nature of the reduced stresses resembles the curves displayed for columns in Figs. 16-31 and 16-34. The key parameter for stress reduction depends on the material properties, geometry of the cross section, and moment gradient. Several of the references cited in this chapter discuss this topic. In this section, only a simple criterion for avoiding the problem of lateral torsional buckling for compact steel beams is given.

According to the AISC ASD specifications, in order for a compact beam to qualify for the maximum allowable bending stress, intermittent lateral supports shall be provided at intervals not exceeding the value

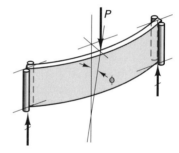

Fig. 16-39   Lateral-torsional buckling of a narrow beam.

$$\frac{76b_f}{\sqrt{F_y}} \quad \text{or} \quad \frac{20{,}000}{(d/A_f)F_y} \quad \text{[in]} \quad (16\text{-}75)$$

where A_f is the area of a compression flange, b_f is the flange width, d is the depth of a beam, and F_y is the yield stress for the material in ksi.

PROBLEMS

Section 16-3

16-1. A rigid bar hinged at the base is held in a vertical position by two springs: One has a stiffness k N/mm and the other, $2k$ N/mm, as shown in the figure. Determine the critical force P_{cr} for this system.

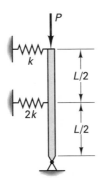

Fig. P16-1

16-2 through 16-5. Rigid-bar segments of equal lengths a are connected at the joints and at the bottoms by frictionless hinges and are maintained in straight positions by torsional springs of the stiffnesses shown in the figures. Determine the eigenvalues for these systems and show the eigenfunctions on separate diagrams. Identify the critical loads.

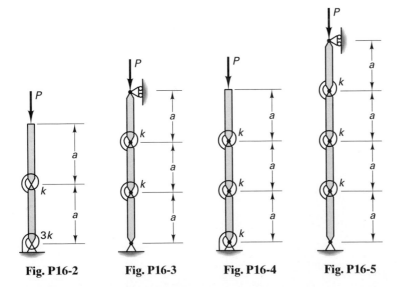

Fig. P16-2   **Fig. P16-3**   **Fig. P16-4**   **Fig. P16-5**

16-6. A weightless prismatic elastic column can be approximated by a series of rigid bars each of length a, with an appropriate torsional spring constant k at each joint, as shown in the figure. Set up the determinantal equation for finding the critical load for a system having n degrees of freedom.

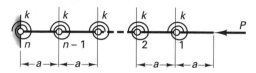

Fig. P16-6

Section 16-5.

16-7. An ideal column is pinned at the base and guyed at the top by four wires, as shown in the figure. The 3000-mm-long column has a solid circular cross section of 80 mm in diameter. For the column and the wires, $E = 200$ GPa and $\sigma_{yp} = 400$ MPa. What should be the diameter of the wires such that a perfectly concentric buckling load P_{cr} could be reached simultaneously with lateral displacement at the top? Assume that the lateral displacement of the top is prevented by one wire only, with the diametrically opposite wire becoming slack, as shown by the dashed curve. Consider the column to be perfectly rigid during lateral displacement of the top. (*Note:* Load eccentricity and column crookedness should be considered in actual applications.)

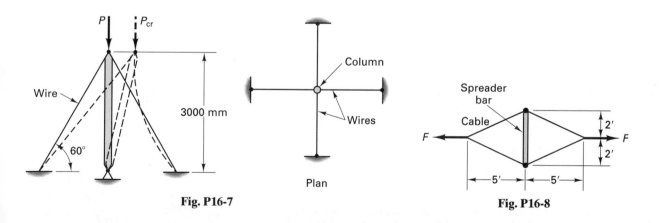

Fig. P16-7   **Fig. P16-8**

16-8. A 1-in round steel bar 4 ft long acts as a spreader bar in the arrangement shown in the figure. If cables and connections are properly designed, what pull F can be applied to the assembly? Use Euler's formula and assume a factor of safety of 3. $E = 29 \times 10^6$ psi.

16-9. A solid steel bar having a 21 mm radius acts as a spreader bar in the system shown in the figure. Based on the Euler formula with a factor of safety of 1.7, what is the capacity of the system based on the spreader bar strength? Let $E = 200$ GPa.

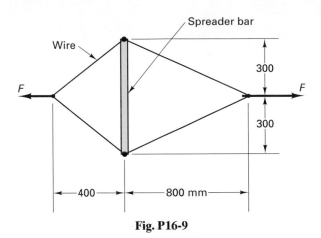

Fig. P16-9

16-10. A boom is made from an aluminum pipe of 60 mm outside diameter and having a 4-mm wall thickness, and is part of an arrangement for lifting weights, as shown in the figure. Determine the magnitude of the force F that could be applied to this planar system as controlled by the capacity of the boom. Assume a factor of safety of 2 for the Euler buckling load. $E = 75$ GPa. All dimensions are shown in mm.

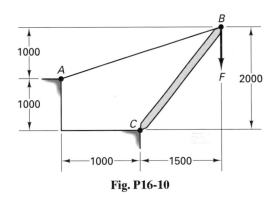

Fig. P16-10

16-11. The mast of a derrick is made of a standard rectangular 4×2-in steel tubing weighing 6.86 lb/ft. ($A = 2.02$ in^2, $I_x = 1.29$ in^4, and $I_z = 3.87$ in^4.) If this derrick is assembled as indicated in the figure, what vertical force F, governed by the size of the mast, can be applied at A? Assume that all joints are pin connected and that the connection details are so made that the mast is loaded concentrically. The top of the mast is braced to prevent sidewise displacement. Use Euler's formula with a factor of safety of 3.3. $E = 29 \times 10^6$ psi.

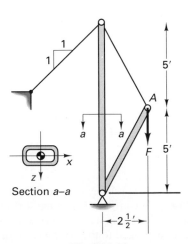

Fig. P16-11

16-12.   What force F can be applied to the system shown in the figure, governed by the 25 × 16-mm aluminum-alloy bar AB? The factor of safety on the Euler buckling load is to be 2.5. Assume the ends are pinned. $E = 70$ GPa.

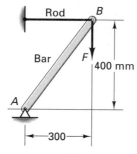

Fig. P16-12

16-13.   Governed by the steel T section, what force F can be applied to the system shown in the figure? The factor of safety on the buckling load must be 2. Assume that the ends are pinned and that the applied force is concentrically applied. $E = 200$ GPa. Neglect the possibility of torsional buckling.

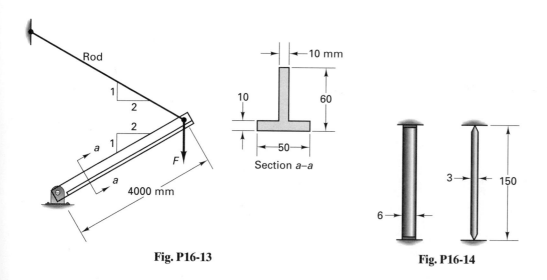

Fig. P16-13   **Fig. P16-14**

16-14.   A thin bar of stainless steel is axially precompressed 100 N between two plates that are fixed at a constant distance of 150 mm apart; see the figure. This assembly is made at 20°C. How high can the temperature of the bar rise, so as to have a factor of safety of 2 with respect to buckling? Assume $E = 200$ GPa and $\alpha = 15 \times 10^{-6}$ per °C.

16-15. What size standard steel pipe should be used for the horizontal member of the jib crane shown in the figure for supporting the maximum force of 20 kN, which includes an impact factor? Use the Euler buckling formula for columns with pinned ends and a factor of safety of 2.5. Neglect the weight of construction. $E = 200$ GPa.

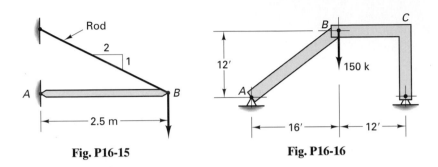

Fig. P16-15   **Fig. P16-16**

16-16. Select a W steel section for member AB for the system shown in the figure to resist a vertical force of 150 k. The system is laterally braced at B and C. Neglect the weight of the members. Assume pinned ends and a factor of safety of 2. $E = 29 \times 10^3$ ksi.

16-17. Select standard steel pipes for members AC and AD shown in the figure to support a vertical load $F = 4.75$ k with a factor of safety of 2.5 on the Euler buckling load. Neglect the weight of the members. $E = 29 \times 10^3$ ksi.

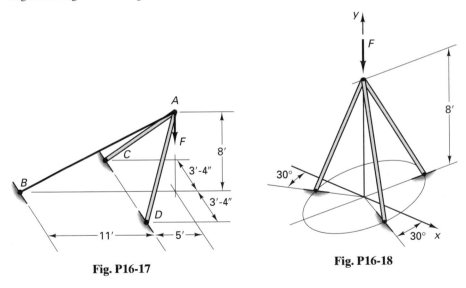

Fig. P16-17   **Fig. P16-18**

16-18. A tripod is to be made up from 3 × 3-in steel angles, each 10 ft long, to support a vertical load $F = 8$ k at the center, as shown in the figure. Using the Euler buckling formula with a factor of safety of 3 to account for impact, determine the required thickness of the angles. Neglect the weight of the angles; assume that they are loaded concentrically and that the ends are pinned. $E = 30 \times 10^6$ psi.

16-19.   A simple beam of flexural rigidity EI_b is propped up at the middle by a slender rod of flexural rigidity EI_c. Estimate the deflection of the beam at the center if a force F double the Euler load for the column is applied to this system.

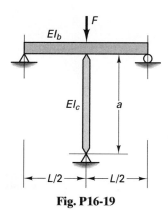

Fig. P16-19

Section 16-6

16-20.   Derive Eq. 16-17a using Eq. 16-5 in the form $EIv'' + Pv = M_o$, where M_o is the moment at the end.

16-21.   Derive Eq. 16-17b using Eq. 16-5 in the form $EIv'' + P(\delta - v)$, where δ is the end deflection.

16-22.   Determine the critical buckling load for the column shown in the figure. (*Hint:* See the preceding problem; enforce continuity conditions at a change in EI.)

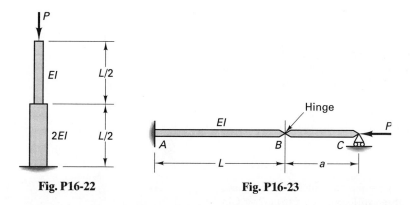

Fig. P16-22   **Fig. P16-23**

16-23.   Determine the transcendental equation for finding the critical buckling load for bar AB of constant EI due to the application of axial force P through rigid link BC. (*Hint:* In a deflection position, note the presence of a shear force at B.)

16-24.   An allowable axial load for a 4-m-long pin-ended column of a certain linearly elastic material is 20 kN. Five different columns made of the same material and having the same cross section have the supporting conditions shown in the figure. Using the column capacity for the 4-m column as the criterion, what are the allowable loads for the five columns shown?

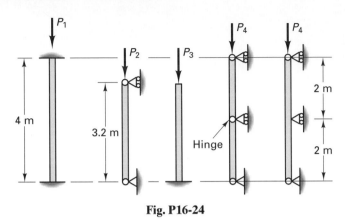

Fig. P16-24

16-25.   Consider the five columns with different boundary conditions in Problem 16-24. All five columns are made of the same linearly elastic material. Using the Euler formula for different boundary conditions, determine columns lengths to carry the same load as the 4-m column with fixed ends.

16-26.   A machine bracket of steel alloy is to be made as shown in the figure. The compression member AB is so arranged that it can buckle as a pin-ended column in the plane ABC, but as a fixed-ended column in the direction perpendicular to this plane. (a) If the thickness of the member is $\frac{1}{2}$ in, what should be its height h to have equal probability of buckling in the two mutually perpendicular directions? (b) If $E = 28 \times 10^6$ and the factor of safety on instability is 2, what force F can be applied to the bracket? Assume that the bar designed in (a) controls the capacity of the assembly.

16-27.   A piece of mechanical equipment is to be supported at the top of a 127-mm nominal-diameter standard steel pipe, as shown in the figure. The mass of the equipment and the supporting platform is 2500 kg. The base of the pipe will be anchored in a concrete pad and the top end will be unsupported. If the factor of safety required against buckling is 2.5, what is the maximum height of the column on which the equipment can be supported? $E = 200$ GPa. (*Note:* The solution becomes inaccurate if the height of the rigid mass is significant in relation to the height of the column.)

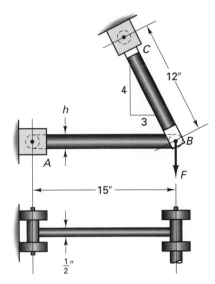

Fig. P16-26

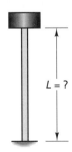

Fig. P16-27

Sections 16-6 through 16-8

16-28.   Find the shortest lengths for columns with pinned ends such that the Euler elastic buckling formula would apply. Consider three different cases: (a) a 2×4-in wooden strut of nominal size (see Table 9 of the Appendix) if $E = 1.8 \times 10^6$ psi and the maximum compression stress is 1500 psi, (b) a solid aluminum-alloy shaft 50 mm in diameter if $E = 70$ GPa and $\sigma_{yp} = 360$ MPa, and (c) a W 14×193 steel section (see Table 4A of the Appendix) if $E = 29 \times 10^3$ ksi and $\sigma_{yp} = 36$ ksi.

16-29. Two grades of steel are in common use for columns in buildings: A36 steel with $\sigma_{yp} = 36$ ksi, and A572 with $\sigma_{yp} = 50$ ksi. For each steel, determine the smallest slenderness ratios for which the Euler elastic buckling formula applies when the column is pinned at both ends and when it is fixed at both ends.

16-30. The stress-strain curve in simple tension for an aluminum alloy is shown in the figure, where, for convenience, $\varepsilon \times 10^3 = e$. The alloy is linearly elastic for stresses up to 280 MPa; the ultimate stress is 350 MPa. (a) Idealize the stress-strain relation by fitting a parabola to the curve so that σ and $d\sigma/de = E_t$ is continuous at the proportional limit and so that the $\sigma = 350$-MPa line is tangent to the parabola. (b) Plot $E_t(\sigma)/E$ against σ/σ_{ult}, where E is the elastic modulus, σ_{ult} the ultimate stress, and E_t the tangent modulus at stress σ. (c) Plot in one graph σ_{cr} against L/r for fixed-fixed and pinned-pinned columns, where σ_{cr} is based on E_t.

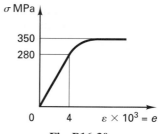

Fig. P16-30

16-31. For some materials, the stress-strain relationship in normalized form can be expressed[1] as $\sigma = 1 - \exp(-c\varepsilon)$, where c is an arbitrary constant. Setting $c = 500$, plot the stress-strain diagram for ε from 0 to 0.01, and the normalized-stress-vs-column slenderness ratio L_e/r from 0 to 200. [*Note:* $\exp(x) = e^x$.]

16-32. Using Eq. 16-24, obtain the average stress P/A for $L/r = 0$ and 75. Assume $ec/r^2 = 0.05$.

Section 16-9

16-33. A high-strength thin-walled steel tube 1250 mm long is loaded as shown in Fig. 16-25. The axial force $P = 25$ kN and the transverse $F = 500$ N. The outside diameter of the tube is 37 mm, and its cross-sectional area is 223 mm². For this tube, $I = 34.2 \times 10^3$ mm⁴ and $E = 200$ GPa. (a) Determine the maximum deflection and bending moment using Eqs. 16-33 and 16-34. (b) Compare the results in (a) with the results using the approximate Eqs. 16-41 and 16-42. (c) Calculate the combined stresses due to the axial force and the maximum bending moment. Neglect local stress concentrations.

16-34. Show that for a beam column loaded by an end moment M_B, as shown in the figure, the deflection is

$$v = \frac{M_B \sin \lambda x}{p \sin \lambda L} - \frac{M_B x}{PL}$$

and the bending moment is

$$M = -\frac{M_B \sin \lambda x}{\sin \lambda L}$$

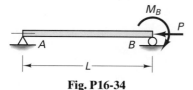

Fig. P16-34

[1]Courtesy of F. C. Filippou.

16-35. Consider the thin-walled tube having the mechanical properties given in Problem 16-33 subjected to an end moment $M_o = 250$ N · m and an axial force $P = 30$ kN, as shown in the figure. (a) Determine the maximum deflection and then the maximum bending moment using an approximate method. Use Table 10 of the Appendix for beam deflection due to an end moment. (b) Compare the results in (a) with those using the accurate expressions found in the preceding example. Note that the maximum moment occurs at $dM/dx = 0$. (c) Calculate the maximum in-span stresses due to the axial force and bending.

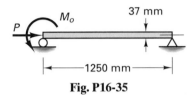

Fig. P16-35

16-36. If an elastic bar is initially curved as shown in the figure, show that the total deflection

$$v = v_o + v_1 = \left(\frac{1}{1 - P/P_{cr}} \right) a \sin \frac{\pi x}{L}$$

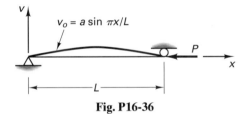

Fig. P16-36

Section 16-10

16-37. Show that since the character of Eqs. 16-45 and 16-46 changes if, instead of a compression axial force, a tensile force is applied, the homogeneous solution of the differential equation for deflection is

$$v = C_1 \sinh \lambda x + C_2 \cosh \lambda x + C_3 x + C_4$$

where constants $C_1, C_2, C_3,$ and C_4 are determined from the boundary conditions.

16-38. Show that if, in Example 16-3, axial force P were tensile, the deflection would be

$$v = \frac{F}{2P\lambda} \operatorname{sech} \frac{\lambda L}{2} \sinh \lambda x - \frac{Fx}{2P}$$

16-39. Verify Eq. 16-48 by superposing the deflections due to the moments applied at each end using the expression for the deflection found in Problem 16-34. This special case demonstrates that the solutions for beam-column deflections can be found by superposition for identical members subjected to the *same* axial force.

16-40.   Show that the equation of the elastic curve for an elastic beam-column of constant EI subjected to a sinusoidal load, as shown in the figure, is

$$v = \frac{1}{1 - P/P_{cr}} \frac{q_o L^4}{\pi^4 EI} \sin \frac{\pi x}{L}$$

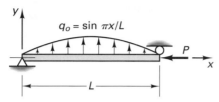

Fig. P16-40

16-41.   Using Eq. 16-45, show that the equation for the bending moment for an elastic beam-column subjected to a uniformly varying increasing load to the right is given as

$$M = -\frac{q_o \sin \lambda x}{\lambda^2 \sin \lambda L}$$

where $q = q_o x/L$.

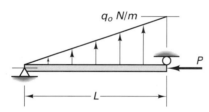

Fig. P16-41

16-42.   (a) Using Eq. 16-45, show that the equation for the bending moment for a uniformly loaded elastic beam-column is given as

$$M = -\frac{q_o}{\lambda^2} \left(\frac{\cos \lambda L - 1}{\sin \lambda L} \sin \lambda x - \cos \lambda x + 1 \right)$$

(b) How can the equation of the elastic curve be easily found from the preceding result? (*Hint:* See Eq. 16-50.)

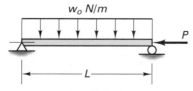

Fig. P16-42

16-43.   Rework Example 16-4 using Eq. 16-45, and show that for $P = 0$, Eq. 16-49 reduces to $v_{max} = M_o L^2/8EI$.

16-44.   Using Eq. 16-55, rederive Eq. 16-16.

16-45.   Using homogeneous Eq. 16-45, determine the critical buckling load for the column of variable stiffness shown in the figure. (*Hint:* Enforce continuity conditions at the change in *EI*.)

16-46.   A pin-ended bar of constant *EI* is supported along its length by an elastic foundation, as shown in the figure. The foundation modulus is k lb/in^2 and is such that when the bar deflects by an amount v, a restoring force kv lb/in is exerted by the foundation normal to the bar. First, satisfy yourself that the governing homogeneous differential equation for this problem is

$$EIv^{iv} + Pv'' + kv = 0$$

Then show that the required eigenvalue of the differential equation is

$$P_{cr} = \frac{\pi^2 EI}{L^2}\left[n^2 + \frac{1}{n^2}\left(\frac{kL^4}{\pi^4 EI} \right) \right]$$

Note that if $k = 0$, the minimum value of P_{cr} becomes the classical Euler buckling load.

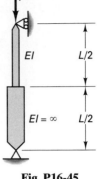

Fig. P16-45

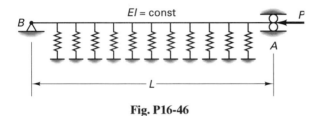

Fig. P16-46

Sections 16-11 and 16-12

16-47.   (a) If a pin-ended solid circular shaft is 1.5 m long and its diameter is 50 mm, what is the shaft's slenderness ratio? (b) If the same amount of material as in (a) is reshaped into a square bar of the same length, what is the slenderness ratio of the bar?

16-48.   The cross section of a compression member for a small bridge is made as shown in Fig. 16-28(a). The top cover plate is $\frac{1}{2} \times 18$ in and the two C 12 $\times$ 20.7 channels are placed 10 in from back to back. If this member is 20 ft long, what is its slenderness ratio? (Check L/r in two directions.)

16-49.   Consider two axially loaded columns made from W 10 $\times$ 112 sections of 50 grade steel with $\sigma_{yp} = 50$ ksi. One of the columns is 12 ft long and the other is 40 ft long. Both columns are braced at the pin ends. Using the AISC ASD, determine the allowable loads for these columns.

16-50.   A 14 $\times$ 193 column of 50 grade ($\sigma_{yp} = 50$ ksi) steel is laterally braced 12 ft apart in the weak direction of buckling and 24 ft apart in the strong direction, as shown in the figure. (a) Determine the allowable axial load for this column per AISC ASD. (b) Is this is a well-balanced design?

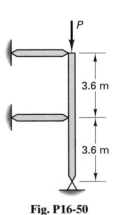

Fig. P16-50

16-51. A standard 12-in-nominal-diameter steel pipe (see Table 7 of the Appendix) supports a water tank, as shown in the figure. Assuming that the effective length of the free-standing pipe column is 30 ft, what weight of water can be supported per AISC ASD? Let $\sigma_{yp} = 50$ ksi. (*Note:* In a complete design, wind load should also be considered.)

16-52. For 50 grade steel, $\sigma_{yp} = 50$ ksi and $E = 29 \times 10^3$ ksi. (a) Determine the ratio L_e/r for the transition point between Eqs. 16-56 and 16-57 for AISC ASD formulas. [These formulas are constructed using the concept shown in Fig. 16-31.] (b) Show that the AISC LRFD Eq. 16-58 reduces to $L_e/r = 75.66\lambda_c$, and then determine the ratio L_e/r for the transition point between Eqs. 16-59 and 16-60.

16-53. (a) Using the AISC LRFD method, determine the nominal axial column strengths (factored loads) $P_n = \phi_c A\sigma_{cr}$, where A is the cross section for the two columns in Problem 16-49. (b) Determine the ratios between the factored and the allowable axial loads for the corresponding columns in Problem 16-49. Such allowable axial loads are 593 k and 153 k, respectively, for the short and the long columns.

16-54. Using the AISC LRFD formulas, rework Problem 16-50 and form the ratio between the factored and the allowable axial loads.

16-55. Using AISC LRFD formulas, rework Problem 16-51.

16-56. Two 50 grade steel C 10 × 15.3 channels form a 24-ft-long square compression member; the channel flanges are turned in and are adequately laced together. Using the AISC ASD formulas, what is the allowable axial force on this member? $\sigma_{yp} = 50$ ksi and $E = 29 \times 10^3$ ksi.

16-57. A compression member is made up from two 50 grade steel C 8 × 11.5 channels arranged as shown in Fig. 16-28(b). (a) Determine the distance back to back of the channels so that the moments of inertia for the section about the two principal axes are equal. (b) If the member is 32 ft long, what is the nominal axial compressive strength of the member according to AISC LRFD provisions? $\sigma_{yp} = 50$ ksi and $E = 29 \times 10^3$ ksi.

16-58. A boom for an excavating machine is made up from four $2\frac{1}{2} \times 2\frac{1}{2} \times \frac{1}{2}$-in steel angles, as shown in Fig. 16-28(c). The out-to-out dimension of the square column, excluding lacing bars, is 14 in. According to AISC ASD formulas, what axial load can be applied to this member if it is 52 ft long? $\sigma_{yp} = 50$ ksi and $E = 29 \times 10^3$ ksi.

16-59. A compression chord of a small truss consists of two 4 × 4 × $\frac{3}{8}$-in steel angles arranged as shown in Fig. 16-28(d). The vertical legs of the angles are separated by spacers $\frac{1}{2}$ in apart. If the length of this member between braced points is 8 ft, what axial load may be applied according to the AISC ASD code? $\sigma_{yp} = 50$ ksi and $E = 29 \times 10^3$ ksi.

16-60. Using Aluminum Association formulas, determine the allowable axial loads for two 8 in × 8 in × 10.72-lb/ft 6061-T6 aluminum-alloy pin-ended columns that are 10 and 30 ft long. For cross-sectional properties of the columns, use Table 4 of the Appendix for W 8 × 31 steel section.

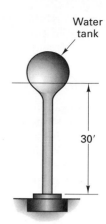

Water tank

30'

Fig. P16-51

16-61. Using the NFPA formulas, determine the allowable axial loads for three 6×6-in Douglas Fir columns of different lengths: 5, 12, and 20 ft. Each column is braced at both ends, and $F_c = 1000$ psi and $E = 1.6 \times 10^6$ psi.

Sections 16-13 and 16-14

16-62. An observation platform 6 ft in diameter is attached to the top of a standard 6-in pipe 20 ft long supported by a footing. Governed by the strength of the pipe, what weight, including a person or persons, can be placed on the platform? Locate the live load 3 ft from the pipe centerline. Neglect the weight of construction. Use Eq. 16-68, with the allowable stress given by the Euler formula with F.S. = 3. $E = 29 \times 10^6$ psi and $\sigma_{yp} = 50$ ksi.

16-63. A W 10×60 column 20 ft long is subjected to an eccentric load of 180 k located as shown in the figure. Using the AISC ASD interaction formula, determine whether this column is adequate. Use 50 grade steel and the same allowable stresses as in Example 16-11.

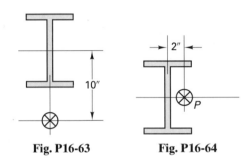

Fig. P16-63   **Fig. P16-64**

16-64. A W 14×90 column made of 50 grade steel ($\sigma_{yp} = 50$ ksi) is 20 ft long and is loaded eccentrically, as shown in the figure. Determine the allowable load P using the AISC ASD formulas. Assume pin-ended conditions. Let $F_b = 37$ ksi.

16-65. A W 10×60 column has an effective length of 20 ft. Using the AISC ASD formulas, determine the magnitude of an eccentric load that can be applied to this column at A, as shown in the figure, in addition to a concentric load of 20 k. The column is braced at top and bottom. The allowable bending stress $F_b = 24$ ksi. Use 50 grade steel.

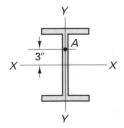

Fig. P16-65

16-66.   What is the magnitude of the maximum beam reaction that can be carried by a W 10×49 column having an effective length of 14 ft, according to the AISC ASD interaction formula? Assume that the beam delivers the reaction at the outside flange of the column, as shown in the figure, and is concentric with the centerline of the column web. The top and bottom of the column are held laterally. Assume $F_y = 50$ ksi and $F_b = 30$ ksi.

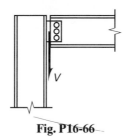

Fig. P16-66

16-67.   Using the AISC ASD code, select a W-shape-column to carry a concentric load of 60 k and an eccentric load of 25 k applied on the Y–Y axis at a distance of 6 in from the X–X axis. The column is braced top and bottom and is 14 ft long. The allowable bending stress is 30 ksi and $\sigma_{yp} = 50$ ksi.

16-68.   A narrow rectangular beam, such as that shown in the figure, can collapse when loaded through lateral instability by twisting and displacing sidewise. It can be shown[2] that for this case, the critical force that may be applied at the end is

$$P_{cr} = 4.013\sqrt{B_1 C}/L^2$$

where $B_1 = hb^3 E/12$ is the flexural stiffness of the beam around the vertical axis and $C = \beta hb^3 G$ is the torsional stiffness. (For rectangular sections, coefficient β is given in a table in Section 6-14.)

A $5 \times \frac{1}{2}$-in narrow rectangular cantilever is made from steel ($\sigma_{yp} = 50$ ksi and $E = 30 \times 10^3$ ksi) and is loaded as shown in the figure. (a) Determine the critical load P_{cr} and the critical length L_{cr}, where both the strength and the stability criteria are equally applicable. (b) Plot P versus L in the neighborhood of P_{cr} and L_{cr} for the two criteria. (Note that the smaller of the P values governs the design.)

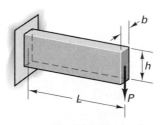

Fig. P16-68

[2]See S. P. Timoshenko and J. M. Gere, *Theory of Elastic Stability*, 2nd ed. (New York: McGraw-Hill, 1961).

17

Energy and Virtual Work

17-1. Introduction

In a few instances in the preceding chapters, the deflection of members was obtained by invoking the law of conservation of energy and equating the internal strain energy to the external work. This Lagrangian approach of employing *scalar functions* can be greatly extended, resulting in some of the most effective procedures for the analysis of deformable bodies. In Part A, the previously encountered concept of elastic strain energy is discussed from a somewhat more general point of view. This is followed by a specialized statement of the law of conservation of energy for deformable bodies, and the reason for the need to develop additional methods based on work and energy concepts to solve deflection problems.

Part B serves as an introduction to the two virtual work methods for deformable bodies. One of these, the method of *virtual forces,* is very useful for determining deflections caused by any kind of deformation and is not limited at all to elastic behavior. This method is one of the best available for calculating deflections of members. The conjugate method of *vir-*

tual displacements, of great importance in the matrix analysis of structures and in finite elements, is also discussed. The duality of these two methods is illustrated by considering discrete structural systems.

Part A ELASTIC STRAIN ENERGY AND EXTERNAL WORK

17-2. Elastic Strain Energy

Consider a general state of stress acting on a cubic element having all edges of unit length. Such an element similar to that of Fig. 1-3(a) is shown in Fig. 17-1. The forces acting on the surfaces of this element are numerically equal to stresses, and the displacements are numerically equal either to the displacements due to shear [see Fig. 5-6(b)] or due to normal stresses (see Fig. 5-10). Therefore, a gradual application (increasing) of the applied forces (stresses) acting through their respective displacements (strains) do *work* equal to one-half of the product of the corresponding quantities. On bringing in the concept of conservation energy, the stored *elastic strain energy density U_o* per unit volume can be expressed as

$$U_o = \frac{1}{2}(\sigma_x \varepsilon_x + \sigma_y \varepsilon_y + \sigma_z \varepsilon_z + \tau_{xy}\gamma_{xy} + \tau_{yz}\gamma_{yz} + \tau_{zx}\gamma_{zx}) \quad (17\text{-}1)$$

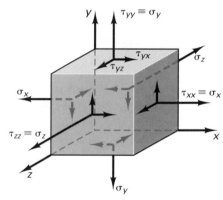

Fig. 17-1 Unit cube with various uniform stresses on each of its facets.

On this basis, the general expression for the total *internal* strain energy in a *linearly elastic* body is

$$U = \frac{1}{2}\iiint_V (\sigma_x \varepsilon_x + \sigma_y \varepsilon_y + \sigma_z \varepsilon_z$$
$$+ \tau_{xy}\gamma_{xy} + \tau_{yz}\gamma_{yz} + \tau_{zx}\gamma_{zx})\, dx\, dy\, dz \quad (17\text{-}2)$$

Integration extends over the volume of a body. Such a general expression is used in elasticity. In engineering mechanics of solid, a less general class of problems is considered and Eq. 17-2 simplifies. An expression

$$U = \frac{1}{2}\iiint_V (\sigma_x \varepsilon_x + \tau_{xy}\gamma_{xy})\, dx\, dy\, dz \quad (17\text{-}3)$$

is sufficient for determining the strain energy in axially loaded bars as well as in bent and sheared beams. Moreover, the last term of Eq. 17-3 written in the appropriate coordinates is all that is needed in the torsion problem of a circular shaft and for thin-walled tubes. These cases include the major types of problems treated in this text.

For linearly elastic material, for uniaxial stress, $\varepsilon_x = \sigma_x/E$, and for pure shear, $\gamma_{xy} = \tau_{xy}/G$. Thus, Eq. 17-3 can be recast in the following form:

$$U = \underbrace{\iiint_V \frac{\sigma_x^2}{2E}\, dx\, dy\, dz}_{\substack{\text{for axial loading and} \\ \text{bending of beams}}} + \underbrace{\iiint_V \frac{\tau_{xy}^2}{2G}\, dx\, dy\, dz}_{\text{for shear in beams}} \qquad (17\text{-}4)$$

or

$$U = \iiint_V \frac{E\varepsilon_x^2}{2}\, dx\, dy\, dz + \iiint_V \frac{G\gamma_{xy}^2}{2}\, dx\, dy\, dz \qquad (17\text{-}5)$$

These equations can be specialized for the solutions encountered in engineering mechanics of solids, where it is generally customary to work with stress resultants P, V, M, and T. In this manner, the triple integrals are reduced to single integrals. Assuming that E and G are constant, some special cases of the last two equations follow.

Strain Energy for Axially Loaded Bars

In this problem, $\sigma_x = P/A$ and $A = \iint dy\, dz$. Therefore, since axial force P and cross-sectional area A can only be functions of x,

$$U = \iiint_V \frac{\sigma_x^2}{2E}\, dV = \int_L \frac{P^2}{2AE}\, dx \qquad (17\text{-}6)$$

where an integration along bar length L gives the required quantity.

If P, A, and E are constant, and, since for such cases, per Eq. 3-4, bar elongation $\Delta = PL/AE$, alternatively,

$$U = \frac{P^2 L}{2AE} = \frac{AE\Delta^2}{2L} \qquad (17\text{-}7)$$

Strain Energy for Beams in Bending

According to Eq. 8-24, the elastic strain energy in pure bending of a beam around one of its principal axes reduces to an integral along the beam length L; that is,

$$U = \iiint_V \frac{\sigma_x^2}{2E}\, dV = \int_L \frac{M^2}{2EI}\, dx \qquad (17\text{-}8)$$

where M is the bending moment and I is the moment of inertia for the cross section.

Strain Energy for Beams in Shear   The expression given by Eq. 14-34 for a rectangular beam subjected to a constant shear can be generalized using the last term in Eq. 17-4 to read

$$U = \iiint_V \frac{\tau^2}{2G} \, dx \, dy \, dz = \alpha \int_L \frac{V^2}{2GA} \, dx \qquad (17\text{-}9a)$$

where factor α depends on the cross-sectional area of a beam and was shown to be 6/5 in Example 14-12 for a rectangular beam.[1] In this equation, both shear V and area A can vary along the span of length L.

Strain Energy for Circular Tubes in Torsion   For this case, the basic expression for the shearing strain energy is analogous to the last term of Eq. 17-4. Such an expression has been used previously in Example 6-11. By substituting $\tau = T\rho/I_p$, Eq. 6-4, after some simplifications, becomes

$$U = \iiint_V \frac{\tau^2}{2G} \, dV = \int_L \frac{T^2}{2GI_p} \, dx \qquad (17\text{-}9b)$$

17-3. Displacements by Conservation of Energy

The law of conservation of energy, which states that energy can be neither created nor destroyed, can be adopted for determining the displacements of elastic systems due to the applied forces. The first law of thermodynamics expresses this principle as

$$\text{work done} = \text{change in energy} \qquad (17\text{-}10)$$

For an adiabatic process[2] and when no heat is generated in the system, with the forces applied in a quasistatic manner,[3] the special form of this law for conservative systems[4] reduces to

$$W_e = U \qquad (17\text{-}11)$$

[1]For a circular cross section, $\alpha = 10/9$, and for I beams and box sections, $\alpha = 1$, provided only web area A_{web} is used in Eq. 17-9a.

[2]No heat is added or subtracted from the system.

[3] These forces are applied to the body so slowly that the kinetic energy can be neglected.

[4]In a conservative system, there are no dissipative forces such as those due to friction. More generally, in a conservative system no work is done in moving the system around any closed path.

where W_e is the total work done by the externally applied forces during the loading process and U is the total strain energy stored in the system.

It is significant to note that the total work W must be zero, and

$$W = W_e + W_i = 0 \qquad (17\text{-}12)$$

where W_e is the external work and W_i is the internal work. Therefore, from Eqs. 17-11 and 17-12, one has

$$U = -W_i \qquad (17\text{-}13)$$

where W_i has a negative sign because the deformations are opposed by the internal forces. (See the discussion in connection with Fig. 17-2.)

Some formulations for determining the internal elastic strain energy U were given in the preceding section. For linearly elastic systems, when a force, or a couple, is gradually applied, the external work W_e is equal to one-half the total force multiplied by the displacement in the direction of its action. The possibility of formulating both W_e and U provides the basis for applying Eq. 17-11 for determining displacements.

This procedure was used in Example 3-9 for finding the deflection of an axially loaded bar, and again in Example 6-11 for determining the twist of a circular shaft. A general relation, Eq. 6-37, was derived using this procedure for twist of a thin-walled hollow member subjected to a torque. Lastly, this method was applied in Example 14-12 for finding the deflection caused by bending and shear in a cantilever loaded by a concentrated force at the end. In all of these cases, the procedure was limited to the determination of elastic deflections caused by a single concentrated force at the point of its application. Otherwise, intractable equations are obtained. For example, for two forces P_1 and P_2, $P_1\Delta_1/2 + P_2\Delta_2/2 = U$, where Δ_1 and Δ_2 are, respectively, the unknown deflections of the two forces. An additional relationship between Δ_1 and Δ_2, except in cases of symmetry, is not available. This requires development of the more general methods discussed in the remainder of this chapter.

Part B   VIRTUAL WORK METHODS

17-4. Virtual Work Principle

Direct use of external work and internal strain energy for determining deflections breaks down if several deflections and/or rotations are sought at different points in a deformed body subjected to one or more forces. It is possible, however, to devise extraordinarily effective means for solving such problems by replacing true or real work and strain energy by external and internal virtual (imaginary) work. Two different procedures for apply-

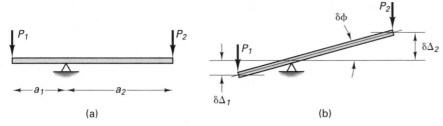

Fig. 17-2   Alternative means for determining static equilibrium.

ing the virtual work principle are described, resulting in the virtual displacement method and the virtual force method.

Virtual Displacement Method   The conventional solution of static equilibrium problems usually follows the concepts introduced by Archimedes in his studies of levers. On this basis, the forces shown in Fig. 17-2(a) are related as

$$P_1 a_1 = P_2 a_2 \qquad (17\text{-}14)$$

An alternative method[5] consists of rotating the lever through an *imaginary* or *virtual angle* $\delta\phi$. Here, as elsewhere, for emphasis, all such virtual quantities are expressed as $\delta\phi$ rather than the $d\phi$ employed in usual differential notation. The rotation shown causes *virtual displacements* $\delta\Delta_1$ and $\delta\Delta_2$ at the points of load application. Then, assuming that the system is conservative, the *virtual work* δW done by real forces moving through virtual displacements in the direction of the applied forces is zero. Such work is positive when the directions of forces and displacements coincide. Applying this principle to the rigid bar shown in Fig. 17-2(b).

$$\delta W = P_1 \delta\Delta_1 - P_2 \delta\Delta_2 = 0 \qquad (17\text{-}15)$$

However, since $\delta\Delta_1 = a_1 \delta\phi$ and $\delta\Delta_2 = a_2 \delta\phi$, and P_1 and P_2 *do not change* during the application of $\delta\phi$,

$$(P_1 a_1 - P_2 a_2) \delta\phi = 0 \qquad (17\text{-}16)$$

Inasmuch as $\delta\phi$ is *perfectly arbitrary,* bearing no relation to the applied forces, the expression in parentheses must be zero, reverting to Eq. 17-14. Stated differently, for a system in equilibrium, the virtual displacement equation simply leads to an *equation of statics* multiplied by an arbitrary function $\delta\phi$.

For deformable bodies, the virtual displacement equation must be generalized. For such systems, the total virtual work δW, consisting of the

[5]This approach apparently was considered by Leonardo da Vinci (1452–1519), Stevinus (1548–1620), Galileo (1564–1642), and Johann Bernoulli, who in 1717 introduced the notion of virtual displacements (velocities) in his letter to Varignon.

external virtual work δW_e and the internal virtual work δW_i, is zero. In the form of an equation,

$$\delta W = \delta W_e + \delta W_i = 0 \qquad (17\text{-}17)$$

This equation can be interpreted by making reference to Fig. 17-3, where a weightless spring supports a rigid mass. This mass applies a force P to the spring, and *the system is in equilibrium.* Then a *virtual displacement* $\delta\Delta$ is imposed on this system, as shown in Fig. 17-3(a). During this displacement, force P and internal forces F, shown on isolated parts in Fig. 17-3(b), *remain constant.*

As can be seen from the isolated mass in Fig. 17-3(b), the *external* virtual work δW_e done by force P is $P\,\delta\Delta$. On the other hand, the *internal* virtual work δW_i done by F is $-F\,\delta\Delta$. Therefore, this internal virtual work is negative.

However, it can be noted that the work done by F acting on the spring, shown in the upper diagram of Fig. 17-3(b), has an opposite sign. Therefore, by calling this *internal* virtual work caused by the *external* force as δW_{ie}, it follows that

$$\delta W_i = -\delta W_{ie} \qquad (17\text{-}18)$$

By substituting this relation into Eq. 17-17,

$$\boxed{\delta W_e = \delta W_{ie}} \qquad (17\text{-}19)$$

Applying Eq. 17-19 to the simple system in Fig. 17-3

$$P\,\delta\Delta = F\,\delta\Delta \quad \text{or} \quad (P - F)\delta\Delta = 0$$

This relation is analogous to Eq. 17-14. Here $\delta\Delta$ is arbitrary, so $P - F = 0$, an equation of equilibrium.

The *virtual displacement method* for deformable systems expressed by Eq. 17-19 establishes the *equations for static equilibrium.*

It is essential to note that during a virtual displacement, the magnitudes and the directions of applied forces do not change. It is to be emphasized that constitutive relations do not enter into the derivation of the virtual work equations.

Virtual Force Method

For deformable bodies, virtual work can be formulated in two alternative ways. In the previous discussion, virtual work was determined by multiplying real forces by virtual displacements. Here the virtual work is obtained as a product of the virtual forces and real displacements. This approach leads to the *virtual force method.* In this method, again, no restrictions are placed on constitutive relations, and problems with thermal deformations, as well as settlement of supports and lack of member fit, can be analyzed.

In the virtual force method, the total virtual force δW^*, consisting of the *external* virtual work δW_e^* and the *internal* work δW_i^*, is zero. In order to differentiate between the virtual work in this method with that in the

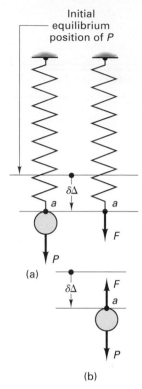

Fig. 17-3   Virtual displacement mass-spring model.

virtual displacement method, the work quantities are identified by aster-
isks. For this case, analogous to Eq. 17-17,

$$\delta W^* = \delta W_e^* + \delta W_i^* = 0 \qquad (17\text{-}20)$$

This equation can be clarified with the aid of Fig. 17-4, where a weightless
spring supports a rigid mass. However, unlike the previous case, virtual
force δP is placed on the system first and is in equilibrium with internal
forces $\delta F = \delta P$, as shown on isolated parts in Fig. 17-4(b). The deformation
of the system is permitted to take place *after* force δP is applied.
Thereafter, δP remains *constant*.

In the next step, *real displacement* Δ is allowed to occur when force δP
does the *external* virtual work:

$$\delta W_e^* = \delta P\, \Delta$$

During the same process, as can be seen from the isolated mass in Fig. 17-4(b),
the *internal* virtual work δW_i^* done by δF is $-\delta F\,\Delta$. Therefore, here, again,
the internal virtual work is negative. However, this sign can be reversed by
considering the *internal* virtual work δW_{ie}^* caused by the *external* force
$\delta P = \delta F$; that is

$$`\delta W_i^* = -\delta W_{ie}^* \qquad (17\text{-}21)$$

Therefore, since from Eq. 17-20,

$$\delta W_e^* = -\delta W_i^*$$

the basic virtual work equation for the *virtual force method* is

$$\boxed{\delta W_e^* = \delta W_{ie}^*} \qquad (17\text{-}22)$$

where δW_e^* is the *external* virtual work and δW_{ie}^* is the *internal* virtual work
calculated in the sense described before.

In applying 17-22 to the simple system in Fig. 17-4, it is known *a priori*
that $\delta F = \delta P$. Then, since the virtual work equation is $\delta P\, \Delta = \delta F\, \Delta_{\text{spr}}$,
$\Delta = \Delta_{\text{spr}}$, an *equation of compatibility*.

It is important to recognize that only one deformable element is considered in each of the simple systems in Figs. 17-2 and 17-3. Typically, there
are several such elements, and calculations for the internal virtual work
must extend over all of them.

To summarize, in the *virtual displacement* method, the use of kinematically admissible (plausible) displacements assures compatibility, and solutions lead to equations for static equilibrium. By contrast, in the *virtual
force* method, the requirements of statics are fulfilled by assuming the virtual force system in equilibrium, and solutions lead to conditions of compatibility for the systems.

In applying Eqs. 17-19 and 17-22, the terms δW_{ie} and δW_{ie}^* will be simply
referred to as the *internal* virtual work. It is to be understood, however,

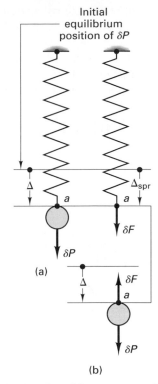

Fig. 17-4 Virtual force mass-spring
model.

that these terms are calculated in accordance with the definition given in connection with Eqs. 17-18 and 17-21.

In the next five sections, self-contained development of the two virtual work methods at an introductory level is given. For more advanced treatment of this important subject, the reader is referred to other texts.[6] In this text, the applications are limited to small deformations.

17-5. Virtual Forces for Deflections

The virtual work principle can be simply stated in words as

$$\boxed{\text{external virtual work} = \text{internal virtual work}} \qquad (17\text{-}23)$$

For the virtual force method, virtual work is obtained by multiplying *virtual forces* by *real displacements*. An algebraic implementation of this equation enables one to calculate deflection (or rotation) of any point (or element) on a deformed body. The deformations may be due to any cause, such as a temperature change, misfit of parts, or external forces deforming a body. *The method is not limited to the solution of elastic problems.* For this reason, this method has an exceptionally broad range of applications. By confining the discussion to typical problems of engineering mechanics of solids involving stress resultants, the basic virtual work equation, corresponding to general Eq. 17-23, can be readily derived. For this purpose, consider, for example, a body such as shown in Fig. 17-5 for which the deflection of some point A in direction AB caused by deformation or distortion of the body is sought. For this, the virtual work equation can be formulated by employing the following sequence of reasoning.

First, apply an imaginary or virtual force δP at A acting in the desired direction AB to the unloaded body. This force causes internal forces throughout the body. These internal forces, designed as δF, Fig. 17-5(a), can be found in any statically determinate systems.

Next, with the virtual force remaining on the body, apply the actual or real forces, Fig. 17-5(b), or introduce the specified deformations, such as those due to a change in temperature. This causes real internal deformations u, which can be computed. Due to these deformations, the virtual force system does external and internal work.

Therefore, since the external work done by virtual force δP moving a real amount Δ in the direction of this force is equal to the total work done on the internal elements by the virtual forces δF's moving their respective real amounts u, the special form of the virtual work equation becomes

---

[6]For rigorous mathematical treatment of virtual work for three-dimensional elastic problems requiring the use of the divergence (Green's) theorem, see J. T. Oden and E. A. Ripperger, *Mechanics of Elastic Structures,* 2nd ed. (New York: McGraw-Hill, 1981). For an extensive exposition of virtual work, see G. A. O. Davies, *Virtual Work in Structural Analysis* (Chichester: Wiley, 1982); and J. Lubliner, *Plasticity Theory* (New York: Macmillan, 1990).

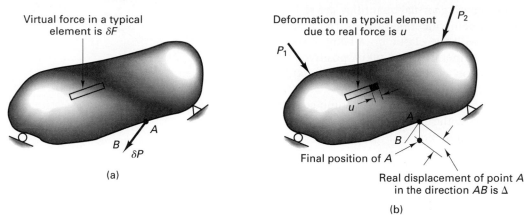

Fig. 17-5 Virtual forces and real displacements.

$$\underbrace{\delta P \cdot \overbrace{\Delta}^{\text{real}} = \sum \delta F \cdot u}_{\text{virtual}} \tag{17-24}$$

Since all virtual forces attain their full values before real deformations are imposed, virtual work is a produce of these quantities. Summation, or, in general, integration, of the right side of the equation indicates that *all internal* virtual work must be included.

Note that in Eq. 17-24, the ratios between δF's and δP remain constant regardless of the value of δP; hence these virtual quantities need not be infinitesimal. Therefore, it is particularly convenient in applications to choose the applied virtual force δP equal to unity and to restate Eq. 17-24 as

$$\underbrace{\bar{1} \cdot \overbrace{\Delta}^{\text{real}} = \sum \bar{p} \cdot u}_{\text{virtual}} \tag{17-25}$$

where

$\bar{1}$ = virtual unit force

Δ = real displacement of a point in the direction of the applied
virtual unit force

$\bar{p}$ = virtual internal forces in equilibrium with the virtual unit force

u = real internal displacements of a body

For simplicity, the symbols designating virtual quantities, are redefined and are barred as shown instead of being identified by δ's. The real deformations can be due to any cause, with the elastic ones being a special case. Tensile forces and elongations of members are taken positive. A positive result indicates that the deflection occurs in the same direction as the applied virtual force.

In determining the angular rotations of a member, a unit couple is used instead of a unit force. In practice, the procedure of using a virtual unit force or a virtual unit couple in conjunction with virtual work is referred to as the *unit-dummy-load method.*

17-6. Virtual Force Equations for Elastic Systems

Equation 17-25 can be specialized for linearly elastic systems to facilitate the solution of problems. This is done here for axially loaded and for flexural members. Application examples follow.

Trusses   A virtual unit force must be applied at a point in the direction of the deflection to be determined.

For linearly elastic bars of constant cross section A subjected to real axial forces F, according to Eq. 3-4, the real axial bar deformations $u = FL/AE$. Therefore, Eq. 17-25 becomes

$$\bar{1} \times \Delta = \sum_{i=1}^{n} \frac{\bar{p}_i F_i L_i}{A_i E_i} \qquad (17\text{-}26)$$

where $\bar{p}_i$ is the axial force in a member due to the virtual unit force and F_i is the force in the same member due to the real loads. The summation extends over all members of a truss.

Beams   If the deflection of a point on an elastic beam is wanted by the virtual work method, a virtual unit force must be applied first in the direction in which the deflection is sought. This virtual force will set up internal bending moments at various sections of the beam designated by $\bar{m}$, as is shown in Fig. 17-6(a). Next, as the real forces are applied to the beam, bending moments M rotate the "plane sections" of the beam $M\,dx/EI$ radians, Eq. 15-1. Hence, the virtual work done on an element of a beam by the virtual moments $\bar{m}$ is $\bar{m}M\,dx/EI$. Integrating this over the length of the beam gives the internal work on the elements. Hence, the special form of Eq. 17-25 for beams becomes

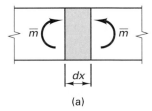

(a)

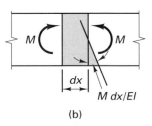

(b)

Fig. 17-6   Beam elements. (a) Virtual bending moments m. (b) Real bending moments M and the rotation of sections they cause.

$$\bar{1} \times \Delta = \int_0^L \frac{\bar{m}M \, dx}{EI} \qquad (17\text{-}27)$$

An analogous expression may be used to find the angular rotation of a particular section in a beam. For this case, instead of applying a virtual unit force, a virtual unit couple is applied to the beam at the section being investigated. This virtual couple sets up internal moments $\bar{m}$ along the beam. Then, as the real forces are applied, they cause rotations $M \, dx/EI$ of the cross sections. Hence, the same integral expression as in Eq. 17-27 applies here. The external work by the virtual unit couple is obtained by multiplying it by the real rotation θ of the beam at this couple. Hence,

$$\bar{1} \times \theta = \int_0^L \frac{\bar{m}M \, dx}{EI} \qquad (17\text{-}28)$$

In Eqs. 17-27 and 17-28, $\bar{m}$ is the bending moment due to the virtual loading, and M is the bending moment due to the real loads. Since both $\bar{m}$ and M usually vary along the length of the beam, both must be expressed by appropriate functions.

Example 17-1

Find the vertical deflection of point B in the pin-jointed steel truss shown in Fig. 17-7(a) due to the following causes: (a) the elastic deformation of the members, (b) a shortening by 0.125 in of member AB by means of a turnbuckle, and (c) a drop in temperature of 120°F occurring in member BC. The coefficient of thermal expansion of steel is 6.5×10^{-6} inch per inch per degree Fahrenheit. Neglect the possibility of lateral buckling of the compression member. Let $E = 30 \times 10^6$ psi.

SOLUTION

(a) A virtual unit force is applied in the upward vertical direction, as shown in Fig. 17-7(b), and the resulting forces $\bar{p}$ are determined and recorded on the same diagram. Then the forces in each member due to the real force are also determined and recorded, Fig. 17-7(c). The solution follows by means of Eq. 17-26. The work is carried out in the table.

Member	$\bar{p}$, lb	F, lb	L, in	A, in²	$\bar{p}FL/A$
AB	−0.833	+2500	60	0.15	−833,000
BC	+0.833	−2500	60	0.25	−500,000

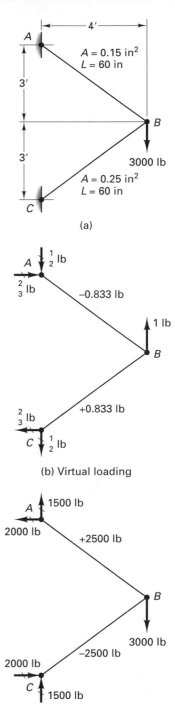

(a)

(b) Virtual loading

(c) Real loading

Fig. 17-7

From this table, $\Sigma \bar{p}FL/A = -1,333,000$. Hence,

$$\bar{1} \times \Delta = \Sigma \frac{\bar{p}FL}{AE} = \frac{-1,333,000}{30 \times 10^6} = -0.0444 \text{ lb-in}$$

and

$$\Delta = -0.0444 \text{ in}$$

The negative sign means that point B deflects down. In this case, "negative work" is done by the virtual force acting upward when it is displaced in a downward direction. Note particularly the units and the signs of all quantities. Tensile forces in members are taken positive, and vice versa.

(b) Equation 17-25 is used to find the vertical deflection of point B due to the shortening of member AB by 0.125 in. The forces set up in the bars by the virtual force acting in the direction of the deflection sought are shown in Fig. 17-7(b). Then, since u is -0.125 in (shortening) for member AB and is zero for member BC,

$$\bar{1} \times \Delta = (-0.833)(-0.125) + (+0.833)(0) = +0.1042 \text{ lb-in}$$

and

$$\Delta = +0.1042 \text{ in up}$$

(c) Again, using Eq. 17-25, and noting that due to the drop in temperature, Eq. 2-11, $\Delta_T = -6.5 \times 10^{-6} \times 120 \times 60 = -0.0468$ in in member BC,

$$\bar{1} \times \Delta = (+0.833)(-0.0468) = -0.0390 \text{ lb-in}$$

and

$$\Delta = -0.0390 \text{ in down}$$

By superposition, the net deflection of point B due to all three causes is $-0.0444 + 0.1042 - 0.0390 = +0.0208$ in up. To find this quantity, all three effects could have been considered simultaneously in the virtual work equation.

Example 17-2

Find the deflection and rotation at the middle of the cantilever beam loaded as shown in Fig. 17-8. EI for the beam is constant.

SOLUTION

The downward virtual force is applied at point A, whose deflection is sought, Fig. 17-8(b). The $\bar{m}$ diagram and the M diagram are shown in Figs. 17-8(c) and (d), respectively. For these functions, the same origin of x is taken at the

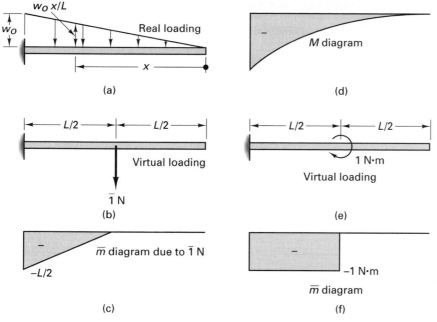

$w_O x/L$

w_O

Real loading

x

(a)

M diagram

−

(d)

L/2   L/2

Virtual loading

$\overline{1}$ N

(b)

L/2   L/2

1 N·m

Virtual loading

(e)

−

$\overline{m}$ diagram due to $\overline{1}$ N

−L/2

(c)

−

−1 N·m

$\overline{m}$ diagram

(f)

Fig. 17-8

free end of the cantilever. After these moments are determined, Eq. 17-27 is applied to find the deflection.

$$M = -\frac{x}{2}\frac{w_o x}{L}\frac{x}{3} = -\frac{w_o x^3}{6L} \qquad 0 \le x \le L$$

$$\overline{m} = 0 \qquad 0 \le x \le L/2$$

$$\overline{m} = -1(x - L/2) \qquad L/2 \le x \le L$$

$$\overline{1} \times \Delta = \int_0^L \frac{\overline{m}M\,dx}{EI} = \frac{1}{EI}\int_0^{L/2}(0)\left(-\frac{w_o x^3}{6L}\right)dx$$

$$+ \frac{1}{EI}\int_{L/2}^L\left(-x + \frac{L}{2}\right)\left(-\frac{w_o x^3}{6L}\right)dx$$

$$= \frac{49w_o L^4}{3840EI}\,N \cdot m$$

The deflection of point A is numerically equal to this quantity. The deflection due to shear has been neglected.

To find the beam rotation at the middle of the beam, a virtual unit couple is applied at A, Fig. 17-8(e). The corresponding $\overline{m}$ diagram is shown in Fig. 17-8(f). The real bending moment M is the same as in the previous part of the problem. The virtual moment $\overline{m} = 0$ for x between 0 and $L/2$, and

$\overline{m} = -1$ for the remainder of the beam. Using these moments, and applying Eq. 17-28, determines the rotation of the beam at A.

$$M = -\frac{w_o x^3}{6L} \qquad \text{and} \qquad \overline{m} = -1 \qquad L/2 \le x \le L$$

$$1 \times \theta = \int_0^L \frac{\overline{m}M\,dx}{EI} = \frac{1}{EI}\int_{L/2}^L (-1)\left(-\frac{w_o x^3}{6L}\right)dx = \frac{15w_o L^3}{384EI}\,\text{N}\cdot\text{m}$$

The rotation of the beam at A is numerically equal to this result.

Example 17-3

An aluminum beam is supported by a pin at one end and an inclined aluminum bar at a third point, as shown in Fig. 17-9(a). Find the deflection at C caused by the application of the downward force of 2 kN at that point. The cross section of the beam is 5000 mm^2 (50×10^{-4} m^2), and that of the bar is 500 mm^2 (5×10^{-4} m^2). The moment of inertia for the beam around the horizontal axis is 60×10^6 mm^4 (60×10^{-6} m^4). Neglect deflection caused by shear. Let $E = 70$ GPa.

SOLUTION

A unit virtual force of 1 kN is applied vertically downward at C. This force causes an axial force in member DB and in part AB of the beam, Fig. 17-9(b). Due to this force, bending moments are also caused in beam AC, Fig. 17-9(c). Similar computations are made and are shown in Figs. 17-9(d) and (e) for the applied real force. The deflection of point C depends on the deformations caused by the axial forces, as well as flexure; hence, the virtual work equation is

$$\overline{1} \times \Delta = \sum \frac{\overline{p}FL}{AE} + \int_0^L \frac{\overline{m}M\,dx}{EI}$$

The first term on the right side of this equation is computed in the table. Then the integral for the internal virtual work due to bending is found. For the different parts of the beam, two origins of x's are used in writing the expressions for $\overline{m}$ and M; see Figs. 17-9(c) and (e), respectively.

Member	$\overline{p}$, kN	F, kN	L, m	A, m^2	$\overline{p}FL/A$
DB	+5	+10	2.5	5×10^{-4}	+250,000
AB	−4	−8	2.0	50×10^{-4}	+12,800

From the table, $\sum \overline{p}FL/A = +262{,}800$, or

$$\sum \overline{p}FL/AE = 3.75 \times 10^{-3}\ \text{kN}\cdot\text{m}$$

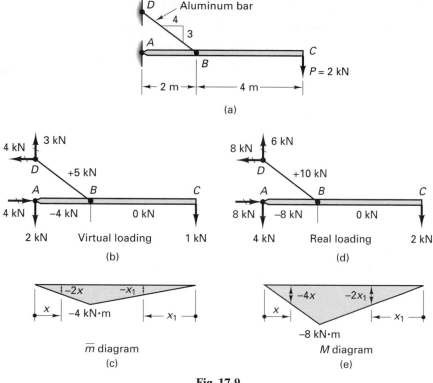

Fig. 17-9

$$\int_0^L \frac{\bar{m}M\,dx}{EI} = \int_0^2 \frac{(-2x)(-4x)\,dx}{EI} + \int_0^4 \frac{(-x_1)(-2x_1)dx_1}{EI}$$

$$= +15.25 \times 10^{-3}\,\text{kN} \cdot \text{m}$$

Therefore, $\bar{1} \times \Delta = (3.75 + 15.25)10^{-3} = 19 \times 10^{-3}\,\text{kN} \cdot \text{m}$ and point C deflects $19 \times 10^{-3}\,\text{m} = 19\,\text{mm}$ down.

Note that the work due to the two types of action was superposed. Also note that the origins for the coordinate system for moments may be chosen as convenient; however, the same origin must be used for the corresponding $\bar{m}$ and M.

Example 17-4

Find the horizontal deflection, caused by concentrated force P, of the end of the curved bar shown in Fig. 17-10(a). The flexural rigidity EI of the bar is constant. Neglect the effect of axial force and shear on the deflection.

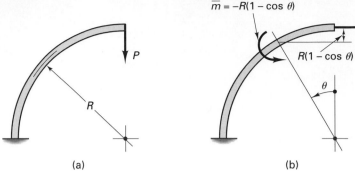

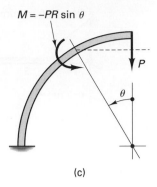

(a)   (b)   (c)

Fig. 17-10

SOLUTION

If the radius of curvature of a bar is large in comparison with the cross-sectional dimensions (Section 10-9), ordinary beam deflection formulas may be used, replacing dx by ds. In this case, $ds = R\,d\theta$.

Applying a horizontal virtual force at the end in the direction of the deflection wanted, Fig. 17-10(b), it is seen that $\overline{m} = -R(1 - \cos\theta)$. Similarly, for the real load, from Fig. 17-10(c), $M = -PR\sin\theta$. Therefore,

$$\overline{1} \times \Delta = \int_0^L \frac{\overline{m}M\,ds}{EI}$$

$$= \int_0^{\pi/2} \frac{-R(1 - \cos\theta)(-PR\sin\theta)R\,d\theta}{EI} = +\frac{PR^3}{2EI}\ \text{N} \cdot \text{m}$$

The deflection of the end to the right is numerically equal to this expression.

17-7. Virtual Forces for Indeterminate Problems

The unit-dummy-load method derived using the virtual force concept can be used to advantage for the solution of statically indeterminate problems. Here the procedure is illustrated on a problem statically indeterminate to the first degree. The basic procedure is essentially the same as that already described in Section 4-3 on the *force* method of analysis for statically indeterminate axially loaded bar systems (see Fig. 4-2). Applications of the *force* (or *flexibility*) method to problems of higher degree of statical indeterminancy are discussed in Sections 19-2 and 19-3. In general, this method is best suited for linearly elastic problems, where superposition is valid.

Example 17-5

(a) Find the forces in the bars of the pin-jointed steel structure shown in Fig. 17-11. (b) Determine the deflection of joint (nodal point) B. Let $E = 30 \times 10^6$ psi.

SOLUTION

(a) The structure can be rendered statically determinate by cutting bar DB at D. Then the forces in the members are as shown in Fig. 17-11(b). In this determinate structure, the deflection of point D must be found. This can be done by applying a vertical virtual force at D, Fig. 17-11(c), and using the virtual force method. However, since the $\bar{f}FL/AE$ term for member BD is zero, the vertical deflection of point D is the same as that of B. In Example 17-1, the latter quantity was found to be 44.4×10^{-3} in down and is so shown in Fig. 17-11(b).

The deflection of point D, shown in Fig. 17-11(b), violates a boundary condition of the problem, and a vertical force must be applied at D to restore it. If f_{DD} is the deflection of point D due to a unit (real) force at D, it defines the flexibility of this system. It is necessary to multiply f_{DD} by a factor X_D to close the gap $\Delta_{DP} = 44.4 \times 10^{-3}$ in at D caused by the force P in the determinate system. This simply means that the deflection Δ_D at D becomes zero. Stated algebraically,

$$\Delta_D = f_{DD}X_D + \Delta_{DP} = 0$$

Hence, the problem resolves into finding f_{DD}. This can be done by applying a 1-lb virtual force at D, then applying a 1-lb real force at the same point, and then using Eq. 17-26. The forces set up in the determinate structure by the virtual and the real forces are numerically the same, Fig. 17-11(c). To differentiate between the two, forces in members caused by a virtual force are designated by $\bar{p}$ and the real force by p. The solution is carried out in the following table:

Member	$\bar{p}$, lb	p, lb	L, in	A, in^2	$\bar{p}pL/A$
AB	-0.833	-0.833	60	0.15	$+278$
BC	$+0.833$	$+0.833$	60	0.25	$+167$
BD	$+1.000$	$+1.000$	40	0.10	$+400$

From the table, $\sum \bar{p}pL/A = +845$. Therefore, since

$$\bar{1} \times \Delta = \sum \frac{\bar{p}pL}{AE} = \frac{+845}{30 \times 10^6} = 28.1 \times 10^{-6} \text{ lb-in}$$

$f_{DD} = 28.1 \times 10^{-6}$ in   and $28.1 \times 10^{-6}X_D - 44.4 \times 10^{-3} = 0$

To close the gap of 44.4×10^{-3} in, the 1-lb real force at D must be increased $0.0444/0.0000281 = 1580$ times. Therefore, the actual force in

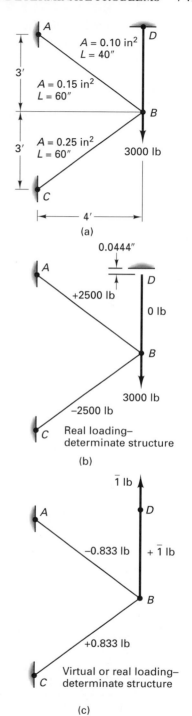

(a)

(b) Real loading–determinate structure

(c) Virtual or real loading–determinate structure

Fig. 17-11

the member DB is 1580 lb. The forces in the other two members may now be determined from statics or by superposition of the forces shown in Fig. 17-11(b) with X_D times the p forces shown in Fig. 17-11(c). By either method, the force in AB is found to be $+1180$ lb (tension), and in BC, -1180 lb (compression).

(b) Three different virtual systems are employed to determine the deflection of nodal point B caused by the applied force. The simplest of the three consists of recognizing that since the force in vertical member BD is known to be 1580 lb, the deflection at B

$$\Delta_B = \frac{FL}{AE} = \frac{1580 \times 40}{0.10 \times 30 \times 10^6} = 21 \times 10^{-3} \text{ in}$$

This solution from the point of view of a virtual force system means that the virtual force in member DB is unity and is zero in the other members.

Alternatively, the virtual force system may consist of active members AB and BC, with a zero virtual force in member BD. Then, by assuming that the virtual unit force acts upward at B, the virtual forces in members AB and BC are as shown in Fig. 17-11(c) [or Fig. 17-7(b)]. (Remember that the force in member BD is assumed to be zero.) From the solution for (a), the real forces in members AB, BC, and BD are known to be, respectively, $+1180$ lb, -1180 lb, and $+1580$ lb. The solution of Eq. 17-26 to obtain the deflection at B is carried out in the following table.

Member	$\bar{p}$, lb	F, lb	L, in	A, in^2	$\bar{p}FL/A$
AB	-0.833	$+1180$	60	0.15	$-393{,}000$
BC	$+0.833$	-1180	60	0.25	$-236{,}000$
BD	0	$+1580$	40	0.10	0

Hence,

$$\Delta_B = \frac{\sum \bar{p}FL/A}{E} = -\frac{629{,}000}{30 \times 10^6} = -21 \times 10^{-3} \text{ in}$$

The negative sign shows that the deflection is downward.

Lastly, let the virtual force system consist of all three bars. The virtual forces in the bars due to a unit downward force can be found by dividing the bar forces due to the applied forces by 3000; for example, for member AB, such a virtual force is $1180/3000 = 0.393$ lb. Again, the solution is carried out in tabular form.

Member	$\bar{p}$, lb	F, lb	L, in	A, in^2	$\bar{p}FL/A$
AB	$+0.393$	$+1180$	60	0.15	$+185{,}000$
BC	-0.393	-1180	60	0.25	$+111{,}000$
BD	$+0.527$	$+1580$	40	0.10	$+333{,}000$

Hence,

$$\Delta_B = \frac{\sum \bar{p}FL/A}{E} = \frac{629,000}{30 \times 10^6} = 21 \times 10^{-3} \text{ in}$$

The results are the same by three entirely different virtual force systems that are in static equilibrium. This is true in general. *Any* self-equilibrating virtual system can be used provided its displacements go through the prescribed real displacements.

In any given case, to make certain that the elastic analysis is applicable, maximum stresses must be determined. For the solution to be correct, these must be in the linearly elastic range for the material used.

17-8. Virtual Displacements for Equilibrium

The virtual work principle can be adapted for developing the virtual displacement method of structural analysis. The derivation of this method can begin by restating the virtual work principle in words:

$$\text{external virtual work } = \text{ internal virtual work} \qquad (17\text{-}23)$$

Virtual work for the virtual displacement method is determined by multiplying the virtual displacements by real forces. This is to be contrasted with the virtual force method, where virtual work is found by multiplying the virtual forces by real displacements. Because of this, a number of differences arise in the virtual work equations.

In the virtual displacement method, both the virtual and the real displacements must be compatible with the special requirements of a problem. This means that the member displacements must conform to the boundary conditions and the displacements of the load points. Since the boundary conditions are simplest to satisfy at pin-ended axially loaded bars, only such problems are considered here. Moreover, the discussion is limited to bar assemblies meeting at a single pinned joint where an external force is applied. Such a joint is referred to as a *nodal point*. Although the discussion is limited to the simplest class of problems, the described procedure provides an introduction to the most widely used method in the matrix analysis of structures and finite elements, where it is indispensable.

In the virtual displacement method, besides an accurate definition of the real and the virtual displacements, member forces must be defined as functions of the nodal displacements. This is achieved with the aid of constitutive relationships. Here such relationships are *strictly limited to linearly elastic behavior.*

As with Archimedes' level, the virtual work equations provide the equations of equilibrium. In this manner, the three basic requirements of equilibrium, compatibility, and constitutive relations are satisfied.

In order to construct the basic virtual work equation, by analogy to Eq. 17-25, one can formulate it by going directly to the *unit-dummy-displacement method*. Here the real external force at its full value moves through a virtual unit displacement in the direction of the force. Simultaneously, the real internal forces at their full values move through the virtual displacements caused by the unit virtual displacement. This yields the following virtual work equation:

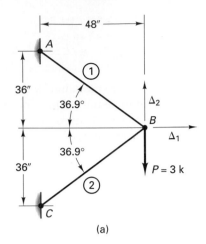

(a)

$$\overset{\text{real}}{\overline{1} \cdot P = \underset{\text{virtual}}{\sum \overline{u} \cdot F}} \qquad (17\text{-}29)$$

where

$\overline{1}$ = virtual unit displacement at a nodal point in the direction of P

P = real external (nodal) force

$\overline{u}$ = virtual internal displacements compatible with the virtual unit displacement

F = real internal forces in equilibrium with P

Deformations of flexural members as well as those of finite elements for a continuum generally require more than one nodal point for their definitions. Therefore, the examples that follow consider only axially loaded pin-ended bars.

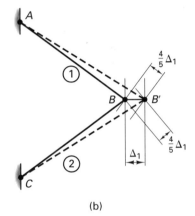

(b)

Example 17-6

Using the virtual displacement method, determine the bar forces in the pin-jointed linearly elastic steel truss of Example 17-1; see Fig. 17-12. $E = 30 \times 10^3$ ksi.

SOLUTION
In this truss, bar AB has the cross-sectional area $A_1 = 0.15$ in^2, and bar BC has an area $A_2 = 0.25$ in^2. Because of this lack of bar symmetry, during a loading process, joint B can move both horizontally and vertically, Figs. 17-12(b) and (c). Hence, this system has two degrees of freedom, or two degrees of kinematic indeterminancy (see Section 4-5). These displacement components for nodal point B are designated, respectively, as Δ_1 and Δ_2, with their positive sense shown in Fig. 17-12(a).

The compatibility requirements for the problem are complied with by permitting nodal point B to move, as shown in Figs. 17-12(b) and (c). A linear combination of these displacements is appropriate.

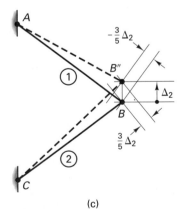

(c)

Fig. 17-12

The constitutive requirements for the problem are defined by the bar stiffnesses, Eq. 3-7, which for bars 1 and 2, respectively, are

$$k_1 = \frac{A_1 E}{L_1} = \frac{0.15 \times 30 \times 10^3}{60} = 75 \text{ k/in}$$

$$k_2 = \frac{A_2 E}{L_2} = \frac{0.25 \times 30 \times 10^3}{60} = 125 \text{ k/in}$$

On this basis, the internal bar forces F_1 and F_2 can be determined as functions of the joint displacements Δ_1 and Δ_2. The bar deformations u_1 and u_2 corresponding to these displacements are

$$u_1 = 0.8\Delta_1 - 0.6\Delta_2 \quad \text{and} \quad u_2 = 0.8\Delta_1 + 0.6\Delta_2$$

Hence,

$$F_1 = k_1 u_1 = 75(0.8\Delta_1 - 0.6\Delta_2) = 60\Delta_1 - 45\Delta_2$$

$$F_2 = k_2 u_2 = 125(0.8\Delta_1 + 0.6\Delta_2) = 100\Delta_1 + 75\Delta_2$$

As this problem is kinematically indeterminate to the second degree, the virtual displacement Eq. 17-29 must be applied twice. The equilibrium equation for forces acting in the horizontal direction follows by taking $\overline{\Delta}_1 = \overline{1}$, causing virtual bar displacements $\overline{u}_1 = \overline{u}_2 = 0.8$. Noting that no horizontal force is applied at B.

$$\overline{1} \times 0 = \overline{u}_1 F_1 + \overline{u}_2 F_2$$

$$0.8(60\Delta_1 - 45\Delta_2) + 0.8(100\Delta_1 + 75\Delta_2) = 0$$

or

$$128\Delta_1 + 24\Delta_2 = 0$$

Similarly, the equilibrium equation for forces acting in the vertical direction is obtained by setting $\overline{\Delta}_2 = \overline{1}$, resulting in virtual bar displacements $\overline{u}_1 = -0.6$ and $\overline{u}_2 = 0.6$. Again, applying Eq. 17-29

$$\overline{1} \times (-3) = \overline{u}_1 F_1 + \overline{u}_2 F_2$$

$$-0.6(60\Delta_1 - 45\Delta_2) + 0.6(100\Delta_1 + 75\Delta_2) = -3$$

or

$$24\Delta_1 + 72\Delta_2 = -3$$

Solving the two reduced equations simultaneously,

$$\Delta_1 = 8.33 \times 10^{-3}\text{in} \quad \text{and} \quad \Delta_2 = -44.4 \times 10^{-3} \text{ in}$$

Hence,

$$F_1 = 60\Delta_1 - 45\Delta_2 = 2.5 \text{ k}$$

$$F_2 = 100\Delta_1 + 75\Delta_2 = -2.5 \text{ k}$$

These results are in complete agreement with those given in Example 17-1 for bar forces as well as for the vertical deflection. The advantages of this method are more apparent in the next example.

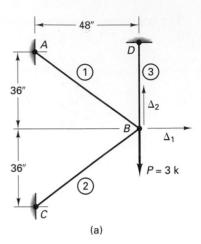

(a)

Example 17-7

Using the virtual displacement method, determine the bar forces in the statically indeterminate pin-jointed linearly elastic steel truss of Example 17-5; see Fig. 17-13. Let $E = 30 \times 10^3$ ksi.

SOLUTION

Although this problem is statically indeterminate to the first degree, as in the previous example of a statically determinate case, the system remains kinematically indeterminate to the second degree. In both cases, nodal point B has two deflection components, a horizontal and a vertical, and both systems have two degrees of freedom. Therefore, the solution becomes only slightly more complicated than that in the previous example. Hence, proceeding as before, and noting that the cross-sectional area for the third bar, DB, is 0.10 in^2,

$$k_3 = \frac{A_3 E}{L_3} = \frac{0.10 \times 30 \times 10^3}{40} = 75 \text{ k/in}$$

From the previous example, $k_1 = 75$ k/in and $k_2 = 125$ k/in.

The displacements of the system in the horizontal and vertical directions are shown in Figs. 17-13(b) and (c). It is to be noted that the length of bar DB is considered not to change because Δ_1 is very small (see Fig. 3-6). Bar deformations u_1 and u_2 due to Δ_1 and Δ_2, respectively, remain the same as in the previous example, whereas u_3 is equal to Δ_2. Summarizing these results,

$$u_1 = 0.8\Delta_1 - 0.6\Delta_2 \qquad u_2 = 0.8\Delta_1 + 0.6\Delta_2 \qquad \text{and} \qquad u_3 = \Delta_2$$

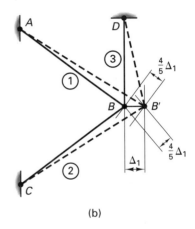

(b)

Hence, recalling the earlier results, and adding only a new term for bar DB,

$$F_1 = 60\Delta_1 - 45\Delta_2 \qquad F_2 = 100\Delta_1 + 75\Delta_2 \qquad F_3 = k_3 u_3 = 75\Delta_2$$

By noting that for the virtual displacement $\Delta_1 = \bar{1}$, $\bar{u}_1 = \bar{u}_2 = 0.8$ and $\bar{u}_3 = 0$, the equilibrium equation for the forces acting in the horizontal direction, based on Eq. 17-29, becomes

$$\bar{1} \times 0 = \bar{u}_1 F_1 + \bar{u}_2 F_2 + \bar{u}_3 F_3$$

However, since $u_3 = 0$, this equation reduces to the one given before, reading

$$128\Delta_1 + 24\Delta_2 = 0$$

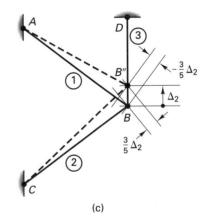

(c)

Fig. 17-13

Since for $\Delta_2 = \bar{1}$, $\bar{u}_1 = -0.6$, $\bar{u}_2 = 0.6$, and $\bar{u}_3 = 1$, the equilibrium equation for the forces acting in the vertical direction, using Eq. 17-29, becomes

$$\bar{1} \times (-3) = \bar{u}_1 F_1 + \bar{u}_2 F_2 + \bar{u}_3 F_3$$

$$0.6(60\Delta_1 - 45\Delta_2) + 0.6(100\Delta_1 + 75\Delta_2) + 75\Delta_2 = -3$$

or

$$24\Delta_1 + 147\Delta_2 = -3$$

Solving the reduced equations simultaneously,

$$\Delta_1 = 3.947 \times 10^{-3}\,\text{in} \qquad \text{and} \qquad \Delta_2 = -21.05 \times 10^{-3}\,\text{in}$$

Hence,

$$F_1 = 60\Delta_1 - 45\Delta_2 = 1.18\,\text{k}$$

$$F_2 = 100\Delta_1 + 75\Delta_2 = 1.18\,\text{k}$$

$$F_3 = 75\Delta_2 = 1.58\,\text{k}$$

These results are in complete agreement with those found earlier in Example 17-5.

The kinematic indeterminancy of this problem would remain the same regardless of the number of bars meeting at joint B.

Problems of higher degree of statical indeterminancy are discussed in Section 19-6 in connection with the *displacement* method of analysis.

17-9. Virtual Work for Discrete Systems

The virtual displacement and virtual methods both stem from the same virtual work principle. It is instructive, therefore, to show the interrelationship between the two methods using discrete structural systems (i.e., on structural systems with a finite number of applied forces, members, and nodal displacements). This is done here by employing matrix notation. The required matrix definitions and operations required for this purpose follow.

A *matrix* is an ordered array of numbers, such as encountered earlier in Eqs. 1-1a, 1-1b, and 5-12. The special matrix in Eq. 1-1a is commonly referred to as a *column vector*. The matrices in Eqs. 1-1b and 5-12 are known as *square matrices*. Here matrices are identified by braces for column vectors and by brackets for square matrices, or are shown in boldface type.

A *matrix product* of a 2×2 square matrix by a 2×1 column vector results in a 2×1 column vector:

$$\begin{bmatrix} a_{11} & a_{12} \\ a_{21} & a_{22} \end{bmatrix} \begin{Bmatrix} b_1 \\ b_2 \end{Bmatrix} = \begin{bmatrix} a_{11}b_1 + a_{12}b_2 \\ a_{21}b_1 + a_{22}b_2 \end{bmatrix}$$

A product of a 4×4 symmetric square matrix by a 4×1 column vector is displayed in Eq. 4-13.

The *transpose* of a column vector such as $\mathbf{P}$ is denoted by $\mathbf{P}^T$ and is obtained by interchanging the rows and columns of $\mathbf{P}$. Therefore, if

$$
\mathbf{P} = \begin{Bmatrix} P_1 \\ P_2 \\ \vdots \\ P_n \end{Bmatrix} \quad \text{and} \quad \Delta = \begin{Bmatrix} \Delta_1 \\ \Delta_2 \\ \vdots \\ \Delta_n \end{Bmatrix}
$$

then

$$
\mathbf{P}^T = [P_1 \, P_2 \, P_3 \cdots P_n] \quad \text{and} \quad \Delta^T = [\Delta_1 \, \Delta_2 \, \Delta_3 \cdots \Delta_n]
$$

The following products of these two functions lead to the same *scalar function:*

$$
\mathbf{P}^T \Delta = P_1 \Delta_1 + P_2 \Delta_2 + P_3 \Delta_3 + \cdots + P_n \Delta_n
$$

$$
\mathbf{\Delta}^T \mathbf{P} = \Delta_1 P_1 + \Delta_2 P_2 + \Delta_3 P_3 + \cdots + \Delta_n P_n
$$

These scalar functions are associated with the work term in the discussion that follows.

The *transpose of the product* of the two matrices needed in the subsequent development is defined[7] as the product of the transposed matrices taken in the reverse order. That is, if $\mathbf{F} = \mathbf{b}\mathbf{P}$,

$$
\mathbf{F}^T = \mathbf{P}^T \mathbf{b}^T
$$

The *duality* of the virtual force and virtual displacement methods can be readily shown with the aid of this matrix notation. By recalling, first, Eq. 17-23 in words, a parallel development employing virtual work is given. For the virtual force method, the forces are virtual and the displacements are real; whereas for the virtual displacement method, the forces are real and the displacements are virtual. Except for forming the virtual work in a different manner, the matrix operations for the two methods are identical. The following is an outline for the two methods.

---

[7]For proof, see any text on linear algebra, such as B. Noble, *Applied Linear Algebra*, 3rd ed. (Englewood Cliffs, NJ: Prentice Hall, 1988).

External Virtual Work = Internal Virtual Work   (17-23)

Virtual Force Method	**Virtual Displacement Method**

$$\delta W_e^* = \delta W_{ie}^* \qquad (17\text{-}22)$$

$$\delta W_e = \delta W_{ie} \qquad (17\text{-}19)$$

Statics:

Kinematics

$$\overline{\mathbf{F}} = \mathbf{b}\overline{\mathbf{P}} \qquad (17\text{-}30a)$$

$$\overline{\mathbf{u}} = \mathbf{a}\overline{\boldsymbol{\Delta}} \qquad (17\text{-}30b)$$

{**F**} = internal member forces

[**b**] = force transformation matrix

{**P**} = external forces at nodes

{**u**} = member distortions

[**a**] = displacement transformation matrix

{**Δ**} = nodal displacements

$$\delta W_e^* = \overline{\mathbf{P}}^T\boldsymbol{\Delta} \quad \text{and} \quad \delta W_{ie}^* = \overline{\mathbf{F}}^T\mathbf{u}$$

$$\delta W_e = \overline{\boldsymbol{\Delta}}^T\mathbf{P} \quad \text{and} \quad \delta W_{ie} = \overline{\mathbf{u}}^T\mathbf{F}$$

Equating:

Equating:

$$\overline{\mathbf{P}}^T\boldsymbol{\Delta} = \overline{\mathbf{F}}^T\mathbf{u}$$

$$\overline{\boldsymbol{\Delta}}^T\mathbf{P} = \overline{\mathbf{u}}^T\mathbf{F}$$

From Eq. 17-30a:

From Eq. 17-30b:

$$\overline{\mathbf{F}}^T = \overline{\mathbf{P}}^T\mathbf{b}^T$$

$$\overline{\mathbf{u}}^T = \overline{\boldsymbol{\Delta}}^T\mathbf{a}^T$$

Hence,

Hence,

$$\overline{\mathbf{P}}^T\boldsymbol{\Delta} = \overline{\mathbf{P}}^T\mathbf{b}^T\mathbf{u} \quad \text{or} \quad \overline{\mathbf{P}}^T(\boldsymbol{\Delta} - \mathbf{b}^T\mathbf{u}) = \mathbf{0}$$

$$\overline{\boldsymbol{\Delta}}^T\mathbf{P} = \overline{\boldsymbol{\Delta}}^T\mathbf{a}^T\mathbf{F} \quad \text{or} \quad \overline{\boldsymbol{\Delta}}^T(\mathbf{P} - \mathbf{a}^T\mathbf{F}) = \mathbf{0}$$

and

and

$$\boldsymbol{\Delta} = \mathbf{b}^T\mathbf{u} \qquad (17\text{-}31a)$$

$$\mathbf{P} = \mathbf{a}^T\mathbf{F} \qquad (17\text{-}31b)$$

Since $\overline{\mathbf{P}}^T$ and $\overline{\boldsymbol{\Delta}}^T$ are perfectly arbitrary, bearing no relation to the applied forces, the preceding expressions in parentheses must vanish, and Eqs. 17-31a and 17-31b are in *real variables* only.

In the outline, the internal forces {**F**} are determined by conventional statics and are related to the externally applied nodal forces {**P**} by the matrix [**b**]. Similarly, member distortions (deformations) {**u**} are related by kinematics to the nodal displacements {**Δ**} through a displacement transformation matrix [**a**]. Symbols designating virtual quantities are barred.

The parallel development in the two methods is striking, but whereas the virtual force method leads to *equations of compatibility,* the virtual displacement method determines the *equations of equilibrium.*

An example illustrating the application of these procedures follows. It is confined to a statically determinate problem, as additional matrix operations are required for statically indeterminate problems; such procedures are discussed in texts on finite element analysis.[8]

---

[8]See, for example, J. L. Meek, *Matrix Structural Analysis* (New York: McGraw-Hill, 1971).

Example 17-8

(a) Using the virtual force method in matrix notation, determine the displacement components for nodal point B for the pin-ended elastic truss system shown in Fig. 17-14. (b) Using the virtual displacement method in matrix notation, find nodal forces P_1 and P_2 for static equilibrium of the same system if the *elastic* elongation of bar AB is $5L/AE$ and that of bar BC is $25L/AE$. For both bars, lengths L and cross-sectional areas A are the same, and E is constant.

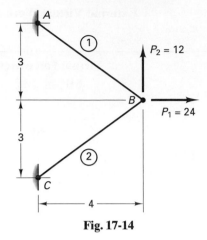

Fig. 17-14

SOLUTION

(a) From statics,

$$F_{AB} = F_1 = \frac{5}{8}P_1 - \frac{5}{6}P_2 \quad \text{and} \quad F_{BC} = F_2 = \frac{5}{8}P_1 + \frac{5}{6}P_2$$

Hence,

$$\mathbf{F} = \begin{Bmatrix} F_1 \\ F_2 \end{Bmatrix} = \mathbf{bP} = \begin{bmatrix} \dfrac{5}{8} & -\dfrac{5}{6} \\ \dfrac{5}{8} & \dfrac{5}{6} \end{bmatrix} \begin{Bmatrix} P_1 \\ P_2 \end{Bmatrix}$$

By using Eq. 3-4, the constitutive relations for the bars are

$$u_1 = \frac{F_1 L}{AE} = \left(\frac{5}{8} \times 24 - \frac{5}{6} \times 12 \right) \frac{L}{AE} = \frac{5L}{AE}$$

$$u_2 = \frac{F_2 L}{AE} = \left(\frac{5}{8} \times 24 + \frac{5}{6} \times 12 \right) \frac{L}{AE} = \frac{25L}{AE}$$

Hence,

$$\mathbf{u} = \begin{Bmatrix} u_1 \\ u_2 \end{Bmatrix} = \begin{Bmatrix} 5 \\ 25 \end{Bmatrix} \frac{L}{AE}$$

By using Eq. 17-31a, for the compatibility of the system,

$$\boldsymbol{\Delta} = \begin{Bmatrix} \Delta_1 \\ \Delta_2 \end{Bmatrix} = \mathbf{b}^T \mathbf{u} = \begin{bmatrix} \dfrac{5}{8} & \dfrac{5}{8} \\ -\dfrac{5}{6} & \dfrac{5}{6} \end{bmatrix} \begin{Bmatrix} 5 \\ 25 \end{Bmatrix} \frac{L}{AE} = \begin{Bmatrix} 18.75 \\ 16.67 \end{Bmatrix} \frac{L}{AE}$$

(b) Compatible bar deformations as functions of nodal displacements, with the aid of Figs. 17-13(b) and (c), are determined to be

$$u_1 = \frac{4}{5}\Delta_1 - \frac{3}{5}\Delta_2 \quad \text{and} \quad u_2 = \frac{4}{5}\Delta_1 + \frac{3}{5}\Delta_2$$

Hence,

$$\mathbf{u} = \begin{Bmatrix} u_1 \\ u_2 \end{Bmatrix} = \mathbf{a\Delta} = \begin{bmatrix} \dfrac{4}{5} & -\dfrac{3}{5} \\ \dfrac{4}{5} & \dfrac{3}{5} \end{bmatrix} \begin{Bmatrix} \Delta_1 \\ \Delta_2 \end{Bmatrix}$$

From constitutive relations for *linearly elastic* bars, since $u_1 = 5L/AE$ and $u_2 = 25L/AE$,

$$F_1 = \frac{AE}{L}u_1 = 5 \quad \text{and} \quad F_2 = \frac{AE}{L}u_2 = 25$$

Hence, using Eq. 17-31b, for static equilibrium, the joint forces are

$$\mathbf{P} = \begin{Bmatrix} P_1 \\ P_2 \end{Bmatrix} = \mathbf{a}^T\mathbf{F} = \begin{bmatrix} \dfrac{4}{5} & \dfrac{4}{5} \\ -\dfrac{3}{5} & \dfrac{3}{5} \end{bmatrix} \begin{Bmatrix} 5 \\ 25 \end{Bmatrix} = \begin{Bmatrix} 24 \\ 12 \end{Bmatrix}$$

This result corresponds to the joint forces given for part (a). This means that the two processes are completely reversible for *elastic* systems.

In the matrix analyses of structures and especially in finite element applications, equations similar to the previous ones contain a large number of unknowns. The use of computers is essential for the solution of such systems of equations.

PROBLEMS

Sections 17-2 and 17-3

17-1. A solid circular bar bent 90° at two points is built in at one end, as shown in the figure. Application of force P at the free end causes an axial force, direct shear, bending, and torsion in the three bar segments. (a) Using Eq. 17-11, obtain the expression for the deflection of the free end. Constants A, I, J, E, and G are given for the bar. (*Hint:* See Examples 3-9 and 14-12.) (b) If $L = 100$ mm and the diameter $d = 40$ mm, in percentage, what amount of deflection is due to each of the four causes enumerated earlier? Assume $E/G = 2.5$. (c) Repeat part (b) for $L = 500$ mm and $d = 40$ mm. Neglect the effect of local stress concentrations on deflection.

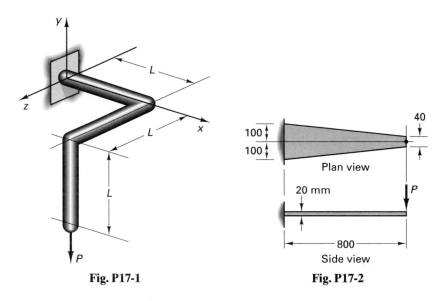

Fig. P17-1   **Fig. P17-2**

17-2. Using Eq. 17-11, determine the vertical deflection, in mm, of the free end of the cantilever shown in the figure due to the application of force $P = 500$ N. Consider only flexural deformation. $E = 200$ GPa.

17-3. Using Eq. 17-11 and taking advantage of symmetry, determine the flexural deflections at the load points due to the application of both forces P for the elastic beam shown in the figure.

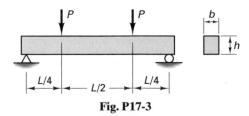

Fig. P17-3

17-4.   Using Eq. 17-11 and taking advantage of symmetry, determine the flexural deflections at the load points due to the application of both forces P for the elastic beam shown in the figure. The moment of inertia of the cross section in the middle half of the beam is I_o.

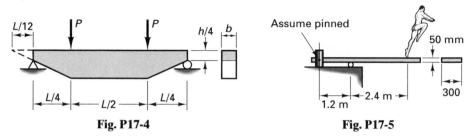

Fig. P17-4   **Fig. P17-5**

17-5.   A man weighing 80 kg jumps onto a diving board, as shown in the figure, from a height of 0.6 m. What maximum bending stress will this cause in the board? The diving board is 50 × 300 mm cross section, and its $E = 12$ GPa. Use Eq. 17-11 to determine the deflection characteristics of the board.

Sections 17-5 and 17-6

All problems for these two sections should be solved using the virtual force method. For planar problems, the following notation applies: Δ_V and Δ_H are, respectively, the vertical and the horizontal deflections, and θ is the rotation of an element at a specified point. In each case, clearly indicate the *direction* and *sense* of the computed quantity.

Trusses.   *Consider axial deformations only.*

17-6.   In Example 17-1, determine Δ_H for point B due to the enumerated three causes.

17-7.   For the planar mast and boom arrangement shown in the figure, (a) determine Δ_V of load W caused by lengthening rod AB a distance of 0.5 in. (b) By how much must rod BC be shortened to bring weight W to its original position?

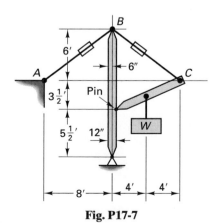

Fig. P17-7

17-8. A pin-joined system of three bars, each having the same cross section A, is loaded as shown in the figure. (a) Determine Δ_V and Δ_H of joint B due to applied force P. (b) If by means of a turnbuckle the length of member AC is shortened by 12 mm, what Δ_V and Δ_H take place at point B?

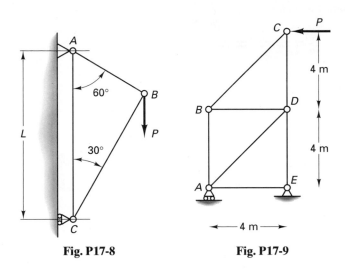

Fig. P17-8   **Fig. P17-9**

17-9. For the planar truss shown in the figure, determine Δ_V and Δ_H of joint C due to applied force $P = 10$ kN. For simplicity, assume $AE = 1$ for all members.

17-10. For the truss in Problem 17-9, determine the relative deflection between joints B and E caused by applied force $P = 10$ kN. (*Hint:* Place equal and opposite unit forces, one at joint B and the other at joint E, along a line joining them.)

17-11. For the truss shown in the figure, determine Δ_V of joint B due to applied vertical force $P = 9$ k at B. For simplicity, assume L/AE is unity for all members.

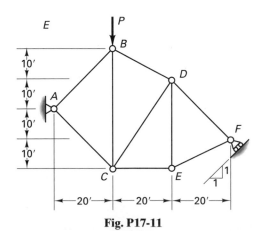

Fig. P17-11

Beams. *Consider flexural deformations only.*

17-12.   A simply supported beam of length L and constant EI supports a downward uniformly distributed load w_o. Find the maximum Δ_V due to w_o.

17-13.   For the beam in Problem 17-3, find the maximum Δ_V due to the two applied forces.

17-14.   For the beam in Problem 17-3, find Δ_V and/or θ, as assigned, at the left force P due to both applied forces.

17-15.   A simply supported beam of length L and constant EI supports a downward, uniformly distributed load w_o. Determine Δ_V and/or θ, as assigned, due to w_o at a distance $L/3$ from the left support.

17-16 and 17-17.   Determine Δ_V and/or θ, as assigned, at the center of the span due to the applied loads shown in the figures. EI is constant.

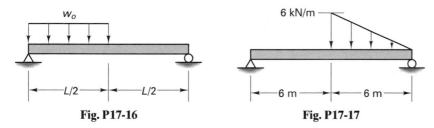

Fig. P17-16   **Fig. P17-17**

17-18.   Find Δ_V and/or θ, as assigned, at the point of application of force P for the beam of variable cross section shown in the figure.

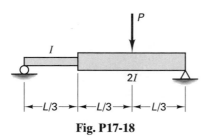

Fig. P17-18

17-19.   For the cantilever shown in the figure, determine (a) Δ_V at the applied force, and (b) Δ_V at the tip. EI is constant.

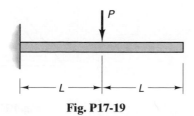

Fig. P17-19

17-20. Find the deflection at the point of application of force P. EI is constant.

17-21. For the overhanging beam shown in the figure, find Δ_V and/or θ, as assigned, at the point of application of couple M_o. EI is constant.

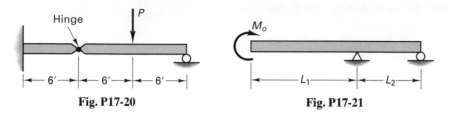

| Fig. P17-20 | Fig. P17-21 |

Rigid Frames. *Consider flexural deformations only.*

17-22. A planar bent bar of constant EI has the dimensions shown in the figure. Determine Δ_V, Δ_H, or θ, as assigned, at the tip due to the application of force P. Comment on the virtual force method in comparison to the geometric approach based on the differential equations and superposition discussed in Chapter 14.

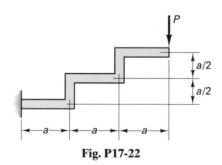

Fig. P17-22

17-23 through 17-29. For the planar frames shown in the figures, determine Δ_V, Δ_H, or θ for point A, as assigned, due to the applied loading. For all cases, assume EI constant. [*Hint:* For ease of solution, for each frame segment, locate the origin of x to obtain the simplest expressions for $m(x)$ and $M(x)$.]

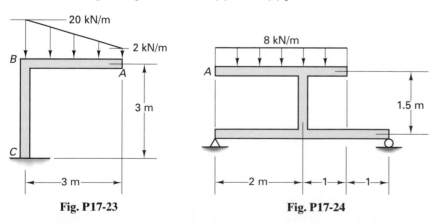

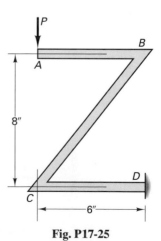

| Fig. P17-23 | Fig. P17-24 | Fig. P17-25 |

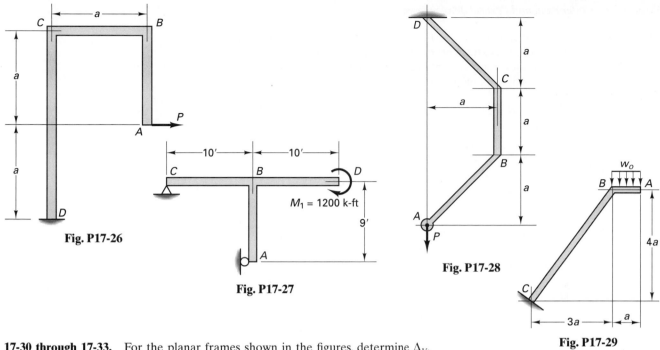

Fig. P17-26

Fig. P17-27

Fig. P17-28

Fig. P17-29

17-30 through 17-33.   For the planar frames shown in the figures, determine Δ_V, Δ_H, or θ for points A and B, as assigned, due to the applied loading. For all cases, EI is constant.

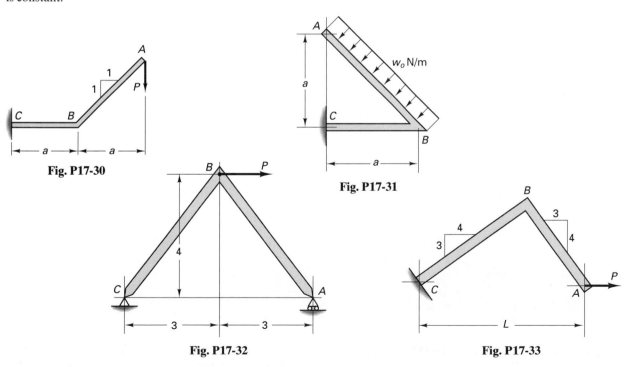

Fig. P17-30

Fig. P17-31

Fig. P17-32

Fig. P17-33

Frames. *Consider axial and flexural deformations.*

17-34. Two steel wires BC and CD ($A = 0.10$ in^2 each) are arranged as shown in the figure. At D the wire CD is attached to a rigid support; at B the wire CB is attached to a vertical cantilever AB ($A = 2$ in^2, $I = 6$ in^4). Determine the vertical deflection at C caused by applying the force $P = 1600$ lb. Neglect the contribution of shear deformation.

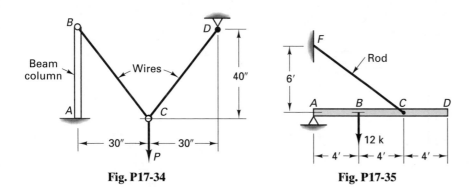

Fig. P17-34   **Fig. P17-35**

17-35. For the aluminum-alloy, planar structural system shown in the figure, determine the vertical deflection of D due to the applied force of 12 k. For the rod, $A = 0.5$ in^2; for the beam, $A = 4$ in^2 and $I = 15$ in^4. Let $E = 10 \times 10^3$ ksi.

17-36. In the preceding problem, it was determined that due to the applied force of 12 k, end D moves 1.57 in up. If, without removing this force, it is necessary to return point D to its initial position to make a connection, what is the required change in the length of rod CF? This change in length can be accomplished by means of a turnbuckle.

17-37. An inclined steel bar 2 m long, having a cross section of 4000 mm^2 and an I of 8.53×10^6 mm^4, is supported as shown in the figure. The inclined steel hanger DB has a cross section of 600 mm^2. Determine the downward deflection of point C due to the application of the vertical force of $2\sqrt{2}$ kN. Let $E = 200$ GPa.

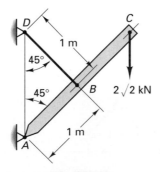

Fig. P17-37

17-38. A planar system consists of an inclined cantilever and rods BC and CD, as shown in the figure. Determine Δ_V and/or Δ_H, as assigned, of joint C due to the application of force $P = 300$ N. The cross-sectional area of each rod is 10 mm^2 and that of the cantilever 400 mm^2. For the cantilever, $I = 10^4$ mm^4. For each member, $E = 200$ GPa.

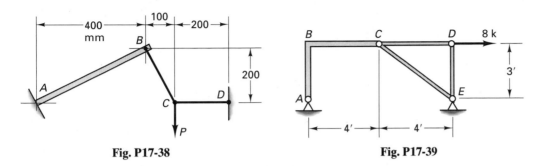

Fig. P17-38   Fig. P17-39

17-39. A planar structure consists of a moment-resisting frame ABC and a truss CDE with pinned joints. Determine Δ_V and/or Δ_H at C, as assigned, due to the horizontal force 8 k at D. For all members, $EI = 800$ k-ft^2 and $EA = 500$ k. Work the problem using the units of k and ft.

17-40. For the data given in Problem 17-39, determine the rotation of member CD due to the applied force at D. (*Hint:* Apply equal and opposite forces at C and D, generating a unit couple.)

Curved Members. *Neglect deformations due to direct shear.*

17-41. A U-shaped member of constant EI has the dimensions shown in the figure. Determine the deflection of the applied forces away from each other due to flexure.

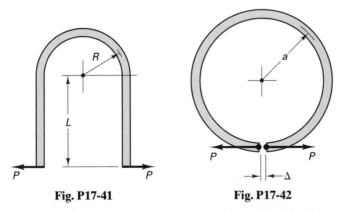

Fig. P17-41   Fig. P17-42

17-42. In order to install a split ring used as a retainer on a machine shaft, it is necessary to open a gap of Δ by applying forces P, as shown in the figure. If EI of the cross section of the ring is constant, determine the required magnitude of forces P. Consider only flexural effects.

Deformations in Three dimensions. *Neglect deformations due to direct shear.*

17-43.   A bar having a circular cross section is bent into a semicircle and is built in at one end, as shown in the figure. Determine the deflection of the free end caused by the application of force P acting normal to the plane of the semicircle. Neglect the contribution of shear deformation.

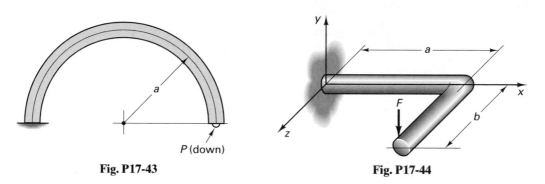

Fig. P17-43

Fig. P17-44

17-44.   A solid circular bar is bent into the shape shown in the figure and is built in at one end. Determine the three translations, Δ_x, Δ_y, and Δ_z, and the three rotations, θ_{xy}, θ_{yz}, and θ_{zx}, of the free end due to applied force P. Constants A, I, J, E, and G for the bar are given.

Section 17-7

17-45.   A system of steel rods, each having a cross-sectional area of 130 mm², is arranged as shown in the figure. At 10°C, joint D is 3 mm away from its support. (a) At what temperature can the connection be made without stressing any of the members? Let $E = 200$ GPa and $\alpha = 12 \times 10^{-6}/°C$. (b) What stresses will develop in the members if, after making the connections at D, the temperature drops to $-10°C$?

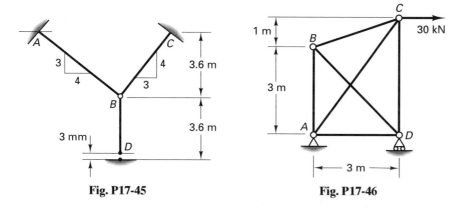

Fig. P17-45

Fig. P17-46

17-46.   Find the force in bar AC for the planar truss shown in the figure due to the 30-kN horizontal force at C. For member AC, let the relative $L/AE = 0.50$, and for all other members, unity.

17-47. (a) For the planar truss shown in the figure, determine the axial forces in all members due to the 18-kN vertical force at B. (b) By using at least two different virtual systems, find the vertical deflection at B caused by the applied force at B. Let the relative values of L/A be as follows: 1 for AB, 2 for DB, and 3 for CB. Consider member BC to be redundant.

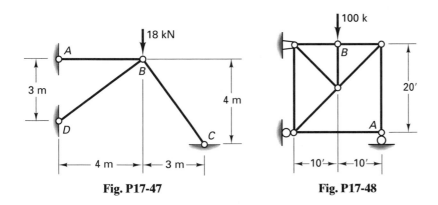

Fig. P17-47 Fig. P17-48

17-48. For the planar truss shown in the figure, determine the reaction at A, treating it as redundant, due to the applied vertical force at B. For all members, L/A is unity.

17-49. For the beam shown in the figure, (a) determine the reaction at A, treating it as redundant. (b) Determine the moment at B, treating it as redundant. (*Hint:* Use the solution given to Problem 14-51.)

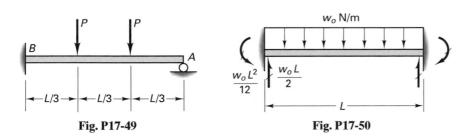

Fig. P17-49 Fig. P17-50

17-50. A uniformly loaded beam fixed at both ends has the reactions shown in the figure. By using a simply supported beam with a unit load in the middle as a virtual system, determine the maximum deflection for the real beam.

17-51. A small pipe expansion joint in a plane can be idealized as shown in the figure. Hinge support points A and B are immovable. Derive an expression for the horizontal abutment reactions R caused by the change in temperature ΔT in the pipe. The coefficient of thermal expansion for the pipe is α and its flexural rigidity is EI. Consider flexural deformations only.

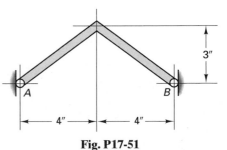

Fig. P17-51

17-52. A circular ring of a linearly elastic material is loaded by two equal and opposite forces P, as shown in the figure. For this ring, both A and I are constant. (a) Determine the largest bending moment caused by the applied forces, and plot the entire moment diagram. (b) Find the decrease in diameter AB caused by the applied forces. Consider only flexural deformations. (*Hint:* Take advantage of symmetry and consider the moment at A as redundant.)

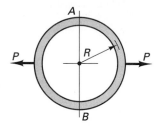

Fig. P17-52

Section 17-8

17-53. Using the virtual displacement method, (a) determine the forces in members BD and BC in Problem 17-47 assuming that member BA is removed from the system, and (b) find the forces in all three members in the complete framing.

17-54. For the elastic truss shown in the figure and using the virtual displacement method, (a) determine the forces in members AC, AD, and AE assuming that AB is inactive due to the applied force at A, and (b) find the forces in all four members in the complete framing. The relative values L/A are as follows: 0.40 for AB and AD, 0.20 for AC, and 0.80 for AE.

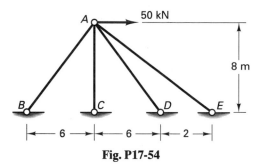

Fig. P17-54

18

Classical Energy Methods

18-1. Introduction

This chapter discusses the classical energy methods for solving problems similar to those solved using virtual work methods, which were discussed, in the preceding chapter. These methods are based on considering the internal strain energy or the complementary strain energy and the corresponding external work. The derived equations are specialized for *linear elastic systems* and are known as Castigliano's theorems. Illustrative examples are provided for both statically determinate and indeterminate cases. In many cases the numerical solutions are identical to those of the virtual work methods. The latter approach, because of its wide use in finite element formulations, is now generally favored.

A brief discussion of elastic energy concepts for determining column buckling loads concludes the chapter.

18-2. General Remarks

Elastic strain energy equations for applications in engineering mechanics of solids were summarized in Section 17-2. The direct use of these equations in determining deflections in conjunction with the law of conservation of energy and in equating the total elastic energy of the system to the total work done by the externally applied forces is very limited. This was pointed out in the Section 17-3. An effective approach to enlarging the scope of possible applications was discussed in Part B of the preceding chapter. Here an alternative classical approach based on elastic strain energy and complementary strain energy is considered. This requires the derivation of appropriate theorems.

18-3. Strain Energy and Complementary Strain Energy Theorems

In Section 2-5, it was indicated that some materials during loading and unloading respond in a nonlinear manner along the same stress-strain curve, Fig 2-13(b). Such materials are elastic, although they do not obey Hooke's law. It is advantageous to consider such *nonlinear elastic* materials in deriving the two theorems based on strain energy concepts. In this manner, the distinction between elastic strain energy and complementary strain energy is clearly evident. The derivation of the two basic theorems for nonlinear and linear elastic systems is essentially the same. These theorems are specialized in the next section for the solution of the linearly elastic problems considered in this text.

As a rudimentary example for deriving the theorems, consider the axially loaded bar show in Fig. 18-1(a). The nonlinear elastic stress-strain diagram for the material of this bar is shown in Fig. 18-1(b). By multiplying the normal stress σ in the bar by the cross sectional area A of the bar, one obtains axial force P. Similarly, the product of the axial strain ε by bar length L gives bar elongation Δ. The P-Δ diagram in Fig. 18-1(c), except for scale, corresponds in detail to the σ-ε diagram. Since in engineering mechanics of solids it is customary to work with *stress resultants*, only the P-Δ diagram is considered in the following discussion.

According to the diagram in Fig. 18-1(c), when force P_1 is increased by dP_1, the bar elongates $d\Delta_1$. Therefore, neglecting infinitesimals of higher order, the increment the external work $dW_e = P_1\, d\Delta_1$. According to Eq. 17-11, this increment in the external work must equal the increase in the strain energy of the system, since $dW_e = dU$. The narrow vertical strip in Fig. 18-1(c) corresponds to $P_1\, d\Delta_1$, and the area under the curve is the total strain energy U, which is equal to W_e. State mathematically,

$$W_e = U = \int_0^{\Delta} P_1\, d\Delta_1 \qquad (18\text{-}1)$$

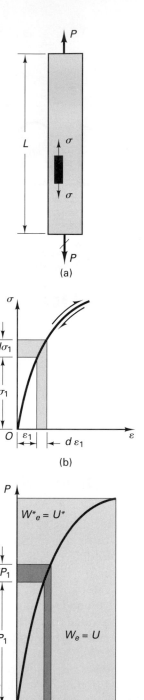

Fig. 18-1   Work and complementary work, and strain energy and complementary strain energy.

A derivative of this relation with respect to the upper limit gives

$$\frac{dU}{d\Delta} = P \tag{18-2}$$

A generalization of this procedure, which follows, establishes the first basic theorem.

An analogous expression can be formulated by increasing Δ_1, by $d\Delta_1$, causing a force increment dP_1, Fig. 18-1(c). Then, by *defining* an increment in the *complementary* external work $dW_e^* = \Delta_1\, dP_1$, it can be noted that this quantity is represented by the horizontal dark strip in the figure. By analogy to U, the integral of this infinitesimal area above the curve *defines* the *complementary strain energy* U^*, and it follows that $U^* = W_e^*$. On this basis, one can write

$$U^* = W_e^* = \int_0^P \Delta_1\, dP_1 \tag{18-3}$$

A derivative of this relation with respect to the upper limit gives

$$\frac{dU^*}{dP} = \Delta \tag{18-4}$$

This is the prototype of the second basic theorem.[1]

In order to generalize these results for problems where several forces (and/or moments) are applied simultaneously, consider the externally statically determinate body shown in Fig. 18-2. The stress resultants in such a member, or group of members, in any given problem must be related to displacement by the *same nonlinear (or linear) function*. On this basis, a general theorem corresponding to Eq. 18-4 is derived.

The complementary strain energy U^* for a statically determinate body, such as shown in Fig. 18-3(a), is defined to be a function of the externally applied forces, $P_1, P_2, \ldots, P_k, \ldots, P_n; M_1, M_2, \ldots, M_p$; that is,

$$U^* = U^*(P_1, P_2, \ldots, P_k, \ldots, P_n; M_1, M_2, \ldots, M_j, \ldots, M_p) \tag{18-5}$$

An infinitesimal increase in this function δU^* is given by the total differential as

$$\delta U^* = \frac{\partial U^*}{\partial P_1} \delta P_1 + \frac{\partial U^*}{\partial P_2} \delta P_2 + \cdots + \frac{\partial U^*}{\partial P_k} \delta P_k + \cdots + \frac{\partial U^*}{\partial M_j} \delta M_j + \cdots \tag{18-6}$$

In this expression, δP's and δM's are used instead of ordinary differentials to emphasize the *linear independence* of these quantities. From this point

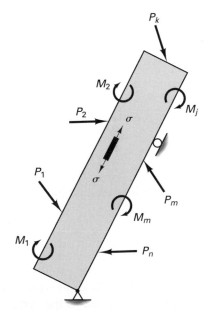

Fig. 18-2 Statically determinate member.

[1]The concept of complementary energy and derivation of this equation is generally attributed to F. Engesser's 1889 paper. See S. P. Timoshenko, *History of Strength of Materials* (New York: McGraw-Hill, 1953), 292.

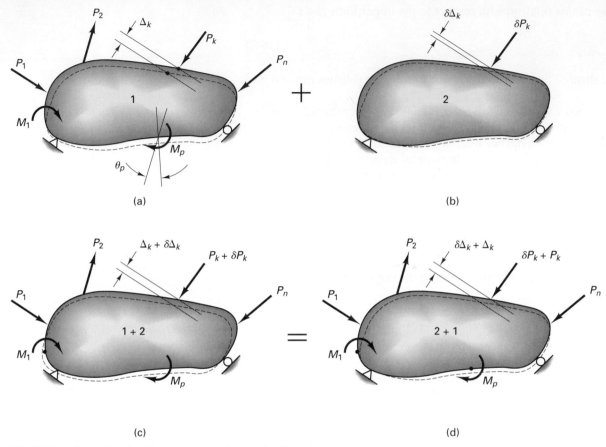

Fig. 18-3   Alternative loading sequences for an elastic system.

of view, if on force P_k were increase by δP_k, the complementary strain energy increment would be

$$\delta U^* = \frac{\partial U^*}{\partial P_k} \delta P_k \qquad (18\text{-}7)$$

The addition of the incremental force δP_k is illustrated in Fig. 18-3(c). If the order of load application were reversed, Fig. 18-3(d), infinitesimal force δP_k would be applied to the system first, Fig. 18-3(b). Then, being already applied to the system, it would do work by moving through a deflection Δ_k caused by the application of the loads shown in Fig 18-3(a). This work may be likened to the horizontal strip in Fig. 18-1(c), and, by definition, is an increment in the *complementary work* δW_e^*. Hence,

$$\delta W_e^* = \Delta_k \, \delta P_k \qquad (18\text{-}8)$$

However, since $W_e^* = U_e^*$, setting Eqs. 18-7 and 18-8 equal, and canceling δP_k,

$$\Delta_k = \frac{\partial U^*}{\partial P_k} \tag{18-9}$$

which is the generalization of Eq. 18-4 and gives deflection Δ_k in the direction of force P_k.

By retaining a derivative with respect to M_j in Eq. 18-6 and proceeding as before,

$$\theta_j = \frac{\partial U^*}{\partial M_j} \tag{18-10}$$

where θ_j is the rotation in the direction of M_j.

In an analogous manner to the previous derivation, strain energy U can be defined as a function of displacement Δ_k and/or rotation θ_j, as well as known members' constitutive relations, (see Eq. 17-7). On this basis,

$$U = U(\Delta_1, \Delta_2, \ldots, \Delta_k, \ldots, \Delta_n; \theta_1, \theta_2, \ldots, \theta_j, \ldots, \theta_m) \tag{18-11}$$

The total differential for this case is

$$\delta U = \frac{\partial U}{\partial \Delta_1} \delta\Delta_1 + \frac{\partial U}{\partial \Delta_2} \delta\Delta_2 + \cdots + \frac{\partial U}{\partial \Delta_k} \delta\Delta_k + \cdots + \frac{\partial U}{\delta\theta_j} \delta\theta_j + \cdots \tag{18-12}$$

If only one displacement were allowed to occur with the other remaining fixed, the last relation reduces to

$$\delta U = \frac{\partial U}{\partial \Delta_k} \delta\Delta_k \tag{18-13}$$

For this case, external work $\delta W_e = P_k \, \delta\Delta_k$ and corresponds to the vertical narrow strip in Fig. 18-1(c). Therefore, since $\delta W_e = \delta U$, after substitution of the previous quantities into this relation and simplifications,

$$P_k = \frac{\partial U}{\partial \Delta_\kappa} \tag{18-14}$$

This relation is a generalization if Eq. 18-2 and gives the external force acting at point k if U is expressed as a continuous function of displacements and rotations. A similar expression can be written for an external moment acting at a point by taking a derivative of U with respect to a rotation angle such as θ_j.

In the next section, the general expressions are specialized for linearly elastic materials.

18-4. Castigliano's Theorems

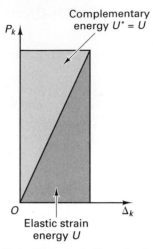

Fig. 18-4   Energies in linearly elastic materials.

Castigliano's theorems[2] apply to *linearly elastic systems for small deformations*. The mathematical statements of these theorems are the same as those derived in the previous section for nonlinear elastic materials. However, as shown in Fig. 18-4, for linearly elastic material, the elastic strain energy U is equal to the complementary strain energy U^*; that is,

$$U = U^* \qquad (18\text{-}15)$$

The external work W_e is also equal to the complementary external work W_e^*. Therefore, using Eqs. 18-9 and 18-10, because of Eq. 18-15, one can express the *second* Castigliano's theorem for linearly elastic material as

$$\Delta_k = \frac{\partial U^*}{\partial P_k} = \frac{\partial U}{\partial P_k} \qquad (18\text{-}16)$$

$$\theta_j = \frac{\partial U^*}{\partial M_j} = \frac{\partial U}{\partial M_j} \qquad (18\text{-}17)$$

In both equations, if U is expressed as a function of externally applied forces, Δ_k (or θ_j) is the deflection (or rotation) in the direction of the force (or moment) P_k (or M_j).

The expression for the *first* Castigliano's theorem remains the same as before for nonlinear elastic materials, and Eq. 18-14 is repeated here for reference:

$$P_k = \frac{\partial U}{\partial \Delta_k} \qquad (18\text{-}18)$$

where, if U is expressed as a function of displacements, P_k is the force (or moment) in the direction of the deflection (or rotation) Δ_k (or θ_k).

It should be further noted from Eqs. 17-5–17-9 that the strain energy U for linearly elastic materials is of quadratic form. Therefore, in applying Castigliano's theorems, it is advantageous to form derivatives of U before carrying out a complete solution of the problem.

It is also important to note that if a deflection (rotation) is required where no force (moment) is acting, a *fictitious* force (moment) must be applied at the point question. Then, after applying Eq. 18-16 or 18-17, the fictitious force is set equal to zero in order to obtain the desired results.

---

[2]These theorems were first derived by Italian engineer C. A. Castigliano in 1879. Extension of the theorems to the nonlinear elastic cases developed in the preceding section, as noted earlier, is generally attributed to F. Engesser of Karlsruhe. Further developments of this approach are due to H. M. Westergaard and J. H. Argyris. See J. H. Argyris, "Energy theorems and structural analysis," *Aircraft Engineering,* **26** (1954) and **27** (1955). These articles, combining joint papers with S. Kelsey, were republished in book form by Butterworth & Co. in 1960.

Several examples follow illustrating the application of Castigliano's second theorem to statically determinate linearly elastic problems. An application of Castigliano's first theorem for a statically indeterminate case is given in Example 18-8, where the use of the theorem is more appropriate.

Example 18-12

By applying Castigliano's second theorem, verify the results of Examples 3-9, 6-11, and 14-12.

SOLUTION

In all these examples, the expressions for the internal strain energy U have been formulated. Therefore, a direct application of Eq. 18-16 or 18-17 is all that is necessary to obtain the required results. In all cases, the material obeys Hooke's law.

Deflection of an axially loaded bar (P = constant):

$$U = \frac{P^2L}{2AE} \quad \text{hence,} \quad \Delta = \frac{\partial U}{\partial P} = \frac{PL}{AE}$$

Angular rotation of a circular shaft (T = Constant):

$$U = \frac{T^2L}{2I_pG} \quad \text{hence,} \quad \varphi \equiv \theta = \frac{\partial U}{\partial T} = \frac{TL}{I_pG}$$

Deflection of a rectangular cantilever due to end load P:

$$U = \frac{P^2L^3}{6EI} + \frac{3P^2L}{5AG} \quad \text{hence,} \quad \Delta = \frac{\partial U}{\partial P} = \frac{PL^3}{3EI} + \frac{6PL}{5AG}$$

Example 18-2

The bracket of Example 1-3 is shown schematically in Fig. 18-5. Verify the deflection of point B caused by applied force $P = 3$ kips using Castigliano's second theorem with the result found in Example 3-4. Assume that each bar is of constant cross-sectional area, with $A_{AB} = A_1 = 0.125$ in^2 and $A_{BC} = A_2 = 0.219$ in^2. As before, let $E = 10.6 \times 10^3$ ksi.

SOLUTION

From Eq. 17-7, the elastic strain energy is

$$U = U^* = \sum_{k=1}^{2} \frac{P_k^2 L_k}{2A_k E_k} = \frac{P_1^2 L_1}{2A_1 E} + \frac{P_2^2 L_2}{2A_2 E} \qquad (18\text{-}19a)$$

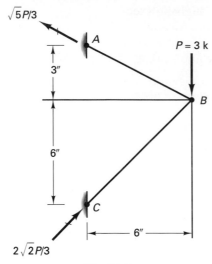

$\sqrt{5}P/3$

A

$P = 3\,\text{k}$

3"

B

6"

C

6"

$2\sqrt{2}P/3$

Fig. 18-5

By differentiating with respect to P, an expression for the vertical deflection Δ at B is determined.

$$\Delta = \frac{\partial U^*}{\partial P} = \frac{P_1 L_1}{A_1 E}\frac{\partial P_1}{\partial P} + \frac{P_2 L_1}{A_2 E}\frac{\partial P_2}{\partial P} \qquad (18\text{-}19b)$$

By statics, the forces in bars as *functions* of applied force P are

$$P_{AB} = P_1 = \frac{\sqrt{5}}{3}P \qquad \text{and} \qquad P_{BC} = P_2 = -\frac{2\sqrt{2}}{3}P$$

Here $A_1 = 0.125$ in^2, $A_2 = 0.219$ in^2, $L_1 = 3\sqrt{5}$ in, and $L_2 = 6\sqrt{2}$.

Substituting the preceding quantities into Eq 18-18b and carrying out the necessary operations, the deflection Δ for $P = 3$ kips is found.

$$\Delta = \frac{(\sqrt{5}P/3) \times (3\sqrt{5})}{0.125 \times 10.6 \times 10^3}\left(\frac{\sqrt{5}}{3}\right) + \frac{(-2\sqrt{2}P/3) \times (6\sqrt{2})}{0.219 \times 10.6 \times 10^3}\left(-\frac{2\sqrt{2}}{3}\right)$$

$$= 0.002813P + 0.003249P = 0.006062P = 18.2 \times 10^{-3}\,\text{in}$$

This is more easily obtained result, except for a small discrepancy because of roundoff errors, is in agreement with that found by an entirely different method in Example 3-4.[3]

---

[3] A solution of this problem by the virtual force method requires the use of Eq. 17-26. For a downward virtual unit force applied at B, $\bar{p}_1 = \sqrt{5}/3$ and $\bar{p}_2 = -2\sqrt{2}/3$, resulting in an identical expression for Δ.

Example 18-3

A linearly elastic prismatic beam is loaded as shown in Fig. 18-6. Using Castigliano's second theorem, find the deflection due to bending caused by applied force P at the center.

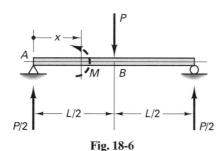

Fig. 18-6

SOLUTION

The expression for the internal strain energy in bending is given by Eq 17-8. Since, according to Castigliano's theorem, the required deflection is a derivative of this function, it is advantageous to differentiate the expression for U before integrating. In problems where M is a complex function, this scheme is particularly useful. For this purpose, the following relation becomes applicable:

$$\Delta = \frac{\partial U}{\partial P} = \int_0^L \frac{M}{EI} \frac{\partial M}{\partial P} \, dx \qquad (18\text{-}20)$$

Proceeding on this basis, one has, from A to B:

$$M = +\frac{P}{2}x \qquad and \qquad \frac{\partial M}{\partial P} = \frac{x}{2}$$

On substituting these relations[4] into Eq. 18-20 and observing the symmetry of the problem,

$$\Delta = 2\int_0^{L/2} \frac{Px^2}{4EI} \, dx = +\frac{PL^3}{48EI}$$

The positive sign indicates that the deflection takes place in the direction of applied force P.

---

[4]Note again that for a downward virtual unit force at the middle of the span, $\overline{m} = x/2$, corresponding to $\partial M / \partial P$.

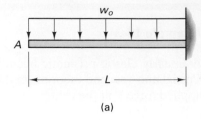

(a)

Example 18-4

Using Castigliano's second theorem, determine the deflection and the angular rotation of the end of a uniformly loaded cantilever, Fig. 18-7(a). EI is a constant.

SOLUTION

No forces are applied at the end of the cantilever where the displacements are to be found. Therefore, in order to able to apply Castigliano's theorem, a fictitious force[5] must be added corresponding to the displacement sought. Thus, as shown in Fig. 18-7(b), in addition to the specified loading force R_A has been introduced. This permits determining $\partial U/\partial R_A$, which with $R_A = 0$ gives the vertical deflection of point A. Applying Eq. 18-20 in this manner, one has

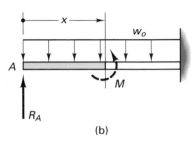

(b)

$$M = -\frac{w_o x^2}{2} + R_A x \qquad \text{and} \qquad \frac{\partial M}{\partial R_A} = +x$$

$$\Delta_A = \frac{\partial U}{\partial R_A} = \frac{1}{EI}\int_0^L \left(-\frac{w_o x^2}{2} + R_A x\right)^{\!\!\nearrow 0}(+x)\, dx = -\frac{w_o L^4}{8EI}$$

where the negative sign shows that the deflection is in the opposite direction to that assumed for the force R_A. If R_A in the integration were not set equal to zero, the end deflection due to w_o and R_A would be found.

The angular rotation of the beam at A can be found in an analogous manner. A fictitious moment M_A is applied at the end, Fig 18-7(c), and the calculations are made in the same manner as before:

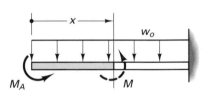

(c)

Fig. 18-7

$$M = -\frac{w_o x^2}{2} - M_A \qquad \text{and} \qquad \frac{\partial M}{\partial M_A} = -1$$

$$\Delta_A = \frac{\partial U}{\partial M_A} = \frac{1}{EI}\int_0^L \left(-\frac{w_o x^2}{2} - M_A\right)^{\!\!\nearrow 0}(-1)\, dx = +\frac{w_o L^3}{6EI}$$

where the sign indicates that the sense of the rotation of the end coincides with the assumed sense of the fictitious moment M_A.

---

[5]Application of a fictitious force or a fictitious couple at A precisely corresponds, respectively, to the application of a virtual unit force or a virtual unit coupe at A in the virtual force method.

Example 18-5

Using Castigliano's second theorem, determine the horizontal deflection for the elastic frame shown in Fig. 18-8(a). Consider only the deflection caused by bending. The flexural rigidity EI of both members is equal and constant.

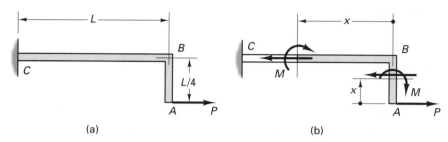

(a)   (b)

Fig. 18-8

SOLUTION

The strain energy function is scalar. Therefore, the separate strain energies for the different elements of an elastic system can be added algebraically. After the total strain energy is determined, its partial derivative with respect to a force gives the displacement of that force. For the problems at hand, Eq. 18-20 is appropriate.

From A to B:

$$M = +Px \quad \text{and} \quad \partial M/\partial P = +x$$

From B to C[6]:

$$M = +\frac{PL}{4} \quad \text{and} \quad \frac{\partial M}{\partial P} = +\frac{L}{4}$$

$$\Delta_A = \frac{\partial U}{\partial P} = \frac{1}{EI}\int_0^{L/4}(+Px)(+x)dx$$

$$+ \frac{1}{EI}\int_0^{L}\left(+\frac{PL}{4}\right)\left(+\frac{L}{4}\right)dx = +\frac{13PL^3}{192EI}$$

Note the free choice in location of the x-coordinate axes and the sign convention for bending moments. If the elastic strain energy included the energy due to the axial force in member BC and the shear energy in member AB, the deflection caused by these effects would also be found. However, deflection Δ_A due to bending is generally dominant.

---

[6]The reader should check the correspondence of the $\partial M/\partial P$ terms with those caused by a horizontal virtual unit force applied at A.

If the vertical deflection of point A were required, a fictitious vertical force F at A would have to be applied. Then, as in the preceding example, $\partial U / \partial F$, with $F = 0$, would give the desired result. In a similar manner, the rotation of any normal section for this beam may be obtained.

18-5. Statically Indeterminate Systems

Castigliano's second theorem can be generalized for statically indeterminate linear elastic systems. The necessary modifications consist of expressing the strain energy not only to be a function of n externally applied forces (and/or moments) $P_1, P_2, P_3, \ldots, P_n$, but also of p statically indeterminate *redundant forces* (and/or moments) $X_1, X_2, \ldots, X_p$. A possible system of such forces is shown in Fig. 18-9. The necessary number of selected supports for maintaining static equilibrium of the primary section (Section 4-3) are excluded from the enumeration of the redundant forces. On this basis, strain energy U for an indeterminate system can be defined as

$$U^* = U = U(P_1, P_2, P_3, \ldots, P_n; X_1, X_2, \ldots, X_j, \ldots, X_p) \qquad (18\text{-}21)$$

Using this function and Castigliano's second theorem, p displacements (and/or rotations) at the points of application of redundant forces (and/or couples) X_j in the direction of these forces can be found. If these displacements are zero,

$$\frac{\partial U}{\partial X_j} = 0 \qquad (j = 1, 2, 3, \ldots, p) \qquad (18\text{-}22)$$

These p equations are equal to the degree of statical indeterminancy of the system.[7] By solving these equations simultaneously, the magnitudes of the redundant are obtained.

Castigliano's first theorem can be used directly for the solution of statically indeterminate problems.

Several examples follow that illustrate these procedures.

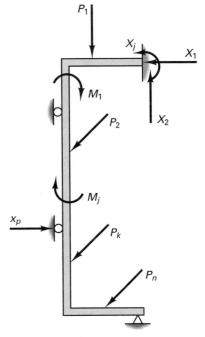

Fig. 18-9 Statically indeterminate system.

Example 18-6

Using Castigliano's second theorem, verify the bar forces found in Example 4-3 caused by applied force P. The planar system of three elastic bars is repeated in Fig. 18-10(a). The cross-sectional area A of each bar is the same, and their elastic modulus is E.

---

[7]Italian mathematician L.F. Menabrea (1809–1896) proved that the total work for a problem solved in this manner is a minimum. His theorem is known as the *principle of least work*. Castigliano employed this principle in the solution of statically indeterminate problems.

SOLUTION

It is convenient to visualize the system to be cut at B and to designate the unknown force in bar BC by X. From statics, the forces in the inclined bars then have the magnitudes shown in Fig. 18-10(b). Hence, using Eq. 18-19a, with an appropriate change, the complementary strain energy is

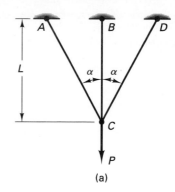

(a)

$$U^* = U = \frac{X^2 L}{2AE} + 2\left[\frac{(P - X)^2 L}{2 \times 2^2 AE \cos^3 \alpha}\right]$$

Since the deflection of the system at point B is zero, by applying Eq. 18-22,

$$\frac{\partial U}{\partial X} = \frac{XL}{AE} \times 1 + \frac{(P - X)L}{2AE \cos^3 \alpha} \times (-1) = 0$$

$$X = \frac{P}{1 + 2\cos^3 \alpha}$$

The expression is identical to that given for F_1 in Eq. 4-5. Here the procedure for obtaining the result is more direct.

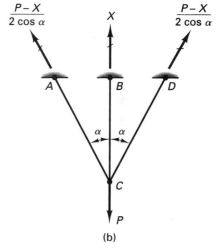

(b)

Fig. 18-10

Example 18-7

Consider an elastic uniformly loaded beam clamped at one end and simply supported at the other, as represented in Fig. 18-7(b). Determine the reaction at A. Use Eq. 18-22.

SOLUTION

The solution is analogous to that of Example 18-4 except that R_A must be treated as the unknown and not permitted to vanish. The key kinematic condition per Eq. 18-22 is

$$\Delta_A = \partial U / \partial R_A = 0$$

which states that no deflection occurs at A due to the applied load w_o and R_A.

$$M = -\frac{w_o x^2}{2} + R_A x \qquad \text{and} \qquad \frac{\partial M}{\partial R_A} = +x$$

$$\Delta_A = \frac{\partial U}{\partial R_A} = \frac{1}{EI}\int_0^L \left(-\frac{p_o x^2}{2} + R_A x\right)(+x)\, dx = -\frac{w_o L^4}{8EI} + \frac{R_A L^3}{3EI} = 0$$

Therefore, $R_A = +3w_o L/8$, the result found in Example 14-5.

Example 18-8

Consider an elastic beam fixed at both ends and subjected to a uniformly increasing load to one end, as shown in Fig. 18-11. Determine the reactions at end A using Eq. 18-22. EI for the beam is constant.

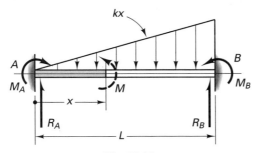

Fig. 18-11

SOLUTION

This problem is statically indeterminate to the second degree. It is convenient to take reactions R_A and M_A as the redundant forces and to express M as a function of these forces as well as of the applied load. The kinematic conditions require that the vertical displacement and the rotation at A be zero. These two conditions can be fulfilled by applying Eq. 18-22 twice and setting deflection Δ_A and rotation θ_A and A equal to zero. This provides two simultaneous equations for determining R_A and M_A. Proceeding in this manner,

$$M = M_A + R_A x - kx^3/6$$

Hence,

$$\frac{\partial M}{\partial M_A} = 1 \quad \text{and} \quad \frac{\partial M}{\partial R_A} = x$$

$$\Delta_A = \frac{\partial U}{\partial R_A} = \int_0^L \frac{M}{EI}\frac{\partial M}{\partial R_A}\,dx = \frac{1}{EI}\int_0^L \left(M_A + R_A x - \frac{1}{6}kx^3\right)x\,dx = 0$$

$$\theta_A = \frac{\partial U}{\partial M_A} = \int_0^L \frac{M}{EI}\frac{\partial M}{\partial M_A}\,dx = \frac{1}{EI}\int_0^L \left(M_A + R_A x - \frac{1}{6}kx^3\right)(1)\,dx = 0$$

Carrying out the indicated operations and simplifying,

$$M_A/2 + R_A L/3 = kL^3/30$$

$$M_A + R_A L/2 = kL^3/24$$

Solving these two equations simultaneously,

$$R_A = 3kL^2/20 \quad \text{and} \quad M_A = -kL^3/30 \qquad (18\text{-}23)$$

where the negative sign of M_A shows that this end moment has a counter-clockwise sense.

Example 18-9

Rework Example 18-6 using Castigliano's first theorem. See Fig. 18-12.

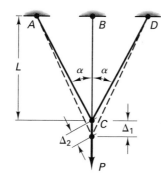

Fig. 18-12

SOLUTION

In applying Castigliano's first theorem, the elastic strain energy in all three bars must be expressed in terms of the vertical elongation Δ_1 of the center bar. For small deflections,

$$\Delta_2 = \Delta_1 \cos \alpha$$

Using Eq. 17-7 expressed as a function of displacement Δ_1 and noting that $L_{AC} = L_{DC} = L/\cos \alpha$

$$U = \sum_{k=1}^{3} \frac{A_k E_k \Delta_k^2}{2L_k} = \frac{AE \Delta_1^2}{2L} + 2\frac{AE \Delta_1^2 \cos^3 \alpha}{2L} \qquad (18\text{-}24)$$

and

$$\frac{\partial U}{\partial \Delta_1} = \frac{AE}{L}\Delta_1 + 2\frac{AE}{L}\cos^3 \alpha \, \Delta_1 = P$$

Hence,

$$\Delta_1 = \frac{PL}{AE}\frac{1}{1 + 2\cos^3 \alpha}$$

Then the force in the vertical bar using Eq. 3-5 is

$$X = k\Delta_1 = \frac{AE}{L}\Delta_1 = \frac{P}{1 + 2\cos^3\alpha}$$

This result is in agreement with that found in Example 18-6.

This type of solution is easily extended to any number of symmetrically inclined bars with Δ_1 remaining as the only unknown, regardless of the degree of indeterminacy.

If the inclined bars lack symmetry or the applied force forms an angle with the vertical, the problem is more complex. In such cases, the elongation in each bar is determined from two separate displacements at the load point. This procedure is analogous to that shown in Example 17-7 and illustrated in Fig. 17-13. Further discussion of this approach can be found in Section 20-2, where the *displacement* method of analysis is considered.

18-6. Elastic Energy for Buckling Loads

Stability problems can be treated in a very general manner using the energy or the virtual work methods. As an introduction to such methods, the basic criteria for determining the stability of equilibrium are derived in this chapter for conservative linearly elastic systems using an energy method.

To establish the stability criteria, a function Π, called the *total potential* of the system, must be formulated. This function is expressed as the sum of the internal energy U (strain energy) and the potential energy Ω (omega) of the external forces that act on a system; that is,

$$\Pi = U + \Omega \tag{18-25}$$

Disregarding a possible additive constant, $\Omega = -W_e$ (i.e., the loss of potential energy during the application of the forces is equal to the work done on the system by the external forces). Hence, Eq. 18-25 can be rewritten as

$$\Pi = U - W_e \tag{18-26}$$

As is know from classical mechanics, for equilibrium, total potential Π must be stationary,[8] therefore, its variation $\delta\Pi$ must equal zero. That is,

$$\boxed{\delta\Pi = \delta U - \delta W_e = 0} \tag{18-27}$$

For conservative, elastic systems, this relation is in agreement with Eq. 17-11. This condition can be used to determine the position of equilibrium.

[8]In terms of the ordinary functions, this simply means that a condition exists where the derivative of a function with respect to an independent variable is zero and the function itself has a maximum, a minimum, a minimax, or a constant value.

However, Eq. 18-27 cannot discern the type of equilibrium and thereby establish the condition for the stability of equilibrium. Only by examining the high-order terms in the expression for the change $\Delta\Pi$ in the total potential Π can this be determined. Therefore, the more complete expression for the increment in Π as given by Taylor's expansion must be examined. Such an expression is

$$\Delta\Pi = \delta\Pi + \frac{1}{2!}\delta^2\Pi + \frac{1}{3!}\delta^3\Pi + \cdots \qquad (18\text{-}28)$$

Since for any type equilibrium, $\partial\Pi = 0$, it is the first nonvanishing term of this expansion that determines the type of equilibrium. For linear elastic systems, the second term suffices. Thus, from Eq. 18-28, the stability criteria are

$$\boxed{\begin{array}{l}\delta^2\Pi > 0 \\ \delta^2\Pi < 0 \\ \delta^2\Pi = 0\end{array}} \quad \begin{array}{l}\text{for stable equilibrium} \\ \text{for unstable equilibrium} \\ \text{for neutral equilibrium associated} \\ \quad \text{with the critical load}\end{array} \qquad (18\text{-}29)$$

The meaning of these expressions be may clarified by referring to Fig. 18-13 where the curve represents the potential function Π. The origin of this function is shown below the curve, since the absolute value of Π is arbitrary. Three different possible positions of equilibrium for the ball are shown in this figure.[9] The first derivative of Π at points of equilibrium is zero for all three cases; it is the second derivative that determines the type of equilibrium.

For simple functions of Π, the procedures for forming the derivatives, differentials, and variations are alike. If, however, the function of Π is expressed by integrals, the problem becomes mathematically much more complicated, requiring the use of the calculus of variations or finite elements. The treatment of such problems is beyond the scope of this text.[10]

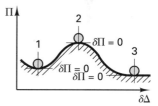

Fig. 18-13 Different equilibrium conditions.

Example 18-10

Using the energy method, verify the critical load found before a rigid bar with a torsional spring at the base, Fig. 16-7(a).

---

[9]A point on a curve resulting from a combination , for example, of the curve to the left of position 1 with that of the curve to the right of position 2 defines a *minimax*. In stability analysis, such a point corresponds to the condition of *unstable* equilibrium.

[10]H. L. Langhaar, *Energy Methods in Applied Mechanics* (New York: Wiley, 1962); K. Washizu, *Variational Methods in Elasticity and Plasticity,* 2nd ed. (New York: Pergamon, 1975); J. S. Przemieniecki, "Discrete-element methods for stability analysis of complex structures," *Aeron. J.* **72** (1968), 1077.

SOLUTION

For a displaced position of the bar, the strain energy in the spring is $k\theta^2/2$. For the same displacement, force P lowers an amount $L - L \cos \theta = L(1 - \cos \theta)$. Therefore,

$$\Pi = U - W_e = \frac{1}{2} k\theta^2 - PL(1 - \cos \theta)$$

If the study of the problem is confined to small (infinitesimal) displacements and $\cos \theta = 1 - \theta^2/2! + \theta^4/4! + \cdots$, the total potential Π to a consistent order of accuracy simplifies to

$$\Pi = \frac{k\theta^2}{2} - \frac{PL\theta^2}{2}$$

Note especially that the $\frac{1}{2}$ in the last term is due to the *expansion of the cosine into the series*. Full external force P acts on the bar as θ is permitted to change.

Having the expression for the total potential, one must solve two distinctly different problems. In the first problem, a position of equilibrium is found. For this purpose, Eq. 18-27 is applied:

$$\delta\Pi = \frac{d\Pi}{d\theta} \delta\theta = (k\theta - PL\theta)\delta\theta = 0 \qquad \text{or} \qquad (k - PL)\theta \, \delta\theta = 0$$

At this point of the solution, k, P, and L must be considered constant, and $\delta\theta$ cannot be zero. Therefore, an equilibrium position occurs at $\theta = 0$.

In the second, distinctly different, phase of the solution, according to the last part of Eq. 18-29 for neutral equilibrium,

$$\delta^2\Pi = \frac{d^2\Pi}{d\theta^2} \delta\theta^2 + \frac{d\Pi}{d\theta} \delta^2\theta = 0$$

$$(k - PL)(\delta\theta)^2 + (k - PL)\theta \, \delta^2\theta = 0$$

For equilibrium at $\theta = 0$, the second term on the left side vanishes: whereas, since $\delta^2\theta$ cannot be zero, the first term yields $P = k/L$, which is the critical buckling load.

PROBLEMS

Section 18-4

18-1. Using Castigliano's second theorem, in Example 18-2, determine the horizontal deflection of B due to the applied vertical force $P = 3$ k.

The following problems are for solution by Castigliano's second theorem:

18-2. Rework Problem 17-8.

18-3. Rework Problem 17-19.

18-4. Rework Problem 17-16.

18-5. Rework Problem 17-17.

18-6. Rework Problem 17-21.

18-7. Rework Problem 17-23.

18-8. Rework Problem 17-33.

18-9. Rework Problem 17-25.

18-10. Rework Problem 17-29.

18-11. Rework Problem 17-30.

18-12. Rework Problem 17-31.

18-13. Rework Problem 17-35.

18-14. Rework Problem 17-36.

Section 18-5

18-15. Using Eq. 18-22, determine the forces in the elastic bar system shown in the figure due to applied force P. L/AE is the same for each bar.

18-16. A two-span continuous beam is loaded with a uniformly distributed downward load w_o N/m. If the left span is L and the right one is $2L$, what is the reaction at the middle support? Use Eq. 18-22 to obtain the solution. Draw shear and moment diagrams for this beam.

18-17. Without taking advantage of symmetry and using Eq. 18-22, determine the reaction components on the left for the beam in Problem 17-50 due to applied load w_o.

18-18. Assuming that in Example 18-7 end B is simply supported, determine the reaction with the aid of Eq. 18-22.

18-19. Rework Example 18-8 after assuming that the cross section of bar BC is twice as large as that of bar AC or DC.

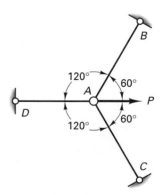

Fig. P18-15

Section 18-6

18-20.   Using Eq. 18-27 and 18-29 for neutral equilibrium, determine the critical buckling load in Problem 16-1.

18-21.   Using Eq. 18-29 for neutral equilibrium, determine the critical Eular buckling load P_{cr} for an elastic column of constant EI with pinned ends, as shown in Fig. 16-13. Assume that the deflected shape for a slightly bent column in a neighboring equilibrium position is $v = A \sin \pi x/L$, where A is an arbitrary constant. (*Hint*: Axial shortening of a column due to lateral deflection v is given by

$$\Delta_v = \frac{1}{2} \int_0^L \left(\frac{dv}{dx} \right)^2 dx$$

and heuristically[1] the external work $\delta W_e = P \, \Delta_v$. By noting from Eq. 16-5 that $M = -Pv$, the expression for δU then follows from Eq. 17-8.)

18-22.   Find an approximate solution to the preceding problem by assuming the deflected shape of the column to be a parabola, $v = A(x^2 - xL)$, *satisfying the kinematic boundary conditions*. (*Note*: Energy solutions are not very sensitive to the assumed deflected shape provided one takes $M = -Pv$ and ***not*** as $M = EIv''$, where the second derivative of an assumed function is used. Numerous approximate solutions of column-buckling problems can be found in this manner).

---

[1]For further study of this problem, see K. Marguerre, *Neuere Festigkeitsprobleme des Ingenieurs* (Berlin/Göttingen/Heidelberg: Springer, 1980), 189–229.

19

Elastic Analysis of Systems

19-1. Introduction

The force and displacement methods for solving linearly elastic statically indeterminate problems previously encountered in this text are extended in this chapter to more complex cases. These two methods are particularly important in the matrix analysis of structures and in finite element formulations. They are directly applicable in satisfying elastic design criteria often based on the maximum allowable stress. Such a criterion is referred to as the *limit state* for the maximum stress. In other cases, the limit state may be the maximum allowable deflection or the effect of system stiffness on vibrations. Such criteria are *serviceability* limit states.

If the *strength* of a member or members for emergency overloads is the only controlling parameter, the elastic maximum stress limit state may lead to an unduly conservative design. For *ductile* materials, where the fatigue problem does not arise, merely reaching the maximum stress at a point or a few points of a member does not necessarily exhaust the strength capacity of a system. The ultimate strength of such systems can be reasonably well approximated by considering the material rigid and ideally plastic. A few such cases were encountered earlier. This approach is discussed in the next chapter for beams and frames.

19-2. Two Basic Methods for Elastic Analysis

Structural systems that experience only small deformations and are composed of linearly elastic materials are linear structural systems. The principle of superposition is applicable for such structures and forms the basis for two of the most effective methods for the analysis of indeterminate systems.

In the first of these methods, a statically indeterminate system is reduced initially to one that is determinate by removing redundant (superfluous) reactions or internal forces for maintaining static equilibrium; see Fig. 4-1. Then these redundant forces are considered as externally applied, and their magnitudes are so adjusted as to satisfy the prescribed deformation conditions at their points of application. Once the redundant reactions are determined, the system is statically determinate and can be analyzed for strength or stiffness characteristics by the methods introduced earlier. This widely used method is commonly referred to as the *force method,* or the flexibility method; see Section 4-3.

In the second method, referred to as the *displacement method,* or the stiffness method, the joint displacements of a structure are treated as the unknowns; see Sections 4-4 and 4-5. The system is first reduced to a series of members whose *joints* are imagined to be completely restrained from any movement. The joints are then released to an extent sufficient to satisfy the force equilibrium conditions at each joint. This method is extremely well suited to computer coding and, hence, is even more widely used in practice than the force method, especially for the analysis of large-scale structures.

While some of the older classical methods continue to have some utility, the force and displacement methods are the two modern approaches to the solution of indeterminate structural systems.

19-3. Force Method

The first step in the analysis of structural systems using the force method is the determination of the degree of statical indeterminacy, which is the same as the number of redundant reactions, as discussed in Sections 1-8 and 4-3. The redundant reactions[1] are temporarily removed to obtain a statically determinate structure, which is referred to as the *released* or *primary* structure. Then, since this structure is artificially reduced to statical determinacy, it is possible to find any desired displacement by the methods previously dis-

---

[1]In the analysis of beams and frames, the bending moments at the supports are often treated as redundants. In such cases, rotations of tangents at the supports are considered instead of deflections.

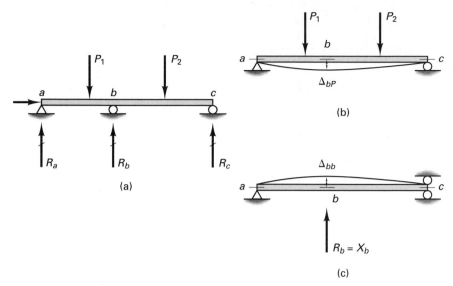

Fig. 19-1 Superposition for the force method.

cussed. For example, the beam shown in Fig. 19-1(a) is indeterminate to the first degree. For this beam to remain in stable static equilibrium, only one of the vertical reactions can be removed. Removing the vertical reactions at b, Fig. 19-1(b), deflection Δ_{bP} at b caused by applied forces P can be calculated. By reapplying the removed redundant reaction R_b to the *unloaded* member, Fig. 19-1(c), deflection Δ_{bb} at b due to R_b can be found. Since the deflection at b of the given beam must be zero, by *superposing* the deflections and requiring that $\Delta_{bP} + \Delta_{bb} = 0$, the magnitude of $R_b = X_b$ can be determined.

This procedure can be generalized to any number of redundant reactions. However, it is essential in such cases to recognize that *the displacement of every point on the primary structure is affected by each reapplied redundant force*. This also holds true for the rotation of elements. As an example, consider the beam in Fig. 19-2(a).

By removing any two of the redundant reactions, such as R_b and R_c, the beam becomes determinate and the deflections at b and c can be computed, Fig. 19-2(b). These deflections are designated Δ_{bP} and Δ_{cP}, respectively, where the first letter of the subscript indicates the point where the deflection occurs, and the second the cause of the deflection. By reapplying R_b to the same beam, the deflections at b and c due to R_b at b can be found, Fig. 19-2(c). These deflections are designated Δ_{bb} and Δ_{cb}, respectively. Similarly, Δ_{bc} and Δ_{cc}, due to R_c, can be established, Fig. 19-2(d). Superposing the deflections at each support and setting the sum equal to zero, since points b and c actually do not deflect, one obtains two equations:

$$\Delta_b = \Delta_{bP} + \Delta_{bb} + \Delta_{bc} = 0$$
$$\Delta_c = \Delta_{cP} + \Delta_{cb} + \Delta_{cc} = 0 \qquad (19\text{-}1)$$

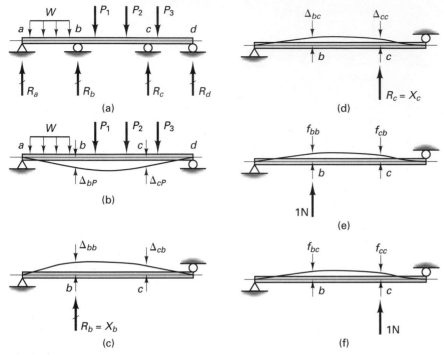

Fig. 19-2   Superposition for a continuous beam.

These can be rewritten in a more meaningful form using *flexibility coeffi-cients* f_{bb}, f_{bc}, f_{cb}, and f_{cc}, which are defined as the deflections shown in Figs. 19-2(e) and (f) due to unit forces applied in the direction of the redun-dants. Then, since a linear structural system is being considered, the deflec-tion at point b due to the redundants can be expressed as

$$\Delta_{bb} = f_{bb}X_b \quad \text{and} \quad \Delta_{bc} = f_{bc}X_c \tag{19-2}$$

and, similarly, at point c as

$$\Delta_{cb} = f_{cb}X_b \quad \text{and} \quad \Delta_{cc} = f_{cc}X_c \tag{19-3}$$

where X_b and X_c are the redundant quantities. Using this notation, Eq. 19-1 becomes

$$\Delta_b = f_{bb}X_b + f_{bc}X_c + \Delta_{bP} = 0$$
$$\Delta_c = f_{cb}X_b + f_{cc}X_c + \Delta_{cP} = 0 \tag{19-4}$$

where the only unknown quantities are X_b and X_c; simultaneous solution of these equations constitutes the solution of the problem.

Generalizing the preceding results for determining the unknown forces for systems with n redundants, using superposition, the following *compati-bility equations*[2] can be formed:

---

[2]Sometimes these expressions are referred to as the Maxwell-Mohr equations.

$$\Delta_a = f_{aa}X_a + f_{ab}X_b + \cdots + f_{an}X_n + \Delta_{aP}$$

$$\Delta_b = f_{ba}X_a + f_{bb}X_b + \cdots + f_{bn}X_n + \Delta_{bP}$$

$$\vdots \qquad\qquad (19\text{-}5)$$

$$\Delta_n = f_{na}X_a + f_{nb}X_b + \cdots + f_{nn}X_n + \Delta_{nP}$$

When the redundant supports are immovable, the left column of the equation is zero. Alternatively, such deflections can be prescribed.[3] The terms for deflections in the right column can be calculated for the primary structure. The flexibility coefficients[4] f_{ij} are for the whole primary system. All quantities in these equations represent either deflections or angular rotations, depending on whether they are associated with forces or couples.

For the force method, it is customary to express Eq. 19-5 in matrix form as

$$\begin{bmatrix} f_{aa} & f_{ba} & \cdots & f_{an} \\ f_{ba} & f_{bb} & \cdots & f_{bn} \\ \cdots & \cdots & \cdots & \cdots \\ f_{na} & f_{nb} & \cdots & f_{nn} \end{bmatrix} \begin{Bmatrix} X_a \\ X_b \\ \cdots \\ X_n \end{Bmatrix} = \begin{Bmatrix} \Delta_a - \Delta_{aP} \\ \Delta_b - \Delta_{bP} \\ \cdots \\ \Delta_n - \Delta_{nP} \end{Bmatrix} \qquad (19\text{-}6a)$$

Because the square matrix is made up of the flexibility coefficients, this method is often called the *flexibility method* of structural analysis.

It should be clearly understood that the previous equations are applicable only to linearly elastic systems that undergo small displacements. It should be noted further that the matrix exhibited by Eq. 19-6 is a *system* or *global* flexibility matrix. Such matrices can be readily constructed directly only for the simpler problems. For treatment of more complex problems, the reader is referred to texts on finite elements or structural matrix analysis cited previously in Sections 3-3 and 17-9.

Before proceeding with examples, it is shown next that the matrix of the flexibility coefficients f_{ij} is *symmetric* (i.e., $f_{ij} = f_{ji}$).

19-4. Flexibility Coefficients Reciprocity

According to the definition of flexibility coefficients, for linearly elastic systems, the displacement Δ_i at i due to forces P_i at i and P_j at j patterned after Eq. 19-5 can be expressed as

$$\Delta_i = f_{ii}P_i + f_{ij}P_j \qquad (19\text{-}6b)$$

---

[3]If an elastic support is provided at the ith point, the flexibility coefficient at the support is increased by adding the flexibility of such a support.

[4]The flexibility coefficients are also called the *deflection influence coefficients*.

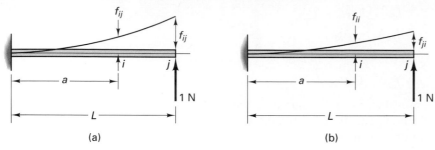

Fig. 19-3   Reciprocal deflections $f_{ij} = f_{ji}$.

Similarly, the deflection at j is

$$\Delta_j = f_{ji}P_i + f_{jj}P_j \qquad (19\text{-}6c)$$

where f_{ii}, f_{ij}, f_{ji} and f_{jj} are the flexibility coefficients of a given system.

If the strain energy of the system due to the application of these forces is U, according to Castigliano's second theorem, Eq. 18-16, the same qualities are also given as

$$\Delta_i = \frac{\partial U}{\partial P_i} \quad \text{and} \quad \Delta_j = \frac{\partial U}{\partial P_j}$$

By taking partial derivatives of Δ_i with respect to P_j in Eq. 19-5a and the preceding equation, the following equality is obtained:

$$\frac{\partial \Delta_i}{\partial P_j} = f_{ij} = \frac{\partial^2 U}{\partial P_j \, \partial P_i}$$

And, similarly,

$$\frac{\partial \Delta_j}{\partial P_i} = f_{ji} = \frac{\partial^2 U}{\partial P_i \partial P_j}$$

However, since the order of differentiation is immaterial,

$$\boxed{f_{ij} = f_{ji}} \qquad (19\text{-}7)$$

As illustrated in Fig. 19-3, this relation states that the displacement at any point i due to a unit force at any point j is equal to the displacement of j due to a unit force at i, provided the directions of the forces and deflections in each of the two cases coincide. It can be noted that this relationship holds true for several cases considered earlier in applications of virtual force equations in Section 17-6. For example, in calculating flexibility coefficients, using Eq. 17-26, by setting F_i equal to unit force p_i, its role with $\bar{p}_j$ is interchangeable. This is also true in the use of Eqs. 17-27 and 17-28.

The derived relationship is often called *Maxwell's theorem of reciprocal displacements.*[5]

---

[5] This relationship was discovered by James Clerk Maxwell in 1864. The more general case was demonstrated by E. Betti in 1872.

Example 19-1

For the simply supported elastic beam shown in Fig. 19-4, show that the rotation of the tangent to the elastic curve at the support i, caused by applying a unit force at j, is equal to the deflection at j caused by applying a unit couple at i.

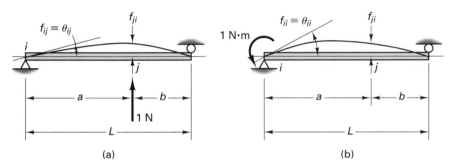

(a)   (b)

Fig. 19-4

SOLUTION

The deflection of the beam due to a concentrated force P at j is given by Eq. 14-27, applicable for $0 \leq x \leq a$. The derivative of this equation with respect to x gives the slope of the elastic curve. The slope of this function at $x = 0$ gives the rotation θ_{ij}, defining f_{ij}, when the applied force $P = -1$:

$$v = -\frac{Pb}{6EIL}(L^2x - b^2x - x^3) \quad \text{and} \quad v' = -\frac{Pb}{6EIL}(L^2 - b^2 - 3x^2)$$

$$v'(0) = \theta(0) = -\frac{Pb}{6EIL}(L^2 - b^2) = -\frac{Pab}{6EIL}(a + 2b)$$

and

$$\theta_{ij} \equiv f_{ij} = \frac{ab}{6EIL}(a + 2b) \tag{19-8}$$

The equation for an elastic curve for a beam subjected to an end moment is derived next. By proceeding as before, the deflection at j is found. Assuming that a counterclockwise moment M_o is applied at i,

$$M = -M_o + M_ox/L \quad \text{and} \quad EIv'' = M = -M_o + M_ox/L$$

$$EIv' = -M_ox + M_ox^2/2L + C_3$$

Hence,

$$EIv = -M_o x^2/2 + M_o x^3/6L + C_3 x + C_4$$

From $v(0) = 0$, $C_4 = 0$, and from $v(L) = 0$, $C_3 = M_o L/3$, and

$$EIv = \frac{M_o x}{6L}(-3Lx + x^2 + 2L^2) \qquad (19\text{-}9)$$

Therefore, for $v(a)$ and $M_o = 1$,

$$f_{ji} = \frac{a}{6EIL}(-3La + a^2 + 2L^2) = \frac{ab}{6EIL}(a + 2b) \qquad (19\text{-}10)$$

This result is identical to that given by Eq. 19-8.

Example 19-2

A two-span continuous elastic beam on simple supports carries a uniformly distributed load, as shown in Fig. 19-5. Determine the reactions and plot shear and moment diagrams. EI for the beam is constant.

SOLUTION

Reaction R_b at b is removed to make the beam statically determinate. The deflection at b for the primary structure, using Eq. 14-22, is

$$\Delta_{bP} = -\frac{5w_o(2L)^2}{384EI} = -\frac{5w_o L^4}{24EI}$$

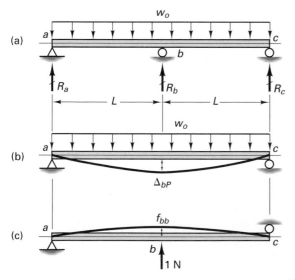

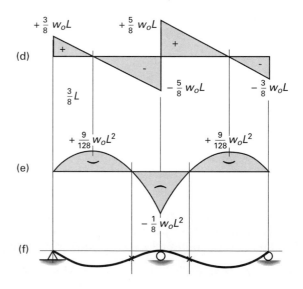

Fig. 19-5

The deflection at b due to a concentrated force is given by Eq. 14-30. Therefore, by setting $P = 1$, the flexibility coefficient is

$$f_{bb} = \frac{1 \times (2L)^3}{48EI} = \frac{L^3}{6EI}$$

By using Eq. 19-5 and assuming that the supports are immovable,

$$\Delta_b = f_{bb}X_b + \Delta_{bP} = 0 \quad \text{and} \quad X_b \equiv R_b = -\Delta_{bP}/f_{bb} = 5w_oL/4$$

From statics, $R_a = R_c = 3w_oL/8$ and the shear and moment diagrams are as in Fig. 19-5(d) and (e), respectively. The elastic curve is shown in Fig. 19-5(f).

Example 19-3

A two-span continuous beam is clamped at one end and simply supported at two other points; see Fig. 19-6(a). Determine the reactions caused by the application of a uniformly distributed load w_o. EI for the beam is constant.

SOLUTION

This beam is statically indeterminate to the second degree. Therefore, two redundants must be removed to proceed. A convenient choice is to remove M_a and R_b, resulting in a simply supported beam, Fig. 19-6(b). Using the results found in Example 14-3 and summarized in Table 10 of the Appendix,

$$\Delta_{aP} \equiv \theta_{aP} = -\frac{w_o(2L)^3}{24EI} = -\frac{w_oL^3}{3EI}$$

$$\Delta_{bP} = -\frac{5w_o(2L)^3}{384EI} = -\frac{5w_oL^4}{24EI}$$

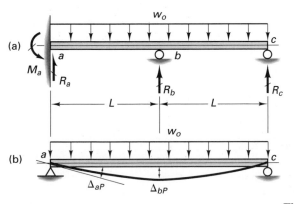
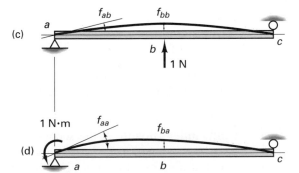

Fig. 19-6

One set of flexibility coefficients is determined by applying a unit force at b, Fig. 19-6(c), and determining the rotation at a and the deflection at b using the equations in Table 10 of the Appendix. This process is repeated by applying a unit moment at a, Fig. 19-6(d), and finding the rotation at a and the deflection at b. Thus,

$$f_{ab} = \frac{(2L)^2}{16EI} = \frac{L^2}{4EI} \quad \text{and} \quad f_{bb} = \frac{(2L)^3}{48EI} = \frac{L^3}{6EI}$$

$$f_{aa} = \frac{(2L)}{3EI} = \frac{2L}{3EI} \quad \text{and} \quad f_{ba} = \frac{L[(2L)^2 - L^2]}{6EI(2L)} = \frac{L^2}{4EI}$$

Note that, as is to be expected, $f_{ab} = f_{ba}$.

Forming two equations for compatibility of displacements at a and b using Eq. 19-5,

$$\Delta_a \equiv \theta_a = \Delta_{aP} + f_{aa}X_a + f_{ab}X_b = 0$$

$$\Delta_b = \Delta_{bP} + f_{ba}X_a + f_{bb}X_b = 0$$

Substituting the relevant quantities from before, the required equations are

$$\frac{2L}{3EI}X_a + \frac{L^2}{4EI}X_b = \frac{w_o L^3}{3EI}$$

$$\frac{L^2}{4EI}X_a + \frac{L^3}{6EI}X_b = \frac{5w_o L^4}{24EI}$$

Solving these two equations simultaneously,

$$X_a = M_a = 0.0714w_o L^2 \quad \text{and} \quad X_b = R_b = 1.143w_o L$$

The positive signs of these quantities indicate agreement with the assumed direction of unit forces.

Example 19-4

Consider the planar elastic pin-ended bar system shown in Fig. 19-7(a). Determine the bar forces caused by the application of inclined force $P = 10\sqrt{5}$ kN at joint e. All bars can resist either tensile or compressive forces. For simplicity in calculations, let L/EA for each member be unity.

SOLUTION

This problem is statically indeterminate to the second degree, and, in this solution, bars ae and ce are assumed to be redundant. Therefore, the bar system with the bars cut at a and c, shown in Fig. 19-7(b), is the *primary* system. The bar forces for this condition are shown on the diagram in parentheses. In this primary system, the possible displacements that may develop at a and c are noted and must be removed to restore the required

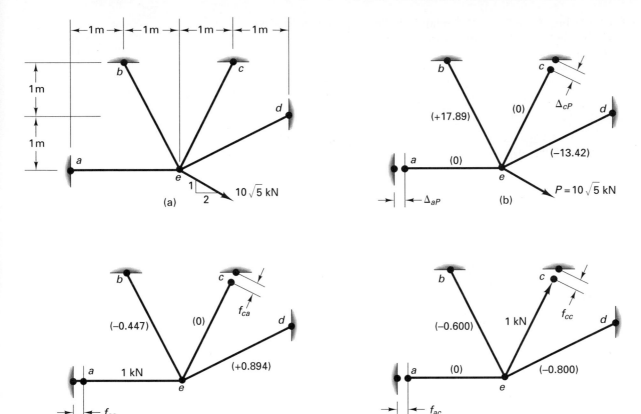

Fig. 19-7

compatibility conditions. Therefore, the behavior of the *unloaded* primary system due to the application of unit axial forces is studied first, as shown in Figs. 19-7(c) and (d). Again, the axial bar forces for each case are shown directly on the figures. Note that when the force in bar *ae* is unity, the force in bar *ce* is zero, Fig. 19-7(c); conversely, when the force in the bar *ce* is unity, the force in bar *ae* is zero.

Calculations for the required deflections and flexibility coefficients are carried out in tabular form using the virtual force method and following the solution pattern of Example 17-5.

Bar	F, kN	$\bar{p}_a$ or p_a	$\bar{p}_c$ or p_c	$\bar{p}_a F$	$\bar{p}_b F$	$\bar{p}_a p_a$	$\bar{p}_c p_c$	$\bar{p}_a p_c$ or $\bar{p}_c p_a$
ae	0	+1	0	0	0	+1	0	0
be	+17.89	−0.447	−0.60	−8.00	−10.73	+0.20	+0.36	+0.268
ce	0	0	+1	0	0	0	+1	0
de	−13.42	+0.894	−0.80	−12.00	+10.73	+0.80	+0.64	−0.716
			Sum:	−20.00	0	+2.00	+2.00	−0.448

Since for each bar $L/AE = 1$, the relative deflections and flexibility coefficients according to Eq. 17-26 are

$$\Delta_{aP} = -20 \quad \Delta_{cP} = 0 \quad f_{aa} = f_{cc} = 2$$

and

$$f_{ac} = f_{ca} = -0.448$$

Therefore, for bar forces $F_{ac} = X_a$ and $F_{cc} = X_c$, the required conditions of compatibility at a and c, using Eq. 19-5, gives

$$\Delta_a = f_{aa}X_a + f_{ac}X_c + \Delta_{aP} = 2X_a - 0.448X_c - 20 = 0$$

and

$$\Delta_c = f_{ca}X_a + f_{cc}X_c + \Delta_{cP} = -0.448X_a + 2X_c + 0 = 0$$

By solving these two equations simultaneously,

$$F_{ae} = X_a = +10.52 \text{ kN} \quad \text{and} \quad F_{ce} = X_b = +2.36 \text{ kN}$$

Using superposition, the forces in the other two bars are

$$F_{be} = 17.89 + 10.52 \times (-0.447) + 2.36 \times (-0.600) = +11.77 \text{ kN}$$

and

$$F_{de} = -13.42 + 10.52 \times 0.894 + 2.36 \times (-0.800) = -5.90 \text{ kN}$$

Computer solutions are commonly used for problems with a high degree of indeterminacy.

19-5. Introduction to the Displacement Method

In the force method discussed in Section 19-3, the redundant forces were assumed to be unknowns. In the displacement method, on the other hand, the displacement—both linear and/or angular—of the joints or nodal points are taken as the unknowns. The first step in applying this method is to prevent these joint displacements, which are called *kinematic indeterminants* or *degrees of freedom*. The suppression of these degrees of freedom results in a modified system that is composed of a series of members, each of whose end points is restrained from translations and rotations. Calculation of reactions at these artificially restrained ends due to externally applied loads can be carried out using any of the previously described methods. The results of such calculations are usually available for a large variety of loading conditions, and a few are given in Table 11 of the Appendix. In beam analysis by this method, counterclockwise moments and upward reactions acting *on either end of a member* are taken as positive. *This beam sign convention differs from that used previously in this text* and is necessary for a consistent formulation of the superposition equations.

Sometimes this sign convention is referred to as "analyst's" to distinguish it from "designer's," used previously throughout. The designer's sign convention conveniently differentiates between tensile and compressive regions in flexural members.

The procedure for applying a displacement method for a beam with one degree of kinematic indeterminancy is illustrated in Fig. 19-8(a). First, the support at b is restrained, Fig. 19-8(b), reducing the problem to that of a fixed-end beam. Both the vertical reactions and end moments in such a beam can be found by methods discussed previously. Moment M_{bP} is an example of such a reactive force at an end, where the first letter of the subscript designates the location and the second identifies the cause. Such end moments and reactions are referred to as *fixed-end actions* at beam ends. For general use, fixed-end actions are identified here by a letter A with two subscripts. For the preceding case, $A_{bP} \equiv M_{bP}$. Subscript P refers to *any kind* of applied lateral load.

Next, moment M_{bb} at b, Fig. 19-8(c), is determined as a function of the applied rotation θ_b. In this notation, the first letter of the subscript identifies the location of the fixed-end force (moment) and the second identifies the location of the applied displacement. Two basic cases for end moments and reactions caused either by applied end rotation or displacement are given in Table 11 of the Appendix.

Finally, an equation for static equilibrium is written. In this case, since the beam is simply supported at b, the total moment M_b must be zero. For general use, such force quantities are identified as P_b (i.e., $M_b \equiv P_b$). Therefore, assuming that the system is linearly elastic and undergoes small displacement, for equilibrium at joint b,

$$M_b = M_{bP} + M_{bb} = 0 \qquad (19\text{-}11a)$$

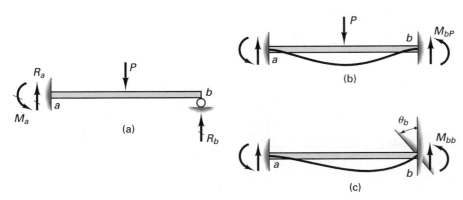

Fig. 19-8

or, in generalized notation,

$$P_b = A_{bP} + A_{bb} = 0 \qquad (19\text{-}11b)$$

Example 19-5

Using a displacement method, determine the reactions for a uniformly loaded beam fixed at one end and simply supported at the other, Fig. 19-9(a). EI is constant.

SOLUTION

Since joint rotation at b is the only kinematic unknown at the supports, Fig. 19-9(a), this beam is kinematically indeterminate to the first degree. Using Table 11 in the Appendix, the fixed-end actions due to the applied load, Fig. 19-9(b), and the end moments and reactions due to θ_b, Fig. 19-9(c), are

$$M_{aP} \equiv A_{aP} = w_o L^2/12 \quad \text{and} \quad M_{bP} \equiv A_{bP} = -w_o L^2/12$$

$$M_{ab} \equiv A_{ab} = 2EI\theta_b/L \quad \text{and} \quad M_{bb} \equiv A_{bb} = 4EI\theta_b/L$$

$$R_{ab} = 6EI\theta_b/L^2 \qquad \text{and} \quad R_{bb} = -6EI\theta_b/L^2$$

For moment equilibrium at the end b, using Eq. 19-11a,

$$M_b \equiv P_b = M_{bP} + M_{bb} = -\frac{w_o L^2}{12} + \frac{4EI}{L}\theta_b = 0$$

Hence,

$$\theta_b = w_o L^2/48EI$$

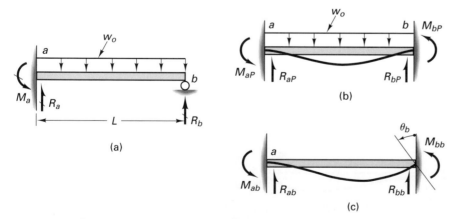

Fig. 19-9

Using this θ_b in the superposition equations,

$$M_a = M_{aP} + M_{ab} = \frac{w_oL^2}{12} + \frac{2EI}{L}\theta_b = \frac{w_oL^2}{8}$$

$$R_a = R_{aP} + R_{ab} = \frac{w_oL}{2} + \frac{6EI}{L}\theta_b = \frac{5w_oL}{8}$$

$$R_b = R_{bP} + R_{bb} = \frac{w_oL}{2} - \frac{6EI}{L}\theta_b = \frac{3w_oL}{8}$$

The sign of M_a is opposite from that of the designer's beam sign convention.

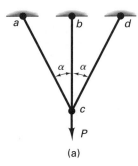

(a)

Example 19-6

Three elastic pin-jointed bars are symmetrically arranged in a plane to form the system shown in Fig. 19-10(a). The cross-sectional area A of each bar is the same, and the elastic modulus is E. Verify the bar forces found in Examples 4-3, 18-6, and 18-9 caused by applied force P.

SOLUTION

Because of symmetry, this system has only one degree of kinematic freedom and joint c can only be displaced in the vertical direction. In this solution, first, the joint is restrained from displacement, Fig. 19-10(b). Here all of the fixed-end actions are zero, and $A_{cP} \equiv P_{cP} = 0.$[6]

Force P_{cc} for the system is determined next as a function of deflection Δ_1 for bar bc. As in Example 18-8, for geometric compatibility at joint c, $\Delta_2 = \Delta_1 \cos \alpha$. Hence, using Eq. 3-7, the bar forces F_1 and F_2 in members bc and ac (or dc), respectively, are

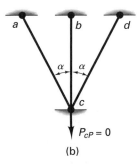

(b)

$$F_1 = k_1\Delta_1 = \frac{AE}{L}\Delta_1 \quad \text{and} \quad F_2 = k_2\Delta_1 \cos \alpha = \frac{AE}{L/\cos \alpha}\Delta_1 \cos \alpha$$

Then for vertical force equilibrium at joint c,

$$P_c = P_{cP} + F_1 + 2F_2 \cos \alpha = P$$

Substituting the values of P_{cP}, F_1, and F_2 into the preceding equation, and solving for Δ_1, one finds

$$\Delta_1 = \frac{PL}{AE(1 + 2\cos^3 \alpha)}$$

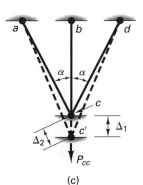

(c)

Fig. 19-10

---

[6]If an axial force were applied somewhere between b and c, P_{cP} would not be zero. For example, if a downward force P_1 were applied at a distance $L_{bc}/4$ above c, per Eq. 4-10, the fixed-end downward force at c would be $R_{cP} = 3P_1/4$.

By substituting this value of Δ_1 into the relations for the bar forces, the results in Example 4-12 are verified.

If in this example there were no symmetry about the vertical axis (either due to lack of symmetry in the structure itself or due to the application of force P at an angle), a horizontal displacement would also have developed at the joint. Two force equilibrium equations, one in the horizontal direction and the other in the vertical direction, must then be set up and solved simultaneously for the horizontal and vertical displacements. Such cases are illustrated in Figs. 17-12 and 17-13, and are also considered in the next section.

It should be noted that adding additional bars to the system, as shown in Fig. 19-11, does not increase the kinematic indeterminancy, and it remains at two. In the force method, on the other hand, the number of statical redundants increases, as does the number of simultaneous equations for determining redundants. However, this does not imply that the displacement method always involves the solution of fewer equations compared with the force method. Consider, for example, the case of a propped cantilever with an overhand; see Fig. 19-12. This beam is statically indeterminate only to the first degree, but kinematically indeterminate to the third degree (rotations at b and c, and a vertical deflection at c); hence, only one equation is needed for solution by the force method, but three simultaneous equations are required using the displacement method.

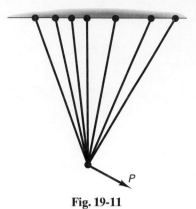

Fig. 19-11

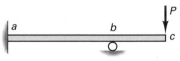

Fig. 19-12

19-6.   Further Remarks on the Displacement Method

The displacement method is extended to problems with several degrees of kinematic indeterminancy in this section. For this purpose, consider the beam shown in Fig. 19-13(a), where the guided support at c allows for vertical displacement but no rotation of the beam. The other degree of freedom of this beam is the rotation of its tangent at support b. This beam is thus kinematically indeterminate to the second degree. Upon restraining these two degrees of freedom, one obtains a system consisting of two fixed-end beams, ab and bc, Fig. 19-13(b). The effect of the externally applied loads on these two fixed-end beams is to produce a set of reactive forces at the supports. The fixed-end action (moment) A_{bP} at b is the *sum* of the fixed-end moments in beams ba and bc at b caused by the applied loads. Similarly, the fixed-end action A_{cP} is the vertical reaction at c restraining vertical displacement. Since the support is capable of developing a moment at c, it does not enter the problem at this level.

Next the support at b is rotated through an angle θ_b, giving rise to the fixed-end actions (moments) A_{bb} and A_{cb} at points b and c, respectively, as shown in Fig. 19-13(c). Similarly, A_{bc} and A_{cc} are caused by the vertical displacement Δ_c at c, Fig. 19-13(d).

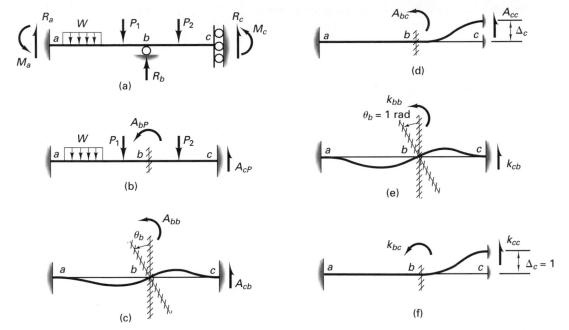

Fig. 19-13

Since no external moment M_b is applied at b, nor a vertical reaction P_c at c, the resultant forces $M_b \equiv P_b$ and P_c at these points are equal to zero. These two forces may be found by superposing three separate analyses, shown in Figs. 19-13(b)–(d), leading to two simultaneous equilibrium equations:

$$P_b = A_{bP} + A_{bb} + A_{bc} = 0$$
$$P_c = A_{cP} + A_{cb} + A_{cc} = 0 \tag{19-12}$$

These equations can be rewritten in more meaningful form using *stiffness coefficients* k_{bb}, k_{bc}, and k_{cc}, defined as the fixed-end actions shown in Figs. 19-13(e) and (f) due to the unit displacements (linear or angular) corresponding to the kinematic indeterminants. Then for a linear system, the moments at b and the vertical reactions at c, caused by displacements $\Delta_b = \theta_b$ and Δ_c, are

$$A_{bb} = k_{bb}\,\Delta_b \quad \text{and} \quad A_{bc} = k_{bc}\,\Delta_c \tag{19-13}$$
$$A_{cb} = k_{cb}\,\Delta_b \quad \text{and} \quad A_{cc} = k_{cc}\,\Delta_c \tag{19-14}$$

By substituting these relations into Eq. 19-12,

$$P_b = k_{bb}\,\Delta_b + k_{bc}\,\Delta_c + A_{bP} = 0$$
$$P_c = k_{cb}\,\Delta_b + k_{cc}\,\Delta_c + A_{cP} = 0 \tag{19-15}$$

These equations can be solved simultaneously for unknowns Δ_b and Δ_c.

By extending this approach to systems having n degrees of kinematic indeterminancy, the force equilibrium equations for determining the unknown nodal displacements Δ_i are

$$P_a = k_{aa}\Delta_a + k_{ab}\Delta_b + \cdots + k_{an}\Delta_n + A_{aP}$$
$$P_b = k_{ba}\Delta_a + k_{bb}\Delta_b + \cdots + k_{bn}\Delta_n + A_{bP}$$
$$\vdots$$
$$P_n = k_{na}\Delta_a + k_{nb}\Delta_b + \cdots + k_{nn}\Delta_n + A_{nP}$$

(19-16)

where terms $P_a, P_b, \ldots, P_n$ correspond to the *external* forces applied *at the nodal points.* In the absence of such forces, these terms are zero. The stiffness coefficients k_{ij} are associated either with a displacement or a rotation. The fixed-end actions $A_{aP}, A_{bP}, \ldots, A_{nP}$ are caused by the externally applied loads.

In matrix form, Eq. 19-16 for the displacement method can be written as

$$
\begin{bmatrix}
k_{aa} & k_{ab} & \cdots & k_{an} \\
k_{ba} & k_{bb} & \cdots & k_{bn} \\
\cdots & \cdots & \cdots & \cdots \\
k_{na} & k_{nb} & \cdots & k_{nn}
\end{bmatrix}
\begin{Bmatrix}
\Delta_1 \\
\Delta_2 \\
\cdots \\
\Delta_n
\end{Bmatrix}
=
\begin{Bmatrix}
P_a - A_{aP} \\
P_b - A_{bP} \\
\cdots \\
P_n - A_{nP}
\end{Bmatrix}
$$

(19-17)

Because the square matrix consists entirely of stiffness coefficients, the displacement method is often referred to as the *stiffness method.* For general procedures for constructing the stiffness matrix, the reader is referred to previously cited texts on finite elements or structural matrix analysis in Sections 3-3 and 17-9. In this text, only the simpler problems are considered.

Before proceeding with further examples, it will be shown that the stiffness matrix is *symmetric* (i.e., $k_{ij} = k_{ji}$) and that it is related to the flexibility matrix.

19-7. Stiffness Coefficients Reciprocity

For linearly elastic systems, an analogous relationship for stiffness coefficients can be obtained similar to that found in Section 19-4 for flexibility coefficients. Thus, if the system's elastic energy is U, according to Castigliano's first theorem, Eq. 18-18, the displacement of forces P_i and P_j in the respective directions of Δ's are

$$P_i = \frac{\partial U}{\partial \Delta_i} \quad \text{and} \quad P_j = \frac{\partial U}{\partial \Delta_j}$$

(19-18)

Alternatively, it can be seen from Eq. 19-16 that a partial derivative of P_i with respect to Δ_j is k_{ij}. Similarly, a partial derivative of P_j with respect to Δ_i

is k_{ji}. Carrying out these operations with Eqs. 19-18 establishes the following equalities:

$$\frac{\partial P_i}{\partial \Delta_j} = \frac{\partial^2 U}{\partial \Delta_j \, \partial \Delta_i} = k_{ij}$$

and

$$\frac{\partial P_j}{\partial \Delta_i} = \frac{\partial^2 U}{\partial \Delta_i \, \partial \Delta_j} = k_{ji} \qquad (19\text{-}19)$$

Since the order of differentiation for the mixed derivatives is immaterial,

$$\boxed{k_{ij} = k_{ji}} \qquad (19\text{-}20)$$

This relation proves that the matrix of stiffness coefficients is *symmetric*, a very important property for the analysis of structural systems.

The relationship between the stiffness and flexibility coefficients is illustrated in the next example. It is more complex than that for systems with one degree of kinematic and static indeterminancy.

Example 19-7[7]

Show the relationship between the flexibility and the stiffness matrices for the two-spring system shown in Fig. 19-14. The externally applied forces are P_1 and P_2, and the linearly elastic flexibilities and stiffnesses for each spring are shown in the figure.

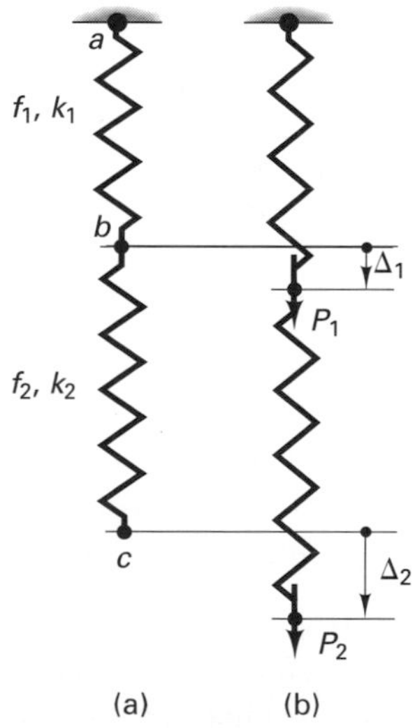

SOLUTION
The displacement of nodal points b and c for the loaded system can be written using spring flexibilities as

$$\Delta_1 = (P_1 + P_2)f_1 \quad \text{and} \quad \Delta_2 = (P_1 + P_2)f_1 + P_2 f_2$$

where force $P_1 + P_2$ acts on spring ab.

Similarly, the equilibrium equations for each nodal point b and c, using spring stiffnesses, are

$$P_1 = k_1 \Delta_1 - k_2(\Delta_2 - \Delta_1) \quad \text{and} \quad P_2 = k_2(\Delta_2 - \Delta_1)$$

where the stretch of the spring bc is $\Delta_2 - \Delta_1$.

Fig. 19-14

[7]Adapted from M. F. Rubinstein, *Matrix Computer Analysis of Structures* (Englewood Cliffs, NJ: Prentice Hall, 1966), 60–63.

Recasting these equations into matrix form gives

$$\begin{Bmatrix} \Delta_1 \\ \Delta_2 \end{Bmatrix} = \begin{bmatrix} f_1 & f_1 \\ f_1 & f_1 + f_2 \end{bmatrix} \begin{Bmatrix} P_1 \\ P_2 \end{Bmatrix}$$

and

$$\begin{Bmatrix} P_1 \\ P_2 \end{Bmatrix} = \begin{bmatrix} k_1 + k_2 & -k_2 \\ -k_2 & k_2 \end{bmatrix} \begin{Bmatrix} \Delta_1 \\ \Delta_2 \end{Bmatrix}$$

Next it can be noted that the individual spring flexibilities can be replaced by the reciprocals of the spring constants. Then the flexibility matrix, expressed in terms of spring constants, is multiplied by the stiffness matrix using the rules of matrix multiplication, giving

$$\begin{bmatrix} \dfrac{1}{k_1} & \dfrac{1}{k_1} \\[2ex] \dfrac{1}{k_1} & \dfrac{1}{k_1} + \dfrac{1}{k_2} \end{bmatrix} \begin{bmatrix} k_1 + k_2 & -k_2 \\ -k_2 & k_2 \end{bmatrix} = \begin{bmatrix} 1 & 0 \\ 0 & 1 \end{bmatrix}$$

This shows that a product of a flexibility matrix by a stiffness matrix leads to an *identity* matrix. All diagonal elements of this *unit* matrix are unity, and all others are zero.

This result means that a flexibility matrix is an *inverse* of a stiffness matrix or vice versa. For these symmetric matrices, this can be symbolically written as

$$[\mathbf{f}] = [\mathbf{k}]^{-1} \quad \text{or} \quad [\mathbf{k}] = [\mathbf{f}]^{-1} \tag{19-21}$$

For problems with single degrees of static and kinematic indeterminacy, these expressions degenerate into simple reciprocals of these quantities.

Example 19-8

Using the displacement method, calculate the rotations at b and c for the continuous beam of constant EI loaded as shown in Fig. 19-15(a), and determine the moments at a and b.

SOLUTION

At supports b and c, the beam is free to rotate, making the system kinematically indeterminate to the second degree. By temporarily restraining these supports against rotations, a system of two fixed-end beams is obtained, Fig. 19-15(b). The fixed-end actions for these beams can be obtained with the aid of Table 11 in the Appendix. In the following, the first letter of the subscript outside the brackets identifying a beam designates the end where the fixed-end action applies.

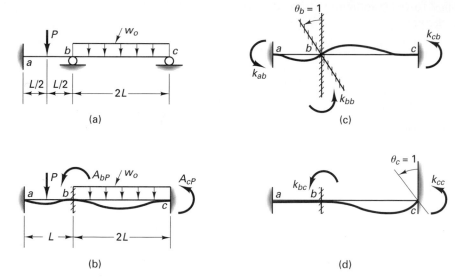

Fig. 19-15

For beam ab:

$$[A_{aP}]_{ab} = + PL/8 \quad \text{and} \quad [A_{bP}]_{ba} = - PL/8$$

For beam bc:

$$[A_{bP}]_{bc} = + w_o(2L)^2/12 = + w_oL^2/3 \quad \text{and} \quad [A_{cP}]_{cb} = - w_oL^2/3$$

For joint b:

$$A_{bP} = [A_{bP}]_{ba} + [A_{bP}]_{bc} = - PL/8 + w_oL^2/3$$

The *stiffness coefficients* can be calculated by subjecting the temporarily fixed ends b and c to unit rotations *one at a time*, Figs. 19-15(c) and (d). Again, using formulas in Table 11 of the Appendix and noting that the two adjoining spans contribute to the stiffness of the joint at b, one has

$$k_{bb} = \left[\frac{4EI}{L} \right]_{ba} + \left[\frac{4EI}{2L} \right]_{bc} = \frac{6EI}{L} \qquad k_{bc} = \left[\frac{2EI}{2L} \right]_{bc} = \frac{EI}{L}$$

$$k_{cb} = \left[\frac{2EI}{2L} \right]_{cb} = \frac{EI}{L} \qquad\qquad k_{cc} = \left[\frac{4EI}{2L} \right]_{cc} = \frac{2EI}{L}$$

Similarly, for the member ab, due to a unit rotation at b,

$$k_{ba} = \left[\frac{4EI}{L} \right]_{ba} = \frac{4EI}{L} \quad \text{and} \quad k_{ab} = \left[\frac{2EI}{L} \right]_{ab} = \frac{2EI}{L}$$

Since there are no externally applied forces (moments) at b and c, for equilibrium at these joints, Eqs. 19-15 become

$$P_b = \frac{6EI}{L}\Delta_b + \frac{EI}{L}\Delta_c - \frac{PL}{8} + \frac{w_o L^2}{3} = 0$$

$$P_c = \frac{EI}{L}\Delta_b + \frac{2EI}{L}\Delta_c - \frac{w_o L^2}{3} = 0$$

By solving these two equations simultaneously,

$$\Delta_b \equiv \theta_b = \frac{L^2}{11EI}\left(\frac{P}{4} - w_o L\right) \quad \text{and} \quad \Delta_c \equiv \theta_c = \frac{L^2}{11EI}\left(-\frac{P}{8} + \frac{7}{3}w_o L\right)$$

By substituting these displacement values into the member superposition equations, the end moments in all members are found:

$$M_{ab} = [A_{aP}]_{ab} + k_{ab}\theta_b = \frac{15}{88}PL - \frac{2}{11}w_o L^2$$

$$M_{ba} = [A_{bP}]_{ba} + k_{ba}\theta_b = -\frac{3}{88}PL - \frac{4}{11}w_o L^2$$

$$M_{bc} = [A_{bP}]_{bc} + k_{bc}\theta_b + k_{cb}\theta_c = +\frac{3}{88}PL + \frac{4}{11}w_o L^2$$

$$M_{cb} = [A_{cP}]_{cb} + k_{cb}\theta_b + k_{cc}\theta_c = 0$$

Note that with the analyst's beam sign convention employed in this solution, $M_{ba} + M_{bc} = 0$, since they are of opposite sign.

Example 19-9

Rework Example 19-4 using the displacement method of analysis; see Fig. 19-16(a).

SOLUTION

In this problem, since nodal point e can move horizontally and vertically, the system has two degrees of freedom. As noted in Example 19-4, this system is also statically indeterminate to the second degree. Each additional bar emanating from e would increase the statical indeterminacy by one; however, the kinematic degree of indeterminacy would remain at two.

The horizontal and vertical positive displacements, Δ_1 and Δ_2, shown in Figs. 19-16(b) and (c), respectively, are the unknowns. For displacement Δ_1, if end e of bar ie is *constrained* to move only horizontally, as in the upper diagram of Fig. 19-16(d), the bar elongates by $\Delta_1 \sin \alpha_i$. This would develop a bar axial force $P_1^i = k^i \Delta_1 \sin \alpha_i$, where the bar spring constant $k^i = A_i E_i / L_i$.

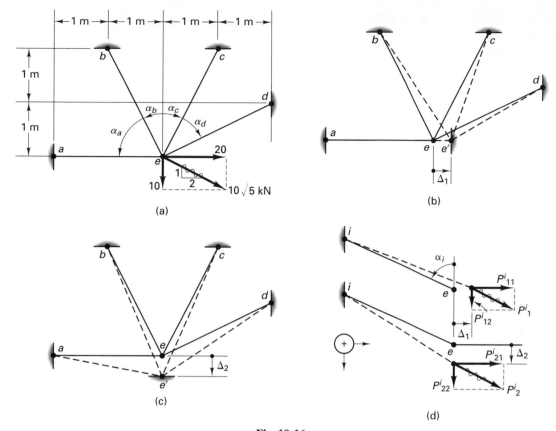

Fig. 19-16

This bar force, P_1^i, can be resolved, respectively, into horizontal and vertical components $P_{11}^i = P_1^i \sin \alpha_i$ and $P_{12}^i = P_1^i \cos \alpha_i$. Therefore,

$$P_{11}^i = \left(\frac{A_i E_i}{L_i} \sin^2 \alpha_i \right) \Delta_1 = k_{11}^i \Delta_1$$

$$P_{12}^i = \left(\frac{A_i E_i}{L_i} \sin \alpha_i \cos \alpha_i \right) \Delta_1 = k_{12}^i \Delta_1$$

(19-22a)

where k_{11}^i and k_{12}^i are bar stiffnesses for a horizontal displacement Δ_1.

By the same reasoning, if end e of bar ie is *constrained* to move Δ_2 in the vertical direction only, as shown in the lower diagram of Fig. 19-16(d), the respective horizontal and vertical force components for the bar are

$$P_{22}^i = \left(\frac{A_i E_i}{L_i} \cos^2 \alpha_i \right) \Delta_2 = k_{22}^i \Delta_2$$

$$P_{21}^i = \left(\frac{A_i E_i}{L_i} \cos \alpha_i \sin \alpha_i \right) \Delta_2 = k_{21}^i \Delta_2$$

(19-22b)

where k_{21}^i and k_{22}^i are bar vertical and horizontal stiffnesses, respectively, for vertical displacement Δ_2.

To solve this problem, these equations must be applied to each of the four bars and summed to obtain the horizontal and vertical stiffnesses of the system. This is carried out in the following table:

Bar	α_i, degrees	$\sin \alpha_i$	$\cos \alpha_i$	$\sin^2 \alpha_i$	$\cos^2 \alpha_i$	$\sin \alpha_i \cos \alpha_i$
ae	90.	1.	0.	1.	0.	0.
be	26.565	0.4472	0.8944	0.200	0.800	0.400
ce	−26.565	−0.4472	0.8944	0.200	0.800	−0.400
de	−63.435	−0.8944	0.4472	0.800	0.200	−0.400
			Sum:	2.200	1.800	−0.400

The relative bar stiffness $A_i E_i / L_i$ for each bar is unity. Therefore, from the table, the system's horizontal stiffness $k_{11} = \Sigma k_{11}^i = \Sigma \sin^2 \alpha_i = 2.2$, and, similarly, $k_{22} = \Sigma \cos^2 \alpha_i = 1.8$ and $k_{12} = k_{21} = \Sigma \sin \alpha_i \cos \alpha_i = -0.4$.

Writing these results in matrix form,

$$\begin{bmatrix} k_{11} & k_{12} \\ k_{21} & k_{22} \end{bmatrix} \begin{Bmatrix} \Delta_1 \\ \Delta_2 \end{Bmatrix} = \begin{Bmatrix} P_1 \\ P_2 \end{Bmatrix} \quad \text{or} \quad \begin{bmatrix} 2.2 & -0.4 \\ -0.4 & 1.8 \end{bmatrix} \begin{Bmatrix} \Delta_1 \\ \Delta_2 \end{Bmatrix} = \begin{Bmatrix} 20 \\ 10 \end{Bmatrix}$$

The solution for this matrix equation gives $\Delta_1 = 10.536$ and $\Delta_2 = 7.895$. Therefore, again, since for each bar $A_i E_i / L_i = 1$,

$$F_i = \Delta_1 \sin \alpha_i + \Delta_2 \sin \alpha_2$$

Using this equation, $F_{ae} = +10.53$ kN, $F_{be} = +11.77$ kN, $F_{ce} = +2.35$ kN, and $F_{de} = -5.88$ kN. These results agree with those found in Example 19-4 by the force method.

In contrast to the force method, application of the displacement method to a similar problem with more bars is only slightly more complex.

PROBLEMS

Sections 19-3 and 19-4

19-1. Show that for a linearly elastic simply supported beam, the angle of rotation θ_{ji} of the elastic curve at j due to a couple acting at i (see the figure) is equal to the angle of rotation θ_{ij} at i due to the same couple at j. (*Hint:* Use the results in Example 19-1, and determine θ_{ij} by the moment area or singularity functions.)

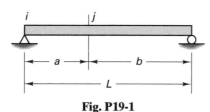

Fig. P19-1

19-2. For the planar elastic structure shown in the figure, (a) determine the reactions, and (b) draw the final moment diagram. Both members have the same constant *EI*. (*Hint:* Use the virtual force method for finding deflections.)

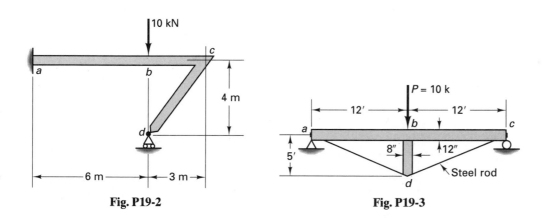

Fig. P19-2   **Fig. P19-3**

19-3. A 10×12-in (actual size) rectangular wooden beam is braced by a 1-in round steel rod and an 8×8-in (actual size) wooden post, as shown in the figure. Determine the force that would develop in the post by applying a concentrated force $P = 10$ k at the center of the span. For wood, $E_w = 1500$ ksi and for steel, $E_{st} = 30 \times 10^3$ ksi. For purposes of calculation, consider post *bd* to be 5 ft long.

19-4. Using the force method, rework Example 19-3. Consider the reactions at b and c as redundants. (*Hint:* Use the solution given in Problem 14-51.)

19-5.   For a planar structure consisting of rod *ab* and frame *bcde*, as shown in the figure, (a) determine the reactions, and (b) plot the bending-moment diagram for the frame. All members are of the same material. *EI* for the frame is constant and *AE* for the rod is *IE*/5. Assume the force in the bar as redundant. Work in k-ft units.

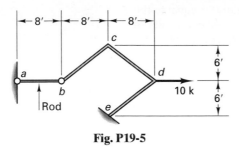

Fig. P19-5

19-6.   Assuming elastic behavior and using the force method, rework Problem 4-23.

19-7.   Using the force method, rework Problem 17-54. Consider the forces in *AB* and *AD* as redundants.

19-8.   For the planar system of six elastic bars shown in the figure, determine the forces in the vertical bars due to applied force $P = 30$ kN. The bars are pinned at the ends. The cross-sectional area A of each bar is 100 mm² and $E = 200$ GPa. (*Hint:* Take advantage of symmetry and use Eq. 4-5.)

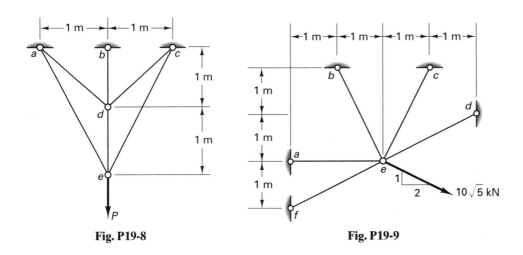

Fig. P19-8   **Fig. P19-9**

19-9.   The planar pin-ended bar system of Example 19-4 is augmented by adding member *fe*, as shown in the figure. (a) Assuming members *ae, ce,* and *fe* as redundants, determine the numerical values for a 3 × 3 square matrix of the flexibility coefficients and set up the corresponding column vectors as in Eq. 19-6. (b) If assigned, find the forces in all bar members.

19-10.   Rework Example 19-4 after assuming that $L/AE = 1$ for members *ae* and *be*, and $L/AE = 2$ for members *ce* and *de*.

19-11.   For the planar structure shown in the figure, determine the reactions at the support, and, if assigned, plot the moment diagram. Neglect axial and shear deformations, and assume *EI* for the members is constant. (*Hint:* Use the virtual force method for finding deflections.)

19-12.   A nominal 4-in-diameter steel pipe weighing 10.79 lb per foot is bent into the form of one-quarter of a circle to a radius of $R = 100$ in and is connected to two pressure vessels, as shown in the figure. In operation this pipe can rise 500°F above its surroundings. For the material of the pipe, $E = 29 \times 10^6$ psi, and $\alpha = 6.5 \times 10^{-6}$ per °F. (a) Assuming that the pipe supports at *A* and *B* provide completely fixed conditions, set up superposition equations for the solution of this problem. Results found in Example 17-4, Fig. 17-10, are useful for this purpose. Derive additional flexibility coefficients using an energy method. Consider only flexural effects in establishing these quantities. (b) Solve the preceding equations simultaneously, and plot the bending-moment diagram for the pipe caused by the change in temperature.

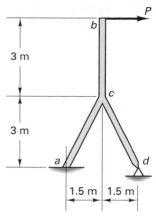

Fig. P19-11

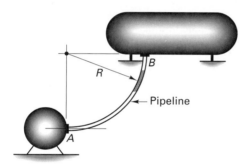

Fig. P19-12

Sections 19-5 and 19-6

19-13.   Rework Example 19-8 assuming that end *c* is fixed.

19-14.   Using the displacement method, determine the rotation of the elastic curve at *b* and the moments at *a*, *b*, and *c* for the continuous beam shown in the figure. *EI* is constant.

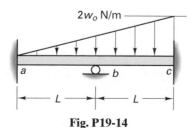

Fig. P19-14

19-15.   Rework Problem 19-14 assuming that end c is simply supported.

19-16.   Determine the deflection and rotation at the end of the cantilever shown in the figure due to applied force P. Use the displacement method. (*Hint:* Both equations of equilibrium pertain to end b; one requires that $M_b = 0$ and the other that $R_b = -P$.)

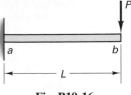

Fig. P19-16

19-17.   Let the following conditions apply for the continuous beam ac shown in Fig. 19-13(a): (a) Both spans are of equal length L, (b) span ab is loaded with a uniformly distributed downward load w_o, (c) span bc is loaded with a concentrated downward force P in the middle of the span, and (d) EI is constant. The boundary conditions remain as shown. Determine the rotation at b and the vertical displacement at c due to the applied loads. Calculate the moments at a, b, and c.

19-18.   A propped cantilever of constant EI is loaded with a concentrated force $P = 100$ N, as shown in the figure. (a) Using the force method, determine the reaction at b. Then calculate the rotation of the elastic curve at b and c and the deflection at c. (*Hint:* For rotations and deflection, use the moment-area method.) (b) Using the displacement method, determine the rotations at b and c, and the deflection at c. Then calculate the moments at a and b, and the reaction at b. (*Hint:* The three external forces applied at b and c are $M_b = 0$, $M_c = 0$, and $R_c = -100$ N.)

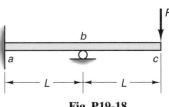

Fig. P19-18

19-19.   Rework Example 19-9 assuming that $L/AE = 1$ for members ae and be and $L/AE = 2$ for members ce and de.

19-20.   Using the displacement method, find the bar forces for the pin-ended bar system given in Problem 19-9.

20

Plastic Limit
Analysis

20-1. Introduction

In 1638 Galileo Galilei described[1] his experiment with a wooden cantilever beam built into a wall, as shown in Fig. 20-1. He assumed that the strained beam tension fibers were inextensible, leading to the conclusion of uniform stress distribution across the beam section.[2] A host of distinguished scientists, such as Mariotte, Newton, Euler, and Musschenbrock, tried to clarify the problem with particular reference to the elasticity of material. At the basic level, a French educator, Navier (1785–1836), following Mariotte's stress-strain experiments (1620–1684), resolved the problem correctly for elastic materials. Henceforth, the kinematic hypothesis that plane sections remain plane during bending became the working hypothesis in the analysis of beams and columns (see Sections 8-2 and 9-4). Simultaneously with this hypothesis the idea of linearly elastic material behavior became firmly

[1]Galileo Galilei, *Discorsi e demonstazioni matematiche,* 1638; see the English translation, *Two New Sciences,* by H. Crew and A. de Silvio (New York: Macmillan, 1933).

[2]S. P. Timoshenko, *History of Strength of Materials* (New York: McGraw-Hill, 1953), 12.

Fig. 20-1   Galileo's experiment with a wooden beam, circa 1638 (courtesy of Dover Publications, from *A History of the Theory of Elasticity and the Strength of Materials,* I. Todhunter and K. Pearson, 1960).

entrenched in engineering practice. Virtually all codes are based on these concepts. Moreover, important strides in the mathematical theory of elasticity and computer technology made adherence to the linear elastic concepts attractive.

It is entirely correct to employ linear elastic theory in many instances. For this approach, machine design for cyclic fatigue loadings is an excellent field of applications. However, for quasi-static loadings or for catastrophic overloads, as well as for missiles, better approximations of material behavior are necessary. Throughout this text an attempt was made to draw the reader's attention to the possible different levels of approximations of stress-strain relations (see Sections 2-8, 4-6, 6-13, and 10-5). Finally, a simplified approach on ideal plastic behavior is beginning to emerge as a working tool for some applications.

First developed in Europe[3] and advocated in the early 1960s by T. R. Higgins[4] in the United States,[5] this approach is now actively pursued throughout the world. The need to modify seismic design along these lines

[3]G. Kazinczy, "Experiments with clamped girders," *Betonszembe,* **2,** nos. 4, 5, and 6 (1914) (in Hungarian); H. Maier-Lebnitz, "Contributions to the problems of ultimate carrying capacity of structural steel," *Die Bautechnik,* **1,** no. 6 (in German); A. A. Gvozdev, *Analysis of Carrying Capacity of Structures by Limite Equilibrium Method* (Moscow: Stroiizdat, 1949) (in Russian).

[4]AISC private communication (1953).

[5]P. G. Hodge, Jr., *Plastic Analysis of Structures* (New York: McGraw-Hill, 1959).

was brought out by the unsatisfactory behavior of buildings after the recent strong earthquakes in California (Loma Prieta in 1989 and Northridge in 1994), as well as in Japan (Hyogoken-Nabu [Kobe] in 1995). These events clearly showed that extrapolations of the elastic solutions into the inelastic range of structural behavior are unrealistic. A far better approximation of the actual behavior of a structure near collapse can be obtained by assuming plastic behavior of members and joints. Plastic limit analysis for ductile materials can provide a good indication as to where the members or joints are excessively stressed. These analyses, novel to designers, are often referred to as push-over analyses. An approach to obtaining such solutions is the purpose of this chapter.

20-2. Plastic Limit Analysis of Beams[6]

Procedures for determining ultimate load for axially loaded bar systems of elastic, ideally plastic material are given in Examples 4-7 and 4-12. These ultimate loads are the plastic limit states. In the process of obtaining the loads, the entire range of elastic-plastic system behavior under an increasing load is considered. As can be seen from Fig. 4-13 or Fig. 4-18, there are three distinct regions of response. At first, these systems respond in a linear manner. Then a part of the structural system yields as the remainder continues to deform elastically. This is the range of contained plastic flow. Finally, a structure continues to yield at no further increase in applied load. At this stage of behavior of ideally plastic structures, the deformations become unbounded. This condition is the plastic limit state. In this analytical idealization, the effects of strain hardening and changes in structure geometry are neglected.

As is shown in the previous examples, a direct calculation of the plastic limit state for ideally plastic materials is both possible and rather simple. From the practical point of view, such calculations provide an insight into the collapse mode of ductile structures. However, such direct solutions for plastic limit load do not provide complete information on inelastic behavior. If at a service or working load some prior yielding had occurred, the deflections and distribution of forces remain unknown. Only step-by-step computer solutions, or solutions for simple cases, as in Examples 4-7 and 4-12, can provide a complete history of force and deflection distributions.

The same general behavior is exhibited by elastic, ideally plastic beams and frames, and here the objective is to develop simplified procedures for determining directly the plastic limit states for such members. By bypassing the elastic and the elastic-plastic stages of loading and determining the plastic limit loads, the procedure becomes relatively simple. Some previously established results are reexamined for background.

---

[6]For further details, see J. Lubliner, *Plasticity Theory* (New York: Macmillan, 1990).

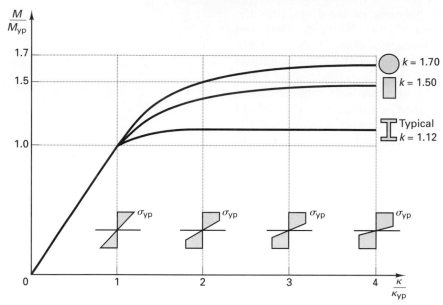

Fig. 20-2   Moment-curvature relations for circular, rectangular, and I cross sections. $M_p/M_{yp} = k$, the shape factor.

Typical moment-curvature relationships, normalized with respect to M_{yp}, for elastic, perfectly plastic beams are shown in Fig. 20-2 for three different cross sections. Basic results for a rectangular beam were established in Example 14-14 (see Fig. 14-25). Results for the other two cases can be found using the same procedure. Curves normalized with respect to M_p are shown in Fig. 20-3. The behavior of an idealized cross section with large flanges and a negligibly thin web is added in this diagram.

In both diagrams, as the cross sections plastify, a rapid ascent of the curves toward their respective asymptotes occurs. This means that shortly after reaching the elastic capacity of a beam, a rather constant moment, very near to M_p, is both achieved and maintained. This is particularly true for the important case of an I beam. As can be noted from Fig. 20-3, for this cross section the elastic-plastic behavior is essentially confined to the range between B' and C; for the remainder, the moment is essentially M_p. The influence of the elastic core next to the beam neutral axis is more pronounced for members with rectangular or round cross sections, whose shape factors, k, are larger than those for an I beam, Fig. 20-2. Nevertheless, in the plastic limit analysis of members subjected to bending, it is generally assumed that *an abrupt transition from elastic to ideally plastic behavior occurs at M_p.* Therefore, member behavior between M_{yp} and M_p is considered to be elastic. It is further assumed that when M_p is reached, a *plastic hinge* is formed in the member. In contrast to a frictionless hinge permitting free rotation, it is postulated that the plastic hinge allows large rotations to occur at a *constant plastic moment M_p.*

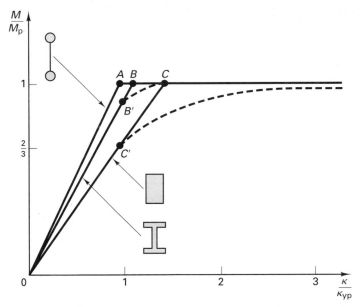

Fig. 20-3   Moment-curvature idealizations for plastic analyses of beams of different cross sections.

In a plastic limit analysis of beams, the elastic displacements in relation to the plastic ones are small and can be neglected. Detailed analyses have shown[7] that it is sufficiently accurate to consider beams rigid-plastic, with plasticity confined to plastic hinges at *points*. In reality, plastic hinges extend along short lengths of beams and depend on loading conditions.

The approximate theory discussed here is applicable to beams as well as columns subjected to moderate axial forces. When a cross section lacks biaxial symmetry, the positive and negative moments differ in their magnitudes and should be accounted for in the analysis. A method for determining the reduced plastic capacity of members in the presence of axial forces is discussed in Section 9-4.

By inserting a plastic hinge at a plastic limit load into a statically determinate beam, a kinematic mechanism permitting an unbounded displacement of the system can be formed. This is commonly referred to as the *collapse mechanism*.[8] For each degree of static indeterminacy of a beam, an additional plastic hinge must be added to form a collapse mechanism. The insertion of plastic hinges must be such as to obtain a kinematically *admissible* (plausible) collapse mechanism. The use of kinematically admissible collapse mechanisms is illustrated in the examples to follow.

[7]See, for example, L. S. Beedle, *Plastic Design of Steel Frames* (New York: Wiley, 1966) or S. J. Moy, *Plastic Methods for Steel and Concrete Structures* (New York: Wiley, 1981).

[8]In seismic analyses, the plastic hinges dissipate energy. Therefore, it is preferable to call such mechanisms *energy-dissipating mechanisms*.

In plastic limit design, it is necessary to multiply working loads by a load factor larger than unity to obtain design *factored loads*. This is analogous to the use of a factor of safety in elastic analyses. This issue is discussed in Section 1-11.

There are two common methods of plastic limit analysis. One is based on conventional statics and the other on virtual work. In either method the bending moments anywhere along a member cannot exceed the plastic moment M_p, and the conditions of equilibrium must always be satisfied. The procedure for forming kinematically admissible mechanisms, somewhat similar to continuity conditions in elastic analysis, is illustrated in the following examples.

Example 20-1

A concentrated force P is applied at the middle of a simply supported prismatic beam, as shown in Fig. 20-4(a). If the beam is of a ductile material, what is the plastic limit load P_{ult}? Obtain the solution using (a) the

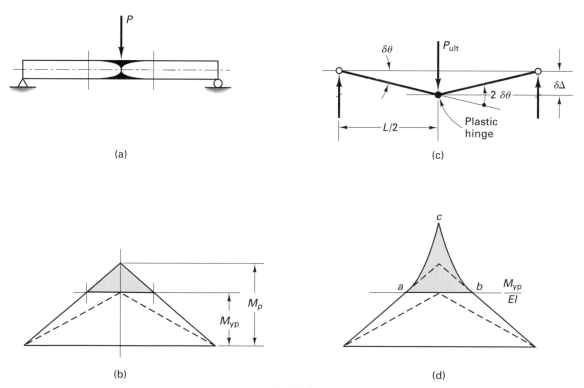

(a)

(c)

(b)

(d)

Fig. 20-4

equilibrium method and (b) the virtual work method. Consider only flexural behavior (i.e., neglect the effect of shear forces). Neglect beam weight.

SOLUTION
(a) The shape of the moment diagram is the same regardless of the load magnitude. For any value of P, the maximum moment $M = PL/4$, and if $M \le M_{yp}$, the beam behaves elastically. When the moment is at M_{yp}, the force at yield

$$P_{yp} = 4M_{yp}/L$$

When M_{yp} is exceeded, contained yielding of the beam commences and continues until the plastic moment M_p is reached, Fig. 20-4(b).

The curvature diagram prior to reaching M_p at the middle of the beam resembles that shown in Fig. 20-4(d). Since the elastic curvature can at most be M_{yp}/EI, it is exceeded as shown above line ab. At M_p, the fully plastic part of the beam near the middle is shown in black in Fig. 20-4(a). This region is considerably narrower for I beams than for the rectangular cross section implied in this figure because most of the bending moment is carried in the flanges. The curvature at the middle of the beam becomes very large as it rapidly approaches M_p and continues to grow without bound (see Fig. 20-3). By setting the plastic moment M_p equal to $PL/4$ with $P = P_{ult}$, one obtains the result sought:

$$P_{ult} = 4M_p/L$$

Note that consideration of the actual plastic region indicated in Fig. 20-4(a) is unnecessary in this calculation. A comparison of this result with $P_{yp} = 4\,M_{yp}/L$ shows that

$$P_{ult} = \frac{M_p}{M_{yp}} P_{yp} = kP_{yp}$$

where the difference between the two forces depends only on the shape factor k.

(b) An admissible virtual kinematic mechanism assuming a rigid-plastic beam is shown in Fig. 20-4(c). The external virtual work is $P_{ult}\,\delta\Delta$, where from geometry $\delta\Delta = L\,\delta\theta/2$. The internal virtual work is caused by rotating M_p through an angle of $2\,\delta\theta$. Hence, per Eq. 17-19, equating the expressions for work,

$$P_{ult}\,\delta\Delta = P_{ult}L\,\delta\theta/2 = M_p(2\,\delta\theta)$$

On solving the last two expressions for P_{ult}, as before,

$$P_{ult} = 4M_p/L$$

Example 20-2

A prismatic beam of ductile material, fixed at one end and simply supported at the other, carries a concentrated force in the middle, as shown in Fig. 20-5(a). Determine the plastic limit load P_{ult} using (a) the equilibrium method and (b) the virtual displacement method. Compare the result with that of an elastic solution. Neglect beam weight.

SOLUTION

(a) The results of an elastic analysis are shown in Fig. 20-5(b). The same results are replotted in Fig. 20-5(c) from horizontal base line AB. In both diagrams, the shaded portions of the diagrams represent the net result. Note that the auxiliary ordinates $PL/4$ have precisely the value of the maximum moment in a simple beam with concentrated force in the middle.

By setting the maximum elastic moment equal to M_{yp}, one obtains force P_{yp} at impending yield

$$P_{yp} = \frac{16M_{yp}}{3L}$$

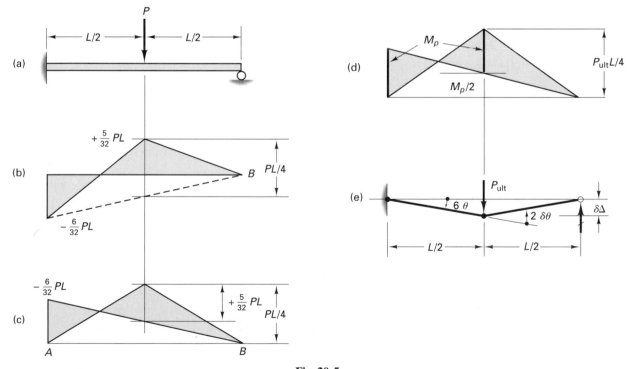

Fig. 20-5

When the load is increased above P_{yp}, the moment at the built-in end increases and can reach but cannot exceed M_p. This is also true of the moment at the middle of the span. These limiting conditions are shown in Fig. 20-5(d). At the plastic limit load, it is necessary to have a kinematically admissible mechanism. With the two plastic hinges and a roller on the right, this condition is satisfied, Fig. 20-5(e).

From the geometric construction in Fig. 20-5(d), in the middle of the span, $M_p + M_p/2 = P_{ult}L/4$. Hence,

$$P_{ult} = 6M_p/L$$

Comparing this result with P_{yp}, one has

$$P_{ult} = \frac{9M_p}{8M_{yp}} P_{yp} = \frac{9}{8} k P_{yp}$$

The increase in P_{ult} over P_{yp} is due to two causes: the shape factor k and the *equilization of the maximum moments.* [Compare the moment diagrams in Figs. 20-5(c) and (d).]

(b) For the virtual displacement shown in Fig. 20-5(e), the external virtual work at the plastic limit load is $P_{ult}\ \delta\Delta$. The internal virtual work takes place in the plastic hinges at the left support and in the middle of the span. Equating these expressions of work per Eq. 17-19,

$$P_{ult}\ \delta\Delta = P_{ult}L\ \delta\theta/2 = M_p\ \delta\theta + M_p(2\ \delta\theta)$$

giving, as before,

$$P_{ult} = 6M_p/L$$

Example 20-3

A prismatic beam of ductile material is loaded as shown in Fig. 20-6(a). Using the virtual displacement method, determine the plastic limit loads. Neglect the weight of the beam.

SOLUTION

In this case, several kinematic displacement mechanisms are possible, and the solution is found by a trial-and-error process. The correct mechanism is one where the assumed virtual displacement generates a compatible moment diagram.

An admissible mechanism is shown in Fig. 20-6(b). By equating the external and the internal virtual work per Eq. 17-19 and identifying the plastic limit loads for this case as P_1 and $2P_1$, one has

$$(2P_1)(L\ \delta\theta/4) = M_p\ \delta\theta + M_p 2\ \delta\theta + M_p\ \delta\theta$$

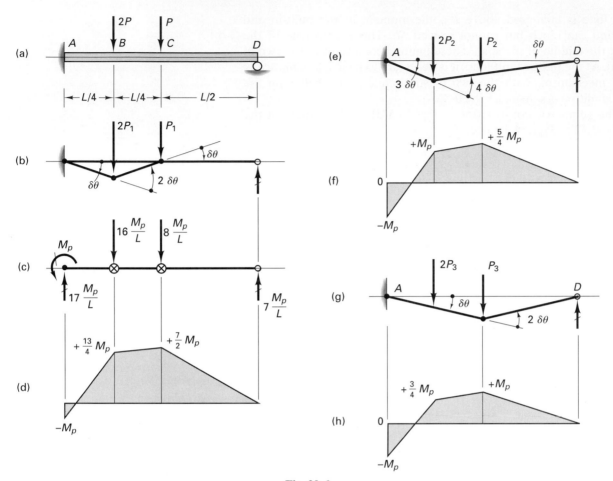

Fig. 20-6

where the three terms on the right apply, respectively, to the plastic hinges at A, B, and C. The solution of this equation gives

$$P_1 = 8M_p/L \qquad \text{and} \qquad 2P_1 = 16M_p/L$$

By applying the forces to the beam and assuming hinges B and C rigid, Fig. 20-6(c), the resulting bending moment diagram is as shown in Fig. 20-6(d). This diagram shows that with P_1 and $2P_1$, the moments at B and C are greater than M_p. This is an *upper bound* solution asserts that a load found on the basis of an assumed admissible kinematic mechanism is always greater than or, at best, equal to the plastic limit load.[9]

---

[9]For proof, see any of the cited references on plastic analysis, and H. J. Greenberg and W. Prager, "Limit design of beams and frames," *Trans. ASCE,* **117** (1952), 447–458.

By reducing P_1 and $2P_1$ by a ratio of $2/7$, the conditions for the plastic moment capacity of the member and that of equilibrium *are satisfied*. Since such a solution occurs prior to the full development of a kinematic mechanism, it gives the *lower bound*[10] for the applied loads.

Based on this reasoning, the results obtained with the assumed mechanism have the following lower and upper bounds:

$$\frac{2}{7} \times 8 \frac{M_p}{L} = \frac{16}{7} \frac{M_p}{L} < P_1 < 8 \frac{M_p}{L}$$

A similar relation applies for $2P_i$. These bounds are rather far apart, and alternative mechanisms, shown in Figs. 20-6(e) and (g), are tried.

By following the earlier procedure, the results for the mechanism in Fig. 20-6(e) give $P_2 = 3.5 M_p/L$ and $2P_2 = 7M_p/L$. The moment diagram corresponding to these forces is shown in Fig. 20-6(f). These results establish better bounds for the solution, which are

$$\frac{4}{5} \times 3.5 \frac{M_p}{L} = 2.8 \frac{M_p}{L} < P_2 < 3.5 \frac{M_p}{L}$$

By carrying out a solution for the mechanism in Fig. 20-6(g), it can be shown that $P_3 = 3M_p/L$ and $2P_3 = 6M_p/L$. The moment diagram for these forces in Fig. 20-6(h) confirms the correct choice of the mechanism, since the moments at A and C are each equal to M_p. Therefore, the solution is "exact."

The mechanism in Fig. 20-6(b) is not a good choice for this problem. However, even this solution, as can be seen from Fig. 20-6(c), indicates that the plastic hinges within the span should be at C. By taking advantage of such observations, the exact result could have been obtained more quickly.

This problem can be easily solved by the equilibrium method. For such a solution, assuming the beam simply supported, the moment diagram is prepared first. Then an inclined line, as shown in Fig. 20-5(d) is drawn such that equal moments M_p develop at A and C.

Example 20-4

A prismatic beam of ductile material, fixed at one end and simply supported at the other, carries a uniformly distributed load, as shown in Fig. 20-7(a). Find the plastic limit load w_{ult} using (a) the equilibrium method and (b) the virtual force method.

[10]Proof and formal statement of the lower bound theorem can be found in the previously cited references.

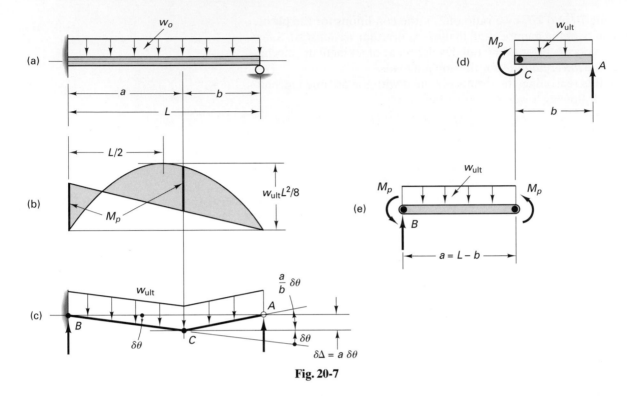

Fig. 20-7

SOLUTION

(a) In this problem, two plastic hinges are required to create a collapse mechanism. One of these hinges is at the built-in end. The location of the hinge associated with the maximum positive moment is not known, since the moment varies gradually and there is no distinct peak. However, one can assume an admissible mechanism, such as that shown in Fig. 20-7(c), which is compatible with the moment diagram of Fig. 20-7(b).

For purposes of analysis, the beam with the assumed plastic hinges is separated into two parts, as shown in Figs. 20-7(d) and (e). Then, by noting that no shear is possible at C, since it is the point of maximum moment for a continuous function, one can write two equations of static equilibrium:

$$\sum M_A = 0 \curvearrowright + \qquad M_p - w_{ult}b^2/2 = 0$$

$$\sum M_B = 0 \curvearrowleft + \qquad 2M_p - w_{ult}(L - b)^2/2 = 0$$

Simultaneous solution of these equations locates the plastic hinge C at $b = (\sqrt{2} - 1)L$. Either one of these equations yields the limit load

$$w_{ult} = \frac{2M_p}{b^2} = \frac{2M_p}{[(\sqrt{2} - 1)L]^2}$$

(b) On the *average,* the uniformly distributed plastic limit load w_{ult} goes through a virtual displacement of $\delta\Delta/2$, Fig. 20-7(c). Hence, for use in Eq. 17-19,

$$\delta W_e = w_{ult} L \frac{\delta\Delta}{2} = w_{ult} L \frac{a\,\delta\theta}{2}$$

The internal virtual work is done by plastic moments M_p at plastic hinges B and C, going through their respective rotations, Fig. 20-7(c). Hence,

$$\delta W_{ie} = M_p \delta\theta + M_p \left(1 + \frac{a}{b}\right)\delta\theta$$

By equating the previous two relations and solving for w_{ult}, after some simplifications,

$$w_{ult} = \frac{2M_p}{L}\left(\frac{2L - a}{La - a^2}\right)$$

The unknown distance a can be found by taking a derivative of w_{ult} with respect to a and setting it equal to zero. Thus,

$$\frac{dw_{ult}}{da} = 0$$

After carrying out the differentiation and simplifications,

$$-a^2 + 4aL - 2L^2 = 0$$

By solving this quadratic equation and retaining the root falling within the span,

$$a = (2 - \sqrt{2})L \quad\text{and}\quad b = L - a = (\sqrt{2} - 1)L$$

as before. Hence, w_{ult} found previously applies to this solution as well.

The virtual work solutions for distributed loads, such as those just shown, are somewhat complex for routine applications. Two alternative procedures, however, are possible. In one, the distributed load can be approximated by a series of concentrated forces, where possible plastic hinge locations are more easily identified. Alternatively, the location of a plastic hinge can be estimated, leading to a simple solution. The accuracy of such a solution can be judged by calculating the upper and the lower bounds, as has been illustrated in Example 12-3.

Example 20-5

Rework the previous example by assuming that a plastic hinge for a positive bending moment occurs in the middle of the span; see Fig. 20-8. Determine the bounds on this approximate solution.

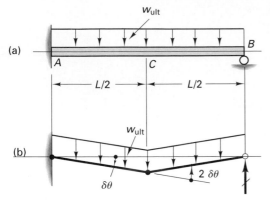

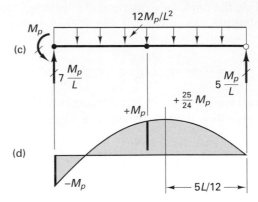

Fig. 20-8

SOLUTION

By applying Eq. 17-19 (i.e., equating the external and internal virtual work),

$$w_{ult}L\left(\frac{L\,\delta\theta}{2}\,\frac{1}{2}\right) = M_p(\delta\theta + 2\,\delta\theta)$$

where $L\,\delta\theta/2$ is the maximum deflection at C, and the factor of $\frac{1}{2}$ reduces this to an average deflection for the distributed load. Solution of the last equation gives an upper bound for the plastic limit load w_{ult} for the assumed mechanism, and

$$w_{ult} = 12M_p/L^2$$

By assuming the plastic hinge C rigid and applying the above load to the beam, Fig. 20-8(c), the resulting moment diagram is as shown in Fig. 20-8(d). Since, in this diagram, the maximum positive bending moment exceeds M_p, the applied load in Fig. 20-8(c) must be reduced by a factor of 24/25 to obtain the lower-bound solution. Therefore, the lower-bound solution for the plastic limit load is $(24/25)12M_p/L^2 = 11.52M_p/L^2$.

Summarizing, the bounds for this solution are

$$11.52\frac{M_p}{L^2} < w_{ult} < 12\frac{M_p}{L^2}$$

By taking the plastic hinge at the point of the maximum positive moment in Fig. 20-8(d) and repeating the calculations, nearly an exact plastic limit load is found.

Example 20-6

A prismatic uniformly loaded beam is fixed at both ends, as shown in Fig. 20-9(a). (a) Determine the plastic limit load using the equilibrium method, and compare the results with elastic analysis. (b) Verify the plastic limit load using the virtual work method.

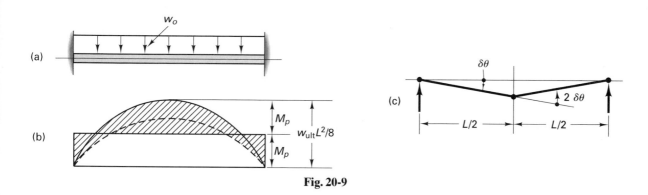

Fig. 20-9

SOLUTION

According to the analysis in Example 15-8, Fig. 15-11(c), the maximum bending moments occur at the built-in ends and are equal to $w_o L^2/12$. The maximum positive moment develops at the middle of the span and is $w_o L^2/24$. Therefore, at yield, based on the maximum moment,

$$M_{yp} = w_{yp}L^2/12 \qquad \text{or} \qquad w_{yp} = 12M_{yp}/L^2$$

By increasing the load, plastic hinges develop at the supports. The collapse mechanism is not formed, however, until a plastic hinge also develops in the middle of the span, Fig. 20-9(c).

The maximum moment for a simply supported uniformly loaded beam is $w_o L^2/8$. Therefore, as can be seen from Fig. 20-9(b), to obtain the limit load in a clamped beam, this quantity must be equated to $2M_p$, with $w_o = w_{ult}$. Hence,

$$w_{ult}L^2/8 = 2M_p \qquad \text{or} \qquad w_{ult} = 16M_p/L^2$$

Comparing this result with w_{yp}, one has

$$w_{ult} = \frac{4M_p}{3M_{yp}} w_{yp} = \frac{4}{3} k w_{yp}$$

As in Example 20-2, the increase in w_{ult} over w_{yp} depends on shape factor k and the *equlization* of the maximum moments.

(b) Because of symmetry, the precise location of the plastic hinges is as shown in Fig. 20-9(c). By writing a virtual work equation, Eq. 17-19, one has

$$w_{ult}L\left(\frac{L\,\delta\theta}{2}\,\frac{1}{2}\right) = M_p(\delta\theta + 2\,\delta\theta + \delta\theta)$$

and $w_{ult} = 16M_p/L^2$ as before.

20-3. Continuous Beams and Frames

The procedures discussed in the preceding section, and illustrated by examples, can be extended to the simpler cases for plastic limit analysis of continuous beams and frames. Usually, the kinematic mechanisms in continuous beams, associated with a collapse mode, occur locally in only one beam. For the two-span continuous beam shown in Fig. 20-10(a), the plastic moment at the middle support is limited to $(M_p)_{min}$ of the smaller beam. Then, whether the kinematic mechanism would develop in the right or the left span depends on the relative beam sizes as well as the magnitudes of the applied loads. The solution in either case follows the procedure discussed in Examples 20-2, 20-3, and 20-4.

The beams, restrained at both ends, usually develop the kinematic mechanisms shown in Fig. 20-10(d) for the two left spans in Fig. 20-10(c). The solution of such problems resembles that of Example 20-6 except that the end moments for each span are not necessarily equal. For example, for the left span of Fig. 20-10(c), the plastic moment on the left is determined by the large beam, whereas that on the right depends on the plastic moment of the center span beam.

Plastic limit analysis of frames may become rather complex as the number of members, joints, and different loading conditions increases. For analysis of such problems, the reader is referred to the previously cited texts. As a reasonably simple illustration of the plastic limit state frame analysis, an example follows.

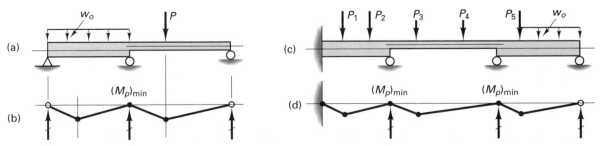

Fig. 20-10   Collapse mechanisms for continuous beams.

Example 20-7

Consider a rigid jointed planar frame of ductile material fixed at A and pinned at E, and loaded as shown in Fig. 20-11(a). All members are of the same size and can develop full M_p (i.e., the effect of the axial forces on M_p can be neglected). Determine the plastic limit loads.

SOLUTION

The solution to this problem is obtained by assuming different kinematically admissible mechanisms and searching for the one that satisfies both equilibrium and plastic member capacity.

A virtual work solution for an assumed mechanism provides an upper bound for the plastic limit loads. With these loads, a static analysis is then performed on members or parts of the frame separated at plastic hinges. Since the moment at each plastic hinge is M_p, a complete moment diagram can be

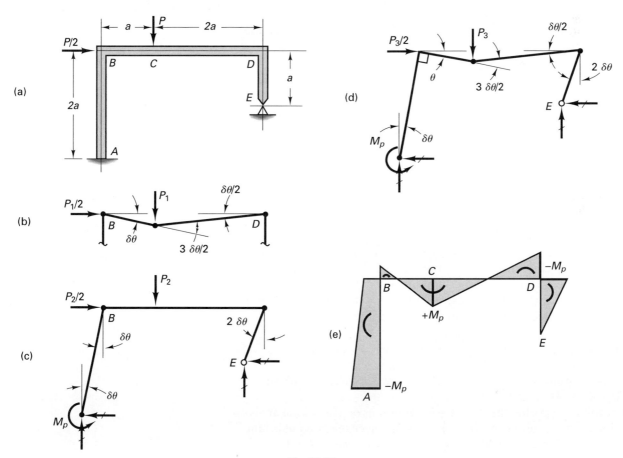

Fig. 20-11

constructed for the frame. The lower-bound solution is obtained by reducing the upper-bound loads by a factor such that nowhere is M_p exceeded.

The virtual work equation for the admissible kinematic (beam) mechanism in Fig. 20-11(b) is

$$P_1 a\, \delta\theta = M_p(\delta\theta + \delta\theta/2) \qquad \text{and} \qquad P_1 = 3M_p/2a$$

Applying P_1 and $P_2/2$ to the frame and separating it at joints B and D, where the moments are M_p, the moment diagram for the frame is found (not shown). This solution, using the designer's sign convention, as shown in Fig. 7-22(b), gives the following moments at critical points $A, B, C,$ and D:

$$M_A = -2M_p \qquad M_B = -M_p \qquad M_C = M_p \qquad \text{and} \qquad M_D = -M_p$$

Since M_A is twice as large as M_p, the upper-bound solution found before must be reduced by a factor of 2 in order to obtain the lower-bound solution. On this basis, for the assumed mechanism, the bounds for the solution are

$$\frac{3M_p}{2a} < P_1 < \frac{3M_p}{a}$$

By proceeding in the same manner using the (sway) mechanism for the frame shown in Fig. 20-11(c),

$$\frac{P_2}{2}\, 2a\, \delta\theta = M_p(\delta\theta + \delta\theta + 2\, \delta\theta) \qquad \text{and} \qquad P_2 = \frac{4M_p}{a}$$

For this upper-bound solution, the moments at the critical points are

$$M_A = -M_p \qquad M_B = M_p \qquad M_C = 3M_p \qquad \text{and} \qquad M_D = -M_p$$

Since M_C is three times greater than M_p, the upper bound solution for the assumed mechanism must be reduced by a factor of 3 to obtain the lower-bound solution. Hence, for this case,

$$\frac{4M_p}{3a} < P_2 < \frac{4M_p}{a}$$

This solution is no better than the first. However, it is possible to *combine* the previous two mechanisms, such as to eliminate the plastic hinge at B, leading to better results. For a proper combination of these mechanisms, the internal plastic work in hinges can be reduced. Such a mechanism is shown in Fig. 20-11(d). The virtual work equation for this case is

$$\frac{P_3}{2}\, 2a\, \delta\theta + P_3 a\, \delta\theta = M_p\!\left(\delta\theta + \frac{3\, \delta\theta}{2} + \frac{\delta\theta}{2} + 2\, \delta\theta\right) \quad \text{and} \quad P_3 = \frac{5M_p}{2a}$$

The moment diagram corresponding to P_3 is shown in Fig. 20-11(e), where $M_A = -M_p, M_C = M_p,$ and $M_D = -M_p$.

The last solution satisfies the three basic conditions of plastic limit analysis, consisting of the requirements of an admissible mechanism, equilibrium, and all moments being at most M_p. Therefore, this is an exact solution.

PROBLEMS

Section 20-2

20-1. Rework Example 20-3 after removing the concentrated force P at C.

20-2. A ductile prismatic beam is simply supported at one end and fixed at the other, as shown in the figure. (a) Determine the position x where the smallest concentrated force P would cause a collapse mechanism. (b) Find the ultimate moments for the critical position of applied force P.

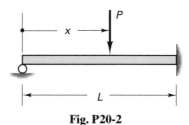

Fig. P20-2

20-3. A ductile prismatic beam is fixed at both ends. For a concentrated force P placed at the third point of the span, as shown in the figure, determine the plastic limit load P_{ult}. Demonstrate that the result satisfies both the upper- and lower-bound criteria.

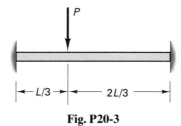

Fig. P20-3

20-4. A T beam fixed at both ends is loaded by a uniformly distributed load w including its own weight. (a) What load w_1 can this beam carry when the stress in the middle just reaches yield and plastic moment point hinges develop at the built-in ends? The yield strength of the material is 50 ksi. (b) What is the midspan deflection due to w_1? Let $E = 30 \times 10^3$ ksi. (c) What is the plastic limit load w_{ult}?

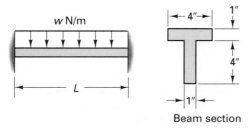

Fig. P20-4

20-5. A prismatic beam of ductile material, fixed at one end and simply supported at the other, carries a uniformly increasing load, as shown in the figure. Determine the plastic limit load W_{ult} using the virtual force method and assuming that one of the plastic hinges forms in the middle of the span. Check the result using the equilibrium method.

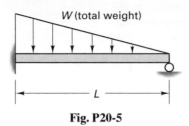

Fig. P20-5

20-6. A prismatic beam of ductile material is partially loaded, as shown in the figure. (a) Determine the upper- and lower-bound solutions by assuming a plastic hinge in the middle of the span. Let $M_p = 1000$ in-lb. (b) If assigned to by instructor, refine the solution by placing the plastic hinge at the point of maximum positive moment found for the lower-bound solution in part (a).

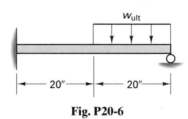

Fig. P20-6

20-7 and 20-8. Beams of variable cross sections and ductile material are loaded as shown in the figures. The plastic bending capacity of the larger left sides of the beams is $2M_p$ and that of the right sides is M_p. Determine the plastic limit loads for the two cases.

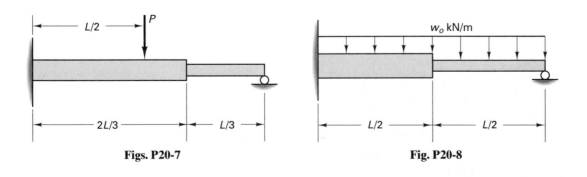

Figs. P20-7   **Fig. P20-8**

20-9 and 20-10. Rework the preceding two problems after assuming that the beams are clamped at both ends.

Section 20-3

20-11. Using limit analysis, calculate the value of P that would cause flexural collapse of the two-span beam shown. The beam has a rectangular cross section 120 mm wide and 300 mm deep. The yield stress is 15 MPa. Neglect the weight of the beam.

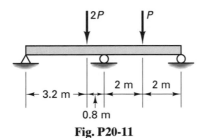

Fig. P20-11

20-12. Using limit analysis, select a steel W section for the loading condition shown in the figure. Let $\sigma_{yp} = 40$ ksi, the shape factor be 1.10, and the load factor be 2. The beam size is the same throughout.

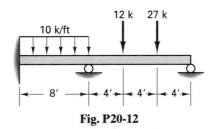

Fig. P20-12

20-13. Determine the ultimate plastic moment for the governing factored load for the prismatic continuous beam of ductile material shown in the figure.

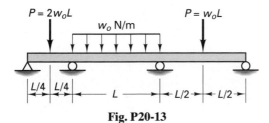

Fig. P20-13

20-14. For the structure shown in the figure, assume that at collapse, plastic hinges form at $A, B,$ and $C.$ Based on this assumption, establish the upper and lower bound on load $w_{ult}.$ The plastic moment for beam AC is 150 and that for column DE is 50. Assume that all quantities are given in a consistent system of units.

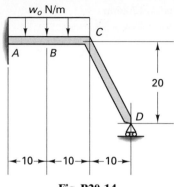

Fig. P20-14

20-15. Rework Example 20-7 assuming that the horizontal force at B is P and column DE is fixed at $E.$ The vertical force P remains at $C.$

20-16. A portal frame pinned at A and F carries three concentrated forces $P,$ each as shown in the figure. If M_p of all members is the same throughout, obtain the collapse value of $P.$ Substantiate your results by applying both the upper- and lower-bound theorems.

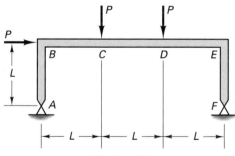

Fig. P20-16

Appendix

Tables

Acknowledgment: Data for Tables 3 through 9 are taken from *AISC Manuals of Steel Construction* and are reproduced by permission of the American Institute of Steel Construction, Inc. The tables are compiled for use with this text. Original sources should be consulted for actual design.

TABLE 1A. TYPICAL PHYSICAL PROPERTIES OF, AND ALLOWABLE STRESSES FOR, SOME COMMON MATERIALS[a]
(IN U.S. CUSTOMARY SYSTEM OF UNITS)

| Material | Unit Weight, lb/in³ | Ultimate Strength, ksi | | | Yield Strength,[g] ksi | | Allow Stresses,[i] psi | | Elastic Moduli ×10⁻⁶ psi | | Coef. of Thermal Expans. ×10⁻⁶ per °F |
		Tens.	Comp.[c]	Shear	Tens.[h]	Shear	Tens. or Comp.	Shear	Tens. or Comp.	Shear	
Aluminum alloy (extruded) 2024-T4	0.100	60	—	32	44	25			10.6	4.00	12.9
6061-T6		38	—	24	35	20			10.0	3.75	13.0
Cast iron Gray	0.276	30	120	—[e]	—	—			13	6	5.8
Malleable		54	—	48	36	24			25	12	6.7
Concrete[b] 8 gal/sack	0.087	—	3	—[e]	—	—	−1,350[f]	66	3	—	6.0
6 gal/sack		—	5	—	—	—	−2,250[f]	86	5	—	
Magnesium alloy, AM100A	0.065	40	—	21	22	—	±24,000	14,500	6.5	2.4	14.0
Steel 0.2% Carbon (hot-rolled)	0.283	65	—	48	36	24					
0.6% Carbon (hot-rolled)		100	—	80	60	36					
0.6% Carbon (quenched)		120	—	100	75	45			30[k]	12	6.5
3½% Ni, 0.4% C		200	—	150	150	90					
Wood Douglas fir (coast)	0.018	—	7.4[d]	1.1[f]	—	—	±1,900[j]	120[f]	1.76	—	—
Southern pine (longleaf)	0.021	—	8.4[d]	1.5[f]	—	—	±2,250[j]	135[f]	1.76	—	—

[a]Mechanical properties of metals depend not only on composition but also on heat treatment, previous cold working, etc. Data for wood are for clear 2 × 2-in specimens at 12% moisture content. True values vary.

[b]8 gal/sack means 8 gallons of water per 94-lb sack of Portland cement. Values are for 28-day-old concrete.

[c]For short blocks only. For ductile materials, the ultimate strength in compression is indefinite; may be assumed to be the same as that in tension.

[d]Compression parallel to grain on short blocks. Compression perpendicular to the grain at proportional limit 950 psi, 1190 psi, respectively. Values from *Wood Handbook*, U.S. Dept. of Agriculture.

[e]Fails in diagonal tension.

[f]Parallel to grain.

[g]For most materials, at 0.2% set.

[h]For ductile materials, compressive yield strength may be assumed the same.

[i]For static loads only. Much lower stresses required in machine design because of fatigue properties and dynamic loadings.

[j]In bending only. No tensile stress is allowed in concrete. Timber stresses are for select or dense grade.

[k]AISC recommends the value of 29 × 10⁶ psi.

TABLE 1B. TYPICAL PHYSICAL PROPERTIES OF, AND ALLOWABLE STRESSES FOR, SOME COMMON MATERIALS[a] (IN SI SYSTEM OF UNITS)

Material	Unit Mass $\times 10^3$ kg/m³	Ultimate Strength, MPa Tens.	Comp.[c]	Shear	Yield Strength,[g] MPa Tens.[h]	Shear	Allow Stresses,[i] MPa Tens. or Comp.	Shear	Elastic Moduli, GPa Tens. or Comp.	Shear	Coef. of Thermal Expans. $\times 10^{-6}$ per °C
Aluminum alloy (extruded) 2024-T4	2.77	414	—	220	300	170	—	—	73	27.6	23.2
6061-T6		262	—	165	241	138	—	—	70	25.9	23.4
Cast iron Gray	7.64	210	825	—[e]	—	—	—	—	90	41	10.4
Malleable		370	—	330	250	165	—	—	170	83	12.1
Concrete[b] 0.70 water-cement ratio	2.41	—	20	—[e]	—	—	-9.31^j	0.455	20	—	10.8
0.53 water-cement ratio		—	35	—	—	—	-15.5^j	0.592	35	—	
Magnesium alloy, AM100A	1.80	275	—	145	150	—	±165	100	45	17	25.2
Steel 0.2% Carbon (hot-rolled)	7.83	450	—	330	250	165	—	—			
0.6% Carbon (hot-rolled)		690	—	550	415	250	—	—	200	83	11.7
0.6% Carbon (quenched)		825	—	690	515	310	—	—			
3½% Ni, 0.4% C		1380	—	1035	1035	620	—	—			
Wood Douglas fir (coast)	0.50	—	51^d	7^f	—	—	$\pm13.1^k$	0.825^f	12.1	—	—
Southern pine (longleaf)	0.58	—	58^d	10^f	—	—	$\pm15.5^k$	0.930^f	12.1	—	—

[a]Mechanical properties of metals depend not only on composition but also on heat treatment, previous cold working, etc. True values vary. Where SI values are not yet available, a soft conversion of values currently accepted in industry was used in constructing this table.

[b]Water-cement ratio by weight for concrete with a 75 to 100 mm slump. Values are for 28-day-old concrete.

[c]For short blocks only. For ductile materials, the ultimate strength in compression is indefinite; may be assumed to be the same as that in tension.

[d]Compression parallel to grain on short blocks. Compression perpendicular to the grain at proportional limit 6.56 MPa, 8.20 MPa, respectively. Soft conversion of values from *Wood Handbook*, U.S. Dept. of Agriculture.

[e]Fails in diagonal tension

[f]Parallel to grain

[g]For most materials, at 0.2% offset.

[h]For ductile materials, compressive yield strength may be assumed the same.

[i]For static loads only. Much lower stresses required in machine design because of fatigue properties and dynamic loadings.

[j]No tensile stress is allowed in concrete.

[k]In bending only. Timber stresses are for select and dense grade.

Note: Data in all tables with gray overlay are in SI system of units.

TABLE 2.   USEFUL PROPERTIES OF AREAS

Areas and moments of inertia of areas around centroidal axes

RECTANGLE

$A = bh$
$I_o = bh^3/12$

CIRCLE

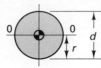

$A = \pi R^2$
$I_o = I_p/2 = \pi R^4/4$

TRIANGLE

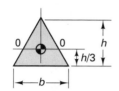

$A = bh/2$
$I_o = bh^3/36$

SEMICIRCLE

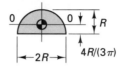

$A = \pi R^2/2$
$I_o = 0.110 R^4$

THIN TUBE

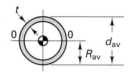

$A = 2\pi R_{av} t$
$I_o = I_p/2 \approx \pi R_{av} t$

HALF OF THIN TUBE

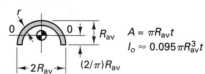

$A = \pi R_{av} t$
$I_o \approx 0.095 \pi R_{av}^3 t$

Areas and Centroids of areas

TRIANGLE

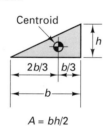

$A = bh/2$

TRIANGLE

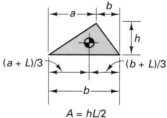

$A = hL/2$

PARABOLA

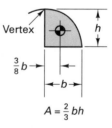

$A = \frac{2}{3} bh$

PARABOLA: $y = -ax^2$

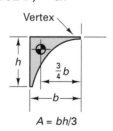

$A = bh/3$

$y = -ax^n$

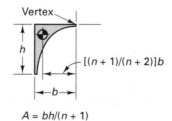

$[(n + 1)/(n + 2)]b$

$A = bh/(n + 1)$

PARABOLA

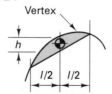

The area for any segment of a parabola is $A = \frac{2}{3} hl$

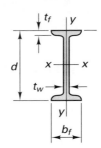

TABLE 3. AMERICAN STANDARD STEEL S SHAPES DIMENSIONS AND PROPERTIES
U.S. CUSTOMARY UNITS AND SI UNITS (ABRIDGED LIST)

Designation*	Area A	Depth d	Web Thickness t_w	Flange Width b_f	Flange Thickness t_f	Axis X–X I_x	Axis X–X r_x	Axis Y–Y I_y	Axis Y–Y r_y
$in \times lb/ft$	in^2	in	in	in	in	in^4	in	in^4	in
S 24 × 100	29.30	24.00	0.747	7.245	0.870	2 390	9.01	47.7	1.27
× 80	23.50	24.00	0.500	7.000	0.870	2 100	9.47	42.2	1.34
S 20 × 96	28.20	20.30	0.800	7.200	0.920	1 670	7.71	50.2	1.33
× 75	22.00	20.00	0.635	6.385	0.795	1 280	7.62	29.8	1.16
S 18 × 70	20.60	18.00	0.711	6.251	0.691	926	6.71	24.1	1.08
× 54.7	16.10	18.00	0.461	6.001	0.691	804	7.07	20.8	1.14
S 12 × 50	14.70	12.00	0.687	5.477	0.659	305	4.55	15.7	1.03
× 31.8	9.35	12.00	0.350	5.000	0.544	218	4.83	9.36	1.00
S 10 × 35	10.30	10.00	0.594	4.944	0.491	147	3.78	8.36	0.90
× 25.4	7.46	10.00	0.311	4.661	0.491	124	4.07	6.79	0.95
S 8 × 23	6.77	8.00	0.441	4.171	0.426	64.9	3.10	4.31	0.80
× 18.4	5.41	8.00	0.271	4.001	0.426	57.6	3.26	3.73	0.83
$mm \times kg/m$	mm^2	mm	mm	mm	mm	$10^6\ mm^4$	mm	$10^6\ mm^4$	mm
S 610 × 149	18 900	610	18.90	184.0	22.1	995	229	19.9	32.4
× 119	15 200	610	12.70	178.0	22.1	874	240	17.6	34.0
S 510 × 143	18 200	516	20.30	183.0	23.4	695	195	20.9	33.9
× 112	14 200	508	16.10	162.0	20.2	533	194	12.4	29.6
S 460 × 104	13 300	457	18.10	159.0	17.6	385	170	10.0	27.4
× 81.4	10 400	457	11.70	152.0	17.6	335	179	8.66	28.9
S 310 × 74	9 480	305	17.40	139.0	16.7	127	116	6.53	26.2
× 47	6 030	305	8.89	127.0	13.8	90.7	123	3.90	25.4
S 250 × 52	6 650	254	15.10	126.0	12.5	61.2	95.9	3.48	22.9
× 38	4 810	254	7.90	118.0	12.5	51.6	104	2.83	24.3
S 200 × 34	4 370	203	11.20	106.0	10.8	27.0	78.6	1.79	20.2
× 27	3 490	203	6.88	102.0	10.8	24.0	82.9	1.55	21.1

American Standard I-shape beams are referred to as S shapes and are designated by the letter S followed by the depth in inches or millimeters, with the weight per linear foot or mass in kilograms per meter given last. For example, S 24 × 100 means that this S shape is 24 in deep and weighs 100 lb/ft. Alternatively, the same shape S 610 × 149 is 610 mm deep and has a mass of 149 kg/m.

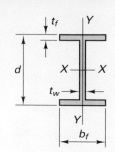

TABLE 4A. AMERICAN STANDARD STEEL W SHAPES DIMENSIONS AND PROPERTIES U.S. CUSTOMARY UNITS (ABRIDGED LIST)

Designation*	Area A	Depth d	Web Thickness t_w	Flange Width b_f	Flange Thickness t_f	Axis X–X I_x	Axis X–X r_x	Axis Y–Y I_y	Axis Y–Y r_y
$in \times lb/ft$	in^2	in	in	in	in	in^4	in	in^4	in
W36 × 245	72.1	36.08	0.800	16.510	1.350	16100	15.0	1010	3.75
230	67.6	35.90	0.760	16.470	1.260	15000	14.9	940	3.73
150	44.2	35.85	0.625	11.975	0.940	9040	14.3	270	2.47
135	39.7	35.55	0.600	11.950	0.790	7800	14.0	225	2.38
W33 × 201	59.1	33.68	0.715	15.745	1.150	11500	14.0	749	3.56
130	38.3	33.09	0.580	11.510	0.855	6710	13.2	218	2.39
118	34.7	32.86	0.550	11.480	0.740	5900	13.0	187	2.32
W30 × 191	56.1	30.68	0.710	15.040	1.185	9170	12.8	673	3.46
173	50.8	30.44	0.655	14.985	1.065	8200	12.7	598	3.43
W27 × 161	47.4	27.59	0.660	14.020	1.080	6280	11.5	497	3.24
146	42.9	27.38	0.605	13.965	0.975	5630	11.4	443	3.21
94	27.7	26.92	0.490	9.990	0.745	3270	10.9	124	2.12
84	24.8	26.71	0.460	9.960	0.640	2850	10.7	106	2.07
W18 × 60	17.6	18.24	0.415	7.555	0.695	984	7.47	50.1	1.69
50	14.7	17.99	0.355	7.495	0.570	800	7.38	40.1	1.65
46	13.5	18.06	0.360	6.060	0.605	712	7.25	22.5	1.29
35	10.3	17.70	0.300	6.000	0.425	510	7.04	15.3	1.22
W16 × 26	7.68	15.69	0.250	5.500	0.345	301	6.26	9.59	1.12
W14 × 193	56.8	15.48	0.890	15.710	1.440	2400	6.50	931	4.05
159	46.7	14.98	0.745	15.565	1.190	1900	6.38	748	4.00
99	29.1	14.16	0.485	14.565	0.780	1110	6.17	402	3.71
90	26.5	14.02	0.440	14.520	0.710	999	6.14	362	3.70
W12 × 72	21.1	12.25	0.430	12.040	0.670	597	5.31	195	3.04
65	19.1	12.12	0.390	12.000	0.605	533	5.28	174	3.02
50	14.7	12.19	0.370	8.080	0.640	394	5.18	56.3	1.96
45	13.2	12.06	0.335	8.045	0.575	350	5.15	50.0	1.94
40	11.8	11.94	0.295	8.005	0.515	310	5.13	44.1	1.93
W10 × 112	32.9	11.36	0.755	10.415	1.250	716	4.66	236	2.68
60	17.6	10.22	0.420	10.080	0.680	341	4.39	116	2.57
49	14.4	9.98	0.340	10.000	0.560	272	4.35	93.4	2.54
45	13.3	10.10	0.350	8.020	0.620	248	4.33	53.4	2.01
39	11.5	9.92	0.315	7.985	0.530	209	4.27	45.0	1.98
33	9.71	9.73	0.290	7.960	0.435	170	4.19	36.6	1.94
W8 × 67	19.7	9.00	0.570	8.280	0.935	272	3.72	88.6	2.12
58	17.1	8.75	0.510	8.220	0.810	228	3.65	75.1	2.10
40	11.7	8.25	0.360	8.070	0.560	146	3.53	49.1	2.04
31	9.13	8.00	0.285	7.995	0.435	110	3.47	37.1	2.02
28	8.25	8.06	0.285	6.535	0.465	98.0	3.45	21.7	1.62
24	7.08	7.93	0.245	6.495	0.400	82.8	3.42	18.3	1.61
21	6.16	8.28	0.250	5.270	0.400	75.3	3.49	9.77	1.26
18	5.26	8.14	0.230	5.250	0.330	61.9	3.43	7.97	1.23

American standard wide-flange shapes are designated by the letter W followed by the nominal depth in inches with the weight in pounds per linear foot given last.

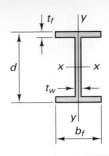

TABLE 4B. AMERICAN STANDARD STEEL W SHAPES DIMENSIONS AND PROPERTIES SI UNITS (ABRIDGED LIST)

Designation[*]	Area A	Depth d	Web Thickness t_w	Flange		Axis X–X		Axis Y–Y	
				Width b_f	Thickness t_f	I_x	r_x	I_y	r_y
$mm \times kg/m$	mm^2	mm	mm	mm	mm	$10^6 \ mm^4$	mm	$10^6 \ mm^4$	mm
W920 × 365	46500	916	20.3	419	34.3	6710	380	421	95.2
342	43600	912	19.3	418	32.0	6250	379	390	94.6
223	28500	911	15.9	304	23.9	3770	364	112	62.7
201	25600	903	15.2	304	20.1	3250	356	94.4	60.7
W840 × 299	38100	855	18.2	400	29.2	4790	355	312	90.5
193	24700	840	14.7	292	21.7	2780	335	90.3	60.5
176	22400	835	14.0	292	18.8	2460	331	78.2	59.1
W760 × 284	36200	779	18.0	382	30.1	3810	324	280	87.9
257	32800	773	16.6	381	27.1	3420	323	250	87.3
W690 × 240	30600	701	16.8	356	27.4	2610	292	206	82.0
217	27700	695	15.4	355	24.8	2340	291	185	81.7
140	17800	684	12.4	254	18.9	1360	276	51.7	53.9
125	16000	678	11.7	253	16.3	1190	273	44.1	52.5
W460 × 89	11400	463	10.5	192	17.7	410	190	20.9	42.8
74	9460	457	9.02	190	14.5	333	188	16.6	41.9
68	8730	459	9.14	154	15.4	297	184	9.41	32.8
52	6640	450	7.62	152	10.8	212	179	6.34	30.9
W410 × 39	4960	399	6.35	140	8.80	126	159	4.02	28.5
W360 × 287	36600	393	22.6	399	36.6	997	165	388	103
237	30200	380	18.9	395	30.2	788	162	310	101
147	18800	360	12.3	370	19.8	463	157	167	94.2
134	17100	356	11.2	369	18.0	415	156	151	94.0
W310 × 107	13600	311	10.9	306	17.0	248	135	81.2	77.3
97	12300	308	9.91	305	15.4	222	134	72.9	77.0
74	9480	310	9.40	205	16.3	165	132	23.4	49.7
67	8530	306	8.51	204	14.6	145	130	20.7	49.3
60	7600	303	7.49	203	13.1	129	130	18.3	49.1
W250 × 167	21300	289	19.2	265	31.8	300	119	98.8	68.1
89	11400	260	10.7	256	17.3	143	112	48.4	65.2
73	9310	253	8.64	254	14.2	113	110	38.8	64.6
67	8560	257	8.89	204	15.7	104	110	22.2	50.9
58	7400	252	8.00	203	13.5	87.3	109	18.8	50.4
49	6260	247	7.37	202	11.0	70.6	106	15.1	49.1
W200 × 100	12700	229	14.5	210	23.7	113	94.3	36.6	53.7
86	11000	222	13.0	209	20.6	94.7	92.8	31.4	53.4
59	7580	210	9.14	205	14.2	61.2	89.9	20.4	51.9
46	5890	203	7.24	203	11.0	45.5	87.9	15.3	51.0
42	5320	205	7.24	166	11.8	40.9	87.7	9.01	41.2
36	4570	201	6.22	165	10.2	34.4	86.8	7.64	40.9
31	3980	210	6.35	134	10.2	31.3	88.7	4.10	32.1
27	3400	207	5.84	133	8.40	25.8	87.1	3.29	31.1

Notes: American Standard wide-flange shapes in SI Units are designated by the letter W followed by the nominal depth in millimeters, with the mass in kilograms per meter given last.

TABLE 5.   AMERICAN STANDARD STEEL CHANNELS DIMENSIONS AND PROPERTIES
U.S. CUSTOMARY UNITS AND SI UNITS (ABRIDGED LIST)

Designation*	Area A	Depth d	Web Thickness t_w	Flange Width b_f	Flange Thickness t_f	Axis X-X I_x	Axis X-X r_x	Axis Y-Y I_y	Axis Y-Y r_y	Axis Y-Y $\bar{x}$	Axis Y-Y e_0
in × lb/ft	in^2	in	in	in	in	in^4	in	in^4	in	in	in
C 15 × 50	14.70	15.00	0.716	3.716	0.650	404	5.24	11.0	0.867	0.799	0.583
× 33.9	9.96	15.00	0.400	3.400	0.650	315	5.62	8.13	0.904	0.787	0.896
C 12 × 30	8.82	12.00	0.510	3.170	0.501	162	4.29	5.14	0.763	0.674	0.618
× 20.7	6.09	12.00	0.282	2.942	0.501	129	4.61	3.88	0.799	0.698	0.870
C 10 × 30	8.82	10.00	0.673	3.033	0.436	103	3.42	3.94	0.669	0.649	0.369
× 15.3	4.49	10.00	0.240	2.600	0.436	67.4	3.87	2.28	0.713	0.634	0.796
C 8 × 18.75	5.51	8.00	0.487	2.527	0.390	44.0	2.82	1.98	0.599	0.565	0.431
× 11.5	3.38	8.00	0.220	2.260	0.390	32.6	3.11	1.32	0.625	0.571	0.697
mm × kg/m	mm^2	mm	mm	mm	mm	$10^6\ mm^4$	mm	$10^6\ mm^4$	mm	mm	mm
C 380 × 74	9 480	381	18.20	94.4	16.50	168	133	4.58	22.0	20.30	14.8
× 50	6 430	381	10.20	86.4	16.50	131	143	3.38	22.9	19.99	22.8
C 310 × 45	5 690	305	13.00	80.5	12.70	67.4	109	2.14	19.4	17.12	16.0
× 31	3 930	305	7.16	74.4	12.70	53.7	117	1.61	20.2	17.73	22.1
C 250 × 45	5 690	254	17.10	77.0	11.10	42.9	86.8	1.64	17.0	16.48	9.37
× 23	2 900	254	6.10	66.0	11.10	28.1	98.4	0.949	18.1	16.10	20.2
C 200 × 28	3 550	203	12.40	64.2	9.90	18.3	71.8	0.824	15.2	14.35	10.95
× 17	2 180	203	5.59	57.4	9.90	13.6	79.0	0.549	15.9	13.94	17.7

Note: Channels are designated by the letter C followed by their depth in inches or millimeters, with the weight in pounds per linear foot or mass in kilograms per meter given last. For example, C 15×50 means that the channel is 15 in deep and weighs 50 lb/ft. Alternatively, the same shape C 380 × 74 is 380 mm deep and has a mass of 74 kg/m. In the table, $\bar{x}$ designates the distance from the back of a channel to the centroid of the section, and e_0 locates the shear center.

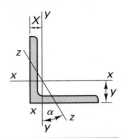

TABLE 6A. AMERICAN STANDARD STEEL ANGLES EQUAL AND UNEQUAL LEGS DIMENSIONS AND PROPERTIES U.S. CUSTOMARY UNITS (ABRIDGED LIST)

Size and Thickness	Weight per foot	Area A	Axis X–X			Axis Y–Y			Axis Z–Z	
			I_x	r_x	y	I_y	r_y	x	r_z	$\tan \alpha$
in	lb/ft	in²	in⁴	in	in	in⁴	in	in	in	
L 8 × 8 × 1	51.0	15.00	89.0	2.44	2.37	89.0	2.44	2.37	1.56	1.000
× ½	26.4	7.75	48.6	2.50	2.19	48.6	2.50	2.19	1.59	1.000
L 8 × 6 × 1	44.2	13.00	80.8	2.49	2.65	38.8	1.73	1.65	1.28	0.543
× ½	23.0	6.75	44.3	2.56	2.47	21.7	1.79	1.47	1.30	0.558
L 6 × 6 × 1	37.4	11.00	35.5	1.80	1.86	35.5	1.80	1.86	1.17	1.000
× ½	19.6	5.75	19.9	1.86	1.68	19.9	1.86	1.68	1.18	1.000
L 6 × 4 × ¾	23.6	6.94	24.5	1.88	2.08	8.68	1.12	1.08	0.860	0.428
× ½	16.2	4.75	17.4	1.91	1.99	6.27	1.15	0.987	0.870	0.440
L 4 × 4 × ½	12.8	3.75	5.56	1.22	1.18	5.56	1.22	1.18	0.782	1.000
× ⅜	9.8	2.86	4.36	1.23	1.14	4.36	1.23	1.14	0.788	1.000
L 4 × 3 ½ × ⅜	9.1	2.67	4.18	1.25	1.21	2.95	1.06	0.955	0.727	0.755
× 5/16	7.7	2.25	3.56	1.26	1.18	2.55	1.07	0.932	0.730	0.757
L 4 × 3 × ½	11.1	3.25	5.05	1.89	1.25	2.42	0.827	0.864	0.639	0.543
× ¼	5.8	1.69	2.77	1.28	1.24	1.36	0.896	0.736	0.651	0.558
L 3 × 2 × ½	7.7	2.25	1.92	0.924	1.08	0.672	0.546	0.583	0.428	0.414
× 5/16	5.0	1.46	1.32	0.948	1.02	0.470	0.567	0.516	0.432	0.435
L 2 ½ × 2 ½ × ½	7.7	2.25	1.23	0.739	0.806	1.23	0.739	0.806	0.487	1.000
× 5/16	5.0	1.46	0.849	0.761	0.740	0.849	0.761	0.740	0.489	1.000

Note: x and y locate the centroid of a section.

TABLE 6B. AMERICAN STANDARD STEEL ANGLES EQUAL AND UNEQUAL LEGS DIMENSIONS AND PROPERTIES SI UNITS (ABRIDGED LIST)

Size and Thickness	Mass per Meter	Area A	Axis X–X			Axis Y–Y			Axis Z–Z	
			I_x	r_x	y	I_y	r_y	x	r_z	$\tan \alpha$
mm	kg/m	mm²	$10^6\,mm^4$	mm	mm	$10^6\,mm^4$	mm	mm	mm	
L 203 × 203 × 25.4	75.9	9 680	36.9	61.7	60.1	36.9	61.7	60.1	39.6	1.000
× 12.7	39.3	5 000	20.2	63.6	50.5	20.2	63.6	50.5	40.4	1.000
L 203 × 152 × 25.4	65.8	8 390	33.5	63.2	67.4	16.0	43.7	41.9	32.5	0.543
× 12.7	34.2	4 350	18.4	65.0	62.8	8.96	45.4	37.3	33.0	0.558
L 152 × 152 × 25.4	55.7	7 100	14.6	45.3	47.2	4.6	45.3	47.2	29.7	1.000
× 12.7	29.2	3 710	8.22	47.1	42.7	8.22	47.1	42.7	30.0	1.000
L 152 × 102 × 19.0	35.1	4 480	10.1	47.5	52.5	3.65	28.5	27.5	21.8	0.428
× 12.7	24.1	3 060	7.20	48.5	50.2	2.64	29.4	25.2	22.1	0.440
L 102 × 102 × 12.7	19.0	2 420	2.34	31.1	30.2	2.34	31.1	30.2	19.9	1.000
× 9.5	14.6	1 840	1.84	31.6	29.0	1.84	31.6	29.0	20.0	1.000
L 102 × 89 × 9.5	13.5	1 720	1.76	32.0	30.8	1.25	27.0	24.3	18.5	0.755
× 7.9	11.3	1 450	1.50	32.2	30.2	1.07	27.2	23.7	18.5	0.757
L 102 × 76 × 12.7	16.5	2 100	2.12	31.8	33.9	1.00	21.8	20.9	16.2	0.543
× 6.4	8.6	1 090	1.16	32.6	31.6	0.560	22.7	18.6	16.5	0.558
L 76 × 51 × 12.7	11.5	1 450	0.795	23.4	27.4	0.283	14.0	14.9	10.9	0.414
× 7.9	6.1	766	0.450	24.2	25.1	0.198	14.5	13.2	11.0	0.435
L 64 × 64 × 12.7	11.5	1 450	0.524	19.0	20.6	0.524	19.0	20.6	12.4	1.000
× 7.9	7.4	945	0.362	19.6	18.9	0.362	19.6	18.9	12.4	1.000

Note: x and y locate the centroid of a section.

TABLE 7. AMERICAN STANDARD STEEL PIPES DIMENSIONS AND PROPERTIES U.S. CUSTOMARY UNITS AND SI UNITS (ABRIDGED LIST)

Nominal Diameter		Dimensions			Weight per Foot	Properties			
		Outside Diameter	Inside Diameter	Wall Thickness		A	I	S	r
in	mm	in	in	in	lb/ft	in^2	in^4	in^3	in
$\frac{1}{2}$	13	0.840	0.622	0.109	0.85	0.250	0.017	0.041	0.261
$\frac{3}{4}$	19	1.050	0.824	0.113	1.13	0.333	0.037	0.071	0.334
1	25	1.315	1.049	0.133	1.68	0.494	0.087	0.133	0.421
$1\frac{1}{4}$	32	1.660	1.380	0.140	2.27	0.669	0.195	0.235	0.540
$1\frac{1}{2}$	38	1.900	1.610	0.145	2.72	0.799	0.310	0.326	0.623
2	51	2.375	2.067	0.154	3.65	1.070	0.666	0.561	0.787
$2\frac{1}{2}$	64	2.875	2.469	0.203	5.79	1.700	1.530	1.060	0.947
3	75	3.500	3.068	0.216	7.58	2.230	3.020	1.720	1.160
$3\frac{1}{2}$	89	4.000	3.548	0.226	9.11	2.680	4.790	2.390	1.340
4	102	4.500	4.026	0.237	10.79	3.170	7.230	3.210	1.510
5	127	5.563	5.047	0.258	14.62	4.300	15.20	5.450	1.880
6	152	6.625	6.065	0.280	18.97	5.580	28.10	8.500	2.250
8	203	8.625	7.981	0.322	28.55	8.400	72.50	16.80	2.940
10	254	10.750	10.020	0.365	40.48	11.90	161.0	29.90	3.670
12	310	12.750	12.000	0.375	49.56	14.60	279.0	43.80	4.380
mm	in	mm	mm	mm	kg/m	mm^2	$10^6\ mm^4$	$10^3\ mm^3$	mm
13	$\frac{1}{2}$	21.3	15.8	2.77	1.3	161	0.007	0.667	6.640
19	$\frac{3}{4}$	26.7	20.9	2.87	1.7	215	0.015	1.160	8.490
25	1	33.4	26.6	3.38	2.5	319	0.037	2.190	10.70
32	$1\frac{1}{4}$	42.2	35.1	3.56	3.4	431	0.081	3.820	13.70
38	$1\frac{1}{2}$	48.3	40.9	3.68	4.0	516	0.129	5.340	15.80
51	2	60.3	52.5	3.91	5.4	693	0.277	9.190	20.00
64	$2\frac{1}{2}$	73.0	62.7	5.16	8.6	1 100	0.637	17.50	24.10
75	3	88.9	77.9	5.49	11.3	1 440	1.260	28.30	29.60
89	$3\frac{1}{2}$	102.0	90.1	5.74	13.6	1 730	2.080	40.80	34.70
102	4	114.0	102.0	6.02	16.1	2 050	2.980	52.30	38.10
127	5	141.0	128.0	6.55	21.8	2 770	6.230	88.40	47.40
152	6	168.0	154.0	7.11	28.2	3 600	11.50	137.0	56.50
203	8	219.0	203.0	8.18	42.5	5 420	29.60	270.0	73.90
254	10	273.0	255.0	9.27	60.2	7 680	65.10	477.0	92.10
310	12	324.0	305.0	9.52	73.3	9 410	116.0	716.0	111.0

Note: $S = I/(d_o/2)$

TABLE 8.   SELECTED PLASTIC MODULI AROUND THE X–X AND THE Y–Y AXES FOR AMERICAN STANDARD STEEL W SHAPES U.S. CUSTOMARY UNITS AND SI UNITS (ABRIDGED LIST)

	Plastic Moduli			*Plastic Moduli*	
Designation	Z_x	Z_y	*Designation*	Z_x	Z_y
in × lb/ft	*in³*	*in³*	*mm × kg/m*	*10³ mm³*	*10³ mm³*
W 36 × 150	581	70.9	W 920 × 223	9.540	1 160
W 27 × 94	278	38.8	W 690 × 140	4 550	636
W 18 × 60	123	20.6	W 460 × 89	2 010	339
W 12 × 65	96.8	44.1	W 310 × 97	1 590	725
W 10 × 33	38.8	14.0	W 250 × 49	633	228
W 8 × 34	23.2	8.57	W 200 × 36	380	141

TABLE 9.   PROPERTIES OF STRUCTURAL LUMBER (ABRIDGED LIST). SECTIONAL PROPERTIES OF AMERICAN STANDARD DRESSED (S4S)* SIZES.

Nominal Size	Standard Dressed Size	Area of Section	Moment of Inertia	Section Modulus	Weight per Foot	Nominal Size	Standard Dressed Size	Area of Section	Moment of Inertia	Section Modulus	Weight per Foot
in	*in × in*	*in²*	*in⁴*	*in³*	*lb*	*in*	*in × in*	*in²*	*in⁴*	*in³*	*lb*
2 × 4	$1\frac{1}{2} \times 3\frac{1}{2}$	5.25	5.36	3.06	1.46	6 × 10	$9\frac{1}{2}$	52.3	393	82.7	14.5
6	$5\frac{1}{2}$	8.25	20.8	7.56	2.29	12	$11\frac{1}{2}$	63.3	697	121	17.5
8	$7\frac{1}{4}$	10.9	47.6	13.1	3.02	8 × 8	$7\frac{1}{2} \times 7\frac{1}{2}$	56.3	264	70.3	15.6
10	$9\frac{1}{4}$	13.9	98.9	21.4	3.85	10	$9\frac{1}{2}$	71.3	536	113	19.8
12	$11\frac{1}{4}$	16.9	178	31.6	4.69	12	$11\frac{1}{2}$	86.3	951	165	23.9
3 × 4	$2\frac{1}{2} \times 3\frac{1}{2}$	8.75	8.93	5.10	2.43	10 × 10	$9\frac{1}{2} \times 9\frac{1}{2}$	90.3	679	143	25.1
6	$5\frac{1}{2}$	13.8	34.7	12.6	3.82	12	$11\frac{1}{2}$	109	12044	209	30.3
8	$7\frac{1}{4}$	18.1	79.4	21.9	5.04	14	$13\frac{1}{2}$	128	1948	289	35.6
10	$9\frac{1}{4}$	23.1	165	35.7	6.42	12 × 12	$11\frac{1}{2} \times 11\frac{1}{2}$	132	1458	253	36.7
12	$11\frac{1}{4}$	28.1	297	52.7	7.81	14	$13\frac{1}{2}$	155	2358	349	43.1
4 × 4	$3\frac{1}{2} \times 3\frac{1}{2}$	12.3	12.5	7.15	3.40	16	$15\frac{1}{2}$	178	3569	460	49.5
6	$5\frac{1}{2}$	19.3	48.5	17.6	5.35	14 × 14	$13\frac{1}{2} \times 13\frac{1}{2}$	182	2768	410	50.6
8	$7\frac{1}{4}$	25.4	111	30.7	7.05						
10	$9\frac{1}{4}$	32.4	231	49.9	8.94	16 × 16	$15\frac{1}{2} \times 15\frac{1}{2}$	240	4810	621	66.7
12	$11\frac{1}{4}$	39.4	415	73.8	10.9	18 × 18	$17\frac{1}{2} \times 17\frac{1}{2}$	306	7816	893	85.0
6 × 6	$5\frac{1}{2} \times 5\frac{1}{2}$	30.3	76.3	27.7	8.40	20 × 20	$19\frac{1}{2} \times 19\frac{1}{2}$	380	12049	1236	106
8	$7\frac{1}{2}$	41.3	193	51.6	11.4	24 × 24	$23\frac{1}{2} \times 23\frac{1}{2}$	552	25415	2163	153

*Surfaced four sides. All properties and weights given are for dressed sizes only. The weights given are based on an assumed average weight of 40 lb per cubic foot. Based on a table compiled by the National Forest Products Association.

TABLE 10.   DEFLECTIONS AND SLOPES OF ELASTIC CURVES FOR VARIOUSLY LOADED BEAMS

Loading	Equation of Elastic Curve	
	Maximum Deflection	Slope at End

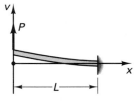

$$v = \frac{P}{6EI}(2L^3 - 3L^2x + x^3)$$

$$v_{\max} = v(0) = \frac{PL^3}{3EI}$$

$$\theta(0) = -\frac{PL^2}{2EI}$$

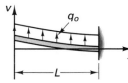

$$v = \frac{q_o}{24EI}(x^4 - 4L^3x + 3L^4)$$

$$v_{\max} = v(0) = \frac{q_oL^4}{8EI}$$

$$\theta(0) = -\frac{q_oL^3}{6EI}$$

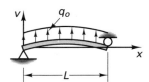

$$v = \frac{q_ox}{24EI}(L^3 - 2Lx^2 + x^3)$$

$$v_{\max} = v(L/2) = \frac{5q_oL^4}{384EI}$$

See Example 14-3.

$$\theta(0) = -\theta(L) = \frac{q_oL^3}{24EI}$$

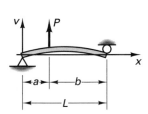

When $0 \le x \le a$, then

$$v = \frac{Pbx}{6EIL}(L^2 - b^2 - x^2)$$

When $a = b = \dfrac{L}{2}$, then

$$v = \frac{Px}{48EI}(3L^2 - 4x^2)$$

$$v_{\max} = v(L/2) = \frac{PL^3}{48EI}$$

See Example 14-6.

$$\left(0 \le x \le \frac{L}{2}\right)$$

$$\theta(0) = -\theta(L) = \frac{PL^2}{16EI}$$

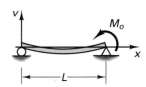

$$v = \frac{M_ox}{6EIL}(L^2 - x^2)$$

$$v_{\max} = v(L/\sqrt{3}) = -\frac{M_oL^2}{9\sqrt{3}EI}$$

See Example 19-1.

$$\theta(0) = -\frac{\theta(L)}{2} = -\frac{M_oL}{6EI}$$

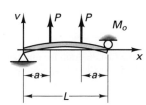

$$v_a = v(a) = \frac{Pa^2}{6EI}(3L - 4a)$$

$$v_{\max} = v(L/2) = \frac{Pa}{24EI}(3L^2 - 4a^2)$$

$$\theta(0) = \frac{Pa}{2EI}(L - a)$$

TABLE 11.   FIXED-END ACTIONS OF PRISMATIC BEAMS[*]

Loading	Moments[*]	Reactions[*]

$$M_{ab} = -M_{ba} = -\frac{q_o L^2}{12}$$

$$R_a = R_b = -\frac{q_o L}{2}$$

$$M_{cd} = -\frac{Pab^2}{L^2}$$

$$M_{dc} = \frac{Pba^2}{L^2}$$

$$R_c = -\frac{Pb^2}{L^3}(3a + b)$$

$$R_d = -\frac{Pa^2}{L^3}(a + 3b)$$

$$M_{ab} = -\frac{q_o L^2}{30}$$

$$M_{ba} = \frac{q_o L^2}{20}$$

$$R_a = -\frac{3q_o L}{20}$$

$$R_b = -\frac{7q_o L}{20}$$

$$M_{ab} = \frac{2EI}{L}\theta_b = K_{ab}\theta_b$$

$$M_{ba} = \frac{4EI}{L}\theta_b = K_{ba}\theta_b$$

$$R_a = -\frac{6EI}{L^2}\theta_b$$

$$R_b = -\frac{6EI}{L^2}\theta_b$$

$$M_{ab} = -\frac{6EI}{L^2}\Delta$$

$$M_{ba} = -\frac{6EI}{L^2}\Delta$$

$$R_a = -\frac{12EI}{L^3}\Delta$$

$$R_b = \frac{12EI}{L^3}\Delta$$

$$M_{bc} = M_o\left(-1 + 4\frac{a}{L} - \frac{3a^2}{L^2}\right)$$

$$M_{cb} = \frac{M_o a}{L}\left(2 - 3\frac{a}{L}\right)$$

$$R_b = \frac{6M_o a}{L^2}\left(1 - \frac{a}{L}\right)$$

$$R_c = -\frac{6M_o a}{L^2}\left(1 - \frac{a}{L}\right)$$

[*]For all the cases tabulated, the positive senses of the end moments and reactions are the same as those shown in the first diagram for uniformly distributed loading. *The special sign convention used here is that adopted for the displacement method in Section 19-5.*

Answers to Alternate Odd-Numbered Problems

Chapter 1

1.1 $\dfrac{\partial \sigma_x}{\partial x} + \dfrac{\partial \tau_{yx}}{\partial y} + \dfrac{\partial \tau_{zx}}{\partial z} + x = 0.$

1.5 Axial force 99 kN 15.9 mm from top.

1.9 $\sigma_{max} = 1.5$ GPa.

1.13 **(a)** Max. Force 9 kg, Max. Stress 38.9 MPa,
    (b) Max. Force 9 kg, Max. Axial Stress 8.07 MPa.

1.17 **(a)** $\sigma_{a-a} = 150$ MPa, $\tau_{a-a} = 86.6$ MPa,
        $\sigma_{b-b} = 50$ MPa, $\tau_{b-b} = 86.6$ MPa.

1.21 $\tau = 3.13$ MPa.

1.25 $\tau = 21$ ksi, $\sigma = 9.1$ ksi.

1.29 **(a)** $P_1 = 5$ kN,
    (b) $P_1 = 110$ kN.

1.33 $\tau_A = 23.1$ GPa, $\tau_B = 21.6$ GPa.

1.37 $\tau_A = 184$ MPa, $\tau_B = 300$ MPa.

1.41 $\sigma_1 = 14.5$ MPa, $\sigma_2 = 12.1$ MPa, $\sigma_3 = 9.24$ MPa.

1.45 $d = D.$

1.49 $A_{FC} = 572$ mm^2, $A_{BC} = 2580$ mm^2.

1.53 $A_{AB} = 58.9$ cm^2, $A_{BC} = 88.4$ cm^2, $A_{BE} = 40.4$ cm^2,
      $A_{BD} = 50$ cm^2, $A_{CD} = 124$ cm^2, $A_{DE} = 165$ cm^2.

1.57 $d_{AB} = d_{AC} = 2.93$ cm.

Chapter 2

2.1 $E = 202 \times 10^9$ N/m^2.

2.5

	Compression			Tension		
Strain $\varepsilon(\%)$	−0.1	−1	−4	0.1	1	4
eng. stress σ	18	72	128	18	72	95
true stress $\bar{\sigma}$	18.0	71.3	122.9	18.0	72.7	95.7
true area (A_0)	1.00	1.01	1.04	1.00	0.99	0.96

2.9 **(a)** $d = 0.49$ mm,
    (b) $\Delta = 2.25$ mm.

2.15 186 MPa for steel, 150 MPa for aluminum.

Chapter 3

3.1 For $\sigma \leq 100$ MPa $d \geq 11.3$ mm,
    for $\varepsilon \leq 0.1\%$ $d \geq 16.8$ mm.

3.5 **(a)** Axial force diagram   **(b)** Strain diagram

29.4 N (3 kg) 187×10^{-4}

    (c) Displacement diagram

0.52 mm

3.9 $P = 32.3$ kN, $\Delta_{rem} = 54$ mm.

3.13 **(a)** $\Delta = \dfrac{FL}{4AE},$

    (b) $\Delta = 1.56$ mm.

3.17 $\Delta = 9.20$ mm.

3.21 $\Delta = \left(\dfrac{W}{AE}\right)^{\frac{1}{n}} \left(\dfrac{n}{n+1}\right) L.$

3.25 $\dfrac{L_A}{L_B} = \ln 3 = 1.1.$

3.29 $\Delta x = 0.0109$ in, $\Delta y = 3.52 \times 10^{-3}$ in.

3.33 **(a)** $K = 4.0 \times 10^6$ N/m,
    (b) $\Delta = 4.0$ mm.

3.37 $P = 30.3$ kN.

3.41 $k_1 = 1.63 \Rightarrow$, $\sigma_{1max} = 301.55$ MPa,
    $k_2 = 2.30 \Rightarrow$, $\sigma_{2max} = 425.5$ MPa.

3.45 $\Delta_B = 0.018$ in.

3.49 $\Delta = 3.42$ mm.

Chapter 4

4.1 $R_1 = -70$ kN, $R_2 = 120$ kN.

4.5 $R_1 = -1.2\,P$, $R_2 = -0.2P$.

4.9 $f = 256$ Hz.

4.13 (a) $R_1 = -bP/L$, $R_2 = -aP/L$.

4.17 $F_{st} = 9/17$ kips, $F_{al} = 4/17$ kips.

4.21 $R_A = 5.57$ kN, $R_B = 5.14$ kN, $R_C = 6.43$ kN.

4.25 (b) $R_1 = 10P/7$, $R_2 = -11P/7$.

4.29 (a) $\sigma_{st} = 15$ ksi,
(b) $\Delta_{al} = 0.01$ in,
(c) $P_{ult} = 400$ kips.

4.33 First bar yields: at $\Delta = \dfrac{\sigma_{yp} L}{3E}$,

second bar yields: at $\Delta_1 = \dfrac{\sigma_{yp} L}{E \cos^2 \alpha}$.

4.37 $\Delta = 2Iw^2 L^3/(3gE)$.

Chapter 5

5.1 $k_s = 51.2$ N/mm.

5.5 $\sigma_x = 3.52$ MPa.

5.9 $G = 72$ MPa.

5.13 For glass: $G_g = 26.64$ MPa, $K_g = 38.7$ MPa,
for steel: $G_s = 80$ GPa, $K_s = 133$ GPa,
for lead: $G_l = 5.17$ GPa, $K_l = 50$ GPa,

5.17 (a) $t = 4.66$ mm, use 5 mm plate,
(b) $\Delta_d = 6.72$ mm.

5.21 $\Delta_c = 0.080$ in, $\Delta_d = 0.025$ in.

5.25 $\sigma_{1a} = 5.93$ MPa.

5.29 $\sigma_{+max}/\sigma_{+ave} = (1 + \beta^2)/(1 + \beta)$.

5.37 (a) $p = 7.26$ ksi
(b) $\sigma_r = -7.26$ ksi, $\sigma_t = 16.6$ ksi,
(c) $p_i = 32.2$ ksi,

Chapter 6

6.1 $\tau_{max} = 1.79 \times 10^7$ N/m^2.

6.5 (a) $\tau_{max} = 162$ MPa,
(b) $d = 79.4$ mm.

6.9 $T_{allow} = 457$ N · m.

6.13 $r = 0.31$ in.

6.17 (a) $c = 0.12$ in, $D_0 = 0.24$ in,
(b) $k_t = 4.34 \times 10^6$ in · lb/rad.

6.21 10 hp.

6.25 $f_t = 9.57 \times 10^5\, G$ rad/N · m.

6.29 (a) $\tau_{st} = 32$ kPa, $\tau_{al} = 30$ kPa,
(b) $f_t = 1.54 \times 10^{-6}$ rad/N · m.

6.33 (a) $T_a = 3/7$, $T_b = 4/7$, $\phi_{ab} = L/(7GI_{p1})$,
(b) $\phi_{ab} = \phi_{ba} = L/(7GI_{p1})$.

6.37 (a) $T_B = t_0 L/3$,

(b) $\phi_x = -\dfrac{1}{JG}\left(\dfrac{t_0 L}{6}x + \dfrac{t_0 x^3}{6L}\right)$.

6.41 (a) $JG\phi\left(\dfrac{L}{2}\right) = C_1\dfrac{L}{2} - \dfrac{t_0 x^2}{8}$,

(b) $\phi_{max} = \dfrac{9}{128}\dfrac{t_0 x^2}{JG}$.

6.45 $\tau = 509$ MPa.

6.49 (a) $\tau_{max} = 395$ MPa,
(b) $\Delta\theta = 0.89 \times 10^{-4}$ rad.

6.53 $T_{ult} = 5a^3 \tau_{yp}/6$.

6.57 Triangle & circle: $a = 2.92r$,
Ellipse & circle: $a = 1.50r$, $b = 0.748r$.

Chapter 7

7.1 $R_{AX} = 0.422$ k, $R_{AY} = 5.11$ k, $R_B = 13.2$ k.

7.5 $V_b = -6$ k, $M_b = 12$ k · ft.

7.9 $P_a = -333$ lb, $V_a = -111$ lb, $M_a = 666$ lb · ft,

7.13 $P_a = 87.7$ kN, $V_a = 31$ kN, $M_a = 26.7$ kN · ft.

7.17 $P_a = -3$ k, $V_a = -3$ k, $M_a = 6$ k · ft.

7.21 $V(0) = 3P$, $M(0) = -2PL$.

7.25 $V(L) = -P/2$, $M(L) = -Pa/2$.

7.29 $R_A = R_B = w_0 L/2$, $M = w_0 Lx/2 - w_0 Lx^2/2 + M_A$.

7.33 $P(\theta) = P(\cos\theta - \sin\theta)/2$, $V(\theta) = -P(\cos\theta + \sin\theta)/2$,
$M(\theta) = PR(1 + \sin\theta - \cos\theta)/2$.

7.37 $V(0) = kL^2/3$, $M(0) = -kL^4/4$.

7.41 $V(x) = const = -M_1/L$, $M(L) = -M_1$.

7.45 $V(x) = 2$, $M(x) = 2x$,   for $0 \le x \le 3$,
$V(x) = 10$, $M(x) = 10x - 24$,   for $3 \le x \le 6$,
$V(x) = -2$, $M(x) = -2x + 48$,   for $6 \le x \le 9$,
$V(x) = -10$, $M(x) = -10x + 120$,   for $9 \le x \le 12$.

7.49 $V(0) = 540$ kN, $M(0) = -2160$ kN $\cdot$ m.

7.53 $V_{max} = 4.5$ kN, $M_{max} = 2.0$ kN $\cdot$ m.

7.57 $V_{max} = 12.0$ k, $M_{min} = -39.0$ k $\cdot$ ft.

7.61 $V_{min} = -3q_0a/2$, $M_{max} = 5q_0a^2/8$.

7.65 $V_{min} = -20$ kN, $M_{max} = 40$ kN $\cdot$ m.

7.69 $V_{max} = 25$ k, $M_{max} = 67$ k $\cdot$ ft.

7.73 $P_{min} = -68$ kN, $V_{min} = -24$ kN, $M_{max} = 20$ kN $\cdot$ m.

7.77 $V_{max} = 2P/3$, $M_{max} = 4Pa/3$.

7.81 $P_{min} = -50$ k, $V_{max} = 2$ k, $M_{max} = 70$ k $\cdot$ in.

7.85 $M_{max} = 4.17$ k $\cdot$ f, $M_{min} = -24$ k $\cdot$ ft.

7.91 $V_{min} = -65q_1a/72$, $M_{min} = -11q_1a^2/24$.

Chapter 8

8.1   367 kN $\cdot$ m.

8.5   1000 k $\cdot$ ft.

8.9   (a) $I_x = 60.8a^4$, $I_x/c = 13.5a^3$, $I_y = 0.75a^4$, $I_y/c = 1.5a^3$,
(b) $I_x = 16.8a^4$, $I_x/c = 6.7a^3$, $I_y = 4.75a^4$, $I_y/c = 3.17a^3$,
(c)   both axes: $I = 10.8a^4$, $I/c = 4.3a^3$.

8.13 $M_c = 310$ k $\cdot$ in, $M_t = 231$ k $\cdot$ in.

8.17 $T = 80$ kN, $e = 71.8$ mm.

8.21 $\sqrt{2}$.

8.25   26.9 k.

8.29   926 N $\cdot$ m.

8.33   15 mm.

8.37   1.7.

8.41   1.80.

8.45   2320 k $\cdot$ in.

8.49 $\sigma_{al} = \pm 26.8$ MN/m^2, $\sigma_{st} = \pm 40.3$ MN/m^2,

8.53   11.9 kN/m.

8.57 $M_0 = 11.8$ k $\cdot$ in, $M_i = 7.0$ k $\cdot$ in.

Chapter 9

9.1 $\sigma_{max} = 4.19$ MPa.

9.5 $\sigma_{max} = 72.6$ kPa.

9.9 $\sigma_B = 12.6$ MPa, $\sigma_C = -30.6$ MPa,
$\sigma_D = 12.6$ MPa, $x = 29.2$ mm.

9.13 $\sigma_{max} = -21.0$ ksi.

9.17 $F_x = 4$ kN, $F_y = 120$ kN,

9.21   922 ksi.

9.25   R/4.

9.29   (a) $b^2h^2/24$,
(b) $-b^2h^2/72$.

9.33 $\sigma_B = -36.3$ MPa, $\sigma_F = -61.6$ MPa, $\beta = 77.2°$

Chapter 10

10.1 $A_{fghi} = 7500$ mm^2, $\bar{y}_1 = 100$ mm, $\bar{y}_2 = 25$ mm^2.

10.5 $q = 3715$ N/mm, $S = 64.6$ mm.

10.9 $T = 2870$ Pa.

10.13 $t_{max} = \dfrac{4}{3} \dfrac{V}{A}$.

10.17 $\tau_1 = 136$ MPa, $\tau_2 = 143$ MPa.

10.21 $Q = 265000$ mm^3, $V = 2.03 \times 10^5$N, $M = 4.31 \times 10^4$ N $\cdot$ m.

10.25 $V = 5.2$ kN, $\tau = 0.73$ MPa.

10.29 $(\sigma_{upper})_L = 0$, $(\sigma_{bottom})_L = 16$ MPa, $(\sigma_{bottom})_R = 17.3$ MPa,
$\tau_{upper} = 1$ MPa, $V_1 = 20$ kN.

10.33   (a) $I = 1.82 \times 10^6$ mm^4,
(b) $\tau_{aa} = 5.49$ MPa, $\tau_{bb} = 7.7$ MPa, $\tau_{cc} = 18.7$ MPa.

10.37   (a) $\bar{y} = 150$ mm, $P_t = 1.89$ kN,
(b)   Force per/bolt $= 118$ kN/bolt.

10.41 $e = 15.9$ mm from center of plate

10.45   Shear center at centroid.

10.49   due to bending $\sigma_A = 0$, $\sigma_B = 0.70$ MPa,
due to shear $\tau_A = 0.104$ MPa, $\tau_B = 0$,
due to torsion $\tau_A = \tau_B = 0.05$ MPa,
total $\tau_A = 0.154$ MPa, $\tau_B = 0.05$.

10.53 $F_{max} = 1.24$ kN.

Chapter 11

11.1　$\sigma_A = P_1/A$, $\sigma_B = P_1/A + M_y/I$, $\sigma_C = P_1/A$, $\tau_C = VQ/(It)$,
$\tau_D = T_r/I_p$, $\tau_E = T_r/I_p = P_1Q/(It)$.

11.5　(a)　$\sigma = -5.92$ ksi,　$\tau = -5.24$ ksi,
　　　(b)　$\sigma = -12.1$ ksi,　$\tau = 5.24$ ksi.

11.9　State of stress of 242 kN/m^2 > 225 kN/m^2 is not permissible.

11.13　$\sigma_{x'} = 22.9$ ksi,　$\tau_{x'y'} = 6.99$ ksi.

11.17　(a)　$\sigma_1 = 18.3$ ksi,　$\sigma_2 = -38.3$ ksi,
　　　(b)　$\tau_{max} = 28.3$ ksi,　$\sigma = -10$ ksi,
　　　(c)　$\sigma_1 + \sigma_2 = -20$ ksi $= \sigma_x + \sigma_y$.

11.21　(a)　$\sigma_1 = 16.1$ ksi,　$\sigma_2 = -56.1$ ksi,
　　　(b)　$\tau_{max} = 36.1$ ksi,　$\sigma = -20$ ksi,
　　　(c)　$\sigma_1 + \sigma_2 = -40$ ksi $= \sigma_x + \sigma_y$.

11.25　(a)　$\theta_1 = 26.6°$,　$\sigma_1 = 6$ ksi,　$\sigma_2 = -4$ ksi,
　　　(b)　$\tau = 5$ ksi,　$\theta_2 = 71.6°$,　$\sigma = 1$ ksi.

11.29　(a)　$\sigma_1 = -9.5$ MPa,　$\sigma_2 = -60.5$ MPa,　$\theta = 50.7°$,
　　　(b)　$\tau_{max} = 25.5$ MPa,　$\sigma = -35$ MPa.

11.33　$\sigma_\theta = -15$ ksi,　$\tau_\theta = 8.7$ ksi

11.39　$\tau = -4.58$ ksi,　$\theta = 14.8°$.

11.43　(a)　$\alpha = 10°$,　$\sigma_x = -\dfrac{P}{0.352\alpha}$.
　　　(b)　$\alpha = 45°$,　$\sigma_x = -P/2\alpha$.

11.51　$\beta = -(\varepsilon_x - \varepsilon_y)\sin\theta\cos\theta + \gamma_{xy}\cos\theta$

11.55　$\varepsilon_1 = 1130$ μm/m,　$\varepsilon_2 = -128$ μm/m,　$\theta = 4.58°$.

11.59　$\sigma_1 = 81.8$ MPa,　$\sigma_2 = 11.5$ MPa,　$\theta = 4.58°$.

Chapter 12

12.1　$\bar{\sigma} = 6$,

$$\begin{pmatrix} 6 & 0 & 0 \\ 0 & 6 & 0 \\ 0 & 0 & 6 \end{pmatrix} + \begin{pmatrix} 4 & 4 & -6 \\ 4 & -12 & 8 \\ -6 & 8 & 8 \end{pmatrix}$$

12.5　(a)　The three criteria have the same σ_{yp}.
　　　(b)　Maximum normal stress criterion: $\sigma_{yp} = 111$ MPa,
　　　　　Distortion-energy criterion: $\sigma_{yp} = 143$ MPa,
　　　　　Maximum shear stress criterion: $\sigma_{yp} = 80.8$ MPa,
　　　(c)　Maximum normal stress criterion: $\sigma_{yp} = 100$ MPa,
　　　　　Distortion-energy criterion: $\sigma_{yp} = 152$ MPa,
　　　　　Maximum shear stress criterion: $\sigma_{yp} = 87.5$ MPa.

12.9　(a)　$\sigma_1 = 50$ ksi,　$\sigma_2 = 20$ ksi,　$\sigma_3 = -10$ ksi,
　　　(b)　$\sigma_1 = 57.7$ ksi,　$\sigma_2 = 23.1$ ksi,　$\sigma_3 = -11.5$ ksi.

Chapter 13

13.1　$\sigma_\theta = -15/2$ MPa,　$\tau_\theta = -15\sqrt{3}/2$ MPa.

13.5　$N = 97.7$ MN,　$\sigma_\theta = 97.7$ MPa,　$S = 33.8$ MN,　$\tau_\theta = 33.8$ MPa.

13.9　$p = 1.2$ MPa,　$T = 15.1$ kN · m.

13.13　$p = 117$ lb,　$A_y = 58.9$ lb.

13.17　(a)　$\sigma_A = 333$ MPa,　$\tau_A = 578$ MPa,
　　　(b)　$\sigma_1 = 768$ MPa,　$\sigma_2 = -435$ MPa.

13.21　$\sigma_A = 13.3$ psi,　$\tau_A = 1.42$ psi,　$\sigma_B = 9.91$ psi,　$\tau_B = 1.52$ psi.

13.25　$p = 764$ lb.

13.29　$y + 27x/8 = 0$.

13.33　$\Delta = [3(\alpha_2 - \alpha_1)\delta T\, L_2]/(4h)$.

13.37　$\sigma_{max} = 1180$ psi $< \sigma_{awb} = 1250$ psi,
　　　$\tau_{max} = 85.7$ psi $< \tau_{aw} = 95.0$ psi.

13.41　$w = 2.13$ kN/m.

13.45　S 10 × 25.4.

13.49　$d(x) = (x/l)^4/d_0$.

13.53　$d = 0.161$ m.

13.57　$\tau_{max} = 500$ lb.

Chapter 14

14.1　$\sigma_{max} = 200$ MPa.

14.5　$q(x) = -kx$.

14.9　$v(x) = -\dfrac{P}{6EI}(x^3 - 3L^2x + 2L^3)$.

14.13　$v(x) = -\dfrac{k}{EI}\left(\dfrac{L}{\pi}\right)^4 \sin\left(\dfrac{\pi x}{L}\right)$.

14.17　$v(x) = -\dfrac{P}{48EI}(4x^3 - 3L^2x)$　for $0 \le x \le 42$.

14.21　$v(x) = \dfrac{Px^3}{12EI} - \dfrac{PLx^2}{16EI}$　for $0 \le x \le L$.

14.25　$EIv(x) = -\dfrac{kL^4}{\pi^4}\sin\dfrac{px}{L} + \dfrac{kL^4}{2\pi^3}x^3 - \dfrac{3kL^2}{2\pi^3}x^2 + \dfrac{kL^3}{\pi^3}x$.

14.29　$EIv(x) = \dfrac{5P}{96}x^3 - \dfrac{PL^2}{32}x$　for $0 \le x \le L/2$,

$EIv(x) = \dfrac{5P}{96}x^3 - \dfrac{P}{6}\left(x - \dfrac{L}{2}\right)^3 - \dfrac{PL^2}{32}x$　for $L/2 \le x \le L$.

14.33 $E_s Iv(x) = \dfrac{P}{12}x^3 - \dfrac{5PL^2}{48}x$ for $(0 \le x \le L/2)$,

$E_A Iv(x) = \dfrac{P}{12}(L-x)^3 - \dfrac{7PL^2}{144}(L-x)$ for $L/2 \le x \le L$.

14.37 $v_B = 0.210$ in.

14.41   **(a)** $I_s = 830$ in^4,   use 18 I70
  (b) $I_{AI} = 2490$ in^4,   use 24I,
  (c) $\sigma_s = 14.15$ ksi, $\sigma_{AI} = 6.14$ ksi.

14.45 $EIv(x) = \dfrac{5w_0 a}{48}x^3 - \dfrac{95w_0 a^3}{96}x - \dfrac{w_0}{24}(x-a)^4 +$

$+ \dfrac{w_0}{24}(x-2a)^4$ for $2a \le x \le 4a$,

for $0 \le x \le a$ take first two terms,
for $a \le x \le 2a$ take first three terms.

14.49 $EIv(x) = -\dfrac{k}{120}x^5 + \dfrac{ka^2}{18}x^3 - \dfrac{41ka^4}{360}x$ for $0 \le x \le a$,

$EIv(x) = -\dfrac{k}{120}x^5 + \dfrac{ka^2}{24}(x-a)^4 + \dfrac{k}{120}(x-a)^5$

$+ \dfrac{ka^2}{18}x^3 - \dfrac{41ka^4}{360}x$ for $a \le x \le 2a$.

14.53   For 6 k load: $v_C = -0.061$ in,
  for 3 k/ft load $v_{C\,total} = -0.391$ in.

14.57 $v_{CX} = \dfrac{13PL^3}{192EI}$, $v_{CY} = \dfrac{PL^3}{8EI}$.

14.61 $P_S = 8.13$ lb.

14.65 $X = 531$ N, in sides wires $= 485$ N.

14.69 $\delta T = 96.8°$ F.

14.73 $\gamma = 11.2°$, $22.5° + 11.2°$.

14.77   **(a)** $P = 11bh^2\sigma_{yp}/(12L)$.

Chapter 15

15.1 $v_A = -\dfrac{744P}{EI}$, $\theta_A = -\dfrac{57P}{EI}$ rad.

15.5 $v_A = \dfrac{25Pa^3}{108EI}$, $\theta_A = \dfrac{19Pa^2}{108EI}$ rad.

15.9 $v_A = \dfrac{4M_1 a^2}{9EI}$, $\theta_A = -\dfrac{M_1 a}{3EI}$ rad.

15.13 $v_C = \dfrac{11PL^3}{768EI}$.

15.17 $v_{max} = -\dfrac{4a^2 M_1}{9\sqrt{3}EI}$.

15.21 $v_{max} = 0.10$ in, $v_{center} = 0.0905$ in.

15.25 $v_C = 1240/EI$.

15.29 $M_C = 23.5$ kN $\cdot$ m.

15.33 $R_A = 4P/3$, $R_B = 2P/3$.

15.37   **(b)** $\tau_{max} = 680$ kN/m$^2 < \tau_{all}$.

15.41 $\dfrac{v_f}{v_s} = \dfrac{1}{5}$.

15.45 $V_{max} = 41.9$ k, $M_{max} = 40.2$ k $\cdot$ ft.

15.49 $V_{max} = 282$ kN, $M_{min} = -504$ kN $\cdot$ m.

15.53 $V_{max} = 12.6$ k, $M_{min} = -25.5$ k $\cdot$ ft.

Chapter 16

16.1 $P_{CR} = 3k/2$.

16.5 $0.586k/a$, $2k/a$, $3.41k/a$.

16.9 $F = 876$ kN.

16.13 $F = 5980$ N.

16.17   Use 2 in pipe. $L/r = 152$.

16.21 $P_{CR} = \pi^2 EI/(4L^2)$

16.25 $L_2 = 2$ m, $L_3 = 1$ m, $L_4 = L_5 = L_1 = 4$ m.

16.29   For pined-pined columns $(L/r)_1 = 89.2, (L/r)_2 = 75.7$;
  For fixed-fixed columns $(L/r)_1 = 178, (L/r)_2 = 151$.

16.33   **(a)** $v_{max} = 7.01$ mm, $M_{max} = 332 \times 10^3$ N $\cdot$ mm,
  (b) $v_{max} = 7.06$ mm, $M_{max} = 333 \, 10^3$ n $\cdot$ mm,
  (c) $\sigma_{max} = 42$ ksi.

16.37 $v_1 = C_1 \sinh(\lambda x) + C_2 \cosh(\lambda x) + C_3 x + C_4$.

16.41 $M = -\dfrac{q_0 \sin(\lambda x)}{\lambda^2 \sin(\lambda L)}$.

16.45 $P_{CR} = 1.67\,\pi^2 EI/L^2$.

16.49 $P_{allow} = 153$ kips.

16.53   **(a)** $P_{al} = 1110$ kips, $P_{n2} = 219$ kips,
  (b) $\dfrac{P_{n1}}{P_{allow}} = 1.87$, $\dfrac{P_{n2}}{P_{allow}} = 1.43$.

16.57   **(a)** $2b = 4.94$ in,
  (b) $P_n = 94.6$ kips.

16.61 $P_{allow} = 10.8$ kips.

16.65 $P_{allow} \leq 173$ kips.

Chapter 17

17.1   (a) $\Delta = \dfrac{PL}{AE} + \dfrac{2PL^3}{3EI} + \dfrac{20PL}{9GA} + \dfrac{PL^3}{GI}$,

    (b) $\Delta = \dfrac{4PL}{\pi d^2 E}$,

        $\dfrac{\Delta_1}{\Delta} = 0.5\%$, $\dfrac{\Delta_2}{\Delta} = 33.6\%$, $\dfrac{\Delta_3}{\Delta} = 2.8\%$, $\dfrac{\Delta_4}{\Delta} = 63.3\%$,

    (c) $\dfrac{\Delta_1}{\Delta} = 0.02\%$, $\dfrac{\Delta_2}{\Delta} = 34.7\%$, $\dfrac{\Delta_3}{\Delta} = 0.1\%$, $\dfrac{\Delta_4}{\Delta} = 65.1\%$.

17.5 $\sigma_{max} = 59.3$ MPa.

17.9 $\Delta_h = 546$ mm, $\Delta_v = 120$ mm.

17.13 $\Delta_{max} = \dfrac{11PL^3}{384EI}$.

17.17 $v_c = \dfrac{518}{EI}$.

17.21 $\dfrac{M_0}{EI}\left(L_1 + \dfrac{L_2}{3}\right)$, $\dfrac{2M_0 L_1}{6EI}(L_1 + 2L_2)$.

17.25 $\theta_A = 66P/EI$.

17.29 $\theta = \dfrac{61w_0 a^3}{6EI}$.

17.33 $\Delta_V = 0.145\dfrac{PL^3}{EI}$, $\Delta_H = 0.108\dfrac{PL^3}{EI}$.

17.37 $\Delta_C = 0.604$ mm.

17.41 $\Delta = \dfrac{P}{EI}\left[\dfrac{2L^3}{3} + R\left(L^2\pi + \dfrac{R^2\pi}{2} + 4LR\right)\right]$.

17.45   (a) $T = 85.7°$,
    (b) $F = 398$ lb, $\sigma_{BD} = 1940$ psi,
        $\sigma_{BC} = 1550$ psi, $\sigma_{AB} = 1170$ psi.

17.49   (a) $R_A = 2P/3$,
    (b) $M_B = PL/3$.

17.53   (a) $F_{BD} = -10.8$ kN, $F_{BC} = -14.4$ kN,
    (b) $F_{AB} = 2.57$ kN, $F_{BD} = -12.9$ kN, $F_{BC} = -12.9$ kN,

Chapter 18

18.1 $\Delta_H = 0.0133$ in.

18.5 $\Delta_V = 518/(EI)$.

18.9 $\Delta_H = -224P/(EI)$.

18.13 $\Delta_D = 1.57$.

18.17 $R_A = w_0 L/2$, $M_A = w_0 L^2/12$.

18.21 $P_{CR} = \pi^2 EI/L^2$.

Chapter 19

19.1 $EIv' = (2L^2 + 3a - 6La)/6$, $\theta_C = (2L^2 - 3a^2 + 6La)/(6L)$.

19.5 $R_A = 3$ kips.

19.9 $\begin{bmatrix} 2.00 & 0.89 & -0.80 \\ 0.89 & 2.00 & -0.45 \\ -0.80 & -0.45 & 2.00 \end{bmatrix} = \begin{Bmatrix} x_a \\ x_b \\ x_d \end{Bmatrix} = \begin{bmatrix} 13.40 \\ 20.00 \\ 0 \end{bmatrix}$

19.13 $M_{ab} = PL/6 - w_0 L^2/9$, $M_{ba} = PL/24 + w_0 L^2/9$,
    $M_{bc} = PL/24 + 2w_0 L^2/9$, $M_{cb} = -PL/48 + 7w_0 L^2/18$.

19.17 $M_{ab} = -3PL/20 + 7w_0 L^2/60$, $M_{ba} = 3PL/10 + w_0 L^2/60$,
    $M_{bc} = 3PL/10 + w_0 L^2/60$, $M_{cb} = -PL/5 + w_0 L^2/60$.

Chapter 20

20.1 $P = 14M_p/(3L)$.

20.5 $W_{ult} = 12 M_p/L$.

20.9 $P_{ult} = 10.5 M_p/L$.

20.13 $M_{ult} = w_0 L^2/6$.

Index